Technical Index for the Linguistic Atlas of the Gulf States

Linguistic Atlas of the Gulf States

Volume Three
Technical Index for the Linguistic Atlas of the Gulf States

Lee Pederson, Editor
Susan Leas McDaniel, Associate Editor
Carol M. Adams, Assistant Editor
Caisheng Liao, Assistant Editor

Cartography by Borden D. Dent
Graphics Programming by William H. McDaniel

The University of Georgia Press
Athens and London

The work of the LAGS Project and the publication of this book
were made possible through the generous assistance of the
Research Tools Program of the National Endowment for the Humanities
and Emory University.

The editors and the publisher express their grateful appreciation.

The paper in this book meets the guidelines for permanence and durability
of the Committee on Production Guidelines for Book Longevity
of the Council on Library Resources.

Printed in the United States of America
92 91 90 89   5 4 3 2 1

Library of Congress Cataloging-in-Publication Data
(Revised for vol. 3)

Linguistic atlas of the Gulf States.

   Vol. 2: Carol M. Adams, assistant editor.
   Includes index.
   Bibliography: v. 1, p. [315]-363.
   Contents: v. 1. Handbook for the Linguistic atlas of
the Gulf States - v. 2. General index for the Linguistic
atlas of the Gulf States - v. 3. Technical index for the
the Linguistic atlas of the Gulf States.
   1. English language - Dialects - Gulf States - Atlases.
I. Pederson, Lee, 1930 -
PE2970.G85L56 1986   912'.142'0976   83-24139
ISBN 0-8203-0715-7 (v.1: alk. paper)
ISBN 0-8203-0972-9 (v.2: alk. paper)
ISBN 0-8203-1182-0 (v.3: alk. paper)

British Library Cataloging-in-Publication Data available.

Linguistic Atlas of the Gulf States

Lee Pederson, Director

Index Editors

Lee Pederson
Susan Leas McDaniel
Carol Adams
Caisheng Liao

Editorial Assistants

Nancy-Laurel Pettersen
Mary Zeigler

Computer Consultants

William H. McDaniel, BellSouth Services
John J. Nitti, University of Wisconsin

Contents

Introduction

This technical index reorganizes the LAGS data base as entries in a set of microcomputer files. The book combines orthographic evidence recorded in the *Concordance* (1986) with phonological evidence recorded in the *Basic Materials* (1981) to identify all linguistic texts reported in the maps of the atlas. As summaries of ASCII files, these index entries list responses of 914 primary informants to 1297 work sheet items. The files combine with sorting and mapping programs to form the LAGS disk/text, an Automatic Atlas in Microform (AAM).

The evidence includes 390 lexical, 209 grammatical, 423 graphophonemic, and 74 systematic phonetic files, plus 201 lexical files from the Urban Supplement. The four cartographic volumes (4-7) will include the analytic maps of Volume 4 (Regional Matrix) and Volume 5 (Social Matrix), the synthetic maps of Volume 6 (Thematic Maps), and the summary regional and social legends of Volume 7 (Legendry). These maps will suggest the analytic range and descriptive variety of AAM, and the kinds of information a user can generate with the files and programs.

An Automatic Atlas in Microform (AAM)

The LAGS disk/text is an Automatic Atlas in Microform (AAM) with programs and files combined on a single optical disk, two dozen 5 1/4" high-density diskettes, or six dozen low-density, double-sided diskettes. As a LAGS textual analogue, this format gives users a complete set of materials, all edited data as an immediately readable unit. The sorting and mapping programs realize plans outlined in seven reports (*LAGS Working Papers: Third Series*, 1986), published with the Concordance and summarized in the introduction to the *General Index* (1988), and in four *Journal of English Linguistics* essays: "Systematic Phonetics" (1985), "A Graphic Plotter Grid" (1986), "An Automatic Book Code" (1987), and "Electronic Matrix Maps" (1988).

AAM offers a research tool for virtually instantaneous analysis of evidence recorded in a regional dialect survey. In a few seconds, programs will search files, tabulate incidence, and map findings in print, on screen, or in newly created files. This analogue sustains the transparency of LAGS description. As the protocols, concordance, and indexes identify all evidence observed in the field records (the tape-recorded interviews), the files and programs of AAM identify the full range of descriptive method used in the interpretation. The analytical regional and social maps lay the foundation for the synthetic interpretations that follow. The terminal summaries of the Legendry identify all observed regional and social characteristics projected through those maps. This transparent method conceals nothing: its operations keep the materials of inventory, analysis, and description available for immediate appraisal. That resource gives users of the disk/text an electronic evaluation procedure. AAM becomes a convenient critical tool that demonstrates the range, system, and economy of its own resources.

In those ways and on its own terms, AAM combines the requirements of Hjelmslev's empirical principle for complete, consistent, and simple description. The presentation, however, extends beyond its immediate interpretations to become an independent research instrument, an electronic atlas in microform that can be read through as many different programs as a reader finds useful. And, given the format and rationale of files and programs, a reader may create additional evidence with little difficulty. These materials can include more files from the Basic Materials and Concordance, as well as further programs to refine regional and social observations.

As the terminal link in the textual chain, AAM, the disk/text (D), points steadily back through the book/text (B) and fiche/text (F) to the tape/text (T) that preserves the complete data base: T >< F >< B >< D. That descriptive unity explains the interdependence of these components, as if they were links in a chain. AAM, therefore, remains inseparable from the tape/text and analogues of the book and fiche texts. And, in all formats (analogues), behind every graphic text stands a phonetic string to unite form and meaning with sound.

Files

AAM files include lexical (L), urban (U), graphophonemic (P), grammatical (G), and systematic phonetic (S) sets. Each file is numbered according to the page and line on which the item occurs in the LAGS work sheets and reports appropriate responses of primary informants in a 914-line data base. For example, file **010.8 L porch** represents the item investigated on page 10, line 8, of the LAGS protocol, synonyms for *porch*, with *L* indicating that this is a lexical file. For each file, a list summarizes the contents as tabulated variants and multiple responses. Certain lexical, urban, and grammatical lists also contain inappropriate or substitute responses, which are not tabulated in the list or recorded in the file. The lists give book/text readers an inventory of variants and disk/text (AAM) users a code book.

LEXICAL FILES. In all lexical files, variants are coded alphabetically. A simple lexical file, such as **095.7 L lagniappe**, records a set of variants, coded A-Z, aa-au, and a set of combinations, indicating multiple responses from a single informant, not reproduced in the book/text. By consulting the code list, the reader ascertains that the letter *S*, for example, represents the response *lagniappe*, which occurs 86 times in the data base, either as the sole response or in specific combinations from the following list:

A+O+ar (1)	E+am (2)	O+aj (1)	S+au (1)
B+E (1)	E+an (2)	O+al (1)	T+W (1)
B+ar (1)	E+ar (2)	O+al+am (1)	aa+ad (1)
C+S (1)	F+I (1)	O+am (2)	aa+af (1)
E+H (1)	H+O (1)	O+ar (2)	ag+ah (1)
E+J (1)	K+O+Q+S (1)	R+S (1)	ak+al (1)
E+O (5)	M+ap (1)	S+Y (1)	al+am (1)
E+O+P (1)	O+S (4)	S+am (1)	al+an (1)
E+S (2)	O+S+ar (1)	S+ao (1)	an+au (1)
E+ak (4)	O+ab (1)	S+ar (1)	

URBAN FILES. The 201 lexical files of the Urban Supplement are coded in the same manner as those described above. However, the data base for the Urban Supplement consists of only 145 records; therefore, special mapping programs based upon its smaller size are necessary. The Urban Supplement terms are included in the Concordance, General Index, and Technical Index, but will be used only selectively in subsequent volumes. The single exception is the file **111.9 P helicopter**, which occurs as a phonological file.

PHONOLOGICAL (ABC) FILES. The ABC files, identified in the heading by the letter *P*, include all basic LAGS pronunciation items (underlined entries in the work sheets) and additional items identified during the course of the investigation. Rather than being represented by a one or two-letter code, as with lexical files, the ABC entries include the complete string, alphabetized in the list using the standard ASCII collating sequence. Recorded between carets (< >) as graphophonemic strings, ABC notation identifies vowels and consonants under four degrees of stress. Each polysyllabic string concludes with the designation (=) to indicate (1) primary, (2) secondary, (3) tertiary, and (4) weak stress. The code also includes fifteen stressed vowels:

<a>	pat	<ai>	bait	<ie>	bite
<e>	pet	<ee>	beet	<ow>	bout
<i>	pit	<ue>	boot	<oy>	boy
<o>	pot	<oe>	boat	<ui>	buoy
<oo>	put	<aw>	bought	<u>	putt

two weakly stressed vowels and five syllabic consonants:

<A>	coda	<koedA=14>	<M>	bottom	<botM=14>
<I>	Cody	<koedI=14>	<N>	bacon	<baikN=14>
			<NG>	baking	<baikNG=14>
			<L>	bottle	<botL=14>
			<R>	butter	<butR=14>

and twenty-four consonants:

<p>	pill	<f>	fill	<m>	mill
<b>	bill	<v>	villa	<n>	sin
<t>	till	<th>	ether	<ng>	sing
<d>	dill	<dh>	either	<l>	lieu
<k>	kill	<s>	sue	<r>	rill
<g>	gill	<z>	zoo	<w>	will
<ch>	chill	<sh>	shoe	<y>	you
<j>	pledger	<zh>	pleasure		
		<h>	hill		

The code writes the sequence <h> + <w> as <wh> (<wheet>) and <ng> + <k> as <nk> (<drink>) to reflect rules of English spelling and phonotactics, respectively. Deleted consonants and vowels appear between parens (<(A)rown(d)>). Any of the five resonants that occur as weakly stressed syllabics (<m, n, ng, l, r>) can appear between square brackets as vocalized units. For example, when realized as nasalized vowels and signifying vowel plus consonant, they occur in the weakly stressed syllables of *bottom* <bot[M]=14>, *bacon* <baik[N]=14>, and *baking* <baik[NG]=14>, respectively. When realized as an unrounded high-back vowel, the lateral <l> is bracketed, as in *milk* <mi[l]k> and *hospital* <hospit[L]=134>. When realized as a rounded or unrounded mid-central monophthong or diphthong, the lateral <r> is bracketed in *spur* <spu[r]>, *hurry* <hu[r]I=14>, and *coder* (homophonous with *coda*) <coed[R]=14>. Finally, braces mark subphonemic distinctions in ABC files. Figure 1A records the first 15 lines of a LAGS Idiolect Synopsis, illustrating stressed vowels in five environments, before 1) voiceless consonants, 2) voiced consonants or open juncture, 3) nasals, 4) /l/ laterals, and 5) /r/ laterals. Figure 1B rewrites the narrow phonetics of Figure 1A as ABC strings, with braces marking these special designations:

Figure 1A: IDIOLECT SYNOPSIS VOWELS

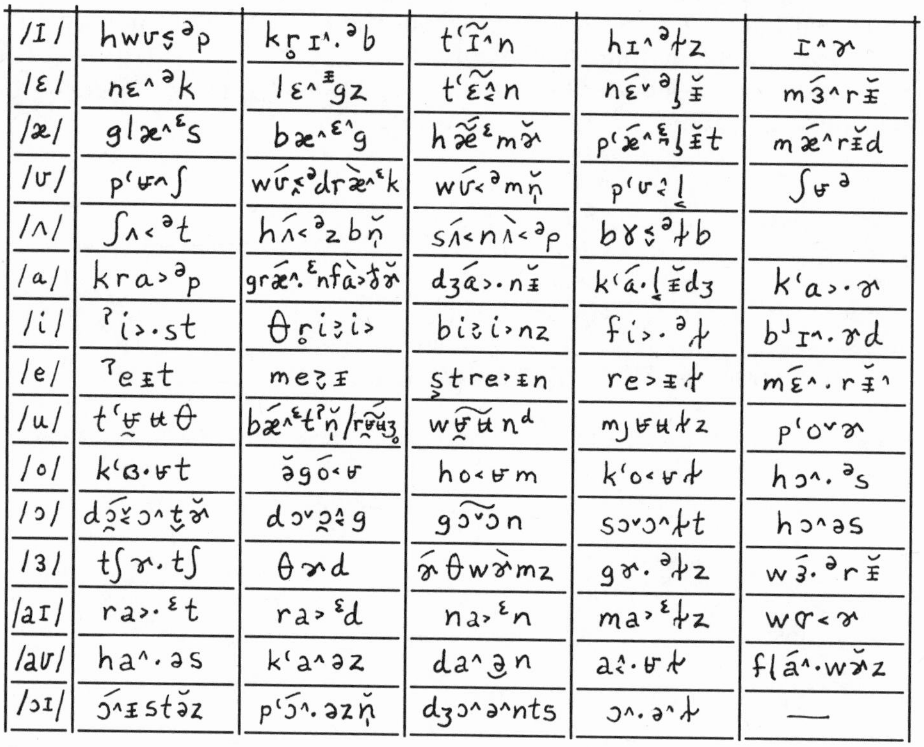

/I/	hwʊṣᵊp	k̥rɪ^.ᵊb	t'Ĩ^n	hɪ^ᵊʈz	I^ɚ
/ɛ/	nɛ^ᵊk	lɛ^ᵻgz	t'ɛ̃ᵌn	nɛ̃ᵛᵊ|ᵛ̆ᵻ	m3^rᵻ̆
/æ/	glæ^ᵋs	bæ^ᵋ^g	hæ̃ᵋmɚ̆	p'æ̃^ᵋ|ᵻ̆t	mæ^rᵻ̆d
/ʊ/	p'ʊ^ʃ	wʊ̃ʐᵊdræ^ᵋk	wʊ̃<ᵊmn̩̆	p'ʊ̰|	ʃʊᵊ
/ʌ/	ʃʌ<ᵊt	hʌ̃<ᵊzbn̩̆	sʌ̃<nʌ̃<ᵊp	bɤṣᵊʈb	
/a/	kra>ᵊp	græ^.ᵋnfà>ðɚ̆	dʒá>.nᵻ	k'á.|ᵻ̆dʒ	k'a>.ɚ
/i/	ʔi>.st	θ̥ṛiᶾi>	biᶾi>nz	fi>.ᵊʈ	bʲɪ^.ɚd
/e/	ʔeᵻt	meᶾᵻ	ʂtre>ɪn	re>ᵻʈ	mɛ̃^.rᵻ^
/u/	t'ʉ̃ʉθ	bæ^ᵋt'n̩̆/rʊ̃ʒ	wʉ̃ʉnᵈ	mʲʉʉz	p'oɚ
/o/	k'ɞ.ʊt	ᵊgo<ʊ	ho<ʊm	k'o<ʊʈ	hoᵊ^.ᵊs
/ɔ/	dᵌᶾʊ<ʈɚ̆	dᵛ̃ᶾᵌg	gᶜ̃ᶜn	sᵛɔ^ʈ	hᵃ^ᵊs
/ɝ/	tʃɚ.tʃ	θɚd	ɚ̃θwɚ̃mz	gɚ.ᵊʈz	wᶾᵊ.ᵊrᵻ̆
/aɪ/	ra>.ᵋt	ra>ᵋd	na>ᵋn	ma>ᵋʈz	wɒ<ɚ
/aʊ/	ha^.ᵊs	k'a^ᵊz	da^ᵊn	aᶾ.ʊʈ	flá^.wᶾ̆z
/ɔɪ/	ᵊ̃ᶾᵻstᵛ̆z	p'ᶾᵛ.ᵊzn̩̆	dʒᵌ^ᵊ^nts	ᵊ̃ᵛᶜʈ	—

Figure 1B: AUTOMATIC BOOK CODE CONVERSION

<i> whoop	krib	t{i}n	hilz	ir
<e> nek	legz	t{e}n	ne{l}I=14	murI=14
<a> glas	bag	h{a}[m]mR=14	pa{l}It=14	marId=14
<oo> poosh	woodrak=13	woomN=14	pool	shoo[r]
<u> shut	huzbN(d)=14	sunup=13	b{oo}lb	---
<o> krop	gran(d)fadhR=134	jonI=14	kolIj=14	kor
<ee> {?}eest	th{r}ee	beenz	feel(d)	byird
<ai> {?}ait	mai	{s}train	rail	merI=14
<ue> tueth	batNr{ue}{zh}=141	w{ue}nd	myuelz	poer
<oe> koet	Agoe=41	hoem	koel(d)	haw[r]s
<aw> dawtR=14	dawg	g{aw}n	sawlt	haw[r]s
<ur> church	thurd	urthwurmz=13	gurlz	wurI=14
<ie> r{ie}t	r{ie}d	n{ie}n	m{ie}lz	w{o}r
<ow> h{ow}s	k{ow}z	d{ow}n	owl	fl{ow}Rz=14
<oy> oyst[R]z=14	p{oy}zN=14	j{oy}nts	{oy}l	----

{a}, {e}, {i}, {aw}, {ue} for nasalized vowels
{ie}, {ow}, {oy} for short glides or long monophthongs
{l} for "clear" <l> (front-vowel timbre)
{o} for a low-back vowel
{oo} for an unrounded vowel
{r} for devoiced retroflex laterals
{s} for a retracted fricative (palatalized)
{zh} for a devoiced fricative
{?} for glottal stops

GRAMMATICAL FILES. With the exception of verb files that record principal parts, grammatical files use the same alphabetic code as lexical files, but are identified in the header as *G* rather than *L*. Salutations, animal calls, and other syntactic structures are routinely classified as *G* files, although they often have lexical components. An example of a grammatical file is **024.9 G inceptives**. A second type includes verb files, such as **048.7 G eat**. Recorded in ABC notation, with limited use of the subphonemic braces ({ }), each item in a verb file is preceded by a symbol to indicate its form or tense:

<!>	infinitive
<&>	present indicative, third person singular
<@>	present participle
<*>	preterit
<#>	past participle

SYSTEMATIC PHONETICS FILES. These 74 files register the phonetic features of 15 stressed vowels in five environments, as recorded in the LAGS Idiolect Synopses, Basic Materials (1981, Fiche 6-16) and illustrated above as Figure 1. The Systematic Phonetics Code (SPC) concentrates on the essential elements of notation--the features all LAGS scribes were trained to observe.

SPC includes a consonantal and a syllabic code. Only the latter is included in the current files because ABC notation identifies all systematic phonetic contrasts among consonantal sets. The syllabic code includes primary, secondary, and tertiary components, ordered to reflect a hierarchy of phonological signals and designed to resolve itself into ultimate units through mechanical deduction. Primary (positional) features include 20 components, each of which represents a point on the LAGS vowel quadrant:

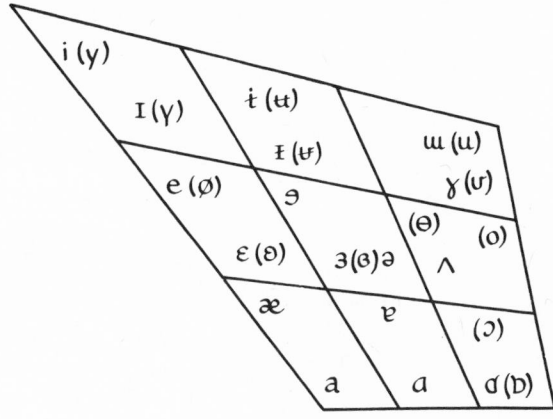

Each of those primary features is a complex, implying vocalization and indicating lingual and mandible actions. Secondary (conditional) features include six more considerations: unmarked, tense, long, nasal, retroflex, and round, with the last five of these listed in all possible combinations within the code. All secondary features are phonologically, geographically, or socially contrastive within the LAGS collection. Finally, tertiary (modificational) features include the narrowest markings of LAGS phonetic notation, indicating vowels in raised, lowered, retracted, or advanced positions (relative to the norms established on the quadrant), vowels weakly realized in articulation (transcribed above the baseline in the protocol/synopsis notation), and vowels distinguished by glottalization. Like secondary features, these also record all possible combinations. SPC includes:

I. Primary Features (Positional)

	Front	Central 1	Central 2	Back 1	Back 2
High 1	A		B		C
High 2	D		E		F
Mid 1	G	H		I	J
Mid 2	K	L	M	N	
Low 1	O		P		Q
Low 2	R		S		T

II. Secondary Features (Conditional):

A. Unmarked	L. C + E	W. C + D + E	
B. Tense	M. C + F	X. C + D + F	
C. Long	N. D + E	Y. C + E + F	
D. Nasal	O. D + F	Z. D + E + F	
E. Retroflex	P. E + F	1. B + C + D + E	
F. Round	Q. B + C + D	2. B + C + D + F	
G. B + C	R. B + C + E	3. B + C + E + F	
H. B + D	S. B + C + F	4. B + D + E + F	
I. B + E	T. B + D + E	5. C + D + E + F	
J. B + F	U. B + D + F	6. B + C + D + E + F	
K. C + D	V. B + E + F		

III. Tertiary Features (Modificational):

A.	Unmarked	M.	J + D	Y.	S + G
B.	Raised	N.	J + E	Z.	S + H
C.	Lowered	O.	J + F	1.	S + I
D.	Advanced	P.	J + G	2.	S + J
E.	Retracted	Q.	J + H	3.	S + K
F.	B + D	R.	J + I	4.	S + L
G.	B + E	S.	Glottal	5.	S + M
H.	C + D	T.	S + B	6.	S + N
I.	C + E	U.	S + C	7.	S + O
J.	Weak	V.	S + D	8.	S + P
K.	J + B	W.	S + E	9.	S + Q
L.	J + C	X.	S + F	0.	S + R

The same code records the incidence of diphthongs and triphthongs with the nuclear, core, or most prominent element in a syllabic complex written in uppercase letters and the non-nuclear, peripheral, or glide elements written in lowercase letters. Thus, the diphthong underlying <oo> in *whip* in Figure 1, a lower high-back (F), rounded (F), lowered and advanced (H) followed by a mid-central (m), unmarked (a), and weakly realized (j) offglide yields the string |FFHmaj|. Figure 1C records the 73 syllabic nuclei of the texts of Figure 1A in SPC notation.

Figure 1C: SYSTEMATIC PHONETICS CONVERSION

<i>	FFHmaj	DCBmaj	DDB	DABmaj	DABmea
<e>	KABmaj	KABeaj	KDF	KACmaj	LAD
<a>	OABkaj	OABkak	ODBkdj	OABkbj	OAB
<oo>	EFB	FFFmaj	FFDmaj	FFF	EFAmaj
<u>	NADmaj	NADmaj	NAD	FAHmaj	---
<o>	SAEmaj	SAE	SCE	SCA	SCEmea
<ee>	AGW	abiABE	abiABE	AGEmaj	DCBmea
<ai>	GBSeaa	GBIeaa	GBEeaa	GBEeaa	KCB
<ue>	eaaBJA	edaBUA	edaBUA	efaBJA	JJCmea
<oe>	LMAefa	JJDefa	JJDefa	JJDefa	QMBmaj
<aw>	QAHqfb	QFCqaf	QOCqoa	QFCqfb	QFBmaa
<ur>	MLA	MEH	MEA	MLAmaj	LCAmaj
<ie>	RCEkaj	RAEkaj	RAEkaj	RAEkaj	TADmea
<ow>	RCBmaa	RABmaa	RABmfa	RCFefa	RCB
<oy>	QFBeaa	QMBmaa	QFBmab	QMBmab	---

Mapping Programs

AAM programs sort data for several preliminary lists and map correlations in five formats. The latter include five graphic charts: three summary matrix maps -- SECTOR TOTALS, LAND REGION TOTALS, and SOCIAL TOTALS -- and two graphic plotter grids, the LAGSMAP and CODEMAP formats.

SECTOR TOTALS. This program reports incidence according to the 16 LAGS sectors (Figure 2) including East Tennessee (ET), Upper Georgia (UG), Lower Georgia (LG), East Florida (EF), Middle Tennessee (MT), Upper Alabama (UA), Lower Alabama (LA), Eastern Gulf sector of West Florida and Gulf Alabama (EG), West Tennessee (WT), Upper Mississippi (UM), Lower Mississippi (LM), Western Gulf sector of Gulf Mississippi and East Louisiana (WG), Arkansas (AR), West Louisiana (WL), Upper Texas (UT), and Lower Texas (LT):

AR	WT	MT	ET
WL	UM	UA	UG
UT	LM	LA	LG
LT	WG	EG	EF

The program lists the 180 occurrences of entry **gallery** (code **at**) in file **010.8 L porch** in this way:

9	4	1	0
33	10	3	1
20	28	12	1
16	24	17	1

LAND REGION TOTALS. This program reports incidence according to six land regions and their subdivisions (Figure 3):

A) Highlands:
   A1: ET Blue Ridge, A2: UG Blue Ridge, A3: ET/MT Cumberland Plateaus, A4: UA Cumberland Plateaus, A5: MT/UA Lower Plateaus (Nashville Basin), A6: AR Ozark/Ouachita Mountains;
B) Piedmont:
   B1: UG Eastern Piedmont, B2: UA/LA Western Piedmont;
C) Coastal:
   C1: LG Upper Atlantic, C2: EF Lower Atlantic, C3: EF/EG East Gulf, C4: WG West Gulf;
D) Plains:
   D1: LG/EF Eastern Coastal, D2: UA/LA/UM Black Belt, D3: WT Upper-Central, D4: UM Mid-Central, D5: LM Lower-Central, D6: AR/WL Ouachita, D7: UT Middle Western, D8: LT Lower Western;
E) Piney Woods:
   E1: UG/LG Georgia Wire Grass, E2: EF/EG Eastern Pine Flats; E3: LA/EG Alabama Wire Grass, E4: LM/WG Mississippi Piney Woods, E5: WL/UT Western Pine Flats;
F) Delta:
   F1: AR St. Francis Basin; F2: AR/WT/UM Upper Mississippi Basin; F3: UM/LM Yazoo Basin, F4: WL/WG/LM Lower Mississippi Basin, F5: WG/WL Atchafalaya Basin, F6: WL Red River Basin.

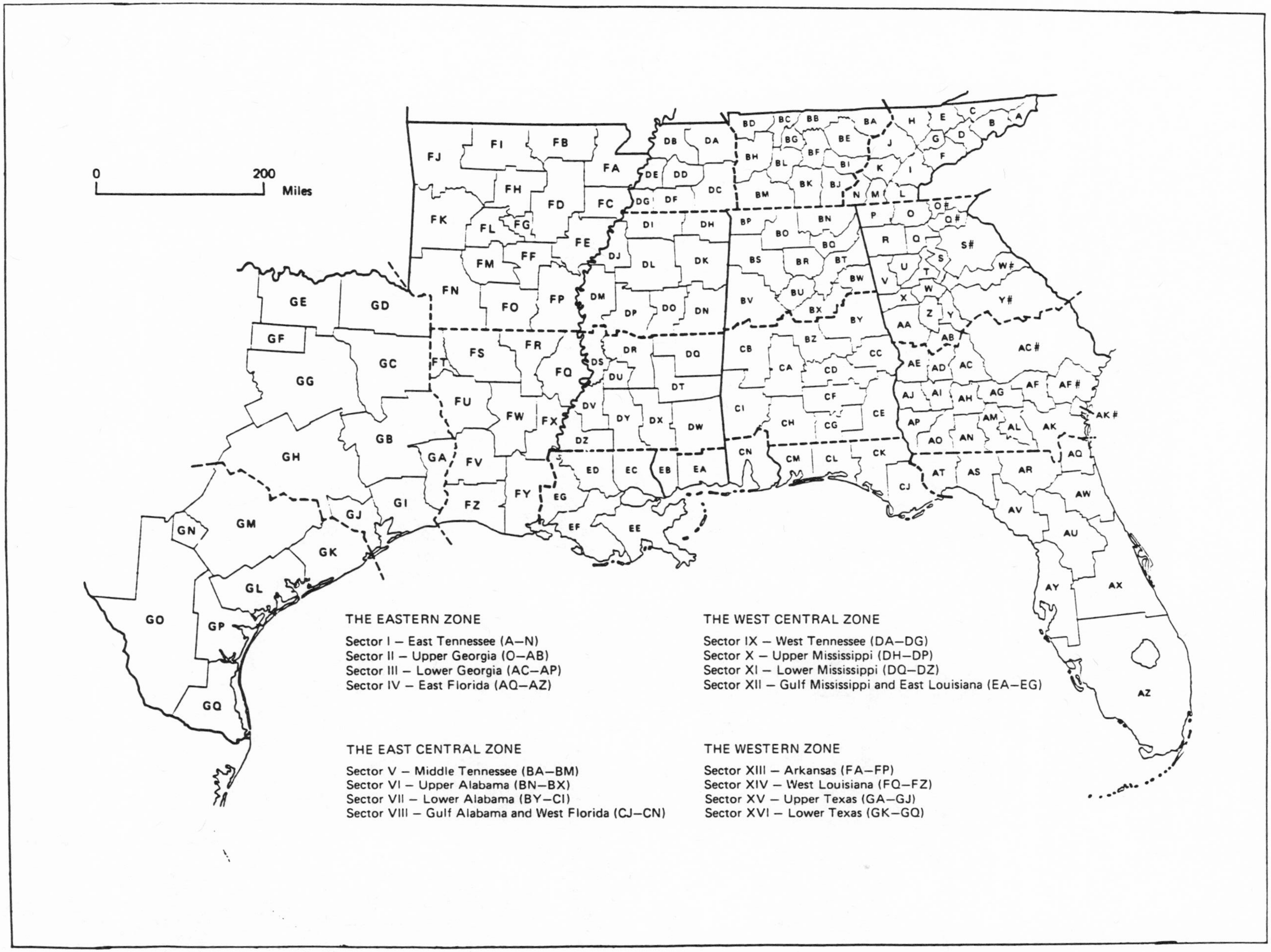

THE WEST CENTRAL ZONE

Sector IX – West Tennessee (DA–DG)
Sector X – Upper Mississippi (DH–DP)
Sector XI – Lower Mississippi (DQ–DZ)
Sector XII – Gulf Mississippi and East Louisiana (EA–EG)

THE WESTERN ZONE

Sector XIII – Arkansas (FA–FP)
Sector XIV – West Louisiana (FQ–FZ)
Sector XV – Upper Texas (GA–GJ)
Sector XVI – Lower Texas (GK–GQ)

THE EASTERN ZONE

Sector I – East Tennessee (A–N)
Sector II – Upper Georgia (O–AB)
Sector III – Lower Georgia (AC–AP)
Sector IV – East Florida (AQ–AZ)

THE EAST CENTRAL ZONE

Sector V – Middle Tennessee (BA–BM)
Sector VI – Upper Alabama (BN–BX)
Sector VII – Lower Alabama (BY–CI)
Sector VIII – Gulf Alabama and West Florida (CJ–CN)

Miles

200

0

Figure 2

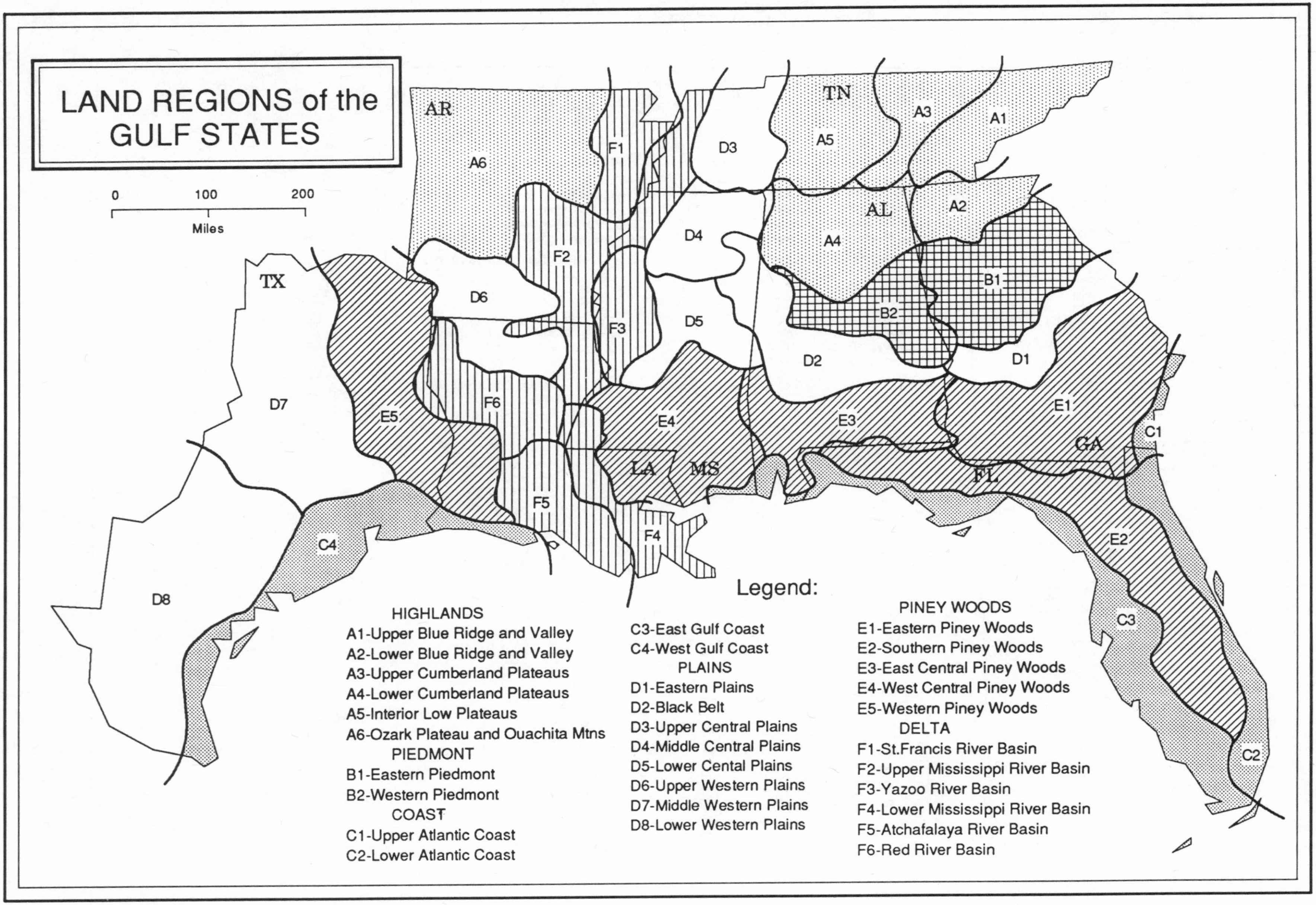
LAND REGIONS of the GULF STATES
0
100
200
Miles
AR
TN
AL
TX
LA
MS
GA
FL
A1
A2
A3
A4
A5
A6
B1
B2
C1
C2
C3
C4
D1
D2
D3
D4
D5
D6
D7
D8
E1
E2
E3
E4
E5
F1
F2
F3
F4
F5
F6
Legend:
HIGHLANDS
A1-Upper Blue Ridge and Valley
A2-Lower Blue Ridge and Valley
A3-Upper Cumberland Plateaus
A4-Lower Cumberland Plateaus
A5-Interior Low Plateaus
A6-Ozark Plateau and Ouachita Mtns
PIEDMONT
B1-Eastern Piedmont
B2-Western Piedmont
COAST
C1-Upper Atlantic Coast
C2-Lower Atlantic Coast
C3-East Gulf Coast
C4-West Gulf Coast
PLAINS
D1-Eastern Plains
D2-Black Belt
D3-Upper Central Plains
D4-Middle Central Plains
D5-Lower Cental Plains
D6-Upper Western Plains
D7-Middle Western Plains
D8-Lower Western Plains
PINEY WOODS
E1-Eastern Piney Woods
E2-Southern Piney Woods
E3-East Central Piney Woods
E4-West Central Piney Woods
E5-Western Piney Woods
DELTA
F1-St.Francis River Basin
F2-Upper Mississippi River Basin
F3-Yazoo River Basin
F4-Lower Mississippi River Basin
F5-Atchafalaya River Basin
F6-Red River Basin

Figure 3

The land region matrix records incidence, as, for example, of *gallery*, in 31 units with regional and subregional percentages:

A 7/207 3%   B 1/84 1%   C 26/109 24%   D 36/175 21%   E 50/184 27%   F 60/155 39%

A1 0/49 0%   B1 1/59 2%   C1 0/12 0%   D1 0/16 0%   E1 1/55 2%   F1 0/15 0%
A2 0/20 0%   B2 0/25 0%   C2 0/23 0%   D2 4/25 16%   E2 4/32 13%   F2 11/49 22%
A3 0/21 0%   C3 10/46 22%   D3 1/17 6%   E3 13/33 39%   F3 9/13 69%
A4 3/37 8%   C4 16/28 57%   D4 1/22 5%   E4 19/37 51%   F4 17/41 41%
A5 1/39 3%   D5 8/26 31%   E5 13/27 48%   F5 12/24 50%
A6 3/41 7%   D6 8/17 47%   F6 11/23 48%
                                                   D7 5/23 22%
                                                   D8 9/29 31%

SOCIAL TOTALS.   This program reports incidence according to nine sets of social characteristics in nine fields: 1) Racial Caste: 1A Black, 1B White; 2) Sex: 2A Female, 2B Male; 3) Perspective: 3A Insular, 3B Worldly; 4) Age Group: 4A 13-30, 4B 31-60, 4C 61-99; 5 Alternate Age Group: 5A 13-45, 5B 46-70, 5C 71-99; 6) Education: 6A Elementary School, 6B High School, 6C College; 7) Social Class: 7A Lower, 7B Middle, 7C Upper; 8) Speech Type: 8A Folk, 8B Common, 8C Cultured; 9) Informant Type: 9A I, 9B II, 9C III. Fields 3 and 9 are Linguistic Atlas of New England classifications; field 8 summarizes fieldworkers' and scribes' remarks; field 7 conflates LAGS social classification according to Warner's *Four Factor Index*.   The *Basic Materials* (1981) and the *Handbook* (1986) elaborate these fields. The matrix program maps them in those A) fields, according to the B) distribution of the 914 primary informants, as in C) **gallery**:

A) Fields					B) Informants					C) **gallery**			
1A	4A	4B	4C		197	108	224	582		48	4	45	131
1B	5A	5B	5C		717	197	317	400		132	25	63	92
2A	6A	6B	6C		422	350	333	231		77	78	62	40
2B	7A	7B	7C		492	295	513	106		103	73	85	22
3A	8A	8B	8C		529	344	352	218		123	79	62	39
3B	9A	9B	9C		385	349	348	217		57	79	63	38

LAGSMAP. This program records incidence according to grid coordinates explained in the essay "A Graphic Plotter Grid." As designed, the form will map a single variant (Figure 4), or as many as three variants from a single file, as, for example, **gallery (at)**, **piazza (bp)**, and **veranda (dv)** in **010.8 L porch** (Figure 5). Or it will map entries from different files. Figure 6 maps three words frequently heard in Louisiana, **gallery (at) (010.8)**, **pirogue (bi) (024.6)**, and **lagniappe (S) (095.7)**.

CODEMAP. This program reports incidence according to the nine fields of the SOCIAL TOTALS matrix, as explained in the essay "Electronic Matrix Maps." The program will map any ASCII file item according to the nine fields in these configurations:

Figure 4: **gallery**

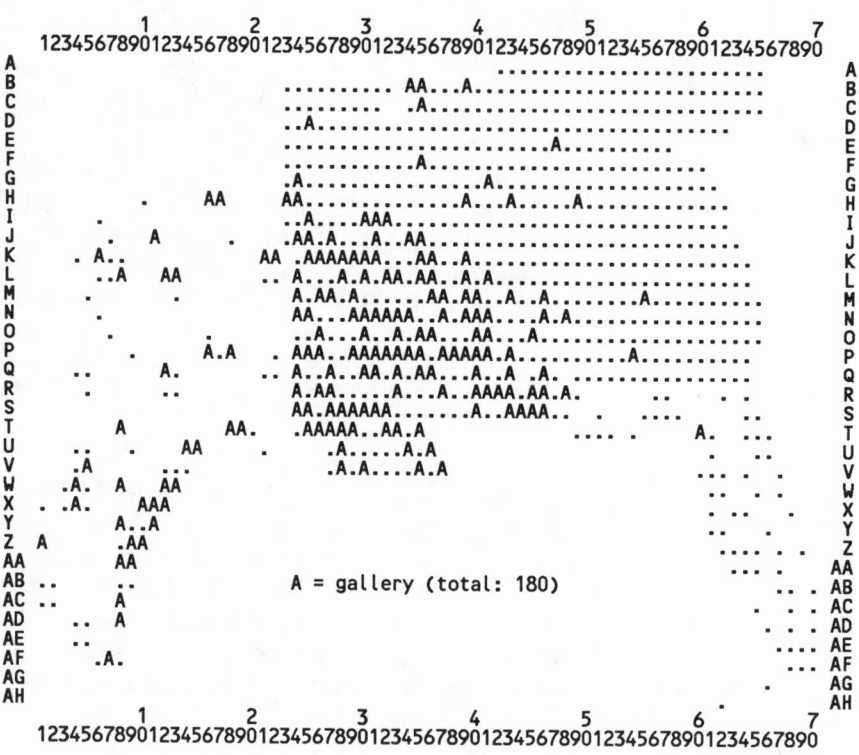

Figure 5: Three *Porch* Synonyms

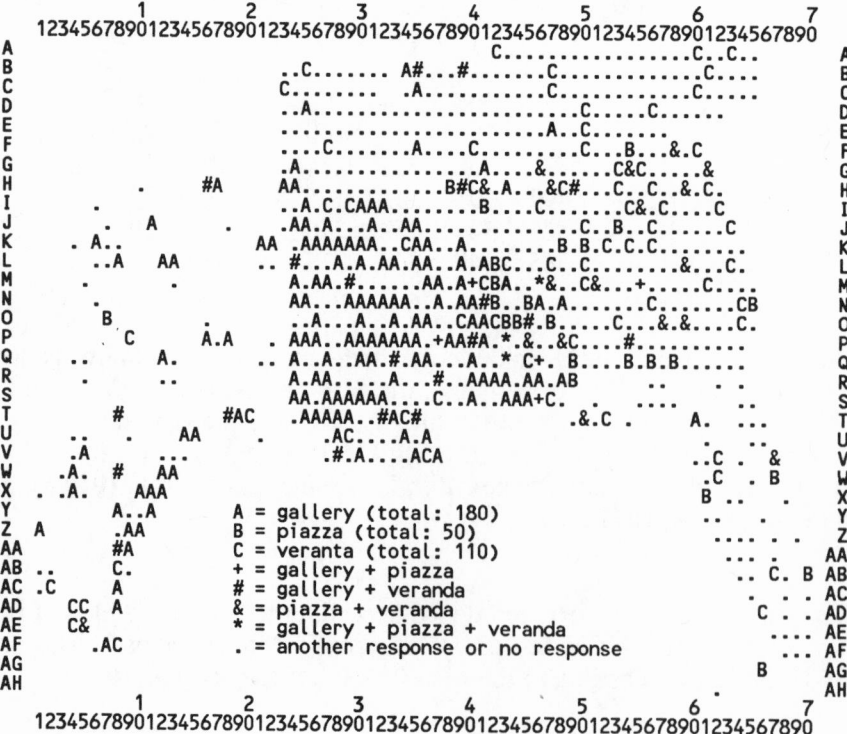

Figure 6: Three Louisiana Words

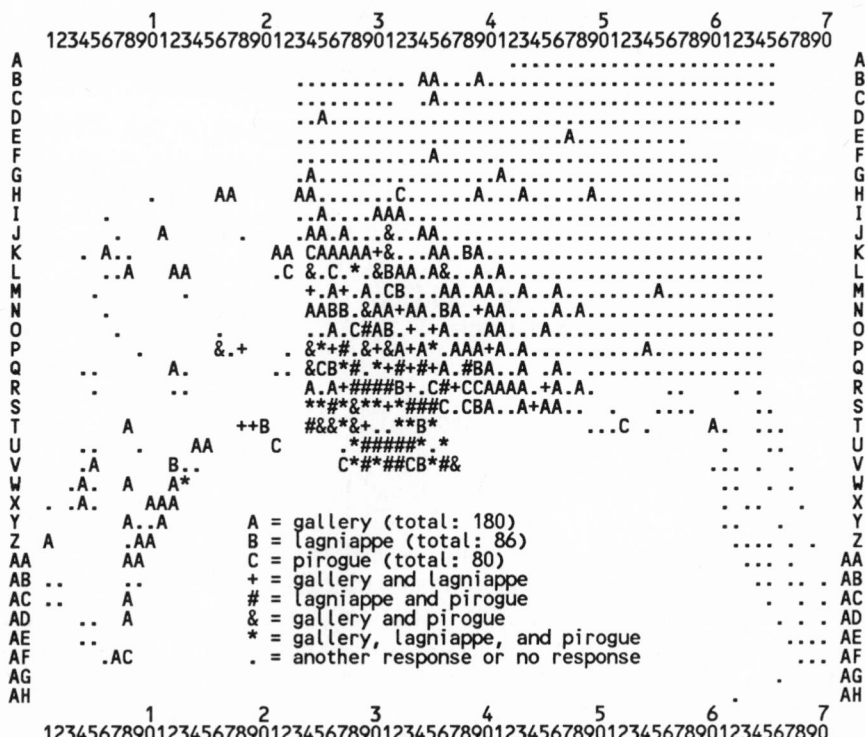

Figure 7: {010.8} gallery (180)

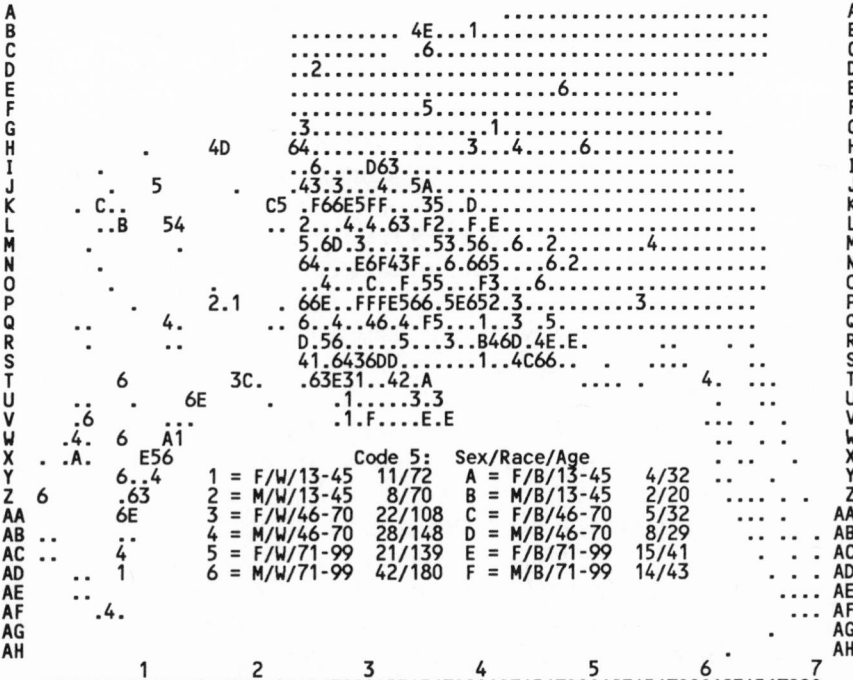

Code 1: Race (1), Age (4), and Social Class (7)
Code 2: Race (1), Age (5), and Social Class (7)
Code 3: Race (1), Age (4), and Education (6)
Code 4: Race (1), Age (5), and Education (6)
Code 5: Race (1), Age (5), and Sex (2)
Code 6: Race (1), Sex (2), and Education (6)
Code 7: Race (1), Sex (2), and Social Class (7)
Code 8: Race (1), Sex (2), and Speech Type (8)
Code 9: Race (1), LANE Type (9), and LANE Perspective (3)

For example, Code 5 in Figure 7 records incidence according to racial caste, sex, and the second age grouping, reporting information of SOCIAL TOTALS fields 1, 2, and 5.

The Technical Index

All of the 1297 files are included in the Technical Index, in numerical order according to protocol page and line. Appendix I lists the files in the order in which they appear. Appendix II is an alphabetical list of the work-sheet items in this volume.

In the index, each file begins with a boldface header line that contains the page and line number, the letter that designates the type of file (e.g., *L* for lexical), and the title of the file. Most of these titles come from the LAGS work sheets, except in a few cases where responses from the Gulf States indicate that another title is more appropriate. For instance, file **044.3 L** is called *wheat bread* in the work sheets but *loaf bread* in the Technical Index because the file itself records all bread in loaves. Beneath this header is the line "No Response (53)." This line indicates that 53 of the 914 primary informants did not respond to the item, or that the fieldworker did not ask the question. The total of 53 does not include inappropriate responses such as *whole wheat flour*. The "No Response" total for Systematic Phonetics files is sometimes (0) because when the target word did not appear in a given protocol, a substitute word containing the designated vowel in a similar environment was sought. The rest of the file consists of the responses themselves, here from A to ca, *American bread* to *yeast-rising bread*. Each response is followed by a total in parentheses, e.g., *ab light bread (482)*. Parentheses as part of the entry indicate that an item may have appeared in alternate ways. For example, *P graham (bread) (8)* may have occurred in the concordance as *graham*, with *bread* implied, or as *graham bread*. Editorial glosses appear in square brackets. In some cases, subfiles, such as **[walkway to separate kitchen]** may occur within main files (here, **009.9 L kitchen**).

In general, responses to lexical and grammatical items that informants report as heard in the speech of others are not included in the files because the regional and social distribution might be affected. However, responses used by members of the informant's family, particularly parents or grandparents, do appear on the list. Some facetious responses and instances of misspeaking also occur. These generally do not have editorial glosses but may be confirmed in the General Index or Concordance. Users of the disk/text who wish to consider "heard" responses may use the Concordance to add these terms to the files.

ABC files and the grammatical files that report principal parts of verbs contain additional headers to indicate subphonemic elements recorded in the files. For example, file **041.2 P furrow** has the symbol *{f}* in its header to indicate that in the pronunciation <{f}urA = 14>, the initial *f* is bilabial. The meaning of symbols in braces may vary from one file to another, so the reader should consult the header for each file. Most of the items from pages 86-87 (names of states, cities, and countries) do not contain braces because of the complexity of many of the responses and subsequent length of the files.

The LAGS Concordance conventions appear throughout the Technical Index to indicate deletions, parts of speech, and foreign language terms. These are the most common:

[F]	French	[adj.]	adjective
[G]	German	[n.]	noun
[S]	Spanish	[v.]	verb
[C-0]	deleted copula	[M-i]	deleted pronoun plural
[D-0]	deleted article	[M-k]	deleted pronoun possessive
[J-0]	deleted conjunction	[N-i]	deleted noun plural
[M-0]	deleted pronoun	[N-k]	deleted noun possessive
[N-0]	deleted noun	[V-p]	deleted 3rd person sing. present
[P-0]	deleted preposition	[V-r]	deleted preterit
[R-0]	deleted relative	[V-t]	deleted past participle
[X-0]	deleted auxiliary		

The Concordance conventions and other aspects of the Concordance are described in the Introduction to the *General Index* (1988). Users of the Technical Index should consult the General Index, Concordance, and Basic Materials for verification and additional information concerning items in the lists.

Although the Technical Index aims to represent every item in the LAGS work sheets with at least one file (and sometimes as many as four), the files for a few items would not produce contrastive results. These are mentioned in the index as headers only. Those entries include:

030.7	names of local streams
105.1	major sections of the city
105.4	ethnic neighborhoods
105.5	ethnic neighborhoods [stratified]
105.6	ethnic commerce centers
106.1	upper-class neighborhoods
106.2	middle-class neighborhoods
106.3	lower-class neighborhoods
106.4	local landmarks
107.6	main streets in the city
107.7	neighborhood streets
131.1	local culture
131.2	secondary responses to language

Each file in the Technical Index has been edited according to the individual nature of the work-sheet item. While striving for consistency among files, editors have been more concerned with each file as a separate entity. Hence, some variations in alphabetizing and in treatment of items do occur in this index. Whereas an item may be broken down by definitions, such as **044.5-6 L corn breads**, or divided into sections, such as **022.1 L sawhorse**, most files are simple lists of variants, sometimes combined for the sake of simplicity and for ease in mapping. The user who desires to work closely with a particular file should consult the Protocols in the Basic Materials in the case of ABC and SPC files, and both the Concordance and the Protocols for Lexical and Grammatical files. The Technical Index should serve as a guide to the contents of the other analogues and not as a substitute for them.

The Technical Index

001.1A P one

No Response (10)

<wawn> (6)

<wo[n]> (1)

<woe[n]> (1)

<woen> (2)

<won> (105)

<woon> (7)

<wu(n)> (2)

<wu[n]> (6)

<wun> (838)

001.1B P two

No Response (1)

<chew> (1)

<chue> (1)

<due> (1)

<tew> (164)

<too> (6)

<tue> (805)

001.1 S two

No Response (0)

|BJA| (2)

|BJAeaj| (1)

|BJAefj| (1)

|BJAffd| (1)

|BJCeab| (1)

|BJE| (1)

|BSA| (3)

|BSAeaa| (1)

|BSAmaj| (2)

|CJAffa| (1)

|CJD| (8)

|CJDmaj| (1)

|CJDmak| (1)

|CJH| (1)

|CSC| (1)

|CSD| (1)

|EAC| (1)

|EFBeaa| (1)

|EFBmaj| (2)

|EMB| (2)

|FFAmaj| (1)

|FFBkak| (1)

|FFCeaa| (1)

|FFD| (1)

|FFDeaa| (1)

|FFDeaj| (4)

|FFDmaj| (1)

|FFFeaj| (2)

|FFFefj| (1)

|FFFmaj| (1)

|FMB| (1)

|FMDeaj| (1)

|FMF| (2)

|FMFeaa| (1)

|FMFmaj| (1)

|FSBmaj| (1)

|JJAefj| (1)

|JJBefa| (1)

|NABean| (1)

|cjdCJD| (1)

|cjhCJA| (1)

|eaaBBA| (3)

|eaaBGA| (1)

|eaaBJA| (42)

|eaaBJC| (1)

|eaaBSA| (2)

|eaaCJD| (1)

|eacBJA| (2)

|eadBSA| (1)

|ecaBBA| (1)

|ecaBJA| (9)

|ecaBSD| (1)

|ecbBJA| (1)

|eccBJA| (1)

|edaBUA| (2)

|efaBJA| (442)

|efaBJAeaj| (2)

|efaBJAkaj| (1)

|efaBJAmaj| (2)

|efaBJC| (2)

|efaBJD| (1)

|efaBJJ| (1)

|efaBSA| (64)

|efaEFA| (1)

|efbBJA| (2)

|efcBJA| (15)

|efcBJC| (2)

|efcBSA| (1)

|efcCJD| (1)

|efdBJA| (4)

|efdCJD| (1)

|efeCJA| (1)

|efhBJA| (1)

|efhBJJ| (1)

|emaBJA| (6)

|emaBJJ| (1)

|emaCJD| (1)

|embBJA| (1)

|emcBJA| (6)

|emcBJD| (1)

|emcBJJ| (2)

|emdBJA| (3)

|emhBJA| (1)

|eoaBUA| (2)

|eocBUA| (1)

|faaBJE| (1)

|facBJA| (1)

|fadBJA| (3)

|fadCJD| (2)

|ffaBJA| (1)

|ffaCJA| (6)

|ffaCJD| (1)

|ffbBJA| (2)

|ffbBJJ| (1)

|ffcBJA| (4)

|ffdBJA| (14)

|ffdBJAmaj| (1)

|ffdBSA| (1)

|ffdCJA| (1)

|ffdCJD| (118)

|ffdCJDeaj| (2)

|ffdCJDmaj| (2)

|ffdCJH| (1)

|ffdCJM| (5)

|ffdCJMeaj| (1)

|ffdCSD| (22)

|fffCJD| (1)

|fffFFF| (1)

|ffhBJA| (1)

|ffhCJD| (8)

|ffhCJH| (1)

|ffhCSD| (2)

|fmbBJA| (2)

|fmdBJA| (4)

|fmdCJD| (3)

|fmdCJDmaj| (1)

|focBUA| (1)

|fxhCUD| (1)

|mffBJA| (1)

001.2A P three

{r}   flap

No Response (4)

<free> (2)

<shree> (2)

<sree> (7)

<s{r}ee> (1)

<th(r)ee> (1)

<thrai> (1)

<three> (644)

<th{r}ee> (304)

<tree> (24)

<t{r}ee> (1)

001.2 S three

No Response (0)

|ABA| (6)

|ABAeaa| (1)

|ABAeaj| (37)

|ABAeam| (1)

|ABC| (11)

|ABCeaj| (2)

|ABCeak| (1)

|ABE| (315)

|ABEeaj| (3)

|ABI| (28)

|ABIeaa| (1)

|AGA| (6)

|AGAeaa| (3)

|AGAeaj| (8)

|AGC| (5)

|AGCeaj| (1)

|AGE| (95)

|AGG| (1)

|AGI| (2)

|BBA| (17)

|BBD| (1)

|BBDeaj| (1)

|BGA| (11)
|BGE| (1)
|abcABA| (14)
|abcABE| (1)
|abcBBA| (2)
|abeABA| (3)
|abiABA| (8)
|abiABE| (23)
|abiABI| (1)
|agiABE| (1)
|daaABA| (7)
|daaABC| (9)
|daaABE| (1)
|daaABG| (1)
|daaABI| (1)
|daaBBA| (1)
|dabABA| (15)
|dabABB| (2)
|dabABC| (5)
|dabABE| (1)
|dabBBJ| (1)
|dacABA| (2)
|dacABC| (1)
|dacABE| (1)
|dacBBA| (8)
|dacBBJ| (1)
|daeABA| (6)
|daeABC| (2)
|daeABE| (106)
|daeAGE| (9)
|dagABE| (4)
|dahABE| (1)
|dahBBA| (3)
|dahBBJ| (4)
|daiABA| (3)
|daiABE| (9)
|daiABI| (2)
|daiAGE| (1)
|dcaABA| (2)
|dcaBBA| (2)
|dcaBBJ| (1)
|dcbBBA| (1)
|dccABA| (2)
|dceABE| (1)
|dceBBA| (3)
|dciABA| (1)
|eaaBBA| (45)
|eaaBBD| (1)
|eaaBGA| (3)
|eacBBA| (5)
|eacBBD| (1)
|eacBGD| (1)
|eadABA| (2)
|eadBBD| (1)
|eaeBBJ| (3)
|eahBBA| (17)
|eahBBD| (1)
|eahBBJ| (1)
|eahBGA| (1)

|echBBA| (1)

001.2B P four
No Response (9)
<faw(r)> (1)
<faw[r]> (5)
<fawr> (9)
<foe(r)> (175)
<foe[r]> (354)
<foer> (506)
<foewA=14> (3)
<foewR=14> (3)
<foo[r]> (1)
<fue[r]> (1)
<fur> (1)

001.3A P five
{v} devoiced
No Response (12)
<fav> (1)
<fie(v)> (80)
<fiev> (838)
<fie{v}> (22)

001.3 S five
No Response (0)
|PCAeaa| (2)
|PCAmaj| (1)
|PCHeaj| (1)
|PFGdaj| (1)
|RAA| (8)
|RAAdaa| (1)
|RAAeaa| (2)
|RAAead| (1)
|RAAeaj| (10)
|RAAeak| (1)
|RAAkaj| (9)
|RAAmaj| (1)
|RAAmak| (3)
|RAB| (3)
|RABeaa| (5)
|RABeaj| (15)
|RABkab| (1)
|RABkaj| (12)
|RAE| (4)
|RAEdab| (1)
|RAEeaa| (35)
|RAEeab| (2)
|RAEeaj| (72)
|RAEeak| (1)
|RAEeal| (2)
|RAEkaj| (63)
|RAEkak| (2)
|RAEkal| (1)
|RAEkan| (1)
|RAEkap| (1)
|RAEmaj| (4)
|RAEmam| (1)
|RAG| (3)
|RAGdan| (1)
|RAGeaa| (21)
|RAGeab| (2)

|RAGeaj| (58)
|RAGeal| (1)
|RAGkaj| (5)
|RAIeaj| (2)
|RAIkak| (1)
|RCA| (50)
|RCAdaj| (1)
|RCAeaa| (11)
|RCAeaj| (54)
|RCAkaj| (40)
|RCAmaj| (12)
|RCAraj| (2)
|RCB| (9)
|RCBeaa| (16)
|RCBeaj| (31)
|RCBkaj| (15)
|RCBmaj| (2)
|RCE| (13)
|RCEbbj| (1)
|RCEeaa| (29)
|RCEeab| (2)
|RCEeaj| (45)
|RCEeal| (6)
|RCEeaq| (1)
|RCEkab| (1)
|RCEkaj| (86)
|RCEkak| (5)
|RCEkan| (3)
|RCEmaj| (9)
|RCEraj| (1)
|RCG| (2)
|RCGeaa| (39)
|RCGeaj| (39)
|RCGkaj| (5)
|RCGkak| (1)
|RCGmaj| (5)
|RDGrdbedj| (1)
|SADmaj| (1)
|SAFeaj| (3)
|SCAdaj| (1)
|SCAeaj| (1)
|SCAmaj| (1)
|SCDeaa| (1)
|SCDmaj| (2)
|SCFeaa| (3)
|SCFeal| (1)
|SCFmaj| (1)
|SKBeda| (1)

001.3B P six
{s} palatal
No Response (22)
<seeks> (1)
<shiksh> (1)
<sik(s)> (15)
<siks> (857)
<siksh> (1)
<sik{s}> (17)
<thiks> (1)
<thikth> (1)

<t{s}ik{s}> (1)
<{s}iks> (12)
<{s}ik{s}> (6)

001.4A P seven
{v}   bilabial
No Response (28)
<se(v)M=14> (1)
<se(vI)m> (33)
<se(vN)> (1)
<sebM=14> (209)
<sebN=14> (4)
<sedN=14> (1)
<sevId=14> (1)
<sevM=14> (8)
<sevN=14> (720)
<sev[N]=14> (3)
<sevin=13> (1)
<sevun=13> (2)
<se{v}M=14> (51)
<se{v}N=14> (20)
<shaivM=14> (1)
<shevN=14> (1)
<sibM=14> (5)
<sivM=14> (2)
<sivN=14> (9)
<siv[N]=14> (1)
<theven=13> (1)
<thibM=14> (1)
<tsevN=14> (1)

001.4B P eight
No Response (23)
<ai(t)> (2)
<ait> (884)
<eet> (1)
<et> (5)
<hait> (2)

001.4 S eight
No Response (0)
|GAAeaj| (1)
|GB1eaa| (1)
|GB1eaj| (1)
|GB1eal| (1)
|GBA| (1)
|GBAbbj| (1)
|GBAdae| (3)
|GBAea2| (3)
|GBAeaa| (16)
|GBAeab| (1)
|GBAeaj| (47)
|GBAeak| (1)
|GBAeas| (1)
|GBBeab| (1)
|GBBeaj| (23)
|GBC| (2)
|GBCdaa| (1)
|GBCdae| (6)
|GBCeaa| (39)
|GBCeab| (1)
|GBCeac| (1)

|GBCeaj| (49)
|GBDdab| (1)
|GBE| (4)
|GBEeaa| (196)
|GBEeab| (2)
|GBEeaj| (192)
|GBEeak| (1)
|GBEeal| (1)
|GBFeaa| (1)
|GBFeaj| (8)
|GBGeaa| (1)
|GBGeab| (1)
|GBGeaj| (10)
|GBI| (5)
|GBIdae| (1)
|GBIeaa| (51)
|GBIeab| (2)
|GBIeac| (1)
|GBIeaj| (49)
|GBIeak| (1)
|GBImaj| (1)
|GBSeaa| (4)
|GBSeaj| (1)
|GBTeaj| (5)
|GBU| (1)
|GBUeaa| (6)
|GBUeaj| (2)
|GBW| (1)
|GBWeaa| (4)
|GBWeaj| (3)
|GG1| (1)
|GG1bbj| (1)
|GG1eaj| (1)
|GGA| (3)
|GGAdaj| (1)
|GGAeaa| (4)
|GGAead| (1)
|GGAeaj| (21)
|GGAeak| (2)
|GGCeaa| (4)
|GGCeaj| (3)
|GGEdae| (1)
|GGEeaa| (24)
|GGEeaj| (22)
|GGEeak| (1)
|GGFeaj| (2)
|GGI| (2)
|GGIbbj| (1)
|GGIeaa| (8)
|GGIeaj| (7)
|GGSeaa| (1)
|GGSeaj| (2)
|GGTeaj| (1)
|GGUeaj| (1)
|GGWeaj| (1)
|HAHeaj| (2)
|KABeaa| (2)
|KABeaj| (2)
|KACeaa| (2)

|KAGmaj| (2)
|KASabaeaa| (1)
|KATeaa| (1)
|KBBeaj| (1)
|KC1eaa| (1)
|KC1eaj| (1)
|KCAeaa| (5)
|KCAeak| (1)
|KCSeaa| (6)
|KCSeaj| (3)
|KCUeaa| (2)
|KCWeaa| (1)
|KGA| (1)
|OABeaa| (1)
|OABeaj| (1)
|gbaGBF| (1)
|gbcGBAabj| (1)
|kabGBA| (2)
|kacGGB| (1)

001.5A P nine
No Response (36)
<nan> (1)
<nie(n)> (1)
<nie[n]> (13)
<nien> (866)

001.5A S nine
No Response (0)
|ODImdj| (1)
|PCHeaa| (1)
|PKAeda| (2)
|RAA| (4)
|RAAdaj| (1)
|RAAeaa| (4)
|RAAeaj| (3)
|RAAeak| (1)
|RAAkaj| (4)
|RAAkak| (1)
|RAAmaj| (1)
|RABdab| (1)
|RABeaa| (2)
|RABeab| (1)
|RABeaj| (18)
|RABkaj| (15)
|RABkak| (2)
|RAE| (4)
|RAEeaa| (46)
|RAEeab| (4)
|RAEeaj| (54)
|RAEeal| (1)
|RAEkaj| (60)
|RAEkak| (1)
|RAEkan| (1)
|RAEmaj| (1)
|RAEmak| (1)
|RAG| (2)
|RAGdaj| (1)
|RAGeaa| (36)
|RAGeab| (2)
|RAGeaj| (38)

|RAGkaj| (3)
|RAGkak| (1)
|RCA| (36)
|RCAeaa| (2)
|RCAeaj| (27)
|RCAeam| (1)
|RCAkaj| (25)
|RCAmaa| (1)
|RCAmaj| (7)
|RCB| (9)
|RCBeaa| (12)
|RCBeaj| (21)
|RCBkaj| (11)
|RCBmaj| (3)
|RCE| (15)
|RCEeaa| (24)
|RCEeaj| (35)
|RCEeak| (1)
|RCEkab| (1)
|RCEkaj| (61)
|RCEkak| (1)
|RCEmaj| (2)
|RCGeaa| (29)
|RCGeab| (1)
|RCGeaj| (31)
|RCGeal| (1)
|RCGkaj| (6)
|RCGmaj| (2)
|RCGmak| (1)
|RDA| (2)
|RDAeda| (3)
|RDAedj| (3)
|RDAkdj| (2)
|RDAmdj| (10)
|RDBkdj| (1)
|RDBmdj| (1)
|RDE| (1)
|RDEdde| (1)
|RDEeda| (8)
|RDEedj| (5)
|RDEedl| (2)
|RDEkdj| (18)
|RDEkdk| (4)
|RDEkdn| (1)
|RDEmdj| (8)
|RDEmdk| (2)
|RDGeda| (1)
|RDGedb| (1)
|RDGedj| (1)
|RDGkdj| (1)
|RDGmdm| (1)
|RDIedl| (1)
|RKA| (5)
|RKAeda| (11)
|RKAedj| (15)
|RKAedl| (1)
|RKAkda| (1)
|RKAkdj| (6)
|RKAmdj| (19)

|RKArdp| (1)
|RKBeda| (1)
|RKBedj| (3)
|RKBkdj| (2)
|RKE| (4)
|RKEeda| (5)
|RKEedj| (4)
|RKEedl| (3)
|RKEkdj| (27)
|RKEkdk| (2)
|RKEkdn| (1)
|RKEmdj| (8)
|RKEmdk| (1)
|RKEmdm| (1)
|RKGeda| (2)
|RKGedj| (3)
|RKGkdj| (2)
|RKGkdn| (1)
|RKGmdk| (1)
|RKIkdj| (1)
|SADmaj| (1)
|SAFeaa| (1)
|SAFeab| (1)
|SAFeaj| (3)
|SAFmak| (1)
|SCFeaa| (1)
|SCFeab| (1)
|SDDeda| (1)
|SFGeaj| (1)
|SKAeda| (1)
|SKAedj| (3)
|SKAmdj| (2)
|SKBmdj| (1)
|SKDedj| (1)
|SKDmdj| (1)
|TCDeaj| (1)

001.5B P ten
No Response (23)
<tain> (5)
<tan> (2)
<te[n]> (3)
<ten> (516)
<ti[n]> (2)
<tin> (428)
<tind> (1)

001.5B S ten
No Response (0)
|DAA| (1)
|DAAmaj| (4)
|DAB| (9)
|DABdac| (4)
|DABeak| (1)
|DABmaj| (5)
|DAC| (5)
|DACdab| (8)
|DACmaa| (1)
|DACmaj| (2)
|DACmak| (1)
|DAE| (58)

|DAEeaj| (4)
|DAEeak| (2)
|DAEeal| (2)
|DAEmaj| (12)
|DAEmak| (2)
|DAG| (12)
|DAGeaj| (1)
|DAGmaj| (5)
|DAI| (57)
|DAIeaj| (1)
|DAImaj| (5)
|DCBeak| (1)
|DCBmaj| (1)
|DCE| (4)
|DCEeaj| (2)
|DCEeak| (1)
|DCEmaj| (3)
|DCGmaj| (1)
|DCI| (1)
|DCIeaj| (2)
|DCImaj| (3)
|DCImak| (1)
|DDA| (2)
|DDAmdj| (3)
|DDB| (1)
|DDBmdj| (3)
|DDC| (6)
|DDCddb| (1)
|DDE| (3)
|DDEmdj| (1)
|DDFmdj| (1)
|DDG| (2)
|DDI| (9)
|DDImdj| (4)
|DKA| (6)
|DKAedj| (1)
|DKBeda| (1)
|DKBedj| (1)
|DKBkdj| (1)
|DKBmdj| (4)
|DKC| (3)
|DKCmdj| (1)
|DKE| (1)
|EAA| (1)
|EABeaa| (1)
|EABeac| (1)
|EAC| (5)
|EACeab| (10)
|EACeaf| (1)
|EADmaj| (1)
|EAFmaj| (1)
|EAH| (4)
|EAHeab| (2)
|EAHmaj| (1)
|ECC| (1)
|EDC| (1)
|GGCkaj| (1)
|GKA| (1)
|KAA| (38)

|KAAeaj| (6)
|KAAkak| (1)
|KAAmaj| (10)
|KAB| (77)
|KABdaj| (1)
|KABeaj| (8)
|KABmaj| (11)
|KABmak| (9)
|KAC| (16)
|KACmaj| (11)
|KAD| (2)
|KADmaj| (1)
|KAE| (56)
|KAEdan| (1)
|KAEmaj| (10)
|KAEmak| (1)
|KAF| (69)
|KAFdaj| (1)
|KAFeaj| (6)
|KAFgbj| (1)
|KAFmaj| (6)
|KAFmak| (1)
|KAG| (2)
|KAGmaj| (3)
|KAI| (2)
|KAImaj| (3)
|KBAmaj| (1)
|KCA| (11)
|KCAdan| (1)
|KCAeaj| (2)
|KCAmaj| (1)
|KCBmaj| (1)
|KCBmak| (1)
|KCCeaj| (2)
|KCCkab| (1)
|KCCmaj| (3)
|KCE| (1)
|KCF| (3)
|KCFmaj| (1)
|KCGkaj| (1)
|KDA| (25)
|KDAedj| (1)
|KDAkdk| (2)
|KDAmdj| (8)
|KDB| (33)
|KDBmdj| (6)
|KDC| (6)
|KDCmdj| (2)
|KDD| (2)
|KDE| (13)
|KDF| (66)
|KDFedj| (3)
|KDFedl| (1)
|KDFmdj| (4)
|KDG| (3)
|KDI| (1)
|KKA| (14)
|KKAmdj| (3)
|KKB| (10)

|KKBmdj| (3)
|KKC| (1)
|KKCkda| (2)
|KKCkdj| (1)
|KKCmdj| (1)
|KKD| (2)
|KKE| (4)
|KKEmdj| (1)
|KKF| (2)
|KQB| (1)
|KQCkda| (1)

001.6A P eleven
{v} bilabial
No Response (73)
<(i)le(vI)m> (12)
<(i)lebM=14> (122)
<(i)lebN=14> (2)
<(i)levM=14> (3)
<(i)levN=14> (286)
<(i)lev[N]=14> (3)
<(i)le{v}M=14> (25)
<(i)le{v}N=14> (13)
<(i)libM=14> (1)
<AlaivN=414> (1)
<Ale(vI)m=41> (3)
<AlebM=414> (26)
<AlevN=414> (146)
<Alev[N]=414> (1)
<Ale{v}M=414> (2)
<Ale{v}N=414> (2)
<Ile(vI)m=41> (2)
<IlebM=414> (21)
<IlevAd=414> (1)
<IlevM=414> (1)
<IlevN=414> (192)
<Ilev[N]=414> (1)
<Ile{v}N=414> (2)
<IlivN=414> (2)
<ailevN=314> (1)
<eelavN=314> (1)
<eelevN=134> (4)
<eelevN=314> (37)
<elevN=314> (2)
<ilebM=314> (3)
<ilevN=134> (2)
<ilevN=214> (1)
<ilevN=314> (32)
<ulevN=314> (1)
001.6B P twelve
{v} devoiced
No Response (42)
<tve[1]v> (1)
<twa(1)v> (1)
<twai(1)v> (3)
<twai[1]v> (9)
<twailv> (3)
<twail{v}> (2)
<twal(v)> (1)
<twalv> (1)

<twe(1)v> (36)
<twe(lv)> (1)
<twe[1](v)> (7)
<twe[1]v> (357)
<twe[1]{v}> (9)
<twel(v)> (73)
<twelb> (2)
<twelf> (3)
<twelv> (411)
<twel{v}> (23)
<twerv> (1)
<twi(1)v> (2)
<twi[1](v)> (1)
<twi[1]v> (9)
<twil(v)> (1)
<twilv> (2)
<twulv> (1)
001.7A P thirteen
{r} weakly retroflex
No Response (102)
<surteen=13> (1)
<thertteen=13> (1)
<the{r}tteen=13> (1)
<thu[r]teen=13> (120)
<thu[r]teen=31> (7)
<thu[r]ttN=14> (1)
<thu[r]tteen=13> (82)
<thu[r]tteen=31> (5)
<thurtee[n]=13> (2)
<thurteen=11> (2)
<thurteen=13> (235)
<thurteen=21> (3)
<thurteen=31> (29)
<thurttN=14> (1)
<thurtteen=11> (1)
<thurtteen=13> (225)
<thurtteen=21> (6)
<thurtteen=31> (10)
<thu{r}tN=14> (1)
<thu{r}teen=13> (56)
<thu{r}teen=21> (1)
<thu{r}teen=31> (3)
<thu{r}tteen=13> (41)
<thu{r}tteen=21> (2)
<thu{r}tteen=31> (1)
<tu[r]teen=13> (1)
<turteen=13> (1)
<tu{r}teen=13> (1)
<tu{r}teen=31> (1)
001.7B P fourteen
{r} weakly retroflex
No Response (82)
<faw(r)teen=13> (1)
<faw(r)tteen=13> (1)
<faw[r]tN=14> (2)
<faw[r]teen=13> (3)
<faw[r]tteen=13> (1)
<fawrteen=13> (3)
<fawrttN=14> (1)

<fawrtteen=13> (8)
<faw{r}teen=13> (2)
<faw{r}tteen=13> (2)
<foe(r)tN=14> (1)
<foe(r)teen=11> (1)
<foe(r)teen=13> (144)
<foe(r)teen=21> (3)
<foe(r)teen=31> (11)
<foe(r)ttN=14> (1)
<foe(r)tteen=11> (1)
<foe(r)tteen=13> (66)
<foe(r)tteen=21> (1)
<foe(r)tteen=31> (6)
<foe(r)tten=13> (1)
<foe[r]tN=14> (1)
<foe[r]teen=13> (79)
<foe[r]teen=21> (1)
<foe[r]teen=31> (2)
<foe[r]ttN=14> (1)
<foe[r]tteen=13> (101)
<foe[r]tteen=21> (1)
<foerteen=11> (6)
<foerteen=13> (176)
<foerteen=21> (2)
<foerteen=31> (14)
<foertteen=13> (125)
<foertteen=21> (4)
<foertteen=31> (1)
<foe{r}teen=13> (59)
<foe{r}teen=31> (2)
<foe{r}ttN=14> (1)
<foe{r}tteen=13> (38)
<foe{r}tteen=21> (1)
<foe{r}tteen=31> (1)
<foo[r]tteen=13> (1)
<hoerteen=31> (1)

001.8A P twenty
{t} flap
No Response (73)
<fwen(t)I=14> (1)
<twe(n){t}I=14> (3)
<twe[n](t)I=14> (1)
<twe[n]{t}I=14> (6)
<twen(t)A=14> (1)
<twen(t)I=14> (232)
<twen(t)ee=13> (1)
<twen(tI)> (1)
<twendI=14> (2)
<twennI=14> (80)
<twennee=13> (8)
·<twentI=14> (116)
<twentee=13> (14)
<twen{t}I=14> (102)
<twi[n]{t}I=14> (2)
<twin(t)I=14> (133)
<twin(t)ee=13> (1)
<twinnI=14> (62)
<twinnee=13> (1)
<twintI=14> (52)

<twintee=13> (1)
<twin{t}I=14> (30)
<twoon(t)I=14> (2)
<twoontI=14> (1)
<twu(n){t}I=14> (2)
<twun(t)I=14> (30)
<twun(t)ee=13> (1)
<twunnI=14> (13)
<twunnee=13> (1)
<twuntI=14> (13)
<twun{t}I=14> (3)

001.8B P twenty-seven
{t} flap
{v} bilabial
No Response (204)
<twe(n){t}IsevN=1434> (1)
<twe(n){t}IsevN=2414> (1)
<twe(n){t}Ise{v}M=3414> (1)
<twe[n](t)IsevN=2414> (1)
<twe[n]{t}IsebM=2414> (1)
<twe[n]{t}IsebM=3414> (1)
<twe[n]{t}IsevN=2414> (2)
<twe[n]{t}Ise{v}N=2414> (1)
<twen(n)Ise(vI)m=143> (1)
<twen(n)Ise(vI)m=341> (1)
<twen(t)AsebM=2414> (1)
<twen(t)Ise(vI)m=341> (5)
<twen(t)IsebM=1414> (3)
<twen(t)IsebM=1434> (3)
<twen(t)IsebM=2414> (14)
<twen(t)IsebM=3414> (17)
<twen(t)IsebN=3414> (1)
<twen(t)Isef[N]=2414> (1)
<twen(t)IsevN=1414> (4)
<twen(t)IsevN=1434> (7)
<twen(t)IsevN=2414> (44)
<twen(t)IsevN=3414> (73)
<twen(t)Isev[N]=2414> (2)
<twen(t)Isev[N]=3414> (1)
<twen(t)Ise{v}M=1434> (1)
<twen(t)Ise{v}M=3414> (9)
<twen(t)Ise{v}N=1434> (1)
<twen(t)Ise{v}N=2414> (1)
<twen(t)Ise{v}N=3414> (1)
<twen(t)eesebM=2314> (1)
<twen(tI)sevN=214> (2)
<twen(tI)sevN=314> (4)
<twennIse(vI)m=141> (1)
<twennIse(vI)m=341> (2)
<twennIsebM=1414> (1)
<twennIsebM=2414> (2)
<twennIsebM=3414> (2)
<twennIsevN=1414> (1)
<twennIsevN=1424> (1)
<twennIsevN=1434> (6)
<twennIsevN=2414> (19)
<twennIsevN=3414> (17)
<twennIse{v}M=2414> (1)
<twennIse{v}N=2414> (1)

<twennIsibM=2414> (1)
<twenneesebM=2314> (1)
<twenneesevN=1314> (1)
<twenneesevN=2314> (2)
<twent(I)sevN=314> (5)
<twent(I)se{v}M=314> (2)
<twentIse(vI)m=341> (1)
<twentIsebM=1434> (1)
<twentIsebM=2414> (2)
<twentIsebM=3414> (2)
<twentIsevN=1414> (4)
<twentIsevN=1434> (4)
<twentIsevN=2414> (29)
<twentIsevN=3414> (32)
<twentIse{v}M=3414> (1)
<twentIsivN=3414> (1)
<twenteesevN=1314> (1)
<twenteesevN=1324> (1)
<twenteesevN=2314> (5)
<twen{t}AsebM=3414> (1)
<twen{t}AsevN=3414> (2)
<twen{t}Ise(vI)m=341> (1)
<twen{t}IsebM=2414> (1)
<twen{t}IsebM=3414> (6)
<twen{t}IsebN=3414> (1)
<twen{t}IsevN=1414> (1)
<twen{t}IsevN=1434> (1)
<twen{t}IsevN=2414> (9)
<twen{t}IsevN=3414> (34)
<twen{t}Ise{v}M=3414> (3)
<twen{t}Ise{v}N=3414> (2)
<twen{t}IsivN=1414> (1)
<twi[n](t)IsevN=3414> (1)
<twi[n]{t}IsevN=2414> (1)
<twi[n]{t}IsevN=3414> (2)
<twin(t)Ise(vI)m=341> (3)
<twin(t)Iseb(M)=341> (1)
<twin(t)IsebM=1414> (2)
<twin(t)IsebM=1434> (2)
<twin(t)IsebM=2414> (3)
<twin(t)IsebM=3414> (29)
<twin(t)IsebN=3414> (1)
<twin(t)IsevN=1414> (1)
<twin(t)IsevN=1424> (1)
<twin(t)IsevN=1434> (3)
<twin(t)IsevN=2414> (9)
<twin(t)IsevN=3414> (86)
<twin(t)Ise{v}N=3414> (1)
<twin(t)eesevN=2314> (1)
<twinnIsebM=1434> (1)
<twinnIsebM=3414> (3)
<twinnIsevN=1434> (3)
<twinnIsevN=2414> (6)
<twinnIsevN=3414> (31)
<twinnIsevin=3413> (1)
<twintIsebM=2414> (1)
<twintIsebM=3414> (1)
<twintIsevN=1434> (5)
<twintIsevN=2414> (3)

<twintIsevN=3414> (26)
<twin{t}IsebM=3414> (2)
<twin{t}IsevN=3414> (13)
<twin{t}Ise{v}M=2414> (1)
<twoon(t)IsevN=3414> (1)
<twoon(t)Ise{v}M=3414> (1)
<twoontIsevN=3414> (1)
<twu[n](t)IsevN=3414> (1)
<twun(t)IsebM=3414> (1)
<twun(t)IsevN=2414> (1)
<twun(t)IsevN=3414> (28)
<twun(t)Ise{v}M=3414> (10)
<twun(t)Ise{v}N=3414> (1)
<twun(t)IsivN=3414> (1)
<twun(t)eesevN=2314> (1)
<twundIsevN=3414> (2)
<twunnIsebM=1424> (1)
<twunnIsevM=3414> (1)
<twunnIsevN=1434> (1)
<twunnIsevN=2414> (1)
<twunnIsevN=3414> (7)
<twunnIse{v}N=3414> (2)
<twuntIsevM=1434> (1)
<twuntIsevM=3414> (1)
<twuntIsevN=2414> (1)
<twuntIsevN=3414> (7)
<twun{t}IsevN=3414> (1)

001A.1A P thirty
{r}   weakly retroflex
{t}   flap
{?}   glottal
No Response (57)
<dhu[r]tI=14> (1)
<dhurtI=14> (1)
<surtI=14> (1)
<sur{t}I=14> (1)
<thertI=14> (2)
<thu[r]dI=14> (2)
<thu[r]tI=14> (203)
<thu[r]tIz=14> (1)
<thu[r]{?}I=14> (1)
<thu[r]{t}I=14> (28)
<thur(t)I=14> (1)
<thurdI=14> (5)
<thurtI=14> (470)
<thurtIz=14> (2)
<thurtee=13> (10)
<thur{?}I=14> (1)
<thur{t}I=14> (56)
<thu{r}tI=14> (100)
<thu{r}tIz=14> (1)
<thu{r}{t}I=14> (27)
<tu[r]tI=14> (5)
<turtI=14> (4)
<tur{t}I=14> (2)
<tu{r}tI=14> (3)

001A.1B P forty
{r}   weakly retroflex
{t}   flap

{?}   glottal
No Response (66)
<faw(r)tI=14> (110)
<faw(r)tIz=14> (1)
<faw(r){t}I=14> (13)
<faw[r]tI=14> (62)
<faw[r]tee=13> (1)
<faw[r]{t}I=14> (20)
<fawr(t)I=14> (3)
<fawrtI=14> (88)
<fawrtIz=14> (1)
<fawrtee=13> (1)
<fawr{?}I=14> (1)
<fawr{t}I=14> (10)
<faw{r}tI=14> (28)
<faw{r}{t}I=14> (5)
<fo(r)tI=14> (3)
<foe(r)tI=14> (44)
<foe(r){t}I=14> (5)
<foe[r]tA=14> (1)
<foe[r]tI=14> (156)
<foe[r]{t}I=14> (13)
<foerdI=14> (1)
<foertI=14> (245)
<foertIz=14> (1)
<foertee=13> (2)
<foer{t}I=14> (16)
<foe{r}tI=14> (60)
<foe{r}tee=13> (1)
<foe{r}{t}I=14> (5)
<fortI=14> (9)
<fo{r}tI=14> (2)
<fo{r}{t}I=14> (1)
<furtI=14> (1)

001A.2A P seventy
{t}   flap
{v}   bilabial
No Response (92)
<se(vI)m(t)I=14> (1)
<se(vI)mdI=14> (1)
<se(vI)mtI=14> (21)
<se(vI)ndI=14> (2)
<se(vI)ntI=14> (2)
<seb(N)nI=14> (1)
<seb(N)tI=14> (1)
<sebM(tI)=14> (1)
<sebMdI=144> (61)
<sebMdIz=144> (1)
<sebMnI=144> (3)
<sebMtA=144> (1)
<sebMtI=144> (115)
<sebMtee=143> (1)
<sebM{t}I=144> (9)
<sebN(t)I=144> (1)
<sebN(tI)=14> (1)
<sebNdI=144> (4)
<sebNtI=144> (13)
<sebN{t}I=144> (5)
<sevN(t)I=144> (12)

<sevNdI=144> (109)
<sevNnI=144> (2)
<sevNtI=144> (375)
<sevNtee=143> (14)
<sevN{t}I=144> (17)
<sev[N]tI=144> (2)
<sev[N]{t}I=144> (3)
<se{v}MdI=144> (26)
<se{v}MtI=144> (12)
<se{v}M{t}I=144> (2)
<se{v}NdI=144> (8)
<se{v}NtI=144> (8)
<sib(N)mI=14> (1)
<sibMdI=144> (1)
<sibMtI=144> (3)
<sidN(t)I=144> (1)
<sivN(t)I=144> (2)
<sivNdI=144> (1)
<sivNtI=144> (2)
<sivN{t}I=144> (1)
<siv[N]tI=144> (1)
<si{v}MdI=144> (1)
<si{v}NtI=144> (1)
<sub(N)nI=14> (1)
<subMtI=144> (1)

001A.2B P hundred
{R}   weakly retroflex
{r}   weakly retroflex
{t}   flap
{?}   glottal
No Response (55)
<(h)und(r)Ad=14> (1)
<(h)undRd=14> (1)
<ho[n]d(r)At=14> (1)
<ho[n]dRd=14> (1)
<ho[n]drId=14> (1)
<hon(d)Rd=14> (1)
<hon(d){R}d=14> (1)
<hon(dr)I(d)=14> (1)
<hon(dr)Id=14> (1)
<hond(r)Ad=14> (7)
<hond(r)Id=14> (1)
<hondRd=14> (9)
<hondRt=14> (3)
<hondrAd=14> (1)
<hondrId=14> (7)
<hond{R}d=14> (2)
<hon{t}(r)Ad=14> (2)
<hoon(dr)Ad=14> (1)
<hu[n]{t}(r)A(d)=14> (1)
<hu[n]{t}(r)Ad=14> (1)
<hun(d)Rd=14> (30)
<hun(d)Rt=14> (9)
<hun(d)[R]d=14> (1)
<hun(d)rAd=14> (1)
<hun(d)rI(d)=14> (1)
<hun(d)rId=14> (1)
<hun(d)red=13> (1)
<hun(d){R}d=14> (10)

<hun(d){R}t=14> (2)
<hun(d){t}Ad=14> (1)
<hun(dr)Ad=14> (13)
<hun(dr)At=14> (1)
<hun(dr)I(d)=14> (1)
<hun(dr)Id=14> (3)
<hun(dr)It=14> (1)
<hund(r)Ad=14> (66)
<hund(r)Adz=14> (1)
<hund(r)At=14> (2)
<hund(r)Id=14> (69)
<hund(r)Idz=14> (1)
<hund(r)It=14> (1)
<hundR(d)=14> (3)
<hundRd=14> (151)
<hundRdz=14> (1)
<hundRt=14> (26)
<hundR{?}=14> (1)
<hundrAd=14> (50)
<hundrI(d)=14> (2)
<hundrId=14> (292)
<hundrIdz=14> (2)
<hundrIt=14> (8)
<hundrI{?}=14> (1)
<hundrRd=14> (2)
<hundred=13> (3)
<hundr{R}d=14> (4)
<hundu{r}d=13> (1)
<hund{R}d=14> (75)
<hund{R}dz=14> (2)
<hund{R}t=14> (1)
<hund{t}Ad=14> (1)
<hund{t}Id=14> (1)
<hund{t}{R}d=14> (1)
<hunjrId=14> (2)
<hunn(r)Ad=14> (2)
<hunn(r)Id=14> (1)
<hunn(r)Nt=14> (1)
<hunnRd=14> (4)
<hunnRt=14> (1)
<hunt(r)Id=14> (1)
<hun{?}Rd=14> (1)
<hun{t}(r)Ad=14> (20)
<hun{t}(r)At=14> (1)
<hun{t}(r)Id=14> (3)
<hun{t}Rd=14> (18)
<hun{t}Rt=14> (1)
<hun{t}rId=14> (2)
<hun{t}{R}d=14> (9)

001A.2C P thousand
　{?}　glottal
　No Response (112)
<dhowzN(d)=14> (4)
<thowdN(d)=14> (9)
<thowdhN(d)=14> (7)
<thowdzN(d)=14> (1)
<thowsN(d)=14> (4)
<thowzN(d)=14> (693)
<thowzN(d)z=14> (19)

<thowzNd=14> (42)
<thowzNt=14> (2)
<thowzN{?}=14> (1)
<thowz[N](d)=14> (1)
<thowzhN(d)=14> (7)
<thowzundz=13> (1)
<thow{?}N(d)=14> (17)
<thow{?}Nt=14> (1)
<towzN(d)=14> (7)
<towzN(d)z=14> (2)

001A.2D P million
　{d}　flap
　No Response (283)
<me(1)yN=14> (1)
<meelyN=14> (1)
<mi(1)yNt=14> (1)
<mi(1)yNz=14> (6)
<mi(1)yN=14> (79)
<mi[1]y[N]=14> (1)
<mi[1]yNz=14> (2)
<mi[1]yN=14> (34)
<milIyN=144> (1)
<milyIt=14> (1)
<milyM=14> (1)
<milyN=14> (473)
<milyNt=14> (1)
<milyNz=14> (22)
<mily[N]=14> (5)
<mil{d}N=14> (2)
<mi{d}yN=14> (1)

001A.3A P first
　{r}　weakly retroflex
　No Response (55)
<firs(t)> (1)
<foorst> (1)
<fu[r](s)t> (1)
<fu[r]s(t)> (107)
<fu[r]st> (99)
<furs(t)> (225)
<fursh(t)> (4)
<fursht> (6)
<furst> (349)
<fu{r}s(t)> (45)
<fu{r}st> (66)

001A.3B P second
　{?}　glottal
　No Response (111)
<sakN(d)=14> (8)
<sakNt=14> (13)
<sekN(d)=14> (387)
<sekNG(d)=14> (2)
<sekNd=14> (53)
<sekNt=14> (332)
<sekN{?}=14> (2)
<sek[N](d)=14> (3)
<sek[N]{?}=14> (1)
<sekawnt=13> (1)
<sigN(d)=14> (1)
<sikN(d)=14> (1)

<sookNt=14> (1)
<thekNt=14> (1)

001A.3C P third
　{r}　weakly retroflex
　{?}　glottal
　No Response (138)
<dhu[r]d> (1)
<dhurd> (1)
<dhu{r}d> (1)
<therd> (1)
<third> (1)
<thoord> (1)
<thu[r]d> (180)
<thurd> (489)
<thurdz> (1)
<thurt> (2)
<thur{?}> (1)
<thu{r}d> (93)
<thu{r}t> (1)
<tu[r]d> (2)
<turd> (2)
<tu{r}d> (1)

001A.3 S third
　No Response (4)
|DFImla| (1)
|EMAeaj| (1)
|EMDeaj| (1)
|FMAmea| (1)
|KCEmea| (1)
|KFEmaj| (1)
|LAA| (5)
|LAAdaj| (1)
|LAAeaa| (1)
|LAAeaj| (8)
|LAAeal| (1)
|LAAmaj| (1)
|LAAmak| (1)
|LAAmea| (17)
|LAAmej| (6)
|LABmaj| (1)
|LABmea| (3)
|LACmea| (9)
|LADmea| (7)
|LAE| (1)
|LAEeaj| (1)
|LAElabmea| (1)
|LAEmak| (1)
|LAEmea| (12)
|LAH| (1)
|LAImea| (1)
|LCA| (12)
|LCAeaj| (8)
|LCAeal| (2)
|LCAmak| (1)
|LCAmea| (8)
|LCAmej| (1)
|LCBeaj| (1)
|LCBmea| (2)
|LCBmej| (1)

|LCDeaj| (1)
|LCDeal| (1)
|LCDmea| (3)
|LCE| (1)
|LCEeal| (1)
|LCEmea| (4)
|LCEmej| (1)
|LCEmpa| (1)
|LCFmej| (1)
|LCGmaj| (1)
|LEA| (22)
|LEAmaj| (7)
|LEAmak| (2)
|LEAmej| (2)
|LED| (1)
|LEE| (6)
|LEG| (1)
|LFA| (4)
|LFAeaj| (20)
|LFAkaj| (1)
|LFAmaj| (19)
|LFAmak| (7)
|LFAmea| (4)
|LFAmej| (4)
|LFAmfk| (1)
|LFBeaj| (1)
|LFBmaj| (1)
|LFBmea| (1)
|LFBmej| (1)
|LFBmejeaj| (1)
|LFCeaj| (3)
|LFCkak| (2)
|LFDeaj| (1)
|LFDmej| (1)
|LFE| (2)
|LFEeal| (1)
|LFEmea| (2)
|LFGeaj| (1)
|LFHeaj| (1)
|LLA| (2)
|LLAmaj| (1)
|LLB| (1)
|LLEmaj| (1)
|LMA| (6)
|LMAeaa| (1)
|LMAeaj| (34)
|LMAeal| (1)
|LMAmaj| (34)
|LMAmak| (8)
|LMAmea| (3)
|LMAmej| (4)
|LMAmfj| (4)
|LMAmpa| (1)
|LMBeaj| (2)
|LME| (1)
|LMEmea| (4)
|LMGeaj| (1)
|LPA| (10)
|LPAmaj| (3)

|LPE| (1)
|LYA| (3)
|LYAeaj| (3)
|LYAmaj| (1)
|LYAmea| (1)
|MCAeaa| (3)
|MCAeaj| (2)
|MCCeaj| (1)
|MEA| (222)
|MEAmaj| (1)
|MEAmea| (1)
|MEAnca| (1)
|MEB| (2)
|MEC| (3)
|MED| (19)
|MEE| (4)
|MEF| (1)
|MEH| (4)
|MEI| (1)
|MLA| (202)
|MLAmaj| (4)
|MLB| (7)
|MLC| (3)
|MLD| (4)
|MLE| (8)
|MLS| (1)
|MMA| (2)
|MPA| (12)
|MPB| (1)
|MRA| (1)
|MYA| (7)
|MYB| (1)
|MYD| (1)
|NADmea| (1)
|NCDmea| (1)
|PABmea| (1)
|PAJmea| (1)

001A.3D P fourth
{r}   weakly retroflex
No Response (160)
<faw[r]th> (4)
<fawrth> (7)
<faw{r}th> (1)
<foe(r)dh> (1)
<foe(r)f> (7)
<foe(r)s> (1)
<foe(r)t> (1)
<foe(r)th> (69)
<foe(r)v> (1)
<foe(rth)> (3)
<foe[r](th)> (6)
<foe[r]f> (5)
<foe[r]s> (2)
<foe[r]t> (6)
<foe[r]th> (256)
<foer(th)> (6)
<foerf> (2)
<foers> (2)
<foert> (2)

<foerth> (278)
<foe{r}(th)> (1)
<foe{r}f> (1)
<foe{r}s> (1)
<foe{r}t> (2)
<foe{r}th> (94)
<foors> (1)

001A.3E P fifth
No Response (179)
<fi(f)s> (1)
<fi(f)th> (361)
<fi(fth)> (1)
<fif(th)> (196)
<fift> (79)
<fifth> (98)
<fisth> (1)
<fitth> (1)
<fiv(th)> (2)

001A.3F P sixth
No Response (181)
<seks(th)> (1)
<si(k)st> (1)
<sik(s)t> (1)
<sik(s)th> (12)
<sik(sth)> (7)
<siks(th)> (429)
<sikst> (81)
<siksth> (197)
<sikts> (2)
<siktth> (1)
<thik(s)th> (2)

001A.3G P seventh
{t}   flap
{v}   bilabial
No Response (182)
<se(vI)m(th)> (1)
<se(vI)mf> (1)
<se(vI)mth> (10)
<se(vI)nt> (2)
<sebM(th)=14> (13)
<sebMf=14> (1)
<sebMp=14> (1)
<sebMt=14> (7)
<sebMth=14> (69)
<sebN(th)=14> (1)
<sebNdh=14> (1)
<sebNf=14> (1)
<sebNt=14> (3)
<sebNth=14> (7)
<sev(N)th> (1)
<sevMt=14> (3)
<sevMth=14> (3)
<sevN(th)=14> (26)
<sevNdh=14> (1)
<sevNf=14> (1)
<sevNt=14> (68)
<sevNth=14> (451)
<sevNz=14> (1)
<sevN{t}=14> (1)

<sev[N](th)=14> (2)
<sev[N]th=14> (1)
<sevunth=13> (2)
<sewNth=14> (1)
<se{v}M(th)=14> (4)
<se{v}Mt=14> (2)
<se{v}Mth=14> (30)
<se{v}N(th)=14> (1)
<se{v}Nt=14> (1)
<se{v}Nth=14> (10)
<sibM(th)=14> (1)
<sivNth=14> (3)
<thebMth=14> (1)
<thevNth=14> (1)
<the{v}Nth=14> (1)

001A.3H P eighth
No Response (168)
<ais> (2)
<ait> (112)
<aith> (633)

001A.3I P ninth
No Response (212)
<nie(n)t> (1)
<nie(n)th> (7)
<nie[n](th)> (2)
<nie[n]t> (3)
<nie[n]th> (19)
<nien(th)> (44)
<nienIth=14> (1)
<niens> (2)
<nient> (59)
<nienth> (568)
<nients> (2)

001A.3J P tenth
No Response (203)
<tainth> (1)
<te(n)th> (1)
<te(n)ths> (1)
<te[n](th)> (1)
<te[n]t> (1)
<te[n]th> (1)
<ten(th)> (19)
<tent> (35)
<tenth> (342)
<tents> (1)
<ti[n]th> (3)
<tin(th)> (12)
<tint> (16)
<tinth> (283)

001A.4 P once
No Response (223)
<wawns> (1)
<wawnst> (1)
<wawnts> (3)
<wons> (11)
<wonst> (7)
<wonts> (28)
<wu[n]s> (2)
<wu[n]st> (1)

<wu[n]ts> (7)
<wun(s)> (1)
<wuns> (52)
<wunst> (85)
<wunt(s)> (4)
<wunth> (4)
<wunts> (504)
<wuntsh> (1)
<wuntst> (48)
<wunz> (1)

001A.5 P twice
No Response (167)
<trwies> (1)
<twies> (615)
<twiesh> (3)
<twiest> (166)
<twieth> (1)
<twiez> (1)

001A.6A P January
{d}   flap
{r}   weakly retroflex
No Response (115)
<chanyAwarI=1434> (1)
<dyanyIwerI=1434> (1)
<ja(n)yIwerI=1434> (1)
<ja[n]yAweree=1423> (1)
<ja[n]yIwe(r)I=1434> (1)
<ja[n]yIwu[r](I)=143> (1)
<ja[n]yIwurI=1434> (2)
<ja[n]yIwu{r}(I)=143> (1)
<jainyuewerI=1324> (1)
<jan(y)Awer(I)=143> (1)
<jan(y)AwerI=1434> (1)
<jan(y)AwirI=1434> (1)
<jan(y)AwurI=1434> (1)
<jan(y)IwarI=1434> (1)
<jan(y)IwerI=1434> (5)
<jan(y)Iwur(I)=143> (1)
<jan(y)IwurI=1424> (1)
<jan(y)IwurI=1434> (1)
<jan(yI)werI=134> (1)
<jan(yI)wurI=134> (3)
<jandyIwerI=1434> (1)
<janew(w)RI=1344> (1)
<janew(w)urI=1324> (1)
<janj(Iw)urI=124> (1)
<janjAwerI=1434> (1)
<janjAwerIs=1434> (1)
<janjIwe[r](I)=143> (1)
<janjIwer(I)=143> (1)
<janjIwerI=1434> (1)
<janjIwu[r](I)=143> (1)
<janjai(werI)=13> (1)
<janjuew(er)I=134> (1)
<janjuewerI=1324> (1)
<jany(Iw)erI=134> (3)
<jany(Iw)urI=134> (2)
<janyA(w)arI=1434> (1)
<janyA(w)erI=1434> (6)

<janyA(w)eree=1423> (1)
<janyAwarI=1434> (1)
<janyAwaree=1423> (1)
<janyAwa{r}(I)=143> (1)
<janyAwer(I)=143> (8)
<janyAwerA=1434> (2)
<janyAwerI=1424> (3)
<janyAwerI=1434> (152)
<janyAweree=1423> (9)
<janyAweri=1423> (1)
<janyAwe{r}(I)=143> (2)
<janyAwe{r}I=1434> (5)
<janyAwirI=1434> (2)
<janyAwu[r]I=1434> (1)
<janyAwur(I)=143> (1)
<janyAwurI=1424> (1)
<janyAwurI=1434> (8)
<janyAwu{r}(I)=143> (1)
<janyAwu{r}I=1434> (3)
<janyI(w)erI=1434> (10)
<janyIrerI=1434> (1)
<janyIwa(r)I=1434> (1)
<janyIwa(rI)=143> (1)
<janyIwai(rI)=143> (8)
<janyIwarI=1434> (8)
<janyIwe(r)I=1434> (9)
<janyIwe[r](I)=143> (3)
<janyIwe[r]I=1434> (6)
<janyIwer(I)=143> (4)
<janyIwerA=1434> (1)
<janyIwerI=1424> (1)
<janyIwerI=1434> (246)
<janyIwerI=3414> (1)
<janyIweree=1423> (2)
<janyIwe{d}I=1434> (2)
<janyIwe{r}(I)=143> (1)
<janyIwe{r}I=1434> (6)
<janyIwi[r]I=1434> (1)
<janyIwir(I)=143> (1)
<janyIwirI=1434> (1)
<janyIwi{r}I=1434> (1)
<janyIwu[r](I)=143> (1)
<janyIwur(I)=143> (7)
<janyIwurI=1434> (53)
<janyIwu{r}(I)=143> (10)
<janyIwu{r}I=1434> (11)
<janyewwurI=1324> (1)
<janyi(we)rA=124> (1)
<janyoowarI=1324> (1)
<janyoowaree=1323> (1)
<janyoowe(r)I=1324> (1)
<janyoowe[r](I)=132> (1)
<janyoowerI=1234> (1)
<janyoowerI=1324> (8)
<janyooweree=1323> (2)
<janyoowurI=1324> (1)
<janyue(w)RI=1344> (1)
<janyue(w)erI=1324> (3)
<janyue(w)urI=1324> (1)

<janyuewR(I)=134> (1)
<janyuewai(rI)=132> (1)
<janyuewai{d}I=1324> (1)
<janyuewarI=1324> (1)
<janyuewerI=1234> (1)
<janyuewerI=1324> (52)
<janyueweree=1323> (1)
<janyuewu[r]I=1324> (1)
<janyuewurI=1324> (9)
<janyuwerI=1324> (1)
<jen(y)AwerI=1434> (1)
<jen(yI)verI=134> (1)
<jenjuewurI=1324> (1)
<jeny(Iw)erI=134> (1)
<jenyAwerI=1434> (5)
<jenyAweree=1423> (1)
<jenyAwirI=1434> (1)
<jenyAwuree=1423> (1)
<jenyI(w)erI=1434> (1)
<jenyIwa(r)I=1434> (1)
<jenyIwai(rI)=143> (2)
<jenyIwarI=1434> (1)
<jenyIwe[r]I=1434> (1)
<jenyIwerI=1434> (17)
<jenyIwirI=1434> (1)
<jenyIwur(I)=143> (1)
<jenyIwurI=1434> (2)
<jenyue(w)RI=1344> (1)
<jenyuewerI=1234> (1)
<jenyuewerI=1324> (7)
<jenyuewurI=1324> (1)
<ji[n]yIwurI=1434> (1)
<jin(y)AwurI=1434> (1)
<jinew(w)erI=1234> (1)
<jinyIwerI=1434> (2)
<jinyIwurI=1434> (1)
<jinyuewe[r](I)=132> (1)
<jonyIwerI=1434> (1)
<jonyIwurI=1434> (2)
<yanyIwurI=1434> (1)
<yanyoowerI=1324> (1)
<zhan(yI)wurI=134> (1)

001A.6B P February

{b} fricative
{d} flap
{R} weakly retroflex
{r} weakly retroflex
{?} glottal
No Response (114)
<fav(r)Iwai(rI)=143> (1)
<fe(b)r(uew)er(I)=13> (1)
<fe(b)yAwerI=1434> (1)
<fe(b)yIwerI=1434> (1)
<feb(r)A(w)erI=1434> (3)
<feb(r)A(w)urI=1434> (1)
<feb(r)ArerI=1434> (1)
<feb(r)Avai(rI)=143> (1)
<feb(r)Awai(rI)=143> (1)
<feb(r)AwairI=1434> (1)

<feb(r)AwarI=1434> (1)
<feb(r)Awaree=1423> (1)
<feb(r)Awa{r}(I)=143> (1)
<feb(r)Awe(r)I=1434> (1)
<feb(r)Awe[r](I)=143> (1)
<feb(r)Awe[r]I=1434> (1)
<feb(r)Awer(I)=143> (9)
<feb(r)AwerI=1424> (3)
<feb(r)AwerI=1434> (92)
<feb(r)Aweree=1423> (1)
<feb(r)Awe{r}(I)=143> (2)
<feb(r)Awe{r}I=1434> (3)
<feb(r)AwirI=1434> (1)
<feb(r)Awu[r](I)=143> (1)
<feb(r)Awur(I)=143> (1)
<feb(r)AwurI=1434> (11)
<feb(r)Awu{r}I=1434> (1)
<feb(r)I(w)erI=1434> (2)
<feb(r)Iwa(r)I=1434> (1)
<feb(r)Iwai(rI)=143> (3)
<feb(r)IwarI=1434> (1)
<feb(r)Iwe(r)I=1434> (2)
<feb(r)Iwe(rI)=143> (1)
<feb(r)Iwe[r](I)=143> (3)
<feb(r)Iwe[r]I=1434> (1)
<feb(r)Iwer(I)=143> (3)
<feb(r)IwerA=1434> (1)
<feb(r)IwerI=1434> (49)
<feb(r)Iwe{r}I=1434> (1)
<feb(r)Iwu[r](I)=143> (1)
<feb(r)Iwu[r]I=1434> (2)
<feb(r)Iwur(I)=143> (1)
<feb(r)IwurI=1434> (35)
<feb(r)Iwu{r}I=1434> (2)
<feb(r)ewwerI=1324> (1)
<feb(r)ewwurI=1324> (3)
<feb(r)oowe[r](I)=132> (1)
<feb(r)oowerI=1234> (1)
<feb(r)oowerI=1324> (8)
<feb(r)oowirI=1324> (1)
<feb(r)ue(w)eree=1323> (1)
<feb(r)uewRI=1344> (1)
<feb(r)uewerI=1324> (12)
<feb(r)uewe{r}ee=1323> (1)
<feb(r)uewurI=1324> (3)
<feb(rue)wai(rI)=13> (1)
<feb(rue)we(r)I=134> (1)
<feb(rue)wer(I)=13> (3)
<feb(rue)werI=134> (11)
<feb(rue)weree=123> (2)
<feb(rue)we{r}(I)=13> (1)
<feb(rue)we{r}I=134> (2)
<feb(rue)wurI=134> (3)
<feb(ruew)urI=134> (1)
<febrAweri=1423> (1)
<febrAwurI=1434> (1)
<febrIwerI=1434> (2)
<febre(we)rI=134> (1)
<febroo(w)erI=1324> (2)

<febroowerI=1234> (1)
<februe(w)erI=1324> (6)
<februewerI=1324> (3)
<febvIwerI=1434> (1)
<febvIwur(I)=143> (1)
<febvIwu{r}(I)=143> (1)
<febyAw(er)A=144> (1)
<febyAwRee=1443> (1)
<febyAwarI=1434> (2)
<febyAwe(r)I=1434> (1)
<febyAwe[r]I=1434> (1)
<febyAwer(I)=143> (3)
<febyAwerA=1434> (1)
<febyAwerI=1424> (2)
<febyAwerI=1434> (69)
<febyAweree=1423> (6)
<febyAwe{r}(I)=143> (2)
<febyAwe{r}I=1434> (3)
<febyAwirI=1434> (1)
<febyAwurA=1434> (1)
<febyAwurI=1434> (6)
<febyI(w)erI=1434> (7)
<febyI(w)urI=1434> (2)
<febyIwai(rI)=143> (2)
<febyIwairI=1434> (1)
<febyIwai{r}(I)=143> (1)
<febyIwarI=1434> (1)
<febyIwe(r)I=1434> (2)
<febyIwe[r](I)=143> (1)
<febyIwe[r]I=1434> (3)
<febyIwer(I)=143> (2)
<febyIwerI=1434> (93)
<febyIwerI=2414> (1)
<febyIwe{r}I=1434> (1)
<febyIwi{r}(I)=143> (1)
<febyIwu[r](I)=143> (1)
<febyIwu[r]I=1434> (3)
<febyIwur(I)=143> (3)
<febyIwurI=1434> (25)
<febyIwurI=2414> (1)
<febyIwu{r}(I)=143> (4)
<febyIwu{r}I=1434> (3)
<febyRwurI=1434> (1)
<febyewwurI=1324> (1)
<febyoo(w)erI=1324> (1)
<febyoo(w)e{d}I=1324> (1)
<febyoowerI=1324> (7)
<febyooweree=1323> (1)
<febyoowurI=1324> (1)
<febyue(w)erI=1234> (1)
<febyue(w)erI=1324> (7)
<febyue(w)eree=1323> (1)
<febyue(w)urI=1324> (1)
<febyuewRI=1344> (1)
<febyuewai(rI)=132> (1)
<febyuewerI=1324> (59)
<febyuewe{r}I=1324> (1)
<febyuewurA=1324> (1)
<febyuewurI=1324> (14)

<febyui(w)erI=1324> (1)
<feby{R}werI=1424> (1)
<fev(r)AwerI=1434> (2)
<fev(r)Awu{r}(I)=143> (1)
<fev(r)IwerI=1434> (3)
<fev(r)Iweree=1423> (1)
<fev(r)Iwu[r]I=1434> (2)
<fev(r)IwurI=1434> (1)
<fev(r)Iwu{r}(I)=143> (1)
<fev(r)ue(w)erI=1324> (1)
<fev(r)uewerI=1324> (1)
<fev(rue)werI=134> (1)
<fev(rue)wu[r]I=134> (1)
<fev(rue)wurI=134> (1)
<fevyAwerI=1434> (1)
<fevyIwarI=1434> (1)
<fevyIwerI=1434> (4)
<fevyIwe{r}I=1434> (1)
<fevyuewerI=1324> (2)
<fe{?}(r)uewerI=1324> (1)
<fe{?}(rue)werI=134> (3)
<fe{b}(r)Awe(r)I=1434> (1)
<fe{b}(r)Awe[r]I=1434> (1)
<fe{b}(r)AwerI=1434> (12)
<fe{b}(r)Awe{r}I=1434> (2)
<fe{b}(r)Iwa(r)I=1434> (1)
<fe{b}(r)Iwe[r]I=1434> (1)
<fe{b}(r)IwerI=1434> (10)
<fe{b}(r)Iwe{r}(I)=143> (1)
<fe{b}(r)Iwe{r}I=1434> (1)
<fe{b}(r)Iwu[r](I)=143> (1)
<fe{b}(r)Iwu[r]I=1434> (1)
<fe{b}(r)Iwur(I)=143> (1)
<fe{b}(r)IwurI=1434> (4)
<fe{b}(r)Iwu{r}(I)=143> (3)
<fe{b}(r)Iwu{r}I=1434> (1)
<fe{b}(r)oowerI=1324> (2)
<fe{b}(r)ooweree=1323> (1)
<fe{b}(r)ue(w)erI=1324> (1)
<fe{b}(r)uewerI=1324> (2)
<fe{b}(r)ueweree=1323> (1)
<fe{b}(rue)werI=134> (2)
<fe{b}(rue)werI=214> (1)
<fe{b}(rue)wurI=134> (1)
<fe{b}(rue)wu{r}(I)=13> (1)
<fe{b}(ruew)urI=134> (1)
<fe{b}vIwur(I)=143> (1)
<fe{b}vIwurI=1434> (1)
<fe{b}vIwu{r}I=1434> (1)
<fe{b}yAwerI=1434> (4)
<fe{b}yAwur(I)=143> (1)
<fe{b}yIrerI=1434> (1)
<fe{b}yIwai(rI)=143> (1)
<fe{b}yIwarI=1434> (1)
<fe{b}yIwe[r](I)=143> (1)
<fe{b}yIwerI=1434> (7)
<fe{b}yIwe{r}(I)=143> (1)
<fe{b}yIwu[r]I=1434> (1)
<fe{b}yIwu{r}(I)=143> (1)

<fe{b}yuewerI=1324> (2)
<fib(r)Aw(er)ee=143> (1)
<fib(r)AwurI=1434> (1)
<fib(r)ue(w)er(I)=132> (1)
<fib(r)uewerI=1324> (1)
<fibyIwerI=1434> (1)
<fizh(r)AwirI=1434> (1)
<fi{b}yuewerI=1324> (1)
<fueeb(r)uewerI=31324> (1)

001A.6C P March
{o} low-back
{r} weakly retroflex
No Response (117)
<maw(r)ch> (11)
<maw[r]ch> (23)
<mawrch> (61)
<maw{r}ch> (15)
<mo(r)ch> (37)
<mo(r)sh> (1)
<mo[r]ch> (82)
<mo[r]t> (1)
<morch> (295)
<morsh> (2)
<mort> (1)
<mo{r}ch> (64)
<m{o}(r)ch> (16)
<m{o}[r]ch> (65)
<m{o}rch> (108)
<m{o}{r}ch> (21)

001A.6D P April
{d} flap
{r} devoiced
No Response (116)
<aip(r)L=14> (92)
<aip(r)[L]=14> (7)
<aipRl=14> (19)
<aiprL=14> (365)
<aiprRl=14> (5)
<aipr[L]=14> (20)
<aipril=13> (1)
<aipwL=14> (4)
<aip{d}L=14> (3)
<aip{r}L=14> (275)
<aip{r}Rl=14> (1)
<aip{r}[L]=14> (3)
<eprL=14> (3)
<ep{r}L=14> (2)

001A.6E P May
No Response (130)
<mai> (784)
<mieai=31> (1)

001A.6 S May
No Response (0)
|GACeaa| (1)
|GACeaj| (1)
|GBAdae| (2)
|GBAdag| (1)
|GBAeaa| (17)
|GBAeab| (2)

|GBAead| (1)
|GBAeaf| (1)
|GBAeaj| (29)
|GBAeak| (1)
|GBAecaabj| (1)
|GBAgbk| (2)
|GBBeaa| (2)
|GBBeaj| (8)
|GBCdae| (1)
|GBCeaa| (28)
|GBCeab| (3)
|GBCead| (1)
|GBCeaj| (41)
|GBCkab| (1)
|GBDeaj| (1)
|GBE| (2)
|GBEdae| (2)
|GBEeaa| (193)
|GBEeab| (4)
|GBEead| (1)
|GBEeae| (1)
|GBEeaf| (1)
|GBEeaj| (57)
|GBEeak| (2)
|GBEmaj| (1)
|GBFeaa| (1)
|GBFeab| (1)
|GBFeaj| (2)
|GBGeaa| (4)
|GBGeaj| (1)
|GBHeaj| (1)
|GBIeaa| (71)
|GBIeab| (4)
|GBIeaj| (35)
|GBIeal| (1)
|GGAeaa| (9)
|GGAeab| (1)
|GGAeaj| (27)
|GGBeaj| (4)
|GGBeak| (1)
|GGCbbj| (2)
|GGCeaa| (14)
|GGCeab| (1)
|GGCeaj| (14)
|GGCeak| (1)
|GGDeaa| (1)
|GGE| (2)
|GGEeaa| (107)
|GGEeab| (6)
|GGEeaj| (30)
|GGEgbbeaj| (1)
|GGFeaa| (2)
|GGFeab| (1)
|GGFeaj| (2)
|GGGeaa| (1)
|GGIbba| (1)
|GGIeaa| (34)
|GGIeab| (5)
|GGIeaj| (23)

|GHAeda| (1)
|GHCeda| (1)
|GHEeda| (4)
|GHEedj| (1)
|GHIeda| (1)
|GHIedj| (2)
|GJIeab| (1)
|GQAedj| (2)
|GQCeda| (1)
|GQEeda| (2)
|GQIeda| (2)
|GQIedj| (1)
|HAHeaa| (1)
|HAHeaj| (2)
|HCCeaa| (1)
|HCHeaa| (2)
|HCHeaj| (1)
|KAAeaj| (1)
|KABabc| (1)
|KABeaa| (4)
|KABeab| (1)
|KABeaj| (4)
|KAFeaj| (1)
|KAIeaj| (1)
|KBBeaa| (1)
|KBBeaj| (1)
|KBBmak| (1)
|KBGeaj| (1)
|KCA| (1)
|KCAbba| (1)
|KCAeaa| (6)
|KCAeaj| (2)
|KCBeaa| (7)
|KCCeaa| (4)
|KCEeaa| (3)
|KCEeaj| (3)
|KCFeaj| (3)
|KCIeaa| (1)
|KCIeaj| (2)
|KDBedj| (1)
|KGAeaa| (1)
|KGBeaj| (1)
|KKAedj| (2)
|KKBedj| (1)
|OAAeaa| (1)
|OABeaj| (1)
|OAFdab| (1)
|OAFeaj| (1)
|OCBeaa| (1)
|OGBeab| (1)
|gbcGBB| (1)
|kabGBA| (2)
|kabGBB| (2)
|kabGBC| (1)

001A.6F P June
No Response (120)
<chuen> (3)
<druen> (1)
<dyoon> (1)

<dyuen> (1)
<jeen> (1)
<jewn> (130)
<joon> (4)
<jue[n]> (11)
<juen> (643)
<jyuen> (3)

001A.6G P July
No Response (96)
<chuelie=13> (1)
<dAlie=41> (1)
<duelie=31> (1)
<dyuelie=13> (2)
<jAlie=41> (88)
<jIlie=41> (4)
<jewlie=13> (10)
<jewlie=21> (4)
<jewlie=31> (10)
<jilie=31> (1)
<joelie=31> (1)
<joolie=13> (5)
<joolie=21> (1)
<joolie=31> (31)
<juelie=12> (6)
<juelie=13> (345)
<juelie=21> (29)
<juelie=31> (270)
<julie=13> (1)
<julie=21> (1)
<julie=31> (6)
<zhAlie=41> (1)

001A.6H P August
No Response (124)
<awgA(s)t=14> (1)
<awgA(st)=14> (1)
<awgAs(t)=14> (280)
<awgAsh(t)=14> (2)
<awgAst=14> (167)
<awgAth(t)=14> (1)
<awgAtht=14> (1)
<awgIs(t)=14> (157)
<awgIst=14> (61)
<awgRs(t)=14> (1)
<awgoos(t)=13> (27)
<awgoost=13> (35)
<awgos(t)=13> (1)
<awgus(t)=13> (16)
<awgust=13> (15)
<oegAs(t)=14> (1)
<oegAth(t)=14> (1)
<oegoost=13> (1)
<ogAs(t)=14> (7)
<ogAst=14> (5)
<ogIs(t)=14> (6)
<ogIst=14> (3)
<ogoest=13> (1)
<ugIs(t)=14> (1)

001A.6I P September
{b}   fricative

{d}   flap
{R}   weakly retroflex
No Response (111)
<sAptembR=414> (2)
<sAptembur=413> (1)
<sAptemb{R}=414> (1)
<sAptem{b}{R}=414> (1)
<sIptembR=414> (3)
<sIptemb[R]=414> (4)
<sIptemb{R}=414> (3)
<sIptimbR=414> (2)
<sIptimb[R]=414> (1)
<sIptimb{R}=414> (1)
<se(p)temb[R]=314> (1)
<se(p)tim{b}R=314> (1)
<semptemb{R}=314> (1)
<septImb[R]=144> (2)
<septe[m]b{R}=314> (1)
<septem(b)R=134> (7)
<septem(b)R=314> (4)
<septem(b)[R]=134> (25)
<septem(b)[R]=214> (1)
<septem(b)[R]=314> (4)
<septem(b){R}=134> (1)
<septem(b){R}=314> (1)
<septembR=124> (1)
<septembR=134> (73)
<septembR=214> (2)
<septembR=314> (98)
<septemb[R]=124> (1)
<septemb[R]=134> (65)
<septemb[R]=214> (9)
<septemb[R]=314> (92)
<septembur=123> (1)
<septemb{R}=134> (20)
<septemb{R}=214> (2)
<septemb{R}=314> (38)
<septemm[R]=134> (1)
<septem{b}R=134> (1)
<septem{b}R=314> (3)
<septem{b}[R]=134> (2)
<septem{b}{R}=134> (3)
<septem{b}{R}=314> (1)
<septem{d}[R]=314> (1)
<septim(b)R=314> (1)
<septim(b)[R]=314> (1)
<septimbR=134> (44)
<septimbR=214> (5)
<septimbR=314> (114)
<septimb[R]=134> (35)
<septimb[R]=214> (6)
<septimb[R]=314> (53)
<septimbu[r]=123> (1)
<septimbur=313> (1)
<septimb{R}=134> (6)
<septimb{R}=214> (2)
<septimb{R}=314> (7)
<septiml[R]=314> (1)
<septimmR=314> (1)

<septimm[R]=134> (1)
<septim{b}R=134> (2)
<septim{b}R=314> (2)
<septim{b}[R]=134> (3)
<septim{b}[R]=214> (1)
<septim{b}[R]=314> (4)
<septim{b}{R}=134> (1)
<septim{b}{R}=214> (1)
<septim{b}{R}=314> (4)
<septim{d}R=134> (2)
<septim{d}R=314> (4)
<septim{d}[R]=134> (2)
<septim{d}[R]=314> (3)
<siptembR=314> (1)
<siptemb[R]=134> (1)
<siptemb[R]=314> (1)
<siptemmR=314> (1)
<siptimbR=134> (1)
<siptimb[R]=124> (1)
<siptimb[R]=314> (1)
<siptimb{R}=314> (1)
<siptim{d}R=314> (1)
<suptembR=314> (1)
<suptemb[R]=314> (1)
<theptimbR=314> (1)
<thiptimm[R]=134> (1)
<zeptemb[R]=214> (1)

001A.6J P October
{b} fricative
{d} flap
{R} weakly retroflex
No Response (354)
<AktoebR=414> (7)
<Aktoeb[R]=414> (4)
<Aktoeb{R}=414> (2)
<Aktoe{b}R=414> (2)
<awktoebR=134> (1)
<awktoebR=214> (1)
<awktoebR=314> (5)
<awktoeb[R]=134> (2)
<awktoeb[R]=314> (3)
<awktoeb{R}=314> (3)
<awktoe{b}R=314> (1)
<o(k)toebR=314> (1)
<o(k)toeb[R]=314> (3)
<o(k)toe{b}R=314> (1)
<oektoebR=314> (1)
<oktoebR=124> (3)
<oktoebR=134> (104)
<oktoebR=214> (8)
<oktoebu[r]=123> (1)
<oktoeb[R]=124> (3)
<oktoeb[R]=134> (100)
<oktoeb[R]=214> (17)
<oktoeb[R]=314> (165)
<oktoebw[R]=314> (1)
<oktoeb{R}=124> (1)
<oktoeb{R}=134> (29)
<oktoeb{R}=214> (4)

<oktoeb{R}=314> (55)
<oktoevR=314> (1)
<oktoev[R]=314> (2)
<oktoew[R]=134> (1)
<oktoe{b}R=134> (3)
<oktoe{b}R=314> (2)
<oktoe{b}[R]=134> (7)
<oktoe{b}[R]=314> (12)
<oktoe{d}R=134> (2)
<oktoe{d}R=314> (1)
<orktoebR=314> (1)
<uktoebR=314> (1)

001A.6K P November
{b} fricative
{d} flap
{R} weakly retroflex
No Response (117)
<nAvembR=414> (4)
<nAvemb[R]=414> (7)
<nAvemb{R}=414> (1)
<nAvimbR=414> (4)
<nAvimb[R]=414> (1)
<nAvim{b}R=414> (1)
<noevMbR=144> (2)
<noeve(m)b{R}=314> (1)
<noeve(m){b}[R]=314> (1)
<noeve[m]b[R]=134> (1)
<noevem(b)R=134> (2)
<noevem(b)R=314> (1)
<noevem(b)[R]=134> (5)
<noevem(b)[R]=314> (2)
<noevem(b){R}=214> (1)
<noevem(b){R}=314> (2)
<noevem(bR)=13> (1)
<noevembR=124> (1)
<noevembR=134> (78)
<noevembR=214> (6)
<noevembR=314> (128)
<noevembur=213> (1)
<noevemb[R]=124> (3)
<noevemb[R]=134> (94)
<noevemb[R]=214> (4)
<noevemb[R]=314> (109)
<noevemb{R}=134> (20)
<noevemb{R}=214> (5)
<noevemb{R}=314> (48)
<noevemm[R]=124> (1)
<noevemm[R]=134> (1)
<noevemm[R]=314> (1)
<noevemw[R]=134> (1)
<noevem{b}R=134> (1)
<noevem{b}R=214> (1)
<noevem{b}R=314> (3)
<noevem{b}[R]=134> (3)
<noevem{b}[R]=314> (4)
<noevem{b}{R}=134> (1)
<noevem{b}{R}=314> (4)
<noevem{d}R=314> (1)
<noevem{d}[R]=314> (1)

<noevi(m)b[R]=134> (1)
<noevi[m]bR=214> (1)
<noevim(b)[R]=134> (1)
<noevim(bR)=31> (1)
<noevimbR=134> (37)
<noevimbR=214> (8)
<noevimbR=314> (79)
<noevimb[R]=134> (30)
<noevimb[R]=214> (2)
<noevimb[R]=314> (43)
<noevimb{R}=134> (4)
<noevimb{R}=314> (7)
<noevimmR=314> (2)
<noevimm[R]=314> (2)
<noevim{b}R=314> (1)
<noevim{b}[R]=314> (3)
<noevim{b}{R}=134> (1)
<noevim{b}{R}=214> (1)
<noevim{b}{R}=314> (1)
<noevim{d}R=114> (1)
<noevim{d}R=134> (2)
<noevim{d}R=214> (1)
<noevim{d}R=314> (3)
<noevim{d}[R]=214> (1)
<noevim{d}[R]=314> (3)
<noe{b}embR=134> (1)
<noe{b}emb[R]=314> (1)
<noe{b}imbR=134> (1)
<noe{b}imbR=314> (1)
<snoevemb[R]=314> (1)

001A.6L P December
{b} fricative
{d} flap
{R} weakly retroflex
No Response (129)
<dIsembR=414> (11)
<dIsemb[R]=414> (12)
<dIsemb{R}=414> (8)
<dIsemmR=414> (1)
<dIsem{b}R=414> (1)
<dIsem{b}{R}=414> (1)
<dIsimbR=414> (17)
<dIsimb[R]=414> (1)
<dIsim{b}R=414> (1)
<deese(m)b[R]=134> (1)
<deese[m]mR=134> (1)
<deese[m]m[R]=134> (1)
<deeseembR=134> (1)
<deeseem{d}[R]=314> (1)
<deesem(b)R=134> (3)
<deesem(b)R=314> (1)
<deesem(b)[R]=134> (15)
<deesem(b){R}=134> (1)
<deesem(bR)=13> (1)
<deesembR=124> (1)
<deesembR=134> (120)
<deesembR=214> (6)
<deesembR=314> (76)
<deesemb[R]=114> (1)

<deesemb[R]=124> (5)
<deesemb[R]=134> (122)
<deesemb[R]=214> (5)
<deesemb[R]=314> (59)
<deesemb{R}=134> (36)
<deesemb{R}=214> (1)
<deesemb{R}=314> (29)
<deesemmR=134> (1)
<deesemm[R]=134> (4)
<deesemm[R]=214> (1)
<deesem{b}R=134> (5)
<deesem{b}R=314> (1)
<deesem{b}[R]=134> (7)
<deesem{b}[R]=314> (6)
<deesem{b}{R}=134> (4)
<deesem{b}{R}=314> (3)
<deesem{d}[R]=314> (1)
<deesi[m]m[R]=314> (1)
<deesim(b)[R]=134> (2)
<deesim(b)[R]=314> (2)
<deesimb(R)=31> (1)
<deesimbR=124> (1)
<deesimbR=134> (41)
<deesimbR=214> (7)
<deesimbR=314> (61)
<deesimbu[r]=213> (1)
<deesimb[R]=134> (31)
<deesimb[R]=214> (1)
<deesimb[R]=314> (33)
<deesimb{R}=134> (5)
<deesimb{R}=314> (4)
<deesimm[R]=134> (1)
<deesim{b}R=134> (3)
<deesim{b}R=214> (1)
<deesim{b}R=314> (4)
<deesim{b}[R]=134> (4)
<deesim{b}[R]=214> (1)
<deesim{b}[R]=314> (3)
<deesim{b}{R}=134> (1)
<deesim{b}{R}=214> (1)
<deesim{d}R=314> (2)
<deesim{d}[R]=134> (1)
<deesim{d}[R]=214> (1)
<deesim{d}[R]=314> (3)
<deethimbR=134> (1)
<disembR=314> (1)
<disemb[R]=314> (1)
<disimbR=314> (1)

002.1A P Sunday
{d} flap
No Response (67)
<sawndai=13> (1)
<sendI=14> (1)
<son(d)ai=13> (1)
<sondI=14> (12)
<sondai=13> (2)
<su(n)dI=14> (1)
<su[n]dI=14> (2)
<sun(d)I=14> (2)

<sun(d)ai=13> (1)
<sundA=14> (1)
<sundI=14> (704)
<sundIz=14> (8)
<sundai=11> (1)
<sundai=13> (81)
<sundee=13> (23)
<sungdI=14> (1)
<sunnI=14> (5)
<sunnai=13> (2)
<sun{d}I=14> (9)

002.1B P Sabbath
{b} fricative
No Response (574)
<sab(I)th> (1)
<sabA(th)=14> (1)
<sabAf=14> (1)
<sabAs=14> (5)
<sabAt=14> (4)
<sabAth=14> (196)
<sabIch=14> (1)
<sabIf=14> (1)
<sabIs=14> (8)
<sabIt=14> (8)
<sabIth=14> (101)
<sabeth=13> (1)
<sabith=13> (1)
<sabuth=13> (3)
<samIth=14> (1)
<sapawth=13> (1)
<sa{b}Adh=14> (1)
<sa{b}Ath=14> (2)
<sa{b}If=14> (1)
<sa{b}Ith=14> (2)
<sebIth=14> (1)
<sebith=13> (1)

002.1C P Monday
{d} flap
No Response (110)
<mo[n]nA=14> (1)
<mondI=14> (32)
<mondIz=14> (1)
<mondai=13> (4)
<mondee=13> (2)
<mu[n]nI=14> (1)
<mun(d)I=14> (1)
<mun(d)ai=13> (2)
<mundA=14> (4)
<mundI=14> (634)
<mundIz=14> (2)
<mundai=13> (91)
<mundee=13> (21)
<munnI=14> (1)
<munnai=13> (4)
<mun{d}I=14> (6)

002.1D P Tuesday
{d} flap
No Response (111)
<chew(z)dI=14> (1)

<chewzdI=14> (7)
<chewzdai=13> (1)
<chuezdI=14> (6)
<tewshdI=14> (1)
<tewz(d)I=14> (2)
<tewzd(I)> (1)
<tewzdI=14> (536)
<tewzdIz=14> (1)
<tewzdai=13> (17)
<tewzdee=13> (1)
<tewzhdI=14> (2)
<tewz{d}I=14> (1)
<thewzdI=14> (2)
<thuezdI=14> (1)
<tueewzdI=214> (1)
<tuesdI=14> (1)
<tuez(d)I=14> (1)
<tuezdI=14> (214)
<tuezdai=13> (3)
<tuezdaiz=13> (1)
<tuezdee=13> (1)
<tuezhdI=14> (1)
<tue{d}dI=14> (1)

002.1E P Wednesday
{d} flap
No Response (124)
<venIsdai=143> (1)
<venzdI=14> (1)
<wanzdI=14> (2)
<wanzdai=13> (1)
<we(n)zdI=14> (1)
<we[n]sdI=14> (1)
<we[n]zdI=14> (15)
<we[n]zdai=13> (1)
<we[n]zhdI=14> (1)
<we[n]z{d}I=14> (1)
<wen(z)dI=14> (7)
<wen(z)dai=13> (2)
<wendhdI=14> (1)
<wendzdI=14> (1)
<wenthdI=14> (2)
<wentzdI=14> (1)
<wenz(d)I=14> (5)
<wenzdI=14> (400)
<wenzdai=13> (55)
<wenzdee=13> (16)
<wenz{d}I=14> (1)
<whenzdI=14> (1)
<wi[n]zdI=14> (39)
<winsdI=14> (3)
<winthdI=14> (1)
<wintsdI=14> (1)
<winz(d)I=14> (3)
<winzdI=14> (193)
<winzdai=13> (28)
<winzdee=13> (4)
<winztI=14> (1)
<wu[n]zdI=14> (1)
<wunzdI=14> (1)

002.1F P Thursday
  {d}   flap
  {r}   weakly retroflex
  No Response (125)
  <dhurzdI=14> (1)
  <dhu{r}zdI=14> (1)
  <therzdI=14> (2)
  <therzdee=13> (1)
  <thu[r](z)dI=14> (1)
  <thu[r](z)dai=13> (1)
  <thu[r]z(d)I=14> (1)
  <thu[r]zdI=14> (162)
  <thu[r]zdai=13> (6)
  <thu[r]zdaiz=13> (1)
  <thu[r]z{d}I=14> (1)
  <thur(z)tI=14> (1)
  <thursdI=14> (1)
  <thursdai=13> (1)
  <thurthdai=13> (1)
  <thurz(d)I=14> (4)
  <thurzdI=14> (403)
  <thurzdIz=14> (1)
  <thurzdai=13> (67)
  <thurzdee=13> (23)
  <thurzhdI=14> (2)
  <thurzhdai=13> (1)
  <thurz{d}I=14> (1)
  <thu{r}sdI=14> (5)
  <thu{r}zdI=14> (87)
  <thu{r}zdai=13> (6)
  <thu{r}zdee=13> (1)
  <thu{r}z{d}I=14> (1)
  <turzdI=14> (4)
  <tu{r}zdI=14> (1)
  <zhur(z)dai=13> (1)
002.1G P Friday
  {d}   flap
  No Response (98)
  <friedA=14> (4)
  <friedI=14> (693)
  <friedIz=14> (2)
  <friedai=13> (71)
  <friedee=13> (20)
  <frietI=14> (1)
  <frie{d}I=14> (24)
  <frie{d}ai=13> (1)
002.1H P Saturday
  {d}   flap
  {R}   weakly retroflex
  {r}   weakly retroflex
  {t}   voiced
  {?}   glottal
  No Response (75)
  <sa(t)RdI=144> (30)
  <sa(t)Rdai=143> (2)
  <sa(t)R{d}I=144> (3)
  <sa(t)[R]dI=144> (7)
  <sa(t)[R]{t}I=144> (1)
  <sa(t)r(d)I=14> (1)

  <sa(t)rdI=14> (43)
  <sa(t)rdIz=14> (1)
  <sa(t)rdai=13> (2)
  <sa(t)rdee=13> (2)
  <sa(t)rtI=14> (1)
  <sa(t)r{d}I=14> (1)
  <sa(t)r{t}I=14> (5)
  <sa(t){R}dI=144> (7)
  <sa(t){R}dai=143> (1)
  <sa(t){r}dI=14> (11)
  <sa(t){r}dIz=14> (1)
  <sa(t){r}{t}I=14> (2)
  <sa(tR)dI=14> (14)
  <sa(tR){d}I=14> (2)
  <sa(tR){t}I=14> (1)
  <sad(R)dI=14> (14)
  <sad(R){d}I=14> (1)
  <sadNdai=143> (1)
  <sadRdai=143> (1)
  <sad[R]dI=144> (3)
  <sai(t)rdI=14> (1)
  <sar{d}Rdai=143> (1)
  <satRdI=144> (6)
  <satRdai=143> (2)
  <sat[R]dI=144> (5)
  <sat[R]dee=143> (2)
  <sat{R}dI=144> (8)
  <sa{?}RdI=144> (7)
  <sa{?}Rdai=143> (3)
  <sa{d}RdI=144> (77)
  <sa{d}Rdai=143> (8)
  <sa{d}Rdee=143> (2)
  <sa{d}R{d}I=144> (1)
  <sa{d}[R]dI=144> (45)
  <sa{d}[R]dIz=144> (1)
  <sa{d}[R]dai=143> (7)
  <sa{d}{R}dI=144> (16)
  <sa{d}{R}dai=143> (2)
  <sa{t}(R)dI=14> (13)
  <sa{t}(Rd)I=14> (1)
  <sa{t}RdI=144> (209)
  <sa{t}RdIz=144> (1)
  <sa{t}Rdai=143> (51)
  <sa{t}Rdee=143> (8)
  <sa{t}R{t}I=144> (1)
  <sa{t}urdI=134> (6)
  <sa{t}[R]dI=144> (101)
  <sa{t}[R]dIz=144> (4)
  <sa{t}[R]dai=143> (15)
  <sa{t}[R]daiz=143> (2)
  <sa{t}[R]dee=143> (1)
  <sa{t}{R}dI=144> (58)
  <sa{t}{R}dai=143> (12)
  <se(t)RdI=144> (1)
  <se(t)[R]dI=144> (1)
  <se(t)rdI=14> (3)
  <sedRdI=144> (1)
  <se{d}RdI=144> (1)
  <se{d}Rdai=143> (1)

  <se{d}[R]dee=143> (1)
  <si(tR)dI=14> (1)
  <tha{d}Rdai=143> (1)
002.2 P morning
  {r}   weakly retroflex
  No Response (51)
  <maw(r)n(NG)> (2)
  <maw(r)nN=14> (82)
  <maw(r)nNG=14> (12)
  <maw(r)n[N]=14> (2)
  <maw[r]nN=14> (64)
  <maw[r]nNG=14> (19)
  <maw[r]nNGz=14> (1)
  <maw[r]n[N]=14> (1)
  <mawr(n)NG=14> (1)
  <mawrnN=14> (97)
  <mawrnNG=14> (76)
  <mawrnNz=14> (1)
  <mawrning=13> (1)
  <maw{r}nN=14> (37)
  <maw{r}nNG=14> (21)
  <maw{r}ning=13> (1)
  <mo(r)nN=14> (1)
  <moe(r)[n]N=14> (1)
  <moe(r)nN=14> (32)
  <moe(r)nNG=14> (5)
  <moe(r)n[N]=14> (1)
  <moe[r]n(NG)> (2)
  <moe[r]nN=14> (104)
  <moe[r]nNG=14> (40)
  <moe[r]nNz=14> (1)
  <moe[r]n[N]=14> (6)
  <moer[n][N]=14> (1)
  <moernN=14> (158)
  <moernNG=14> (134)
  <moernNGz=14> (1)
  <moern[N]=14> (3)
  <moe{r}nN=14> (31)
  <moe{r}nNG=14> (22)
  <mornN=14> (1)
  <mornNG=14> (6)
  <mo{r}nN=14> (2)
002.3 L afternoon
  No Response (151)
  A   afternoon (638)
  B   afternoon day (1)
  C   evening (244)
  D   fall of the evening (1)
  E   heat of the day (1)
  F   late afternoon (3)
  G   late evening (1)
  H   midafternoon (3)
  I   midevening (1)
  J   noon (1)
  K   PM (2)
  L   second and third watch (1)
002.4 G good day
  No Response (458)
  A   au revoir [F] (3)

B   be good (1)
C   buenos dias [S] (1)
D   bye (25)
E   bye-bye (10)
F   bye now (2)
G   catch you later (2)
H   farewell (2)
I   glad to see you (1)
J   good-bye (223)
K   good-bye now (1)
L   good day [greeting] (25)
M   good day [parting] (195)
N   have a good day (14)
O   have a nice day (4)
P   hello (29)
Q   hi (9)
R   how are you? (1)
S   how do you do? (3)
T   how [X-0] you doing? (1)
U   howdy (14)
V   howdy do? (2)
W   hurry back (1)
X   I got to be going (1)
Y   (I) hope you have a good day
    (2)
Z   (I'll) be (a-)seeing you (4)
aa   (I'll) see you (7)
ab   (I'll/we'll) see you later (40)
ac   later on (1)
ad   pleasant afternoon (1)
ae   so long (24)
af   take it easy (1)
ag   talk to you later (1)
ah   top of the day (1)

002.5 P evening
{v}   bilabial
No Response (129)
<aivnN=14> (1)
<ee(v)nNG=14> (1)
<ee(v)nN=14> (41)
<ee(vnI)n> (2)
<eebnN=14> (1)
<eebnNG=14> (1)
<eed(n)N=14> (1)
<eednN=14> (1)
<eev(n)N=14> (2)
<eevNN=144> (3)
<eevNNG=144> (5)
<eevNin=143> (1)
<eevdid=13> (1)
<eevnN=14> (461)
<eevnNG=14> (288)
<eevnNz=14> (2)
<eevn[N]=14> (13)
<eevnin=13> (3)
<eevning=13> (3)
<eevnun=13> (1)
<ee{v}nN=14> (3)
<ee{v}nNG=14> (1)

003.1 G good night
No Response (341)
A   be good (1)
B   bonsoir [F] (1)
C   bye (4)
D   bye-bye (2)
E   good-bye (13)
F   good evening [meeting] (10)
G   good evening [parting] (11)
H   good night [meeting] (5)
I   good night [parting] (485)
J   have a good night (2)
K   night (3)
L   night-night (2)
M   see you again (1)
N   see you later (3)
O   see you tomorrow (2)
P   so long (2)

003.2 L sunrise
No Response (135)
A   break of dawn (2)
B   break of day (12)
C   can see [n.] (2)
D   crack of dawn (6)
E   crack of day (1)
F   dawn (125)
G   dawn time (1)
H   day (21)
I   day bust (1)
J   daybreak (70)
K   daylight (162)
L   first light (1)
M   good light (1)
N   light (6)
O   rise of the sun (1)
P   sun (4)
Q   sunbreak (2)
R   sunlight (5)
S   sunrise (343)
T   sunup (406)

003.2 S sun
No Response (0)
|FAC| (1)
|FAH| (1)
|KAB| (1)
|LAA| (1)
|LAB| (1)
|LAC| (23)
|LAClaa| (1)
|LAD| (5)
|LAE| (14)
|LAEfaj| (1)
|LAF| (1)
|LAG| (2)
|LAH| (1)
|LKAmdj| (1)
|LKE| (1)
|LKEmdj| (2)
|LMBmaj| (1)

|MAA| (1)
|MAE| (1)
|MAG| (1)
|MCA| (1)
|MDA| (1)
|MKA| (2)
|NAA| (58)
|NAAmaj| (8)
|NAB| (4)
|NACmaj| (1)
|NAD| (455)
|NADfaj| (22)
|NADmaj| (56)
|NAE| (1)
|NAF| (16)
|NAFfaj| (1)
|NAG| (2)
|NAH| (43)
|NAHmaj| (7)
|NAI| (1)
|NCA| (14)
|NCB| (1)
|NCD| (9)
|NCDfaj| (10)
|NCDmaj| (6)
|NCFfaj| (1)
|NCH| (1)
|NCHfaj| (2)
|NCHmaj| (1)
|NDA| (11)
|NDAmdj| (2)
|NDB| (1)
|NDD| (49)
|NDDmdj| (14)
|NDFmdj| (1)
|NDG| (1)
|NDH| (3)
|NDHmdj| (2)
|NFA| (1)
|NFB| (1)
|NKA| (21)
|NKAmdj| (5)
|NKB| (1)
|NKD| (10)
|NKDmdj| (2)
|NKH| (2)
|NMF| (1)
|PAEmaj| (1)

003.3 G rise
<!>   infinitive
<&>   present 3rd singular
<@>   present participle
<*>   preterit
<#>   past participle
No Response (192)
<!Ariez=41> (5)
<!raith> (1)
<!raiz> (7)
<!rie(z)> (3)

<!ried> (1)
<!riedh> (1)
<!ries> (3)
<!rieth> (1)
<!riez> (475)
<!riezd> (2)
<!roez> (1)
<!roz> (6)
<&raizAth=14> (1)
<&riez> (5)
<&riezIz=14> (41)
<&rozIz=14> (1)
<@AriezN=414> (1)
<@riezN=14> (22)
<@riezNG=14> (5)
<@rozing=13> (1)
<*airoez=13> (1)
<*Ariz=41> (1)
<*Aroez=41> (11)
<*loez> (1)
<*raizd> (1)
<*riez> (6)
<*riezd> (7)
<*riz> (51)
<*rizAt=14> (1)
<*rizd> (1)
<*rizN=14> (3)
<*rodh> (1)
<*roe(z)> (3)
<*roes> (2)
<*roeth> (1)
<*roez> (467)
<*roz> (1)
<#Ariz=41> (1)
<#ArizN=414> (9)
<#Aroez=41> (3)
<#AroezN=414> (1)
<#raith> (1)
<#raizd> (1)
<#reez> (1)
<#reezN=14> (2)
<#rid> (1)
<#ridN=14> (2)
<#riez> (4)
<#riezd> (12)
<#riezN=14> (1)
<#risN=14> (4)
<#riz> (37)
<#rizM=14> (1)
<#riz[N]=14> (1)
<#rizN=14> (354)
<#roe(z)> (2)
<#roed> (1)
<#roedhN=14> (1)
<#roez> (111)
<#roezd> (1)
<#roezN=14> (3)
<#roz> (1)

003.4 L sunset

No Response (168)
A can't see [n.] (1)
B dark (85)
C darkness (1)
D dusk (35)
E dusk dark (3)
F dusky dark (3)
G eveningtide (1)
H gray time (1)
I nightfall (2)
J setting of the sun (1)
K sundown (497)
L sunset (253)
M twilight (6)

003.5 P yesterday

{d} flap
{R} weakly retroflex
{r} weakly retroflex
No Response (147)
<(y)est[R]dI=144> (1)
<yastRdee=143> (1)
<yast[R]dI=144> (4)
<yast[R]dai=143> (4)
<ye(s)t[R]dai=143> (1)
<yes(t)RdI=144> (2)
<yes(t)[R]dI=144> (2)
<yes(t)[R]dai=143> (8)
<yes(t){R}dai=143> (1)
<yes(tR)dI=14> (15)
<yes(tR)dai=13> (7)
<yes(tR){d}I=14> (1)
<yeshtRdI=144> (1)
<yeshtRdai=143> (1)
<yeshtR{d}I=144> (1)
<yesht[R]dI=144> (2)
<yesht[R]dai=143> (4)
<yesh{d}[R]dI=144> (1)
<yess[R]dai=143> (1)
<yest(R)dI=14> (3)
<yest(R)dai=13> (2)
<yest(Rd)I=14> (1)
<yest(Rd)ai=13> (1)
<yestRdI=144> (81)
<yestRdai=143> (170)
<yestRdee=143> (3)
<yestR{d}I=144> (1)
<yest[R]dI=144> (148)
<yest[R]dai=143> (226)
<yest[R]dee=143> (5)
<yest[R]{d}I=144> (2)
<yest[R]{d}ai=143> (3)
<yesth[R]dai=143> (1)
<yestu[r]dI=134> (4)
<yestu[r]dai=132> (1)
<yesturdI=134> (1)
<yestu{r}(dai)=13> (1)
<yest{R}dI=144> (32)
<yest{R}dai=143> (60)
<yest{d}u[r]{d}I=134> (1)

<yes{R}dI=144> (1)
<yes{d}(R)dai=13> (1)
<yes{d}Rdai=143> (1)
<yes{d}[R]dI=144> (3)
<yes{d}[R]dai=143> (6)
<yes{d}{R}dI=144> (1)
<yetht[R]{d}ai=143> (1)
<yis(t)[R]dI=144> (1)
<yis(t)[R]dai=143> (1)
<yis(tR)dI=14> (1)
<yis(tR)dai=13> (1)
<yishtRdai=143> (1)
<yist(R)dI=14> (1)
<yist(R)dai=13> (2)
<yistRdI=144> (11)
<yistRdai=143> (6)
<yistRdee=143> (1)
<yist[R]dI=144> (16)
<yist[R]dai=143> (7)
<yist[R]dee=143> (1)
<yist[R]{d}I=144> (1)
<yisti(r){d}I=134> (1)
<yistu[r]dI=134> (1)
<yisturdI=134> (1)
<yist{R}dI=144> (1)
<yus(t)[R]dai=143> (1)
<yustR(d)I=144> (1)
<yustRdI=144> (2)
<yust[R]dI=144> (2)
<yust[R]dai=143> (1)
<yust{R}dai=143> (1)

003.6 G Sunday a week [past]

No Response (311)
A couple of Sundays ago (2)
B couple of weeks ago (1)
C fortnight ago (1)
D just a week's Sunday (1)
E last past Sunday (1)
F last Sunday a week ago (4)
G last Sunday but a week ago (1)
H last Sunday was a week ago (4)
I last Sunday week (3)
J last Sunday week ago (2)
K last Sunday's a week ago (4)
L last week before Sunday (1)
M second Sunday (1)
N Sunday a week (13)
O Sunday a/the week ago (50)
P Sunday afore last (1)
Q Sunday before (13)
R Sunday before last (207)
S Sunday before last Sunday (4)
T Sunday before last week (1)
U Sunday before that (1)
V Sunday before this one (1)
W Sunday gone (1)
X Sunday is a week ago (1)
Y Sunday last (2)
Z Sunday past (9)

aa Sunday two weeks ago (4)
ab Sunday was a week ago (33)
ac Sunday week (28)
ad Sunday week ago (27)
ae Sunday's a week ago (7)
af this past Sunday (1)
ag this past Sunday a week ago (1)
ah two or three Sundays ago (1)
ai two Sundays ago (12)
aj two weeks ago (20)
ak two weeks ago come Sunday (1)
al two weeks ago from today (1)
am two weeks ago last Sunday (2)
an two weeks ago next Sunday (1)
ao two weeks ago Sunday (4)
ap two weeks ago this Sunday (1)
aq two weeks ago today (2)
ar week ago from Sunday (1)
as week ago last Sunday (9)
at week ago Sunday (33)
au week ago this past Sunday (1)
av week before (8)
aw week before last (52)
ax week before last Sunday (5)
ay week before Sunday (3)
az week before that (2)
ba week before then (1)
bb weekend before last (1)

003.7 G Sunday a week [future]

No Response (300)
A coming Sunday, the (2)
B coming within two weeks (1)
C couple of Sundays (1)
D following Sunday, the (7)
E following week, the (3)
F following week of next Sunday (1)
G next Sunday (3)
H next Sunday a week (1)
I next Sunday coming (1)
J next Sunday week (7)
K not next Sunday, but the Sunday afterwards (1)
L not this Sunday, but the next (1)
M second Sunday from now (1)
N second week (2)
O Sunday a week (17)
P Sunday a week away (1)
Q Sunday a week from now (6)
R Sunday after, the (3)
S Sunday after next (115)
T Sunday after next Sunday (3)
U Sunday after Sunday (2)
V Sunday after that, after next (1)
W Sunday after this coming one (1)
X Sunday after this coming Sunday (2)
Y Sunday after this one coming (2)
Z Sunday coming (3)

aa Sunday gone (1)
ab Sunday next (2)
ac Sunday two weeks (7)
ad Sunday two weeks from now (1)
ae Sunday week (301)
af Sunday week, the (1)
ag this coming Sunday week (1)
ah this next-coming Sunday (1)
ai this one coming Sunday (1)
aj tomorrow week (4)
ak two Sundays from now (2)
al two weeks from now (3)
am two weeks from Sunday (7)
an two weeks from today (6)
ao two weeks hence (1)
ap two weeks later (3)
aq week after (1)
ar week after next (24)
as week after Sunday (1)
at week after this Sunday (1)
au week after today (1)
av week beyond this Sunday (1)
aw week following, the (1)
ax week from next Sunday (3)
ay week from Sunday (51)
az week from this coming Sunday (3)
ba week from this Sunday (9)
bb week from tomorrow (1)
bc week later, a (1)
bd week next Sunday, a (2)
be week Sunday, a (1)

003.8 L fortnight

No Response (437)
A about fifteen days (1)
B about two weeks (5)
C bimonthly (1)
D couple of weeks (33)
E fifteen days (73)
F first (part) of the month (2)
G fortnight (32)
H fourteen days (4)
I half (of) a/the month (105)
J little better than two weeks, a (1)
K semimonthly (1)
L three weeks (4)
M two or three weeks (3)
N two weeks (270)
O two weeks or so (1)
P two-week period (1)
Q week or two, a (1)

003.8 P fortnight

{r} weakly retroflex
{?} glottal
No Response (778)
<faw(r)tniet=13> (1)
<faw[r]tniet=13> (1)
<faw[r]{?}niet=21> (1)
<fawrtniet=13> (1)

<fawrtniet=21> (1)
<fo[r]tniet=13> (1)
<foe(r)tniet=13> (6)
<foe(r)tniet=21> (1)
<foe[r](t)niet=13> (1)
<foe[r]tniet=11> (2)
<foe[r]tniet=13> (22)
<foe[r]tniet=21> (1)
<foer(t)niet=13> (1)
<foer(t)niet=31> (1)
<foerdnie(t)=13> (1)
<foerthniet=13> (3)
<foertnAt=14> (1)
<foertnIt=14> (3)
<foertnie(t)=13> (1)
<foertniet=11> (4)
<foertniet=13> (67)
<foertniet=21> (1)
<foertniet=31> (1)
<foertniets=13> (1)
<foe{r}tniet=13> (14)

004.1 P tomorrow

{d} flap
{R} weakly retroflex
{r} weakly retroflex
No Response (164)
<(t)AmorA=414> (1)
<(tA)mawrA=14> (1)
<(tA)morA=14> (7)
<(tA)moroe=13> (2)
<(tA)mo{r}A=14> (1)
<dAmorA=414> (3)
<dIma[r]A=414> (1)
<tAmaw(rA)=41> (1)
<tAmaw(r)A=414> (1)
<tAmawr(A)=41> (1)
<tAmawrA=414> (36)
<tAmawroe=413> (9)
<tAmaw{r}(A)=41> (1)
<tAmaw{r}A=414> (1)
<tAmerA=414> (1)
<tAmo(r)A=414> (1)
<tAmo[r](A)=41> (3)
<tAmoerA=414> (1)
<tAmoeroe=413> (1)
<tAmor(A)=41> (5)
<tAmorA=414> (315)
<tAmorI=414> (2)
<tAmoroe=413> (51)
<tAmo{r}(A)=41> (5)
<tAmo{r}A=414> (6)
<tImarwA=414> (1)
<tImawrA=414> (7)
<tImawroe=413> (1)
<tImo[r](A)=41> (5)
<tImoerA=414> (1)
<tImor(A)=41> (1)
<tImorA=414> (191)
<tImorI=414> (8)

<tIImorR=414> (1)
<tIImoroe=412> (1)
<tIImoroe=413> (38)
<tIImo{d}oe=413> (1)
<tIImo{r}(A)=41> (4)
<tIImo{r}A=414> (3)
<toomarA=314> (1)
<toomaroe=313> (1)
<toomawrA=314> (1)
<toomawroe=313> (2)
<toomorA=314> (11)
<toomoroe=313> (16)
<toomorue=313> (1)
<toomo{r}(A)=31> (2)
<toomo{r}A=314> (1)
<tuemarA=314> (1)
<tuemawrA=134> (1)
<tuemorA=314> (4)
<tuemoroe=313> (2)
<tuemor{R}=314> (1)
<tuemo{r}(A)=31> (1)
<tuemo{r}{d}A=314> (1)
<tumawrA=314> (1)
<tumorA=314> (2)
<tumoroe=312> (3)
<{d}Amawroe=413> (1)
<{d}AmorA=414> (1)

004.2 G what time is it?

No Response (307)
A can you tell me the time? (1)
B could you give me the time (please)? (4)
C could you tell me the time? (1)
D could you tell me the time of day? (1)
E do you have the correct time? (1)
F do you have the time (please)? (23)
G do you have your watch, please? (1)
H do you know the time? (2)
I do you know what time of day it is? (1)
J for the time is it (1)
K give me the time (2)
L give me the time of day (1)
M have you got a watch? (1)
N have you got the time? (1)
O have you got the time of day? (2)
P have you the time? (1)
Q how late is it getting to be? (1)
R tell me the time (please)? (2)
S what is the hour? (3)
T what is the time of day? (2)
U what is the time of the day? (1)
V what is the time? (5)
W what time? (3)

X what time do you got? (2)
Y what time do you have? (40)
Z what time do you have now? (1)
aa what time have you? (13)
ab what time have you got? (2)
ac what time is it by your watch? (1)
ad what time is it getting to be? (1)
ae what time is it (please)? (397)
af what time is [M-0]? (2)
ag what time it is? (1)
ah what time it is, [X-0] you reckon? (1)
ai what time of day have you? (2)
aj what time of day is it? (20)
ak what time of day is it getting to be? (1)
al what time of day was it? (1)
am what time of day [X-0] we got? (1)
an what time of day [X-0] you got there? (1)
ao what time of the day is it? (2)
ap what time was it? (1)
aq what time [X-0] it happen to be? (1)
ar what time [X-0] you got? (13)
as what time [X-0] you got on your watch? (1)
at what time [X-0] you have? (7)
au what [X-0] the clock got? (1)
av what's the correct Central Standard? (1)
aw what's the hour? (1)
ax what's the time? (7)
ay what's the time of day? (1)
az what's your clock got there? (1)
ba will you give me the time? (1)
bb will you give me the time of day? (1)
bc would you give me the time, please? (1)
bd would you mind giving me the time, please? (1)
be would you mind telling me the time, please? (1)
bf would you tell me what time it is? (1)
bg [M-0] time is it? (3)
bh [X-0] you got any time on you? (1)
bi [X-0] you got the time? (1)
bj [X-0] you got the time of day? (1)
bk [X-0] [M-0] got the correct time? (1)

004.3 P watch
{r} weakly retroflex

No Response (166)
<voch> (1)
<wach> (1)
<wawch> (38)
<waw{r}ch> (1)
<woch> (694)
<wochIz=14> (10)
<wocht> (1)
<woech> (1)
<wosh> (2)
<woshIz=14> (1)
<wot> (5)
<wots> (2)

004.4 G half past (seven)
No Response (161)
A half after (12)
B half after (seven) (21)
C half after the hour of (seven) (1)
D half an hour before (seven) (1)
E half an hour till (seven) (1)
F half an hour until (1)
G half of the hour (1)
H half past (150)
I half past (seven) (295)
J half past the hour (10)
K halfway before (seven) (1)
L halfway past (seven) (2)
M middle of the hours (1)
N on the half hour (3)
O seven and a half (1)
P (seven)-thirty (633)
Q thirty minutes after (seven) (2)
R thirty minutes before (seven) (1)
S thirty minutes past (seven) (5)
T thirty minutes past the hour (2)
U thirty minutes till (2)
V thirty minutes till (seven) (6)
W thirty minutes to (seven) (1)
X thirty minutes to the hour (1)

004.4 P half (past)
{a} upglide
{b} fricative
{e} upglide
{f} bilabial
{v} devoiced
{?} glottal
No Response (407)
<ha(f)> (65)
<haf> (332)
<hap> (4)
<ha{?}> (1)
<ha{b}> (1)
<ha{f}> (1)
<ha{v}> (3)
<hef> (2)
<ho(f)> (1)
<h{a}(f)> (11)
<h{a}f> (90)
<h{a}p> (1)

<h{a}{f}> (1)
<h{e}f> (1)

004.5 G quarter of (eleven)

No Response (188)

A fifteen before (1)
B fifteen minutes before (1)
C fifteen minutes of (2)
D fifteen minutes of being an hour (1)
E fifteen minutes till (37)
F fifteen minutes to (33)
G fifteen minutes until (3)
H fifteen minutes [P-0] (1)
I fifteen till (60)
J fifteen to (11)
K fifteen until (1)
L forty-five after (2)
M forty-five minutes after (6)
N forty-five minutes past (2)
O forty-five past (1)
P quarter before (3)
Q quarter before, a (1)
R quarter of (68)
S quarter of, a (19)
T quarter of an hour to (1)
U quarter of till (1)
V quarter till (254)
W quarter till, a (41)
X quarter till to (1)
Y quarter to (190)
Z quarter to, a (32)
aa quarter until (1)
ab quarter until, a (1)
ac quarter [P-0] (9)
ad seven fifteen earlier [=7:45] (1)
ae three quarters (4)
af three quarters after (1)
ag three quarters of an hour (1)

004.5 P quarter

{d} flap
{R} weakly retroflex
{r} weakly retroflex

No Response (299)

<kaw[r]t[R]=14> (1)
<koe(rt){R}=14> (1)
<kwaw(r)tR=14> (29)
<kwaw(r)t[R]=14> (122)
<kwaw(r)t[R]z=14> (1)
<kwaw(r)t{R}=14> (22)
<kwaw(r){d}R=14> (8)
<kwaw(r){d}[R]=14> (23)
<kwaw(r){d}{R}=14> (2)
<kwaw[r]tR=14> (5)
<kwaw[r]t[R]=14> (19)
<kwaw[r]t{R}=14> (2)
<kwaw[r]{d}R=14> (3)
<kwaw[r]{d}[R]=14> (5)
<kwaw[r]{d}{R}=14> (2)
<kwawrd[R]=14> (1)

<kwawrtR=14> (110)
<kwawrtRz=14> (1)
<kwawrt[R]=14> (5)
<kwawrt{R}=14> (15)
<kwawr{d}R=14> (11)
<kwawr{d}[R]=14> (1)
<kwaw{r}tR=14> (5)
<kwaw{r}t[R]=14> (13)
<kwaw{r}t{R}=14> (10)
<kwaw{r}{d}R=14> (1)
<kwaw{r}{d}[R]=14> (6)
<kwaw{r}{d}{R}=14> (1)
<kwo(r)tR=14> (4)
<kwo(r)t[R]=14> (23)
<kwo(r)t[R]z=14> (1)
<kwo(r)t{R}=14> (3)
<kwo[r]t[R]=14> (9)
<kwoe(r)tR=14> (3)
<kwoe(r)t[R]=14> (9)
<kwoe(r){d}R=14> (1)
<kwoe(r){d}[R]=14> (1)
<kwoe[r]tR=14> (1)
<kwoe[r]t[R]=14> (16)
<kwoe[r]{d}R=14> (2)
<kwoe[r]{d}{R}=14> (1)
<kwoertR=14> (67)
<kwoert[R]=14> (4)
<kwoert{R}=14> (2)
<kwoer{d}R=14> (1)
<kwoe{r}tR=14> (1)
<kwoe{r}t[R]=14> (3)
<kwoe{r}t{R}=14> (5)
<kwoe{r}{d}R=14> (1)
<kwoe{r}{d}{R}=14> (1)
<kwortR=14> (37)
<kwort[R]=14> (2)
<kwo{r}t[R]=14> (2)
<kwurtR=14> (1)

004.6 L (for quite a) while

No Response (202)

A bit (9)
B bit of years (1)
C coon's age (1)
D few years (1)
E first little while (1)
F good bit (1)
G good little while (2)
H good long time (1)
I good long while (13)
J good while (27)
K good while ago (1)
L little bit (1)
M little run (1)
N little while (27)
O little while ago (1)
P long, long time (1)
Q long spell (1)
R long time (31)
S long while (4)

T number of years (2)
U period (1)
V pretty good little while (2)
W pretty good while (19)
X short spell (1)
Y short while (7)
Z some bit (1)
aa some spell (1)
ab some time (73)
ac some while (2)
ad spell (43)
ae time (5)
af very short while (1)
ag while (539)
ah while ago (51)
ai while back (9)
aj while long (1)

004.7 P this year

{r} weakly retroflex
{s} palatal
{y} palatal
{?} glottal

No Response (210)

<desh(y)i[r]=13> (1)
<dhIshshir=41> (1)
<dhIshyi[r]=41> (1)
<dhIsyi[r]=41> (1)
<dhIsyir=41> (2)
<dhIsyi{r}=41> (1)
<dheesyeer=13> (1)
<dhis(y)i[r]=13> (1)
<dhis(y)ir=13> (1)
<dhish(y)e[r]=13> (3)
<dhish(y)ee[r]=13> (4)
<dhish(y)eer=13> (3)
<dhish(y)i(r)=13> (1)
<dhish(y)i[r]=13> (57)
<dhish(y)i[r]=31> (2)
<dhish(y)ir=13> (72)
<dhish(y)ir=21> (1)
<dhish(y)ir=31> (5)
<dhish(y)irz=13> (1)
<dhish(y)i{r}=13> (19)
<dhish(y)i{r}=31> (1)
<dhish(y)i{r}z=13> (1)
<dhishir=13> (1)
<dhishshi[r]=13> (1)
<dhishshi{r}=13> (1)
<dhishyee[r]=13> (3)
<dhishyeer=13> (1)
<dhishyer=13> (1)
<dhishyi(r)=13> (1)
<dhishyi[r]=13> (16)
<dhishyi[r]=31> (1)
<dhishyir=13> (19)
<dhishyi{r}=13> (14)
<dhisshee[r]=13> (1)
<dhisshe{r}=31> (1)
<dhisshi[r]=13> (4)

<dhisshir=13> (48)
<dhisshi{r}=13> (9)
<dhissir=13> (1)
<dhistyi[r]=13> (1)
<dhisye[r]=13> (4)
<dhisye[r]=31> (1)
<dhisyee[r]=13> (2)
<dhisyeer=13> (2)
<dhisyer=13> (3)
<dhisye{r}=13> (2)
<dhisyi[r]=11> (2)
<dhisyi[r]=13> (88)
<dhisyi[r]=21> (6)
<dhisyi[r]=31> (8)
<dhisyir=11> (2)
<dhisyir=13> (155)
<dhisyir=21> (8)
<dhisyir=31> (13)
<dhisyi{r}=11> (2)
<dhisyi{r}=13> (41)
<dhisyi{r}=21> (2)
<dhisyi{r}=31> (6)
<dhisyu{r}=31> (1)
<dhis{y}ir=13> (1)
<dhizzhi[r]=13> (1)
<dhi{s}ye{r}=13> (1)
<dhi{s}yi[r]=13> (5)
<dhi{s}yir=13> (21)
<dhi{s}yir=21> (1)
<dhi{s}yir=31> (1)
<dhi{s}yi{r}=13> (4)
<dish(y)ee[r]=13> (2)
<dish(y)i[r]=13> (4)
<dish(y)ir=13> (3)
<dishshir=13> (1)
<dishye[r]=13> (1)
<dishyi[r]=13> (3)
<disshir=13> (1)
<disshi{r}=13> (2)
<disye[r]=13> (1)
<disyee[r]=31> (1)
<disyi[r]=13> (14)
<disyi[r]=31> (1)
<disyir=13> (2)
<disyi{r}=13> (2)
<dizhyi[r]=13> (1)
<jish(y)i[r]=13> (1)
<nisyi[r]=13> (2)
<thish(y)ir=13> (2)
<thisshi[r]=13> (1)
<thisshir=13> (2)
<thisshi{r}=13> (3)
<thisyi[r]=13> (3)
<thisyir=13> (1)
<thi{s}yir=31> (1)
<thi{s}yi{r}=13> (2)
<tish(y)ir=13> (2)
<ti{s}yir=13> (1)
<{?}ishyi{r}=13> (1)

005.1 G years (old)
No Response (100)
A   year[N-i] (99)
B   years (761)
005.2 P a year ago
{r}   weakly retroflex
No Response (310)
<(A)hi{r}Agoe=143> (1)
<(A)yeerAgoe=143> (1)
<(A)yeerIgoe=341> (1)
<(A)yerAgoe=143> (2)
<(A)yi(r)Agoe=143> (1)
<(A)yi(r)Agoe=341> (5)
<(A)yi[r]Agoe=143> (1)
<(A)yi[r]Agoe=341> (2)
<(A)yirAgoe=141> (1)
<(A)yirAgoe=142> (1)
<(A)yirAgoe=143> (10)
<(A)yirAgoe=241> (1)
<(A)yirAgoe=341> (9)
<(A)yirIgoe=142> (1)
<(A)yirIgoe=143> (2)
<(A)yi{r}Agoe=143> (3)
<(A)yi{r}Agoe=341> (2)
<(A)yurAgoe=143> (1)
<Aye(r)Agoe=4143> (1)
<Aye(r)Agoe=4341> (3)
<Aye[r]Agoe=4143> (2)
<AyeerAgoe=4341> (2)
<Ayee{r}Agoe=4143> (1)
<AyerAgoe=4143> (9)
<AyerAgoe=4241> (2)
<AyerAgoe=4341> (5)
<AyerIgoe=4143> (3)
<Aye{r}Agoe=4143> (2)
<Ayi(r)Agoe=4141> (1)
<Ayi(r)Agoe=4142> (1)
<Ayi(r)Agoe=4143> (5)
<Ayi(r)Agoe=4341> (5)
<Ayi[r](A)goe=413> (1)
<Ayi[r]Agoe=4141> (3)
<Ayi[r]Agoe=4142> (2)
<Ayi[r]Agoe=4143> (15)
<Ayi[r]Agoe=4241> (5)
<Ayi[r]Agoe=4341> (2)
<AyirAgoe=4141> (3)
<AyirAgoe=4142> (5)
<AyirAgoe=4143> (181)
<AyirAgoe=4241> (62)
<AyirAgoe=4341> (89)
<AyirIgoe=4141> (1)
<AyirIgoe=4143> (3)
<AyirIgoe=4341> (5)
<Ayi{r}Agoe=4141> (1)
<Ayi{r}Agoe=4142> (2)
<Ayi{r}Agoe=4143> (24)
<Ayi{r}Agoe=4241> (4)
<Ayi{r}Agoe=4341> (9)
<Ayi{r}Igoe=4341> (1)

<Iyi{r}Agoe=4143> (1)
<Iyi{r}Igoe=4143> (1)
<aiyi(r)Agoe=3143> (1)
<aiyirAgoe=3141> (1)
<aiyirAgoe=3142> (1)
<aiyirAgoe=3143> (1)
<aiyirAgoe=3241> (1)
<aiyiraigoe=3231> (1)
<wonyi(r)Agoe=2341> (1)
<wonyi[r]Agoe=3241> (1)
<woonyirAgoe=3143> (1)
<wu[n]yi(r)Agoe=3241> (1)
<wunyee(r)Agoe=2143> (1)
<wunyeerAgoe=2143> (1)
<wunyeerAgoe=3143> (2)
<wunye{r}Agoe=3142> (1)
<wunyi(r)AgA=1244> (1)
<wunyi(r)Agoe=1341> (1)
<wunyi(r)Agoe=1343> (1)
<wunyi(r)Agoe=2143> (1)
<wunyi(r)Agoe=2341> (2)
<wunyi[r]Agoe=1141> (1)
<wunyi[r]Agoe=2341> (1)
<wunyi[r]Agoe=3143> (2)
<wunyi[r]Agoe=3241> (1)
<wunyirAgoe=1341> (2)
<wunyirAgoe=1342> (2)
<wunyirAgoe=2141> (1)
<wunyirAgoe=2143> (13)
<wunyirAgoe=2341> (21)
<wunyirAgoe=3143> (9)
<wunyirAgoe=3241> (17)
<wunyirAgoe=3341> (2)
<wunyirIgoe=3241> (1)
<wunyireegoe=2133> (1)
<wunyi{r}Agoe=1342> (1)
<wunyi{r}Agoe=2143> (1)
<wunyi{r}Agoe=2341> (3)
005.2 S ago
No Response (0)
|IJA| (3)
|JBHefa| (1)
|JBHefj| (1)
|JGDefa| (1)
|JJA| (3)
|JJAefa| (13)
|JJAefc| (1)
|JJAefj| (32)
|JJAffd| (18)
|JJAfmd| (1)
|JJAjjb| (18)
|JJAjjf| (6)
|JJAjjk| (1)
|JJAlfj| (8)
|JJBbja| (1)
|JJBefj| (7)
|JJCefa| (1)
|JJCefj| (34)
|JJCjja| (3)

|JJCjjb| (5)
|JJD| (28)
|JJDefa| (359)
|JJDefc| (1)
|JJDefh| (1)
|JJDefj| (79)
|JJDefl| (1)
|JJDffd| (40)
|JJDffm| (21)
|JJDjjb| (1)
|JJDjjk| (2)
|JJDjjo| (1)
|JJDlfj| (2)
|JJFefa| (15)
|JJFefj| (12)
|JJH| (2)
|JJHefa| (17)
|JJHefj| (32)
|JJHffd| (2)
|JSA| (1)
|JSAefj| (1)
|JSAffj| (1)
|JSAjjb| (1)
|JSAjjf| (1)
|JSCefj| (2)
|JSD| (3)
|JSDeaj| (1)
|JSDefa| (37)
|JSDefj| (3)
|JSDffd| (4)
|JSDffj| (4)
|JSDfoa| (1)
|JSDmaj| (1)
|JSFefa| (2)
|JSHefa| (3)
|JUC| (1)
|KFAffd| (1)
|KMAdfj| (1)
|KMAefj| (2)
|KMAffj| (1)
|LCAfaa| (1)
|LFA| (1)
|LFAeaj| (1)
|LFAefa| (14)
|LFAefj| (1)
|LFAffa| (1)
|LFCefa| (1)
|LFEeaj| (1)
|LFEefa| (5)
|LFEefj| (2)
|LFEjjd| (1)
|LFGefa| (3)
|LFGefj| (1)
|LMAeaa| (1)
|LMAefa| (2)
|LMAefj| (1)
|LMAffa| (9)
|LMAffj| (9)
|LMDefa| (1)

|LMDffa| (4)
|LMEefa| (3)
|LMEffj| (2)
|LMGefj| (1)
|MAA| (1)
|QFBjjm| (1)

005.3 P clouds

{a}   low-front
{d}   devoiced
{l}   devoiced
{ow}   inglide
{r}   devoiced
{z}   devoiced
No Response (210)
<k(l)owdz> (1)
<klad> (1)
<kladz> (2)
<klad{z}> (1)
<klow(d)zh> (1)
<klowd> (10)
<klowds> (1)
<klowdz> (48)
<klowd{z}> (24)
<klowts> (1)
<klow{d}s> (1)
<klow{d}{z}> (3)
<kl{a}dz> (1)
<kl{ow}d> (1)
<kl{ow}dz> (4)
<k{l}ow(d)s> (1)
<k{l}ow(d)z> (1)
<k{l}ow(d){z}> (1)
<k{l}ow(dz)> (1)
<k{l}owd> (47)
<k{l}owd(z)> (7)
<k{l}owds> (3)
<k{l}owdz> (351)
<k{l}owd{z}> (142)
<k{l}owths> (1)
<k{l}ow{d}sh> (1)
<k{l}ow{d}z> (3)
<k{l}ow{d}{z}> (12)
<k{l}{a}dz> (2)
<k{l}{ow}d> (4)
<k{l}{ow}d(z)> (1)
<k{l}{ow}dz> (33)
<k{l}{ow}d{z}> (7)
<k{l}{ow}{d}s> (1)
<k{r}owd> (1)
<prowdz> (1)

005.4 L nice day

No Response (228)
A   balmy day (3)
B   beautiful (day) (172)
C   beautiful bright day (1)
D   beautiful clear day (2)
E   beautiful cool afternoon (1)
F   beautiful kind of day (1)
G   beautiful sky (1)

H   beautiful sun (1)
I   beautiful sunny day (1)
J   beautiful sunshine day (3)
K   beautiful sunshiny day (6)
L   blue sky(s) (3)
M   blue-sky day (2)
N   bluebird day (1)
O   bright (day) (30)
P   bright-looking day (1)
Q   bright sunny cloudless day (1)
R   bright sunny day (6)
S   bright sunshiny day (7)
T   brilliant day (1)
U   calm (day) (2)
V   clear (day) (179)
W   clear and cloudless (1)
X   clear as a bell (1)
Y   clear as a crystal (1)
Z   clear as a whistle (1)
aa   clear beautiful day (1)
ab   clear hot day (1)
ac   clear sky (1)
ad   clear sunny day (1)
ae   cloudless (day) (6)
af   comfortable day (1)
ag   cool (evening) (2)
ah   fair (day) (90)
ai   fair and beautiful day (1)
aj   fair and pretty (1)
ak   fair pretty day (1)
al   fair sky (1)
am   fair to partly fair (1)
an   fine (day) (27)
ao   good (day) (21)
ap   good spell of weather (1)
aq   good sunshiny weather (1)
ar   gorgeous day (3)
as   great day (1)
at   hazy day (1)
au   heavenly day (1)
av   high sky (1)
aw   hot (day) (6)
ax   hot broiling day (1)
ay   light day (1)
az   lovely day (7)
ba   mild (day) (5)
bb   moderate (1)
bc   muggy day (1)
bd   nice (day) (89)
be   nice beautiful day (1)
bf   nice bright day (1)
bg   nice clear day (1)
bh   nice large day (1)
bi   nice spring day (1)
bj   nice sunny day (2)
bk   nice sunshine day (1)
bl   nice sunshiny day (2)
bm   partly fair (1)
bn   perfect (day) (4)

bo   pleasant (day) (34)
bp   pretty (day) (135)
bq   pretty and fair (1)
br   pretty blue day (1)
bs   pretty blue sky (1)
bt   pretty blue-sky day (1)
bu   pretty clear day (1)
bv   pretty fair day (5)
bw   pretty sunshine day (3)
bx   pretty sunshiny day (2)
by   scorcher (1)
bz   shiny pretty day (1)
ca   spring-like (1)
cb   sulky day (1)
cc   sultry (1)
cd   summer day (1)
ce   sunny (day) (49)
cf   sunshine day (3)
cg   sunshining (2)
ch   sunshiny (day) (40)
ci   technicolor day (1)
cj   typical Florida day (1)
ck   warm clear day (1)
cl   warm day (1)
cm   weather-breeding day (1)
cn   wonderful (1)

005.5 L gloomy day
No Response (234)
A   awful (1)
B   backwards weather (1)
C   bad (day) (101)
D   bad cloudy day (1)
E   bad damp day (1)
F   bad-looking (day) (4)
G   bad rainy day (1)
H   bad spell (1)
I   bad weather day (1)
J   black day (1)
K   bloomy-looking (1)
L   blue day (2)
M   blurred (1)
N   blurry Blue Monday (1)
O   blusterous (1)
P   blustery (day) (11)
Q   changeable (1)
R   chilly (1)
S   cloudy (day) (322)
T   cloudy and bad weather (1)
U   cloudy bad day (1)
V   cloudy bloomy day (1)
W   cloudy dreary day (1)
X   cloudy foggy morning (1)
Y   cloudy gloomy day (1)
Z   cloudy hazy day (1)
aa   cloudy rainy day (2)
ab   cloudy sky (1)
ac   cloudying bad (1)
ad   cold (3)
ae   cold dreary day (1)

af   cold freezing snow weather (1)
ag   cruddy day (1)
ah   crummy day (1)
ai   damp day (3)
aj   damp drizzly wet day (1)
ak   damp rainy day (1)
al   dark (day) (27)
am   dark and gloomy day (1)
an   dark cloudy (day) (5)
ao   dark dreary-looking day (1)
ap   dark gloomy day (2)
aq   dark kind of day (1)
ar   dense (1)
as   depressing (1)
at   dingy-looking sky (1)
au   dismal (day) (7)
av   dismal black (1)
aw   disturbed weather (1)
ax   dizzy day (1)
ay   drab day (2)
az   drabby (1)
ba   dreadful (1)
bb   dreary (day) (128)
bc   dreary drizzly day (1)
bd   dreary-looking day (2)
be   dreary-old rainy day (1)
bf   dreary raining depressing day (1)
bg   dreary rainy day (1)
bh   dreary-type day (1)
bi   drizzly day (2)
bj   dull (day) (7)
bk   dull gloomy day (1)
bl   eerie (1)
bm   falling weather (3)
bn   foggy (day) (3)
bo   foul (day) (5)
bp   gloom (day) (1)
bq   gloomy (day) (127)
br   gloomy dark day (1)
bs   gloomy-looking (day) (2)
bt   gory day (1)
bu   gray (day) (4)
bv   hazy (day) (22)
bw   hazy clouds (1)
bx   hazy cloudy (1)
by   heavy (1)
bz   heavy dark cloudy day (1)
ca   horrible day (1)
cb   hot (1)
cc   humid (2)
cd   icky day (1)
ce   inclement (5)
cf   lousy (day) (6)
cg   low (1)
ch   mean (day) (2)
ci   messy (day) (7)
cj   miserable (day) (8)
ck   miserable-looking weather (1)
cl   misty (4)

cm   morbid (1)
cn   mucky (2)
co   muddy (1)
cp   muggy (day) (10)
cq   murky (day) (6)
cr   nasty (day) (11)
cs   nasty-looking day (1)
ct   nasty-old day (1)
cu   overcast (day) (32)
cv   overcloudy (1)
cw   partly cloudy (6)
cx   rainy (day) (78)
cy   rainy bad day (1)
cz   rainy cloudy day (1)
da   rainy-looking (day) (3)
db   rotten (day) (2)
dc   rough (day) (16)
dd   rough-looking sky (1)
de   rough rainy day (1)
df   sloppy day (1)
dg   smoggy day (1)
dh   smoky (day) (2)
di   solid cloudy (1)
dj   sorry (1)
dk   squally (1)
dl   stormy (day) (48)
dm   sulky day (1)
dn   terrible day (5)
do   terrible-looking day (1)
dp   threatening (weather) (5)
dq   threatening-looking (1)
dr   ugly (day/weather) (20)
ds   ugly-looking day (1)
dt   unchangeable (1)
du   uncomfortable (1)
dv   unfair (1)
dw   unfavorable (2)
dx   unpleasant (day) (4)
dy   unsettle (day) (3)
dz   unsettled (4)
ea   wet (day) (4)
eb   windy (1)

005.6 L (the weather is) changing
No Response (290)
A   about to rain (3)
B   about to storm (1)
C   air will turn around (1)
D   becoming bad (1)
E   becoming cloudy (1)
F   becoming overcast (1)
G   beginning to change (1)
H   beginning to cloud up (1)
I   beginning to get bad (1)
J   beginning to look rainy (1)
K   beginning to look stormy (1)
L   betwixt and between (1)
M   blowing up a good little bit of wind (1)
N   blowing up a rain (1)

O   blustering (1)
P   blustery (weather) (6)
Q   breaking (4)
R   building (1)
S   building up (9)
T   building up in the west (1)
U   change [n.] (4)
V   change in the weather (13)
W   change of (the) weather (2)
X   changeable (weather) (12)
Y   changing (227)
Z   changing for (the) worse (3)
aa   changing rapidly (1)
ab   changing to wet (1)
ac   changing up (3)
ad   changing weather (3)
ae   clabbering up (1)
af   clamber up for a storm (1)
ag   cloud looks like snow (1)
ah   cloud up and rain (1)
ai   clouding over (1)
aj   clouding up (57)
ak   clouding up fast (1)
al   clouding up to rain (1)
am   clouds are boiling (1)
an   clouds are breaking (1)
ao   clouds are changing (1)
ap   clouds (are) gathering (8)
aq   clouds (are) gathering up (1)
ar   clouds (are) getting thicker (1)
as   clouds are heavy (1)
at   clouds are thickening up (1)
au   cloud's coming up (3)
av   cloudy-looking mighty bad (1)
aw   cloudying up (1)
ax   cold wave is coming (1)
ay   coming a bad spell (1)
az   coming a (big) rain (3)
ba   coming a little snap (1)
bb   coming a real cold spell (1)
bc   coming a storm (3)
bd   coming a windstorm (1)
be   coming up (1)
bf   coming up a cloud (2)
bg   coming up a little storm (1)
bh   coming up a rain (1)
bi   coming up a thunderstorm (2)
bj   darkening up (1)
bk   falling weather (4)
bl   fixing to bluster up (1)
bm   fixing to break (1)
bn   fixing to change (5)
bo   fixing to go to raining (1)
bp   fixing to have a bad spread of
     weather (1)
bq   fixing to have a thunderstorm
     (1)
br   fixing to have one (1)
bs   fixing to make up (1)

bt   fixing to rain (7)
bu   foul weather (is coming) (1)
bv   funny weather (1)
bw   gathering (9)
bx   gathering clouds (2)
by   gathering in (1)
bz   gathering time (1)
ca   getting a little fierce (1)
cb   getting a storm (1)
cc   getting bad (39)
cd   getting bad and cloudy (1)
ce   getting bad weather (1)
cf   getting badder (1)
cg   getting blustery (1)
ch   getting cloudy (14)
ci   getting dangerous (1)
cj   getting down (1)
ck   getting heavy (1)
cl   getting overcast (1)
cm   getting ready now to be bad (1)
cn   getting ready to rain (3)
co   getting ready to storm (2)
cp   getting rough (6)
cq   getting stormy (6)
cr   getting tough (1)
cs   getting worse (19)
ct   going right to raining (1)
cu   going through a change (1)
cv   going to be a storm (2)
cw   going to be bad (weather) (8)
cx   going to be foul (1)
cy   going to be mean (1)
cz   going to be rain (1)
da   going to be rough (1)
db   going to change (20)
dc   going to cloud up and rain (2)
dd   going to come a awful rain (1)
de   going to get a rain (1)
df   going to get bad (3)
dg   going to get rough (1)
dh   going to get stormy (1)
di   going to get worse (1)
dj   going to have a norther (1)
dk   going to have a storm (1)
dl   going to have some bad weather
     (1)
dm   going to have (some) rain (2)
dn   going to have some weather (1)
do   going to make a change (1)
dp   going to rain (31)
dq   going to rain or snow (1)
dr   going to snow (1)
ds   going to start falling (1)
dt   going to storm (3)
du   going to turn cold (2)
dv   going to turn off bad (1)
dw   hanging clouds (1)
dx   in for a change (1)
dy   inclement (weather) (4)

dz   knotting up (1)
ea   looking bad (11)
eb   looking like bad weather (1)
ec   looking like rain (10)
ed   looking rainy (2)
ee   looking rough (2)
ef   looking stormy (1)
eg   making a change (5)
eh   making a sudden change (1)
ei   making up (2)
ej   making up a cloud (1)
ek   making up a/the rain (2)
el   making up for a rain (2)
em   might have some rain (1)
en   might rain (2)
eo   miserable-looking weather (1)
ep   rain's coming (1)
eq   rain's on its way (1)
er   rainy-looking (2)
es   rough weather coming in (1)
et   scary (1)
eu   starting to look bad (1)
ev   storm (1)
ew   storm (is) coming (2)
ex   storm (is) coming up (4)
ey   storm (is) gathering (2)
ez   storm (is) making up (1)
fa   storming (2)
fb   storming up (there) (3)
fc   stormy (day/weather) (14)
fd   sudden change (2)
fe   thickening up (2)
ff   threatening (67)
fg   threatening-looking (1)
fh   threatening rain (16)
fi   threatening raining (1)
fj   threatening to rain (8)
fk   threatening to storm (1)
fl   threatening weather (7)
fm   tornado making up (1)
fn   turning (10)
fo   turning bad (11)
fp   turning cold(er) (5)
fq   turning darker(1)
fr   turning foul (1)
fs   turning off cold (1)
ft   turning out bad (1)
fu   turning out in another direction
     (1)
fv   turning to rain (1)
fw   uncertain (3)
fx   unlikely (1)
fy   unpredictable (1)
fz   unsettle (1)
ga   unsettled (5)
gb   unstable (2)
gc   weather breeder (1)
gd   weather change [n.] (1)
ge   weather changed [v.] (2)

gf   weather's on the change (1)
gg   windy (1)
gh   windy spell (1)
gi   working up rain (1)

005.7 L (going to) clear up

No Response (204)
A   be a beautiful day (1)
B   be a pretty day (1)
C   be beautiful (1)
D   be better weather (1)
E   be brighter (1)
F   be clear (2)
G   be fair (4)
H   be nice (1)
I   be pretty (1)
J   blow over (2)
K   break (42)
L   break away (8)
M   break in the weather (1)
N   break off (47)
O   break off in the west (1)
P   break out (1)
Q   break through (2)
R   break up (25)
S   breaking of clouds (1)
T   breaking weather (1)
U   brighten up (4)
V   broke off and fairing (1)
W   calm off (1)
X   change (31)
Y   change for the better (3)
Z   change to fair (1)
aa   change up (1)
ab   changeable (2)
ac   changing weather (1)
ad   clear [v.] (91)
ae   clear away (5)
af   clear off (99)
ag   clear out (2)
ah   clear up (300)
ai   clearing of the weather (1)
aj   come out (2)
ak   come out nice (1)
al   come out of the clouds (1)
am   different from yesterday (1)
an   disperse (1)
ao   end (1)
ap   fair [v.] (5)
aq   fair clear (1)
ar   fair off (90)
as   fair off from a rain (1)
at   fair up (46)
au   get better (7)
av   get calm (1)
aw   get fair (2)
ax   get pretty (1)
ay   get real good (1)
az   have a break (1)
ba   have some sun today (1)

bb   improve (2)
bc   let up (2)
bd   lighten up (3)
be   look better (1)
bf   moderate (11)
bg   move out (1)
bh   move over (1)
bi   open up (1)
bj   over (2)
bk   over with (1)
bl   pass off (1)
bm   pass over (4)
bn   quit (2)
bo   quit raining (1)
bp   settle (1)
bq   shape up (1)
br   shine (1)
bs   slack up (1)
bt   turn beautiful (1)
bu   turn good (1)
bv   turn into a clear day (1)
bw   turn off pretty (2)
bx   turn out a pretty day (1)
by   turn out to be a nice day (1)
bx   turn out to be a pretty day (1)
ca   turn out to be pretty (1)
cb   warm up (1)

006.1 L heavy rain

No Response (111)
A   April shower (1)
B   beating rain (3)
C   biggest rain, the (1)
D   blockbuster (1)
E   blowing rain (2)
F   chunk floater (7)
G   chunk mover (2)
H   clod buster (1)
I   clod crusher (1)
J   cloud buster (4)
K   cloudburst (147)
L   cloudburster (1)
M   cloudbuster (1)
N   dam buster (1)
O   dash rain (1)
P   deluge (17)
Q   det shower (1)
R   dog strangler (1)
S   doozer (1)
T   downfall (3)
U   downflow (1)
V   downing pour (1)
W   downpour (337)
X   downpour of rain (2)
Y   downpour rain (2)
Z   downspout (1)
aa   downwash (1)
ab   drencher (1)
ac   drenching rain (1)
ad   flash flood (20)

ae   flash-flood-like (1)
af   float chunker (1)
ag   flood (138)
ah   flood-like (1)
ai   flood of rain (1)
aj   flood rain (14)
ak   flood washer (1)
al   flooded rain (1)
am   flooding rain (1)
an   flopdown (1)
ao   fluid (1)
ap   flush cloud (1)
aq   flush rain (1)
ar   fodder shower (3)
as   fresh, a (1)
at   freshes (1)
au   freshet (2)
av   frog croaker (1)
aw   frog drownder (2)
ax   frog drowner (1)
ay   frog strangle (1)
az   frog strangler (18)
ba   general rain (1)
bb   gosling drownder (1)
bc   gully buster (3)
bd   gully thumper (1)
be   gully wash (2)
bf   gully washer (144)
bg   gully water (1)
bh   gusher (1)
bi   gut buster (1)
bj   hailstorm (4)
bk   heavy dew (1)
bl   hell of a rain (1)
bm   high water (1)
bn   hull digger (1)
bo   leaf mover (1)
bp   lighter(d)-knot floater (3)
bq   lighterd-knot sweeper (1)
br   log mover (1)
bs   lot of rain (2)
bt   monsoon (1)
bu   monsoon rain (1)
bv   Noah, a (1)
bw   off-and-on showers (1)
bx   overflow (5)
by   passing rain (1)
bz   (po)tato choker (1)
ca   (po)tato washer (1)
cb   pour, a (3)
cc   pourdown (33)
cd   pourdown rain (4)
ce   pourdown shower (1)
cf   pouring rain [n.] (4)
cg   pouring-down rain [n.] (3)
ch   rain (173)
ci   rain pour (1)
cj   rain shower (1)
ck   rainfall (5)

cl   rainspout (2)
cm   rainsquall (1)
cn   rainstorm (31)
co   sand soaker (1)
cp   shower (143)
cq   shower of rain (3)
cr   shower rain (2)
cs   showering rain (1)
ct   sloosh (1)
cu   sloosh of rain (1)
cv   soaking rain (1)
cw   spring shower (2)
cx   squall (6)
cy   storm (47)
cz   storm-like (1)
da   storm rain (1)
db   stormy weather (1)
dc   strangler (1)
dd   stump mover (2)
de   sudden shower (1)
df   summer shower (1)
dg   surprising shower (1)
dh   toad choker (1)
di   toad strangler (20)
dj   toad stringer (3)
dk   toad-frog strangler (1)
dl   torrent(s) (5)
dm   torrential downpour (4)
dn   torrential rain (3)
do   trash lifter (3)
dp   trash mover (11)
dq   tropical storm (1)
dr   turd floater (1)
ds   turtle strangler (1)
dt   typhoon (1)
du   wash, a (2)
dv   washer (3)
dw   washing rain (3)
dx   washout (14)
dy   washup (1)
dz   waterspout (18)
ea   young Noah, a (1)

006.2 L thunderstorm
No Response (150)
A   afternoon shower (1)
B   bad cloud (1)
C   bad rain (1)
D   bad storm (4)
E   bad weather (5)
F   banshee (1)
G   bluster [n.] (1)
H   blustery weather (1)
I   cloudburst (8)
J   devil's tossing watermelons (1)
K   drum a-beating (1)
L   electric (2)
M   electric cloud (3)
N   electric storm (83)
O   electrical (4)

P   electrical cloud (1)
Q   electrical storm (166)
R   electricity storm (4)
S   equinox storm (1)
T   good blow (1)
U   heavy storm (2)
V   lightning storm (31)
W   lot of thunder and lightning (1)
X   northeaster storm (1)
Y   rainstorm (17)
Z   rough weather (1)
aa   severe storm (1)
ab   squall (3)
ac   storm (153)
ad   storm cloud (1)
ae   storm-like (1)
af   storming (2)
ag   stormy (8)
ah   stormy time (1)
ai   stormy weather (11)
aj   summer thunderstorm (1)
ak   thunder-and-lightning storm (3)
al   thundercloud (7)
am   thundercloud rain (1)
an   thundering storm (1)
ao   thundershower (43)
ap   thundersquall (1)
aq   thunderstorm (383)
ar   tropical storm (1)
as   turbulent weather (1)
at   violent storm (1)
au   windstorm (14)

006.3 G blow
<!>   infinitive
<&>   present 3rd singular
<@>   present participle
<*>   preterit
<#>   past participle
No Response (151)
<!blaw> (1)
<!bloe> (466)
<!blue> (1)
<!broe> (1)
<&bloez> (28)
<@AbloeN=414> (4)
<@AbloewN=414> (3)
<@b(1)oeN=14> (1)
<@bloeing=13> (3)
<@bloeN=14> (59)
<@bloeNG=14> (17)
<@bloewN=14> (18)
<@bloewNG=14> (4)
<*bAloo=41> (1)
<*blew> (18)
<*bloe> (17)
<*bloed> (182)
<*blue> (488)
<*blued> (3)
<*dloe> (1)

<#blawn> (6)
<#bloe> (2)
<#bloed> (99)
<#bloeN=14> (1)
<#bloen> (318)
<#blue> (24)
<#broen> (1)

006.4 G (the wind's) from (the south)
No Response (483)
A   from (359)
B   out of (91)
C   out [P-0] (12)

006.5 L winds
No Response (318)
A   blizzard (1)
B   blue norther (13)
C   blue south wind (1)
D   blue whistler (1)
E   cloudy norther (1)
F   cold front (3)
G   cold winds from the north (1)
H   cool front (1)
I   cyclone (13)
J   dry wind (1)
K   east (wind) (33)
L   east and north (wind) (4)
M   east and west (wind) (2)
N   east-northeast (wind) (2)
O   east west (wind) (1)
P   easter (1)
Q   easterly (wind) (2)
R   eastern (wind) (1)
S   eastern north wind (1)
T   easternly (wind) (1)
U   eastnorth (wind) (2)
V   eastsouth (wind) (2)
W   gale (3)
X   hawk (1)
Y   high dry cold wind (1)
Z   hurricane (23)
aa   north (wind) (48)
ab   north and east (wind) (2)
ac   north and south (wind) (2)
ad   north-northeast (wind) (2)
ae   north to the east (wind) (1)
af   northeast (wind) (343)
ag   northeaster (13)
ah   northeasterly (wind) (24)
ai   northeastern (wind) (11)
aj   northeasterner (wind) (1)
ak   northeasternly (wind) (1)
al   norther (24)
am   northerly (wind) (2)
an   northern (wind) (3)
ao   northernly (wind) (1)
ap   northwest (wind) (339)
aq   northwester (12)
ar   northwesterly (wind) (28)
as   northwestern (wind) (12)

at   northwesterner (1)
au   south (wind) (50)
av   south and east (wind) (4)
aw   south and north (wind) (1)
ax   south and west (wind) (3)
ay   south breeze (1)
az   south-southeast (wind) (2)
ba   south-southwest (wind) (1)
bb   south to the west (wind) (1)
bc   southeast (wind) (337)
bd   southeaster (12)
be   southeasterly (wind) (24)
bf   southeasterly breeze (1)
bg   southeastern (wind) (14)
bh   southerly (wind) (9)
bi   southern (wind) (5)
bj   southernly (wind) (2)
bk   southwest (wind) (355)
bl   southwester (14)
bm   southwesterly (wind) (24)
bn   southwestern (wind) (15)
bo   southwesterner (1)
bp   squall (1)
bq   storm (1)
br   tornado (31)
bs   twister (4)
bt   west (wind) (39)
bu   west and north (wind) (4)
bv   west and south (wind) (1)
bw   west-northwest (1)
bx   west storm (1)
by   westerly (wind) (4)
bz   westerner (1)
ca   westernly (wind) (1)
cb   westnorth (wind) (3)
cc   westsouth (wind) (1)
cd   whirlwind (1)
ce   windstorm (6)

006.6 L drizzle

No Response (167)
A   all-day rain (4)
B   continual rain (1)
C   dew shower (1)
D   dripping (4)
E   drizzle [n.] (296)
F   drizzle [v.] (77)
G   drizzle of rain (1)
H   drizzle rain [n.] (3)
I   drizzle rain [v.] (1)
J   drizzled rain [n.] (1)
K   drizzling rain [n.] (6)
L   drizzling rain [v.] (4)
M   drizzly (2)
N   drizzly weather (1)
O   dropping (1)
P   dropping rain (1)
Q   dry drizzle (2)
R   dust settler (1)
S   fine mist (13)

T   fine rain (1)
U   foggy rain (2)
V   gale (1)
W   gentle rain (5)
X   God's pissing on me (1)
Y   good shower (1)
Z   ground soaker (1)
aa   heavy dew (2)
ab   heavy mist (1)
ac   light drizzle (6)
ad   light mist (2)
ae   light rain (40)
af   light shower (30)
ag   light sprinkle (7)
ah   little drizzles (1)
ai   little mist rain (1)
aj   little small shower (1)
ak   little sprinkle (3)
al   mist [n.] (228)
am   mist [v.] (47)
an   mist of rain (4)
ao   mist rain [n.] (2)
ap   mist-like (1)
aq   misting rain [n.] (21)
ar   misting rain [v.] (2)
as   misty [n.] (1)
at   misty [adj.] (24)
au   misty moisture (1)
av   misty morning (1)
aw   misty rain (10)
ax   misty shower (1)
ay   misty weather (1)
az   mizzle (1)
ba   nice gentle rain (1)
bb   partial shower (1)
bc   peppering down (2)
bd   rain shower (1)
be   rain slowly (1)
bf   scattering of rain (1)
bg   set rain [n.] (1)
bh   shower (54)
bi   sizzle (1)
bj   slow drizzle (6)
bk   slow gentle rain (2)
bl   slow rain (27)
bm   slow shower (2)
bn   slow soaking rain (2)
bo   small rain (2)
bp   soaking rain (3)
bq   spit a couple of times (1)
br   sprinkle [n.] (282)
bs   sprinkle [v.] (131)
bt   sprinkle of rain (3)
bu   sprinkle rain (1)
bv   sprinkling [n.] (1)
bw   sprinkling rain [n.] (11)
bx   sprinkling rain [v.] (1)
by   spry [n.] (1)
bz   sprying [n.] (1)

ca   surface rain (1)
cb   trickle (1)
cc   weepy weather (1)

006.7A P fog

{f}   bilabial
{o}   low-back
No Response (206)
<faw(g)> (2)
<fawg> (313)
<fawgz> (1)
<fawk> (4)
<flog> (1)
<foeg> (2)
<fog> (222)
<fogz> (2)
<frog> (1)
<f{o}g> (159)
<f{o}gd> (1)
<{f}awg> (3)
<{f}og> (6)
<{f}{o}g> (5)

006.7B P foggy

{f}   bilabial
{o}   low-back
No Response (244)
<fawgA=14> (2)
<fawgI=14> (294)
<fawgI[R]=144> (1)
<fawgee=13> (2)
<fawgeeR=134> (1)
<fawggI=14> (9)
<foegI=14> (4)
<fogI=14> (217)
<foggI=14> (21)
<fogiR=134> (1)
<fogyee=13> (1)
<fugI=14> (1)
<f{o}gI=14> (108)
<f{o}gIR=144> (1)
<f{o}ggI=14> (6)
<{f}awgI=14> (1)
<{f}ogI=14> (4)
<{f}oggI=14> (1)

007.1 L drought

No Response (140)
A   almost too dry (1)
B   arid (1)
C   drought (666)
D   drought weather (1)
E   dry [adj.] (17)
F   dry [n.] (2)
G   dry drought (7)
H   dry graft (1)
I   dry hot spell (1)
J   dry period (2)
K   dry season (13)
L   dry spell (389)
M   dry spell of weather (1)
N   dry streak (2)

O   dry summer (1)
P   dry time (3)
Q   dry weather (45)
R   dry year (1)
S   few dry days, a (1)
T   hard dry spell of weather (1)
U   hot dry spell (1)
V   little drought (2)
W   long drought (3)
X   long dry period (1)
Y   long dry spell (13)
Z   mighty dry (2)
aa   miserable weather (1)
ab   need some rain (1)
ac   plumb dry (1)
ad   rather dry (1)
ae   real dry (1)
af   real dry spell (1)
ag   real dry weather (1)
ah   secheresse [F] (2)
ai   severe drought (2)
aj   short drought (2)
ak   short dry spell (1)
al   terrible dry spell (1)
am   turned off so dry (1)
an   very dry spell (1)

007.1 P drought
{a}   low-front
{ow}   inglide
No Response (238)
<d[r]owt> (1)
<drath> (2)
<draw(t)> (1)
<drawt> (4)
<drawth> (11)
<drawts> (1)
<droth> (1)
<drow(t)> (3)
<drowf> (2)
<drowft> (1)
<drowfth> (1)
<drows> (14)
<drowt> (246)
<drowth> (368)
<drowths> (1)
<drowts> (2)
<drowtth> (8)
<dr{a}ft> (1)
<dr{a}t> (4)
<dr{a}th> (11)
<dr{ow}f> (1)
<dr{ow}s> (1)
<dr{ow}t> (4)
<dr{ow}th> (10)

007.2 L (the wind is) picking up
No Response (240)
A   a-breezing up (1)
B   a-getting higher (2)
C   a-getting to be heavy (1)

D   a-getting up (1)
E   a-gusting (1)
F   a-picking up (1)
G   a-rising (8)
H   becoming blustery (1)
I   began to rise (2)
J   beginning to blow (7)
K   beginning to blow harder (3)
L   beginning to breeze (1)
M   beginning to come up (1)
N   beginning to get stronger (1)
O   beginning to pick up (1)
P   beginning to rise (1)
Q   being high (1)
R   blowing harder (76)
S   blowing heavier (1)
T   blowing stronger (6)
U   blowing up (5)
V   blowing up a cloud (1)
W   blowing up a rain (1)
X   blowing up a storm (3)
Y   blustering (1)
Z   breezing up (1)
aa   building (7)
ab   building up (11)
ac   changing (4)
ad   coming more harder (1)
ae   coming up (24)
af   coming up harder (1)
ag   coming up strong (1)
ah   developing (2)
ai   freshened up (1)
aj   freshening (2)
ak   freshening up (1)
al   gaining (1)
am   gaining speed (1)
an   gathering (1)
ao   gets high (1)
ap   gets higher (2)
aq   gets stronger (1)
ar   getting bad (1)
as   getting bigger (1)
at   getting faster (1)
au   getting gusty (4)
av   getting harder (11)
aw   getting harder and harder (2)
ax   getting heavier (1)
ay   getting high (10)
az   getting higher (16)
ba   getting more windy (1)
bb   getting rough (3)
bc   getting rougher (2)
bd   getting stiffer (1)
be   getting stormy (2)
bf   getting stouter (3)
bg   getting strong (9)
bh   getting stronger (52)
bi   getting stronger and stronger (1)
bj   getting swift (1)

bk   getting up (30)
bl   getting worse (4)
bm   getting worse and worser (1)
bn   getting worser (1)
bo   goes to blowing (1)
bp   going to blow up rain (1)
bq   gone to blowing (1)
br   gushed up (1)
bs   gusting (8)
bt   gusting up (2)
bu   has come up (1)
bv   has raised (1)
bw   has risen (2)
bx   higher and higher (1)
by   increasing (51)
bz   increasing its velocity (1)
ca   kicking up (1)
cb   made a sudden change (1)
cc   making up for a storm (1)
cd   picking up (163)
ce   picking up speed (6)
cf   picking up strength (2)
cg   picks up strength (1)
ch   raising (5)
ci   raising up (1)
cj   rises (1)
ck   rising (115)
cl   rising higher (1)
cm   rising up (2)
cn   riz (2)
co   rose (1)
cp   shifting (2)
cq   speeding up (1)
cr   springed up (1)
cs   started blowing (1)
ct   starting (1)
cu   starting to blow (5)
cv   starting to blow harder (1)
cw   starting to pick up (1)
cx   stirring (4)
cy   stirring up (1)
cz   strengthening (1)
da   stronger (1)
db   tightening up (1)
dc   whipping up (2)
dd   whipping up a breeze (1)
de   whipping up a gale (1)
df   worser (1)

007.3 L (the wind is) letting up
No Response (232)
A   abating (5)
B   backing off (2)
C   basing down (1)
D   blowing away (1)
E   blowing less (1)
F   blowing out (2)
G   breaking (1)
H   breaking down (1)
I   breaking off (1)

J   calming (25)
K   calming down (128)
L   ceased blowing (2)
M   ceaseded (5)
N   ceaseded down (2)
O   ceaseding down (1)
P   ceasing (61)
Q   ceasing down (3)
R   ceasing to blow (1)
S   changing (again) (2)
T   clearing up (2)
U   coming down (1)
V   deceasing (2)
W   decreasing (23)
X   diminishing (10)
Y   dissipating (1)
Z   dropping (5)
aa drying down (1)
ab dwindling (1)
ac dwindling out (1)
ad dying (17)
ae dying away (4)
af dying down (147)
ag dying off (1)
ah dying out (8)
ai easing (3)
aj easing off (2)
ak easing up (7)
al ending (2)
am fairing off (2)
an falling (5)
ao falling off (1)
ap getting a calm spell (1)
aq getting better (1)
ar getting breezier (1)
as getting calm (and still) (11)
at getting lighter (5)
au getting low (1)
av getting lower (1)
aw getting mild (2)
ax getting milder (2)
ay getting on weaker (1)
az getting quiet (1)
ba getting quieter (1)
bb getting settled (1)
bc getting slower (2)
bd getting softer (1)
be getting still (4)
bf getting weak (2)
bg getting weaker (8)
bh giving away (1)
bi going away (2)
bj going down (11)
bk going on down (1)
bl gone (1)
bm having a calm (1)
bn laying (75)
bo laying down (4)
bp lessening (3)

bq letting off (1)
br letting up (33)
bs lifting (1)
bt lightening (1)
bu lightening down (1)
bv lightening up (4)
bw low wind (1)
bx lull, a (2)
by lulling (4)
bz lulling down (2)
ca lying (9)
cb lying down (1)
cc lying low (1)
cd moderating (1)
ce moderating down (1)
cf over (4)
cg passing off (1)
ch passing on off (1)
ci playing out (1)
cj quietening (1)
ck quietening down (6)
cl quieting (3)
cm quieting down (12)
cn quieting off (2)
co quit blowing (3)
cp quitting (3)
cq receding (3)
cr settling (6)
cs settling down (11)
ct shifting (1)
cu slackening (rain) (1)
cv slacking off (6)
cw slacking up (3)
cx stilled (1)
cy slowing (1)
cz slowing down (35)
da stopping (5)
db stopping blowing (3)
dc subsiding (15)
dd tailing off (1)
de tapering off (2)
df weakening (3)

007.4 L snappy

No Response (257)
A   air's got a edge on it (1)
B   airish (72)
C   airy (5)
D   bad chilly (1)
E   balmy (3)
F   balmy weather (1)
G   bracing (1)
H   brisk (39)
I   brisk morning (2)
J   brisk weather (1)
K   brisky (3)
L   chill, a (2)
M   chillier (2)
N   chillish (1)
O   chilly (437)

P   chilly day (3)
Q   chilly morning (2)
R   chilly night (1)
S   chilly weather (1)
T   cool (202)
U   cool air (1)
V   cool clear morning (1)
W   cool day (2)
X   cool morning (3)
Y   cool night (1)
Z   cool spell (2)
aa cool weather (2)
ab cooler (12)
ac coolish (1)
ad coolly (1)
ae crisp (15)
af crisp day (1)
ag crispy (2)
ah crispy weather (1)
ai damp (2)
aj edgy (2)
ak exhilarating (1)
al fall-like (1)
am fallish (1)
an fine (1)
ao fine morning (2)
ap foggy-like (1)
aq fresh (4)
ar fresh air (1)
as freshet (1)
at frisky (2)
au frisky morning (1)
av frosty (5)
aw frosty morning (2)
ax getting an edge (1)
ay good brisk frosty morning (1)
az good weather (1)
ba invigorating (2)
bb March weather (1)
bc mild (7)
bd nice (6)
be nice brisk morning (1)
bf nice cool morning (1)
bg nice day (2)
bh nice weather (1)
bi nip, a (1)
bj nip in the air (1)
bk nippy (59)
bl nippy morning (1)
bm penetrating (1)
bn pinching (1)
bo pinchy (3)
bp pleasant (18)
bq pleasant day (1)
br pleasant morning (1)
bs pleasant weather (1)
bt refreshing (1)
bu sharp (5)
bv snappish (1)

bw snappy (19)
bx snappy cold (1)
by springy (1)
bz zesty (1)

007.5 L frost

No Response (171)
A bad frost (2)
B bad hard freeze (1)
C big freeze (4)
D big frost (21)
E biting frost (1)
F black frost (6)
G blight frost (1)
H first frost (1)
I fog (1)
J freeze [n.] (226)
K freeze frog (1)
L freeze time (1)
M freezing, a (1)
N freezing weather (2)
O frost [n.] (610)
P frost [v.] (7)
Q frost cold (1)
R frost freeze (1)
S frosty [adj.] (4)
T frosty morning (1)
U frosty night (1)
V good frost (2)
W half froze (1)
X hard freeze (53)
Y hard frost (13)
Z harder freeze (1)
aa heavy (3)
ab heavy freeze (2)
ac heavy frost (53)
ad hoarfrost (5)
ae hoary frost (4)
af Jack Frost (21)
ag killer-diller (1)
ah killing freeze (2)
ai killing frost (76)
aj late freeze (1)
ak late frost (1)
al light (3)
am light freeze (20)
an light frost (55)
ao nipping frost (1)
ap ordinary frost (1)
aq overnight freeze (1)
ar partial freeze (1)
as partially freeze (1)
at severe freeze (1)
au severe frost (1)
av slight freeze (1)
aw small freeze (1)
ax terrible freeze (1)
ay touch of frost (1)
az white frost (9)

007.6 L froze over

No Response (264)
A crusted over (2)
B double-freeze [v.] (1)
C friz over (2)
D frosted over (1)
E froze (283)
F froze all over (1)
G froze around the edges (2)
H froze dry (1)
I froze off (1)
J froze out (1)
K froze over (356)
L froze over solid (1)
M froze over with ice (1)
N froze plumb over (1)
O froze solid (5)
P froze up (64)
Q iced (2)
R iced over (26)
S iced up (6)
T iceded (1)
U partially froze (2)
V ponded up (1)
W skimmed (2)
X skimmed over (8)
Y skimping over (1)

007.7 G freeze

<!> infinitive
<&> present 3rd singular
<@> present participle
<*> preterit
<#> past participle
No Response (131)
<!fleez> (1)
<!free(z)> (1)
<!freedh> (3)
<!freedz> (1)
<!frees> (1)
<!freez> (612)
<!freezh> (3)
<!frez> (1)
<!froes> (2)
<!reefreez=31> (1)
<&freez> (1)
<&freezIz=14> (32)
<@freezing=13> (1)
<@freezN=14> (30)
<@freezNG=14> (7)
<*f(r)oez> (2)
<*f(r)oezh> (1)
<*frawz> (2)
<*freez> (2)
<*freezd> (5)
<*frez> (2)
<*friz> (2)
<*froe(z)> (2)
<*froedh> (2)
<*froes> (1)
<*froesh> (2)

<*froez> (616)
<*froezd> (3)
<*froezh> (8)
<*froezN=14> (8)
<*froezs> (1)
<*fruz> (2)
<#f(r)ozN=14> (1)
<#frawz> (1)
<#frawzhN=14> (1)
<#frawzN=14> (1)
<#freezd> (1)
<#freezN=14> (1)
<#frez> (1)
<#froe(z)> (2)
<#froe(z)N=14> (1)
<#froedhN=14> (2)
<#froedN=14> (1)
<#froesN=14> (1)
<#froez> (169)
<#froezd> (6)
<#froezen=13> (1)
<#froezh> (2)
<#froezhN=14> (6)
<#froez[N]=14> (2)
<#froezN=14> (389)
<#froezNd=14> (2)
<#froezun=13> (1)

007.8 L sitting room

No Response (119)
A back parlor (1)
B best room (2)
C big den (1)
D big house (4)
E big room (9)
F chambre en avant [F] (1)
G company parlor (1)
H company room (6)
I den (83)
J double parlor (1)
K drawing room (3)
L drilling room (1)
M family house (1)
N family parlor (1)
O family room (32)
P family sitting room (1)
Q fire (1)
R fireplace room (7)
S fireroom (5)
T formal living room (1)
U front bedroom (4)
V front parlor (2)
W front room (141)
X gossiping room (1)
Y great big room (1)
Z great room (3)
aa guest room (17)
ab hall (2)
ac heater room (1)
ad house (2)

ae living area (3)
af living room (669)
ag living-room parlor (1)
ah main family room (1)
ai main sitting room (1)
aj middle room (1)
ak music room (2)
al other room (1)
am parlor (298)
an parlor room (1)
ao receiving room (1)
ap reception room (3)
aq sala [S] (1)
ar salon, un [F] (1)
as service room (1)
at setting room (16)
au side room (1)
av sit room (1)
aw sitting room (97)

007.9 G (nine) feet (high)

No Response (187)
A feet (577)
B feets (1)
C foot[N-i] (259)
D foots (2)

008.1 L chimney

No Response (56)
A brick chimley (8)
B brick chimney (8)
C cat and clay (chimney) (1)
D cat chimley (1)
E cattail chimley (2)
F cheminee [F] (1)
G chimenea [S] (1)
H chimley (387)
I chimney (511)
J chimney funnel (1)
K chimney piece (1)
L chink chimney (1)
M clay chimley (1)
N clay chimney (1)
O coal-burning chimley (1)
P dirt and stick chimley (1)
Q dirt chimley (11)
R dirt chimney (2)
S double chimley (6)
T double chimney (4)
U double stack chimley (1)
V double-fireplace chimley (1)
W hay chimley (1)
X (lamp) chimley (2)
Y mud and stick chimney (1)
Z mud chimley (3)
aa mud chimney (4)
ab one-end chimney (1)
ac rock chimley (8)
ad rock chimney (2)
ae semi-brick chimley (1)
af smokestack (1)

ag stack (1)
ah stack chimley (19)
ai stack chimney (8)
aj stick and clay chimney (2)
ak stick and daub chimley (1)
al stick and dirt chimley (14)
am stick and dirt chimney (1)
an stick and mud chimley (1)
ao stick and mud chimney (1)
ap stone chimney (1)
aq (stove) chimley (1)
ar (stove) chimney (1)
as straw and dirt (chimney) (1)
at thatch chimley (1)
au two-stack chimney (1)

008.1 P chimney

No Response (60)
<chemAlI=144> (1)
<chemblI=14> (1)
<chemlI=14> (36)
<chemlIz=14> (4)
<chemnI=14> (29)
<chi(m)blI=14> (1)
<chi[m]bnI=14> (1)
<chi[m]nI=14> (1)
<chimAlI=144> (4)
<chimAnI=144> (10)
<chimIII=144> (3)
<chimInI=144> (6)
<chimblA=14> (1)
<chimblI=14> (20)
<chimblIz=14> (1)
<chimbliz=13> (1)
<chimlA=14> (1)
<chimlI=14> (322)
<chimlIz=14> (22)
<chimlai=13> (4)
<chimlee=13> (4)
<chimnI=14> (470)
<chimnIz=14> (16)
<chimnai=13> (1)
<chimnaiz=13> (1)
<chimnee=13> (5)
<klimlI=14> (1)
<shimlI=14> (2)
<shimnI=14> (3)

008.2 P hearth

{o} low-back
{r} weakly retroflex
{?} glottal
No Response (169)
<ha(r)f> (1)
<ha(r)t> (1)
<ha(r)th> (10)
<ha(rth)> (1)
<ha[r]th> (8)
<hai(r)th> (1)
<harth> (4)
<haw(r)th> (4)

<haw[r]th> (9)
<hawrth> (23)
<haw{r}fs> (1)
<haw{r}th> (3)
<ha{r}th> (1)
<he(r)th> (1)
<hee(r)th> (1)
<herth> (2)
<he{r}th> (1)
<hi{r}th> (1)
<ho(r)dth> (1)
<ho(r)t> (1)
<ho(r)th> (27)
<ho[r]th> (63)
<ho[r]tth> (1)
<hoorth> (1)
<horIth=14> (1)
<horf> (1)
<hort> (5)
<horth> (287)
<hortth> (2)
<ho{r}(th)> (1)
<ho{r}dh> (1)
<ho{r}dhz> (1)
<ho{r}t> (1)
<ho{r}th> (57)
<hu[r]s> (1)
<hu[r]t> (1)
<hu[r]th> (25)
<hu[r]ths> (1)
<hu[r]tth> (1)
<hurf> (1)
<hurs> (1)
<hurst> (1)
<hurth> (127)
<hurtth> (1)
<hur{?}> (1)
<hu{r}th> (22)
<hu{r}tth> (3)
<h{o}(r)th> (7)
<h{o}[r]th> (23)
<h{o}rf> (1)
<h{o}rp> (1)
<h{o}rt> (1)
<h{o}rth> (68)
<h{o}{r}th> (9)

008.3 L andirons

No Response (118)
A amble irons (1)
B andirons (322)
C anvils (1)
D chenet [F] (1)
E chenille [F] (1)
F dog firedogs (1)
G dog horns (1)
H dog irons (283)
I dog sticks (1)
J dogfire (1)
K dogs (43)

L   fire holders (1)
M   fire irons (52)
N   fire logs (1)
O   fire rack (1)
P   fire tongs (4)
Q   firedogs (210)
R   firehorses (2)
S   fireplace dogs (1)
T   fireplace irons (2)
U   firewood blocks (1)
V   firewood dogs (1)
W   granite dogs (1)
X   gridirons (1)
Y   handirons (7)
Z   hearth (1)
aa   horses (3)
ab   hounds (1)
ac   iron bars (2)
ad   iron block (1)
ae   iron dogs (4)
af   iron firedogs (1)
ag   iron horses (1)
ah   irons (33)
ai   ironstones (1)
aj   jacks (1)
ak   Kamin Eisen [G] (1)
al   log dogs (3)
am   log holders (2)
an   log irons (2)
ao   metal stand (1)
ap   out irons (1)
aq   parilla, la [S] (1)
ar   rack (4)
as   rail benders (1)
at   stand irons (1)
au   stand(s) (4)
av   timber holders (1)
aw   trestles (1)
ax   wood dogs (3)
ay   wood holders (1)
az   wood irons (1)

008.4 L mantel
No Response (72)
A   arch (1)
B   arch rock (1)
C   board (6)
D   chimenea [S] (1)
E   chimney (1)
F   chimney breast (1)
G   chimney shelf (2)
H   chimneypiece (1)
I   clock shelf (1)
J   corniche, la [F] (1)
K   fire mantel (2)
L   fire shelf (2)
M   fireboard (69)
N   fireplace mantel (1)
O   fireplace shelf (3)
P   ledge (1)

Q   mantel (570)
R   mantel board (51)
S   mantel log (1)
T   mantel place (1)
U   manteling (1)
V   mantelpiece (240)
W   mantelshelf (36)
X   manteltree (1)
Y   medicine shelf (1)
Z   oak (1)
aa   shelf (59)
ab   shelf mantel (1)
ac   shelf over the fireplace (1)
ad   stone mantel (1)
ae   whatnot shelf (2)
af   wooden mantel (1)

008.5 L backlog/forestick
No Response (69)
A   ash log (1)
B   back chunk (3)
C   back piece (1)
D   backlog (326)
E   backstand (1)
F   backstick (129)
G   base log (1)
H   base of the wood (1)
I   big log (19)
J   big piece of wood (1)
K   big round stick (1)
L   big stick (7)
M   big stick of wood (2)
N   big wood (1)
O   big-old backlog (1)
P   big-old chunk (2)
Q   big(-old) hunk of oak (2)
R   big-old knot (1)
S   bigger log (1)
T   billet (2)
U   billet wood (1)
V   block (2)
W   block of oakwood (1)
X   block of wood (1)
Y   buche, une [F] (1)
Z   butt cut (1)
aa   butt stick (1)
ab   chimley backlog (1)
ac   chimley wood (1)
ad   chunk (11)
ae   chunk of fire (2)
af   chunk of wood (20)
ag   cypress log (3)
ah   eight-foot log (1)
ai   fire back (1)
aj   fire log (15)
ak   fire stick (1)
al   fireplace wood (2)
am   forestick (14)
an   front log (4)
ao   front stick (4)

ap   front wood (2)
aq   great big green log (1)
ar   great big stick (3)
as   great big stout green backstick
     (1)
at   great big-old backstick of wood
     (1)
au   great big-old log (1)
av   green log (1)
aw   green stick (1)
ax   green wood (2)
ay   heavy log (1)
az   heavy wood (2)
ba   hickory log (2)
bb   hind stick (1)
bc   hollow log (3)
bd   house wood (1)
be   hunk (1)
bf   Kneppel [G] (1)
bg   knot (1)
bh   large backlog (1)
bi   large log (1)
bj   leno [S] (3)
bk   lick log (2)
bl   log (448)
bm   log of wood (5)
bn   log wood (1)
bo   loggerhead (1)
bp   long log (1)
bq   long wood (1)
br   oak, the (2)
bs   oak chunk (1)
bt   oak log (13)
bu   overnight log (1)
bv   palmetto log (1)
bw   piece of wood (7)
bx   pine log (3)
by   pretty good log (1)
bz   quarter log (1)
ca   slab (2)
cb   split log (1)
cc   split wood (1)
cd   stick of firewood (1)
ce   stick of wood (12)
cf   stick wood (1)
cg   stump (2)
ch   tronco [S] (1)
ci   wood log (1)
cj   Yule log (5)

008.5 P log
{aw}   unrounded onset
{o}   low-back
No Response (148)
<law(g)> (4)
<lawg> (464)
<lawgz> (55)
<loeg> (4)
<loegz> (1)
<log> (105)

<logz> (16)
<lok> (1)
<lugz> (1)
<l{aw}(g)> (1)
<l{aw}g> (128)
<l{aw}gz> (18)
<l{o}g> (9)
<l{o}gz> (2)

008.6 L lightwood

No Response (49)
A black pine knots (1)
B burrs (1)
C cedar (3)
D cedar kindling (1)
E cedar shavings (1)
F cedar shingles (1)
G cedar splinters (1)
H chip kindling (1)
I chips (38)
J chips of wood (1)
K chunks of wood (1)
L cypress (4)
M cypress chips (1)
N cypress kindling (1)
O cypress shingles (1)
P cypress wood (1)
Q dead pine (1)
R deadwood (1)
S driftwood (2)
T dross (1)
U dry cedar (1)
V dry chips (1)
W dry hardwood (1)
X dry kindling (6)
Y dry wood (3)
Z fat (1)
aa fat chips (1)
ab fat kindling (4)
ac fat kindling wood (1)
ad fat lighter (4)
ae fat lighter splinters (1)
af fat lighter wood (1)
ag fat lighterd (39)
ah fat lighterd limbs (1)
ai fat lighterd pine (2)
aj fat lighterd pinewood (1)
ak fat lighterd splinters (9)
al fat lighterd wood (1)
am fat lightwood (8)
an fat lightwood splinters (1)
ao fat piece of lighterd (1)
ap fat pine (41)
aq fat pine splinters (2)
ar fat pinewood (1)
as fat splinters (8)
at fatty wood (1)
au fatwood (35)
av fatwood pine (1)
aw fatwood tinder (1)

ax fine pine kindling (1)
ay fine wood (1)
az fire kindling (1)
ba firewood (22)
bb heart of pine (3)
bc heart of the pine (2)
bd hearts (2)
be huisache wood (1)
bf kindle [n.] (1)
bg kindle wood (2)
bh kindling (574)
bi kindling-like, a (2)
bj kindling pieces (1)
bk kindling pine (1)
bl kindling splinters (1)
bm kindling wood (52)
bn kindlings (5)
bo knots (4)
bp knotty pine (1)
bq lena [S] (1)
br light piece of wood (1)
bs light pieces (1)
bt lighter (18)
bu lighter knots (17)
bv lighter pine (1)
bw lighter wood (10)
bx lighterd (102)
by lighterd heart (1)
bz lighterd knots (43)
ca lighterd pine (5)
cb lighterd splinters (9)
cc lighterd wood (7)
cd lighting wood (2)
ce lightning (1)
cf lightning wood (1)
cg lightwood (90)
ch lightwood kindling (1)
ci little chips of pine (1)
cj little pieces of pine (1)
ck little stuff (1)
cl little wood (4)
cm lumps (1)
cn madera [S] (1)
co mesquite (4)
cp pebbles (1)
cq pecan limbs (1)
cr piece of lighter (2)
cs pine (89)
ct pine chips (2)
cu pine fat (1)
cv pine hearts (1)
cw pine kindling (4)
cx pine knots (64)
cy pine lighter (1)
cz pine lighterd (1)
da pine resin (2)
db pine richerd (1)
dc pine shavings (2)
dd pine splinters (6)

de pine sticks (1)
df pine tar (1)
dg pinewood (11)
dh pitch (2)
di pitch pine (3)
dj pitch wood (1)
dk pulp (1)
dl pure fatwood (1)
dm pure rich-pine (1)
dn red cedar (1)
do resin (8)
dp resin lighterd knots (1)
dq resin pine (1)
dr rich [n.] (1)
ds rich kindling (1)
dt rich lighterd (5)
du rich lighterd pine (1)
dv rich lighterd splinters (1)
dw rich piece of pine (1)
dx rich pine splinters (1)
dy rich pinewood (1)
dz rich resin pine (1)
ea rich splinters (2)
eb rich wood (3)
ec rich-pine (43)
ed rich-pine knots (2)
ee richerd (1)
ef rose-comb lighterd knot (1)
eg scrap wood (1)
eh shavings (19)
ei shingles (1)
ej slits of pine (1)
ek small kindling (1)
el small sticks of wood (2)
em small stuff (1)
en small wood (6)
eo soft pine (1)
ep splinter lighterd (1)
eq splinter wood (2)
er splinters (106)
es splinters of pinewood (1)
et splints (2)
eu starter (2)
ev starting wood (1)
ew sticks (1)
ex straight-grain wood (1)
ey stuff (1)
ez tar lighterd (1)
fa tinder (7)
fb tinderwood (1)
fc turpentine chips (1)
fd twigs (5)
fe white pinewood (1)
ff wood (10)
fg wood chips (3)
fh wood shavings (1)

008.6 S wood

No Response (0)
|CSAffj| (1)

|EAC| (1)
|ECAmaj| (1)
|EFA| (13)
|EFAmaj| (6)
|EFB| (8)
|EFBmaj| (8)
|EFC| (9)
|EFCmaj| (3)
|EFD| (2)
|EFE| (2)
|EFF| (2)
|EFFmaj| (1)
|EFGmaj| (3)
|EFH| (1)
|EFHeaj| (1)
|EFHmaj| (1)
|EFI| (1)
|EFIefb| (1)
|EMA| (12)
|EMAmaa| (1)
|EMAmaj| (6)
|EMBmaj| (6)
|EMCmaj| (4)
|EMFmaj| (1)
|EOD| (1)
|FAD| (4)
|FCA| (1)
|FFA| (45)
|FFAfaj| (3)
|FFAmaj| (10)
|FFB| (6)
|FFBffa| (1)
|FFBffc| (1)
|FFBmaa| (1)
|FFBmaj| (4)
|FFC| (16)
|FFCffa| (1)
|FFCmaj| (3)
|FFD| (255)
|FFDbjdmaj| (1)
|FFDbjj| (2)
|FFDcjm| (1)
|FFDefj| (1)
|FFDfaj| (1)
|FFDmaj| (229)
|FFF| (30)
|FFFbjj| (1)
|FFFbjjmaj| (1)
|FFFefk| (1)
|FFFfaj| (1)
|FFFmaj| (35)
|FFG| (2)
|FFGmaj| (4)
|FFH| (9)
|FFHcjq| (1)
|FMA| (37)
|FMAmaj| (4)
|FMBmaa| (1)
|FMBmaj| (4)

|FMCmaj| (3)
|FMD| (18)
|FMDefj| (1)
|FMDfaj| (1)
|FMDmaj| (48)
|FMF| (1)
|FMFmaj| (21)
|FMFmfj| (1)
|FMFmfk| (1)
|FMHmaj| (3)
|FXA| (1)
|FXAmdj| (1)
|fmdCSD| (1)

008.7A P soot

No Response (84)
<(s)mut> (1)
<(s)uet> (1)
<set> (1)
<shmut> (1)
<smoot> (1)
<smu(t)> (1)
<smuj> (1)
<smuk> (1)
<smut> (154)
<sook> (1)
<soot> (390)
<sud> (1)
<sues> (1)
<suet> (37)
<sut> (380)
<thmut> (1)

008.7B P white

No Response (22)
<w(h)ie(t)> (1)
<w(h)iet> (191)
<w(h)iets> (1)
<what> (1)
<whiet> (733)
<whiets> (7)

008.7C P ashes

{a}   upglide
{z}   devoiced
{?}   glottal
No Response (131)
<achI{z}=14> (1)
<aishIs=14> (1)
<aishIz=14> (2)
<aishI{z}=14> (1)
<ash> (18)
<ashIs=14> (6)
<ashIt=14> (1)
<ashIz=14> (570)
<ashI{z}=14> (85)
<ashiz=13> (4)
<a{?}Iz=14> (1)
<esh> (1)
<eshIz=14> (1)
<hashIz=14> (2)
<{a}sh> (5)

<{a}shIz=14> (93)
<{a}shI{z}=14> (3)

008.8 P chair

No Response (62)
<cha(r)> (9)
<cha(r)z> (5)
<cha[r]> (71)
<cha[r]z> (35)
<chai[r]> (2)
<chai[r]z> (4)
<chair> (6)
<chairz> (3)
<char> (171)
<charz> (52)
<che(r)> (5)
<che(r)z> (2)
<che[r]> (119)
<che[r]z> (48)
<chee[r]> (1)
<cher> (206)
<cherz> (97)
<chi[r]> (25)
<chi[r]z> (8)
<chir> (44)
<chirz> (22)
<chur> (18)
<churz> (8)
<chye[r]> (1)
<shar> (1)
<sharz> (1)
<she[r]z> (1)

009.1 L sofa

No Response (75)
A   bamboo couch (1)
B   bed couch (1)
C   bed sofa (1)
D   bunk (1)
E   campaign sofa (1)
F   chesterfield (3)
G   cot (1)
H   couch (509)
I   davender (1)
J   davenette (43)
K   davenport (127)
L   daybed (18)
M   divan (124)
N   do-for (8)
O   double-bed couch (1)
P   fainting couch (3)
Q   flopper (1)
R   foldaway bed (1)
S   folding couch (1)
T   French sofa (1)
U   granddaddy (1)
V   hideaway (2)
W   hideaway bed (7)
X   horsehair couch (1)
Y   horsehair sofa (1)
Z   Irish sofa (1)

aa　little sofa (1)
ab　living-room couch (1)
ac　lounge (39)
ad　love chair (1)
ae　love seat (121)
af　lovers' seat (1)
ag　sectional (3)
ah　sedan (1)
ai　settee (194)
aj　settee bed (1)
ak　settee chair (1)
al　settle (1)
am　short couch (1)
an　sleeper (1)
ao　sleeper couch (1)
ap　sleeping couch (1)
aq　sleigh bed (1)
ar　sofa (637)
as　sofa [F] (2)
at　sofa [S] (1)
au　sofa bed (10)
av　sofa chair (2)
aw　sofa lounge (1)
ax　studio (1)
ay　studio cot (2)
az　studio couch (14)
ba　velvet sofa (1)
bb　Victorian love seat (1)

009.1 P sofa
{R}　weakly retroflex
No Response (259)
<sawfA=14> (1)
<shoevA=14> (1)
<soefA=14> (545)
<soefAdh=14> (1)
<soefAz=14> (49)
<soefI=14> (24)
<soefIz=14> (3)
<soefM=14> (1)
<soefR=14> (25)
<soefRz=14> (3)
<soefee=13> (1)
<soefo=13> (2)
<soefo=31> (1)
<soefu=13> (1)
<soef{R}=14> (5)
<soef{R}z=14> (3)
<soevA=14> (1)
<sufA=14> (2)
<thoefA=14> (1)

009.2 L chest of drawers/dresser
No Response (102)
A　antique chest (1)
B　bedroom safe (1)
C　built-in dresser (1)
D　bureau (164)
E　bureau drawer(s) (5)
F　cedarrobe (5)
G　chest (70)

H　chest in drawers (1)
I　chest of [N-0] (1)
J　chest of drawers (450)
K　chest on chest (1)
L　chest with drawers (1)
M　chester (7)
N　chester drawers (1)
O　chiffonier (26)
P　chifforobe (101)
Q　clothes chest (1)
R　clothes drawer (1)
S　clothespress (1)
T　commode (2)
U　comoda [S] (1)
V　convenience (1)
W　drawers (4)
X　dresser (575)
Y　dresser drawer(s) (19)
Z　dresserette (1)
aa　dressing table (11)
ab　gentleman's chifforobe (1)
ac　highball (1)
ad　highboy (16)
ae　lingerie chest (1)
af　lowboy (3)
ag　marble-top dresser (2)
ah　nightstand (7)
ai　nine-drawer dresser (1)
aj　old-time dresser (1)
ak　safe (2)
al　sideboard (4)
am　toilette [F] (1)
an　triple dresser (3)
ao　vanity (22)
ap　vanity chest (1)
aq　vanity dresser (3)
ar　wardrobe (1)
as　wash table (1)
at　washstand (47)
au　washstand dresser (1)
av　window dresser (1)

009.3 L bedroom
No Response (167)
A　attic (1)
B　back bedroom (10)
C　back room (3)
D　bedchamber (1)
E　bedroom (728)
F　best bedroom (1)
G　boudoir (1)
H　boys' bedroom (1)
I　chamber (2)
J　family bedroom (1)
K　family room (1)
L　fireroom (1)
M　front bedroom (7)
N　front room (4)
O　guest bedroom (7)
P　guest room (5)

Q　master bedroom (10)
R　middle bedroom (3)
S　my room (2)
T　parents' bedroom (1)
U　shed bedroom (1)
V　shed room (3)
W　side room (3)
X　sleeping alcove (1)
Y　sleeping area (1)
Z　sleeping gallery (1)
aa　sleeping porch (7)
ab　sleeping room (14)
ac　slumber chamber (1)
ad　upstairs bedroom (1)

009.3 P bedroom
{ai}　lax onset
{d}　devoiced
{e}　inglide
{oo}　inglide
{r}　labial
{t}　flap
{ue}　unrounded onset
{z}　devoiced
{zh}　devoiced
{?}　glottal
No Response (178)
<baidrum=13> (1)
<bedIruemz=143> (1)
<bedra[m]=13> (1)
<bedrewm=13> (9)
<bedrewmz=13> (1)
<bedrewmzh=13> (1)
<bedrewm{z}=13> (2)
<bedroem=13> (1)
<bedroom(z)=13> (1)
<bedroom=13> (26)
<bedrooms=13> (1)
<bedroomz=13> (5)
<bedroom{z}=13> (1)
<bedrue[m]=13> (5)
<bedruem(z)=13> (7)
<bedruem=13> (383)
<bedruemz=13> (54)
<bedruem{z}=13> (26)
<bedruim=13> (1)
<bedrum=13> (1)
<bedr{oo}m=13> (1)
<bedr{ue}m=13> (8)
<bedr{ue}m{z}=13> (1)
<bed{r}uem=13> (8)
<bed{r}uemth=13> (1)
<betroom=13> (1)
<betruem=13> (5)
<betruemz=13> (2)
<betrum=13> (1)
<be{?}room=13> (1)
<be{?}ruem=13> (1)
<be{d}room{z}=13> (1)
<be{d}ruem=13> (17)

<be{d}ruemz=13> (3)
<be{d}ruem{z}=13> (2)
<be{d}r{oo}m=13> (1)
<be{d}r{ue}m=13> (1)
<be{t}ruem=13> (3)
<bidrewm=13> (6)
<bidrewms=13> (1)
<bidrewmz=13> (1)
<bidrim=13> (1)
<bidroo[m]=13> (1)
<bidroom=13> (1)
<bidrue[m]=13> (1)
<bidruem=13> (9)
<bidruembsh=13> (1)
<bidruemz=13> (1)
<bidruem{zh}=13> (1)
<bidruem{z}=13> (1)
<bidrum=13> (1)
<bid{r}uem=13> (1)
<bitruem=13> (2)
<bitruem{z}=13> (1)
<bitr{oo}m=13> (1)
<b{ai}d> (1)
<b{ai}droem=13> (1)
<b{ai}droom=13> (3)
<b{ai}druem=13> (22)
<b{ai}druemz=13> (3)
<b{ai}druem{z}=13> (2)
<b{ai}drum=13> (2)
<b{ai}{d}ruem=13> (1)
<b{e}(d)rewm=13> (1)
<b{e}d> (1)
<b{e}drewm=13> (3)
<b{e}drewmz=13> (1)
<b{e}droom=13> (3)
<b{e}drue[m]=13> (1)
<b{e}druem=13> (97)
<b{e}druemz=13> (20)
<b{e}druem{z}=13> (1)
<b{e}dr{oo}m=13> (1)
<b{e}dr{ue}m{z}=13> (1)
<b{e}d{r}uem=13> (1)
<b{e}d{z}> (1)
<b{e}truem(z)=13> (1)
<b{e}truem=13> (5)
<b{e}truemz=13> (2)
<b{e}{d}ruem=13> (4)
<b{e}{d}ruem{z}=13> (1)
<b{e}{t}ruem=13> (1)

009.4 L furniture

No Response (144)

A   bedroom furnishing (1)
B   bedroom furniture (3)
C   bedroom suite (14)
D   dining-room furniture (1)
E   dining-room suite (2)
F   furnishings (15)
G   furniture (660)
H   furniture set (1)

I   house fixings (3)
J   house fixtures (1)
K   house furnishings (1)
L   house furniture (3)
M   house plunder (4)
N   household belongings (1)
O   household effects (1)
P   household furnishing (3)
Q   household furniture (2)
R   household goods (7)
S   household supplies (1)
T   household things (1)
U   kitchen furniture (1)
V   living-room furniture (12)
W   living-room set (1)
X   living-room suite (9)
Y   muebles [S] (1)
Z   outfit (1)
aa   plunder (15)
ab   set of furniture (1)
ac   suite (2)
ad   suite of furniture (4)
ae   yard furniture (1)

009.4 P furniture

{R}   weakly retroflex
{r}   weakly retroflex
No Response (166)

<f[R]nichew[r]=431> (1)
<fo(r)nIch[R]=144> (3)
<fo(r)nIch{R}=144> (1)
<foo[r]nIch[R]=144> (1)
<foorn(Ich)R=14> (1)
<fo{r}nIch[R]=144> (1)
<fu[r]n(I)ch[R]=14> (2)
<fu[r]n(I)ch{R}=14> (1)
<fu[r]n(I)t[R]=14> (1)
<fu[r]n(I)tuew[R]=134> (1)
<fu[r]n(I)ty[R]=14> (1)
<fu[r]nIchR=144> (6)
<fu[r]nIch[R]=144> (96)
<fu[r]nIch[R]z=144> (1)
<fu[r]nIchi[r]=143> (1)
<fu[r]nIcho(r)=143> (1)
<fu[r]nIchoo(r)=143> (3)
<fu[r]nIchoo[r]=143> (7)
<fu[r]nIchu[r]=142> (1)
<fu[r]nIchu[r]=143> (5)
<fu[r]nIchue(r)=143> (1)
<fu[r]nIchue[r]=143> (2)
<fu[r]nIchu{r}=143> (1)
<fu[r]nIchyue[r]=143> (1)
<fu[r]nIch{R}=144> (9)
<fu[r]nIj[R]=144> (1)
<fu[r]nIsh[R]=144> (7)
<fu[r]nIsh{R}=144> (1)
<fu[r]nIt[R]=144> (6)
<fu[r]nItew(r)=143> (2)
<fu[r]nItew[r]=143> (6)
<fu[r]nItewr=143> (1)

<fu[r]nItoo[r]=143> (4)
<fu[r]nItoo[r]=341> (1)
<fu[r]nIty[R]=144> (17)
<fu[r]nItyi(r)=143> (1)
<fu[r]nItyoo[r]=143> (1)
<fu[r]nItyue(r)=143> (1)
<fu[r]nItyue[r]=143> (2)
<fu[r]nIzh[R]=144> (1)
<fu[r]neechR=134> (1)
<fu[r]nichR=134> (2)
<fu[r]nich[R]=134> (18)
<fu[r]nichoo[r]=132> (1)
<fu[r]nich{R}=134> (1)
<fu[r]nish[R]=134> (2)
<furNchR=144> (1)
<fur[n]IchR=144> (2)
<fur[n]Ich{R}=144> (1)
<furn(I)chR=14> (3)
<furn(I)ch[R]=14> (2)
<furn(I)jR=14> (1)
<furn(I)toor=13> (1)
<furn(I)tyoo{r}=13> (1)
<furnAchR=144> (2)
<furnAchur=143> (3)
<furnAchu{r}=143> (1)
<furnAch{R}=144> (1)
<furnAtyR=144> (1)
<furnAtyoor=143> (1)
<furnAtyuer=143> (1)
<furnAtyur=143> (1)
<furnIch(R)=14> (1)
<furnIchR=144> (159)
<furnIch[R]=144> (32)
<furnIch[R]z=144> (1)
<furnIchew[r]=143> (2)
<furnIchewr=143> (3)
<furnIchi[r]=241> (1)
<furnIchir=143> (2)
<furnIchoo(r)=143> (1)
<furnIchoo[r]=143> (6)
<furnIchoor=143> (16)
<furnIchoor=341> (1)
<furnIchoo{r}=143> (3)
<furnIchu[r]=143> (3)
<furnIchuer=143> (4)
<furnIchur=143> (33)
<furnIchu{r}=143> (4)
<furnIchy[R]=144> (1)
<furnIchyoor=143> (1)
<furnIch{R}=144> (29)
<furnIjR=144> (1)
<furnItR=144> (12)
<furnIt[R]=144> (1)
<furnItew(r)=143> (1)
<furnItew[r]=143> (4)
<furnItew[r]=341> (1)
<furnItewr=143> (22)
<furnItewr=341> (1)
<furnItew{r}=143> (2)

<furnIti[r]=143> (1)
<furnItir=143> (1)
<furnItir=341> (1)
<furnItoo[r]=143> (2)
<furnItoor=143> (11)
<furnItoo{r}=143> (1)
<furnItue[r]=143> (3)
<furnItuer=143> (2)
<furnItue{r}=143> (1)
<furnItur=143> (2)
<furnItyR=144> (15)
<furnIty[R]=144> (1)
<furnItyir=143> (2)
<furnItyoo[r]=143> (1)
<furnItyoor=143> (15)
<furnItyoor=241> (1)
<furnItyoo{r}=143> (3)
<furnItyu[r]=143> (2)
<furnItyuer=143> (3)
<furnItyue{r}=143> (2)
<furnItyur=143> (4)
<furnIty{R}=144> (1)
<furnRchur=143> (1)
<furnichR=134> (14)
<furnich[R]=134> (7)
<furnichoor=123> (1)
<furnichoor=132> (2)
<furnich{R}=134> (1)
<furnishR=134> (2)
<furnish[R]=134> (1)
<fu{r}n(I)ch[R]=14> (1)
<fu{r}n(I)chue(r)=13> (1)
<fu{r}n(I)too{r}=13> (1)
<fu{r}n(I)ty[R]=14> (2)
<fu{r}n(I)tyue{r}=13> (1)
<fu{r}n(I)ty{R}=14> (1)
<fu{r}n(I)t{R}=14> (3)
<fu{r}nAch[R]=144> (1)
<fu{r}nAch{R}=144> (2)
<fu{r}nIchR=144> (4)
<fu{r}nIch[R]=144> (33)
<fu{r}nIchoo(r)=143> (1)
<fu{r}nIchoo[r]=143> (1)
<fu{r}nIchu[r]=143> (1)
<fu{r}nIch{R}=144> (16)
<fu{r}nIsh[R]=144> (1)
<fu{r}nIt[R]=144> (4)
<fu{r}nItew[r]=143> (1)
<fu{r}nItew{r}=143> (1)
<fu{r}nIti[r]=143> (1)
<fu{r}nItoo[r]=143> (1)
<fu{r}nItoor=143> (2)
<fu{r}nItoo{r}=143> (1)
<fu{r}nItue(r)=143> (1)
<fu{r}nItue[r]=143> (1)
<fu{r}nItue{r}=143> (2)
<fu{r}nItu{r}=143> (2)
<fu{r}nIty[R]=144> (4)
<fu{r}nItyoo(r)=143> (1)

<fu{r}nItyoo[r]=143> (1)
<fu{r}nItyoo{r}=143> (3)
<fu{r}nItyue[r]=143> (1)
<fu{r}nItyuer=143> (1)
<fu{r}nItyue{r}=143> (3)
<fu{r}nItyu{r}=143> (3)
<fu{r}nIty{R}=144> (5)
<fu{r}nIt{R}=144> (2)
<fu{r}nIzh[R]=144> (1)
<fu{r}nich[R]=134> (1)

009.5 L window shades
No Response (161)
A blind shades (1)
B blinds (90)
C canvas curtains (1)
D cortinas [S] (1)
E curtain blinds (1)
F curtains (21)
G drapes (1)
H green shades (1)
I green window shades (1)
J night shades (1)
K pull-down shades (3)
L rideau [F] (2)
M roller curtains (2)
N roller shades (6)
O shade blinds (1)
P shades (516)
Q sun shades (1)
R transparentes [S] (1)
S window blinds (15)
T window curtains (2)
U window rollers (1)
V window shades (209)

009.5 P window
{A} rounded
{b} fricative
{d} devoiced
{R} weakly retroflex
{t} flap
No Response (683)
<wendA=14> (1)
<wi(n)dA=14> (1)
<win(d)A=14> (1)
<windA=14> (167)
<windAz=14> (1)
<windI=14> (3)
<windR=14> (10)
<windRz=14> (6)
<windoe=13> (19)
<windu=13> (1)
<wind{A}=14> (5)
<wind{R}=14> (15)
<win{d}A=14> (1)
<win{t}A=14> (5)
<win{t}R=14> (1)
<{b}indA=14> (1)

009.6 L clothes closet
No Response (81)

A anteroom (1)
B built-in closet (6)
C built-in clothes closet (1)
D built-in locker (1)
E cabinet (2)
F cedar closet (2)
G cedar-lined closet (1)
H chifforobe (2)
I cloakroom (1)
J closet (742)
K closet-like (1)
L clothes closet (107)
M clothes cupboard (1)
N clothes locker (1)
O clothes room (1)
P clothes wardrobe (1)
Q clothespress (1)
R clothing room (1)
S cupboard (1)
T double closet (1)
U dressing room (5)
V hang closet (1)
W Kleiderschrank [G] (1)
X locker (9)
Y ropero [S] (1)
Z side room (1)
aa walk-in (1)
ab walk-in closet (13)
ac walk-in locker (1)
ad wardrobe (22)

009.7 L wardrobe
No Response (161)
A armoire (100)
B armoire, un [F] (4)
C bureau (7)
D bedroom safe (1)
E cabinet (9)
F caboose (1)
G cedar cabinet (1)
H cedar chest (8)
I cedar chifforobe (2)
J cedar closet (4)
K cedar wardrobe (2)
L (cedar)robe (1)
M cedarrobe (16)
N chest (3)
O chiffonette (1)
P chiffonier (6)
Q chiffonrobe (1)
R chifforobe (324)
S closet (10)
T clothes cabinet (2)
U clothes chest (6)
V clothes closet (15)
W clothes rack (5)
X clothes shelves (2)
Y clothespress (15)
Z cupboard (4)
aa divan (1)

ab dresser (1)
ac hanging robe (1)
ad high top (1)
ae highboy (2)
af homemade closet (1)
ag homemade clothespress (1)
ah Kleiderschrank [G] (1)
ai man's robe (3)
aj portable closet (2)
ak press (1)
al quilt pack (1)
am rack (4)
an robe (1)
ao roll-around closet (1)
ap ropero [S] (1)
aq safe closet (1)
ar Schrank [G] (2)
as standing trunk (1)
at storage closet (1)
au tall boy (1)
av tally (1)
aw wardrobe (447)
ax wardrobe chest (1)
ay wardrobe closet (1)
az wardrobe trunk (1)
ba wardroom (1)

009.8 L attic

No Response (128)
A air space (1)
B attic (643)
C attic room (5)
D attic space (3)
E basement (1)
F ceiling (1)
G chimley (1)
H cock loft (1)
I crawl space (1)
J doghouse (3)
K dormer room (2)
L full attic (1)
M garret (11)
N garret loft (3)
O grenier [F] (1)
P gutter (1)
Q half story (2)
R junk room (1)
S loft (215)
T loft overhead (1)
U loft room (1)
V open attic (1)
W overhead (1)
X room upstairs (1)
Y scuttle hole (2)
Z scuttling hole (1)
aa second floor (1)
ab shed room (1)
ac sky parlor (1)
ad space, the (1)
ae stand-up attic (1)

af storage attic (1)
ag storage room (2)
ah storage space (1)
ai top of the house (2)
aj upper room (1)
ak upstairs (44)
al upstairs apartment (1)
am upstairs attic (1)
an upstairs building (1)
ao upstairs room (2)
ap walk-up attic (1)

009.9 L kitchen

No Response (99)
A big room (1)
B breakfast nook (2)
C breakfast room (2)
D cook shack (1)
E cookhouse (8)
F cooking room (1)
G cookroom (13)
H cuisine, la [F] (1)
I detached kitchen (2)
J dining room (1)
K eating room (1)
L ell, an (1)
M gallery (1)
N galley (5)
O kitchen (689)
P kitchen [separate] (133)
Q kitchen area (1)
R kitchen building (1)
S kitchen part (1)
T kitchen-type thing (1)
U kitchenette (4)
V lean-to (3)
W lean-to kitchen (1)
X log house (1)
Y log kitchen (1)
Z off kitchen (1)
aa offset (2)
ab offset kitchen (1)
ac out kitchen (1)
ad outdoor kitchen (1)
ae outside kitchen (5)
af pantry (1)
ag separate kitchen (1)
ah shed (1)
ai shotgun kitchen (1)
aj side house (1)
ak side room (1)
al storeroom (1)
am stove room (13)
an summer kitchen (13)

[walkway to separate kitchen]

ba alleyway (1)
bb breezeway (9)
bc breezeway-type deal (1)
bd brick walk (1)
be catwalk (2)

bf covered hall (1)
bg covered walkway (1)
bh dog run (1)
bi dogtrot (1)
bj gangway (1)
bk hall-like (1)
bl hallway (2)
bm plank walk (2)
bn runway (1)
bo walk (2)
bp walk area (1)
bq walkway (9)

010.1 L pantry

No Response (123)
A anteroom (1)
B back room (2)
C boutique, la [F] (1)
D broom closet (1)
E buffet (1)
F built-in closet (1)
G built-in storage area (1)
H butler's (1)
I butler's pantry (8)
J cabin (1)
K cabin(et) (1)
L cabinet (3)
M can house (2)
N can room (1)
O closet (26)
P cupboard (12)
Q depense [F] (1)
R despensa [S] (1)
S extra room (1)
T food closet (3)
U fruit closet (1)
V garde-manger [F] (1)
W grocery bin (1)
X grocery room (3)
Y keeping room (1)
Z kind of a pantry thing (1)
aa kitchen cabinet (1)
ab kitchen closet (20)
ac kitchen cupboard (1)
ad kitchen pantry (2)
ae larder (3)
af locker (2)
ag meal room (6)
ah outer pantry (1)
ai pantr(y) (1)
aj pantry (572)
ak pantry room (4)
al room (2)
am safe (1)
an side room (2)
ao side storage room (1)
ap storage closet (3)
aq storage place (2)
ar storage room (33)
as storeroom (34)

at   stowaway closet (1)
au   utensil room (1)
av   utility (closet) (1)
aw   utility pantry (1)
ax   utility room (19)
ay   walk-in pantry (3)

010.2 L junk

No Response (186)
A   (ac)cumulation (1)
B   antique furniture (1)
C   antique stuff (3)
D   antique trash (1)
E   antique(s) (36)
F   attic junk (1)
G   bad junk (1)
H   bric-a-brac (2)
I   bunch of junk (4)
J   bunch of trash (1)
K   cast-off furniture (1)
L   crap (2)
M   debarrasser [F] (1)
N   discard(s) (3)
O   discarded stuff (1)
P   Early Attic (1)
Q   family heirlooms (1)
R   fatras [F] (1)
S   garbage (29)
T   gewgaws (1)
U   good junk (2)
V   heirlooms (1)
W   junk (575)
X   junk and stuff (1)
Y   junk furniture (1)
Z   junk lumber (1)
aa   junk stuff (2)
ab   keepsakes (2)
ac   knickknack stuff (1)
ad   little dab of junk (1)
ae   lot of junk (2)
af   mess (2)
ag   no-for-good junk (1)
ah   no-good stuff (1)
ai   odds and ends (9)
aj   old antique stuff (2)
ak   old antiques (1)
al   old antiques and things (1)
am   old junk (12)
an   old junk and stuff (1)
ao   old junk whatnot (1)
ap   old plunder (3)
aq   old relics (1)
ar   old rubbish (1)
as   old stuff (5)
at   old things (1)
au   pack-rat stuff (1)
av   pack-rat things (1)
aw   piece of things (1)
ax   pile of junk (1)
ay   plunder (57)

az   relics (6)
ba   rubbish (20)
bb   rummage (9)
bc   salvage stuff (1)
bd   scrap(s) (4)
be   stuff (10)
bf   surplus junk (1)
bg   things (1)
bh   this and that (1)
bi   throwaway junk (1)
bj   throwaways (3)
bk   trash (83)
bl   treasures (2)
bm   waste (1)
bn   white elephants (1)
bo   wore/worn-out furniture (3)
bp   worthless junk (1)

010.3 L junk room

No Response (221)
A   anteroom (1)
B   antique room (1)
C   attic (32)
D   back porch (2)
E   backroom (1)
F   barn (6)
G   barn dairy room (1)
H   basement (11)
I   big room (1)
J   boxroom (1)
K   carport (1)
L   catchall (6)
M   catchall place (1)
N   catchall room (6)
O   cellar (4)
P   chambre (de) debarras [F] (1)
Q   closet (12)
R   collect all (1)
S   cookhouse (1)
T   cornhouse (1)
U   cotton shed (1)
V   crib (2)
W   den (2)
X   devil's den (1)
Y   extra house (1)
Z   fruit room (1)
aa   garage (17)
ab   garage closet (1)
ac   garbage house (1)
ad   garret (1)
ae   garret loft (1)
af   glory hole (1)
ag   junk collector (1)
ah   junk corner (1)
ai   junk heap (1)
aj   junk hole (1)
ak   junk house (49)
al   junk pile (4)
am   junk place (2)
an   junk room (295)

ao   junk shop (1)
ap   junkyard (3)
aq   kickhole (1)
ar   laundry room (2)
as   little room (2)
at   locker (1)
au   locker room (1)
av   loft (5)
aw   lumber room (4)
ax   meal room (1)
ay   meat house (1)
az   no-good room (1)
ba   Noah's Ark (1)
bb   old kitchen (1)
bc   old room (1)
bd   outbuilding (2)
be   outhouse (11)
bf   pack room (1)
bg   packhouse (2)
bh   packinghouse (1)
bi   pantry (5)
bj   playroom (1)
bk   plunder house (4)
bl   plunder porch (1)
bm   plunder room (40)
bn   pump house (2)
bo   rubbish room (1)
bp   rummage room (2)
bq   Rumpelkammer [G] (2)
br   rumpus room (1)
bs   salvage room (1)
bt   scrap pen (1)
bu   sewing room (3)
bv   shed (8)
bw   shed room (2)
bx   Siberia (1)
by   side closet (1)
bz   side room (8)
ca   smokehouse (25)
cb   spare room (2)
cc   storage area (1)
cd   storage building (1)
ce   storage closet (6)
cf   storage house (13)
cg   storage place (1)
ch   storage room (124)
ci   storage section (1)
cj   storage space (1)
ck   store closet (1)
cl   storehouse (4)
cm   storehouse place (1)
cn   storeroom (109)
co   stowaway (1)
cp   stowaway house (1)
cq   syrup house (1)
cr   tool shed (1)
cs   trash room (1)
ct   trash-catching place (1)
cu   trunk room (1)

cv   utility room (54)
cw   wagon shed (1)
cx   well house (1)
cy   woodhouse (1)
cz   woodshed (1)
da   workshop (2)

010.4 L clean up (the house)

No Response (205)

A   adjust things (1)
B   brush (it) out (2)
C   brush up the house (1)
D   chores (12)
E   clean (the house) (235)
F   clean around (1)
G   clean day (1)
H   clean (it) off (1)
I   clean (it) out (6)
J   clean up (the house) (317)
K   cleaning day (1)
L   clear this out (1)
M   daily chores (2)
N   dirty work (1)
O   do (the) chores (10)
P   do (the) cleaning (2)
Q   do (the) housecleaning (2)
R   do the housekeeping (1)
S   do (the) housework (17)
T   do the sweeping (1)
U   do the work (1)
V   do up her house (1)
W   do your house (1)
X   dress my house (1)
Y   dust (it) (16)
Z   dust around (1)
aa   fall cleaning (1)
ab   fix it like she wants (1)
ac   fool around (1)
ad   general cleanup (1)
ae   get all the junk out of it (1)
af   get the house cleaned up (1)
ag   get this house in order (1)
ah   give it a work over (1)
ai   go about her daily duty (1)
aj   go over some of the rooms (1)
ak   go over the house with a dust
       mop (1)
al   house chores (1)
am   house sweeping [n.] (1)
an   houseclean(ing) (37)
ao   household chores (1)
ap   household duties (1)
aq   housekeep(ing) (9)
ar   housework chores (1)
as   housework(ed) (36)
at   keep (the) house (19)
au   keep (the house) clean (7)
av   look after the house (1)
aw   make the menage (1)
ax   make the toilet (1)

ay   mop (the floor) (10)
az   mop up (2)
ba   morning chores (1)
bb   neatening up (1)
bc   neating up (1)
bd   pick the things up (1)
be   pick up (the house) (16)
bf   piddling (2)
bg   piddling around (2)
bh   put things in order (1)
bi   rearrange (the house) (2)
bj   redd up (2)
bk   scald (2)
bl   scour (7)
bm   scrub (it) (13)
bn   scrub up (1)
bo   set the house in order (1)
bp   shovel (it) out (2)
bq   shovel-out day (1)
br   spring clean(ing) (7)
bs   stir the dust (1)
bt   straighten (the house) (12)
bu   straighten out (1)
bv   straighten up (the house) (63)
bw   sweep (the house) (46)
bx   sweep clean (2)
by   sweep out (the house) (6)
bz   sweep (the house) up (10)
ca   tend to the housework (1)
cb   tidy (the house) (5)
cc   tidy up (the house) (31)
cd   vacuum [v.] (3)
ce   vacuum up (1)
cf   wash [v.] (2)
cg   work [v.] (1)
ch   work it over (1)

010.5 G behind

No Response (229)

A   back behind (7)
B   back of (108)
C   backside of (1)
D   behind (623)
E   (be)hind (6)
F   in back of (15)
G   in behind (2)
H   in the back of (7)
I   on back of (1)

010.5 P broom

No Response (141)

<brew[m]> (1)
<brewm> (26)
<broem> (1)
<broom> (56)
<broomz> (3)
<brue(m)> (1)
<brue[m]> (7)
<bruem> (643)
<bruemb> (2)
<bruemz> (31)

<brum> (9)
<bur[m]> (1)

010.6 L laundry

No Response (110)

[process]

A   boil (the) clothes (5)
B   boil the dirt out (1)
C   clean [v.] (4)
D   clothes washing [n.] (1)
E   do (the) clothes (4)
F   do (the) laundry (12)
G   do (the) wash (7)
H   do (the) washing (11)
I   family wash (1)
J   family washing (1)
K   get the clothes done up (1)
L   iron [v.] (280)
M   iron (the) clothes (2)
N   ironing [n.] (312)
O   launder [v.] (5)
P   laundering (1)
Q   laundry [n.] (359)
R   laundry [v.] (3)
S   laundry work (5)
T   lavage [F] (2)
U   press [v.] (17)
V   pressing [n.] (5)
W   wash [n.] (111)
X   wash [v.] (178)
Y   wash (the) clothes (31)
Z   wash the laundry (1)
aa   washing [n.] (408)
ab   washing of clothes, the (1)
ac   weekly wash (2)

[place]

ba   Chinese laundry (3)
bb   cleaner(s) (25)
bc   clothes cleaners (1)
bd   dry cleaner(s) (7)
be   launderette (7)
bf   Laundromat (25)
bg   laundry (106)
bh   laundry place (1)
bi   laundry shop (1)
bj   laundry-washing business (1)
bk   pressing shop (1)
bl   wash place (2)
bm   washamateria (1)
bn   washateria (16)
bo   washer (1)
bp   washer carriage (1)
bq   washette (2)
br   washhouse (2)
bs   washingmat (1)

010.7 L stairway

No Response (123)

[inside]

A   back steps (1)
B   backstairs (2)

C   disappearing stair (1)
D   flight of stairs (6)
E   flight of steps (1)
F   front stairs (1)
G   front steps (1)
H   hall steps (1)
I   inside stairs (4)
J   inside stairway (4)
K   set of stairs (2)
L   set of stairway (1)
M   staircase (46)
N   staircasing (1)
O   stairs (387)
P   stairsteps (89)
Q   stairway (250)
R   stairwell (7)
S   steps (143)
T   winding staircase (1)
U   winding stairsteps (1)
V   winding steps (1)
[outside]
aa   back doorstep (1)
ab   back stairway (1)
ac   back steps (7)
ad   backstairs (3)
ae   doorstep(s) (61)
af   fire escape (10)
ag   fire stairs (1)
ah   front doorstep (2)
ai   front stairway (1)
aj   front steps (15)
ak   front stoop (1)
al   ground steps (1)
am   outdoor spiral stairs (1)
an   outdoor staircase (2)
ao   outdoor stairs (1)
ap   outdoor stairway (1)
aq   outdoor steps (1)
ar   outside staircase (1)
as   outside stairs (21)
at   outside stairway (11)
au   outside steps (2)
av   pair of steps (3)
aw   porch steps (2)
ax   round spindle stairway (1)
ay   spiral staircase (1)
az   staircase (3)
ba   stairs (56)
bb   stairsteps (13)
bc   stairway (24)
bd   steps (421)
be   stoop (4)
bf   wooden steps (1)

010.7 P stairs

{dh}   devoiced
{r}   weakly retroflex
{z}   devoiced
{zh}   devoiced
No Response (223)

<Apstai[r]z=41> (1)
<Apsta{r}z=41> (1)
<oopsta[r](z)=31> (1)
<sta(r)step=13> (1)
<sta(r)steps=13> (8)
<sta(r)wai=13> (11)
<sta(r)waiz=13> (1)
<sta(r)z> (9)
<sta[r]> (3)
<sta[r]kais=13> (3)
<sta[r]step=13> (4)
<sta[r]steps=13> (12)
<sta[r]steps=21> (1)
<sta[r]wai=13> (30)
<sta[r]waiz=13> (2)
<sta[r]z> (56)
<sta[r]{z}> (4)
<stai[r]wai=13> (1)
<stai[r]z> (1)
<stairz> (4)
<stair{dh}> (1)
<stair{z}> (4)
<stai{r}steps=13> (1)
<stai{r}{zh}> (1)
<star> (1)
<star(z)> (2)
<starkais=13> (5)
<starsteps=13> (26)
<starsteps=21> (1)
<starwai=13> (80)
<starwaiz=13> (5)
<starz> (147)
<star{z}> (17)
<sta{r}> (2)
<sta{r}kais=13> (1)
<sta{r}steps=13> (6)
<sta{r}wai=13> (18)
<sta{r}wais=13> (1)
<sta{r}waiz=13> (1)
<sta{r}z> (32)
<sta{r}{z}> (2)
<ste(r)stips=13> (1)
<ste(r)wai=13> (1)
<ste(r)z> (3)
<ste(r){z}> (2)
<ste[r]> (1)
<ste[r]kais=13> (1)
<ste[r]step=13> (1)
<ste[r]steps=13> (1)
<ste[r]wai=13> (5)
<ste[r]z> (24)
<ster> (1)
<sterkais=13> (6)
<sterstep=13> (1)
<stersteps=13> (2)
<sterwai=13> (24)
<sterwai{z}=13> (1)
<sterwelz=13> (1)
<sterz> (56)

<sterzh> (1)
<ster{z}> (10)
<ste{r}wai=13> (1)
<ste{r}z> (5)
<sti(r)wai=13> (1)
<stirz> (1)
<stir{z}> (1)
<sto[r]steps=13> (1)
<storkais=13> (2)
<storsteps=13> (2)
<storwai=13> (1)
<storz> (3)
<stor{z}> (1)
<sto{r}steps=13> (1)
<sto{r}wai=13> (2)
<sto{r}z> (1)
<sturstep=13> (1)
<ther{z}> (1)
<upshtai(r){zh}=21> (1)
<upsta(r)z=13> (1)
<upsta(r)z=31> (2)
<upsta[r](z)=21> (1)
<upsta[r]z=31> (2)
<upstarz=13> (1)
<upstarz=31> (3)
<upsta{r}z=31> (1)
<upste[r]z=13> (2)
<upste[r]z=21> (1)
<upste[r]z=31> (2)
<upster{z}=13> (2)
<upste{r}z=31> (2)
<upsto[r](z)=31> (1)
<upstorz=31> (1)

010.8 L porch

No Response (35)
A   airplane sleeping porch (1)
B   attic porch (1)
C   back gallery (6)
D   back piazza (2)
E   back porch (317)
F   back shed (1)
G   back stoop (2)
H   balcon [F] (1)
I   balcony (131)
J   balcony porch (2)
K   breezeway (5)
L   circle porch (1)
M   close-in porch (1)
N   closed-in porch (1)
O   country-farmhouse porch (1)
P   covered porch (1)
Q   cupola (2)
R   cupola porch (1)
S   deck (10)
T   door porch (1)
U   door stoop (1)
V   doorstep(s) (3)
W   double gallery (1)
X   double porch (2)

Y   downstairs porch (2)
Z   east porch (2)
aa   ell porch (5)
ab   enclose porch (1)
ac   enclosed back porch (1)
ad   entrance (2)
ae   entrance porch (1)
af   entrance porch way (1)
ag   entry (3)
ah   flat porch (2)
ai   flatform (2)
aj   Florida room (3)
ak   freeze out, a (1)
al   front gallery (9)
am   front porch (315)
an   front shed (1)
ao   front stoop (2)
ap   front veranda (2)
aq   galeria [S] (2)
ar   galerie, la [F] (7)
as   Galerie [G] (1)
at   gallery (180)
au   garret (2)
av   glassed-in porch (2)
aw   half porch (1)
ax   hangover (1)
ay   hip-roof porch (1)
az   kitchen porch (4)
ba   L-shaped porch (3)
bb   landing (3)
bc   lean-to (1)
bd   lean-to porch (2)
be   ledge (1)
bf   long porch (4)
bg   lounge (1)
bh   lower gallery (1)
bi   middle porch (1)
bj   north porch (2)
bk   open porch (7)
bl   outdoor sitting room (1)
bm   outside walkway (1)
bn   parlor (1)
bo   patio (9)
bp   piazza (50)
bq   plateau (1)
br   platform (2)
bs   porch (680)
bt   porch-type thing (1)
bu   portico (21)
bv   portico [S] (1)
bw   post-office gallery (1)
bx   rain porch (1)
by   rear porch (2)
bz   round porch (3)
ca   screen porch (28)
cb   screen-in, a (2)
cc   screen-in back porch (1)
cd   screen-in front porch (1)
ce   screened back porch (1)

cf   screened porch (9)
cg   screened-in back porch (5)
ch   screened-in front porch (1)
ci   screened-in porch (26)
cj   screened-in room (1)
ck   screened-in side porch (1)
cl   second-floor gallery (1)
cm   second-floor porch (1)
cn   second-story porch (4)
co   shed (3)
cp   shed porch (1)
cq   side gallery (1)
cr   side porch (23)
cs   side room (1)
ct   side screen porch (1)
cu   sit out, a (1)
cv   sleeping porch (23)
cw   solarium (2)
cx   south porch (2)
cy   Southern-style porch (1)
cz   step-down, a (1)
da   step-out (1)
db   stoop (98)
dc   straight porch (2)
dd   sun deck (10)
de   sun parlor (4)
df   sun porch (24)
dg   sun-room (3)
dh   suspended porch (1)
di   terrace (9)
dj   two-deck porch (1)
dk   two-story porch (2)
dl   up-and-down back porch (1)
dm   up-and-down front porch (1)
dn   upper gallery (1)
do   upper porch (3)
dp   upstair[N-i] porch (4)
dq   upstairs balcony (1)
dr   upstairs floor (1)
ds   upstairs piazza (1)
dt   upstairs porch (29)
du   utility porch (1)
dv   veranda (110)
dw   walk-out porch (1)
dx   walkway (1)
dy   well porch (2)
dz   west porch (1)
ea   widow's perch (1)
eb   widow's walk (2)
ec   wraparound porch (1)

010.8 P porch
{r}   weakly retroflex
No Response (59)
<paw(r)ch> (2)
<paw[r]ch> (8)
<pawrch> (3)
<po(r)ch> (1)
<poe(r)ch> (45)
<poe(r)chIz=14> (2)

<poe(r)t> (1)
<poeIch=14> (1)
<poe[r]ch> (382)
<poe[r]chIz=14> (6)
<poe[r]t> (4)
<poerch> (367)
<poerchIz=14> (2)
<poert> (1)
<poewich=13> (1)
<poe{r}ch> (157)
<poe{r}chIz=14> (1)
<poo[r]ch> (2)
<poo[r]sh> (1)
<poorch> (1)
<po{r}ch> (1)
<pue[r]ch> (1)

011.1 L shut the door
No Response (134)
A   close (the door) (487)
B   close (the door) back (1)
C   close (the door) down (2)
D   fasten (the door) (3)
E   ferme la porte [F] (1)
F   hook (the door) (1)
G   make shut the door (1)
H   make the door shut (1)
I   pull (the door) to (1)
J   push (the door) close[V-t] (1)
K   push (the door) shut (1)
L   push (the door) to (4)
M   shoot the door (1)
N   shut (the door) (565)
O   shut (the door) back up (1)
P   shut (the door) up (1)
Q   slam (the door) (4)
R   slam (the door) to (2)
[**idiomatic phrases**]
S   close the goddamn door, Eskimo (1)
T   do you live outside? (1)
U   were you born in a barn? (4)
V   were/was you raised in a barn? (3)
W   (you) must have been raised in a barn (1)
X   you weren't born in a barn (1)
011.1A P shut
{?}   glottal
No Response (301)
<shet> (77)
<she{?}> (1)
<shit> (3)
<shoe{?}> (1)
<shoot> (7)
<shot> (1)
<shoth> (1)
<shud> (2)
<shuet> (2)
<shut> (531)

<shuts> (1)
<shu{?}> (3)
<shyet> (1)

011.1 S shut
No Response (0)
|DCE| (1)
|EAA| (1)
|EAD| (1)
|ECC| (1)
|FAA| (1)
|FAC| (1)
|FAD| (1)
|FAH| (3)
|FAHfaj| (1)
|FFA| (1)
|FFH| (1)
|KAA| (13)
|KAB| (2)
|KACmaj| (1)
|KAD| (1)
|KAE| (31)
|KAEmaj| (1)
|KAF| (1)
|KAFeaj| (1)
|KAG| (2)
|KAI| (2)
|KBA| (1)
|KBAmaj| (1)
|KCA| (6)
|KCE| (5)
|KCEmaj| (1)
|KDE| (1)
|KMEmaa| (1)
|LAA| (10)
|LAB| (4)
|LABmaj| (1)
|LAC| (10)
|LAD| (42)
|LADmaj| (3)
|LAE| (19)
|LAElab| (1)
|LAEmaj| (2)
|LAF| (4)
|LAG| (5)
|LAH| (2)
|LAI| (1)
|LCA| (3)
|LCAmaj| (2)
|LCD| (4)
|LCDmaj| (1)
|LCE| (2)
|LCEmaj| (1)
|LFFmaj| (1)
|MAA| (1)
|MAD| (3)
|MAHmaj| (1)
|MCA| (6)
|MCD| (1)
|MCHmaj| (1)

|MCV| (1)
|NAA| (39)
|NAAeaj| (1)
|NAAfaj| (1)
|NAAmaj| (9)
|NAAmak| (1)
|NAB| (13)
|NABmaj| (1)
|NAD| (397)
|NADfaj| (4)
|NADmaj| (82)
|NADnab| (1)
|NAE| (1)
|NAF| (14)
|NAFfal| (1)
|NAFmaj| (1)
|NAG| (6)
|NAGmaj| (6)
|NAH| (28)
|NAHmaj| (5)
|NAHnag| (1)
|NBD| (2)
|NCA| (21)
|NCAfaj| (1)
|NCAmaj| (2)
|NCB| (3)
|NCBfaj| (1)
|NCD| (32)
|NCDfaj| (1)
|NCDmaj| (7)
|NCFfal| (1)
|NCG| (1)
|NCS| (1)
|NFA| (1)
|NFAmaj| (1)
|NFB| (2)
|NFD| (1)
|NFDmaj| (1)
|NFF| (1)
|NFG| (1)
|NFH| (1)
|NFI| (1)
|NKA| (1)
|PAC| (1)
|eajMCA| (1)

011.1B P door
{aw}   raised onset
{d}   devoiced
{o}   raised
{oe}   lowered onset
{R}   weakly retroflex
{r}   weakly retroflex
{t}   flap
{z}   devoiced
No Response (294)
<daw[r]> (2)
<dawr> (2)
<daw{r}> (2)
<doe(r)> (67)

<doe(r)z> (4)
<doe[r]> (160)
<doe[r]z> (7)
<doer> (235)
<doerz> (3)
<doer{z}> (3)
<doewR=14> (3)
<doew[R]=14> (4)
<doew{R}=14> (1)
<doe{r}> (66)
<doe{r}z> (3)
<do{r}> (3)
<do{r}z> (1)
<d{aw}(r)> (3)
<d{aw}[r]> (26)
<d{aw}[r]z> (1)
<d{aw}r> (39)
<d{aw}{r}> (19)
<d{aw}{r}z> (1)
<d{oe}r> (1)
<d{o}r> (1)
<{d}oe(r)> (1)
<{d}oer> (1)
<{t}oer> (1)

011.2 L weatherboards
No Response (139)
A   aluminum siding (23)
B   asbestos siding (5)
C   batten(s) (7)
D   batten board(s) (3)
E   battening (1)
F   bevel siding (1)
G   beveled siding (1)
H   black boarding (1)
I   board(s) (18)
J   board house (3)
K   board siding (1)
L   board-and-batten (18)
M   boarding (1)
N   brick siding (9)
O   bunting-and-batten (1)
P   clabber board (1)
Q   clapboard(s) (82)
R   clapboard house (6)
S   clapboarding (1)
T   clapped (1)
U   corner board (1)
V   covered boards (1)
W   cypress batten (1)
X   drop edge (1)
Y   drop over (1)
Z   drop side (2)
aa   drop side lumber (1)
ab   drop siding (32)
ac   drop-siding board (1)
ad   dropped siding (1)
ae   felt siding (1)
af   gabling (1)
ag   house siding (1)

ah   hurricane siding (1)
ai   insulation board (1)
aj   lap (1)
ak   lap joints (1)
al   lap over [v.] (1)
am   lap siding (5)
an   lap wood (1)
ao   lapboard(s) (6)
ap   lapboarded (2)
aq   lapped (1)
ar   lapped siding (1)
as   lapped-over walls (1)
at   lapping [n.] (1)
au   lapping boards (1)
av   lapping sides (1)
aw   lapstrake (1)
ax   lapstrake aluminum siding (1)
ay   metal weatherboarding (1)
az   novelty boarding (1)
ba   novelty side (1)
bb   novelty siding (6)
bc   novelty weatherboarding (2)
bd   outside sealing (1)
be   outside siding (1)
bf   overlap (1)
bg   overlap siding (1)
bh   particle board (1)
bi   reweatherboard [v.] (1)
bj   rock siding (1)
bk   saddle board (1)
bl   sealing (1)
bm   sealing weatherboarding (1)
bn   sheetlap (1)
bo   shiplap(s) (49)
bp   shiplap siding (3)
bq   shiplapping (1)
br   sideboard (9)
bs   siding(s) (208)
bt   siding boards (1)
bu   siding house (1)
bv   six-inch lap board (1)
bw   slat (1)
bx   slat boards (1)
by   split siding (1)
bz   stripping (3)
ca   strips (1)
cb   V-siding (1)
cc   war blades (1)
cd   weather siding (1)
ce   weather stripping (1)
cf   weatherboard(s) (123)
cg   weatherboard [v.] (9)
ch   weatherboard house (2)
ci   weatherboarded (20)
cj   weatherboarded house (4)
ck   weatherboarding (343)
cl   weatherboarding strips (1)
cm   weatherproof (1)
cn   wide board (1)
co   wide boards and narrow boards (1)
cp   wood siding (2)
cq   wooden siding (1)

011.3 G drive

<!>   infinitive
<&>   present 3rd singular
<@>   present participle
<#>   past participle
No Response (110)
<!drie(v)> (6)
<!driev> (685)
<!droev> (1)
<!drov> (7)
<&driev> (2)
<&drievz> (15)
<@AdrievN=414> (3)
<@drievN=14> (49)
<@drievNG=14> (9)
<@driev[N]=14> (1)
<@drovN=14> (2)
<*driev> (1)
<*drievd> (2)
<*driv> (17)
<*drivN=14> (3)
<*droe(v)> (4)
<*droev> (611)
<*drue(v)> (1)
<*druev> (2)
<*druv> (4)
<#Adroev=41> (1)
<#driev> (2)
<#drievN=14> (1)
<#drievd> (4)
<#driv> (9)
<#drivN=14> (305)
<#driv[N]=14> (1)
<#drivun=13> (2)
<#droe(v)> (2)
<#droe(v)N=14> (1)
<#droev> (142)
<#droevd> (1)
<#droevN=14> (8)
<#druev> (1)
<#druvN=14> (1)
<#reedroev=31> (1)

011.4 P roof

{f}   bilabial
{r}   labial
No Response (97)
<hruef> (1)
<rewf> (36)
<rewfs> (1)
<rew{f}> (6)
<roof> (102)
<roofN=14> (1)
<roo{f}> (1)
<ruef> (620)
<ruefN=14> (21)
<ruefNG=14> (7)
<ruefs> (5)
<ruep> (1)
<rueth> (1)
<ruevz> (1)
<rue{f}> (9)
<ruf> (3)
<{r}ewf> (4)
<{r}ew{f}> (1)
<{r}oof> (2)
<{r}uef> (28)

011.5 L eaves troughs

No Response (241)
A   acorn catchers (1)
B   built-in gutters (2)
C   channels (1)
D   cistern gutters (2)
E   cistern troughs (2)
F   cypress gutters (1)
G   dalle, une [F] (1)
H   drain gutters (2)
I   drain lines (1)
J   drainage (4)
K   drainers (3)
L   drains (14)
M   eaves troughs (7)
N   gullies (17)
O   gutter drains (1)
P   gutter lines (1)
Q   gutter pipes (2)
R   gutter troughs (1)
S   guttering (17)
T   gutters (572)
U   half-moon gutters (1)
V   leaf catchers (1)
W   leaf troughs (1)
X   rain gutters (6)
Y   rain troughs (2)
Z   rudders (1)
aa   runnels (1)
ab   runners (1)
ac   troughs (27)
ad   valleys (6)
ae   water drainers (2)
af   water drains (3)
ag   water gutters (2)
ah   water troughs (7)
ai   wooden gutters (3)
aj   wooden troughs (2)

011.6 L valley [of roof]

No Response (430)
A   alley (11)
B   angle (1)
C   channel (1)
D   comb (1)
E   concave spot (1)
F   corner (2)
G   corner of the house (1)

H   crack (1)
I   crevice (1)
J   divider (1)
K   divider drainage (1)
L   drain (3)
M   eaves valley (1)
N   ell joint (1)
O   Giebel [G] (1)
P   groove (1)
Q   gully (7)
R   gutter (13)
S   hollow (1)
T   joint (1)
U   jointing place (1)
V   junction (1)
W   ridge row (1)
X   roof gutter (1)
Y   roof valley (1)
Z   rudder(s) (1)
aa   trench (1)
ab   triangle (1)
ac   trough (4)
ad   trough roof (1)
ae   valley (308)
af   valley roof (2)
ag   valley trough (1)

011.6 S valley

No Response (10)
|KAAmaj| (1)
|KAC| (3)
|KACmaj| (2)
|KAI| (1)
|KBC| (1)
|KCA| (2)
|KCCmaj| (2)
|KCU| (1)
|OAA| (85)
|OAAcbj| (3)
|OAAkaj| (197)
|OAAkajcba| (1)
|OAAkan| (3)
|OAAkdj| (1)
|OAAmaj| (8)
|OAB| (50)
|OABeaj| (2)
|OABkaj| (65)
|OABkbj| (1)
|OABmaj| (5)
|OAC| (45)
|OACkaj| (7)
|OAD| (9)
|OADkaj| (1)
|OADmaj| (1)
|OAE| (11)
|OAEcbj| (1)
|OAEkaj| (12)
|OAEmaj| (2)
|OAF| (2)
|OAG| (5)

|OAH| (1)
|OAI| (7)
|OAIkaj| (5)
|OAImaj| (1)
|OBA| (1)
|OBAkaj| (1)
|OBBkaj| (1)
|OBBkbj| (2)
|OBD| (1)
|OCA| (129)
|OCAcba| (3)
|OCAkaj| (113)
|OCAkajcba| (1)
|OCAkak| (1)
|OCAkan| (2)
|OCAmaj| (7)
|OCB| (12)
|OCBkaj| (24)
|OCBmaj| (3)
|OCBmak| (1)
|OCC| (5)
|OCCcbj| (1)
|OCCkaj| (3)
|OCCmaj| (1)
|OCD| (10)
|OCE| (3)
|OCEkaj| (4)
|OCEkajcba| (1)
|OCF| (1)
|OCGkaj| (2)
|OCI| (3)
|OCIkaj| (1)
|OCImaj| (1)
|OCSkaj| (2)
|OCT| (1)
|OCWmaj| (1)
|ODA| (1)
|ODAkdj| (1)
|ODB| (1)
|ODBkdj| (1)
|OGA| (2)
|OGAkaj| (5)
|OGEkaj| (1)
|OGEmaj| (1)
|OGF| (2)
|OKA| (1)
|OKAkdj| (1)
|SAFmaj| (1)

011.7 L shed

No Response (119)
A   animal shed (1)
B   backhouse (4)
C   bean house (1)
D   blacksmith shop (4)
E   boathouse (1)
F   buggy house (6)
G   buggy shed (4)
H   buggy shelter (1)
I   butchering shed (1)

J   calf shed (1)
K   car house (6)
L   car porch (1)
M   car shed (8)
N   carpenter shop (1)
O   carport (5)
P   carriage house (3)
Q   chicken house (1)
R   coal house (13)
S   coal shed (4)
T   commissary (2)
U   cook's house (1)
V   cotton house (8)
W   cotton pen (1)
X   cottonseed house (1)
Y   cow shed (1)
Z   doghouse (3)
aa   drop shed (1)
ab   dynamite shed (1)
ac   egg house (1)
ad   ell (1)
ae   equipment room (1)
af   equipment shed (2)
ag   feed room (1)
ah   fertilizer shed (1)
ai   firehouse (1)
aj   fruit house (2)
ak   fuel house (1)
al   garage (60)
am   garden-tool house (1)
an   gear house (4)
ao   gear room (3)
ap   ginhouse (2)
aq   ginhouse shelter (1)
ar   greenhouse (1)
as   harness room (2)
at   hay shed (3)
au   hothouse (2)
av   house (3)
aw   icehouse (1)
ax   implement shed (2)
ay   jelly house (1)
az   junk house (13)
ba   junk shed (3)
bb   kindling house (1)
bc   kindling room (1)
bd   kindling shed (1)
be   lean-in shed (1)
bf   lean-to (13)
bg   lean-to ell (1)
bh   lean-to shed (2)
bi   little extra house (1)
bj   little house (3)
bk   little hush mouth (1)
bl   log house (1)
bm   machine house (1)
bn   machine shed (1)
bo   maintenance shop (1)
bp   maison bois [F] (1)

bq meat house (4)
br metal building (1)
bs milk house (3)
bt milkshed (1)
bu millhouse (1)
bv old kitchen (1)
bw out shed (1)
bx outbuilding (14)
by outdoor building (1)
bz outdoor house (1)
ca outdoor storage room (1)
cb outdoor storeroom (1)
cc outer house (1)
cd outhouse (38)
ce outhouse place (1)
cf packhouse (4)
cg packing room (1)
ch packing shed (1)
ci packinghouse (1)
cj plunder house (1)
ck plunder room (1)
cl potato house (8)
cm (po)tato house (2)
cn pump house (10)
co pump shed (1)
cp rock house (1)
cq root cellar (1)
cr saddle house (1)
cs seed house (2)
ct separator house (1)
cu servant's house (1)
cv servants' quarters (1)
cw shack (10)
cx shanty (1)
cy shed (226)
cz shed house (3)
da shed room (6)
db sheep shed (1)
dc shelter (10)
dd shop (25)
de shop house (3)
df side room (1)
dg side shed (2)
dh side shelter (1)
di slave house (2)
dj smoke room (1)
dk smokehouse (267)
dl springhouse (2)
dm storage building (1)
dn storage house (24)
do storage place (2)
dp storage room (24)
dq storage shed (7)
dr storage shelter (1)
ds storehouse (15)
dt storeroom (18)
du storm house (4)
dv storm pit (1)
dw stovewood house (1)

dx stowaway house (2)
dy sugarhouse (2)
dz supply room (2)
ea tack room (1)
eb tackle room (1)
ec tenant farmhouse (1)
ed tenant house (2)
ee tin house (2)
ef tool building (2)
eg tool shack (2)
eh tool shed (199)
ei tool shelter (3)
ej tool shop (1)
ek toolhouse (123)
el toolroom (11)
em toolroom house (1)
en tractor house (2)
eo tractor shed (9)
ep utility (3)
eq utility building (3)
er utility house (10)
es utility room (17)
et utility shed (4)
eu village shop (1)
ev wagon shed (12)
ew wagon shelter (1)
ex warehouse (2)
ey wash shed (4)
ez washhouse (19)
fa well house (6)
fb well shed (2)
fc west shed (1)
fd wine room (1)
fe wood building (1)
ff wood shack (4)
fg wood shelter (2)
fh woodhouse (114)
fi woodshed (197)
fj work shed (3)
fk working shop (1)
fl workroom (3)
fm workshop (12)

012.1 L outhouse

No Response (112)
A ABC house (1)
B backhouse (37)
C backing (1)
D backy house (2)
E bathhouse (1)
F bathroom (20)
G bathroom outside (1)
H beauty parlor (1)
I big john (1)
J buck privy (1)
K cabinet [F] (1)
L can (1)
M capital (1)
N casita, la [S] (1)
O cesspool (1)

P cesspool toilet (1)
Q chamber (1)
R Chick Sale(s) (7)
S closet (58)
T closet out in the yard (1)
U commode (6)
V commode, la [F] (4)
W convenience (1)
X country toilet (1)
Y cowboy (1)
Z crap house (4)
aa crapper (9)
ab crazy house (1)
ac ditch (1)
ad double header (1)
ae double hole (1)
af dry toilet (4)
ag dump house (1)
ah excusado [S] (1)
ai five-holer (1)
aj flusher (1)
ak four-holer (1)
al garden house (4)
am green house (1)
an greenhouse (1)
ao half-moon house (1)
ap happy house (1)
aq Hauschen [G] (1)
ar head (1)
as house (2)
at house behind the house (1)
au jakes (1)
av john (53)
aw johnny (51)
ax johnny house (22)
ay Kleines Haus [G] (1)
az ladies' room (1)
ba latrine (5)
bb lavato(ry) (1)
bc lavatory (5)
bd little boys' room (2)
be little brown house in the back (1)
bf little brown shack out back (1)
bg little hiding house (1)
bh little house (12)
bi little house behind the big one (1)
bj little house behind the (great) house (2)
bk little house out by the garden (1)
bl little house out in the backyard (1)
bm little john (1)
bn little shack out back (1)
bo little white house outside (1)
bp little(-old) outhouse (5)
bq little(-old) toilet (2)

br   loft (1)
bs   manure parlor (1)
bt   Mrs. Jones (2)
bu   necessary (2)
bv   necessary house (1)
bw   nicho sito [S] (1)
bx   one-holer (13)
by   open toilet (1)
bz   out (1)
ca   out bathroom (1)
cb   out-of-doors toilet (2)
cc   outbuilding (7)
cd   outdoor bathroom (5)
ce   outdoor closet (2)
cf   outdoor crap shop (1)
cg   outdoor facilities (1)
ch   outdoor house (6)
ci   outdoor john (4)
cj   outdoor johnny (2)
ck   outdoor lavatory (3)
cl   outdoor parlor (1)
cm   outdoor privy (8)
cn   outdoor rest room (2)
co   outdoor toilet (146)
cp   outdoors toilet (3)
cq   outer house (3)
cr   outer toilet (1)
cs   outhouse (353)
ct   outhouse toilet (1)
cu   outside (1)
cv   outside bath (2)
cw   outside bathroom (3)
cx   outside building (1)
cy   outside closet (1)
cz   outside commode (1)
da   outside facilities (1)
db   outside house (6)
dc   outside rest room (1)
dd   outside toilet (52)
de   outside toilet facilities (1)
df   outside two-holer (1)
dg   pit toilet (3)
dh   post office (2)
di   private office (1)
dj   privet (4)
dk   privet house (2)
dl   privy (299)
dm   privy house (2)
dn   reading room (4)
do   relaxation house (1)
dp   relief office (1)
dq   rest house (1)
dr   rest room (10)
ds   S house (1)
dt   sanitary toilet (1)
du   Sears building (1)
dv   shanty house (1)
dw   shed (2)
dx   shed house (2)

dy   shed room (1)
dz   SHI house (1)
ea   shit house (25)
eb   shitter (1)
ec   single hole (1)
ed   smokehouse (1)
ee   specialist (1)
ef   square house (1)
eg   step-out house (1)
eh   Sunday house (1)
ei   surface toilet (1)
ej   telephone booth (1)
ek   three-holer (4)
el   throne (1)
em   toilet (254)
en   toilet outside (1)
eo   two-holer (22)
ep   two-seater (2)
eq   Uncle John (1)
er   water closet (2)
es   water toilet (1)
et   wooden bathroom (1)
eu   WPA (1)

012.2 G have/got
   No Response (242)
   A   ain't/hain't got (42)
   B   done[+V] got (3)
   C   don't/didn't got (2)
   D   got [deleted aux.] (368)
   E   gots (1)
   F   have (267)
   G   have get (1)
   H   have/has got (260)

012.3 G hear
   <!>   infinitive
   <&>   present 3rd singular
   <@>   present participle
   <*>   preterit
   <#>   past participle
   {r}   weakly retroflex
   No Response (23)
   <!(h)yi[r]> (1)
   <!hee(r)> (1)
   <!heer> (11)
   <!hee[r]> (7)
   <!hee{r}> (2)
   <!her> (5)
   <!he[r]> (16)
   <!he{r}> (6)
   <!hi(r)> (11)
   <!hir> (317)
   <!hi[r]> (174)
   <!hi{r}> (69)
   <!hye(r)> (3)
   <!hyee[r]> (1)
   <!hyer> (4)
   <!hye[r]> (3)
   <!hye{r}> (6)
   <!hye{r}z> (1)

   <!hyi(r)> (2)
   <!hyir> (27)
   <!hyi[r]> (33)
   <!hyi{r}> (6)
   <!hyur> (1)
   <&hirz> (1)
   <&hi{r}z> (1)
   <@heerN=14> (3)
   <@heerNG=14> (1)
   <@herN=14> (1)
   <@hirN=14> (2)
   <@hirNG=14> (5)
   <@hi[r]N=14> (2)
   <@hi{r}N=14> (1)
   <@hyi(r)N=14> (1)
   <*(h)yoo[r]d> (1)
   <*hee[r]d> (2)
   <*herd> (5)
   <*he[r]d> (1)
   <*he{r}d> (1)
   <*hi(r)> (1)
   <*hi(r)d> (1)
   <*hird> (50)
   <*hi[r]> (1)
   <*hi[r]d> (24)
   <*hi{r}> (2)
   <*hi{r}d> (10)
   <*hoo[r]d> (1)
   <*hu[r](d)> (1)
   <*hu[r]d> (155)
   <*hur(d)> (1)
   <*hurd> (383)
   <*hurt> (1)
   <*hu{r}d> (80)
   <*hyerd> (1)
   <*hyi[r]d> (4)
   <*hyird> (16)
   <*hyi{r}d> (1)
   <*hyurd> (1)
   <#(h)urd> (1)
   <#heer> (2)
   <#heerd> (1)
   <#hee[r]d> (1)
   <#hee{r}d> (1)
   <#herd> (3)
   <#he[r]n> (2)
   <#hir> (1)
   <#hird> (42)
   <#hirn> (1)
   <#hi[r]> (3)
   <#hi[r]d> (22)
   <#hi[r]n> (3))
   <#hi{r}> (1)
   <#hi{r}d> (14)
   <#hoord> (1)
   <#hoo[r]d> (6)
   <#hu[r](d)> (1)
   <#hu[r]d> (169)
   <#hu[r]t> (1)

<#hue[r]d> (1)
<#hur(d)> (2)
<#hurd> (483)
<#hu{r}(d)> (1)
<#hu{r}d> (114)
<#hu{r}t> (1)
<#hyerd> (5)
<#hye{r}d> (3)
<#hyi[r]d> (6)
<#hyi[r]n> (1)
<#hyirId=14> (1)
<#hyird> (26)
<#hyi{r}d> (3)
<#hyu[r]d> (1)
<#hyurd> (2)

012.4 G heard (tell) of

<!>   infinitive
<*>   preterit
<#>   past participle
{r}   weakly retroflex
No Response (324)
<!he[r]ov=13> (1)
<!he[r]tawkA(v)=214> (1)
<!he[r]telAv=314> (1)
<!hi(r)Abowt=143> (1)
<!hi[r]Abowt=143> (1)
<!hi[r]tel=31> (1)
<!hi[r]telA(v)=314> (4)
<!hi[r]telAv=314> (1)
<!hi[r]telov=313> (1)
<!hirA(v)=14> (1)
<!hirov=13> (1)
<!hirtawk=21> (1)
<!hirtel=21> (1)
<!hirtel=31> (1)
<!hirtelA(v)=134> (1)
<!hirtelA(v)=214> (1)
<!hirtelAv=314> (2)
<!hi{r}tel=31> (2)
<!hi{r}telA(v)=314> (1)
<!hyee[r]tawkAv=314> (1)
<!hyi[r]tel=31> (1)
<!hyi[r]telA(v)=314> (1)
<!hyirov=13> (1)
<!hyirtawkA(v)=314> (1)
<!hyirtelA(v)=314> (1)
<!hyi{r}tel=31> (1)
<*ha{r}dAv=14> (1)
<*hee[r]dtawkA(v)=214> (1)
<*herdAv=14> (1)
<*herdtelA(v)=314> (1)
<*hi(r)dteluv=213> (1)
<*hi[r]dA(v)=14> (2)
<*hi[r]dtawk=31> (1)
<*hi[r]dtelA(v)=214> (1)
<*hirAbowt=143> (1)
<*hirdAbowt=143> (1)
<*hirdAv=14> (1)
<*hirdov=13> (1)

<*hirdtawk=21> (1)
<*hirdtawkA(v)=214> (1)
<*hirdtawkA(v)=314> (1)
<*hirdtawkAv=214> (1)
<*hirdtel=31> (1)
<*hi{r}dtawkA(v)=314> (1)
<*hi{r}dtelA(v)=214> (1)
<*hoo[r]duv=13> (1)
<*hu[r]dA(v)=14> (7)
<*hu[r]dAbiet=341> (1)
<*hu[r]dAbowt=143> (4)
<*hu[r]dAv=14> (4)
<*hu[r]dov=13> (8)
<*hu[r]dtawkA(v)=124> (1)
<*hu[r]dtawkov=213> (1)
<*hu[r]dtawkuv=213> (1)
<*hu[r]dtelAv=134> (1)
<*hu[r]dteluv=213> (1)
<*hu[r]dteluv=313> (1)
<*hu[r]du(v)=13> (1)
<*hu[r]duv=13> (3)
<*hurdA(v)=14> (13)
<*hurdAbiet=143> (1)
<*hurdAbowt=143> (1)
<*hurdAv=14> (10)
<*hurdov=13> (8)
<*hurdtawkA(v)=314> (1)
<*hurdtel=21> (1)
<*hurdtel=31> (3)
<*hurdtelA(v)=314> (2)
<*hurdtelAv=134> (1)
<*hurdtelAv=314> (1)
<*hurdtelov=213> (2)
<*hurdtelov=313> (2)
<*hurdteluv=213> (1)
<*hurduv=13> (2)
<*hu{r}dAbowt=143> (3)
<*hu{r}dAv=14> (1)
<*hu{r}dov=13> (2)
<*hu{r}dtelA(v)=214> (1)
<*hu{r}duv=13> (1)
<*hyi[r]dA(v)=14> (1)
<*hyi[r]dAbowt=143> (1)
<*hyi[r]ntawkAv=214> (1)
<*hyirdtelAv=214> (2)
<*hyirdteluv=313> (1)
<#he[r]nsai=13> (1)
<#heerdA(v)=14> (1)
<#heerdtawkA(v)=134> (1)
<#hee{r}duv=13> (1)
<#herduv=13> (1)
<#he{r}dov=13> (1)
<#hi[r]dA(v)=14> (1)
<#hi[r]dAv=14> (1)
<#hi[r]dov=13> (1)
<#hi[r]dtawkuv=213> (1)
<#hi[r]dtel=12> (1)
<#hi[r]dtel=31> (1)
<#hi[r]dtelA(v)=214> (1)

<#hi[r]dtelov=213> (1)
<#hi[r]dtelov=313> (1)
<#hi[r]duv=13> (2)
<#hi[r]tawkA(v)=214> (1)
<#hirdA(v)=14> (2)
<#hirdAv=14> (2)
<#hirdov=13> (3)
<#hirdtelov=213> (1)
<#hirdteluv=313> (1)
<#hirduv=13> (2)
<#hi{r}dAv=14> (1)
<#hi{r}dov=13> (1)
<#hi{r}dtawkuv=213> (1)
<#hi{r}dtelA(v)=214> (1)
<#hi{r}dtelA(v)=314> (1)
<#hi{r}duv=13> (2)
<#hoo(r)dAv=14> (1)
<#hoo[r]dtelA(v)=114> (1)
<#hu[r]dA(v)=14> (14)
<#hu[r]dAbowt=143> (7)
<#hu[r]dAv=14> (15)
<#hu[r]dov=13> (26)
<#hu[r]dtawk=13> (1)
<#hu[r]dtawkA(v)=214> (1)
<#hu[r]dtawkA(v)=314> (2)
<#hu[r]dtawkAbowt=2143> (1)
<#hu[r]dtawkAv=134> (3)
<#hu[r]dtawkAv=314> (3)
<#hu[r]dtel=11> (1)
<#hu[r]dtel=21> (4)
<#hu[r]dtel=31> (2)
<#hu[r]dtelA(v)=214> (1)
<#hu[r]dtelA(v)=314> (1)
<#hu[r]dtelAv=214> (2)
<#hu[r]dtelAv=314> (2)
<#hu[r]dtelev=213> (1)
<#hu[r]dtelov=213> (4)
<#hu[r]duv=13> (12)
<#hue[r]dtelfrum=123> (1)
<#hurdA(v)=14> (33)
<#hurdAbiet=143> (2)
<#hurdAbowt=142> (1)
<#hurdAbowt=143> (10)
<#hurdAbowt=241> (2)
<#hurdAv=14> (89)
<#hurdob=13> (2)
<#hurdov=11> (1)
<#hurdov=12> (3)
<#hurdov=13> (132)
<#hurdov=21> (6)
<#hurdov=31> (7)
<#hurdtawkA(v)=214> (1)
<#hurdtawkAv=214> (1)
<#hurdtawkov=213> (1)
<#hurdtawkov=313> (1)
<#hurdtawkub=213> (1)
<#hurdtawkuv=213> (1)
<#hurdtawkuv=313> (1)
<#hurdtel=21> (2)

<#hurdtel=31> (1)
<#hurdtelA(v)=214> (1)
<#hurdtelAv=134> (2)
<#hurdtelAv=314> (7)
<#hurdtelov=213> (3)
<#hurdtelov=313> (5)
<#hurdteluv=313> (1)
<#hurdu(v)=13> (1)
<#hurduv=12> (3)
<#hurduv=13> (43)
<#hurduv=21> (2)
<#hurduv=31> (2)
<#hu{r}dA(v)=14> (9)
<#hu{r}dAbat=143> (1)
<#hu{r}dAv=14> (12)
<#hu{r}dov=13> (7)
<#hu{r}dov=31> (1)
<#hu{r}dtawkob=123> (1)
<#hu{r}dtawkuv=213> (1)
<#hu{r}dtelA(v)=214> (1)
<#hu{r}dtelAv=214> (3)
<#hu{r}dtelAv=314> (3)
<#hu{r}dtelov=313> (2)
<#hu{r}duv=13> (15)
<#hyerdAv=14> (1)
<#hyerdtelA(v)=314> (1)
<#hyerduv=13> (1)
<#hyi[r]dA(v)=14> (1)
<#hyi[r]dov=13> (1)
<#hyi[r]dtawkA(v)=214> (1)
<#hyirdA(v)=14> (2)
<#hyirdAv=14> (1)
<#hyirdov=13> (1)
<#hyirdtawkAbowt=2143> (1)
<#hyirdtel=31> (2)
<#hyirdtelA(v)=314> (1)
<#hyirdtelAv=314> (1)

012.5 G ain't
No Response (628)
A   ain't (281)
B   hain't (18)

012.6 G interrogative [negative]
No Response (566)
A   ain't he/she/it? (87)
B   ain't I? (2)
C   ain't that right? (4)
D   ain't they? (10)
E   ain't you? (10)
F   ain't [M-0]? (2)
G   am I not? (1)
H   aren't there? (1)
I   aren't they? (14)
J   aren't we? (1)
K   aren't you? (13)
L   can't you? (2)
M   couldn't it? (2)
N   couldn't you? (1)
O   did he not? (1)
P   did I not? (1)

Q   did they not? (2)
R   didn't he/she/it? (11)
S   didn't I? (6)
T   didn't they? (9)
U   didn't you? (8)
V   doesn't it? (14)
W   don't I? (1)
X   don't they? (16)
Y   don't we? (3)
Z   don't you? (31)
aa   don't you know? (3)
ab   don't you see? (9)
ac   don't you think? (1)
ad   don't you think so? (2)
ae   don't[V-p] he/she/it? (16)
af   hadn't he? (1)
ag   hadn't we? (1)
ah   hadn't you? (2)
ai   hain't it? (2)
aj   hain't you? (1)
ak   haven't you? (11)
al   isn't it? (98)
am   isn't that right? (2)
an   wasn't he/she/it? (32)
ao   wasn't that right? (1)
ap   weren't it? (1)
aq   weren't you? (3)
ar   won't they? (1)
as   wouldn't I? (1)
at   wouldn't it? (19)
au   wouldn't it be? (1)
av   wouldn't they? (3)
aw   wouldn't you? (5)
ax   wouldn't you think? (1)
ay   wouldn't [M-0]? (1)

012.7 G do [various inflections]
No Response (461)
A   can do (1)
B   can he do (1)
C   did he do (2)
D   did I do (2)
E   did you do (1)
F   do I (3)
G   do I do (1)
H   do they (3)
I   do they do (1)
J   do you (10)
K   do you do (5)
L   does he/she/it (33)
M   does he do (77)
N   does he does (1)
O   does you (1)
P   doesn't he do (1)
Q   don't they do (1)
R   do[V-p] he/she/it (14)
S   do[V-p] he do (11)
T   he/she/it do[V-p] (20)
U   he/she/it does (99)
V   he don't[V-p] do (1)

W   he never did do (1)
X   he'd do (1)
Y   he'll do (1)
Z   I couldn't do (1)
aa   I did do (1)
ab   I didn't do (3)
ac   I do (318)
ad   I do do (1)
ae   I does (5)
af   I don't do (8)
ag   I never did do (1)
ah   I never do do (1)
ai   I would do (1)
aj   I wouldn't do (1)
ak   I [X-0] do (2)
al   I'll do (2)
am   it doesn't do (1)
an   never did do (1)
ao   she'd do (1)
ap   they do (23)
aq   they do do (1)
ar   they/people does (10)
as   they doos (1)
at   they'd do (1)
au   we do (12)
av   we do do (1)
aw   we does (3)
ax   we don't do (1)
ay   we doos (1)
az   we'll do (1)
ba   will not do (1)
bb   would do (1)
bc   you can do (1)
bd   you could do (1)
be   you didn't do (1)
bf   you do (6)
bg   you does (1)
bh   [X-0] he/she/it do (2)

012.8 G does
No Response (275)
A   do[V-p] (118)
B   does (548)
C   doos (4)

013.1 G doesn't
No Response (173)
A   does not (15)
B   doesn't (353)
C   don't[V-p] (477)

013.2 G interrogative [affirmative]
No Response (736)
A   am I? (1)
B   are there? (1)
C   are they? (5)
D   are we? (1)
E   are you? (7)
F   can they? (1)
G   can you? (2)
H   could I? (1)
I   could we? (1)

J   could you? (1)

K   did I? (4)

L   did it? (3)

M   did they? (2)

N   did you? (8)

O   do they? (12)

P   do we? (1)

Q   do you? (52)

R   do you know? (3)

S   do you think? (1)

T   does he/she/it? (6)

U   has he/she/it? (2)

V   have we? (1)

W   have you? (13)

X   is he/she/it? (26)

Y   is that right? (1)

Z   is that so? (1)

aa is there? (2)

ab is they? (1)

ac is you? (3)

ad was he/she/it? (2)

ae was you? (1)

af were they? (2)

ag would he/she/it? (12)

ah would you? (9)

ai [X-0] you reckon? (2)

aj [X-0] you understand? (1)

013.3 G (don't I) know (it?)

No Response (613)

A   don't I know (3)

B   I ain't knowed (1)

C   (I) didn't know (5)

D   I do not know (2)

E   (I) don't know (220)

F   I know (29)

G   I knows (1)

H   (I) never did know (3)

I   (I) wouldn't know (5)

J   I [X-0] know (1)

013.4 G not sure

No Response (400)

A   ain't clear (1)

B   ain't for sure (1)

C   ain't sure (3)

D   can't say for definitely (1)

E   don't be sure (1)

F   (don't know) for sure (28)

G   don't remember for certain (1)

H   not certain (9)

I   not for sure (28)

J   not positive (15)

K   not sure (349)

L   that's for sure (6)

M   wasn't sure (3)

N   wouldn't be sure (4)

013.4 S sure

No Response (27)

|BJCmea| (1)

|CJCmea| (1)

|CSAmea| (1)

|EAAmaa| (1)

|EAAmaj| (1)

|EAAmea| (10)

|EACmea| (2)

|ECAmea| (4)

|ECAmeb| (1)

|ECAmpa| (1)

|ECDmaa| (1)

|EFA| (2)

|EFAmaa| (25)

|EFAmaj| (10)

|EFAmea| (84)

|EFAmej| (1)

|EFAmla| (2)

|EFBmaa| (4)

|EFBmaj| (1)

|EFBmea| (11)

|EFCmaj| (1)

|EFCmea| (10)

|EFDmaa| (1)

|EFEmaa| (1)

|EFEmaj| (1)

|EFGmea| (2)

|EFHmea| (1)

|EFImea| (3)

|EFJmea| (3)

|EMA| (2)

|EMAkaa| (1)

|EMAmaa| (5)

|EMAmaj| (2)

|EMAmea| (17)

|EMB| (1)

|EMBmaa| (1)

|EMBmaj| (1)

|EMBmea| (3)

|EMCmea| (4)

|EMDmea| (1)

|EMGmea| (2)

|EMHmaa| (1)

|EMHmla| (1)

|FAAmaa| (1)

|FADmaj| (1)

|FADmea| (8)

|FAFmea| (2)

|FAHmea| (1)

|FCBmea| (1)

|FCDmaa| (1)

|FCDmea| (4)

|FFAmaa| (1)

|FFAmaj| (3)

|FFAmajmea| (1)

|FFAmea| (12)

|FFAmej| (2)

|FFBbjj| (1)

|FFBmaa| (5)

|FFBmaj| (3)

|FFBmea| (19)

|FFBmej| (3)

|FFCmaa| (1)

|FFCmea| (16)

|FFD| (4)

|FFDmaa| (46)

|FFDmaj| (33)

|FFDmajmea| (2)

|FFDmea| (154)

|FFDmej| (10)

|FFDmfa| (2)

|FFFeaj| (1)

|FFFmaa| (11)

|FFFmaj| (4)

|FFFmea| (21)

|FFFmej| (1)

|FFGmaa| (1)

|FFH| (1)

|FFHmaa| (2)

|FFHmaj| (5)

|FFHmajmea| (1)

|FFHmea| (32)

|FFHmfa| (2)

|FFIcjjmea| (1)

|FFImea| (2)

|FFKmea| (1)

|FMAmaa| (1)

|FMAmaj| (4)

|FMAmea| (6)

|FMAmej| (1)

|FMBmaa| (4)

|FMBmaj| (1)

|FMBmea| (6)

|FMBmej| (1)

|FMCmaa| (1)

|FMCmea| (1)

|FMD| (6)

|FMDmaa| (8)

|FMDmaj| (4)

|FMDmea| (25)

|FMDmej| (3)

|FMFmaa| (4)

|FMFmea| (3)

|FMFmfa| (1)

|FMFmpj| (1)

|FMGmaj| (1)

|FMHmaa| (1)

|FMHmfj| (1)

|FSBmaj| (1)

|JJAefj| (6)

|JJAmaa| (1)

|JJAmaj| (1)

|JJBefj| (2)

|JJBmaa| (1)

|JJBmea| (2)

|JJCefa| (2)

|JJCefj| (5)

|JJCjjb| (1)

|JJCmaj| (4)

|JJCmea| (4)

|JJDeaj| (1)

|JJDefa| (5)
|JJDefj| (12)
|JJDffd| (3)
|JJDffdmej| (1)
|JJDffm| (1)
|JJDmaa| (3)
|JJDmaj| (1)
|JJDmea| (6)
|JJDmej| (1)
|JJFefa| (1)
|JJFefj| (1)
|JJFefjmea| (1)
|JJFmaa| (2)
|JJFmaj| (4)
|JJFmea| (3)
|JJGefj| (1)
|JJHefa| (1)
|JJHefj| (1)
|JJHmea| (2)
|JSAefj| (1)
|JSC| (2)
|JSCmaa| (1)
|JSCmaj| (1)
|JSCmea| (2)
|JSDefa| (3)
|JSDffj| (1)
|JSDmaj| (1)
|JSDmea| (1)
|JSFefa| (1)
|JSFmaa| (2)
|JSFmaj| (1)
|JSHefa| (1)
|LAAmea| (2)
|LFA| (1)
|LMAefj| (1)
|MCAmea| (1)
|MEA| (15)
|MLA| (8)
|MLD| (1)
|MPA| (1)
|MYA| (1)
|NABmea| (1)
|NABmej| (1)
|QFBefj| (1)
|QFBefjmea| (1)
|QFBmaj| (2)
|QFCmea| (2)
|QMBmea| (1)
|QMCmea| (1)
|eaaCJDmaj| (1)
|eaaEFA| (1)
|eaeBJAmaj| (1)
|eajFMC| (1)
|ecaBJA| (1)
|efaBJA| (1)
|efaBJAmaa| (1)
|efaBJAmaj| (1)
|efaBJAmea| (1)
|ffdBJJ| (1)

|fffBJJ| (1)

013.5 G aux. verb + pres. part.
No Response (354)
A   am I (2)
B   am you (1)
C   are you (9)
D   he/she/it was (25)
E   he/she/it were (1)
F   he/she/it [X-0] (2)
G   he/she/it [X-0] been (3)
H   he'd be (1)
I   he'd been (1)
J   he's (7)
K   he's been (2)
L   I ain't (3)
M   I ain't been (1)
N   I had been (1)
O   I have been (14)
P   I was/wasn't (120)
Q   I were (2)
R   I [X-0] (4)
S   I [X-0] been (57)
T   I'm (82)
U   I's (6)
V   is he/she/it (1)
W   I've been (21)
X   they are (2)
Y   they was (14)
Z   they were (12)
aa   they [X-0] (6)
ab   they [X-0] been (2)
ac   they'd be (1)
ad   they're (2)
ae   they's (1)
af   we have been (2)
ag   we was (16)
ah   we were (24)
ai   we [X-0] (4)
aj   we [X-0] been (3)
ak   we're (3)
al   were we (1)
am   were you (2)
an   we's (1)
ao   we've been (4)
ap   you had been (1)
aq   you was (24)
ar   you were (26)
as   you would be (1)
at   you [X-0] (99)
au   you [X-0] been (2)
av   you'd be (1)
aw   you're (47)
ax   you's (8)
ay   [X-0] we (1)
az   [X-0] you (9)

013.6 G (what) makes (him do it?)
No Response (704)
A   make[V-p]/other [V-p] (169)
B   makes (56)

013.7 G people think/they say
No Response (342)
A   3rd person pl. subject + pl. verb (304)
B   3rd person pl. subject + sing. verb (381)

014.1 P house/houses
{dh}   devoiced
{o}w   central onset
{ow}   raised onset
{s}   voiced
{z}   devoiced
{zh}   devoiced
No Response (16)
<(h){ow}zIz=14> (1)
<(h){ow}zI{z}=14> (1)
<how(s)> (1)
<hows> (579)
<hows(Iz)> (2)
<howsIs=14> (6)
<howsIz=14> (18)
<howsI{z}=14> (3)
<howsh> (4)
<howst> (1)
<howth> (3)
<howthIsh=14> (1)
<howz> (2)
<howzI(z)=14> (4)
<howzIs=14> (5)
<howzIz=14> (321)
<howzIzh=14> (1)
<howzI{z}=14> (21)
<howzez=31> (1)
<howzhAzh=14> (1)
<howzhIzh=14> (2)
<howzhI{zh}=14> (1)
<how{s}Iz=14> (2)
<how{z}I(z)=14> (1)
<how{z}Iz=14> (18)
<how{z}I{z}=14> (8)
<h{ow}(s)> (1)
<h{ow}dh> (1)
<h{ow}s> (348)
<h{ow}sIs=14> (1)
<h{ow}sIz=14> (4)
<h{ow}sI{z}=14> (3)
<h{ow}th> (2)
<h{ow}yIs=14> (1)
<h{ow}z(Iz)> (1)
<h{ow}zIs=14> (1)
<h{ow}zIz=14> (200)
<h{ow}zI{z}=14> (19)
<h{ow}{dh}I{z}=14> (1)
<h{ow}{s}Iz=14> (2)
<h{ow}{z}Iz=14> (7)
<h{o}ws> (27)
<h{o}wzIz=14> (6)

014.1 S house
No Response (0)

|RAIefa| (1)
|RCAeaj| (1)
|RCAfaa| (1)
|RCAffa| (5)
|RCAffd| (1)
|RCAjba| (1)
|RCAjja| (3)
|RCAjjb| (1)
|RCAjjd| (1)
|RCAlfj| (1)
|RCAmaa| (2)
|RCAmae| (1)
|RCAmaj| (2)
|RCBeaa| (6)
|RCBefa| (37)
|RCBefc| (2)
|RCBefj| (1)
|RCBffa| (3)
|RCBffd| (9)
|RCBfff| (1)
|RCBffh| (2)
|RCBffj| (1)
|RCBjbm| (1)
|RCBjbq| (1)
|RCBjja| (2)
|RCBjjb| (4)
|RCBjjc| (3)
|RCBjjd| (11)
|RCBjjf| (3)
|RCBjjh| (1)
|RCBjjk| (1)
|RCBjjm| (2)
|RCBlfa| (1)
|RCBlfj| (3)
|RCBmaa| (4)
|RCBmaj| (1)
|RCBmfa| (2)
|RCBmfj| (1)
|RCDffd| (1)
|RCEeac| (1)
|RCEefa| (1)
|RCEffb| (1)
|RCEffd| (1)
|RCEjjb| (2)
|RCEjjd| (2)
|RCFeaa| (2)
|RCFefa| (7)
|RCFffd| (2)
|RCFjja| (3)
|RCFjjb| (1)
|RCFjjc| (3)
|RCFjjd| (5)
|RCFjjf| (1)
|RCFlfe| (1)
|RCFmaa| (2)
|RCGeac| (1)
|RCGefa| (3)
|RCGffd| (2)
|RCGjbm| (1)

|RCGjjb| (1)
|RCGjjd| (1)
|RCGmaj| (1)
|RCGmfj| (1)
|RDBjud| (1)
|RDBmoa| (1)
|SADefc| (2)
|SADffd| (1)
|SADjjb| (1)
|SAFjjd| (1)
|SAFjjh| (1)
|SCAffa| (1)
|SCAffj| (1)
|SCBefj| (1)
|SCBffj| (1)
|SCBffl| (1)
|SCBqfd| (1)
|SCDffj| (2)

014.2 P barn
{o} low-back
{r} weakly retroflex
No Response (53)
<ba(r)n> (2)
<baw(r)[n]> (3)
<baw(r)n> (29)
<baw[r]n> (37)
<baw[r]nz> (3)
<bawrn> (94)
<bawrnz> (6)
<bawrt> (1)
<bawwN=14> (1)
<baw{r}n> (23)
<ba{r}n> (2)
<bo(r)n> (29)
<bo[r]n> (77)
<bo[r]nz> (1)
<boe(r)n> (1)
<boe[r]n> (3)
<boern> (2)
<boernz> (2)
<bor(n)> (1)
<born> (287)
<bornd> (1)
<borns> (1)
<bornz> (21)
<bo{r}n> (66)
<bo{r}ns> (1)
<bo{r}nz> (3)
<bron> (1)
<b{o}(r)n> (13)
<b{o}[r]n> (72)
<b{o}rn> (148)
<b{o}rnd> (1)
<b{o}rnz> (3)
<b{o}{r}N=14> (1)
<b{o}{r}n> (23)
<b{o}{r}nz> (1)

014.3 L corncrib
No Response (174)

A bin (33)
B corn barn (2)
C corn bin (30)
D corn room (3)
E corn shed (11)
F corn stall (1)
G corncrib (299)
H cornhouse (11)
I crib (406)
J crib house (2)
K crib of corn (1)
L hopper (1)
M house for corn (1)
N Kornspeicher [G] (1)
O little pen (1)
P log crib (3)
Q magasin [F] (2)
R Maishaus [G] (1)
S shed (10)
T stall (1)
U store bin (1)
V troja [S] (1)

014.3 S crib
No Response (0)
|ABImaj| (2)
|AGAmaa| (1)
|AGCmaj| (1)
|AGEmaj| (1)
|AGImaj| (2)
|BGAmaa| (1)
|BGAmaj| (1)
|DAA| (49)
|DAAdar| (1)
|DAAeaj| (1)
|DAAefj| (1)
|DAAmaa| (3)
|DAAmaj| (47)
|DAB| (29)
|DABdac| (1)
|DABdae| (3)
|DABeaa| (1)
|DABefj| (3)
|DABfaq| (1)
|DABmaa| (8)
|DABmaj| (71)
|DAC| (2)
|DACdab| (4)
|DACeae| (1)
|DACefj| (1)
|DACmaa| (6)
|DACmaj| (4)
|DAE| (170)
|DAEeaj| (2)
|DAEmaj| (186)
|DAEmak| (5)
|DAFmaj| (2)
|DAG| (8)
|DAGfaj| (1)
|DAGmaj| (22)

|DAH| (1)
|DAHdab| (1)
|DAHmaj| (5)
|DAI| (12)
|DAIdab| (1)
|DAImaj| (11)
|DAImfj| (1)
|DBB| (1)
|DBBeaa| (1)
|DBBmaj| (1)
|DCA| (36)
|DCAeaj| (4)
|DCAmaa| (1)
|DCAmaj| (18)
|DCB| (1)
|DCBeaa| (2)
|DCBeaj| (10)
|DCBeak| (2)
|DCBmaa| (4)
|DCBmaj| (26)
|DCBmak| (1)
|DCBmej| (1)
|DCE| (10)
|DCEeaj| (4)
|DCEmaj| (46)
|DCEmak| (1)
|DCFmaa| (1)
|DCFmaj| (2)
|DCGeaa| (2)
|DCGeaj| (2)
|DCGmaj| (7)
|DCI| (2)
|DCIeaj| (1)
|DCImaj| (4)
|DDEmdj| (2)
|DGAmaj| (1)
|EAA| (1)
|EAB| (1)
|EABeac| (1)
|EABmaj| (13)
|EAC| (1)
|EACeab| (5)
|EAD| (2)
|EADmaj| (1)
|EAE| (2)
|EAFmaj| (5)
|EAGmaj| (4)
|EAH| (1)
|EAHmaj| (6)
|EAImaj| (1)
|ECA| (2)

014.4 P granary
No Response (660)
<grainArI=144> (57)
<grainArIz=144> (3)
<grainAree=143> (3)
<grainAri=143> (1)
<grainIrI=144> (2)
<grainIree=143> (1)

<grainRI=144> (67)
<grainRIz=144> (1)
<grainRee=143> (8)
<grainrI=14> (86)
<grainrIz=14> (12)
<grainree=13> (6)
<grainurI=134> (2)
<granArI=144> (1)
<granRI=144> (2)
<granrI=14> (1)
<granurI=134> (1)
<grenrI=14> (3)
<grenrIz=14> (1)

014.5 L loft
No Response (157)
A attic (14)
B attic-like (1)
C barn loft (37)
D fodder loft (3)
E hay barn (3)
F hay bin (1)
G hay deck (1)
H hay house (5)
I hay rider (1)
J hay room (1)
K hay shed (4)
L hayloft (191)
M haymow (10)
N hayrack (5)
O loft (556)
P mow (7)
Q open loft (1)
R overhead (4)
S rafters (1)
T shed (2)
U stable loft (1)
V storage space (1)
W top (2)
X top of the barn (1)
Y top story (1)
Z upper barn (1)
aa upper mow (1)
ab upper part (2)
ac upstairs (26)
ad upstairs part (1)

014.6 L haystack
No Response (280)
A berge [F] (1)
B cane stack (1)
C hay in a stack (1)
D hay mound (1)
E hay on the stack (2)
F hay pile (6)
G haycock (2)
H haymow (2)
I hayrack (7)
J hayrick (12)
K hayshock (6)
L haystack (448)

M haystack of hay (1)
N heap (1)
O Heustock [G] (1)
P hubby (1)
Q mound (1)
R mound of hay (1)
S pile (11)
T pile of hay (7)
U rack (7)
V rack of hay (2)
W rick (11)
X rick of hay (4)
Y shock (23)
Z shock of hay (3)
aa stack (146)
ab stack of hay (18)
ac strawstack (2)

014.7 L hay barrack
No Response (725)
A covered haystack (1)
B covered platform (1)
C curing rack (1)
D hay barn (10)
E hay barrack(s) (4)
F hay bin (1)
G hay house (2)
H hay manger (1)
I hay room (1)
J hay shed (23)
K hay shelter (3)
L haymow (2)
M hayrack (29)
N hayrick (5)
O hayshock (1)
P haystack (2)
Q haystack with a top (1)
R lazy-man's manger (1)
S lean-to (2)
T meulon [F] (1)
U open barn (2)
V rack (5)
W rick (6)
X rick of hay (2)
Y shed (22)
Z shelter (6)
aa straw shed (1)
ab tent (2)

014.8 L haycock
No Response (576)
A bunch (2)
B chunk (1)
C clump (1)
D dip pile (1)
E hay pile (6)
F hay row (2)
G hay shocking (1)
H hay windrow (1)
I haycock (7)
J haymow (1)

K   hayrack (2)
L   hayrick (4)
M   hayshock (16)
N   haystack (7)
O   heap (14)
P   heap of hay (3)
Q   heap row (1)
R   little hay pile (1)
S   meule de foin [F] (1)
T   mound (3)
U   noodle shock (1)
V   pile (33)
W   pile of hay (15)
X   rake (1)
Y   raked-up hay (1)
Z   rick (12)
aa rick of hay (3)
ab ridge (1)
ac row (14)
ad shock (78)
ae shock of hay (7)
af shock pile (1)
ag small pile (2)
ah small stack (1)
ai smaller stack (1)
aj stack (4)
ak strawstack (1)
al turn row (1)
am wind heap (1)
an wind rake (1)
ao windroll (1)
ap windrow (125)

015.1 L cow barn
No Response (285)
A   animal barn (1)
B   barn (245)
C   barn shed (6)
D   barn stall (1)
E   calf shed (1)
F   calf stall (1)
G   cattle barn (10)
H   cattle shed (8)
I   cattle shelter (3)
J   covered shelter (1)
K   cow barn (81)
L   cow shed (81)
M   cow shelter (7)
N   cow stable (3)
O   cow stall (23)
P   cow-shed barn (1)
Q   dairy barn (16)
R   dairy building (1)
S   drop shed (1)
T   feeding barn (1)
U   fourteen-foot shed (1)
V   hay barn (1)
W   hay shed (1)
X   hut (1)
Y   lean (1)

Z   lean-to (5)
aa loafing shed (3)
ab milk barn (2)
ac milking barn (3)
ad milking shed (1)
ae milking stall (2)
af milkshed (3)
ag open shed (2)
ah open shelter (1)
ai pole shed (1)
aj porch (1)
ak shack cow shed (1)
al shed (131)
am shed way (1)
an shelter (12)
ao shelter barn (1)
ap side shed (3)
aq sleeping barn (2)
ar stable (32)
as stall (93)
at stock shelter (1)
au stoop (1)
av storage shed (1)

015.2 L stable
No Response (254)
A   barn (131)
B   barn area (1)
C   barn house (1)
D   barn shed (2)
E   barn stable (1)
F   barn stall (2)
G   box stall (1)
H   breeding barn (1)
I   corral (1)
J   double stables (1)
K   horse barn (27)
L   horse shed (6)
M   horse shelter (3)
N   horse stable (22)
O   horse stall (18)
P   lean-to (1)
Q   livery stable (9)
R   log shed (1)
S   lot (2)
T   mare barn (1)
U   mule barn (14)
V   mule shed (1)
W   mule stable (8)
X   mule stall (4)
Y   Pferdestall [G] (1)
Z   riding-horse barn (1)
aa riding stable (2)
ab shed (31)
ac shed with stalls (1)
ad shelter (2)
ae shelter place (1)
af stable (371)
ag stabling (1)
ah stall (172)

ai stall in the barn (1)
aj stalls for the mules (1)
ak stock barn (1)
al stockade (1)

015.3 L milk gap
No Response (344)
A   barn lot (3)
B   barnyard (3)
C   break (8)
D   catch pen (4)
E   cattle gap (2)
F   cattle pen (2)
G   corail [F] (1)
H   corral (12)
I   corral pen (1)
J   cow gap (1)
K   cow lot (41)
L   cow pasture (1)
M   cow pen (197)
N   cow stall (1)
O   cutting pen (1)
P   gap (3)
Q   holding pen (1)
R   horse lot (1)
S   lot (45)
T   milk break (1)
U   milk gap (10)
V   milk lot (9)
W   milk pen (9)
X   milk place (1)
Y   milking corral (1)
Z   milking gap (1)
aa milking lot (3)
ab milking pen (1)
ac milking place (1)
ad open lot (1)
ae parc de betes [F] (1)
af pasture (1)
ag patch (1)
ah pen (47)
ai Penne [G] (1)
aj stanchion (1)
ak stock pen (1)
al temporary pen (1)
am trap (2)
an yard (4)

015.4 L hogpen
No Response (135)
A   barn (1)
B   breeder house (1)
C   breeding pen (1)
D   brooder pen (1)
E   cement feedlot (1)
F   close pen (2)
G   corral (1)
H   dirt pen (1)
I   farrowing house (8)
J   farrowing shed (1)
K   fattening pen (10)

L feed house (1)
M feed pen (1)
N feeder parlor (1)
O feeder pen (1)
P feeding pen (1)
Q feedlot (1)
R floored pen (5)
S hog barn (1)
T hog bed (1)
U hog corral (1)
V hog house (19)
W hog lot (63)
X hog parlor (17)
Y hog pasture (20)
Z hog patch (1)
aa hog place (1)
ab hog runner (1)
ac hog shed (10)
ad hog shelter (6)
ae hog wallow (3)
af hog-fattening pen (1)
ag hogpen (308)
ah hogs' house (2)
ai hollow (1)
aj house (3)
ak lean-to (1)
al lot (46)
am lot pasture (1)
an lot pen (1)
ao parc a cochons [F] (1)
ap parlor (2)
aq patch (2)
ar pen (273)
as pig barn (1)
at pig house (4)
au pig lot (7)
av pig parlor (9)
aw pig pasture (2)
ax pig shelter (2)
ay pig stall (1)
az pigpen (197)
ba pigs' pen (1)
bb pigsty (43)
bc plank pen (1)
bd pound (1)
be rail pen (1)
bf regular pen (1)
bg Schweinepenne [G] (1)
bh shed (21)
bi shelter (6)
bj slop [n.] (1)
bk sty (26)
bl tighter pen, a (1)
bm two-log pen (1)
bn wood pen (1)
bo woods lot (2)
bp yard (3)

015.5A L dairy [storage place]
No Response (115)

A basement (5)
B bored well (1)
C box (4)
D bug-proof safe (1)
E cabinet (1)
F cave spring (1)
G cellar (37)
H cellar house (1)
I channel (1)
J chill box (1)
K churn (2)
L cistern (21)
M cistern house (1)
N coal room (1)
O cold house (1)
P cold spring water (1)
Q cold well (1)
R cool cave (1)
S cool creek (1)
T cooler (14)
U cooling house (2)
V cooling room (1)
W creek (2)
X crock (3)
Y cupboard (1)
Z cyclone cellar (1)
aa dairy (41)
ab dairy case (1)
ac dairy house (5)
ad dairy place (1)
ae dairy room (1)
af deep well (4)
ag dirt cellar (1)
ah dug deep well (1)
ai dug well (6)
aj farm cooler (1)
ak freezer locker (1)
al glass jug (1)
am gully (1)
an home well (1)
ao house over the spring (1)
ap ice cooler (1)
aq icebox (47)
ar jug (3)
as Milchschup(pen) [G] (1)
at milk box (6)
au milk can (1)
av milk closet (2)
aw milk cooler (7)
ax milk dairy (7)
ay milk hole (1)
az milk house (24)
ba milk jug (1)
bb milk pit (1)
bc milk room (4)
bd milk safe (3)
be milk shelf (1)
bf milk trough (2)
bg milk well (1)

bh milkshed (3)
bi open well (2)
bj open-air safe (1)
bk outhouse (1)
bl pantry (1)
bm pit (4)
bn pump house (1)
bo root cellar (5)
bp safe (22)
bq shed (1)
br shelf (1)
bs shelter (1)
bt smokehouse (1)
bu spade well (1)
bv spring (54)
bw spring box (3)
bx spring branch (1)
by spring shed (1)
bz spring water (1)
ca springhouse (67)
cb stone churn (1)
cc storage place (1)
cd storeroom (1)
ce storm cellar (3)
cf storm pit (1)
cg stream (1)
ch trough (2)
ci tub (1)
cj under the house, the (1)
ck underground (1)
cl underground cellar (1)
cm washhouse (1)
cn water cooler (1)
co water well (1)
cp well (98)
cq well house (7)
cr wooden icebox (1)

015.5 P dairy
{ai} lax onset
{r} weakly retroflex
{t} flap
{z} devoiced
{?} glottal
No Response (210)
<dai(rI)> (1)
<daihI=14> (1)
<dairI=14> (183)
<dairIz=14> (18)
<dairee=13> (3)
<dairrI=14> (4)
<dairrIz=14> (2)
<dai{r}I=14> (3)
<dai{r}Iz=14> (1)
<darI=14> (5)
<darrI=14> (1)
<de[r]I=14> (1)
<de[r]ee=13> (1)
<deerI=14> (1)
<der(I)> (1)

<derA=14> (1)
<derI=14> (399)
<derIz=14> (24)
<derI{z}=14> (2)
<deree=13> (15)
<derrI=14> (6)
<derree=13> (2)
<dewI=14> (1)
<de{?}I=14> (1)
<de{r}I=14> (5)
<de{r}rI=14> (9)
<de{t}I=14> (2)
<dirI=14> (18)
<dirIz=14> (3)
<diree=13> (2)
<durI=14> (13)
<durIz=14> (2)
<durI{z}=14> (1)
<duree=13> (1)
<dureez=13> (1)
<du{r}rI=14> (1)
<d{ai}(rI)> (1)
<d{ai}rI=14> (22)
<d{ai}rIz=14> (1)
<d{ai}rrI=14> (1)

015.5B L potato house
No Response (673)
A   bank (24)
B   basement (6)
C   bin (3)
D   bunk (of potatoes) (2)
E   cellar (33)
F   crib (2)
G   dairy (1)
H   dirt kiln (1)
I   dugout (2)
J   hill (9)
K   hole (1)
L   hotbed (1)
M   house (1)
N   kiln (2)
O   mound (3)
P   pile (1)
Q   pit (3)
R   potato bank (24)
S   (po)tato bank (9)
T   potato bed (4)
U   (po)tato bed (1)
V   potato bin (3)
W   potato bunk (4)
X   (po)tato bunk (1)
Y   potato cellar (3)
Z   potato hill (13)
aa   (po)tato hill (4)
ab   potato hole (1)
ac   (po)tato hole (2)
ad   potato house (39)
ae   (po)tato house (7)
af   potato kiln (5)

ag   (po)tato kiln (3)
ah   potato mound (1)
ai   potato pile (2)
aj   (po)tato pit (1)
ak   potato pump (4)
al   potato rick (1)
am   potato room(1)
an   potato shed (1)
ao   potatoes bank (1)
ap   pump (9)
aq   rack (1)
ar   root cellar (5)
as   seed bank (1)
at   shed (1)
au   smokehouse (1)
av   storage bin (1)
aw   storm cellar (2)
ax   storm house (2)
ay   sweet-potato bed (1)
az   sweet-potato house (1)
ba   under the house (3)

015.6 L barnyard
No Response (156)
A   back lot (4)
B   barn lot (73)
C   barnyard (213)
D   barnyard lot (2)
E   basse-cour [F] (1)
F   calf lot (2)
G   catch lot (1)
H   catch pen (2)
I   cattle corral (1)
J   cattle lot (1)
K   cattle pen (2)
L   chicken yard (9)
M   close-up pen (1)
N   corral (42)
O   cow lot (53)
P   cow pen (8)
Q   cow yard (2)
R   farm lot (1)
S   farmyard (6)
T   feeding lot (1)
U   feeding pen (1)
V   feedlot (18)
W   field (3)
X   fold (1)
Y   front lot (1)
Z   grassy lot (1)
aa   grazing area (2)
ab   grazing land (1)
ac   grove (1)
ad   hog lot (7)
ae   horse lot (48)
af   horse pasture (1)
ag   horse pen (2)
ah   lot (398)
ai   milk lot (1)
aj   mule corral (1)

ak   mule lot (8)
al   open lot (1)
am   paddock (2)
an   pasture (1)
ao   pasture lot (1)
ap   pen (20)
aq   pound (1)
ar   puncheon lot (1)
as   runaround pen (1)
at   running room (1)
au   sheepfold (1)
av   stable (1)
aw   stockade (1)
ax   stockyard (2)
ay   stomp lot (1)
az   trap (2)
ba   woodlot (1)
bb   working pen (1)
bc   yard (73)

015.7 L pasture
No Response (85)
A   back levee (1)
B   Bermuda pasture (2)
C   bottom pastureland (1)
D   calf pasture (2)
E   cornfield (1)
F   cow pasture (13)
G   field (22)
H   five-acre pasture (1)
I   free range (4)
J   graze land (2)
K   grazing boundary (1)
L   grazing field (1)
M   grazing land (3)
N   grazing pasture (2)
O   highland (1)
P   hog pasture (4)
Q   horse pasture (1)
R   meadow (14)
S   mule pasture (1)
T   open field (1)
U   open pasture (4)
V   open place (1)
W   open range (18)
X   outside range (2)
Y   pasturage (1)
Z   pasture (789)
aa   pasture field (14)
ab   pasture lot (1)
ac   pastureland (11)
ad   patch (1)
ae   prairie (1)
af   ranch (1)
ag   range (12)
ah   rotation field (1)
ai   Southern pasture (1)
aj   spread (1)
ak   thicket (2)
al   trap (5)

am   winter patch (1)
an   woodland (1)
ao   woodland pasture (1)
ap   woods (7)

015.7 P pasture

{a}   upglide
{ai}   lowered onset
{p}   fricative
{R}   weakly retroflex
{r}   weakly retroflex
{t}   flap
{z}   devoiced
{zh}   devoiced

No Response (96)
<pa(s)chR=14> (2)
<pa(s)chRz=14> (1)
<pa(s)ch{R}=14> (1)
<pa(s)ty{R}=14> (1)
<parIst(y)[R]=144> (1)
<parsht(y)R=14> (1)
<pas(ty)[R]=14> (1)
<paschA{t}=14> (1)
<paschR=14> (222)
<paschRz=14> (7)
<paschR{z}=14> (3)
<pasch[R]=14> (142)
<pasch[R]z=14> (10)
<pasch[R]{z}=14> (1)
<paschoe(r)=13> (1)
<paschoo(r)=13> (1)
<paschoo[r]=13> (4)
<paschoor=13> (5)
<paschoo{r}z=13> (1)
<paschu[r]=13> (1)
<paschur=13> (4)
<paschurz=13> (1)
<paschyR=14> (11)
<paschy[R]=14> (5)
<paschyue{r}z=13> (1)
<paschy{R}=14> (1)
<pasch{R}=14> (36)
<pasch{R}z=14> (4)
<pasch{R}{zh}=14> (1)
<pasch{R}{z}=14> (1)
<pash(t)zhR=14> (1)
<pash(ty)R=14> (2)
<pash(ty)[R]=14> (2)
<pashchR=14> (10)
<pashch[R]=14> (2)
<pashchy[R]=14> (1)
<pashch{R}=14> (2)
<pashch{R}z=14> (1)
<pasht(y)R=14> (1)
<pasht(y)[R]=14> (3)
<pasht(y)i{r}=13> (1)
<pasht(y)rI=14> (1)
<pasht(y)ur=13> (1)
<pasht(y){R}=14> (2)
<pashtyR{zh}=14> (1)

<pashty[R]=14> (3)
<pashty{R}=14> (4)
<pass(y)R=14> (1)
<past(y)R=14> (55)
<past(y)Rz=14> (4)
<past(y)[R]=14> (97)
<past(y)[R]z=14> (3)
<past(y)[R]{z}=14> (1)
<past(y)oo[r]=13> (1)
<past(y)oor=13> (2)
<past(y)rI=14> (1)
<past(y)rIs=14> (1)
<past(y)rIz=14> (1)
<past(y)u[r]=13> (1)
<past(y)ur=13> (2)
<past(y){R}=14> (24)
<past(y){R}z=14> (3)
<pastew(r)=13> (1)
<pastew[R]=134> (1)
<pastew[r]=13> (1)
<pastshoor=13> (1)
<pastyR=14> (26)
<pastyRz=14> (1)
<pasty[R]=14> (33)
<pasty[R]z=14> (3)
<pastyoo[r]=13> (1)
<pastyoor=13> (2)
<pastyoo{t}=13> (1)
<pastyshR=14> (1)
<pastysh{R}=14> (1)
<pastyuer=13> (1)
<pastyur=13> (1)
<pasty{R}=14> (15)
<past{t}R=14> (1)
<pas{t}(y){R}z=14> (1)
<patht(y)[R]=14> (2)
<pa{r}st(y)R=14> (1)
<peschR=14> (1)
<peschR{z}=14> (1)
<pesch[R]=14> (3)
<pest(y)rA=14> (1)
<pestyoo[r]=13> (1)
<p{ai}sch[R]=14> (1)
<p{ai}sch{R}=14> (1)
<p{ai}shchR=14> (1)
<p{ai}sht(y){R}=14> (1)
<p{ai}st(y)[R]=14> (1)
<p{ai}sty{R}=14> (1)
<p{a}s(t)sh{R}=14> (1)
<p{a}schR=14> (19)
<p{a}schRz=14> (2)
<p{a}sch[R]=14> (12)
<p{a}sch[R]z=14> (3)
<p{a}schu{r}=13> (2)
<p{a}schyR=14> (1)
<p{a}schy[R]=14> (1)
<p{a}schy{R}=14> (1)
<p{a}sch{R}=14> (7)
<p{a}sch{R}z=14> (1)

<p{a}sh(ty){R}z=14> (1)
<p{a}shchR=14> (2)
<p{a}shchR{z}=14> (1)
<p{a}shch[R]=14> (2)
<p{a}sht(y){R}=14> (1)
<p{a}shty[R]=14> (2)
<p{a}shty{R}=14> (1)
<p{a}st(y)R=14> (9)
<p{a}st(y)[R]=14> (8)
<p{a}st(y){R}=14> (11)
<p{a}st(y){R}z=14> (2)
<p{a}styR=14> (2)
<p{a}sty[R]=14> (6)
<p{a}sty{R}=14> (4)
<p{a}s{t}(y)[R]=14> (1)
<{p}asch[R]=14> (1)

015.8 L chop cotton

No Response (349)
A   block [v.] (2)
B   block (it) out (2)
C   bunch [v.] (2)
D   bunch my cotton (1)
E   chop by the day (1)
F   chop (it) (158)
G   chop it down (1)
H   chop (it) out (45)
I   chop it up (1)
J   chop on that pretty cotton (1)
K   chop out (1)
L   chop out grasses/weeds (1)
M   chop out (the) cotton (2)
N   chop (the) cotton (231)
O   chop (the) cotton out (8)
P   chop (the) weeds (6)
Q   chop (the) weeds out (6)
R   chop them out (2)
S   chop them up (1)
T   chop through (it) (2)
U   chopping (of cotton) [n.] (3)
V   clean it out (1)
W   clean the weeds out of it (1)
X   cotton chopping (4)
Y   cultivate (it) (4)
Z   cut [v.] (1)
aa   cut fine (1)
ab   cut grass (1)
ac   cut it out (1)
ad   cut (out) the weeds (2)
ae   first hoeing (2)
af   flat-weed it (1)
ag   get the grass out of it (1)
ah   hill cotton [v.] (1)
ai   hoe (it) (133)
aj   hoe (it) out (9)
ak   hoe it thin (1)
al   hoe it up (1)
am   hoe out (Johnson) grass (2)
an   hoe (the) cotton (82)
ao   hoe the grass out (2)

ap   hoe (the) grass (up) (2)
aq   hoe (the) weeds (1)
ar   hoe (the weeds) out (3)
as   hoe your cotton twice (1)
at   hoeing [n.] (2)
au   keep it hoed out (1)
av   scrape (it) (15)
aw   scrape (the) cotton (9)
ax   scrape the cotton out (1)
ay   second it (1)
az   thin [v.] (11)
ba   thin it (down) (21)
bb   thin (it) out (61)
bc   thin out cotton (1)
bd   thin (the) cotton (17)
be   thin the cotton out (4)
bf   trim out the weeds (1)
bg   weed [v.] (3)
bh   weed cotton (1)
bi   weed it (out) (7)
bj   weed out the cotton (1)
bk   weeding of the cotton (1)
bl   work it (7)

015.9 L grass types

No Response (342)
A   American grass (1)
B   Bahia (grass) (3)
C   bamboo briers (1)
D   barnyard weeds (1)
E   bear grass (5)
F   beggar grass (1)
G   beggar-lice (2)
H   beggarweeds (6)
I   bell fountain (1)
J   Bermuda (grass) (78)
K   (Ber)muda grass (19)
L   bitterweed (7)
M   blackbrush (1)
N   bloodweed (2)
O   bluegrass (4)
P   brier bushes/grass (2)
Q   briers (2)
R   broadleaf weeds (1)
S   broom sage (1)
T   buffalo grass (1)
U   buffel grass (1)
V   bull grass (6)
W   bull nettle (2)
X   bullweed (1)
Y   burr (grass) (4)
Z   bush nettle (1)
aa   cane grass (1)
ab   careless weeds (18)
ac   chayote [S] (1)
ad   chickweed (1)
ae   chigger weed (1)
af   clover (3)
ag   coastal grass (1)
ah   cocklebur weeds (1)

ai   cockleburras (1)
aj   cockleburrs (93)
ak   coco (grass) (20)
al   coffeeweeds (17)
am   Colorado grass (1)
an   crabgrass (209)
ao   cresses (1)
ap   crocus grass (1)
aq   crop grass (2)
ar   crowfoot (grass) (9)
as   dock weeds (1)
at   dog fennel (2)
au   fescue (grass) (2)
av   field grass (9)
aw   flagweeds (2)
ax   flat milkweed (1)
ay   forjo (1)
az   foxtail (1)
ba   Fuchsschwanz [G] (1)
bb   goat grass (1)
bc   goat head (1)
bd   goose grass (1)
be   grass burrs (3)
bf   guinea grass (2)
bg   hay grass (2)
bh   Hitler grass (1)
bi   hogweeds (9)
bj   honeysuckle vine (1)
bk   hooded windmill grass (1)
bl   huajillo [S] (1)
bm   hurrah grass (2)
bn   inch-a-night grass (1)
bo   ironweeds (1)
bp   Jimson grass (1)
bq   Jimsonweeds (8)
br   Johnson grass (hay) (158)
bs   Johnson weed (1)
bt   Kelly weed (2)
bu   kudzu (vine) (2)
bv   lamb's quarter (1)
bw   (les)pedeza (1)
bx   lime quarters (1)
by   maiden cane (2)
bz   maypop vine (1)
ca   milkweed (2)
cb   monkey grass (1)
cc   morning glories (15)
cd   morning-glory vine (2)
ce   mule grass (1)
cf   mule-tail weed (1)
cg   mutton grass (1)
ch   nut grass (28)
ci   peavines (1)
cj   pigweed (2)
ck   plankton (1)
cl   plantation weeds (1)
cm   poor dog (1)
cn   poor-land weeds (1)
co   purslane (2)

cp   pussley (14)
cq   quelite [S] (1)
cr   racacha [F] (1)
cs   ragweed (14)
ct   red tea weeds (1)
cu   ribbon grass (1)
cv   ryegrass (3)
cw   sage (grass) (7)
cx   sagebrush (1)
cy   Saint Augustine grass (4)
cz   sandspur (grass/weeds) (15)
da   sassafras sprouts (1)
db   saw briers (2)
dc   sheep sorrel (1)
dd   sheep's-gowan (1)
de   shuckweed (1)
df   slender grama grass (1)
dg   smartweed (3)
dh   snake-grass (1)
di   sour grass (1)
dj   sticker weeds (1)
dk   stickers (1)
dl   stickweed (2)
dm   stinkweed (1)
dn   straw-field grass (1)
do   sunflowers (4)
dp   tara (vine) (2)
dq   tea weeds (4)
dr   Texas grass (1)
ds   thistles (2)
dt   tickle grass (1)
du   tievine (5)
dv   tread-soft briers (1)
dw   trumpet vine (1)
dx   tumbleweed (1)
dy   Uniolas (1)
dz   water grass (13)
ea   water purslane (1)
eb   watercresses (1)
ec   wild beet (1)
ed   wire grass (14)
ee   wood grass (1)

016.1 L field/patch

No Response (53)
A   acre lot (1)
B   acre of cotton (1)
C   acreage (2)
D   acres (3)
E   allotment (2)
F   bean field (2)
G   bean patch/patch of beans (3)
H   bed (3)
I   berry patch (2)
J   blackberry patch (1)
K   bottom (1)
L   brag patch of corn (1)
M   brier patch (6)
N   broom-sage patch (1)
O   butter-bean patch (1)

P   cabbage field (1)
Q   cabbage patch/patch of cabbage (3)
R   cane field (1)
S   cane patch/patch of cane (18)
T   chufa patch (2)
U   collard patch (2)
V   common, the (1)
W   corn patch/patch of corn (43)
X   corner lot (1)
Y   cornfield/field of corn (75)
Z   cotton allotment (1)
aa   cotton field/field of cotton (95)
ab   cotton patch/patch of cotton (98)
ac   cow field (1)
ad   cropland (1)
ae   cucumber field (1)
af   cucumber patch (2)
ag   cut (1)
ah   family peanut patch (1)
ai   farm (5)
aj   Feld [G] (1)
ak   field (721)
al   flower patch (1)
am   fodder field (2)
an   forty-acre field (1)
ao   garden (24)
ap   garden lot (1)
aq   garden patch (9)
ar   garden spot (2)
as   hay patch (2)
at   hayfield/field of hay (8)
au   lettuce patch (1)
av   lot (15)
aw   lot of ground (1)
ax   lowland field (1)
ay   market patch (1)
az   melon patch (2)
ba   newground (1)
bb   oat field (1)
bc   oat patch/patch of oats (3)
bd   palmetto patch (1)
be   pasture (1)
bf   pasture field (2)
bg   patch (326)
bh   patch of crop (1)
bi   patch of land (2)
bj   patch of okra (1)
bk   patch of timber (1)
bl   patch of wheat (1)
bm   patch of woods (3)
bn   pea field (1)
bo   pea patch/patch of peas (43)
bp   peanut field (4)
bq   peanut patch/patch of peanuts (10)
br   pepper patch (1)
bs   piece of land (1)
bt   plot (6)

bu   plot of ground (2)
bv   popcorn patch/patch of popcorn (2)
bw   potato patch/patch of potatoes (42)
bx   rice field (3)
by   roasting-ear field (1)
bz   roasting-ear patch (3)
ca   row (3)
cb   rye patch (1)
cc   sage field (1)
cd   section (2)
ce   small acreage (1)
cf   sorghum patch (1)
cg   square (1)
ch   straw field (1)
ci   strawberry patch (10)
cj   sugarcane field (3)
ck   sugarcane patch (3)
cl   sweet-potato patch/patch of sweet potatoes (8)
cm   tendable land (1)
cn   tobacco acreage (1)
co   tobacco base (1)
cp   tobacco field/field of tobacco (10)
cq   tobacco ground (1)
cr   tobacco lot (2)
cs   tobacco patch/patch of tobacco (32)
ct   tobacco plot/plot of tobacco (2)
cu   tomato patch/patch of tomatoes (6)
cv   truck field (1)
cw   truck garden (1)
cx   truck patch (25)
cy   tung-nut field (1)
cz   turnip patch/patch of turnips (20)
da   vegetable garden (1)
db   vegetable lot (1)
dc   vegetable patch (3)
dd   watermelon field (1)
de   watermelon patch/patch of watermelons (26)
df   weed field (1)
dg   weed patch (1)
dh   wheat field/field of wheat (8)
di   woods row patch (1)
dj   yard (2)

016.1 P field

No Response (103)
<fee[1](d)> (26)
<fee[1](d)z> (4)
<fee[1]d> (11)
<fee[1]dz> (1)
<feel(d)> (412)
<feel(d)s> (1)
<feel(d)z> (44)
<feeld> (364)

<feeldz> (17)
<feelt> (1)
<feld> (1)
<fi[1](d)> (1)
<fild> (1)

016.1 S field

No Response (4)
|AAE| (1)
|AAImajcbj| (1)
|ABA| (1)
|ABAdab| (1)
|ABAeaj| (3)
|ABAmaa| (1)
|ABAmaj| (21)
|ABC| (3)
|ABCmaa| (1)
|ABCmaj| (11)
|ABE| (11)
|ABEcba| (2)
|ABEeaj| (1)
|ABEmaa| (1)
|ABEmaj| (141)
|ABEmajcaa| (1)
|ABEmajcbj| (1)
|ABEmak| (1)
|ABI| (3)
|ABImaj| (26)
|ABImajcbj| (1)
|ACEmaj| (1)
|ACImaj| (1)
|AGA| (2)
|AGAdaj| (1)
|AGAeaa| (3)
|AGAeaj| (2)
|AGAmaa| (11)
|AGAmaacba| (4)
|AGAmaj| (43)
|AGAmajcba| (1)
|AGC| (2)
|AGCeaacba| (1)
|AGCmaa| (1)
|AGCmaj| (7)
|AGCmajcba| (1)
|AGE| (22)
|AGEeajmaa| (1)
|AGEmaa| (4)
|AGEmaj| (275)
|AGEmajcba| (2)
|AGEmajcbj| (1)
|AGEmak| (1)
|AGGmaj| (1)
|AGI| (2)
|AGImaj| (20)
|AQCedacha| (1)
|AQCedjcha| (1)
|BBHmaj| (1)
|BBImaj| (1)
|BGAkfj| (1)
|BGAmaa| (2)

|BGAmaacha| (1)
|BGAmaj| (4)
|BGAmajcba| (1)
|BGDmaj| (3)
|BQAmda| (1)
|DAAmaj| (1)
|DAB| (1)
|DABmaj| (1)
|DAGmaj| (4)
|DCC| (1)
|EAGcba| (1)
|KAGmaj| (1)
|abbABAmaj| (1)
|abcABA| (11)
|abcABAcbj| (1)
|abcABAmaj| (19)
|abcABEmaj| (1)
|abcAGA| (2)
|abcAGAmaj| (5)
|abeABAmaj| (2)
|abeABI| (1)
|abeBBAmaj| (1)
|abeBBJ| (1)
|abiABA| (1)
|abiABAmaj| (1)
|abiABE| (6)
|abiAGE| (1)
|agcABA| (2)
|agcABAmaj| (2)
|ageABEmaj| (1)
|ageABJmaa| (1)
|agiABA| (1)
|daaABA| (4)
|daaABAmaa| (1)
|daaABAmaj| (5)
|daaABC| (2)
|daaABCmaj| (1)
|daaABEmaj| (1)
|daaABEmajcba| (1)
|daaAGA| (2)
|daaabcABA| (1)
|dabABA| (4)
|dabABAmaj| (5)
|dabABC| (1)
|dabABCmaj| (3)
|dabABEmaj| (1)
|dabABJ| (1)
|dabBBJ| (3)
|dacABEcbj| (1)
|dacBBA| (6)
|dacBBC| (1)
|daeABA| (2)
|daeABAmaj| (1)
|daeABB| (1)
|daeABE| (12)
|daeABEmaj| (22)
|daeABEmajcba| (1)
|daeABI| (1)
|daeABImaj| (2)

|daeABNmaj| (1)
|daeAGEmaj| (11)
|daeAGImaj| (1)
|dafABEmaj| (1)
|dagABE| (2)
|dagABEmaj| (1)
|dagBBJmaj| (1)
|dahBBA| (2)
|dahBBJmaj| (1)
|daiABA| (1)
|daiABEmaj| (1)
|dcaABAmcacba| (1)
|dcaBBAmaa| (1)
|dcbABA| (1)
|dcbABCmaj| (1)
|dcbBBJ| (1)
|dceBBAmajcba| (1)
|dcfABAmaj| (1)
|ddaAQA| (1)
|eaaBAA| (1)
|eaaBBA| (19)
|eaaBBAmaj| (14)
|eaaBBDmaj| (2)
|eaaBGA| (4)
|eaaBGAmaa| (1)
|eaaBGAmaj| (1)
|eabBBA| (1)
|eabBBJmaj| (1)
|eacBBJ| (1)
|eadABE| (1)
|eahBBA| (4)
|eahBBAmaj| (3)
|eahBBD| (1)
|eahBBJ| (1)
|eaiBGA| (1)
|ecbBBA| (1)
|ecdBBDmaj| (1)
|ecfABJmaj| (1)
|echBBA| (2)
|echBBJ| (1)

016.2 L picket fence
No Response (119)
A   board fence (2)
B   cedar (1)
C   cedar fence (2)
D   cour bois [F] (1)
E   cypress fence (2)
F   cypress pieu (1)
G   decorative fence (1)
H   fence (70)
I   fence paling (1)
J   fencing (1)
K   fencing-plank fence (1)
L   field fence (2)
M   field fencing (1)
N   garden fence (23)
O   house fence (1)
P   iron picket fence (1)

Q   Kentucky white wooden fence (1)
R   laths (1)
S   lattice fence (1)
T   lawn fence (1)
U   lumber fence (2)
V   oak (1)
W   oak pickets (1)
X   pale fence (11)
Y   palement (1)
Z   palement fence (1)
aa   pales (1)
ab   paling fence (121)
ac   paling garden (1)
ad   paling guards (1)
ae   paling or picket fence (1)
af   paling(s) (113)
ag   panel fence (1)
ah   pasture fence (1)
ai   picket boards (1)
aj   picket fence (497)
ak   picket fencing (1)
al   picket panel fence (1)
am   picket pegs (1)
an   picket(s) (97)
ao   pieu fence (8)
ap   plain fence (1)
aq   plank fence (2)
ar   ranch fence (1)
as   red pickets (1)
at   redwood (1)
au   redwood fence (6)
av   slab fence (1)
aw   slat fence (10)
ax   slat fencing (1)
ay   slat(s) (3)
az   slatted fence (1)
ba   snow fence (1)
bb   spickets (1)
bc   stake fence (2)
bd   trellis fence (1)
be   white fence (2)
bf   white paling fence (1)
bg   white picket fence (6)
bh   white wooden fence (1)
bi   white yard fence (1)
bj   whitewash fence (1)
bk   whitewashed fence (1)
bl   wood fence (13)
bm   wood slat fence (1)
bn   wooden fence (37)
bo   wooden fence with palings (1)
bp   wooden palings (1)
bq   wooden sties (1)
br   wooden-frame fence (1)
bs   wooden-tie fence (1)
bt   yard fence (38)

016.3 L wire fence
No Response (35)

A   American (wire) (7)
B   American fence (1)
C   anchor (chain) (2)
D   barbed (5)
E   barbed(-)wire (fence) (152)
F   barbed-wire fencing (1)
G   barbwire (fence) (671)
H   barbwire fencing (2)
I   block wire (1)
J   cattle fence (2)
K   cattle fencing (1)
L   cattle wire (2)
M   chain fence (5)
N   chain link (fence) (33)
O   chain link wire (1)
P   chain-linked (1)
Q   chain links (1)
R   chicken-coop wire (1)
S   chicken fence (8)
T   chicken netting (1)
U   chicken(-)wire (fence) (101)
V   chicken-yard fence (1)
W   close wire (1)
X   climber fence (1)
Y   cow wire (1)
Z   Cox (fence) (1)
aa cross wire (1)
ab cutoff fence (2)
ac Cyclone (fence) (20)
ad Cyclone fencing (3)
ae Cyclone wire (1)
af electric (fence) (64)
ag electric wire (14)
ah electrical (fence) (1)
ai electrical wire (fence) (3)
aj electricity fence (1)
ak Elwood wire (1)
al fence of chicken wire (1)
am fence wire (8)
an fencing wire (1)
ao field fence (1)
ap field fencing (1)
aq field-fence wire (1)
ar fine-mesh wire (1)
as four-barbwire fence (1)
at four-by-four wire (1)
au four-strand barbwire (fence) (2)
av four-wire fence (1)
aw gap (1)
ax garden fence (3)
ay garden-fence wire (1)
az garden fencing (1)
ba garden netting (1)
bb garden (wire) (13)
bc haywire (1)
bd high wiring (1)
be hog fence (6)
bf hog fencing (1)
bg hog netting (1)

bh hog-pasture fencing (1)
bi hog-proof fence (2)
bj hog-proof (wire) (2)
bk hog-type wire fence (1)
bl hog(-wire fence) (1)
bm hog(-)wire (fence) (110)
bn hog-wire mesh (1)
bo hot wire (4)
bp Hurricane (fence) (7)
bq Hurricane fencing (1)
br Hurricane or Cyclone fence (1)
bs Hurricane-wire fence (2)
bt lawn-wire fence (1)
bu legal fence (1)
bv link-wire fence (1)
bw linked wire (1)
bx mesh (fence) (2)
by mesh wire (9)
bz metal fence (2)
ca net barbwire (1)
cb net fence (5)
cc net type (1)
cd net(-wire fence) (1)
ce net(-)wire (fence) (58)
cf netted fence (1)
cg netting fence (3)
ch netting wire (2)
ci Page (fence) (4)
cj Page chain wire (1)
ck Page(-)wire (fence) (13)
cl panel wire (1)
cm pasture fence (2)
cn pig netting (1)
co Porter wire (1)
cp post-and-wire (fence) (1)
cq poultry fence (1)
cr poultry(-)wire (fence) (10)
cs regular fencing (1)
ct regular wire (fence) (1)
cu regular wire fencing (1)
cv Rio Grande (1)
cw running-wire fence (1)
cx seven-strand barbwire fence (1)
cy seven-strand fence (1)
cz six-string fence (1)
da six-wire fence (1)
db small-mesh wire (1)
dc smooth wire (1)
dd snow fence (1)
de spike fence (1)
df spool wire (1)
dg square wire (1)
dh square-holed fence (1)
di steel fence (3)
dj steel(-)wire (fence) (1)
dk stock fence (1)
dl storm fence (1)
dm straight-line (fence) (1)
dn strip wire (1)

do three strand wire fence (1)
dp web fence (1)
dq web(-)wire (fence) (12)
dr welded wire (1)
ds wire (fence) (346)
dt wire fencing (5)
du wire field fencing (1)
dv wove wire (7)
dw woven fence (3)
dx woven(-)wire (fence) (54)
dy woven wiring (1)
dz yard fence (4)

016.3 S wire

No Response (3)
|OACmea| (1)
|PAAmej| (1)
|PABmea| (1)
|PACmej| (1)
|PAHeajmea| (1)
|PAHkabmea| (1)
|PCAeajmea| (3)
|PCCmea| (1)
|PCHeajmea| (1)
|PCHmea| (1)
|PFCmej| (1)
|RAAdaa| (1)
|RAAdaamaa| (1)
|RAAeaa| (1)
|RAAeaamea| (1)
|RAAeaj| (2)
|RAAeajmaa| (1)
|RAAeajmea| (5)
|RAAeakmea| (1)
|RAAeal| (1)
|RAAkaj| (1)
|RAAkajmea| (3)
|RAAkakmea| (1)
|RAAmaj| (3)
|RAAmea| (7)
|RAAmej| (2)
|RABeajmaa| (1)
|RABeajmea| (2)
|RABeal| (1)
|RABkaj| (1)
|RABmaa| (3)
|RABmaj| (7)
|RABmam| (1)
|RABmea| (24)
|RABmej| (1)
|RAD| (1)
|RAE| (2)
|RAEbbc| (1)
|RAEeaa| (3)
|RAEeaamaa| (5)
|RAEeaamea| (6)
|RAEeabmea| (1)
|RAEeaj| (6)
|RAEeajmaa| (11)
|RAEeajmea| (52)

|RAEeak| (1)
|RAEealmea| (1)
|RAEkaj| (1)
|RAEkajmaa| (10)
|RAEkajmea| (28)
|RAEkajmej| (1)
|RAEkakmea| (3)
|RAEmaa| (33)
|RAEmab| (1)
|RAEmaj| (20)
|RAEmajmea| (2)
|RAEmak| (2)
|RAEmea| (64)
|RAEmej| (5)
|RAErabmea| (2)
|RAGeaa| (1)
|RAGeaamea| (2)
|RAGeaj| (2)
|RAGeajmaa| (5)
|RAGeajmea| (17)
|RAGeal| (1)
|RAGealmea| (1)
|RAGkaj| (1)
|RAGkajmaa| (1)
|RAGkajmea| (4)
|RAGmaa| (11)
|RAGmaj| (7)
|RAGmea| (35)
|RAGmej| (5)
|RAGmek| (1)
|RAGmfa| (2)
|RAImaa| (1)
|RAImea| (2)
|RCA| (1)
|RCAeaamea| (1)
|RCAeaj| (6)
|RCAeajmaa| (2)
|RCAeajmea| (5)
|RCAkajmaa| (1)
|RCAkajmea| (3)
|RCAkanmaa| (1)
|RCAmaa| (6)
|RCAmaj| (12)
|RCAmea| (17)
|RCAmej| (2)
|RCBeaamea| (1)
|RCBeaamej| (1)
|RCBeaj| (1)
|RCBeajmaj| (1)
|RCBeal| (1)
|RCBkajmaa| (3)
|RCBkajmea| (1)
|RCBlfa| (1)
|RCBmaa| (3)
|RCBmaj| (2)
|RCBmea| (9)
|RCBmej| (2)
|RCE| (1)
|RCEeaa| (1)

|RCEeaamea| (3)
|RCEeaj| (4)
|RCEeajmaa| (11)
|RCEeajmea| (13)
|RCEeajmpa| (1)
|RCEeakmaa| (1)
|RCEkaj| (2)
|RCEkajmaa| (12)
|RCEkajmea| (28)
|RCEkakmea| (1)
|RCEmaa| (15)
|RCEmab| (1)
|RCEmaj| (9)
|RCEmajmea| (1)
|RCEmea| (51)
|RCEmej| (2)
|RCEmfa| (2)
|RCEraamea| (1)
|RCEsaj| (1)
|RCFkajmea| (1)
|RCFmea| (2)
|RCGeaa| (1)
|RCGeajmaa| (3)
|RCGeajmea| (6)
|RCGeajmej| (1)
|RCGkajmea| (1)
|RCGmaa| (3)
|RCGmaj| (4)
|RCGmajmaa| (1)
|RCGmea| (17)
|RCImea| (1)
|RFEeajmaa| (1)
|RFEkaj| (1)
|RFEmaj| (1)
|RFEmea| (1)
|RKAedjmda| (1)
|RKAedjmna| (1)
|RKAmdj| (1)
|RKAmna| (2)
|RKEmda| (1)
|RKEmna| (1)
|SAAmaj| (1)
|SAAmea| (1)
|SABmaa| (1)
|SABmaj| (2)
|SABmea| (5)
|SADeaamea| (2)
|SADeaj| (1)
|SADeajmea| (1)
|SADmaa| (1)
|SADmaj| (1)
|SADmea| (19)
|SADsabmea| (1)
|SAEeajmea| (2)
|SAEmaa| (1)
|SAEmajmea| (1)
|SAEmea| (8)
|SAEmej| (1)
|SAF| (1)

|SAFeaj| (1)
|SAFeajmea| (2)
|SAFmaa| (5)
|SAFmaj| (1)
|SAFmea| (21)
|SAGeaamea| (1)
|SAGmea| (3)
|SCAeajmea| (1)
|SCAmaj| (3)
|SCAmea| (1)
|SCAmej| (3)
|SCBmea| (1)
|SCDeajmea| (1)
|SCDmaa| (1)
|SCDmad| (1)
|SCDmea| (9)
|SCEeajeaj| (1)
|SCEeajmaa| (1)
|SCEeajmea| (1)
|SCEmaa| (1)
|SCEmajmea| (1)
|SCEmea| (13)
|SCFmaa| (1)
|SCFmea| (3)
|SCFmej| (1)
|SCGmaj| (1)
|SFD| (1)
|SFF| (1)
|SLAmea| (1)
|SMDmaj| (1)
|SMDmpj| (1)
|SMEmea| (2)
|TAAmea| (1)
|TADmaa| (1)
|TADmaj| (1)
|TADmea| (6)
|TAFmea| (2)
|TCAmaj| (1)
|TCAmajmea| (1)
|TCAmea| (2)
|TCDkajmea| (1)
|TCDmea| (3)
|TFAmea| (2)
|TFAqfjmea| (1)
|TFBtaa| (1)
|TFDeajmea| (1)
|TFDmaj| (1)
|TFDmea| (4)
|TFSmea| (1)
|TMAmea| (2)
|TMBmea| (1)

016.4 L rail fence

No Response (194)

A   Abraham Lincoln fence (1)

B   bar fence (1)

C   bars (1)

D   basket weave (1)

E   board fence (1)

F   bodock fence (1)

G   bold fence (1)
H   bottom rails (1)
I   bull fence (1)
J   cedar (1)
K   cedar fence (1)
L   cedar logs (1)
M   cedar rails (2)
N   cedar-post fence (1)
O   chestnut rail fence (1)
P   chestnut rails (2)
Q   corner fence (1)
R   country fence (2)
S   crisscrossed (1)
T   crooked fence (3)
U   crooked-rail fence (4)
V   cross fence (2)
W   cross-wood fence (1)
X   crossed fence (1)
Y   crossrail fence (1)
Z   crosstied fence (1)
aa   crossties (1)
ab   cypress fence (1)
ac   fat-lighterd rails (1)
ad   fence (4)
ae   fence corners (1)
af   fence rail(s) (9)
ag   fence worm (3)
ah   fencing (1)
ai   field fence (1)
aj   galloping fence (1)
ak   gate fence (1)
al   ground poles (1)
am   ground rail (2)
an   hand-hewn-log rail fence (1)
ao   horizontal fence (1)
ap   in-and-out fence (1)
aq   Kentucky board fence (1)
ar   line fence (1)
as   link fence (1)
at   log (1)
au   log fence (23)
av   lumber fence (1)
aw   mesquite (1)
ax   mesquite-wood fence (2)
ay   oak fence (1)
az   oak rail fence (1)
ba   old-fashion rail fence (1)
bb   old-time rail fence (2)
bc   ornamental fence (1)
bd   pasture fence (3)
be   pieu (2)
bf   pieu fence (5)
bg   pine rail fence (1)
bh   pine railing fence (1)
bi   pockets fence (1)
bj   post and rail (2)
bk   post-and-railing fence (1)
bl   post fence (1)
bm   puncheon fence (2)

bn   rail(s) (101)
bo   rail fence (517)
bp   rail fencing (3)
bq   rail timber (1)
br   rail-type fence (1)
bs   railing(s) (11)
bt   railing fence (12)
bu   ranch fence (1)
bv   rectangle fence (1)
bw   redwood (1)
bx   redwood fence (4)
by   redwood fencing (1)
bz   rickrack (1)
ca   rickrack fence (2)
cb   rider(s) (6)
cc   snake fence (3)
cd   snake-[J-0]-rider fence (1)
ce   split logs (1)
cf   split-out rails (1)
cg   split rail(s) (46)
ch   split-rail fence (49)
ci   split railing (1)
cj   spoke fence (1)
ck   stack rail fence (1)
cl   stake fence (1)
cm   stake-and-lighter (1)
cn   stake-and-rail fence (1)
co   stake-and-ride (2)
cp   stake-and-rider fence (6)
cq   stake-and-rider(s) (14)
cr   stake-[J-0]-rider (1)
cs   stake-rail fence (1)
ct   stakes (3)
cu   stakes-and-riders (1)
cv   stile fence (1)
cw   storm fence (1)
cx   straight fence (3)
cy   straight rails (1)
cz   straight-rail fence (3)
da   tache [F] (1)
db   ten-rail fence (3)
dc   Virginia fence (1)
dd   weaved fence (1)
de   wood fence (4)
df   wood railing (1)
dg   wood rails (1)
dh   wood-rail fence (1)
di   wooden fence (6)
dj   worm(s) (15)
dk   worm board (1)
dl   worm fence (11)
dm   worm kind (1)
dn   worm rail (4)
do   worm style (2)
dp   woven fence (1)
dq   zigzag (24)
dr   zigzag fence (7)
ds   zigzag rail fence (1)
dt   zigzagging (3)

016.5 P post/posts
No Response (77)
<poe(sts)> (1)
<poes(t)> (140)
<poes(t)Iz=14> (29)
<poes(ts)> (245)
<poesh(t)> (2)
<poesh(t)Ish=14> (1)
<poesh(t)s> (1)
<poesh(ts)> (3)
<poesht> (5)
<poesht(s)> (9)
<poeshtsh> (2)
<poest> (568)
<poest(s)> (373)
<poestAz=14> (2)
<poestI(z)=14> (1)
<poestIs=14> (3)
<poestIz=14> (95)
<poesth> (1)
<poests> (85)
<poezd> (1)
<purs(t)> (1)
<pust> (1)
<pust(s)> (1)

016.6 L stone wall
No Response (417)
A   bench terrace (1)
B   chimley fence (1)
C   cobblestone fence (1)
D   cobblestone wall (1)
E   coral fence (1)
F   fence (16)
G   fencerow (1)
H   fieldstone wall (2)
I   graveyard fence (1)
J   hedge out of rocks (1)
K   loose-laid fence (1)
L   retaining wall (2)
M   rock fence (184)
N   rock fencing (1)
O   rock wall (121)
P   rock wall fence (1)
Q   slave wall (1)
R   stack wall (1)
S   stone fence (71)
T   stone wall (98)
U   wall (38)
V   wall fence (2)
W   yard fence (2)

017.1A P china
{n}   flap
{R}   weakly retroflex
No Response (169)
<chanA=14> (3)
<chien(A)> (1)
<chienA=14> (637)
<chienI=14> (93)
<chienR=14> (9)

<chienee=13> (2)
<chienoe=13> (1)
<chien{R}=14> (11)
<chie{n}A=14> (1)
<shainI=14> (1)
<shienA=14> (4)
<tienA=14> (1)

017.1 L china egg

No Response (309)
A   artificial (1)
B   artificial egg (52)
C   artificial glass egg (1)
D   bone-china egg (1)
E   bought nest egg (1)
F   brass egg (1)
G   broken stone plate (1)
H   camphor egg (1)
I   celluloid egg (1)
J   cement egg (2)
K   chalk egg (7)
L   chalk nest egg (1)
M   china (1)
N   china egg (313)
O   china nest egg (7)
P   china nesting egg (1)
Q   china one (1)
R   china thing (1)
S   Chinese egg (1)
T   chinois [F] (1)
U   cinnamon (1)
V   clay egg (1)
W   cymling (8)
X   darning egg (10)
Y   delft egg (3)
Z   doorknob (12)
aa dummy (1)
ab dummy egg (6)
ac egg (42)
ad egg cymling (3)
ae egg gourd (4)
af egg made out of china (2)
ag egg nest (1)
ah fake (1)
ai fake china egg (1)
aj fake egg (3)
ak false egg (21)
al flint rock (1)
am fooler (1)
an glass egg (85)
ao glass nest egg (2)
ap glass one (1)
aq glass-like egg (1)
ar glassed egg (1)
as golf ball (2)
at gourd (23)
au gourd egg (3)
av hatching egg (1)
aw imitation egg (1)
ax laying egg (1)

ay lime egg (1)
az little-old nest egg (1)
ba marble egg (2)
bb medicated egg (1)
bc nest egg (249)
bd nest-egg gourd (7)
be nested egg (1)
bf nesting egg (5)
bg old doorknob (2)
bh old egg concern (1)
bi plastic egg (14)
bj porcelain doorknob (1)
bk porcelain egg (6)
bl rock (1)
bm rotten egg (1)
bn setting egg (8)
bo stone egg (1)
bp tennis ball (1)
bq white doorknob (6)
br white enamel egg (1)
bs white pieces of doorknobs (1)
bt white rock (6)
bu wood nest egg (1)
bv wooden egg (7)

017.1B P china egg

{R}   weakly retroflex
{?}   glottal
No Response (546)
<chien(A)eg=13> (1)
<chienAag=141> (1)
<chienAag=143> (4)
<chienAag=341> (1)
<chienAaig=141> (4)
<chienAaig=142> (1)
<chienAaig=143> (24)
<chienAaig=241> (8)
<chienAaig=341> (6)
<chienAaigz=141> (1)
<chienAaigz=143> (3)
<chienAaigz=241> (1)
<chienAaigz=341> (1)
<chienAe(g)=143> (1)
<chienAeg=141> (25)
<chienAeg=142> (5)
<chienAeg=143> (83)
<chienAeg=241> (23)
<chienAeg=341> (68)
<chienAegs=241> (1)
<chienAegz=141> (4)
<chienAegz=143> (6)
<chienAegz=241> (1)
<chienAegz=341> (6)
<chienAig=143> (1)
<chienA{?}ag=341> (1)
<chienA{?}aig=141> (6)
<chienA{?}aig=143> (4)
<chienA{?}eg=141> (19)
<chienA{?}eg=142> (1)
<chienA{?}eg=143> (10)

<chienA{?}eg=241> (1)
<chienA{?}eg=341> (7)
<chienA{?}egz=141> (1)
<chienA{?}egz=341> (2)
<chienA{?}ig=143> (3)
<chienIagz=143> (1)
<chienIaig=141> (1)
<chienIaig=143> (4)
<chienIaigz=141> (1)
<chienIaigz=143> (1)
<chienIaigz=241> (1)
<chienIeg=141> (5)
<chienIeg=143> (6)
<chienIegz=141> (1)
<chienIyaig=341> (1)
<chienReg=141> (1)
<chienReg=143> (2)
<chienReg=241> (1)
<chienRegz=141> (1)
<chieniaig=132> (1)
<chien{R}eg=141> (2)
<chien{R}eg=143> (1)
<chien{R}eg=341> (1)
<shienAeg=143> (1)
<shienAeg=341> (1)
<shienA{?}aig=141> (1)

017.2 L bucket [wooden]

No Response (54)
A   ash bucket (2)
B   bassin [F] (1)
C   bucket (562)
D   bucket of corn (1)
E   bucket of grease (1)
F   bucket of water (20)
G   cedar bucket (70)
H   cedar pail (4)
I   cedar water bucket (13)
J   cedar well bucket (1)
K   cypress bucket (1)
L   draw bucket (3)
M   drinking bucket (1)
N   eight-pound bucket (2)
O   feed bucket (2)
P   gallon bucket (3)
Q   gallon syrup bucket (1)
R   grease bucket (1)
S   ice bucket (1)
T   lard bucket (1)
U   milk bucket (9)
V   milk pail (3)
W   molasses bucket (1)
X   nail bucket (1)
Y   oak bucket (2)
Z   oaken bucket (14)
aa pail (118)
ab pail bucket (1)
ac pail of water (2)
ad peck bucket (1)
ae piggin (4)

af pine bucket (1)
ag plain-old bucket (1)
ah scrub bucket (1)
ai syrup bucket (3)
aj tar bucket (1)
ak ten-quart water bucket (1)
al twelve-quart water bucket (1)
am wash bucket (1)
an washer bucket (1)
ao water bucket (133)
ap water pail (26)
aq well bucket (19)
ar wood bucket (8)
as wood pail (3)
at wood water bucket (1)
au wooden bucket (73)
av wooden cedar bucket (3)
aw wooden pail (9)
ax wooden water bucket (6)
ay wooden well bucket (2)

017.3 L pail [metal]

No Response (122)
A aluminum bucket (23)
B aluminum milk bucket (1)
C aluminum pail (1)
D aluminum water bucket (1)
E big-old bucket (1)
F brass bucket (1)
G bucket (388)
H bucket of feed (1)
I bucket of milk (3)
J carrying pail (1)
K dinner bucket (1)
L dipper (1)
M eight-pound bucket (1)
N eight-pound lard bucket (1)
O enamel bucket (1)
P enamel milk pail (1)
Q gallon bucket (4)
R gallon pail (1)
S galvanize (5)
T galvanize bucket (8)
U galvanize pail (1)
V galvanized bucket (16)
W galvanized iron bucket (2)
X galvanized pail (3)
Y galvanized tin bucket (1)
Z glazed bucket (1)
aa granite bucket (6)
ab half-bushel bucket (1)
ac iron bucket (1)
ad lard bucket (5)
ae lunch pail (4)
af metal bucket (23)
ag metal pail (3)
ah milk bucket (130)
ai milk pail (117)
aj milking bucket (2)
ak milking pail (7)

al molasses bucket (1)
am pail (345)
an pail bucket (3)
ao pail of food (1)
ap pail of milk (1)
aq paint bucket (1)
ar plain bucket (1)
as porcelain bucket (1)
at pure-old tin or zinc bucket (1)
au stainless-steel pail (1)
av syrup bucket (3)
aw syrup can (1)
ax ten-gallon bucket (1)
ay ten-gallon can (1)
az ten-quart bucket (1)
ba tin bucket (72)
bb tin milk pail (1)
bc tin pail (10)
bd two or three-gallon bucket (1)
be two-gallon bucket (1)
bf water bucket (28)
bg water pail (5)
bh well bucket (4)
bi zinc bucket (8)

017.4 L slop bucket

No Response (187)
A bailed bucket (1)
B barrel (2)
C basket (5)
D big-old bucket (3)
E bucket (100)
F bucket of slop (2)
G can (13)
H candy bucket (1)
I chicken bucket (1)
J dishpan (1)
K feed basket (2)
L feed bucket (7)
M five-gallon bucket (1)
N five-gallon can (3)
O five-gallon drum (1)
P five-gallon pail (1)
Q foot tub (4)
R galvanize bucket (1)
S garbage bag (2)
T garbage barrel (1)
U garbage bucket (3)
V garbage can (69)
W garbage pail (15)
X grass sack (1)
Y grease bucket (1)
Z hog barrel (1)
aa hog bucket (3)
ab hog pail (3)
ac lard bucket (2)
ad lard can (2)
ae little-old bucket can (1)
af oil can (1)
ag pail (22)

ah pan (2)
ai pig bucket (1)
aj pig can (1)
ak pigs' bucket (1)
al plain-old bucket (1)
am plastic bucket (1)
an Schlappkanne [G] (1)
ao scrap bucket (5)
ap scrap can (1)
aq scrap pail (1)
ar slop barrel (3)
as slop bucket (531)
at slop can (34)
au slop cart (1)
av slop jar (10)
aw slop pail (20)
ax slop pan (1)
ay slopping bucket (1)
az special bucket (1)
ba steel container (1)
bb step-on can (1)
bc swill bucket (7)
bd swill pail (3)
be tin can (1)
bf tin tub (1)
bg trash barrel (1)
bh trash bin (1)
bi trash bucket (4)
bj trash can (10)
bk trough (1)
bl tub (6)
bm waste can (1)
bn waste pail (1)
bo wastebasket (2)
bp wheelbarrow (1)
bq wooden bucket (1)
br zinc bucket (1)

017.5 L frying pan

No Response (45)
A aluminum skillet (2)
B bake oven (1)
C baker (37)
D baker's skillet (1)
E baking oven (1)
F baking pan (1)
G baking skillet (1)
H biscuit baker (2)
I black baker (1)
J black iron fryer (1)
K black iron skillet (4)
L black skillet (11)
M bread griddle (1)
N bread hoe (2)
O bread oven (2)
P bread pan (2)
Q cast-iron black skillet (1)
R cast-iron skillet (17)
S corn griddle (1)
T corn-bread griddle (1)

U   corn-bread skillet (1)
V   creeper (1)
W   deep fryer (2)
X   deep-fat fryer (1)
Y   dinner pot (3)
Z   Dutch oven (108)
aa eye hoe (1)
ab fireplace baker (1)
ac flat skillet (1)
ad four, un [F] (1)
ae French oven (1)
af French skillet (1)
ag fryer (15)
ah frying pan (438)
ai frying pan skillet (1)
aj frying skillet (2)
ak frypan (40)
al granite pan (1)
am griddle (18)
an haceros [S] (1)
ao heavy skillet (1)
ap hoe (1)
aq hoecake baker (6)
ar hoecake skillet (2)
as horseshoe spider (1)
at iron fryer (4)
au iron frying pan (5)
av iron griddle (1)
aw iron oven (1)
ax iron pan (2)
ay iron skillet (70)
az iron spider (1)
ba iron vessel (1)
bb leg skillet (1)
bc old-time oven (1)
bd old-time skillet (1)
be oven (58)
bf pan (47)
bg Pfanne [G] (1)
bh poaching skillet (1)
bi poele, la [F] (2)
bj potato oven (2)
bk potato skillet (1)
bl roaster (2)
bm roasting pan (1)
bn roasting skillet (1)
bo shallow baker (1)
bp skillet (631)
bq spider (79)
br steel round skillet (1)
bs steel skillet (1)
bt three-legged iron kettle (1)
bu three-legged skillet (2)
bv tin skillet (3)
bw tripod skillet (1)
bx wrought-iron frying pan (1)

017.6 L kettle
No Response (52)
A   aluminum pot (1)

B   bean pot (4)
C   black boiling pot (1)
D   black cast pot (1)
E   black cast-iron pot (1)
F   black dinner kettle (1)
G   black iron pot (4)
H   black kettle (8)
I   black pot (42)
J   black tub (1)
K   black washpot (4)
L   boil pot (2)
M   boiler (20)
N   boiler pan (1)
O   boiling pot (14)
P   brass kettle (3)
Q   brass pot (1)
R   camp pot (1)
S   cast-iron kettle (1)
T   cast-iron pot (11)
U   cast-iron washpot (2)
V   cauldron (7)
W   cazo [S] (1)
X   chaudiere, la [F] (1)
Y   clothes pot (3)
Z   cook pot (4)
aa cooking kettle (1)
ab cooking pot (7)
ac copper kettle (3)
ad country kettle (1)
ae crock (1)
af crock pot (1)
ag dinner kettle (7)
ah dinner pot (17)
ai doughnut kettle (1)
aj drum (1)
ak granite pot (1)
al graniteware pot (1)
am iron black pot (1)
an iron crock (1)
ao iron kettle (38)
ap iron pot (88)
aq iron washpot (4)
ar kettle (355)
as kettle pot (1)
at laundry tub (2)
au lye pot (1)
av metal pot (1)
aw metal tub (1)
ax number-three tin tub (1)
ay number-three tub (1)
az number-three washtub (1)
ba old-fashion iron pot (1)
bb old-timey black cook pot (1)
bc old-timey cast iron pot (1)
bd old-timey pot (1)
be old-timey washpot (1)
bf paila [S] (1)
bg pot (265)
bh potbelly kettle (1)

bi preserving kettle (1)
bj round kettle (2)
bk round pot (1)
bl salt pot (2)
bm scalding pot (3)
bn soap kettle (1)
bo soup kettle (2)
bp steam kettle (1)
bq steel pot (1)
br stew boiler (1)
bs stewer (4)
bt stewing pot (1)
bu stewpot (5)
bv sugar boiler (1)
bw sugar kettle (7)
bx syrup boiler (1)
by syrup kettle (22)
bz thirty-gallon washpot (1)
ca three-legged iron kettle (1)
cb tin pot (1)
cc tin tub (3)
cd tub (32)
ce twenty-gallon kettle (1)
cf vat (3)
cg Waschtopf [G] (1)
ch wash boiler (3)
ci wash kettle (57)
cj wash pan (2)
ck wash skillet (1)
cl washing pot (1)
cm washing tub (1)
cn washpot (397)
co washtub (32)
cp water kettle (5)
cq wood tub (1)
cr wooden drum (1)
cs wooden tub (1)
ct wrought-iron pot (1)
cu zinc tub (2)

017.6 P kettle
{L} labial
{r} flap
{t} voiced
{?} glottal
No Response (215)
<kai{t}L=14> (1)
<kai{t}Lz=14> (1)
<ka{r}L=14> (2)
<ka{r}Lz=14> (1)
<ka{t}L=14> (1)
<ka{t}Lz=14> (1)
<ka{t}[L]=14> (1)
<ke(tA)l> (1)
<kedL=14> (1)
<kee{t}L=14> (1)
<ketL=14> (7)
<ket{L}=14> (1)
<ke{?}L=14> (11)
<ke{?}[L]z=14> (1)

<ke{r}L=14> (123)
<ke{r}Lz=14> (6)
<ke{r}u[1]=13> (2)
<ke{r}[L]=14> (13)
<ke{r}[L]z=14> (2)
<ke{r}{L}=14> (1)
<ke{t}L=14> (279)
<ke{t}Lz=14> (31)
<ke{t}[L]=14> (23)
<ke{t}[L]z=14> (1)
<ke{t}ul=13> (1)
<ke{t}{L}=14> (1)
<ki(tA)l> (2)
<kidL=14> (1)
<kitL=14> (5)
<kit[L]=14> (1)
<ki{?}L=14> (4)
<ki{?}Lz=14> (1)
<ki{r}L=14> (64)
<ki{r}Lz=14> (5)
<ki{r}[L]=14> (6)
<ki{r}[L]j=14> (1)
<ki{r}[L]z=14> (2)
<ki{t}L=14> (119)
<ki{t}Lz=14> (17)
<ki{t}[L]=14> (7)
<kyetL=14> (1)
<kye{r}L=14> (1)
<kye{t}L=14> (7)
<kyid[L]=14> (1)
<kyitL=14> (1)
<kyi{r}L=14> (2)
<kyi{r}Lz=14> (1)
<kyi{t}L=14> (9)
<kyi{t}Lz=14> (1)
<kyi{t}[L]=14> (1)

017.7 L vase

No Response (133)
A basin (1)
B basket (1)
C bottle (2)
D bowl (4)
E box (3)
F bucket (7)
G bud vase (9)
H can (2)
I cement container (1)
J churn (1)
K clay pot (4)
L Coca-Cola bottle (1)
M container (1)
N crock (5)
O crock bowl (1)
P crock pot (1)
Q crockerware pot (1)
R cup (1)
S cupboard (1)
T cut-glass vase (1)
U flower bed (1)

V flower bin (1)
W flower bottle (1)
X flower bowl (5)
Y flower box (5)
Z flower bucket (3)
aa flower can (1)
ab flower container (1)
ac flower decanter (1)
ad flower jar (2)
ae flower pail (1)
af flower pit (1)
ag flower planter (1)
ah flower stand (1)
ai flower tray (1)
aj flower urn (1)
ak flower vase (41)
al flowerpot (257)
am flowers vase (1)
an frame (1)
ao frog (2)
ap fruit jar (4)
aq glass (5)
ar glass jar (1)
as glass of water (1)
at gray pot (1)
au green glass jar (1)
av hanging basket (1)
aw jar (15)
ax jar of water (1)
ay jardiniere (3)
az jug (2)
ba little jar of a thing (1)
bb mold (1)
bc pail (2)
bd pair of vases (1)
be pan (1)
bf pitcher (6)
bg planter (25)
bh planter's pot (1)
bi pot (89)
bj potholder (1)
bk pottery (1)
bl slop jar (1)
bm spittoon (3)
bn stone vase (1)
bo tar cup (1)
bp terrarium (2)
bq tin can (2)
br urn (6)
bs vase (687)
bt vase of flowers (2)
bu vat (1)
bv vessel (1)
bw window box (1)

017.7 P vase

{f} lax
{v} bilabial
No Response (189)
<bais> (2)

<vail> (1)
<vais> (560)
<vaisIz=14> (82)
<vaish> (1)
<vaith> (1)
<vaiyAs=14> (1)
<vaiz> (15)
<vas> (5)
<vawz> (1)
<ves> (26)
<vesIz=14> (3)
<vies> (1)
<vos> (2)
<voz> (2)
<{f}ais> (2)
<{f}es> (2)
<{v}ais> (17)
<{v}aisIz=14> (2)
<{v}aith> (1)
<{v}es> (4)
<{v}oz> (1)

017.8A P spoon

{p} fricative
No Response (136)
<(s)puenz> (1)
<shpuen> (2)
<spew[n]> (1)
<spewn> (35)
<spewndh> (1)
<spewnz> (6)
<spoon> (5)
<spue[n]> (7)
<spue[n]z> (1)
<spuen> (594)
<spuens> (1)
<spuenz> (120)
<s{p}uen> (1)
<thpewn> (2)
<thpuen> (2)

017.8B P knife/knives

{b} fricative
{f} bilabial
{ie} monophthong/short glide
{v} devoiced
{z} devoiced
No Response (81)
<dief> (1)
<diev> (1)
<nie(f)> (4)
<nie(v)s> (1)
<nie(v)z> (8)
<nie(v){z}> (2)
<nie(vz)> (5)
<nief> (505)
<nief(s)> (3)
<niefs> (22)
<nief{z}> (1)
<niet> (1)
<niev> (6)

<niev(z)> (6)
<nievdh> (2)
<nievs> (2)
<nievsh> (1)
<nievz> (219)
<niev{z}> (85)
<nie{f}> (3)
<nie{f}(s)> (1)
<nie{v}(z)> (2)
<nie{v}s> (3)
<nie{v}z> (1)
<nie{v}{z}> (28)
<nowf> (1)
<n{ie}(f)> (5)
<n{ie}(v)z> (24)
<n{ie}(v){z}> (4)
<n{ie}(vz)> (1)
<n{ie}f> (252)
<n{ie}f(s)> (3)
<n{ie}fs> (9)
<n{ie}v> (5)
<n{ie}v(z)> (7)
<n{ie}vz> (211)
<n{ie}v{z}> (24)
<n{ie}{b}z> (1)
<n{ie}{b}{z}> (1)
<n{ie}{f}> (3)
<n{ie}{v}(z)> (2)
<n{ie}{v}s> (1)
<n{ie}{v}z> (4)
<n{ie}{v}{z}> (5)

017.8C P fork

{f}   bilabial
{r}   weakly retroflex
{?}   glottal
No Response (125)
<faw(r)k> (53)
<faw(r)ks> (15)
<faw[r]k> (46)
<faw[r]ks> (4)
<fawrk> (82)
<fawrks> (18)
<faw{r}k> (37)
<faw{r}ks> (3)
<faw{r}{?}> (1)
<fo(r)k> (2)
<fo(r)ks> (1)
<fo[r]k> (1)
<fo[r]ks> (1)
<foe(r)k> (23)
<foe(r)ks> (8)
<foe[r]k> (85)
<foe[r]ks> (19)
<foerk> (249)
<foerks> (57)
<foerkz> (1)
<foe{r}k> (41)
<foe{r}ks> (8)
<fork> (20)

<forks> (5)
<for{?}> (1)
<fo{r}k> (4)
<fo{r}ks> (1)
<{f}aw(r)k> (1)
<{f}aw[r]k> (2)
<{f}oerk> (3)
<{f}oerksh> (1)
<{f}oer{?}> (1)

018.1 P wash

{aw}   inglide
{o}   inglide
{r}   weakly retroflex
No Response (27)
<(w)orsh> (1)
<warsh> (2)
<wawrsh> (33)
<wawsh> (97)
<wawshAz=14> (1)
<wawshN=14> (1)
<wawshNG=14> (1)
<waw{r}sh> (20)
<waw{r}sht> (1)
<whosh> (1)
<woch> (1)
<woersh> (1)
<worsh> (39)
<worsht> (2)
<wosh> (435)
<woshIz=14> (3)
<woshN=14> (2)
<woshNG=14> (2)
<wosht> (15)
<wo{r}sh> (24)
<wo{r}sht> (1)
<w{aw}sh> (49)
<w{aw}shN=14> (1)
<w{o}ch> (1)
<w{o}sh> (192)
<w{o}shN=14> (2)
<w{o}sht> (5)
<w{o}st> (1)

018.2 P rinses

{z}   devoiced
No Response (50)
<rai(n)ch> (1)
<rainch> (4)
<rainchN=14> (1)
<rains> (1)
<raints> (1)
<ranch> (8)
<ranchIz=14> (3)
<ranshN=14> (1)
<rantcht> (1)
<rants> (2)
<rantsIz=14> (1)
<rantst> (2)
<re[n]ch> (1)
<reench> (3)

<reenchN=14> (1)
<reents> (1)
<reentsI{z}=14> (1)
<rench> (73)
<renchIz=14> (12)
<renchN=14> (6)
<rengch> (2)
<rens> (1)
<rensN=14> (1)
<rensh> (2)
<rent(s)> (1)
<rents> (40)
<rentsIz=14> (4)
<rentsN=14> (2)
<rentst> (7)
<ri(n)ch> (3)
<ri(n)chIz=14> (1)
<ri(n)chI{z}=14> (1)
<ri(n)sIz=14> (1)
<ri[n]ch> (1)
<ri[n]s> (1)
<ri[n]tsIz=14> (1)
<rinch> (157)
<rinchIz=14> (31)
<rinchN=14> (9)
<rincht> (12)
<ringch> (1)
<rins> (26)
<rinsIz=14> (13)
<rinsI{z}=14> (1)
<rinsh> (2)
<rinshIz=14> (1)
<rinst> (3)
<rints> (209)
<rintsAz=14> (1)
<rintsIz=14> (134)
<rintsI{z}=14> (6)
<rintsN=14> (11)
<rintsNG=14> (5)
<rintsin=13> (1)
<rintst> (19)
<rintz> (1)
<rintzIz=14> (1)
<rint{z}NG=14> (1)
<rinz> (6)
<rinzIz=14> (2)
<rin{z}> (2)

018.3 L dishcloth

No Response (161)
A   cheesecloth (1)
B   cloth (11)
C   cotton dishcloth (1)
D   cup towel (1)
E   dish towel (32)
F   dish-wash cloth (1)
G   dishcloth (208)
H   dishrag (494)
I   dishwasher (1)
J   dishwashing cloth (1)

K   fertilize sack (1)
L   kitchen towel (1)
M   lavette [F] (1)
N   piece of cloth (2)
O   rag (36)
P   rinse cloth (1)
Q   small towel (1)
R   soapy rag (1)
S   towel (2)
T   towel rag (1)
U   Waschlappen [G] (1)
V   wash towel (1)
W   washcloth (48)
X   washing rag (1)
Y   washrag (43)
Z   wet dishrag (1)
aa white, clean rag (1)

018.4 L dish towel

No Response (153)
A   clean cloth (1)
B   clean rag (1)
C   cloth (16)
D   cup towel (49)
E   dish towel (250)
F   dish-cleaning towel (1)
G   dishcloth (60)
H   dishes cloth (1)
I   dishrag (40)
J   dry cloth (52)
K   dry dishrag (2)
L   dry rag (29)
M   dry towel (7)
N   dryer (2)
O   dryer cloth (1)
P   drying cloth (154)
Q   drying dish towel (1)
R   drying dishcloth (1)
S   drying rag (86)
T   drying towel (40)
U   flour sack (3)
V   hand dish towel (1)
W   hand towel (2)
X   kitchen cloth (1)
Y   kitchen dry towel (1)
Z   kitchen towel (4)
aa rag (18)
ab salt sack (1)
ac scrub cloth (1)
ad sugar sack (1)
ae tea towel (13)
af terry dishcloth (1)
ag towel (73)
ah wash towel (1)
ai washcloth (2)
aj washrag (2)
ak wipe cloth (2)
al wiping cloth (2)
am wiping rag (1)
an wore-out shirt (1)

018.5 L washcloth

No Response (219)
A   bath cloth (71)
B   bath rag (25
C   bath towel (2)
D   bathing bath cloth (1)
E   cloth (6)
F   face rag (23)
G   face towel (27)
H   facecloth (44)
I   feed sack (1)
J   hand cloth (1)
K   hand rag (1)
L   napkin (2)
M   piece of Lowell (1)
N   rag (15)
O   toallito [S] (1)
P   towel (2)
Q   wash towel (11)
R   washcloth (275)
S   washrag (324)
T   wet rag (1)

018.6 L bath towel

No Response (171)
A   bath towel (179)
B   bathroom towel (1)
C   beach towel (3)
D   body towel (3)
E   cloth (1)
F   dry rag (1)
G   dry towel (4)
H   drying cloth (1)
I   drying rag (4)
J   drying towel (11)
K   face towel (19)
L   fingertip towel (1)
M   guest towel (2)
N   hand towel (42)
O   hook towel (1)
P   old shirt (1)
Q   rag (4)
R   tea towel (1)
S   tow sack (1)
T   towel (579)
U   Turkey towel (1)
V   Turkish towel (2)

018.6 P towel

No Response (144)
<ta(1)> (1)
<ta[1]> (7)
<tal> (2)
<tawL=14> (10)
<tel> (1)
<tiewLz=14> (1)
<to[1]> (1)
<tow(1)> (3)
<tow(1)z> (1)
<towL=14> (269)
<towLz=14> (26)

<towR=14> (2)
<tow[L]=14> (35)
<tow[L]z=14> (5)
<tow[1]> (68)
<tow[1]z> (7)
<towl> (325)
<towlz> (24)
<towvL=14> (1)
<towv[L]=14> (1)

018.7 L faucet

No Response (77)
[at sink]
A   faucet (664)
B   hydrant (48)
C   kitchen faucet (2)
D   knob (1)
E   pet cock (1)
F   robinet [F] (1)
G   spicket (125)
H   spigot (38)
I   spocket (1)
J   spout (11)
K   spraucet (1)
L   sprocket (1)
M   tap (23)
N   valve (1)
O   water faucet (16)
P   water spicket (4)
Q   water turner (1)
R   waterspout (2)
[outside]
aa faucet (303)
ab hose faucet (1)
ac hydrant (219)
ad outdoor faucet (1)
ae outdoor spigot (1)
af outlet faucet (1)
ag outside faucet (10)
ah outside hydrant (1)
ai outside spicket (4)
aj sill cock (1)
ak spicket (157)
al spigot (33)
am spout (2)
an standard (1)
ao tap (7)
ap valve (2)
aq water faucet (10)
ar water fountain (1)
as water hydrant (6)
at water spicket (3)
au water tap (1)
av yard faucet (1)
aw yard spicket (1)
[on container]
ba beer faucet (1)
bb bung (8)
bc bunghole (4)
bd cedar faucet (1)

be   faucet (217)
bf   faucet thing (1)
bg   fountain (1)
bh   hydrant (9)
bi   knob (1)
bj   nozzle (4)
bk   peg (2)
bl   pet cock (1)
bm   spicket (110)
bn   spigot (58)
bo   spit (1)
bp   spout (60)
bq   sprocket (1)
br   tap (24)
bs   valve (1)
bt   water faucet (5)
bu   water hydrant (1)
bv   water spicket (2)
bw   waterspout (1)
bx   wooden faucet (5)
by   wooden spicket (2)

018.8 G burst

<!>   infinitive
<&>   present 3rd singular
<@>   present participle
<*>   preterit
<#>   past participle
{r}   weakly retroflex
{t}   flap
{?}   glottal
No Response (221)
<!barst> (1)
<!boost> (1)
<!boo[r]st> (1)
<!bur(s)t> (1)
<!burs(t)> (18)
<!bursh(t)> (1)
<!bursht> (3)
<!burshtId=14> (1)
<!burst> (197)
<!burs{?}> (1)
<!burtht> (1)
<!bus(t)> (57)
<!bush(t)> (1)
<!busht> (1)
<!bust> (183)
<!bustIz=14> (1)
<!busts> (1)
<!bu[r]s(t)> (10)
<!bu[r]st> (43)
<!bu{r}s(t)> (5)
<!bu{r}sht> (1)
<!bu{r}st> (39)
<&burs(t)> (1)
<&burstIz=14> (3)
<&burstIz=14> (1)
<&bus(t)> (2)
<&bus(t)Iz=14> (1)
<&bust> (5)

<&bustIz=14> (10)
<@burstN=14> (2)
<@burstNG=14> (1)
<@bustN=14> (5)
<@bustNG=14> (1)
<@bu[r]stN=14> (2)
<@bu{r}stNG=14> (1)
<*be{r}s(t)> (1)
<*boo[r]st> (1)
<*brustId=14> (1)
<*bu[r]s(t)> (2)
<*bu[r]st> (19)
<*bu[r]stI(d)=14> (1)
<*bu[r]stId=14> (11)
<*burs(t)> (4)
<*bursht> (1)
<*burshtId=14> (1)
<*burst> (100)
<*burstId=14> (82)
<*bus(t)> (4)
<*bus(t)I(d)=14> (1)
<*bus(t)Id=14> (1)
<*bust> (12)
<*bustA(d)=14> (1)
<*bustI(d)=14> (3)
<*bustId=14> (175)
<*bu{r}s(t)> (1)
<*bu{r}st> (17)
<*bu{r}stId=14> (15)
<#bu[r]s(t)> (1)
<#bu[r]st> (7)
<#bu[r]stId=14> (7)
<#burs(t)> (1)
<#bursht> (5)
<#burshtId=14> (1)
<#burst> (33)
<#burstId=14> (38)
<#burstid=13> (1)
<#bus(t)> (6)
<#bus(t)Id=14> (1)
<#bust> (6)
<#bustId=14> (97)
<#bustN=14> (1)
<#bus{t}Id=14> (1)
<#bu{r}st> (6)
<#bu{r}stId=14> (8)

019.1 P barrel

{b}   fricative
{r}   weakly retroflex
No Response (47)
<ba(r)L=14> (49)
<ba(r)Lz=14> (15)
<ba(r)[L]=14> (2)
<ba(r)[L]z=14> (1)
<ba(r)[L]zh=14> (1)
<ba(r)[l]> (1)
<ba(r)[l]z> (2)
<ba(r)l> (20)
<ba(r)lz> (3)

<ba(r)oel=13> (1)
<ba(r)yL=14> (1)
<ba[r](L)z> (1)
<ba[r]L=14> (15)
<ba[r]Lz=14> (8)
<ba[r][1]> (1)
<ba[r]l> (38)
<ba[r]lz> (12)
<bai[r](1)> (1)
<bai[r][L]=14> (3)
<bai[r]yaw(1)=13> (1)
<bairL=14> (1)
<bairoe[1]=13> (1)
<bar(L)> (1)
<barL=14> (429)
<barLz=14> (112)
<bar[L]=14> (14)
<bar[L]z=14> (2)
<bar[L]zh=14> (1)
<barl> (29)
<barlz> (5)
<baroelz=13> (1)
<baru[1]=13> (1)
<barul=13> (1)
<ba{r}L=14> (34)
<ba{r}Lz=14> (10)
<ba{r}l> (25)
<ba{r}lz> (4)
<be(r)L=14> (1)
<be(r)lz> (1)
<be[r]l> (2)
<ber(1)> (1)
<berL=14> (71)
<berLz=14> (21)
<ber[L]=14> (10)
<ber[L]z=14> (2)
<ber[1]> (1)
<berel=13> (1)
<berl> (2)
<beru[1]=13> (1)
<berul=13> (1)
<be{r}L=14> (2)
<bo(r)L=14> (1)
<bo[r]Lz=14> (1)
<borL=14> (6)
<borLz=14> (4)
<borlz> (1)
<bo{r}Lz=14> (1)
<burL=14> (7)
<burLz=14> (3)
<bu{r}L=14> (1)
<{b}arL=14> (1)

019.2 L stand

No Response (395)
A   barrel (95)
B   bin (2)
C   bottle (12)
D   box (of lard) (1)
E   bucket (141)

F   can (221)
G   carton (2)
H   case (3)
I   churn (3)
J   container (2)
K   cruet (1)
L   demijohn (1)
M   dip bucket (1)
N   display stand (1)
O   drum (10)
P   earthen jug (1)
Q   frame (1)
R   fruit jar (1)
S   glass bowl (1)
T   glass container (1)
U   glass jar (5)
V   glass jug (1)
W   half barrel (1)
X   hogshead (8)
Y   jar (25)
Z   jug (55)
aa   keg (21)
ab   larder (1)
ac   manteca [S] (1)
ad   metal container (1)
ae   metal (syrup) can (1)
af   metal tin can (1)
ag   milking churn (1)
ah   molasses gate barrel (1)
ai   package (1)
aj   pail (9)
ak   pitcher (20)
al   pot (1)
am   rack (1)
an   ruster (1)
ao   shelf (2)
ap   stand (122)
aq   stone churn (1)
ar   stone jar (1)
as   stone jug (3)
at   tin (5)
au   tin can (12)
av   tin pail (2)
aw   tin (syrup) bucket (6)
ax   tray (3)
ay   tub (18)
az   vat (2)
ba   washtub (1)
bb   wooden barrel (3)
bc   wooden bucket (1)
bd   wooden container (1)
be   wooden pail (1)
bf   wooden tray (1)
bg   wooden tub (2)

019.3 L funnel

No Response (172)
A   cone (2)
B   faucet (13)
C   fruit-jar filler (1)

D   fun(nel) (1)
E   funnel (723)
F   gourd (1)
G   scoop (1)
H   spicket (1)
I   spout (6)
J   strainer (3)
K   syrup funnel (1)
L   tunnel (2)

019.4 L whip

No Response (130)
A   black snake (2)
B   black-snake whip (1)
C   board whip (1)
D   box plait (1)
E   buggy quirt (1)
F   buggy switch (5)
G   buggy whip (124)
H   bullwhip (6)
I   cow whip (9)
J   crop (10)
K   four plait (1)
L   goad (2)
M   hickory (1)
N   horsewhip (10)
O   lash (3)
P   little-old switch thing (1)
Q   mule whip (1)
R   ox whip (2)
S   oxgoad (1)
T   plaited deal (1)
U   pole (for oxen) (1)
V   pop whip (1)
W   prod (1)
X   quirt (13)
Y   rawhide whip (2)
Z   riding crop (2)
aa   riding strap (1)
ab   riding switch (1)
ac   riding whip (2)
ad   rope (2)
ae   saddle whip (1)
af   six-plait (1)
ag   slapstick (1)
ah   stick (3)
ai   stock and whip (1)
aj   strap (2)
ak   switch (35)
al   wagon whip (1)
am   whip (666)
an   willow wand (1)

019.4 P whip

{v}   bilabial
{w}   devoiced
No Response (136)
<(wh)ip> (1)
<v(h)ip> (1)
<w(h)eep> (1)
<w(h)ep> (2)

<w(h)ip> (133)
<w(h)ipNG=14> (1)
<w(h)ips> (2)
<wheep> (2)
<whip> (578)
<whipN=14> (1)
<whips> (15)
<whoop> (54)
<whoops> (1)
<whoopt> (2)
<whoorp> (1)
<whu[r]p> (1)
<whuef> (1)
<whup> (14)
<whurp> (1)
<{v}(h)ip> (1)
<{w}(h)ip> (3)

019.4 S whip

No Response (0)
|ABI| (1)
|DAA| (55)
|DAAeaj| (2)
|DAAmaa| (3)
|DAAmaj| (42)
|DAB| (20)
|DABdae| (1)
|DABeaj| (1)
|DABmaa| (8)
|DABmaj| (30)
|DAC| (4)
|DACdab| (1)
|DACmaa| (1)
|DACmaj| (1)
|DAD| (1)
|DAE| (223)
|DAEeaj| (3)
|DAEefj| (1)
|DAEmaa| (2)
|DAEmaj| (149)
|DAEmak| (3)
|DAG| (11)
|DAGmaj| (24)
|DAGmak| (1)
|DAH| (2)
|DAHmaa| (2)
|DAHmaj| (4)
|DAI| (9)
|DAImaj| (4)
|DAS| (1)
|DBE| (1)
|DCA| (46)
|DCAeaj| (1)
|DCAkaj| (1)
|DCAmaj| (11)
|DCB| (3)
|DCBeaj| (8)
|DCBmaa| (2)
|DCBmaj| (4)
|DCC| (3)

|DCE| (19)
|DCEeaj| (3)
|DCEkae| (1)
|DCEmaj| (36)
|DCEmak| (1)
|DCEmam| (1)
|DCG| (1)
|DCGmaj| (4)
|DCI| (2)
|DCIeaj| (1)
|DCImaj| (2)
|DDAmda| (1)
|DFA| (1)
|DFAefj| (1)
|DFC| (1)
|DFE| (6)
|DFEmaj| (1)
|DFEmak| (1)
|DME| (1)
|EAA| (5)
|EAB| (2)
|EABmaa| (1)
|EABmaj| (8)
|EAC| (4)
|EACdag| (1)
|EACmaj| (4)
|EAD| (20)
|EADeab| (1)
|EADmaj| (1)
|EAE| (1)
|EAEmaj| (1)
|EAFmaj| (1)
|EAG| (1)
|EAGmaj| (1)
|EAH| (2)
|EAHeab| (1)
|EAHmaa| (1)
|EAHmaj| (7)
|EAI| (1)
|EAImaj| (2)
|ECA| (3)
|ECAmaj| (1)
|ECC| (1)
|EFA| (10)
|EFAmaj| (2)
|EFC| (1)
|EFCmaj| (1)
|EFCmej| (1)
|EFD| (2)
|EFDmaj| (1)
|EFE| (1)
|EFF| (1)
|EFFmaj| (1)
|EFG| (1)
|EFH| (2)
|EMA| (3)
|FAD| (1)
|FCA| (1)
|FFA| (1)

|FFB| (2)
|FFBbjj| (1)
|FFC| (1)
|FFD| (8)
|FFDmaj| (8)
|FFHmaj| (3)
|FMA| (1)
|FMB| (1)
|FMD| (1)
|FMDmaj| (1)
|KAA| (1)
|KAGefa| (1)
|LFBeaj| (1)
|NAD| (1)
|NADmaj| (3)
|NAF| (2)
|NAFmaj| (1)
|PAG| (1)
|abcABA| (1)

019.5 L paper bag
No Response (88)
A   bag (340)
B   brown bag (5)
C   brown paper bag (7)
D   brown paper sack (4)
E   brown sack (2)
F   craft bag (1)
G   craft sack (1)
H   crocus sack (1)
I   flour sack (1)
J   grocery bag (25)
K   grocery sack (6)
L   lunch sack (1)
M   pack (1)
N   paper bag (354)
O   paper pep (1)
P   paper poke (33)
Q   paper sack (220)
R   poke (81)
S   poke bag (1)
T   pooch (1)
U   poocher (1)
V   sack (193)
W   sandwich sack (1)
X   shopping bag (6)

019.5 P paper
{p}   fricative
{R}   weakly retroflex
No Response (123)
<paib[R]=14> (1)
<paip(R)> (1)
<paipR=14> (349)
<paipRd=14> (1)
<paipRz=14> (1)
<paip[R]=14> (356)
<paip[R]z=14> (1)
<paip{R}=14> (107)
<paip{R}z=14> (1)
<pai{p}R=14> (2)

<pepR=14> (4)
<pep[R]=14> (3)
<pyaip[R]=14> (1)
<{p}aipR=14> (2)
019.5 S bag
No Response (0)
|KAC| (1)
|KACeaj| (1)
|OAA| (7)
|OAAeaa| (2)
|OAAeaj| (64)
|OAAeal| (3)
|OAAgba| (1)
|OAAgbj| (8)
|OAAkaj| (141)
|OAAkak| (9)
|OAAkbj| (2)
|OAAkbk| (2)
|OAB| (9)
|OABeaj| (35)
|OABeal| (1)
|OABgbj| (7)
|OABgbk| (1)
|OABkaj| (69)
|OABkak| (15)
|OABkbj| (24)
|OABkbk| (2)
|OABmaj| (2)
|OAC| (1)
|OACeaj| (4)
|OACkaj| (10)
|OACkak| (1)
|OADgbj| (1)
|OADkaj| (1)
|OAE| (2)
|OAEeaa| (1)
|OAEeaj| (2)
|OAEkaj| (3)
|OAEmak| (1)
|OAFeaj| (1)
|OAG| (1)
|OAGeaa| (1)
|OAGeaj| (2)
|OAGeak| (1)
|OAGkaj| (1)
|OAGkbk| (1)
|OAHeaj| (1)
|OAIeaj| (1)
|OAIkaj| (1)
|OBA| (2)
|OBAeaa| (5)
|OBAeaj| (40)
|OBAgbk| (1)
|OBAkaj| (1)
|OBBeaj| (4)
|OBBgbj| (1)
|OBD| (1)
|OCA| (23)
|OCAeaj| (44)

|OCAeal| (4)
|OCAgba| (7)
|OCAgbj| (18)
|OCAkaa| (3)
|OCAkaj| (168)
|OCAkak| (15)
|OCAkbj| (4)
|OCB| (6)
|OCBeaj| (9)
|OCBgbj| (1)
|OCBkaj| (36)
|OCBkak| (1)
|OCBkbj| (2)
|OCCeaa| (1)
|OCCeaj| (3)
|OCCgbj| (1)
|OCCkaj| (9)
|OCEeaj| (3)
|OCEgbj| (4)
|OCEkaa| (3)
|OCEkaj| (12)
|OCFkaj| (1)
|OCIbbj| (1)
|OCIkaj| (1)
|ODAedj| (1)
|ODBkdj| (1)
|OGA| (4)
|OGAbbj| (1)
|OGAeaa| (5)
|OGAeab| (1)
|OGAeaj| (9)
|OGAkaj| (4)
|OGAkak| (1)
|OGBeaj| (1)
|OGBkaj| (2)
|OGD| (1)
|OGDkaj| (1)
|OKAedj| (1)
|OKAkdj| (1)
|RCBeaj| (1)

019.6 L cloth sack

No Response (161)
A   bag (77)
B   bag of beans (1)
C   bag of cloth (2)
D   bag of fertilizer (2)
E   bag of flour (12)
F   bag of meal (1)
G   bag of sugar (7)
H   bagging sack (1)
I   bale sack (1)
J   bran sack (1)
K   cambric sack (1)
L   chicken-feed sack (1)
M   close bag (1)
N   cloth bag (80)
O   cloth poke (1)
P   cloth sack (110)
Q   clothes bag (1)

R   clover sack (1)
S   cotense [S] (1)
T   cotton bag (9)
U   cotton-cloth sack (1)
V   cotton-picking sack (2)
W   cotton sack (37)
X   cow-feed sack (1)
Y   double-end sack (1)
Z   eight-barrel sack (1)
aa feed bag (4)
ab feed sack (13)
ac fertilize sack (2)
ad fertilizer bag (2)
ae fertilizer sack (2)
af fifty-pound bag (7)
ag fifty-pound sack (of flour) (8)
ah five-pound bag (1)
ai five-pound sack (2)
aj flour bag (10)
ak flour poke (2)
al flour sack (146)
am flowery sack (1)
an forty-eight-pound sack (2)
ao hundred-pound bag (8)
ap hundred-pound sack (14)
aq laundry bag (1)
ar light sack (1)
as meal bag (1)
at meal poke (1)
au meal sack (17)
av muslin sack (1)
aw oat sack (2)
ax osnaburg sack (2)
ay pick sack (4)
az picking sack (1)
ba poke (3)
bb poke of flour (3)
bc pound bag of rice (1)
bd print sack (2)
be printed sack (1)
bf reinforced sack (1)
bg sack (358)
bh sack of bran (2)
bi sack of coffee (3)
bj sack of cotton (1)
bk sack of cottonseed (1)
bl sack of flour (56)
bm sack of meal (5)
bn sack of oats (2)
bo sack of sugar (14)
bp seed sack (2)
bq sugar bag (2)
br sugar sack (21)
bs ten-pound bag (1)
bt tobacco sack (1)
bu tomato sack (1)
bv towel sack (1)
bw twelve-pound sack (1)
bx twenty-five-pound bag (3)

by twenty-five-pound sack (2)
bz twenty-four-pound bag (1)
ca twenty-four-pound flour sack (1)
cb twenty-four-pound sack (of flour) (4)
cc two-bushel sack (1)
cd white cloth sack (1)
ce white cotton bag (1)
cf white cotton sack (1)
cg white flour sack (1)
ch white sack (6)

019.7 L tow sack

No Response (70)
A   bag (17)
B   bag sack (1)
C   bagging sack (9)
D   bark sack (1)
E   blue upper (1)
F   bran sack (1)
G   burlap [n.] (95)
H   burlap bag (109)
I   burlap sack (93)
J   burlap tow sack (1)
K   burly sack (1)
L   chicken-feed sack (1)
M   chop bag (1)
N   coal sack (1)
O   coffee sack (2)
P   corn bag (1)
Q   cornsack (32)
R   cotense [S] (1)
S   crocus [n.] (6)
T   crocus bag (22)
U   cro(cus) sack (2)
V   croc(us) sack (1)
W   crocus sack (235)
X   croker [n.] (1)
Y   croker bag (36)
Z   croker sack (120)
aa dumping sack (1)
ab feed bag (2)
ac feed sack (44)
ad fertilize sack (4)
ae fertilizer bag (1)
af fertilizer sack (1)
ag frog sack (1)
ah grain sack (2)
ai granny sack (1)
aj grass bag (4)
ak grass sack (74)
al Grassack [G] (1)
am guano [n.] (4)
an guano sack (12)
ao gunny [n.] (2)
ap gunnysack (108)
aq hamper sack (1)
ar hay sack (1)
as heavy sack (1)
at hemp sack (2)

au   hopsack (2)
av   Irish-potato bag (1)
aw   jute bag (9)
ax   jute bagging (1)
ay   jute sack (8)
az   lime sack (1)
ba   Manila sack (1)
bb   morral [S] (1)
bc   oat sack (1)
bd   onion sack (4)
be   pea sack (1)
bf   peanut sack (1)
bg   peat sack (1)
bh   pick sack (1)
bi   poke (1)
bj   poke sack (1)
bk   pooch (1)
bl   potato bag (9)
bm   potato burlap (1)
bn   potato sack (25)
bo   rough sack (2)
bp   rye sack (1)
bq   sac a pique en cre(ole) [F] (1)
br   sac de pique [F] (1)
bs   sack (52)
bt   sea-grass sack (1)
bu   seed bag (1)
bv   seed sack (2)
bw   shipping bag (1)
bx   shipping sack (1)
by   short sack (1)
bz   sugar sack (2)
ca   toad sack (1)
cb   tote sack (12)
cc   tow bag (10)
cd   tow sack (315)
ce   towed sack (1)
cf   tung-oil sack (1)
cg   wheat bag (1)
ch   white feed sack (1)
ci   woven bag (1)

019.8 L turn (of corn/wood)
No Response (213)
A   arm (2)
B   arm of wood (7)
C   armful (108)
D   armful (of clothes) (1)
E   armful (of corn) (1)
F   armful (of flowers) (1)
G   armful (of fodder) (2)
H   armful (of groceries) (4)
I   (arm)ful (of wood) (3)
J   armful (of wood) (140)
K   armfuls (2)
L   armload (75)
M   armload (of corn) (4)
N   armload (of wood) (111)
O   armsful (of wood) (2)
P   bag of corn (1)

Q   barrel (1)
R   brasse de bois [F] (1)
S   bunch of corn (1)
T   bundle (of corn) (2)
U   bundle (of wood) (9)
V   burlap bag full (1)
W   bushel (79)
X   bushel and a half (1)
Y   bushel measure (1)
Z   bushel (of corn) (117)
aa   bushel (of wood) (1)
ab   bushel sack full (1)
ac   carload of feed (1)
ad   chance (1)
ae   crow's nest (1)
af   double armful (1)
ag   drag (1)
ah   few sticks, a (1)
ai   fifty-pound bag (1)
aj   five pecks (1)
ak   four or five bushels (1)
al   four pecks (1)
am   gag of corn (1)
an   grinding (of corn) (1)
ao   grist (3)
ap   grist of corn (2)
aq   half (2)
ar   half a bag (1)
as   half a bushel (of corn) (30)
at   half a load (61)
au   half a rick (3)
av   half a truck (1)
aw   half a wagon (3)
ax   half a wagonload (1)
ay   half bushel (9)
az   half cart (1)
ba   half full (1)
bb   half load (22)
bc   half of a load (3)
bd   handful (1)
be   hopperful (of corn) (1)
bf   hundred pound of corn (1)
bg   hundred pound (of wood) (1)
bh   jack of wood (1)
bi   jag (21)
bj   jag of a load (1)
bk   jag (of corn) (2)
bl   jag (of wood) (13)
bm   jagful (1)
bn   jib of wood (1)
bo   light load (2)
bp   load (43)
bq   load full (1)
br   load (of corn) (17)
bs   load (of wood) (83)
bt   measure (1)
bu   mess (of corn) (2)
bv   milling (of corn) (5)
bw   moudage, un [F] (1)

bx   pack of wood (1)
by   paper sack full of corn (1)
bz   part load (7)
ca   part of a load (21)
cb   partial load (8)
cc   peck (42)
cd   peck (of corn) (27)
ce   pen (1)
cf   pickup load (1)
cg   piece (1)
ch   piece (of a) load (23)
ci   pile of wood (2)
cj   rack (1)
ck   rack of wood (1)
cl   ration (of) corn (1)
cm   rick (5)
cn   rick and a half (1)
co   rick (of wood) (10)
cp   sack (3)
cq   sack (of corn) (14)
cr   sackful (2)
cs   sackful (of corn) (2)
ct   shirttail of wood (1)
cu   short load (2)
cv   small load (3)
cw   slack load (1)
cx   stack (1)
cy   three or four bushels (1)
cz   ton (2)
da   ton (of corn) (4)
db   ton (of wood) (2)
dc   tote [n.] (2)
dd   trailer load (1)
de   truckload (4)
df   turn (46)
dg   turn (of corn) (139)
dh   turn of fodder (1)
di   turn (of meal) (13)
dj   turn of turnips (1)
dk   turn (of vegetables) (1)
dl   turn of water (1)
dm   turn (of wheat) (5)
dn   turn (of wood) (83)
do   two bushels (6)
dp   two-horse wagonload (1)
dq   wagon box of corn (1)
dr   wagon full (of corn) (1)
ds   wagon of corn (1)
dt   wagonload (17)
du   wagonload (of corn) (11)
dv   wagonload of cotton (1)
dw   wagonload (of wood) (3)
dx   wash pan full (1)
dy   washtubful (1)
dz   wheelbarrow load (of wood) (1)
ea   wheelbarrowful (1)
eb   yard (of wood) (1)

019.9 L light bulb
No Response (132)

A   bulb (526)
B   burner (3)
C   electric bulb (20)
D   electric globe (1)
E   electric light bulb (5)
F   electric light globe (1)
G   globe (27)
H   lamp (1)
I   lamp bulb (5)
J   lamp globe (2)
K   light bug (1)
L   light bulb (421)
M   light globe (4)
N   plug (1)
O   sixty-watt bulb (1)

019.9 P bulb

{b}   fricative
No Response (157)
<baw[1]b> (1)
<bloob> (1)
<boelbz> (1)
<bolb> (4)
<bolbz> (1)
<boo(1)b> (22)
<boo(1)bz> (1)
<boo[1]b> (59)
<boo[1]bz> (3)
<bool(b)> (1)
<boolb> (31)
<bu(lb)> (2)
<bu(1)b> (59)
<bu(1)bz> (2)
<bu[1](b)> (1)
<bu[1]b> (346)
<bu[1]bz> (15)
<bul(b)> (6)
<bulb> (274)
<bulbz> (12)
<{b}oo[1](b)> (1)
<{b}u[1]b> (1)

019.9 S bulb

No Response (18)
|EAC| (3)
|EACcbj| (1)
|EFA| (1)
|EFAcbj| (1)
|EFC| (1)
|EMAmaa| (1)
|FAA| (1)
|FAAffm| (1)
|FAAmaa| (1)
|FAAmaj| (6)
|FABcbj| (1)
|FABmaj| (1)
|FAC| (3)
|FACmaj| (3)
|FADmaj| (1)
|FAH| (11)
|FAHcbj| (5)

|FAHfam| (2)
|FAHmaj| (7)
|FBA| (1)
|FCA| (3)
|FCAcba| (1)
|FCAmaa| (1)
|FCAmaacba| (2)
|FCAmaj| (10)
|FCAmajcba| (1)
|FCAncamaj| (1)
|FCBmaj| (2)
|FCC| (2)
|FCCfam| (1)
|FCCfaq| (1)
|FCCmaa| (1)
|FCCmaj| (2)
|FCDcbj| (1)
|FCDfal| (1)
|FCF| (1)
|FCH| (2)
|FCHcbj| (1)
|FCHfaj| (1)
|FCHmaj| (3)
|FCHmfj| (1)
|FFAfaj| (1)
|FFCfaj| (1)
|FFCmaa| (1)
|FFDcba| (2)
|FFDfal| (1)
|FFDmaj| (2)
|FFDmfj| (1)
|FFFmaj| (1)
|FFHcbj| (2)
|FFHmaj| (2)
|FMA| (1)
|FMAfaj| (2)
|FMG| (1)
|LAA| (1)
|LAAmaj| (1)
|LAC| (2)
|LACefj| (1)
|LADmaj| (1)
|LAE| (3)
|LAEfaj| (1)
|LAEmaj| (1)
|LCA| (2)
|LCAcba| (1)
|LCAmaj| (2)
|LCAmajcba| (2)
|LCE| (2)
|LCEmajcba| (1)
|LCGcbj| (2)
|LFEmaj| (1)
|LMBmaj| (1)
|MAA| (2)
|MAE| (1)
|MAG| (1)
|MCA| (1)
|MCAcba| (1)

|MCB| (1)
|NAA| (19)
|NAAcba| (2)
|NAAcbj| (1)
|NAAefa| (1)
|NAAefj| (1)
|NAAfaj| (26)
|NAAfajcba| (1)
|NAAmaa| (1)
|NAAmaj| (16)
|NAAmajcba| (2)
|NAAmfa| (1)
|NAB| (15)
|NABcba| (2)
|NABcbj| (2)
|NABefj| (7)
|NABfaj| (14)
|NABfak| (1)
|NABfal| (1)
|NABmaj| (12)
|NAC| (1)
|NACmaj| (1)
|NAD| (99)
|NADcba| (7)
|NADcbj| (20)
|NADfaj| (43)
|NADfajcbj| (1)
|NADmab| (1)
|NADmaj| (138)
|NADmajcba| (2)
|NADmak| (1)
|NADmfj| (3)
|NAE| (1)
|NAEfaj| (1)
|NAEmaj| (3)
|NAF| (13)
|NAFcbj| (2)
|NAFfaj| (2)
|NAFfal| (1)
|NAFmaj| (6)
|NAG| (3)
|NAGcbj| (2)
|NAGfaj| (1)
|NAGmaj| (7)
|NAGmajcbj| (1)
|NAH| (12)
|NAHcba| (1)
|NAHcbj| (2)
|NAHfaj| (1)
|NAHmaj| (7)
|NAHnab| (1)
|NAHnak| (1)
|NAI| (1)
|NBAmaj| (1)
|NBD| (2)
|NBDfaj| (2)
|NCA| (9)
|NCAcbj| (1)
|NCAcbs| (1)

|NCAefj| (2)
|NCAfaa| (1)
|NCAfaj| (4)
|NCAmaacba| (2)
|NCAmaj| (13)
|NCAmajcba| (1)
|NCB| (4)
|NCBfaj| (1)
|NCBfal| (1)
|NCBfam| (1)
|NCBmaa| (1)
|NCBmaj| (5)
|NCBnaj| (1)
|NCD| (21)
|NCDcba| (6)
|NCDcbj| (13)
|NCDfaj| (20)
|NCDmaacba| (1)
|NCDmaj| (44)
|NCF| (3)
|NCFcbj| (1)
|NCFfaj| (1)
|NCFmaj| (2)
|NCFmao| (1)
|NCH| (6)
|NCHcbj| (1)
|NCHfaj| (1)
|NCHmaj| (2)
|NCHmajcba| (1)
|NDDnfb| (1)
|NFA| (3)
|NFAcbj| (1)
|NFAfaj| (1)
|NFAmaj| (4)
|NFB| (5)
|NFBcbj| (1)
|NFBfaj| (1)
|NFBmaj| (1)
|NFD| (4)
|NFDfaj| (1)
|NFDmaj| (5)
|NFDmajcbj| (1)
|NFE| (1)
|NFF| (2)
|NFFmaj| (4)
|NFFmajcba| (1)
|NFG| (1)
|NFGmaj| (3)
|NFHmaj| (1)
|NFI| (1)
|NGA| (1)
|NGAfaj| (1)
|NGAmaj| (1)
|NMAfaj| (1)
|NMAmaj| (1)
|NMBcbj| (1)
|NMBmaj| (4)
|NMDmaj| (4)
|NMEmaj| (2)

|NMFcba| (1)
|NMFcbj| (1)
|NMFfaj| (1)
|NMGmaj| (2)
|PCC| (1)
|PCG| (1)
|SBEmaj| (1)

020.1 L clothes basket
No Response (132)
A basin (1)
B basket (519)
C basket of clothes (2)
D bucket (5)
E clothes bag (2)
F clothes basket (195)
G clothes boiler (1)
H clothes box (1)
I clothes bucket (1)
J clothes sack (1)
K cotton basket (1)
L dishpan (13)
M foot tub (12)
N galvanized tub (1)
O hamper (2)
P hamper bag (1)
Q hamper basket (3)
R hand basket (1)
S homemade basket (2)
T laundry bag (7)
U laundry basket (55)
V pail (3)
W pan (10)
X rinsing tub (1)
Y sack (1)
Z tub (29)
aa wash basket (13)
ab wash pan (2)
ac washtub (7)
ad wicker basket (3)
ae wire basket (1)
af wooden tub (1)
ag woven basket (1)
ah zinc pan (1)
ai zinc tub (1)
aj zinc washtub (1)

020.1 P basket
{b} fricative
{?} glottal
No Response (166)
<ba(s)kIt=14> (1)
<baiskIt=14> (2)
<bas(k)It=14> (1)
<bas(kIt)> (1)
<basgIt=14> (4)
<bashkIts=14> (2)
<bask(It)> (1)
<baskAt=14> (1)
<baskI(t)=14> (4)
<baskI(t)s=14> (1)

<baskIs=14> (1)
<baskIt=14> (673)
<baskIts=14> (48)
<baskI{?}=14> (1)
<basket=13> (1)
<baskit=13> (3)
<bastI(t)=14> (1)
<bastIt=14> (2)
<bastkIt=14> (1)
<bastkit=13> (1)
<bathkIt=14> (1)
<beskIt=14> (6)
<{b}athkIt=14> (1)

020.2 P keg
No Response (109)
<kag> (192)
<kagdh> (1)
<kagz> (77)
<kai(g)> (1)
<kaig> (61)
<kaigz> (20)
<kang> (1)
<ke(g)> (2)
<keeg> (1)
<keg> (380)
<kegs> (5)
<kegz> (89)
<kig> (6)
<kigz> (1)
<kog> (1)
<kyagz> (1)
<kyeg> (3)
<kyegs> (1)
<kyegz> (1)
<kyig> (1)
<tag> (1)

020.3 P hoops
{?} glottal
No Response (186)
<hewp> (1)
<hip> (1)
<hoep> (1)
<hoo(p)z> (1)
<hook> (2)
<hooks> (11)
<hoop> (207)
<hoops> (318)
<hoopsh> (5)
<hoo{?}> (1)
<huek> (1)
<hueks> (2)
<huep> (116)
<hueps> (83)
<huks> (1)
<hup> (5)
<hups> (2)
<whoop> (2)
<whoops> (1)

020.4 L cork

No Response (110)
A bottle cork (1)
B bottle stopper (8)
C bottle top (5)
D bouchon [F] (1)
E bum (1)
F bung (4)
G bung stopper (1)
H cob (9)
I cob stopper (1)
J copper cork (1)
K corcho [S] (1)
L cork (612)
M cork concern (1)
N cork cork (1)
O cork stopper (92)
P cork stopple (1)
Q cork top (1)
R corncob (13)
S corn(cob) stopper (1)
T corncob stopper (1)
U cote de mais [F] (1)
V glass bottle top (1)
W glass cork (3)
X glass stopper (18)
Y glass top (2)
Z paper stopper (1)
aa peg (4)
ab plastic cork (1)
ac plug (3)
ad rag stopper (1)
ae rubber stopper (4)
af stop(per) (4)
ag stopper (420)
ah stopple (2)
ai top (29)
aj wooden plug (1)
ak wooden stopper (5)

020.4 P cork
{o} low-back
{r} weakly retroflex
{?} glottal
No Response (168)
<kark> (1)
<kaw(r)k> (39)
<kaw(r)t> (1)
<kaw[r]k> (45)
<kawrIk=14> (1)
<kawrk> (84)
<kawrks> (2)
<kawr{?}> (1)
<kaw{r}k> (37)
<ko(r)k> (4)
<ko[r]k> (3)
<ko[r]ks> (1)
<koe(r)k> (15)
<koe[r]k> (118)
<koe[r]ks> (1)
<koer(k)> (2)

<koerk> (315)
<koerks> (8)
<koe{r}k> (53)
<koe{r}ks> (2)
<kork> (8)
<ko{r}k> (3)
<ku(r)k> (1)
<kwaw[r]k> (1)
<kwoe[r]k> (1)
<k{o}(r)k> (5)
<k{o}[r]k> (1)
<k{o}rk> (18)
<k{o}rks> (1)
<k{o}{r}k> (3)

020.5 L harmonica
No Response (76)
A bull harp (1)
B French harp (292)
C harm (1)
D harmonica (430)
E harmonica harp (1)
F harp (334)
G harpoon (1)
H Hohner (1)
I Jew's harp (11)
J juice harp (10)
K mouth harmonica (1)
L mouth harp (72)
M mouth music (2)
N mouth organ (87)
O musica de voca [S] (1)
P switch harp (1)
Q wind harp (1)

020.6 L Jew's harp
No Response (183)
A banjo harp (1)
B fiddle (1)
C French harp (7)
D harp (14)
E jaw harp (2)
F jaws harp (1)
G Jew's box (1)
H Jew's harp (419)
I Jew[N-k] harp (10)
J Jewish harp (2)
K juice harp (276)
L kazoo (1)
M mouth harp (4)
N mouth organ (5)
O zoon bug (1)

020.7 P hammer
{R} weakly retroflex
{r} weakly retroflex
No Response (97)
<ha[m]mR=14> (57)
<ha[m]mRz=14> (6)
<ha[m]m[R]=14> (93)
<ha[m]m[R]z=14> (2)
<ha[m]mu{r}=13> (2)

<ha[m]m{R}=14> (31)
<ha[m]m{R}z=14> (1)
<haimmR=14> (1)
<hamR=14> (103)
<hamRd=14> (2)
<hamRz=14> (5)
<ham[R]=14> (75)
<ham[R]d=14> (1)
<ham[R]z=14> (6)
<hammR=14> (199)
<hammRsh=14> (1)
<hammRz=14> (8)
<hammRzh=14> (1)
<hamm[R]=14> (147)
<hamm[R]z=14> (8)
<hammur=13> (1)
<hamm{R}=14> (41)
<hamur=13> (1)
<ham{R}=14> (31)
<he[m]mR=14> (1)
<he[m]m[R]=14> (2)
<he[m]m{R}=14> (1)
<hemR=14> (3)
<hem[R]=14> (2)
<hemmR=14> (6)
<hemm[R]=14> (4)
<hemm{R}=14> (1)

020.7 S hammer
No Response (0)
|KAB| (1)
|KAC| (5)
|KDC| (1)
|KDCmdj| (1)
|KKB| (1)
|KKC| (2)
|OAA| (49)
|OAAeaj| (1)
|OAAkaj| (154)
|OAAlaj| (1)
|OAB| (73)
|OABkaj| (75)
|OABkbj| (1)
|OABmaj| (2)
|OAC| (24)
|OACkaj| (3)
|OAD| (1)
|OAE| (13)
|OAEkaj| (4)
|OAG| (3)
|OAGkaj| (1)
|OAI| (1)
|OAIkaj| (2)
|OAIkan| (1)
|OBAmaj| (1)
|OCA| (45)
|OCAeaj| (2)
|OCAkaj| (81)
|OCAmaj| (2)
|OCAmak| (1)

|OCB| (8)
|OCBkaj| (17)
|OCE| (1)
|OCEkaa| (1)
|OCEkaj| (1)
|OCGkaj| (1)
|OCIkaj| (3)
|ODA| (29)
|ODAkdj| (71)
|ODAkdn| (2)
|ODAmdj| (1)
|ODB| (7)
|ODBkdj| (30)
|ODC| (3)
|ODCkdj| (4)
|ODDkdj| (1)
|ODE| (6)
|ODEkdj| (1)
|ODFkdj| (1)
|ODGkdj| (2)
|ODH| (1)
|ODI| (1)
|ODIkdj| (1)
|OGA| (1)
|OGB| (1)
|OGBkaj| (2)
|OHA| (1)
|OHAmda| (1)
|OHBkhj| (1)
|OKA| (73)
|OKAedj| (1)
|OKAkdj| (53)
|OKAkdn| (2)
|OKAmdj| (3)
|OKB| (10)
|OKBkdj| (7)
|OKBkhj| (1)
|OKC| (2)
|OKE| (2)
|OKI| (1)
|OKImdj| (2)
|OQA| (1)
|OQAkdj| (2)
|OQAmdj| (1)
|OQB| (1)

020.8 L tongue [of wagon]
No Response (194)
A   buggy pole (1)
B   buggy tongue (2)
C   coupling pole (7)
D   coupling tongue (3)
E   fleche [F] (1)
F   fleche du wagon [F] (1)
G   lancia [S] (1)
H   palonnier [F] (1)
I   pole (15)
J   shaft (17)
K   stake (1)
L   staves (1)

M   stoke (1)
N   tee (1)
O   tongue (611)
P   tongue of a/the wagon (2)
Q   wagon tongue (103)
R   whippletree (1)
S   yoke (4)
T   Zunge [G] (1)

020.9 L shafts [of buggy]
No Response (339)
A   brancard [F] (5)
B   buggy shafts (22)
C   double pole (1)
D   double shaft (1)
E   hames (1)
F   horse trace (1)
G   lancias [S] (1)
H   loony shaft (1)
I   poles (2)
J   shafts (531)
K   sidepieces (1)
L   staves (2)
M   stays (1)
N   strides (1)
O   thills (1)
P   timbers (1)
Q   trace (5)
R   trees (1)
S   two bars (1)
T   wagon shaft (1)
U   wooden shaft(s) (2)

021.1 L rim/felly
No Response (199)
A   band (18)
B   buggy tire (1)
C   cerc(le) [F] (1)
D   feather (2)
E   felly (49)
F   felly [=rim] (16)
G   felly [=tire] (2)
H   felly [section of wheel] (73)
I   felly band (1)
J   frame (1)
K   hoop (7)
L   iron band (11)
M   iron part (2)
N   iron rim (16)
O   iron tire (16)
P   llantas [S] (1)
Q   metal band (1)
R   metal rim (12)
S   metal ring (1)
T   metal strip (1)
U   metal tire (4)
V   outer rim (2)
W   outer rung (1)
X   outer wheel (1)
Y   outside rim (1)
Z   rim (226)

aa   rim [=felly] (3)
ab   rim [metal] (161)
ac   rim [wooden] (132)
ad   rimming (2)
ae   ring (5)
af   spinner (1)
ag   steel band (4)
ah   steel plate (1)
ai   steel rim (10)
aj   steel ring (2)
ak   steel tire (8)
al   tire [metal] (213)
am   tire [wooden] (3)
an   tread (1)
ao   two-piece felly (1)
ap   wagon felly (3)
aq   wagon rim (4)
ar   wagon tire (27)
as   wheel (2)
at   wheel casing (1)
au   wheel rim (2)
av   wheel tire (1)
aw   wood rim (9)
ax   wood tire (1)
ay   wooden felly (2)
az   wooden rim (7)
ba   wooden tire (1)

021.2 L singletree
No Response (295)
A   balancin [S] (1)
B   base (1)
C   crosstree (3)
D   leveler (1)
E   Schwengel [G] (1)
F   single (2)
G   singletree (549)
H   singletree-looking thing (1)
I   swingle (1)
J   swingletree (55)
K   swivel tree (2)
L   T bar (1)
M   trace tree (1)
N   tree (5)
O   wagon tree (2)
P   whiffletree (4)
Q   whippletree (7)

021.3 L doubletree
No Response (406)
A   big swingletree (1)
B   bigger singletree (1)
C   breast tree (1)
D   cross member (1)
E   crossbar (2)
F   crosstree (1)
G   coupling pole (1)
H   double (7)
I   double one (2)
J   double pole (1)
K   double singletree (38)

L   double swingletree (8)
M   doubletree (418)
N   evener (6)
O   hammeltree (1)
P   scale (1)
Q   single doubletree (1)
R   singletree (1)
S   singletree two (1)
T   spreader (2)
U   stretcher (1)
V   stretcher rig (1)
W   swivel tree (1)
X   triple tree (2)
Y   triple singletree (1)
Z   two-by-six (1)
aa   whiffletree (2)

021.4 L hauling

No Response (138)
A   a-hauling (8)
B   car(ry) (1)
C   carried (2)
D   carry (6)
E   carrying (38)
F   cart off (1)
G   carting (9)
H   delivering (17)
I   delivers (1)
J   (did) hauling [n.] (1)
K   drawing (3)
L   expressing (1)
M   (freight/public) hauling [n.] (2)
N   haul (236)
O   haul across (1)
P   haul ass (1)
Q   haul away (3)
R   haul in (6)
S   haul off (8)
T   haul off (and do something) (3)
U   haul out (5)
V   haul up (10)
W   hauled (67)
X   hauled away (1)
Y   hauled in (6)
Z   hauled off (6)
aa   hauled out (2)
ab   hauled up (1)
ac   hauler [n.] (3)
ad   hauling (517)
ae   hauling in (2)
af   hauling off (3)
ag   hauling out (1)
ah   hauling up (1)
ai   hauls (6)
aj   logged off (1)
ak   logging (5)
al   (long) hauls [n.] (3)
am   making a run (1)
an   move (1)
ao   moving (11)

ap   moving along (1)
aq   pull (1)
ar   pulled (1)
as   pulling (2)
at   run [n.] (1)
au   running (1)
av   snake (1)
aw   taking (1)
ax   taking (a load) (1)
ay   tote (1)
az   toting (4)
ba   transferring (1)
bb   transporting (7)

021.5 G drag

<!>   infinitive
<&>   present 3rd singular
<@>   present participle
<*>   preterit
<#>   past participle
No Response (203)
<!chrag> (1)
<!drag> (494)
<!dragz> (1)
<!dreg> (12)
<!drug> (2)
<!jrag> (2)
<&dragz> (3)
<@dragN=14> (43)
<@dragNG=14> (11)
<*dra(g)> (1)
<*drag> (8)
<*dragd> (181)
<*dragt> (2)
<*dreg> (1)
<*dregd> (2)
<*drug> (423)
<*drugd> (6)
<*jrug> (3)
<#drag> (4)
<#dragd> (138)
<#dragt> (2)
<#drawn> (1)
<#dregd> (2)
<#drug> (223)
<#drugd> (10)
<#jrug> (1)
<#trug> (1)

021.6 L plow

No Response (60)
A   airplane (1)
B   arado [S] (2)
C   beam (1)
D   bedder (2)
E   blackland plow (1)
F   boll weevil sweep (1)
G   bottom plow (11)
H   break(er/ing) plow (35)
I   bull tongue (plow) (46)
J   buster (plow) (13)

K   buzzard wing sweep (1)
L   camping planter (1)
M   cast plow (2)
N   charrue [F] (1)
O   charrue double [F] (2)
P   charrue simple [F] (2)
Q   chisel plow (2)
R   chopper (3)
S   colter (1)
T   combination stock (1)
U   common plow (2)
V   corn planter (2)
W   cotton planter (4)
X   cricket (1)
Y   cultivator (plow) (49)
Z   cutaway (2)
aa   cutting plow (2)
ab   deadening plow (1)
ac   diamond (2)
ad   disc (plow) (34)
ae   double bit (1)
af   double-bladed plow (1)
ag   double buster (1)
ah   double(-)foot(ed) (plow) (3)
ai   double hill plow (1)
aj   double-horse plow (2)
ak   double-mule plow (1)
al   double plow (stock) (20)
am   double scrape (1)
an   double shovel (plow) (67)
ao   double stock (4)
ap   drag (scraper) (2)
aq   five-foot(ed) plow (2)
ar   flat-bottom turner (1)
as   flat-bottom (turning) plow (4)
at   flat-break plow (1)
au   flatland plow (1)
av   four-foot (plow) (1)
aw   furrow opener (1)
ax   furrowing plow (2)
ay   gang plow (7)
az   garden plow (10)
ba   gee whiz (plow) (6)
bb   go-devil (7)
bc   gopher (plow) (2)
bd   grasshopper (stock) (3)
be   half plow (1)
bf   half shovel (plow) (16)
bg   half turner (1)
bh   hand plow (10)
bi   hill plow/sweep (5)
bj   hillside (plow) (18)
bk   horse-drawn plow (1)
bl   horse plow (2)
bm   job-down plow (1)
bn   landside (plow) (3)
bo   lay(ing)-off (plow) (9)
bp   left-hand (turning plow) (5)
bq   levee plow (1)

br level-land plow (3)
bs lister (1)
bt magnolia (1)
bu middle breaker (3)
bv middle splitter (3)
bw middlebuster (143)
bx moldboard (plow) (11)
by mule (plow) (5)
bz newground plow (5)
ca one-horse (single plow) (9)
cb one little-old horse plow (1)
cc one-mule planter (1)
cd one-row (plow) (4)
ce one-stock plow (1)
cf one-stop plow (1)
cg open(ing) plow (2)
ch planter (10)
ci planting plow (1)
cj plow (stock/tool) (574)
ck pony plow/turner (1)
cl potato plow (1)
cm push plow (4)
cn ratchet stock (2)
co reversible (turning) plow (2)
cp riding (one-row) cultivator (2)
cq riding (sulky) plow (4)
cr right-hand (turning) plow (4)
cs root plow (2)
ct round shovel (5)
cu row plow (1)
cv scoop (stock) (2)
cw scooter (plow) (42)
cx scrape(r) (20)
cy scratcher (5)
cz share plow (1)
da shovel (plow) (31)
db side plow/sweep (2)
dc single bit (1)
dd single-bladed plow (1)
de single(-)foot(ed) (2)
df single (plow) (stock) (28)
dg single-point plow (1)
dh single shaft (plow) (1)
di single shovel (plow) (6)
dj single stock (plow) (21)
dk single stop (1)
dl single turning plow (1)
dm singletree plow (1)
dn sixteen-inch bottom plow (1)
do slap-wing plow (1)
dp slat wing (plow) (1)
dq sodbuster (1)
dr solid (wing) (plow) (2)
ds spading plow (1)
dt stalk-cutter (1)
du steel(-)beam (turning) (plow) (15)
dv steel middlebuster (1)
dw steel (wing) plow (5)

dx stock plow (1)
dy straddle jack (1)
dz straight (plow) (8)
ea straight-top plow (1)
eb stump puller (1)
ec subsoil plow (1)
ed subsoiler (4)
ee sulky plow (2)
ef sweep (plow) (60)
eg sweeping plow (1)
eh terrace plow (1)
ei three-bottom plow (1)
ej three-foot (plow) (3)
ek three-team plow (1)
el throw-out plow (1)
em til(ler) plow (1)
en tobacco plow (1)
eo tractor plow (4)
ep turn (plow) (54)
eq turner (plow) (11)
er turning (plow) (264)
es twelve-inch middlebuster (1)
et twister (3)
eu two-bottom plow (1)
ev two-horse (plow) (20)
ew two-mule riding plow (1)
ex two-row planter (4)
ey two-way plow (1)
ez walking (plow) (6)
fa wheat planter (1)
fb wheel plow (2)
fc wing (turning) plow (4)
fd wood(en)-beam plow (3)

021.6 P plow

{l} devoiced
{ow} monophthong/inglide
{p} fricative
{r} devoiced
No Response (96)
<p[l]ow> (1)
<p[l]{ow}> (1)
<pla> (2)
<plai> (1)
<plow> (211)
<plowth> (1)
<plowz> (17)
<pl{ow}> (61)
<pl{ow}z> (2)
<prawz> (1)
<prow> (1)
<pr{ow}z> (1)
<p{l}ai> (4)
<p{l}az> (1)
<p{l}ow> (469)
<p{l}owz> (29)
<p{l}{ow}> (99)
<p{l}{ow}z> (6)
<p{r}ow> (4)
<p{r}owz> (1)

<{p}[l]{ow}> (1)
<{p}{l}owz> (1)

021.7 L harrow

No Response (212)
A A (harrow) (7)
B bed harrow (2)
C Bermuda digger (1)
D big-tooth harrow (1)
E black-gum log (1)
F bog (harrow) (4)
G bottom harrow (1)
H bung disk (1)
I bush-and-bog (harrow) (2)
J chisel harrow (1)
K clod buster (2)
L clod masher (2)
M culti-mulcher (1)
N cultivating harrow (2)
O cultivator (harrow) (47)
P cutaway (harrow) (12)
Q cutter (1)
R cutting (harrow) (7)
S digger (1)
T disc-and-bog harrow (1)
U disc (harrow) (220)
V disc breaker (1)
W disc cultivator (1)
X disc machine (1)
Y double-A harrow (2)
Z double cutting harrow (1)
aa double (harrow) (3)
ab double set (2)
ac drag (harrow) (62)
ad drag-tooth harrow (1)
ae drag-type tooth harrow (1)
af dray harrow (1)
ag farrow (1)
ah fine-tooth harrow (2)
ai five-teeth harrow (1)
aj flat harrow (1)
ak forty-disc tandem (1)
al fourteen-tooth harrow (1)
am furrow (1)
an gang harrow (2)
ao gee harrod (1)
ap gee whiz (harrow) (41)
aq gee-whiz Joe harrow (1)
ar go-devil (harrow) (6)
as griffe [F] (1)
at groundbreaker (2)
au grove disc (1)
av hard-tooth harrow (1)
aw harrow (481)
ax harrow plow (1)
ay harrower (1)
az hipper (1)
ba homemade harrow (2)
bb iron harrow (2)
bc iron-tooth harrow (2)

bd Joe (harrow) (15)
be Joe-tooth harrow (1)
bf mule (harrow) (6)
bg mule-drawn (harrow) (2)
bh newground harrow (1)
bi offset disc harrow (1)
bj old-fashion disc (1)
bk one-horse harrow (2)
bl one-row cultivator (1)
bm orchard harrow (1)
bn peg-tooth(ed) harrow (5)
bo pulverizer (2)
bp rake (3)
bq revolving harrow (1)
br riding (one-row) cultivator (5)
bs roller (1)
bt rolling cutter (1)
bu root cutter (1)
bv rotary cutaway (1)
bw row harrow (2)
bx scrape (1)
by scraper (3)
bz scratcher (2)
ca section drag (1)
cb section (harrow) (45)
cc side harrow (29)
cd single gee-whiz (1)
ce single (harrow) (2)
cf single set (1)
cg slip scrape (1)
ch smack tooth (1)
ci smoothing harrow (1)
cj snag harrow (1)
ck spike harrow (1)
cl spike(d)-tooth harrow (7)
cm spoon harrow (1)
cn spring harrow (1)
co spring-tooth cultivator (1)
cp spring(-)tooth (harrow) (39)
cq steel drag (1)
cr steel harrow (1)
cs store-bought harrow (1)
ct straight-tooth harrow (2)
cu stribble (1)
cv subsoiler (4)
cw subsoiling plow (1)
cx sweep (3)
cy till [n.] (1)
cz tiller (2)
da tooth harrow (1)
db top harrow (8)
dc tractor harrow (1)
dd tractor-pulled harrow (1)
de trencher (1)
df two-horse disc harrow (1)
dg V harrow (4)
dh V type (1)
di walker cultivator (1)
dj walking cultivator (4)

dk wood harrow (1)
dl wooden harrow (5)

021.7 P harrow
{o} low-back
{R} weakly retroflex
{r} weakly retroflex
No Response (250)
<(h)arA=14> (2)
<(h)orA=14> (1)
<ha[R]=14> (4)
<ha[r](A)> (4)
<hai(rA)> (1)
<hair(A)z> (1)
<hairAz=14> (1)
<hairoe=13> (1)
<har(A)> (11)
<har(A)z> (1)
<harA=14> (334)
<harAwR=144> (1)
<harAz=14> (36)
<harI=14> (1)
<harR=14> (3)
<haroe=12> (1)
<haroe=13> (45)
<haroez=13> (2)
<haroo=13> (2)
<harooz=13> (1)
<harrA=14> (40)
<harrAz=14> (2)
<harroe=13> (8)
<har{R}=14> (3)
<har{R}z=14> (1)
<hawr(A)> (1)
<hawrA=14> (3)
<ha{r}(A)> (7)
<ha{r}A=14> (5)
<ha{r}Az=14> (1)
<ha{r}oe=13> (1)
<ha{r}rA=14> (13)
<ha{r}rAz=14> (3)
<her(A)> (2)
<herA=14> (23)
<herAz=14> (2)
<heroe=13> (6)
<herrA=14> (3)
<herroe=13> (2)
<ho(rA)> (1)
<ho[r](A)> (2)
<hor(A)> (31)
<hor(A)z> (4)
<horA=14> (61)
<horAz=14> (10)
<horI=14> (2)
<horo=13> (1)
<horoe=13> (5)
<horrA=14> (3)
<horroe=13> (2)
<ho{r}(A)> (6)
<ho{r}A=14> (2)

<ho{r}rA=14> (7)
<huroe=13> (1)
<h{o}r(A)> (4)
<h{o}r(A)z> (2)
<h{o}rA=14> (12)
<h{o}rAz=14> (2)
<h{o}rR=14> (2)
<h{o}roe=13> (1)
<h{o}rrA=14> (1)

021.8 L axle
No Response (233)
A axle (631)
B ax(le) (2)
C axle part (1)
D axletree (1)
E buggy axle (2)
F car axle (1)
G eje [S] (1)
H front axle (1)
I main axle (1)
J tongue (1)
K wagon axle (3)
L wheel axle (1)

022.1 L sawhorse
No Response (159)
[X-frame]
A bench (1)
B block (1)
C brace (2)
D brake (1)
E break (1)
F buck (2)
G buck bench (1)
H buck horse (1)
I bucking horse (1)
J bucksaw (1)
K bucksaw rack (2)
L carpenter's bench (1)
M carpenter's horse (1)
N carriage (2)
O chop block (9)
P chopping block (5)
Q cradle (5)
R crib (1)
S cross (1)
T cross log (1)
U crossbar (1)
V crossbuck (1)
W crossties (1)
X draw horse (1)
Y fork (1)
Z frame (4)
aa hand stick (1)
ab holder (1)
ac horse (49)
ad horseshoe (1)
ae jack (8)
af log frame (1)
ag log holder (1)

ah   log horse (1)
ai   log rack (1)
aj   log scaffold (1)
ak   rack (63)
al   rack for wood (1)
am   ramp (1)
an   rick (3)
ao   saw bench (3)
ap   saw block (3)
aq   saw jack (5)
ar   saw rack (28)
as   saw tree (1)
at   sawbuck (44)
au   sawhorse (108)
av   sawing rack (2)
aw   scaffold (3)
ax   see horse (1)
ay   some kind of a cross (1)
az   stob (1)
ba   support (2)
bb   trestle (3)
bc   triangle chopper (1)
bd   wood bench (1)
be   wood brace (1)
bf   wood buck (1)
bg   wood frame (3)
bh   wood sawhorse (1)
bi   wood scaffold (1)
bj   wood stand (1)
bk   wood-chopping place (1)
bl   wooden horse (3)
bm   woodhorse (1)
bn   woodrack (60)
bo   workhorse (1)
bp   X-frame (5)
bq   yard rack (1)
br   yoke (1)

[A-frame]

ca   A-frame (17)
cb   bench (2)
cc   bracing (1)
cd   buck (1)
ce   bucksaw (1)
cf   burro [S] (1)
cg   carpenter horse (5)
ch   carpenter trestle (1)
ci   carpenter's bench (1)
cj   carpenter's horse (3)
ck   carriage (1)
cl   cotton rack (1)
cm   cutting horse (1)
cn   draw horse (2)
co   frame (2)
cp   horse (187)
cq   horse bench (1)
cr   horse frame (1)
cs   horses, les (1)
ct   jack (2)
cu   jack frame (1)

cv   jack horse (2)
cw   johnny horse (1)
cx   quilting horse (1)
cy   rack (2)
cz   saddle horse (1)
da   saw bench (7)
db   saw dog (1)
dc   saw rack (3)
dd   sawbuck (3)
de   sawhorse (236)
df   scaffold (5)
dg   scaffolding (5)
dh   see horse (1)
di   set of horses (1)
dj   trestle (8)
dk   trestle bench (1)
dl   trestle horse (2)
dm   triangle (1)
dn   wood frame (1)
do   wood jack (1)
dp   wooden horse (9)
dq   woodhorse (5)
dr   woodrack (2)
ds   work bench (5)
dt   workhorse (14)

[unspecified]

ea   bench (5)
eb   block (2)
ec   brace (2)
ed   buck (1)
ee   bucksaw (4)
ef   burro [S] (3)
eg   caballos [S] (1)
eh   carpenter burro (1)
ei   carpenter horse (2)
ej   carpenter's horse (1)
ek   chop block (1)
el   chopping block (15)
em   cradle (2)
en   frame (3)
eo   horse (59)
ep   jack (2)
eq   knockdown (1)
er   log frame (1)
es   lumber horse (1)
et   quilting horse (1)
eu   rack (16)
ev   rack for wood (1)
ew   rack to saw wood in (1)
ey   Sagebock [G] (1)
ez   saw (1)
fa   saw bench (3)
fb   saw dog (1)
fc   saw frame (3)
fd   saw jack (1)
fe   saw rack (8)
ff   saw rick (1)
fg   sawbuck (6)
fh   sawhorse (89)

fi   scaffold (3)
fj   see horse (1)
fk   stand (1)
fl   trestle (6)
fm   two-legged sawhorse (1)
fn   wood block (1)
fo   wood cradle (1)
fp   wood frame (1)
fq   wood rick (1)
fr   wooden horse (4)
fs   wooden house (1)
ft   wooden trestle (1)
fu   woodhorse (6)
fv   woodrack (15)
fw   work bench (3)
fx   workhorse (3)
fy   workhorse bench (1)

022.2 P brush

{oo}   unrounded
{r}   weakly retroflex
{u}   upglide
No Response (106)
<b(r){u}sh> (1)
<bresh> (67)
<breshIz=14> (1)
<brish> (1)
<broos> (1)
<broosh> (18)
<brosh> (3)
<bru(sh)> (1)
<bruch> (1)
<brush> (666)
<brushIz=14> (5)
<bru{r}sh> (1)
<br{oo}sh> (19)
<br{u}sh> (70)
<br{u}shIz=14> (1)
<bursh> (2)
<b{r}{u}sh> (1)

022.3 P strap

{o}   low-back
No Response (149)
<s(t)rap> (2)
<s(t)rop> (1)
<sh(t)rop> (1)
<shtrap> (5)
<shtrop> (3)
<st(r)ap> (1)
<st(r)op> (1)
<straip> (1)
<strap> (547)
<straps> (7)
<strawp> (9)
<strep> (1)
<stroep> (1)
<strop> (243)
<strops> (1)
<strurp> (1)
<str{o}p> (21)

022.4 P cartridge

{o}   low-back
{R}   weakly retroflex
{r}   weakly retroflex
{t}   flap
{?}   glottal

No Response (206)

<ka(r)d(r)Ij=14> (1)
<ka(r)t(r)Azh=14> (1)
<ka(r)trIjIz=144> (1)
<ka(r){t}rIjIz=144> (1)
<kaw(r)d(r)IjIz=144> (1)
<kaw(r)t(r)Ij=14> (1)
<kaw(r)tRij=143> (1)
<kaw(r)tRj=14> (1)
<kaw(r)tRjIz=144> (1)
<kaw(r)trI(j)=14> (1)
<kaw(r)trIj=14> (4)
<kaw(r)trIjIz=144> (1)
<kaw(r)trij=13> (2)
<kaw(r)t{R}j=14> (1)
<kaw(r)t{R}jIz=144> (1)
<kaw(r]trIj=14> (1)
<kaw[r]t(r)Ij=14> (1)
<kaw[r]trIj=14> (1)
<kaw[r]trIsh=14> (1)
<kawrt(r)Ij=14> (1)
<kawrt(r)IjIz=144> (1)
<kawrtrIj=14> (10)
<kawrtrIjIz=144> (4)
<kawrtrij=13> (1)
<kawrtrijIz=134> (1)
<kaw{r}trIj=14> (2)
<kaw{t}(r)IjIz=144> (1)
<ka{r}trIjIz=144> (1)
<ko(r)Atrij=143> (1)
<ko(r)chArij=143> (1)
<ko(r)chrIj=14> (2)
<ko(r)ch{R}jIz=144> (1)
<ko(r)d(r)Ij=14> (5)
<ko(r)d(r)IjIz=144> (1)
<ko(r)d(r)ij=13> (1)
<ko(r)dArij=143> (1)
<ko(r)drIj=14> (1)
<ko(r)drijIz=134> (1)
<ko(r)d{R}jIz=144> (1)
<ko(r)p(r)Ij=14> (1)
<ko(r)t(r)Aj=14> (3)
<ko(r)t(r)AjIz=144> (2)
<ko(r)t(r)Ij=14> (17)
<ko(r)t(r)IjIz=144> (9)
<ko(r)t(r)Ijiz=143> (1)
<ko(r)t(r)ijIs=134> (1)
<ko(r)t(r)ijIz=134> (8)
<ko(r)tAlIj=144> (1)
<ko(r)tArIj=144> (6)
<ko(r)tArij=143> (2)
<ko(r)tArijIz=1434> (1)
<ko(r)tRIj=144> (2)

<ko(r)tRIjIz=1444> (1)
<ko(r)tRIjiz=1443> (1)
<ko(r)tRij=143> (1)
<ko(r)tRj=14> (4)
<ko(r)tRjIs=144> (1)
<ko(r)tRjIz=144> (6)
<ko(r)tRjiz=143> (1)
<ko(r)tRrijIz=1434> (1)
<ko(r)trId=14> (1)
<ko(r)trIj=14> (44)
<ko(r)trIjA=144> (1)
<ko(r)trIjIz=144> (25)
<ko(r)trIjiz=143> (1)
<ko(r)trIks=14> (1)
<ko(r)trIzhIs=144> (1)
<ko(r)trij=13> (16)
<ko(r)trijIz=134> (18)
<ko(r)trizhIz=134> (1)
<ko(r)ttrIj=14> (1)
<ko(r)tu{r}j=13> (1)
<ko(r)t{R}ij=143> (1)
<ko(r)t{R}jAz=144> (1)
<ko(r)t{R}jIz=144> (9)
<ko(r)t{t}Ij=14> (1)
<ko(r)t{t}IjIz=144> (3)
<ko(r)t{t}ij=13> (1)
<ko(r){?}(r)IjIz=144> (1)
<ko(r){t}(r)Ad=14> (1)
<ko(r){t}(r)Aj=14> (1)
<ko(r){t}(r)AjIz=144> (2)
<ko(r){t}(r)I(j)=14> (1)
<ko(r){t}(r)Id=14> (2)
<ko(r){t}(r)Ij=14> (14)
<ko(r){t}(r)IjAz=144> (1)
<ko(r){t}(r)IjIz=144> (14)
<ko(r){t}(r)Ijiz=143> (1)
<ko(r){t}ArIj=144> (4)
<ko(r){t}ArIjIz=1444> (1)
<ko(r){t}Arij=143> (4)
<ko(r){t}ArijIz=1434> (2)
<ko(r){t}IrAj=144> (2)
<ko(r){t}IrIj=144> (1)
<ko(r){t}IrIjIz=1444> (1)
<ko(r){t}RIj=144> (2)
<ko(r){t}RIjIz=1444> (1)
<ko(r){t}Rij=143> (2)
<ko(r){t}Rj=14> (1)
<ko(r){t}RjIz=144> (2)
<ko(r){t}[R]jIz=144> (1)
<ko(r){t}rAjIz=144> (1)
<ko(r){t}rIj=14> (5)
<ko(r){t}rIjIz=144> (6)
<ko(r){t}rijIz=134> (2)
<ko(r){t}rijiz=133> (1)
<ko(r){t}trIj=14> (1)
<ko(r){t}{R}j=14> (1)
<ko(r){t}{R}jIz=144> (1)
<ko(r){t}{R}rIj=144> (1)
<ko(r){t}{t}IjIz=144> (1)

<ko(r){t}{t}ijIz=134> (1)
<ko(rt)lIj=14> (1)
<ko(rt)rij=13> (1)
<ko[r](t)lIjIz=144> (1)
<ko[r]t(r)Aj=14> (1)
<ko[r]t(r)Ij=14> (3)
<ko[r]t(r)IjIs=144> (1)
<ko[r]t(r)IjIz=144> (2)
<ko[r]t(r)Izh=14> (1)
<ko[r]t[R]jIz=144> (1)
<ko[r]trAj=14> (1)
<ko[r]trIch=14> (3)
<ko[r]trIj=14> (16)
<ko[r]trIjAz=144> (1)
<ko[r]trIjIz=144> (6)
<ko[r]trij=13> (2)
<ko[r]trijIz=134> (1)
<ko[r]t{t}Ij=14> (2)
<ko[r]t{t}IjIz=144> (1)
<ko[r]{?}(r)Ij=14> (1)
<ko[r]{t}(r)Aj=14> (1)
<ko[r]{t}(r)Ij=14> (9)
<ko[r]{t}(r)IjIz=144> (15)
<ko[r]{t}Rj=14> (1)
<ko[r]{t}rIj=14> (4)
<ko[r]{t}rIjIz=144> (1)
<ko[r]{t}trI(j)=14> (1)
<ko[r]{t}trij=13> (1)
<ko[r]{t}{t}IjIz=144> (2)
<koertrij=13> (1)
<kor(t)rijIz=134> (1)
<kor(tr)Ij=14> (1)
<korchrIj=14> (1)
<korchrIjIz=144> (1)
<kord(r)AjIz=144> (1)
<kord(r)Ij=14> (2)
<kordrIjIz=144> (1)
<korj(r)AjIz=144> (1)
<korj(r)IjIz=144> (1)
<kort(r)Ij=14> (8)
<kort(r)IjIz=144> (3)
<kort(r)ij=13> (1)
<kort(r)ijIz=134> (1)
<kort(r){R}j=14> (1)
<kortArIj=144> (2)
<kortArij=143> (1)
<kortRIj=144> (1)
<korthrIjIz=144> (1)
<korth{t}Ij=14> (1)
<kortlIj=14> (2)
<kortrI(j)=14> (1)
<kortrIch=14> (1)
<kortrIchA=144> (1)
<kortrIj=14> (80)
<kortrIjIz=144> (19)
<kortrIjiz=143> (1)
<kortrIz=14> (1)
<kortrid=13> (1)
<kortrij=13> (30)

<kortrijIz=134> (15)
<kortrizh=13> (1)
<kortrujIz=134> (1)
<kort{R}rIj=144> (1)
<kort{t}Ij=14> (1)
<kort{t}IjIz=144> (1)
<kor{t}(r)Ij=14> (3)
<kor{t}ArIj=144> (1)
<kor{t}rijIz=134> (1)
<ko{r}t(r)AjIz=144> (1)
<ko{r}t(r)Ij=14> (1)
<ko{r}t(r)IjAz=144> (1)
<ko{r}t(r)IjIz=144> (2)
<ko{r}t(r)ijIz=134> (1)
<ko{r}t(rI)zhIz=14> (1)
<ko{r}trAj=14> (1)
<ko{r}trAjIz=144> (1)
<ko{r}trIj=14> (10)
<ko{r}trIjIz=144> (5)
<ko{r}trij=13> (5)
<ko{r}trijIz=134> (1)
<ko{r}t{t}rIjIz=144> (1)
<ko{r}{t}(r)Ij=14> (3)
<ko{r}{t}(r)IjIz=144> (3)
<k{o}(r)d(r)Ij=14> (3)
<k{o}(r)d(r)IjIz=144> (1)
<k{o}(r)t(r)AjIz=144> (2)
<k{o}(r)t(r)Ij=14> (7)
<k{o}(r)t(r)IjIz=144> (1)
<k{o}(r)t(r)ij=13> (1)
<k{o}(r)tArIj=144> (1)
<k{o}(r)tArIjIz=1444> (1)
<k{o}(r)tRIj=144> (1)
<k{o}(r)tRij=143> (1)
<k{o}(r)tRj=14> (2)
<k{o}(r)trAj=14> (1)
<k{o}(r)trIj=14> (10)
<k{o}(r)trIjIs=144> (1)
<k{o}(r)trid=13> (1)
<k{o}(r)trij=13> (2)
<k{o}(r)trijIz=134> (1)
<k{o}(r)t{t}Ij=14> (1)
<k{o}(r){t}RjIz=144> (1)
<k{o}[r]trAj=14> (1)
<k{o}[r]trIch=14> (1)
<k{o}[r]trIj=14> (3)
<k{o}[r]{t}(r)Ij=14> (1)
<k{o}[r]{t}(r)IjIz=144> (1)
<k{o}r(tr)IjIz=144> (1)
<k{o}rt(r)Ij=14> (2)
<k{o}rt(r)ij=13> (1)
<k{o}rtRIj=144> (1)
<k{o}rtrIj=14> (24)
<k{o}rtrIjIz=144> (5)
<k{o}rtrij=13> (4)
<k{o}rtrijIz=134> (4)
<k{o}rt{r}Ajiz=143> (1)
<k{o}r{?}(r)Ij=14> (1)
<k{o}{r}d(r)Ij=14> (1)

<k{o}{r}d(r)ij=13> (1)
<k{o}{r}t(r)IchIz=144> (1)
<k{o}{r}trIj=14> (1)

022.5 L seesaw
No Response (86)
A   balance seesaw (1)
B   bandy billa (1)
C   banky bow (1)
D   boggum by (1)
E   hobby (1)
F   horse buggy (1)
J   jenny horse (1)
H   jigsaw (1)
I   Johnny mowers (1)
J   jump board (1)
K   riding board (1)
L   riding horse (5)
M   ridy-horse (29)
N   ridy-horsey (1)
O   rocking horse (1)
P   rocky horse (3)
Q   sawbuck (1)
R   sawhorse (8)
S   see board (1)
T   see horse (14)
U   seesaw (771)
V   seesaw horse (2)
W   seesawsy (1)
X   spring board (2)
Y   swing (1)
Z   teeter (2)
aa   teeter saw (1)
ab   teeter-totter (44)
ac   teeterboard (3)
ad   teetering plank (1)
ae   windmill (1)

022.6 L joggling board
No Response (700)
A   balance (1)
B   balance beam (1)
C   balance board (1)
D   bounce board (1)
E   bouncer board (1)
F   bouncing board (9)
G   bump board (1)
H   hobbyhorse (1)
I   joggling board (13)
J   jump board (27)
K   jump plank (1)
L   jumping board (24)
M   jumping horse (2)
N   jumping jack (1)
O   jumping plank (1)
P   limber board (1)
Q   limber jack (2)
R   springboard (47)
S   springer board (1)
T   swinging board (1)
U   teeter-totter (2)

V   tumblebuck (1)
022.7 L flying jenny
No Response (215)
A   carrousel (8)
B   fly jenny (1)
C   flying Dutchman (1)
D   flying horse (6)
E   flying-horse thing (1)
F   flying jenny (300)
G   flying mare (3)
H   ginning wheel (1)
I   go-around (1)
J   hobbyhorse (2)
K   horse (1)
L   jenny (7)
M   jenny stripe (1)
N   Maypole (1)
O   merry-go-ride (1)
P   merry-go-round (400)
Q   ocean well (1)
R   riding horse (2)
S   riding something (1)
T   ridy-horse (4)
U   ring around (1)
V   roundhouse board (1)
W   runaround (1)
X   see horse (1)
Y   seesaw (2)
Z   sky scooter (1)
aa   spin wheel (1)
ab   spinning board (1)
ac   spinning jenny (9)
ad   spinning saw (1)
ae   spinning wheel (5)
af   swing around (1)
ag   swinger (1)
ah   swinger-go-round (1)
ai   swinging horse (1)
aj   swinging jenny (1)
ak   tee-tottle (1)
al   teeter-totter (4)
am   turnaround (1)
an   turning horse (1)
ao   turnstyle (1)
ap   volador [S] (3)
aq   vomit wheel (1)
ar   wagon wheel (1)
as   wheel (3)
at   wheelhorse (1)
au   whirl jenny (1)
av   whirlaround (3)
aw   whirligig (21)
ax   whirlimajig (1)
ay   whirling dervish (1)
az   whirling horse (1)
ba   whirling seat (1)
bb   whirliwig (1)
bc   whirlybird (2)
bd   windmill (1)

be   wing jenny (1)

022.8 L seesawing

No Response (360)
A   balancing (1)
B   banky-boating (1)
C   bobbing up and down (1)
D   bouncing up and down (1)
E   get on the seesaw (1)
F   going up and down (12)
G   going up in the air (1)
H   gwine up and gwine down (1)
I   jigging up and down (1)
J   jumping (1)
K   on a seesaw (2)
L   out on the seesaw (1)
M   playing on a/the seesaw (9)
N   playing riding horses (2)
O   playing seesaw (9)
P   riding (it) (7)
Q   riding (the ridy horse) (1)
R   riding a rocky horse (2)
S   riding a/the sawhorse (1)
T   riding a/the seesaw (10)
U   riding on a/that ridy-horse (2)
V   riding on a seesaw (1)
W   riding the see horse (1)
X   rocking together (1)
Y   seesaw bouncing (1)
Z   seesawing (493)
aa   seesawing back and to (1)
ab   seesawing up and down (1)
ac   tee(ter)-tottering (1)
ad   teeter-tottering (5)
ae   teetering (5)
af   teetering and tottering (2)
ag   tottering (1)

022.9 L swing

No Response (181)
A   bag swing (9)
B   balance [F] (1)
C   board swing (1)
D   bouncing swing (1)
E   chain swing (1)
F   double swing (1)
G   grapevine swing (3)
H   hand swing (1)
I   homemade swing (1)
J   inner-tube swing (1)
K   monkey swing (1)
L   old-time swing (1)
M   picnic swing (2)
N   porch swing (1)
O   rope swing (12)
P   rubber tire (1)
Q   sack swing (2)
R   sandbag (1)
S   swing (692)
T   swing board (1)
U   swing seat (1)

V   swing set (3)
W   swing tire (1)
X   swinger (10)
Y   tire swing (11)
Z   tree swing (9)
aa   two-boy swing (1)
ab   vine (3)
ac   vine swing (1)
ad   yard swing (1)

023.1 L coal scuttle

No Response (272)
A   ash bucket (2)
B   ash hopper (1)
C   bucket (135)
D   charcoal bucket (1)
E   coal bin (3)
F   coal bucket (221)
G   coal hamper (1)
H   coal hod (17)
I   coal hopper (1)
J   coal pail (4)
K   coal pot (2)
L   coal scoop (2)
M   coal scut(tle) (1)
N   coal scuttle (139)
O   coal shuttle (14)
P   coal tub (1)
Q   coal vase (1)
R   galvanize bucket (1)
S   gutter (1)
T   hamper (1)
U   hod (12)
V   hopper (2)
W   little bucket (1)
X   pail (12)
Y   scutter (1)
Z   scuttle (175)
aa   scuttle bucket (4)
ab   shuttle (8)
ac   tin bucket (2)
ad   tub (1)
ae   vase (1)

023.2 L stovepipe/flue

No Response (199)
A   brick flue (4)
B   brick stove flue (1)
C   chimley (5)
D   chimley/chimney pipe (4)
E   chimney flue (1)
F   double flue (1)
G   draft (1)
H   elbow (5)
I   elbow pipe (1)
J   elbow stovepipe (1)
K   flue (133)
L   flue [=chimney] (44)
M   flue [=stovepipe] (30)
N   flue [pipe goes into] (101)
O   flue [on stove] (10)

P   flue connection (1)
Q   flue-like (1)
R   flue line (1)
S   flue pipe (2)
T   flume (1)
U   heater flue (1)
V   heater pipe (2)
W   kitchen flue (1)
X   metal pipe (1)
Y   piece of pipe (1)
Z   pipe (220)
aa   piping (4)
ab   smoke pipe (6)
ac   smokestack (8)
ad   stack (3)
ae   stove flue (16)
af   stove flue [=chimney] (7)
ag   stove flue [=stovepipe] (3)
ah   stove joint (3)
ai   stove smokestack (1)
aj   stove stack (1)
ak   stovepipe (462)
al   stovepiping (2)
am   vent (5)
an   vent pipe (2)
ao   ventilation pipe (1)

023.3 L wheelbarrow

No Response (85)
A   Arkansas steam shovel (1)
B   barrow (3)
C   brick barrow (1)
D   Chinese buggy (1)
E   colonel's car (1)
F   country Cadillac (1)
G   dolly (2)
H   garden [J-0] yard wheelbarrow (1)
I   Georgia buggy (9)
J   Georgia buggy [two wheels] (13)
K   Georgia buggy [=wheelbarrow] (12)
L   Georgia truck (1)
M   Georgia wagon (1)
N   hand truck (1)
O   iron-wheel wheelbarrow (1)
P   Mexican hydraulic lift (1)
Q   Schubkarren [G] (1)
R   truck (4)
S   two-handed truck (1)
T   two-wheel cart (1)
U   two-wheel wheelbarrow (1)
V   wheel (25)
W   wheel sow (1)
X   wheelbarrel (11)
Y   (wheel)barrow (1)
Z   wheelbar(row) (184)
aa   wheelbarrow (632)
ab   wheelbarrow car(rier) (1)

023.3 P wheelbarrow

No Response (112)
<v(h)eelbarA=134> (1)
<v(h)ilbarA=134> (1)
<w(h)ee[l]barA=134> (1)
<w(h)ee[l]berA=134> (2)
<w(h)eelba(r)Az=134> (1)
<w(h)eelba(rA)=13> (2)
<w(h)eelba[r](A)=13> (1)
<w(h)eelba[r](A)=31> (1)
<w(h)eelbarA=134> (48)
<w(h)eelbarAz=134> (2)
<w(h)eelbarL=134> (3)
<w(h)eelbaroe=123> (6)
<w(h)eelbaw[r](A)=13> (1)
<w(h)eelbawr(A)=13> (1)
<w(h)eelberA=134> (16)
<w(h)eelberAz=134> (1)
<w(h)eelbo[r](A)=13> (6)
<w(h)eelbo[r]A=134> (1)
<w(h)eelbor(A)=13> (7)
<w(h)eelborA=134> (14)
<w(h)eelborI=134> (1)
<w(h)eelborL=134> (1)
<w(h)eelboroe=123> (1)
<w(h)i(1)beroe=123> (1)
<w(h)i[1]berA=134> (1)
<w(h)i[1]borA=134> (1)
<w(h)ilbar(A)=13> (1)
<w(h)ilbarA=134> (3)
<w(h)ilbaroe=123> (3)
<w(h)ilberoe=123> (1)
<w(h)ilborAz=134> (1)
<w(h)ilborL=134> (1)
<whee(1)barA=134> (1)
<wheeLbor(A)=143> (1)
<whee[1]ba(rA)z=13> (1)
<whee[1]barA=134> (12)
<whee[1]barA=314> (2)
<whee[1]barAz=134> (1)
<whee[1]berA=134> (2)
<whee[1]beroe=123> (1)
<whee[1]beroez=123> (1)
<whee[1]bo[r](A)=13> (1)
<whee[1]bor(A)=13> (1)
<whee[1]borA=134> (3)
<wheelRba(rA)=143> (1)
<wheelRbor(A)=143> (1)
<wheelba(rA)=13> (2)
<wheelba[r](A)=13> (2)
<wheelba[r]A=134> (1)
<wheelbar(A)=13> (16)
<wheelbar(A)z=13> (1)
<wheelbarA=114> (1)
<wheelbarA=134> (254)
<wheelbarA=314> (4)
<wheelbarAz=134> (3)
<wheelbarI=134> (1)
<wheelbarL=134> (5)
<wheelbarLz=134> (1)

<wheelbarR=134> (1)
<wheelbaraw=123> (1)
<wheelbaroe=123> (7)
<wheelbaw(rA)=13> (2)
<wheelbaw[r](A)=13> (1)
<wheelbawr(A)=13> (6)
<wheelbawrA=134> (3)
<wheelbe[r](A)=13> (1)
<wheelber(A)=13> (1)
<wheelber(A)z=13> (1)
<wheelberA=134> (59)
<wheelberA=314> (1)
<wheelberAz=134> (2)
<wheelberL=314> (1)
<wheelberR=134> (1)
<wheelberoe=123> (4)
<wheelbo[r](A)=13> (32)
<wheelbor(A)=13> (102)
<wheelbor(A)z=13> (5)
<wheelborA=134> (104)
<wheelborA=314> (1)
<wheelborAz=134> (5)
<wheelborI=134> (1)
<wheelborIz=134> (1)
<wheelboroe=123> (1)
<wheelbur(A)=13> (1)
<wheelburA=134> (2)
<whi[1]ba(rA)=13> (1)
<whi[1]barA=134> (1)
<whi[1]ber(A)=13> (1)
<whilbarA=134> (28)
<whilbaroe=123> (3)
<whilbawr(A)=13> (1)
<whilberA=134> (3)
<whilberoe=123> (2)
<whilbo[r](A)=13> (1)
<whilbor(A)=13> (5)
<whilborA=114> (1)
<whilborA=134> (4)
<whilburA=134> (1)

023.4 L whetstone
No Response (134)
A Arkansas hard stone (1)
B Arkansas soft stone (1)
C Arkansas stone (2)
D butcher stone (1)
E carbon rock (1)
F Carborundum (1)
G Carborundum file (2)
H Carborundum stone (3)
I emerald board (1)
J emery (10)
K emery rock (19)
L emery sharpener (1)
M emery stone (7)
N eye stone (1)
O flint (3)
P flint rock (3)
Q flint stone (3)

R grind rock (1)
S grinding stone (2)
T hack cutter (1)
U hack whetter (1)
V hand rock (1)
W handstone (1)
X hard rock (1)
Y hone (55)
Z honing rock (2)
aa honing stone (3)
ab knife grinder (1)
ac knife rock (3)
ad knife sharpener (12)
ae knife stone (1)
af lathe (1)
ag limestone (1)
ah little rock (2)
ai little stone (1)
aj oil rock (4)
ak oilstone (12)
al piece of granite (1)
am piece of stone (1)
an pocket stone (1)
ao razor hone (5)
ap razor rock (6)
aq razor stone (2)
ar rock (46)
as rock sharpener (1)
at rockwhet (1)
au sandrock (2)
av sandstone (1)
aw sawing sharpener (1)
ax Schleifstein [G] (1)
ay scythe stone (1)
az scythes rock (1)
ba sharpen rock (2)
bb sharpen stone (1)
bc sharpener (9)
bd sharpening rock (4)
be sharpening stone (11)
bf sickle rock (1)
bg slab (1)
bh slip stone (1)
bi stone (60)
bj stone rock (2)
bk sweet stone (1)
bl whet (2)
bm whet knife (1)
bn whetrock (398)
bo whetstone (259)
bp whetstone rock (1)
bq whetter (1)
br whetting rock (1)
bs whetting stone (5)
bt whittle rock (1)
bu whittling rock (1)
bv whittling stone (2)
023.5 L grindstone
No Response (185)

A anvil wheel (1)
B ax grinder (6)
C ax sharpener (2)
D ax wheel (1)
E bed stone (1)
F big whetrock (2)
G big whetstone on a wheel (1)
H blade sharpen(er) (1)
I Carborundum stone (1)
J cement stone (1)
K emery (5)
L emery grindstone (1)
M emery rock (8)
N emery stone (8)
O emery wheel (38)
P grease wheel (1)
Q grind, a (1)
R grind rock (103)
S grind wheel (3)
T grinder (30)
U grinder stone (1)
V grinding mill (1)
W grinding rock (92)
X grinding stone (103)
Y grinding wheel (25)
Z grindstone (374)
aa ground machine (1)
ab honing wheel (1)
ac knife grinder (2)
ad knife sharpen(er) (1)
ae limestone (1)
af mill rock (1)
ag millstone (1)
ah oilstone (1)
ai rock (3)
aj sand-grit wheel (1)
ak sandrock (1)
al sharpen rock (1)
am sharpener (2)
an sharpening rock (2)
ao sharpening stone (4)
ap sharpening wheel (4)
aq sickle grinder (1)
ar soapstone (1)
as spinning stone (1)
at stone (19)
au stone grinder (2)
av stone wheel (3)
aw turning stone (1)
ax waterwheel (1)
ay wheel (8)
az wheel file (1)
ba whet wheel (1)
bb whetrock (6)
bc whetstone (4)

023.6 L car
No Response (45)
A A-Model (1)
B auto (22)

C auto buggy (2)
D automobile (355)
E car (833)
F char [F] (1)
G chariot (1)
H Chevrolet (1)
I Chrysler roadster (1)
J courtesy car (1)
K Dodge (1)
L Dort (1)
M dune buggy (1)
N electric car (1)
O family car (1)
P flip-flop (1)
Q flivver (1)
R Ford (1)
S Ford automobile (1)
T Ford car (1)
U gas burner (1)
V heap (1)
W horseless buggy (2)
X hot rod (1)
Y Hup automobile (1)
Z jalopy (5)
aa jeep (3)
ab jeep car (1)
ac jigger (1)
ad jitney (2)
ae John Henry (1)
af Jordan automobile (1)
ag limousine (3)
ah machine (7)
ai Model-A (1)
aj Model-A coupe (1)
ak Model-T (2)
al Model-T car (1)
am Model-T Ford (2)
an motor (1)
ao motor buggy (2)
ap motor vehicle (1)
aq motorcar (1)
ar passenger car (1)
as rattletrap Ford (1)
at ride (2)
au riding car (1)
av roadster (1)
aw sedan (1)
ax station wagon (2)
ay T-Model (8)
az T-Model car (2)
ba T-Model Ford (2)
bb three-wheel car (1)
bc Tin Lizzie (2)
bd Tin-Pan Lizzie (1)
be touring car (1)
bf touring Ford (1)
bg vehicle (21)
bh wheels (5)

023.6 P car

{aw} unrounded onset
{o} low-back
{r} weakly retroflex
No Response (85)
<ka[r]> (1)
<karz> (1)
<kaw(r)> (17)
<kaw(r)z> (3)
<kaw[r]> (23)
<kawr> (32)
<kawrz> (10)
<kaw{r}> (10)
<kaw{r}z> (3)
<ka{r}> (1)
<ko(r)> (39)
<ko(r)z> (6)
<ko[r]> (83)
<ko[r]z> (6)
<kor> (289)
<korz> (51)
<ko{r}> (76)
<ko{r}z> (4)
<ko{r}zh> (1)
<kyo(r)> (1)
<kyo[r]> (1)
<k{aw}(r)> (2)
<k{aw}r> (1)
<k{aw}{r}> (1)
<k{o}(r)> (24)
<k{o}(r)z> (1)
<k{o}[r]> (88)
<k{o}[r]z> (6)
<k{o}r> (112)
<k{o}rz> (16)
<k{o}{r}> (15)
<k{o}{r}z> (4)

023.6 S car
No Response (0)
|PAAmaa| (1)
|PACmea| (1)
|PACmej| (1)
|PAEmej| (1)
|PAGmej| (1)
|PAImea| (1)
|PCAmaa| (1)
|PCAmaj| (2)
|PCAmea| (7)
|PCC| (1)
|PCImaj| (1)
|PDAmnj| (1)
|PKA| (2)
|QFCmea| (1)
|QMCmaj| (1)
|SAAmajmea| (1)
|SAAmea| (8)
|SAAmej| (8)
|SAB| (6)
|SABmaa| (1)
|SABmaj| (6)

|SABmea| (29)
|SABmej| (9)
|SADmaa| (1)
|SADmea| (2)
|SAE| (4)
|SAEmaa| (3)
|SAEmaj| (20)
|SAEmajmea| (1)
|SAEmea| (107)
|SAEmej| (15)
|SAEtaa| (4)
|SAEtaj| (1)
|SAEtca| (1)
|SAFmaj| (1)
|SAFmea| (7)
|SAFmej| (1)
|SAG| (1)
|SAGmaa| (2)
|SAGmaj| (5)
|SAGmea| (20)
|SAGmej| (1)
|SBAmej| (1)
|SBBmej| (2)
|SCA| (2)
|SCAjjjmea| (1)
|SCAmaj| (5)
|SCAmajmea| (1)
|SCAmea| (28)
|SCAmej| (5)
|SCAmpa| (1)
|SCApca| (1)
|SCB| (2)
|SCBmaa| (3)
|SCBmaj| (6)
|SCBmea| (16)
|SCBmej| (1)
|SCDmaj| (1)
|SCDmea| (5)
|SCE| (6)
|SCEmaa| (12)
|SCEmaj| (25)
|SCEmajmea| (2)
|SCEmea| (127)
|SCEmej| (12)
|SCEsam| (1)
|SCEtadmea| (1)
|SCFmaj| (2)
|SCFmea| (3)
|SCG| (1)
|SCGmaa| (4)
|SCGmaj| (4)
|SCGmea| (23)
|SDFmdj| (1)
|SFBmaj| (1)
|SFEmaa| (1)
|SFEmea| (2)
|SFEmfj| (2)
|SGT| (1)
|SKAmdj| (1)

|SKB| (1)
|SKEmna| (1)
|SKGmna| (1)
|SMEmaj| (1)
|SMGmaj| (1)
|SMGmea| (3)
|SOE| (1)
|SXEmnj| (1)
|TAA| (1)
|TAAmaa| (1)
|TAAmaj| (2)
|TAAmea| (12)
|TAAmej| (1)
|TABmea| (2)
|TAD| (4)
|TADmaa| (4)
|TADmaj| (24)
|TADmajmea| (1)
|TADmea| (37)
|TADmej| (2)
|TADpanmea| (1)
|TADtabmea| (1)
|TADtafmea| (1)
|TADtfjmea| (1)
|TAFmea| (6)
|TAFmej| (1)
|TAFmla| (1)
|TAFtfa| (1)
|TAFtfj| (1)
|TAGmea| (1)
|TCA| (5)
|TCAmaa| (1)
|TCAmaj| (17)
|TCAmea| (20)
|TCAmfj| (1)
|TCBmaa| (1)
|TCBmea| (1)
|TCD| (4)
|TCDmaa| (10)
|TCDmaj| (22)
|TCDmea| (33)
|TCDmej| (2)
|TCDtff| (1)
|TCEmaj| (1)
|TCFmaa| (1)
|TCFmea| (3)
|TCGmaa| (1)
|TFAmaj| (2)
|TFAmea| (4)
|TFB| (1)
|TFBmaj| (6)
|TFBmea| (2)
|TFBqfjmea| (1)
|TFBtaj| (1)
|TFDmaj| (7)
|TFDmajmea| (1)
|TFDmea| (5)
|TFDqfomea| (1)
|TFDtfbmea| (1)

|TFFmea| (1)
|TFFtad| (1)
|TKAmna| (1)
|TMA| (3)
|TMAmaa| (1)
|TMAmaj| (3)
|TMAmea| (11)
|TMBmaa| (2)
|TMBmaj| (1)
|TMBmea| (3)
|TMBqfc| (1)
|TMBtaamaj| (1)
|TMBtab| (1)
|TMD| (1)
|TMDmaj| (1)
|TMDmea| (5)
|TMF| (1)
|TMFmaa| (1)
|TMFmea| (1)
|TMFqfl| (1)

023.7 G grease

  <!> infinitive
  <&> present 3rd singular
  <@> present participle
  <*> preterit
  <#> past participle
  {?} glottal
No Response (196)
<!greedh> (4)
<!grees> (53)
<!greesh> (1)
<!greez> (527)
<!greezh> (1)
<!griz> (1)
<&greezIz=14> (1)
<@greesN=14> (2)
<@greezN=14> (16)
<@greezNG=14> (3)
<@gree{?}N=14> (1)
<*gree(z)d> (1)
<*greedh> (1)
<*greedhd> (1)
<*grees> (1)
<*greesd> (4)
<*greesh> (1)
<*greest> (27)
<*greez> (22)
<*greezd> (346)
<*greezt> (2)
<*grezd> (1)
<*kreest> (1)
<#greedh> (2)
<#grees> (1)
<#greest> (6)
<#greez> (5)
<#greezd> (55)
<#grizd> (1)

023.8 P greasy
No Response (170)

<greesI=14> (128)
<greesee=13> (1)
<greezI=14> (628)
<greezee=13> (3)

024.1 P oil
{ie}   centered onset
{oy}   inglide
{r}   weakly retroflex
{?}   glottal
No Response (56)
<awL=14> (1)
<awl> (16)
<awrl> (3)
<awwL=14> (1)
<aw{r}l> (3)
<oewL=14> (1)
<oewel=13> (1)
<oewil=13> (1)
<orl> (1)
<oy(1)> (12)
<oy[1]> (7)
<oyl> (331)
<oyyL=14> (3)
<urL=14> (1)
<u{r}l> (2)
<{?}awl> (1)
<{?}oy[1]> (1)
<{?}oyl> (7)
<{?}{oy}[1]> (2)
<{?}{oy}l> (12)
<{ie}l> (8)
<{ie}ld> (1)
<{oy}(1)> (3)
<{oy}[1]> (19)
<{oy}l> (536)
<{oy}lee=13> (1)
<{oy}yL=14> (1)

024.1 S oil
No Response (6)
|J2Cmdj| (1)
|J2Hmdj| (1)
|JJCeaamaj| (2)
|JJCeac| (1)
|JJCeacmaj| (1)
|JJCmab| (1)
|JJDeaj| (1)
|JJDmaj| (1)
|JJH| (1)
|JJHeaa| (2)
|JJHeaacba| (1)
|JJHeab| (1)
|JJHeaj| (5)
|JJHeal| (2)
|JJHmab| (1)
|JJHmaj| (5)
|JJHmajcbj| (1)
|JJHmak| (1)
|JSCeaa| (2)
|JSCeaamaa| (1)

|JSCeajmaa| (1)
|JSCeajmadcba| (1)
|JSCkaa| (1)
|JSCkae| (1)
|JSCmaa| (2)
|JSCmab| (4)
|JSCmaj| (1)
|JSCmak| (1)
|JSHeaj| (2)
|JSHmaj| (1)
|JSHmajcba| (1)
|JSImaa| (1)
|JSU| (1)
|JSUeaa| (1)
|JSUffamaa| (1)
|JSUffjmaacba| (1)
|JSUkaa| (1)
|JSUmaj| (1)
|JSUmajcba| (1)
|JSZmaj| (1)
|LCAeej| (1)
|LMDmaj| (1)
|PAImab| (1)
|QAAmaa| (1)
|QACeaa| (1)
|QACmaa| (1)
|QADeal| (1)
|QADmaj| (1)
|QAF| (1)
|QAFeac| (1)
|QCCjjbmaj| (1)
|QCUmaj| (1)
|QFAeaa| (7)
|QFAeaaamaj| (2)
|QFAead| (1)
|QFAeaj| (11)
|QFAeak| (1)
|QFAeal| (4)
|QFAjjbmak| (1)
|QFAmaa| (2)
|QFAmab| (3)
|QFAmaj| (6)
|QFAmea| (1)
|QFAqff| (1)
|QFBdab| (1)
|QFBeaa| (58)
|QFBeaacba| (1)
|QFBeaamaj| (4)
|QFBeab| (3)
|QFBeabmaj| (1)
|QFBeac| (20)
|QFBeacmaj| (4)
|QFBead| (1)
|QFBeaj| (36)
|QFBeajcba| (1)
|QFBeal| (4)
|QFBefj| (1)
|QFBefjmaa| (1)
|QFBjjamaj| (1)

|QFBjjdmaj| (1)
|QFBkab| (5)
|QFBmaa| (46)
|QFBmab| (70)
|QFBmaj| (55)
|QFBmajcba| (1)
|QFBmak| (18)
|QFBmeb| (1)
|QFCabemaa| (1)
|QFCeaa| (14)
|QFCeaamaj| (2)
|QFCeab| (2)
|QFCeac| (5)
|QFCead| (1)
|QFCeaj| (7)
|QFCkaa| (2)
|QFCkab| (4)
|QFCkaj| (1)
|QFCkak| (1)
|QFCmaa| (29)
|QFCmab| (11)
|QFCmaf| (1)
|QFCmaj| (21)
|QFCmak| (1)
|QFCqfa| (1)
|QFCqfaeaa| (1)
|QFCqfb| (1)
|QFCqfbcbj| (1)
|QFCqfbeaa| (1)
|QFCqfbeaj| (4)
|QFCqfbeal| (6)
|QFCqfbmaj| (1)
|QFD| (1)
|QFDbba| (1)
|QFDeaa| (1)
|QFDeaj| (7)
|QFDmaa| (1)
|QFDmaj| (8)
|QFFeaa| (1)
|QFFeaj| (7)
|QFFeal| (1)
|QFFmab| (1)
|QFFmaj| (4)
|QFFmak| (1)
|QFGmaj| (1)
|QFHeaj| (2)
|QFHmab| (3)
|QFHmaj| (4)
|QFHmak| (1)
|QFI| (1)
|QFSeaa| (1)
|QFTmaj| (1)
|QFUkak| (1)
|QFVeaj| (1)
|QFXeaj| (1)
|QFXmaj| (1)
|QFZefj| (1)
|QMAdaa| (1)
|QMAeaa| (11)

|QMAeac| (1)
|QMAead| (1)
|QMAeaj| (18)
|QMAeal| (3)
|QMAmaa| (1)
|QMAmab| (1)
|QMAmaj| (11)
|QMAmajcba| (1)
|QMAmak| (1)
|QMBeaa| (14)
|QMBeaamaj| (2)
|QMBeac| (2)
|QMBeaj| (14)
|QMBeal| (6)
|QMBmaa| (21)
|QMBmab| (14)
|QMBmaj| (32)
|QMBmajcba| (2)
|QMBmajcbj| (1)
|QMBmak| (6)
|QMBmao| (1)
|QMC| (1)
|QMCeaa| (6)
|QMCeac| (3)
|QMCeaj| (3)
|QMCmaa| (15)
|QMCmab| (1)
|QMCmaj| (11)
|QMCmea| (1)
|QMDdan| (1)
|QMDeaa| (2)
|QMDeaj| (6)
|QMDeam| (1)
|QMDmaj| (8)
|QMDmak| (1)
|QMFeaa| (3)
|QMFeaj| (4)
|QMFmaa| (1)
|QMFmaj| (4)
|QMFmajcba| (1)
|QMFmak| (1)
|QMHeaj| (1)
|QMHmab| (1)
|QMHmaj| (6)
|QMHqfbeaj| (1)
|QMSbbj| (1)
|QMSeaj| (1)
|QMSjjjcba| (1)
|QMSmaj| (1)
|QMSmajcba| (1)
|QMTeaa| (1)
|QMTeaj| (1)
|QMXeaj| (1)
|QXAedjmdacha| (1)
|RAGqfamaj| (1)
|RCEmej| (1)
|RMAmaj| (1)
|TABmaa| (2)
|TABqfbeaa| (1)

|TABqfbkaj| (1)
|TCA| (1)
|TCAeaa| (1)
|TCAeajmaj| (1)
|TCAmaa| (3)
|TCSmaj| (1)
|TCTmaj| (1)
|TFBeaa| (1)
|TFBmaa| (3)
|TFBqfa| (1)
|TFDqfamaa| (1)
|TFDqfb| (1)
|TKAmdacha| (1)
|TKSmda| (1)
|TMAeaamcacga| (1)
|TMBmaa| (1)
|TMSeaa| (2)
|TMSmaa| (1)
|qfcQMA| (2)
|qfcQMBmaj| (3)
|qfcQMBmak| (2)

024.2 L kerosene

No Response (48)
A   alcohol (1)
B   caffeine (1)
C   carbon oil (1)
D   coal oil (457)
E   coalosene (1)
F   fuel (1)
G   fuel oil (5)
H   gasoline (2)
I   insurance oil (2)
J   K oil (4)
K   kerosene (630)
L   kerosene oil (49)
M   lamp oil (31)
N   mineral spirits (1)
O   oil (47)
P   petroleum (1)
Q   rock oil (1)
R   shoo-ants oil (1)
S   whale oil (7)
T   white gas (1)

024.3 L makeshift lamp

No Response (392)
A   African lamp (1)
B   all-night-long torch (1)
C   black fire pot (1)
D   bottle (3)
E   bottle lamp (13)
F   bottle light (6)
G   bottle wick (1)
H   burner (1)
I   camp light (1)
J   cloth torch (1)
K   coal-oil bottle (2)
L   coal-oil lamp (3)
M   coal-oil torch (1)
N   fire jack (1)

O   flambeau (151)
P   flambeau deal (1)
Q   flambeau light (2)
R   flambeau pot (1)
S   flamdozier (1)
T   flame (1)
U   flamethrower (1)
V   flare (10)
W   fusee (1)
X   glut (1)
Y   grease lamp (20)
Z   grease light (5)
aa   hand lamp (1)
ab   headlight (2)
ac   homemade lamp (8)
ad   homemade lantern (1)
ae   homemade light (1)
af   homemade torch (1)
ag   hunting lamp (1)
ah   jack lamping (1)
ai   jar lamp (1)
aj   jumbo (1)
ak   kerosene candle (1)
al   kerosene lamp (2)
am   kerosene torch (1)
an   lamp (44)
ao   lamp jug (1)
ap   lantern (37)
aq   light (12)
ar   lighter (1)
as   lighter knot (1)
at   lighter-wood torch (1)
au   lighterd torch (1)
av   makeshift [n.] (3)
aw   makeshift coal-oil lamp (1)
ax   makeshift lamp (1)
ay   makeshift light (1)
az   mantle (1)
ba   mechon [S] (1)
bb   nigger rigging (1)
bc   night-light (1)
bd   oil lamp (1)
be   pine light (1)
bf   pine torch (7)
bg   pine-knot torch (1)
bh   pitch pot (1)
bi   rag lamp (3)
bj   rag smoke (1)
bk   rag torch (1)
bl   smoke pot (4)
bm   smudge (1)
bn   smudge pot (22)
bo   smudge torch (1)
bp   splinter light (1)
bq   splinters (1)
br   splinters of fat pine (1)
bs   tallow lamp (1)
bt   torch (164)
bu   torch lamp (1)

bv   torchlight (2)
bw   wick (2)
bx   wick lamp (3)

024.4 P tube
{ue}   central
No Response (159)
<chewb> (1)
<chueb> (1)
<chy{ue}b> (3)
<ch{ue}b> (2)
<teeb> (1)
<tew(b)> (2)
<tewb> (311)
<tewbs> (1)
<tewbz> (18)
<toob> (2)
<tueb> (71)
<tuebz> (2)
<ty{ue}(b)> (2)
<ty{ue}b> (200)
<ty{ue}bz> (5)
<t{ue}(b)> (1)
<t{ue}b> (136)
<t{ue}bs> (1)
<t{ue}bz> (5)
<t{ue}bzh> (1)
<t{ue}p> (1)

024.5 P launch
{aw}   unrounded onset
{o}   low-back
No Response (363)
<lanch> (2)
<lanchNG=14> (1)
<lants> (1)
<law[n]ch> (2)
<lawnch> (255)
<lawnchAz=14> (1)
<lawnchIz=14> (2)
<lawnchN=14> (16)
<lawnchNG=14> (6)
<lawnchd> (1)
<lawnchj> (1)
<lawncht> (5)
<lawnj> (1)
<lawnsh> (2)
<liench> (1)
<lo[n]sh> (1)
<loench> (2)
<loens> (1)
<lonch> (145)
<lonchIz=14> (1)
<lonchN=14> (9)
<lonchNG=14> (5)
<loncht> (5)
<lonts> (2)
<lownch> (2)
<loynch> (1)
<loyncht> (1)
<lunch> (5)

<l{aw}nch> (54)
<l{aw}nchN=14> (2)
<l{aw}nchNG=14> (1)
<l{o}nch> (19)
<l{o}nchN=14> (1)
<l{o}ncht> (1)

024.6 L rowboat
No Response (108)
A   aluminum boat (13)
B   aluminum fishing boat (3)
C   aluminum flat-bottom boat (1)
D   bateau (118)
E   blunt-nose boat (1)
F   boat (206)
G   box boat (1)
H   butt head (1)
I   butt-head boat (1)
J   butt-headed boat (1)
K   canoe (220)
L   canoe boat (2)
M   canoe type (1)
N   canoe-type boat (1)
O   cayuco [S] (1)
P   cypress boat (5)
Q   cypress skiff (1)
R   D-line skiff (1)
S   dinghy (9)
T   double hull (1)
U   double-ended pirogue (1)
V   double-ender (5)
W   dugout (17)
X   dugout boat (1)
Y   fish boat (3)
Z   fishing boat (111)
aa   fishing rig (1)
ab   flat [n.] (3)
ac   flat bottom (8)
ad   flat johnboat (1)
ae   flat-bedded boat (1)
af   flat-bottom aluminum boat (3)
ag   flat-bottom bateau (1)
ah   flat-bottom boat (45)
ai   flat-bottom fishing boat (1)
aj   flat-bottom homemade boat (1)
ak   flat-bottom rowboat (1)
al   flatboat (22)
am   freshwater boat (1)
an   freshwater fishing boat (1)
ao   gopher (1)
ap   hand boat (1)
aq   homemade boat (5)
ar   homemade cypress boat (1)
as   hook-and-line boat (1)
at   Indian canoe (1)
au   joe boat (4)
av   john (2)
aw   johnboat (43)
ax   kayak (1)
ay   Lafitte skiff (3)

az   lifeboat (1)
ba   log boat (1)
bb   long john (1)
bc   model hull (1)
bd   oar boat (5)
be   one-man boat (1)
bf   open boat (2)
bg   paddle boat (34)
bh   paddling boat (3)
bi   pirogue (80)
bj   pirogue boat (1)
bk   plank boat (1)
bl   plywood (boat) (1)
bm   pram (1)
bn   pulling skiff (1)
bo   push boat (1)
bp   round-bottom boat (2)
bq   rowboat (269)
br   rowing boat (1)
bs   schooner (1)
bt   shallow-draft boat (1)
bu   sharp-nose boat (1)
bv   skiff (139)
bw   skiff boat (8)
bx   skiffer (1)
by   slip (1)
bz   spike boat (1)
ca   square-pointed boat (1)
cb   triple hull (1)
cc   tub (1)
cd   two-man boat (2)
ce   V boat (1)
cf   V hull (1)
cg   V Schale [G] (1)
ch   V type (1)
ci   V-bottom boat (1)
cj   water boat (1)
ck   wood boat (5)
cl   wooden boat (24)
cm   wooden-bottom boat (1)

024.7 G aux. verb + going
No Response (423)
A   he/she/it ain't going (4)
B   he/she/it is/isn't going (3)
C   he/she/it was/wasn't going (51)
D   he/she/it were going (1)
E   he/she/it [X-0] going (43)
F   he/she/it [X-0] gwine (1)
G   he/she/it's been going (1)
H   he/she/it's going (99)
I   I ain't going (16)
J   I ain't gwine (1)
K   I am going (29)
L   I be[V-q] going (1)
M   I was/wasn't going (50)
N   I were going [subjunctive] (1)
O   I [X-0] been going (1)
P   I [X-0] going (10)
Q   I'm going (246)

R I'm gwine (1)
S I's going (4)
T they ain't going (1)
U they are/aren't going (30)
V they be[V-q] going (1)
W they is going (1)
X they was/wasn't going (11)
Y they were/weren't going (17)
Z they [X-0] going (50)
aa they [X-0] gwine (1)
ab they're going (17)
ac they's going (7)
ad we ain't going (1)
ae we are/aren't going (44)
af we had been going (1)
ag we was/wasn't going (5)
ah we were/weren't going (16)
ai we [X-0] going (39)
aj we're going (33)
ak we's going (2)
al you ain't going (4)
am you are/aren't going (2)
an you was/wasn't going (14)
ao you were/weren't going (10)
ap you [X-0] going (67)
aq you're going (14)
ar you's going (2)

024.8 G am I/are they (going)

No Response (806)
A ain't I (2)
B (a)m I (1)
C am I (57)
D am I not (1)
E are they (24)
F are we (2)
G are you (22)
H aren't I (1)
I aren't they (1)
J is I (1)
K is I'm (1)
L is she (2)
M is you (1)
N [X-0] we (2)
O [X-0] you (10)

024.9 G inceptives

No Response (648)
A commence to [+ v.] (1)
B get a-[+ v.] (1)
C get to [+ v.] (85)
D go to [+ v.] (207)
E start to [+ v.] (20)
F take to [+ v.] (1)

025.1 G here are (your clothes)

No Response (501)
A here are (180)
B here is (21)
C here [C-0] (27)
D here's (126)

025.2 G there are (many people)

No Response (474)
A there ain't (7)
B there are/were (160)
C there hain't (1)
D there is/was (142)
E there [C-0] (21)
F there're (1)
G there's (178)
H [T-0] ain't (1)
I [T-0] was (1)

025.3 G I am not (going to hurt you)

No Response (438)
A I ain't (231)
B I am not (23)
C I hain't (2)
D I [X-0] not (2)
E I'm not (227)

025.4 G am I not?

No Response (750)
A ain't I? (33)
B am I not? (39)
C aren't I? (82)
D hain't I? (1)

025.5 G we were (going anyway)

No Response (586)
A we was/wasn't/is/isn't (104)
B we were/weren't/are/aren't (219)
C we [X-0] (12)
D we're (11)
E we's (10)

025.6 G those were (the good-old days)

No Response (547)
A that was [+ pl.] (11)
B that's [+ pl.] (4)
C them are (3)
D them be[V-q] (1)
E them is (7)
F them was (21)
G them were (2)
H them [C-0] (3)
I them's (12)
J these are (15)
K these is (3)
L these was (3)
M these were (3)
N this is [+ pl.] (1)
O those are (32)
P those is (1)
Q those was (2)
R those were (109)

025.7 G (it wasn't) I

No Response (422)
A I (49)
B me (245)

025.8 G deletions

No Deletions (62)
B [B-0] deleted adverb (9)
C [C-0] deleted copula (413)
D [D-0] deleted article (447)

J [J-0] deleted conjunction (354)
M [M-0] deleted pronoun (205)
N [N-0] deleted noun (3)
P [P-0] deleted preposition (627)
R [R-0] deleted relative pronoun (257)
T [T-0] deleted dummy subject ["there"] (33)
V [V-0] deleted verb (29)
X [X-0] deleted auxiliary (696)

026.1 G be [finite]

No Response (797)
A be[V-p] (56)
B be[V-q] (70)
C bees (28)
D beeses (1)

026.2 L sample

No Response (231)
A bit (1)
B block (2)
C color sample (2)
D example (9)
E fabric sample (3)
F fabric scrap (1)
G guide (3)
H match [n.] (3)
I match piece (1)
J matching scrap (1)
K material (2)
L patch (9)
M patch of cloth (3)
N pattern (2)
O pattern patch (1)
P piece (6)
Q piece of (your) cloth (6)
R piece of goods (2)
S piece of material (1)
T piece to see by (1)
U quilt scraps (1)
V reference (1)
W remnant (7)
X sample (592)
Y sample of the material (1)
Z sampler (1)
aa sampling [n.] (1)
ab scrap (56)
ac scrap of a rag (1)
ad scrap of cloth (3)
ae scrap of material (4)
af scrap piece (4)
ag scrap sample (1)
ah something [P-0] go by (1)
ai splotch (1)
aj square (3)
ak square piece of cloth (1)
al swatch (42)
am swatch of cloth (7)
an swatch of material (2)
ao switch (1)

ap   test [n.] (1)
aq   trimming (1)
ar   wad (1)

026.2 P sample
{a}   upglide
{L}   labial
{R}   weakly retroflex
No Response (274)
<sa(m)pL=14> (2)
<sa[m]pL=14> (18)
<saimpL=14> (3)
<saimp[L]=14> (1)
<sambL=14> (1)
<samb[L]=14> (1)
<samb[L]z=14> (1)
<samp(L)> (1)
<sampL=14> (516)
<sampLz=14> (7)
<samp[L]=14> (24)
<sampaw(l)=13> (1)
<sampool=13> (1)
<sampul=13> (2)
<samp{L}=14> (28)
<samp{R}=14> (1)
<sempL=14> (11)
<semp[L]=14> (3)
<s{a}mpL=14> (19)
<s{a}mp[L]=14> (1)
<zampL=14> (1)

026.3A P pretty
{i}   central
{r}   labial
{t}   flap
No Response (289)
<p(r)i{t}I=14> (1)
<p(r)oor{t}I=14> (1)
<p(r)ootI=14> (13)
<p(r)oo{t}A=14> (1)
<p(r)oo{t}I=14> (3)
<p(r)utI=14> (6)
<p(r)u{t}I=14> (1)
<poortI=14> (23)
<por{t}I=14> (1)
<pretI=14> (9)
<pre{t}I=14> (3)
<pridI=14> (1)
<printI=14> (1)
<pritI=14> (229)
<pritee=13> (1)
<pri{t}I=14> (45)
<prootI=14> (30)
<proo{t}I=14> (4)
<prurtI=14> (7)
<prutI=14> (12)
<pru{r}tI=14> (1)
<pru{t}I=14> (1)
<pr{i}dI=14> (1)
<pr{i}tI=14> (44)
<pr{i}tee=13> (1)

<pr{i}ttI=14> (1)
<pr{i}{t}I=14> (8)
<purdI=14> (5)
<purdee=13> (1)
<purt(I)> (1)
<purtI=14> (134)
<purtee=13> (1)
<pur{t}I=14> (15)
<pu{r}tI=14> (14)
<pwitI=14> (2)
<pwootI=14> (1)
<pwoo{t}I=14> (1)
<p{i}r{t}I=14> (1)
<p{r}i(t)I=14> (1)
<p{r}itI=14> (49)
<p{r}i{t}I=14> (2)
<p{r}ootI=14> (14)
<p{r}utI=14> (4)
<p{r}{i}tI=14> (9)
<p{r}{i}{t}I=14> (1)

026.3B P prettier
p{r}   labial
u{r}   weakly retroflex
{i}   central
{R}   weakly retroflex
{t}   flap
No Response (554)
<p(r)ootIR=144> (1)
<p(r)ootI[R]=144> (5)
<p(r)ootI{R}=144> (1)
<p(r)ootee[R]=134> (1)
<p(r)ooti[R]=134> (2)
<p(r)oo{t}I[R]=144> (2)
<p(r)utI[R]=144> (2)
<p(r){i}tIR=144> (1)
<poortIR=144> (2)
<poortI[R]=144> (1)
<poortI{R}=144> (1)
<pretIR=144> (2)
<pretI[R]=144> (2)
<pretI{R}=144> (3)
<preti[R]=134> (1)
<pridI[R]=144> (1)
<pridiR=134> (1)
<pridiyR=134> (1)
<pritIR=144> (58)
<pritI[R]=144> (35)
<pritIur=143> (3)
<pritIur=341> (1)
<pritIu{r}=143> (1)
<pritIyR=144> (1)
<pritI{R}=144> (17)
<priteeR=134> (1)
<pritee[R]=134> (1)
<pritiR=134> (34)
<priti[R]=134> (9)
<pritiu{r}=231> (1)
<pritiyR=134> (2)
<priti{R}=134> (1)

<prittIr{R}=144> (1)
<prittIur=143> (1)
<pri{t}IR=144> (5)
<pri{t}I[R]=144> (7)
<pri{t}Iu[r]=143> (1)
<pri{t}Iur=143> (1)
<pri{t}Iur=241> (1)
<pri{t}IyR=144> (1)
<pri{t}I{R}=144> (2)
<pri{t}iR=134> (3)
<pri{t}i{R}=134> (1)
<prootIR=144> (2)
<prootI[R]=144> (6)
<prootI{R}=144> (5)
<prootiR=134> (1)
<proo{t}IR=144> (2)
<proo{t}I[R]=144> (2)
<prurtIR=144> (1)
<prutIR=144> (2)
<prutI[R]=144> (1)
<prutiR=134> (2)
<pruti[R]=134> (1)
<pru{r}tIR=144> (1)
<pru{r}tI{R}=144> (1)
<pru{t}I[R]=144> (1)
<pr{i}(ti)[R]=14> (1)
<pr{i}tIR=144> (3)
<pr{i}tI[R]=144> (5)
<pr{i}tIur=143> (1)
<pr{i}tIur=341> (1)
<pr{i}tI{R}=144> (6)
<pr{i}tiR=134> (3)
<pr{i}ti[R]=134> (5)
<pr{i}{t}I{R}=144> (1)
<pu[r]tIR=144> (1)
<purdIR=144> (1)
<purdI[R]=144> (1)
<purdiR=134> (1)
<purtIR=144> (10)
<purtI[R]=144> (2)
<purtI{R}=144> (4)
<purteeR=134> (2)
<purtiR=134> (16)
<purti[R]=134> (2)
<purti{R}=134> (2)
<pur{t}I{R}=144> (1)
<pur{t}iR=134> (1)
<pu{r}dIu{r}=143> (1)
<pu{r}tIR=144> (8)
<pu{r}tI[R]=144> (5)
<pu{r}tI{R}=144> (1)
<pu{r}tiR=134> (3)
<pu{r}ti[R]=134> (2)
<pu{r}{t}Iu{r}=143> (1)
<pwitI{R}=144> (1)
<p{r}it(i)R=14> (1)
<p{r}itIR=144> (5)
<p{r}itI[R]=144> (3)
<p{r}itI{R}=144> (1)

<p{r}iteeR=134> (1)
<p{r}itiR=134> (2)
<p{r}iti[R]=134> (6)
<p{r}iti{R}=134> (1)
<p{r}i{t}I[R]=144> (1)
<p{r}ootI[R]=144> (1)
<p{r}utI[R]=144> (1)
<p{r}uti[R]=134> (1)
<p{r}{i}tI[R]=144> (3)
<p{r}{i}tI{R}=144> (1)
<p{r}{i}ti[R]=134> (1)

026.4 L apron

No Response (111)
A   allover apron (1)
B   apron (794)
C   bib apron (4)
D   cobbler (1)
E   cook apron (2)
F   cooking apron (1)
G   coverall apron (1)
H   dustcoat (1)
I   duster (4)
J   gathered apron (1)
K   hip apron (1)
L   hostess (1)
M   hostess's apron (1)
N   housecoat (15)
O   (Mother) Hubbard apron (1)
P   pinafore (1)
Q   smock (19)
R   stain apron (1)
S   tea apron (1)
T   utility (1)
U   waist apron (3)
V   wraparound (1)

026.4 P apron

{ai}   lowered/lax onset
{R}   weakly retroflex
{r}   weakly retroflex
No Response (115)
<aib{R}nz=14> (1)
<aip(r)N=14> (67)
<aip(r)Nz=14> (3)
<aip(r)[N]=14> (4)
<aipR(n)=14> (2)
<aipR[n]=14> (1)
<aipRn=14> (157)
<aipRnz=14> (11)
<aipoo{r}n=13> (1)
<aippRn=14> (1)
<aipprN=14> (1)
<aiprN=14> (406)
<aiprNs=14> (1)
<aiprNz=14> (23)
<aiprRn=14> (2)
<aipr[N]=14> (8)
<aipren=13> (1)
<aiprin=13> (1)
<aiproon=13> (1)

<aipr{R}n=14> (15)
<aipurn=13> (1)
<aip{R}(n)=14> (1)
<aip{R}n=14> (44)
<aip{R}nz=14> (1)
<apRn=14> (3)
<aprN=14> (1)
<aprNz=14> (1)
<ep(r)N=14> (1)
<eprN=14> (6)
<haiprN=14> (1)
<naipR(n)=14> (1)
<naipRn=14> (4)
<naiprN=14> (7)
<naipr[N]=14> (1)
<naiprun=13> (1)
<naip{R}n=14> (1)
<{ai}p(r)N=14> (4)
<{ai}pRn=14> (6)
<{ai}pprN=14> (1)
<{ai}prN=14> (17)
<{ai}prin=13> (1)
<{ai}prun=13> (1)
<{ai}p{R}(n)=14> (1)
<{a}ip(r)N=14> (1)

026.5A P pen

No Response (182)
<bin> (1)
<pain> (3)
<pan> (4)
<panz> (1)
<pe[n]> (6)
<peen> (25)
<peenz> (1)
<pen> (346)
<pend> (2)
<penz> (7)
<pi[n]> (3)
<pin> (341)
<pinz> (10)
<pyen> (1)
<pyin> (2)

026.5B P pin

No Response (201)
<pe[n]> (2)
<peen> (37)
<peenz> (2)
<pen> (105)
<penz> (13)
<pi[n]> (1)
<pi[n]s> (1)
<pin> (522)
<pinz> (40)
<pyin> (1)

026.6A P ten cents

No Response (364)
<(t)insents=21> (1)
<te[n]sen(t)s=21> (1)
<te[n]sents=21> (1)

<te[n]sents=31> (1)
<teensant(s)=13> (1)
<teense[n]t(s)=13> (1)
<teenseents=21> (1)
<teensents=11> (1)
<teensents=21> (1)
<teensin(ts)=13> (1)
<teensints=21> (1)
<tensNts=14> (1)
<tensen(t)pees=321> (1)
<tensen(t)s=11> (10)
<tensen(t)s=13> (11)
<tensen(t)s=21> (3)
<tensen(t)s=31> (2)
<tensen(t)z=13> (1)
<tensen(t)z=31> (1)
<tensen(ts)=11> (1)
<tensen(ts)=31> (1)
<tensent(s)=11> (9)
<tensent(s)=13> (11)
<tensent(s)=21> (2)
<tensent(s)=31> (10)
<tensentpees=132> (1)
<tensentpees=213> (1)
<tensents=11> (31)
<tensents=12> (3)
<tensents=13> (42)
<tensents=21> (49)
<tensents=31> (73)
<tensin(t)s=13> (1)
<tensin(t)s=21> (1)
<tensint(s)=11> (3)
<tensint(s)=13> (1)
<tensint(s)=21> (1)
<tensint(s)=31> (1)
<tensints=11> (1)
<tensints=13> (3)
<tensints=21> (1)
<tensints=31> (6)
<tenzint(s)=13> (1)
<ti[n]sints=13> (1)
<tinsaints=13> (1)
<tinsen(t)s=11> (1)
<tinsen(t)s=13> (1)
<tinsen(t)s=21> (1)
<tinsen(t)s=31> (2)
<tinsen(ts)=31> (1)
<tinsent(s)=11> (3)
<tinsent(s)=12> (1)
<tinsent(s)=13> (4)
<tinsent(s)=31> (4)
<tinsents=11> (6)
<tinsents=13> (21)
<tinsents=21> (23)
<tinsents=31> (34)
<tinsi[n]ts=13> (1)
<tinsin(t)s=11> (1)
<tinsin(t)s=13> (3)
<tinsin(t)s=21> (1)

<tinsin(ts)=13> (2)
<tinsint(s)=11> (5)
<tinsint(s)=13> (4)
<tinsint(s)=21> (3)
<tinsint(s)=31> (2)
<tinsintpees=213> (1)
<tinsints=11> (16)
<tinsints=13> (26)
<tinsints=21> (36)
<tinsints=31> (53)
<tinsintstoe[r]=213> (1)
<tissents=13> (1)

026.6B P tin

No Response (220)
<teem> (1)
<teen> (37)
<ten> (20)
<ti[n]> (12)
<tin> (641)

026.6 S tin

No Response (0)
|ABC| (2)
|ABCeaa| (1)
|ABCeaj| (1)
|ABCeak| (1)
|ABEmaj| (4)
|ABI| (3)
|ABIeaj| (1)
|ABIeak| (1)
|ABImaj| (5)
|AGCmaj| (1)
|AGIeaj| (1)
|AQAeda| (2)
|AQIedj| (1)
|DAA| (18)
|DAAkaj| (1)
|DAAmaj| (12)
|DAB| (45)
|DABbbj| (1)
|DABbbl| (1)
|DABdaa| (1)
|DABdac| (6)
|DABeab| (1)
|DABead| (1)
|DABeaj| (1)
|DABeak| (4)
|DABmaj| (37)
|DABmak| (1)
|DAC| (21)
|DACdab| (20)
|DACmaj| (4)
|DACmak| (7)
|DADmaj| (1)
|DAE| (101)
|DAEeaj| (11)
|DAEeak| (4)
|DAEeal| (2)
|DAEmaj| (43)
|DAEmak| (10)

|DAF| (1)
|DAFmaj| (2)
|DAG| (25)
|DAGeaj| (3)
|DAGeak| (1)
|DAGmaj| (13)
|DAHmaj| (1)
|DAI| (39)
|DAIeam| (1)
|DAImaj| (11)
|DBB| (1)
|DBE| (1)
|DBG| (1)
|DCA| (8)
|DCAmaj| (5)
|DCAmak| (1)
|DCB| (2)
|DCBeaj| (4)
|DCBeak| (9)
|DCBeal| (1)
|DCBmaj| (5)
|DCBmak| (1)
|DCC| (2)
|DCCmak| (1)
|DCE| (9)
|DCEeaa| (1)
|DCEeaj| (8)
|DCEmaj| (5)
|DCEmak| (4)
|DCGeaj| (6)
|DCGmaj| (1)
|DCGmak| (1)
|DCIeaj| (3)
|DDA| (12)
|DDAedj| (1)
|DDAmdj| (14)
|DDB| (33)
|DDBddc| (4)
|DDBeda| (2)
|DDBedj| (1)
|DDBmda| (1)
|DDBmdj| (27)
|DDC| (14)
|DDCddb| (6)
|DDCmdj| (4)
|DDCmdk| (1)
|DDD| (1)
|DDE| (20)
|DDEmdj| (7)
|DDF| (6)
|DDFmdj| (1)
|DDG| (4)
|DDGmdj| (5)
|DDHddb| (2)
|DDI| (20)
|DDImdj| (11)
|DGAmak| (1)
|DGBmak| (1)
|DHBeda| (2)

|DKA| (14)
|DKAeda| (2)
|DKAedj| (1)
|DKAkdj| (1)
|DKAmdj| (7)
|DKB| (4)
|DKBeda| (2)
|DKBedj| (8)
|DKBmda| (2)
|DKBmdj| (14)
|DKBmdk| (1)
|DKC| (7)
|DKCmdj| (3)
|DKE| (4)
|DKEedj| (1)
|DKEmdj| (4)
|DKFmda| (1)
|DKFmdj| (1)
|DKG| (1)
|DKGedj| (1)
|DKGmdj| (1)
|DKI| (4)
|DKIedj| (1)
|DKImdj| (1)
|DQAmdj| (1)
|DQB| (1)
|EAA| (4)
|EAAeab| (1)
|EAB| (1)
|EABeac| (4)
|EAC| (2)
|EACeab| (15)
|EAD| (4)
|EADeab| (1)
|EADeac| (1)
|EADmaj| (1)
|EAH| (1)
|EAHeab| (2)
|EAHmaj| (1)
|ECAmaj| (1)
|EDBedc| (1)
|EDCedb| (1)
|EHBedc| (1)
|EKB| (1)
|KABeaj| (1)
|KABmak| (1)
|KAF| (6)
|KAFeaj| (1)
|KAFmaj| (1)
|KCA| (1)
|KCFeaj| (1)
|KDA| (1)
|KDB| (2)
|KDBmdj| (1)
|KDD| (2)
|KDF| (2)
|KDFmdj| (1)
|KKA| (2)
|KKB| (1)

|KKCkka| (1)
|KKF| (1)
|KKFmdj| (1)

027.1 P coat

{aw}   upglide
{oe}   monophthong/inglide
{R}   weakly retroflex
{?}   glottal
No Response (107)
<koet> (683)
<koets> (31)
<koe{?}> (5)
<k{aw}t> (2)
<k{oe}t> (37)
<oevRkoet=143> (8)
<oevRkoets=143> (1)
<oev[R]koet=143> (24)
<oev[R]koet=341> (1)
<oev[R]koets=143> (2)
<oev{R}koet=143> (8)
<raink{oe}t=13> (1)
<topkoet=13> (5)
<{oe}vRkoet=143> (1)
<{oe}v[R]koet=143> (1)
<{oe}v[R]k{oe}t=143> (1)

027.1 S coat

No Response (0)
|IJE| (1)
|ISA| (1)
|JBDeaa| (1)
|JBDefa| (1)
|JBHefj| (1)
|JGDefa| (1)
|JJA| (1)
|JJAefa| (7)
|JJAefj| (29)
|JJAffd| (12)
|JJAffh| (1)
|JJAffj| (1)
|JJAfma| (1)
|JJAjjb| (20)
|JJAjjf| (7)
|JJAlfj| (8)
|JJBefa| (2)
|JJBefj| (5)
|JJBefk| (1)
|JJBfak| (1)
|JJBffa| (1)
|JJBffj| (1)
|JJCefa| (2)
|JJCefj| (28)
|JJCffd| (3)
|JJCjja| (7)
|JJCjjb| (4)
|JJCjjk| (3)
|JJClfj| (2)
|JJCmaj| (2)
|JJD| (4)
|JJDefa| (245)

|JJDefc| (1)
|JJDefj| (143)
|JJDffa| (1)
|JJDffb| (1)
|JJDffd| (68)
|JJDffh| (1)
|JJDffm| (15)
|JJDlfj| (2)
|JJDlfn| (1)
|JJDmaa| (2)
|JJDmaj| (2)
|JJFefa| (1)
|JJFefj| (24)
|JJFffm| (1)
|JJG| (1)
|JJGefj| (2)
|JJHefa| (7)
|JJHefj| (29)
|JJHffd| (3)
|JJUefj| (1)
|JSA| (2)
|JSAefj| (2)
|JSAffa| (4)
|JSAffd| (1)
|JSAffm| (1)
|JSAjjb| (1)
|JSAjjh| (1)
|JSBffa| (2)
|JSBffj| (1)
|JSC| (1)
|JSCefa| (1)
|JSCmaj| (2)
|JSD| (3)
|JSDeaa| (2)
|JSDefa| (43)
|JSDefb| (1)
|JSDefj| (7)
|JSDfaj| (1)
|JSDff2| (2)
|JSDffa| (1)
|JSDffc| (2)
|JSDffd| (7)
|JSDffj| (6)
|JSDffm| (1)
|JSDffo| (1)
|JSDlfj| (2)
|JSDmaj| (2)
|JSDmfa| (1)
|JSFefa| (1)
|JSHefj| (3)
|KFAefa| (1)
|KFEefa| (1)
|KMAef2| (1)
|KMAefj| (3)
|LAAeaa| (1)
|LFAefa| (15)
|LFAefj| (4)
|LFAffa| (2)
|LFAffd| (2)

|LFAffj| (1)
|LFDefa| (2)
|LFEefa| (21)
|LFEefj| (1)
|LFGefa| (3)
|LFGefj| (16)
|LMAeaj| (1)
|LMAefa| (3)
|LMAff2| (1)
|LMAffa| (4)
|LMAffj| (5)
|LMDeaa| (1)
|LMDefa| (1)
|LMDffa| (2)
|LMDffj| (1)
|LMEefa| (1)
|LMEffj| (1)
|LMGefj| (1)
|LMSffa| (1)
|QFHjjc| (1)
|TFBefj| (1)

027.2 G (buttons) on it

No Response (493)
A   down (it) (4)
B   on (it) (392)
C   onto (it) (11)
D   to (it) (17)

027.3 L vest

No Response (125)
A   chaleco [S] (3)
B   cravat (1)
C   derringer (1)
D   jacket (45)
E   reversible vest (1)
F   suit vest (1)
G   vest (773)
H   waistcoat (30)

027.4 L trousers

No Response (66)
A   allover suit (1)
B   apron overalls (1)
C   baggy pants (1)
D   bell-bottom trousers (1)
E   bell top (1)
F   bib overalls (6)
G   blue denim pants (1)
H   blue denims (2)
I   blue jeans (80)
J   blue overalls (1)
K   breeches (208)
L   buckskin pants (1)
M   cords (1)
N   corduroy pants (1)
O   cotton trousers (1)
P   country boy's overalls (1)
Q   coverall suit (1)
R   coveralls (105)
S   coverhauls (5)
T   creek-water breeches (1)

U   denim overalls (1)
V   denims (1)
W   dress pair of pants (1)
X   dress pants (5)
Y   dress pantses (1)
Z   drip-dry pants (1)
aa   Duck Heads (3)
ab   ducking breeches (1)
ac   ducking overalls (1)
ad   ducking pants (1)
ae   ducking suit (1)
af   duds (1)
ag   dungarees (18)
ah   everyday pants (2)
ai   Farmer Brown (1)
aj   fatigues (1)
ak   flannel trousers (1)
al   heavy goods (1)
am   homemade pants (1)
an   ice-cream pants (1)
ao   jean breeches (2)
ap   jean pants (3)
aq   jeans (80)
ar   jeans breeches (1)
as   jump suit (15)
at   jumper suit (2)
au   jumper(s) (9)
av   khaki breeches (1)
aw   khaki pants (13)
ax   khaki(s) (21)
ay   knee breeches (1)
az   knee-length pants (1)
ba   knee pants (7)
bb   knickerbottoms (1)
bc   knickers (4)
bd   knit pants (1)
be   knits (1)
bf   knockabout clothes (1)
bg   leather breeches (1)
bh   Levi's (8)
bi   long breeches (1)
bj   long pants (3)
bk   made overhauls (1)
bl   N and W (1)
bm   overall pants (3)
bn   overalls (451)
bo   overhaul pants (3)
bp   overhaul suit (2)
bq   overhauls (98)
br   painter's overalls (1)
bs   pair of breeches (3)
bt   pair of jeans (2)
bu   pair of overalls (3)
bv   pair of pants (34)
bw   pair of trousers (1)
bx   pair of Unionalls (1)
by   pantalones [S] (2)
bz   pantaloons (2)
ca   pants (703)

cb   pantses (3)
cc   peg leg (1)
cd   peg pants (2)
ce   peg-top pants (1)
cf   pinstriped overalls (1)
cg   pistol-legged breeches (1)
ch   Red Fox (1)
ci   riding breeches (1)
cj   roll pants (1)
ck   seersuckers (1)
cl   short breeches (1)
cm   short pants (5)
cn   slacks (104)
co   snickers (1)
cp   striped trousers (1)
cq   Sunday-go-to-meeting pants (1)
cr   Sweetwater breeches (1)
cs   tight-legged jeans (1)
ct   trous(ers) (4)
cu   trousers (435)
cv   tux pants (1)
cw   two-pants suit (1)
cx   Union Hauls (1)
cy   Unionalls (4)
cz   unions (1)
da   waist breeches (1)
db   waist pants (1)
dc   waist trousers (1)
dd   whistle breeches (1)
de   white-duck trousers (1)
df   white ducks (1)
dg   work clothes (8)
dh   work overalls (1)
di   work pants (15)
dj   work trousers (1)

027.4 P overalls
{o}   low-back
{R}   weakly retroflex
No Response (365)
<awvR{o}[l]z=143> (1)
<awv[R]{o}lz=143> (1)
<oe(vR)aw[l]z=13> (1)
<oevA)raw[l]zh=13> (1)
<oev(A)rawlz=13> (1)
<oev(A)r{o}lz=13> (1)
<oev(R)awlz=13> (3)
<oevAraw[l]z=143> (1)
<oevArawl(z)=143> (4)
<oevArawlz=143> (56)
<oevArawlz=241> (1)
<oevAr{o}lz=143> (2)
<oevIraw(1)z=143> (1)
<oevIraw[1]z=143> (1)
<oevIrawl(z)=143> (2)
<oevIrawlz=143> (6)
<oevIro[1]z=143> (1)
<oevIr{o}lz=143> (1)
<oevRaw(1)z=143> (4)
<oevRaw[1]dz=143> (1)

<oevRaw[l]z=143> (12)
<oevRaw[l]zh=143> (1)
<oevRawl(z)=143> (6)
<oevRawlz=143> (162)
<oevRawlz=241> (1)
<oevRawlz=341> (1)
<oevRhaw[l]z=143> (2)
<oevRhawl(z)=143> (2)
<oevRhawlpants=2431> (1)
<oevRhawlsuet=1431> (2)
<oevRhawlz=143> (20)
<oevRh{o}[l]z=143> (1)
<oevRh{o}lz=143> (4)
<oevRo[l]z=143> (2)
<oevRolz=143> (5)
<oevRolz=341> (1)
<oevRrawlz=143> (1)
<oevR{o}[l](z)=143> (1)
<oevR{o}[l]dh=143> (1)
<oevR{o}[l]z=143> (10)
<oevR{o}lz=142> (1)
<oevR{o}lz=143> (37)
<oevR{o}lzh=143> (1)
<oev[R]aw[l](z)=143> (1)
<oev[R]aw[l]z=143> (1)
<oev[R]awl(z)=143> (5)
<oev[R]awlz=142> (1)
<oev[R]awlz=143> (39)
<oev[R]awlz=341> (1)
<oev[R]haw(1)z=143> (1)
<oev[R]haw[1]z=143> (2)
<oev[R]hawl(z)=143> (3)
<oev[R]hawlpants=1432> (1)
<oev[R]hawls=143> (1)
<oev[R]hawlz=143> (42)
<oev[R]hawlz=241> (1)
<oev[R]h{o}[1](z)=143> (1)
<oev[R]h{o}lz=143> (2)
<oev[R]owlz=143> (1)
<oev[R]rawlz=143> (1)
<oev[R]{o}lz=143> (2)
<oevirawlz=132> (1)
<oev{R}awl(z)=143> (3)
<oev{R}awlz=143> (52)
<oev{R}haw(1)z=143> (1)
<oev{R}haw[1]z=143> (1)
<oev{R}hawlz=143> (13)
<oev{R}h{o}lz=143> (4)
<oev{R}rawlz=143> (7)
<oev{R}r{o}lz=143> (1)
<oev{R}{o}lpants=2431> (1)
<oev{R}{o}lz=143> (2)
<ovR{o}lz=143> (1)
<uvRolz=241> (1)

027.5 G bring
<!>   infinitive
<&>   present 3rd singular
<@>   present participle
<*>   preterit

<#>   past participle
No Response (105)
<!braing> (13)
<!braink> (1)
<!brang> (22)
<!breeng> (26)
<!breengg> (2)
<!breng> (210)
<!b(r)ing> (1)
<!bring> (465)
<!bri[ng]> (1)
<!burng> (1)
<&brangz> (1)
<&braingz> (1)
<&breengz> (1)
<&brengz> (1)
<&bringz> (16)
<@braingN=14> (1)
<@brangN=14> (1)
<@breengNG=14> (1)
<@brengN=14> (3)
<@bringN=14> (7)
<@bringNG=14> (2)
<*braing> (1)
<*brang> (4)
<*brawd> (2)
<*b(r)awt> (4)
<*braw(t)> (3)
<*brawt> (577)
<*breeng> (1)
<*breng> (4)
<*bring> (1)
<*bringd> (1)
<*broeng> (1)
<*broe(t)> (1)
<*broet> (14)
<*brot> (25)
<*brung> (13)
<*bwawt> (1)
<#b(r)awd> (1)
<#b(r)awt> (2)
<#brawt> (403)
<#broet> (5)
<#brot> (24)
<#brung> (8)
<#brut> (1)

027.6 G fit
<!>   infinitive
<&>   present 3rd singular
<@>   present participle
<*>   preterit
<#>   past participle
No Response (269)
<!fit> (64)
<&fit> (1)
<&fits> (12)
<@fitNG=14> (1)
<*fet> (2)
<*fid> (2)

<*fidId=14> (1)
<*fit> (495)
<*fitId=14> (103)
<*fitIt=14> (1)
<#fit> (6)
<#fitId=14> (10)

027.7 P new suit
No Response (372)
<newsew(t)=11> (1)
<newsewt=11> (24)
<newsewt=13> (10)
<newsewt=21> (8)
<newsewt=31> (3)
<newshuet=21> (1)
<newsue(t)=11> (1)
<newsuet=11> (44)
<newsuet=12> (2)
<newsuet=13> (84)
<newsuet=21> (66)
<newsuet=31> (33)
<newsuets=21> (1)
<noosuet=31> (1)
<nuesewt=13> (1)
<nuesewt=21> (1)
<nuesewt=31> (1)
<nuesuet=11> (11)
<nuesuet=12> (1)
<nuesuet=13> (30)
<nuesuet=21> (27)
<nuesuet=31> (26)
<nyewsewt=11> (1)
<nyewsewt=31> (2)
<nyewsuet=11> (1)
<nyewsuet=13> (6)
<nyewsuet=21> (2)
<nyewsuet=31> (19)
<nyisewt=31> (1)
<nyoosue(t)=31> (1)
<nyuesewt=11> (2)
<nyuesewt=13> (4)
<nyuesewt=21> (1)
<nyuesewt=31> (3)
<nyuesuet=11> (14)
<nyuesuet=12> (2)
<nyuesuet=13> (29)
<nyuesuet=21> (16)
<nyuesuet=31> (65)
<nyuesuets=31> (1)

027.8 L bulge
No Response (272)
A   bag [v.] (6)
B   bag down (2)
C   bag out (3)
D   blow out (2)
E   bug out (1)
F   bulge (470)
G   bulge out (159)
H   bulk [v.] (2)
I   bulk out (5)

J   bulk up (1)
K   droop (2)
L   flare [v.] (1)
M   poke out (8)
N   pooch (2)
O   pooch out (15)
P   pop out (1)
Q   protrude (2)
R   pucker (2)
S   pucker out (2)
T   puff (2)
U   puff out (22)
V   puff up (2)
W   puffle (1)
X   pull (1)
Y   punch out (4)
Z   push out (3)
aa   sag (6)
ab   sag down (1)
ac   set out (1)
ad   stand out (1)
ae   stick out (41)
af   stretch out (1)
ag   strut (2)
ah   swag (2)
ai   swag down (1)
aj   swell (1)
ak   swell out (1)
al   swell up (1)
am   toot out (1)

027.8 P bulge
No Response (272)
<boelj> (1)
<bolj> (3)
<boo(1)j> (5)
<boo(1)jI=14> (1)
<boo(1)jId=14> (1)
<boo(1)jN=14> (1)
<boo(1)zh> (1)
<boo[1]dsh> (1)
<boo[1]j> (26)
<boo[1]jI=14> (1)
<boo[1]jN=14> (2)
<boo[1]jd> (2)
<boo[1]sh> (1)
<boo[1]zh> (2)
<boolch> (6)
<boold> (1)
<boolg> (1)
<boolj> (208)
<booljI=14> (9)
<booljIz=14> (3)
<booljN=14> (13)
<booljNG=14> (5)
<booljd> (8)
<boolsh> (1)
<boolyA=14> (1)
<boolz> (1)
<boolzh> (8)

<boolzhI=14> (1)
<bu(1)j> (8)
<bu(1)jI=14> (1)
<bu(1)jN=14> (1)
<bu[1]d> (1)
<bu[1]j> (29)
<bu[1]jd> (1)
<bu[1]zh> (3)
<bue[1]j> (1)
<buelj> (9)
<bueljI=14> (1)
<bueljN=14> (2)
<bueljd> (2)
<bul(j)> (2)
<bulch> (6)
<bulg> (1)
<bulj> (217)
<buljI=14> (11)
<buljIz=14> (2)
<buljN=14> (14)
<buljNG=14> (13)
<buljd> (4)
<buls> (1)
<bulz> (1)
<bulzh> (10)
<bulzhNG=14> (1)

027.9 G shrink

<!>   infinitive
<&>   present 3rd singular
<@>   present participle
<*>   preterit
<#>   past participle
No Response (172)
<!preesrink=31> (1)
<!reeshrenk=31> (1)
<!shraink> (4)
<!shrank> (3)
<!shreenk> (44)
<!shremp> (1)
<!shren(k)> (1)
<!shrenk> (53)
<!shrink> (349)
<!shrunk> (1)
<!shwenk> (2)
<!shwink> (2)
<!sraink> (2)
<!sran(k)> (1)
<!srank> (1)
<!sreenk> (13)
<!srenk> (14)
<!srink> (132)
<!strink> (3)
<!swank> (1)
<!sweenk> (2)
<!swenk> (5)
<!swink> (19)
<!swunk> (1)
<!trink> (1)
<&shreenks> (3)

<&shrinks> (18)
<&shrinkz> (1)
<&sreenks> (2)
<&srenks> (3)
<&srinks> (6)
<&swinks> (1)
<@shrenkN=14> (1)
<@shrinkN=14> (7)
<@shrinkNG=14> (1)
<@sreenkN=14> (1)
<@sreenkNG=14> (1)
<@srenkN=14> (2)
<@srinkN=14> (2)
<*preesrunk=31> (1)
<*sh(r)ank> (1)
<*shraink> (8)
<*shrank> (105)
<*shreenkt> (2)
<*shremp> (1)
<*shrenk> (13)
<*shrenkt> (1)
<*shrink> (5)
<*shrinkt> (12)
<*shrun(k)> (2)
<*shrunk> (253)
<*shrunkt> (2)
<*skrunk> (1)
<*sraink> (2)
<*srank> (18)
<*sreenkt> (3)
<*srenk> (3)
<*srenkt> (2)
<*srink> (3)
<*srinkt> (12)
<*srinst> (1)
<*srunk> (82)
<*sru[n]kt> (1)
<*streenkt> (1)
<*strink> (1)
<*strunk> (2)
<*swancht> (1)
<*swankt> (1)
<*swawnk> (1)
<*sweenkt> (1)
<*swenk> (5)
<*swenkt> (2)
<*swenktId=14> (1)
<*swinch> (1)
<*swinkt> (10)
<*swunk> (3)
<*tsrunk> (1)
<#ch(r)unk> (1)
<#preeshrinkt=31> (1
<#preeshrunk=13> (1)
<#preeshrunk=21> (1)
<#preeshrunk=31> (4)
<#preesrunk=13> (1)
<#preesrunk=31> (2)
<#prIshrunk=41> (1)

<#shraink> (1)
<#shrangt> (1)
<#shrank> (16)
<#shrawnk> (1)
<#shreenkN=14> (1)
<#shreenkt> (1)
<#shrenk> (7)
<#shrenkt> (4)
<#shrink> (1)
<#shrinkN=14> (3)
<#shrinkt> (9)
<#shrunk> (250)
<#shrunkN=14> (22)
<#shru[n]gk> (1)
<#skrunk> (1)
<#sraink> (2)
<#srank> (8)
<#sreenk> (1)
<#sreenkt> (3)
<#srenk> (3)
<#srenkN=14> (1)
<#srenkt> (3)
<#srink> (1)
<#srinkN=14> (2)
<#srinkt> (3)
<#srunk> (74)
<#srunkN=14> (5)
<#sru[n]gk> (1)
<#sru[n]k> (2)
<#streenkt> (1)
<#strink> (1)
<#strunk> (1)
<#swancht> (1)
<#swankt> (1)
<#swawnk> (1)
<#swemp> (1)
<#swenk> (4)
<#swink> (3)
<#swinkt> (5)
<#swinktId=14> (1)
<#swunk> (9)
<#swunkN=14> (1)

028.1 L dress up

No Response (152)
[of women]
A   admire herself (2)
B   be beautiful (1)
C   beautify (herself) (10)
D   beauty up (3)
E   deck out (4)
F   dike (2)
G   dike out (3)
H   dike up (9)
I   doll up (57)
J   dress (nice/well) (99)
K   dress her hair (1)
L   dress herself out nice (1)
M   dress in finery (1)
N   dress to go out (1)

O   dress to kill (1)
P   dress up (315)
Q   dude up (3)
R   fancy up (1)
S   fix (3)
T   fix (her) face (10)
U   fix her hair (1)
V   fix up (nice/pretty) (21)
W   fixed up raring to roam (1)
X   foxed up (1)
Y   get fancy (1)
Z   get on a dike (1)
aa   get pretty (3)
ab   get ready (12)
ac   get sharp (1)
ad   groom (4)
ae   gussied up (3)
af   kill time (1)
ag   loaded for bear (1)
ah   look at herself (3)
ai   look (good/pretty) (7)
aj   look groomy (1)
ak   make a nice showing (1)
al   make (her) face (1)
am   make herself (attractive) (7)
an   make (herself) body beautiful
     (1)
ao   make herself show up (1)
ap   make up (18)
aq   make up her face (5)
ar   paint herself (1)
as   paint up (1)
at   pamper (1)
au   party [v.] (1)
av   pimpoter [F] (1)
aw   powder (1)
ax   powder and paint her face (1)
ay   powder her nose (1)
az   powder up (1)
ba   preen (4)
bb   prettify (1)
bc   pretty it up (1)
bd   pretty up (17)
be   primp (411)
bf   primp out (1)
bg   primp up (67)
bh   prince up (2)
bi   priss around (1)
bj   put on (1)
bk   put on a lot of makeup (1)
bl   put on an Indian face (1)
bm   put on cosmetics (1)
bn   put on her face (1)
bo   put on her lip rouge (1)
bp   put on (her) makeup (7)
bq   put on (her) war paint (3)
br   put on pretty clothes (1)
bs   put on the dog (3)
bt   put on the glad rags (1)

bu   rag [v.] (1)
bv   rouged up (1)
bw   show off (4)
bx   slick down (2)
by   slick up (2)
bz   spread on (1)
ca   spruce up (13)
cb   style up (1)
cc   tidy up (1)
cd   togged up (1)
ce   tricked out (1)
cf   try to look good (1)
cg   use makeup (1)
ch   wear nice clothes (1)
ci   well-dressed (8)
[of men]
da   clean up (2)
db   deck out (3)
dc   dike out (3)
dd   dike up (3)
de   doll up (15)
df   dress (nice/well) (27)
dg   dress up (123)
dh   dressed fit to kill (1)
di   dude up (11)
dj   fix (1)
dk   fix his hair (1)
dl   fix up (4)
dm   fuss over his appearance (1)
dn   get ready (10)
do   get sharp (1)
dp   get together (1)
dq   groom (himself) (14)
dr   gussied up (1)
ds   look neat (1)
dt   look sharp (1)
du   look slick (1)
dv   pose (1)
dw   preen (3)
dx   pretty hisself up (1)
dy   primp (141)
dz   primp up (12)
ea   put on (his) monkey suit (1)
eb   put on style in a big way (1)
ec   put on the dog (3)
ed   rerag (1)
ee   rigged up (1)
ef   sharp up (2)
eg   sheik down (1)
eh   sheik up (2)
ei   shine up (2)
ej   show off (2)
ek   slick down (his hair) (3)
el   slick up (8)
em   spruce up (7)
en   style up (1)
eo   tidy up (1)
ep   togged up (1)
028.2 L purse

No Response (87)
A   bag (25)
B   bag [=change purse] (2)
C   bag [=handbag] (7)
D   billfold (80)
E   billfolder (5)
F   carrying bag (1)
G   chain purse (1)
H   change bag (1)
I   change pocketbook (1)
J   change pouch (1)
K   change purse (118)
L   cloth pouch (1)
M   clutch purse (1)
N   coin case (1)
O   coin bag (4)
P   coin pouch (2)
Q   coin purse (155)
R   evening purse (1)
S   hand pocketbook (1)
T   hand purse (3)
U   hand sack (1)
V   hand satchel (2)
W   handbag (113)
X   knapsack (1)
Y   leather bank (1)
Z   leather pocketbook (2)
aa   leather pouch (1)
ab   little evening bag (1)
ac   little leather pouch (1)
ad   little-old pocketbook (1)
ae   money bag (2)
af   money coin (1)
ag   money poke (1)
ah   money pouch (3)
ai   money purse (3)
aj   money sack (5)
ak   penny purse (1)
al   pocket (2)
am   pocket purse (2)
an   pocketbook (237)
ao   pocketbook [=change purse] (51)
ap   pocketbook [=handbag] (37)
aq   pocketbook [=man's billfold] (3)
ar   pouch (6)
as   pouch [=change purse] (4)
at   pouch [=handbag] (1)
au   purse (517)
av   purse [=change purse] (44)
aw   purse [=handbag] (71)
ax   purse chain (1)
ay   reticule (1)
az   sack (1)
ba   satchel (10)
bb   shopping bag (1)
bc   shopping book (1)
bd   shoulder bag (7)

be small pocketbook (3)
bf small purse (1)
bg snap pocketbook (1)
bh snap-on pocketbook (1)
bi (to)bacco sack (2)
bj tote bag (3)
bk valise (1)
bl wallet (49)

028.2 P purse
{r} weakly retroflex
{s} palatal
No Response (137)
<pirz> (1)
<poe{r}s> (1)
<poors> (1)
<pu[r](s)> (2)
<pu[r]s> (147)
<pu[r]sIz=14> (8)
<pu[r]sh> (1)
<pur(s)> (1)
<purs> (486)
<pursIz=14> (16)
<pursh> (4)
<pur{s}> (15)
<pur{s}Iz=14> (1)
<pu{r}s> (92)
<pu{r}sIs=14> (1)
<pu{r}sIz=14> (3)
<pu{r}sh> (1)
<pu{r}{s}> (1)

028.3 P bracelet
{ai} lowered/lax onset
{r} labial
{s} palatal
{?} glottal
No Response (145)
<bAraislIt=414> (1)
<blaislIt=14> (1)
<brais(1)It=14> (2)
<braisAlet=341> (1)
<braishlIt=14> (2)
<braishlIts=14> (1)
<braislAt=14> (1)
<braislA{?}=14> (1)
<braislI{?}=14> (1)
<braislI(t)=14> (10)
<braislI(t)s=14> (3)
<braislIt=14> (567)
<braislIts=14> (49)
<braislI{?}=14> (1)
<braisle(t)=13> (1)
<braislet=13> (9)
<braislit=13> (11)
<braizlIt=14> (1)
<brai{s}lIt=14> (38)
<brai{s}lIts=14> (2)
<braslIt=14> (3)
<bresAlet=341> (1)
<breslIt=14> (9)

<breslIts=14> (1)
<brislIt=14> (1)
<brizlIt=14> (1)
<bruslIt=14> (1)
<br{ai}slIt=14> (31)
<br{ai}slIts=14> (1)
<br{ai}slI{?}=14> (1)
<br{ai}slit=13> (1)
<br{ai}thlIt=14> (1)
<br{ai}{s}lIt=14> (1)
<b{r}aish(1)At=14> (1)
<b{r}aislIt=14> (15)

028.4 L string of beads
No Response (215)
A bead necklace (4)
B beaded necklace (3)
C beads (347)
D chain of beads (4)
E cluster of beads (1)
F collar (1)
G doodads (1)
H double string (1)
I glass beads (1)
J necklace (396)
K necklace of beads (4)
L pair (4)
M pair of beads (53)
N pair of pearls (1)
O pearl beads (3)
P pearl necklace (4)
Q pearls (40)
R rope beads (1)
S rope of beads (1)
T row of beads (2)
U set of beads (4)
V set of pearls (1)
W strand (5)
X strand of beads (20)
Y strand of pearls (4)
Z string (20)
aa string of [N-0] (2)
ab string of beads (338)
ac string of gold beads (1)
ad string of pearls (27)
ae two strands (2)

028.5 L suspenders
No Response (80)
A braces (6)
B bretelles [F] (2)
C elastics (1)
D gallus (21)
E gallu(ses) (1)
F galluses (377)
G straps (2)
H strops (2)
I suspender (14)
J (su)spender (2)
K suspender strops (1)
L suspender-like (1)

M suspenders (688)
N (su)spenders (78)
O (sus)penders (1)
P trouser holder (1)

028.6 L umbrella
No Response (115)
A bumbershoot (6)
B para agua, un [S] (1)
C para un sol [S] (1)
D parasol (271)
E parasol [for sun] (41)
F parasol, un [S] (1)
G parasol umbrella (1)
H rain (um)brella (1)
I shower stick (2)
J sunshade (4)
K umbersol (1)
L umbrel(la) (17)
M umbrella (766)

028.6 P umbrella
{R} weakly retroflex
{r} labial
{t} flap
No Response (129)
<MbRelA=4414> (1)
<MbrelA=414> (11)
<MbrellA=414> (2)
<Mbrel{R}=414> (1)
<MbrulA=414> (4)
<Mb{r}elA=414> (1)
<embArelA=3414> (1)
<emburelR=2314> (1)
<hombArelA=1434> (1)
<hombArel{R}=1434> (1)
<hum(b)ArelA=1434> (1)
<humbrelA=314> (1)
<numbrelA=134> (2)
<ombArelA=1434> (3)
<ombArelA=3414> (1)
<ombIrelA=1434> (1)
<ombRrelA=1434> (1)
<ombralA=134> (1)
<ombrelA=134> (4)
<ombrelA=314> (5)
<ombrulA=134> (1)
<ombrulA=314> (1)
<oombrelA=134> (1)
<u(m)bArelA=1434> (1)
<um(b)Arel(A)=143> (1)
<um(b)ArelA=1434> (13)
<um(b)ArelA=3414> (1)
<um(b)ArelAs=3414> (1)
<um(b)Aru[1](A)=143> (1)
<um(b)RelA=1434> (1)
<um(b)RrelA=3414> (1)
<um(b)re{t}A=134> (1)
<um(b){r}elA=314> (1)
<umb(r)elA=134> (1)
<umb(r)elA=314> (1)

<umb(r)ulR=134> (1)
<umbArel(A)=143> (2)
<umbArelA=1424> (4)
<umbArelA=1434> (102)
<umbArelA=2414> (3)
<umbArelA=3414> (15)
<umbArelAz=1434> (3)
<umbArelR=1434> (5)
<umbArelR=3414> (1)
<umbArel{R}=3414> (2)
<umbArezA=1434> (1)
<umbArilA=1434> (4)
<umbArulA=3414> (2)
<umbA{r}elA=1434> (2)
<umbA{r}elA=3414> (1)
<umbIrelA=1434> (16)
<umbIrelA=2414> (1)
<umbIrelA=3414> (3)
<umbIrelAz=1434> (2)
<umbIrilA=1434> (1)
<umbI{t}elA=1434> (1)
<umbRel(A)=143> (1)
<umbRelA=1434> (6)
<umbRelA=2414> (1)
<umbRellA=1424> (1)
<umbRellA=1434> (2)
<umbRrelA=3414> (1)
<umbRulA=1434> (1)
<umbbrelA=134> (1)
<umbralA=134> (2)
<umbralA=314> (2)
<umbre[1](A)=13> (1)
<umbre[1]A=134> (3)
<umbre[1]A=314> (1)
<umbrel(A)=13> (7)
<umbrel(A)=31> (1)
<umbrelA=124> (4)
<umbrelA=134> (272)
<umbrelA=214> (11)
<umbrelA=314> (127)
<umbrelAz=134> (7)
<umbrelAz=314> (2)
<umbrelR=134> (10)
<umbrelR=314> (5)
<umbrellA=134> (5)
<umbrellA=214> (2)
<umbrellA=314> (3)
<umbreloe=313> (1)
<umbrelyA=134> (1)
<umbrel{R}=134> (5)
<umbrel{R}z=134> (1)
<umbrel{R}z=314> (1)
<umbre{t}A=134> (1)
<umbrilA=134> (3)
<umbrilA=314> (4)
<umbroellA=214> (1)
<umbru[1]A=314> (1)
<umbrudhA=134> (1)
<umbrulA=134> (18)

<umbrulA=214> (2)
<umbrulA=314> (9)
<umbrulAz=134> (1)
<umbrulR=314> (1)
<umbwelA=134> (1)
<umb{R}relA=1434> (1)
<umb{r}elA=134> (14)
<umb{r}elA=314> (2)
<umb{t}elA=314> (1)
<ummArelA=1434> (1)
<ummRrilA=1434> (1)
<umpbrelA=134> (1)
<umpbrelA=314> (1)
<um{t}Arel(A)=143> (1)
<um{t}ArelA=1434> (1)
<unbRelA=1434> (1)
<unbrelA=134> (2)
<unbrelA=314> (1)
<unbrellA=134> (1)
<unb{r}elA=314> (1)

028.7 L bedspread

  No Response (121)
  A bed covering (2)
  B bedcover (12)
  C bedspread (479)
  D Bettdecke [G] (1)
  E chenille (1)
  F chenille spread (1)
  G (counter)pane (1)
  H counterpane (231)
  I counterpiece (1)
  J couvre-pied [F] (1)
  K cover (26)
  L coverlet (78)
  M dress bedspread (1)
  N electric spread (1)
  O spade (1)
  P spread (298)
  Q spread cover (1)
  R throw cover (1)
  S tuft(ed) spread (1)
  T yo-yo bedspread (1)

028.8 P pillow

  {p} fricative
  {R} weakly retroflex
  {r} weakly retroflex
  {t} flap
  No Response (74)
<peelR=14> (1)
<pelA=14> (5)
<pelAz=14> (1)
<pi[1](A)> (2)
<pi[1]A=14> (6)
<pi[1][L]=14> (1)
<pilA=14> (528)
<pilAs=14> (1)
<pilAz=14> (79)
<pilI=14> (1)
<pilIz=14> (1)

<pilR=14> (44)
<pilRz=14> (19)
<pillA=14> (21)
<pillAz=14> (1)
<pillI=14> (1)
<pilloe=13> (5)
<piloe=12> (1)
<piloe=13> (105)
<piloez=13> (15)
<pilyA=14> (1)
<pilu{r}=13> (1)
<pil{R}=14> (34)
<pil{R}z=14> (8)
<pi{t}A=14> (1)
<poollAz=14> (1)
<pulA=14> (1)
<pyilA=14> (1)
<pyiloe=13> (1)
<{p}ilA=14> (1)

028.9 G all the way (across)

  No Response (264)
  A all (across/around) (11)
  B all the way (420)
  C all the [N-0] (3)
  D all ways (1)
  E all [D-0] way (20)
  F clam (1)
  G clean (84)
  H clear (92)
  I clear right (1)
  J completely (3)
  K entirely (1)
  L flam (1)
  M flat (1)
  N full (length) (2)
  O jam (1)
  P plumb (170)
  Q plumb right (3)
  R right (22)
  S slam (18)
  T slap (7)
  U smack (1)
  V straight (across/around) (10)
  W straight clean (1)
  X straight out (1)
  Y way (across) (2)
  Z whole (length/width) (3)
  aa whole way (2)

029.1 L quilt

  No Response (97)
  A afghan (1)
  B bed quilt (1)
  C bedcover (1)
  D bedspread (1)
  E blanket (3)
  F bowtie quilt (1)
  G Cinderella quilt (1)
  H colchas [S] (1)
  I comfort (121)

J   comfort quilt (1)
K   comforter (73)
L   counterpane (2)
M   coverlet (7)
N   crazy quilt (8)
O   dollar quilt (1)
P   down comfort (2)
Q   down comforter (1)
R   downies (1)
S   eiderdown (2)
T   feather bed (1)
U   flower-garden quilt (1)
V   heavy quilt (1)
W   homemade quilt (7)
X   old-time quilt (1)
Y   patch quilt (5)
Z   patchwork quilt (9)
aa piece quilt (3)
ab pieced bedcover (1)
ac quilt (766)
ad spread (1)
ae string quilt (1)
af tack comfort (1)
ag tack quilt (1)
ah wagon-wheel quilt (1)
ai wool comfort (1)

029.2 L pallet

No Response (128)
A   air mattress (1)
B   Baptist pallet (6)
C   bed (3)
D   bed down, a (3)
E   bed on the floor (7)
F   bed pad (1)
G   bedroll (5)
H   bedticking (1)
I   blanket (1)
J   bunk (8)
K   cot (1)
L   do-away bed (1)
M   down a bed (1)
N   down bed (1)
O   down pallet (1)
P   feather bed (4)
Q   fill mattress (1)
R   flat bed (1)
S   floor pack (1)
T   floor pallet (2)
U   hard-shell pallet (1)
V   laid-down bed (1)
W   made-down bed (3)
X   make down [n.] (1)
Y   mat(s) (7)
Z   mattress (13)
aa mattress (and) blanket (2)
ab mattress bed (1)
ac mattress quilt (1)
ad Methodist pallet (3)
ae pad (12)

af pad-like (1)
ag padding (1)
ah paillet [F] (1)
ai pallet (700)
aj pallet on the floor (8)
ak pat (1)
al put-down-on-the-floor bed (2)
am quilt (3)
an roll (1)
ao shuck bed (1)
ap shuck mattress (1)
aq sleeping bag (24)
ar sleeping pad (1)
as straw mattress (1)
at straw tick (2)
au throw bed (1)
av tick (2)
aw trial bed (1)

029.3 P fertile

{f}   bilabial
{L}   labial
{r}   weakly retroflex
{t}   flap
{?}   glottal
No Response (450)
<foo(r)tL=14> (1)
<foor{t}L=14> (1)
<fu[r]tL=14> (60)
<fu[r]t[L]=14> (2)
<fu[r]{t}L=14> (8)
<furdL=14> (3)
<furtL=14> (280)
<furt[L]=14> (4)
<furtiel=13> (1)
<furto[l]=13> (1)
<furt{L}=14> (2)
<fur{?}L=14> (1)
<fur{t}L=14> (33)
<fur{t}[L]=14> (6)
<fu{r}dL=14> (1)
<fu{r}tL=14> (39)
<fu{r}{t}L=14> (18)
<fu{r}{t}[L]=14> (1)
<{f}ur{t}L=14> (2)
<{f}ur{t}[L]=14> (5)
<{f}u[r]{t}L=14> (1)
<{f}u[r]{t}[L]=14> (2)

029.4 L bottomland

No Response (178)
A   backwater land (1)
B   bank(s) (12)
C   barrio [S] (1)
D   basin (4)
E   bay field(s) (1)
F   bed (2)
G   black bottom (soil) (2)
H   blackland(s) (5)
I   bog (1)
J   bottom(s) (213)

K   bottom country (2)
L   bottom dirt (1)
M   bottom field(s) (5)
N   bottom ground (1)
O   bottom pasture (1)
P   bottom places (1)
Q   bottom section (1)
R   bottom soil (1)
S   bottomland(s) (403)
T   branch bottom(s) (6)
U   branch side (1)
V   built-up land (1)
W   clay bottom (1)
X   coastal plain (2)
Y   coulee (1)
Z   creek bed (6)
aa creek(-)bottom (land) (42)
ab cropland (1)
ac damp land (1)
ad delta bottomlands (1)
ae delta (land) (28)
af delta section (1)
ag easement (1)
ah fertile bottomland (1)
ai flat(s) (19)
aj flat lowland (2)
ak flatland (31)
al flatwoods (land) (2)
am floodland (5)
an floodplain(s) (5)
ao hammock (land) (5)
ap hollow (land) (2)
aq lake bottom (1)
ar level land (1)
as low bottom(s) (4)
at low flatland (1)
au low foundation (1)
av low ground (4)
aw low-lying (land) (4)
ax low marshy land (1)
ay low pastureland (1)
az low piece of land (1)
ba low place (4)
bb low spot (1)
bc low wetland (1)
bd lower bottom (1)
be lower flat (1)
bf lower land (2)
bg lowland(s) (145)
bh lowland bottom (1)
bi lowland field (1)
bj made land (2)
bk marsh (3)
bl marsh field (1)
bm marshland (2)
bn Mississippi bottom(s) (2)
bo Mississippi Delta (2)
bp moisture land (1)
bq muck farms (1)

br   muckland (3)
bs   newground (2)
bt   overflow land (5)
bu   rice field (1)
bv   rice land (1)
bw   rich ground (1)
bx   rich piece of bottomland (1)
by   rich river-bottom land (1)
bz   river basin (1)
ca   river-bottom farm (1)
cb   river(-)bottom (land) (60)
cc   river flat (2)
cd   river land (3)
ce   river valley (2)
cf   riverbank (1)
cg   riverbed(s) (12)
ch   riverfront land (1)
ci   rocky bottom (1)
cj   sand ridge (1)
ck   sand(-)soak (land) (1)
cl   savannas (1)
cm   seeps [n.] (1)
cn   slough (2)
co   sobby (bottom)land (1)
cp   swale (1)
cq   swamp fields (1)
cr   swampland (4)
cs   valley(s) (21)
ct   wash place (1)
cu   wet bottomland (1)
cv   wet-natured land (1)
cw   wetland (7)

029.5 L meadow

No Response (347)
A   basin land (1)
B   blackjack country (1)
C   blackland prair(ie) (1)
D   bottom(s) (6)
E   bottomland (2)
F   clover land (1)
G   coastal prairie (1)
H   cow pasture (1)
I   dale (1)
J   delta(s) (5)
K   field (of grass) (17)
L   flat(s) (5)
M   flat country (2)
N   flat field (1)
O   flat piece of land (1)
P   flatland(s) (13)
Q   glade (2)
R   glen (1)
S   grass prairie (1)
T   grassland(s) (18)
U   grassy lowlands (1)
V   grassy piece of land (1)
W   graze land (1)
X   grazer patch (1)
Y   grazing field (2)

Z   grazing land (8)
aa   grazing pasture (1)
ab   green (1)
ac   green meadow (1)
ad   green pasture (1)
ae   hammock land (1)
af   hay bottom (1)
ag   hay land (1)
ah   hay meadow (19)
ai   hay pasture (1)
aj   hayfield(s) (30)
ak   hollow (3)
al   lawn (1)
am   lea (1)
an   level fields (1)
ao   light land (1)
ap   low country (1)
aq   lowland (field) (20)
ar   marsh(es) (2)
as   marshland (5)
at   meadow(s) (247)
au   meadow field (1)
av   meadowland (9)
aw   no-good land (2)
ax   open country (1)
ay   open field (1)
az   open land (1)
ba   pasture (129)
bb   pasture ground (1)
bc   pasture-type land (1)
bd   pastureland (43)
be   plain(s) (9)
bf   plain land (1)
bg   pond side (1)
bh   poor land (8)
bi   prairie(s) (71)
bj   prairie country (1)
bk   prairie ground (1)
bl   prair(ie) land (12)
bm   prair(ie) meadow (1)
bn   ranchland (1)
bo   raw land (1)
bp   round prairie (1)
bq   sage field (2)
br   sandy hammock (1)
bs   savanna (1)
bt   seepy place (1)
bu   slags (1)
bv   straw field (1)
bw   stubble, a (1)
bx   swag (2)
by   swamp (3)
bz   timothy field (1)
ca   valley (6)
cb   wasteland (2)
cc   weak land (1)
cd   wetland(s) (3)
ce   wheat field (1)

029.6 L swamp

No Response (110)
A   backwater (2)
B   bay (4)
C   baygall (4)
D   bayhead (1)
E   bayou (3)
F   bayou land (2)
G   bog (31)
H   bog swamp (1)
I   boggy land (5)
J   boggy place (3)
K   boggy-type land (1)
L   boghole (1)
M   bottomland (2)
N   brake (2)
O   brake land (1)
P   branch head (1)
Q   brushy swamp (1)
R   catfish swamp (1)
S   cedar swamp (1)
T   crawfish ground (1)
U   crawfish land (2)
V   crawfishy area (1)
W   crawfishy land (1)
X   creek swamp (3)
Y   cypress brakes (1)
Z   cypress swamp (7)
aa   cypress-tree land (1)
ab   damp land (2)
ac   damp place (1)
ad   dry swamp (1)
ae   flat(s) (3)
af   flat ponds (1)
ag   flat swamp (1)
ah   flatland (1)
ai   flooded land (1)
aj   fresh marsh (1)
ak   frog level (1)
al   frog pond (4)
am   glade (2)
an   gooey land (1)
ao   gummy land (1)
ap   hammock (4)
aq   hog wallow (1)
ar   lagoon (6)
as   live-oak pond (1)
at   low ground (2)
au   low place (3)
av   lower land (1)
aw   lowland(s) (21)
ax   mango swamps (1)
ay   mangrove swamp (1)
az   marsh (35)
ba   marshland (8)
bb   marshy ground (2)
bc   marshy land (8)
bd   marshy place (1)
be   marshy swamp (1)
bf   marshy swampland (1)

bg mashy land (1)
bh mashy place (1)
bi mire (1)
bj moisture places (1)
bk muck (2)
bl muck land (1)
bm mucky land (3)
bn mud flats (1)
bo mud lashes (1)
bp mud mashy place (1)
bq muddy swamp (1)
br mudhole (3)
bs mushy place (1)
bt myrtle swamp (1)
bu overflow (1)
bv overflow land (2)
bw pin-oak glades (1)
bx pine swamp (1)
by pond (28)
bz pond-like, a (1)
ca pondy place (2)
cb pony land (1)
cc poor land (2)
cd prairie (2)
ce prairie tremblante [F] (1)
cf quarry (1)
cg reed brakes (4)
ch river swamp (8)
ci seepage (1)
cj seepish land (1)
ck seepy place (2)
cl sinkhole (2)
cm slag (1)
cn slash (5)
co slash land (1)
cp slosh (1)
cq sloshy place (1)
cr slough(s) (41)
cs slough-like (2)
ct slough of water (1)
cu slush (2)
cv sobby land (1)
cw soggy bottom (1)
cx soggy land (4)
cy spillover area (1)
cz spring land (1)
da spring seep (1)
db stagnant water (1)
dc surfaced land (1)
dd swag (2)
de swamp (585)
df swamp area(s) (3)
dg swamp country (3)
dh swamp ground (1)
di swamp-like, a (1)
dj swamp marshy land (1)
dk swamp place (1)
dl swamp water (2)
dm swampland (117)

dn swampy area (6)
do swampy ground (3)
dp swampy land (45)
dq swampy low swaggy place (1)
dr swampy place (7)
ds swampy-type land (1)
dt swampy water (1)
du swampy wet place (1)
dv tadpoly land (1)
dw timber swamp (1)
dx trembling prairie (1)
dy wasteland (3)
dz water-sob place (1)
ea wet bottom (field) (2)
eb wet flat (1)
ec wet marsh (1)
ed wet-natured land (2)
ee wet place (1)
ef wet spot (1)
eg wetland (13)
eh wilderness (1)
ei willow swamp (1)
ej woods land (2)

029.6 P swamp

{o} low-back onset
{?} glottal
No Response (178)
<shwawmp> (1)
<swaw(m)p> (1)
<swaw[m]p> (1)
<swaw[m]plan(d)=13> (1)
<swawm(p)> (1)
<swawm(p)lan(d)=13> (1)
<swawmp> (294)
<swawmpI=14> (28)
<swawmplan(d)=13> (24)
<swawmplan(d)z=13> (1)
<swawmpland=13> (5)
<swawmps> (34)
<swo(m)p> (1)
<swo[m]p> (2)
<swoemp> (2)
<swoemplan(d)=13> (1)
<swomb> (1)
<swomp> (185)
<swompI=14> (27)
<swompIlan(d)=143> (1)
<swompIland=143) (2)
<swomplan(d)=13> (10)
<swomplan(d)=21> (1)
<swomplan(d)z=13> (1)
<swompland=13> (7)
<swomps> (22)
<swump> (4)
<swumpI=14> (1)
<swumps> (2)
<sw{o}[m]{?}> (1)
<sw{o}mp> (80)
<sw{o}mpI=14> (4)

<sw{o}mplan(d)=13> (4)
<sw{o}mpland=13> (2)
<sw{o}mps> (10)
<thwawmp> (1)

029.7 L marsh

No Response (505)
A bay (2)
B baygall (1)
C bayou (6)
D beach (1)
E bog (6)
F boggy land (2)
G brackish land (1)
H brackish water (1)
I brine (1)
J bulrush (1)
K coastal prairie (1)
L dunes, the (1)
M flat, a (2)
N flat marshy place (1)
O flatland (2)
P graze land (1)
Q hammock (1)
R inlet (1)
S intercoastal thing (1)
T lagoon (3)
U Louisiana marsh (1)
V lowland(s) (2)
W marsh (272)
X marsh area (2)
Y marsh region (1)
Z marsh swamp (1)
aa marshland (82)
ab marshy area (1)
ac marshy land (25)
ad marshy place (4)
ae mire (1)
af morass (1)
ag muck (1)
ah mucky place (1)
ai mud pond (1)
aj mudhole place (1)
ak ocean meadow (1)
al prairie (2)
am prairie marsh (1)
an rice land (1)
ao salt flats (1)
ap salt grass (1)
aq salt marsh (8)
ar saltwater flats (1)
as saltwater marsh (2)
at saltwater swamp (1)
au savanna (1)
av saw-grass flats (1)
aw scrap land (1)
ax sea marsh (1)
ay sea-rim marsh (1)
az seep (1)
ba shore crest (1)

bb   sinkhole (1)
bc   soddy ground (1)
bd   swamp (10)
be   swampland (3)
bf   swampy land (1)
bg   tidal marsh (1)
bh   tidal marshland (1)
bi   tide wood (1)
bj   tidelands (2)
bk   wasteland (2)
bl   wet grass (1)
bm   wet place (1)
bn   wetland(s) (5)

029.8 L soil types

No Response (146)
A   beach (soil) (2)
B   Black Belt (soil) (5)
C   black buckshot (3)
D   black clay (8)
E   black gumbo (land) (11)
F   black loam (soil) (9)
G   black loamy land (1)
H   black muck soil (1)
I   black mucky clay (1)
J   black sandy land (1)
K   blackjack (land) (4)
L   blackland (prairie/soil) (79)
M   blue buckshot land (1)
N   blue clay (2)
O   brown loam (2)
P   buck(-)dough (land) (2)
Q   buckshot (land) (81)
R   buckshotty (land/soil) (4)
S   caliche (dirt) (5)
T   chert (bottomland) (4)
U   cherty lands (1)
V   clay buckshot (1)
W   clay (land/soil) (296)
X   clay-like (1)
Y   clay loam (11)
Z   clay sand (2)
aa   clayey (1)
ab   corduroy land (1)
ac   crawdad land (2)
ad   crawfish (clay/land/soil) (22)
ae   crawfishy (land) (23)
af   creek sand (1)
ag   delta (land/soil) (4)
ah   dipper land (1)
ai   gray loam (1)
aj   gray sand (2)
ak   gumbo (land/mud/soil) (104)
al   gumbo clay (4)
am   hill gumbo (1)
an   ice-cream land (1)
ao   jumbo land/soil (1)
ap   lime(-)(rock)(soil) (6)
aq   limestone (rock/soil) (7)
ar   limy (land/soil) (2)

as   loam (land/soil) (217)
at   loamus soil (1)
au   loamy (land/soil) (60)
av   loess (3)
aw   marl (soil) (5)
ax   Mississippi loam (1)
ay   muck (soil) (22)
az   muck-like, a (1)
ba   muck loam (1)
bb   muck-type soil (1)
bc   muckland(s) (11)
bd   mucky (black) (land/soil) (11)
be   mucky-type black soil (1)
bf   mulatto (1)
bg   Natchez loam (1)
bh   palmetto land (2)
bi   peat (moss/muck) (4)
bj   post oak (flats/land/prairie) (7)
bk   post-oaky dirt (1)
bl   post-oaky-type sand (1)
bm   prairie (land/mud/soil) (10)
bn   prairie gumbo (1)
bo   red clay (79)
bp   red clay-like (1)
bq   red Georgia clay (1)
br   red gumbo (1)
bs   red mulatto (2)
bt   red sand (3)
bu   redbud land (4)
bv   river sand (3)
bw   rocky loam (1)
bx   salitre [S] (1)
by   salt-heavy land (1)
bz   salt land (1)
ca   salty land/soil (3)
cb   sand (land/soil) (100)
cc   sand clay (3)
cd   sand loam (4)
ce   sandsoap land (1)
cf   sandstone (land) (2)
cg   sandy (land/soil) (278)
ch   sandy chocolate loam (1)
ci   sandy clay (3)
cj   sandy-like (1)
ck   sandy loam (land/soil) (122)
cl   sandy-loam-type soil (1)
cm   sandy loamy land (1)
cn   sandy-stone land (1)
co   sharky clay (1)
cp   silk clay loam (1)
cq   silt loam (1)
cr   slate (land) (3)
cs   slaty land (1)
ct   soapstone (clay) (3)
cu   soddy (soil) (2)
cv   stiff land (8)
cw   sweet dirt (1)
cx   Tift loam (1)
cy   white clay (6)

cz   white glady buckshotty soil (1)
da   white loamy land (1)
db   white muck (1)
dc   white sand (4)
dd   white sandy land (2)
de   yellow clay (4)
df   yellow gumbo (1)

029.8 P loam

No Response (534)
<lawm> (7)
<loeM=14> (2)
<loem> (298)
<loemI=14> (43)
<loen> (4)
<lowm> (3)
<luem> (19)
<luemAs=14> (1)
<luemI=14> (3)
<lum> (2)
<lumI=14> (1)

030.1 P draining

No Response (179)
<drai[n]> (1)
<drain> (383)
<drainN=14> (100)
<drainNG=14> (78)
<draind> (29)
<draint[N]=14> (1)
<drainz> (9)
<dran> (1)
<dree[n]> (1)
<dreen> (122)
<dreenN=14> (16)
<dreenNG=14> (2)
<dreend> (7)
<dreenz> (5)
<drenN=14> (1)
<drend> (1)
<drin> (1)
<jrain> (3)
<zhran> (1)

030.2 L canal

No Response (133)
A   barge canal (1)
B   bevel ditch (1)
C   blind ditch (2)
D   boat slip (1)
E   borrow ditch (1)
F   canal (212)
G   canal ditch (1)
H   canal-like (1)
I   canal something (1)
J   canal-type thing (1)
K   cement culvert (1)
L   channel (33)
M   coastal canal (1)
N   covered ditch (1)
O   creek (1)
P   culvert (4)

Q   cut [n.] (2)
R   dence (1)
S   ditch (586)
T   diversion ditch (1)
U   drain [n.] (27)
V   drain canal (1)
W   drain ditch (22)
X   drain tile (1)
Y   drainage (16)
Z   drainage canal (5)
aa   drainage ditch (75)
ab   drainage ditching (1)
ac   drainage furrow (1)
ad   drainage structure (1)
ae   dredge [n.] (3)
af   dredge ditch (8)
ag   dredged ditch (1)
ah   farm ditch (1)
ai   furrow (1)
aj   government drainage ditch (1)
ak   gully (10)
al   gutter (4)
am   hand ditch (1)
an   hand-ditched canal (1)
ao   hillside ditch (1)
ap   intercoastal canal (2)
aq   irrigation canal (1)
ar   irrigation ditch (9)
as   lateral ditch (1)
at   levee (1)
au   natural channel (1)
av   open ditch (1)
aw   outlet (1)
ax   pipeline canal (1)
ay   raw sand ditch (1)
az   road ditch (2)
ba   sandbag ditch (1)
bb   ship channel (2)
bc   sleven ditch (1)
bd   slough (4)
be   steamboat channel (1)
bf   straight ditch (1)
bg   tile (4)
bh   trapping ditch (1)
bi   trench (106)
bj   trough (2)
bk   tunnel (3)
bl   valley (1)
bm   W-Fourteen diversion canal (1)
bn   water ditch (1)
bo   water furrow (1)
bp   waterway (1)

030.3 L creek [tidal]
No Response (554)
A   back bay (1)
B   backwater (6)
C   basin (3)
D   bay (51)
E   bayou (105)

F   bayou bank (1)
G   bog (1)
H   bottomland (1)
I   brackish water (4)
J   brake (2)
K   branch (8)
L   cove (7)
M   creek (100)
N   dry creek (1)
O   estuary (3)
P   flats (1)
Q   floodland (1)
R   ford (1)
S   gulf (2)
T   inlet (31)
U   lagoon (7)
V   lake (5)
W   marsh (1)
X   mouth (1)
Y   mud flat (1)
Z   neck (2)
aa   outlet (1)
ab   pass (1)
ac   pond (4)
ad   saltwater creek (1)
ae   saltwater marsh (1)
af   shallow(s) (2)
ag   slip (1)
ah   slough (34)
ai   slough way (1)
aj   spillway (4)
ak   stream (9)
al   tidal basin (2)
am   tidal marsh (1)
an   tidal pool (2)
ao   tidal stream (2)
ap   tide creek (1)
aq   tidewater creek (1)
ar   tributaries (2)
as   tunnel of water (1)
at   waterway (1)
au   wet-weather branch (1)
av   wet-weather spring (2)

030.4 L ravine
No Response (355)
A   arroyo [S] (8)
B   bayou (1)
C   borrow pit (1)
D   branch (1)
E   canal (12)
F   canyon (36)
G   canyon-like (1)
H   channel (8)
I   chasm (1)
J   coulee (3)
K   coupe [F] (3)
L   cove (2)
M   creek (1)
N   creek bed (1)

O   crevasse [F] (2)
P   crevice (4)
Q   cutoff (1)
R   deep ditch (1)
S   deep gully (1)
T   deep thing (1)
U   ditch (78)
V   drain [n.] (4)
W   drain ditch (1)
X   drainage ditch (1)
Y   draw (8)
Z   dry bed (1)
aa   dry branch (1)
ab   dry creek (1)
ac   dry ditch (1)
ad   furrow (1)
ae   gap (1)
af   glade (1)
ag   gorge (40)
ah   gulch (10)
ai   gully (194)
aj   gully land (1)
ak   gully wash (3)
al   hollow (49)
am   inner hollow (1)
an   low place (1)
ao   pond (1)
ap   ravine (193)
aq   ravine-like (1)
ar   resaca [S] (2)
as   riddle (1)
at   rift (1)
au   river gorge (1)
av   riverbed (1)
aw   sinkhole (2)
ax   slash (1)
ay   slough (3)
az   spring bed (1)
ba   suckhole (2)
bb   sump hole (1)
bc   trench (8)
bd   trough (1)
be   underground wash (1)
bf   valley (22)
bg   wash [n.] (34)
bh   wash drain (1)
bi   wash hole (1)
bj   washed-out place (3)
bk   washed-through (land) (1)
bl   washout (17)
bm   washout place (1)
bn   waterfalls (1)

030.5 L gully
No Response (266)
A   alley (1)
B   alley-type thing (1)
C   brake (1)
D   channel (3)
E   coulee (2)

F   coupe [F] (1)
G   crack (1)
H   crevice (1)
I   culvert (1)
J   dip (1)
K   ditch (152)
L   drain (9)
M   drainage (3)
N   eroded land (1)
O   erosion ditch (1)
P   foot ditch (1)
Q   gorge (2)
R   gulch (4)
S   gullied hill (1)
T   gullied land (1)
U   gully (448)
V   gully type (1)
W   gully wash (1)
X   gutter (5)
Y   hole (5)
Z   hollow (1)
aa low place (1)
ab mud ditch (1)
ac mud puddle (1)
ad mudhole (3)
ae passage (1)
af pothole (4)
ag rain ditch (1)
ah rain-out area (1)
ai run (3)
aj runoff (1)
ak rut (15)
al sand gully (1)
am sink (2)
an slide (1)
ao swag (2)
ap tire rut (1)
aq trench (30)
ar wash (38)
as wash hole (2)
at wash place (2)
au washaway (1)
av washed place (1)
aw washed-out area (1)
ax washed-out ditch (1)
ay washed-out gully (1)
az washed-out place (2)
ba washout (73)
bb washout place (1)
bc water channel (1)
bd water ditch (1)
be water drain (1)
bf water furrow (2)
bg water gully (1)
bh water hole (1)

030.6 L creek

No Response (35)
A   alley (1)
B   artesian well (3)

C   ba(you) (1)
D   bay(ou) (2)
E   bayou (62)
F   boiling spring (2)
G   branch (455)
H   branch head (2)
I   branch of a creek (3)
J   branch of the bayou (1)
K   branch of water (1)
L   branch spring (2)
M   branch to the river (1)
N   brook (110)
O   canal (5)
P   canal branch (1)
Q   channel (2)
R   clear creek (1)
S   confluence (1)
T   contributors (1)
U   coulee (9)
V   coulee [F] (2)
W   coulees of water (1)
X   creek (739)
Y   creek of water (1)
Z   creek run (1)
aa cutoff (1)
ab ditch (24)
ac drain (8)
ad draw (3)
ae dribble (1)
af dry branch (2)
ag dry creek (1)
ah dry-weather branch (2)
ai everlasting spring (1)
aj everlasting stream (1)
ak feeder stream (1)
al flat stream (1)
am flowing stream (1)
an flowing well (2)
ao fork (1)
ap fork(s) [=two streams] (5)
aq free-running branch (1)
ar fresh stream (1)
as freshet (2)
at freshwater bayou (1)
au freshwater creek (1)
av freshwater flowing stream (1)
aw freshwater stream (1)
ax gully (8)
ay gutter (1)
az head of the creek (2)
ba heads (1)
bb hollow (3)
bc little bayou (1)
bd little branch (5)
be little creek (9)
bf little river (3)
bg little spring (1)
bh little stream (4)
bi little trickle (1)

bj main run (1)
bk marsh creek (1)
bl mountain spring (1)
bm mountain stream (1)
bn natural stream (1)
bo neck of the branch (1)
bp prong (3)
bq race (1)
br ravine (7)
bs reed brake (1)
bt resaca [S] (2)
bu riddle (1)
bv rill (5)
bw river (2)
bx rivulet (14)
by run (7)
bz running creek (1)
ca running ditch (1)
cb running stream (5)
cc running water(s) (3)
cd seep (2)
ce slough (14)
cf slough-like (1)
cg small branch (1)
ch small creek (2)
ci small river (2)
cj small stream (14)
ck small stream of water (5)
cl source [F] (1)
cm spring (172)
cn spring branch (35)
co spring creek (1)
cp spring runner (1)
cq spring stream (1)
cr spring water (3)
cs springhead (2)
ct springhead branch (1)
cu stream (335)
cv stream of water (17)
cw stream water (1)
cx tributary (14)
cy trickle (3)
cz wash (1)
da wash hole (1)
db water spring (2)
dc water stream (1)
dd waterway (1)
de wet-weather branch (5)
df wet-weather creek (1)
dg wet-weather spring (2)
dh wet-weather stream (3)

030.6 P creek

No Response (131)
<kree(k)> (1)
<kreek> (707)
<kreeks> (59)
<krik> (41)
<kriks> (2)

030.7 names of local streams

030.8 L hill

No Response (67)
A alto [S] (1)
B bald [n.] (1)
C bald hill (1)
D bald knob (5)
E bank (7)
F bench (1)
G bench land (1)
H bluff (4)
I bump (3)
J butte [F] (2)
K chenier [F] (2)
L clay hills (4)
M clay ridge (1)
N cote, une [F] (2)
O creek swamp hill (1)
P crest (4)
Q dam (1)
R dividing ridge (1)
S double-S hill (1)
T elevation (1)
U escarpment (1)
V foothill(s) (6)
W front ridge (1)
X gopher mound (1)
Y grade (2)
Z gravel ridge (1)
aa gray hill (1)
ab high place (1)
ac high plains (1)
ad highland (5)
ae hill (791)
af hill country (10)
ag hill knob (3)
ah hill land (17)
ai hill-like (2)
aj hill-like thing (1)
ak hill place (1)
al hill section (3)
am hillock (2)
an hillside (33)
ao hillside land (1)
ap hilltop (2)
aq hilly country (5)
ar hilly ground (1)
as hilly land (17)
at hilly place (1)
au hilly section (1)
av hummock (1)
aw hump (8)
ax incline (10)
ay Indian knoll (1)
az Indian mound (7)
ba knob (131)
bb knob hill (7)
bc knob of land (1)
bd knoll (106)
be loam (1)

bf lump (2)
bg mold (1)
bh mole (1)
bi molehill (1)
bj mound (85)
bk mound of dirt (1)
bl mound of earth (2)
bm pine hills (3)
bn potato hill (1)
bo potato knob (1)
bp raise [n.] (1)
bq red-clay hill (1)
br ridge (33)
bs ridge country (1)
bt rise (44)
bu rising (4)
bv rocky hills (3)
bw rolling ground (1)
bx rolling land (2)
by rolling section (1)
bz rolly land (1)
ca sandhill country (1)
cb sandhill(s) (6)
cc second bottom (1)
cd shelf (1)
ce slope (20)
cf sloping land (1)
cg steep hill (2)
ch steep incline (1)
ci tableland (1)
cj terrace (3)
ck town knob (1)
cl upgrade (1)
cm upland (2)
cn wethill (1)

030.8A P hill

{l}   dark
{w}   lateral
No Response (101)
<hee[l]> (6)
<hee[l]z> (1)
<heel> (11)
<heelz> (3)
<hee{l}> (9)
<hel> (1)
<he{l}> (2)
<hi[l]> (55)
<hi[l]z> (9)
<hil> (290)
<hils> (1)
<hilz> (67)
<hilzh> (1)
<hi{l}> (338)
<hi{l}z> (30)
<hi{w}> (16)
<hi{w}z> (2)
<hyil> (1)

030.8 S hill

No Response (0)

|ABAmaj| (1)
|ABCaba| (1)
|ABCabacba| (1)
|ABCmaj| (5)
|ABCmajcba| (1)
|ABEmaj| (1)
|ABImaj| (5)
|AGAmaacba| (2)
|AGAmaj| (1)
|AGEmaj| (1)
|AGImaj| (3)
|BGAmaj| (1)
|DAA| (29)
|DAAeaj| (1)
|DAAeak| (1)
|DAAmaj| (21)
|DAAmajcba| (1)
|DAB| (20)
|DABbbl| (1)
|DABcba| (2)
|DABcbj| (1)
|DABdac| (3)
|DABdae| (1)
|DABmaa| (8)
|DABmab| (1)
|DABmaj| (185)
|DABmajcba| (6)
|DAC| (3)
|DACmaj| (4)
|DAD| (1)
|DAE| (20)
|DAEabecba| (1)
|DAEcba| (6)
|DAEcbj| (1)
|DAEmaj| (156)
|DAEmajcba| (10)
|DAEmak| (1)
|DAFmaj| (1)
|DAG| (1)
|DAGcba| (2)
|DAGmaa| (1)
|DAGmaj| (37)
|DAHdae| (1)
|DAHefj| (1)
|DAHmaj| (2)
|DAI| (4)
|DAImaj| (26)
|DCA| (21)
|DCAcba| (1)
|DCAeal| (1)
|DCAmaacba| (1)
|DCAmaj| (14)
|DCAmajcba| (1)
|DCB| (1)
|DCBcba| (1)
|DCBcbj| (1)
|DCBeaa| (3)
|DCBeaacba| (2)
|DCBeac| (1)

|DCBeaj| (3)
|DCBeajcba| (2)
|DCBeajcia| (1)
|DCBkfj| (1)
|DCBmaa| (9)
|DCBmaacba| (1)
|DCBmaj| (95)
|DCBmajcba| (9)
|DCBmak| (1)
|DCBmam| (1)
|DCBmamcba| (1)
|DCBmancba| (1)
|DCC| (4)
|DCCmaj| (5)
|DCD| (1)
|DCE| (1)
|DCEcba| (1)
|DCEmaj| (53)
|DCFmaa| (1)
|DCFmaj| (5)
|DCFmak| (1)
|DCGmaj| (28)
|DCImaj| (10)
|DDBmdj| (1)
|DGBmaj| (2)
|DGEmaj| (2)
|DKBedacha| (1)
|DKBmda| (1)
|DKBmdj| (1)
|DKBmdjcha| (1)
|EABbbjmaj| (1)
|EABcba| (1)
|EABmaj| (17)
|EACmaj| (2)
|EAD| (2)
|EAFmaj| (1)
|EAGcba| (1)
|EAHcba| (1)
|EAHmaj| (4)
|ECBmaj| (4)
|ECBmca| (1)
|ECHmaj| (1)
|KAFeaj| (1)
|KAFmaj| (1)
|KCFmaj| (1)

030.8B P knob
{b}   devoiced
{o}   low-back onset
{r}   weakly retroflex
{?}   glottal
No Response (418)
<dawrnob=13> (2)
<do(r)nob=13> (2)
<do[r]nob=21> (1)
<doe(r)nob=13> (9)
<doe[r]no(b)=13> (1)
<doe[r]no(b)=21> (1)
<doe[r]nob=13> (19)
<doe[r]nobz=13> (2)

<doe[r]n{o}b=13> (1)
<doe[r]tnob=31> (1)
<doernawb=13> (2)
<doernob=13> (48)
<doernob=21> (1)
<doernobz=13> (3)
<doernub=13> (1)
<doern{o}b> (1)
<doern{o}b=13> (1)
<doe{r}nob=11> (1)
<doe{r}nob=13> (7)
<doe{r}nob=31> (1)
<nawb> (17)
<nawbz> (4)
<naw{b}> (1)
<naw{b}sh> (1)
<no(b)> (3)
<nob> (274)
<nobz> (24)
<nop> (2)
<no{?}> (1)
<no{b}> (10)
<nub> (3)
<n{o}b> (47)
<n{o}bz> (7)

030.9 P Gulf of Mexico
{oo}   unrounded
No Response (629)
<dAgu(1)f=41> (1)
<dAgulf=41> (1)
<dIgu[1]f=41> (3)
<dIgulf=41> (3)
<dhAgu[1]f=41> (2)
<dhAgu[1]fAvmeksIkoe=434143> (1)
<dhAgulf=41> (13)
<dhAgulfA(v)meksIkoe=414143> (1)
<dhAgulfAvmeksIkoe=414143> (1)
<dhAgulfAvmeksIkoe=434143> (1)
<dhAgulfovmeksIkoe=413143> (1)
<dhIgo[1]f=41> (1)
<dhIgolf=41> (1)
<dhIgu(1)f=41> (1)
<dhIgu[1]f=41> (2)
<dhIgulf=41> (7)
<gaw(1)f> (1)
<golf> (3)
<golfAvmeksIkoe=34143> (1)
<goo(1)fA(v)meksIkoe=34143> (1)
<goo[1]f> (4)
<goolf> (1)
<goolfA(v)meksIkoe=34143> (2)
<gu(1)f> (9)
<gu(1)fA(v)meks(I)koe=1423> (1)
<gu(1)fA(v)meks(I)koe=3413> (1)
<gu(1)fA(v)meksIkoe=24143> (4)
<gu(1)fA(v)meksIkoe=34143> (13)
<gu(1)fAvmeksIkoe=34143> (1)
<gu[1]f> (47)
<gu[1]fA(v)meks(I)koe=1423> (1)

<gu[1]fA(v)meksIkoe=24143> (4)
<gu[1]fA(v)meksIkoe=34142> (1)
<gu[1]fA(v)meksIkoe=34143> (3)
<gu[1]fAvmeksIkoe=14143> (2)
<gu[1]fAvmeksIkoe=24143> (1)
<gu[1]fAvmeksIkoe=34143> (2)
<gulf> (41)
<gulfA(v)me(k)sIkoe=24143> (1)
<gulfA(v)meksAkoe=24143> (1)
<gulfA(v)meksIkoe=14143> (17)
<gulfA(v)meksIkoe=14243> (1)
<gulfA(v)meksIkoe=24143> (14)
<gulfA(v)meksIkoe=34142> (1)
<gulfA(v)meksIkoe=34143> (30)
<gulfA(v)muchIkoe=34143> (1)
<gulfA(v)muksIkoe=34143> (1)
<gulfAvmaksIkoe=14143> (1)
<gulfAvmeks(I)koe=1413> (1)
<gulfAvmeksIkoe=14143> (8)
<gulfAvmeksIkoe=24143> (9)
<gulfAvmeksIkoe=34143> (13)
<g{oo}(1)f> (1)
<g{oo}[1]f> (1)
<g{oo}lf> (1)
<meksIkoe=143> (10)

031.1 P mountain
{r}   flap
{t}   glottal
No Response (105)
<mow(n)tN=14> (9)
<mow(n)tNG=14> (1)
<mow(n)tNz=14> (1)
<mow(n){r}in=13> (1)
<mow(n){t}N=14> (12)
<mow(n){t}Nz=14> (1)
<mow[n](t)N=14> (1)
<mow[n]tN=14> (6)
<mow[n]{r}N=14> (2)
<mow[n]{r}ing=13> (1)
<mow[n]{t}N=14> (48)
<mow[n]{t}NG=14> (1)
<mow[n]{t}Nz=14> (1)
<mown(tN)z> (1)
<mown(t)N=14> (2)
<mown(t)[N]=14> (1)
<mownd[N]=14> (1)
<mownd{t}N=14> (1)
<mownt(N)> (1)
<mowntN=14> (153)
<mowntNG=14> (3)
<mowntNGz=14> (1)
<mowntNs=14> (1)
<mowntNz=14> (21)
<mownt[N]=14> (1)
<mowntin=13> (4)
<mown{r}N=14> (12)
<mown{r}Nz=14> (1)
<mown{t}(N)> (3)
<mown{t}N=14> (432)

<mown{t}NG=14> (4)
<mown{t}NGz=14> (3)
<mown{t}Ns=14> (2)
<mown{t}Nz=14> (103)
<mown{t}Nzh=14> (1)
<mown{t}[N]=14> (4)
<mown{t}in=13> (2)
<mown{t}ing=13> (1)
<mown{t}inz=13> (1)
<mowtNGz=14> (1)

031.2 L cliff
No Response (256)
A   bench (1)
B   bluff (92)
C   buttress (1)
D   canyon wall (1)
E   cliff (576)
F   cliff of rock (2)
G   cliffside (2)
H   crag (1)
I   crest (1)
J   drop (1)
K   drop-off (10)
L   edge (4)
M   embankment (2)
N   escarpment (2)
O   face (8)
P   fall (1)
Q   falloff (1)
R   hanging-out cliff (1)
S   hillside (2)
T   incline (2)
U   jump-off (3)
V   ledge (39)
W   mountain cliff (1)
X   mountainside (1)
Y   palisade (1)
Z   peak (4)
aa   plateau (4)
ab   precipice (17)
ac   promontory (1)
ad   ridge (7)
ae   ridge country (1)
af   rock cliff (10)
ag   rock ledge (1)
ah   rocky cliff (1)
ai   rocky side (1)
aj   sharp cliff (1)
ak   sheer drop (1)
al   shelf (1)
am   side (2)
an   slope (17)
ao   steep [n.] (2)
ap   steep place (1)
aq   steepside (1)
ar   tableland (1)
as   terrace (1)

031.2 P cliff/cliffs
{f}   bilabial

No Response (322)
<kleef> (1)
<kleefs> (1)
<klef> (4)
<klefs> (1)
<kleth> (1)
<kli(f)s> (2)
<klif> (511)
<klif(s)> (8)
<klifs> (279)
<klift> (54)
<klifts> (1)
<kliths> (1)
<kliv> (1)
<kli{f}> (9)
<kli{f}s> (5)

031.3 L notch
No Response (363)
A   channel (1)
B   cut (12)
C   dip (4)
D   divide (7)
E   dock (1)
F   draw (4)
G   gap (125)
H   gulch (2)
I   low gap (4)
J   low pass (1)
K   low place (3)
L   mountain cut (1)
M   mountain pass (7)
N   mountain road (1)
O   notch (59)
P   open space (2)
Q   pass (110)
R   path (1)
S   swag (5)
T   trail (7)

031.3 P notch
{o}   low-back
No Response (582)
<nawch> (5)
<niech> (1)
<noch> (274)
<nochAz=14> (1)
<nochIz=14> (20)
<nochN=14> (1)
<noch[NG]=14> (1)
<nocht> (9)
<not> (1)
<n{o}ch> (16)
<n{o}chIz=14> (3)

031.4 L wharf
No Response (283)
A   anchor [n.] (1)
B   arbor (1)
C   bank (2)
D   boat depot (1)
E   boat dock (56)

F   boat land(ing) (2)
G   boat landing (36)
H   boat launching pad (1)
I   boat ramp (4)
J   boat slip (2)
K   boat stop (1)
L   boatyard (1)
M   channel (1)
N   city dock (1)
O   dirt bank (1)
P   dock (384)
Q   dockboard (1)
R   dry dock (1)
S   ferry landing (1)
T   fish dock (2)
U   fisherman's landing (1)
V   flatform (1)
W   floating dock (1)
X   freight depot (2)
Y   harbor (43)
Z   jetty (1)
aa   landing (64)
ab   landing place (2)
ac   landing port (1)
ad   launching [n.] (1)
ae   launching dock (1)
af   launching pad (1)
ag   levee (11)
ah   loading dock (7)
ai   loading port (1)
aj   loading ramp (1)
ak   log landing (1)
al   mail-boat landing (1)
am   marina (5)
an   pier (87)
ao   platform (2)
ap   port (51)
aq   railroad dock (1)
ar   ramp (6)
as   river landing (1)
at   river port (1)
au   riverfront (1)
av   runway (1)
aw   seaport (3)
ax   sea wharf (1)
ay   ship base (1)
az   ship channel (1)
ba   ship dock (1)
bb   ship house (1)
bc   ship landing (2)
bd   shipping dock (1)
be   shipping lock (1)
bf   shipping port (2)
bg   shipyard (4)
bh   shoal (1)
bi   shore (1)
bj   shrimp dock (1)
bk   slip (1)
bl   stage flat (1)

bm   station (1)
bn   stop [n.] (1)
bo   unloading dock (2)
bp   wharf (130)

031.5 L waterfall

No Response (292)
A   cascade (3)
B   cascade falls (1)
C   cataract (3)
D   cliff (1)
E   down, a (1)
F   drop (2)
G   drop-off (3)
H   falling water (1)
I   fall(s) (149)
J   freshet (1)
K   high fall (1)
L   overflow (2)
M   pour off (1)
N   pourover (3)
O   rapid falls (1)
P   rapid(s) (11)
Q   riffle (1)
R   shoals (6)
S   spillway (8)
T   water fill (1)
U   water flow (1)
V   water sinkhole (1)
W   water spill (1)
X   waterfalling (1)
Y   waterfall(s) (488)

031.6 L road materials/surfaces

No Response (29)
A   (a)dobe (road) (2)
B   all-weather road (2)
C   amesite (2)
D   asbestos (4)
E   asphalt (road) (426)
F   asphalt concrete (1)
G   asphalt pave (2)
H   asphalt (pavement) (3)
I   asphalt top (1)
J   asphalted (2)
K   asphalting (1)
L   base dirt (1)
M   Benton County chert (1)
N   billy-goat road (1)
O   bituminous (1)
P   black asphalt (1)
Q   black-bottom road (1)
R   black cement (1)
S   black dirt (2)
T   black hard-surface road (1)
U   black oil (3)
V   black road (2)
W   black tar (4)
X   blacktop (road/street) (352)
Y   blacktop clay (1)
Z   blacktop paving (1)

aa   blacktopped (road) (9)
ab   blacktopping (5)
ac   block road (1)
ad   blue gravel (1)
ae   board road (1)
af   bodock block (1)
ag   brick (road/street) (26)
ah   caliche (road) (19)
ai   car road (1)
aj   cement (road) (264)
ak   cement blocks (1)
al   cement brick (1)
am   cement lime (1)
an   cement paving (5)
ao   cement slab (5)
ap   cement-surface road (1)
aq   cemented (3)
ar   chert (road) (20)
as   cinders (2)
at   clamshell (2)
au   clay (road) (45)
av   clay-base road (1)
aw   clay dirt (1)
ax   coal tar (6)
ay   cobblestone (13)
az   cold mix (1)
ba   conbrick (1)
bb   concrete (road) (418)
bc   concrete blocks (3)
bd   concrete pave (1)
be   concrete pavement (1)
bf   concrete slab (road) (2)
bg   concreted (1)
bh   concretement (1)
bi   coquina (1)
bj   coquina shell (1)
bk   corduroy road (5)
bl   cover stone (1)
bm   creek gravel (1)
bn   creosote (3)
bo   creosote oil (1)
bp   creosote wood-block road (1)
bq   creosoted wood blocks (1)
br   crush bottles (1)
bs   crush rock (2)
bt   crush stone (1)
bu   crushed rock (7)
bv   crushed shells (1)
bw   crushed-stone road (1)
bx   dirt (road/street) (654)
by   dust (road) (4)
bz   dusty road (1)
ca   Georgia shale (1)
cb   graded (road) (13)
cc   granite (1)
cd   gravel (road) (589)
ce   gravel(-)rock (road) (3)
cf   gravel top (1)
cg   graveled (road) (7)

ch   gravels (8)
ci   ground limestone (1)
cj   ground-rock road (1)
ck   gum (1)
cl   gutter rock (1)
cm   hard clay (1)
cn   hard road (9)
co   hard-pave road (1)
cp   hard(-)surface (road) (13)
cq   hardtop (road) (10)
cr   hardtopped road (2)
cs   hot mix (3)
ct   hot top (1)
cu   lime (1)
cv   lime(-)rock (road) (6)
cw   limestone (6)
cx   log road (3)
cy   macadam (road) (22)
cz   macadam paving (1)
da   macadamize (road) (3)
db   macadamized (road) (9)
dc   marl (2)
dd   mud (road/street) (19)
de   muddy (road) (3)
df   natural (1)
dg   oil (road) (15)
dh   oily road (1)
di   oolite limestone (1)
dj   oystershell (road) (8)
dk   pale road (2)
dl   paled road (1)
dm   paling (1)
dn   paper-wood road (1)
do   pave (road) (50)
dp   paved (road/street) (140)
dq   pavement (road) (57)
dr   paving (6)
ds   pea gravel (3)
dt   pebbles (4)
du   pebblestone (1)
dv   phosphate (1)
dw   pike (road) (7)
dx   pine tar (3)
dy   pitch (4)
dz   plank mix (1)
ea   plank road (2)
eb   plant mix (2)
ec   pole road (2)
ed   post road (1)
ee   pulpwood road (1)
ef   red clay (2)
eg   red clay gravel (1)
eh   red gravel (2)
ei   red rock (1)
ej   red-soil road (1)
ek   redtop road (1)
el   resin (1)
em   road oil (1)
en   rock (road) (80)

eo rock bottom (1)
ep rock pavement (1)
eq rocky road (2)
er rut road (1)
es salt (1)
et sand (road) (40)
eu sand(-)clay (road) (2)
ev sand gravel (1)
ew sand-graded road (1)
ex sandrock (3)
ey sandy (road) (5)
ez sawdust road (1)
fa seashell road (1)
fb sediment road (1)
fc shale (1)
fd shell (road) (49)
fe shell-dust road (1)
ff slab (1)
fg slag (road) (23)
fh slagged road (1)
fi soft dirt (1)
fj soft gravel (1)
fk soil (1)
fl soil cement (1)
fm stone (road) (5)
fn surface(d) road (4)
fo tar (road/street) (384)
fp tar belt road (1)
fq tar blocks (1)
fr tar covering (1)
fs tar on gravel (1)
ft tar surface (1)
fu tar-surfaced (1)
fv Tarmac (1)
fw tarred (1)
fx Tarvia (1)
fy Tarviated road (1)
fz topping (road) (2)
ga unimproved (2)
gb unpave road (1)
gc unpaved (road) (6)
gd vitrified-brick road (1)
ge vulcanized road (1)
gf wash gravel (2)
gg washboard road (3)
gh white asphalt (1)
gi white chalk (1)
gj white clay (1)
gk white gravel (1)
gl white pavement (1)
gm white rock (1)
gn white sand (2)
go white slag (1)
gp wood (road) (2)
gq wood blocks (1)
gr wooden blocks (2)
gs woods road (3)

031.6A P tar
{o} low-back

{r} weakly retroflex
No Response (579)
<taw(r)> (8)
<taw[r]> (4)
<tawr> (17)
<taw{r}> (1)
<ter> (1)
<to(r)> (11)
<to[r]> (36)
<tor> (142)
<to{r}> (20)
<t{o}(r)> (15)
<t{o}[r]> (32)
<t{o}r> (50)
<t{o}{r}> (2)

031.6B P dirt
{r} weakly retroflex
{t} flap
{?} glottal
No Response (298)
<du[r]t> (158)
<du[r]{?}> (1)
<dur(t)> (2)
<durt> (377)
<dur{?}> (4)
<dur{t}> (4)
<du{r}t> (76)

031.6C P gravel
{L} labial
{v} bilabial
No Response (305)
<dravL=14> (1)
<graivL=14> (1)
<gravL=14> (548)
<gravLd=14> (11)
<gravLz=14> (8)
<gravR=14> (1)
<grav[L]=14> (21)
<gravool=13> (1)
<gravul=13> (1)
<grav{L}=14> (10)
<grawL=14> (2)
<gra{v}L=14> (1)
<gra{v}[L]=14> (1)
<grevL=14> (4)
<grovL=14> (2)
<gruvL=14> (1)

031.7 L byway
No Response (101)
A access (road) (4)
B alternate road (1)
C auxiliary road (1)
D back dirt road (1)
E back lane (1)
F back road/street (26)
G back-street pave road (1)
H backcountry road (1)
I beach road (1)
J billy-goat road (1)

K black hard-surface road (1)
L blacktop road (3)
M blanket road (1)
N blind road (1)
O branch off [n.] (2)
P branch road (12)
Q bypass (9)
R byroad (25)
S byway (9)
T caliche road (6)
U cart road (1)
V CC road (1)
W chemin travers [F] (1)
X chert road (6)
Y city road/street (4)
Z clay road (22)
aa cobblestone street (1)
ab community dirt road (1)
ac community road (7)
ad corduroy road (5)
ae cote, le [F] (1)
af country road/highway (128)
ag country side road (1)
ah county farm road (1)
ai county grade (1)
aj county-maintained road (2)
ak county road (41)
al cow path (1)
am cross street (1)
an crosscountry road (1)
ao crossroad(s) (20)
ap cutoff (road) (11)
aq dead(-)end (road) (3)
ar detour (road) (5)
as dirt country road (1)
at dirt road/street (464)
au dirt trail (1)
av dirt wagon road (1)
aw drive (1)
ax driveway (1)
ay dust road (2)
az dusty road (1)
ba egress road (1)
bb exit road (1)
bc farm road (19)
bd farm-to-market road (53)
be feeder road (4)
bf field road (10)
bg fork (2)
bh front road (1)
bi graded road (4)
bj gravel road/street (196)
bk gravel trail (1)
bl graveled road (3)
bm hard road (4)
bn hard-surface road (1)
bo hardtop (3)
bp headland (1)
bq horse-and-wagon road (1)

br   horse path (1)
bs   improved country road (1)
bt   in road (1)
bu   intersection road (1)
bv   junction road (1)
bw   lane (35)
bx   lead-in road (1)
by   leading road (1)
bz   little road (8)
ca   little short road (1)
cb   log road (3)
cc   logging road (1)
cd   military road (3)
ce   mountain road (2)
cf   mud road/street (9)
cg   narrow road (2)
ch   narrow small road (1)
ci   neighborhood road (4)
cj   no-name road (1)
ck   nowhere road (1)
cl   off road/street (3)
cm   one-way street (1)
cn   out road (2)
co   outside road (1)
cp   oystershell road (2)
cq   paper-wood road (1)
cr   parish road (10)
cs   pass (1)
ct   path (road) (19)
cu   pave road/street (4)
cv   paved (road/street) (11)
cw   pavement road (1)
cx   pig trail (1)
cy   pike (road) (5)
cz   plantation road (3)
da   pole road (1)
db   post road (1)
dc   primary road (1)
dd   public road (30)
de   pulpwood road (1)
df   ranch road (1)
dg   residential street (1)
dh   ridge road (1)
di   right-of-way (1)
dj   rock road (21)
dk   route (road) (3)
dl   rural country road (1)
dm   rural road (7)
dn   sand road (12)
do   sand trail (1)
dp   sawdust road (1)
dq   seashell road (1)
dr   second-class road (1)
ds   second-place road (1)
dt   secondary (road) (10)
du   service road (7)
dv   settlement road (13)
dw   shell-dust road (1)
dx   shell road (24)

dy   shortcut (road) (4)
dz   side road/street (202)
ea   sidetrack road (1)
eb   sled road (1)
ec   slim road (1)
ed   small road (1)
ee   spur (of the road) (2)
ef   stagecoach road (1)
eg   state road/street (18)
eh   straight-out road (1)
ei   subgrade (1)
ej   third road (1)
ek   thoroughfare (1)
el   three-packed road (1)
em   three-path road (6)
en   three-pathed road (1)
eo   three-track road (1)
ep   three-trail road (2)
eq   through road (2)
er   trail (road) (28)
es   turn road (1)
et   turnoff (road) (7)
eu   ungraded road (1)
ev   unimproved (1)
ew   unpave(d) road (5)
ex   valley road (1)
ey   wagon road (9)
ez   wagon trail (1)
fa   ward road (1)
fb   wood block road (1)
fc   woods road (4)
fd   WPA road (2)

031.8 L lane

No Response (163)
A   access road (3)
B   alley (20)
C   alley road (2)
D   alleyway (1)
E   alligator trail (1)
F   asphalt drive (1)
G   avenue (6)
H   back road/street (3)
I   bicycle trail (1)
J   big road (1)
K   branch-off road (1)
L   branch road (4)
M   brechas [S] (1)
N   buggy road (1)
O   byroad (6)
P   byway (4)
Q   car driveway (1)
R   cattle crossing (3)
S   cattle gap (1)
T   cattle gate (1)
U   cattle pass (2)
V   cattle path (2)
W   cattle road (1)
X   cattle thing (1)
Y   cattle trail (4)

Z   cattle underpass (1)
aa   community road (2)
ab   concrete driveway (1)
ac   country lane (3)
ad   country road (5)
ae   country side road (1)
af   county road (2)
ag   cow lane (1)
ah   cow pass (2)
ai   cow-pasture road (1)
aj   cow trail (19)
ak   cow(s') path (30)
al   cutoff (2)
am   dead end (road) (3)
an   dirt road (30)
ao   drive (52)
ap   drive-in (5)
aq   drive out (1)
ar   driveway (351)
as   entrance (road) (3)
at   entranceway (1)
au   exit (1)
av   farm road (15)
aw   fence road (1)
ax   field road (13)
ay   footpath (5)
az   front drive (1)
ba   gap (1)
bb   gap through (1)
bc   gravel driveway (1)
bd   graveled road (1)
be   halfway road (1)
bf   haul road (1)
bg   hog path (1)
bh   hog trail (1)
bi   home road (1)
bj   horse lane (1)
bk   horse trail (2)
bl   house trail (1)
bm   individual (little) road (2)
bn   lane (328)
bo   lane road (4)
bp   laneway (1)
bq   lawn (1)
br   little road (8)
bs   lovers' lane (3)
bt   main drive (1)
bu   meadow road (1)
bv   narrow road (4)
bw   narrow strip (1)
bx   neighborhood lane (1)
by   neighborhood road (1)
bz   off road (1)
ca   out road (2)
cb   outlet (1)
cc   parkway (1)
cd   pass (8)
ce   pasture road (4)
cf   path (174)

cg   path-like, a (2)
ch   pathway (10)
ci   pavement road (1)
cj   pig path (2)
ck   pig trail (6)
cl   plantation road (3)
cm   private drive (10)
cn   private driveway (4)
co   private lane (2)
cp   private road (70)
cq   property road (1)
cr   (rac)coon trail (1)
cs   ranch road (1)
ct   right-of-way (2)
cu   road field (1)
cv   road (to the farm/house) (23)
cw   runway (1)
cx   sand road (2)
cy   sendero (road) [S] (1)
cz   settlement road (2)
da   shaded lane (1)
db   shady drive (1)
dc   shady road (1)
dd   sheep path (1)
de   short cutoff (1)
df   side drive (1)
dg   side lane (1)
dh   side road (9)
di   spur (1)
dj   three-path road (3)
dk   three-trail road (1)
dl   township road (1)
dm   track (3)
dn   trail (80)
do   trail road (3)
dp   trailway (1)
dq   tramroad (1)
dr   travel path (1)
ds   turn road (3)
dt   turnaround (1)
du   turnoff (road) (8)
dv   turnout (1)
dw   two-rutted road (1)
dx   wagon road (5)
dy   walk (3)
dz   walkway (4)
ea   welcome road (1)
eb   wire road (1)

031.9A L sidewalk
No Response (198)
A   banquette [F] (30)
B   board sidewalk (2)
C   boardwalk (11)
D   brick walk (1)
E   briquette [F] (1)
F   catwalk (1)
G   cement pavement (1)
H   cement walk (2)
I   concrete sidewalk (1)

J   concrete walk (1)
K   dirt sidewalk (2)
L   palement (1)
M   pathway (1)
N   pave (1)
O   pave walk (1)
P   paved sidewalk (1)
Q   pavement (24)
R   plank walk (6)
S   plank walkway (1)
T   side (1)
U   sidewalk (686)
V   street (1)
W   walk (13)
X   walking street (1)
Y   walkway (11)
Z   wooden bridge (1)

031.9B L parkway
No Response (714)
A   allee [F] (1)
B   bank(s) (3)
C   beautifying place (1)
D   block (1)
E   border (2)
F   boulevard (5)
G   channel (1)
H   city property (1)
I   curb (8)
J   curbing (5)
K   ditch line (1)
L   divider (1)
M   divider strip (1)
N   easement (4)
O   edges (2)
P   enfilade [F] (1)
Q   esplanade (2)
R   grass (5)
S   grass between the pavement and
     the street (1)
T   grass cot (1)
U   grass median (1)
V   grass strip (15)
W   grassplot (4)
X   grassy place (1)
Y   grassy strip (1)
Z   gutter (1)
aa   hedge (1)
ab   intermediate (1)
ac   land (1)
ad   lawn (13)
ae   margin (1)
af   median (16)
ag   median strip (1)
ah   medium (5)
ai   meridian (1)
aj   neutral ground (9)
ak   neutral strip (4)
al   park (1)
am   park strip (1)

an   parking (3)
ao   parking strip (1)
ap   parkway (13)
aq   parquette (1)
ar   part of the lawn (1)
as   patch of Bermuda grass (1)
at   path (2)
au   piece of grass (1)
av   right-of-way (5)
aw   road (1)
ax   shoulder (6)
ay   shoulder of the road (1)
az   small lawn (1)
ba   sod belt (1)
bb   strip (2)
bc   strip of grass (9)
bd   swale (1)
be   terrace (2)
bf   tree belt (1)
bg   tree lawn (2)
bh   walk (1)

032.1 G throw
<!>   infinitive
<&>   present 3rd singular
<@>   present participle
<*>   preterit
<#>   past participle
No Response (160)
<!sroe> (2)
<!th(r)aw> (1)
<!th(r)oe> (99)
<!th(r)oed> (1)
<!th(r)oer> (1)
<!th(r)oez> (1)
<!thAroe=41> (1)
<!thraw> (1)
<!throe> (246)
<!troe> (10)
<&th(r)oez> (5)
<&throez> (3)
<@th(r)oeN=14> (7)
<@thrawN=14> (1)
<@throeN=14> (3)
<@throeNG=14> (1)
<@throewN=14> (2)
<@throewNG=14> (1)
<@troeN=14> (1)
<*srue> (1)
<*th(r)oe> (1)
<*th(r)oed> (87)
<*th(r)ue> (21)
<*threw> (7)
<*throe> (3)
<*throed> (122)
<*throo> (1)
<*throo> (1)
<*thrue> (379)
<*thrued> (1)
<*troed> (3)

<*true> (7)
<#th(r)oed> (7)
<#th(r)oen> (1)
<#throed> (16)
<#throen> (28)
<#throend> (1)
<#thrue> (2)

032.1A L rock

No Response (253)
A   fieldstone (1)
B   pebble (7)
C   rock (613)
D   stone (95)

032.1B L threw (the rock)

No Response (116)
A   cast (2)
B   chalk(ed) it (1)
C   chuck(ed) (7)
D   chunk(ed) (the dog with the rock) (16)
E   chunk(ed) (the rock at the dog) (161)
F   chunk(ed) after (the dog) (1)
G   chunk(ed) at (the dog) (17)
H   chunk(ed) out (1)
I   fetched it (at him) (1)
J   flew it (1)
K   flung (8)
L   heaved (it) (3)
M   hummed it (2)
N   hurled (7)
O   pitch(ed) (59)
P   rock [v.] (1)
Q   shied (1)
R   sling/slung (7)
S   threw/throwed (767)
T   toss(ed) (19)
U   whiz (1)

032.2 G (not) at home

No Response (159)
A   at home (199)
B   home (168)

032.2 S home

No Response (0)
|ISA| (1)
|J2Afoa| (4)
|J2Ajub| (1)
|J2Bfoa| (1)
|J2Cfod| (3)
|J2Cjub| (1)
|J2Cmdj| (1)
|J2Deda| (1)
|J2Deoa| (23)
|J2Deoj| (4)
|J2Dfod| (3)
|J2Dfoj| (8)
|J2Dfom| (1)
|J2Heoa| (8)
|J2Hfoa| (1)

|J2Hfoc| (1)
|J2Hfod| (3)
|J2Hfoh| (3)
|J2Hfom| (1)
|JBHeaa| (1)
|JBHeaj| (1)
|JBHefj| (2)
|JHHeoj| (1)
|JHHmoa| (1)
|JJAefa| (1)
|JJAefj| (11)
|JJAffd| (2)
|JJAffj| (1)
|JJAjjb| (14)
|JJAjjf| (3)
|JJAjjk| (1)
|JJBefj| (4)
|JJBffj| (1)
|JJC| (1)
|JJCefa| (3)
|JJCefj| (24)
|JJCffd| (1)
|JJCjja| (15)
|JJCjjb| (10)
|JJCjjk| (1)
|JJClfj| (1)
|JJD| (3)
|JJDcjj| (1)
|JJDeaa| (1)
|JJDefa| (188)
|JJDefj| (30)
|JJDffd| (31)
|JJDffh| (1)
|JJDffm| (8)
|JJDjjf| (1)
|JJDjjk| (1)
|JJDjjo| (1)
|JJDlfj| (1)
|JJFefa| (3)
|JJFefj| (5)
|JJFffm| (1)
|JJHefa| (39)
|JJHefc| (1)
|JJHefj| (26)
|JJHfad| (1)
|JJHffd| (3)
|JJHffm| (1)
|JJHfod| (1)
|JJHjjk| (1)
|JQDeoa| (1)
|JSA| (1)
|JSAefa| (1)
|JSAefj| (8)
|JSAjbb| (1)
|JSAjjb| (4)
|JSAjjf| (1)
|JSCefe| (1)
|JSCefj| (11)
|JSCffd| (1)

|JSD| (2)
|JSDefa| (91)
|JSDefb| (1)
|JSDefj| (12)
|JSDema| (1)
|JSDffd| (4)
|JSDffm| (1)
|JSDlfj| (2)
|JSFefa| (6)
|JSFffd| (1)
|JSGefa| (1)
|JSHefa| (25)
|JSHefj| (13)
|JSHffa| (1)
|JSHffj| (1)
|JSHmfj| (1)
|JUAeoa| (2)
|JUAfod| (1)
|JUC| (1)
|JUCeoa| (1)
|JUCeoj| (3)
|JUCfoc| (2)
|JUCfod| (6)
|JUCjua| (5)
|JUCjub| (1)
|JUD| (1)
|JUDeda| (1)
|JUDeoa| (42)
|JUDeoj| (9)
|JUDexa| (1)
|JUDfoa| (1)
|JUDfod| (22)
|JUDfom| (4)
|JUFeoa| (1)
|JUFeoj| (1)
|JUH| (1)
|JUHeoa| (10)
|JUHeoj| (1)
|JUHfoa| (4)
|JUHfoc| (2)
|JUHfod| (11)
|JUHfoh| (6)
|LFAefa| (6)
|LFEefj| (3)
|LFEffd| (1)
|LFEjjm| (1)
|LFGefa| (5)
|LFGefj| (1)
|LFHefa| (1)
|LMAefa| (1)
|LMAffj| (4)
|LMEefj| (1)
|LMGefa| (1)
|LMGefj| (2)
|LOAeoa| (3)
|LOAfoa| (1)
|LOEeoa| (1)
|LXAedj| (1)
|LXAeoa| (1)

|LXAfoa| (12)
|LXAfoj| (9)
|LXDfoa| (1)
|LXIfoj| (1)
|QCBjjc| (1)
|QOBfod| (1)
|QOBjua| (1)
|QODfoa| (1)
|QOHfod| (1)
|QXFeof| (1)

032.3 L black coffee

No Response (205)
A   as is (2)
B   bare (1)
C   barefoot (coffee) (10)
D   barefooted (coffee) (38)
E   bitter (5)
F   black and rich (2)
G   black as your hat (1)
H   black (coffee) (559)
I   black straight coffee (1)
J   blank (1)
K   cafe negro [S] (1)
L   cafe noir [F] (2)
M   cafe solo [S] (1)
N   coffee from the pot (1)
O   coffee with no milk (1)
P   cowboy style (1)
Q   cup walking, a (1)
R   dark (coffee) (5)
S   flatfoot (1)
T   French coffee (2)
U   Java (9)
V   Joe (1)
W   just as it is (1)
X   Kilgore coffee (1)
Y   mud (4)
Z   naked (coffee) (6)
aa   plain black (coffee) (4)
ab   plain (coffee) (71)
ac   pure (coffee) (5)
ad   reverent (1)
ae   sawmill coffee (1)
af   solid coffee (1)
ag   straight black (coffee) (6)
ah   straight (coffee) (230)
ai   straight-old black coffee (1)
aj   straight up (1)
ak   strong (coffee) (14)
al   without cream/milk (214)

032.3 P without

{t}   flap
{?}   glottal
No Response (342)
<(wi)dhowt> (2)
<(wi)dowt> (1)
<(wi)thowt> (1)
<w(i)thowt> (1)
<wAdhowt=41> (4)

<wAthowt=41> (7)
<wIdhowt=41> (10)
<wIdhow{t}=41> (2)
<wIdowt=41> (4)
<wIthowt=41> (14)
<wI{t}owt=41> (1)
<wI{t}ow{t}=41> (1)
<widhowt=13> (5)
<widhowt=31> (362)
<widhow{?}=31> (1)
<widhow{t}=31> (3)
<widow(t)=31> (2)
<widowt=13> (1)
<widowt=31> (28)
<wifowt=31> (1)
<withowt=13> (7)
<withowt=31> (126)
<withow{?}=31> (2)
<witowt=31> (2)
<wi{?}owt=31> (1)
<wi{t}owt=31> (2)
<woofowt=31> (1)

032.4 P with

{r}   weakly retroflex
{t}   flap
{?}   glottal
No Response (201)
<wi(th)> (50)
<wid> (84)
<widh> (362)
<wif> (3)
<wim> (1)
<wis> (3)
<wit> (63)
<with> (349)
<wiv> (2)
<wi{?}> (4)
<wi{r}th> (1)
<wi{t}> (10)
<wudh> (1)
<wuth> (1)

032.5 G (coming) toward

No Response (208)
A   at (33)
B   for (3)
C   on at (1)
D   to (128)
E   toward (368)
F   towards (314)

032.5 P toward

{o}   low-back
{R}   weakly retroflex
{r}   weakly retroflex
{t}   flap
No Response (292)
<tAawrd=41> (1)
<tAoerdz=41> (1)
<tAwaw(r)dz=41> (3)
<tAwaw[r]d=41> (8)

<tAwaw[r]dz=41> (10)
<tAwawrd=41> (19)
<tAwawrdz=41> (18)
<tAwaw{r}d=41> (4)
<tAwaw{r}dz=41> (2)
<tAwo(r)d=41> (2)
<tAwo(r)dz=41> (1)
<tAwo[r]d=41> (1)
<tAwoe[r]d=41> (3)
<tAwoe[r]dz=41> (5)
<tAwoerd=41> (23)
<tAwoerdz=41> (14)
<tAwoe{r}d=41> (1)
<tAwoe{r}dz=41> (4)
<tAword=41> (2)
<tAwu[r]dz=41> (1)
<tAw{o}(r)dz=41> (2)
<tAw{o}[r]ds=41> (1)
<tAw{o}[r]ts=41> (1)
<tAw{o}rd=41> (2)
<tAw{o}{r}d=41> (1)
<tAw{o}{r}dz=41> (1)
<tIoe(r)dz=41> (1)
<tIwaw(r)d=41> (2)
<tIwaw(r)dz=41> (2)
<tIwaw[r]dz=41> (1)
<tIwawrd=41> (2)
<tIwawrdz=41> (1)
<tIwaw{r}dz=41> (2)
<tIwo(r)d=41> (4)
<tIwo(r)dz=41> (2)
<tIwo[r]d=41> (1)
<tIwo[r]dz=41> (1)
<tIwoe(r)d=41> (1)
<tIwoe(r)dz=41> (3)
<tIwoe[r]d=41> (5)
<tIwoe[r]dz=41> (9)
<tIwoerd=41> (7)
<tIwoerdz=41> (6)
<tIwoe{r}d=41> (2)
<tIwoe{r}dz=41> (2)
<tIwordz=41> (2)
<tIwu[r]dz=41> (1)
<tIw{o}rdz=41> (1)
<taw(r)d> (3)
<taw(r)dz> (1)
<taw[R]lj=14> (1)
<taw[R]t=14> (1)
<taw[r]d> (7)
<taw[r]dz> (2)
<taw[r]t> (1)
<tawrd> (23)
<tawrdz> (9)
<taw{r}d> (7)
<taw{r}dz> (3)
<ti{r}dz> (1)
<toe(r)d> (6)
<toe(r)dz> (8)
<toe[R]d=14> (4)

<toe[r]d> (56)
<toe[r]dz> (15)
<toe[r]t> (1)
<toer(d)> (1)
<toerd> (136)
<toerds> (1)
<toerdz> (36)
<toerj> (2)
<toewRd=14> (1)
<toewRdz=14> (1)
<toew[R]d=14> (1)
<toewawrdz=31> (1)
<toewo[r]dz=13> (1)
<toew{R}d=14> (1)
<toew{R}dz=14> (1)
<toe{R}dz=14> (1)
<toe{r}ch> (1)
<toe{r}d> (18)
<toe{r}dz> (7)
<toow[R]d=14> (1)
<toowaw[r]dz=13> (1)
<toowo(r)dz=31> (1)
<toowoerd=31> (1)
<toowoe{r}dz=13> (1)
<tooword=31> (1)
<toowu[r]d=31> (1)
<tue(r)d> (1)
<tueoerd=13> (1)
<tueoerd=31> (1)
<tuewRd=14> (1)
<tuewaw(r)dz=31> (1)
<tuewawrdz=31> (1)
<tuewo(r)dz=13> (1)
<tuewo(r)dz=31> (1)
<tuewo[r]dz=31> (2)
<tuewoe[r]dz=31> (1)
<tuew{o}rdz=31> (1)
<tuwo{r}dz=31> (1)
<tu{r}dz> (1)
<twaw(r){t}> (1)
<twaw[r]d> (4)
<twaw[r]dz> (4)
<twawrd> (12)
<twawrdz> (1)
<twaw{r}dz> (2)
<two(r)d> (1)
<twoe(r)d> (1)
<twoe(r)dz> (1)
<twoe[R]d=14> (2)
<twoe[r]ch> (1)
<twoe[r]d> (20)
<twoe[r]dz> (16)
<twoe[r]ts> (1)
<twoerd> (15)
<twoerdz> (15)
<twoert> (1)
<twoe{r}d> (2)
<twoe{r}dz> (4)
<twordz> (1)

<two{r}d> (1)
<two{r}dz> (1)
<tw{o}[r]d> (1)
<tw{o}[r]dz> (1)

032.6 G (ran) across
No Response (228)
A bumped into (19)
B came across (1)
C chanced into (1)
D chanced upon (2)
E happened up on (3)
F lucked upon (1)
G jumped into (1)
H met up with (11)
I (ran) across (65)
J (ran) against (1)
K (ran) into (560)
L (ran) on (2)
M (ran) onto (4)
N (ran) through (1)
O (ran) up (1)
P (ran) up on (34)
Q (ran) up to (1)
R (ran) up with (8)
S (ran) upon (15)
T struck up with (1)
U stumbled upon (1)
V walked into (1)
W walked up on (1)

032.7 G (named) for
No Response (184)
A after (624)
B by (1)
C for (139)
D from (3)
E like (1)

033.1 P dog
{g} devoiced
{?} glottal
<aw> variants:
{au} inglide
{aw} upglide
{ou} unrounded onset
No Response (43)
<dawg> (28)
<daw{g}> (1)
<doe(g)> (1)
<doeg> (4)
<dog> (14)
<dogz> (2)
<dok> (1)
<do{g}> (2)
<do{g}z> (1)
<d{au}d> (1)
<d{au}f> (1)
<d{au}g> (35)
<d{au}gz> (2)
<d{au}{g}> (3)
<d{aw}(g)> (21)

<d{aw}g> (560)
<d{aw}gz> (92)
<d{aw}gzh> (1)
<d{aw}k> (1)
<d{aw}{?}> (1)
<d{aw}{g}> (24)
<d{aw}{g}z> (3)
<d{ou}(g)> (3)
<d{ou}g> (105)
<d{ou}gs> (2)
<d{ou}gz> (8)
<d{ou}{g}> (8)
<d{ou}{g}z> (1)

033.1 S dog
No Response (0)
|JSHmfj| (1)
|PAAqfb| (1)
|PCC| (1)
|QACqfb| (1)
|QADqfb| (1)
|QAEmaj| (1)
|QAHjjb| (1)
|QAHqaa| (1)
|QAHqab| (1)
|QAHqfb| (3)
|QCCqab| (1)
|QCCqfb| (2)
|QCHjjb| (2)
|QCHjjc| (2)
|QCHqfb| (1)
|QFAefj| (1)
|QFAjbc| (1)
|QFAjja| (1)
|QFAjjb| (1)
|QFAjjc| (19)
|QFAjjd| (2)
|QFAjjh| (1)
|QFAjjl| (2)
|QFAlfa| (1)
|QFAlfj| (6)
|QFAqfb| (13)
|QFAqfc| (1)
|QFAqfd| (1)
|QFAqff| (1)
|QFB| (2)
|QFBjja| (2)
|QFBjjb| (6)
|QFBjjc| (10)
|QFBjjd| (7)
|QFBjjf| (1)
|QFBjjl| (3)
|QFBjjm| (2)
|QFBjjq| (1)
|QFBjsb| (1)
|QFBjsc| (4)
|QFBjsd| (2)
|QFBlfb| (1)
|QFBqfj| (1)
|QFC| (3)

|QFCffc| (1)
|QFCjja| (5)
|QFCjjb| (36)
|QFCjjc| (45)
|QFCjjd| (2)
|QFCjjh| (2)
|QFCjjl| (4)
|QFCjsb| (1)
|QFCqab| (2)
|QFCqaf| (3)
|QFCqfa| (16)
|QFCqfb| (204)
|QFCqffmaj| (1)
|QFCqfj| (2)
|QFCqfk| (1)
|QFCqmb| (25)
|QFCtfb| (1)
|QFDjjd| (3)
|QFDjjm| (3)
|QFDlfa| (1)
|QFDlfj| (4)
|QFDqfa| (1)
|QFDqfb| (1)
|QFF| (1)
|QFFjjh| (2)
|QFFjjm| (2)
|QFFjjq| (1)
|QFFjsb| (1)
|QFH| (1)
|QFHjjb| (2)
|QFHjjc| (2)
|QFHjjq| (1)
|QFHqfb| (44)
|QFHqfd| (2)
|QFHqff| (1)
|QFHqfj| (3)
|QFHqfk| (1)
|QMAjbj| (1)
|QMAjja| (3)
|QMAjjb| (1)
|QMAjjc| (2)
|QMAjjd| (1)
|QMAjjj| (13)
|QMAjjl| (1)
|QMAlfe| (1)
|QMAlfj| (2)
|QMAlfk| (1)
|QMAmaj| (3)
|QMAqfa| (1)
|QMAqfb| (4)
|QMAqff| (2)
|QMAqfk| (1)
|QMB| (1)
|QMBjja| (2)
|QMBjjc| (3)
|QMBjjd| (4)
|QMBjjj| (1)
|QMBjjl| (1)
|QMBmaj| (1)

|QMBqfa| (1)
|QMC| (10)
|QMCJJB| (1)
|QMCjjb| (13)
|QMCjjc| (11)
|QMCmaj| (2)
|QMCqad| (1)
|QMCqfa| (9)
|QMCqfb| (60)
|QMCqff| (2)
|QMCqfk| (2)
|QMD| (3)
|QMDefj| (2)
|QMDjjm| (1)
|QMDqfb| (1)
|QMFjjd| (1)
|QMFjjh| (1)
|QMFjjm| (1)
|QMH| (4)
|QMHjjb| (2)
|QMHjjc| (1)
|QMHmaj| (1)
|QMHqab| (1)
|QMHqfa| (1)
|QMHqfb| (31)
|QMHqfj| (1)
|QMHqfk| (1)
|SABjjc| (1)
|SABqfm| (1)
|SAEjjc| (1)
|SAEmaj| (1)
|SAEqfa| (3)
|SAEqfb| (2)
|SAGqfa| (9)
|SAGqfd| (1)
|SAGqfj| (7)
|SAI| (1)
|SCAmaa| (1)
|SCAtab| (1)
|SCDqfb| (1)
|SCE| (1)
|SCEqfa| (2)
|SCGqfa| (5)
|SCGqfb| (1)
|SCGqfj| (2)
|SFEqfb| (1)
|SFEqfj| (1)
|SFGqfk| (1)
|SMGqfa| (1)
|TAAQFAmaj| (1)
|TAAjja| (1)
|TAAtfa| (1)
|TAB| (1)
|TABjjb| (1)
|TABjjc| (2)
|TABqfb| (2)
|TABqfc| (1)
|TADjjc| (3)
|TADqfb| (10)

|TADqfc| (1)
|TADqfj| (1)
|TADtfb| (1)
|TAFjjc| (1)
|TAFqfb| (1)
|TCA| (1)
|TCAjja| (2)
|TCAjsaffa| (1)
|TCAmaa| (1)
|TCAqfa| (1)
|TCAqfj| (1)
|TCBqfb| (1)
|TCBqfj| (1)
|TCDjja| (2)
|TCDjjj| (2)
|TCDmaa| (1)
|TCDqfb| (8)
|TCDqfj| (1)
|TCFqfb| (2)
|TCFqfk| (1)
|TFAqfb| (1)
|TFBjja| (2)
|TFBjjb| (2)
|TFBjjc| (2)
|TFBmaj| (1)
|TFBqfa| (1)
|TFBqfb| (17)
|TFBqfc| (2)
|TFBqfk| (1)
|TFDjjc| (2)
|TFDqfb| (2)
|TFDqfj| (1)
|TFFjjb| (1)
|TFFqfb| (1)
|TMA| (1)
|TMAmaj| (1)
|TMAqfj| (1)
|TMB| (4)
|TMBjja| (1)
|TMBjjc| (1)
|TMBqfa| (1)
|TMBqfb| (5)
|TMBqfj| (2)
|TMD| (1)
|TMDqfb| (1)

033.2 G calls to dogs to attack

No Response (200)
A   attack (12)
B   attack him (1)
C   bite him (1)
D   catch (4)
E   catch him/it/them (83)
F   catch-him(x3) (1)
G   fetch him (1)
H   fight (1)
I   get after him (1)
J   get him/it/them (170)
K   get-him(x2) (6)
L   get him off (1)

M   get on him (3)
N   get that dog (1)
O   go (1)
P   go after him (1)
Q   go and get him/it (3)
R   go at him (1)
S   go catch him (2)
T   go find him (1)
U   go get him/them (43)
V   grab him (1)
W   hiss him (4)
X   hit (1)
Y   hooey (1)
Z   jowl him (1)
aa   jump (1)
ab   jump on him (2)
ac   kill (7)
ad   kill him (1)
ae   run him away (1)
af   sic (14)
ag   sic(x3) (2)
ah   sic him/them (435)
ai   sic-him/them(x2)/(x3) (6)
aj   sic it psst (1)
ak   sook-him(x3) (1)
al   take him (3)
am   whooey (1)
an   wushel (1)

033.3 L mongrel

No Response (95)
A   all-American (dog) (3)
B   alley dog (3)
C   asthma dog (2)
D   bad dog (1)
E   barker (1)
F   barking dog (1)
G   barking little devil (1)
H   bastard (1)
I   bird dog (1)
J   biscuit catcher (1)
K   biscuit eater (3)
L   bitch (1)
M   bread eater (1)
N   bucero [S] (1)
O   bull feist (1)
P   bum (1)
Q   carpenter dog (1)
R   Catahoula (3)
S   Catahoula cur (8)
T   Catahoula dog (4)
U   Catahoula hound (1)
V   Catahoula leopard (1)
W   catch dog (1)
X   combination dog (2)
Y   common cur (2)
Z   common dog (16)
aa   common hound (1)
ab   common-old breed of dog (1)
ac   common stray dog (1)

ad   crooch (1)
ae   crossbreed (dog) (14)
af   crossbreeded dog (1)
ag   crossed-up dog (1)
ah   cur (dog) (222)
ai   cur-looking dog (1)
aj   damn old dog (1)
ak   dime a dozen (1)
al   dog (26)
am   dog dog (2)
an   drop (1)
ao   dud (1)
ap   duke's mixture (9)
aq   dumb dog (2)
ar   dunghill (1)
as   feist (dog) (343)
at   feisty [n.] (1)
au   feisty (little) dog (17)
av   feisty little rascal (1)
aw   fido (1)
ax   Fifty-Seven Heinz (1)
ay   fifty-seven variety(s) (7)
az   flea raiser (1)
ba   fleabag (2)
bb   fox feist (1)
bc   fox-terrier feist (1)
bd   full-blooded feist (1)
be   fuss box (1)
bf   fuss maker (1)
bg   glass-eyed cur (1)
bh   good-for-nothing (dog) (8)
bi   Grant cur (1)
bj   guard dog (2)
bk   gyp (dog) (4)
bl   half-and-half (4)
bm   half-and-half feist (1)
bn   half-breed (31)
bo   half-breed dog (3)
bp   Heinz (variety) (8)
bq   Heinz Fifty-Seven (39)
br   Heinz Fifty-Seven cur (1)
bs   Heinz Fifty-Seven variety(s) (4)
bt   Heinz Forty-Seven varieties (1)
bu   Heinz Sixty-Seven (1)
bv   Heinz Variety Fifty-Seven (1)
bw   hog dog (5)
bx   hooey dog (1)
by   hound (dog) (114)
bz   hound-colored feist (1)
ca   house dog (17)
cb   hybrid (2)
cc   Jiggs's dog (1)
cd   knotty dog (1)
ce   kyoodle (11)
cf   lapdog (5)
cg   lazy dog/hound (3)
ch   leopards dog (1)
ci   loafer (1)
cj   loafing dog (2)

ck   loudmouth (2)
cl   Maggie's dog (1)
cm   mangy (old) dog (2)
cn   March and May dog (1)
co   meat eater (1)
cp   meat hound (1)
cq   miniature dog (1)
cr   mix [n.] (1)
cs   mix-blooded dog (1)
ct   mix bred (1)
cu   mix breed (80)
cv   mix-breed dog (11)
cw   mix breed of dog (1)
cx   mix dog (11)
cy   mix hound (1)
cz   mix-up (1)
da   mixblood (1)
db   mixed (10)
dc   mixed breed (30)
dd   mixed-breed dog (5)
de   mixed dog (7)
df   mixed-up breed (3)
dg   mixed-up cur dog (1)
dh   mixed-up (dog) (7)
di   mixture (7)
dj   monger (1)
dk   Mongolian dog (1)
dl   mongrel (dog) (186)
dm   mongrel hound (1)
dn   mongrel pup (1)
do   mutt (132)
dp   natural (1)
dq   no-account (dog) (8)
dr   no-account for nothing (1)
ds   no breed of dog (1)
dt   no-good darned old cur (1)
du   no-good (dog) (17)
dv   no-good mongrel (1)
dw   no-good mutt (1)
dx   no-good one (1)
dy   no-winner Pedro (1)
dz   noisy dog (1)
ea   noisy little rascal (1)
eb   noisy old dog (1)
ec   nondescript (2)
ed   nuisance (8)
ee   off brand (2)
ef   off breed (3)
eg   old dog (2)
eh   old son (1)
ei   old whelp (1)
ej   outlaw (dog) (2)
ek   pain in the neck (1)
el   part Chihuahua (1)
em   part dog (1)
en   pest (6)
eo   pet (1)
ep   pickaninny (1)
eq   plain dog (5)

er   plain-old dog (3)
es   plain-old hound (1)
et   poll-blood (1)
eu   pooch (2)
ev   pot cur (1)
ew   pot ham (1)
ex   pot hound (4)
ey   potlicker (hound) (19)
ez   pup (2)
fa   rascal (2)
fb   rattail (1)
fc   rattan dog (1)
fd   rattlehead (1)
fe   regular dog (1)
ff   riffraff (1)
fg   rotty dog (1)
fh   runt (1)
fi   Russian soccer (1)
fj   Sandy's dog (1)
fk   scrub (dog) (4)
fl   Seymour (1)
fm   shit eater (1)
fn   sit-on dog (1)
fo   sleep hound (1)
fp   society dog (1)
fq   sooner (dog) (37)
fr   sooner hound (1)
fs   sorry-ass dog (1)
ft   sorry cur (dog) (2)
fu   sorry (dog) (8)
fv   soup hound (4)
fw   spit feist (1)
fx   spitz (3)
fy   spitz feist (1)
fz   squirt (1)
ga   straggling dog (1)
gb   straight dog (1)
gc   stray (dog) (39)
gd   street dog (1)
ge   strooch (1)
gf   surface dog (1)
gg   toy dog (1)
gh   toy feist (1)
gi   trailer (1)
gj   tramp (dog) (3)
gk   trash (1)
gl   trig (1)
gm   useless dog (2)
gn   who, sir; me, sir (1)
go   whining dog (1)
gp   wild dog (1)
gq   Winn Parish cur (3)
gr   worthless (dog) (8)
gs   worthless hound (2)
gt   worthless no-good dog (1)
gu   yapper (4)
gv   yapping dog (4)
gw   yard dog (10)
gx   yellow dog (3)

033.3 P feist

{f}   bilabial
{ie}   monophthong/inglide
No Response (570)
<boolfiest=21> (1)
<fief(t)> (1)
<fies(t)> (95)
<fies(t)Iz=14> (4)
<fies(t)dawg=11> (2)
<fies(t)dawg=13> (12)
<fies(t)dawg=21> (1)
<fies(t)dawgz=13> (1)
<fiest> (130)
<fiestdawg=11> (1)
<fiestdawg=13> (4)
<fiestdawg=31> (1)
<fiests> (4)
<fiethst> (1)
<fieth(t)> (1)
<fows(t)> (1)
<fows(t)dawg=13> (1)
<fw{ie}s(t)> (1)
<f{ie}s(t)> (26)
<f{ie}s(t)Iz=14> (1)
<f{ie}s(t)dawg=13> (2)
<f{ie}s(t)dawgz=31> (1)
<f{ie}st> (54)
<f{ie}stIz=14> (1)
<f{ie}stdawg=13> (2)
<f{ie}stdawgz=13> (1)
<{f}ies(t)> (4)
<{f}iest> (4)

033.4 G bite

<!>   infinitive
<&>   present 3rd singular
<@>   present participle
<*>   preterit
<#>   past participle
{?}   glottal
No Response (132)
<!bie(t)> (2)
<!biet> (594)
<!bit> (1)
<!dawgbiet=13> (1)
<&biet> (3)
<&biets> (10)
<@bietN=14> (8)
<@bietNG=14> (5)
<*beet> (1)
<*bid> (1)
<*biet> (3)
<*bit> (512)
<*bitN=14> (1)
<*dawgbit=13> (2)
<*snaikbit=13> (1)
<#antbit=13> (1)
<#beet> (2)
<#beetN=14> (1)
<#bidN=14> (1)

<#biet> (4)
<#bit> (303)
<#bitN=14> (369)
<#bitNd=14> (1)
<#daw(g)bit=13> (1)
<#dawgbeet=13> (1)
<#dawgbiet=13> (1)
<#dawgbit=11> (1)
<#dawgbit=12> (1)
<#dawgbit=13> (203)
<#dawgbit=21> (3)
<#dawgbit=31> (3)
<#dawgbitN=114> (1)
<#dawgbitN=124> (1)
<#dawgbitN=134> (26)
<#dawgbitN=214> (1)
<#dawgbi{?}N=134> (1)
<#doegbit=13> (4)
<#fraws(t)bit=13> (3)
<#skwurlbit=13> (1)
<#snaikbit=11> (1)
<#snaikbit=13> (26)
<#snaikbit=21> (2)
<#snaikbitN=134> (4)

033.5 L bull

No Response (102)
A   beast (8)
B   beef, a (4)
C   big boy (1)
D   boar (1)
E   bobtail bull (1)
F   boeuf [F] (4)
G   boy, the (2)
H   boy cow (3)
I   breeder (1)
J   breeding bull (1)
K   breeding cattle (1)
L   breeding male (1)
M   brute (2)
N   bull (548)
O   bull [taboo] (241)
P   bull calf (3)
Q   bull cow (8)
R   bull steer (1)
S   bull yearling (2)
T   bullock (1)
U   bully (1)
V   bully bull (1)
W   cow (4)
X   daddy, the (1)
Y   eunuch (1)
Z   fighting bull (1)
aa   gentleman (1)
ab   gentleman cow (6)
ac   he, a (2)
ad   he cow (5)
ae   he male (1)
af   head of the herd (1)
ag   heifer (2)

ah herd bull (4)
ai herd sire (1)
aj herd stock (1)
ak husbandry (1)
al king of the woods (1)
am leader (3)
an magnolia (1)
ao male (132)
ap male animal (3)
aq male beast (1)
ar male bull (1)
as male calf (3)
at male cow (86)
au male of a cow (1)
av male ox (1)
aw male yearling (2)
ax males cow (1)
ay man, the (1)
az man cow (3)
ba mean-old male (1)
bb moo ah (1)
bc Ochs [G] (1)
bd ox(en) (12)
be papa cow (1)
bf preacher cow (1)
bg ranger (1)
bh scrub bull (1)
bi sire (8)
bj stag (3)
bk steer (67)
bl steer cow (1)
bm stock (1)
bn stock breeder (1)
bo stock bull (3)
bp stock cow (14)
bq stock male (3)
br stud (4)
bs surly (2)
bt taureau [F] (2)
bu top bull (1)
bv top cow (2)
bw toro [S] (7)
bx yearling (13)
by yearling steer (1)

033.6 P cow

<ow> variants:
{ao} raised onset/unrounded glide
{au} raised onset
{ou} unrounded glide
{uu} centered onset
No Response (26)
<ka> (4)
<kaz> (1)
<ko> (1)
<kow> (260)
<kowz> (122)
<kowzh> (1)
<kyow> (3)
<ky{ao}> (2)

<ky{au}> (3)
<ky{ou}> (2)
<k{ao}> (69)
<k{ao}z> (12)
<k{au}> (216)
<k{au}z> (112)
<k{ou}> (93)
<k{ou}(z)> (1)
<k{ou}z> (19)
<k{uu}> (4)
<k{uu}z> (2)

033.6 S cow

No Response (0)
|KCCjjd| (1)
|OAAefa| (1)
|OAAjja| (1)
|OAAjjb| (1)
|OAAjjc| (1)
|OAAjjd| (8)
|OAAjjh| (1)
|OAAmaa| (2)
|OAAmab| (2)
|OAAmae| (2)
|OAAmag| (1)
|OAAmfe| (1)
|OABefa| (3)
|OABefc| (1)
|OABjja| (1)
|OABjjb| (4)
|OABjjd| (9)
|OABjjf| (1)
|OABmaa| (1)
|OACeaa| (3)
|OACefa| (28)
|OACefb| (2)
|OACefc| (1)
|OACefj| (9)
|OACffd| (12)
|OACffh| (1)
|OACffm| (5)
|OACjbd| (9)
|OACjbm| (1)
|OACjja| (5)
|OACjjb| (11)
|OACjjc| (2)
|OACjjd| (56)
|OACjjf| (9)
|OACjjh| (1)
|OACjjhefj| (1)
|OACjjk| (1)
|OACjjl| (2)
|OACjjm| (6)
|OAClfg| (1)
|OACmaa| (1)
|OACmab| (2)
|OACmae| (1)
|OACmaj| (3)
|OACmfa| (6)
|OACmfj| (2)

|OACqfo| (1)
|OADmaj| (1)
|OAGjjd| (3)
|OAGjjf| (1)
|OAGjjq| (1)
|OAHffh| (1)
|OAHjjm| (1)
|OAIeaa| (12)
|OAIefa| (13)
|OAImaa| (2)
|OCAefa| (2)
|OCAefj| (1)
|OCAffa| (1)
|OCAffd| (1)
|OCAffj| (4)
|OCAffl| (1)
|OCAfma| (1)
|OCAjjd| (7)
|OCAjjj| (1)
|OCAjjl| (1)
|OCAjjm| (1)
|OCAlfa| (3)
|OCAlfj| (2)
|OCAmaa| (2)
|OCAmaj| (2)
|OCBefa| (1)
|OCBjjd| (4)
|OCCeaa| (1)
|OCCefa| (12)
|OCCefj| (3)
|OCCfad| (1)
|OCCffa| (1)
|OCCffd| (1)
|OCCffh| (2)
|OCCffm| (2)
|OCCjbj| (1)
|OCCjja| (2)
|OCCjjb| (1)
|OCCjjd| (27)
|OCCjjf| (4)
|OCCjjh| (1)
|OCCjjj| (1)
|OCCjjl| (1)
|OCClfa| (2)
|OCClfj| (2)
|OCCmaa| (1)
|OCCmaj| (3)
|OCCmfa| (2)
|OCEefj| (1)
|OCEfaa| (1)
|OCEjbj| (1)
|OCEjjd| (1)
|OCGjbd| (1)
|OCGjjd| (1)
|OCGjjm| (1)
|OCIjbh| (1)
|OCIjjd| (1)
|OCImfa| (1)
|ODAfod| (1)

|ODCjuo| (1)
|OKCjuj| (2)
|OKCmdj| (1)
|PACefe| (1)
|PAFefa| (1)
|PAHefc| (1)
|PAHffd| (1)
|PCAffd| (1)
|PCDffj| (1)
|RAAefc| (1)
|RAAffa| (5)
|RAAffh| (1)
|RAAjja| (1)
|RAAjjb| (2)
|RAAjjd| (2)
|RAAmaj| (1)
|RABeaa| (16)
|RABefa| (69)
|RABefc| (5)
|RABefe| (1)
|RABefj| (2)
|RABfaa| (1)
|RABfah| (1)
|RABffa| (8)
|RABffd| (13)
|RABffh| (1)
|RABffm| (1)
|RABjba| (1)
|RABjbd| (1)
|RABjbm| (1)
|RABjja| (13)
|RABjjb| (29)
|RABjjc| (1)
|RABjjd| (49)
|RABjjdjjk| (1)
|RABjjf| (5)
|RABjsd| (1)
|RABlfa| (1)
|RABlfejjm| (1)
|RABmaa| (11)
|RABmab| (2)
|RABmad| (1)
|RABmae| (2)
|RABmaj| (2)
|RABmfa| (2)
|RABmfb| (1)
|RABmfj| (1)
|RACjjd| (1)
|RAEeaa| (1)
|RAEefa| (2)
|RAEefc| (2)
|RAEefe| (1)
|RAEffa| (1)
|RAEffd| (1)
|RAEjbd| (1)
|RAEjbm| (1)
|RAEjja| (1)
|RAEjjb| (11)
|RAEjjd| (2)

|RAEjjo| (1)
|RAElfa| (1)
|RAEmab| (1)
|RAEmaj| (1)
|RAEmfj| (1)
|RAFeaa| (13)
|RAFeae| (1)
|RAFefa| (16)
|RAFefc| (2)
|RAFjja| (4)
|RAFjjb| (1)
|RAFjjc| (2)
|RAFjjd| (9)
|RAFjjm| (1)
|RAFlfj| (1)
|RAFmaa| (5)
|RAFmaj| (1)
|RAGefa| (8)
|RAGefc| (3)
|RAGfaf| (1)
|RAGffd| (1)
|RAGffh| (1)
|RAGjja| (2)
|RAGjjb| (1)
|RAGjjd| (2)
|RAGlfj| (1)
|RAGmaa| (1)
|RAIefa| (1)
|RCAefa| (2)
|RCAfaa| (1)
|RCAffa| (3)
|RCAffd| (2)
|RCAffj| (1)
|RCAjjb| (2)
|RCAjjd| (2)
|RCAjjf| (2)
|RCAjjh| (1)
|RCAjjj| (1)
|RCAlfa| (1)
|RCAlfj| (1)
|RCAmaa| (3)
|RCBeaa| (4)
|RCBeac| (1)
|RCBeaj| (1)
|RCBefa| (37)
|RCBefc| (6)
|RCBefj| (1)
|RCBfaa| (1)
|RCBfad| (3)
|RCBfaj| (1)
|RCBffa| (2)
|RCBffd| (2)
|RCBfff| (1)
|RCBffm| (2)
|RCBjbd| (1)
|RCBjja| (3)
|RCBjjc| (1)
|RCBjjd| (13)
|RCBjjf| (1)

|RCBjjm| (1)
|RCBlfj| (3)
|RCBmaa| (2)
|RCBmaj| (2)
|RCBmfj| (1)
|RCCjjd| (1)
|RCCjjm| (1)
|RCEefa| (1)
|RCEffd| (1)
|RCEffj| (1)
|RCEjja| (1)
|RCEjjb| (2)
|RCEjjd| (3)
|RCEmfj| (1)
|RCFeaa| (2)
|RCFefa| (5)
|RCFjja| (2)
|RCFjjb| (3)
|RCFjjd| (2)
|RCFjjh| (1)
|RCFlfa| (2)
|RCFlfj| (1)
|RCGefa| (6)
|RCGefj| (1)
|RCGjjm| (1)
|RCGmaj| (1)
|RKEfoa| (1)
|SADefc| (1)
|SADffd| (1)
|SADjja| (1)
|SADjjb| (1)
|SAEjjd| (1)
|SAFefa| (1)
|SCAefj| (1)
|SCAfaj| (1)
|SCAffj| (1)
|SCDjjb| (1)
|SCFjjd| (1)

033.7 L pair

No Response (216)
A   brace (2)
B   brace [horses] (2)
C   brace [mules] (3)
D   bull train (1)
E   couple (2)
F   couple of mules (2)
G   couple of oxen (2)
H   couple of oxteams (1)
I   cow train (1)
J   double, a [horses] (1)
K   double, a [oxen] (1)
L   double plow [mules] (1)
M   double mules (1)
N   double stock (1)
O   double string (2)
P   double team (15)
Q   double team [horses] (6)
R   double team [mules] (20)
S   double yoke (1)

T   double yoke of oxen (2)
U   drove, a [mules] (1)
V   five-mule team (1)
W   four hitch (1)
X   four-horse team (2)
Y   four-mule team (5)
Z   four up, a [mules] (1)
aa   four-up team (1)
ab   full team [mules] (1)
ac   hitch [horses/mules] (1)
ad   horse team (1)
ae   lead team (1)
af   log team [mules] (1)
ag   log-wagon team [mules] (1)
ah   logging team (1)
ai   long team of oxen (1)
aj   matched team (1)
ak   mix team [mule + horse] (1)
al   mule team (20)
am   mule train (1)
an   oxen team (3)
ao   oxteam (21)
ap   pair (92)
aq   pair [donkeys] (1)
ar   pair [horses] (26)
as   pair [mules] (249)
at   pair [oxen] (43)
au   plow team [mules] (1)
av   set (1)
aw   set of mules (2)
ax   six up [mules] (1)
ay   six up [horses] (1)
az   six-up team (2)
ba   span (3)
bb   span [horses] (5)
bc   span [mules] (11)
bd   span [oxen] (4)
be   spike team (2)
bf   stand of mules (1)
bg   string of oxen (1)
bh   tandem (1)
bi   team (184)
bj   team [horses] (67)
bk   team [mules] (213)
bl   team [oxen] (77)
bm   three-mule team (1)
bn   triple mules (1)
bo   twelve-up team (1)
bp   two-ox team (1)
bq   two pair(s) (5)
br   two pair(s) [horses] (1)
bs   two pair(s) [mules] (14)
bt   two pair(s) [oxen] (4)
bu   two team(s) (11)
bv   two team(s) [horses] (4)
bw   two team(s) [mules] (10)
bx   two team(s) [oxen] (2)
by   two yoke(s) (2)
bz   two yoke(s) [oxen] (11)

ca   wagon team (1)
cb   yoke (14)
cc   yoke [beeves] (1)
cd   yoke [cattle] (4)
ce   yoke [mules] (1)
cf   yoke [oxen] (112)
cg   yoke [steers] (15)

033.7A P pair
{e}   inglide
{r}   weakly retroflex
No Response (558)
<pa(r)> (41)
<pa[r]> (70)
<pai[r]> (1)
<pair> (1)
<par> (145)
<parz> (3)
<pa{r}> (31)
<pe(r)> (2)
<pe[r]> (15)
<per> (48)
<pe{r}> (5)
<pe{r}z> (1)
<pur> (1)
<p{e}[R]=14> (1)
<p{e}r> (1)

033.7B P mules
{z}   palatal
{zh}   alveolar
No Response (157)
<mIyue[l]s=41> (1)
<mIyue[l]{z}=41> (1)
<mew(1)z> (2)
<mew(1){z}> (1)
<mew[l]> (4)
<mew[l]z> (3)
<mew[l]zh> (1)
<mew[l]{z}> (5)
<mewl> (21)
<mewlz> (52)
<mewl{z}> (21)
<mye[l]> (1)
<myew(1)z> (1)
<myew[l]> (5)
<myew[l]dh> (1)
<myew[l]z> (4)
<myew[l]{zh}> (1)
<myew[l]{z}> (2)
<myewl> (8)
<myewldz> (1)
<myewlj> (1)
<myewls> (1)
<myewlz> (24)
<myewlzh> (1)
<myewl{z}> (3)
<myi[l]z> (2)
<myool> (3)
<myoolz> (1)
<myue(1)z> (13)

<myue(1){z}> (1)
<myue[l]> (10)
<myue[l]th> (1)
<myue[l]z> (14)
<myue[l]{zh}> (1)
<myue[l]{z}> (7)
<myuel> (150)
<myuel(z)> (2)
<myueld> (1)
<myueldh> (1)
<myuels> (2)
<myuelz> (342)
<myuel{z}> (63)

033.7 S mule
No Response (5)
|B2A| (6)
|BBA| (4)
|BGAcba| (2)
|BGAmaj| (2)
|BJA| (116)
|BJAcba| (3)
|BJAcbj| (1)
|BJAefa| (2)
|BJAefj| (4)
|BJAffa| (1)
|BJAmaa| (1)
|BJAmaj| (24)
|BJC| (1)
|BJCefb| (1)
|BJCmaj| (1)
|BJD| (1)
|BJEmaj| (1)
|BJH| (1)
|BSA| (53)
|BSAefa| (1)
|BSAefk| (1)
|BSAmaj| (20)
|BSD| (1)
|BSDefj| (1)
|BUA| (8)
|BUAmdj| (2)
|C2D| (2)
|CBD| (2)
|CFD| (1)
|CGD| (1)
|CGDmaj| (1)
|CJA| (1)
|CJD| (23)
|CJDcba| (5)
|CJDmaj| (11)
|CJH| (1)
|CSA| (1)
|CSAmaj| (2)
|CSD| (21)
|CSDcba| (3)
|CSDcbj| (1)
|CSDmaj| (15)
|CUD| (2)
|ECEcba| (1)

|fmdCSAcba| (1)
|fmgCSJ| (1)
|fmiBJJ| (1)
|fodBUA| (2)
|fodCUD| (5)

033.8 P calf

{a}   upglide
{e}   upglide
{f}   bilabial
{v}   devoiced
{z}   devoiced
No Response (116)
<ka(f)> (2)
<ka(v)z> (1)
<ka[1]f> (1)
<ka[1]vz> (1)
<kaf> (545)
<kafN=14> (1)
<kafs> (2)
<kafz> (1)
<kaif> (11)
<kaivz> (3)
<kai{f}> (3)
<kai{v}{z}> (1)
<kav> (3)
<kav(z)> (1)
<kavz> (23)
<ka{f}> (7)
<kef> (9)
<kevz> (2)
<kif> (1)
<kyaf> (4)
<kya{f}> (1)
<kyef> (1)
<ky{a}f> (1)
<ky{a}vz> (2)
<k{a}(f)> (1)
<k{a}f> (172)
<k{a}v> (2)
<k{a}vz> (9)
<k{e}f> (8)
<k{e}v> (1)

033.9 L calve

No Response (178)
A   avoir un veau [F] (1)
B   be fresh (29)
C   be in (1)
D   bear [v.] (3)
E   bear (you) a calf (3)
F   birth (him) (5)
G   birth (a baby) calf (9)
H   born [v.] (2)
I   born a cow (1)
J   break a calf (1)
K   bring (a baby) (2)
L   bring (me a little) calf (69)
M   bring in (1)
N   calve (124)
O   come back in the pen (1)

P   come fresh (17)
Q   come in (and give milk) (66)
R   come in fresh (with a calf) (11)
S   come in(to) the pen (9)
T   come in with a/her calf (1)
U   come to (the) pail (4)
V   come to the pen (4)
W   coming (1)
X   deliver (12)
Y   deliver (a) calf (3)
Z   domino [v.] (1)
aa   drop (it) [v.] (16)
ab   drop a baby (1)
ac   drop (a) calf (110)
ad   dug it up in a field (1)
ae   farrow (2)
af   find (a little baby) calf (82)
ag   find her (a) calf (3)
ah   find one (2)
ai   foal (of cow) (10)
aj   fold (2)
ak   freshen (94)
al   freshen time (1)
am   get a calf (1)
an   give birth (26)
ao   give birth to a calf (7)
ap   go to the pen (1)
aq   going to cow (1)
ar   hatch (1)
as   hatching day is nigh (1)
at   have a foal (1)
au   have a litter (1)
av   have (a little) baby (8)
aw   have (a little baby) calf/cow
     (282)
ax   have (a little one) (6)
ay   have birth (1)
az   looking for a calf (1)
ba   milk [v.] (1)
bb   put down (1)
bc   raise (a calf) (2)
bd   spring [v.] (21)
be   suckle (9)
bf   yield [v.] (1)

034.1 L stallion
No Response (193)
A   boy (2)
B   boy horse (6)
C   breed horse (1)
D   breeder (1)
E   breeding horse (1)
F   breeding stock (1)
G   breeding-stock horse (1)
H   colt (8)
I   etalon [F] (3)
J   fellow horse (1)
K   four-year-old (1)
L   gentleman horse (1)
M   he horse (8)

N   horse (67)
O   horse colt (1)
P   jack (2)
Q   male (19)
R   male horse (50)
S   man horse (1)
T   mare (5)
U   Morgan stallion (1)
V   papa horse (2)
W   pony (1)
X   seed horse (1)
Y   sire (2)
Z   stable horse (10)
aa   stag (3)
ab   stallion (386)
ac   stallion [taboo] (15)
ad   stallion horse (3)
ae   stock horse (6)
af   stock stud (1)
ag   stud (315)
ah   stud [taboo] (40)
ai   stud colt (1)
aj   stud pony (1)
ak   studhorse (108)
al   studhorse [taboo] (11)

034.2A P horse/horses
{aw}   unrounded onset
{oe}   lowered onset
{r}   weakly retroflex
{z}   devoiced
{ʔ}   glottal
No Response (19)
<(h)aw(r)s> (1)
<(h)aw(r)sIz=14> (1)
<(h)aw[r]s> (1)
<haw(r)s> (104)
<haw(r)sAz=14> (1)
<haw(r)sI(z)=14> (1)
<haw(r)sIs=14> (3)
<haw(r)sIz=14> (81)
<haw(r)sI{z}=14> (10)
<haw[r]s> (121)
<haw[r]sI(z)=14> (1)
<haw[r]sIs=14> (1)
<haw[r]sIz=14> (58)
<haw[r]sI{z}=14> (3)
<haw[r]sh> (1)
<hawrs> (138)
<hawrsI(z)=14> (1)
<hawrsIs=14> (2)
<hawrsIz=14> (134)
<hawrsI{z}=14> (21)
<hawrsh> (1)
<hawrshI{z}=14> (1)
<haw{r}s> (72)
<haw{r}s(Iz)> (1)
<haw{r}sIs=14> (1)
<haw{r}sIz=14> (57)
<haw{r}sI{z}=14> (4)

<haw{r}shI{z}=14> (1)
<ho(r)s> (1)
<ho(r)sIz=14> (1)
<ho[r]s> (3)
<hoe(r)s> (2)
<hoe(r)sI{z}=14> (1)
<hoe(r)sh> (1)
<hoe[r]s> (3)
<hoe[r]sIz=14> (1)
<hoe[r]sI{z}=14> (2)
<hoe[r]sh> (1)
<hoers> (4)
<hoersIz=14> (2)
<hoors> (1)
<hors> (16)
<horsI(z)=14> (1)
<horsIz=14> (20)
<horsI{z}=14> (2)
<ho{r}s> (2)
<ho{r}sIz=14> (5)
<h{aw}(r)s> (6)
<h{aw}(r)sIz=14> (9)
<h{aw}[r]s> (2)
<h{aw}[r]sIz=14> (2)
<h{aw}rs> (9)
<h{aw}rsIz=14> (3)
<h{aw}{r}s> (1)
<h{oe}(r)s> (14)
<h{oe}(r)sAz=14> (1)
<h{oe}(r)sIs=14> (2)
<h{oe}(r)sIz=14> (15)
<h{oe}(r)sI{z}=14> (1)
<h{oe}(r)sh> (1)
<h{oe}[r]s> (143)
<h{oe}[r]s(Iz)> (1)
<h{oe}[r]sAz=14> (1)
<h{oe}[r]sIz=14> (107)
<h{oe}[r]sI{z}=14> (10)
<h{oe}[r]sh> (2)
<h{oe}[r]shI(z)=14> (1)
<h{oe}[r]shIsh=14> (1)
<h{oe}[r]th> (1)
<h{oe}[r]z(Iz)> (1)
<h{oe}r(s)> (1)
<h{oe}rs> (287)
<h{oe}rsA{z}=14> (1)
<h{oe}rsI(z)=14> (1)
<h{oe}rsIs=14> (3)
<h{oe}rsIz=14> (255)
<h{oe}rsI{z}=14> (27)
<h{oe}rsh> (7)
<h{oe}rthIz=14> (1)
<h{oe}{r}(s)> (1)
<h{oe}{r}s> (59)
<h{oe}{r}s(Iz)> (1)
<h{oe}{r}sI(z)=14> (1)
<h{oe}{r}sIts=14> (1)
<h{oe}{r}sIz=14> (30)
<h{oe}{r}sh> (1)

<{?}aw(r)sIz=14> (1)

034.2 S horse

No Response (0)
|J2Cmna| (1)
|JJCmea| (3)
|JJHmaj| (1)
|JJHmea| (8)
|JSCmaa| (3)
|JSCmea| (7)
|JSDmaa| (1)
|JSHffjmaa| (1)
|JSHmaa| (1)
|JSHmea| (3)
|JSHmfb| (1)
|QABmea| (2)
|QADmea| (2)
|QAHmea| (1)
|QCBmea| (3)
|QCDmaa| (1)
|QCDmaj| (1)
|QCH| (1)
|QCHmea| (1)
|QFAjjc| (1)
|QFAlfj| (6)
|QFAmaa| (6)
|QFAmaj| (5)
|QFAmea| (11)
|QFAmej| (10)
|QFAqfb| (3)
|QFAqfd| (1)
|QFB| (2)
|QFBeaj| (1)
|QFBefjmaa| (4)
|QFBefjmea| (23)
|QFBjbl| (1)
|QFBjjamaj| (1)
|QFBjjd| (1)
|QFBjjl| (1)
|QFBjjlmea| (1)
|QFBmaa| (26)
|QFBmaj| (32)
|QFBmak| (1)
|QFBmea| (175)
|QFBmeb| (1)
|QFBmej| (12)
|QFBmek| (1)
|QFBmfa| (1)
|QFBmfj| (1)
|QFCefjmea| (3)
|QFCjjb| (1)
|QFCjjcmea| (1)
|QFCmaa| (9)
|QFCmaj| (18)
|QFCmak| (1)
|QFCmea| (69)
|QFCmej| (2)
|QFCqak| (1)
|QFCqfa| (2)
|QFCqfamaa| (1)

|QFCqfb| (40)
|QFCqfbmaj| (5)
|QFCqfbmea| (16)
|QFCqfbmej| (2)
|QFCqfbmek| (1)
|QFCqmbmaj| (1)
|QFCqmbmak| (1)
|QFD| (1)
|QFDefjmea| (2)
|QFDlfj| (1)
|QFDmaj| (5)
|QFDmea| (8)
|QFDmej| (3)
|QFF| (1)
|QFFefjmea| (3)
|QFFmaj| (1)
|QFFmea| (13)
|QFFmej| (4)
|QFFmfj| (1)
|QFHmea| (8)
|QFHmej| (2)
|QFHqfb| (2)
|QMA| (4)
|QMAjjj| (1)
|QMAmaa| (7)
|QMAmaj| (3)
|QMAmea| (13)
|QMAmej| (3)
|QMAmek| (1)
|QMAqfb| (2)
|QMB| (2)
|QMBjjc| (1)
|QMBjjjmaa| (1)
|QMBjjmmea| (1)
|QMBmaa| (20)
|QMBmaj| (32)
|QMBmajmea| (2)
|QMBmak| (1)
|QMBmam| (1)
|QMBmea| (73)
|QMBmej| (9)
|QMC| (4)
|QMCjjl| (1)
|QMCmaa| (6)
|QMCmaj| (14)
|QMCmak| (2)
|QMCmea| (23)
|QMCmej| (2)
|QMCmpa| (1)
|QMCqfa| (1)
|QMCqfb| (6)
|QMCqfbmaj| (1)
|QMCqfbmea| (1)
|QMCqfk| (1)
|QMDjjj| (1)
|QMDlfj| (1)
|QMDmaa| (3)
|QMDmaj| (5)
|QMDmea| (3)

|QMDmej| (2)
|QMFmaa| (1)
|QMFmaj| (1)
|QMFmea| (9)
|QMFmej| (1)
|QMGmea| (1)
|QMH| (2)
|QMHmaj| (1)
|QMHmea| (5)
|QMHmej| (2)
|QODmna| (1)
|QXAmna| (1)
|SAEmea| (1)
|SAGmea| (1)
|SAGqfa| (2)
|SCEmea| (1)
|SCGmea| (1)
|SFEmea| (1)
|SFGmea| (3)
|SFGmej| (1)
|SMEmea| (1)
|TABqfb| (1)
|TABqfjmea| (1)
|TADqfbmaa| (2)
|TCAmea| (3)
|TFAmea| (2)
|TFBmea| (1)
|TFBqfa| (1)
|TFBqfbmaa| (1)
|TFBqfbmea| (1)
|TFDmea| (1)
|TFFmea| (1)
|TMA| (1)
|TMAeaj| (1)
|TMAmea| (3)
|TMB| (1)
|TMBmaj| (1)
|TMBmea| (1)

034.2B P mare

{r}   weakly retroflex
{z}   devoiced
No Response (225)
<ma(r)> (14)
<ma[r]> (119)
<ma[r]z> (8)
<mai(r)> (1)
<mai[r]> (7)
<mair> (20)
<mai{r}> (1)
<mar> (296)
<marA=14> (1)
<marz> (15)
<mar{z}> (1)
<ma{r}> (73)
<ma{r}s> (1)
<ma{r}z> (2)
<me(r)> (1)
<me[r]> (17)
<mer> (89)

<merz> (2)
<me{r}> (9)
<mier> (3)
<mierz> (2)
<mi{r}> (1)
<mor> (4)
<morz> (1)
<mur> (3)
<mu{r}> (1)
<mye[r]> (1)

034.3 G ride

<!>   infinitive
<&>   present 3rd singular
<@>   present participle
<*>   preterit
<#>   past participle
No Response (95)
<!rad> (1)
<!rid> (1)
<!ried> (681)
<!riedz> (1)
<!riet> (1)
<!rod> (9)
<!roed> (1)
<&riedz> (5)
<@rieding=13> (1)
<@riedN=14> (44)
<@riedNG=14> (14)
<@rodN=14> (1)
<@rodNG=14> (1)
<*rid> (16)
<*ried> (4)
<*roe(d)> (2)
<*roed> (591)
<*roet> (1)
<#reedN=14> (1)
<#ri(d)N=14> (1)
<#rid> (18)
<#rid[N]=14> (1)
<#ridN=14> (355)
<#ried> (2)
<#ritN=14> (2)
<#rod> (1)
<#roe(d)> (1)
<#roeAd=14> (1)
<#roed> (211)

034.4 G fell off (the horse)

No Response (236)
A   bucked (me) off (4)
B   bucked me offen there (1)
C   bucked off (a horse) (2)
D   (fell) down (3)
E   fell down (from a horse) (1)
F   (fell/was thrown) from (the
     horse) (14)
G   (fell/was thrown) off (372)
H   (fell/was thrown) off (the horse)
     (219)

I   (fell/was thrown) off of (the
     horse) (59)
J   (fell/was thrown) offen (the
     horse) (8)
K   fell out (1)
L   (was) pitched off (1)
M   (was) pitched off the horse (1)
N   slid off (him) (1)
O   slid off of (it) (2)
P   slipped off (2)
Q   threw (me) off (10)
R   went off/off I went (3)

034.5A G fell out of bed

No Response (288)
A   (fell) down (1)
B   (fell) down from the bed (1)
C   (fell) from (the bed) (7)
D   (fell) off (72)
E   (fell) off (the bed) (196)
F   (fell) off in the floor (1)
G   (fell) off of (the bed) (34)
H   (fell) offen (the bed) (7)
I   (fell) out (15)
J   (fell) out of (bed) (156)
K   (fell) out of (the bed) (69)
L   (fell) out [P-0] (the bed) (35)
M   (fell) outen (the bed) (1)
N   rolled off (12)
O   rolled off (the bed) (26)
P   rolled off of (the bed) (5)
Q   rolled offen (it) (1)
R   rolled out (3)
S   rolled out of (the bed) (10)
T   rolled out [P-0] the bed (1)
U   slipped off the bed (1)
V   tumbled off (1)
W   tumbled out (2)
X   tumbled out (of bed) (1)

034.5B G fall

<!>   infinitive
<&>   present 3rd singular
<@>   present participle
<*>   preterit
<#>   past participle
No Response (293)
<!fawl> (72)
<!faw[1]> (1)
<!fol> (1)
<&fawlz> (1)
<@fawlN=14> (5)
<*fal> (1)
<*fawld> (1)
<*fel> (418)
<*fe[1]> (2)
<*fil> (2)
<*ful> (1)
<#faw(1)N=14> (1)
<#fawl> (2)
<#fawlN=14> (163)

<#fa[1]N=14> (1)
<#fel> (105)
<#fel[N]=14> (1)
<#felN=14> (3)
<#fil> (1)
<#folN=14> (9)

034.6 P horseshoes

{aw}   low-back
{dh}   devoiced
{oe}   lowered
{r}   weakly retroflex
{z}   devoiced
{zh}   devoiced
No Response (176)
<haw(r)sshue=13> (3)
<haw(r)sshuez=13> (7)
<haw(rs)shew=13> (2)
<haw(rs)shewdh=13> (1)
<haw(rs)shewz=13> (2)
<haw(rs)shew{zh}=13> (1)
<haw(rs)shew{z}=13> (2)
<haw(rs)shue(z)=13> (1)
<haw(rs)shue=13> (14)
<haw(rs)shuez=12> (1)
<haw(rs)shuez=13> (34)
<haw(rs)shuez=21> (1)
<haw(rs)shue{z}=13> (6)
<haw[r](s)shew=13> (1)
<haw[r](s)shewsh=13> (1)
<haw[r](s)shewz=13> (4)
<haw[r](s)shew{dh}=13> (1)
<haw[r](s)shew{z}=13> (2)
<haw[r](s)shue(z)=13> (1)
<haw[r](s)shue=13> (12)
<haw[r](s)shuez=13> (32)
<haw[r](s)shue{z}=13> (3)
<haw[r]sshewz=13> (1)
<haw[r]sshue(z)=13> (1)
<haw[r]sshue=13> (2)
<haw[r]sshuez=13> (10)
<hawr(s)shee{z}=13> (1)
<hawr(s)shewz=13> (11)
<hawr(s)shewzh=13> (1)
<hawr(s)shew{dh}=13> (1)
<hawr(s)shew{z}=13> (2)
<hawr(s)shue=13> (17)
<hawr(s)shues=13> (1)
<hawr(s)shuez=13> (58)
<hawr(s)shuez=31> (1)
<hawr(s)shue{z}=13> (2)
<hawrshshewz=13> (1)
<hawrshshew{z}=13> (3)
<hawrshshue(z)=13> (1)
<hawrshshue=13> (2)
<hawrshshuez=13> (3)
<hawrshshuez=21> (1)
<hawrshshue{z}=13> (1)
<hawrsshewz=13> (1)
<hawrsshew{z}=11> (1)

<hawrsshew{z}=13> (1)
<hawrsshue=13> (5)
<hawrsshuez=13> (22)
<hawrsshue{z}=13> (2)
<haw{r}(s)shewz=13> (2)
<haw{r}(s)shue=13> (6)
<haw{r}(s)shuez=13> (31)
<haw{r}(s)shue{z}=13> (3)
<haw{r}sshue=13> (1)
<haw{r}sshues=13> (1)
<haw{r}sshuez=13> (6)
<haw{r}sshue{z}=13> (1)
<ho(rs)shue=13> (1)
<ho(rs)shuez=13> (3)
<ho[r](s)shewz=13> (1)
<ho[r](s)shue=13> (2)
<hoe[r]shshewsh=13> (1)
<hoer(s)shuez=13> (1)
<hoersshuez=13> (1)
<hor(s)shue=13> (5)
<hor(s)shuez=13> (9)
<hor(s)shue{z}=13> (2)
<horsshewz=21> (1)
<horsshew{z}=13> (1)
<ho{r}(s)shewz=13> (1)
<ho{r}(s)shue=13> (1)
<h{aw}(r)sshuez=13> (1)
<h{aw}(rs)shew=13> (1)
<h{aw}(rs)shuez=13> (2)
<h{aw}(rs)shue{z}=13> (1)
<h{aw}[r](s)shuez=13> (1)
<h{aw}r(s)shewz=13> (1)
<h{aw}r(s)shue=13> (1)
<h{aw}r(s)shuez=13> (1)
<h{aw}r(s)shue{z}=13> (1)
<h{aw}rshshew=13> (1)
<h{oe}(rs)shue=13> (1)
<h{oe}(rs)shuez=13> (6)
<h{oe}(rs)shue{z}=13> (2)
<h{oe}[r](s)shew=13> (3)
<h{oe}[r](s)shewdh=13> (1)
<h{oe}[r](s)shewz=13> (5)
<h{oe}[r](s)shew{z}=13> (4)
<h{oe}[r](s)shue(z)=13> (4)
<h{oe}[r](s)shue=13> (18)
<h{oe}[r](s)shuez=13> (51)
<h{oe}[r](s)shue{z}=13> (5)
<h{oe}[r]shshew=13> (1)
<h{oe}[r]shshew{z}=13> (1)
<h{oe}[r]shshue{dh}=13> (1)
<h{oe}[r]sshew=13> (2)
<h{oe}[r]sshewz=13> (2)
<h{oe}[r]sshue=13> (4)
<h{oe}[r]sshuez=13> (6)
<h{oe}[r]sshuez=31> (1)
<h{oe}[r]stshuez=13> (1)
<h{oe}r(s)chue=13> (1)
<h{oe}r(s)chuez=13> (1)
<h{oe}r(s)shew=13> (3)

<h{oe}r(s)shew=21> (1)
<h{oe}r(s)shewz=13> (10)
<h{oe}r(s)shew{z}=13> (9)
<h{oe}r(s)shue(z)=13> (3)
<h{oe}r(s)shue=13> (13)
<h{oe}r(s)shuez=11> (1)
<h{oe}r(s)shuez=13> (104)
<h{oe}r(s)shue{z}=13> (16)
<h{oe}rshshew=13> (1)
<h{oe}rshshuez=13> (1)
<h{oe}rsshewz=13> (2)
<h{oe}rsshue=13> (7)
<h{oe}rsshuez=11> (1)
<h{oe}rsshuez=13> (31)
<h{oe}rsshuez=21> (1)
<h{oe}rsshue{z}=13> (3)
<h{oe}{r}(s)shew=13> (2)
<h{oe}{r}(s)shewz=13> (8)
<h{oe}{r}(s)shue(z)=13> (1)
<h{oe}{r}(s)shue=13> (6)
<h{oe}{r}(s)shuez=13> (21)
<h{oe}{r}(s)shue{z}=13> (2)
<h{oe}{r}sshewz=13> (1)
<h{oe}{r}sshue=13> (1)
<h{oe}{r}sshuez=11> (1)
<h{oe}{r}sshuez=13> (2)
<kaw(rs)shuez=13> (1)

034.7 P hoof/hoofs

{f} voiced
{v} devoiced
{z} devoiced
No Response (134)
<(h)oof> (1)
<hawf> (1)
<hewf> (4)
<hewfs> (2)
<hewfsh> (1)
<hewv{z}> (1)
<hof> (1)
<hoo(f)> (1)
<hoo(f)s> (2)
<hoof> (457)
<hoof(s)> (16)
<hoofs> (255)
<hoofth> (1)
<hoofz> (1)
<hoov> (4)
<hoov(z)> (1)
<hoovz> (79)
<hoov{z}> (30)
<hoo{f}z> (1)
<hoo{v}> (1)
<hoo{v}s> (2)
<hoo{v}{z}> (5)
<hu(f)s> (1)
<hue(f)> (1)
<hue(f)s> (1)
<huef> (196)
<huef(s)> (9)

<huefs> (130)
<huefth> (1)
<huev> (2)
<huev(z)> (1)
<huevs> (2)
<huevz> (47)
<huev{z}> (14)
<hue{v}s> (1)
<hue{v}{z}> (5)
<huf> (42)
<huf(s)> (7)
<hufIz=14> (1)
<hufs> (28)
<hufsh> (1)
<huvz> (1)
<hu{v}{z}> (1)
<hwoofs> (1)
<ruef> (1)
<ruefs> (1)
<swuef> (1)

034.8 L quoits

No Response (309)
A   chunking the horseshoes (2)
B   game of horseshoes (2)
C   hoop game (1)
D   horse pitch (1)
E   horseshoe pitching (6)
F   horseshoe ring (2)
G   horseshoeing (it) (2)
H   horseshoe(s) (398)
I   horseshoes for pitching (1)
J   horseshoe(s) game (56)
K   looping (1)
L   pitch(ing) a horseshoe (2)
M   pitching rings (2)
N   pitching shoes (1)
O   pitch(ing) (the/those) horseshoes (123)
P   pitch(ing) (them) (6)
Q   pitch(ing) them/those shoes (2)
R   play pitch horseshoes (1)
S   play rings (1)
T   play throwing horseshoes over the stob (1)
U   play(ing) horseshoe(s) (21)
V   playing with the horse (1)
W   quoits (13)
X   ring game (1)
Y   ring-out stobs (1)
Z   ring that shoe (1)
aa   ring that stob (1)
ab   ring (the) hoop (2)
ac   ring the horseshoes (1)
ad   ring the stob around (1)
ae   ring-tossing (1)
af   ringers (2)
ag   ring(ing) it/that (4)
ah   ringing shoes (1)
ai   ringing your stob (1)

aj ring(s) (6)
ak ringtoss (15)
al ringtoss game (1)
am rope the peg (1)
an shoes (2)
ao shoot rings (1)
ap throw them horseshoes (1)
aq throwing a horseshoe (3)
ar throw(ing) horseshoes (13)
as toss some shoes (1)
at tossing shoes (1)
au toss(ing) (the) rings (2)

034.9 L ram

No Response (279)
A belier [F] (1)
B big male sheep (1)
C billy (1)
D billy sheep (1)
E boar sheep (1)
F boy sheep (2)
G buck (95)
H buck [taboo] (6)
I buck sheep (5)
J bull sheep (1)
K doe (2)
L ewe (8)
M goat (4)
N he [n.] (1)
O he male (1)
P he sheep (1)
Q lamb (4)
R male (10)
S male sheep (20)
T mouton [F] (1)
U mutton (3)
V ram (498)
W ram [taboo] (5)
X sheep (10)
Y wether (5)
Z wether sheep (1)

035.1 L ewe

No Response (289)
A billy (1)
B doe (24)
C ewe (517)
D EWE (4)
E ewe sheep (1)
F female (14)
G female sheep (8)
H girl (2)
I lamb (7)
J lee (1)
K mamma (1)
L mamma sheep (1)
M mammy sheep (3)
N mother sheep (2)
O mouton [F] (1)
P nanny (14)
Q nanny sheep (1)

R ram (3)
S she (1)
T she lamb (1)
U she sheep (1)
V sheep (7)
W wether (1)
X youth (1)

035.1 P ewe

No Response (374)
<(y)aw> (1)
<(y)ee> (3)
<(y)eev> (1)
<(y)eez> (1)
<(y)ew> (5)
<(y)oe> (1)
<(y)or> (1)
<(y)ue> (2)
<doe> (24)
<eewee=13> (1)
<eeyu=13> (1)
<ew> (1)
<ewee=13> (1)
<goe> (1)
<joe> (1)
<yaw> (2)
<yee> (2)
<yeeb> (1)
<yeez> (1)
<yew> (144)
<yewI=14> (1)
<yews> (1)
<yewz> (7)
<yoe> (96)
<yoez> (9)
<yoo> (2)
<yue> (256)
<yueI=14> (1)
<yuel> (1)
<yuewI=14> (1)
<yuez> (9)

035.2 P wool

{l} dark
No Response (120)
<woo[l]> (77)
<wool> (199)
<woo{l}> (507)
<woo{l}z> (1)
<wue[l]> (2)
<wuel> (1)
<wue{l}> (13)
<wul> (3)
<wu{l}> (2)

035.3 L boar

No Response (162)
A barrow hog (1)
B boar (552)
C boar [taboo] (62)
D boar hog (89)
E boar hog [taboo] (18)

F boar pig (9)
G boar pig [taboo] (1)
H boy hog (4)
I boy one (1)
J boy pig (1)
K breeding hog (3)
L breeding stock (2)
M bull (1)
N daddy pig (1)
O Eber [G] (1)
P gentleman pig (1)
Q he (1)
R he hog (5)
S hog (27)
T male (64)
U male [taboo] (1)
V male hog (88)
W male pig (6)
X man hog (2)
Y man pig (1)
Z old male (2)
aa old male hog (2)
ab papa (1)
ac papa hog (2)
ad pig (6)
ae Russian boar (1)
af sow (1)
ag stag (1)
ah stock hog (20)
ai stud (1)
aj swine (2)
ak verrat [F] (2)

035.4 L barrow

No Response (416)
A altered pig (1)
B barred hog (1)
C bar(row) (131)
D barrow (296)
E bar(row) hog (6)
F barrow hog (3)
G boar (4)
H boar hog (2)
I castrated boar (2)
J castrated hog (4)
K castrated male hog (1)
L castrated pig (2)
M common pig (1)
N cut boar (1)
O cut hog (3)
P fattening hog (2)
Q gelding (1)
R gilt (5)
S grease hog (1)
T hog (21)
U it (1)
V male (6)
W male hog (4)
X meat hog (9)
Y neuter, a (3)

Z   ordinary hog (1)
aa   ox (1)
ab   pig (3)
ac   rig (2)
ad   shoat (6)
ae   stag (40)
af   sterile hog (1)
ag   virgin (1)

035.4 P barrow
{aw}   unrounded onset
{oe}   upglide
{r}   weakly retroflex
{t}   flap
No Response (443)
<ba[R]=14> (1)
<ba[r](A)> (3)
<ba[r]rA=14> (1)
<bar(A)> (1)
<barA=14> (116)
<barAz=14> (12)
<baroe=13> (21)
<barrA=14> (17)
<barroe=13> (4)
<bawr(A)> (8)
<bawrA=14> (6)
<baw{r}(A)> (2)
<ba{r}(A)> (3)
<ba{r}rA=14> (6)
<ba{t}A=14> (1)
<berA=14> (10)
<berAz=14> (1)
<beroe=13> (2)
<berroe=13> (1)
<bo[r](A)> (7)
<bor(A)> (70)
<bor(A)z> (2)
<bor(A){z}> (1)
<borA=14> (103)
<borAz=14> (8)
<borI=14> (2)
<boroo=13> (1)
<borrA=14> (5)
<borrI=14> (1)
<bor{R}z=14> (1)
<bow(r)wA=14> (1)
<bo{r}(A)> (14)
<bo{r}A=14> (1)
<bo{r}I=14> (1)
<bo{r}rA=14> (3)
<b{aw}(rA){z}> (1)
<b{aw}[r](A)> (4)
<b{aw}r(A)> (28)
<b{aw}r(A){z}> (1)
<b{aw}rA=14> (18)
<b{aw}rAz=14> (2)
<b{aw}rrA=14> (3)
<b{aw}{r}(A)> (5)
<b{oe}[r](A)> (1)

035.5 P hogs

{aw}   unrounded onset
{g}   devoiced
{oe}   lowered onset
{z}   devoiced
No Response (87)
<(h)awg{z}> (1)
<haw(g)> (3)
<haw(g)z> (2)
<haw(gz)> (1)
<hawg> (146)
<hawg(z)> (5)
<hawgsh> (2)
<hawgz> (297)
<hawg{z}> (71)
<hawks> (1)
<haw{g}> (8)
<haw{g}s> (1)
<haw{g}z> (1)
<haw{g}{z}> (9)
<ho(g)> (1)
<hoeg> (3)
<hog> (58)
<hogs> (1)
<hogz> (108)
<hog{z}> (8)
<howgz> (2)
<ho{g}> (2)
<ho{g}s> (1)
<ho{g}{z}> (2)
<h{aw}(gz)> (1)
<h{aw}g> (50)
<h{aw}gs> (1)
<h{aw}gsh> (1)
<h{aw}gz> (93)
<h{aw}g{z}> (27)
<h{aw}{g}> (2)
<h{aw}{g}{z}> (2)
<h{oe}gs> (1)
<h{oe}gsh> (1)
<h{oe}gz> (1)
<h{oe}g{z}> (1)

035.6 P bristles
{dh}   devoiced
{i}   high central
{oo}   high central
{r}   labial
{t}   flap
{z}   devoiced
No Response (214)
<(b)risL=14> (1)
<b(r){i}s[L]s=14> (1)
<breesL{z}=14> (1)
<bresL=14> (2)
<bresLz=14> (1)
<bresL{z}=14> (1)
<bri(s)L=14> (1)
<brisL(z)=14> (19)
<brisL=14> (68)
<brisLs=14> (1)

<brisLz=14> (230)
<brisL{z}=14> (63)
<bris[L](z)=14> (1)
<bris[L]=14> (3)
<bris[L]d=14> (1)
<bris[L]z=14> (3)
<bris[L]{dh}=14> (1)
<bris[L]{z}=14> (5)
<brish[L]z=14> (1)
<brish[L]{z}=14> (1)
<briskL=14> (1)
<brisk[L]z=14> (1)
<brissL(z)=14> (1)
<brissL=14> (5)
<brissLz=14> (6)
<brissL{z}=14> (6)
<briss[L](z)=14> (1)
<briss[L]z=14> (2)
<briss[L]{z}=14> (3)
<bristL(z)=14> (1)
<bristL=14> (2)
<bristLz=14> (8)
<bris{t}L=14> (1)
<britLz=14> (2)
<briz[L]{z}=14> (1)
<brizhL=14> (1)
<bri{t}Lz=14> (2)
<bro{t}L(z)=14> (1)
<brusL=14> (1)
<brusLz=14> (3)
<br{i}sL(z)=14> (11)
<br{i}sL=14> (25)
<br{i}sLz=14> (117)
<br{i}sL{z}=14> (55)
<br{i}s[L](z)=14> (1)
<br{i}s[L]=14> (2)
<br{i}s[L]z=14> (3)
<br{i}s[L]{z}=14> (1)
<br{i}shL=14> (1)
<br{i}ssL=14> (5)
<br{i}ssLz=14> (8)
<br{i}ssL{z}=14> (1)
<br{i}ss[L]{z}=14> (1)
<br{oo}sLz=14> (3)
<br{oo}sL{z}=14> (1)
<bwish[L](z)=14> (1)
<b{r}isL=14> (3)
<b{r}isLt=14> (1)
<b{r}isLz=14> (11)
<b{r}is[L]=14> (1)
<b{r}is[L]{z}=14> (2)
<b{r}ish[L]{z}=14> (1)
<b{r}{i}sLz=14> (1)

035.7 P tusks
{oo}   unrounded
{r}   weakly retroflex
{z}   devoiced
No Response (154)
<chushIz=14> (1)

<husks> (1)
<krushIz=14> (1)
<kushIz=14> (1)
<tawsh(s)> (1)
<tawsh[L]=14> (1)
<techIz=14> (1)
<teshIz=14> (1)
<teshI{z}=14> (1)
<toosh> (2)
<tooshIz=14> (4)
<tooshI{z}=14> (1)
<tos(ks)> (1)
<toshIz=14> (2)
<tu(s)ks> (2)
<tu[r]ch> (1)
<tu[r]chIz=14> (1)
<tu[r]s(ks)> (1)
<tu[r]sh(s)> (2)
<tu[r]sh> (4)
<tu[r]shI(s)=14> (1)
<tu[r]shIz=14> (3)
<tu[r]shI{z}=14> (2)
<tu[r]shk> (1)
<tuch(s)> (2)
<tuch> (2)
<tuchIs=14> (1)
<tuchIz=14> (13)
<tuchI{z}=14> (3)
<tuesh> (1)
<tuf(k)> (1)
<tuf(k)s> (3)
<tursIz=14> (1)
<tursh(s)> (3)
<tursh> (2)
<turshI(s)=14> (2)
<turshIz=14> (4)
<turshI{z}=14> (1)
<tus(k)> (3)
<tus(k)Iz=14> (3)
<tus(k)s> (2)
<tus(ks)> (48)
<tusL=14> (1)
<tush(s)> (37)
<tush> (31)
<tushA{z}=14> (1)
<tushI(s)=14> (1)
<tushIsh=14> (1)
<tushIz=14> (222)
<tushI{z}=14> (27)
<tushk> (1)
<tushtIz=14> (1)
<tusk(s)> (155)
<tusk> (68)
<tuskIz=14> (5)
<tusks> (112)
<tussIz=14> (1)
<tust(s)> (6)
<tustks> (1)
<tusts> (1)

<tuth(s)> (1)
<tuzhI{z}=14> (1)
<tu{r}shIz=14> (5)
<t{oo}sh> (2)
<t{oo}shIz=14> (2)
<t{oo}shI{z}=14> (1)
<t{oo}sk(s)> (2)
<t{oo}sks> (1)

035.8 P trough/troughs

{aw}   unrounded onset
{dh}   devoiced
{f}   bilabial
{oe}   lowered onset
{r}   devoiced
{v}   devoiced
{z}   devoiced
No Response (110)
<ch(r)awf> (1)
<chrawf> (3)
<chrawfs> (1)
<chrawvz> (1)
<chraw{f}> (1)
<ch{r}awf> (1)
<srawf> (1)
<strawf(s)> (1)
<tawft> (1)
<tawrf> (1)
<travz> (1)
<traw(f)> (3)
<traw(f)s> (3)
<traw(f)z> (8)
<traw(f){z}> (2)
<traw(fs)> (3)
<traw(v)z> (2)
<trawdh{z}> (2)
<trawf> (303)
<trawf(s)> (18)
<trawfs> (132)
<trawft> (103)
<trawft(s)> (2)
<trawfth> (1)
<trawfts> (4)
<trawfz> (1)
<traws> (1)
<trawt> (2)
<trawth> (11)
<trawths> (2)
<trawthz> (1)
<trawv(z)> (2)
<trawvz> (75)
<trawv{z}> (17)
<traw{dh}s> (1)
<traw{f}> (3)
<traw{v}s> (1)
<traw{v}z> (5)
<traw{v}{z}> (10)
<tro(f)z> (1)
<troef> (1)
<troeft> (1)

<troeth> (1)
<troevzh> (1)
<trof> (19)
<trof(s)> (3)
<trofs> (13)
<troft> (1)
<troth> (1)
<trovz> (3)
<trow(f)> (4)
<trow(f)z> (2)
<trow(f){z}> (2)
<trowf> (6)
<trowf(s)> (1)
<trowfs> (1)
<trowvz> (1)
<tro{v}{z}> (1)
<tr{aw}dh{z}> (2)
<tr{aw}f> (45)
<tr{aw}fs> (11)
<tr{aw}ft> (2)
<tr{aw}th> (6)
<tr{aw}th(s)> (1)
<tr{aw}ths> (4)
<tr{aw}vz> (15)
<tr{aw}v{z}> (2)
<tr{aw}{f}s> (2)
<tr{aw}{v}z> (1)
<tr{aw}{v}{z}> (2)
<tr{oe}dh{z}> (2)
<tr{oe}f> (2)
<tr{oe}th> (1)
<tr{oe}{v}sh> (1)
<t{r}av(z)> (1)
<t{r}avz> (1)
<t{r}aw(f)> (1)
<t{r}aw(f)s> (2)
<t{r}aw(f)z> (2)
<t{r}aw(f){z}> (2)
<t{r}aw(fs)> (1)
<t{r}awdh{z}> (1)
<t{r}awf> (219)
<t{r}awf(s)> (13)
<t{r}awfs> (69)
<t{r}awft> (40)
<t{r}awfts> (2)
<t{r}awth> (1)
<t{r}awths> (1)
<t{r}awv> (1)
<t{r}awv(s)> (2)
<t{r}awvz> (55)
<t{r}awv{z}> (22)
<t{r}aw{v}> (1)
<t{r}aw{v}(s)> (3)
<t{r}aw{v}{z}> (11)
<t{r}a{v}z> (1)
<t{r}o(f)> (1)
<t{r}oef> (2)
<t{r}oefs> (3)
<t{r}of> (13)

<t{r}ofs> (9)
<t{r}oft> (1)
<t{r}ovz> (6)
<t{r}ov{z}> (1)
<t{r}owf> (1)
<t{r}{aw}(f)z> (1)
<t{r}{aw}f> (36)
<t{r}{aw}fs> (19)
<t{r}{aw}ft> (2)
<t{r}{aw}v> (1)
<t{r}{aw}vz> (7)
<t{r}{aw}v{z}> (6)
<t{r}{aw}{v}> (1)
<t{r}{aw}{v}{z}> (3)
<{f}(r)awf> (1)

035.9 L wild hog

No Response (208)
A   African type (1)
B   Arkansas razorback (2)
C   Arkansas razorback hog (2)
D   boar (74)
E   boar hog (2)
F   bougre barrow (1)
G   bush hog (1)
H   field dodger (1)
I   flatwood hog (1)
J   guinea pig (1)
K   hazel splitter (1)
L   hill hog (1)
M   hog (2)
N   jabalina [S] (23)
O   jabalina hog (1)
P   mix breed of hogs (1)
Q   mountain hog (2)
R   mountain rooter (2)
S   native hog (1)
T   peccary (4)
U   pine root(er) (1)
V   pine rooter (14)
W   pine-hill rooter (2)
X   pine-ridge rooter (1)
Y   pinewood rooter (1)
Z   pinewoods rooter (1)
aa piney rooter (4)
ab piney-wood hog (2)
ac piney-wood rooter (22)
ad piney woods (2)
ae piney-woods hog (4)
af piney-woods rooter (54)
ag poor hog (2)
ah range hog (3)
ai razorback (98)
aj razorback boar (1)
ak razorback hog (15)
al razorback pig (1)
am razorback rooter (1)
an ridge runner (1)
ao ridge runner hog (1)
ap rooter (5)

aq rooter hog (1)
ar Russian boar (1)
as Russian wild boar (2)
at sembel breed (1)
au scrub hog (2)
av sinner hog (1)
aw swamp hog (3)
ax swine (1)
ay tusher (1)
az tusker (1)
ba warthog (1)
bb wild (6)
bc wild black boar (1)
bd wild boar (170)
be wild boar hog (4)
bf wild gilt (2)
bg wild hog (457)
bh wild male (2)
bi wild one (4)
bj wild pig (30)
bk wild range hog (1)
bl wild rooter (1)
bm wild sow (3)
bn wild stag (1)
bo wood hog (1)
bp wood rooter (1)
bq woods hog (6)
br woods rooter (1)

036.1 L castrate

No Response (173)
A   after (1)
B   alt(er) (3)
C   alter (46)
D   alterate (1)
E   alteration (1)
F   alternate (1)
G   barrowing (1)
H   caponize (3)
I   casperate (1)
J   casteraise (1)
K   casterize (12)
L   castracize (1)
M   castr(ate) (1)
N   castrate (508)
O   castrate on (1)
P   castration (3)
Q   catharize (1)
R   change (20)
S   circumcise (3)
T   clamp (2)
U   clip (2)
V   cut (202)
W   cut his nuts out (3)
X   cut something off (2)
Y   cut the seed out (1)
Z   cut up (1)
aa cutting his seeds out (1)
ab cutting something out (1)
ac deball (2)

ad deflower (2)
ae denatured (1)
af denude (1)
ag denut (4)
ah desex (1)
ai do something to them (1)
aj doctor (2)
ak dress (2)
al emasculate (2)
am emasculation (1)
an fix (25)
ao fix off (1)
ap fix up (2)
aq geld (18)
ar get the seeds out (1)
as had his marbles taken out (1)
at have a operation (1)
au kill (1)
av lancelate (1)
aw make over (1)
ax make sterile (2)
ay make tame (1)
az mark (42)
ba neuter (30)
bb operate (1)
bc operate on (22)
bd pinch (4)
be removing its testicles (1)
bf robbed of his privilege (1)
bg service (1)
bh shaving (1)
bi spade (23)
bj spay (75)
bk spray (1)
bl stab (1)
bm sterile (1)
bn sterilize (8)
bo stunt (1)
bp take his sex out (1)
bq take his tonsils out (1)
br take the nuts out (2)
bs take their balls out (1)
bt tend to (3)
bu trim (16)
bv trimmed up (1)
bw undergone a seed change (1)
bx unsexed (1)
by veterinary work (1)
bz work (2)
ca work on (51)
cb work over (1)

036.2 L bawl [of calf]

No Response (245)
A   baa (17)
B   baby moo (1)
C   bawl (210)
D   bawling calf (1)
E   bay (1)
F   bellow (96)

G blare (1)
H bleat (236)
I bleating sound (1)
J boo (1)
K bray (2)
L cry (35)
M crying calf (1)
N crying noise (1)
O groan (1)
P holler (32)
Q low (43)
R maa (5)
S mew (2)
T moo (43)
U nanny (1)
V noo (1)
W squall (5)
X squeal (4)
Y stunning (1)
Z wail (2)
aa weep (1)
ab whine (8)
ac whinny (3)
ad yakking (1)
ae yell (3)

036.3 L low [of cow]
No Response (217)
A baa (1)
B bawl (77)
C bay (1)
D bellow (61)
E bleat (8)
F blow (1)
G bray (1)
H burp (1)
I groan (1)
J grunt (1)
K holler (8)
L hum (1)
M low (277)
N lower (1)
O lowing sound (1)
P maa (1)
Q mew (5)
R moan (4)
S moo (347)
T moo noise (1)
U mooing sound (2)
V whimper (1)
W whine (1)

036.4 L whinny [of horse]
No Response (192)
A a-nickering (3)
B a-whinkering (1)
C bellow (3)
D bleat (2)
E blow (2)
F blowing his nose (1)
G bray (57)

H braying noise (1)
I cry (1)
J grinning sound (1)
K grunt (1)
L hee-haw (4)
M hennit [v.] [F] (1)
N hennit [n.] [F] (1)
O hinny [n.] (2)
P holler (12)
Q horselaugh (2)
R laugh [v.] (1)
S laugh [n.] (1)
T laughing noise (1)
U low (2)
V minny (1)
W moo (1)
X nanny (1)
Y neeing (1)
Z neigh [v.] (214)
aa neigh [n.] (5)
ab neighing sound (2)
ac nicker (251)
ad nighing (1)
ae ninny (2)
af nipping (1)
ag nuzzling (1)
ah shaying (1)
ai sigh (1)
aj snicker (3)
ak snort (18)
al snout (1)
am snuffling (2)
an soft whinny (1)
ao squeal (5)
ap squealing noise (1)
aq trill [n.] (1)
ar whicker [v.] (75)
as whicker [n.] (2)
at whickering [n.] (1)
au whickering noise (1)
av whickering sound (1)
aw whicking (1)
ax whigger (1)
ay whimper (6)
az whine (7)
ba whining sound (1)
bb whinker (14)
bc whinny [v.] (202)
bd whinny [n.] (12)
be whinny-like (1)
bf whiny (1)
bg wince (1)
bh yell (1)

036.5 L cattle
No Response (193)
A animals (160)
B barnyard animals (1)
C breeding stock (1)
D cattle (286)

E critters (4)
F domestic animals (3)
G farm animals (9)
H head of stock (1)
I herd (12)
J herd of cattle (3)
K livestock (118)
L plowing stock (1)
M stock of cattle (1)
N stock(s) (399)
O work animals (1)
P work stock (4)

036.6 L fowls
No Response (341)
A animals (9)
B barnyard fowls (2)
C birds (35)
D bunch of chickens (1)
E chicken(s) (161)
F covey of birds (1)
G domestic fowls (1)
H feathered animals (1)
I feathered fowl (1)
J feathered friends (1)
K flock(s) (60)
L flock of chickens (2)
M fowl(s) (248)
N game (1)
O hens (1)
P livestock (1)
Q pets (1)
R poultry (85)
S stock (7)
T wildfowl (1)

036.7 L setting hen
No Response (185)
A a-setting [v.] (5)
B breeding hen (1)
C brood hen (3)
D brooder (4)
E brooder hen (4)
F brooder one (1)
G brooding hen (7)
H broodish (1)
I broody [adj.] (2)
J broody hen (5)
K cackling (1)
L cackling (hen) (1)
M cluck (3)
N clucker (2)
O clucking (1)
P clucking hen (2)
Q clueca [S] (1)
R couveuse [F] (1)
S hatching (1)
T hatching hen (2)
U hen (38)
V hen that's laying (1)
W hen that's setting (1)

D   chicken hash (1)
E   chicken innards (1)
F   chicken stock (1)
G   chicken trash (1)
H   chitlins (12)
I   chitterlings (1)
J   cow intestines (1)
K   eatable parts (1)
L   entrail(s) (93)
M   giblet(s) (64)
N   gizzards (1)
O   grinding, the (1)
P   gut part (1)
Q   gut(s) (53)
R   hash (20)
S   haslet(s) (96)
T   hog guts (2)
U   hog hash (1)
V   hog haslet (4)
W   innards (26)
X   inside(s) (14)
Y   internals (1)
Z   intestines (12)
aa   light of the entrails (1)
ab   lights (2)
ac   lights and (the) liver(s) (5)
ad   liver [J-0] (the) light(s) (8)
ae   liver(s) and (the) lights (85)
af   liver hash (1)
ag   main parts (1)
ah   maw (3)
ai   middling (1)
aj   offal(s) (3)
ak   organ meat(s) (4)
al   organs (4)
am   orts (1)
an   paunch (2)
ao   pizzles (1)
ap   plucks (1)
aq   remnant(s) (1)
ar   scraps (1)
as   trimmings (1)
at   tripe (1)

037.3 L chitterlings

No Response (107)
A   beef chitlins (1)
B   big and little guts (1)
C   bowels (1)
D   cases (3)
E   casings (22)
F   chitlin(s) (637)
G   chitterling(s) (138)
H   city fish (1)
I   cow chitlins (1)
J   crackling(s) (7)
K   entrail(s) (104)
L   gut sausage (1)
M   gut(s) (66)
N   hog chitlins (11)

O   hog chitterlings (1)
P   hog entrails (1)
Q   hog gut(s) (9)
R   hog intestines (2)
S   hog's chitlins (1)
T   hog's guts (1)
U   hog's intestines (1)
V   innards (2)
W   inner tubes (1)
X   integrals (1)
Y   intestinal tract (2)
Z   intestine part (1)
aa   intestines (130)
ab   little chitlin (1)
ac   little entrails (1)
ad   little gut(s) (2)
ae   marrow guts (1)
af   paunch (4)
ag   pig intestines (1)
ah   pizzles (1)
ai   sausage casing (1)
aj   shitlins (3)
ak   small entrails (1)
al   small intestine(s) (5)
am   smaller chitlins (1)
an   soul food (1)
ao   tripas [S] (4)
ap   tripe(s) (2)

037.3 P chitterlings

{d}   devoiced
{l}   clear
{R}   weakly retroflex
{t}   flap
{z}   devoiced
{?}   glottal
No Response (172)
<cheetRlNG{z}=144> (1)
<cheetlNz=14> (2)
<cheetlN{z}=14> (1)
<cheetl[N]{z}=14> (1)
<chetAlN{z}=144> (1)
<chetlNz=14> (1)
<chi(t)lNz=14> (2)
<chi(t){l}N{z}=14> (1)
<chichAlingz=143> (1)
<chidAlNz=144> (1)
<chidA{l}ints=143> (1)
<chidlNz=14> (2)
<chidlinz=13> (1)
<chid{l}Nz=14> (1)
<chiklN{z}=14> (1)
<chillN(z)=14> (1)
<chillNz=14> (3)
<chit(1)N(z)=14> (1)
<chit(1)NGz=14> (1)
<chit(1)Nz=14> (2)
<chitAlN(z)=144> (11)
<chitAlNGz=144> (2)
<chitAlNG{z}=144> (1)

<chitAlNs=144> (1)
<chitAlNz=144> (25)
<chitAlN{z}=144> (10)
<chitAl[N]z)=144> (1)
<chitAlingz=143> (3)
<chitAling{z}=143> (2)
<chitAlinz=143> (2)
<chitAlin{d}{z}=143> (1)
<chitIlNz=144> (7)
<chitL(N)z=14> (1)
<chitLlNz=144> (1)
<chitRlNGz=144> (5)
<chitRlNG{z}=144> (1)
<chitRlNz=144> (1)
<chitRlendz=143> (1)
<chitRli(nz)=143> (1)
<chitRlingz=143> (4)
<chitRling{z}=143> (1)
<chitRrNz=144> (1)
<chit[1]Nz=14> (1)
<chitlId{z}=14> (1)
<chitlIts=14> (1)
<chitlN(z)=14> (31)
<chitlNGz=14> (10)
<chitlNG{z}=14> (1)
<chitlNdz=14> (1)
<chitlNz=14> (417)
<chitlN{z}=14> (113)
<chitl[N]{z}=14> (2)
<chitleengz=13> (1)
<chitlendz=13> (1)
<chitlenz=13> (1)
<chitlingz=13> (3)
<chitlins=13> (1)
<chitlinz=13> (21)
<chitlin{z}=13> (3)
<chitlits=13> (1)
<chiturlNG{z}=134> (1)
<chit{R}lNGz=144> (1)
<chit{R}lNz=144> (2)
<chit{l}N(z)=14> (1)
<chit{l}Nz=14> (5)
<chit{l}N{z}=14> (2)
<chit{t}AlNz=144> (2)
<chit{t}Nz=14> (2)
<chit{t}RlNGz=144> (1)
<chi{?}lNz=14> (1)
<chi{?}lN{z}=14> (2)
<chi{?}lenz=13> (1)
<chi{?}{l}ints=13> (1)
<chi{t}AlNG(z)=144> (1)
<chi{t}AlNGz=144> (1)
<chi{t}AlNz=144> (7)
<chi{t}AlN{z}=144> (3)
<chi{t}Alinz=143> (1)
<chi{t}A{l}ins=143> (1)
<chi{t}IlNGz=144> (1)
<chi{t}RlNGz=144> (1)
<chi{t}RlNz=144> (1)

<chi{t}Rlinz=143> (1)
<chi{t}lN(z)=14> (4)
<chi{t}lNz=14> (15)
<chi{t}lN{z}=14> (4)
<chi{t}linz=13> (1)
<chi{t}{R}lN{z}=144> (1)
<chi{t}{R}lindz=143> (1)
<chi{t}{R}rNz=144> (1)
<chi{t}{l}Nz=14> (2)
<chi{t}{l}N{z}=14> (1)
<kitlinz=13> (1)
<sheetlN(z)=14> (1)
<shitAlNz=144> (1)
<shitlNz=14> (5)
<shi{t}lN{z}=14> (1)
<titlNz=14> (1)

037.4 L feeding time

No Response (306)
A afternoon chores (1)
B chore(s) (17)
C chore(s) time (29)
D dinnertime (6)
E eating time (2)
F evening chores (1)
G evening time (1)
H evening work (1)
I feed time (41)
J feeding hours (1)
K feeding time (409)
L feeding-up time (2)
M hog-feeding time (1)
N milk time (4)
O milking time (22)
P night chores (1)
Q night work (8)
R night-work time (1)
S outside chores (1)
T outside work (1)
U stock-feeding time (1)
V straight time (1)
W suppertime (5)
X time for chores (1)
Y time for work (1)
Z (time to) do (the) chores (36)
aa (time to) do (the) chores up (1)
ab (time to) do (the) night work (8)
ac (time to) do the outside work (1)
ad (time to) do the work (2)
ae (time to) do up (the) chores (2)
af (time to) do up (the) night work (5)
ag (time to) do up (the) work (3)
ah (time to) feed (22)
ai (time to) feed the (stock) (41)
aj (time to) feed up (15)
ak (time to) get ready for feeding (1)

al (time to) get (the) chores (done) (2)
am (time to) get (the) outside chores done (1)
an (time to) get the stock fed (1)
ao (time to) go and feed up (the livestocks) (2)
ap (time to) go do the chores (1)
aq (time to) go feed (5)
ar (time to) go feed the (stock) (3)
as (time to) go feed up (the stock) (7)
at (time to) go milk (1)
au (time to) go milk her and feed her (1)
av (time to) go out and feed (1)
aw (time to) go to work (1)
ax (time to) milk (1)
ay (time to) slop (the) hogs (3)
az (time to) tend the cattle (1)
ba (time to) tend to the things (1)
bb (time to) work (1)
bc work time (5)

037.5 G calls to cows

No Response (282)
A aa/aw (2)
B bossy (1)
C cahey hey (1)
D chal-bal (1)
E chaw (1)
F choo/chuh (cow) (2)
G co (boss/cow) (16)
H co-ah (1)
I co-a(n)k (3)
J co-ant(sy) (2)
K co-atch (1)
L co-ay/co-eh (cow) (6)
M co-ench/co-inch (11)
N co-et/co-it (7)
O co-up (3)
P co, wench (2)
Q coey (co/cow) (17)
R come along (1)
S come (boss/cow) (6)
T come here (cow) (15)
U come on (cow) (46)
V come to barn here (1)
W coo (3)
X cooey/cuey/coy (cow) (11)
Y core (1)
Z cow (1)
aa ee-oo/eh-ooh (2)
ab eeh (1)
ac go-it (1)
ad hark (1)
ae haw (2)
af hee-ah/hee-ok (2)
ag here (boss/cow) (21)

ah here, sook (1)
ai hey (cow) (7)
aj ho (cow) (7)
ak ho-eh/hoey (2)
al hoo (cow) (21)
am hoo-ba/hoo-ha (2)
an hoo-oke sookey (1)
ao hoo sug (1)
ap hoo-wee/hoowee (2)
aq hooey (7)
ar hook sook (2)
as hoop(y)/hoopee (4)
at ki-yea (1)
au kope (2)
av kwo cow (1)
aw kwo-it (2)
ax kwope (1)
ay kwoy (2)
az kwup (1)
ba moo (cow) (7)
bb moop (1)
bc oh (4)
bd oh-a (1)
be ooey (1)
bf ooh (2)
bg poc (1)
bh poy (1)
bi pshaw/shaw (2)
bj salt (1)
bk saw (boss/cow) (237)
bl shamoshack (1)
bm shoo (2)
bn sir (1)
bo so (cow) (36)
bp sob (1)
bq soey (1)
br sog (1)
bs soke (oke) (4)
bt soo (boss/cow) (160)
bu sooey (cow) (13)
bv sook (boss/cow) (194)
bw sookoo (1)
bx sooky (cow) (14)
by sooky kwo aa (1)
bz sow, heifer (1)
ca suck (3)
cb suh (1)
cc sute (1)
cd swoo (cow) (4)
ce swook (1)
cf venganse [S] (1)
cg whoa/wo (cow) (21)
ch whoo (wa) (9)
ci whooey (1)
cj whook (2)
ck wo-ah (1)
cl woey (1)
cm woo (cow) (13)
cn wu wee (1)

co   yea yet (1)
cp   yee-wye (1)
cq   yoo (2)
cr   yoody-roo (1)

037.6 G calls to calves

No Response (682)
A   baa (1)
B   bossy (1)
C   calfa, soke (1)
D   calfy (3)
E   casoo (1)
F   co sooky (1)
G   coey, come on (1)
H   coey, cow (1)
I   come here (2)
J   come here, calf (1)
K   come in, calfy (1)
L   come on (9)
M   come on, baby (calf) (7)
N   come on, calf(y) (10)
O   come on here (boys) (2)
P   come on, little girl (1)
Q   come on, sweetie (1)
R   cooey (1)
S   here (1)
T   here, calf(y) (3)
U   here, cow (1)
V   ho, calf (1)
W   ho, sook, calf (1)
X   ho-wuh (1)
Y   hoo (1)
Z   hoo-cow (1)
aa   hoo hee here (1)
ab   keebo (1)
ac   kwo-it (1)
ad   minny (1)
ae   moo (1)
af   ninny (1)
ag   saw, calf (1)
ah   saw, heifer (1)
ai   she-calf (2)
aj   sheek (1)
ak   soo (2)
al   soo, baby (1)
am   soo, calf(y) (90)
an   soo, cow (4)
ao   sooey (1)
ap   sook (17)
aq   sook, baby (1)
ar   sook, calf(y) (65)
as   sookaa sook (1)
at   sooky (6)
au   sooky sook, calf (1)
av   sweetie (1)
aw   whoa, calf (1)
ax   wo (1)

037.7 G gee/haw

No Response (312)
A   ah (1)

B   aw [left] (1)
C   bike [right] (1)
D   ee [right] (1)
E   gee (221)
F   gee [left] (47)
G   gee [right] (275)
H   gee haw (6)
I   go [left] (2)
J   ha [left] (2)
K   haw (221)
L   haw [left] (279)
M   haw [right] (45)
N   hee (6)
O   hee [left] (1)
P   hee [right] (3)
Q   hey (1)
R   hey [right] (1)
S   ho (2)
T   ho [left] (1)
U   ho [right] (1)
V   jay (1)
W   left (2)
X   nay (5)
Y   right (2)
Z   wah (1)
aa   whoa (1)
ab   whoa [left] (2)
ac   whoa, come, gee (1)
ad   whoa, come, haw (1)
ae   whoa, gee [right] (1)
af   whoa, haw [left] (2)
ag   whoa you then [left] (1)
ah   wocam [left] (1)
ai   yea (14)
aj   yea [right] (12)
ak   yea, gee [right] (1)
al   yee (1)
am   yee [right] (4)

037.8 G calls to horses

No Response (638)
A   click (5)
B   cluck (1)
C   co (8)
D   co-up (2)
E   colt (1)
F   come (horsey) (5)
G   come here (boy) (32)
H   come in (here) (3)
I   come on (boy) (31)
J   come on in (2)
K   come up (here) (2)
L   coop/koop (3)
M   coop cup coop (1)
N   cowee (1)
O   cup coal (1)
P   get up (1)
Q   ha (1)
R   hee (1)
S   here (boy) (9)

T   het (1)
U   hey (3)
V   hoey (1)
W   kope (horsey) (42)
X   kope coop (1)
Y   kope gope (1)
Z   kope hope (1)
aa   kope kwope (1)
ab   kup/cup (3)
ac   kup coop (1)
ad   kup kope (1)
ae   kwope (14)
af   kwup (2)
ag   kwup kup (1)
ah   kwup wup (1)
ai   look out (1)
aj   wa (1)
ak   wee (1)
al   whistle/whistling (113)
am   whu (1)
an   whup (1)
ao   woop (3)
ap   wope (1)
aq   wup (1)

038.1 G get up [to horse]

No Response (169)
A   all right, let's go (2)
B   click (to him) (42)
C   cluck (to him) (17)
D   clucking sounds (1)
E   come (1)
F   come on (boy/horse) (17)
G   come on up (1)
H   come out (1)
I   come up (84)
J   come up here/there (4)
K   faster (1)
L   gee (4)
M   gee haw (1)
N   gee up (2)
O   get (2)
P   get along there (1)
Q   get going (3)
R   get gone (1)
S   get in there (1)
T   get on out (1)
U   get on up (1)
V   get on up here/there (now) (2)
W   get out (of here) (4)
X   get up (horse/horsey/sir) (484)
Y   get up here/there (sir) (20)
Z   get up, now (1)
aa   giddap (6)
ab   giddyup (horse) (165)
ac   giddyup there (2)
ad   go (horse) (9)
ae   go (a)head (1)
af   go faster (1)
ag   go on (1)

ah   go to it (1)
ai   ha (2)
aj   here (1)
ak   hey (now) (2)
al   ho up (1)
am   hurry, get up (1)
an   hya (1)
ao   let's go (boy) (13)
ap   step up (1)
aq   whistle (1)
ar   yea (1)
as   yup (1)

038.2A G whoa [to horse]
No Response (176)
A   gee (2)
B   gee, whoa up (1)
C   go (1)
D   halt (6)
E   haw (5)
F   hey (1)
G   ho (27)
H   ho haw (1)
I   hold it (3)
J   hoo (2)
K   hoop hup hoop (1)
L   hope (2)
M   mo (1)
N   oh (1)
O   stand still (1)
P   stand there (1)
Q   stop (10)
R   whoa (boy/horse) (694)
S   whoa now (2)
T   whoa up (1)
U   whoa, yeah (2)
V   whoaee (1)
W   whoop (1)
X   woo (1)
Y   woop (1)

038.2B G back up [to horse]
No Response (639)
A   back (78)
B   back (over) here (2)
C   back up (152)
D   back up (in) here/there (10)
E   back up now (1)
F   back, whoa (3)
G   come around (1)
H   come on, back (2)
I   gee (2)
J   get back, boy (1)
K   get back here (1)
L   get back in there (1)
M   get in there (1)
N   get that wagon back here (1)
O   go back (1)
P   hack (2)
Q   haw there (1)
R   here (1)

S   ho (1)
T   ho, back (2)
U   move back (1)
V   whoa (4)
W   whoa, back (here) (22)
X   whoa, back up (here) (5)
Y   whoa, yea, haw (1)
Z   yea (7)
aa   yea, back (4)
ab   yea, back up (1)
ac   yea, wup, yea (1)
ad   yee, back (1)

038.3 G calls to pigs
No Response (285)
A   a-ooh pig (1)
B   beaup (1)
C   chinny, here, chinny (1)
D   cho, pig (1)
E   choo/chu (pig/piggy) (4)
F   chooey (1)
G   chook (1)
H   choop (1)
I   click (1)
J   co, pig (2)
K   come here (pig/piggy) (4)
L   come on (pig/piggy) (22)
M   come on, soo/sooey (2)
N   come, pig/piggy (3)
O   coo (1)
P   cooey (1)
Q   go, pig (2)
R   goo (1)
S   goop (1)
T   grunt (1)
U   gur (1)
V   hee (hoo) (2)
W   hee ooh (hee)/he ooh (3)
X   here (pig/piggy) (20)
Y   here, sooky (1)
Z   hey (1)
aa   hiyi (1)
ab   ho (hoey), pig (2)
ac   hoggy (2)
ad   hoo (13)
ae   hoo hooey (2)
af   hoo oh (hoo/pig) (2)
ag   hoo pee (1)
ah   hoo, pig/piggy (hoo/hooey) (21)
ai   hooey/huey (11)
aj   hoop(s) (pig) (7)
ak   hoopoly (1)
al   hoopy (1)
am   hope hoey (1)
an   hope, pig (1)
ao   hoy, pig/piggy (hoy) (2)
ap   kahoops (1)
aq   kope (1)
ar   kup (1)
as   kwaw, pig (1)

at   kwoo, pig (1)
au   kwoop (1)
av   moo, piggy (1)
aw   oh, hog (1)
ax   oh, pig/piggy (oh) (3)
ay   oh wee (1)
az   ooey (1)
ba   ooey, pig, sook (1)
bb   oogy (1)
bc   ooh (2)
bd   ooh, pig/piggy (pig) (6)
be   ooh sooey (1)
bf   oop, pig (1)
bg   pee/pi (4)
bh   pee hoo (1)
bi   pee ooh ee (1)
bj   pee, pig (1)
bk   pee whoa, pig (1)
bl   pee w(h)oo (pig) (2)
bm   pew, pig (1)
bn   pig/pigs (89)
bo   pig, here, pig (1)
bp   pig, ho (1)
bq   pig-hog (1)
br   pig, hoo (1)
bs   pig, hooey (2)
bt   pig, pew (1)
bu   pig, piggo, pig (1)
bv   pig, piggy (5)
bw   pig, pigoo (piggy) (2)
bx   pig, sooky (1)
by   pig, whoa, ye (1)
bz   pig, w(h)oop (pig) (2)
ca   pig, woo, pig (1)
cb   pig, wuh (1)
cc   pig, you, pig (2)
cd   pigawee (1)
ce   piggo (2)
cf   piggo, pig (ooey/piggo) (2)
cg   piggoee oee pig (1)
ch   piggy/piggies (130)
ci   piggy a-piggy (1)
cj   piggy, come (1)
ck   piggy pee (1)
cl   piggy pig (piggy) (7)
cm   piggy pigoo (2)
cn   piggy po (1)
co   piggy wiggy (wig) (1)
cp   piggy woo (piggy) (2)
cq   pigoey (1)
cr   pigoo/piggoo (pig/piggy) (9)
cs   pigooey/pigoy (pig) (5)
ct   piyoop, pig (1)
cu   pyoo woo (1)
cv   shoo (pig) (2)
cw   shooey (1)
cx   soo (7)
cy   soo, hog (2)
cz   soo, pig/piggy (29)

da sooey (192)
db sooey, get on (1)
dc sooey, hog (sooey) (2)
dd sooey ooey soo (1)
de sooey, pig/piggy (14)
df sooey soody (1)
dg sook (1)
dh sooky (sook sooky) (3)
di sow, sully, sow (1)
dj sowee/swee (3)
dk swoo, pig (1)
dl ti-woo (1)
dm wee, pig (1)
dn whoa (1)
do whoa ho (1)
dp whoa/wo, pig/piggy (5)
dq w(h)oo (9)
dr w(h)oo, pig/piggy (54)
ds whoo wee (1)
dt whoo whooey (1)
du w(h)ooey (4)
dv whooey, piggy (2)
dw w(h)oop (pig/piggy) (9)
dx whoop, pig (2)
dy whoopa (1)
dz whope (1)
ea woo sook (1)
eb woopy (1)
ec yee hoo (1)
ed yee, pig (1)
ee yo wo, pig (1)
ef yoo/you, pig (2)
eg yooey (1)

038.4 G calls to sheep
No Response (819)
A baa (8)
B co, nanny (1)
C co, sheepy (2)
D come here, little sheep (1)
E come on, levies (1)
F come on, sheepy (2)
G come, baa (1)
H come, batty (1)
I coo (1)
J coo, sheep (21)
K coo, sheepy (17)
L here, sheep (1)
M here, sheepy (1)
N hooey shooey (1)
O lamb (1)
P maa (1)
Q mouton [F] (1)
R naa (1)
S poo, sheepy (1)
T sheep (12)
U sheep sheepy (1)
V sheep sheepy sheep (1)
W sheepy (17)
X sheepy sheep (2)

Y whoo-hee (1)
038.5 G calls to chickens
No Response (241)
A bee (1)
B biddy (biddies) (9)
C bok/buck (3)
D cachicky (1)
E chee (chick) (2)
F chick(s) (298)
G chick check (1)
H chick chicken (3)
I chick chickeroo (1)
J chick chicko (3)
K chick chickoo (chick) (8)
L chick chicks chicky (1)
M chick chicky (chick) (48)
N chick gehee chicky (1)
O chick twoo chick (1)
P chicka chick/chicky (3)
Q chickabies (1)
R chicken(s) (10)
S chicken chick/chicky (4)
T chicken chicka chicky (1)
U chicko (4)
V chickoo (chick/chicky) (11)
W chicky (128)
X chicky chick (chicky) (24)
Y chicky GRUNT(C) chicka (1)
Z chiddy/chitty (2)
aa chitty kitty gitty (1)
ab click (7)
ac cloo (1)
ad cluck (7)
ae clucking noise(s) (2)
af come and get it (2)
ag come chee (1)
ah come, chicky (1)
ai come here, chickens (1)
aj come here, guinea (1)
ak come on (and get your food) (2)
al come on, chick/chicky (17)
am come on, jays (1)
an diddle (1)
ao hee (1)
ap here (1)
aq here, biddy (chick) (3)
ar here, chick (chicky) (71)
as here, chickadee chick (1)
at here, chicken(s) (3)
au here, chicky/chickies (chick) (7)
av here you are (1)
aw kee (2)
ax keep (1)
ay kiddy/kitty (5)
az kwa (1)
ba oo-eh biddy wenny (1)
bb pee/pi (3)
bc pitta pee (1)

bd piup (1)
be poo (1)
bf pook pookaw (1)
bg sh/sha (4)
bh shoo (chicken) (36)
bi show (1)
bj whoop (1)
bk wip chicky (1)
038.6 L harness [v.]
No Response (152)
A breast (the horse) up (1)
B dress (the horse) (1)
C fix (the horse) up (1)
D gear (the horse) (7)
E gear (the horse) up (25)
F gear up (the horse) (12)
G get (the horse) up (1)
H harness (the horse) (306)
I harness (the horse) up (58)
J harness up (the horse) (23)
K hitch (the horse) (69)
L hitch (the horse) up (134)
M hitch up (the horse) (63)
N hook (the horse) (9)
O hook (the horse) up (16)
P hook up (the horse) (12)
Q rig [v.] (1)
R suit up (1)
S tack up (1)
T trace (the horse) (2)
U yoke (the ox) up (1)
038.6 P harness
{aw} unrounded onset
{oe} lowered onset
{r} weakly retroflex
{t} flap
{z} devoiced
No Response (294)
<haw(r)nIs=14> (11)
<haw(r)nis=13> (1)
<haw[r]n(Is)> (1)
<haw[r]nAs=14> (2)
<haw[r]nIs=14> (12)
<haw[r]nIsIz=144> (2)
<haw[r]nIz=14> (1)
<hawrnIs=14> (42)
<hawrnIsIz=144> (4)
<hawrnIsh=14> (1)
<hawrnIst=14> (1)
<hawrnIth=14> (1)
<hawrnis=13> (1)
<hawrnisN=134> (1)
<haw{r}nAs=14> (1)
<haw{r}nIs=14> (12)
<ho(r)nIs=14> (72)
<ho(r)nIsAz=144> (1)
<ho(r)nIsIz=144> (7)
<ho(r)nIsd=14> (1)
<ho(r)nIst=14> (1)

<ho(r)nis=13> (2)
<ho(r)nisIz=134> (1)
<ho[r]IsIz=144> (1)
<ho[r]nAs=14> (4)
<ho[r]nIs=14> (28)
<ho[r]nIsIz=144> (4)
<ho[r]nIsI{z}=144> (1)
<hoe[r]nIs=14> (1)
<hornAs=14> (12)
<hornAsN=144> (1)
<hornIs=14> (244)
<hornIsIz=144> (2)
<hornIsI{z}=144> (1)
<hornIsh=14> (3)
<hornIst=14> (1)
<hornes=13> (2)
<hornis=13> (4)
<hornish=13> (1)
<ho{r}nAs=14> (1)
<ho{r}nIs=14> (40)
<ho{r}nis=13> (1)
<ho{t}(n)Is=14> (1)
<hu[r]nIs=14> (4)
<hu[r]nIsIz=144> (1)
<hurnIs=14> (2)
<hu{r}nAs=14> (1)
<h{aw}(r)nIs=14> (16)
<h{aw}[r]nAs=14> (2)
<h{aw}[r]nIs=14> (12)
<h{aw}nIs=14> (6)
<h{aw}rnAs=14> (4)
<h{aw}rnIs=14> (61)
<h{aw}rnIsIz=144> (1)
<h{aw}rnI{z}=14> (1)
<h{aw}rnes=13> (1)
<h{aw}{r}nIs=14> (6)
<h{aw}{t}[n]Is=14> (1)
<h{oe}rnIs=14> (6)

039.1 L lines

No Response (176)
A   bridle(s) (10)
B   bridle reins (4)
C   buggy line(s) (4)
D   buggy reins (1)
E   checklines (29)
F   checkreins (1)
G   cross lines (1)
H   double line (1)
I   driving lines (3)
J   driving reins (1)
K   guideline(s) (2)
L   harness reins (2)
M   jerk line (1)
N   lead lines (1)
O   leather lines (1)
P   line(s) (392)
Q   long line (1)
R   long reins (1)
S   plowline(s) (109)

T   ranges (1)
U   rein(s) (324)
V   rope(s) (19)
W   rope lines (1)
X   short line (1)
Y   strap(s) (6)
Z   string (1)
aa   strips (1)
ab   trace line (1)
ac   traces (4)
ad   wagon lines (11)

039.2 L reins

No Response (242)
A   bridle(s) (100)
B   bridle and rein (1)
C   bridle line(s) (5)
D   bridle rein(s) (98)
E   bridle rope (1)
F   bridle strap(s) 3
G   bridle strop (1)
H   checkrein(s) (2)
I   hitch lines (1)
J   hitch reins (1)
K   leather reins (2)
L   line(s) (46)
M   rein(s) (500)
N   riding bridle (2)
O   riding rein(s) (3)
P   rings (2)
Q   rope(s) (4)
R   short bridle (1)
S   strap(s) (6)
T   strops (1)

039.3 P stirrups

{r}   weakly retroflex
No Response (166)
<s(t)urAp=14> (1)
<sh(t)urApth=14> (1)
<shturAps=14> (1)
<starIps=14> (1)
<stawrIp=14> (1)
<ste(r)Ap=14> (1)
<ste(rI)ps> (1)
<ste[r](I)ps> (1)
<ster(I)p> (1)
<ster(I)ps> (1)
<sterA(p)s=14> (1)
<sterAp(s)=14> (1)
<sterAp=14> (9)
<sterAps=14> (26)
<sterIp(s)=14> (1)
<sterIp=14> (1)
<sterIps=14> (14)
<sterups=13> (1)
<ste{r}(I)ps> (1)
<sti[r]Ap=14> (1)
<stir(I)p(s)> (1)
<stir(I)p> (2)
<stir(I)ps> (2)

<stirAp=14> (9)
<stirAps=14> (22)
<stirIp=14> (4)
<stirIps=14> (11)
<stiroop=13> (1)
<stoo(r)Ip=14> (1)
<stoo(rI)p(s)> (1)
<stoorAp=14> (1)
<stoorAps=14> (5)
<storAp(s)=14> (1)
<storAps=14> (1)
<stu[r](I)p(s)> (2)
<stu[r](I)p> (13)
<stu[r](I)ps> (30)
<stu[r](Ip)> (1)
<stu[r]Ap(s)=14> (1)
<stu[r]Aps=14> (5)
<stu[r]Ip(s)=14> (1)
<stu[r]Ip=14> (5)
<stu[r]Ips=14> (2)
<stu[r]rIps=14> (1)
<stur(I)p(s)> (2)
<stur(I)p> (32)
<stur(I)ps> (84)
<stur(I)psh> (1)
<stur(Ip)z> (1)
<sturA(ps)=14> (1)
<sturAbz=14> (1)
<sturAp(s)=14> (19)
<sturAp=14> (46)
<sturAps=14> (188)
<sturApsh=14> (1)
<sturIp(s)=14> (8)
<sturIp=14> (20)
<sturIps=14> (84)
<sturIpsh=14> (1)
<sturIts=14> (1)
<sturoops=13> (1)
<sturrAps=14> (3)
<sturripsh=13> (1)
<sturup=13> (1)
<sturups=13> (5)
<stu{r}(I)p(s)> (1)
<stu{r}(I)p> (5)
<stu{r}(I)ps> (27)
<stu{r}(Ips)> (1)
<stu{r}Ap=14> (9)
<stu{r}Aps=14> (18)
<stu{r}Ip(s)=14> (1)
<stu{r}Ip=14> (3)
<stu{r}Ips=14> (5)
<stu{r}rAps=14> (2)

039.4 L lead horse

No Response (595)
A   dominant animal (1)
B   driving horse (1)
C   forward horse (1)
D   furrow horse (3)
E   furrow mule (2)

F gee (horse) (6)
G gee side (1)
H gentleman (1)
I haw (horse) (3)
J head ox (1)
K inside (2)
L lead, the (23)
M lead horse (153)
N lead mule (12)
O lead ox(en) (3)
P leader (15)
Q left horse (2)
R left-hand horse (2)
S line mule (1)
T male horse (1)
U near, the (2)
V near horse (6)
W near lead (1)
X near leader (1)
Y near mule (1)
Z near side (1)
aa nigh horse (1)
ab outside horse (1)
ac plow horse (2)
ad port horse (1)
ae right horse (2)
af right-hand animal (1)
ag right mule (1)
ah starboard (horse) (1)
ai swing horse (1)

039.5 G a little way
No Response (235)
A bit over, a (1)
B few blocks, a (1)
C few feet, a (1)
D few miles, a (5)
E few steps, a (8)
F few yards, a (1)
G hair jump, a (1)
H hop and a jump, a (1)
I hop (and) (a) skip, a (4)
J hop, skip, and (a) jump (3)
K hop, step, and jump (1)
L jump (away), a (5)
M little bit (away/off/over) (38)
N little distance (away/over) (33)
O little drive (1)
P little farther way (1)
Q little hop (1)
R little jump (2)
S little piece (away/off/over) (206)
T little step (1)
U little stretch (1)
V little trip (1)
W little walk (1)
X little way (off/over) (74)
Y little ways (away/off/over) (198)
Z piece, a (away) (47)
aa reach, a (1)

ab short distance (away) (62)
ac short piece (18)
ad short throw (1)
ae short way (over) (9)
af short ways (15)
ag skip and a hop, a (2)
ah small distance (2)
ai small piece (2)
aj small way (1)
ak step, a (away) (6)
al stone cast, a (1)
am stone's throw, a (6)
an tad, a (1)
ao three shakes of a sheep's tail (1)
ap way, a (off) (5)
aq ways, a (off) (11)
ar whoop and a holler (1)

040.1 G a long way
No Response (158)
A big good bit (1)
B distance, a (6)
C fair piece (1)
D far out (1)
E far piece (43)
F far trip (1)
G far way (5)
H farther piece (1)
I good distance (11)
J good little piece (5)
K good little step (1)
L good little ways (1)
M good long way (3)
N good long ways (9)
O good piece (39)
P good way (4)
Q good ways (27)
R great distance (3)
S great piece (1)
T great way (1)
U greater way (1)
V journey, a (2)
W long distance (38)
X long drive (3)
Y long hike (1)
Z long journey (5)
aa long piece (4)
ab long ride (1)
ac long space (1)
ad long stretch (3)
ae long trip (8)
af long walk (1)
ag long way (174)
ah long ways (210)
ai lot farther/further, a (3)
aj lots more (2)
ak mite to go yet, a (1)
al nice little stretch (1)
am piece, a (9)
an piece further, a (1)

ao piece of a way (1)
ap place, a (1)
aq pretty far distance (1)
ar pretty far piece (2)
as pretty good distance (6)
at pretty good (little) piece (16)
au pretty good long way (1)
av pretty good walk (1)
aw pretty good ways (6)
ax pretty long way (1)
ay quite a bit (3)
az quite a (little) distance (29)
ba quite a (little) piece (6)
bb quite a (little) ways (20)
bc quite a way (9)
bd quite some distance (1)
be right smart piece (2)
bf smart distance, a (1)
bg some (little) distance (3)
bh trip, a (2)
bi way, a (10)
bj way around (1)
bk way back (2)
bl way off (11)
bm way on (out) (2)
bb way out (2)
bo way over (there/yonder) (3)
bp ways, a (29)

040.2 G anywhere
No Response (191)
A anyplace (93)
B anywhere (595)
C anywheres (35)

040.3 P backward
{d} devoiced
{dh} devoiced
{R} weakly retroflex
{r} weakly retroflex
{z} devoiced
No Response (249)
<bak(w)Rd=14> (3)
<bak(w)Rdz=14> (38)
<bak(w)Rd{z}=14> (11)
<bak(w)R{d}s=14> (1)
<bak(w)R{d}{z}=14> (2)
<bak(w)[R](d){z}=14> (1)
<bak(w)[R]d=14> (2)
<bak(w)[R]dz=14> (8)
<bak(w)[R]d{z}=14> (4)
<bak(w)[R]t=14> (1)
<bak(w)[R]{d}=14> (1)
<bak(w)[R]{d}{z}=14> (1)
<bak(w){R}d=14> (1)
<bak(w){R}dz=14> (10)
<bak(w){R}d{z}=14> (2)
<bakw(R)d{z}=14> (1)
<bakwR(d)z=14> (1)
<bakwR(d){z}=14> (2)
<bakwRd=14> (61)

<bakwRds=14> (1)
<bakwRdz=14> (70)
<bakwRd{z}=14> (63)
<bakwRj=14> (2)
<bakwR{d}=14> (12)
<bakwR{d}s=14> (2)
<bakwR{d}{z}=14> (12)
<bakw[R](d)=14> (2)
<bakw[R](d)s=14> (2)
<bakw[R](d)sh=14> (1)
<bakw[R](d)z=14> (2)
<bakw[R](d){z}=14> (1)
<bakw[R]d=14> (66)
<bakw[R]ds=14> (1)
<bakw[R]dz=14> (77)
<bakw[R]d{dh}=14> (1)
<bakw[R]d{z}=14> (62)
<bakw[R]t=14> (2)
<bakw[R]ts=14> (1)
<bakw[R]{d}=14> (14)
<bakw[R]{d}s=14> (3)
<bakw[R]{d}z=14> (1)
<bakw[R]{d}{z}=14> (17)
<bakwu[r]d=13> (4)
<bakwu[r]dz=13> (2)
<bakwu[r]d{z}=13> (1)
<bakwu[r]{d}{z}=13> (1)
<bakwurd=13> (16)
<bakwurds=13> (1)
<bakwurdz=13> (20)
<bakwurd{z}=13> (2)
<bakwurt=13> (1)
<bakwu{r}d=12> (1)
<bakwu{r}d=13> (2)
<bakwu{r}dz=13> (1)
<bakwu{r}{d}{z}=13> (1)
<bakw{R}(d)s=14> (2)
<bakw{R}d=14> (29)
<bakw{R}dz=14> (34)
<bakw{R}d{z}=14> (14)
<bakw{R}{d}=14> (1)
<bakw{R}{d}s=14> (1)
<bakw{R}{d}sh=14> (1)
<bakw{R}{d}{z}=14> (2)
<bekw[R]{d}s=14> (1)

040.4 P forward

{aw}   unrounded onset
{d}   devoiced
{f}   bilabial
{oe}   lowered onset
{R}   weakly retroflex
{r}   weakly retroflex
{t}   flap
{z}   devoiced
No Response (265)
<fa(r)wRd=14> (1)
<fa[r]wRd=14> (1)
<fa[r]w[R]d=14> (1)
<fa[r]w[R]d{z}=14> (1)

<faw(r)wRd=14> (11)
<faw(r)wRdz=14> (4)
<faw(r)wRd{z}=14> (4)
<faw(r)wR{d}=14> (3)
<faw(r)wR{d}{z}=14> (1)
<faw(r)w[R](d)=14> (1)
<faw(r)w[R]d=14> (27)
<faw(r)w[R]dz=14> (5)
<faw(r)w[R]d{z}=14> (2)
<faw(r)w[R]j=14> (1)
<faw(r)w[R]{d}=14> (5)
<faw(r)w[R]{d}{z}=14> (1)
<faw(r)wu[r]{d}=13> (1)
<faw(r)wurd=13> (1)
<faw(r)w{R}d=14> (7)
<faw(r)w{R}dz=14> (2)
<faw(r)w{R}d{z}=14> (2)
<faw(rw)Rd=14> (2)
<faw(rw)Rd{z}=14> (2)
<faw(rw)R{d}=14> (1)
<faw(rw)[R]d=14> (2)
<faw[r]wRd=14> (2)
<faw[r]w[R](d)=14> (1)
<faw[r]w[R]d=14> (24)
<faw[r]w[R]dz=14> (3)
<faw[r]w[R]d{z}=14> (2)
<faw[r]w[R]t=14> (1)
<faw[r]w[R]ts=14> (1)
<faw[r]w[R]{d}=14> (3)
<faw[r]wu[r]d{z}=13> (1)
<faw[r]wurd=13> (1)
<faw[r]w{R}d=14> (4)
<fawr(w)[R]d=14> (2)
<fawrwRd=14> (29)
<fawrwRdz=14> (4)
<fawrwRd{z}=14> (4)
<fawrwR{d}=14> (1)
<fawrw[R]d=14> (7)
<fawrw[R]dz=14> (5)
<fawrw[R]d{z}=14> (2)
<fawrwurd=13> (4)
<fawrw{R}d=14> (6)
<fawrw{R}dz=14> (3)
<fawrw{R}d{z}=14> (1)
<faw{r}(w)[R]dz=14> (1)
<faw{r}wRd=14> (2)
<faw{r}w[R]d=14> (2)
<faw{r}w[R]dz=14> (1)
<faw{r}w[R]{d}=14> (1)
<faw{r}w{R}d=14> (5)
<faw{r}w{R}d{z}=14> (1)
<fa{r}w[R]d=14> (1)
<fo(r)wRd=14> (8)
<fo(r)wRdz=14> (2)
<fo(r)wRd{z}=14> (2)
<fo(r)wR{d}=14> (2)
<fo(r)w[R](d)=14> (2)
<fo(r)w[R]d(z)=14> (2)
<fo(r)w[R]d=14> (20)

<fo(r)w[R]dz=14> (8)
<fo(r)w[R]d{z}=14> (2)
<fo(r)w[R]t=14> (1)
<fo(r)w[R]{d}=14> (1)
<fo(r)w[R]{d}sh=14> (1)
<fo(r)wu[r]d=13> (2)
<fo(r)wurd=13> (1)
<fo(r)w{R}d=14> (6)
<fo(r)w{R}ds=14> (1)
<fo(r)w{R}dz=14> (3)
<fo(rw)Rd=14> (1)
<fo(rw)rd> (1)
<fo(rw)r{d}> (1)
<fo[r](w)[R]dz=14> (1)
<fo[r](w)rdz> (1)
<fo[r]wRdz=14> (1)
<fo[r]wR{d}=14> (2)
<fo[r]w[R](d)=14> (1)
<fo[r]w[R](d){z}=14> (1)
<fo[r]w[R]d=14> (19)
<fo[r]w[R]dz=14> (5)
<fo[r]w[R]d{z}=14> (6)
<fo[r]w[R]t=14> (1)
<fo[r]w[R]{d}=14> (7)
<fo[r]w[R]{d}s=14> (1)
<fo[r]w[R]{d}{z}=14> (1)
<fo[r]wu[r]dz=13> (1)
<fo[r]wu[r]{d}{z}=13> (1)
<fo[r]wurdz=13> (1)
<fo[r]w{R}d=14> (1)
<fo[r]w{R}dz=14> (1)
<fo[r]w{R}t=14> (1)
<fo[r]w{R}{d}{z}=14> (1)
<foe(r)w[R]d=14> (2)
<foerwRd=14> (2)
<foerwRdz=14> (1)
<foerw[R]d=14> (1)
<for(w)R{d}=14> (1)
<for(w)[R]d=14> (1)
<for(w)[R]dz=14> (1)
<forwR(d)z=14> (1)
<forwRd=14> (27)
<forwRdz=14> (10)
<forwRd{z}=14> (1)
<forwR{d}=14> (1)
<forwR{d}{z}=14> (1)
<forw[R](d)=14> (1)
<forw[R]d=14> (8)
<forw[R]dz=14> (3)
<forwurd=13> (3)
<forwurdz=13> (4)
<forwu{r}d=13> (1)
<forw{R}d=14> (3)
<forw{R}dz=14> (2)
<fow(r)wRd=14> (1)
<fow(r)wR{d}=14> (1)
<fow(r)w[R]d=14> (1)
<fow(r)w[R]d{z}=14> (1)
<fow(r)w{R}dz=14> (1)

<fowrwRdz=14> (1)
<fo{r}(w)[R]d=14> (1)
<fo{r}(wR)dz> (1)
<fo{r}r[R]dz=14> (1)
<fo{r}wR(d)=14> (2)
<fo{r}wRd=14> (4)
<fo{r}wR{d}=14> (1)
<fo{r}w[R]d=14> (2)
<fo{r}w[R]dz=14> (3)
<fo{r}w{R}d=14> (1)
<fo{r}w{R}dz=14> (1)
<fu[r]w{R}d=14> (1)
<f{aw}(r)wRd=14> (5)
<f{aw}(r)wRd{z}=14> (1)
<f{aw}(r)w[R](d)=14> (2)
<f{aw}(r)w[R]d=14> (9)
<f{aw}(r)w[R]{d}=14> (3)
<f{aw}(r)wurd=13> (1)
<f{aw}(r)w{R}d=14> (5)
<f{aw}(r)w{R}dz=14> (1)
<f{aw}(r)w{R}d{z}=14> (1)
<f{aw}(rw)[R]d=14> (2)
<f{aw}[r]wRd=14> (1)
<f{aw}[r]w[R]d=14> (5)
<f{aw}[r]w[R]dz=14> (2)
<f{aw}[r]w[R]d{z}=14> (1)
<f{aw}[r]w[R]{d}=14> (1)
<f{aw}[r]w[R]{d}{z}=14> (1)
<f{aw}[r]w[R]{t}=14> (1)
<f{aw}r(w)[R](d)=14> (1)
<f{aw}rwRd=14> (4)
<f{aw}rwRdz=14> (2)
<f{aw}rwRd{z}=14> (1)
<f{aw}rwR{d}=14> (1)
<f{aw}rwR{d}{z}=14> (1)
<f{aw}rw[R]d=14> (5)
<f{aw}rw[R]dz=14> (1)
<f{aw}rw[R]d{z}=14> (1)
<f{aw}rw[R]{d}=14> (1)
<f{aw}rw{R}d=14> (1)
<f{aw}{r}(w)u[r]d=13> (1)
<f{aw}{r}wRd{z}=14> (1)
<f{aw}{r}wR{d}=14> (2)
<f{aw}{r}w{R}d=14> (2)
<f{oe}(r)wRd=14> (1)
<f{oe}(r)wRd{z}=14> (5)
<f{oe}(r)w[R]d=14> (2)
<f{oe}(r)w[R]d{z}=14> (2)
<f{oe}(r)w[R]{d}=14> (1)
<f{oe}(r)w[R]{t}=14> (1)
<f{oe}(r)w{R}d=14> (1)
<f{oe}(r)w{R}dz=14> (1)
<f{oe}(rw)Rd{z}=14> (1)
<f{oe}(rw)rd> (1)
<f{oe}(rw){R}d=14> (1)
<f{oe}(rw){R}dz=14> (2)
<f{oe}[r](wR)dz> (1)
<f{oe}[r]wRd=14> (2)
<f{oe}[r]wRd{z}=14> (1)

<f{oe}[r]wR{d}=14> (1)
<f{oe}[r]wR{d}{z}=14> (1)
<f{oe}[r]w[R]d=14> (24)
<f{oe}[r]w[R]ds=14> (1)
<f{oe}[r]w[R]dz=14> (5)
<f{oe}[r]w[R]d{z}=14> (2)
<f{oe}[r]w[R]t=14> (1)
<f{oe}[r]w[R]{d}=14> (3)
<f{oe}[r]w[R]{d}s=14> (1)
<f{oe}[r]w[R]{d}{z}=14> (1)
<f{oe}[r]wu[r]d=13> (1)
<f{oe}[r]w{R}d=14> (2)
<f{oe}rwR(d)=14> (1)
<f{oe}rwRd=14> (34)
<f{oe}rwRdz=14> (5)
<f{oe}rwRd{z}=14> (9)
<f{oe}rwR{d}=14> (7)
<f{oe}rwR{d}{z}=14> (2)
<f{oe}rw[R]d=14> (5)
<f{oe}rw[R]dz=14> (3)
<f{oe}rw[R]d{z}=14> (2)
<f{oe}rwurd=13> (3)
<f{oe}rwurdz=13> (1)
<f{oe}rw{R}d=14> (6)
<f{oe}rw{R}d{z}=14> (1)
<f{oe}rw{R}{d}=14> (1)
<f{oe}{r}(w)Rd{z}=14> (1)
<f{oe}{r}wRd=14> (2)
<f{oe}{r}wR{d}=14> (2)
<f{oe}{r}w[R]d=14> (6)
<f{oe}{r}w[R]t=14> (1)
<f{oe}{r}wu{r}{d}=13> (1)
<f{oe}{r}w{R}d=14> (4)
<f{oe}{r}w{R}dz=14> (1)
<f{oe}{r}w{R}d{z}=14> (1)
<{f}aw(r)wRdz=14> (1)
<{f}aw(r)wR{d}{z}=14> (1)
<{f}aw(r)w[R](d)=14> (1)
<{f}aw[r]w[R]d=14> (1)
<{f}awrwR{d}{z}=14> (1)
<{f}o[r]wRd{zh}=14> (1)
<{f}o[r]w[R]d=14> (1)
<{f}o[r]w[R]{d}=14> (1)
<{f}o[r]w[R]{d}{z}=14> (1)
<{f}oe(r)wRd=14> (1)
<{f}{aw}(r)w{R}d{z}=14> (1)
<{f}{aw}[r]w[R]d=14> (2)
<{f}{aw}rw[R]d{z}=14> (1)
<{f}{oe}(r)wR{d}=14> (1)
<{f}{oe}[r]wR{t}=14> (1)
<{f}{oe}rwRdz=14> (1)
<{f}{oe}rwRd{z}=14> (1)

040.5 G ne'er (a one)
No Response (497)
A ary (a one) (3)
B e'er (a one) (5)
C e'er [D-0] (one) (2)
D nary (a one) (30)
E nary [D-0] (one) (8)

F ne'er a (one) (51)
G ne'er [D-0] (one) (45)
H not a (one) (144)

040.5 P ne'er (a)
{R} weakly retroflex
{r} weakly retroflex
No Response (793)
<na(r)> (2)
<na(r)A=14> (12)
<na(r)I=14> (4)
<na[r]> (6)
<na[r]A=14> (2)
<na[r]I=14> (1)
<na[r]n> (1)
<nair> (1)
<nar> (8)
<narA=14> (12)
<narI=14> (21)
<narn> (2)
<na{R}=14> (2)
<na{r}> (5)
<na{r}A=14> (1)
<na{r}N=14> (1)
<ne(r)A=14> (1)
<nerA=14> (11)
<nerI=14> (26)
<nirI=14> (1)
<norI=14> (2)
<nurA=14> (1)
<nurI=14> (1)
<nurN=14> (1)
<nyerA=14> (1)

040.6 G (didn't do) anything
No Response (569)
A anything (139)
B nothing (219)

040.7 G (didn't like it) anyway
No Response (411)
A anyhow (77)
B anyway (314)
C anyways (7)
D at all (211)
E nohow (37)
F noway (39)
G noways (7)
H nowhere (1)

040.8 G (didn't give me) any
No Response (435)
A any (341)
B none (173)

040.9 G duratives
No Response (629)
A at night (151)
B at nights (1)
C at nighttime (1)
D by night (2)
E during the daytime (1)
F during the night (5)
G during the time (1)

H   during the week (1)
I   in the afternoon (1)
J   in the dark (1)
K   in the evening (2)
L   in the morning (2)
M   in the mornings (4)
N   in the night (12)
O   in the nighttime (1)
P   of a afternoon (1)
Q   of a day (3)
R   of a daytime (2)
S   of a evening (12)
T   of a morning (50)
U   of a night (35)
V   of a nights (2)
W   of a noon (1)
X   of a summer (1)
Y   of a summertime (1)
Z   of a Sunday (morning) (4)
aa   of a weekend (1)
ab   of a winter (1)
ac   of a wintertime (1)
ad   of an evening (3)
ae   of evenings (1)
af   of mornings (1)
ag   of Sundays (1)
ah   of the evening (2)
ai   of the night (1)
aj   of [D-0] afternoon (1)
ak   of [D-0] day (1)
al   of [D-0] morning (1)
am   over in the night (1)
an   [P-0] a morning (2)

041.1 G like as not
No Response (740)
A   apt (to) (25)
B   apt as not (17)
C   chances are (1)
D   for sure (2)
E   liable (to) (32)
F   like as not (27)
G   likely (17)
H   likely as not (9)
I   maybe (1)
J   more likely (than not) (2)
K   more than apt (11)
L   more than likely (14)
M   most likely (4)
N   perhaps (1)
O   probably (36)
P   sooner or later (2)
Q   sure as I'm born (1)
R   sure enough (1)

041.2 P furrows
{f}   bilabial
{R}   weakly retroflex
{r}   weakly retroflex
{t}   flap
{v}   devoiced

{z}   devoiced
{zh}   devoiced
No Response (256)
<burAz=14> (1)
<bu{t}ooz=13> (1)
<faw[r](A)z> (1)
<fawrA=14> (2)
<fawrAz=14> (1)
<fa{r}rA=14> (1)
<fer(A)> (2)
<fer(A)z> (1)
<ferA=14> (1)
<ferAz=14> (2)
<feroe=13> (2)
<fir(A)> (1)
<foo[r](A)> (1)
<foorA=14> (2)
<foorI=14> (1)
<forA=14> (2)
<foroe=13> (1)
<foroez=13> (1)
<fru{r}Az=14> (1)
<fu[r](A)> (26)
<fu[r](A)z> (6)
<fu[r](Az)> (1)
<fu[r]A=14> (13)
<fu[r]Az=14> (4)
<fu[r]oe=31> (1)
<fu[r]roe=13> (1)
<fu[r]{r}A=14> (1)
<fur(A)> (34)
<fur(A)z> (27)
<fur(A){z}> (6)
<fur(Az)> (2)
<furA(z)=14> (4)
<furA=14> (197)
<furAs=14> (1)
<furAz=14> (130)
<furA{z}=14> (10)
<furI=14> (1)
<furIz=14> (1)
<furiz=13> (1)
<furoe=13> (25)
<furoes=13> (1)
<furoez=13> (21)
<furoe{z}=13> (8)
<furrA=14> (30)
<furrAz=14> (11)
<furrA{z}=14> (6)
<furrIz=14> (1)
<furroe=13> (2)
<furroez=13> (2)
<furrow=13> (1)
<furuz=13> (3)
<fur{R}z=14> (1)
<furu{z}=13> (1)
<fur{R}=14> (1)
<fur{t}A{z}=14> (1)
<fu{r}(A)> (15)

<fu{r}(A)z> (5)
<fu{r}(A){z}> (2)
<fu{r}A=14> (13)
<fu{r}As=14> (1)
<fu{r}Az=14> (4)
<fu{r}A{z}=14> (2)
<fu{r}oez=13> (1)
<fu{r}rA=14> (11)
<fu{r}rAz=14> (6)
<fu{r}rA{z}=14> (3)
<fu{r}roe=13> (8)
<fu{r}roez=13> (1)
<fu{r}{R}=14> (1)
<fu{r}{t}oez=13> (1)
<fu{t}oe=13> (1)
<{f}aw[r](A)> (1)
<{f}oo[r](A)> (1)
<{f}ur(A){z}> (1)
<{f}ur(A){zh}> (1)
<{f}urA=14> (3)
<{f}uroe=13> (1)
<{f}uroe{z}=13> (1)
<{f}urrA=14> (2)
<{f}urrA{z}=14> (2)
<{f}urroe=13> (1)
<{f}urroe{z}=13> (1)
<{v}oroe{z}=13> (1)

041.3 P crop
{aw}   low-back
{k}   fricative
{r}   devoiced
{t}   flap
<o> variants:
{o}   low-back
{ou}   inglide
No Response (159)
<krap> (1)
<krop> (207)
<krops> (24)
<kr{aw}p> (5)
<kr{aw}ps> (1)
<kr{ou}p> (79)
<kr{ou}ps> (5)
<kr{o}p> (16)
<kr{o}ps> (2)
<kwap> (1)
<kw{ou}p> (1)
<k{r}aps> (1)
<k{r}op> (305)
<k{r}ops> (26)
<k{r}{aw}p> (3)
<k{r}{ou}p> (117)
<k{r}{ou}ps> (6)
<k{r}{o}p> (35)
<k{r}{o}ps> (3)
<k{t}op> (1)
<k{t}ops> (1)
<{k}(r)op> (1)

041.3 S crop

No Response (0)
|PAA| (40)
|PAC| (7)
|PACpab| (1)
|PAD| (2)
|PAE| (2)
|PAG| (1)
|PCA| (27)
|PCC| (6)
|PFA| (2)
|RCA| (7)
|SAA| (15)
|SAAmaj| (3)
|SAApaj| (1)
|SAB| (53)
|SABmaj| (3)
|SABpaj| (1)
|SAD| (10)
|SADmaj| (1)
|SADsab| (1)
|SAE| (263)
|SAEmaj| (108)
|SAEsab| (3)
|SAEsak| (1)
|SAF| (9)
|SAG| (64)
|SAGmaj| (7)
|SBA| (1)
|SCA| (39)
|SCAmaj| (17)
|SCAmal| (1)
|SCB| (5)
|SCBmaj| (4)
|SCD| (10)
|SCE| (52)
|SCEmaj| (53)
|SCErae| (1)
|SCF| (2)
|SCFmaj| (1)
|SCGmaj| (1)
|SCGmfj| (1)
|SDB| (1)
|SDE| (1)
|SFE| (8)
|SFEmaj| (2)
|SFG| (2)
|TAA| (8)
|TAB| (3)
|TAD| (27)
|TADmaj| (6)
|TADmfj| (1)
|TADtfa| (1)
|TADtfb| (1)
|TAF| (3)
|TAFmaj| (1)
|TAG| (1)
|TCA| (4)
|TCB| (1)
|TCD| (4)

|TCDmaj| (1)
|TCEmaj| (1)
|TFA| (3)
|TFAmaj| (1)
|TFBqfa| (1)
|TFD| (4)
|TFF| (1)
|TMD| (1)

041.4 L cleared (the land)
No Response (144)
A   blew the stumps up (1)
B   broke (4)
C   broke up (1)
D   bulldozed off (1)
E   burned (2)
F   burned off (6)
G   burned up (1)
H   bush-hogged (7)
I   bushed (2)
J   chopped (1)
K   clean-cut [v.] (1)
L   cleaned (26)
M   cleaned off (23)
N   cleaned out (13)
O   cleaned up (114)
P   cleared (526)
Q   cleared away (1)
R   cleared off (31)
S   cleared out (12)
T   cleared up (88)
U   cropped (1)
V   cut (1)
W   cut a road/roadway (3)
X   cut a route (1)
Y   cut a trail (2)
Z   cut down (6)
aa   cut off (1)
ab   cut out (1)
ac   cut over (1)
ad   cut sprouts (1)
ae   ditched (1)
af   double-cut (1)
ag   dozed (2)
ah   dragged out (2)
ai   dropped off (1)
aj   got rid of the trash (1)
ak   got that brush away (1)
al   graded (1)
am   grubbed (19)
an   grubbed out (2)
ao   grubbed up (5)
ap   hoed (1)
aq   improved (2)
ar   knocked off (1)
as   landscaped (1)
at   made a trail (1)
au   made newground (1)
av   plowed (2)
aw   plowed up (1)

ax   raked (2)
ay   ridded the trees off (1)
az   root-plowed (1)
ba   sawed the trees out (1)
bb   scrubbed (1)
bc   scrubbed off (1)
bd   shrubbed (2)
be   shrubbed off (2)
bf   shrubbed out (1)
bg   sprouted (1)
bh   stripped (1)
bi   trimmed up (1)
bj   underbrushed (1)
bk   weeded (1)

041.5 L second cutting
No Response (383)
A   aftermath (5)
B   another cutting (of grass) (3)
C   best cutting (1)
D   bumper (1)
E   chaff (2)
F   come-up crop, a (1)
G   cover (crop) (7)
H   cutover (1)
I   dead (Bermuda/sage) grass (15)
J   dead hay (1)
K   double crop (2)
L   double hay (1)
M   dried Johnson grass (1)
N   dried-up hay (1)
O   dry grass (3)
P   fodder (1)
Q   free stand (1)
R   good cutting (1)
S   grass (4)
T   growing wild (1)
U   harvest (1)
V   hay (meadow) (34)
W   last cutting (1)
X   late crop (1)
Y   lattermath (2)
Z   leftover(s) (2)
aa   litter (2)
ab   mess, a (1)
ac   middle cutting (1)
ad   mill, a (1)
ae   mistake, a (1)
af   mulch (6)
ag   native (3)
ah   natural crop (1)
ai   new crop (2)
aj   new growth (3)
ak   new-mown (1)
al   offals (1)
am   old (dry/dead) grass (6)
an   old hay (crop) (2)
ao   old hay grass (1)
ap   old stalks (1)
aq   peanut hay (1)

ar   pumice (1)
as   recropping (1)
at   recut(ting) (2)
au   regrowth (2)
av   reharvest (1)
aw   reseeding (1)
ax   residue (1)
ay   second bloom (1)
az   second cover (1)
ba   second crop (96)
bb   second cut (8)
bc   second-cut hay (1)
bd   second cutting (169)
be   second growth (39)
bf   second harvest (7)
bg   second mowing (3)
bh   second time (around) (7)
bi   second yield (1)
bj   seconds (1)
bk   seed crop (2)
bl   self-sown (1)
bm   something that volunteered (1)
bn   stajoles [S] (1)
bo   straggler, a (1)
bp   straw (4)
bq   stubble [n.] (21)
br   stubble [adj.] (2)
bs   stubble crop (2)
bt   stubs (1)
bu   thatch (1)
bv   trash (3)
bw   two crops (1)
bx   two cuttings (7)
by   unwanted vegetables (1)
bz   voluntary (1)
ca   volunteer (196)
cb   volunteer [adj.] (22)
cc   volunteer crop (38)
cd   volunteered [adj.] (1)
ce   volunteered crop (1)
cf   waste (2)
cg   weed(s) (4)
ch   wheat straw (1)
ci   whey (1)
cj   wild [adj.] (6)
ck   wild crop (6)

041.6 L sheaf
No Response (299)
A   armful (1)
B   bag (1)
C   bale (17)
D   binding (1)
E   bunch (9)
F   bundle (494)
G   hame (1)
H   hands (7)
I   heap (3)
J   heap row (1)
K   oat bundle (1)

L   pile (3)
M   roll, a (1)
N   shaft (4)
O   sheaf (87)
P   sheath (6)
Q   shock (32)
R   shock pile (1)
S   square bundle (1)
T   stack (14)
U   stalks (1)
V   stock (2)
W   three hands (1)
X   wad, a (1)
Y   wheat sheaf (1)

041.7 L shock
No Response (441)
A   bale (19)
B   binder (1)
C   bunch (4)
D   bundle (34)
E   cap (7)
F   cap bundle (6)
G   capped sheaves (1)
H   corn pile (2)
I   corn shock (2)
J   hand, a (1)
K   heap (7)
L   hooder (2)
M   huddle (1)
N   mound (1)
O   pile (20)
P   rick (2)
Q   sheaf (8)
R   sheath (1)
S   shock (207)
T   shuck (2)
U   stack (126)
V   stalk heap (1)
W   stalk stand (1)
X   stook (1)
Y   wheat stack (4)

041.8 G bushels
No Response (233)
A   bushel[N-i] (131)
B   bushels (498)

042.1 G oats are
No Response (472)
A   oats [pl./count noun] (76)
B   oats [sing./mass noun] (62)
C   oats are/were (115)
D   oats is/was (33)
E   oats [X-0] (1)

042.1 P thrashed
{d}   devoiced
{R}   weakly retroflex
{r}   devoiced
{t}   flap
{tt}   trill
No Response (351)

<dh{r}ash> (1)
<flashN=14> (1)
<fra(sh)> (1)
<shrash> (1)
<th(r)ash> (1)
<th(r)eshN=14> (1)
<thrash> (94)
<thrashIz=14> (2)
<thrashN=14> (15)
<thrashNG=14> (2)
<thrashR=14> (3)
<thrash[R]=14> (3)
<thrasht> (59)
<thrash{R}=14> (2)
<threk> (1)
<thresh> (32)
<threshN=14> (3)
<threshNG=14> (1)
<thresht> (11)
<thrush> (1)
<thwasht> (1)
<th{r}ash> (62)
<th{r}ash(t)> (1)
<th{r}ashAz=14> (1)
<th{r}ashIz=14> (1)
<th{r}ashN=14> (15)
<th{r}ashNG=14> (3)
<th{r}ashR=14> (4)
<th{r}ashRz=14> (1)
<th{r}ash[R]=14> (5)
<th{r}asht> (41)
<th{r}ash{R}z=14> (1)
<th{r}as{d}> (1)
<th{r}esh> (25)
<th{r}eshN=14> (5)
<th{r}eshNG=14> (3)
<th{r}esht> (8)
<th{r}etht> (1)
<th{r}osh> (1)
<th{r}ush> (3)
<th{r}ushN=14> (1)
<th{r}usht> (1)
<th{tt}ash> (4)
<th{tt}ashR=14> (1)
<th{tt}esh> (4)
<th{tt}eshN=14> (1)
<th{tt}esht> (2)
<th{t}ash> (50)
<th{t}ashIz=14> (2)
<th{t}ashN=14> (8)
<th{t}ashNG=14> (4)
<th{t}ashR=14> (2)
<th{t}ash[R]=14> (3)
<th{t}ashd> (1)
<th{t}asht> (50)
<th{t}ash{t}> (1)
<th{t}esh> (17)
<th{t}eshN=14> (1)
<th{t}eshNG=14> (3)

<th{t}eshR=14> (1)
<th{t}esht> (16)
<th{t}esh{d}> (1)
<th{t}est> (2)
<trash> (4)
<trashIz=14> (1)
<t{r}ash> (5)
<t{r}ashNG=14> (1)
<t{r}eshR=14> (1)
<t{r}osht> (1)
<t{t}ash> (2)

042.2 G you and I
No Response (462)
A   I and you (5)
B   me and you (91)
C   you and I (301)
D   you and me (88)
E   you and myself (2)

042.3 G both of us
No Response (279)
A   all of us (2)
B   all two of us (3)
C   both of us (300)
D   both [P-0] us (2)
E   pair of us, the (1)
F   two of us, (the) (28)
G   us both (3)
H   us two (1)
I   we both of us (2)

042.4 G he and I
No Response (315)
A   he and I (208)
B   he and me (4)
C   he and myself (2)
D   her and I (6)
E   her and me (2)
F   him and I (22)
G   him and me (17)
H   him and myself (6)
I   I and [noun] (10)
J   I and her (1)
K   I and him (2)
L   me and [noun] (188)
M   me and he (1)
N   me and her (51)
O   me and him (103)
P   me and she (1)
Q   she and I (61)
R   [noun] and I (146)
S   [noun] and me (21)
T   [noun] and myself (9)

042.5A G (it's) I
No Response (496)
A   I (77)
B   me (376)

042.5B G (it's) he
No Response (589)
A   he (85)
B   him (260)

042.5C G (it's) she
No Response (592)
A   her (240)
B   she (100)

042.5D G (it's) they
No Response (628)
A   them (250)
B   they (46)

042.6 G (as tall) as I am
No Response (391)
A   as I (83)
B   as I am/was (388)
C   as I are (1)
D   as I is (8)
E   as I'm (1)
F   as me (55)
G   as myself (1)

043.1 G (as tall) as he is
No Response (447)
A   as he/she (110)
B   as he am (1)
C   as he/she are (3)
D   as he/she is/was (318)
E   as him/her (47)

043.2 G (better) than I can
No Response (461)
A   than I (140)
B   than I can (261)
C   than me (68)

043.3 G the farthest
No Response (334)
A   all the far (3)
B   all the further (7)
C   (as) far (as) (253)
D   as further (as) (1)
E   farest (6)
F   farther (41)
G   fartherest (34)
H   farthest (71)
I   further (197)
J   furtherest (32)
K   furthest (45)

043.4A G yours
No Response (426)
A   yourn (23)
B   yournses (1)
C   yours (480)

043.4B G ours
No Response (362)
A   ourn (12)
B   ours (544)

043.4C G theirs
No Response (454)
A   theirn (3)
B   theirs (454)
C   theirsn (2)
D   them's (1)

043.4D G his
No Response (396)

A   his (485)
B   hisn (42)

043.4E G hers
No Response (414)
A   hern (17)
B   hers (483)
C   hersen (1)

043.5 G you-all
No Response (253)
A   all [P-0] y'all (1)
B   all of you (12)
C   all of y(ou) ones (1)
D   guys (1)
E   y'all (376)
F   y'all guys (1)
G   you (92)
H   you-all (380)
I   you folks (4)
J   you guys (1)
K   you ones (8)
L   you oneses (1)
M   you people (3)

043.6 G you-all's
No Response (507)
A   all of your (1)
B   all y'all's (1)
C   y'all[M-k] (9)
D   y'all's (118)
E   y'all'ses (2)
F   you-all[M-k] (3)
G   you-all's (60)
H   you folks's (1)
I   your (298)
J   your-all's (10)
K   yournses (1)
L   yours (1)

043.7A G who-all
No Response (439)
A   who (265)
B   who-all (307)
C   who and all (1)
D   who was all (1)
E   who's all (1)

043.7B G who-all's
No Response (671)
A   who[M-k] (6)
B   who-all[M-k] (11)
C   who-all's (61)
D   whom (1)
E   whose (192)
F   whose-all (9)

043.8 G what-all
No Response (363)
A   what (331)
B   what-all (348)

044.1 G themselves
No Response (236)
A   their own self[M-i] (5)
B   their own selves (2)

C   theirself[M-i] (125)
D   theirselves (135)
E   themself[M-i] (63)
F   themselves (423)

044.2 G himself

No Response (203)
A   himself (464)
B   his own self (6)
C   hisself (309)

044.3 L loaf bread

No Response (53)
A   American bread (1)
B   baker's bread (6)
C   bakery bread (2)
D   black bread (1)
E   bread (403)
F   brown bread (22)
G   butter bread (2)
H   country-style light bread (1)
I   crack-wheat bread (1)
J   cracked(-)wheat (bread) (4)
K   dark (bread) (5)
L   enrich bread (1)
M   flour bread (15)
N   flour light bread (1)
O   foundation bread (1)
P   graham (bread) (8)
Q   graham-flour (bread) (1)
R   hallah (2)
S   home-baked bread (1)
T   homemade bread (40)
U   homemade light bread (9)
V   homemade loaf bread (3)
W   homemade-style bread (1)
X   homemade wheat bread (1)
Y   homemade yeast bread (1)
Z   Jewish white bread (1)
aa   leaven(ed) bread (7)
ab   light bread (482)
ac   light loaf bread (1)
ad   light salt bread (1)
ae   loaf (23)
af   loaf bread (137)
ag   loaf light bread (2)
ah   loaf of bread (70)
ai   loaf of light bread (2)
aj   loafed bread (1)
ak   long loaf (1)
al   pain americain [F] (1)
am   pan bread (1)
an   plain bread (8)
ao   plain flour bread (1)
ap   plain self-rising bread (1)
aq   pone (7)
ar   pone bread (5)
as   pone light bread (1)
at   pone of bread (5)
au   pone of light bread (1)
av   pone of wheat bread (1)

aw   rise loaf (1)
ax   risen bread (1)
ay   rising bread (3)
az   salt bread (1)
ba   salt-raising (1)
bb   salt-rising (bread) (17)
bc   salt-rising light bread (1)
bd   sandwich bread (6)
be   sandwich loaf (1)
bf   Schnitsbrot [G] (1)
bg   self-rising bread (3)
bh   short loaf (1)
bi   sliced bread (3)
bj   sliced white bread (1)
bk   sour bread (4)
bl   sourdough (bread) (16)
bm   sourdough light bread (1)
bn   store-bought bread (1)
bo   (un)leaven(ed) bread (5)
bp   wasp(-)nest (bread) (4)
bq   wheat (bread) (166)
br   wheat loaf (1)
bs   white bread (144)
bt   white loaf (of bread) (2)
bu   whole bread (3)
bv   whole loaf (1)
bw   whole(-)wheat (bread) (93)
bx   yeast bread (75)
by   yeast light bread (1)
bz   yeast-rise bread (1)
ca   yeast-rising bread (1)

044.4 L other flour breads

No Response (145)

[biscuits]

A   angel biscuits (1)
B   beaten biscuits (1)
C   biscuit bread (23)
D   biscuit buns (1)
E   biscuit roll (1)
F   biscuits (646)
G   brown biscuits (1)
H   buttermilk biscuits (6)
I   canned biscuits (1)
J   cathead biscuits (2)
K   catheads (2)
L   choke biscuits (1)
M   clabber biscuits (2)
N   Coon biscuits (1)
O   drop biscuits (2)
P   flour biscuits (1)
Q   hoecake biscuits (1)
R   homemade biscuits (8)
S   icebox biscuits (1)
T   potato biscuits (1)
U   puffs (1)
V   soda biscuits (1)
W   sour-milk biscuits (1)
X   sourdough biscuits (1)
Y   Southern biscuits (1)

Z   spoon biscuits (1)
aa   spoon bread (1)
ab   stepmother biscuits (1)
ac   whole cake (1)

[hoecakes]

ad   batter bread (1)
ae   battercakes (2)
af   biscuit hoecakes (2)
ag   buckwheat-cake bread (1)
ah   buckwheat cakes (1)
ai   flapjacks (3)
aj   flat cakes (3)
ak   flitters (2)
al   flop cake (1)
am   flour bread (1)
an   flour hoecakes (3)
ao   galette [F] (5)
ap   hoecakes (52)
aq   johnny bread (1)
ar   johnnycake (6)
as   johnnycake bread (1)
at   nigger cakes (1)
au   pancake bread (1)
av   spoon bread (1)
aw   spread wide (1)
ax   turnover bread (1)
ay   wheat hoecakes (1)

[muffins]

az   blueberry muffins (3)
ba   bran muffins (1)
bb   cake muffins (3)
bc   egg bread (2)
bd   English muffins (3)
be   flour muffins (2)
bf   muffin bread (2)
bg   muffin cakes (1)
bh   muffin ring (1)
bi   muffins (66)
bj   popovers (2)
bk   whole-wheat muffins (1)

[rolls/buns]

bl   bagels (1)
bm   brown-and-serve rolls (2)
bn   buns (42)
bo   butter rolls (1)
bp   buttermilk rolls (1)
bq   crescent rolls (2)
br   crescents (1)
bs   dinner rolls (3)
bt   egg rolls (1)
bu   French rolls (1)
bv   hamburger buns (5)
bw   hard rolls (2)
bx   home rolls (1)
by   homemade rolls (2)
bz   hot-dog bread (1)
ca   hot-dog buns (4)
cb   light rolls (4)
cc   light-bread rolls (1)

cd   onion buns (1)
ce   onion rolls (4)
cf   Parker House rolls (2)
cg   potato rolls (1)
ch   quick rolls (1)
ci   roll bread (1)
cj   rolls (231)
ck   soft rolls (1)
cl   twist(ed) rolls (2)
cm   whole-wheat rolls (1)
cn   wienie rolls (1)
co   yeast rolls (5)
[miscellaneous]
cp   brioche [F] (1)
cq   camp bread (1)
cr   cap bread (1)
cs   cap loaf (1)
ct   chicken dumplings (2)
cu   cholah (1)
cv   cowboy bread (1)
cw   creole bread (1)
cx   croquignole [F] (1)
cy   Cuban bread (4)
cz   doughboy bread (1)
da   dumplings (30)
db   eating bread (1)
dc   flour dumplings (2)
dd   French bread (51)
de   German bread (1)
df   hardtack (1)
dg   Italian bread (4)
dh   lost bread (2)
di   monkey bread (1)
dj   New Orleans bread (2)
dk   oven bread (1)
dl   pan of bread (1)
dm   quick bread (6)
dn   round bread (2)
do   Sally Lunn (1)
dp   scones (1)
dq   twist loaf (1)
dr   Yorkshire bread (1)
044.5-6 L corn breads
No Response (40)
A   Anadama bread (1)
B   Arkansas wedding cake (1)
C   ash bread (12)
D   ash hoecake (1)
E   ash pone (3)
F   ash-cooked corn bread (1)
G   ashcake (72)
H   ashcake corn bread (1)
I   ashes cake (1)
J   ashy cake (1)
K   bake bread [n.] (2)
L   bake corn bread [n.] (1)
M   baked bread [n.] (1)
N   baked corn bread (1)
O   baker bread (1)

P   bass bread (1)
Qa   batter bread (7)
Qb   batter bread [=hoecake] (1)
R   batter corn bread (1)
Sa   battercake (22)
Sb   battercake [=corn dodger] (1)
T   big pone (3)
Ua   biscuit (1)
Ub   biscuit [=dumpling] (1)
V   bollos [S] (1)
W   bracken bread (1)
X   bread (6)
Y   breadsticks (1)
Z   buttermilk bread (1)
aa   cake bread (1)
ab   cakes (1)
ac   Camp Fire Girls' corn bread (1)
ad-a   chicken dressing (6)
ad-b   chicken dressing [=cush] (1)
ad-c   chicken dressing [boiled with greens/chicken] (1)
ae   chicken dumplings (2)
af   chitlin bread (1)
ag   cold-water corn bread (2)
ah   Conch flitters (1)
ai   convict bread (1)
aj   cook bread [n.] (1)
ak   corn balls (1)
al-a   corn bread (798)
al-b   corn bread [=pone/dodger] (9)
al-c   corn bread [with corn] (1)
al-d   corn bread [=crackling bread] (1)
al-e   corn bread [=hoecake] (1)
al-f   corn bread [=hush puppies] (1)
am   corn bread with cracklings (1)
an   corn-bread battercakes (3)
ao   corn-bread buns (1)
ap   corn-bread cakes (2)
aq   corn-bread dodgers (2)
ar   corn-bread dressing (5)
as   corn-bread dumplings (9)
at   corn-bread flapjacks (1)
au   corn-bread fritters (2)
av   corn-bread hotcakes (1)
aw   corn-bread muffins (33)
ax   corn-bread pancakes (2)
ay   corn-bread patties (10)
az   corn-bread pone (1)
ba   corn-bread slapjack (1)
bb   corn-bread sticks (14)
bc-a   corn cake(s) (32)
bc-b   corn cake [=pone] (1)
bc-c   corn cake [=ashcake] (2)
bc-d   corn cake [=pancake] (9)
bc-e   corn cake(s) [=dodgers/fried] (2)
bd   corn cups (1)
be-a   corn dodger (78)

be-b   corn dodger [=pone] (36)
be-c   corn dodger [=small pone] (6)
be-d   corn dodger [=hoecake] (9)
be-e   corn dodger [=corn bread] (57)
be-f   corn dodger [=corn sticks] (4)
be-g   corn dodger [=fried corn bread] (7)
be-h   corn dodger [=cornmeal dumpling] (33)
be-i   corn dodger [=corn bread balls] (4)
be-j   corn dodger [=corn bread biscuit] (1)
be-k   corn dodger [=spoon bread] (1)
be-l   corn dodger [=hush puppy] (28)
be-m   corn dodger [like hush puppy] (8)
be-n   corn dodger [=pan of corn bread] (3)
be-o   corn dodger [=dog bread] (1)
be-p   corn dodger [muffin-shaped] (2)
be-q   corn dodger [=fried patty] (4)
be-r   corn dodger [=pancake] (5)
be-s   corn dodger [=cold corn bread] (1)
be-t   corn dodger [=small cakes/ round cakes] (5)
be-u   corn dodger [=hot-water corn bread] (1)
be-v   corn dodger [=corn dog/looks like hot dog] (1)
be-w   corn dodger [=made in ashes] (3)
be-x   corn dodger [similar to mush] (1)
bf   corn dodger bread (2)
bg   corn-dodger style (corn bread) (1)
bh-a   corn dog (11)
bh-b   corn dog [=hot dog wrapped in cornmeal] (12)
bh-c   corn dog [=corn stick] (1)
bh-d   corn dog [=small balls of corn bread] (1)
bh-e   corn dog [=dumpling] (1)
bh-f   corn dog [not hot dog] (1)
bi   corn dumpling (40)
bj   corn flitters (9)
bk   corn fritters (39)
bl   corn hoecake (2)
bm   corn huskes (1)
bn   corn light bread (9)
bo   corn loaf (4)
bp   corn muffins (103)
bq-a   corn mush (4)

bq-b   corn mush [=spoon bread] (3)
br   corn pancakes (1)
bs   corn patties (6)
bt   corn pokes (1)
bu-a   corn pone (92)
bu-b   corn pone [=dodger] (4)
bu-c   corn pone [=(large) loaf] (8)
bu-d   corn pone [=small loaf] (8)
bu-e   corn pone [=corn bread] (8)
bu-f   corn pone [=thin cake/flat] (2)
bu-g   corn pone [round] (1)
bu-h   corn pone [=hot-water bread] (5)
bu-i   corn pone [=sticks of corn bread] (7)
bu-j   corn pone [cooked in fire/ashes/on hearth] (13)
bu-k   corn pone [=creamed corn] (1)
bu-l   corn pone [=corn pudding] (1)
bu-m   corn pone [=spoonbread] (1)
bu-n   corn pone [made in skillet/on stove] (9)
bu-o   corn pone [=large cake] (5)
bu-p   corn pone [=mushy cornmeal] (1)
bu-q   corn pone [like hush puppies] (2)
bu-r   corn pone [like pancakes] (2)
bu-s   corn pone [=hush puppies] (1)
bv-a   corn pudding [=corn pone] (1)
bv-b   corn pudding [=mush] (1)
bv-c   corn pudding [=hoecake] (1)
bw   corn puppies (1)
bx   corn roll (2)
by   corn-stick type (corn bread) (1)
bz   corn sticks (134)
ca   corn sweet bread (1)
cb   corn tortillas (2)
cc   corn wienie (1)
cd   cornmeal balls (3)
ce   cornmeal bread (3)
cf   cornmeal cakes (2)
cg   cornmeal dodger (1)
ch   cornmeal dumplings (22)
ci   cornmeal flitters (1)
cj-a   cornmeal fritters [=fried corn bread] (1)
cj-b   cornmeal fritters [made in muffin pan] (1)
ck   cornmeal muffins (14)
cl   cornmeal mush (3)
cm   cornmeal patties (2)
cn   cornmeal sticks (1)
co-a   corny dog (2)
co-b   corny dog [=hot dog in cornmeal batter] (4)

co-c   corny dog [=meal fried in skillet/small] (1)
co-d   corny dog [made with spice/peppers] (1)
cp   country homemade corn bread (1)
cq   crackling bread (131)
cr   crackling corn bread (19)
cs   cumpfolos (1)
ct-a   cush (4)
ct-b   cush [=spoon bread] (2)
ct-c   cush [=cornmeal mush] (2)
ct-d   cush [fried] (1)
cu   cush bread (1)
cv-a   cush-cush (5)
cv-b   cush-cush [in ball/baked] (1)
cv-c   cush-cush [=mush] (2)
cv-d   cush-cush [may have cracklings] (1)
cw   cushion (1)
cx-a   dodger (13)
cx-b   dodger [=corn bread] (1)
cx-c   dodger [=pone of bread] (8)
cx-d   dodger [chunks/round] (2)
cx-e   dodger [=hoecake] (1)
cx-f   dodger [=spoon bread] (1)
cx-g   dodger [=dumpling] (2)
cx-h   dodger [=hush puppy] (4)
cx-i   dodger [fried in grease] (1)
cx-j   dodger [=muffin] (2)
cy   dodger balls (1)
cz   dodger corn bread (2)
da   dodger of bread (1)
db   dodger of corn bread (2)
dc   dodging bread (1)
dd-a   dog bread [=corn dodger] (2)
dd-b   dog bread [=hot-water bread] (2)
dd-c   dog bread [=hoecake] (1)
de   doodads (1)
df   dough bread [=dumplings] (1)
dg   doughballs (1)
dh   doughboys [=hush puppies] (4)
di   doughty bread (1)
dj   dress(ing) (1)
dk-a   dressing (44)
dk-b   dressing [=mush] (1)
dk-c   dressing [=cush] (1)
dl   drop biscuits (1)
dm-a   dumpling(s) (50)
dm-b   dumpling [=corn dodger] (5)
dm-c   dumpling [boiled in cheesecloth] (3)
dm-d   dumpling [boiled/with onions/green pepper] (2)
dm-e   dumplings [like noodles/strips of bread] (2)
do   egg and bread (1)
dp   egg bread (72)

dq   egg-bread muffin (1)
dr   egg corn bread (2)
ds   egg muffins (1)
dt   fatty bread (1)
du   fish corn bread (1)
dv   fish doughs (1)
dw   fish sticks (1)
dx   fish-grease biscuits (1)
dy   five-finger bread (1)
dz   flat bread (1)
ea   flat cake (1)
eb   flitters (2)
ec   foot pone (1)
ed   French duck (1)
ee-a   fried bread (4)
ee-b   fried bread [=hoecake] (3)
ef   fried corn batter (1)
eg-a   fried corn bread (12)
eg-b   fried corn bread [=hoecakes] (1)
eg-c   fried corn bread [=hush puppies] (2)
eg-d   fried corn bread [=corn pone] (1)
eg-e   fried corn bread [thin and crisp] (1)
eg-f   fried corn bread [=hot-water bread] (1)
eh   fried corn cakes (2)
ei   fried cornmeal (1)
ej   fried hoecake (1)
ek   fried mush (1)
el   friedcakes (2)
em-a   fritter(s) (15)
em-b   fritter [=hoecake] (2)
em-c   fritter [=cornmeal pancake] (6)
em-d   fritter [fried/like hush puppies] (2)
em-e   fritter [=hot-water corn cakes] (1)
em-f   fritter [=corn dodger] (1)
en   fry bread [n.] (2)
eo   good, quick light bread, a (1)
ep   gosh (1)
eq   grated bread (1)
er   griddle bread (3)
es   griddle cake(s) (3)
et   grits corn bread (1)
eu   gritted (bread) (1)
ev   gritted bread (1)
ew   gritted-cornmeal bread (1)
ex   heavy bread (1)
ey-a   hoecake(s) (239)
ey-b   hoecake [=cookie] (1)
ez   hoecake bread (22)
fa   hoecake corn bread (4)
fb   hoecake of bread (5)
fc-a   hoecake of corn bread (3)

fc-b   hoecake of corn bread [=corn
       dodger] (2)
fd   hokey-dokey (1)
fe   hot battercakes (1)
ff   hot bread (1)
fg   hot corn dodger (1)
fh   hot dodgers (1)
fi   hot tamale (1)
fj   hot-roll corn bread (1)
fk   hot-water bread (26)
fl-a   hot-water corn bread (13)
fl-b   hot-water corn bread [=fried
       mush] (1)
fl-c   hot-water corn bread [=corn
       pone] (5)
fl-d   hot-water corn bread [=hush
       puppies] (1)
fl-e   hot-water corn bread [=corn
       dodger] (1)
fm   hot-water corn cakes (1)
fn   hotcakes (10)
fo-a   hush puppies (475)
fo-b   hush puppies [=pancakes] (2)
fo-c   hush puppies [=corn dodgers]
       (17)
fo-d   hush puppies [=dough boys]
       (1)
fo-e   hush puppies [stiff dough fried
       in strips] (1)
fo-f   hush puppies [like dog bread]
       (1)
fo-g   hush puppies [=hot-water
       bread] (2)
fp   hush puppy things (1)
fq   johnny bread (1)
fr-a   johnnycakes (24)
fr-b   johnnycakes [sweet] (7)
fs   lacy bread (3)
ft   light bread (1)
fu   little hoecakes (1)
fv   little-old pieces of corn bread (1)
fw   little pone of corn bread (2)
fx   little round dodgers (1)
fy   loaf of corn bread (1)
fz   lost John (1)
ga   meal batter (1)
gb   meal bread (1)
gc   meal dumplings (4)
gd   meal mush (1)
ge   menablers (1)
gf   Mexican bread (3)
gg   Mexican corn bread (7)
gh   Mexican cornmeal (1)
gi   Mexican-style corn bread (1)
gj   milk bread (4)
gk   molasses cake (1)
gl-a   muffin (120)
gl-b   muffin [=corn dodger] (2)
gm   muffin bread (8)

gn   muffin cakes (1)
go   muffin ring(s) (4)
gp   mush bread (1)
gq   old crackling corn bread (1)
gr   old hard corn bread (1)
gs   old-fashion pone (1)
gt   old-timey corn bread (1)
gu   old-timey hoecake (1)
gv   old-timey poor-folks' bread (1)
gw   onion bread (1)
gx   onion dumplings (1)
gy   onion-and-egg bread (1)
gz   oven bread (2)
ha   oyster dressing (1)
hb-a   pan [=pone] (1)
hb-b   pan [=corn bread] (1)
hb-c   pan (of corn bread) (1)
hc   pan bread (2)
hd   pan of bread (2)
he   pan of corn bread (6)
hf   pancakes (16)
hg   panic bread (1)
hh   pat-a-cake (2)
hi   patties (3)
hj   patties of bread (1)
hk   patty bread (1)
hl   pistolets (1)
hm   plain bread (7)
hn   plain brick (1)
ho-a   plain corn bread (7)
ho-b   plain corn bread [=pone/
       dodger] (2)
hp   plain cornmeal bread (1)
hq   plain hoecake (3)
hr-a   pone(s) (115)
hr-b   pone [=loaf] (12)
hr-c   pone [large cake] (11)
hr-d   pone [=dodger] (6)
hr-e   pone [patty shape] (2)
hr-f   pone [lump-shaped] (6)
hr-g   pone [=hoecake] (2)
hr-h   pone [=hushpuppy] (1)
hs   pone bread (47)
ht   pone cake (1)
hu   pone corn bread (8)
hv   pone of bread (24)
hw-a   pone of corn bread (16)
hw-b   pone of corn bread [=corn
       dodger] (3)
hw-c   pone of corn bread [baked in
       skillet] (3)
hx   poor do (2)
hy   poor soul (1)
hz   poor-boy corn bread (1)
ia   poor-folks bread (1)
ib   poor-man's bread (1)
ic   pot dodger (4)
id   pot liquor (1)
ie-a   potato bread (2)

ie-b   potato bread [with sweet
       potatoes] (1)
ie-c   potato bread [with Irish
       potatoes] (1)
if   pronto puff (1)
ig   puff cakes (1)
ih   puppy dog (1)
ii   raisin corn bread (1)
ij   regular-old corn bread (1)
ik   right on corn bread (2)
il   rings (1)
im   river bread (1)
in   roasted bread (1)
io   Sally Lunn (1)
ip   saltwater corn bread (2)
iq   salty (corn bread) (1)
ir   scalded bread (2)
is   scalded hoecake (1)
it   scalded hot hoecake (1)
iu   shortbread (1)
iv-a   shortening bread (4)
iv-b   shortening bread [=crackling
       bread] (6)
iw   skillet bread (2)
ix   skillet corn bread (1)
iy   snow bread (1)
iz   soda corn bread (1)
ja   sour bread (1)
jb   sour corn bread (1)
jc   sourdough bread (1)
jd   Southern spoon bread (1)
je   Southern sweet bread (1)
jf-a   spoon bread (45)
jf-b   spoon bread [fried by spoonful]
       (3)
jf-c   spoon bread [served with
       spoon] (31)
jf-d   spoon bread [=Sally Lunn] (1)
jf-e   spoon bread [=cush] (1)
jf-f   spoon bread [=drop biscuits]
       (1)
jg   squaw bread (1)
jh   stick bread (1)
ji   sticks (7)
jj   sticks of corn bread (1)
jk   stone bread (1)
jl   stove fingers (1)
jm   straight-out corn bread (1)
jn   stuffing (4)
jo   Sunday muffin (1)
jp   sweet bread (2)
jq   sweet corn bread (2)
jr   syrup cake (2)
js   taco (1)
jt   thin hoecake (1)
ju   tortilla (9)
jv   turkey stuffing (1)
jw   turn mush (1)
jx   turnover(s) (2)

jy   turnover bread (1)
jz   turnover corn bread (1)
ka   water bread (4)
kb   white corn bread (2)
kc   whole cake (1)
kd   yeast cake (1)
ke   yeast corn bread (1)
kf   yeast-rising bread (1)
kg   yellow corn bread (3)

045.1 L store-bought bread
No Response (207)
A   bake bread [n.] (2)
B   baker('s) bread (41)
C   baker shop (bread) (1)
D   bakery (bread) (90)
E   bakery-made (1)
F   bakery-shop bread (2)
G   bakery-type bread (1)
H   bought (bread) (115)
I   bought biscuits (4)
J   bought light bread (4)
K   boughten (bread) (4)
L   bread (10)
M   bread from the bakery (1)
N   bread from the store (1)
O   brought-home bread (1)
P   bum bread (2)
Q   commercial (bread) (4)
R   commercial light bread (1)
S   company bread (1)
T   factory bread (3)
U   factory-made (bread) (7)
V   light bread (158)
W   light rolls (1)
X   loaf (4)
Y   loaf bread (94)
Z   loaf of bread (21)
aa   loaf of light bread (3)
ab   manufactured bread (1)
ac   manufactury bread (1)
ad   market bread (2)
ae   outside bread (1)
af   packaged (2)
ag   ready-made (bread) (3)
ah   regular bread (2)
ai   salt-rising bread (1)
aj   sandwich bread (4)
ak   slice bread [n.] (3)
al   sliced bread (2)
am   spider webs (1)
an   store bread (20)
ao   store-bought biscuits (1)
ap   store-bought (bread) (210)
aq   store-bought loaf bread (1)
ar   store-bought wheat bread (1)
as   store-boughten (bread) (7)
at   white bread (7)

045.2 L doughnut
No Response (136)

A   animal dip (1)
B   beignet [F] (15)
C   biscuit (1)
D   bunuelos [S] (1)
E   cake doughnut (10)
F   cake-like doughnut (1)
G   candied (doughnut) (1)
H   cartwheel (1)
I   cherry (doughnut) (1)
J   chocolate (doughnut) (4)
K   chocolate-covered doughnut (2)
L   chocolate top [n.] (1)
M   cinnamon bar (1)
N   cinnamon bun (1)
O   cinnamon (doughnut) (1)
P   cinnamon roll (2)
Q   cinnamon stick (1)
R   cinnamon twist (doughnut) (2)
S   coffee bread (1)
T   coffee cake (4)
U   cookie (1)
V   cream-filled (doughnut) (1)
W   cream puff (1)
X   croquignole [F] (9)
Y   cruller (10)
Z   doorknob (1)
aa   doughboy (1)
ab   doughnut (762)
ac   doughnut center (1)
ad   doughnut hole (10)
ae   doughnut twist (1)
af   dropped cookie (1)
ag   dunker (2)
ah   egg ball (1)
ai   figurine (1)
aj   fill(ed) doughnut (4)
ak   flat cake (1)
al   flitter (1)
am   flour doughnut (1)
an   French doughnut (1)
ao   French Market doughnut (2)
ap   French pastry (1)
aq   fried beignet (1)
ar   fried bread (1)
as   fried dough (1)
at   fried fritter (1)
au   fritter (4)
av   frosted doughnut (1)
aw   glaze(d) (doughnut) (5)
ax   hole (of the doughnut) (5)
ay   homemade doughnut (2)
az   honey (doughnut) (1)
ba   honey-drip (doughnut) (1)
bb   hot cross bun (2)
bc   jelly doughnut (5)
bd   jelly-fill(ed) doughnut (2)
be   jelly roll (7)
bf   Krapfen [G] (1)
bg   Krepletz [G] (1)

bh   lemon (doughnut) (1)
bi   long john (2)
bj   muffin (6)
bk   pastry (4)
bl   plain (doughnut) (4)
bm   puff (1)
bn   raise(d) doughnut (5)
bo   sinker (3)
bp   solid doughnut (1)
bq   spoon bread (1)
br   square doughnut (1)
bs   strip (1)
bt   suet cake (1)
bu   sugar-covered (doughnut) (1)
bv   sugar-top doughnut (1)
bw   sweet biscuit (1)
bx   sweet bread (1)
by   sweet cake (doughnut) (2)
bz   sweet doughnut (1)
ca   sweet loaf (1)
cb   sweet roll (8)
cc   sweeten bread (1)
cd   sweeten cake (1)
ce   tea cake (17)
cf   twist (doughnut) (6)
cg   twisted doughnut (2)
ch   yeast cake (1)
ci   yeast doughnut (8)

045.3 L pancakes
No Response (88)
A   batter bread (1)
B   battercakes (150)
C   beignets [F] (6)
D   buckwheat bread (1)
E   buckwheat cakes (12)
F   buckwheat pancakes (2)
G   cakes (1)
H   corn cakes (13)
I   corn flitters (3)
J   corn fritters (8)
K   corn pancakes (1)
L   corn patties (1)
M   corn-bread battercakes (2)
N   corn-bread flitters (1)
O   corn-bread fritters (1)
P   corn-bread hotcakes (1)
Q   corn-bread pancakes (1)
R   cornmeal cakes (1)
S   crepes (4)
T   deceivers (1)
U   flap flitters (1)
V   flapcakes (2)
W   flapjackety (1)
X   flapjacks (221)
Y   flatjacks (1)
Z   flatter cakes (1)
aa   flipjacks (2)
ab   flips (1)
ac   flitter cakes (3)

ad flitters (73)	<{?}eest> (47)	|abeABE| (1)
ae flour cakes (1)	**045.5 S yeast**	|abiABA| (6)
af flour flitters (1)	No Response (0)	|abiABE| (5)
ag flour fritters (1)	|ABA| (3)	|abuABA| (2)
ah flour hoecakes (1)	|ABAbbl| (1)	|agaBBA| (11)
ai fried battercakes (1)	|ABAdab| (1)	|agaBBC| (1)
aj fried flapjacks (1)	|ABAeaa| (1)	|agcABA| (1)
ak fried hobbies (1)	|ABAeaj| (13)	|agcBBA| (1)
al fried pancakes (1)	|ABAeak| (1)	|ageABE| (1)
am fritter cakes (2)	|ABE| (107)	|ageABN| (3)
an fritters (46)	|ABEeaj| (1)	|ageBBJ| (1)
ao frog (1)	|ABEeak| (1)	|agiABA| (2)
ap griddle bread (1)	|ABI| (11)	|agiABE| (5)
aq griddle cakes (29)	|ABW| (3)	|ahcAHE| (1)
ar hobbies (1)	|ACE| (1)	|bbcABC| (1)
as hoecakes (28)	|AG1| (1)	|bbhABE| (1)
at hot stack (1)	|AGA| (10)	|bbvABA| (1)
au hotcakes (213)	|AGAabk| (1)	|bgdABA| (1)
av hush puppies (1)	|AGAdab| (2)	|daaABA| (15)
aw Indian bread (1)	|AGAeaa| (7)	|daaABC| (2)
ax johnnycakes (4)	|AGAeab| (1)	|daaABE| (1)
ay pancake bread (1)	|AGAeaj| (10)	|daaAGA| (2)
az pancakes (642)	|AGAeak| (1)	|daaBBA| (2)
ba pat-a-cakes (5)	|AGAeba| (1)	|dabABA| (18)
bb Pfannkuchen [G] (1)	|AGB| (1)	|dabABC| (5)
bc potato pancakes (2)	|AGC| (11)	|dabABE| (5)
bd rice pancakes (1)	|AGE| (153)	|dabABI| (1)
be shortcakes (3)	|AGEbba| (1)	|dabABJ| (1)
bf skillet cakes (1)	|AGEbbj| (2)	|dabAGA| (2)
bg slapjacks (7)	|AGEeaj| (4)	|dacABA| (2)
bh stack cakes (1)	|AGEeak| (2)	|dacAGG| (1)
bi stack of cakes (1)	|AGEmaj| (1)	|dacBBA| (4)
bj stacked cakes (1)	|AGG| (1)	|dadABD| (1)
bk syrup soppers (1)	|AGI| (6)	|daeABA| (7)
bl tortilla (2)	|AGIbbj| (1)	|daeABE| (112)
bm wheat cakes (7)	|AGS| (1)	|daeABG| (1)
bn wheat hoecakes (1)	|AGW| (20)	|daeABI| (5)
bo wheat pancakes (1)	|ASAeaj| (1)	|daeABN| (6)
bp whole-wheat pancakes (1)	|BBD| (2)	|daeAGA| (1)
bq yellow pancakes (1)	|BGA| (3)	|daeAGE| (29)
045.4 G pounds	|BGD| (1)	|daeAGI| (1)
No Response (141)	|DABmaj| (1)	|daeBBA| (1)
A pound[N-i] (215)	|DAG| (1)	|daeBBJ| (1)
B pounds (592)	|DCAeaj| (1)	|dafABE| (2)
045.5 P yeast	|DCE| (1)	|dagABA| (3)
{?} glottal	|EAA| (1)	|dagABC| (1)
No Response (153)	|KAA| (1)	|dagABE| (11)
<(y)ees(t)> (78)	|ab1ABA| (1)	|dagABG| (2)
<(y)eest> (120)	|ab1ABE| (1)	|dagABI| (1)
<heesht> (1)	|abaABA| (1)	|dagAGE| (1)
<leest> (1)	|abaBBA| (14)	|dagBBJ| (1)
<yaist> (1)	|abaBBC| (1)	|dahABA| (1)
<yees(t)> (85)	|abaBBJ| (1)	|daiABE| (5)
<yeest> (481)	|abcABA| (33)	|daiABI| (2)
<yees{?}> (1)	|abcABJ| (1)	|daiAGE| (1)
<yest> (1)	|abcAGA| (1)	|dasABA| (1)
<yist> (3)	|abcAGE| (1)	|datABE| (3)
<{?}ees(t)> (19)	|abcBBA| (2)	|datAGA| (1)
<{?}eesh(t)> (1)	|abeABA| (2)	|dawABE| (7)

|dawAGE| (2)
|dayABE| (1)
|dayAGE| (1)
|dazBBA| (1)
|dbbABE| (1)
|dbeABE| (2)
|dcaABA| (12)
|dcaABE| (1)
|dcbABA| (2)
|dcbABC| (1)
|dcbABE| (2)
|dcbAGE| (1)
|dcbBBJ| (1)
|dccBBA| (1)
|dceABE| (6)
|dceAGE| (1)
|dceBBA| (1)
|dcgABE| (1)
|dcgABG| (1)
|dciABE| (1)
|dcsABA| (2)
|dcsBBA| (2)
|dcwABE| (2)
|dcwBBA| (1)
|ddaAHA| (3)
|ddzBHA| (1)
|dgaABA| (1)
|dgtABE| (1)
|eaaABA| (1)
|eaaABE| (6)
|eaaAGE| (1)
|eaaBAA| (1)
|eaaBBA| (35)
|eaaBBD| (2)
|eaaBGA| (2)
|eabBBD| (1)
|eacABE| (1)
|eacBBA| (2)
|eacBBD| (5)
|eacBBJ| (2)
|eadABA| (1)
|eadABE| (4)
|eadAGI| (1)
|eadBBD| (1)
|eadBGH| (1)
|eaeBBA| (3)
|eahABE| (2)
|eahBBA| (3)
|eahBBD| (2)
|eaiABI| (1)
|eaiBBA| (1)
|eajABE| (1)
|eauABE| (1)
|ebcABA| (1)
|ebcABJ| (1)
|ebdABA| (1)
|ebsBBA| (1)
|ecaBGA| (1)
|eccBBA| (1)

|ecsBBA| (2)
|efaABE| (1)
|egbBBA| (1)
|ehaBHA| (1)
|kbfABE| (1)

045.6 L yolk
No Response (119)
A   egg yellow (2)
B   egg yolk (3)
C   meat (1)
D   oeuf [F] (1)
E   red (2)
F   red [adj.] (1)
G   red part (1)
H   white yolk (1)
I   yel(low) (1)
J   yellow (233)
K   yel(low) of the egg (1)
L   yellow of an/the egg (10)
M   yellow part (7)
N   yellow yolk (2)
O   yolk (670)
P   yolk [=egg white] (21)
Q   yolk of the egg (6)

045.7 P yellow
{l}   clear
{R}   weakly retroflex
{t}   flap
{?}   glottal
No Response (86)
<ya[l]A=14> (1)
<yalA=14> (36)
<yalR=14> (9)
<yaloe=13> (3)
<yal{R}=14> (5)
<ya{l}A=14> (6)
<ya{l}oe=13> (1)
<ye[l]A=14> (1)
<yel(A)> (1)
<yelA=14> (466)
<yelAz=14> (2)
<yelI=14> (4)
<yelR=14> (41)
<yelRz=14> (2)
<yeloe=13> (102)
<yeloo=13> (2)
<yel{R}=14> (22)
<ye{l}A=14> (115)
<ye{l}R=14> (11)
<ye{l}Rz=14> (1)
<ye{l}oe=13> (7)
<ye{l}{R}=14> (2)
<ye{t}A=14> (1)
<yilA=14> (9)
<yilR=14> (2)
<yiloe=13> (2)
<yi{l}A=14> (1)
<yolA=14> (1)
<yol{R}=14> (1)

<yo{l}A=14> (1)
<yulA=14> (49)
<yulR=14> (1)
<yuloe=13> (9)
<yulu=13> (1)
<yul{R}=14> (5)
<yu{l}A=14> (1)
<{?}eloe=13> (1)

046.1 P eggs
{a}   upglide
{e}   upglide
{g}   devoiced
{z}   devoiced
{?}   glottal
No Response (108)
<ag> (3)
<agz> (2)
<ag{z}> (1)
<ai(g)> (1)
<aig> (49)
<aig(z)> (1)
<aigs> (1)
<aigsh> (1)
<aigz> (134)
<aig{z}> (19)
<aik> (1)
<ai{?}> (1)
<ai{g}> (5)
<ai{g}z> (1)
<ai{g}{z}> (6)
<a{g}> (1)
<e(g)> (2)
<eg> (43)
<eg(z)> (1)
<egs> (3)
<egz> (155)
<eg{z}> (81)
<eigz> (1)
<e{?}s> (1)
<e{g}> (4)
<e{g}s> (1)
<e{g}{z}> (13)
<ig> (2)
<igz> (1)
<ig{z}> (1)
<i{g}{z}> (2)
<{a}g> (1)
<{a}gz> (10)
<{a}g{z}> (1)
<{a}{g}> (1)
<{e}(g)> (1)
<{e}g> (65)
<{e}g(z)> (1)
<{e}gs> (2)
<{e}gz> (234)
<{e}g{z}> (43)
<{e}{?}> (1)
<{e}{g}> (3)
<{e}{g}s> (1)

<{e}{g}{z}> (7)

046.2 L poached egg

No Response (224)
A   baked egg (1)
B   boiled (egg) (3)
C   broiled egg (1)
D   broke and boiled (2)
E   busted egg (1)
F   coddle [v.] (2)
G   coddled (egg) (6)
H   crack egg (1)
I   dropped egg (3)
J   hulled egg (1)
K   open egg (1)
L   poach [v.] (155)
M   poach (egg) (24)
N   poached (egg) (500)
O   posted egg (1)
P   sheared (1)
Q   sick person's egg (1)
R   three-minute egg (1)
S   toasted egg (4)

046.3 L salt pork

No Response (153)
A   Alabama ham (1)
B   Arkansas chicken (1)
C   back (1)
D   bacon (92)
E   bac(on) fat (1)
F   bacon fat (2)
G   bacon meat (2)
H   bacon salt (1)
I   belly (4)
J   belly meat (2)
K   boar flank (1)
L   boil meat (3)
M   boiled meat (1)
N   boiling bacon (4)
O   boiling meat (34)
P   boiling pork (2)
Q   boiling white meat (1)
R   Canadian bacon (1)
S   chunk meat (2)
T   cooking meat (3)
U   country cured side bacon (1)
V   cured bacon (2)
W   cured meat (6)
X   cured hog meat (1)
Y   cured piece of side meat (1)
Z   cured pork (1)
aa dried meat (2)
ab dry pork (1)
ac dry salt (9)
ad dry salt bacon (1)
ae dry salt meat (7)
af dry salt pork (1)
ag fat (17)
ah fat bacon (10)
ai fat belly (3)

aj fat (meat) (1)
ak fat meat (63)
al fat off of a middling (1)
am fat off the middlings (1)
an fat part of this side meat (1)
ao fat pork (4)
ap fat pork meat (1)
aq fat salt pork (5)
ar fat side (1)
as fat white meat (1)
at fat-lean pork (1)
au fatback (335)
av fatback meat (3)
aw flank (1)
ax fried meat (2)
ay green meat (2)
az grunt meat (1)
ba ham hock (1)
bb ham with the buttons on (1)
bc hog back (1)
bd hog meat (4)
be home cure (1)
bf leaf fat (2)
bg leaf lard (2)
bh lean (1)
bi lean fatback (1)
bj lean meat (12)
bk lean salt pork (1)
bl lean streak (1)
bm lean streaked meat (1)
bn meat (2)
bo meat and lard (1)
bp middling (31)
bq middling meat (12)
br middlings (6)
bs pickle meat (4)
bt pickle pork (2)
bu pickled meat (1)
bv piece of bacon (1)
bw piece of cheap meat (1)
bx piece of meat (3)
by piece of pork (1)
bz plain-old fat (1)
ca plate meat (1)
cb pork (31)
cc pork bacon (1)
cd pork bellies (2)
ce pork belly (1)
cf pork fat (1)
cg pork loin (1)
ch pork meat (3)
ci pork rind (1)
cj salt back (2)
ck salt bacon (27)
cl salt meat (121)
cm salt pork (153)
cn salt side (3)
co salt side meat (2)
cp salt side pork (1)

cq salt-cured (meat) (1)
cr salted (1)
cs salted meat (4)
ct salted side meat (1)
cu salty meat (1)
cv sawmill chicken (1)
cw scutter back (1)
cx season meat (1)
cy seasoning (4)
cz seasoning bacon (1)
da seasoning meat (9)
db seasoning pork (1)
dc side (2)
dd side back (1)
de side meat (85)
df side of salt meat (1)
dg side of salt pork (1)
dh side-plate meat (1)
di side pork (2)
dj sideback (1)
dk slab bacon (2)
dl smoke bacon (3)
dm smoke meat (2)
dn smoke pork (1)
do sow bellies (2)
dp sow bosom (2)
dq sow's belly (1)
dr sowbelly (127)
ds sowbelly meat (1)
dt sowbelly with the buttons on (1)
du streak [P-0] lean (1)
dv streak meat (1)
dw streak of fat (4)
dx streak of fat and streak of lean (1)
dy streak of fat streak of lean (1)
dz streak of lean (85)
ea streak of lean and a streak of fat (1)
eb streak of lean and streak of fat (2)
ec streak of lean bacon (1)
ed streak of lean meat (1)
ee streak of lean or strip of fat (1)
ef streak of lean streak of fat (27)
eg streak of the lean (1)
eh streaked (6)
ei streaked bacon (1)
ej streaked lean (4)
ek streaked meat (18)
el streaked pork (1)
em streaks of lean (1)
en stripe back (1)
eo tenderloin (5)
ep Tennessee chicken (2)
eq white back (3)
er white bacon (25)
es white fat (1)
et white meat (54)

eu white pork (3)
ev white salt bacon (1)
ew white salt meat (2)
ex white salt pork (1)
ey white side (8)
ez white side meat (1)
fa white side of bacon (1)
fb white sowbelly (1)
fc whiteback (1)

046.4 L side (of bacon)
No Response (209)
A bacon (64)
B bacon middling (1)
C bacon slab (1)
D chunk meat (2)
E half a hog (1)
F half a middling (1)
G half of the hog (1)
H middle (1)
I middling(s) (293)
J middling meat (31)
K middling of bacon (2)
L middling of meat (5)
M middling part (2)
N middling side (1)
O middlings slab (1)
P midsection (1)
Q piece of meat (2)
R pork side (3)
S salt side (1)
T salt side pork (1)
U side(s) (181)
V side bacon (3)
W side meat (104)
X side of (a/the) hog (17)
Y side of a pork (1)
Z side of bacon (110)
aa side of meat (17)
ab side of middling (2)
ac side of pork (3)
ad side of salt meat (2)
ae side-plate meat (1)
af side pork (3)
ag side slab (1)
ah siding (2)
ai slab (51)
aj slab bacon (6)
ak slab meat (3)
al slab of bacon (35)
am slab part (1)
an sparerib (1)
ao streaked meat (3)
ap streaky meat (1)
aq white bacon (1)
ar whole middling (1)
as whole side (of a hog) (6)
at whole slab (of bacon) (2)

046.5 L smoked meat
No Response (329)

A bacon (353)
B bacon meat (2)
C bacon squares (2)
D bulk bacon (1)
E Canadian bacon (9)
F chunk (of) meat (2)
G country bacon (1)
H country-cured ham (2)
I country-cured side bacon (1)
J country ham (2)
K country meat (1)
L country pork (1)
M cured (4)
N cured bacon (6)
O cured ham (meat) (4)
P cured hog meat (1)
Q cure(d) meat (13)
R cured piece of side meat (1)
S cured pork (1)
T cured side (1)
U dried salt pork (1)
V dry meat (1)
W dry pork (1)
X dry salt (1)
Y dry salt bacon (1)
Z dry salt meat (1)
aa fried bacon (1)
ab fried ham (1)
ac fried meat (2)
ad ham (104)
ae ham meat (3)
af hickory-smoked (ham) (1)
ag hog ham (1)
ah hunk of meat (1)
ai middling (10)
aj middling meat (1)
ak middling of bacon (1)
al piece of bacon (1)
am piece of meat (1)
an pork bacon (1)
ao rasher (1)
ap rasher of bacon (1)
aq salt bacon (7)
ar salt-fried meat (1)
as salt ham (1)
at salt meat (13)
au salt pork (11)
av salt side meat (1)
aw salted bacon (1)
ax salted meat (2)
ay side bacon (2)
az side meat (17)
ba side of bacon (6)
bb side of meat (1)
bc slab (15)
bd slab bacon (16)
be slab meat (1)
bf slab of bacon (16)
bg slab of country ham (1)

bh smoked (3)
bi smoke(d) bacon (30)
bj smoked country ham (1)
bk smoke(d) ham (12)
bl smoke(d) meat (28)
bm smoked middling meat (1)
bn smoke(d) pork (4)
bo smoked salted meat (1)
bp smoke(d) shoulder (2)
bq smoked side (3)
br smoked side meat (2)
bs smoked stuff (1)
bt streak of lean (16)
bu streaked bacon (2)
bv streaked meat (5)
bw sugar-cured (2)
bx sugar-cured bacon (1)
by sugar-cured ham (2)
bz sugar-cured meat (3)
ca thick bacon (1)
cb unsliced (bacon) (4)
cc white bacon (4)
cd white pork (1)
ce white salt pork (1)

046.6 L bacon rind
No Response (232)
A bacon end(s) (2)
B bacon rind (38)
C bacon skin (8)
D belly part (1)
E chitlins (1)
F crackling(s) (3)
G crust (3)
H edge(s) (2)
I end(s) (6)
J hard skin (1)
K hide (8)
L hog rind (1)
M hog skin (1)
N meat skin (9)
O outside (1)
P pieces (1)
Q pork rind (8)
R pork skin (2)
S rim (3)
T rind (332)
U scrap meat skin (1)
V scraps (3)
W scribblings (1)
X skin (380)
Y stem (1)
Z strip (1)
aa trimming(s) (5)

046.7 L bacon
No Response (213)
A bacon (575)
B bacon meat (2)
C bacon slices (1)
D bacon strip(s) (2)

E   bought bacon (1)
F   breakfast bacon (93)
G   breakfast meat (1)
H   breakfast middling (1)
I   Cincinnati bacon (1)
J   cured bacon (2)
K   cured meat (1)
L   fatback (1)
M   fried meat (1)
N   frying bacon (1)
O   ham (1)
P   lean meat (1)
Q   middling meat (1)
R   presliced (1)
S   ready slice (1)
T   side meat (8)
U   sliced (4)
V   slice(d) bacon (51)
W   sliced meat (1)
X   slices of bacon (1)
Y   smoky breakfast bacon (1)
Z   streaked bacon (1)
aa   streaked meat (2)
ab   strip bacon (2)
ac   striped part (1)
ad   strips of bacon (1)
ae   thin bacon (1)
af   thin part of the side (1)

046.8A P sausage
{d}   devoiced
{j}   devoiced
{o}   upglide
{oe} lowered onset
{R}   weakly retroflex
{r}   weakly retroflex
{z}   devoiced
{zh} devoiced
{?}   glottal
No Response (91)
<sasIch=14> (1)
<sasIt=14> (1)
<sawchI(j)=14> (1)
<sawchIj=14> (1)
<sawfIj=14> (1)
<sawfI{j}=14> (1)
<sawfsIj=14> (1)
<sawrsIj=14> (1)
<sawrsh{R}(j)=14> (1)
<sawsAs=14> (1)
<sawsI(j)=14> (3)
<sawsIch=14> (25)
<sawsId=14> (15)
<sawsIdz=14> (2)
<sawsIj=14> (307)
<sawsIjIz=144> (4)
<sawsIjsh=14> (1)
<sawsIs=14> (3)
<sawsIsh=14> (2)
<sawsIt=14> (16)

<sawsIts=14> (1)
<sawsIzh=14> (7)
<sawsI{?}=14> (1)
<sawsI{d}=14> (3)
<sawsI{j}=14> (106)
<sawsI{zh}=14> (1)
<sawsej=13> (2)
<sawsejIz=134> (1)
<sawshI(j)=14> (1)
<sawshIch=14> (1)
<sawshId=14> (2)
<sawshIdh=14> (1)
<sawshIz=14> (1)
<sawshI{d}=14> (1)
<sawshI{j}=14> (4)
<sawshI{z}=14> (1)
<sawshsI{j}=14> (1)
<sawsij=13> (16)
<sawsit=13> (1)
<sawtI{j}=14> (1)
<sawzIj=14> (1)
<saw{r}sij=13> (1)
<shawshI{j}=14> (2)
<siesI{j}=14> (1)
<sochI(j)=14> (1)
<soesI{j}=14> (1)
<sorsI(j)=14> (1)
<sorsIt=14> (1)
<sosAt=14> (1)
<sosIch=14> (10)
<sosId=14> (2)
<sosIj=14> (127)
<sosIjIz=144> (4)
<sosIjI{z}=144> (2)
<sosIsh=14> (2)
<sosIt=14> (4)
<sosIzh=14> (3)
<sosI{d}=14> (2)
<sosI{j}=14> (46)
<sosI{zh}=14> (2)
<sosI{z}=14> (1)
<soshA{z}=14> (1)
<soshI(j)=14> (1)
<soshIj=14> (2)
<soshIst=14> (1)
<soshIz=14> (2)
<soshI{?}=14> (1)
<soshI{j}=14> (1)
<sosij=13> (1)
<soysIt=14> (1)
<so{r}sIj=14> (1)
<susIch=14> (1)
<s{oe}sAzhIdh=144> (1)
<s{oe}sIj=14> (2)
<s{o}sId=14> (1)
<s{o}sIj=14> (78)
<s{o}sIjIz=144> (2)
<s{o}sIsh=14> (1)
<s{o}sIt{z}=14> (1)

<s{o}sI{j}=14> (30)
<s{o}sij=13> (6)
046.8B P butcher
{oo} unrounded
{R}   weakly retroflex
No Response (203)
<bichR=14> (2)
<bich[R]=14> (1)
<bich{R}=14> (2)
<boochR=14> (322)
<boochRN=144> (2)
<boochRNG=144> (2)
<boochRd=14> (7)
<boochRz=14> (7)
<boochR{z}=14> (1)
<booch[R]=14> (233)
<booch[R]d=14> (2)
<booch[R]z=14> (5)
<booch{R}=14> (95)
<booch{R}N=144> (1)
<booch{R}t=14> (1)
<booch{R}z=14> (2)
<booshR=14> (1)
<boosh[R]=14> (1)
<bootchR=14> (1)
<bootch[R]=14> (8)
<bootch{R}=14> (2)
<buchR=14> (5)
<buch[R]=14> (5)
<buch[R]d=14> (1)
<buch{R}=14> (3)
<buechR=14> (3)
<buech[R]=14> (1)
<buech{R}=14> (1)
<bueshR=14> (1)
<b{oo}ch[R]=14> (2)
046.9 L spoiled [meat]
No Response (140)
A   age[V-t] (1)
B   aged out (2)
C   bad (20)
D   cankered (3)
E   canky (1)
F   contaminated (1)
G   decayed (1)
H   deteriorated (1)
I   faisande [F] (1)
J   flabby (1)
K   funky (1)
L   hard (2)
M   mold (2)
N   mold[V-t] (1)
O   molded (6)
P   moldy (3)
Q   musty (1)
R   nasty (1)
S   no good (2)
T   old (33)
U   putrified (1)

V   rance [F] (2)
W   rancy (1)
X   rancid (124)
Y   rank (59)
Z   ripe (1)
aa rot(s) (3)
ab rot[V-t] (1)
ac rotted (4)
ad rotten (22)
ae rough (1)
af ruin[V-t] (6)
ag ruined (38)
ah sour(s) (14)
ai soured (14)
aj spoil(s) (102)
ak spoil[V-p/r/t] (56)
al spoiled (480)
am spoilt (76)
an stale (25)
ao stark (1)
ap stink(s) (2)
aq stout (1)
ar strong (52)
as swump (1)
at taint(s) (7)
au taint[V-t] (1)
av tainted (89)
aw tainty (1)
ax tint of rotteness (1)
ay tinted (1)
az turn[V-p] (1)
ba turned (1)

046.9 P spoiled
{d}   devoiced
{l}   devoiced
{o}   upglide
{oy} inglide
{r}   weakly retroflex
No Response (215)
<pfoyl{d}> (1)
<sb{oy}l> (1)
<spaw(l)t> (1)
<spawlld=14> (1)
<spawld> (14)
<spawl{d}> (1)
<spawrld> (1)
<spaw{r}l{d}> (1)
<spiel> (3)
<spield> (2)
<spoe(ld)> (1)
<spoe[l]d> (1)
<spoy(l)> (1)
<spoy(ld)> (2)
<spoy(l)d> (2)
<spoy(l)t> (1)
<spoyLd=14> (1)
<spoy[l]> (2)
<spoy[l](d)> (1)
<spoy[l]d> (3)

<spoyl> (26)
<spoyl(d)> (6)
<spoylN=14> (2)
<spoyld> (166)
<spoylt> (16)
<spoylz> (4)
<spoyl{d}> (27)
<spoy{l}d> (2)
<sp{oy}(ld)> (1)
<sp{oy}(l)t> (1)
<sp{oy}(l){d}> (1)
<sp{oy}[l]> (5)
<sp{oy}[l](d)> (2)
<sp{oy}[l]d> (1)
<sp{oy}[l]t> (3)
<sp{oy}[l]{d}> (1)
<sp{oy}l> (43)
<sp{oy}l(d)> (13)
<sp{oy}lN=14> (1)
<sp{oy}lNG=14> (1)
<sp{oy}ld> (235)
<sp{oy}lt> (47)
<sp{oy}lz> (11)
<sp{oy}l{d}> (41)
<sp{oy}{l}> (1)
<sp{oy}{l}(d)> (1)
<sp{o}ld> (3)
<sp{o}lt> (1)
<sp{o}l{d}> (1)
<thp{oy}ld> (1)

047.1 L headcheese
No Response (114)
A   bought cheese (1)
B   cheese (6)
C   cheesehead (2)
D   fromage [F] (1)
E   head sausage (1)
F   head souse (5)
G   headcheese (86)
H   headhog cheese (1)
I   hog cheese (8)
J   hog souse (5)
K   hog's head cheese (53)
L   hog's head souse (2)
M   hoghead (2)
N   hoghead and cheese (1)
O   hoghead cheese (260)
P   hoghead chow (1)
Q   hoghead fry (1)
R   hoghead mush (2)
S   hoghead sausage (1)
T   hoghead side (1)
U   hoghead souse (44)
V   louder (1)
W   mincemeat (1)
X   press meat (55)
Y   pressed meat (11)
Z   Schwademagen [G] (1)
aa souse (296)

ab souse meat (201)
ac south meat (4)
ad Sulze [G] (1)

047.2 L liver sausage
No Response (490)
A   blood pudding (1)
B   braunschweiger (1)
C   cheese spread (1)
D   goose liver (7)
E   goose-liver cheese (1)
F   goose-liver sausage (1)
G   hash (48)
H   haslet (6)
I   haslet stew (1)
J   hog haslet (1)
K   hog pudding (1)
L   liver cheese (42)
M   liver dumplings (1)
N   liver hash (23)
O   liver loaf (17)
P   liver mush (17)
Q   liver paste (4)
R   liver pate (1)
S   liver pudding (103)
T   liver roll (1)
U   liver sausage (40)
V   liver spread (2)
W   liverelle (1)
X   liverwurst (60)
Y   pate (7)
Z   pate de foie gras [F] (1)
aa pate de maison [F] (1)
ab pate ordinaire [F] (1)
ac picadillo [S] (2)
ad pudding (6)
ae sausage (2)
af Schwademagen [G] (1)

047.3 L blood sausage
No Response (702)
A   black pudding (2)
B   blood boudin (4)
C   blood cheese (5)
D   blood pie (11)
E   blood pudding (98)
F   blood ring (4)
G   blood sausage (55)
H   boudin [F] (24)
I   dark boudin (1)
J   hog pudding (1)
K   hot tamale (2)
L   morcilla [S] (1)
M   pudding (8)
N   pudding pie (1)
O   red boudin (9)
P   red sausage (1)
Q   sausage (6)
R   white blood pudding (1)
S   white boudin (1)

047.4 L scrapple

No Response (824)
A　cheese, a (1)
B　cornmeal pudding (1)
C　cripple (2)
D　fried souse (2)
E　hash (5)
F　liver bread (1)
G　Panamagen [G] (1)
H　Philadelphia scrapple (2)
I　ponhaws (3)
J　poor joe (1)
K　press meat (1)
L　scramble (1)
M　scrapple (50)

047.5 L rancid [butter]
No Response (180)
A　aged (2)
B　aromatic (1)
C　bad (20)
D　bitter (2)
E　blinky (2)
F　cankered (4)
G　cheese-like (1)
H　cheesy (2)
I　curdled (4)
J　fermented (1)
K　funky (35)
L　funny (1)
M　loud (2)
N　mildewed (1)
O　molded (7)
P　moldy (9)
Q　mushroomy-like (1)
R　musty (3)
S　nasty (1)
T　no-good (5)
U　old (89)
V　puffed (1)
W　putrid (2)
X　rance [F] (4)
Y　ranc(id) (7)
Z　rancid (348)
aa　rank (138)
ab　rankid (1)
ac　rankish (1)
ad　ranky (3)
ae　rotten (6)
af　ruined (23)
ag　sanging (1)
ah　sour (51)
ai　soured (25)
aj　spoiled/spoilt (118)
ak　spunky (1)
al　stale (40)
am　stout (13)
an　strong (78)
ao　tainted (20)
ap　tarnished (1)
aq　turned (1)

ar　white (1)
as　yukky (1)

047.6 L curdled milk
No Response (143)
A　blink [v.] (4)
B　blink [n.] (2)
C　blinked [v./adj.] (7)
D　blinking (1)
E　blinking stage (1)
F　blinks [v.] (2)
G　blinky (11)
H　blinky milk (1)
I　buttermilk (145)
J　clabber [adj.] (1)
K　clabber [v.] (36)
L　clabber [n.] (463)
M　clabber buttermilk (1)
N　clabber milk (76)
O　clabbered [v./adj.] (64)
P　clabbered buttermilk (1)
Q　clabbered milk (65)
R　clabbering (2)
S　clabbers [n.] (2)
T　clabbers [v.] (23)
U　clabbers milk (1)
V　crud [v.] (1)
W　crudded milk (1)
X　cruddy (1)
Y　cruds (1)
Z　curd (11)
aa　curdle (7)
ab　curdle milk (4)
ac　curdled (25)
ad　curdled milk (17)
ae　curdles [v.] (8)
af　curds (13)
ag　drip clabber (1)
ah　lump milk (1)
ai　natural clabber (1)
aj　sour [adj.] (19)
ak　sour [v.] (7)
al　sour buttermilk (3)
am　sour clabber (1)
an　sour cream (9)
ao　sour milk (63)
ap　soured (5)
aq　soured milk (3)
ar　thick (2)
as　thick buttermilk (1)
at　thick milk (1)
au　turn milk (1)
av　whey (2)
aw　wheyed (1)

048.1 L cottage cheese
No Response (286)
A　buttermilk cheese (1)
B　caille [F] (1)
C　caille goutte [F] (2)
D　caso [S] (1)

E　cheese (54)
F　clabber cheese (42)
G　clabber cottage cheese (1)
H　clabbered cheese (6)
I　clabbered-milk cheese (1)
J　college cheese (1)
K　cook case (1)
L　cook cheese (3)
M　cottage (3)
N　cottage cheese (468)
O　cream cheese (62)
P　cream cottage cheese (1)
Q　creole cream cheese (1)
R　curd (17)
S　curd cheese (2)
T　curdled cheese (1)
U　curds (6)
V　drip cheese (1)
W　drip clabber (1)
X　dry cheese (1)
Y　Dutch cheese (2)
Z　farmers cheese (2)
aa　homemade cheese (5)
ab　Kase [G] (1)
ac　Kochkase [G] (1)
ad　milk cheese (3)
ae　pot cheese (2)
af　smearcase (4)
ag　sour cheese (2)
ah　sour milk (1)
ai　sour-cream cheese (1)
aj　sour-milk cheese (2)
ak　white cheese (8)

048.2A P strain
{a}　long upglide
{ai}　lowered onset
{r}　devoiced
{s}　palatal
No Response (234)
<s(t)rain> (1)
<shkr{ai}n> (1)
<shtrain> (2)
<shtr{ai}n> (1)
<sht{r}ain> (1)
<st(r)ain> (2)
<st(r)aind> (1)
<strain> (278)
<strainN=14> (8)
<strainNG=14> (4)
<strainR=14> (7)
<strainRz=14> (2)
<strain[R]=14> (1)
<straind> (18)
<straing> (1)
<strainz> (2)
<streen> (2)
<stren> (1)
<str{ai}n> (19)
<str{ai}nN=14> (1)

<str{ai}nNG=14> (1)
<str{ai}n[R]=14> (1)
<str{a}n> (4)
<st{r}ain> (131)
<st{r}ainN=14> (2)
<st{r}ainNG=14> (6)
<st{r}ainR=14> (6)
<st{r}ain[R]=14> (1)
<st{r}aind> (16)
<st{r}{ai}n> (4)
<thtraind> (1)
<{s}train> (126)
<{s}trainN=14> (3)
<{s}trainNG=14> (2)
<{s}trainR=14> (1)
<{s}trainRz=14> (1)
<{s}train[R]=14> (2)
<{s}traind> (5)
<{s}tr{ai}n> (6)
<{s}tr{ai}nR=14> (1)
<{s}tr{a}n> (1)
<{s}t{r}ain> (10)
<{s}t{r}ainR=14> (1)

048.2 S strain
No Response (0)
|GACeaj| (1)
|GAEeaj| (1)
|GBA| (3)
|GBAdab| (1)
|GBAdad| (1)
|GBAdae| (3)
|GBAeaa| (22)
|GBAeaj| (28)
|GBBeaa| (1)
|GBBeab| (1)
|GBBeaj| (4)
|GBCabc| (1)
|GBCeaa| (20)
|GBCeaj| (39)
|GBE| (4)
|GBEdaa| (1)
|GBEdae| (2)
|GBEeaa| (240)
|GBEeab| (4)
|GBEeac| (1)
|GBEeaj| (69)
|GBFeaa| (6)
|GBFeab| (1)
|GBFeaj| (6)
|GBFmaj| (1)
|GBGeaa| (1)
|GBGeaj| (2)
|GBGeal| (1)
|GBI| (1)
|GBIeaa| (51)
|GBIeaj| (27)
|GBImaj| (1)
|GCCeaa| (1)
|GDIeda| (1)

|GGAeaa| (1)
|GGAeab| (1)
|GGAeaj| (12)
|GGAeak| (1)
|GGB| (2)
|GGBeaa| (3)
|GGBeaj| (3)
|GGCbbj| (1)
|GGCeaa| (10)
|GGCeaj| (12)
|GGEeaa| (76)
|GGEeab| (2)
|GGEeaj| (12)
|GGEeak| (2)
|GGGeaa| (2)
|GGGeaj| (3)
|GGIeaa| (10)
|GGIeaj| (8)
|GHAeda| (2)
|GHAedb| (1)
|GHAedj| (6)
|GHBedj| (3)
|GHC| (2)
|GHCeda| (1)
|GHCedj| (15)
|GHD| (1)
|GHEeda| (11)
|GHEedj| (4)
|GHFedj| (1)
|GHI| (5)
|GHIeda| (35)
|GHIedj| (16)
|GHW| (1)
|GQAedj| (8)
|GQCedj| (3)
|GQEeda| (6)
|GQEedb| (1)
|GQEedj| (6)
|GQFedl| (1)
|GQI| (2)
|GQIeda| (14)
|GQIedj| (7)
|HACeaa| (1)
|HAHeaa| (1)
|KABeaa| (1)
|KABeaj| (1)
|KABmaj| (1)
|KACeaa| (1)
|KACeaj| (1)
|KAGeaa| (1)
|KAIeaa| (1)
|KCAeaa| (2)
|KCBeaa| (1)
|KCEeaa| (1)
|KDCedj| (2)
|KKAeda| (12)
|KKAedj| (6)
|KKCedj| (1)
|KKEeda| (2)

|KKEedj| (1)
|KKIedj| (2)
|LAFeaj| (1)
|OABeaa| (1)
|OAGeaa| (1)
|ODFeda| (1)
|ODFedj| (2)
|OHBedj| (1)
|abcABA| (1)
|gbcGBA| (1)
|kabGBA| (5)
|kkcKDA| (1)

048.2B P milk
{?} glottal
No Response (497)
<me[1]k> (2)
<mee[1]k> (12)
<meelk> (6)
<melk> (5)
<mi(1)g> (1)
<mi[1](k)> (1)
<mi[1]g> (1)
<mi[1]k> (129)
<mil(k)> (2)
<milk> (275)
<mil{?}> (2)
<myi[1]k> (1)
<myilk> (3)

048.3 L cobbler
No Response (188)
A   Betty (3)
B   brown Betty (4)
C   cobbler (535)
D   cobbler pie (59)
E   crisp (3)
F   crunch (1)
G   deep pie (15)
H   deep-dish cobbler (1)
I   deep-dish (pie) (63)
J   deep-pan (pie) (3)
K   dish pie (1)
L   dooby (1)
M   doolunkum (1)
N   duff (1)
O   dumpling (30)
P   dumpling pie (1)
Q   Dutch (pie) (1)
R   Dutch-oven pie (1)
S   family pie (18)
T   family's pie (1)
U   fried pie (9)
V   half-moon pie (2)
W   layer pie (1)
X   lazy pie (1)
Y   pan pie (9)
Z   pandowdy (11)
aa   parch (1)
ab   pastry (1)
ac   patty (1)

ad   pie (255)
ae   pie cobbler (1)
af   plate pie (3)
ag   poor-man's cobbler (1)
ah   poor-man's pie (2)
ai   potpie (6)
aj   roll (1)
ak   scuffle (1)
al   slickum (1)
am   sling (1)
an   slump (1)
ao   sonker (1)
ap   spread pie (1)
aq   stack pie (5)
ar   stew (1)
as   streusel (2)
at   strudel (9)
au   turnover (8)
av   upside-down pie (1)
aw   vinegar cobbler (1)
ax   vinegar pie (3)

048.4 L food

No Response (223)
A   eats (15)
B   chow (10)
C   commodities (1)
D   fat (1)
E   feed (1)
F   food (641)
G   foodstuff (4)
H   fuel (1)
I   groceries (34)
J   grub (35)
K   rations (5)
L   stuff (1)
M   victuals (166)

048.5 L sweet sauce

No Response (500)
A   ambrosia (1)
B   covering (1)
C   cream (3)
D   cream sauce (7)
E   creme patissiere [F] (1)
F   custard sauce (2)
G   dessert topping (1)
H   dip (32)
I   dip sauce (1)
J   drawn sauce (1)
K   dressing (16)
L   hard butter sauce (1)
M   hard sauce (3)
N   pap (1)
O   pudding sauce (1)
P   hush puppy (1)
Q   liquor (1)
R   mixer (1)
S   sauce (283)
T   seasoning (1)
U   sugar syrup (3)

V   sweet cream (1)
W   sweet milk (2)
X   sweet sauce (3)
Y   syllabub (1)
Z   syrup (76)
aa   topping (30)
ab   white sauce (2)

048.6 L snack

No Response (201)
A   a-snacking (2)
B   aftermeal/after meal (3)
C   between meal (1)
D   between-meal lunch (1)
E   between-meal snack (10)
F   bite (19)
G   bite of lunch (1)
H   bite or two, a (2)
I   bite to eat (8)
J   bite [P-0] something to eat (2)
K   brunch (4)
L   coffee break (1)
M   eating between meals (3)
N   evening snack (1)
O   garbage (1)
P   in-between-meal snack (1)
Q   in-between snack (4)
R   junk (2)
S   Klatsch [G] (1)
T   knack (1)
U   knacking (1)
V   knickknack (18)
W   knickknack snack (1)
X   knickknacking (1)
Y   light snack (1)
Z   light supper (1)
aa   little bite (2)
ab   little bite of something (1)
ac   little bite to eat (1)
ad   little lunch, a (5)
ae   little snack (3)
af   little something I can nibble on, a (1)
ag   little treat (1)
ah   lunch (57)
ai   lunch between meals (2)
aj   luncheon (1)
ak   lunching (1)
al   merienda [S] (2)
am   mid-meal (1)
an   mid-meal lunch (1)
ao   midday snack (1)
ap   midevening snack (1)
aq   midmorning snack (1)
ar   morning snack (1)
as   mouth of something to eat (1)
at   munchy/munchies (2)
au   nibbled (1)
av   nibbling (4)
aw   refreshments (1)

ax   sandwich (3)
ay   smack (4)
az   small snack (1)
ba   snack [n.] (624)
bb   snack [v.] (1)
bc   snack around (1)
bd   snack between meals (2)
be   snack in between meals (1)
bf   snacked (1)
bg   snacking (12)
bh   something to eat (2)
bi   Sunday brunch (1)
bj   Sunday-night snack (1)
bk   sweets (1)
bl   tad (1)
bm   taste, a (2)
bn   tea party (1)
bo   tidbit (1)
bp   trash (1)

048.7 G eat

<!>   infinitive
<&>   present 3rd singular
<@>   present participle
<*>   preterit
<#>   past participle
No Response (28)
<!ait> (1)
<!ee(t)> (1)
<!eed> (2)
<!eet> (813)
<!eets> (6)
<!et> (1)
<!it> (1)
<!yeet> (2)
<&eets> (10)
<@eet[NG]=14> (1)
<@eeting=13> (2)
<@eetN=14> (11)
<@eetNG=14> (16)
<*ait> (561)
<*aitN=14> (1)
<*eet> (160)
<*eetN=14> (3)
<*et> (68)
<*it> (4)
<#ait> (81)
<#aitN=14> (10)
<#ee(t)> (1)
<#ee(t)N=14> (3)
<#eed> (1)
<#eedN=14> (2)
<#eet> (206)
<#eet[N]=14> (1)
<#eetId=14> (1)
<#eetN=14> (484)
<#et> (38)
<#etN=14> (1)
<#it> (3)
<#yeetN=14> (2)

048.8 L make (some coffee)
No Response (450)
A   boil (93)
B   brew (37)
C   cook (4)
D   draw (2)
E   drip (8)
F   dripolate (1)
G   fix (31)
H   make (279)
I   percolate (33)
J   perk (87)
K   perkle (1)
L   put on (5)

048.8 P coffee
{f}   bilabial
{o}   upglide
{oe}   lowered onset
{r}   weakly retroflex
No Response (101)
<kafI=14> (1)
<kawfA=14> (3)
<kawfI=14> (666)
<kawfIz=14> (1)
<kawfee=13> (13)
<kawffI=14> (14)
<kawffee=13> (1)
<kaw{f}I=14> (7)
<koefI=14> (5)
<koevI=14> (2)
<kofI=14> (31)
<kowfI=14> (1)
<ko{r}fI=14> (1)
<kufI=14> (1)
<k{oe}fI=14> (18)
<k{oe}ffI=14> (4)
<k{oe}{f}I=14> (4)
<k{o}fI=14> (87)
<k{o}fee=13> (2)
<k{o}ffI=14> (1)
<k{o}{f}I=14> (2)

048.9 G break
<!>   infinitive
<&>   present 3rd singular
<@>   present participle
<*>   preterit
<#>   past participle
No Response (116)
<!brai(k)> (2)
<!braig> (3)
<!braik> (634)
<!bree(k)> (1)
<!brek> (9)
<!bruk> (1)
<&braiks> (10)
<@braiking=13> (1)
<@braikN=14> (6)
<@braikNG=14> (5)
<@brekN=14> (1)

<*b(r)oek> (3)
<*b(r)oekN=14> (1)
<*broe(k)> (2)
<*broek> (631)
<*broekN=14> (4)
<*broek[N]=14> (1)
<*brook> (1)
<*brue(k)> (1)
<*bruk> (2)
<#broeg> (1)
<#broek> (217)
<#broekN=14> (401)
<#broek[N]=14> (1)
<#broekt> (1)
<#brook> (1)
<#bwoek> (1)

048.9A P glass
{a}   upglide
{e}   upglide
{l}   clear
No Response (193)
<gAlas=41> (1)
<g[l]as> (1)
<glas> (493)
<glasIz=14> (18)
<glash> (1)
<glassIz=14> (1)
<glaz> (1)
<gles> (4)
<glos> (2)
<gl{a}s> (151)
<gl{a}sIz=14> (8)
<gl{e}s> (2)
<gras> (1)
<g{l}as> (35)
<g{l}asIz=14> (1)
<g{l}{a}s> (4)

048.9 S glass
No Response (0)
|GGCkaa| (1)
|KCA| (1)
|KCCeaa| (1)
|OAA| (18)
|OAAdaj| (1)
|OAAeaa| (3)
|OAAeac| (1)
|OAAeaj| (44)
|OAAeal| (2)
|OAAeam| (1)
|OAAgbj| (7)
|OAAgbk| (1)
|OAAkaa| (1)
|OAAkaj| (176)
|OAAkak| (5)
|OAAkbj| (9)
|OAAmaj| (1)
|OAB| (17)
|OABeaj| (22)
|OABgbj| (8)

|OABgbl| (2)
|OABkaj| (90)
|OABkak| (1)
|OABkbb| (1)
|OABkbj| (21)
|OABkbk| (2)
|OABmak| (1)
|OAC| (2)
|OACeaj| (3)
|OACgbj| (2)
|OACkaj| (15)
|OAE| (3)
|OAEkaj| (15)
|OAFeaj| (3)
|OAFkaj| (1)
|OAG| (1)
|OAGkaj| (1)
|OAI| (2)
|OAIkaj| (6)
|OASkaj| (1)
|OBA| (2)
|OBAeaa| (3)
|OBAeaj| (34)
|OBAgbj| (2)
|OBAkaj| (15)
|OBAkbj| (3)
|OBAmaj| (1)
|OBB| (1)
|OBBeaj| (4)
|OBBkaj| (2)
|OBBkak| (1)
|OBBkbj| (2)
|OBDeaj| (1)
|OBDkaj| (1)
|OBFeaj| (1)
|OCA| (22)
|OCAeaj| (18)
|OCAeal| (5)
|OCAgba| (1)
|OCAgbj| (6)
|OCAgbl| (1)
|OCAkaa| (4)
|OCAkaj| (126)
|OCAkak| (10)
|OCAkbj| (1)
|OCAkbk| (1)
|OCAmaj| (2)
|OCB| (9)
|OCBeaj| (4)
|OCBkaj| (27)
|OCBkan| (1)
|OCBkbj| (4)
|OCCkaj| (2)
|OCCmaj| (1)
|OCE| (3)
|OCEkaj| (3)
|OCFkaj| (1)
|OCI| (3)
|OCIkaj| (3)

|OCS| (1)
|OGA| (6)
|OGAeaa| (10)
|OGAeaj| (22)
|OGAkaj| (36)
|OGAkak| (1)
|OGAkao| (1)
|OGAkbj| (1)
|OGB| (1)
|OGBeaj| (1)
|OGBkaj| (4)
|OGBmaj| (1)
|OGEkaj| (1)
|OKAkdj| (1)
|PCA| (1)
|SCG| (1)
|cbaOCAkaj| (1)

048.9B P water
{o}   upglide
{oe}   lowered onset
{R}   weakly retroflex
{r}   weakly retroflex
{t}   flap
No Response (64)
<wawd[R]=14> (2)
<wawr(t)[R]=14> (1)
<wawtR=14> (170)
<wawt[R]=14> (220)
<wawt{R}=14> (58)
<waw{r}tR=14> (1)
<waw{r}t{R}=14> (1)
<waw{t}R=14> (32)
<waw{t}[R]=14> (50)
<waw{t}{R}=14> (6)
<woe{t}[R]=14> (1)
<wotR=14> (170)
<wot[R]=14> (64)
<wot{R}=14> (29)
<wo{t}R=14> (27)
<wo{t}[R]=14> (16)
<wo{t}{R}=14> (7)
<w{oe}tR=14> (1)
<w{oe}t[R]=14> (2)
<w{oe}{t}R=14> (3)
<w{oe}{t}[R]=14> (3)
<w{oe}{t}{R}=14> (1)
<w{o}dR=14> (1)
<w{o}tR=14> (45)
<w{o}t[R]=14> (27)
<w{o}t{R}=14> (10)
<w{o}{t}R=14> (4)
<w{o}{t}[R]=14> (3)

049.1 G drink
<!>   infinitive
<&>   present 3rd singular
<@>   present participle
<*>   preterit
<#>   past participle
No Response (80)

<!draink> (12)
<!drank> (13)
<!dreenk> (5)
<!drenk> (167)
<!drenks> (2)
<!drin(k)> (2)
<!drink> (517)
<!drinks> (2)
<!jrink> (3)
<&dranks> (1)
<&drenks> (1)
<&drinks> (8)
<@drainkN=14> (2)
<@drankN=14> (1)
<@drenkN=14> (11)
<@drink> (1)
<@drinkN=14> (15)
<@drinkNG=14> (4)
<*draink> (25)
<*drainkt> (2)
<*dran(k)> (3)
<*dran(k)t> (1)
<*drank> (410)
<*drankt> (8)
<*dreenk> (1)
<*dren(k)t> (3)
<*dreng> (1)
<*drenk> (79)
<*drenkN=14> (2)
<*drenkt> (9)
<*drin(k)> (1)
<*drin(k)t> (1)
<*drink> (24)
<*drinkId=14> (1)
<*drinkN=14> (1)
<*drinkt> (23)
<*drunk> (60)
<*dwinkt> (1)
<*jrank> (2)
<#draink> (11)
<#drainkt> (2)
<#drai[ng](k)> (1)
<#dran(k)t> (1)
<#drank> (195)
<#drankN=14> (9)
<#drankt> (8)
<#dren(k)t> (3)
<#dren(k)tN=14> (1)
<#drenk> (42)
<#drenkN=14> (4)
<#drenkt> (10)
<#drink> (23)
<#drinkN=14> (6)
<#drinkt> (22)
<#droonk> (1)
<#drun(k)> (1)
<#drunk> (237)
<#drunk[N]=14> (1)
<#drunkN=14> (6)

<#drunkt> (1)
<#dru[ng]k> (1)
<#jrank> (2)
<#jrunk> (1)

049.2 G sit down
No Response (298)
A   be seated (83)
B   bring your chair (1)
C   come and sit down (3)
D   come and take a seat (1)
E   come on and sit down (1)
F   come sit down (1)
G   everybody be seated (1)
H   find you a place (1)
I   get a seat (1)
J   get seated (2)
K   get you a chair (1)
L   go ahead and sit (1)
M   go ahead and sit down (2)
N   grab a chair (1)
O   have a chair (8)
P   have a seat (128)
Q   have you a seat (2)
R   have your seat (1)
S   hunker down to the table (1)
T   hunt you a seat (1)
U   let's be seated (6)
V   let's have a seat (1)
W   let's sit down (6)
X   make yourself at home (1)
Y   please be seated (7)
Z   please have a seat (1)
aa   please sit (1)
ab   please sit down (4)
ac   pull up a chair (3)
ad   pull you up a chair (2)
ae   seat yourself (1)
af   set a while (1)
ag   set down (71)
ah   set down there (1)
ai   set here (1)
aj   set right down (2)
ak   sit (14)
al   sit around (2)
am   sit down (353)
an   sit here (2)
ao   sit over here (1)
ap   sit over there (2)
aq   sit right down (1)
ar   sit there (1)
as   take a chair and set down (1)
at   take a seat (and sit down in it) (5)
au   take your seat (2)
av   why don't y'all be seated? (1)
aw   will you have a seat? (1)
ax   won't you be seated please? (1)
ay   won't you have a seat? (1)
az   won't you sit down? (6)

ba   would you be seated? (1)
bb   would you please have a seat?
(2)
bc   y'all be seated (1)
bd   y'all have a seat (2)
be   you-all come sit down (1)
bf   you-all go ahead and sit down
(1)
bg   you-all go set down (1)
bh   you-all have a seat (1)
bi   you-all sit down (1)

049.3 G sit

<!>   infinitive
<&>   present 3rd singular
<@>   present participle
<*>   preterit
<#>   past participle
{t}   flap
{?}   glottal
No Response (141)
<!se(t)> (56)
<!sed> (2)
<!see(t)> (2)
<!seet> (3)
<!set> (134)
<!se{t}> (3)
<!si(t)> (233)
<!sid> (1)
<!sit> (402)
<!sits> (1)
<!si{?}> (6)
<!si{t}> (12)
<!su(t)> (2)
<!sut> (2)
<!thi{t}> (1)
<&sets> (9)
<&si(t)s> (1)
<&sits> (22)
<&thi(t)> (1)
<@AsetN=414> (4)
<@setN=14> (40)
<@seting=13> (1)
<@se{?}N=14> (1)
<@sidN=14> (1)
<@sitN=14> (31)
<@sitNG=14> (15)
<@siting=13> (1)
<*sa(t)> (30)
<*sat> (279)
<*sa{?}> (2)
<*sa{t}> (4)
<*se(t)> (49)
<*sed> (4)
<*see(t)> (1)
<*set> (115)
<*se{?}> (4)
<*si(t)> (35)
<*sid> (2)
<*sit> (46)

<*si{?}> (1)
<*si{t}> (1)
<*so(t)> (2)
<*sot> (7)
<*sut> (1)
<#sa(t)> (9)
<#sat> (186)
<#sa{?}> (2)
<#sa{t}> (1)
<#se(t)> (23)
<#sed> (3)
<#set> (72)
<#si(t)> (30)
<#sidN=14> (1)
<#sit> (43)
<#sitN=14> (5)
<#si{?}> (1)
<#so(t)> (1)
<#su(t)> (1)
<#sut> (1)
<#thi(t)> (1)

049.4 G help yourself

No Response (314)
A   come and help yourself (2)
B   dig in (5)
C   dive in (3)
D   fix your own plate (1)
E   get it yourself (3)
F   get some (2)
G   get you some (1)
H   get you something to eat (1)
I   get yours (2)
J   go ahead (5)
K   go ahead and begin (1)
L   go ahead and dip (1)
M   go ahead and get some (4)
N   go ahead and help yourself (6)
O   go ahead and make yourself at
home (1)
P   go ahead and reach (4)
Q   go ahead and take it (1)
R   go ahead and take some out (1)
S   go ahead and use it (1)
T   go ahead and use your
boardinghouse reach (1)
U   go help yourself (1)
V   have some (45)
W   help the plates (2)
X   help your own self (2)
Y   help your plate (7)
Z   help yourself (485)
aa   jump in and help yourself (1)
ab   just help yourself (4)
ac   make a long arm and reach for
what you want (1)
ad   pass it yourself (1)
ae   pitch in and help yourself (1)
af   please have some (1)
ag   please help yourself (3)

ah   reach and get it (6)
ai   reach and get what you want (1)
aj   reach and help yourself (1)
ak   reach for it (4)
al   serve your plate (1)
am   serve yourself (57)
an   take it (1)
ao   take out (5)
ap   take some (9)
aq   take your share (1)
ar   try it (1)
as   wait on your own self (1)
at   wait on yourself (6)
au   y'all help yourself[M-i] (2)

049.5 G help

<!>   infinitive
<&>   present 3rd singular
<@>   present participle
<*>   preterit
<#>   past participle
{l}   flap
No Response (59)
<!halp> (3)
<!he(1)p> (248)
<!he[1]p> (261)
<!help> (335)
<!helps> (1)
<!helpt> (1)
<!he{l}p> (1)
<!hi(1)p> (5)
<!hi[1]p> (8)
<!hilp> (1)
<!hoe(1)p> (3)
<!hoelp> (1)
<!hulp> (3)
<!hye(1)p> (1)
<&he(1)ps> (6)
<&he[1]ps> (7)
<&he[1]psh> (1)
<&helps> (6)
<&hulps> (1)
<@he(1)pN=14> (1)
<@he[1]pN=14> (12)
<@he[1]pNG=14> (3)
<@helpN=14> (5)
<@helpNG=14> (1)
<@hi[1]pN=14> (1)
<@hulpNG=14> (1)
<*(h)e[1]pt> (1)
<*hai(1)pt> (1)
<*halpt> (1)
<*he(1)p> (21)
<*he(1)pt> (115)
<*he[1]p> (16)
<*he[1]pt> (198)
<*help> (21)
<*helpt> (239)
<*hi(1)p> (1)
<*hi(1)pt> (1)

<*hi[1]pt> (3)
<*hilp> (1)
<*hoe(1)p> (26)
<*hoe(1)pt> (8)
<*hoe[1]p> (2)
<*hoelp> (17)
<*hulpt> (2)
<*hyelpt> (1)
<#hai[1]p> (1)
<#hai[1]pt> (1)
<#he(1)p> (9)
<#he(1)pt> (59)
<#he[1]p> (18)
<#he[1]pt> (100)
<#help> (12)
<#helpt> (159)
<#hi(1)pt> (1)
<#hi[1]pt> (2)
<#hilpt> (1)
<#hoe(1)p> (15)
<#hoe(1)pt> (8)
<#hoe[1]pt> (3)
<#hoelp> (7)

049.6 G I don't care for any

No Response (240)
A   don't feed me (that) (1)
B   don't give me none (1)
C   excuse me (1)
D   get that away from me (1)
E   I appreciate it (1)
F   I believe I'll pass on that (1)
G   I believe not (1)
H   I can't cut it (1)
I   I can't digest it (1)
J   I can't do nothing with it (1)
K   I can't eat (that) (6)
L   I don't aim to eat (1)
M   I don't believe (1)
N   I don't believe I can eat (any) (2)
O   I don't believe I care for (any) (9)
P   I don't believe I do (1)
Q   I don't believe I want (to eat any) (5)
R   I don't believe I [V-0] a meal right now (1)
S   I don't believe I'd care for that (2)
T   I don't believe I'd have some (1)
U   I don't believe I'd take (any) (2)
V   I don't believe I('d) want (any) (7)
W   I don't believe I'll have (any) (5)
X   I don't believe I'll partake of that (1)
Y   I don't care (1)
Z   I don't care about (it) (7)

aa   I don't care for (any) (384)
ab   I don't care to (eat) (4)
ac   I don't choose to have this (1)
ad   I don't eat (that) (25)
ae   I don't like (that) (47)
af   I don't need it (1)
ag   I don't prefer that (1)
ah   I don't think I care for any (1)
ai   I don't think I'd like any (1)
aj   I don't think I'd want any (1)
ak   I don't think I'll have any (1)
al   I don't want (any) (138)
am   I don't want to eat (now) (3)
an   I never cared that much for (it) (1)
ao   I never did care for (them) (3)
ap   I never eat that (1)
aq   I never touch the stuff (1)
ar   I won't eat them (1)
as   I won't have it (1)
at   I wouldn't care for (any) (49)
au   I wouldn't choose (that) (3)
av   I wouldn't like it (1)
aw   I wouldn't want any of it (1)
ax   I'll eat that some other time (1)
ay   I'll let somebody else enjoy that (1)
az   I('ll) pass (5)
ba   I'm not allowed to eat (that) (1)
bb   I'm not hungry (9)
bc   I'm sorry (1)
bd   it doesn't agree with me (1)
be   maybe some other time (1)
bf   no, thank you (95)
bg   no, thank you, I don't (1)
bh   no, thank you, I wouldn't (1)
bi   no, thanks (15)
bj   noway (1)
bk   pass it on (1)
bl   thank you (very much) (27)

050.1 L warmed-over

No Response (482)
A   carried-over food (1)
B   coldovers (1)
C   cooked-over food (3)
D   hand-me-down food (1)
E   hash (2)
F   leave overs (1)
G   leftover food (6)
H   leftovers (387)
I   (left)overs (1)
J   old food (1)
K   remainders (1)
L   repeat [n.] (1)
M   rerun [n.] (2)
N   scraps (2)
O   second serving (1)
P   secondhanded food (2)
Q   seconds (5)

R   warm-ups (3)
S   warmed-over dinner (1)
T   warmed-over food (15)
U   warmed-over meal (2)
V   warmed-over stuff (1)
W   warmed-over supper (2)
X   warmed overs (14)
Y   warmed-up food (5)
Z   warmed-up leftovers (2)

050.2 P chew

No Response (163)
<chaw> (2)
<chawN=14> (1)
<chee> (1)
<cheez> (1)
<chew> (183)
<chewNG=14> (2)
<chewd> (1)
<chewz> (1)
<choo> (3)
<chow> (1)
<chue> (529)
<chueN=14> (9)
<chueNG=14> (4)
<chued> (5)
<chuewN=14> (2)
<chuewNG=14> (1)
<chuez> (2)
<chyoo> (1)
<chyue> (5)
<shue> (2)
<tew> (1)
<tyue> (1)

050.3 L mush

No Response (266)
A   broth (1)
B   chicken dressing (1)
C   cold sandwich (1)
D   corn gruel (1)
E   corn mush (28)
F   corn pudding (3)
G   corn-bread mush (4)
H   corn-bread pudding (2)
I   cornmeal gruel (1)
J   cornmeal mush (59)
K   cornmeal pudding (2)
L   cornmeal soup (3)
M   cream of wheat (1)
N   cush (65)
O   cush-cush (28)
P   dog mush (1)
Q   dressing (1)
R   fried mush (8)
S   goulash (1)
T   gruel (54)
U   Indian pudding (2)
V   Indian-corn pudding (1)
W   liver mush (1)
X   meal gruel (2)

Y   meal mush (2)
Z   mull (1)
aa   mush (459)
ab   mush meal (1)
ac   mush-mush (1)
ad   poor do (1)
ae   poor-man's pudding (1)
af   pudding (2)
ag   turn mush [n.] (1)
050.4 P vegetables
{d}   devoiced
{e}   upglide
{j}   devoiced
{L}   labial
{t}   flap
{v}   bilabial
{z}   devoiced
{zh}   devoiced
No Response (142)
<bechtAbLz=144> (1)
<vaijtIbLz=144> (1)
<vaj(t)AbLz=144> (1)
<vajtIbLz=144> (1)
<vashtIbLz=144> (1)
<ve(j)tIbLz=144> (1)
<ve(j)tIbL{z}=144> (1)
<ve(j){t}(I)bL(z)=14> (1)
<vech(t)AbL=144> (1)
<vech(t)AbLz=144> (2)
<vech(t)IbLz=144> (1)
<vech(tI)bL=14> (1)
<vechAtibL=1434> (1)
<vechItAbL{z}=1444> (1)
<vechdAbL=144> (1)
<vechdAbLz=144> (3)
<vechdAbL{z}=144> (1)
<vechdIbLz=144> (1)
<vechtAbL=144> (4)
<vechtAbLz=144> (26)
<vechtAbL{z}=144> (8)
<vechtAbulz=143> (3)
<vechtIbL(z)=144> (2)
<vechtIbL=144> (3)
<vechtIbLz=144> (23)
<vechtIbL{z}=144> (3)
<vechtibL{z}=134> (1)
<ved(t)AbL{z}=144> (1)
<vedItibulz=1423> (1)
<vedshtAbLs=144> (1)
<vedshtAbL{z}=144> (2)
<vedshtIbLz=144> (2)
<vedshtIbL{z}=144> (1)
<vedshtIbool=143> (1)
<vedshtIbueL{z}=1434> (1)
<vedstAbLz=144> (1)
<vej(t)A(b)L{z}=144> (1)
<vej(t)AbL(z)=144> (1)
<vej(t)AbL=144> (3)
<vej(t)AbLdh=144> (1)

<vej(t)AbLz=144> (6)
<vej(t)AbL{z}=144> (1)
<vej(t)IbL(z)=144> (3)
<vej(t)IbL=144> (8)
<vej(t)IbLz=144> (20)
<vej(t)IbL{z}=144> (4)
<vej(t)Ib[L](z)=144> (2)
<vej(t)Ib[L]=144> (2)
<vej(t)Ib[L]z=144> (1)
<vej(t)Ib[L]{z}=144> (1)
<vej(t)Ib{L}z=144> (1)
<vej(t)ibL(z)=134> (1)
<vej(tIb)[L]z=14> (1)
<vej(tI)bL=14> (1)
<vej(tI)bLz=14> (2)
<vejAtAbLz=1444> (1)
<vejAtIbLz=1444> (1)
<vejAtaibLz=3414> (1)
<vejIdIbulz=1443> (1)
<vejItAbLz=1444> (5)
<vejItAbL{z}=1444> (1)
<vejItAb[L]{z}=1444> (1)
<vejItAbulz=1443> (1)
<vejItIbLz=1444> (10)
<vejItIbulz=1443> (1)
<vejItIbul{z}=1443> (1)
<vejItaibL=1434> (1)
<vejItaibLz=1434> (1)
<vejItebL=1434> (2)
<vejItebLz=1434> (1)
<vejIteb[L]z=1434> (1)
<vejItibLz=1434> (2)
<vejItoobL=1434> (1)
<vejItubLz=1434> (1)
<vejItubL{z}=1434> (1)
<vejIt{e}bLz=1434> (2)
<vejdAbLz=144> (2)
<vejdIbL(z)=144> (1)
<vejdIbL=144> (1)
<vejdIbLz=144> (1)
<vejdIb[L]z=144> (1)
<vejit(bLz)=13> (1)
<vejitAbLz=1344> (3)
<vejitAbL{z}=1344> (1)
<vejitAb[L]{z}=1344> (1)
<vejitubL=1324> (1)
<vejitubLz=1334> (1)
<vejt(Ib)L=14> (1)
<vejtAbL=144> (11)
<vejtAbLdh=144> (1)
<vejtAbLs=144> (1)
<vejtAbLz=144> (99)
<vejtAbL{z}=144> (1)
<vejtAb[L]z=144> (3)
<vejtAb[L]{z}=144> (1)
<vejtAbulz=143> (4)
<vejtAbul{z}=143> (1)
<vejtAb{L}z=144> (1)
<vejtIbL(z)=144> (3)

<vejtIbL=144> (28)
<vejtIbLz=144> (134)
<vejtIbL{z}=144> (44)
<vejtIb[L]=144> (1)
<vejtIb[L]z=144> (4)
<vejtIb[L]{z}=144> (5)
<vejtIbuel=143> (1)
<vejtIbuelz=143> (1)
<vejtIbuel{z}=143> (1)
<vejtIbulz=143> (2)
<vejtIbul{z}=143> (1)
<vejtIb{L}z=144> (1)
<vejtI{v}L{z}=144> (1)
<vejtebL=134> (1)
<vejtebL=314> (1)
<vejtebLz=134> (1)
<vejtibL=134> (2)
<vejtibLz=134> (12)
<vejtobLz=134> (1)
<vejtobL{z}=134> (1)
<vejtubLz=134> (1)
<vejt{e}bLz=134> (1)
<vejztAbLz=144> (1)
<vej{d}IbLz=144> (1)
<vej{t}AbL=144> (1)
<vej{t}AbLz=144> (1)
<vej{t}IbLz=144> (1)
<vej{t}IbL{z}=144> (2)
<vesh(t)Ab[L]{z}=144> (1)
<vesh(tI)bL=14> (1)
<veshitAbLz=1344> (1)
<veshtAbLdh=144> (1)
<veshtAbLz=144> (2)
<veshtAbL{z}=144> (2)
<veshtAbulz=143> (1)
<veshtIbL=144> (3)
<veshtIbLz=144> (4)
<veshtIbL{z}=144> (2)
<veshtIbuel=143> (1)
<veshtIbul=143> (1)
<vestAbLz=144> (1)
<vestAb[L]{z}=144> (1)
<vestIbLz=144> (1)
<vetstAbLz=144> (1)
<vetstIbLz=144> (1)
<vezh(t)AbL(z)=144> (1)
<vezh(t)AbLz=144> (1)
<vezh(t)ibLz=134> (1)
<vezhItob[L]s=1434> (1)
<vezhItubL{z}=1434> (1)
<vezhd(I)bLz=14> (1)
<vezhdAbL=144> (1)
<vezhitAbLz=1344> (1)
<vezht(I)bLz=14> (1)
<vezht(I)bL{z}=14> (1)
<vezhtAbL=144> (1)
<vezhtAbLz=144> (8)
<vezhtAb{L}z=144> (1)
<vezhtIbL(z)=144> (1)

<vezhtIbL=144> (3)
<vezhtIbLz=144> (8)
<vezhtIbL{z}=144> (4)
<vezhtIb[L]z=144> (1)
<vezhtIb[L]{z}=144> (2)
<vezhtibLz=134> (1)
<veztAbL{z}=144> (1)
<veztIbLz=144> (1)
<ve{d}shtAbulz=143> (1)
<ve{d}shtIbLz=144> (1)
<ve{d}shtIbL{z}=144> (1)
<ve{d}shtIbuel{z}=143> (2)
<ve{j}(t)AbL{z}=144> (1)
<ve{j}(t)IbL=144> (1)
<ve{j}(t)IbLz=144> (1)
<ve{j}(t)IbL{z}=144> (3)
<ve{j}(t)Ib[L]{z}=144> (1)
<ve{j}ItIbLz=1444> (1)
<ve{j}tAbL(z)=144> (1)
<ve{j}tAbL=144> (4)
<ve{j}tAbLz=144> (22)
<ve{j}tAbL{d}{z}=144> (1)
<ve{j}tAbL{z}=144> (2)
<ve{j}tAb[L]z=144> (1)
<ve{j}tAbul{z}=143> (2)
<ve{j}tIbL(z)=144> (1)
<ve{j}tIbL=144> (8)
<ve{j}tIbLt=144> (1)
<ve{j}tIbLz=144> (28)
<ve{j}tIbL{z}=144> (19)
<ve{j}tIb[L]z=144> (1)
<ve{j}tIb[L]{z}=144> (4)
<ve{j}tIbul{z}=143> (1)
<ve{j}tibLz=134> (1)
<ve{j}{d}IbL{z}=144> (1)
<ve{t}tAbLz=144> (1)
<ve{zh}(t)IbL{z}=144> (1)
<ve{zh}htAbLz=144> (1)
<ve{zh}tIbL=144> (2)
<ve{zh}tIbL{z}=144> (2)
<ve{zh}tIb[L]=144> (1)
<ve{zh}tIb[L]{z}=144> (1)
<ve{zh}{d}IbLz=144> (1)
<ve{z}tIbL{z}=144> (1)
<vichtAbL{z}=144> (1)
<vidsii(tI)bL(z)=14> (1)
<vid{zh}tAbLdh=144> (1)
<vijigAbLz=1344> (1)
<vijtAbLs=144> (1)
<vijtIbL=144> (1)
<vijtIbLz=144> (2)
<vizhtIbLz=144> (1)
<vi{j}tAbL{z}=144> (1)
<vi{zh}tibL=134> (1)
<vujtIbLz=144> (1)
<v{e}chtAbLz=144> (3)
<v{e}dtAbLz=144> (1)
<v{e}j(t)AbL=144> (1)
<v{e}j(t)AbLz=144> (5)

<v{e}j(tI)bLz=14> (2)
<v{e}jdAbL=144> (2)
<v{e}jdAbLz=144> (1)
<v{e}jtAbL=144> (1)
<v{e}jtAbLz=144> (19)
<v{e}jtAbL{z}=144> (1)
<v{e}jtAbulz=143> (1)
<v{e}jtIbLz=144> (1)
<v{e}sht(I)bLz=14> (1)
<v{e}zhtIbL{z}=144> (1)
<v{e}{j}tAbL=144> (1)
<v{e}{j}tAbLz=144> (2)
<we{j}tIbL{z}=144> (1)
<{v}echtIbLdh=144> (1)
<{v}echtIb[L]z=144> (1)
<{v}echtIb[L]{z}=144> (1)
<{v}edsh(t)IbL{z}=144> (1)
<{v}ejItAbLs=1444> (1)
<{v}eshtAb[L]{z}=144> (1)
<{v}eshtIb[L]{z}=144> (2)
<{v}eshtIbu[l]sh=143> (1)
<{v}id(t)Ab[L]=144> (1)
<{v}i{j}tAbLsh=144> (1)
<{v}i{j}tIbLsh=144> (1)

050.5 L garden

No Response (57)
A back-door garden (1)
B backyard (1)
C backyard garden (1)
D city garden (1)
E community garden (1)
F dirt garden (1)
G fall garden (1)
H family garden (4)
I flower bed (3)
J flower garden (15)
K garden (819)
L garden area (1)
M garden farm (1)
N garden patch (5)
O garden place (1)
P garden plot (4)
Q garden spot (13)
R herb garden (1)
S home garden (5)
T house garden (1)
U kitchen garden (3)
V Mexican garden (1)
W orchard (1)
X patch (10)
Y patch garden (1)
Z patch of ground (1)
aa plant bed (1)
ab plastic garden (1)
ac plot (2)
ad rock garden (1)
ae rose garden (2)
af spring garden (2)
ag summer garden (3)

ah table garden (1)
ai truck garden (4)
aj truck patch (29)
ak vegetable garden (45)
al vegetable patch (7)
am victory garden (2)
an yard (2)
ao year-round garden (1)
ap year-round vegetable garden (1)

050.5 P garden

{d} devoiced
{o} low-back
{oe} lowered onset
{r} weakly retroflex
{t} flap
{z} devoiced
{?} glottal

No Response (57)
<gaw(r)dN=14> (6)
<gaw(r)dNG=14> (1)
<gaw[r]dN=14> (21)
<gaw[r]dNz=14> (1)
<gawrdN(z)=14> (1)
<gawrdN=14> (63)
<gawrdNz=14> (3)
<gawr{t}N=14> (1)
<gawr{?}Nz=14> (1)
<gaw{r}dN=14> (8)
<gaw{r}tN=14> (1)
<go(r)dN=14> (61)
<go(r)dNz=14> (1)
<go(r)dN{z}=14> (1)
<go(r){d}N=14> (1)
<go[r]dN=14> (59)
<go[r]dNz=14> (3)
<go[r]{d}N=14> (1)
<gor(d)N=14> (2)
<gor(d)Nz=14> (1)
<gordN=14> (418)
<gordNG=14> (1)
<gordNz=14> (13)
<gordN{z}=14> (1)
<gord[N]=14> (1)
<gordun=13> (1)
<gor{d}N=14> (4)
<gor{d}Nz=14> (1)
<gor{t}N=14> (3)
<go{r}(d)N=14> (1)
<go{r}d(N)> (1)
<go{r}dN=14> (77)
<go{r}dNz=14> (2)
<gyo(r)dN=14> (3)
<gyo[r]dN=14> (1)
<gyo{r}dN=14> (1)
<gy{o}rdNz=14> (1)
<g{oe}[r]dN{z}=14> (1)
<g{o}(rd)N=14> (1)
<g{o}(r)dN=14> (18)
<g{o}[r]dN=14> (41)

<g{o}[r]dNz=14> (7)
<g{o}[r]dN{z}=14> (1)
<g{o}[r]d[N]=14> (1)
<g{o}[r]tN=14> (1)
<g{o}rdN=14> (115)
<g{o}rdNz=14> (5)
<g{o}rdN{z}=14> (1)
<g{o}{r}dN=14> (12)

050.6A L grits
No Response (224)
A coarse grits (3)
B corn grits (5)
C fine grits (2)
D Georgia ice cream (1)
E grist (1)
F grits (661)
G ground hominy (2)
H heart of the corn (1)
I homemade grits (1)
J homily (1)
K homily grits (1)
L hominy (6)
M hominy grits (48)
N little hominy (2)
O yellow grits (4)

050.6B L hominy
No Response (300)
A big hominy (16)
B coarse hominy (1)
C corn hominy (1)
D homily (25)
E hominies (1)
F hominy (523)
G hominy corn (3)
H lye corn (9)
I lye homily (6)
J lye hominy (59)
K lyed corn (4)
L lyed hominy (3)
M white hominy (1)
N whole-grained hominy (1)
O yellow hominy (1)

050.7 P rice
{ie} monophthong/short glide
No Response (107)
<ries> (603)
<rieth> (2)
<r{ie}s> (215)
<r{ie}sh> (1)

050.8 L moonshine
No Response (104)
[whiskey and wine]
A aguardiente (1)
B apple cider (2)
C applejack (2)
D backing(s) (3)
E bad booze (1)
F bad moonshine (1)
G bad whiskey (2)

H barn liquor (1)
I bathtub gin (12)
J bathtub whiskey (1)
K bayou water (1)
L black pot (1)
M blackberry wine (4)
N blind tiger (1)
O blind-tiger liquor (1)
P blue john (1)
Q bootleg (100)
R bootleg booze (1)
S bootleg liquor (13)
T bootleg moonshine (1)
U bootleg stuff (1)
V bootleg whiskey (48)
W bootlegged liquor (1)
X bootlegged whiskey (3)
Y bootlegging (whiskey) (3)
Z booze (30)
aa brand XXX (1)
ab brandy (3)
ac brew (1)
ad brier(-)patch (whiskey) (2)
ae buck head (1)
af bug-eyed (1)
ag bulk (1)
ah bulkhead (1)
ai bust skull (4)
aj busthead (4)
ak cane buck (3)
al cane-skimming whiskey (1)
am cane(-)skimmings (liquor) (3)
an cat (whiskey) (2)
ao cheap booze (1)
ap cheap whiskey (7)
aq Christmas whiskey (1)
ar cider (2)
as coal-oil johnny (1)
at corn (1)
au corn buck (5)
av corn gin (1)
aw corn juice (1)
ax corn lightning (1)
ay corn liquor (40)
az corn mash (1)
ba corn squeezings (10)
bb corn whiskey (49)
bc crystal (1)
bd crystal clear (1)
be dewberry wine (1)
bf dram, a (1)
bg dry rot (1)
bh explode [n.] (1)
bi eye-opener (1)
bj firewater (2)
bk four hundred and ten rebreak (1)
bl glucken (1)
bm Golden Pa liquor (1)
bn good whiskey (1)

bo gosh (2)
bp grape (1)
bq grape jack (1)
br grape whiskey (1)
bs grape wine (5)
bt gray mule (1)
bu grease lightning (1)
bv green whiskey (1)
bw groundhog whiskey (1)
bx gunpowder whiskey (1)
by gut rot (2)
bz happy juice (1)
ca hard cider (1)
cb hog and hair (1)
cc hog and hominy (1)
cd home brew (14)
ce homemade liquor (6)
cf homemade scald cat (1)
cg homemade shine (2)
ch homemade whiskey (7)
ci homemade wine (4)
cj hootch (3)
ck horse piss (1)
cl hundred-and-ten proof (1)
cm illegal liquor (1)
cn illegal whiskey (1)
co illicit whiskey (1)
cp jake leg (1)
cq Joe Louis (3)
cr joy juice (1)
cs julep (1)
ct Kickapoo Joy Juice (1)
cu knockum (1)
cv laughing water (1)
cw lightning (2)
cx liquor (38)
cy low(-)grade (whiskey) (2)
cz low wine (4)
da malt liquor (1)
db mash (whiskey) (19)
dc moonshine (483)
dd moonshine gosh (1)
de moonshine liquor (8)
df moonshine whiskey (26)
dg (mo)squito juice (1)
dh mountain dew (15)
di mountain juice (1)
dj muscadine (wine) (4)
dk mustang wine (1)
dl nectar (1)
dm old moonshine (1)
dn old rum liquor (1)
do old whiskey (1)
dp outlaw (1)
dq outlawed whiskey (1)
dr packing ham (1)
ds panther piss (1)
dt peach brandy (5)

du   please don't fight in the house (1)
dv   poison liquor (1)
dw   poison whiskey (3)
dx   poontang (2)
dy   popeyed (1)
dz   popskull (16)
ea   pot liquor (1)
eb   prune-and-raisin wine (1)
ec   punch (1)
ed   pure corn (whiskey) (3)
ee   pure grain alcohol (1)
ef   recipe, the (1)
eg   red-eye (6)
eh   roasting-ear cordial (1)
ei   rotgut (whiskey) (67)
ej   rum (6)
ek   rye (whiskey) (7)
el   saki (2)
em   scald cat (1)
en   scrap iron (1)
eo   shake a leg (1)
ep   sheep dip (1)
eq   shimmy (1)
er   shine (15)
es   shinny (whiskey) (30)
et   sizzling (1)
eu   skag (1)
ev   skaw (1)
ew   skimmings (1)
ex   skull bust(er) (2)
ey   slop (3)
ez   snake piss (1)
fa   something grain (1)
fb   sorry grade of whiskey (1)
fc   sorry whiskey (1)
fd   sorry wildcat whiskey (1)
fe   sour mash (whiskey) (3)
ff   spirits (1)
fg   splo (whiskey) (10)
fh   squeezings (1)
fi   squirrel whiskey (1)
fj   still whiskey (1)
fk   stomach buster (1)
fl   stoop/stop (2)
fm   stump (3)
fn   stump fit (1)
fo   stump-hole juice (1)
fp   stump juice (7)
fq   stump liquor (5)
fr   stump rum (4)
fs   stump water (5)
ft   stump whiskey (1)
fu   sugar whiskey (1)
fv   sweet cider (1)
fw   Sweet Lucy (2)
fx   syrup liquor (1)
fy   tanglefoot (1)
fz   thicket whiskey (1)

ga   unstamp whiskey (1)
gb   whiskey (159)
gc   white corn (liquor) (2)
gd   white corn whiskey (3)
ge   white jack (1)
gf   white lightning (298)
gg   white liquor (3)
gh   white meal (1)
gi   white mule (whiskey) (12)
gj   white whiskey (7)
gk   wildcat (19)
gl   wildcat liquor (1)
gm   wildcat piss (1)
gn   wildcat stuff (1)
go   wildcat whiskey (10)
gp   wine home brew (1)
gq   wood alcohol (2)
[beer]
ha   bad beer (1)
hb   beer (47)
hc   bootleg beer (1)
hd   brew (9)
he   buck (9)
hf   California beer (1)
hg   California seed beer (1)
hh   cane beer (4)
hi   cane skimmings (3)
hj   corn beer (3)
hk   corn buck (1)
hl   green beer (1)
hm   home brew (beer) (239)
hn   homemade beer (9)
ho   homemade brew (3)
hp   locust beer (2)
hq   loggerhead beer (1)
hr   malt (1)
hs   malt liquor (1)
ht   persimmon beer (7)
hu   potato beer (1)
hv   second beer (1)
hw   seed beer (1)
hx   skimmings (2)
hy   spruce beer (1)
hz   thicklen (1)

051.1 G smell (that)
No Response (306)
A   smell (357)
B   smell of (43)
C   taste (7)
D   taste of (16)
051.2 G molasses is
No Response (562)
A   molasses [pl.] (46)
B   molasses [sing.] (43)
C   molasses are/were (42)
D   molasses is/was (238)
E   molasses [C-0] (6)
051.2 L molasses
No Response (144)

A   black joe (4)
B   black molasses (4)
C   black syrup (1)
D   blackjack molasses (1)
E   blackstrap (11)
F   blackstrap molasses (20)
G   cane juice (2)
H   cane molasses (3)
I   cane syrup (4)
J   colored-folks' molasses (1)
K   flapjack molasses (1)
L   homemade syrup (1)
M   long sweetening (4)
N   Louisiana molasses (1)
O   (mo)lasses (20)
P   molas(ses) (3)
Q   molasses (693)
R   ribbon-cane molasses (2)
S   sorghum (135)
T   sorghum molas(ses) (1)
U   sorghum molasses (61)
V   sorghum molasses syrup (1)
W   sorghum stuff (1)
X   sorghum syrup (12)
Y   sugarcane molasses (3)
Z   sumac molasses (1)
aa   sweetening (2)
ab   syrup (42)
ac   thick syrup (1)
051.2 P molasses
{a}   upglide
{e}   upglide
{R}   weakly retroflex
{z}   devoiced
{?}   glottal
No Resposne (174)
<(mA)lasI(z)=14> (1)
<(mA)lasIs=14> (1)
<(mA)lasIz=14> (10)
<(mA)lasI{z}=14> (1)
<(mA)l{a}sIz=14> (6)
<MlasIs=414> (1)
<MlasIz=414> (10)
<MlasI{z}=414> (1)
<Ml{a}sIz=414> (2)
<bAlasI(z)=414> (1)
<mAlaisI{z}=414> (2)
<mAlas(Iz)=41> (2)
<mAlasA(z)=414> (1)
<mAlasI(z)=414> (15)
<mAlasIdh=414> (1)
<mAlasIs=414> (55)
<mAlasIt=414> (1)
<mAlasIz=414> (449)
<mAlasI{?}=414> (2)
<mAlasI{z}=414> (72)
<mAlashI{z}=414> (1)
<mAlasiz=413> (2)
<mAlaskIz=414> (1)

<mAlassAz=414> (1)
<mAlassId=414> (1)
<mAlassIdh=414> (1)
<mAlassIs=414> (4)
<mAlassIz=414> (11)
<mAlassI{z}=414> (2)
<mAlassis=413> (1)
<mAlassiz=413> (1)
<mAlathsI(z)=414> (1)
<mAlazIz=414> (5)
<mAla{z}Is=414> (1)
<mAlesIz=414> (3)
<mAlessIz=414> (1)
<mAlosI(z)=414> (1)
<mAlosIs=414> (1)
<mAlosIz=414> (1)
<mAlussIz=414> (1)
<mAl{a}s(Iz)=41> (1)
<mAl{a}sIs=414> (3)
<mAl{a}sIts=414> (1)
<mAl{a}sIz=414> (64)
<mAl{a}sI{z}=414> (3)
<mAl{a}zIz=414> (1)
<mAl{e}sIz=414> (2)
<mAl{e}sI{z}=414> (3)
<mIlasAz=414> (1)
<mIlasIdh=414> (1)
<mIlasIs=414> (2)
<mIlasIz=414> (14)
<mIlasI{z}=414> (1)
<mIlassId=414> (1)
<mIlassI{z}=414> (1)
<mIl{a}sIz=414> (2)
<mIl{a}sI{z}=414> (2)
<mIl{e}sI{z}=414> (1)
<mLasIz=414> (4)
<mLlasIz=414> (5)
<mLl{a}sIz=414> (7)
<mL{a}sIz=414> (13)
<malasI{z}=314> (1)
<milasIs=314> (1)
<moelasIz=134> (1)
<moelasIz=314> (3)
<moelasI{z}=314> (2)
<molasIt=314> (1)
<molasIz=314> (1)
<molasI{z}=314> (1)
<muel{a}sIz=314> (7)
<mulaisIz=314> (1)
<mulasIz=214> (1)
<mulasIz=314> (6)
<mulasI{z}=314> (1)
<mul{a}sIz=314> (2)
<mul{a}sI{z}=314> (1)
<m{R}lasIz=414> (1)

051.3 L syrup
No Response (85)
A bought syrup (1)
B cane syrup (47)

C corn syrup (17)
D country syrup (1)
E Georgia cane syrup (2)
F Georgia syrup (1)
G green-cane syrup (1)
H homemade maple syrup (1)
I homemade syrup (2)
J honeydew syrup (1)
K light and heavy syrup (1)
L long sweetening (5)
M Louisiana (2)
N Louisiana pure cane syrup (2)
O Louisiana syrup (2)
P maple syrup (110)
Q molasses (2)
R pancake syrup (2)
S pure-old cane syrup (1)
T ribbon-cane syrup (13)
U simple syrup (1)
V sirop (de batterie) [F] (2)
W soft molasses (1)
X sopping (1)
Y sorghum (4)
Z sorghum syrup (35)
aa South Georgia syrup (1)
ab sugar syrup (4)
ac sugarcane syrup (16)
ad syrup (765)
ae table syrup (1)
af thin syrup (1)
ag tree molasses (1)
ah waffle syrup (1)

051.3 P syrup
{p} fricative
{r} weakly retroflex
{t} flap
{?} glottal
No Response (94)
<sar(A)p> (1)
<se(r)Ap=14> (1)
<seer(A)p> (1)
<seerAp=14> (2)
<ser(A)p> (6)
<serAp=14> (42)
<serIp=14> (7)
<se{r}Ip=14> (1)
<shurAp=14> (1)
<shurIp=14> (1)
<siRp=14> (1)
<si[r](A)p> (1)
<sir(A)p> (8)
<sir(A)ps> (1)
<sirAp=14> (93)
<sirIp=14> (18)
<sirup=13> (1)
<si{r}Ap=14> (1)
<si{t}oep=31> (1)
<soo[r](A)p> (1)
<soor(A)p> (1)

<soorAp=14> (8)
<su[r](A)p> (50)
<su[r]Ap=14> (14)
<su[r]A{?}=14> (1)
<su[r]Ip=14> (10)
<sur(A)p> (143)
<surAp=14> (390)
<surA{p}=14> (1)
<surIp=14> (70)
<suri(p)=13> (1)
<surrAp=14> (12)
<surrIp=14> (1)
<surup=13> (1)
<suryIp=14> (1)
<su{r}(A)p> (42)
<su{r}Ap=14> (28)
<su{r}Ip=14> (6)
<su{r}Ips=14> (1)
<su{r}rAp=14> (10)
<su{r}rIp=14> (2)
<su{r}{t}Ap=14> (1)
<su{t}Ap=14> (1)
<su{t}Ip=14> (1)
<syirA(p)=14> (1)
<thurAp=14> (1)

051.4 P genuine
No Response (256)
<janyIwien=143> (1)
<je[n]jAwien=143> (1)
<je[n]yAwin=143> (1)
<je[n]yIwien=143> (1)
<jeenyAwN=144> (1)
<jeenyIwien=143> (3)
<jeenyueien=132> (1)
<jeenyuewN=134> (5)
<jeenyuewien=132> (2)
<jen(y)AwN=144> (1)
<jen(y)Awien=143> (1)
<jen(y)Awin=143> (1)
<jen(y)IwN=144> (1)
<jen(y)uewN=134> (1)
<jen(yA)wien=13> (2)
<jenjAwN=144> (1)
<jenjAwien=143> (2)
<jenjIwN=144> (1)
<jenjIwien=143> (1)
<jenjuewN=134> (1)
<jeny(A)N=14> (1)
<jenyA(N)=14> (1)
<jenyAN=144> (1)
<jenyAien=143> (2)
<jenyAwN=144> (49)
<jenyAwen=143> (3)
<jenyAwien=142> (1)
<jenyAwien=143> (48)
<jenyAwien=341> (23)
<jenyAwin=143> (12)
<jenyAwun=143> (1)
<jenyIien=143> (1)

<jenyIwN=144> (41)
<jenyIwien=142> (1)
<jenyIwien=143> (42)
<jenyIwien=241> (1)
<jenyIwien=341> (18)
<jenyIwin=143> (5)
<jenyewwN=134> (1)
<jenyewwien=132> (1)
<jenyewwien=231> (1)
<jenyooN=134> (2)
<jenyooien=133> (1)
<jenyoowN=134> (4)
<jenyoowien=123> (2)
<jenyoowien=132> (4)
<jenyoowien=231> (5)
<jenyueN=134> (4)
<jenyuewN=134> (25)
<jenyuewie[n]=132> (1)
<jenyuewien=123> (2)
<jenyuewien=132> (24)
<jenyuewien=133> (1)
<jenyuewien=231> (13)
<jenyuewien=321> (1)
<jenyuewieng=132> (1)
<jenyuewin=123> (1)
<jenyuewoon=132> (1)
<ji(n)yIwin=143> (1)
<ji[n](yA)wN=14> (1)
<ji[n]yoowie[n]=132> (1)
<jin(y)Iwien=143> (1)
<jin(y)ueien=231> (1)
<jin(y)uien=123> (1)
<jinewwN=134> (2)
<jinewwien=231> (1)
<jinjAwien=241> (1)
<jinjIwien=341> (1)
<jinjiwien=132> (1)
<jinjuewN=134> (2)
<jiny(A)N=14> (1)
<jiny(A)[N]=14> (1)
<jinyAN=144> (2)
<jinyAin=143> (1)
<jinyAwN=144> (45)
<jinyAwien=142> (2)
<jinyAwien=143> (27)
<jinyAwien=241> (3)
<jinyAwien=341> (12)
<jinyAwin=143> (6)
<jinyIien=341> (1)
<jinyIwN=144> (40)
<jinyIwie[n]=143> (1)
<jinyIwien=143> (26)
<jinyIwien=241> (1)
<jinyIwien=341> (15)
<jinyIwin=143> (3)
<jinyewwN=134> (1)
<jinyewwien=132> (2)
<jinyooien=132> (2)
<jinyoowN=134> (1)

<jinyoowien=132> (3)
<jinyoowien=133> (1)
<jinyueN=134> (5)
<jinyueien=132> (1)
<jinyueien=231> (1)
<jinyuewN=134> (47)
<jinyuewie[n]=132> (1)
<jinyuewien=132> (23)
<jinyuewien=133> (1)
<jinyuewien=231> (21)
<jinyuewin=123> (4)
<jinyuewin=132> (3)
<jinyuewin=133> (1)
<jinyuewun=132> (1)

051.5 P bulk
{b}   fricative
{o}   upglide
{oo} unrounded
{ue} unrounded
{?}   glottal
No Response (418)
<baw(1)kI=14> (1)
<boo(1)k> (5)
<boo(1)ks> (2)
<boo[1]k> (38)
<boo[1]ks> (2)
<boolk> (225)
<boolkI=14> (3)
<boolks> (3)
<boolts> (1)
<bu(1)k> (4)
<bu(1)ks> (1)
<bu[1]k> (34)
<bu[1]ks> (2)
<bue(1)k> (2)
<bue(1)ks> (1)
<buelk> (3)
<bulk> (163)
<bulkI=14> (4)
<bulks> (2)
<bul{?}> (1)
<b{oo}[1]k> (7)
<b{oo}[1]kI=14> (1)
<b{oo}lk> (6)
<b{o}[1]k> (1)
<b{ue}lk> (2)
<{b}oo[1]k> (1)

051.6 P jelly
{e} upglide
{l}   clear
No Response (152)
<che{l}I=14> (2)
<jai{l}I=14> (2)
<jalI=14> (1)
<ja{l}I=14> (6)
<ja{l}Iz=14> (1)
<je[1]I=14> (3)
<jelA=14> (2)
<jelI=14> (136)

<jelIz=14> (12)
<jelee=13> (1)
<jelII=14> (2)
<jellai=13> (1)
<jellee=13> (3)
<jel{l}I=14> (4)
<jel{l}Iz=14> (1)
<jel{l}ee=13> (2)
<je{l}A=14> (4)
<je{l}I=14> (510)
<je{l}Iz=14> (37)
<je{l}ee=13> (6)
<je{l}eez=13> (2)
<jilII=14> (2)
<ji{l}I=14> (13)
<ji{l}ee=13> (1)
<jow{l}I=14> (1)
<julII=14> (3)
<ju{l}I=14> (17)
<j{e}{l}I=14> (1)
<yellee=13> (1)
<zhye{l}I=14> (1)

051.7 P salt/pepper
{e} upglide
{o} unrounded onset
{oe} lowered onset
{p} fricative
{R} weakly retroflex
{r} weakly retroflex
{t} flap
{?} glottal
No Response (150)
<pep(R)N(d)sawlt=341> (1)
<pepR=14> (108)
<pepRN(d)sawlt=1441> (1)
<pepRN(d)sawlt=1443> (1)
<pepRN(d)sawlt=2441> (3)
<pepRN(d)sawlt=3441> (2)
<pepRN(d)s{o}lt=1441> (1)
<pepRN(d)s{o}lt=3441> (1)
<pepRz=14> (3)
<pep[R](Nd)sawlt=143> (1)
<pep[R]=14> (105)
<pep[R]N(d)sa[1]t=3441> (1)
<pep[R]N(d)saw(1)t=3441> (1)
<pep[R]N(d)sawlt=1441> (4)
<pep[R]N(d)sawlt=2441> (1)
<pep[R]N(d)sawlt=3441> (2)
<pep[R]z=14> (2)
<peppR=14> (13)
<pepp[R]=14> (8)
<pepp[R]en(d)sawlt=1431> (1)
<pepp[R]o(nd)saw[1]t=1423> (1)
<peppur=13> (1)
<pepp{R}=14> (1)
<pepur=13> (1)
<pep{R}=14> (37)
<pep{R}N(d)saw[1]t=3441> (1)
<pep{R}N(d)sawlt=1441> (1)

<pep{R}N(d)sawlt=2441> (1)
<pep{R}N(d)sawlts=1441> (1)
<pip[R]=14> (1)
<pyepR=14> (1)
<pyep[R]=14> (4)
<pyip[R]=14> (1)
<p{e}pR=14> (8)
<p{e}p{R}=14> (2)
<saw(lt)N(d)pepR=1434> (1)
<saw(1)k> (1)
<saw(1)t> (58)
<saw(1)tN(d)pepR=1414> (3)
<saw(1)tN(d)pepR=2414> (1)
<saw(1)tN(d)pepR=3414> (22)
<saw(1)tN(d)pep[R]=1414> (2)
<saw(1)tN(d)pep[R]=1434> (1)
<saw(1)tN(d)pep[R]=2414> (2)
<saw(1)tN(d)pep[R]=3414> (6)
<saw(1)tN(d)peppR=3414> (3)
<saw(1)tN(d)pepp[R]=1414> (1)
<saw(1)tN(d)pep{R}=1414> (1)
<saw(1)tN(d)pep{R}=3414> (8)
<saw(1)tN(d)pyep[R]=3414> (1)
<saw(1)tN(d)p{e}pR=3414> (3)
<saw(1)tN(d){p}epR=1414> (1)
<saw(1){?}N(d)peppR=2414> (1)
<saw[1](t)> (1)
<saw[1]t> (35)
<saw[1]tN(d)pepR=1414> (3)
<saw[1]tN(d)pepR=3414> (6)
<saw[1]tN(d)pep[R]=3414> (6)
<saw[1]tN(d)pepp[R]=1424> (1)
<saw[1]tN(d)pepp[R]=1434> (1)
<saw[1]tN(d)pep{R}=3414> (1)
<saw[1]tN(d)perpR=1414> (1)
<saw[1]tN(d)pipR=1414> (1)
<saw[1]tN(d)pippR=1424> (1)
<saw[1]tN(d)pupR=3414> (1)
<saw[1]ten(d)pep[R]=1314> (1)
<saw[1]{?}> (1)
<sawl(t)> (3)
<sawl(t)M(d)pep[R]=1424> (1)
<sawlt> (192)
<sawlt[N](d)peppR=1414> (1)
<sawltI=14> (1)
<sawltN(d)pap[R]=2414> (1)
<sawltN(d)pepR=1414> (39)
<sawltN(d)pepR=1424> (1)
<sawltN(d)pepR=1434> (6)
<sawltN(d)pepR=2414> (20)
<sawltN(d)pepR=3414> (41)
<sawltN(d)pep[R]=1414> (22)
<sawltN(d)pep[R]=1434> (2)
<sawltN(d)pep[R]=2414> (14)
<sawltN(d)pep[R]=3414> (32)
<sawltN(d)peppR=1414> (2)
<sawltN(d)peppR=1434> (1)
<sawltN(d)peppR=3414> (2)
<sawltN(d)pepp[R]=1434> (1)

<sawltN(d)pepp[R]=3414> (1)
<sawltN(d)peppu{r}=1413> (1)
<sawltN(d)pepp{R}=1414> (1)
<sawltN(d)pepp{R}=1424> (1)
<sawltN(d)pepp{R}=1434> (1)
<sawltN(d)pepur=2413> (1)
<sawltN(d)pep{R}=1414> (9)
<sawltN(d)pep{R}=1434> (1)
<sawltN(d)pep{R}=2414> (7)
<sawltN(d)pep{R}=3414> (9)
<sawltN(d)pipR=3414> (1)
<sawltN(d)pyep[R]=1414> (1)
<sawltN(d)p{e}pR=3414> (2)
<sawltN(d)p{e}pur=2413> (1)
<sawltN(d)p{e}p{R}=3414> (1)
<sawltan(d)pepR=1314> (1)
<sawltan(d)pepR=2314> (3)
<sawltan(d)pep[R]=1314> (1)
<sawltan(d)pep[R]=2314> (2)
<sawltan(d)pep{R}=1314> (1)
<sawltan(d)pep{R}=1324> (1)
<sawltan(d)pep{R}=2314> (1)
<sawltandpepR=2314> (1)
<sawlten(d)pep[R]=1314> (1)
<sawlten(d)pep[R]=2314> (1)
<sawltendpepR=1314> (1)
<sawltin(d)pepR=1314> (1)
<sawltin(d)pepR=2314> (1)
<sawlto{r}pep[R]=1314> (1)
<sawltsN(d)pepR=3414> (1)
<sawl{?}N(d)pipp[R]=1424> (1)
<shawltN(d)pep{R}=1414> (1)
<slawlt> (1)
<so(1)t> (2)
<so(1)tN(d)peppR=3414> (1)
<so[1]tN(d)pepR=1414> (1)
<so[1]tN(d)pep[R]=2414> (1)
<so[1]tN(d)pep[R]=3414> (1)
<so[1]tN(d)pepp[R]=2414> (1)
<soel(t)N(d)pep[R]=3414> (1)
<sol(t)N(d)pep[R]=3414> (1)
<solt> (3)
<soltN(d)pep[R]=2414> (1)
<soltN(d)pep{R}=1414> (1)
<soltN(d)pep{R}=3414> (1)
<s{oe}lt> (1)
<s{o}(1)t> (14)
<s{o}(1)tN(d)pepR=1414> (3)
<s{o}(1)tN(d)pepR=2414> (1)
<s{o}(1)tN(d)pepR=3414> (6)
<s{o}(1)tN(d)pep[R]=3414> (2)
<s{o}(1)tN(d)pep{R}=3414> (2)
<s{o}(1)tN(d)p{e}pR=3414> (4)
<s{o}(1)tN(d)p{e}p[R]=3414> (2)
<s{o}[1]t> (4)
<s{o}[1]tN(d)pebR=1414> (1)
<s{o}[1]tN(d)pepR=1414> (1)
<s{o}[1]tN(d)pepR=1434> (1)
<s{o}[1]tN(d)pep[R]=1414> (1)

<s{o}[1]tN(d)pep[R]=3414> (1)
<s{o}[1]tN(d)peppR=1414> (1)
<s{o}l(t)> (1)
<s{o}lt> (35)
<s{o}ltM(d)peppR=1424> (1)
<s{o}ltN(d)pep[R]=1414> (1)
<s{o}ltN(d)pep[R]=3414> (2)
<s{o}ltN(d)pepR=1414> (6)
<s{o}ltN(d)pepR=1434> (1)
<s{o}ltN(d)pepR=3414> (8)
<s{o}ltN(d)peppR=1414> (1)
<s{o}ltN(d)peppR=1424> (2)
<s{o}ltN(d)peppR=1434> (1)
<s{o}ltN(d)pepur=1423> (1)
<s{o}ltN(d)pep{R}=3414> (2)
<s{o}ltN(d)pippR=1424> (1)
<s{o}ltN(d)pipp[R]=1434> (1)
<s{o}ltan(d)pepR=1314> (1)
<s{o}lten(d)pepR=3214> (1)
<s{o}l{?}> (1)
<s{o}l{?}N(d)pepp[R]=1424> (1)
<s{o}l{t}N(d)pep[R]=1414> (1)

051.7 S salt

No Response (0)
|JJH| (1)
|JSC| (1)
|PACjjb| (1)
|PAEqfb| (1)
|PAIqfb| (1)
|QAC| (1)
|QACjjc| (2)
|QAD| (2)
|QADqfa| (1)
|QAHqfb| (4)
|QAHqff| (1)
|QFA| (4)
|QFAjjc| (10)
|QFAjjd| (1)
|QFAjjf| (1)
|QFAlfa| (4)
|QFAlfe| (1)
|QFAlfj| (17)
|QFAqfb| (10)
|QFAqfk| (4)
|QFAqfm| (1)
|QFB| (4)
|QFBcba| (1)
|QFBjjc| (1)
|QFBjjdcbj| (1)
|QFBjjh| (1)
|QFBjjjcba| (1)
|QFBjjk| (1)
|QFBjjl| (3)
|QFBjjlcba| (1)
|QFBjjm| (3)
|QFBjjmcbj| (1)
|QFBjsc| (1)
|QFC| (27)
|QFCjja| (2)

|QFCjjb| (1)
|QFCjjc| (4)
|QFCjjccba| (1)
|QFCjjdcbj| (1)
|QFCjjj| (1)
|QFCjjl| (1)
|QFCmaj| (1)
|QFCqfa| (16)
|QFCqfacba| (2)
|QFCqfb| (252)
|QFCqfbcba| (5)
|QFCqfbcbj| (11)
|QFCqfbmaj| (1)
|QFCqfj| (1)
|QFCqfk| (13)
|QFCqfkcba| (1)
|QFCqmb| (7)
|QFCqmbmaj| (1)
|QFD| (4)
|QFDefj| (3)
|QFDjjl| (1)
|QFDjjm| (1)
|QFDlfj| (4)
|QFDlfn| (1)
|QFDqfb| (1)
|QFF| (2)
|QFFcba| (1)
|QFFcbj| (1)
|QFFjjm| (2)
|QFFjjq| (1)
|QFH| (4)
|QFHcbj| (1)
|QFHjjb| (1)
|QFHqfb| (20)
|QFHqfbcba| (1)
|QFHqfbcbj| (1)
|QFHqff| (1)
|QFHqfk| (1)
|QMA| (4)
|QMAcba| (2)
|QMAjja| (2)
|QMAjjj| (1)
|QMAjjjcba| (7)
|QMAjjjcbs| (2)
|QMAlfa| (1)
|QMAlfj| (1)
|QMAmajcba| (1)
|QMAqfb| (2)
|QMAqfd| (1)
|QMAqff| (1)
|QMBcba| (1)
|QMBjjjcbs| (1)
|QMBjjm| (1)
|QMC| (5)
|QMCcba| (1)
|QMCma2| (1)
|QMCmaj| (2)
|QMCqfa| (3)
|QMCqfb| (21)

|QMCqfbcba| (4)
|QMCqfbcbj| (1)
|QMCqfbmaj| (1)
|QMCqff| (1)
|QMCqfk| (6)
|QMD| (1)
|QMDlfa| (1)
|QMDlfj| (1)
|QMFjjl| (1)
|QMHqfb| (5)
|QMHqfbcbj| (1)
|QMSjjj| (1)
|SAE| (1)
|SAEmaj| (1)
|SAEqfa| (4)
|SAG| (1)
|SAGmaj| (1)
|SAGqfa| (12)
|SAGqfacba| (1)
|SAGqfc| (1)
|SAGqfh| (1)
|SAGqfj| (12)
|SCBmfjcba| (1)
|SCE| (2)
|SCEcba| (1)
|SCEjjjcba| (1)
|SCEtaa| (1)
|SCGqfa| (4)
|SCGqfacbj| (2)
|SFE| (2)
|SFGcba| (1)
|SFGqfa| (1)
|TAAqfacba| (1)
|TAAqfb| (2)
|TAAqfk| (1)
|TABjjqcbj| (1)
|TABqfa| (1)
|TABqfacba| (1)
|TABqfb| (8)
|TABqfj| (1)
|TABqfl| (1)
|TADjjb| (1)
|TADjjc| (1)
|TADqfa| (1)
|TADqfb| (23)
|TADqfj| (2)
|TADqfjcbj| (1)
|TADqfk| (1)
|TADtfb| (1)
|TAEqfb| (1)
|TAFqfb| (1)
|TCA| (9)
|TCAcba| (2)
|TCAjja| (2)
|TCAjjacba| (1)
|TCAmaj| (1)
|TCAmajcba| (1)
|TCB| (1)
|TCBqfb| (1)

|TCD| (1)
|TCDmaacba| (1)
|TCDqfb| (1)
|TCDqfj| (1)
|TFA| (10)
|TFAcba| (6)
|TFAqaj| (3)
|TFAqfa| (15)
|TFAqfacba| (1)
|TFAqfb| (5)
|TFAqfj| (40)
|TFAqfjcba| (2)
|TFAqfk| (1)
|TFAqfkcba| (1)
|TFB| (30)
|TFBcba| (2)
|TFBcbj| (1)
|TFBjja| (1)
|TFBjjc| (2)
|TFBjjl| (2)
|TFBqfa| (11)
|TFBqfb| (20)
|TFBqfc| (1)
|TFBqfdcba| (1)
|TFBqfh| (1)
|TFBqfj| (18)
|TFBqfk| (3)
|TFBqfkcba| (1)
|TFBqfm| (1)
|TFC| (1)
|TFCqfb| (1)
|TFCqfc| (1)
|TFD| (3)
|TFDmaj| (1)
|TFDqfa| (1)
|TFDqfj| (1)
|TFF| (1)
|TFFqfa| (1)
|TKA| (1)
|TMA| (1)
|TMAmaj| (1)
|TMAqfb| (1)
|TMAqfc| (1)
|TMAqfj| (2)
|TMB| (5)
|TMBcba| (3)
|TMBcbj| (1)
|TMBmajcba| (1)
|TMBqfa| (1)
|TMBqfb| (3)
|TMBqfc| (1)
|TMBqfjcba| (1)
|TMBtfa| (1)
|TMFmaj| (1)
|TOAcha| (2)

051.8 G a/an (apple)
No Response (189)
A a (370)
B an (439)

C [D-0] (11)

052.1 G those (boys)

No Response (133)

A them (415)

B them there (8)

C those (454)

052.2 G over there

No Response (94)

A (a)cross yonder (way) (4)

B (a)round yonder (1)

C back in yonder (2)

D back there/here (7)

E back up yonder (ways) (4)

F back yonder (way) (41)

G down there/here (9)

H down yonder (74)

I here and yonder (10)

J here, there, and yonder (4)

K here, yonder, and everywhere (1)

L in there (14)

M in yonder (33)

N out there/here (50)

O out yon(der) (5)

P out yonder (95)

Q over down yonder (1)

R over the yonders (1)

S over there/here (563)

T over yon(der) (way) (5)

U over yonder (234)

V over yonders (1)

W there/here (51)

X up back yonder (1)

Y up there (18)

Z up through yonder (1)

aa up yonder (63)

ab yon(der) (2)

ac yon(der) way (1)

ad yonder (108)

ae yonder way (5)

052.3 G this way

No Response (175)

A that way (78)

B thataway (228)

C thataways (3)

D this here way (1)

E this way (456)

F thisaway (237)

G whichaway (22)

052.4 G what's that?

No Response (314)

A beg (your) pardon, (I) (78)

B come again (with that/on that) (18)

C come by with that again (1)

D come over that again (1)

E como? [S] (1)

F could you (please) repeat that/it (again)? (5)

G do how? (2)

H do/does/done what (now)? (45)

I do/done which? (7)

J excuse me (4)

K give it to me again now (1)

L GRUNT(H) (7)

M GRUNT(R) (227)

N how is/was that/it (now)? (12)

O how you said/say (again)? (1)

P how [C-0] that (now)? (4)

Q how [X-0] you put/say that? (2)

R how'd you have it? (1)

S how's that (again)? (42)

T how's was that? (1)

U I can't hear you (1)

V I can't understand you (2)

W I didn't catch/get that/it (4)

X I didn't hear (you) (22)

Y I didn't (quite) understand (you/-that) (33)

Z I don't follow you (1)

aa I'm sorry (7)

ab let's get that again (1)

ac ma'am? (37)

ad once again/more (2)

ae one more time (1)

af pardon (me) (53)

ag pass that by me again (1)

ah please (1)

ai repeat it/that (again), (please) (19)

aj repeat what you [X-0] just saying (1)

ak repeat your question (1)

al repeat yourself again (1)

am run that back (through again) (2)

an run that by me again (5)

ao say how, (now)? (2)

ap say it/that (once) again/over (20)

aq say/said what, (now)? (34)

ar say which? (4)

as sir? (25)

at sorry (1)

au speak louder (1)

av speak that again (1)

aw speak up (3)

ax talk louder (3)

ay tell me again (2)

az what, (now)? (197)

ba what do/did you say (now)? (67)

bb what is/was that (again)? (9)

bc what which? (1)

bd what [C-0] that? (1)

be what [X-0] you call it (now)? (2)

bf what [X-0] you say/mean? (14)

bg what [X-0] [M-0] say? (9)

bh what's that? (18)

bi which, (now)? (18)

bj which is that? (1)

bk who? (3)

bl will you repeat that? (2)

bm would you mind saying it again? (1)

bn would you repeat that (again), (please)? (7)

bo would you say that over (again)? (2)

bp you'll have to speak that again (1)

053.1 P poor

{oe} lowered onset

{p} fricative

{r} weakly retroflex

No Response (206)

<paw(r)> (1)

<paw[r]> (1)

<pawr> (14)

<paw{r}> (2)

<poe(r)> (70)

<poe[r]> (73)

<poer> (61)

<poe{r}> (35)

<poo(r)> (3)

<poo[r]> (137)

<poor> (236)

<poo{r}> (56)

<pue(r)> (2)

<pue[r]> (23)

<puer> (27)

<pue{r}> (6)

<pur> (20)

<pu{r}> (1)

<p{oe}(r)> (8)

<p{oe}[r]> (15)

<p{oe}r> (25)

<p{oe}{r}> (4)

<{p}oor> (3)

<{p}oo{r}> (1)

053.1 S poor

No Response (99)

|BJA| (1)

|BJAmaj| (1)

|BJAmfa| (1)

|BJC| (1)

|BJCmaa| (1)

|BJCmaj| (1)

|BSAmaj| (1)

|BSAmea| (2)

|CJCmea| (1)

|CJD| (1)

|CJDmea| (3)

|CJHmea| (1)

|CSFmaj| (1)

|CSHmaa| (1)

|CSHmea| (1)

|EAAmea| (2)
|EABmea| (2)
|EACmea| (2)
|EAFmea| (1)
|EAHmea| (1)
|ECAmea| (2)
|EFAmaa| (3)
|EFAmaj| (2)
|EFAmajmea| (1)
|EFAmea| (16)
|EFBmaa| (4)
|EFBmaj| (3)
|EFBmea| (13)
|EFCmaa| (2)
|EFCmaj| (1)
|EFCmea| (4)
|EFGmea| (2)
|EFHmea| (1)
|EFImaa| (5)
|EFImea| (7)
|EMAmaa| (1)
|EMAmaj| (1)
|EMAmea| (3)
|EMBmea| (4)
|EMCmaa| (1)
|EMCmea| (1)
|EMDmea| (2)
|EMGmea| (4)
|EMImaa| (1)
|EMImea| (1)
|FADmaa| (1)
|FADmea| (1)
|FAHmea| (2)
|FFAmaa| (2)
|FFAmaj| (2)
|FFAmea| (5)
|FFBmaa| (4)
|FFBmaj| (4)
|FFBmea| (12)
|FFBmej| (1)
|FFCmaa| (3)
|FFCmea| (13)
|FFDmaa| (37)
|FFDmaj| (17)
|FFDmajmea| (6)
|FFDmea| (80)
|FFDmej| (7)
|FFF| (1)
|FFFmaa| (7)
|FFFmaj| (3)
|FFFmea| (21)
|FFFmej| (1)
|FFGmea| (4)
|FFHmaa| (18)
|FFHmaj| (9)
|FFHmea| (30)
|FFHmej| (1)
|FFImaj| (1)
|FFImea| (11)

|FJAmac| (1)
|FJAmej| (1)
|FMAmea| (4)
|FMBmaa| (6)
|FMBmaj| (2)
|FMBmea| (6)
|FMCmaa| (1)
|FMCmea| (3)
|FMDmaa| (5)
|FMDmaj| (1)
|FMDmea| (30)
|FMDmej| (2)
|FMFmaa| (3)
|FMFmaj| (2)
|FMFmea| (14)
|FMFmfa| (1)
|FMGmaa| (1)
|FMHmaa| (1)
|FMHmaj| (1)
|FMHmea| (9)
|FMHmfa| (1)
|FMImaa| (1)
|FMImea| (1)
|FSAmea| (1)
|IJAlfj| (1)
|JBCmaj| (1)
|JJAefj| (3)
|JJAffd| (2)
|JJAjjb| (1)
|JJAmaj| (3)
|JJAmea| (2)
|JJAmej| (1)
|JJBefa| (1)
|JJBefjmea| (1)
|JJBmaj| (1)
|JJBmea| (3)
|JJBmej| (1)
|JJCefa| (2)
|JJCefj| (2)
|JJCefjmea| (1)
|JJCffd| (1)
|JJCjjb| (1)
|JJCmaa| (4)
|JJCmaj| (6)
|JJCmea| (9)
|JJCmpa| (1)
|JJDefa| (10)
|JJDefamea| (1)
|JJDefamej| (1)
|JJDefj| (16)
|JJDefjmea| (1)
|JJDefl| (1)
|JJDffd| (1)
|JJDffdmea| (3)
|JJDffm| (1)
|JJDmaa| (2)
|JJDmaj| (5)
|JJDmea| (5)
|JJDmfj| (1)

|JJFefa| (1)
|JJFefj| (8)
|JJFefjmaa| (1)
|JJFefjmea| (5)
|JJFmaa| (4)
|JJFmaj| (4)
|JJFmea| (5)
|JJFmej| (1)
|JJGmaa| (1)
|JJGmaj| (1)
|JJGmea| (1)
|JJH| (1)
|JJHefa| (1)
|JJHefj| (2)
|JJHffm| (1)
|JJHmaj| (3)
|JJHmea| (1)
|JSA| (1)
|JSAffamea| (1)
|JSAffj| (1)
|JSAmaa| (3)
|JSAmaamej| (1)
|JSAmea| (4)
|JSAmej| (1)
|JSBefa| (1)
|JSBffj| (1)
|JSBmaa| (1)
|JSBmea| (3)
|JSC| (1)
|JSCefa| (1)
|JSCefj| (2)
|JSCffj| (1)
|JSCmaa| (3)
|JSCmaj| (4)
|JSCmea| (10)
|JSDefj| (1)
|JSDffj| (3)
|JSDlfj| (1)
|JSDmaa| (4)
|JSDmaj| (1)
|JSDmea| (6)
|JSDmej| (1)
|JSFefj| (1)
|JSFmaa| (2)
|JSFmea| (3)
|JSHmaj| (1)
|JSHmea| (1)
|JSHmej| (1)
|JSHmpa| (1)
|LCBmea| (1)
|LCDmea| (1)
|LFE| (1)
|LFImaa| (1)
|LMG| (1)
|MABmea| (1)
|MACmea| (1)
|MEA| (2)
|MLA| (1)
|QAFmaj| (1)

C   that is, his father (1)
D   that's father (3)
E   who his father (1)
F   whom his father (1)
G   whose father (189)
H   [J-0] his father (17)
I   [R-0] father (5)

054.1 L cherry seed

No Response (149)
A   bone (1)
B   bottom (1)
C   cherry core (1)
D   cherry kernel (1)
E   cherry pit (5)
F   cherry seed (18)
G   cherrystone (6)
H   church (1)
I   core (22)
J   heart (13)
K   hueso [S] (1)
L   inside (1)
M   kernel (30)
N   kernel seed (1)
O   noyau [F] (3)
P   nut (1)
Q   pit (287)
R   pith (1)
S   seed (460)
T   stone (51)

054.2 L peach seed

No Response (146)
A   almond [inside seed] (2)
B   bone (2)
C   core (8)
D   core [inside seed] (4)
E   germ (1)
F   goody [inside seed] (4)
G   heart (3)
H   heart [inside seed] (5)
I   inside [inside seed] (1)
J   kernel (96)
K   kernel [inside seed] (84)
L   noyau [F] (2)
M   nut [inside seed] (2)
N   peach core [inside seed] (1)
O   peach kernel (12)
P   peach pit (8)
Q   peach seed (115)
R   peach stone (13)
S   pit (101)
T   pit [inside seed] (7)
U   pit of the stone [inside] (1)
V   plug (1)
W   seed (482)
X   seed [inside seed] (7)
Y   stone (82)
Z   white kernel [inside seed] (1)

054.3 L cling peach

No Response (233)

A   canning peach (2)
B   clear seed (1)
C   cling (131)
D   cling free (1)
E   cling peach (108)
F   cling pit peach (1)
G   cling seed (24)
H   cling seed peach (1)
I   cling seeded peach (1)
J   cling sing peach (1)
K   cling-type peach (1)
L   clinger (2)
M   clinging (2)
N   clinging stone (1)
O   clinging type (1)
P   clingstone (122)
Q   clingstone peach (9)
R   crouch peach (1)
S   early peach (1)
T   eating type (1)
U   English peach (1)
V   freestone (1)
W   green peach (5)
X   hairless peach (1)
Y   hard cling peach (1)
Z   hard core (1)
aa   hard peach (7)
ab   hard stone (1)
ac   hateful peach (1)
ad   honey peach (1)
ae   Indian (2)
af   Indian peach (37)
ag   Indian pickled peach (1)
ah   June peach (2)
ai   lemon peach (2)
aj   May peach (1)
ak   native peach (1)
al   November peach (1)
am   peach (38)
an   peche au noyau [F] (1)
ao   pickle peach (4)
ap   pickled peach (1)
aq   pickling peach (6)
ar   pitted peach (1)
as   plum (9)
at   plum peach (90)
au   plum seed (7)
av   plum seed peach (7)
aw   plum seeded (1)
ax   plum stone (5)
ay   plum stone peach (3)
az   preserving peach (2)
ba   press (44)
bb   press peach (78)
bc   press seed (4)
bd   press stone (3)
be   press stone peach (3)
bf   pressed [n.] (1)
bg   pressed peach (3)

bh   pressing peach (1)
bi   prince peach (1)
bj   red peach (2)
bk   ruddy Indian peach (1)
bl   seed peach (1)
bm   soft meat (1)
bn   soft peach (2)
bo   stone (1)
bp   stone peach (2)
bq   summer peach (1)
br   sweet peach (1)
bs   tan peach (1)
bt   tight peach (1)
bu   white peach (2)
bv   white press (2)
bw   yellow cling (2)
bx   yellow cling peach (2)
by   yellow peach (2)
bz   yellow press (2)

054.4 L freestone peach

No Response (233)
A   break peach (1)
B   breaking-open peach (1)
C   busting-open peach (1)
D   canning peach (1)
E   clay stone peach (1)
F   clear (2)
G   clear cut (1)
H   clear one (1)
I   clear peach (3)
J   clear seed (180)
K   clear seed peach (43)
L   clear seeded (1)
M   clear seeded peach (2)
N   clear sing peach (1)
O   clear stone (35)
P   clear stone peach (4)
Q   clears peach (1)
R   cling free (3)
S   cling peach (1)
T   eating peach (2)
U   Firestone peach (1)
V   free (5)
W   free cling (2)
X   free seed (6)
Y   free seed peach (1)
Z   freestone (290)
aa   freestone Indian peach (1)
ab   freestone peach (35)
ac   juice peach (1)
ad   loose peach (1)
ae   mellow peach (2)
af   open heart (1)
ag   open peach (4)
ah   open seed (3)
ai   open stone (29)
aj   peach (4)
ak   peche a jus [F] (1)
al   peche au jus [F] (1)

<wolnuts=13> (11)
<wo{r}nIts=14> (1)
<wulnuts=13> (1)
<w{oe}lnAts=14> (1)
<w{oe}lnut=13> (1)
<w{o}(l)nAks=14> (1)
<w{o}(l)nAt=14> (1)
<w{o}(l)nuts=13> (1)
<w{o}[l]nAt=14> (4)
<w{o}[l]nAts=14> (6)
<w{o}[l]nut=13> (6)
<w{o}[l]nuts=13> (8)
<w{o}lnA(t)=14> (1)
<w{o}lnAt=14> (6)
<w{o}lnAts=14> (34)
<w{o}lnAtsh=14> (1)
<w{o}lnIt=14> (1)
<w{o}lnIts=14> (2)
<w{o}lnut=13> (4) ·
<w{o}lnuts=13> (11)

054.9A P almonds
{d}   devoiced
{dh}   devoiced
{o}   low-back
{R}   weakly retroflex
{z}   devoiced
No Response (435)
<a[l]m[N](d)=14> (1)
<a[l]mN(d)z=14> (1)
<a[l]mN(d)=14> (1)
<a[l]mN(d){z}=14> (2)
<almN(d)=14> (34)
<almN(d)z=14> (40)
<almN(d){z}=14> (3)
<almN(dz)=14> (1)
<almNd=14> (7)
<almNdz=14> (2)
<almNd{z}=14> (1)
<almon(d)=13> (1)
<amN(d)=14> (7)
<amN(d)z=14> (16)
<amN(d){z}=14> (6)
<amNdz=14> (1)
<amN{d}=14> (1)
<amN{d}{z}=14> (1)
<am![N](d)=14> (1)
<amm[N](d)=14> (1)
<awNd=14> (1)
<aw[l]mN(d)z=14> (1)
<awl(m)N(d){z}=14> (1)
<awlmN(d)=14> (15)
<awlmN(d)z=14> (12)
<awlmN(d){z}=14> (4)
<awlmNd=14> (4)
<awlmNdz=14> (1)
<awlmNd{z}=14> (1)
<awlm{R}n(d)z=14> (1)
<awmN(d)=14> (2)
<awmN(d)z=14> (3)

<awmN(d){dh}=14> (1)
<awmNdz=14> (1)
<elmN{d}{z}=14> (1)
<emN(d)z=14> (1)
<o[l]mN(d)=14> (2)
<o[l]mN(d)z=14> (1)
<o[l]mN(d){z}=14> (2)
<o[l]mN{d}{z}=14> (2)
<olmN(d)=14> (30)
<olmN(d)s=14> (1)
<olmN(d)z=14> (49)
<olmN(d){z}=14> (10)
<olmNd=14> (5)
<olmNdz=14> (6)
<olmN{d}=14> (1)
<olmN{d}s=14> (1)
<om[N](d){z}=14> (1)
<om[N](d)=14> (1)
<omN(d)z=14> (43)
<omN(d)=14> (46)
<omN(d){z}=14> (28)
<omNdz=14> (4)
<omNd=14> (8)
<omNd{z}=14> (1)
<omNt=14> (1)
<omN{d}z=14> (1)
<omN{d}=14> (1)
<omN{d}{z}=14> (1)
<oml[N](d)=14> (1)
<{o}lmN(d)z=14> (10)
<{o}lmN(d)=14> (18)
<{o}lmN(d){z}=14> (7)
<{o}lmNd=14> (1)
<{o}lm[N](d){z}=14> (1)
<{o}mN(d)s=14> (1)
<{o}mN(d)=14> (8)
<{o}mN(d)z=14> (9)
<{o}mN(d){z}=14> (7)

054.9B P pecans
{d}   devoiced
{o}   low-back
{oe}   lowered onset
{p}   fricative
{z}   devoiced
{zh}   devoiced
No Response (143)
<(pI)kon{z}> (1)
<(pI)k{o}n{z}> (2)
<bAkon=41> (2)
<bAkon{z}=41> (1)
<bAk{o}n=41> (1)
<bIkon=41> (3)
<bIkonz=41> (1)
<bIkon{z}=41> (1)
<beekon=31> (1)
<bikonz=31> (1)
<p(I)kon> (3)
<p(I)konz> (7)
<p(I)kon{z}> (3)

<pAkanz=41> (1)
<pAkawn=41> (8)
<pAkawnz=41> (9)
<pAkon=41> (27)
<pAkonz=41> (85)
<pAkonzh=41> (1)
<pAkon{zh}=41> (1)
<pAkon{z}=41> (15)
<pAk{oe}n=41> (1)
<pAk{o}n=41> (3)
<pAk{o}nz=41> (7)
<pAk{o}n{z}=41> (2)
<pIkan=41> (3)
<pIkanz=41> (15)
<pIkan{z}=41> (4)
<pIkawn=41> (7)
<pIkawnz=41> (11)
<pIkawn{z}=41> (5)
<pIkien=41> (1)
<pIko[n]=41> (1)
<pIko[n]{z}=41> (1)
<pIkon=41> (78)
<pIkondz=41> (1)
<pIkons=41> (3)
<pIkonz=41> (208)
<pIkon{z}=41> (47)
<pIk{oe}n=41> (1)
<pIk{o}[n]=41> (1)
<pIk{o}n=41> (9)
<pIk{o}nz=41> (19)
<pIk{o}n{z}=41> (10)
<peekNz=14> (1)
<peek[N]z=14> (1)
<peekan=13> (17)
<peekan=31> (1)
<peekanz=13> (30)
<peekanz=31> (2)
<peekan{z}=13> (5)
<peekan{z}=31> (2)
<peekaw[n]=13> (2)
<peekawn=31> (1)
<peekawnz=13> (1)
<peekawn{z}=13> (1)
<peekenz=13> (2)
<peekkanz=13> (1)
<peekon=13> (18)
<peekon=31> (4)
<peekondh=13> (1)
<peekonz=13> (32)
<peekonz=31> (10)
<peekon{d}{z}=13> (1)
<peekon{z}=13> (5)
<peekon{z}=31> (5)
<peekyan=13> (1)
<peek{o}n=31> (1)
<peek{o}nz=13> (3)
<peek{o}nz=31> (1)
<pika(n){z}=13> (1)
<pikan=13> (2)

<pikanz=13> (1)
<pikanz=31> (2)
<pikawn=31> (2)
<pikk{o}n=31> (1)
<pikon=13> (1)
<pikon=31> (1)
<pikonz=31> (27)
<pikon{z}=31> (6)
<pikyan{z}=31> (1)
<pik{o}n=31> (1)
<pik{o}nz=31> (3)
<pokawnz=13> (1)
<pookonz=13> (1)
<pukan=13> (1)
<pukaw[n]=13> (1)
<pukawn=13> (4)
<pukawn=31> (1)
<pukawnz=13> (2)
<pukawnz=31> (1)
<pukawn{z}=13> (1)
<pukon=13> (1)
<pukon=31> (2)
<pukonz=13> (1)
<pukonz=21> (1)
<puk{o}nz=31> (1)
<puk{o}n{z}=13> (1)
<{p}Ikon=41> (1)

055.1A P oranges

{d}   devoiced
{j}   devoiced
{o}   low-back
{oe}   lowered onset
{r}   weakly retroflex
{z}   devoiced
{zh}   devoiced
No Response (121)
<arNj=14> (1)
<aw(r)Nj=14> (3)
<aw(r)NjIz=144> (1)
<aw(r)N{j}=14> (1)
<aw(r)irnjIz=134> (1)
<aw(r)njIz=14> (3)
<aw[r]Nj=14> (1)
<aw[r]nj> (2)
<aw[r]njIz=14> (15)
<aw[r]njIzh=14> (1)
<aw[r]nyI{zh}=14> (1)
<aw[r]n{j}> (1)
<awrNj=14> (11)
<awrNjI(z)=144> (1)
<awrNjIdh=144> (1)
<awrNjIz=144> (18)
<awrNjI{z}=144> (1)
<awrNjiz=143> (1)
<awrNzhIz=144> (1)
<awrN{j}Iz=144> (1)
<awranjIz=134> (1)
<awrenj=13> (1)
<awrinjIz=134> (4)

<awrin{j}=13> (3)
<awrnch> (2)
<awrnj> (12)
<awrnjIdh=14> (1)
<awrnjIth=14> (1)
<awrnjIz=14> (33)
<awrnjI{z}=14> (1)
<awrnji{z}=13> (1)
<awrn{j}> (1)
<awrn{j}I{z}=14> (1)
<aw{r}N{d}Idh=144> (1)
<aw{r}nj> (1)
<aw{r}njAz=14> (1)
<aw{r}njIz=14> (6)
<o(r)Nj=14> (1)
<o(r)NjIz=144> (1)
<o(r)N{j}=14> (1)
<o(r)i(n)j=13> (1)
<o(r)injIz=134> (2)
<o(r)njIz=14> (3)
<o[r]NjIz=144> (4)
<o[r][n]{zh}> (1)
<o[r]nj> (8)
<o[r]njIz=14> (9)
<o[r]n{j}> (3)
<oe[r]Nj=14> (1)
<oerNj=14> (1)
<oerinj=13> (1)
<oerinjIz=134> (2)
<or(n)jIz=14> (1)
<orNchIz=144> (1)
<orNdIz=144> (1)
<orNj=14> (53)
<orNjAz=144> (1)
<orNjIs=144> (1)
<orNjIz=144> (53)
<orNjI{z}=144> (6)
<orNjiz=143> (2)
<orN{j}=14> (20)
<orN{j}Is=144> (1)
<orN{j}I{z}=144> (1)
<or[N]{j}=14> (1)
<or[n]jI{z}=14> (1)
<oren{j}=13> (1)
<ori[n]jI{z}=134> (1)
<orinj=13> (12)
<orinjIs=134> (1)
<orinjIz=134> (44)
<orinjIzh=134> (1)
<orinjI{z}=134> (9)
<orin{j}=13> (9)
<orin{j}I{z}=134> (2)
<orin{zh}=13> (1)
<ornNj=14> (1)
<ornj> (26)
<ornjAz=14> (2)
<ornjIz=14> (64)
<ornjI{z}=14> (3)
<ornjiz=13> (1)

<orn{j}> (1)
<orunj=13> (2)
<o{r}Nj=14> (3)
<o{r}NjIz=144> (3)
<o{r}nj> (7)
<o{r}njIz=14> (19)
<u(r)enj=13> (1)
<u[r]n{j}> (1)
<urinj=13> (1)
<urnjIz=14> (1)
<{oe}(r)N{zh}=14> (1)
<{oe}(r)injIz=134> (1)
<{oe}(r)njI(z)=14> (1)
<{oe}(r)njIz=14> (1)
<{oe}NjIz=144> (1)
<{oe}[r]Nj=14> (8)
<{oe}[r]NjIz=144> (2)
<{oe}[r]N{j}=14> (1)
<{oe}[r]nd> (1)
<{oe}[r]nj> (11)
<{oe}[r]njAz=14> (1)
<{oe}[r]njIs=14> (1)
<{oe}[r]njIz=14> (21)
<{oe}[r]njI{z}=14> (1)
<{oe}[r]njiz=13> (2)
<{oe}[r]n{j}> (2)
<{oe}ern{j}=13> (1)
<{oe}rNch=14> (1)
<{oe}rNj=14> (12)
<{oe}rNjIs=144> (1)
<{oe}rNjIz=144> (22)
<{oe}rNjI{z}=144> (1)
<{oe}rNjez=143> (1)
<{oe}rNjiz=143> (1)
<{oe}rN{j}=14> (7)
<{oe}rN{j}i{z}=143> (1)
<{oe}ranj=13> (1)
<{oe}renj=13> (1)
<{oe}ri[n]jI{z}=134> (1)
<{oe}rinj=13> (2)
<{oe}rinjIz=134> (5)
<{oe}rinjI{z}=134> (1)
<{oe}rin{j}=13> (1)
<{oe}rin{j}I{z}=134> (1)
<{oe}rnch> (1)
<{oe}rnj> (16)
<{oe}rnjAz=14> (1)
<{oe}rnjIz=14> (21)
<{oe}rnjI{z}=14> (2)
<{oe}rnjiz=13> (1)
<{oe}rn{j}> (2)
<{oe}winjIz=134> (1)
<{oe}{r}Nj=14> (2)
<{oe}{r}NjIz=144> (2)
<{oe}{r}nj> (2)
<{oe}{r}njIz=14> (11)
<{oe}{r}n{j}> (1)
<{o}(r)Nch=14> (1)
<{o}(r)Nj=14> (1)

<{o}(r)in(j)=13> (1)
<{o}(r)injIz=134> (1)
<{o}(r)njIs=14> (1)
<{o}(r)njIz=14> (1)
<{o}(r)njI{z}=14> (1)
<{o}[r]Nch=14> (3)
<{o}[r]Nj=14> (1)
<{o}[r]NjIz=144> (2)
<{o}[r][n]zhIz=14> (1)
<{o}[r]nch> (1)
<{o}[r]nchIz=14> (1)
<{o}[r]nj> (2)
<{o}[r]njIs=14> (1)
<{o}[r]njIz=14> (4)
<{o}[r]nzhIz=14> (1)
<{o}rNch=14> (5)
<{o}rNj=14> (11)
<{o}rNjIs=144> (1)
<{o}rNjIz=144> (11)
<{o}rNjiz=143> (1)
<{o}rN{j}=14> (3)
<{o}rN{j}Iz=144> (1)
<{o}rinj=13> (4)
<{o}rinjIz=134> (2)
<{o}rin{j}=13> (2)
<{o}rnj> (7)
<{o}rnjIz=14> (18)
<{o}rnjI{z}=14> (2)
<{o}wNjIz=144> (1)
<{o}{r}N(j)=14> (1)
<{o}{r}NchIz=144> (1)
<{o}{r}Nj=14> (1)
<{o}{r}NjIz=144> (2)
<{o}{r}nch> (1)
<{o}{r}nchIz=14> (1)
<{o}{r}nj> (1)
<{o}{r}njIz=14> (5)

055.1B P all gone
　{g}　devoiced
　{o}　low-back
　{oe}　lowered onset
　No Response (240)
<aw(1)gawn=21> (3)
<aw(1)gawn=31> (4)
<aw[1]gaw[n]=21> (1)
<aw[1]gaw[n]=31> (1)
<aw[1]gawn=12> (1)
<aw[1]gawn=13> (2)
<aw[1]gawn=21> (6)
<aw[1]gawn=31> (13)
<aw[1]goen=31> (1)
<aw[1]g{oe}n=31> (1)
<aw[1]g{o}n=12> (1)
<aw[1]g{o}n=31> (1)
<awlgaw[n]=11> (1)
<awlgaw[n]=21> (1)
<awlgaw[n]=31> (2)
<awlgawn=11> (8)
<awlgawn=13> (23)

<awlgawn=21> (51)
<awlgawn=31> (152)
<awlgoen=21> (1)
<awlgoen=31> (6)
<awlgon=21> (1)
<awlgon=31> (4)
<awlg{oe}n=21> (2)
<awlg{oe}n=31> (1)
<awlg{o}n=13> (1)
<awlg{o}n=21> (1)
<awlg{o}n=31> (3)
<gaw[n]> (3)
<gawn> (224)
<goen> (5)
<gon> (7)
<gown> (1)
<goyn> (1)
<gun> (1)
<g{oe}n> (16)
<g{o}[n]> (1)
<g{o}n> (44)
<hawlgawn=13> (1)
<h{o}lg{oe}n=31> (1)
<o(1)gawn=31> (1)
<o(1)gon=31> (1)
<o[1]gown=31> (1)
<olgawn=13> (1)
<olgawn=31> (4)
<olgon=21> (1)
<olgon=31> (1)
<olg{o}n=21> (1)
<{oe}lgawn=31> (1)
<{oe}lg{oe}n=21> (1)
<{o}(1)gawn=31> (1)
<{o}(1)g{oe}n=31> (1)
<{o}(1)g{o}n=21> (2)
<{o}[1]gawn=21> (2)
<{o}[1]g{oe}n=31> (1)
<{o}[1]g{o}n=21> (1)
<{o}[1]g{o}n=31> (1)
<{o}[1]{g}{o}n=31> (1)
<{o}lgawn=11> (2)
<{o}lgawn=13> (7)
<{o}lgawn=21> (4)
<{o}lgawn=31> (17)
<{o}lgont=31> (1)
<{o}lg{oe}n=21> (1)
<{o}lg{o}[n]=21> (1)
<{o}lg{o}n=12> (1)
<{o}lg{o}n=13> (1)
<{o}lg{o}n=21> (7)
<{o}lg{o}n=31> (16)

055.1 S gone
　No Response (5)
|J2C| (3)
|J2Deoa| (3)
|J2Heoa| (3)
|J2Hmdj| (1)
|JJHefj| (6)

|JJHffd| (1)
|JJHmfj| (1)
|JJHmfk| (1)
|JSC| (1)
|JSHefa| (2)
|JSHefj| (2)
|JSHffm| (1)
|JUCeoa| (1)
|JUDfod| (3)
|JUHeoa| (1)
|JUHfoc| (1)
|JUHmoj| (1)
|LFDjjc| (1)
|NFHmaj| (1)
|PAEjjc| (1)
|PAEqfm| (1)
|PFEqfa| (1)
|QAAjjb| (1)
|QAC| (1)
|QACjjc| (1)
|QACqab| (1)
|QACqff| (1)
|QADqfb| (1)
|QADqfd| (1)
|QADqfk| (1)
|QAHmaj| (1)
|QAHqfb| (4)
|QCAqfj| (1)
|QCHqfb| (1)
|QCHqff| (1)
|QDAjub| (1)
|QDCjub| (1)
|QDCqob| (1)
|QDDjuc| (1)
|QDHjua| (1)
|QDHqoa| (1)
|QDHqob| (1)
|QFA| (1)
|QFAjja| (1)
|QFAjjc| (3)
|QFAjjd| (1)
|QFAlfa| (1)
|QFAlfj| (4)
|QFAqfb| (16)
|QFAqff| (1)
|QFB| (9)
|QFBefa| (1)
|QFBjja| (3)
|QFBjjb| (3)
|QFBjjc| (24)
|QFBjjd| (17)
|QFBjjh| (2)
|QFBjjl| (4)
|QFBjjq| (1)
|QFBjsc| (7)
|QFBjsd| (3)
|QFBjud| (1)
|QFBmaj| (1)
|QFC| (10)

|TFAqfb| (2)
|TFAtfb| (1)
|TFB| (3)
|TFBjjb| (1)
|TFBjjc| (1)
|TFBmaj| (1)
|TFBqfa| (3)
|TFBqfb| (6)
|TFBqfj| (2)
|TFDjjc| (1)
|TFDqfb| (1)
|TKAjua| (6)
|TKAmda| (1)
|TKAmdj| (1)
|TKAqob| (1)
|TKDjua| (1)
|TMAmaa| (1)
|TMB| (3)
|TMBqfb| (2)
|TMBqfj| (2)
|TOAqob| (1)
|TOAqoj| (1)
|TOBqoa| (1)
|TOBqob| (2)
|TOBqok| (1)
|TXA| (1)
|TXB| (1)
|TXBjuj| (1)
|TXBqoamdj| (1)
|TXBqoc| (1)
|TXBqol| (1)

055.2 P radishes
{e} upglide
{t} flap
{z} devoiced
{?} glottal
No Response (159)
<ledIsh=14> (1)
<ra(d)Ish=14> (1)
<ra(d)IshIz=144> (1)
<radAshIz=144> (3)
<radAshI{z}=144> (1)
<radIs=14> (1)
<radIsh(Iz)=14> (6)
<radIsh=14> (156)
<radIshAz=144> (1)
<radIshIt=144> (1)
<radIshIz=144> (146)
<radIshI{z}=144> (6)
<radIshiz=143> (19)
<raddIsh=14> (1)
<radish=13> (46)
<radishAz=134> (2)
<radishI(z)=134> (1)
<radishIs=134> (1)
<radishIz=134> (74)
<radishI{z}=134> (19)
<raidIsh=14> (1)
<ralIsh=14> (1)

<ralishIz=134> (1)
<ratIsh=14> (1)
<ra{t}Ish=14> (11)
<ra{t}IshIz=144> (6)
<ra{t}dIsh=14> (1)
<ra{t}ish=13> (2)
<ra{t}ishIz=134> (1)
<ra{t}ishI{z}=134> (1)
<red(i)shIz=14> (1)
<redAshIz=144> (3)
<redIs=14> (1)
<redIsh(Iz)=14> (2)
<redIsh=14> (100)
<redIshAz=144> (1)
<redIshIz=144> (70)
<redIshI{z}=144> (3)
<redIshiz=143> (2)
<redIshi{z}=143> (1)
<redis=13> (1)
<redish=13> (16)
<redishAz=134> (1)
<redishI(z)=134> (1)
<redishIsh=134> (1)
<redishIz=134> (23)
<redishI{z}=134> (10)
<relAshiz=143> (1)
<relIsh=14> (1)
<re{t}IshIz=144> (1)
<re{t}IshI{z}=144> (1)
<ritIshI{?}=144> (1)
<rodIsh=14> (1)
<rodish=13> (1)
<rudAshA(z)=144> (1)
<rudIshI{z}=144> (1)
<rudish=13> (1)
<r{e}(dI)sh> (1)
<r{e}dIsh=14> (2)

055.3 L cherry tomato
No Response (35)
A acorn tomato (1)
B baby tomato (8)
C bell tomato (5)
D bullet tomato (1)
E bunch tomato (1)
F canning tomato (2)
G cherry (tomato) (192)
H cherry-type tomato (1)
I cocktail tomato (9)
J cooking tomato (1)
K domino (1)
L dwarf tomato (4)
M fig tomato (3)
N grape tomato (2)
O gravy tomato (1)
P hogpen tomato (1)
Q hybrid tomato (1)
R icebox tomato (2)
S Italian pear tomato (1)
T lemon tomato (1)

U little-bitty (to)mato (5)
V little-old tomato (1)
W little ornamental tomato (1)
X little thumb tomato (1)
Y little tomato (12)
Z love apple (4)
aa love tomato (1)
ab marble [n.] (1)
ac marble tomato (4)
ad mimmyto (1)
ae miniature [n.] (4)
af miniature tomato (3)
ag nest tomato (1)
ah old-fashion tomato (1)
ai outhouse tomato (3)
aj party tomato (1)
ak patio (tomato) (6)
al pear (tomato) (31)
am pear-shape tomato (1)
an pee wee tomato (1)
ao pendaligne (1)
ap pimento (1)
aq pink tomato (1)
ar pinto (to)mato (1)
as plum tomato (48)
at potted egg (tomato) (1)
au preserving tomato (1)
av privy tomato (1)
aw red tomato (1)
ax rose tomato (1)
ay running tomato (4)
az salad (tomato) (89)
ba salad-type tomato (1)
bb sallet tomato (2)
bc small tomato (13)
bd soup tomato (6)
be sour tomato (1)
bf sugar tomato (1)
bg sweet tomato (1)
bh teeny toe (1)
bi teeny tomato (1)
bj Texas tomato (1)
bk Thumbellina tomato (1)
bl Tiny Tim (2)
bm Tom Thumb (tomato) (2)
bn tom toe (2)
bo tom(-)tom (tomato) (4)
bp tom tomato (4)
bq tomate figue [F] (1)
br tommy (1)
bs tommy tomato (1)
bt tommyquat (1)
bu tommyto (183)
bv tommyto thing (1)
bw tommyto tomato (10)
bx toy tomato (1)
by tree tomato (6)
bz volunteer [n.] (3)
ca volunteer tomato (3)

cb   wild tomato (5)
055.3 P tomatoes
{d}   devoiced
{dh}   devoiced
{e}   upglide
{R}   weakly retroflex
{t}   voiced
{z}   devoiced
{?}   glottal
No Response (88)
<(tA)maidAz=14> (3)
<(tA)maidIz=14> (1)
<(tA)maidR=14> (2)
<(tA)maitAz=14> (1)
<(tA)maitA{z}=14> (1)
<(tA)maitR=14> (1)
<(tA)mai{t}Az=14> (7)
<(tA)mai{t}A{z}=14> (2)
<(tA)mai{t}Iz=14> (1)
<(tA)mai{t}{R}z=14> (1)
<dAmaitA=414> (1)
<dAmai{t}A=414> (1)
<dAm{e}dIz=414> (1)
<dAm{e}tIz=414> (1)
<dImai{t}A{z}=414> (1)
<pAmai{t}A=414> (1)
<shAmai{t}A{z}=414> (1)
<tAb{e}tA=414> (1)
<tAb{e}tA{z}=414> (1)
<tAmaidA=414> (14)
<tAmaidAz=414> (102)
<tAmaidA{z}=414> (1)
<tAmaidIz=414> (2)
<tAmaidR=414> (2)
<tAmaidRz=414> (5)
<tAmaidoe=413> (2)
<tAmaidoez=413> (1)
<tAmaidoe{z}=413> (2)
<tAmaitA=414> (4)
<tAmaitAz=414> (13)
<tAmaitA{z}=414> (7)
<tAmaitIz=414> (1)
<tAmaitRz=414> (4)
<tAmaitR{z}=414> (2)
<tAmaitoez=413> (4)
<tAmaituz=413> (1)
<tAmai{?}(Az)=41> (1)
<tAmai{t}A(z)=414> (1)
<tAmai{t}A=414> (36)
<tAmai{t}As=414> (1)
<tAmai{t}AsIz=4144> (1)
<tAmai{t}Az=414> (283)
<tAmai{t}AzI{z}=4144> (1)
<tAmai{t}Azh=414> (1)
<tAmai{t}A{z}=414> (25)
<tAmai{t}Iz=414> (8)
<tAmai{t}R=414> (3)
<tAmai{t}Rz=414> (26)
<tAmai{t}R{z}=414> (5)

<tAmai{t}oe=413> (2)
<tAmai{t}oez=413> (15)
<tAmai{t}oe{z}=413> (4)
<tAmai{t}tAz=414> (1)
<tAmai{t}toez=413> (1)
<tAmai{t}urz=413> (1)
<tAmai{t}{R}=414> (1)
<tAmai{t}{R}z=414> (22)
<tAmai{t}{R}{z}=414> (1)
<tAma{t}Az=414> (1)
<tAme{t}Az=414> (1)
<tAmitAz=414> (1)
<tAmotAz=414> (1)
<tAm{e}dA=414> (1)
<tAm{e}dAz=414> (1)
<tAm{e}tA=414> (1)
<tAm{e}tAdh=414> (1)
<tAm{e}tAs=414> (1)
<tAm{e}tAz=414> (4)
<tAm{e}tA{z}=414> (5)
<tAm{e}tI{dh}=414> (1)
<tAm{e}tI{z}=414> (1)
<tAm{e}tRz=414> (1)
<tAm{e}toe{z}=413> (1)
<tAm{e}{t}A=414> (1)
<tAm{e}{t}Az=414> (5)
<tAm{e}{t}A{z}=414> (3)
<tAm{e}{t}oez=413> (1)
<tImadAz=414> (1)
<tImai(t)oez=413> (1)
<tImaidAz=414> (2)
<tImaidA{z}=414> (1)
<tImaidoez=413> (2)
<tImaidoe{z}=413> (1)
<tImaid{R}{z}=414> (1)
<tImaitAz=414> (1)
<tImaitA{z}=414> (1)
<tImaitoez=413> (3)
<tImai{t}A=414> (5)
<tImai{t}Az=414> (83)
<tImai{t}A{z}=414> (35)
<tImai{t}Iz=414> (13)
<tImai{t}I{z}=414> (2)
<tImai{t}R=414> (1)
<tImai{t}Rz=414> (3)
<tImai{t}R{z}=414> (3)
<tImai{t}oe=413> (2)
<tImai{t}oez=413> (7)
<tImai{t}oe{z}=413> (4)
<tImai{t}{R}=414> (1)
<tImai{t}{R}z=414> (7)
<tImai{t}{R}{z}=414> (3)
<tIma{t}Az=414> (1)
<tImotoe{z}=413> (1)
<tImu{t}oe=413> (1)
<tIm{a}{t}Iz=414> (1)
<tIm{e}dAz=414> (1)
<tIm{e}{t}Az=414> (1)
<tMaitoez=413> (1)

<tMai{t}Az=414> (2)
<tMai{t}oez=413> (1)
<tM{e}tA=414> (1)
<tM{e}tA{dh}=414> (1)
<tM{e}tA{z}=414> (1)
<toemaidoez=133> (1)
<toemai{t}A=134> (1)
<toemai{t}Az=314> (1)
<toemai{t}{R}z=314> (1)
<toomai{t}oe=313> (1)
<tumaidAz=314> (1)
<tumai{t}Az=314> (4)
<tumai{t}A{z}=314> (1)
<t{R}mai{t}Rz=414> (1)
<t{R}mai{t}{R}=414> (1)
<t{R}mai{t}{R}z=414> (1)
<t{R}mai{t}{R}{z}=414> (2)
<{d}AmaitA{z}=414> (1)
<{d}Am{e}tI{z}=414> (1)
055.4 L potatoes
No Response (98)
A   bakers (1)
B   baking (1)
C   baking potatoes (7)
D   Ball potatoes (1)
E   boiling potatoes (1)
F   brown potatoes (1)
G   Bruce Reds (1)
H   bunch potatoes (1)
I   Burbank (3)
J   California white (1)
K   cobblers (7)
L   Early Bliss (1)
M   Early Rose (3)
N   eating potatoes (1)
O   elephants (1)
P   fall potatoes (2)
Q   great big jumbo potatoes (1)
R   Green Mountain (1)
S   hog potatoes (1)
T   Idaho bakers (2)
U   Idaho potatoes (43)
V   Idaho whites (2)
W   Idahoes (19)
X   Irish (18)
Y   Irish cobblers (8)
Z   Irish (po)tatoes (6)
aa   Irish potatoes (559)
ab   Irish white potatoes (1)
ac   Kennebec (7)
ad   little red potatoes (1)
ae   new (1)
af   new Irish potatoes (2)
ag   new ones (1)
ah   new potatoes (45)
ai   new red potatoes (1)
aj   nigger-killer potatoes (1)
ak   old potatoes (1)
al   old whites (1)

am   Piggy Bank (1)
an   pink Irish potatoes (1)
ao   pink potatoes (1)
ap   pink-skin potatoes (1)
aq   potatoes (542)
ar   (po)tatoes (75)
as   queen potatoes (1)
at   red (2)
au   red (po)tatoes (2)
av   Red Bliss (3)
aw   Red Bliss potatoes (1)
ax   red Irish potatoes (2)
ay   red ones (5)
az   red potatoes (38)
ba   red russets (1)
bb   Red Triumph (1)
bc   red-eye potatoes (1)
bd   red-skinned potatoes (1)
be   regular potatoes (1)
bf   russet potatoes (5)
bg   russets (5)
bh   seed potatoes (1)
bi   Sequoia (1)
bj   small potatoes (1)
bk   spring potatoes (1)
bl   spuds (25)
bm   straight potatoes (1)
bn   summer potatoes (2)
bo   Triumph (3)
bp   Triumph potatoes (2)
bq   white (3)
br   white cobblers (1)
bs   white Idaho (2)
bt   white Irish potatoes (1)
bu   white ones (3)
bv   white potatoes (73)
bw   white russet (2)
bx   White Star (1)
by   yams (1)
bz   young potatoes (1)

055.5 L sweet potatoes
No Response (154)
A   above-the-ground potatoes (1)
B   All Gold (1)
C   Allen (1)
D   Arkansas yams (1)
E   Arkansas Yellow (1)
F   blue yams (1)
G   Boones (1)
H   Boston potatoes (1)
I   botah (1)
J   Brizina potatoes (1)
K   buck yams (1)
L   bunch potatoes (1)
M   bunch yams (7)
N   burnt yams (1)
O   Centennials (3)
P   chokers (1)
Q   Coleman yams (1)

R   Colorado potatoes (1)
S   Contenders (1)
T   creole yams (1)
U   Cubas (1)
V   Dooley potatoes (1)
W   Dooley yams (8)
X   Dooleys (3)
Y   fart fruit (1)
Z   Florida yams (1)
aa   forked-leaf yams (1)
ab   Georgia potatoes (1)
ac   Georgia Reds (5)
ad   Gold Rush potatoes (1)
ae   Gold Rushes (1)
af   ground potatoes (1)
ag   jams (1)
ah   jumbos (1)
ai   Key West (1)
aj   Louisiana Improved (1)
ak   Louisiana yam (5)
al   Moody (1)
am   Moody (po)tatoes (1)
an   music roots (4)
ao   Nancy Hall (19)
ap   Nancy yams (1)
aq   nigger chokers (2)
ar   nigger killers (4)
as   nigger legs (1)
at   Norton yam potatoes (1)
au   Nuggets (1)
av   pink potatoes (1)
aw   pink yams (1)
ax   poot root (1)
ay   Porto Acorns (1)
az   Porto Rican potatoes (2)
ba   Porto Rican sweet potatoes (1)
bb   Porto Ricans (12)
bc   Porto Rico (31)
bd   Porto Rico potatoes (6)
be   Porto Rico sweet potatoes (1)
bf   Porto Rico yams (1)
bg   (Porto) Rico yams (2)
bh   (po)tato yams (1)
bi   potatoes (4)
bj   (po)tatoes (2)
bk   pumpkin yams (4)
bl   Queen of the South (1)
bm   red Porto Rico potatoes (1)
bn   red potatoes (12)
bo   red Spanish (2)
bp   red yams (5)
bq   Southern Queen sweet potatoes (1)
br   Southern Queens (2)
bs   Spanish potatoes (1)
bt   Spanish sweet potatoes (1)
bu   Spanish yam (1)
bv   spuds (1)
bw   strings (1)

bx   sugar yams (1)
by   Suss Kartoffel [G] (1)
bz   sweet potatoes (737)
ca   sweet (po)tatoes (7)
cb   Texas Longs (1)
cc   tramps (1)
cd   two-by-fours (1)
ce   upper-ground potatoes (1)
cf   white potatoes (5)
cg   white sweet potatoes (5)
ch   white yams (3)
ci   yam potatoes (11)
cj   yam (po)tatoes (1)
ck   yam yam (1)
cl   yammy-yammy (1)
cm   yams (398)
cn   yellow ones (2)
co   yellow potatoes (1)
cp   yellow yam potatoes (2)
cq   yellow yams (31)
cr   yellow-skin yams (1)

055.6 P onions
{dh}   devoiced
{n}   palatal
{oe}   lowered onset
{oo}   unrounded
{z}   devoiced
{zh}   devoiced
No Response (80)
\<awnIoen=143\> (1)
\<awnyN=14\> (1)
\<awnyNz=14\> (2)
\<awny[N](z)=14\> (1)
\<enyNz=14\> (1)
\<hunyN=14\> (2)
\<hunyN{z}=14\> (1)
\<h{oo}nyNz=14\> (1)
\<ingRnz=14\> (1)
\<ingRn{z}=14\> (1)
\<o[n]yNz=14\> (1)
\<o[n]yoontz=13\> (1)
\<oenyN=14\> (1)
\<oenyN{z}=14\> (1)
\<onyN=14\> (4)
\<onyNz=14\> (11)
\<onyN{z}=14\> (4)
\<oonyNz=14\> (5)
\<u[n]yN=14\> (2)
\<u[n]yNz=14\> (4)
\<u[n]yN{z}=14\> (1)
\<un(y)Nz=14\> (1)
\<unIyN{z}=144\> (1)
\<undyNz=14\> (1)
\<ungyNz=14\> (1)
\<unjNz=14\> (1)
\<unj[N]=14\> (1)
\<unyN(z)=14\> (2)
\<unyN=14\> (172)
\<unyNs=14\> (2)

<unyNth=14> (1)
<unyNz=14> (439)
<unyNzh=14> (1)
<unyN{dh}=14> (1)
<unyN{zh}=14> (1)
<unyN{z}=14> (162)
<uny[N](z)=14> (1)
<uny[N]=14> (2)
<uny[N]z=14> (2)
<uny[N]{z}=14> (1)
<unyenz=13> (1)
<unyin=13> (1)
<unyinz=13> (4)
<unyunz=13> (1)
<unyun{z}=13> (2)
<urnyN{z}=14> (1)
<u{n}(y)Nz=14> (6)
<u{n}(y)N=14> (1)
<u{n}(y)N{z}=14> (1)
<u{n}yNz=14> (5)
<u{n}yN=14> (3)
<{oe}nyNz=14> (1)
<{oo}nyN=14> (4)
<{oo}nyNz=14> (3)
<{oo}nyN{z}=14> (3)

055.7 L spring onions

No Response (250)
A   baby onions (1)
B   Bermuda onions (9)
C   Bermudas (1)
D   boots (1)
E   bunch of onions (1)
F   bunch onions (3)
G   button onions (1)
H   buttons (3)
I   chives (8)
J   cluster onions (1)
K   cocktail onions (1)
L   creole onions (3)
M   early onions (1)
N   echalotes [F] (1)
O   evergreen multiplying shallots (1)
P   evergreen onions (10)
Q   evergreens (1)
R   flat Dutch onions (1)
S   fresh onions (10)
T   garden onions (5)
U   green kind (1)
V   green ones (1)
W   green onions (298)
X   green shoots (1)
Y   green spring onions (1)
Z   green tops (2)
aa   green-onion tops (1)
ab   green-top onions (1)
ac   guinea nest (1)
ad   leaf onions (1)
ae   little butts (1)
af   little ones (1)

ag   mist onions (1)
ah   multipliers (9)
ai   multiply (3)
aj   multiply onions (6)
ak   multiplying (4)
al   multiplying onions (49)
am   multiplying variety (1)
an   nest-egg onions (1)
ao   nest eggs (1)
ap   nest onions (31)
aq   new onions (3)
ar   onion bulbs (1)
as   onion buttons (2)
at   onion plants (2)
au   onion sets (18)
av   onion slips (1)
aw   onion sprouts (1)
ax   onion stalks (1)
ay   onion tops (3)
az   onions (14)
ba   onions with green tops (1)
bb   pearl onions (3)
bc   red onions (1)
bd   salad onions (8)
be   sallet onions (4)
bf   scallions (52)
bg   scallops (2)
bh   sconions (1)
bi   sets (15)
bj   Seven Sisters (1)
bk   shallot onions (12)
bl   shallots (178)
bm   shell (1)
bn   shoats (1)
bo   silver skins (1)
bp   slip onions (1)
bq   slips (3)
br   spring buttons (1)
bs   Spring Maid onions (1)
bt   spring onions (91)
bu   stick-up onions (1)
bv   sweet onions (3)
bw   table onions (1)
bx   tender onions (2)
by   white globes (1)
bz   white nest onions (1)
ca   white onions (1)
cb   wild (1)
cc   wild onions (16)
cd   winter onions (6)
ce   winter shallots (1)
cf   young onions (12)

055.7 P shallots

{aw}   lower low-back
{o}   lower low-back
{r}   weakly retroflex
{?}   glottal
No Response (726)
<shAlots=41> (4)

<shalA(t)s=14> (1)
<shalAlunyNz=3414> (1)
<shalAps=14> (1)
<shalAt(s)=14> (1)
<shalAt=14> (5)
<shalAts=14> (30)
<shalAtunyN=1434> (1)
<shalIt=14> (2)
<shalIts=14> (15)
<shalawts=31> (1)
<shaleez=13> (1)
<shallAt=14> (1)
<shallAts=14> (1)
<shallots=13> (1)
<shaloe(t)z=13> (2)
<shaloet=31> (2)
<shaloets=13> (7)
<shaloets=21> (1)
<shalot=13> (1)
<shalots=13> (3)
<shalotunyN=1324> (1)
<shal{aw}ts=13> (1)
<shal{aw}ts=31> (1)
<shal{o}ts=31> (1)
<sharIts=14> (1)
<shelAt=14> (4)
<shelAts=14> (22)
<shelIt=14> (2)
<shelIts=14> (9)
<shelItunyNz=1414> (1)
<shelawts=31> (1)
<shelaw{?}(s)=31> (1)
<shellots=13> (1)
<sheloedlunyN=1324> (1)
<sheloek=13> (1)
<sheloet=13> (5)
<sheloets=13> (15)
<sheloetunyN=1324> (1)
<sheloetunyNz=1324> (3)
<shelootunyNz=2314> (1)
<shelot=13> (7)
<shelots=13> (19)
<shelots=31> (2)
<shelotunyNz=1314> (1)
<shelut=13> (1)
<sheluts=13> (1)
<shel{aw}ts=13> (1)
<shetlawt=13> (1)
<sholAts=14> (4)
<sholI(t)s=14> (1)
<sholIts=14> (1)
<sholItunyN=2414> (1)
<sholoet=31> (1)
<sholots=13> (1)
<sho{r}lIt(s)=14> (1)
<sho{r}lIts=14> (1)
<shuloe(t)=13> (1)
<shulot=31> (1)
<sh{o}lIts=14> (1)

<sh{o}lawt=31> (1)
<so(lA)ths> (1)

055.8 P okra

{oe}   lowered onset
{R}   weakly retroflex
{r}   devoiced
No Response (204)
<hoekrI=14> (1)
<hoek{r}A=14> (1)
<oek(r)A=14> (2)
<oek(r)I=14> (1)
<oekArA=144> (1)
<oekR=14> (1)
<oekrA=14> (252)
<oekrAz=14> (2)
<oekrI=14> (209)
<oekrIz=14> (1)
<oekrai=13> (2)
<oekree=13> (17)
<oekwA=14> (1)
<oekwai=13> (1)
<oekwee=13> (1)
<oek{R}=14> (1)
<oek{r}A=14> (91)
<oek{r}Az=14> (1)
<oek{r}I=14> (79)
<oek{r}Iz=14> (1)
<oek{r}ee=13> (1)
<oek{r}{R}=14> (1)
<oelk{r}I=14> (1)
<ukrA=14> (1)
<{oe}krA=14> (38)
<{oe}krI=14> (30)
<{oe}krai=13> (2)
<{oe}kree=13> (2)
<{oe}k{r}A=14> (10)
<{oe}k{r}I=14> (8)

055.9 P shriveled

{d}   devoiced
{R}   flap
{r}   devoiced
{v}   bilabial
{z}   devoiced
No Response (474)
<chrivLz=14> (1)
<sh(r)eevL=14> (1)
<sh(r)ivL=14> (2)
<shrevLd=14> (1)
<shribLz=14> (2)
<shrivL=14> (135)
<shrivLd=14> (58)
<shrivLs=14> (1)
<shrivLt=14> (1)
<shrivLz=14> (21)
<shrivL{d}=14> (10)
<shrivL{z}=14> (1)
<shriv[L]=14> (7)
<shriv[L]{d}=14> (1)
<shriv{R}=14> (1)

<shrizL=14> (3)
<shri{v}[L]=14> (1)
<shri{v}[L]d=14> (1)
<shruvL=14> (1)
<shwivL=14> (1)
<shwivLd=14> (1)
<shwivLt=14> (1)
<shwivLz=14> (1)
<shwizL=14> (1)
<sh{r}idhL=14> (1)
<sh{r}ivL=14> (4)
<sh{r}ivLd=14> (2)
<sh{r}ivLz=14> (3)
<skwivLz=14> (1)
<srivL=14> (36)
<srivLNG=144> (2)
<srivLd=14> (13)
<srivLz=14> (3)
<srivrL=14> (1)
<srwivrN=14> (1)
<swidlN=14> (1)
<swivL=14> (78)
<swivLI=144> (1)
<swivLN=144> (2)
<swivLd=14> (34)
<swivLz=14> (8)
<swivL{d}=14> (4)
<swiv[L]d=14> (2)
<swiv[L]{d}=14> (1)
<swizLd=14> (1)
<swoovLd=14> (1)
<swuvL=14> (1)
<s{r}ivL=14> (2)
<s{r}ivLd=14> (1)
<s{r}ivLz=14> (1)

055A.1 G cabbages

No Response (241)
A   cabbage (542)
B   cabbage[N-i] (147)
C   cabbages (108)

055A.2 L shell [v.]

No Response (175)
A   break the shell (1)
B   break them out (1)
C   bust (1)
D   bust them hulls open (1)
E   crack (1)
F   cut (1)
G   dip (1)
H   dish (1)
I   hand-shell (1)
J   hull (58)
K   hulled (1)
L   hulling (6)
M   hulling [n.] (1)
N   husk (1)
O   open (2)
P   peel (10)
Q   peeling (1)

R   pop (2)
S   pull open (1)
T   shade (1)
U   shell (584)
V   shelled (17)
W   shelling (32)
X   shuck (10)
Y   shucking (1)
Z   skin (2)
aa   snap (2)
ab   split (2)
ac   splitting (1)
ad   take them out of [D-0] shell (1)

055A.3 L butter bean

No Response (110)
A   baby lima (13)
B   baby lima bean (2)
C   bean (37)
D   bunch (3)
E   bunch bean (11)
F   bunch butter bean (12)
G   bunch lima (1)
H   bunch one (1)
I   bush bean (1)
J   bush butter bean (1)
K   bush lima (1)
L   butter (1)
M   butter bean (699)
N   calico (2)
O   calico bean (1)
P   calico butter bean (1)
Q   colored bean (1)
R   colored butter bean (3)
S   colored-spotted lima (1)
T   elephant ear (1)
U   Fordhook (10)
V   Fordhook bean (3)
W   Fordhook lima (3)
X   Fordhook lima bean (1)
Y   Fordhurst (1)
Z   garden bean (1)
aa   green bean (2)
ab   green butter bean (6)
ac   green lima (1)
ad   green lima bean (1)
ae   half-a-dollar bean (1)
af   hook (1)
ag   hull (1)
ah   hull bean (1)
ai   jumbo (1)
aj   lima (61)
ak   lima bean (387)
al   lima butter bean (3)
am   long-stem lima (1)
an   muddy butter bean (1)
ao   October (5)
ap   October bean (7)
aq   peanut bean (1)
ar   pieded (1)

B   beet leaves (1)
C   beet tops (5)
D   blue-stem collards (1)
E   cabbage collard (1)
F   carrot green(s) (1)
G   coarse greens (1)
H   collard greens (115)
I   collard leaves (1)
J   collard sallet (1)
K   collards (229)
L   collards greens (1)
M   cress(es) (2)
N   dandelion greens (5)
O   dandelions (5)
P   dock (3)
Q   dry-land cresses (1)
R   field cresses (1)
S   green salad (3)
T   green sallet (1)
U   green tops (1)
V   greens (337)
W   horse food (1)
X   kale (38)
Y   kale greens (1)
Z   kohlrabi (3)
aa   lamb's-quarter (1)
ab   leaves (1)
ac   light greens (1)
ad   mixed greens (1)
ae   mustard (205)
af   mustard greens (138)
ag   mustard salad (3)
ah   mustard sallet (3)
ai   nightshade (1)
aj   peppergrass (2)
ak   poke (21)
al   poke greens (8)
am   poke salad (64)
an   poke salad greens (3)
ao   poke sallet (53)
ap   purpletop (1)
aq   radish leaves (1)
ar   radish tops (4)
as   radishes (1)
at   rake (1)
au   rape (15)
av   rape sallet (1)
aw   rutabaga (1)
ax   rutabaga greens (1)
ay   rutabaga salad (1)
az   rutabaga tops (1)
ba   salad (45)
bb   salad greens (13)
bc   salad part (1)
bd   salad turnips (1)
be   saladox (1)
bf   sallet (48)
bg   sallet part (1)
bh   sass (2)

bi   spinach (106)
bj   spinach greens (2)
bk   tender greens (1)
bl   tender mustard (1)
bm   top part (1)
bn   tops (7)
bo   tops of a radish (1)
bp   tripe (1)
bq   turnip greens (439)
br   turnip heads (1)
bs   turnip leaves (1)
bt   turnip salad (34)
bu   turnip sallet (18)
bv   turnip tops (15)
bw   turnips (12)
bx   vegetable greens (2)
by   watercress(es) (3)
bz   wild cress (1)
ca   wild greens (6)
cb   winter collards (1)
cc   winter green (1)

055A.6 P heads
{d}   devoiced
{e}   upglide
{t}   flap
{z}   devoiced
No Response (284)
<(h)edz> (1)
<(h)ed{z}> (1)
<haid(z)> (2)
<haidz> (1)
<haid{z}> (4)
<haits> (1)
<hai{d}{z}> (2)
<he(dz)> (1)
<hed> (70)
<hed(z)> (109)
<heds> (1)
<hedz> (282)
<hed{z}> (49)
<he{d}s> (1)
<he{d}z> (2)
<he{d}{z}> (8)
<he{t}(z)> (2)
<hid> (1)
<hid(z)> (4)
<hidz> (5)
<hid{z}> (2)
<hit{z}> (1)
<hi{t}(z)> (1)
<hud(z)> (1)
<hudz> (3)
<hud{z}> (1)
<h{e}d> (14)
<h{e}d(z)> (15)
<h{e}dz> (63)
<h{e}d{z}> (11)
<h{e}{d}> (1)
<h{e}{d}(z)> (1)

<h{e}{d}{z}> (2)
<kedz> (1)
<ted{z}> (1)
055A.7 G heads (of children)
No Response (669)
A   head [livestock] (126)
B   heads [children] (47)
C   heads [livestock] (15)
D   head[N-i] [children] (68)
055A.8 P passel
{a}   upglide
{L}   devoiced
{o}   low-back
No Response (610)
<parsL=14> (1)
<pasL=14> (235)
<pas[L]=14> (5)
<passL=14> (53)
<pass[L]=14> (2)
<pasuel=13> (1)
<pas{L}=14> (1)
<pesL=14> (1)
<pessL=14> (1)
<p{a}sL=14> (7)
<p{o}sL=14> (2)
056.1 L shuck
No Response (94)
A   cob (1)
B   corn husk (7)
C   corn shuck (23)
D   cornhouse (1)
E   covering (1)
F   hull (2)
G   husk [n.] (130)
H   husk [v.] (6)
I   husking [v.] (2)
J   leaf (2)
K   peel (1)
L   roasting-ear shuck (1)
M   sheaf (1)
N   shell [n.] (3)
O   shell [v.] (8)
P   shelled [v.] (1)
Q   shock [n.] (5)
R   shock [v.] (2)
S   shocking [v.] (1)
T   shocks [v.] (1)
U   shuck [n.] (671)
V   shuck [v.] (60)
W   shucked [v.] (7)
X   shucking [v.] (6)
Y   silk (1)
Z   skin (3)
aa   slip-shuck [v.] (1)
056.2 L roasting ears
No Response (51)
A   baking ears (1)
B   Bantam (1)
C   Bantam corn (2)

D   big corn (1)
E   boil corn (25)
F   boiled corn (35)
G   boiled corn on the cob (1)
H   boiled on the cob (1)
I   boiled roasting ears (2)
J   boiling corn (3)
K   brier corn (1)
L   clear corn (1)
M   cob corn (1)
N   corn (258)
O   corn in the cob (2)
P   corn in the ear (1)
Q   corn off the cob (2)
R   corn on the cob (205)
S   corn on [D-0] cob (5)
T   corn [P-0] [D-0] cob (1)
U   cut corn (1)
V   dwarf corn (1)
W   ear(s) (8)
X   ear corn (5)
Y   ear(s) of corn (13)
Z   early corn (10)
aa   early roasting ears (1)
ab   early tender corn (1)
ac   eating corn (2)
ad   field corn (64)
ae   freezer corn (1)
af   fresh corn (9)
ag   fresh corn on the cob (1)
ah   fried corn (3)
ai   fried roasting ears (1)
aj   frozen corn (1)
ak   garden corn (2)
al   golden corn (1)
am   green corn (16)
an   horse corn (2)
ao   hybrid (1)
ap   hybrid corn (2)
aq   hybrid field corn (1)
ar   Indian corn (2)
as   Indian-type corn (1)
at   late corn (2)
au   late roasting ears (1)
av   maize (6)
aw   milo corn (1)
ax   milo maize (1)
ay   mule corn (1)
az   mutton corn (6)
ba   new corn (1)
bb   ninety-day corn (1)
bc   nubbins (1)
bd   off the cob (2)
be   on the cob (6)
bf   pencil-cob corn (1)
bg   popcorn (5)
bh   red corn (1)
bi   refrigerator corn (1)
bj   roasted (2)

bk   roasted ears (4)
bl   roasting corn (5)
bm   roasting ear(s) (532)
bn   roasting ear of corn (2)
bo   roasting-ear corn (20)
bp   roasting-ear stage (5)
bq   row corn (1)
br   seed corn (2)
bs   shell corn (1)
bt   short corn (1)
bu   soft corn (1)
bv   squirrel corn (1)
bw   stewed corn (1)
bx   strawberry corn (1)
by   strawberry popcorn (1)
bz   sugar corn (5)
ca   sweet (2)
cb   sweet corn (226)
cc   sweet ear (1)
cd   table corn (2)
ce   tasting stage (1)
cf   tender corn (3)
cg   white (4)
ch   white corn (33)
ci   white sweet (1)
cj   white sweet corn (1)
ck   white tender corn (1)
cl   whole grain corn (2)
cm   whole-kernel corn (3)
cn   yellow (5)
co   yellow corn (39)
cp   yellow field corn (2)
cq   yellow garden corn (1)
cr   yellow hybrid (1)
cs   yellow sweet corn (1)
ct   young corn (9)
cu   young roasting-ear corn (1)

056.3 P tassel
{a}   upglide
{e}   upglide
{o}   low-back
No Response (168)
<taizL=14> (1)
<tasL=14> (296)
<tasLN=144> (2)
<tasLd=14> (1)
<tasLz=14> (9)
<tas[L]=14> (28)
<tas[L]z=14> (1)
<taslNG=14> (1)
<tassL=14> (70)
<tassLz=14> (4)
<tass[L]=14> (9)
<tass[L]z=14> (1)
<tath[L]=14> (1)
<taws(L)> (2)
<tawsL=14> (171)
<tawsLN=144> (1)
<tawsLz=14> (8)

<taws[L]=14> (10)
<taws[L]z=14> (3)
<tawsh[L]=14> (1)
<tawssL=14> (6)
<tawss[L]=14> (1)
<tawz[L]=14> (1)
<tesL=14> (3)
<tosL=14> (98)
<tosLz=14> (2)
<tos[L]=14> (3)
<toslA=14> (1)
<tossL=14> (4)
<towsL=14> (1)
<tusL=14> (1)
<t{a}sL=14> (1)
<t{e}ssL=14> (1)
<t{o}sL=14> (36)
<t{o}sLz=14> (3)
<t{o}s[L]=14> (3)
<t{o}ssL=14> (2)
<t{o}ss[L]=14> (2)
<t{o}thL=14> (1)

056.4 L corn silk
No Response (167)
A   angel hair (1)
B   awn (1)
C   barbe, la [F] (2)
D   beard (7)
E   bottom (1)
F   corn beards (1)
G   corn hair (2)
H   corn silk (60)
I   corn silks (14)
J   hair (31)
K   hairs (2)
L   husk (1)
M   moustache (3)
N   red silk (1)
O   shoot (1)
P   silk (402)
Q   silk hair (1)
R   silks (256)
S   straw (1)
T   string (2)
U   string silk stuff (1)
V   strings (4)
W   stringy stuff (3)
X   stringy white stuff (1)
Y   threads (3)
Z   whiskers (7)

056.5 P pumpkin
{o}   low-back
{oe}   lowered onset
{oo}   unrounded
{p}   fricative
No Response (171)
<numpkNz=14> (1)
<paw[m](p)kN=14> (2)
<pawnkNz=14> (1)

<pawnk[N]=14> (1)
<po[m](p)kN=14> (3)
<pom(p)kN=14> (1)
<pom(p)kNz=14> (2)
<pom(p)kin=13> (1)
<pomp(k)N=14> (1)
<pompkN=14> (7)
<pompkNz=14> (2)
<pompkin=13> (1)
<pompwIt=14> (1)
<ponkN=14> (16)
<ponkNz=14> (3)
<ponkinz=13> (1)
<poom(p)kN=14> (1)
<poonkN=14> (2)
<pu[m](p)gNz=14> (1)
<pu[m](p)kN=14> (15)
<pu[m](p)kNz=14> (3)
<pu[m]pkN=14> (1)
<pu[m]pkNz=14> (1)
<pum(p)kN=14> (58)
<pum(p)kNz=14> (13)
<pum(p)kin=13> (3)
<pumpAkN=144> (1)
<pumpkN=14> (230)
<pumpkNs=14> (1)
<pumpkNz=14> (66)
<pumpk[N]=14> (1)
<pumpk[N]z=14> (2)
<pumpkin=13> (9)
<pumpkinz=13> (5)
<pumpkyN=14> (1)
<punkN=14> (231)
<punkNs=14> (2)
<punkNz=14> (82)
<punk[N]=14> (3)
<punk[N]z=14> (1)
<punkin=13> (6)
<p{oe}(n)kNts=14> (1)
<p{oo}m(p)kN=14> (1)
<p{oo}mpkN=14> (1)
<p{o}nkNz=14> (1)
<{p}unkN=14> (1)
<{p}unkin=13> (1)

056.6 P squash
{ie} low-central onset
{o} low-back
{oy} upglide/inglide
{r} weakly retroflex
{u} upglide
No Response (126)
<sk(w)osh> (3)
<skwash> (4)
<skwawchIz=14> (1)
<skwawrsh> (1)
<skwawsh> (130)
<skwawshAz=14> (1)
<skwawshIz=14> (4)
<skwaw{r}sh> (3)

<skwoch> (1)
<skwochIz=14> (1)
<skworsh> (7)
<skworshIz=14> (1)
<skwosh> (486)
<skwoshIz=14> (25)
<skwoysh> (3)
<skwo{r}sh> (3)
<skwursh> (1)
<skwush> (4)
<skw{ie}sh> (29)
<skw{oy}sh> (9)
<skw{o}(sh)> (1)
<skw{o}sh> (93)
<skw{o}shIz=14> (2)
<skw{o}t> (1)
<skw{o}{r}sh> (1)
<skw{o}{r}shIz=14> (1)
<skw{u}sh> (1)
<thkwawsh> (1)
<thkw{o}sh> (1)

056.7 L muskmelon
No Response (127)
A alligator melon (1)
B breakfast melon (9)
C cantaloupe (719)
D cantaloupe melon (1)
E Crenshaw (4)
F Crenshaw melon (1)
G creole mushmelon (1)
H Golden Honeymoon mushmelon (1)
I Honey Ball (1)
J mushmelon (340)
K muskmelon (91)
L Pecos (1)
M Rocky Ford (3)
N Rocky Ford cantaloupe (1)
O Rocky Ford melon (1)
P smell melon (2)
Q sugar melon (1)

056.8 L mushroom
No Response (165)
A champignon [F] (6)
B dry-land fish (5)
C frog house (1)
D frog umbrella (1)
E frogstool (2)
F mushroom (734)
G spring chicken (2)
H spring mushroom (1)
I stool (1)
J toad-frog (1)
K toadstool (14)
L woodfish (1)

056.8 P mushroom
{oo} urounded
{r} weakly retroflex
{u} upglide

{z} devoiced
No Response (165)
<bushruembsh=13> (1)
<meshruemz=13> (2)
<mooshrewm=13> (1)
<mooshruem=13> (1)
<mooshruemz=13> (1)
<moshruemz=13> (1)
<murshruem=13> (1)
<murshruemz=13> (3)
<musIruen=143> (1)
<mush(r)uem=13> (1)
<mushAruem=143> (6)
<mushAruem=341> (1)
<mushAruemz=143> (3)
<mushAruen=143> (2)
<mushAruenz=143> (1)
<mushIrewm=143> (1)
<mushIroom=143> (2)
<mushIrue[m]z=143> (1)
<mushIruem=141> (1)
<mushIruem=143> (24)
<mushIruem=341> (1)
<mushIruemz=143> (15)
<mushIruen=143> (5)
<mushIruenz=143> (5)
<mushLruemz=143> (1)
<mushrM=14> (2)
<mushrMz=14> (2)
<mushrewm=13> (19)
<mushrewmsh=13> (1)
<mushrewmz=11> (1)
<mushrewmz=13> (10)
<mushrewn=13> (1)
<mushrimz=13> (1)
<mushroom=13> (17)
<mushroomz=13> (4)
<mushroom{z}=13> (1)
<mushrue[m]=13> (2)
<mushruem=11> (1)
<mushruem=13> (261)
<mushruem=21> (2)
<mushruem=31> (1)
<mushruemdh=13> (1)
<mushruemz=13> (268)
<mushruemz=21> (3)
<mushruem{z}=13> (1)
<mushruen=13> (3)
<mushruenz=13> (5)
<mushrum=13> (1)
<mushyewm=13> (1)
<muskruem=13> (1)
<musrewmz=13> (1)
<musruem=13> (4)
<musruemz=13> (1)
<muszhruen=13> (1)
<muzhruem=13> (1)
<mu{r}shruem=13> (1)
<mu{r}shruemz=13> (1)

<m{oo}shAruem=143> (1)
<m{oo}shIruemz=143> (1)
<m{oo}shmew[m]=13> (1)
<m{oo}shrimz=13> (1)
<m{oo}shrue(m)=13> (1)
<m{oo}shruem=13> (2)
<m{oo}shruemz=13> (4)
<m{oo}shruenz=13> (1)
<m{oo}sruem=13> (1)
<m{u}shIruem=143> (1)
<m{u}shIruemz=143> (1)
<m{u}shrewm=13> (3)
<m{u}shrewnz=13> (1)
<m{u}shroomz=13> (1)
<m{u}shroon=13> (1)
<m{u}shruem=13> (24)
<m{u}shruemz=13> (21)
<m{u}shruen=13> (1)
<m{u}zhruem=13> (2)
<puzhruem=13> (1)

056.9 L watermelon

No Response (107)
A   African watermelon (1)
B   Alabama melon (1)
C   Alabama Striped Back (1)
D   Alabama Sweet (1)
E   All Heart (2)
F   alligator (1)
G   amber (1)
H   Apple Honey (1)
I   Archy Gray (1)
J   Arkansas Black (1)
K   banana (1)
L   big green (1)
M   big striper (1)
N   Black Beauty (1)
O   Black Diamond (21)
P   Black Giant (1)
Q   black melon (1)
R   black rind (1)
S   black seed (melon) (2)
T   black seed Golden Jubilee (1)
U   Black Snake (1)
V   Black Spanish (1)
W   blue one (2)
X   blue rind (1)
Y   Boss Talbott (1)
Z   cabin melon (1)
aa   Calhoun Sweet (3)
ab   Cannonball (11)
ac   Charleston (3)
ad   Charleston Gray (19)
ae   Charleston Green (1)
af   Charleston Red (1)
ag   Chufa Gray (1)
ah   citron (3)
ai   Colorado Rattlesnake (1)
aj   Congo (22)
ak   Congo Gray (1)

al   Congolean (1)
am   cotton-patch (water)melon (2)
an   cream color (1)
ao   cream meat (1)
ap   cream watermelon (1)
aq   Crimson Sweet (1)
ar   Crisscross (1)
as   Cuban Queen (5)
at   dark green (2)
au   Darlington (1)
av   Diamond (1)
aw   Diamondback (2)
ax   Dixie Gem (1)
ay   Dixie Queen (22)
az   Dixie Rattlesnake (1)
ba   Dixie Sweet (1)
bb   Early Dixie (1)
bc   favorite (1)
bd   Florida Favorite (4)
be   Florida Giant (1)
bf   Florida Gray (1)
bg   Florida Rattlesnake (1)
bh   Florida Sweet (1)
bi   Frigidaire watermelon (2)
bj   Garrison (2)
bk   Garrison Gray (1)
bl   Garrisonian (1)
bm   Gastonian (1)
bn   Georgia Rattlesnake (23)
bo   Georgia Sweet (2)
bp   Georgia (water)melon (3)
bq   Globe watermelon (1)
br   Golden Honey (1)
bs   golden something (1)
bt   Gray Irish (1)
bu   Gray Stone (2)
bv   Gray Strand (1)
bw   gray (water)melon (9)
bx   green (watermelon) (2)
by   green and white striped (1)
bz   Green England (1)
ca   green stripe (1)
cb   Guinea-Nest watermelon (1)
cc   Guinea watermelon (3)
cd   Hester melon (1)
ce   Honey Boy (1)
cf   honeycomb (1)
cg   Honeycorn (1)
ch   honeydew (1)
ci   ice-cold watermelon (1)
cj   ice-cream (water)melon (3)
ck   Ice Gray (1)
cl   ice rind (1)
cm   icebox (water)melon (33)
cn   Irish Gray (11)
co   Jones melon (1)
cp   Jubilee (5)
cq   jumbo (1)
cr   Kleckley Sweet (13)

cs   Knots (3)
ct   Kolb Gem (2)
cu   lemon watermelon (1)
cv   long one (2)
cw   long stripe melon (1)
cx   mammoth (1)
cy   Marlon melon (1)
cz   McGuire (1)
da   mellow melon (1)
db   melon (4)
dc   midget (1)
dd   mirliton (1)
de   Mitchell Yellow Meat (1)
df   Moon and (the) Star(s) (3)
dg   Mountain Dew (2)
dh   Mountain Gray (1)
di   Mountain Hoosier (1)
dj   Mountain Sprout (2)
dk   Mountain Sweet (2)
dl   Nancy (1)
dm   oblong (1)
dn   orange flesh (1)
do   penitentiary stripe (1)
dp   pink (1)
dq   pink-meat watermelon (1)
dr   Pride of Georgia (1)
ds   pumpkin (water)melon (2)
dt   pungo (1)
du   purple stripe (1)
dv   rattlesnake color (1)
dw   Rattlesnake (water)melon (70)
dx   Razorback (1)
dy   red (melon) (6)
dz   red(-)meat(ed) (water)melon
      (27)
ea   red seed (1)
eb   refrigerator melon (5)
ec   Reyuda Wonder (1)
ed   round (water)melon (2)
ee   Ruby Red (1)
ef   salmon (water)melon (2)
eg   Savanna Sweet (1)
eh   Scrimshaw (1)
ei   seed watermelon (1)
ej   seedless (1)
ek   semiround (1)
el   shipping (water)melon (2)
em   Smith melon (1)
en   snake (water)melon (2)
eo   Snider (1)
ep   solid(-)green (kind) (2)
eq   solid melon (1)
er   Southern Queen (1)
es   speckled (1)
et   Star melon (1)
eu   Stone Mountain (melon) (48)
ev   Stonewall Jackson (1)
ew   Stony Mountain (1)
ex   strawberry melon (1)

ey   streak-backed (1)
ez   streaked one (1)
fa   striped gooseneck (1)
fb   stripe(d) (water)melon (36)
fc   sugar (watermelon) (1)
fd   Sugar Baby (3)
fe   sugar(-)meat(ed) (3)
ff   Sugar Town (1)
fg   Sugarloaf (1)
fh   Sweet Valikia (1)
fi   sweet watermelon (1)
fj   Sweet William (1)
fk   Sweetheart (melon) (3)
fl   Tendersweet (1)
fm   Texas Giant (1)
fn   Texas Sweet (1)
fo   thick rind (1)
fp   thin rind (1)
fq   Thomas melon (1)
fr   Thompson (1)
fs   Thurmond Grey (2)
ft   Tom Watkins (1)
fu   Tom Watson (35)
fv   Unknown watermelon (1)
fw   watermelon (783)
fx   Watkins Green (1)
fy   Watson (water)melon (5)
fz   Wheeler watermelon (1)
ga   white (melon) (2)
gb   white-meated (2)
gc   white rind (1)
gd   white seed (1)
ge   white striped watermelon (2)
gf   Wonder (1)
gg   yellow (watermelon) (8)
gh   yellow-meat(ed) (water)melon
     (64)
gi   yellowbelly (1)

057.1 L toadstool

No Response (280)
A   angel mushroom (1)
B   black mushroom (1)
C   champignon [F] (1)
D   devil mushroom (1)
E   devil stool (1)
F   fairy seat (1)
G   fairy stool (2)
H   frog bed (1)
I   frog bench (3)
J   frog bread (1)
K   frog breath (1)
L   frog hat (1)
M   frog house (4)
N   frog nest (1)
O   frog noodle (1)
P   frog stuff (1)
Q   frog toad outfit (1)
R   frog toadstool (1)
S   frog umbrella (1)

T   frog's umbrella (1)
U   frogstool (86)
V   mushroom (31)
W   poison mushroom (14)
X   poisonous mushroom (4)
Y   puffball (1)
Z   stool (2)
aa   tadpole stool (1)
ab   toad (2)
ac   toad-frog (1)
ad   toad-frog house (2)
ae   toad-frog stool (4)
af   toadstool (503)
ag   toadystool (1)
ah   umbrella (2)
ai   wild mushroom (3)
aj   wild toadstool (1)

057.2 P swallow (it)

{aw}   low-back
{o}   low-back
{R}   weakly retroflex
{r}   weakly retroflex
No Response (171)
<shwo[1]oe=13> (1)
<shwolA=14> (1)
<shwolRIt=144> (1)
<shwollRIt=144> (1)
<swalA=14> (1)
<swalAwit=143> (1)
<swalR=14> (1)
<swaloewIt=134> (1)
<swal{R}=14> (1)
<swawlA=14> (1)
<swawlAIt=144> (1)
<swawlAit=341> (1)
<swawlRIt=144> (1)
<swawloeNG=134> (1)
<swo[1]Ait=141> (1)
<swol(A)It=14> (57)
<swol(A)N=14> (1)
<swol(A)it=13> (5)
<swol(A)rIt=14> (2)
<swolA(I)t=14> (10)
<swolA=14> (189)
<swolAIt=144> (45)
<swolAd=14> (1)
<swolAdIt=144> (2)
<swolAit=141> (2)
<swolAit=143> (28)
<swolArIt=144> (2)
<swolAwIt=144> (14)
<swolAwNG=144> (1)
<swolAwit=143> (8)
<swolAz=14> (1)
<swolI=14> (2)
<swolR(I)t=14> (11)
<swolR=14> (23)
<swolRI(t)=144> (1)
<swolRIt=144> (76)

<swolRd=14> (3)
<swolRit=143> (15)
<swolRit=341> (1)
<swoll(A)it=13> (1)
<swollA=14> (4)
<swollAIt=144> (2)
<swollAit=142> (1)
<swollRIt=144> (1)
<swollRd=14> (1)
<swolloe=13> (1)
<swolloeIt=134> (3)
<swollu{r}=13> (1)
<swolo=13> (1)
<swoloe=13> (35)
<swoloeIt=134> (29)
<swoloed=13> (1)
<swoloeit=123> (2)
<swoloeit=132> (5)
<swoloeit=133> (5)
<swoloerIt=134> (1)
<swoloewIt=134> (21)
<swoloewit=132> (5)
<swoloewit=133> (1)
<swoloez=13> (1)
<swoloe{r}It=134> (1)
<swoluelt=134> (1)
<swoluewIt=134> (1)
<swol{R}(I)t=14> (1)
<swol{R}=14> (14)
<swol{R}It=144> (14)
<swol{R}it=143> (9)
<swol{R}rIt=144> (2)
<swol{R}wIt=144> (1)
<swo{r}l{R}=14> (1)
<sw{aw}l(A)It=14> (1)
<sw{aw}lA=14> (9)
<sw{aw}lAit=143> (1)
<sw{aw}lAwIt=144> (1)
<sw{aw}lAz=14> (1)
<sw{aw}lRIt=144> (4)
<sw{aw}lRit=143> (1)
<sw{aw}loe=13> (5)
<sw{aw}loeIt=134> (1)
<sw{aw}l{R}=14> (1)
<sw{aw}l{R}It=144> (1)
<sw{o}[1](A)> (1)
<sw{o}l(A)It=14> (2)
<sw{o}lA=14> (20)
<sw{o}lAIt=144> (3)
<sw{o}lAit=143> (1)
<sw{o}lAwit=143> (1)
<sw{o}lR=14> (6)
<sw{o}lRIt=144> (6)
<sw{o}lloeIt=134> (1)
<sw{o}loe=13> (5)
<sw{o}loeIt=134> (1)
<sw{o}loeit=133> (1)
<sw{o}loewIt=134> (1)
<sw{o}l{R}It=144> (1)

<seeg{o}[r]=31> (1)

<sw{o}l{R}wIt=144> (1)
<thwol(A)N=14> (1)
<thwollRIt=144> (1)
<twollR=14> (1)

057.3A P cigars
  {o} low-back
  {r} weakly retroflex
  {z} devoiced
No Response (220)
<s(I)ga[r]> (1)
<sAgaw{r}z=41> (1)
<sAgorz=41> (2)
<sAgor{z}=41> (2)
<sAgo{r}z=41> (1)
<sIgaw[r]z=41> (1)
<sIgawrz=41> (1)
<sIgo(r)=41> (1)
<sIgo(r)z=41> (2)
<sIgo[r]=41> (3)
<sIgo[r]z=41> (3)
<sIgor=41> (11)
<sIgorz=41> (35)
<sIgor{z}=41> (9)
<sIgo{r}=41> (6)
<sIgo{r}z=41> (8)
<sIgo{r}{z}=41> (1)
<sIg{o}(r)=41> (2)
<sIg{o}(r)z=41> (1)
<sIg{o}[r]z=41> (2)
<sIg{o}[r]{z}=41> (1)
<sIg{o}r=41> (1)
<sIg{o}rz=41> (7)
<sIg{o}r{z}=41> (2)
<saigorz=31> (1)
<seegaw(r)=13> (1)
<seegaw[r]z=13> (1)
<seega{r}=12> (1)
<seego(r)=13> (1)
<seego(r)z=13> (2)
<seego[r]=13> (2)
<seego[r]=31> (1)
<seego[r]z=13> (5)
<seego[r]z=31> (1)
<seegor=13> (4)
<seegorz=13> (11)
<seegorz=31> (6)
<seegor{z}=13> (2)
<seegor{z}=21> (1)
<seegor{z}=31> (1)
<seego{r}=13> (1)
<seego{r}=31> (1)
<seego{r}z=13> (4)
<seego{r}z=31> (2)
<seeg{o}(r)=13> (3)
<seeg{o}(r)z=13> (3)
<seeg{o}(r)z=31> (1)
<seeg{o}(r){z}=31> (1)
<seeg{o}[r]=12> (1)
<seeg{o}[r]=13> (1)

<seeg{o}[r]=31> (1)
<seeg{o}[r]z=31> (2)
<seeg{o}[r]{z}=31> (1)
<seeg{o}r=13> (3)
<seeg{o}rz=13> (5)
<seeg{o}rz=31> (2)
<seeg{o}r{z}=31> (1)
<seeg{o}{r}=12> (1)
<seeg{o}{r}=31> (1)
<seeg{o}{r}z=13> (1)
<segor{z}=13> (1)
<sigaw(r)=13> (1)
<sigaw(r)=31> (2)
<sigaw(r)z=31> (2)
<sigaw[r]=21> (1)
<sigaw[r]z=13> (1)
<sigaw[r]z=31> (2)
<sigawr=13> (3)
<sigawr=21> (1)
<sigawr=31> (2)
<sigawrz=13> (2)
<sigawrz=31> (8)
<sigawr{z}=31> (1)
<sigaw{r}=13> (2)
<sigaw{r}=31> (1)
<sigaw{r}z=31> (1)
<sigaw{r}{z}=31> (1)
<sigo(r)=13> (7)
<sigo(r)=21> (1)
<sigo(r)=31> (3)
<sigo(r)z=13> (7)
<sigo(r)z=31> (7)
<sigo(r){z}=12> (1)
<sigo(r){z}=13> (3)
<sigo[r]=13> (11)
<sigo[r]=21> (2)
<sigo[r]=31> (6)
<sigo[r]z=13> (14)
<sigo[r]z=21> (1)
<sigo[r]z=31> (12)
<sigo[r]zh=13> (1)
<sigo[r]{z}=13> (6)
<sigo[r]{z}=21> (1)
<sigo[r]{z}=31> (1)
<sigor=13> (17)
<sigor=21> (2)
<sigor=31> (28)
<sigordh=12> (1)
<sigorz=12> (2)
<sigorz=13> (54)
<sigorz=21> (7)
<sigorz=31> (78)
<sigor{z}=12> (1)
<sigor{z}=13> (16)
<sigor{z}=21> (1)
<sigor{z}=31> (24)
<sigo{r}=12> (1)
<sigo{r}=13> (17)
<sigo{r}=31> (6)

<sigo{r}z=13> (12)
<sigo{r}z=21> (1)
<sigo{r}z=31> (21)
<sigo{r}{z}=13> (1)
<sigo{r}{z}=31> (2)
<sig{o}(r)=13> (7)
<sig{o}(r)=31> (1)
<sig{o}(r)z=13> (11)
<sig{o}(r)z=31> (3)
<sig{o}(r){z}=13> (1)
<sig{o}(r){z}=31> (1)
<sig{o}[r]=13> (5)
<sig{o}[r]=31> (3)
<sig{o}[r]z=12> (1)
<sig{o}[r]z=13> (7)
<sig{o}[r]z=31> (17)
<sig{o}[r]{z}=13> (2)
<sig{o}[r]{z}=31> (1)
<sig{o}r=13> (8)
<sig{o}r=31> (4)
<sig{o}rz=12> (1)
<sig{o}rz=13> (8)
<sig{o}rz=21> (1)
<sig{o}rz=31> (17)
<sig{o}r{z}=13> (6)
<sig{o}r{z}=31> (4)
<sig{o}{r}=13> (1)
<sig{o}{r}=31> (2)
<sig{o}{r}z=13> (6)
<sig{o}{r}z=31> (3)
<thigo{r}=13> (1)
<wigo{r}{z}=13> (1)

057.3B P cigarettes
  {R} weakly retroflex
  {?} glottal
No Response (197)
<sIgArets=441> (3)
<sIgRets=441> (3)
<sIgRrets=441> (1)
<see(g)Arets=143> (1)
<seeg(A)rets=13> (3)
<seegAret=143> (2)
<seegArets=143> (3)
<seegArit=143> (1)
<seegArits=341> (1)
<seegIrets=241> (1)
<seegRets=143> (1)
<seegRrets=143> (1)
<segArets=142> (1)
<segArets=143> (1)
<seg{R}rets=143> (1)
<shig(A)rets=13> (1)
<sig(A)ret=13> (1)
<sig(A)rets=12> (1)
<sig(A)rets=13> (18)
<sig(A)rets=31> (1)
<sigArAts=144> (1)
<sigArIt=144> (1)
<sigArIts=144> (3)

<sigArat=143> (1)
<sigAre(t)s=143> (1)
<sigAret(s)=143> (1)
<sigAret=143> (97)
<sigAret=341> (7)
<sigArets=142> (2)
<sigArets=143> (287)
<sigArets=241> (1)
<sigArets=341> (130)
<sigArit=143> (1)
<sigArits=143> (3)
<sigIrIts=144> (1)
<sigIret=143> (2)
<sigIret=341> (1)
<sigIrets=143> (15)
<sigIrets=341> (4)
<sigRe(t)=143> (1)
<sigRet=142> (1)
<sigRet=143> (7)
<sigRet=241> (1)
<sigRet=341> (1)
<sigurets=123> (1)
<sigRets=143> (50)
<sigRets=241> (1)
<sigRets=341> (8)
<sigRit=143> (1)
<sigRits=143> (2)
<sigRi{?}=143> (1)
<sigRret=143> (1)
<sigRret=241> (1)
<sigRrets=143> (12)
<sigRrets=341> (4)
<sigRretth=143> (1)
<sigRre{?}=143> (1)
<sigoret=132> (1)
<sigorets=123> (1)
<sigorets=231> (2)
<sigorets=321> (1)
<sig{R}e(t)s=143> (1)
<sig{R}ets=143> (2)
<sig{R}ets=341> (1)
<sig{R}ret=143> (2)
<sig{R}rets=143> (7)
<sig{R}rets=341> (2)
<thigRrets=341> (1)

057.4 G a-(+ pres. part.)
No Response (356)
A   a-[+pres. part.] (356)

057.5 L obligated
No Response (557)
A   behold(en) (1)
B   beholden (47)
C   beholding (6)
D   bother, a (13)
E   botheration, a (1)
F   bothering you (2)
G   bothersome (1)
H   bounden (1)
I   burden, a (13)

J   dependent (2)
K   heavy on you (1)
L   impairment on you, an (1)
M   imposing (on you) (6)
N   in debt (to you) (17)
O   in his debt (1)
P   indebted (to) (24)
Q   (in)debted (1)
R   intruding on (1)
S   involved (with anybody) (5)
T   leech, a (1)
U   no obligation (1)
V   no trouble to you (1)
W   nuisance, a (1)
X   obligated (229)
Y   obliged (to you) (6)
Z   (o)bliged to you (1)
aa obliging (1)
ab on charity (1)
ac owing (to you) (4)
ad tied up (1)
ae trouble, (any) (5)
af unbeholdens (1)
ag under (any) obligation (4)
ah under obligations (2)
ai upholden (1)
aj worried up (1)
ak worry [n.] (1)

057.6 P can [v./stressed]
{a}   upglide
{e}   upglide
No Response (549)
<ka[n]> (2)
<kain> (1)
<kan> (211)
<ken> (61)
<kin> (98)
<kun> (4)
<k{a}n> (6)
<k{e}n> (2)

057.7 P can't
{a}   upglide
{e}   upglide
{?}   glottal
No Response (75)
<ka[n](t)> (7)
<ka[n]t> (1)
<kai[n](t)> (21)
<kai[n]t> (2)
<kain(t)> (133)
<kaint> (418)
<kain{?}> (1)
<kan(t)> (24)
<kand> (1)
<kant> (319)
<kan{?}> (6)
<kent> (71)
<ken{?}> (1)
<kint> (1)

<kont> (1)
<kyant> (4)
<k{a}[n]t> (1)
<k{a}n(t)> (10)
<k{a}nt> (67)
<k{e}[n](t)> (2)
<k{e}n(t)> (6)
<k{e}nt> (32)
<k{e}n{?}> (1)

057.8 G done [+ v.]
No Response (543)
A   done[+V] (371)

057.9 G done [+ adj./adv.]
No Response (870)
A   done[+A] [adj.] (41)
B   done[+B] [adv.] (3)

058.1 G should (be careful)
No Response (308)
A   belong(s) to (8)
B   (had) better (14)
C   has/have to (4)
D   is to (1)
E   need(s) to (7)
F   ought to (240)
G   ought [P-0] (2)
H   should (372)
I   supposed to (207)

058.2 G dare not
No Response (753)
A   dare not (42)
B   dare to not (1)
C   daren't (6)
D   dasn't (10)
E   don't/didn't dare (30)
F   don't want to take a dare (1)
G   durstn't (1)
H   won't dare (7)
I   won't stand a dare (1)
J   won't take the dare (1)
K   wouldn't dare (34)

058.3 G ought
No Response (309)
A   belong(s) to (2)
B   better (1)
C   ought to (416)
D   ought to better (1)
E   ought to have (17)
F   ought to [X-0] (63)
G   ought to've (2)
H   profess to (1)
I   should (135)
J   should have (124)
K   should [X-0] (1)
L   should've (11)
M   supposed to (104)
N   supposed to have (2)
O   supposed to [X-0] (4)
P   supposed to've (2)

058.4 G ought not

No Response (329)
A ain't supposed to (6)
B aren't supposed to (2)
C didn't ought (2)
D didn't ought not [P-0] have (1)
E don't suppose(d) to (2)
F had better not (1)
G hadn't have didn't (1)
H hadn't ought to (5)
I hadn't ought to [X-0] (3)
J hadn't ought to've (1)
K hain't supposed to (1)
L never should have (1)
M not supposed to (17)
N not supposed to have (1)
O ought not (to) (109)
P ought not to have (64)
Q ought not to [X-0] (21)
R ought not to've (6)
S ought not [P-0] (8)
T ought not [P-0] had (1)
U ought not [P-0] have (26)
V ought not [P-0] [X-0] (11)
W ought to didn't (1)
X ought to not (1)
Y ought to not have (1)
Z ought to not to (1)
aa ought to not to have (1)
ab ought to not [X-0] (1)
ac ought to [X-0] not to [X-0] (1)
ad oughtn't not (to) (1)
ae oughtn't not to [X-0] (1)
af oughtn't (to) (35)
ag oughtn't to have (10)
ah oughtn't to not (1)
ai oughtn't to [X-0] (5)
aj oughtn't to've (1)
ak oughtn't [P-0] (8)
al oughtn't [P-0] have (26)
am oughtn't [P-0] [X-0] (3)
an should have not (2)
ao should have not have (1)
ap should not (17)
aq should not have (27)
ar shouldn't (111)
as shouldn't ever [X-0] (1)
at shouldn't had (1)
au shouldn't have (244)
av shouldn't have ought (to have) (3)
aw shouldn't never (1)
ax shouldn't not have (1)
ay shouldn't ought to (5)
az shouldn't [X-0] (4)
ba wasn't not supposed to (1)
bb wasn't supposed to (16)
bc weren't supposed to (3)
bd wouldn't be supposed to (1)
be [X-0] better not (3)

058.5 P won't
{o} low-back
{oe} lowered onset
{?} glottal
No Response (321)
<wawn(t)> (1)
<wawnt> (8)
<wawn{?}> (1)
<woe(nt)> (1)
<woe[n](t)> (18)
<woe[n]t> (24)
<woe[n]{?}> (1)
<woen(t)> (90)
<woent> (289)
<woen{?}> (4)
<wont> (3)
<wuent> (1)
<wunt> (5)
<w{oe}[n](t)> (7)
<w{oe}[n]t> (5)
<w{oe}n(t)> (14)
<w{oe}nt> (162)
<w{oe}n{?}> (1)
<w{o}nt> (1)

058.6 G might have
No Response (370)
A could (4)
B could did have (1)
C could have (86)
D could [X-0] (2)
E couldn't (1)
F couldn't have (2)
G could've (8)
H may (4)
I may have (14)
J might (119)
K might have (351)
L might have not (2)
M might have not have (1)
N might not (6)
O might not have (4)
P might [X-0] (13)
Q might've (30)
R might've not (1)
S mought (1)
T mought have (3)
U ought to have (1)
V ought to [X-0] (1)
W should (1)
X should have (21)
Y shouldn't have (1)
Z should've (3)
aa would (1)
ab would have (3)

058.7 G might could
No Response (327)
A could (20)
B could might (1)
C couldn't (1)

D may (15)
E may can (8)
F may not can (1)
G may not ought to (1)
H may would (1)
I might (376)
J might can (48)
K might can't (1)
L might could (have) (193)
M might couldn't (2)
N might could've (1)
O might have could (have) (5)
P might have would (have) (3)
Q might not can (1)
R might ought not [P-0] (1)
S might ought to (2)
T might should (have) (3)
U might will (2)
V might would (have) (37)
W might wouldn't (2)
X must can (1)
Y should (1)
Z used to could (23)
aa used to couldn't (1)
ab used to might (1)
ac used to would (7)
ad used to wouldn't (1)
ae used [P-0] could (2)
af would may (1)
ag would might have (1)

059.1 L screech owl
No Response (155)
A barn owl (31)
B barnyard owl (1)
C barred owl (1)
D brown owl (1)
E cat owl (3)
F chouette, la [F] (3)
G crinch owl (2)
H deaf owl (2)
I death owl (4)
J freezing owl (1)
K frog owl (1)
L haunted owl (1)
M hoot owl (1)
N horn owl (1)
O lechuza [S] (2)
P monkey-faced owl (2)
Q moonlight owl (1)
R mouse owl (1)
S nightowl (12)
T owl (394)
U peep owl (1)
V pygmy owl (1)
W quibbling owl (1)
X quivering owl (3)
Y red owl (1)
Z sand owl (1)
aa screak owl (1)

ab   screaming owl (2)
ac   screech (2)
ad   screech owl (456)
ae   screeching owl (8)
af   scrinch owl (23)
ag   scrinching owl (1)
ah   scrooch owl (87)
ai   scrunch owl (1)
aj   shiver owl (2)
ak   shivering owl (17)
al   shriek owl (1)
am   skrink owl (1)
an   snowy owl (1)
ao   squeak owl (4)
ap   squeech owl (5)
aq   squeeching owl (2)
ar   squinch owl (36)
as   squinching owl (2)
at   squink owl (1)
au   squinky owl (1)
av   squint owl (1)
aw   streak owl (1)
ax   streaking owl (1)
ay   swamp owl (2)
az   swinch owl (1)
ba   swink owl (1)
bb   tchi-tchi (1)
bc   tree owl (3)
bd   walleyed owl (1)
be   whistle owl (1)
bf   white owl (1)

059.1 P screech owl
{a}   inglide
{ow}   inglide/unrounded offset
{r}   devoiced
No Response (305)
<(s)kreech{ow}l=13> (1)
<(s)kreeshNGowl=143> (1)
<(s)krinchowl=13> (2)
<(s)kwinchow[1]=13> (1)
<(s)kwinchowl=13> (1)
<s(k)reech{ow}lz=13> (1)
<s(k)weechowl=13> (1)
<s(k)weenkowL=134> (1)
<s(k)winchowl=13> (1)
<shkreechow[1]=13> (1)
<shruech{ow}l=13> (1)
<sk(r)ewchowl=13> (1)
<sk(r)uechowl=13> (3)
<sk(r)uech{ow}l=13> (1)
<skre[n]chowlz=13> (1)
<skrechowl=13> (1)
<skreechNGowl=143> (1)
<skreechNow[1]=143> (1)
<skreechNowlz=143> (1)
<skreecha[1]=13> (1)
<skreechal=13> (1)
<skreechalz=13> (1)
<skreechhow[1]=13> (1)

<skreechow(1)=13> (2)
<skreechow[1]=13> (12)
<skreechow[1]z=13> (1)
<skreechowl=11> (2)
<skreechowl=13> (165)
<skreechowlz=13> (25)
<skreechowwL=134> (1)
<skreech{a}l=13> (5)
<skreech{a}lz=13> (1)
<skreech{a}wL=134> (3)
<skreech{a}wl=13> (1)
<skreech{ow}[1]=13> (1)
<skreech{ow}[1]zh=13> (1)
<skreech{ow}l=13> (60)
<skreech{ow}lz=13> (5)
<skreech{ow}wL=134> (1)
<skreej{ow}l=13> (1)
<skreekNowl=143> (1)
<skreekowl=13> (2)
<skreek{ow}l=13> (1)
<skreenchowl=13> (3)
<skrenchowL=134> (1)
<skrenchowl=13> (1)
<skrenchowlz=13> (1)
<skrewchowl=13> (1)
<skrichow[1]z=11> (1)
<skrichowl=13> (4)
<skrichowlz=13> (3)
<skrich{ow}l=13> (2)
<skrinchNow[1]=143> (1)
<skrinchal=13> (1)
<skrinchow[1]=13> (3)
<skrinchowl=13> (5)
<skrinch{ow}lz=13> (2)
<skrinkow[1]=13> (1)
<skruecha[1]z=13> (1)
<skruechal=13> (1)
<skruechalz=13> (1)
<skruechow(1)=13> (1)
<skruechow[1]=13> (1)
<skruechowl=13> (38)
<skruechowl=21> (1)
<skruechowlz=13> (1)
<skruech{a}l=13> (1)
<skruech{a}wL=134> (1)
<skruech{ow}l=13> (6)
<skruech{ow}lz=13> (3)
<skruenchowl=13> (1)
<skrunchowl=13> (1)
<skwechowl=13> (1)
<skweechNowl=143> (2)
<skweechiewL=134> (1)
<skweechol=13> (1)
<skweechow[1]=13> (1)
<skweechowl=13> (15)
<skweechowlz=13> (1)
<skweechowwL=134> (2)
<skweech{a}[1]=13> (1)
<skweech{a}wL=134> (2)

<skweech{ow}l=13> (6)
<skweek{a}w[L]=134> (1)
<skweencho[1]=13> (1)
<skweenchowL=134> (1)
<skweenchowl=13> (1)
<skweench{ow}l=13> (1)
<skwenchNowlz=143> (1)
<skwichow[1]=13> (1)
<skwichowl=13> (1)
<skwich{ow}l=13> (1)
<skwinchNowl=143> (1)
<skwinchal=13> (1)
<skwinchowL=134> (2)
<skwinchow[1]=13> (6)
<skwinchowl=13> (13)
<skwinchowlz=13> (1)
<skwinchowwL=134> (1)
<skwinchoww[L]=134> (1)
<skwinch{a}[1]=13> (1)
<skwinch{a}l=13> (1)
<skwinch{ow}l=13> (2)
<skwinkIowl=143> (1)
<skwinkowl=13> (1)
<skwishow(1)=13> (1)
<sk{r}eechIowl=143> (1)
<sk{r}eechNowl=143> (1)
<sk{r}eechowLz=134> (1)
<sk{r}eechow[1]=11> (1)
<sk{r}eechow[1]=13> (9)
<sk{r}eechow[1]z=13> (3)
<sk{r}eechowl=13> (73)
<sk{r}eechowlz=13> (15)
<sk{r}eechowwL=134> (3)
<sk{r}eechowwLz=134> (1)
<sk{r}eechskreechowl=113> (1)
<sk{r}eech{a}[1]=13> (1)
<sk{r}eech{ow}l=13> (11)
<sk{r}eech{ow}lz=13> (2)
<sk{r}eech{ow}wLz=134> (1)
<sk{r}eet{ow}l=13> (1)
<sk{r}ichNowl=143> (1)
<sk{r}ichowl=13> (1)
<sk{r}ich{ow}l=13> (2)
<sk{r}ich{ow}lz=13> (1)
<sk{r}inchowL=134> (1)
<sk{r}inchowl=13> (2)
<sk{r}inchowwL=134> (1)
<sk{r}inch{ow}l=13> (1)
<sk{r}uechal=13> (1)
<sk{r}uechowl=13> (10)
<sk{r}uechowlz=13> (4)
<sk{r}uech{ow}l=13> (2)
<streech{ow}l=13> (1)
<streekstreekowl=113> (1)
<st{r}uechowl=13> (1)
<thkruech{ow}[1]=13> (1)
<threcho[1]=13> (1)

059.2 L hoot owl
No Response   (156)

A   barn owl (48)
B   barned owl (1)
C   barnyard owl (1)
D   big-eyed owl (1)
E   big-head owl (2)
F   boo-hoo owl (1)
G   booby owl (1)
H   bottom owl (1)
I   brown owl (1)
J   cat owl (1)
K   cat-looking owl (1)
L   chicken owl (11)
M   cuckoo owl (1)
N   Domineck owl (1)
O   eight hooter (1)
P   French owl (1)
Q   gourd-headed owl (1)
R   gray owl (2)
S   great horn owl (1)
T   great horned owl (6)
U   ground owl (1)
V   hawk owl (1)
W   hawkeye owl (1)
X   hen owl (2)
Y   hoo owl (70)
Z   hoo-hoo owl (9)
aa   hoo-hoo-hoo owl (1)
ab   hoo-hoo-hoo-hoo owl (1)
ac   hoo-hoop owl (1)
ad   hooded owl (1)
ae   hoop owl (1)
af   hoople owl (1)
ag   hoopy owl (1)
ah   hoot owl (482)
ai   hooter owl (1)
aj   hooting owl (84)
ak   hooty owl (4)
al   horn owl (84)
am   horned hoot owl (1)
an   horned owl (44)
ao   horny owl (3)
ap   hornyhead owl (1)
aq   house owl (1)
ar   laughing owl (2)
as   marsh owl (1)
at   monkey owl (1)
au   moonlight owl (1)
av   mountain owl (1)
aw   nightowl (18)
ax   owl (163)
ay   pooch owl (1)
az   quivering owl (1)
ba   rabbit owl (1)
bb   rooster owl (1)
bc   roundhead owl (1)
bd   screech owl (1)
be   shivering owl (1)
bf   skunk owl (1)
bg   snow owl (4)

bh   snowy owl (3)
bi   swamp owl (14)
bj   tecolote, el [S] (1)
bk   timber owl (1)
bl   tree owl (3)
bm   tufted owl (1)
bn   white owl (12)
bo   white-faced owl (1)
bp   whoop owl (1)
bq   whooping owl (12)
br   wood owl (3)
bs   woods owl (1)

059.2 P owl

{a}   raised low-front onset/glide
{o}   lower high-front onset/glide
{ow}   raised low-front onset/
    rounded offset
No Response (92)
<a[1]> (2)
<al> (4)
<alz> (2)
<b{ow}l> (1)
<h{ow}lz> (1)
<iel> (1)
<ieoelz=13> (1)
<iewL=14> (1)
<o[1]> (2)
<oelz> (2)
<ow(1)> (5)
<owL=14> (14)
<owLz=14> (1)
<ow[1]> (20)
<ow[1]z> (1)
<owl> (232)
<owlz> (26)
<owwL=14> (10)
<oww[L]=14> (1)
<{a}[1]> (11)
<{a}[1]zh> (1)
<{a}l> (80)
<{a}lz> (11)
<{a}wL=14> (3)
<{ow}(1)> (8)
<{ow}L=14> (2)
<{ow}[1]> (30)
<{ow}[1]z> (8)
<{ow}l> (261)
<{ow}ldz> (1)
<{ow}lz> (30)
<{ow}wL=14> (18)
<{ow}wLz=14> (1)
<{ow}w[L]=14> (2)
<{o}L=14> (1)
<{o}[1]> (9)
<{o}[1]z> (1)
<{o}l> (48)
<{o}lz> (5)
<{o}wL=14> (4)
<{o}wLz=14> (1)

<{o}w[L]=14> (2)

059.2 S owl
No Response (48)
|OAAefa| (1)
|OAAffj| (1)
|OAAjja| (1)
|OAAjjd| (10)
|OAAjje| (1)
|OAAjjk| (1)
|OAAlfe| (1)
|OAAmaa| (8)
|OAAmae| (1)
|OAAmaj| (1)
|OABefa| (1)
|OABjjd| (5)
|OABjjm| (1)
|OABmaj| (2)
|OABmfacba| (1)
|OACeaa| (7)
|OACefa| (22)
|OACefc| (1)
|OACefe| (1)
|OACefj| (10)
|OACefjcba| (1)
|OACffd| (3)
|OACffm| (11)
|OACjbd| (3)
|OACjbm| (2)
|OACjja| (6)
|OACjjb| (5)
|OACjjc| (4)
|OACjjd| (82)
|OACjjdcba| (11)
|OACjjdcbj| (1)
|OACjjdmaj| (1)
|OACjjf| (2)
|OACjjl| (3)
|OACjjm| (7)
|OACjjmcba| (1)
|OACjjmmaa| (5)
|OACjsd| (2)
|OACkaj| (1)
|OAClfa| (1)
|OAClfe| (1)
|OACmaa| (7)
|OACmaj| (5)
|OACmajcba| (1)
|OACmfa| (8)
|OACmfacba| (1)
|OACmfj| (4)
|OADjjd| (1)
|OAEjjdcba| (1)
|OAEmaj| (1)
|OAGjjd| (2)
|OAGjjdcba| (2)
|OAGmaj| (1)
|OAH| (1)
|OAIeaa| (8)
|OAIefa| (11)

|OAIffd| (1)
|OAIjjd| (3)
|OAIjjdcba| (1)
|OAIjjmmaa| (1)
|OAImaa| (2)
|OAImaj| (2)
|OAImfj| (1)
|OAUjjd| (1)
|OCAeaa| (1)
|OCAefa| (1)
|OCAfajmaa| (1)
|OCAjja| (1)
|OCAjjb| (2)
|OCAjjd| (10)
|OCAjjjcba| (2)
|OCAlfacba| (1)
|OCAlfacbj| (1)
|OCAlfamaa| (2)
|OCAmaa| (4)
|OCAmae| (1)
|OCAmaj| (2)
|OCAmajcba| (5)
|OCAmfj| (1)
|OCBjjd| (1)
|OCBmaa| (1)
|OCBmaj| (1)
|OCBmfa| (1)
|OCC| (3)
|OCCcbj| (1)
|OCCeaa| (2)
|OCCefa| (5)
|OCCefc| (1)
|OCCefj| (5)
|OCCffd| (2)
|OCCffh| (1)
|OCCffjmaacba| (1)
|OCCffm| (1)
|OCCjbd| (1)
|OCCjja| (1)
|OCCjjd| (25)
|OCCjjdcba| (1)
|OCCjjdcbamaj| (1)
|OCCjjdmaj| (1)
|OCCjjf| (1)
|OCCjjjcba| (1)
|OCCjjm| (2)
|OCCmaa| (7)
|OCCmaj| (12)
|OCCmfa| (3)
|OCCmfe| (1)
|OCCmfj| (1)
|OCDjja| (1)
|OCFjba| (1)
|OCGjjd| (1)
|OCGjjh| (1)
|OCIjjd| (1)
|OCIjjm| (1)
|OCIjjmmaa| (1)
|OCImaj| (1)

|OCSmajcba| (2)
|ODBjub| (1)
|OGCjbd| (1)
|OHCjuk| (1)
|OKAchjmdacga| (1)
|PAHjjd| (1)
|RAAffa| (3)
|RAAfff| (1)
|RAAjja| (1)
|RAAjjacba| (1)
|RAAjjamaj| (1)
|RAAjjb| (5)
|RAAjjbmaj| (1)
|RAAjjd| (2)
|RAAmaa| (1)
|RAB| (2)
|RABcba| (1)
|RABeaa| (9)
|RABefa| (28)
|RABefacba| (4)
|RABefe| (1)
|RABefj| (1)
|RABfad| (1)
|RABffa| (6)
|RABffacba| (1)
|RABffd| (6)
|RABffm| (1)
|RABjbd| (1)
|RABjbm| (1)
|RABjbmmaa| (1)
|RABjja| (6)
|RABjjb| (19)
|RABjjbmaj| (1)
|RABjjc| (1)
|RABjjd| (27)
|RABjjdcba| (1)
|RABjjdmaj| (1)
|RABjje| (1)
|RABjjf| (2)
|RABjjh| (1)
|RABjjj| (1)
|RABjjm| (4)
|RABlfj| (2)
|RABmaa| (8)
|RABmaj| (1)
|RABmfa| (1)
|RABqfb| (1)
|RACffa| (1)
|RAE| (3)
|RAEefa| (1)
|RAEefc| (2)
|RAEefe| (2)
|RAEefi| (1)
|RAEefj| (1)
|RAEefjcba| (1)
|RAEfaj| (1)
|RAEffa| (1)
|RAEffacbj| (1)
|RAEffb| (1)

|RAEffc| (1)
|RAEffd| (3)
|RAEffdcbj| (1)
|RAEjja| (1)
|RAEjjacba| (1)
|RAEjjb| (7)
|RAEjjd| (5)
|RAEjjh| (1)
|RAEmaa| (1)
|RAFeaa| (4)
|RAFefa| (10)
|RAFefamaj| (1)
|RAFffd| (1)
|RAFjba| (1)
|RAFjja| (4)
|RAFjjb| (3)
|RAFjjd| (1)
|RAFjjf| (1)
|RAFjjj| (1)
|RAFlfa| (3)
|RAFlfe| (1)
|RAFlfj| (4)
|RAFmaa| (2)
|RAFmfa| (1)
|RAG| (2)
|RAGefa| (3)
|RAGefamaj| (1)
|RAGffd| (1)
|RAGjjb| (1)
|RAGjjd| (1)
|RAGmaj| (1)
|RAGmajcba| (1)
|RAGmfj| (1)
|RAI| (1)
|RAIffd| (1)
|RATjjd| (1)
|RAYjjbffj| (1)
|RCAffa| (1)
|RCAffacba| (1)
|RCAffamaa| (2)
|RCAffb| (1)
|RCAffd| (1)
|RCAjjd| (1)
|RCAlfj| (2)
|RCAmaa| (1)
|RCAmaj| (1)
|RCB| (11)
|RCBcbj| (1)
|RCBcbjmaj| (1)
|RCBcja| (1)
|RCBeaa| (4)
|RCBeaacba| (1)
|RCBeaj| (1)
|RCBefa| (22)
|RCBefacba| (1)
|RCBefc| (3)
|RCBefj| (6)
|RCBffa| (2)
|RCBffamajcba| (1)

|RCBffbcbj| (1)
|RCBffd| (3)
|RCBfff| (1)
|RCBffjmaacba| (1)
|RCBjjb| (3)
|RCBjjc| (2)
|RCBjjd| (10)
|RCBjjf| (1)
|RCBjjh| (2)
|RCBjjm| (4)
|RCBjjmmaa| (2)
|RCBjjo| (1)
|RCBkaj| (1)
|RCBlfacba| (1)
|RCBlfe| (1)
|RCBlfj| (2)
|RCBmaa| (8)
|RCBmaacba| (1)
|RCBmaj| (8)
|RCBmak| (1)
|RCBmfa| (1)
|RCCcbj| (1)
|RCE| (1)
|RCEbjc| (1)
|RCEefa| (3)
|RCEefacba| (1)
|RCEefb| (1)
|RCEffb| (1)
|RCEffm| (1)
|RCEfmd| (1)
|RCEjjacba| (1)
|RCEjjc| (1)
|RCEjjf| (1)
|RCElfj| (1)
|RCEmaa| (2)
|RCEmaj| (3)
|RCFeaa| (1)
|RCFefa| (2)
|RCFefj| (1)
|RCFffd| (1)
|RCFjba| (2)
|RCFjbd| (1)
|RCFjjb| (1)
|RCFjjd| (1)
|RCFlfa| (4)
|RCFlfj| (4)
|RCGefa| (3)
|RCGefj| (1)
|RCGffd| (2)
|RCGffh| (1)
|RCGjjb| (1)
|RCGjjdcba| (1)
|RCSmaacba| (1)
|RCTefamaj| (1)
|RCVlfjmaa| (1)
|RDBjudcha| (1)
|RKAmdjcha| (1)
|SABjjd| (1)
|SAD| (1)

|SADefa| (1)
|SADjjb| (3)
|SCAmaj| (2)
|SCAmajcba| (1)
|SCBmajcba| (1)
|SCDefc| (1)
|SCSmajcba| (1)
|SCVmajcba| (1)
|TCDjjb| (1)

059.3 L woodpecker

No Response (65)
A   ben kins (1)
B   big redheaded one (1)
C   black-throated (1)
D   bluebird (1)
E   carpenter (1)
F   carpentero [S] (1)
G   chab (1)
H   Cham-Chak (3)
I   checkedy-looking bird (1)
J   checker bird (1)
K   checkerwood (1)
L   chuckwood (2)
M   Dominecker peckerwood (1)
N   downy (woodpecker) (3)
O   flicker (12)
P   golly whopper (1)
Q   good god (5)
R   gray-throated (1)
S   guinea sapsucker (1)
T   hairy woodpecker (1)
U   hammer knocker (1)
V   hammered woodpecker (1)
W   hammerhead (2)
X   Indian head (2)
Y   Indian hen (13)
Z   ivory-billed (woodpecker) (4)
aa   ivorybill (7)
ab   ivorybill woodpecker (4)
ac   jenny wood hen (1)
ad   log god (1)
ae   loggerhead (3)
af   lord god (26)
ag   my god (1)
ah   New England woodcock (1)
ai   pecker woodpecker (2)
aj   peckerwood (358)
ak   peckerwood bird (3)
al   pic bois [F] (2)
am   pileate (1)
an   pileated (woodpecker) (10)
ao   red-bellied (1)
ap   red-breasted sapsucker (1)
aq   red-breasted woodpecker (1)
ar   red peckerwood (1)
as   redhead [n.] (64)
at   redhead-and-whitewing
      peckerwood (1)
au   redhead bird (1)

av   redhead peckerwood (13)
aw   redhead sapsucker (2)
ax   redhead woodpecker (12)
ay   redheaded (12)
az   redheaded bird (1)
ba   redheaded peckerwood (22)
bb   redheaded sapsucker (3)
bc   redheaded wood hen (1)
bd   redheaded wooden pecker (1)
be   redheaded woodpecker (48)
bf   redpecker (1)
bg   redwood (1)
bh   regular (woodpecker) (1)
bi   sapsuck (5)
bj   sapsucker (87)
bk   shirttail (2)
bl   small redheaded (1)
bm   speckle (2)
bn   speckle peckerwood (1)
bo   speckle woodpecker (1)
bp   striped woodpecker (1)
bq   tomtit (1)
br   weathercock (1)
bs   white shirt (1)
bt   whitewing (1)
bu   wood bird (1)
bv   wood bunker (1)
bw   wood god (1)
bx   wood hen (18)
by   wood knocker (4)
bz   woodchecker (1)
ca   woodchuck (48)
cb   woodchucker (2)
cc   woodcock (9)
cd   woodpeck (3)
ce   woodpecker (621)
cf   Woody (2)
cg   yellow-bellied sapsucker (2)
ch   yellow breast (1)
ci   yellow-headed woodpecker (1)
cj   yellowhammer (61)
ck   yellowhanger (1)
cl   yellowhead peckerwood (1)

059.4 L skunk

No Response (93)
A   bete puante [F] (3)
B   bete pue [F] (1)
C   black one (1)
D   black skunk (1)
E   black-and-white kitty (1)
F   cat (1)
G   civet (4)
H   civet cat (48)
I   hydrophobi(a) cat (2)
J   kitten (1)
K   KNUKS (1)
L   little flower (1)
M   Mister Poley (1)
N   Mister Skunk (2)

O   musk cat (1)
P   perfume cat (1)
Q   pole kitty (2)
R   polecat (534)
S   pussy with a fluid drive (1)
T   pussycat (2)
U   ringtail (1)
V   sachet kitten (2)
W   sissy cat (1)
X   skunk (653)
Y   skunk cat (1)
Z   stink cat (1)
aa   stink kitty (1)
ab   stinker (1)
ac   striped kitty (1)
ad   striped polecat (1)
ae   wild kitty (1)
af   wood kitty (1)
ag   wood pussy (1)

059.5 L varmint
No Response (230)
A   creature (1)
B   critter (15)
C   marauder (1)
D   night varmint (1)
E   nuisance (2)
F   pest (27)
G   predator (12)
H   prowler (1)
I   raider (2)
J   rodent (28)
K   scavenger (7)
L   scoundrel (3)
M   varmint (670)
N   vermin (5)
O   wild varmint (2)

059.5 P varmints
{o}   low-back
{R}   weakly retroflex
{r}   weakly retroflex
{v}   bilabial
{z}   devoiced
{?}   glottal
No Response (253)
<(v)armNts=14> (1)
<borm[N]ts=14> (1)
<vaw(r)mNt(s)=14> (1)
<vaw(r)mNt=14> (8)
<vaw(r)mNts=14> (11)
<vaw(r)m[N]t=14> (1)
<vaw(r)m[N]ts=14> (3)
<vaw[r]mN(t)z=14> (1)
<vaw[r]mNt=14> (5)
<vaw[r]mNts=14> (2)
<vawm[N]t=14> (1)
<vawrmNt=14> (7)
<vawrmNts=14> (17)
<vawrm[N]t=14> (2)
<vawrm[N]ts=14> (2)

<vawrmi(n)ts=13> (1)
<vawrmoo(n)t=13> (1)
<vaw{r}mNt=14> (3)
<vaw{r}mNts=14> (3)
<va{r}mNts=14> (1)
<vo(r)mN(t)=14> (1)
<vo(r)mN(t){z}=14> (1)
<vo(r)mNks=14> (1)
<vo(r)mNt=14> (15)
<vo(r)mNts=14> (19)
<vo(r)m[N](ts)=14> (1)
<vo(r)m[N]k=14> (2)
<vo(r)m[N]t(s)=14> (1)
<vo(r)m[N]t=14> (7)
<vo(r)m[N]ts=14> (11)
<vo(r)mi(n)t=13> (1)
<vo(r)mi(n)ts=13> (1)
<vo(r)m{R}nts=14> (1)
<vo[r]mN(t)z=14> (1)
<vo[r]mNt=14> (15)
<vo[r]mNts=14> (23)
<vo[r]m[N]k(s)=14> (1)
<vo[r]m[N]t=14> (3)
<vo[r]m[N]ts=14> (2)
<vormN(t)=14> (2)
<vormNt=14> (63)
<vormNts=14> (100)
<vorm[N]t=14> (22)
<vorm[N]ts=14> (39)
<vormi(n)t=13> (1)
<vormi(n)ts=13> (3)
<vormint=13> (1)
<vormints=13> (2)
<vormunts=13> (3)
<vo{r}mNt=14> (25)
<vo{r}mNts=14> (38)
<vo{r}m[N]t(s)=14> (1)
<vo{r}m[N]t=14> (1)
<vo{r}m[N]ts=14> (2)
<vo{r}mints=13> (1)
<vurmN(t)=14> (1)
<vurmNts=14> (1)
<v{o}(r)mNt=14> (4)
<v{o}(r)mNts=14> (7)
<v{o}(r)m[N]t=14> (6)
<v{o}(r)m[N]ts=14> (17)
<v{o}[r]mNt=14> (6)
<v{o}[r]mNts=14> (16)
<v{o}[r]mNtz=14> (1)
<v{o}[r]m[N](t)=14> (1)
<v{o}[r]m[N]t=14> (2)
<v{o}[r]m[N]ts=14> (3)
<v{o}[r]mi(n)ts=13> (1)
<v{o}rmN(t){z}=14> (1)
<v{o}rmN(ts)=14> (2)
<v{o}rmNt=14> (26)
<v{o}rmNts=14> (38)
<v{o}rm[N](t)s=14> (1)

<v{o}rm[N]t=14> (14)
<v{o}rm[N]ts=14> (17)
<v{o}rm[N]tz=14> (1)
<v{o}{r}mN(t)s=14> (1)
<v{o}{r}mNt=14> (7)
<v{o}{r}mNts=14> (5)
<v{o}{r}m[N]ts=14> (2)
<wo(r)m[N]t=14> (1)
<w{o}[r]mNts=14> (1)
<w{o}{r}mNt=14> (1)
<{v}o[r]mNts=14> (2)
<{v}o[r]m[N]t(s)=14> (1)
<{v}o[r]m[N]ts=14> (3)
<{v}ormNts=14> (2)
<{v}orm[N]ts=14> (1)
<{v}{o}rmNts=14> (1)

059.6 L gray squirrel
No Response (95)
A   albino (1)
B   black cat squirrel (1)
C   black squirrel (16)
D   bony (1)
E   boomer (3)
F   brown squirrel (3)
G   burr squirrel (1)
H   bushy-tail (gray) squirrel (2)
I   cat (1)
J   cat squirrel (160)
K   eating squirrel (1)
L   field squirrel (1)
M   fox squirrel (2)
N   gray (1)
O   gray cat squirrel (1)
P   gray one (6)
Q   gray squirrel (394)
R   hunting squirrel (1)
S   mountain squirrel (1)
T   pet squirrel (1)
U   rat squirrel (1)
V   redtail cat squirrel (1)
W   ringtail squirrel (1)
X   rock squirrel (1)
Y   squirrel (638)
Z   tame squirrel (1)
aa   tree squirrel (15)
ab   white squirrel (6)
ac   wild squirrel (2)
ad   wood(s) squirrel (2)

059.7 L fox squirrel
No Response (285)
A   albino squirrel (4)
B   black fox squirrel (8)
C   black one (4)
D   black squirrel (32)
E   boomer (11)
F   brown one (1)
G   brown squirrel (27)
H   cat squirrel (3)
I   fantail squirrel (1)

J fox squirrel (416)
K great squirrel (1)
L half-white squirrel (1)
M Mexican squirrel (1)
N mountain boomer (2)
O nutcracker (1)
P orange one (1)
Q red fox squirrel (20)
R red kind/one (3)
S red squirrel (144)
T reddish squirrel (1)
U redtail squirrel (1)
V solid-black fox squirrel (1)
W Southern squirrel (1)
X squirrel (15)
Y swamp squirrel (1)
Z tree squirrel (5)
aa white one (1)
ab white squirrel (4)
ac wood squirrel (2)
ad yellow squirrel (3)

059.8 L chipmunk

No Response (300)
A boomer (2)
B chipmunk (271)
C chuckmunk (1)
D flying squirrel (4)
E gopher (16)
F gopher rat (3)
G ground squirrel (241)
H groundhog (22)
I mole (1)
J muskrat (5)
K prairie dog (6)
L red chipmunk (1)
M squirrel (1)
N woodchuck (9)
O woods creature (1)

059.9 L fish

No Response (181)
A alligator gar (8)
B amberjack (2)
C angelfish (2)
D App (1)
E Appaloosa (cat) (5)
F Arkansas buffalo (1)
G aronker (1)
H ballyhoo (1)
I barfish (6)
J barracuda (1)
K bass (fish) (377)
L bastard perch (1)
M bezugo (1)
N bigmouth (bass) (11)
O Biloxi bacon (1)
P black bass (19)
Q black bream (1)
R black mullet (1)
S black perch (2)

T black(fish) (13)
U blowfish (2)
V blue bream (3)
W blue cat(fish) (30)
X blue marlin (1)
Y blue perch (1)
Z blue runner (3)
aa bluebill (1)
ab blue(fish) (12)
ac bluegill (43)
ad bluegill bream (2)
ae bluegill cat (1)
af boneless cat (1)
ag bony shad (1)
ah bream (fish) (277)
ai brown bass (1)
aj brown cat (1)
ak brown mullet (1)
al brown trout (4)
am brumalia (1)
an buffalo (fish) (90)
ao bull bream (1)
ap bull cat (1)
aq bull fish (1)
ar bullhead (cat) (3)
as butter cat (1)
at butterfish (3)
au carp (fish) (85)
av cat(fish) (529)
aw cavalla (1)
ax chaetodon (1)
ay champagne (1)
az channel bass (1)
ba channel cat (34)
bb channel mullet (2)
bc choupique (7)
bd chinquapin (1)
be cock fish (1)
bf cod(fish) (3)
bg copperhead (bream) (2)
bh corker (1)
bi cottonfish (1)
bj crappie (fish) (158)
bk creek minnow (1)
bl creek sucker (1)
bm croaker (fish) (35)
bn cypress trout (2)
bo dolphin (7)
bp drum(fish) (37)
bq drummer (1)
br elwise (1)
bs fish gar (1)
bt flap-head cat (1)
bu flat tail (1)
bv flathead (1)
bw flounder (75)
bx flying fish (1)
by forked-tail cat (1)
bz freshwater bream (2)

ca freshwater catfish (2)
cb freshwater drum (1)
cc freshwater mullet (1)
cd frogfish (1)
ce galope (1)
cf gar(fish) (90)
cg gaspergou (22)
ch Georgia cat (1)
ci German carp (1)
cj goggle-eye catfish (1)
ck goggle-eye (fish) (15)
cl goggle-eye(d) perch (12)
cm goldfish (1)
cn goo (fish)/(gasper)gou (12)
co goujon (1)
cp government bream (1)
cq gray(fish) (2)
cr green trout (5)
cs grindle (fish) (19)
ct grinner (10)
cu ground mullet (2)
cv grouper (fish) (22)
cw grunt (6)
cx grunter (1)
cy gulf runner (1)
cz halibut (2)
da hand-painted bream (1)
db hardhead catfish (1)
dc hardtail (1)
dd herring (1)
de hickory shad (1)
df hog molly (4)
dg hog sucker (2)
dh hogfish (4)
di horn trout (1)
dj horny hide (1)
dk hornyhead (12)
dl humpback blue cat (1)
dm jack grindle (1)
dn jack salmon (1)
do jack(fish) (43)
dp jewfish (5)
dq jughead (1)
dr king mackerel (6)
ds kingfish (8)
dt Kitty Mitchell (1)
du ladyfish (3)
dv largemouth (bass) (6)
dw lemonfish (2)
dx ling (1)
dy littlemouth (bass) (2)
dz long gravy (1)
ea mackerel (fish) (38)
eb manta ray (1)
ec marble(-)head (cat) (3)
ed marlin (8)
ee minnow (1)
ef moccasin (2)
eg mott (1)

eh   mountain trout (4)
ei   mud black cat (1)
ej   mud cat(fish) (24)
ek   mud trout (1)
el   muddy cat (1)
em   mudfish (17)
en   mudsucker (1)
eo   mullet (fish) (89)
ep   muskie (4)
eq   muttonfish (1)
er   needlefish (1)
es   nigger fish (1)
et   Northern pike (2)
eu   Northern rock bass (1)
ev   ocean catfish (1)
ew   ocean perch (1)
ex   ocean trout (8)
ey   paddle bill (1)
ez   pan trout (1)
fa   panfish (5)
fb   patassa (1)
fc   perch (fish) (226)
fd   pickerel (2)
fe   pigfish (1)
ff   piggy perch (1)
fg   pike (fish) (19)
fh   pink salmon (1)
fi   pogy (fish) (5)
fj   polliwog (2)
fk   pompano (8)
fl   pond catfish (1)
fm   porgy/porky (3)
fn   porpoise (dolphin) (4)
fo   Portuguese man-of-war (1)
fp   rainbow (trout) (16)
fq   rattlesnake (2)
fr   ray (1)
fs   razor fish (1)
ft   razorback buffalo (1)
fu   red bass (4)
fv   red bream (1)
fw   red cat (1)
fx   red perch (6)
fy   red snapper (57)
fz   red sucker (1)
ga   red tail (1)
gb   redbelly (perch) (8)
gc   redbreast (bream) (4)
gd   redear sunfish (1)
ge   redeye (10)
gf   redfin pike (1)
gg   red(fish) (64)
gh   redhorse (sucker) (7)
gi   reef fish (1)
gj   river perch (1)
gk   rock bass (11)
gl   rock cat (1)
gm   rock gill (1)
gn   rock perch (1)

go   rock(fish) (5)
gp   root perch (1)
gq   runner fish (1)
gr   sacalait (16)
gs   sailfish (6)
gt   salmon (4)
gu   salt mullet (1)
gv   saltwater bass (1)
gw   saltwater bream (1)
gx   saltwater catfish (3)
gy   saltwater mullet (1)
gz   saltwater striped bass (1)
ha   saltwater trout (2)
hb   salty trout (1)
hc   sand bass (2)
hd   sand bream (1)
he   sand perch (2)
hf   sand trout (2)
hg   sauger jack (1)
hh   saw grass (1)
hi   scaly fish (1)
hj   scamp (1)
hk   scissorbill gar (1)
hl   sea bass (4)
hm   sea cat (1)
hn   sea perch (1)
ho   sea trout (5)
hp   seinefish (1)
hq   shad (24)
hr   shark (14)
hs   sheepshead (26)
ht   shellcracker (22)
hu   shiner (3)
hv   shovel-bill cat (1)
hw   shovelhead (1)
hx   silverside (1)
hy   skipjack (2)
hz   smallmouth (bass) (6)
ia   snapper (30)
ib   snook (1)
ic   snooker (1)
id   Spanish mackerel (8)
ie   speckle bass (1)
if   speckle sea trout (1)
ig   speckle(d) cat (2)
ih   speckle(d) perch (17)
ii   speckle(d) trout (34)
ij   spoon-type garfish (1)
ik   spoonbill (catfish) (5)
il   spot(s) (4)
im   spottail (1)
in   spotted cat(fish) (3)
io   squirrelfish (1)
ip   stingaree (6)
iq   stingray (1)
ir   stone toter (1)
is   strawberry (1)
it   stripe (2)
iu   stripe(d) bass (18)

iv   striped trout (1)
iw   stumpknocker (8)
ix   sturgeon (3)
iy   sucker(fish) (41)
iz   sun perch (19)
ja   sunfish (7)
jb   swamp fish (1)
jc   sweetwater trout (1)
jd   swordfish (5)
je   tabby cat (3)
jf   tarpon (13)
jg   toadfish (2)
jh   top minnow (1)
ji   tripe (1)
jj   trout (fish) (290)
jk   tuna (fish) (4)
jl   turbot (2)
jm   Virginia drum (1)
jn   walking catfish (1)
jo   walleye (2)
jp   walleye perch (1)
jq   walleye(d) pike (3)
jr   warmouth (5)
js   warmouth bream (1)
jt   warmouth perch (9)
ju   warmouth trout (1)
jv   warsaw (1)
jw   weakfish (4)
jx   white and black bass (1)
jy   white bass (7)
jz   white cat(fish) (3)
ka   white crappie (1)
kb   white perch (58)
kc   white sucker (3)
kd   white trout (7)
ke   whitefish (2)
kf   whitehead (1)
kg   whities (2)
kh   whiting (16)
ki   widemouth bass (1)
kj   willow cat (2)
kk   yellow-bellied bream (1)
kl   yellow cat(fish) (24)
km   yellow roe mullet (1)
kn   yellow shell (1)
ko   yellow sucker (1)
kp   yellowfish (2)
kq   yellowtail (5)
kr   yellowtail tarpon (1)

060.1 P oysters
{o}   low-back
{oy}   inglide
{R}   weakly retroflex
{r}   weakly retroflex
{s}   palatal
{sh}   alveolar
{t}   flap
{z}   palatal
No Response (145)

<awrshtR=14> (1)
<awrshtRz=14> (1)
<awrsht[R]z=14> (1)
<awrstR(z)=14> (1)
<awsch[R]z=14> (1)
<awsh(t)[R]z=14> (1)
<awsht[R]=14> (1)
<awsht[R]z=14> (3)
<awst[R]z=14> (2)
<awst{R}z=14> (1)
<aw{r}schRz=14> (1)
<aw{r}sch{R}s=14> (1)
<aw{r}shtR{z}=14> (1)
<aw{r}sht[R]z=14> (1)
<aw{r}stRz=14> (2)
<aw{r}{sh}t{R}z=14> (1)
<aw{r}{s}tRz=14> (1)
<aw{r}{s}t[R]=14> (1)
<ieschRz=14> (1)
<ieshst[R]=14> (1)
<iesht[R]z=14> (1)
<iesht{R}=14> (1)
<iestRz=14> (2)
<iest[R]=14> (3)
<iest[R]z=14> (2)
<iesty[R]z=14> (1)
<iest{R}z=14> (1)
<ie{s}t{R}z=14> (1)
<oerstRz=14> (1)
<oer{s}tR=14> (1)
<oer{s}tRz=14> (1)
<oesht[R]zh=14> (1)
<oe{r}stR=14> (1)
<oe{r}stRz=14> (1)
<oe{r}{s}tRz=14> (1)
<ooshtRz=14> (1)
<orst{R}z=14> (1)
<oshtR=14> (1)
<ost[R]z=14> (2)
<ost{R}z=14> (1)
<oyrstRz=14> (1)
<oyrst[R]z=14> (1)
<oys[R]{z}=14> (1)
<oyschR=14> (3)
<oyschRz=14> (19)
<oysch[R]=14> (5)
<oysch[R]z=14> (22)
<oyschoorz=13> (1)
<oysch{R}=14> (1)
<oysch{R}z=14> (1)
<oysh(t)[R]z=14> (1)
<oyshchRd=14> (1)
<oyshchRs=14> (1)
<oyshchRz=14> (1)
<oyshchRzh=14> (1)
<oyshch[R]sh=14> (1)
<oyshch[R]z=14> (2)
<oyshtR=14> (6)
<oyshtRsh=14> (2)

<oyshtRz=14> (11)
<oyshtRzh=14> (1)
<oyshtR{z}=14> (2)
<oysht[R]=14> (20)
<oysht[R]sh=14> (1)
<oysht[R]z=14> (30)
<oyshtu[r]dh=13> (1)
<oyshtu[r]z=13> (1)
<oysht{R}=14> (2)
<oysht{R}z=14> (4)
<oysht{R}zh=14> (1)
<oysh{t}[R]=14> (1)
<oysst[R]sh=14> (1)
<oystR(z)=14> (1)
<oystR=14> (18)
<oystRz=14> (89)
<oystR{z}=14> (2)
<oyst[R]=14> (18)
<oyst[R]z=14> (89)
<oystewrz=13> (1)
<oystk[R]=14> (1)
<oystrAz=14> (1)
<oystur=13> (1)
<oysturz=13> (5)
<oystu{r}z=13> (1)
<oystyRz=14> (1)
<oysty[R]=14> (1)
<oysty[R]z=14> (1)
<oyst{R}=14> (5)
<oyst{R}z=14> (40)
<oyst{R}{z}=14> (1)
<oys{t}[R]z=14> (2)
<oys{t}{R}z=14> (1)
<oy{sh}ch{R}=14> (1)
<oy{sh}stR{z}=14> (1)
<oy{sh}tR=14> (1)
<oy{sh}tRz=14> (6)
<oy{sh}tR{z}=14> (1)
<oy{sh}t[R]z=14> (3)
<oy{sh}t{R}=14> (1)
<oy{sh}t{R}z=14> (1)
<oy{s}chR=14> (1)
<oy{s}chRz=14> (7)
<oy{s}ch[R]=14> (1)
<oy{s}ch[R]z=14> (5)
<oy{s}ch[R]{z}=14> (1)
<oy{s}k[R]z=14> (1)
<oy{s}tR=14> (9)
<oy{s}tRs=14> (1)
<oy{s}tRz=14> (28)
<oy{s}tR{z}=14> (7)
<oy{s}t[R]=14> (6)
<oy{s}t[R]z=14> (18)
<oy{s}tyRz=14> (1)
<oy{s}ty[R]z=14> (1)
<oy{s}t{R}=14> (2)
<oy{s}t{R}z=14> (10)
<oy{s}t{R}{z}=14> (1)
<oy{s}{t}[R]z=14> (2)

<o{r}shtRz=14> (1)
<o{r}sht[R]=14> (2)
<o{r}{s}t[R]=14> (1)
<o{s}tRz=14> (1)
<u{r}st{R}z=14> (1)
<{oy}schR=14> (1)
<{oy}schRz=14> (3)
<{oy}sch[R]=14> (1)
<{oy}sch[R]z=14> (5)
<{oy}sh(t)R=14> (1)
<{oy}sh(t)Rdh=14> (1)
<{oy}shtRz=14> (2)
<{oy}shtR{z}=14> (1)
<{oy}sht[R]=14> (2)
<{oy}sht[R]dh=14> (1)
<{oy}sht[R]z=14> (1)
<{oy}sht[R]zh=14> (2)
<{oy}sht{R}=14> (1)
<{oy}sht{R}{z}=14> (1)
<{oy}stR=14> (6)
<{oy}stRz=14> (38)
<{oy}stR{z}=14> (4)
<{oy}st[R]=14> (8)
<{oy}st[R]z=14> (47)
<{oy}sty[R]=14> (1)
<{oy}sty[R]z=14> (2)
<{oy}st{R}=14> (2)
<{oy}st{R}z=14> (19)
<{oy}st{R}{z}=14> (2)
<{oy}t[R]z=14> (1)
<{oy}{sh}tR=14> (2)
<{oy}{s}tR=14> (5)
<{oy}{s}tRz=14> (7)
<{oy}{s}tR{z}=14> (8)
<{oy}{s}t[R]z=14> (11)
<{oy}{s}tch[R]z=14> (1)
<{oy}{s}ty{R}z=14> (1)
<{oy}{s}t{R}=14> (1)
<{oy}{s}t{R}z=14> (5)
<{o}shtRz=14> (1)
<{o}shtyR=14> (1)
<{o}st[R]z=14> (1)
<{o}st{R}s=14> (1)
<{o}st{R}z=14> (1)

060.1 S oysters

No Response (132)
|FFImaj| (1)
|JJBmaj| (1)
|JJCeaa| (1)
|JJCeab| (1)
|JJCeac| (1)
|JJCefjmaa| (1)
|JJCmab| (1)
|JJCmea| (1)
|JJDeaa| (1)
|JJHeaa| (8)
|JJHeaj| (13)
|JJHeak| (1)
|JJHmaa| (1)

|JSCeaa| (2)
|JSCmab| (1)
|JSHeaa| (1)
|JSHmaj| (1)
|JSImaa| (1)
|JSSmaj| (1)
|JSUeaj| (3)
|JSUmaj| (2)
|JSVeaj| (1)
|JSZmaj| (1)
|LAAeaj| (1)
|LCEeej| (1)
|LLA| (1)
|PACmaj| (1)
|PAEeaa| (1)
|PAGeaj| (1)
|PAIeaa| (1)
|PFEeaa| (1)
|PFEmak| (1)
|QAAmaa| (1)
|QABeaj| (1)
|QABmak| (1)
|QACeaa| (1)
|QACmaa| (1)
|QADeaa| (1)
|QADeaj| (1)
|QCBeac| (1)
|QCCmab| (1)
|QCDeaj| (2)
|QFAdaa| (1)
|QFAeaa| (14)
|QFAeaamej| (1)
|QFAeac| (5)
|QFAeaj| (11)
|QFAeak| (3)
|QFAeal| (2)
|QFAecc| (1)
|QFAkaj| (1)
|QFAmaa| (2)
|QFAmab| (1)
|QFAmaj| (1)
|QFAmal| (1)
|QFAmea| (1)
|QFAmej| (2)
|QFAqfbeaj| (1)
|QFBeaa| (98)
|QFBeaamej| (1)
|QFBeab| (5)
|QFBeac| (41)
|QFBeaj| (56)
|QFBeak| (7)
|QFBeal| (5)
|QFBjjaeaa| (1)
|QFBjjaeaj| (1)
|QFBjjm| (1)
|QFBkab| (1)
|QFBkak| (2)
|QFBmaa| (16)
|QFBmab| (29)

|QFBmaj| (12)
|QFBmajmea| (1)
|QFBmak| (10)
|QFBmea| (1)
|QFBmej| (3)
|QFCeaa| (37)
|QFCeac| (7)
|QFCeaj| (5)
|QFCeal| (1)
|QFCefj| (1)
|QFCkaj| (1)
|QFCkak| (2)
|QFCmaa| (11)
|QFCmab| (8)
|QFCmaj| (6)
|QFCmajmea| (1)
|QFCmea| (1)
|QFCqfakab| (1)
|QFCqfb| (2)
|QFCqfbeaa| (2)
|QFCqfbeaj| (12)
|QFCqfbeal| (2)
|QFCqfbkaj| (1)
|QFCqfbmaj| (1)
|QFCqfk| (1)
|QFDdaj| (1)
|QFDeaa| (10)
|QFDeaj| (8)
|QFDeam| (1)
|QFDefj| (1)
|QFDkab| (1)
|QFDkag| (1)
|QFDmaa| (2)
|QFDmaj| (1)
|QFDqfbeaj| (1)
|QFFeaa| (7)
|QFFeaj| (5)
|QFFeal| (1)
|QFFkab| (1)
|QFFmaa| (1)
|QFFmab| (1)
|QFFmak| (1)
|QFHeaa| (4)
|QFHeaj| (3)
|QFHmaa| (1)
|QFHmaj| (1)
|QFHmak| (1)
|QFHqfbeaj| (1)
|QFHqfbmej| (1)
|QFSeac| (1)
|QFTeaa| (1)
|QFTeac| (1)
|QFXeaa| (2)
|QFXeaj| (1)
|QLAeal| (1)
|QMAdan| (1)
|QMAeaa| (4)
|QMAeac| (2)
|QMAeaj| (15)

|QMAmaa| (2)
|QMAmaj| (4)
|QMAmej| (2)
|QMBeaa| (15)
|QMBeab| (1)
|QMBeac| (14)
|QMBeaj| (10)
|QMBeal| (9)
|QMBmaa| (5)
|QMBmab| (11)
|QMBmaj| (10)
|QMBmak| (6)
|QMBmea| (1)
|QMBmej| (1)
|QMCeaa| (3)
|QMCeaj| (6)
|QMCmaa| (4)
|QMCmaj| (1)
|QMCmak| (1)
|QMCmej| (2)
|QMCqfbeaj| (1)
|QMDeaa| (5)
|QMDeam| (2)
|QMDeao| (1)
|QMDmaj| (3)
|QMFeaa| (5)
|QMFeaj| (2)
|QMFeak| (1)
|QMFeal| (1)
|QMFmaj| (2)
|QMFmak| (1)
|QMHeaa| (1)
|QMHeaj| (1)
|QMHmaj| (1)
|QMHqfb| (2)
|QMSbbj| (1)
|QMSeaj| (2)
|QMTeac| (1)
|QMTmak| (1)
|QSAeaj| (1)
|QYAmej| (1)
|RAEeaj| (1)
|RAEmaj| (1)
|RAIeaj| (1)
|SABmej| (1)
|SAGmej| (1)
|SCEqaj| (1)
|SCFmaj| (1)
|SCGmej| (1)
|SFEeaj| (1)
|SFGeaa| (1)
|SMAmaj| (1)
|SMGeaj| (1)
|TABkaj| (1)
|TABtfakab| (1)
|TAD| (1)
|TADeaa| (1)
|TADkab| (1)
|TADqfcdaa| (1)

|TADqfjmaa| (1)
|TAFkaj| (1)
|TCAeaa| (2)
|TCDtcbkak| (1)
|TCS| (2)
|TCSeaa| (1)
|TCSeaj| (2)
|TCTeaa| (1)
|TFBeaa| (2)
|TFBmab| (1)
|TFDeaa| (1)
|TFSeaa| (1)
|TFTmaj| (1)
|TMAeaa| (1)
|TMAeaj| (2)
|TMBeaa| (1)
|TMSeaa| (4)
|TXSedj| (1)
|ma2TCAeaj| (1)

060.2 L bullfrog
No Response (76)
A bullfrog (754)
B bully frog (1)
C croaker (4)
D croaking frog (1)
E frog (445)
F gopher (1)
G granddaddy (1)
H gray frog (1)
I green frog (1)
J hopper frog (1)
K jumbo frog (1)
L long-legged frog (1)
M pond frog (1)
N prairie green (1)
O spring chicken (2)
P spring frog (1)
Q toad-frog (2)
R water frog (2)
S weed frog (1)

060.3 L spring frog
No Response (269)
A baby frog (2)
B bell frog (1)
C branch frog (1)
D brook frog (1)
E drit drat (1)
F frog (22)
G frog frog (1)
H grass frog (7)
I gray frog (2)
J green frog (71)
K green slimy frog (1)
L green spring frog (1)
M green-tinted frog (1)
N green tree frog (4)
O grenouille [F] (1)
P grit grat (1)
Q ground frog (1)

R jumping frog (1)
S leaper (1)
T leapfrog (7)
U leaping frog (1)
V leopard frog (3)
W little frog (6)
X mile jumper (1)
Y mile leaper (1)
Z peep frog (3)
aa peeper (3)
ab piper (1)
ac pond frog (2)
ad rainbow frog (1)
ae rainfrog (130)
af ring frog (1)
ag running frog (1)
ah sand frog (1)
ai screaking frog (1)
aj spring frog (137)
ak spring peeper (1)
al swamp frog (1)
am thunder frog (2)
an tree frog (400)
ao tree toad (7)
ap water frog (3)
aq weather frog (1)

060.4 L toad
No Response (136)
A common frog (1)
B dirt frog (1)
C dry frog (1)
D dry-land frog (6)
E dry-land toad-frog (1)
F frog (42)
G garden frog (2)
H garden toad (1)
I gray frog (1)
J ground frog (2)
K hill toad (1)
L hop-in-[D-0]-yard toad (1)
M hopping toad (2)
N hoppy toad (2)
O hoptoad (4)
P horn back (1)
Q horn frog (2)
R horn toad (4)
S horned frog (4)
T horned toad (1)
U horny frog (3)
V horny toad (7)
W house-yard frog (1)
X land frog (2)
Y night frog (1)
Z pea frog (1)
aa rough toad (1)
ab scaly back (1)
ac spring toad (1)
ad squat frog (1)
ae striped toad (1)

af toad (256)
ag toad-frog (538)
ah toady (1)
ai toady-frog (15)
aj wart frog (2)
ak yard frog (1)

060.5 L earthworm
No Response (78)
A African red worm (1)
B African worm (1)
C angle (1)
D angleworm (10)
E angling worm (1)
F bait (121)
G bait worm (13)
H black wiggler (1)
I black worm (2)
J bloodworm (2)
K blue wiggler (1)
L blue worm (1)
M bottom worm (1)
N brown wiggler (1)
O brown worm (3)
P buckshot red worm (1)
Q catalpa worm (8)
R catawba (2)
S catawba worm (50)
T coffee worm (1)
U commercial worm (1)
V crawler (3)
W creeper (1)
X cutworm (4)
Y dirt worm (1)
Z earthworm (385)
aa eelworm (8)
ab English red worm (1)
ac English worm (2)
ad fiddle worm (1)
ae fiddler (1)
af fiddler worm (1)
ag fiddling worm (1)
ah fish bait (13)
ai fish-bait worm (2)
aj fishing bait (1)
ak fishing worm (41)
al fishworm (26)
am flathead (2)
an flatworm (2)
ao Florida worm (1)
ap foot-long red worm (1)
aq foot-long worm (1)
ar Georgia wiggler (1)
as giant red worm (1)
at ground worm (14)
au grub (7)
av grubber (1)
aw grubworm (110)
ax grunt worm (1)
ay grunt-nut worm (1)

az house bait (1)
ba jumbo (1)
bb jumper (2)
bc jumping jack (1)
bd king worm (1)
be liver worm (1)
bf long john (2)
bg long jumper (1)
bh Louisiana pink (8)
bi maple worm (1)
bj mudworm (4)
bk multiplier (1)
bl night crawler (80)
bm night creeper (1)
bn night walker (1)
bo night wiggler (1)
bp oak worm (3)
bq pink worm (5)
br pond worm (2)
bs purple worm (1)
bt rainworm (4)
bu red bait (2)
bv red earthworm (4)
bw red wiggler (31)
bx red worm (234)
by redhead (1)
bz Regenwurm [G] (1)
ca roundworm (1)
cb sawyer (10)
cc segmented roundworm (1)
cd sleeker (1)
ce slop worm (7)
cf snakeworm (1)
cg sneaker (1)
ch stump worm (1)
ci swamp bait (1)
cj swamp wiggler (2)
ck swamp worm (1)
cl Tennessee (1)
cm Texas Giant (1)
cn Washington worm (1)
co wee-wee worm (1)
cp white worm (4)
cq wiggle (1)
cr wiggle worm (12)
cs wiggle-tail (1)
ct wiggler (103)
cu wiggler worm (2)
cv wiggly (1)
cw wiggly worm (2)
cx wild wiggler (2)
cy willow worm (1)
cz wood sawyer (1)
da worm (561)
db worm bait (1)
dc worm for bait (1)
dd wriggler (2)
de wriggly worm (1)
df yard worm (1)

dg yellow worm (1)

060.5 S worm
No Response (1)
|EXAmna| (1)
|EXAmnb| (1)
|EXCmna| (1)
|FXAeda| (1)
|J2Cedj| (1)
|KACmea| (1)
|KFAeaj| (1)
|L5A| (1)
|L5Amdk| (1)
|LAA| (4)
|LAAeaa| (3)
|LAAeaj| (5)
|LAAmaj| (1)
|LAAmea| (14)
|LAAmej| (4)
|LAC| (2)
|LACmea| (9)
|LADeaj| (1)
|LADmea| (6)
|LAEmea| (14)
|LAF| (1)
|LAGmea| (2)
|LAGmej| (1)
|LAHmea| (1)
|LAI| (1)
|LCA| (3)
|LCAeaj| (1)
|LCAmaj| (2)
|LCAmea| (11)
|LCAmej| (3)
|LCBmea| (1)
|LCDmea| (1)
|LCDmeb| (1)
|LCEeaj| (1)
|LCEmea| (8)
|LCFmea| (2)
|LCHmej| (1)
|LCI| (1)
|LDA| (1)
|LDAedj| (1)
|LDAmna| (3)
|LDE| (1)
|LEA| (7)
|LEAeaj| (2)
|LEAmaj| (2)
|LEAmej| (3)
|LEAmek| (1)
|LEE| (2)
|LEEmej| (1)
|LEG| (1)
|LFA| (4)
|LFAeaa| (4)
|LFAeaj| (30)
|LFAeak| (1)
|LFAeal| (2)
|LFAkaj| (1)

|LFAkak| (1)
|LFAmaj| (11)
|LFAmak| (3)
|LFAmea| (8)
|LFAmeaeaj| (1)
|LFAmej| (3)
|LFAmfk| (1)
|LFBeaj| (2)
|LFBmea| (2)
|LFCeaj| (1)
|LFCkak| (1)
|LFCmea| (1)
|LFDeaj| (3)
|LFEmaj| (1)
|LFEmak| (1)
|LFEmea| (4)
|LFGeaj| (2)
|LFGeak| (1)
|LFGmea| (1)
|LFHeaj| (1)
|LKA| (3)
|LKAedj| (1)
|LKAedl| (1)
|LKAmna| (1)
|LKEeda| (1)
|LLA| (1)
|LLE| (1)
|LMA| (6)
|LMAeaa| (3)
|LMAeaj| (46)
|LMAeak| (1)
|LMAeal| (1)
|LMAefj| (1)
|LMAmab| (1)
|LMAmaj| (9)
|LMAmak| (8)
|LMAmea| (1)
|LMAmej| (6)
|LMCeaj| (1)
|LMCeajmej| (1)
|LMDeaj| (1)
|LMDmea| (1)
|LMDmej| (2)
|LMEdaj| (1)
|LMEeaj| (1)
|LMEmea| (3)
|LMGeaj| (1)
|LMGmea| (1)
|LMIeaj| (2)
|LNA| (3)
|LNAmdj| (2)
|LNAmdk| (1)
|LNE| (1)
|LOA| (2)
|LOAedl| (1)
|LOAmdk| (2)
|LODmdj| (1)
|LPA| (7)
|LPAmaj| (2)

|LPE| (3)
|LWAmdk| (1)
|LWE| (2)
|LXAedj| (4)
|LXAmdj| (4)
|LXAmdk| (1)
|LXAmnj| (1)
|LYA| (3)
|LYAmea| (1)
|LYCeaj| (1)
|LYE| (1)
|M1A| (1)
|MCAeaa| (1)
|MEA| (219)
|MEAeaj| (1)
|MEAmaj| (1)
|MEAmak| (2)
|MEB| (1)
|MEC| (4)
|MED| (9)
|MEDmaj| (1)
|MEE| (3)
|MEHmea| (1)
|MEI| (1)
|MFA| (1)
|MKA| (2)
|MKAedj| (1)
|MKAmna| (1)
|MKAmnb| (1)
|MKEeda| (1)
|MLA| (141)
|MLAeaj| (2)
|MLAmaj| (11)
|MLAmak| (2)
|MLB| (1)
|MLC| (5)
|MLD| (5)
|MLE| (4)
|MLH| (2)
|MNA| (12)
|MND| (3)
|MPA| (13)
|MPAmaj| (2)
|MPD| (1)
|MPE| (1)
|MWA| (33)
|MWAmdj| (3)
|MWB| (3)
|MWBmna| (1)
|MWCmdj| (1)
|MWE| (4)
|MYA| (14)
|MYD| (1)
|MZA| (1)
|NADmea| (1)
|NADmej| (1)
|NAEeaa| (1)
|NAHmea| (1)
|NAIeaj| (1)

|NAImea| (1)
|NCDmea| (2)
|NCDmej| (1)
|NKAmna| (1)
|QFCeaj| (1)
|QFCqffmea| (1)
|QFDeaj| (1)
|SKBmdj| (1)

060.6 L turtle

No Response (106)
A   alligator snapper (1)
B   alligator snapping turtle (1)
C   (alli)gator tail (1)
D   (alli)gator-tail terrapin (1)
E   (alli)gator-tail turtle (1)
F   alligator terrapin (1)
G   alligator (turtle) (1)
H   alligator turtle (19)
I   Atlantic ridley turtle (1)
J   black turtle (1)
K   box cooter (2)
L   box-shell turtle (1)
M   box (turtle) (1)
N   box tur(tle) (1)
O   box turtle (5)
P   caouaine [F] (3)
Q   chicken turtle (1)
R   common snapper (1)
S   cooter (61)
T   cooter turtle (1)
U   diamond belly (1)
V   diamondback (5)
W   diamondback turtle (4)
X   flatwoods mud turtle (1)
Y   flying turtle (1)
Z   freshwater cooter (1)
aa   freshwater turtle (1)
ab   green sea turtle (1)
ac   green turtle (7)
ad   greenhead (1)
ae   hard back (1)
af   hard-shell (16)
ag   hard-shell cooter (2)
ah   hard-shell snapper (1)
ai   hard-shell turtle (23)
aj   hard-shelled turtle (1)
ak   hardback turtle (1)
al   hardtop mud turtle (1)
am   hawk-neck turtle (1)
an   hawkbill (1)
ao   horseshoe cooter (1)
ap   lady turtle (1)
aq   leatherback (1)
ar   log head (2)
as   logger back (1)
at   loggerhead (57)
au   loggerhead cooter (3)
av   loggerhead turtle (31)
aw   loggerheaded turtle (1)

ax   Mobilian (2)
ay   Mobilian turtle (1)
az   mud terrapin (1)
ba   mud turtle (42)
bb   musher (1)
bc   musk turtle (1)
bd   ocean turtle (1)
be   peace turtle (1)
bf   pond cooter (1)
bg   pond turtle (2)
bh   red snapper (1)
bi   red-eyed turtle (1)
bj   red-neck turtle (1)
bk   redhead (1)
bl   redheaded turtle (1)
bm   ridley (1)
bn   ridley turtle (1)
bo   river turtle (1)
bp   saltwater turtle (2)
bq   sea turtle (51)
br   skillpot (2)
bs   slider (2)
bt   snake turtle (1)
bu   snapper (4)
bv   snapper turtle (3)
bw   snapping jenny (1)
bx   snapping kind (1)
by   snapping terrapin (1)
bz   snapping turtle (85)
ca   snappy turtle (1)
cb   soft-back (2)
cc   soft-back turtle (2)
cd   soft-shell (42)
ce   soft-shell cooter (5)
cf   soft-shell one (1)
cg   soft-shell terrapin (1)
ch   soft-shell turtle (84)
ci   soft-shelled turtle (3)
cj   soft-water turtle (1)
ck   speckle turtle (1)
cl   stink Jenny (1)
cm   stink Jim (2)
cn   stinking Jim (1)
co   stinking Tom (1)
cp   streaked-head (3)
cq   streaked-head turtle (3)
cr   streaked-neck (1)
cs   streaked-neck turtle (1)
ct   streakedy-head turtle (2)
cu   streaker head (1)
cv   streaky head (1)
cw   striped head (1)
cx   striped-headed one (1)
cy   striped leg (1)
cz   striped-neck turtle (1)
da   stripy leg (1)
db   swimming turtle (1)
dc   terrapin (42)
dd   three-rowed turtle (1)

de   tortoise (11)
df   trunkback (1)
dg   turkey (1)
dh   turtle (714)
di   water terrapin (10)
dj   water turtle (15)
dk   white turtle (1)

060.7 L terrapin

No Response (152)
A   bottle turtle (1)
B   box cooter (1)
C   box-hull terrapin (1)
D   box-hull turtle (1)
E   box-shell cooter (1)
F   box-shell terrapin (3)
G   box-shell turtle (3)
H   box terrapin (4)
I   box turtle (12)
J   burying tortoise (1)
K   cooter (36)
L   deer-head turtle (1)
M   dew turtle (1)
N   dirt turtle (1)
O   dried-back turtle (1)
P   dry-land terrapin (26)
Q   dry-land turtle (28)
R   dry-lander (1)
S   dry turtle (1)
T   gopher (164)
U   gopher turtle (3)
V   ground turtle (3)
W   hard-shell (4)
X   hard-shell cooter (1)
Y   hard-shell terrapin (2)
Z   hard-shell turtle (13)
aa   highland (2)
ab   highland gopher (1)
ac   highland terrapin (8)
ad   highland turtle (11)
ae   hill terrapin (2)
af   land gopher (1)
ag   land terrapin (2)
ah   land tortoise (2)
ai   land turtle (36)
aj   loggerhead (2)
ak   loggerhead turtle (3)
al   Maryland terrapin (1)
am   sand gopher (1)
an   sand turtle (1)
ao   sandhill gopher (1)
ap   scooter (1)
aq   stink turtle (1)
ar   stinky-back (1)
as   streaked head (1)
at   streakedy head turtle (1)
au   striped-head terrapin (1)
av   terrapin (458)
aw   terrapin turtle (1)
ax   thunder cooter (1)

ay   tortoise (112)
az   trapdoor (1)
ba   turtle (72)
bb   wood terrapin (1)
bc   woods terrapin (1)
bd   yellow-bellied turtle (1)
be   yellowbelly (2)

060.8 L crawfish

No Response (161)
A   backslider (1)
B   catfish bait (1)
C   clawfish (1)
D   crab (7)
E   crab fish (1)
F   craw mollies (1)
G   crawdab (8)
H   crawdad (160)
I   crawdad [adj.] (1)
J   crawdaddy (3)
K   craw(fish) (1)
L   crawfish (632)
M   crawfish [adj.] (4)
N   crawfishy [adj.] (2)
O   crawly bottom (1)
P   crawpa (1)
Q   craydad (1)
R   crayfish (106)
S   grampus (1)
T   molly (1)
U   red crawfish (1)
V   scabies (1)
W   scissors (1)
X   shrimp (4)

060.9 P shrimp

{s}   palatal
{sh}   alveolar
No Response (183)
<ch(r)imps> (1)
<chrimp> (2)
<sh(r)imp> (1)
<shreemp> (1)
<shremp> (25)
<shri[m]p> (1)
<shrim(p)> (3)
<shrim(p)z> (1)
<shrimp> (303)
<shrimps> (21)
<shtrimps> (1)
<shwimp> (2)
<shwimps> (2)
<shwimp{s}> (1)
<skrimp> (1)
<sreemp> (1)
<srem(p)> (1)
<sremp> (3)
<srimp> (127)
<srimps> (11)
<strimp> (1)
<strimps> (1)

<swamp> (1)
<swemp> (1)
<swimp> (25)
<swimps> (15)
<{sh}remp> (5)
<{sh}remps> (1)
<{sh}rimp> (182)
<{sh}rimps> (12)
<{sh}wemps> (1)
<{sh}wimp> (3)
<{sh}wimps> (1)
<{s}hrimp> (1)
<{s}reemp> (2)
<{s}rimp> (91)
<{s}rimps> (3)
<{s}rimp{s}> (1)
<{s}wimp> (4)
<{s}wimps> (2)

060A.1 L moth

No Response (210)
A   bee moth (1)
B   blackfly (1)
C   bug (13)
D   butterfly (3)
E   butterfly-like thing (1)
F   candle bat (3)
G   candle bug (22)
H   candle flapper (1)
I   candle fly (284)
J   candle-fly-like thing (1)
K   candle miller (1)
L   candle moth (1)
M   candlelight (3)
N   candlelight bug (1)
O   cellar fly (1)
P   clothes moth (1)
Q   electric-light bug (1)
R   firefly (6)
S   fly bug (1)
T   green light bug (1)
U   lamp bug (4)
V   lamp fly (2)
W   light bug (36)
X   light dabber (1)
Y   light fly (1)
Z   light insect (1)
aa   light miller (1)
ab   lightning bug (3)
ac   miller (42)
ad   miller bug (5)
ae   miller fly (6)
af   miller moth (1)
ag   moth (363)
ah   moth miller (1)
ai   night bug (2)
aj   night fly (2)
ak   night miller (1)
al   pest (1)
am   shrimp moth (1)

060A.2 P moth/moths

{dh} devoiced
{f} bilabial
{o} low-back
{oo} unrounded
{th} voiced
{v} devoiced
{z} devoiced
{?} glottal

No Response (133)
<math> (1)
<maw(dh)s> (79)
<maw(dh)z> (100)
<maw(dh){z}> (11)
<maw(th)> (7)
<mawdh(z)> (7)
<mawdh> (4)
<mawdhIz=14> (1)
<mawdhs> (1)
<mawdhz> (62)
<mawdh{z}> (10)
<mawf> (7)
<mawfs> (8)
<maws> (32)
<mawsIz=14> (5)
<mawsts> (1)
<mawt(s)> (1)
<mawt> (13)
<mawth(s)> (19)
<mawth> (395)
<mawthIz=14> (2)
<mawths> (116)
<mawthz> (1)
<mawthzIz=14> (1)
<mawth{z}> (3)
<mawts> (8)
<mawv{z}> (1)
<mawz> (1)
<maw{?}s> (1)
<maw{dh}(z)> (1)
<maw{dh}> (1)
<maw{dh}s> (5)
<maw{dh}z> (3)
<maw{dh}{z}> (11)
<maw{th}(z)> (1)
<maw{th}z> (1)
<maw{th}{z}> (1)
<maw{v}{z}> (1)
<mo(dh)s> (8)
<mo(dh)z> (15)
<mo(dh){z}> (3)
<modhz> (16)
<modh{z}> (8)
<moe(dh)s> (1)
<moedh> (1)
<moes> (2)
<moesIz=14> (1)
<moeth(s)> (1)
<moeth> (5)

<moeths> (2)
<mot> (2)
<moth(s)> (3)
<moth> (100)
<moths> (35)
<mothz> (1)
<mots> (5)
<mow(dh)z> (1)
<mowths> (1)
<mo{dh}{z}> (2)
<muth> (1)
<m{oo}th> (1)
<m{o}(dh)s> (10)
<m{o}(dh)z> (7)
<m{o}(dh)zh> (1)
<m{o}(dh){z}> (1)
<m{o}dh> (1)
<m{o}dhs> (1)
<m{o}dhz> (21)
<m{o}dh{z}> (7)
<m{o}t> (1)
<m{o}th(s)> (7)
<m{o}th> (90)
<m{o}ths> (36)
<m{o}thz> (1)
<m{o}th{z}> (1)
<m{o}vz> (1)
<m{o}{dh}> (1)
<m{o}{dh}z> (1)
<m{o}{dh}{z}> (3)
<m{o}{f}> (1)

060A.3 L firefly

No Response (99)
A   bug light (1)
B   candle bug (1)
C   candle fly (2)
D   candlelight (1)
E   fire flier (1)
F   firebug (14)
G   firefly (149)
H   fly fire (1)
I   fox fire (1)
J   glowworm (7)
K   jack lantern (1)
L   Jack-o'-lantern (1)
M   lamp bug (1)
N   light bug (14)
O   lighten bug (1)
P   lightning bog bug (1)
Q   lightning bug (760)
R   lightning-bug bug (1)
S   limper light (1)
T   linterna [S] (2)
U   luciernagas [S] (1)
V   match (1)
W   moucheron [F] (1)
X   sparkling bug (1)

060A.4 L dragonfly

No Response (158)

A   blue tail (1)
B   damselfly (1)
C   devil doctor (1)
D   devil horse (4)
E   devil's horse (5)
F   devil's little horse (1)
G   doctor snake (2)
H   dragon (1)
I   dragon(fly) (1)
J   dragonfly (277)
K   feeder (snake) (1)
L   hawk (1)
M   helicopter bug (1)
N   horse doctor (4)
O   horsefly (3)
P   jubilee (1)
Q   Katydid (1)
R   (mo)squito (1)
S   mosquito bug (1)
T   (mo)squito bug (1)
U   mosquito catcher (2)
V   mosquito doctor (1)
W   mosquito fly (3)
X   mosquito hawk (242)
Y   (mo)squito hawk (58)
Z   mosquito horse (1)
aa   praying mantis (1)
ab   shepherd needle (1)
ac   skimmers (1)
ad   snake doc(tor) (1)
ae   snake doctor (276)
af   snake doctor fly (1)
ag   snake feeder (55)
ah   snake fly (2)
ai   snake medicine (1)
aj   swamp fly (1)
ak   willow fly (1)
al   wine doctor (1)
am   witch doctor (4)
an   witch's horse (1)

060A.5 L hornet/bee

No Response (161)
A   bee (199)
B   blackhead(ed) (bumblebee) (2)
C   bull-faced bumblebee (1)
D   bumblebee (203)
E   carnation bee (2)
F   carpenter bee (1)
G   ground hornet (1)
H   honeybee (114)
I   hornet (677)
J   hornet bee (1)
K   horse bee (1)
L   Japanese hornet (1)
M   news bee (2)
N   paper hornet (1)
O   red bee (1)
P   red hornet (1)
Q   steady bee (1)

R   stinging bee (1)
S   sweat bee (38)
T   whitehead (1)
U   wood bee (1)
V   woodworker (1)
W   yellow bee (1)
X   yellow hornet (2)

060A.6 L wasp/dirt dauber

No Response (76)
A   black wasp (27)
B   blackjack (1)
C   chien (de) terre, un [F] (1)
D   clay dauber (1)
E   dauber (5)
F   dirt dauber (498)
G   dirt dodger (1)
H   dirt gobbler (1)
I   dirt wasp (4)
J   giddy wasp (1)
K   ground wasp (3)
L   guepe [F] (1)
M   guinea (wasp) (47)
N   mason (1)
O   Mexican wasp (1)
P   mud daub (1)
Q   mud dauber (70)
R   mud dugger (1)
S   mud mason (1)
T   mud wasp (3)
U   paper wasp (2)
V   red jacket wasp (1)
W   red wasp (74)
X   Spanish wasp (2)
Y   spider getter (1)
Z   striped wasp (8)
aa wasp (806)
ab wasp dauber (1)
ac wasper (13)
ad white wasp (1)
ae woods wasp (1)
af yellow wasp (9)
ag zebra wasp (1)

060A.6 P wasps

{aw}   upglide
{o}   low-back
{R}   weakly retroflex
{r}   weakly retroflex
{z}   devoiced
No Response (86)
<was(p)> (1)
<was(ps)> (3)
<washp(s)> (1)
<wasp(s)> (3)
<waspR(z)=14> (1)
<waspRz=14> (1)
<wasps> (1)
<wast> (1)
<wast(s)> (1)
<wasts> (1)

<waw(s)ps> (2)
<wawlts> (1)
<waws(p)> (24)
<waws(ps)> (64)
<waws(p)Iz=14> (17)
<waws(p)I{z}=14> (4)
<waws(p){R}z=14> (1)
<waws(t)Is=14> (1)
<waws(t)Iz=14> (3)
<wawsh(p)> (1)
<wawsh(ps)> (1)
<wawshp> (2)
<wawshp(s)> (2)
<wawshpR{z}=14> (1)
<wawshts> (1)
<wawsp> (58)
<wawsp(s)> (100)
<wawspI(s)=14> (1)
<wawspIz=14> (1)
<wawspR=14> (2)
<wawspRz=14> (6)
<wawsps> (27)
<wawst> (35)
<wawst(s)> (34)
<wawstIs=14> (1)
<wawstIz=14> (21)
<wawstI{z}=14> (4)
<wawsts> (4)
<waw{r}st> (1)
<wies(p)> (1)
<wiesp> (2)
<wo(s)ps> (4)
<woes(p)> (1)
<woesp(s)> (1)
<wos(p)> (7)
<wos(ps)> (23)
<wosh(ps)> (1)
<wosp> (82)
<wosp(s)> (102)
<wospIz=14> (4)
<wospI{z}=14> (1)
<wosps> (94)
<wosp{R}z=14> (1)
<wost> (6)
<wost(s)> (14)
<wostIz=14> (1)
<wothp(s)> (1)
<w{aw}sp> (1)
<w{aw}st(s)> (1)
<w{o}(s)p(s)> (1)
<w{o}s(p)> (3)
<w{o}s(ps)> (11)
<w{o}s(p)Iz=14> (2)
<w{o}s(p)I{z}=14> (2)
<w{o}sfs> (1)
<w{o}sh(ps)> (1)
<w{o}sp> (23)
<w{o}sp(s)> (24)
<w{o}sps> (12)

<w{o}st> (6)
<w{o}st(s)> (4)
<w{o}stIz=14> (4)
<w{o}{r}s(p)> (1)

060A.7 L yellow jacket/fly

No Response (207)
A   black jacket (1)
B   blackjack (1)
C   dog bee (1)
D   jacket (6)
E   yellow bee (1)
F   yellow fly (7)
G   yellow jack (10)
H   yellow jack bee (1)
I   yellow jacket (688)
J   yellow jacket wasp (2)

060A.8 P mosquito

{A}   rounded
{dh}   devoiced
{R}   weakly retroflex
{t}   flap
{z}   devoiced
{zh}   devoiced
No Response (90)
<(mA)skeetA=14> (11)
<(mA)skeetAz=14> (14)
<(mA)skeetA{z}=14> (1)
<(mA)skeetR(z)=14> (1)
<(mA)skeetRz=14> (9)
<(mA)skeetR{z}=14> (4)
<(mA)skeetoez=13> (1)
<(mA)skeetoe{z}=13> (1)
<(mA)skeet{A}z=14> (2)
<(mA)skeet{R}=14> (1)
<(mA)skeet{R}z=14> (5)
<(mA)skee{t}Az=14> (1)
<(mA)skee{t}A{zh}=14> (1)
<(mA)skee{t}R{z}=14> (1)
<(mA)skee{t}{R}s=14> (1)
<(mA)skitR=14> (2)
<(mA)ski{t}R{z}=14> (1)
<MskeetA=414> (1)
<bAskeetA{z}=414> (1)
<mA(s)keetA=414> (1)
<mAshkeetA{z}=414> (1)
<mAskaitA{z}=414> (1)
<mAskeedA=414> (1)
<mAskeedoez=413> (2)
<mAskeetA(z)=414> (1)
<mAskeetA=414> (163)
<mAskeetAs=414> (1)
<mAskeetAz=414> (219)
<mAskeetA{zh}=414> (1)
<mAskeetA{z}=414> (21)
<mAskeetIz=414> (2)
<mAskeetI{z}=414> (1)
<mAskeetR=414> (14)
<mAskeetRz=414> (14)
<mAskeetR{z}=414> (2)

\<mAskeetoe=413> (17)
\<mAskeetoez=413> (25)
\<mAskeetoe{z}=413> (2)
\<mAskeetur=413> (1)
\<mAskeeturz=413> (1)
\<mAskeet{R}=414> (10)
\<mAskeet{R}z=414> (9)
\<mAskeet{R}{z}=414> (2)
\<mAskee{t}A=414> (11)
\<mAskee{t}Az=414> (10)
\<mAskee{t}Azh=414> (1)
\<mAskee{t}A{z}=414> (3)
\<mAskee{t}I=414> (1)
\<mAskee{t}I{z}=414> (1)
\<mAskee{t}R=414> (3)
\<mAskee{t}R{z}=414> (3)
\<mAskee{t}oe=413> (4)
\<mAskee{t}oez=413> (2)
\<mAskee{t}oe{dh}=413> (1)
\<mAskee{t}oe{z}=413> (2)
\<mAskee{t}{R}=414> (1)
\<mAskee{t}{R}s=414> (1)
\<mAskee{t}{R}z=414> (1)
\<mAskee{t}{R}{z}=414> (1)
\<mAski(t)R=414> (1)
\<mAskitA=414> (1)
\<mAskitAz=414> (1)
\<mAskitoez=413> (1)
\<mAskweetoez=413> (1)
\<mIskeedoez=413> (1)
\<mIskeetA=414> (9)
\<mIskeetAz=414> (15)
\<mIskeetA{z}=414> (6)
\<mIskeetIz=414> (8)
\<mIskeetR=414> (2)
\<mIskeetRz=414> (1)
\<mIskeetR{z}=414> (1)
\<mIskeetoe=413> (3)
\<mIskeetoez=413> (6)
\<mIskeet{R}=414> (1)
\<mIskeet{R}z=414> (2)
\<mIskeet{R}{z}=414> (1)
\<mIskee{t}Az=414> (1)
\<mIskee{t}R{z}=414> (2)
\<mIskee{t}i{z}=413> (1)
\<meskeetAs=134> (1)
\<meskeetAz=314> (1)
\<miskeetA=214> (1)
\<miskeetA=314> (3)
\<miskeetAz=314> (1)
\<miskeetoez=313> (1)
\<miskeetooz=313> (1)
\<miskee{t}Iz=314> (1)
\<moeskeetA=314> (1)
\<moeskeetR=214> (1)
\<moeskeetoe{z}=213> (1)
\<moeskee{t}A=314> (2)
\<mooskeetA=314> (3)
\<mooskeetAz=314> (1)

\<mooskeetoe=313> (1)
\<mooskeetue{z}=313> (1)
\<moskeetA=134> (1)
\<moskeetA=314> (3)
\<moskeetAz=314> (1)
\<moskeetoe=312> (1)
\<moskeetoez=123> (1)
\<mushskeetAz=134> (1)
\<muskeedA=134> (1)
\<muskeedAz=134> (1)
\<muskeedoe{z}=313> (3)
\<musket(A)=13> (1)
\<muskeetA=124> (1)
\<muskeetA=134> (37)
\<muskeetA=214> (1)
\<muskeetA=314> (34)
\<muskeetAz=124> (2)
\<muskeetAz=134> (23)
\<muskeetAz=214> (2)
\<muskeetAz=314> (19)
\<muskeetA{z}=134> (2)
\<muskeetA{z}=314> (6)
\<muskeetR=134> (3)
\<muskeetR=214> (1)
\<muskeetR=314> (1)
\<muskeetRz=134> (1)
\<muskeetRz=314> (4)
\<muskeetR{z}=134> (1)
\<muskeetoe=313> (1)
\<muskeetoez=213> (1)
\<muskeetoez=312> (1)
\<muskeetoez=313> (2)
\<muskeetoe{z}=312> (1)
\<musket{A}=314> (1)
\<musket{R}=134> (1)
\<musket{R}z=134> (2)
\<musket{R}z=214> (1)
\<musket{R}z=314> (3)
\<muskee{t}A=134> (1)
\<muskee{t}A=314> (3)
\<muskee{t}Az=314> (1)
\<muskee{t}A{zh}=314> (1)
\<muskee{t}A{z}=314> (1)
\<muskee{t}I{zh}=134> (1)
\<muskee{t}Rz=314> (1)
\<muskee{t}R{z}=314> (1)
\<muskee{t}u{z}=213> (1)
\<muski{t}Adh=134> (1)
\<muskyeetAz=214> (1)
\<m{R}skeetAz=414> (1)

060A.9 L chigger
No Response (210)
A   bete rouge [F] (1)
B   chigger (407)
C   chigger bug (4)
D   chigger flea (1)
E   chinch (4)
F   chinch bug (1)
G   chinker (1)

H   grass bug (2)
I   jigger (11)
J   jiggler (1)
K   red bug (429)
L   red chigger (1)
M   sugar (1)
N   tick (2)

061.1 L grasshopper
No Response (123)
A   black grasshopper (2)
B   black hopper (1)
C   cemetery grasshopper (1)
D   cricket (2)
E   devil's horse (1)
F   Georgia boy (1)
G   Georgia grasshopper (1)
H   Georgia stumper (1)
I   Georgia thumper (7)
J   grass eater (1)
K   grasshopper (755)
L   graveyard horse (1)
M   gray grasshopper (1)
N   green grasshopper (1)
O   green hoppergrass (1)
P   hop [n.] (1)
Q   hopgrasser (1)
R   hopper (5)
S   hopper cricket (2)
T   hoppergrass (145)
U   hopping grass (2)
V   horse grasshopper (1)
W   jiminy cricket (1)
X   locust (1)
Y   sawyer (1)
Z   yellow grasshopper (1)

061.2 L minnow
No Response (181)
A   Arkansas shiner (1)
B   bait (6)
C   bait minnow (1)
D   ballyhoo (1)
E   Baltimore minnow (1)
F   biscuit (1)
G   bream (9)
H   buffalo (1)
I   bull minnow (2)
J   cacaho (1)
K   catfish (3)
L   choker (1)
M   chopa (2)
N   chub (2)
O   cigar minnow (1)
P   creek minnow (1)
Q   croaker (2)
R   cut bait (1)
S   fish bait (4)
T   fly bream (1)
U   golden shiner (1)
V   goldfish (10)

W grouper (1)
X guppy (1)
Y hornyhead (2)
Z little fish (2)
aa mackerel (1)
ab minnow (662)
ac minnow fish (2)
ad Missouri minnow (2)
ae mudminnow (1)
af mullet (8)
ag mullet fish (1)
ah oysters' fish (1)
ai panfish (1)
aj perch (17)
ak piggy (1)
al pilchard (1)
am pogy (1)
an pot-gutted minnow (1)
ao pumpkinseed perch (1)
ap red goldfish (1)
aq redeye (3)
ar redfin (1)
as redfin minnow (1)
at redhorse (1)
au redtail minnow (1)
av roach (2)
aw sand perch (1)
ax sardine (6)
ay shad (10)
az shad minnow (1)
ba shadow (1)
bb shiner (86)
bc shiner minnow (1)
bd silver (2)
be silverfish (1)
bf silverside minnow (1)
bg small fish (1)
bh snail darter (1)
bi spottail (3)
bj steel-back minnow (1)
bk top minnow (3)
bl top water (2)
bm top-water bait (1)
bn top-water minnow (3)
bo toughie (3)
bp toughie minnow (1)
bq trash fish (1)
br white jig (1)

061.3 L spider web

No Response (161)
A cobweb (372)
B dew web (3)
C dust web (2)
D inside spider web (1)
E nest (7)
F smoke web (1)
G soot tag (1)
H spider cob (1)
I spider house (1)

J spider nest (6)
K spider silk (1)
L spider web (556)
M spider's nest (1)
N spider's web (8)
O turtle head (1)
P web (213)
Q webbing (1)

061.4 P roots

{?} glottal
No Response (116)
<rewt> (6)
<rewts> (32)
<rewtsh> (4)
<rhuet> (1)
<rits> (1)
<root> (17)
<roots> (37)
<rue(t)> (1)
<rue(t)s> (2)
<ruet> (152)
<ruet(s)> (2)
<ruetId=14> (2)
<ruets> (554)
<ruetsh> (5)
<rue{?}> (2)
<rut> (2)
<ruts> (1)

061.5 L maple

No Response (377)
A alina tree (1)
B bull maple (1)
C cane maple (1)
D cut-leaf maple (1)
E forest maple (1)
F gum (2)
G gum maple (1)
H gum tree (1)
I hard maple (6)
J hard maple tree (1)
K honey maple (1)
L honey tree (1)
M maple (328)
N maple tree (169)
O maple-syrup tree (1)
P mountain maple (1)
Q nursery maple (1)
R red (maple) (1)
S red maple (3)
T red maple tree (1)
U sap tree (1)
V scaly-bark maple (1)
W scarlet maple (1)
X silver maple (7)
Y silver maple tree (1)
Z silverleaf maple (6)
aa soft maple (2)
ab sugar (maple) (1)
ac sugar maple (96)

ad sugar maple tree (1)
ae sugar tree (28)
af sugar type (1)
ag sugarcane tree (2)
ah swamp maple (5)
ai sweet gum (1)
aj sweet maple (2)
ak syrup tree (3)
al syrup-making kind (1)
am Vermont maple (1)
an water maple (1)
ao white maple (4)
ap wild maple (2)
aq wood maple (1)

061.6 L grove

No Response (566)
A almond grove (1)
B arbor (1)
C body of trees (1)
D boundary (1)
E brake (1)
F bunch (10)
G chenier [F] (1)
H citrus grove (3)
I clump (6)
J cluster (3)
K copse (1)
L cypriere [F] (1)
M forest (23)
N group (4)
O grove (164)
P grow (1)
Q hickory-nut grove (1)
R hummock (1)
S knot (1)
T maple crop of trees (1)
U maple forest (3)
V maple grove (26)
W maple orchard (23)
X maple stand (1)
Y maple trees (1)
Z maple wood lot (1)
aa maple-sugar orchard (1)
ab maple-syrup orchard (1)
ac maple-tree grove (1)
ad mote (1)
ae motte (1)
af orange grove (8)
ag orchard (44)
ah patch (3)
ai peach grove (3)
aj pecan grove (9)
ak pecan orchard (2)
al pine thicket (2)
am plantation (1)
an scope of timber (1)
ao stand (8)
ap sugar grove (5)
aq sugar orchard (3)

ar   sugar-maple grove (2)
as   sugar-maple orchard (1)
at   sugar-tree grove (1)
au   sugar-tree orchard (2)
av   thicket (4)
aw   tree orchard (1)
ax   turpentine grove (1)
ay   turpentine orchard (1)
az   woods (5)

061.7 L sycamore
No Response (235)
A   button willow (2)
B   buttonball (1)
C   buttonwood (3)
D   cotton tree (1)
E   cotton-ball tree (1)
F   cottonwood (1)
G   plane tree (1)
H   red sycamore (1)
I   sevenbark (1)
J   sycamore (tree) (651)
K   white sycamore (1)

061.7 P sycamore
{oe}   lowered onset
{R}   weakly retroflex
{r}   weakly retroflex
{z}   devoiced
No Response (236)
<seekAmoerz=143> (1)
<seekIm{oe}[r]=143> (1)
<seekIm{oe}r=341> (1)
<sigAm{oe}(r)=143> (1)
<sigAm{oe}rz=143> (1)
<sik(I)moe[r]z=13> (1)
<sik(I)m{oe}r{z}=13> (1)
<sikAb{oe}{r}=143> (1)
<sikAmaw(r)=143> (3)
<sikAmawr=143> (8)
<sikAmaw{r}=143> (1)
<sikAmoe(r)=143> (16)
<sikAmoe(r)z=143> (1)
<sikAmoe[r]=142> (1)
<sikAmoe[r]=143> (59)
<sikAmoe[r]=241> (1)
<sikAmoe[r]z=143> (2)
<sikAmoe[r]{z}=143> (2)
<sikAmoer=143> (58)
<sikAmoerz=143> (3)
<sikAmoer{z}=143> (1)
<sikAmoe{r}=143> (22)
<sikAm{oe}(r)=143> (9)
<sikAm{oe}(r){z}=143> (1)
<sikAm{oe}[r]=143> (37)
<sikAm{oe}[r]z=143> (3)
<sikAm{oe}[r]{z}=143> (2)
<sikAm{oe}r=143> (84)
<sikAm{oe}r=241> (1)
<sikAm{oe}rz=143> (9)
<sikAm{oe}r{z}=143> (2)

<sikAm{oe}{r}=143> (32)
<sikAm{oe}{r}z=143> (2)
<sikImA(r)=144> (1)
<sikImaw(r)=143> (3)
<sikImaw[r]z=143> (1)
<sikImawr=143> (3)
<sikImoe(r)=143> (18)
<sikImoe[r]=143> (20)
<sikImoe[r]z=143> (2)
<sikImoe[r]{z}=143> (1)
<sikImoer=143> (10)
<sikImoer=341> (1)
<sikImoe{r}=143> (13)
<sikImoe{r}z=143> (1)
<sikIm{oe}(r)=143> (23)
<sikIm{oe}(r)z=143> (2)
<sikIm{oe}[r]=143> (67)
<sikIm{oe}[r]z=143> (2)
<sikIm{oe}[r]{z}=143> (2)
<sikIm{oe}r=143> (92)
<sikIm{oe}rz=143> (9)
<sikIm{oe}{r}=143> (22)
<sikIm{oe}{r}z=143> (1)
<sikM(oer)=14> (1)
<sikMmoer=143> (1)
<sikMm{oe}[r]=143> (1)
<sikMm{oe}{r}=143> (3)
<sikMoe[r]=143> (1)
<sikMoe{r}=143> (1)
<sikM{oe}[r]=143> (2)
<sikM{oe}{r}=143> (4)
<sikim{oe}r=132> (2)
<sikkImoe(r)=143> (1)
<sikyIm{oe}{r}=143> (1)
<sik{R}m{oe}{r}=143> (1)
<sinkAmoer=143> (1)
<thikAmawr=143> (1)

061.8 L trees
No Response (64)
A   acantha (1)
B   acorn (4)
C   alamo (1)
D   alder (2)
E   alfia (1)
F   alina (1)
G   almond (1)
H   anaqua (4)
I   apple (69)
J   apple, hedge (2)
K   apricot (6)
L   arborvitae (1)
M   ash (84)
N   ash, Arizona (3)
O   ash, prickly (2)
P   ash, punk (1)
Q   ash, sea (1)
R   ash, white (2)
S   aspen (1)
T   autograph (1)

U   avocado (7)
V   bamboo (1)
W   banana (4)
X   banyan (1)
Y   bay (26)
Z   bay, bull (1)
aa   bay, red (1)
ab   bay, stink (1)
ac   bay, sweet (2)
ad   bay, white (3)
ae   bean tree (1)
af   beech (34)
ag   beechnut (1)
ah   beeshang (1)
ai   birch (44)
aj   birch, white (1)
ak   bitternut (1)
al   blackjack (21)
am   blueberry (1)
an   bodock (18)
ao   (bois) connu [F] (2)
ap   bois d'arc [F] (6)
aq   bottle cleaner (1)
ar   boxwood (1)
as   Brazil (2)
at   breadfruit (1)
au   buckeye (1)
av   buckeye ball (1)
aw   buckthorn (1)
ax   buttonbush (1)
ay   buttonwood (2)
az   cabbage (4)
ba   calamondin (1)
bb   calendar (1)
bc   camellia tree (1)
bd   camphor (12)
be   camphor, Japanese (1)
bf   Cape jasmine (3)
bg   castor bean (1)
bh   catalpa (7)
bi   catawba (27)
bj   cedar (176)
bk   cedar, mountain (2)
bl   cedar, red (1)
bm   cedar, saltwater (1)
bn   cedar, stinking (1)
bo   Charley ball (1)
bp   chene gris [F] (1)
bq   cherry (8)
br   cherry, Chinese (1)
bs   cherry, wild (6)
bt   chestnut (52)
bu   chestnut, American (1)
bv   chestnut, Chinese (3)
bw   chicken (2)
bx   china (8)
by   chinaball (12)
bz   chinaberry (54)
ca   chinquapin (21)

cb   cigar (1)
cc   cinnamon (1)
cd   coconut (6)
ce   cork (1)
cf   corkscrew (1)
cg   cotonnier [F] (1)
ch   cotton (3)
ci   cottonwood (97)
cj   cowitch (1)
ck   crab apple (3)
cl   crab apple, ornament (1)
cm   crape myrtle (22)
cn   crybaby (1)
co   cucumber (2)
cp   cypress (131)
cq   cypress, black (1)
cr   cypress, Italian (1)
cs   cypress, white (2)
ct   damson (1)
cu   date (2)
cv   dog (1)
cw   dog thumb (1)
cx   dogwood (164)
cy   dogwood, flowering (1)
cz   dogwood, red (1)
da   dwarf (1)
db   ebony (4)
dc   eight-nut (1)
dd   elder (1)
de   elder, box (8)
df   elderberry (2)
dg   elm (177)
dh   elm, American (1)
di   elm, Chinese (4)
dj   elm, Japanese (1)
dk   elm, piss (2)
dl   elm, red (2)
dm   elm, rock (1)
dn   elm, slippery (1)
do   elm, white (2)
dp   eucalyptus (1)
dq   evergreen (7)
dr   fig (45)
ds   fig, black (1)
dt   fig, strangler (1)
du   fir (5)
dv   fir, California (1)
dw   fish (1)
dx   fork-leaf (1)
dy   fringe (1)
dz   gallberry (1)
ea   ginkgo (1)
eb   grain tree (1)
ec   grandaddy graybeard (1)
ed   granny graybeard (1)
ee   grape (3)
ef   grapefruit (10)
eg   graqueno [S] (1)
eh   guava (2)

ei   gum (76)
ej   gum, beech (1)
ek   gum, black (71)
el   gum, red (6)
em   gum, sweet (162)
en   gum, sweetie (1)
eo   gum, tupelo (8)
ep   gum, white (3)
eq   gum ball (1)
er   gumbo file (1)
es   gumbo-limbo (2)
et   gypsy (1)
eu   hackberry (55)
ev   hackleberry (1)
ew   Haden (1)
ex   hagberry (2)
ey   hall (3)
ez   haw (3)
fa   haw, bird (1)
fb   haw, black (1)
fc   haw, possum (1)
fd   haw, red (5)
fe   hawthorn (2)
ff   hazelnut (2)
fg   hedge (tree) (2)
fh   hemlock (1)
fi   hen-dung (1)
fj   hickory (200)
fk   hickory, scaly-bark (3)
fl   hickory, tight-bark (1)
fm   hickory nut (46)
fn   hickory nut, scaly-bark (2)
fo   hog-acorn (1)
fp   holly (25)
fq   hopper (1)
fr   horehound (1)
fs   horn bean (1)
ft   hornbeam (1)
fu   horse-apple (1)
fv   huisache (10)
fw   ipiliple (1)
fx   ironwood (7)
fy   japonica (1)
fz   jacaranda (1)
ga   junco (1)
gb   juniper (4)
gc   knockaway (1)
gd   knowledge (1)
ge   kumquat (3)
gf   laurel, cherry (2)
gg   lemon (5)
gh   lemon, wild (1)
gi   lime (8)
gj   lime, Spanish (1)
gk   linden (1)
gl   linn (2)
gm   linn wood tree (1)
gn   loblolly (4)
go   locust (23)

gp   locust, black (7)
gq   locust, honey (2)
gr   locust, ironwood (1)
gs   locust, yellow (1)
gt   log tree (1)
gu   longleaf (2)
gv   loquat (2)
gw   magnolia (1)
gx   mahogany (1)
gy   mandarin (1)
gz   mango (8)
ha   maple (79)
hb   maple, curly (1)
hc   maple, cut-leaf (1)
hd   maple, forest (1)
he   maple, hard (1)
hf   maple, Japanese (1)
hg   maple, nursery (1)
hh   maple, red (3)
hi   maple, scaly-bark (1)
hj   maple, silver (6)
hk   maple, silverleaf (10)
hl   maple, soft (3)
hm   maple, sugar (2)
hn   maple, swamp (3)
ho   maple, water (1)
hp   maple, white (5)
hq   maple, wild (1)
hr   maple, wood (1)
hs   marine (1)
ht   mayapple (1)
hu   mayhaw (2)
hv   melaleuca (1)
hw   mesquite (35)
hx   mezquite [S] (1)
hy   mimosa (57)
hz   morita (1)
ia   mosquito (1)
ib   mulberry (53)
ic   mulberry, English (1)
id   mulberry, wild (1)
ie   munguba (1)
if   myrtle tree (2)
ig   no-name (1)
ih   nutmeg (1)
ii   oak (551)
ij   oak, beechnut (1)
ik   oak, black (30)
il   oak, blackjack (13)
im   oak, border (3)
in   oak, cherry-bark (1)
io   oak, chestnut (11)
ip   oak, chinquapin (2)
iq   oak, cotton (1)
ir   oak, cow (1)
is   oak, evergreen (1)
it   oak, giant (1)
iu   oak, green (2)
iv   oak, ground (1)

pr   willow, budding (1)
ps   willow, button (2)
pt   willow, pussy (1)
pu   willow, water (1)
pv   willow, weeping (30)
pw   wonder (1)
px   worm tree (1)
py   yaupon (4)
pz   yew (1)
qa   yew, Japanese (1)

062.1 P cherry
{r}   weakly retroflex
{t}   flap
{z}   devoiced
{?}   glottal
No Response (158)
<chai(r)I=14> (1)
<chairI=14> (4)
<charI=14> (1)
<charee=13> (1)
<che(r)I=14> (7)
<che[r](I)z> (1)
<che[r]I=14> (2)
<cher(I)> (1)
<cherA=14> (2)
<cherI=14> (608)
<cherIz=14> (32)
<cherI{z}=14> (3)
<cheree=13> (9)
<chereez=13> (1)
<che{?}I=14> (1)
<che{r}(I)> (2)
<che{r}A=14> (1)
<che{r}I=14> (14)
<che{r}Iz=14> (2)
<che{t}I=14> (1)
<chirI=14> (15)
<chirIz=14> (1)
<chi{r}(I)> (1)
<chi{r}ee=13> (1)
<churI=14> (44)
<churIz=14> (6)
<churee=13> (1)
<churrI=14> (5)
<chu{r}I=14> (2)
<chu{r}rI=14> (3)
<chu{r}rIz=14> (1)

062.2 L sumac
No Response (458)
A   black sumac (1)
B   burning bush (1)
C   Christmas bush (1)
D   elderberry (2)
E   elm (1)
F   fire bush (1)
G   fire tree (1)
H   flaming sumac (1)
I   hackberry bush (1)
J   heaven bush (1)

K   huckleberry (1)
L   poison elder (1)
M   poison sumac (32)
N   poisonous sumac (1)
O   pokeberry tree (1)
P   red bush (1)
Q   red sumac (2)
R   shoemaker (5)
S   shoemaker bush (1)
T   shoemaker tree (2)
U   sourwood (1)
V   staghorn sumac (1)
W   sumac (379)
X   sumac bush (15)
Y   sumac poison ivory (1)
Z   sumac tree (9)
aa   white sumac (2)
ab   wild grape (1)

062.2 P sumac
No Response (442)
<chuemaik=13> (1)
<chuemak=13> (1)
<sewmaik=13> (1)
<sewmak=13> (7)
<shewmaik=13> (11)
<shewmait=13> (2)
<shewmak=13> (3)
<shewmok=13> (1)
<shoomaik=13> (1)
<shuebaik=13> (1)
<shuemaig=13> (1)
<shuemaik=13> (210)
<shuemaikR=134> (4)
<shuemaikRz=134> (1)
<shuemaik[R]=134> (6)
<shuemaiks=13> (5)
<shuemais=13> (1)
<shuemait=13> (23)
<shuemak=13> (45)
<shuemek=13> (6)
<shuemet=13> (1)
<shuemik=13> (1)
<shuemok=13> (1)
<soomAk=14> (1)
<soomak=13> (3)
<suemAk=14> (5)
<suemaik=13> (6)
<suemak=13> (147)
<suemaks=13> (2)
<suemash=13> (1)
<suemek=13> (3)
<suemich=13> (1)
<suemit=13> (1)
<suemok=13> (4)
<suemuch=13> (1)
<sumak=13> (1)
<tsuemok=13> (1)

062.3 L poison ivy
No Response (160)

A   bowl ivy (1)
B   bramblebush (1)
C   brambles (1)
D   buck vine (1)
E   bull nettle (13)
F   bush ivy (1)
G   bush nettle (1)
H   carriage vine (1)
I   cat's vine (1)
J   cow vine (1)
K   cowitch (11)
L   cowitch vine (13)
M   cowlick (1)
N   dropsy vine (1)
O   five-leaf (1)
P   five-leaf poison vine (3)
Q   four-leaf poison vine (1)
R   ground ivy (2)
S   ivory (3)
T   ivy (27)
U   ivy vine (2)
V   l'herbe a la puce [F] (2)
W   live oak (1)
X   manchineel (1)
Y   nettle(s) (6)
Z   nettle rash (2)
aa   oak (5)
ab   pink elder (1)
ac   poison ash (3)
ad   poison elder (2)
ae   poison itch bush (1)
af   poison ivory (52)
ag   poison ivy (545)
ah   poison oak (496)
ai   poison sumac (33)
aj   poison three-leaf (1)
ak   poison vine (28)
al   poison-ivy bush (1)
am   poison-oak vine (8)
an   poisoned ivy (1)
ao   poisoning oak (1)
ap   poppy nettle (1)
aq   smartweed (1)
ar   sour vine (1)
as   stingarees (1)
at   stinging nettle (11)
au   stinging vine (1)
av   stinging weed (1)
aw   sumac (29)
ax   sumac poison ivory (1)
ay   three-leaf poison vine (3)
az   thunder oak (1)
ba   thunderwood (17)
bb   thunderwood bush (2)
bc   thunderwood tree (1)
bd   white elder (1)
be   white sumac (1)
bf   wild bull nettle (1)
bg   wild ivy (1)

062.3 S poison

No Response (30)
|JJCeaa| (3)
|JJCeac| (1)
|JJCeaj| (1)
|JJCmab| (1)
|JJHeaa| (7)
|JJHeab| (2)
|JJHeaj| (4)
|JJHmaj| (1)
|JSCeaa| (6)
|JSCeac| (2)
|JSCeaj| (4)
|JSCkaa| (1)
|JSCmaj| (2)
|JSDffjeaj| (1)
|JSHeaa| (1)
|JSHeaj| (3)
|JSHmaa| (1)
|PAHeaa| (1)
|QABeaj| (1)
|QACeac| (1)
|QADeab| (1)
|QAHeab| (1)
|QAHeaj| (1)
|QAHqfbeaa| (1)
|QCAeaj| (1)
|QCBeaj| (1)
|QFAdan| (1)
|QFAeaa| (26)
|QFAeab| (1)
|QFAeac| (4)
|QFAead| (2)
|QFAeae| (1)
|QFAeaj| (18)
|QFAeak| (2)
|QFAeal| (2)
|QFAmaa| (5)
|QFAmab| (2)
|QFAmaj| (2)
|QFBdac| (2)
|QFBeaa| (168)
|QFBeab| (10)
|QFBeac| (47)
|QFBead| (1)
|QFBeaj| (44)
|QFBeak| (2)
|QFBeal| (9)
|QFBkab| (6)
|QFBkak| (1)
|QFBmaa| (26)
|QFBmab| (63)
|QFBmaj| (14)
|QFBmak| (9)
|QFCeaa| (43)
|QFCeac| (8)
|QFCeaj| (6)
|QFCeal| (1)
|QFCkab| (3)
|QFCkak| (3)
|QFCmaa| (14)
|QFCmab| (7)
|QFCmaj| (4)
|QFCqfaeaa| (1)
|QFCqfbeaa| (3)
|QFCqfbeaj| (6)
|QFCqfbeal| (2)
|QFCqmbeaj| (2)
|QFDdaj| (1)
|QFDeaa| (18)
|QFDeaj| (6)
|QFDmaj| (4)
|QFDqfbeaa| (1)
|QFFeaa| (19)
|QFFeab| (1)
|QFFeaj| (3)
|QFFkaa| (1)
|QFFkab| (1)
|QFFkak| (1)
|QFFmaa| (1)
|QFFmaj| (1)
|QFHeaa| (3)
|QFHeab| (2)
|QFHeac| (1)
|QFHeaj| (1)
|QFHkaj| (1)
|QMAbbj| (1)
|QMAeaa| (11)
|QMAeac| (1)
|QMAeaj| (21)
|QMAmaa| (1)
|QMAmab| (1)
|QMAmaj| (5)
|QMAmak| (1)
|QMB| (1)
|QMBeaa| (36)
|QMBeab| (1)
|QMBeac| (9)
|QMBeaj| (12)
|QMBeal| (1)
|QMBmaa| (5)
|QMBmab| (13)
|QMBmaj| (5)
|QMBmak| (3)
|QMBmcb| (1)
|QMCeaa| (11)
|QMCeac| (3)
|QMCeaj| (3)
|QMCmaa| (2)
|QMCmaf| (1)
|QMCmaj| (1)
|QMCmea| (1)
|QMD| (1)
|QMDdaj| (1)
|QMDeaa| (2)
|QMDeaj| (2)
|QMDmaa| (2)
|QMDmaj| (4)

|QMFeaa| (5)
|QMFeab| (1)
|QMFeak| (1)
|QMHeaa| (1)
|QMHeaj| (1)
|QXBmdb| (1)
|RAIeal| (1)
|RCE| (1)
|RCEkaj| (1)
|SAE| (1)
|SAGeaa| (1)
|TAAeaa| (2)
|TCAeaa| (1)
|TCAmaj| (1)
|TFAeaj| (1)
|TFBqfamaj| (1)
|TFBqfjkab| (1)
|TFFeaj| (1)
|TMAeaa| (7)
|TMAeaj| (2)
|TMAmaj| (1)
|TXAeda| (1)

062.4 P strawberries

{b} fricative
{o} low-back
{r} weakly retroflex
{t} flap
{z} devoiced
{zh} devoiced
{?} glottal

No Response (148)
<ch(r)awbai(rI)=13> (1)
<s(t)rawbe(r)A=134> (1)
<s(t)rawberIz=134> (5)
<sh(t)rawberIz=134> (1)
<shtrawbairI{z}=134> (1)
<shtrawberI=134> (1)
<shtrawberIz=134> (3)
<shtrawberIzh=134> (1)
<shtrawbi{r}(I){z}=13> (1)
<shtraw{b}erIz=134> (1)
<shtr{o}{b}erIz=134> (1)
<skraw{b}erIz=134> (1)
<st(r)oberIz=134> (1)
<strawb(e)rIz=14> (1)
<strawbai(rI)=13> (2)
<strawbairIz=134> (1)
<strawbarI=134> (2)
<strawbarIz=134> (4)
<strawba{r}Iz=134> (1)
<strawbe(r)I=134> (2)
<strawbe(r)Iz=134> (9)
<strawbe[r](I){z}=13> (1)
<strawbe[r]I=134> (2)
<strawbe[r]Iz=134> (1)
<strawber(I){z}=13> (1)
<strawberAz=134> (4)
<strawberI(z)=134> (1)
<strawberI=134> (119)

<strawberIs=134> (1)
<strawberIz=134> (393)
<strawberIz=214> (1)
<strawberI{z}=134> (34)
<strawbereez=123> (4)
<strawbe{?}Iz=134> (1)
<strawbe{r}(I)=13> (4)
<strawbe{r}I=134> (2)
<strawbe{r}Iz=134> (9)
<strawbe{r}I{z}=134> (1)
<strawbe{t}I=134> (1)
<strawbe{t}Iz=134> (1)
<strawbirIz=134> (3)
<strawbirI{z}=134> (2)
<strawburI=134> (9)
<strawburIz=134> (32)
<strawburI{z}=134> (7)
<strawbureez=123> (1)
<strawbu{r}(I)z=13> (3)
<strawbu{r}I=134> (1)
<strawbu{r}Iz=134> (7)
<strawbu{r}I{z}=134> (1)
<straw{b}erI{z}=134> (1)
<stroberI=134> (2)
<stroberIz=134> (10)
<stroberI{z}=134> (5)
<stroburI=134> (1)
<stroburIz=134> (1)
<stroeberI=134> (2)
<stroeberI{zh}=134> (1)
<stroeburIz=134> (1)
<strowberIz=134> (1)
<str{o}berI=134> (10)
<str{o}berIs=134> (2)
<str{o}berIz=134> (29)
<str{o}berI{z}=134> (6)
<str{o}bereez=123> (1)
<str{o}birI=134> (1)
<str{o}birIz=134> (2)
<str{o}biri{z}=123> (1)
<str{o}burIz=134> (1)
<str{o}burI{z}=134> (3)
<str{o}bu{r}Iz=134> (1)
<str{o}{b}irI{z}=134> (1)
<s{t}(r)awbu{r}I=134> (1)
<s{t}rawberIz=134> (1)

062.5 P raspberries

{b}   fricative
{dh}   devoiced
{r}   weakly retroflex
{t}   flap
{z}   devoiced
No Response (311)
<kArazberI=4134> (1)
<ra(z)berIz=134> (1)
<radhberI=134> (1)
<radhbi{r}Idh=134> (1)
<rasberI=134> (24)
<rasberIs=134> (1)

<rasberIz=134> (18)
<rasberI{z}=134> (1)
<rasbirI=134> (1)
<rasburI=134> (1)
<rasburIz=134> (1)
<rashberI=134> (1)
<rashberIz=134> (1)
<raspberI{z}=134> (2)
<rastberI=134> (1)
<ras{b}irIz=134> (1)
<rawzberI=134> (1)
<razbA(rI)z=14> (1)
<razba(rI)=13> (2)
<razbai(rI)=13> (1)
<razbai(rI)z=13> (2)
<razbairI=134> (1)
<razbarI=134> (1)
<razbarIz=134> (2)
<razbe(r)Iz=134> (1)
<razbe(rI){dh}=13> (1)
<razbe[r](I){z}=13> (1)
<razbe[r]I=134> (1)
<razbe[r]Iz=134> (1)
<razber(I)=13> (1)
<razberA=134> (2)
<razberAz=134> (2)
<razberI=134> (112)
<razberIz=134> (275)
<razberI{z}=134> (13)
<razbereez=123> (1)
<razbe{r}(I)=13> (2)
<razbe{r}(I)z=31> (1)
<razbe{r}I=134> (2)
<razbe{r}Iz=134> (6)
<razbirI=134> (1)
<razbirI{z}=134> (1)
<razbu[r]I{z}=134> (1)
<razburI=134> (16)
<razburIz=134> (35)
<razburI{z}=134> (1)
<razbureez=123> (1)
<razburrI{z}=134> (1)
<razbu{r}(I)z=13> (4)
<razbu{r}I=134> (3)
<razbu{r}Iz=134> (4)
<razpberIz=134> (1)
<raz{b}airI=134> (1)
<ra{dh}birI{dh}=134> (1)
<ra{t}berIz=134> (1)
<ra{t}burIz=134> (1)
<ra{z}berAz=134> (1)
<ra{z}berI=134> (2)
<ra{z}berIz=134> (11)
<ra{z}berI{z}=134> (3)
<ra{z}pberIz=134> (1)
<resberI=134> (1)
<resbe{r}Iz=134> (1)
<rezbai(rI)z=13> (1)
<rezbairI{z}=134> (1)

<rezbarIz=134> (2)
<rezberI=134> (1)
<rezberIz=134> (13)
<rezbu[r]I=134> (1)
<rezburIz=134> (2)
<rez{b}irI=134> (1)
<rozberI=134> (2)

062.6 P poisonous

{oy}   inglide
{p}   fricative
{r}   weakly retroflex
{t}   flap
{z}   devoiced
No Response (195)
<pawIzh(NAs)=14> (1)
<pawdhN(As)=14> (1)
<pawrzN(As)=14> (1)
<pawzN(As)=14> (2)
<pawzNA(s)=144> (1)
<paw{r}zN(As)=14> (2)
<piezN(As)=14> (6)
<poydNAs=144> (1)
<poydhN(As)=14> (1)
<poysNIs=144> (1)
<poyz(A)nAs=14> (63)
<poyz(A)nIs=14> (7)
<poyzInus=143> (1)
<poyzN(As)=14> (326)
<poyzNA(s)=144> (1)
<poyzNAs=144> (116)
<poyzNIs=144> (1)
<poyzNoos=143> (1)
<poyzNus=143> (2)
<poyzhN(As)=14> (1)
<poy{t}N(As)=14> (2)
<poy{z}(A)nAs=14> (4)
<poy{z}N(As)=14> (8)
<poy{z}NAs=144> (3)
<pozinIs=134> (1)
<p{oy}dhN(As)=14> (2)
<p{oy}sN(As)=14> (1)
<p{oy}z(A)nAs=14> (7)
<p{oy}zN(As)=14> (160)
<p{oy}zNAs=144> (38)
<p{oy}zNIs=144> (1)
<p{oy}zNus=143> (1)
<p{oy}z[N](As)=14> (2)
<p{oy}zun(As)=13> (1)
<p{oy}{z}N(As)=14> (7)
<p{oy}{z}NAs=144> (1)
<p{oy}{z}NG(As)=14> (1)
<p{o}zN(As)=14> (1)
<{p}oy{z}N(As)=14> (1)

062.7 L mountain laurel

No Response (603)
A   bay (2)
B   bay laurel (1)
C   bay-leaf laurel (1)
D   calico bush (1)

E   cherry laurel (7)
F   creek ivy (1)
G   creek laurel (1)
H   flowering laurel (1)
I   ivory (2)
J   ivy (20)
K   ivy bush (1)
L   laurel (74)
M   laurel ivy (1)
N   laurel tree (5)
O   mountain hydrangea (1)
P   mountain ivy (1)
Q   mountain laurel (144)
R   sevenbark (1)
S   Texas mountain laurel (1)
T   white laurel (1)

062.8 L rhododendron
No Response (677)
A   azalea (27)
B   cherry laurel (2)
C   elephant ear (1)
D   ivory (1)
E   ivy (2)
F   laurel (5)
G   laurel tree (1)
H   laurier [F] (1)
I   oleander (14)
J   red laurel (1)
K   rhodo-something (1)
L   rhododendron (171)
M   white bay (1)
N   wild azalea (4)

062.9 L magnolia
No Response (250)
A   bay (4)
B   bay tree (4)
C   blue magnolia (1)
D   bull bay (2)
E   china magnolia (1)
F   cucumber (17)
G   cucumber bush (1)
H   cucumber plant (1)
I   cucumber tree (16)
J   flower tree (3)
K   Japanese magnolia (3)
L   Japanese tree (1)
M   magnolia (553)
N   magnolia bay (3)
O   magnolia bush (3)
P   Magnolia grandiflora (1)
Q   magnolia tree (83)
R   mulberry (1)
S   pink magnolia (1)
T   Southern magnolia (1)
U   sweet bay (1)
V   sweet magnolia (1)
W   tulip (1)
X   tulip magnolia (1)
Y   tulip poplar (1)

Z   tulip tree (1)
aa   umbrella tree (1)
ab   wild cucumber (2)
ac   wild magnolia (2)

063.1 L husband
No Response (104)
A   Babe (1)
B   better half (28)
C   boss (24)
D   boss man (1)
E   boyfriend (1)
F   bread toter (1)
G   cat (1)
H   companion (1)
I   Dad (1)
J   dad (1)
K   Daddy (5)
L   daddy (1)
M   Darling (2)
N   dude (1)
O   head of the house (1)
P   helpmate (1)
Q   Honey (2)
R   honey (1)
S   hub (1)
T   hubby (16)
U   husband (793)
V   man (25)
W   master (2)
X   mate (3)
Y   milk-toast (1)
Z   Mister (3)
aa   mister (2)
ab   old husband (1)
ac   old man (186)
ad   old son of a bitch (2)
ae   other half (4)
af   Pa (4)
ag   pain in the you-know-what (1)
ah   Pap (1)
ai   partner (1)
aj   spouse (34)
ak   sugar (1)
al   Sugar Foot (1)
am   Sweetheart (1)
an   sweetie (2)
ao   Sweetie Pie (2)
ap   that thing (1)

063.1 S husband
No Response (0)
|CGA| (1)
|FAA| (2)
|FAAmaj| (3)
|FAC| (2)
|FADmaj| (1)
|FAH| (13)
|FAHmaj| (6)
|FCA| (2)
|FCAmaj| (3)

|FCC| (1)
|FCD| (1)
|FCDmaj| (1)
|FCH| (3)
|FCHmaj| (1)
|FFH| (1)
|FKH| (1)
|FMD| (1)
|KAC| (1)
|LAA| (3)
|LAB| (8)
|LABfaj| (1)
|LABmaj| (2)
|LAC| (12)
|LAD| (4)
|LADmaj| (2)
|LAE| (8)
|LAEmaj| (2)
|LAF| (2)
|LAG| (6)
|LAGfaj| (1)
|LAI| (2)
|LCA| (4)
|LCAmaj| (4)
|LCB| (1)
|LCBmaj| (1)
|LCD| (2)
|LCDmaj| (1)
|LCE| (4)
|LCEfaj| (5)
|LCEmaj| (1)
|LCGmaj| (1)
|LFA| (1)
|LFAmaj| (1)
|LFB| (1)
|LFBmaj| (1)
|LFG| (2)
|LMBfaj| (1)
|LMC| (1)
|MCA| (11)
|MCD| (3)
|NAA| (19)
|NAAfaj| (38)
|NAAmaj| (9)
|NAB| (21)
|NABfaj| (3)
|NABfal| (1)
|NABmaj| (6)
|NACmaj| (1)
|NAD| (209)
|NADfaj| (35)
|NADmaj| (129)
|NADnab| (3)
|NADnap| (1)
|NAE| (1)
|NAEfaj| (1)
|NAEmaj| (1)
|NAF| (26)
|NAFfaj| (4)

|NAFmaj| (6)
|NAG| (19)
|NAGfaj| (2)
|NAGmaj| (10)
|NAH| (20)
|NAHmaj| (6)
|NAHmap| (1)
|NAI| (1)
|NBA| (2)
|NBAfaj| (1)
|NBD| (1)
|NBDfaj| (3)
|NCA| (16)
|NCAfaj| (13)
|NCAmaj| (13)
|NCAmap| (1)
|NCB| (1)
|NCBfaj| (2)
|NCBmaj| (3)
|NCC| (2)
|NCD| (44)
|NCDfaj| (32)
|NCDmaj| (26)
|NCDmap| (1)
|NCF| (5)
|NCFfaj| (2)
|NCFmaj| (2)
|NCG| (1)
|NCGmaj| (3)
|NCH| (1)
|NCHmaa| (1)
|NCHmaj| (2)
|NCImaj| (1)
|NDAfdj| (1)
|NDAmdj| (1)
|NDD| (1)
|NDDmdj| (2)
|NDHmdj| (1)
|NFAfaj| (1)
|NFB| (1)
|NFD| (1)
|NFDfdj| (1)
|NFF| (1)
|NFGmaj| (1)
|NKA| (1)
|NKH| (1)
|NMB| (1)
|NMFfaj| (1)
|PAA| (1)
|PAGmaj| (1)
|SCA| (1)

063.2 L wife

No Response (52)
A aggravator (1)
B air brake (1)
C Baby (2)
D baby (1)
E ball and chain (5)
F battle-ax (6)

G better half (38)
H biscuit maker (1)
I bitch (1)
J Boss (9)
K boss (20)
L boss of the house (1)
M boss woman (1)
N broad (2)
O chick (1)
P child (1)
Q cook (4)
R Darling (3)
S Dear (1)
T Doll (1)
U femme [F] (1)
V Girl (1)
W good woman (1)
X helpmate (1)
Y home wife (1)
Z Honey (5)
aa honey (1)
ab housewife (125)
ac lady (2)
ad lady of the house (1)
ae lesser half (1)
af little lady (1)
ag little woman (4)
ah Love (2)
ai Ma (4)
aj madam (13)
ak Mamma (8)
al Mammy (1)
am master (1)
an mate (2)
ao missus (16)
ap mistress (2)
aq Mistress (2)
ar Mom (2)
as Mommy (1)
at Mother (3)
au mother (2)
av old battle-ax (2)
aw old bitch (1)
ax old boss (1)
ay old cranky (1)
az old hen (1)
ba old hussy (1)
bb old lady (196)
bc old miss (2)
bd old missus (2)
be old son of a bitch (1)
bf old squaw (1)
bg Old Sugar (1)
bh old sweetie (1)
bi Old Woman (1)
bj old woman (37)
bk other half (4)
bl partner (2)
bm Pudding (1)

bn rib (1)
bo spouse (25)
bp squaw (3)
bq Sugar (2)
br Sugar Babe (1)
bs sweetheart (1)
bt Sweetie Pie (1)
bu sweetie pie (1)
bv vieille, la [F] (1)
bw war department (3)
bx warden (1)
by wife (816)
bz woman (28)
ca woman of the house (1)
cb worse half (2)

063.3 L widow

No Response (153)
A sod widow (10)
B sodded widow (1)
C veuve, une [F] (2)
D wid(ow) (1)
E widow (724)
F widow lady (5)
G widow woman (60)
H widower (5)

063.3 P widow

{d} devoiced
{R} weakly retroflex
{t} flap
No Response (151)
<vidoe=13> (2)
<wed{t}A=14> (1)
<weedA=14> (1)
<weedoe=13> (1)
<whidA=14> (3)
<widA=14> (411)
<widAz=14> (6)
<widR=14> (60)
<widRz=14> (1)
<widdA=14> (2)
<widdR=14> (2)
<widdoe=13> (1)
<widd{R}=14> (1)
<widoe=13> (178)
<widue=13> (21)
<wid{R}=14> (24)
<wid{t}A=14> (2)
<wid{t}oe=13> (3)
<witA=14> (3)
<witoe=13> (1)
<wit{R}=14> (2)
<wi{d}A=14> (2)
<wi{d}oe=13> (1)
<wi{t}A=14> (49)
<wi{t}Az=14> (1)
<wi{t}R=14> (4)
<wi{t}dA=14> (1)
<wi{t}oe=13> (15)
<wi{t}ue=13> (4)

<wi{t}{R}=14> (7)
<woodA=14> (1)
<wudA=14> (1)
083.3 S woman
No Response (523)
|EAA| (1)
|EAC| (2)
|EFA| (9)
|EFB| (2)
|EFC| (10)
|EFCmaj| (2)
|EFE| (2)
|EFG| (1)
|EFGmaj| (1)
|EFI| (4)
|EFImaj| (1)
|EMC| (1)
|EME| (1)
|EXA| (1)
|EXC| (1)
|FAC| (2)
|FAD| (1)
|FAH| (4)
|FAHmaj| (2)
|FCA| (1)
|FFA| (14)
|FFB| (1)
|FFBmaj| (1)
|FFC| (12)
|FFD| (68)
|FFDmaj| (35)
|FFF| (8)
|FFFbjj| (1)
|FFFmaj| (1)
|FFH| (38)
|FFHmaj| (4)
|FFI| (10)
|FFImaa| (1)
|FFImaj| (1)
|FMA| (12)
|FMAmej| (1)
|FMD| (8)
|FMDmaj| (7)
|FMH| (1)
|FMHmaj| (1)
|FOD| (7)
|FODmdj| (2)
|FOF| (1)
|FOH| (2)
|FOHmdj| (3)
|FOI| (2)
|FXA| (1)
|FXB| (1)
|FXC| (1)
|FXCmdj| (2)
|FXDmdj| (1)
|J2Bmdj| (1)
|JBFefj| (1)
|JBHefj| (1)

|JJBefj| (2)
|JJCefj| (1)
|JJD| (1)
|JJDefj| (9)
|JJDffd| (4)
|JJDffm| (4)
|JJF| (4)
|JJFefa| (1)
|JJFefj| (9)
|JJGefj| (1)
|JJGefl| (1)
|JJHefa| (1)
|JJHefj| (8)
|JSDefa| (1)
|JSDefj| (1)
|JSFefa| (1)
|JSHefj| (2)
|JUDeoj| (1)
|JUDfom| (1)
|JUFeoa| (1)
|JUFeoj| (1)
|LDE| (1)
|LXAfoj| (1)
|MKA| (1)
|NAA| (1)
|NAD| (2)
|NAF| (1)
|NAG| (1)
|NAGmaj| (1)
|NDD| (1)
|NDF| (3)
|NFA| (1)
|NFGmaj| (1)
|NFI| (2)
|NFImaj| (1)
|NKC| (1)
|NKD| (1)
|NXF| (1)
|PAB| (1)
|PKE| (1)
|QABmaj| (4)
|QAF| (2)
|QFB| (1)
|QFBmaj| (2)
|QFBmfj| (1)
|QOB| (1)
|QOBmdj| (1)
|QXAmdj| (1)
063.4-5 L father
No Response (9)
A   dad (72)
B   Dad (239)
C   Dada (1)
D   daddy (283)
E   Daddy (530)
F   Daddy Man (1)
G   Day (1)
H   Father (62)
I   father (809)

J   old man (32)
K   Pa (81)
L   pa (2)
M   Pap (12)
N   Papa (351)
O   papa (8)
P   papa [S] (1)
Q   Pappy (19)
R   Pop (47)
S   pop (1)
T   Pops (1)
U   Poppy (4)
063.4 P father
{dh}   devoiced
{f}   bilabial
{o}   low-back
{R}   weakly retroflex
{r}   weakly retroflex
{t}   flap
{th}   voiced
{?}   glottal
No Response (106)
<fawdhR=14> (5)
<fawdh[R]=14> (20)
<fawdh{R}=14> (10)
<fawt[R]z=14> (1)
<faw{r}dhR=14> (1)
<faw{t}[R]=14> (1)
<fa{?}[R]=14> (1)
<fa{th}{R}=14> (1)
<fodR=14> (1)
<fod[R]=14> (2)
<fodh(R)> (1)
<fodhR=14> (293)
<fodhRz=14> (6)
<fodh[R]=14> (312)
<fodh[R]z=14> (3)
<fodhe[r]=13> (1)
<fodhrA=14> (1)
<fodh{R}=14> (107)
<fodh{R}z=14> (1)
<fod{R}=14> (1)
<fo{dh}[R]=14> (1)
<fo{th}[R]=14> (1)
<fo{t}R=14> (1)
<fo{t}[R]=14> (2)
<fudhR=14> (1)
<fudh[R]=14> (2)
<fwodh[R]z=14> (1)
<f{o}dhR=14> (36)
<f{o}dh[R]=14> (77)
<f{o}dh{R}=14> (19)
<f{o}dh{R}z=14> (1)
<f{o}thR=14> (1)
<{f}odhR=14> (3)
<{f}odh[R]=14> (10)
<{f}o{dh}[R]=14> (2)
063.4 S father
No Response (1)

|PAA| (4)
|PAC| (3)
|PAG| (2)
|PCA| (6)
|PCC| (11)
|PFC| (1)
|QFCmea| (1)
|SAA| (18)
|SAAmaj| (3)
|SAB| (62)
|SABmaj| (6)
|SAD| (5)
|SAE| (181)
|SAEmaj| (64)
|SAEmak| (1)
|SAEtaa| (2)
|SAEtfa| (1)
|SAF| (11)
|SAG| (55)
|SAGmaj| (3)
|SBB| (2)
|SBF| (1)
|SCA| (67)
|SCAmaj| (6)
|SCB| (30)
|SCBmaj| (2)
|SCD| (6)
|SCE| (126)
|SCEmaa| (1)
|SCEmaj| (60)
|SCFmaj| (2)
|SCG| (5)
|SCGmaj| (4)
|SCGqfj| (1)
|SCW| (1)
|SDB| (1)
|SDEmdj| (1)
|SDF| (1)
|SFBmfj| (1)
|SFD| (1)
|SFE| (6)
|SGA| (2)
|SKAmdj| (1)
|SKD| (1)
|SKE| (1)
|SME| (5)
|SMEmaj| (2)
|SMEtfa| (1)
|TAA| (6)
|TAAtfa| (1)
|TAAtfb| (1)
|TAAtfj| (1)
|TAB| (1)
|TABtfj| (1)
|TAD| (36)
|TADmaj| (15)
|TADsae| (1)
|TADtab| (1)
|TADtfj| (3)

|TAF| (4)
|TAG| (1)
|TCA| (10)
|TCAmaj| (2)
|TCD| (10)
|TCDmaj| (8)
|TCF| (1)
|TFA| (4)
|TFAmaj| (1)
|TFB| (5)
|TFBqfa| (1)
|TFD| (7)
|TFF| (1)
|TFFmaa| (1)
|TMA| (1)
|TMAmaj| (1)
|TMBmaj| (1)
|TMBqfj| (1)
|TMDmaa| (1)
|TMDmaj| (3)
|TMF| (3)
|TMFmaj| (1)

063.6-7 L mother

No Response (17)
A   Ma (97)
B   ma (6)
C   Ma'am (1)
D   Mam(ma) (2)
E   Mamma (552)
F   mamma (72)
G   Mammy (28)
H   mammy (7)
I   Mamou (1)
J   Mima (2)
K   Mimi (1)
L   Mom (124)
M   mom (29)
N   Mommy (25)
O   mommy (1)
P   mother (853)
Q   Mother (221)
R   Mo(ther) (1)
S   Mo(ther) Dear (10)
T   Mum (1)
U   Mummy (2)
V   old lady (7)
W   old woman (2)

063.6 P mother

{b}   fricative
{oo}   unrounded
{R}   weakly retroflex
{t}   flap
No Response (43)
<modhR=14> (4)
<modh[R]=14> (4)
<moedhR=14> (1)
<moodh[R]=14> (5)
<mudR=14> (4)
<mud[R]=14> (3)

<mudh(R)> (2)
<mudhR=14> (364)
<mudhRz=14> (7)
<mudh[R]=14> (390)
<mudh[R]z=14> (3)
<mudh{R}=14> (155)
<mut[R]=14> (1)
<muthR=14> (1)
<muvR=14> (1)
<mu{b}[R]=14> (1)
<mu{t}R=14> (1)
<mu{t}[R]=14> (1)
<mwudh[R]=14> (1)
<m{oo}dh[R]=14> (5)
<{b}udh[R]=14> (1)

063.8 P parents

{p}   fricative
{r}   weakly retroflex
{t}   flap
{z}   devoiced
{?}   glottal
No Response (145)
<pa(r)N(t)s=14> (3)
<pa(r)Nts=14> (20)
<pa(r)N{?}s=14> (1)
<pa(r)[N]ts=14> (1)
<pa(r)n(t)z> (1)
<pa(r)nt> (1)
<pa(r)nts> (3)
<pa(r)u[n]ts=13> (1)
<pa[r]N(t)s=14> (1)
<pa[r]Nts=14> (16)
<pa[r][N]ts=14> (1)
<pa[r]n(t)s> (1)
<pa[r]nt> (1)
<pa[r]nts> (3)
<pai(r)N(t)s=14> (1)
<pai(r)Nts=14> (1)
<pairNts=14> (6)
<pai{r}Nts=14> (1)
<parN(t)s=14> (39)
<parN(t)z=14> (1)
<parN(t){z}=14> (2)
<parNt(s)=14> (1)
<parNt=14> (3)
<parNts=14> (417)
<parNtsIz=144> (1)
<parNtsh=14> (1)
<par[N](t)s=14> (1)
<par[N]ts=14> (2)
<par[n]ts> (1)
<parnts> (2)
<pay(r)N(t)s=14> (1)
<pa{?}Nts=14> (2)
<pa{r}N(t)z=14> (1)
<pa{r}Nt=14> (1)
<pa{r}Nts=14> (30)
<pa{r}[N]t=14> (1)
<pa{r}nts> (5)

<pa{t}Nts=14> (2)
<pe(r)N(t)s=14> (1)
<pe(r)Nts=14> (3)
<pe(r)n(I)ch> (1)
<pe[r]N(t)s=14> (2)
<pe[r]Nts=14> (4)
<pe[r]nts> (3)
<perN(t)s=14> (42)
<perNt(s)=14> (1)
<perNt=14> (1)
<perNts=14> (160)
<perNtsh=14> (2)
<perNtz=14> (1)
<per[N]ts=14> (1)
<per[n](ts)> (1)
<perents=13> (1)
<perints=13> (1)
<pernts> (1)
<pe{r}N(t)s=14> (1)
<pe{r}Nts=14> (17)
<pe{r}nts> (1)
<pe{t}rN{?}s=14> (1)
<pie(r)nts> (1)
<pirNts=14> (1)
<po[r]nts> (1)
<porN(t)s=14> (1)
<porNts=14> (5)
<purN(t)s=14> (1)
<purN(t){z}=14> (1)
<purNts=14> (7)
<pu{r}Nts=14> (1)
<{p}erNts=14> (1)

064.1 L grandfather

No Response (67)
A   (a)buelo [S] (1)
B   (ab)uelito [S] (1)
C   abuelo [S] (2)
D   Abuelo [S] (1)
E   Baby Grandpa (1)
F   Big Dad (1)
G   Big Daddy (15)
H   Big Granddaddy (1)
I   Big Pa (2)
J   Big Papa (2)
K   Big Pop (1)
L   Biggy (1)
M   Compere [F] (1)
N   D Daddy (1)
O   Dad (4)
P   Dada (3)
Q   Daddy (8)
R   Daddy Pa (2)
S   Dodo (1)
T   Fatti [G] (1)
U   Gramp (3)
V   Gramps (13)
W   Grampy (1)
X   Gran (1)
Y   Grand (1)

Z   Grandda (1)
aa Granddad (72)
ab granddad (6)
ac Granddaddy (252)
ad granddaddy (17)
ae grandfa(ther) (3)
af Grandfather (21)
ag grandfather (669)
ah Grandpa (385)
ai grandpa (7)
aj Grandpap (7)
ak Grandpapa (19)
al Grandpappy (3)
am Grandpop (3)
an Grandy (2)
ao Granny (1)
ap Gros Pop [F] (1)
aq old gentleman (1)
ar old Granddaddy (1)
as old grandfather (1)
at Opa [G] (2)
au Pa (9)
av pa (1)
aw Papa (107)
ax papa grande [S] (1)
ay Papo (1)
az Papop (1)
ba Pappy (10)
bb Peapop (1)
bc Pepere [F] (1)
bd Pere [F] (1)
be Pipa (2)
bf Pop (9)
bg Pop Pop (1)
bh Poppy (2)

064.2 L grandmother

No Response (84)
A   (a)buelita [S] (1)
B   (ab)uela [S] (1)
C   abuela [S] (2)
D   Abuela [S] (1)
E   Annie (1)
F   Big Mamma (20)
G   Didi (1)
H   Gaga (1)
I   Ganny (1)
J   GG (1)
K   Goggy (1)
L   Gommo (1)
M   Gram (2)
N   Gran (3)
O   Gran-Gran (1)
P   Grand (1)
Q   grandma (15)
R   Grandma (378)
S   grandmamma (1)
T   Grandmamma (49)
U   Grandmammy (2)
V   Grandmom (5)

W   grandmother (722)
X   Grandmother (32)
Y   Granny (133)
Z   Grosse Mom [F] (1)
aa Gumma (1)
ab Honey Mamma (1)
ac Ma (22)
ad Ma Mia (1)
ae Ma-Mom (2)
af Mam (1)
ag Mama Grande [S] (1)
ah Maman [F] (2)
ai Mamere [F] (1)
aj Mamie (1)
ak Mamma (78)
al Mammy (9)
am Mere [F] (2)
an Mima (10)
ao Mimi (8)
ap Mimmy (1)
aq Mimom (1)
ar Minny (1)
as Mo-moo (1)
at Mom (5)
au Mommy (2)
av Mother (2)
aw mother (1)
ax Mummum (1)
ay Munner (3)
az Mutti [G] (1)
ba My Dear (2)
bb Namoo (1)
bc Nana (8)
bd Nanna (4)
be Nanny (16)
bf Nini (1)
bg Oma [G] (1)
bh She (1)

064.3 L children

No Response (37)
A   babies (2)
B   black children (1)
C   black kids (1)
D   brats (16)
E   brood (1)
F   chaps (21)
G   childer (1)
H   children (804)
I   childrens (11)
J   childs (1)
K   chops (1)
L   crawlers (1)
M   delinquents (1)
N   family (1)
O   farm children (1)
P   grand boys (1)
Q   grand kids (9)
R   grand young ones (3)
S   grandbabies (2)

T   grandchildren (30)
U   grandchilds (1)
V   grands (1)
W   great-grandchildren (4)
X   great-grands (1)
Y   juveniles (1)
Z   kiddos (1)
aa   kids (518)
ab   lap children (1)
ac   little ones (3)
ad   monsters (2)
ae   ninos [S] (1)
af   offspring (10)
ag   offsprings (4)
ah   school kids (1)
ai   schoolchildren (1)
aj   toddlers (2)
ak   tots (2)
al   urchins (1)
am   young ones (160)
an   youngsters (35)

064.4 L pet name
No Response (428)
A   baby name (2)
B   basket name (1)
C   byname (2)
D   byword (1)
E   family name (2)
F   given name (5)
G   hot name (1)
H   little name (1)
I   name (1)
J   nickname (341)
K   pet name (89)
L   play name (1)
M   short name (2)
N   special name (1)
O   sweet name (1)

064.5 L baby carriage
No Response (148)
A   baby buggy (202)
B   baby carriage (227)
C   baby cart (6)
D   baby coop (1)
E   buggy (119)
F   carriage (284)
G   carriage buggy (1)
H   cart (7)
I   commissary (1)
J   crib (1)
K   go-cart (4)
L   perambulator (15)
M   pram (8)
N   push buggy (2)
O   pushcart (5)
P   pushing buggy (1)
Q   red wagon (1)
R   stroll (1)
S   stroller (15)

T   wagon (1)

064.6 L wheel (the baby)
No Response (247)
A   a-rolling (1)
B   air (the baby) (3)
C   air out (the baby) (1)
D   carry (7)
E   carry (the baby) around (2)
F   carry (the baby) for a ride (2)
G   carry (the baby) for a stroll or ride (1)
H   carry (the baby) for a walk (1)
I   give (the baby) a ride (2)
J   give (the baby) a stroll (2)
K   give (the baby) a walk (1)
L   give (the baby) an airing (2)
M   give (the baby) some fresh air (1)
N   give (the baby) some sunshine (1)
O   giving (the baby) a ride (1)
P   go for a ride (1)
Q   go for a stroll (3)
R   go for a walk (2)
S   go out a-walking (1)
T   go out and ride (1)
U   go out and roll (the baby) around (1)
V   go out for a walk (1)
W   go walk (the baby) (1)
X   going for a stroll (1)
Y   going for a walk (1)
Z   haul (1)
aa   have a stroll (1)
ab   let (the baby) get some air (1)
ac   pull (1)
ad   push (188)
ae   push for a walk (1)
af   push (the baby) along (6)
ag   push (the baby) around (12)
ah   push (the baby) around the block (1)
ai   push (the baby) out (1)
aj   pushed (3)
ak   pushed (the baby) around (2)
al   pushing (16)
am   put (the baby) in a stroller (1)
an   ride (56)
ao   ride (the baby) around (1)
ap   riding (4)
aq   riding around (1)
ar   rock (the baby) (1)
as   rode (1)
at   roll (119)
au   roll (the baby) about (1)
av   roll (the baby) around (22)
aw   roll (the baby) in the sun (1)
ax   roll (the baby) out (3)
ay   rolling (8)

az   rolling around (1)
ba   stroll (129)
bb   stroll (the baby) around (6)
bc   stroll with (the baby) (2)
bd   strolling (13)
be   sun (the baby) (1)
bf   sun (the baby) out (1)
bg   take a little jaunt (1)
bh   take a stroll (5)
bi   take a walk (12)
bj   take (the baby) for a buggy ride (1)
bk   take (the baby) for a little walk (1)
bl   take (the baby) for a ride (17)
bm   take (the baby) for a stroll (15)
bn   take (the baby) for a walk (8)
bo   take (the baby) for fresh air (1)
bp   take (the baby) out (8)
bq   take (the baby) out for a joyride (1)
br   take (the baby) out for a ride (3)
bs   take (the baby) out for a stroll (1)
bt   take (the baby) out for a walk (2)
bu   take (the baby) out riding (2)
bv   take (the baby) strolling (3)
bw   take (the baby) to ride (1)
bx   taking a ride (1)
by   taking a stroll (1)
bz   taking (the baby) for a ride (2)
ca   taking (the baby) for a stroll (5)
cb   taking (the baby) for a walk (3)
cc   took (the baby) for a walk (1)
cd   tote (2)
ce   walk (83)
cf   walk (the baby) about (1)
cg   walk (the baby) out (1)
ch   walking (7)
ci   wheel (21)
cj   wheel (the baby) out (1)
ck   wheeling (7)

064.7 G most grown up
No Response (675)
A   eldest (12)
B   grown-uppest (3)
C   grownest (5)
D   largest (2)
E   most adult (1)
F   most grown (3)
G   most grown-up (50)
H   most mature (9)
I   older (1)
J   oldest (148)
K   senior child (1)

064.8 P daughter
{o}   low-back

{oe}   lowered onset
{R}   weakly retroflex
{r}   weakly retroflex
{t}   flap
{z}   devoiced
{zh}   devoiced
No Response (101)
<daw(t)R=14> (1)
<dawdRz=14> (1)
<dawd[R]=14> (1)
<dawtR=14> (213)
<dawtRz=14> (58)
<dawtR{z}=14> (21)
<dawt[R]=14> (212)
<dawt[R]z=14> (52)
<dawt[R]{z}=14> (6)
<dawt{R}=14> (62)
<dawt{R}z=14> (13)
<dawt{R}{z}=14> (3)
<daw{r}dR=14> (1)
<daw{r}tR=14> (1)
<daw{r}t{R}=14> (2)
<daw{t}R=14> (26)
<daw{t}Rz=14> (2)
<daw{t}R{zh}=14> (1)
<daw{t}R{z}=14> (7)
<daw{t}[R]=14> (30)
<daw{t}[R]z=14> (3)
<daw{t}[R]{zh}=14> (1)
<daw{t}[R]{z}=14> (1)
<daw{t}{R}=14> (13)
<daw{t}{R}z=14> (1)
<daw{t}{R}{z}=14> (3)
<da{t}R=14> (1)
<doe{t}R=14> (2)
<doe{t}[R]=14> (2)
<dotR=14> (8)
<dotRz=14> (3)
<dot[R]=14> (1)
<dot[R]z=14> (1)
<dot{R}=14> (4)
<do{t}R=14> (1)
<do{t}{R}=14> (1)
<d{oe}d{R}{z}=14> (1)
<d{oe}t[R]=14> (1)
<d{oe}t[R]{z}=14> (1)
<d{oe}{t}R=14> (1)
<d{oe}{t}[R]=14> (1)
<d{o}tR=14> (38)
<d{o}tRz=14> (10)
<d{o}tR{z}=14> (2)
<d{o}t[R]=14> (8)
<d{o}t[R]z=14> (5)
<d{o}t{R}=14> (14)
<d{o}{t}R=14> (7)
<d{o}{t}Rs=14> (1)
<d{o}{t}R{z}=14> (2)
<d{o}{t}[R]=14> (2)
<d{o}{t}[R]{z}=14> (1)

<d{o}{t}u{r}=13> (1)
<d{o}{t}{R}=14> (1)
<tawt[R]z=14> (1)
064.8 S daughter
No Response (0)
|JJHmfj| (1)
|JSC| (1)
|JSCmaj| (1)
|JSH| (1)
|PAEqfa| (1)
|PAEqfm| (1)
|PFEqfd| (1)
|QAA| (1)
|QAAqfd| (1)
|QACqfb| (2)
|QACqfk| (1)
|QADqfa| (2)
|QAH| (1)
|QAHjjc| (1)
|QAHmaa| (1)
|QAHqfa| (1)
|QAHqfb| (11)
|QCCqfb| (1)
|QCD| (2)
|QCHqfb| (1)
|QFA| (3)
|QFAjja| (1)
|QFAjjc| (20)
|QFAjjd| (1)
|QFAjjj| (1)
|QFAlfa| (2)
|QFAlfe| (1)
|QFAlfj| (3)
|QFAqfb| (14)
|QFAqfk| (3)
|QFB| (8)
|QFBjbl| (1)
|QFBjja| (1)
|QFBjjc| (8)
|QFBjjd| (4)
|QFBjjh| (1)
|QFBjjl| (5)
|QFBjjm| (9)
|QFBmaj| (2)
|QFBmak| (1)
|QFBmea| (1)
|QFBqfd| (1)
|QFC| (16)
|QFCjja| (4)
|QFCjjb| (6)
|QFCjjc| (11)
|QFCjjh| (1)
|QFCjjl| (1)
|QFCmaj| (5)
|QFCqaa| (1)
|QFCqadmaj| (1)
|QFCqaf| (2)
|QFCqfa| (26)
|QFCqfamej| (1)

|QFCqfb| (289)
|QFCqff| (2)
|QFCqfj| (2)
|QFCqfk| (13)
|QFD| (2)
|QFDefj| (1)
|QFDjjm| (1)
|QFDlfa| (1)
|QFDlfj| (1)
|QFDmaj| (1)
|QFDmej| (1)
|QFDqfa| (1)
|QFDqfb| (2)
|QFDqfk| (1)
|QFF| (5)
|QFH| (9)
|QFHjjj| (1)
|QFHmaj| (2)
|QFHqfa| (1)
|QFHqfb| (34)
|QFHqfd| (1)
|QFHqfj| (1)
|QFHqfk| (3)
|QFHqfl| (1)
|QMA| (9)
|QMAjja| (1)
|QMAjjc| (4)
|QMAjjj| (7)
|QMAlfa| (1)
|QMAlfj| (1)
|QMAmaa| (1)
|QMAqfb| (3)
|QMB| (7)
|QMBjjb| (1)
|QMBmaj| (2)
|QMBmfa| (1)
|QMC| (19)
|QMCjbf| (1)
|QMCjja| (1)
|QMCjjb| (2)
|QMCjjc| (2)
|QMCmaj| (8)
|QMCqfa| (2)
|QMCqfb| (49)
|QMCqfd| (1)
|QMCqff| (1)
|QMCqfj| (1)
|QMCqfk| (5)
|QMD| (3)
|QMDjjj| (2)
|QMDlfj| (1)
|QMF| (1)
|QMH| (1)
|QMHqao| (1)
|QMHqfb| (7)
|SAA| (1)
|SAE| (1)
|SAEjjc| (1)
|SAElfj| (1)

|SAEmaj| (1)
|SAEqfb| (2)
|SAG| (2)
|SAGqfa| (3)
|SAGqfb| (1)
|SAGqfj| (11)
|SBA| (1)
|SCE| (1)
|SCEqfj| (1)
|SCGqfa| (2)
|SCGqfj| (2)
|SFB| (1)
|SFEqfj| (1)
|SFG| (2)
|SFGqfa| (1)
|SGB| (1)
|SME| (1)
|SMEmaj| (1)
|TAAjsa| (2)
|TAAqfb| (1)
|TAAqfj| (1)
|TAAtfa| (1)
|TABjjb| (1)
|TABqfb| (14)
|TABqfj| (1)
|TABqfk| (1)
|TAD| (2)
|TADjjc| (3)
|TADqfb| (22)
|TADqfj| (1)
|TADqfk| (1)
|TAFqfb| (2)
|TAGjjd| (1)
|TCA| (3)
|TCAjja| (1)
|TCAmaj| (1)
|TCAqfa| (1)
|TCB| (1)
|TCD| (3)
|TCDjja| (1)
|TCDqfb| (1)
|TCDqfk| (1)
|TCF| (1)
|TFAjjc| (1)
|TFAjjj| (1)
|TFAmaj| (1)
|TFAqfa| (6)
|TFAqfb| (3)
|TFAqfc| (2)
|TFAqff| (1)
|TFAqfj| (2)
|TFB| (8)
|TFBjja| (1)
|TFBjjb| (1)
|TFBjjc| (2)
|TFBmaj| (3)
|TFBqaj| (1)
|TFBqfa| (3)
|TFBqfb| (20)

|TFBqfc| (3)
|TFBqff| (1)
|TFBqfj| (5)
|TFBqfk| (1)
|TFBqfl| (2)
|TFDqfa| (1)
|TFDqfb| (1)
|TFDqfc| (1)
|TFDqfj| (1)
|TFFqff| (1)
|TFHjjc| (1)
|TFT| (1)
|TMA| (4)
|TMAqfj| (1)
|TMB| (3)
|TMBqfj| (1)
|TMBqfk| (2)

064.9 P girl

{L}   dark
{l}   dark
{oo}   unrounded
{r}   weakly retroflex
{z}   devoiced
No Response (60)
<ge[r]lz> (2)
<gerl> (2)
<ge{r}l> (1)
<gi[r][1]> (2)
<gi[r][1]{zh}> (1)
<gir[L]=14> (3)
<gir[1]{z}> (1)
<gir{L}=14> (1)
<gir{l}> (1)
<goo[r](1)z> (1)
<goo[r][1]> (1)
<goo[r]lz> (1)
<goor{l}> (1)
<goo{r}(1)> (1)
<gru[r]{l}> (1)
<gu[r][1]> (16)
<gu[r][1]sh> (1)
<gu[r][1]z> (9)
<gu[r][1]{z}> (3)
<gu[r]l(z)> (1)
<gu[r]l> (60)
<gu[r]lz> (14)
<gu[r]l{z}> (4)
<gu[r]{l}> (66)
<gu[r]{l}z> (12)
<gu[r]{l}{z}> (2)
<gue[r]l> (1)
<gue[r]{l}> (1)
<gur(1)> (6)
<gurL=14> (1)
<gur[L]=14> (1)
<gur[1]> (15)
<gur[1]sh> (1)
<gur[1]z> (6)
<gur[1]{z}> (15)

<gurl> (156)
<gurldh> (1)
<gurlz> (83)
<gurl{z}> (25)
<gur{L}=14> (2)
<gur{l}> (193)
<gur{l}dh> (1)
<gur{l}z> (58)
<gur{l}{z}> (6)
<gu{r}(1)z> (1)
<gu{r}L=14> (1)
<gu{r}[1]> (2)
<gu{r}[1]{z}> (1)
<gu{r}l> (49)
<gu{r}lz> (16)
<gu{r}l{z}> (10)
<gu{r}{l}> (38)
<gu{r}{l}z> (21)
<gu{r}{l}{z}> (2)
<g{oo}[r][1]> (1)
<g{oo}{r}l> (2)

064.9 S girl

No Response (11)
|ECA| (1)
|ECAmaacba| (3)
|ECAmea| (2)
|EFH| (1)
|EFJlyamej| (1)
|EMAeaa| (1)
|FAAmej| (1)
|FCAmajcba| (1)
|KAEmea| (2)
|KFAmaj| (1)
|KFEmfj| (1)
|LAA| (11)
|LAAeaa| (1)
|LAAmaj| (4)
|LAAmea| (28)
|LAAmeamaacba| (1)
|LAAmeamaj| (4)
|LAAmee| (1)
|LAAmej| (3)
|LABmaj| (1)
|LABmea| (4)
|LABmeamaj| (1)
|LABmej| (1)
|LACmea| (1)
|LACmeamaj| (1)
|LADmak| (1)
|LADmea| (7)
|LADmej| (3)
|LAEmea| (16)
|LAFmea| (1)
|LAFmeamaj| (1)
|LAFmej| (1)
|LAGmea| (5)
|LBA| (1)
|LCA| (5)
|LCAeal| (1)

|LCAfaj| (1)
|LCAmaj| (10)
|LCAmea| (11)
|LCAmeacba| (1)
|LCAmej| (5)
|LCBmaa| (1)
|LCBmaj| (1)
|LCBmea| (3)
|LCCmea| (1)
|LCDmea| (1)
|LCDmej| (1)
|LCE| (2)
|LCEmea| (5)
|LCEmeamaj| (2)
|LCEmej| (1)
|LCFmej| (1)
|LCGmea| (1)
|LEA| (6)
|LEAmaj| (6)
|LEAmak| (2)
|LEAmea| (1)
|LEAmej| (3)
|LECmaj| (1)
|LED| (1)
|LEDmaj| (1)
|LEEmaj| (3)
|LEG| (1)
|LEHmaj| (1)
|LFAeaj| (3)
|LFAeajcba| (2)
|LFAeajcbj| (1)
|LFAkaj| (1)
|LFAmaf| (1)
|LFAmaj| (17)
|LFAmajcba| (2)
|LFAmajcbj| (1)
|LFAmak| (1)
|LFAmea| (8)
|LFAmej| (5)
|LFBeaj| (1)
|LFBmaa| (1)
|LFBmaj| (2)
|LFBmea| (1)
|LFBmej| (2)
|LFBmfj| (1)
|LFCeaj| (1)
|LFClakmea| (1)
|LFCmea| (3)
|LFDmaj| (2)
|LFDmea| (2)
|LFDmej| (1)
|LFE| (1)
|LFEeaj| (2)
|LFEmea| (1)
|LFEmej| (1)
|LFGmap| (1)
|LLA| (1)
|LLAmaj| (7)
|LLDmaj| (1)

|LLE| (2)
|LMA| (4)
|LMAeaj| (7)
|LMAeajcba| (2)
|LMAeal| (1)
|LMAmaj| (30)
|LMAmajcba| (8)
|LMAmajcbj| (1)
|LMAmak| (13)
|LMAmea| (3)
|LMAmej| (6)
|LMAmek| (2)
|LMAmfj| (5)
|LMAmfk| (2)
|LMB| (1)
|LMBmaj| (1)
|LMBmea| (4)
|LMBmej| (1)
|LMC| (1)
|LMD| (1)
|LMDmaj| (1)
|LMDmak| (1)
|LMDmej| (1)
|LMEeaj| (1)
|LMEmaj| (4)
|LMEmajcba| (1)
|LMEmea| (4)
|LMEmfj| (2)
|LMFmfj| (1)
|LMGmaa| (1)
|LMGmaj| (1)
|LPA| (2)
|LPAmaj| (4)
|LPAmak| (1)
|LPAmej| (2)
|LPAmfk| (1)
|LPB| (1)
|LPE| (1)
|LPEmaj| (1)
|LYA| (2)
|LYAcbj| (1)
|LYAmaj| (2)
|MAAmeamaj| (1)
|MCAmea| (2)
|MCEmea| (1)
|MEA| (105)
|MEAcba| (10)
|MEAcbj| (2)
|MEAeal| (1)
|MEAmaa| (1)
|MEAmaj| (84)
|MEAmce| (1)
|MEAmej| (1)
|MEBcba| (1)
|MEBmaj| (2)
|MEC| (1)
|MECmaj| (2)
|MED| (34)
|MEDmaj| (22)

|MEE| (4)
|MEEmaj| (1)
|MEF| (1)
|MEH| (1)
|MEI| (3)
|MLA| (65)
|MLAcba| (2)
|MLAcbj| (2)
|MLAmaa| (3)
|MLAmaacba| (3)
|MLAmaj| (88)
|MLAmajcba| (1)
|MLAmca| (1)
|MLAmej| (1)
|MLBmaacba| (1)
|MLBmajcba| (2)
|MLCmaj| (1)
|MLD| (3)
|MLDmaj| (5)
|MLDmak| (1)
|MLE| (2)
|MLEmaacba| (1)
|MLEmaj| (2)
|MLEmajcba| (1)
|MLG| (1)
|MLHmaj| (3)
|MPA| (6)
|MPAmaj| (1)
|MPBmaj| (2)
|MPD| (1)
|MPE| (1)
|MPEmaj| (1)
|MWAmojcha| (1)
|MWBmdjcha| (1)
|MYA| (1)
|MYAmaj| (6)
|MYAmfj| (1)
|NADmea| (1)
|NADmej| (1)
|NAEmea| (1)
|NCAkcacba| (1)
|NCDmea| (2)
|NCDmek| (1)
|NCEmaj| (1)
|NCEmej| (1)
|NCFmea| (1)
|NFDmeamaj| (1)
|NMAmfj| (1)

065.1 L pregnant

No Response (204)
A ate too much (1)
B baby in the oven, has a (1)
C bed, going to (2)
E big, (getting/got) (74)
F big as a barrel (1)
G big as a cow (2)
H big with a baby (1)
I big with child (5)
J big with increase (1)

K bigged (3)
L bigness (1)
M birth a baby, going (to) (1)
N blown up, has (2)
O bring a child, about to (1)
P bring (him) another mouth to
   feed (1)
Q bring birth, about to (1)
R broke a/her foot (2)
S broke her leg (20)
T bun in the oven, (has a) (5)
U burnt, got (1)
V busted up, (got) (1)
W buy a baby, (going to) (2)
X cake in the oven, got a (1)
Y carrying (4)
Z carrying a baby (3)
aa carrying a child (6)
ab carrying a (heavy) load (2)
ac carrying it (1)
ad caught, got (1)
ae caught up (1)
af churn bellies (1)
ag comme ca [F] (1)
ah conceived, has (1)
ai confined, (going/fixing to) be (9)
aj confinement, going to be in (1)
ak delicate state, in a (2)
al divide up, fixing to (1)
am domino, getting ready to/going
    to (4)
an down(ed), (going to be) (1)
ao drop a child (1)
ap due (1)
aq eating pumpkinseed, been (1)
ar eating watermelon, been (1)
as enceinte [F] (2)
at expectant mother, an (1)
au (e)xpected mother, a (1)
av expecting (201)
aw expecting mother, an (1)
ax expecting the stork (1)
ay expecting (to have) a baby (10)
az expecting to mother (1)
ba famille, en [F] (1)
bb family, in (2)
bc family way, in a/the (161)
bd family work, in [D-0] (1)
be far along, quite (1)
bf fat, (getting) (4)
bg find a baby, going/fixing to (1)
bh fix, in a (1)
bi fixed (up good) (2)
bj freshening (1)
bk full (1)
bl getting a baby (1)
bm give birth (to a child), going/
    about to (5)
bn gone, (so many months) (1)

bo grossesse, la [F] (1)
bp growing (1)
bq had it, has (1)
br half pregnant (1)
bs hanky-panky a little too long (1)
bt hatch (one), about to/going to
    (3)
bu hatching (1)
bv have a baby, about/fixing/going
    to (79)
bw have a child, (going to) (2)
bx have a kid, going to (3)
by have a new one in the family,
    going to (1)
bz have one, going to (2)
ca having a baby soon (1)
cb heavy (1)
cc heavy with child (2)
cd hiding a basketball (1)
ce hopped up (1)
cf house-confined (1)
cg impregnate(d) (2)
ch in the house, she'll go (1)
ci infanticipating (1)
cj interesting position, in an (1)
ck kick the bucket, going to (1)
cl knocked up, (got) (44)
cm laid up (1)
cn large, (getting) (2)
co leg broke [adj.] (1)
cp leg broke, (got) her (4)
cq looking for a baby (3)
cr looking for an offspring (1)
cs looking to go to the hospital (1)
ct made her Easter duties before
    Easter (1)
cu mother, going/is to be a (4)
cv mother to be (1)
cw motherhood, in (1)
cx motherly way, in a/the (2)
cy not going out (1)
cz on the nest (1)
da (one) in the oven (2)
db out of order (1)
dc out (of) the way (2)
dd PG (16)
de pleine, elle est [F] (1)
df preg(nant) (1)
dg pregnant (525)
dh pregnant [taboo/crude] (18)
di pregnant [formerly taboo/crude]
    (91)
dj pregnant with a baby (1)
dk prenado [S] (1)
dl pumpkin in her belly, got a (1)
dm pumpkinseed, got a (1)
dn ready for the baby (1)
do ready to deliver (4)
dp ready to get down (2)

dq ready to give birth (1)
dr rocking chair, in a (1)
ds round and big (1)
dt show(ing) (1)
du sowing a watermelon (1)
dv springing (1)
dw stuck, got (1)
dx stung by the trouser worm, got
    (1)
dy swallowed a peach seed (1)
dz swallowed a pumpkinseed (30)
ea swallowed a watermelon (3)
eb swallowed a watermelon seed
    (17)
ec swallowed the seed (1)
ed swelled up (1)
ee that way, (in) (4)
ef thataway (1)
eg took it serious (1)
eh top heavy (1)
ei waiting, in (3)
ej wearing a hatching jacket (1)
ek with a baby (4)
el with a child (2)
em with child (52)
[unmarried]
en beat her in the gutter, somebody
    (1)
eo caught for somebody, got (1)
ep fix, in a (1)
eq fixed up (1)
er in trouble, (got) (16)
es in trouble by herself (1)
et knocked up (14)
eu messed up (1)
ev pregnant (1)
ew ruined (1)
ex slipped up on, got (1)
ey spoil(t) (2)
ez swallowed the whole cabbage (1)
fa tight, (got herself) in a (1)
fb watermelon growing earlier this
    year (1)

065.2 L midwife
No Response (122)
A aide (1)
B baby nurse (1)
C baby snatcher (1)
D birthing lady (1)
E black woman (1)
F chaste woman (1)
G colored lady (1)
H doctor woman (1)
I godmother (4)
J grandma (3)
K Grandmamma (1)
L granny (120)
M granny [v.] (2)
N granny doctor (2)

O   granny lady (4)
P   granny mother (1)
Q   granny nurse (1)
R   granny one (1)
S   granny woman (77)
T   help maid (1)
U   helper (1)
V   housemother (1)
W   housewife (1)
X   inner wife (1)
Y   landlady (1)
Z   maid lady (1)
aa   mammy (3)
ab   Memere [F] (1)
ac   mid lady (3)
ad   mid woman (8)
ae   midway (1)
af   midwife (718)
ag   midwife woman (1)
ah   mother doctor (1)
ai   nanny (2)
aj   Negro mammy (1)
ak   Negro midwife (1)
al   Negro woman (1)
am   nigger midwife (1)
an   nigger woman (1)
ao   nurse (14)
ap   old maid (1)
aq   old woman (2)
ar   older lady (1)
as   practical nurse (3)
at   sage-femme [F] (1)
au   semilegal granny (1)
av   wet nurse (1)
aw   woman doctor (3)

065.3 L resembles (his father)

No Response (148)
A   actions like, has (4)
B   acts (his father) (3)
C   acts (just) like (114)
D   acts similar (1)
E   all over, his father (1)
F   attitude, same (1)
G   behaves like (3)
H   belongs to (him) (1)
I   build, father's (1)
J   built like (1)
K   carbon copy (3)
L   character, same (1)
M   characteristics, has (4)
N   child, his father's (1)
O   chip, same old (1)
P   chip off the old block (47)
Q   clear through, father (1)
R   comes by it honest (3)
S   copies (1)
T   cut out of the same pattern (1)
U   dead ringer (1)
V   disposition, (has father's) (7)

W   does daddy hisself, he (1)
X   double, his father's (1)
Y   exactly like (2)
Z   favors (303)
aa   featured like (1)
ab   features [n.] (12)
ac   features [v.] (7)
ad   futures [v.] (1)
ae   follows his father (1)
af   follows his father's footseps (5)
ag   good dog follows his race (1)
ah   habits, (has) his father's (5)
ai   identical to (2)
aj   image of (33)
ak   images, got his father's (1)
al   imitates (3)
am   inherited (father's traits) (4)
an   just like (115)
ao   kind, is daddy's (1)
ap   like (70)
aq   like father, like son (6)
ar   like mother, like daughter (1)
as   likeness of, the (2)
at   living image (1)
au   looks, has (1)
av   looks and acts like (1)
aw   looks like (230)
ax   made over, father (5)
ay   mannerisms, has (4)
az   manners like (2)
ba   marked like (1)
bb   off of the old tree (1)
bc   over and over, his father (2)
bd   patterned after (1)
be   perfect image (2)
bf   personality, has same (2)
bg   picture of, the (3)
bh   piece off the old block (1)
bi   pulled a hair out of his ass (1)
bj   resembles (217)
bk   same nature (1)
bl   similar (to) (5)
bm   solid image (1)
bn   son like father, (father like son) (2)
bo   spit, the (very) (11)
bp   spit him out, looks like (his father) (2)
bq   spit image (7)
br   spitting image (60)
bs   splitting image (1)
bt   takes after (189)
bu   takes at (his father) (1)
bv   takes behind (1)
bw   takes it after (6)
bx   takes it natural (1)
by   takes on (1)
bz   takes out after (1)
ca   takes up after (1)

cb   temper like, has a (2)
cc   temperament, has father's (1)
cd   thinks like (1)
ce   traits after, has (1)
cf   traits of, has (1)
cg   walks in his footsteps (1)
ch   way(s), has father's (34)
ci   ways and actions, has father's (1)

065.4 L reared

No Response (91)
A   born and raise(d) (38)
B   born and rear(ed) (12)
C   borned and rear(ed) (5)
D   bring/brought up (74)
E   bring up by the hair of the head (1)
F   brought and raised (1)
G   brung (them) up (2)
H   care(d) for (5)
I   grow (them) up (1)
J   growed (children) (1)
K   jerked (them) up (1)
L   juked (them) up (1)
M   look after (5)
N   look out for (1)
O   mother(ed) (7)
P   raise(d) (690)
Q   raise(d) up (64)
R   rear(ed) (162)
S   rear(ed) up (5)
T   see after (1)
U   take and raise (1)
V   take/took care of (17)
W   take/took up (2)
X   tend(ed) (1)

065.5 L whipping

No Response (176)
A   ass whipping [n.] (2)
B   beat (12)
C   beat hell out of (5)
D   beat on (1)
E   beat the hang out of (1)
F   beat the life out of (1)
G   beat the tar out of (1)
H   beat up (4)
I   beat your butt (4)
J   beating [n.] (57)
K   belt [n.] (1)
L   belting [n.] (3)
M   blister [v.] (2)
N   blister your behind (1)
O   blistering [n.] (1)
P   boxing [n.] (1)
Q   break you down (1)
R   break your arm (1)
S   break your neck (1)
T   brush up (1)
U   brushing [n.] (1)
V   burn your fanny (1)

W   bust hell out of (1)
X   cane [v.] (1)
Y   catch it (1)
Z   chastise (3)
aa   chastising [n.] (3)
ab   clubbing [n.] (1)
ac   cut [v.] (1)
ad   cut the blood (1)
ae   dressing down [n.] (1)
af   drub (1)
ag   drubbing [n.] (1)
ah   fan your fanny (1)
ai   ferdootin [n.] (1)
aj   flogging [n.] (3)
ak   frail [v.] (1)
al   frail hell out of (1)
am   frail the tar out of (1)
an   frailing [n.] (3)
ao   fussing [n.] (1)
ap   get a belt (1)
aq   get a belt after (1)
ar   get a board to (1)
as   get a hickory (1)
at   get a limb and wear it out (1)
au   get a peach-tree limb after (1)
av   get a switch to (2)
aw   get on his breeches (1)
ax   get the rod (1)
ay   get your jacket (1)
az   give him mischief (1)
ba   go to the washhouse (1)
bb   hawk [v.] (1)
bc   hit [n.] (1)
bd   hit [v.] (2)
be   horsewhipping [n.] (1)
bf   kick your ass up between your
     shoulders (1)
bg   kick your tail (1)
bh   killing [n.] (4)
bi   knuckle sandwich (1)
bj   larruping [n.] (3)
bk   lashing [n.] (13)
bl   latching [n.] (1)
bm   lick [n.] (4)
bn   licking [n.] (53)
bo   lint your jacket (1)
bp   mark up (2)
bq   nettle [v.] (1)
br   paddle [v.] (8)
bs   paddling [n.] (33)
bt   pat [v.] (1)
bu   peach-limb whipping (1)
bv   punch [n.] (1)
bw   punish (15)
bx   punish(ing) [n.] (2)
by   punishing [n.] (2)
bz   punishment (6)
ca   put a switch on you (1)
cb   put a whipping on you (1)

cc   put the switch to (1)
cd   razor soup (1)
ce   score [v.] (1)
cf   (shel)lacking [n.] (1)
cg   shellacking [n.] (1)
ch   skin you (1)
ci   skin you alive (3)
cj   skinning [n.] (2)
ck   slap [n.] (6)
cl   slap [v.] (2)
cm   slap around (1)
cn   slap hell out of (1)
co   slapping [n.] (2)
cp   slashing [n.] (2)
cq   smack [v.] (2)
cr   smacking [n.] (1)
cs   sock in the jaw (1)
ct   socking [n.] (1)
cu   spank [n.] (1)
cv   spank [v.] (38)
cw   spank hell out of (1)
cx   spanking [n.] (408)
cy   stomping [n.] (1)
cz   strap [v.] (5)
da   strapping [n.] (6)
db   stripe [v.] (1)
dc   striping [n.] (1)
dd   strop [v.] (1)
de   stropping [n.] (1)
df   swap [v.] (2)
dg   switch [n.] (2)
dh   switch [v.] (9)
di   switching [n.] (31)
dj   tail-oiling [n.] (1)
dk   take a belt strap to (1)
dl   take a limb to (1)
dm   take a piece off your butt (1)
dn   take you to the woodshed (1)
do   tan [v.] (3)
dp   tan the hide off (1)
dq   tan up (1)
dr   tan your bottom (1)
ds   tan your breeches (1)
dt   tan your hide (5)
du   tan your hind part (1)
dv   tanning [n.] (10)
dw   tap [n.] (1)
dx   tear [v.] (1)
dy   tear down (1)
dz   tear up (10)
ea   tear your ass up (1)
eb   tear your breeches up (2)
ec   tear your butt (1)
ed   tear your butt up (1)
ee   tear your pants off (1)
ef   tear your tail up (1)
eg   tearing up [n.] (2)
eh   thrash (3)
ei   thrashing [n.] (20)

ej   thrashing out [n.] (3)
ek   threshing [n.] (2)
el   troubling [n.] (1)
em   trounce (1)
en   trouncing [n.] (1)
eo   wallop [v.] (1)
ep   walloping [n.] (2)
eq   warm you up (1)
er   warm your leather (1)
es   wear it out (1)
et   wear you out (7)
eu   wearing out [n.] (1)
ev   whack [v.] (1)
ew   whacking [n.] (2)
ex   whale the daylights out of (1)
ey   whaling [n.] (1)
ez   whip [v.] (135)
fa   whip hell out of him (1)
fb   whip your ass (1)
fc   whip your butt (2)
fd   whipping [n.] (476)
fe   work (over) [v.] (2)
ff   work on the rear end (1)
fg   working [n.] (1)
fh   working over [n.] (2)

065.6 G grow

<!>   infinitive
<&>   present 3rd singular
<@>   present participle
<*>   preterit
<#>   past participle
No Response (63)
<!droe> (2)
<!graw> (2)
<!groe> (542)
<!groed> (1)
<!groez> (1))
<!gru> (1)
<!grue> (3)
<!owtgroe=31> (2)
<&groe> (3)
<&groedh> (2)
<&groez> (57)
<&groezh> (1)
<@AgroeN=414> (1)
<@groein=13> (1)
<@groeing=12> (1)
<@groeing=13> (3)
<@groeN=14> (51)
<@groeNG=14> (17)
<@groewN=14> (6)
<@groewNG=14> (4)
<@grueN=14> (1)
<*(g)roed> (1)
<*droe> (1)
<*grawd> (1)
<*grew> (24)
<*groe> (6)
<*groed> (209)

<*groen> (8)
<*groez> (1)
<*grom> (1)
<*groo> (6)
<*grue> (480)
<*grued> (5)
<*owtgroe=21> (1)
<*owtgroed=21> (1)
<*owtgroed=31> (1)
<#droed> (1)
<#droen> (1)
<#graw[n]> (1)
<#grawn> (23)
<#grew> (1)
<#groe> (3)
<#groeN=14> (6)
<#groe[n]> (3)
<#groed> (154)
<#groen> (587)
<#groend> (1)
<#groewN=14> (1)
<#grown> (1)
<#grue> (10)
<#grued> (2)
<#hoemgroen=13> (1)
<#oevAgrown=143> (1)
<#owtgroed=21> (1)
<#owtgroed=31> (1)
<#owtgroen=31> (1)

065.7 L bastard

No Response (198)
A   baby borned out of wedlock (1)
B   baby without a father (1)
C   back-seat baby (1)
D   baseborn (1)
E   baseborn child (1)
F   bastard (461)
G   bastard baby (2)
H   bastard child (40)
I   bastard kid (1)
J   bastard young one (3)
K   batard [F] (2)
L   bitch (1)
M   born on the wrong side of the blanket (3)
N   born out of wedlock (21)
O   borned out of wedlock (5)
P   brat (1)
Q   brier-patch (1)
R   brier-patch baby (1)
S   bush child (2)
T   bush colt (1)
U   child ain't got no daddy (1)
V   child born out of wedlock (4)
W   child borned out of wedlock (2)
X   child from an unwed mother (1)
Y   child of the woods (1)
Z   child out of wedlock (4)
aa   come by chance (2)

ab   common law (1)
ac   crossbreed (1)
ad   daddyless child (1)
ae   delinquent child (1)
af   derelict (1)
ag   doesn't know who his daddy is (1)
ah   don't know the daddy (1)
ai   fatherless (4)
aj   fatherless child (2)
ak   foster baby (1)
al   grass colt (2)
am   grass young one (1)
an   had no father (1)
ao   half-breed (1)
ap   has no father (1)
aq   hasn't got a daddy (1)
ar   illegal (5)
as   illegal child (1)
at   illegitimate (227)
au   illegitimate [n.] (4)
av   (il)legitimate (16)
aw   (il)legiti(mate) (1)
ax   (ille)gitimate (1)
ay   illegitimate baby (5)
az   (il)legitimate baby (2)
ba   illegitimate bastard (1)
bb   illegitimate child (84)
bc   (il)legitimate child (11)
bd   (ille)gitimate child (2)
be   illegitimate kid (2)
bf   (il)legitime [F] (1)
bg   illicit (1)
bh   just a baby (1)
bi   kid, a (1)
bj   kid out of marriage (1)
bk   kid out of wedlock (1)
bl   little volunteer (1)
bm   loner (1)
bn   love child (10)
bo   ma and pa wasn't married (1)
bp   malignant child (1)
bq   mamma just got out and picked him up (1)
br   mistake, a (1)
bs   not legal (1)
bt   not legitimate (1)
bu   one-night baby (1)
bv   onus child (1)
bw   orphan child (1)
bx   out of family (1)
by   out of lock (1)
bz   out of the wedlock (1)
ca   out-of-wed marriage (1)
cb   out of wedlock (14)
cc   out-of-wedlock child (1)
cd   outcast (2)
ce   outlaw (1)
cf   outside [n.] (1)

cg   outside [adj.] (1)
ch   outside child (11)
ci   outsider (1)
cj   pea dropper (1)
ck   pickup, a (1)
cl   prematured (1)
cm   range child (1)
cn   SOB (1)
co   son of a bitch (2)
cp   sprung up out of wedlock (1)
cq   stray (1)
cr   stray colt (2)
cs   towhead (1)
ct   trash (1)
cu   unexpected (1)
cv   unfortunate child (2)
cw   unlawful (1)
cx   unlawful baby (1)
cy   unlawful child (2)
cz   unlegal bastard (1)
da   unlegal child (4)
db   unlegitimate child (1)
dc   unwanted (1)
dd   unwanted child (2)
de   unwed child (3)
df   unwedded child (2)
dg   unwedlock child (1)
dh   volunteer (3)
di   volunteer baby (1)
dj   wedlock (1)
dk   wedlock child (1)
dl   wild jackass (1)
dm   wildwoods kid (1)
dn   wire-grass colt (1)
do   wood chicken (1)
dp   wood colt (8)
dq   woodling colt (1)
dr   woodman (1)
ds   woods child (1)
dt   woods colt (92)
du   yard child (1)
dv   young one out of wedlock (1)

066.1 G more loving

No Response (750)
A   lovinger (18)
B   more loving (148)
C   more lovinger (1)

066.2 P nephew

{e}   upglide
{f}   bilabial
{v}   bilabial
{ue}   lowered/lax
{z}   devoiced
No Response (170)
<lefyue=13> (1)
<nafyA=14> (1)
<nafyue=13> (1)
<naifyue=13> (2)
<nef(y)ue=13> (1)

<nefI=14> (1)
<nefIyue=143> (1)
<nefee=13> (1)
<nefew13> (1)
<nefew=13> (175)
<nefewz=13> (14)
<nefew{z}=13> (3)
<neffyue=13> (1)
<nefyA=14> (34)
<nefyAz=14> (2)
<nefyI=14> (6)
<nefyee=13> (2)
<nefyew=13> (44)
<nefyewz=13> (1)
<nefyue=13> (397)
<nefyuez=13> (14)
<nefyue{z}=13> (1)
<nefy{ue}=13> (15)
<nepyue=13> (1)
<nevew=13> (2)
<nevyew=13> (1)
<nevyue=13> (3)
<nevyuez=13> (1)
<ne{f}(y)ue=13> (1)
<ne{f}yee=13> (1)
<ne{f}yew=13> (4)
<ne{f}yue=13> (1)
<ne{v}ew=13> (1)
<ne{v}yue=13> (1)
<nifew=13> (3)
<nifyA=14> (1)
<nifyew=13> (1)
<nifyue=13> (5)
<ni{f}yew=13> (2)
<n{e}few=13> (1)
<n{e}fyue=13> (6)

066.3 L orphan

No Response (150)
A fatherless baby (1)
B fatherless child (6)
C homeless young one (1)
D motherless and daddyless child (1)
E motherless and fatherless child (10)
F motherless [J-0] fatherless child (4)
G motherless baby (1)
H motherless child (24)
I motherless child [J-0] fatherless child (1)
J motherless girl (1)
K orphan (681)
L orphan baby (1)
M orphan boy (10)
N orphan child (72)
O orphan girl (1)
P orphan-home child (1)
Q orphan kid (2)

R orphanage (1)
S orphanage child (2)
T orphaned young one (1)
U orphans' boy (1)
V orphans' girl (1)
W orphlet (1)
X urchin (1)
Y waif (1)
Z ward of the state (1)

066.3 P orphan

{d} devoiced
{f} bilabial
{o} low-back
{oe} lowered onset
{R} weakly retroflex
{r} weakly retroflex
{z} devoiced
No Response (174)
<arfN=14> (3)
<aw(r)fN=14> (109)
<aw(r)fNt=14> (5)
<aw(r)fNts=14> (1)
<aw(r)fNz=14> (3)
<aw(r)fN{z}=14> (2)
<aw(r)fRNt=144> (1)
<aw(r)fRn=14> (4)
<aw(r)fin=13> (1)
<aw(r)flN{z}=14> (1)
<aw(r)frN=14> (5)
<aw(r)frNz=14> (1)
<aw(r)frin=13> (1)
<aw(r)ftN=14> (12)
<aw(r)fun=13> (1)
<aw(r)f{R}n=14> (2)
<aw(r)f{R}nz=14> (1)
<aw(r)pN=14> (1)
<aw(r){f}N=14> (1)
<aw[r]fLt=14> (1)
<aw[r]fN=14> (52)
<aw[r]fNt=14> (2)
<aw[r]fRn=14> (2)
<aw[r]finz=13> (1)
<aw[r]frM=14> (1)
<aw[r]ftN=14> (2)
<aw[r]{f}N=14> (1)
<awrfN=14> (86)
<awrfNt=14> (10)
<awrfNts=14> (1)
<awrfNz=14> (2)
<awrfN{z}=14> (2)
<awrfrN=14> (3)
<awr{f}N=14> (1)
<aw{r}fN=14> (41)
<aw{r}fNt=14> (4)
<aw{r}fun=13> (2)
<aw{r}f{R}n=14> (1)
<o(r)fN=14> (4)
<o(r)fNz=14> (1)
<o(r)frN=14> (1)

<o[r]fN=14> (1)
<oe(r){f}len=13> (1)
<oe[r]{f}N=14> (1)
<oerfN=14> (2)
<oerfNt=14> (1)
<oe{r}fN=14> (1)
<orfN=14> (9)
<o{r}fN=14> (1)
<{oe}(r)fN=14> (12)
<{oe}(r)fNdz=14> (1)
<{oe}(r)fNt=14> (1)
<{oe}(r)fRn=14> (1)
<{oe}(r)f[N]=14> (1)
<{oe}(r)frN=14> (1)
<{oe}(r){f}N=14> (1)
<{oe}(r){f}rM=14> (1)
<{oe}[r]fN=14> (77)
<{oe}[r]fNt=14> (8)
<{oe}[r]fNz=14> (1)
<{oe}[r]fRn=14> (1)
<{oe}[r]f[N]=14> (1)
<{oe}[r]frN=14> (2)
<{oe}[r]ftN=14> (3)
<{oe}[r]{f}N=14> (3)
<{oe}rfN=14> (182)
<{oe}rfNt=14> (8)
<{oe}rfNts=14> (1)
<{oe}rfNz=14> (3)
<{oe}rfN{z}=14> (1)
<{oe}rfRn=14> (1)
<{oe}rfR{d}=14> (1)
<{oe}rfrN=14> (2)
<{oe}rftN=14> (1)
<{oe}rfun=13> (1)
<{oe}{r}fN=14> (35)
<{oe}{r}fNt=14> (2)
<{oe}{r}ftN=14> (1)
<{o}(r)fN=14> (7)
<{o}(r)fNt=14> (1)
<{o}(r)fNz=14> (1)
<{o}[r]fN=14> (2)
<{o}rfN=14> (8)
<{o}rfun=13> (1)
<{o}{r}fN=14> (1)

066.4 L guardian

No Response (173)
A (ad)ministrator (2)
B administrator (2)
C (a)dopted parent (3)
D adopted parent (5)
E caretaker (4)
F conservator (1)
G counselor (2)
H custodian (2)
I foster father (2)
J foster-mother (4)
K foster parent (68)
L godfather (13)
M godmother (11)

N   godparent (7)
O   guard(ian) (1)
P   guardian (703)
Q   legal father (1)
R   legal guard(ian) (1)
S   legal guardian (6)
T   legal mother (1)
U   legal tutor (1)
V   matron (1)
W   nurse (1)
X   overseer (1)
Y   sheriff (1)
Z   trustee (1)
aa   tutor (4)

066.4 P guardian
{d}   devoiced
{o}   low-back
{oe}   lowered
(r)   weakly retróflex
{t}   flap
{z}   devoiced
{?}   glottal
No Response (202)
<gard(I)yN=14> (1)
<gaw(r)dIN=144> (6)
<gaw(r)dIyN=144> (1)
<gaw(r)dee(I)n=13> (1)
<gaw(r)deeN=134> (2)
<gaw(r){t}IN=144> (1)
<gaw[r]d(I)yN=14> (1)
<gaw[r]dIN=144> (1)
<gaw[r]dIyN=144> (1)
<gaw[r]{t}IN=144> (2)
<gawr(d)IyN=144> (1)
<gawr(d)eeyN=134> (1)
<gawrd(I)N=14> (1)
<gawrd(I)yN=14> (1)
<gawrdIN=144> (9)
<gawrdIin=143> (1)
<gawrdIyN=144> (9)
<gawrdIy[N]=144> (1)
<gawrdee(I)n=21> (1)
<gawrdee(I)n=31> (1)
<gawrdee(I)nz=31> (1)
<gawrdeeN=134> (3)
<gawrdeeyN=134> (3)
<gawrdiyN=134> (1)
<gawrj(I)N=14> (1)
<gawr{t}IN=144> (1)
<gaw{r}dIN=144> (5)
<gierdiNts=134> (1)
<go(r)d(I)N=14> (2)
<go(r)d(I)yN=14> (1)
<go(r)dIN=144> (13)
<go(r)dINt=144> (1)
<go(r)dIyN=144> (1)
<go(r)dIyN{z}=144> (1)
<go(r)dee(I)n=13> (7)
<go(r)dee(I)n=31> (12)

<go(r)deeN=134> (4)
<go(r)di(I)nz=13> (1)
<go(r)diN=134> (1)
<go(r)diyN=134> (1)
<go(r)dy(I)N=14> (1)
<go(r)rdeeN=134> (1)
<go(r){t}IN=144> (1)
<go(r){t}IyNts=144> (1)
<go(r){t}dIN=144> (1)
<go(r){t}ee(I)n=21> (1)
<go[r]d(I)N=14> (1)
<go[r]d(I)yN=14> (2)
<go[r]dIN=144> (9)
<go[r]dIyN=144> (3)
<go[r]dee(I)n=13> (3)
<go[r]dee(I)n=21> (1)
<go[r]dee(I)n=31> (7)
<go[r]dee(I)nz=13> (1)
<go[r]deeN=134> (3)
<go[r]deeyN=134> (2)
<go[r]zee(I)n=12> (1)
<go[r]zee(I)n=31> (1)
<go[r]{t}IN=144> (1)
<gord(I)N=14> (7)
<gord(I)[N]=14> (1)
<gord(I)yN=14> (6)
<gordAyN=144> (1)
<gordIN=144> (151)
<gordINd=144> (1)
<gordINz=144> (2)
<gordI[N]=144> (5)
<gordIen=143> (1)
<gordIin=143> (2)
<gordIun=143> (1)
<gordIyN=144> (27)
<gordIyNz=144> (2)
<gordIyin=143> (1)
<gordee(I)[n]=31> (1)
<gordee(I)n=12> (1)
<gordee(I)n=13> (27)
<gordee(I)n=21> (8)
<gordee(I)n=31> (49)
<gordee(I)nz=31> (1)
<gordeeN=134> (26)
<gordeeN=314> (1)
<gordeeyN=134> (16)
<gordeeyN=314> (1)
<gordi(I)n=13> (1)
<gordi(I)n{z}=13> (1)
<gordiN=134> (9)
<gordiNz=134> (1)
<gordiN{z}=134> (1)
<gordiyN=134> (8)
<gor{d}Iin=143> (1)
<gor{t}I(N)=14> (1)
<gor{t}IN=144> (8)
<gor{t}eeN=314> (1)
<go{?}dzee(I)n=13> (1)
<go{r}d(I)N=14> (3)

<go{r}d(I)Ns=14> (1)
<go{r}d(I)Nz=14> (1)
<go{r}d(I)yN=14> (1)
<go{r}d(I)yun=13> (1)
<go{r}dIN=144> (31)
<go{r}dIyN=144> (1)
<go{r}dee(I)n=13> (4)
<go{r}dee(I)n=31> (15)
<go{r}deeN=134> (3)
<go{r}deenA=314> (1)
<go{r}deeyNts=314> (1)
<go{r}deeyNz=134> (1)
<go{r}di(I)n=13> (2)
<go{r}diN=314> (1)
<gyordIN=144> (1)
<gyordee(I)n=13> (1)
<gyordee(I)n=31> (1)
<g{oe}(r)diN=134> (1)
<g{oe}rdIyN=144> (1)
<g{o}(r)dIN=144> (8)
<g{o}(r)dIyN=144> (1)
<g{o}(r)dee(I)n=13> (1)
<g{o}(r)dee(I)n=31> (2)
<g{o}(r)deeAs=134> (1)
<g{o}(r)deeN=134> (4)
<g{o}(r)diN=134> (4)
<g{o}(r)diyN=134> (1)
<g{o}(r){t}(I)N=14> (1)
<g{o}[r]d(I)N=14> (2)
<g{o}[r]dIN=144> (10)
<g{o}[r]dIyN=144> (3)
<g{o}[r]dee(I)n=13> (1)
<g{o}[r]dee(I)n=21> (1)
<g{o}[r]deeN=134> (2)
<g{o}[r]deeyN=134> (1)
<g{o}rd(I)yN=14> (2)
<g{o}rdIN=144> (13)
<g{o}rdINts=144> (2)
<g{o}rdINz=144> (1)
<g{o}rdIN{z}=144> (1)
<g{o}rdI[N]=144> (1)
<g{o}rdIin{z}=143> (1)
<g{o}rdIyN=144> (24)
<g{o}rdai(I)n=13> (1)
<g{o}rdee(I)n=12> (1)
<g{o}rdee(I)n=13> (11)
<g{o}rdee(I)n=31> (14)
<g{o}rdeeN=134> (3)
<g{o}rdeeyN=134> (10)
<g{o}rdiN=134> (1)
<g{o}rdiyN=134> (3)
<g{o}r{d}(IN)> (1)
<g{o}{r}d(I)N=14> (1)
<g{o}{r}d(I)yN=14> (1)
<g{o}{r}d(I)yN{z}=14> (1)
<g{o}{r}dIN=144> (3)
<g{o}{r}dIyN=144> (1)
<g{o}{r}dee(I)n=31> (2)
<g{o}{r}deeN=134> (1)

<g{o}{r}deeyNz=134> (1)

066.5 L relatives

No Response (104)
A big family (3)
B blood (2)
C blood kin (5)
D blood relations (1)
E blood relatives (2)
F bunch (1)
G clan (6)
H connections (2)
I family (126)
J family folks (1)
K folks (101)
L kin (63)
M kin line (1)
N kin people (54)
O kindred (1)
P kinfolks (372)
Q kinnery (4)
R kinsmen (4)
S kissing kinfolks (1)
T Machetunim [G] (1)
U Mishpokhe [G] (1)
V people (185)
W rabbit kin (1)
X race of people (1)
Y (re)lations (1)
Z relations (38)
aa relatives (468)

066.6 L no kin

No Response (203)
A ain't a bit of kin (2)
B ain't kin (1)
C ain't no kin (8)
D different set of dogs (2)
E no akin (1)
F no blood kin (6)
G no blood relation (1)
H no kin (413)
I no related (1)
J no relation(s) (209)
K no relationship (1)
L no relative(s) (9)
M none related (1)
N not a bit of kin (1)
O not a bit of relation (1)
P not (a/my) relative(s) (3)
Q not (a/my) relation(s) (2)
R not akin (1)
S not any blood kin (1)
T not any kin (26)
U not any kindry (1)
V not any of my kinfolks (1)
W not any related (1)
X not any relation (9)
Y not any relative (1)
Z not in the family (1)
aa not kin (22)

ab not kinfolks (1)
ac not no kin (1)
ad not related (129)
ae unrelated (3)

066.7 L stranger

No Response (247)
A blue belly (1)
B damn Yankee (10)
C damned old foreigner (1)
D flatland foreigner (1)
E foreign dude (1)
F foreign fellow (1)
G foreign person (3)
H foreigner (149)
I (from) out of state (5)
J from out of town (1)
K immigrant (1)
L lost child (1)
M new face (in town) (2)
N new fellow (1)
O new in town (1)
P new kid (1)
Q new neighbor (1)
R new people (1)
S new person (in town) (1)
T new (to the neighborhood) (2)
U newcomer (54)
V Northern folks (1)
W Northerner (7)
X of [D-0] nations (1)
Y out-of-state person (1)
Z out of towner (3)
aa outlander (1)
ab outside agitator (1)
ac outside people (1)
ad outsider (12)
ae perfect stranger (2)
af rank stranger (5)
ag strange man in town (1)
ah strange people (1)
ai strange somebody, a (1)
aj stranger (605)
ak total stranger (2)
al tourist (2)
am traveler (2)
an visitor (8)
ao Westerner (2)
ap Yankee (49)

[indigent stranger]
aq drifter (2)
ar hermit (1)
as hobo (2)
at tramp (5)
au transient (4)
av vagrant (1)
aw wino (1)

067.1 P Mary
{ai} lax onset/upglide
{r} weakly retroflex

{t} flap
{z} devoiced
No Response (116)
<mai(r)I=14> (1)
<mai[r]I=14> (1)
<mair(I)> (1)
<mairA=14> (2)
<mairI=14> (301)
<mairIz=14> (1)
<mairI{z}=14> (1)
<mairee=13> (5)
<mairrI=14> (6)
<mai{r}I=14> (1)
<mai{r}rI=14> (3)
<mai{t}I=14> (1)
<marI=14> (6)
<maree=13> (1)
<me(r)I=14> (2)
<merA=14> (1)
<merI=14> (410)
<meree=13> (16)
<merrI=14> (4)
<me{r}I=14> (9)
<me{r}rI=14> (11)
<me{t}I=14> (1)
<mirI=14> (9)
<miree=13> (1)
<mi{r}I=14> (2)
<moree=31> (1)
<mu[r]I=14> (1)
<murI=14> (18)
<muree=13> (3)
<mu{r}I=14> (6)
<mu{r}rI=14> (3)
<m{ai}rI=14> (26)

067.1 S Mary
No Response (37)
|DAImea| (3)
|DCCmea| (1)
|DCGmea| (1)
|GBAbbjmea| (1)
|GBAeaa| (1)
|GBAeaj| (9)
|GBAeajmea| (3)
|GBAgbkmea| (1)
|GBAmea| (1)
|GBBeaj| (1)
|GBBmea| (1)
|GBC| (9)
|GBCeaa| (2)
|GBCeaamea| (2)
|GBCeaj| (5)
|GBCeajmea| (2)
|GBCmaj| (3)
|GBCmea| (13)
|GBCmej| (1)
|GBE| (14)
|GBEeaa| (17)
|GBEeaamaj| (1)

|OAGmea| (1)
|OBBmea| (1)
|OCB| (2)
|OGAmaa| (1)
|OGBmea| (1)
|kabGBAmea| (2)
|kabGBJmea| (1)

067.2 P Martha
{o}   low-back
{R}   weakly retroflex
{r}   weakly retroflex
No Response (188)
<maw(r)tA=14> (1)
<maw(r)thA=14> (12)
<maw(r)thI=14> (1)
<maw[r]thA=14> (3)
<maw[r]th{R}=14> (1)
<mawrthA=14> (20)
<mawrthI=14> (2)
<mawrth{R}=14> (1)
<maw{r}thA=14> (9)
<merthA=14> (1)
<mo(r)dhA=14> (7)
<mo(r)dh{R}=14> (1)
<mo(r)tI=14> (1)
<mo(r)thA=14> (80)
<mo(r)thAz=14> (1)
<mo(r)thI=14> (12)
<mo(r)th{R}=14> (1)
<mo[r]dhA=14> (1)
<mo[r]kA=14> (1)
<mo[r]tA=14> (2)
<mo[r]thA=14> (76)
<mo[r]thI=14> (11)
<mo[r]thR=14> (1)
<mo[r]thee=13> (2)
<mo[r]th{R}=14> (1)
<mordhR=14> (1)
<morth(A)> (1)
<morthA=14> (226)
<morthAz=14> (1)
<morthI=14> (33)
<morthR=14> (4)
<morthee=13> (7)
<mortho=13> (2)
<morthrI=14> (1)
<morth{R}=14> (7)
<mo{r}tA=14> (1)
<mo{r}thA=14> (58)
<mo{r}thI=14> (7)
<mo{r}thtI=14> (1)
<mo{r}th{R}=14> (2)
<m{o}(r)dhA=14> (2)
<m{o}(r)thA=14> (32)
<m{o}(r)thI=14> (2)
<m{o}(r)th{R}=14> (2)
<m{o}[r]thA=14> (27)
<m{o}[r]thI=14> (1)
<m{o}rtA=14> (1)

<m{o}rthA=14> (51)
<m{o}rthI=14> (9)
<m{o}rthR=14> (1)
<m{o}rthai=13> (1)
<m{o}{r}thA=14> (15)
<northA=14> (1)

067.3 P Nelly
{l}   clear
{w}   dark lateral
No Response (291)
<nai{l}I=14> (3)
<nai{l}ee=13> (1)
<na{l}I=14> (3)
<ne[1]I=14> (2)
<nelI=14> (96)
<nelIz=14> (1)
<nelee=13> (1)
<nelII=14> (1)
<nellee=13> (1)
<nel{l}I=14> (4)
<ne{l}A=14> (1)
<ne{l}I=14> (458)
<ne{l}Iz=14> (1)
<ne{l}ee=13> (16)
<ne{l}{l}ee=13> (1)
<ne{w}I=14> (13)
<ne{w}lI=14> (3)
<ne{w}lee=13> (1)
<ni{l}I=14> (11)
<nulI=14> (3)
<nu{l}I=14> (5)
<nu{w}I=14> (2)
<nye{l}I=14> (3)

067.3 S Nelly
No Response (0)
|DAC| (1)
|DAI| (3)
|DCA| (3)
|DKA| (2)
|GBCmaj| (2)
|GBImaj| (1)
|GCB| (1)
|GGCkaj| (1)
|KAA| (107)
|KAAead| (1)
|KAAmaj| (25)
|KAAmfj| (1)
|KAB| (67)
|KABkbk| (1)
|KABmaj| (25)
|KAC| (42)
|KACmaj| (15)
|KAD| (2)
|KADmaj| (2)
|KAE| (217)
|KAEcba| (1)
|KAEcbj| (1)
|KAEmaj| (61)
|KAF| (36)

|KAFmaj| (10)
|KAG| (9)
|KAGmaj| (5)
|KAI| (16)
|KAImaj| (10)
|KBA| (12)
|KBAmaj| (3)
|KBB| (5)
|KBE| (2)
|KBF| (2)
|KCA| (59)
|KCAmaj| (9)
|KCB| (18)
|KCBmaj| (11)
|KCC| (4)
|KCCkaj| (2)
|KCCmaj| (11)
|KCCmajcba| (1)
|KCDmaj| (1)
|KCE| (20)
|KCEmaj| (2)
|KCF| (4)
|KCFmaj| (1)
|KCG| (3)
|KCGcbj| (1)
|KCGmaj| (1)
|KCI| (2)
|KCImaj| (2)
|KDA| (12)
|KDAmdj| (2)
|KDB| (5)
|KDC| (2)
|KDD| (1)
|KDE| (1)
|KDEmdj| (2)
|KDF| (5)
|KDI| (2)
|KFE| (1)
|KGA| (2)
|KGAmaj| (2)
|KGB| (1)
|KHB| (1)
|KKA| (10)
|KKAmdj| (1)
|KKB| (2)
|KKC| (5)
|LAD| (8)
|LAH| (1)
|LFDmfj| (1)
|OABkaj| (3)

067.4 P Billy
{l}   clear
{t}   flap
{w}   dark lateral
No Response (228)
<belI=14> (1)
<be{l}I=14> (2)
<bi[1]I=14> (6)
<bidI=14> (1)

<bilI=14> (139)
<bilee=13> (3)
<bilII=14> (3)
<bil{l}I=14> (3)
<bi{l}I=14> (496)
<bi{l}Iz=14> (4)
<bi{l}ee=13> (15)
<bi{l}{l}I=14> (1)
<bi{l}{t}I=14> (1)
<bi{t}I=14> (4)
<bi{w}I=14> (20)
<bi{w}II=14> (2)
<bi{w}lee=13> (1)
<boo{l}I=14> (1)

067.5 P Matthew
{ue} lax
{z} devoiced
No Response (201)
<ma(thyue)> (1)
<machyue=13> (2)
<madh(y)A=14> (1)
<madhew=13> (1)
<madhyue=13> (3)
<madhyuez=13> (1)
<mafew=13> (2)
<mafyue=13> (2)
<matew=13> (2)
<math(y)A=14> (7)
<math(y)As=14> (1)
<math(y)I=14> (4)
<math(y)Is=14> (1)
<math(y)ue=13> (71)
<math(y)uez=13> (2)
<mathAyue=143> (1)
<mathew=13> (171)
<mathewz=13> (3)
<mathew{z}=13> (1)
<mathyA=14> (21)
<mathyAs=14> (1)
<mathyAz=14> (1)
<mathyI=14> (3)
<mathyew=13> (36)
<mathyewz=13> (1)
<mathyew{z}=13> (1)
<mathyue=12> (1)
<mathyue=13> (337)
<mathyues=13> (1)
<mathyuez=13> (18)
<mathyue{z}=13> (3)
<mathy{ue}=13> (6)
<matsyew=13> (1)
<matyew{z}=13> (1)
<matyue=13> (4)
<methew=13> (7)
<methyew=13> (2)
<methyue=13> (2)
<mothew=13> (1)

067.6 L woman teacher
No Response (217)

A   educator (2)
B   female teacher (1)
C   girl marm (1)
D   governess (1)
E   instructor (9)
F   (in)structor (1)
G   lady teacher (8)
H   ma (1)
I   ma'am (1)
J   madam (1)
K   marm (2)
L   matron (2)
M   mistress (8)
N   old maid (4)
O   old-maid schoolteacher (7)
P   old-maid teacher (1)
Q   school ma (1)
R   school madam (5)
S   school maid (1)
T   school maker (1)
U   school matron (2)
V   school miss (2)
W   school woman (1)
X   schoolma'am (15)
Y   schoolmarm (180)
Z   schoolmistress (22)
aa   schoolteacher (310)
ab   severe spinster (1)
ac   sister (3)
ad   spinster (1)
ae   teacher (409)
af   tutor (2)
ag   woman teacher (14)

067.7A P Mrs.
{z} devoiced
{zh} devoiced
No Response (293)
<me(sI)z> (1)
<meezIz=14> (1)
<mi(s)r(I)z> (1)
<mi(s)rIz=14> (2)
<mi(sI)dh> (1)
<mi(sI)z> (213)
<mi(sI){z}> (22)
<midhIdh=14> (1)
<mis(Iz)> (63)
<misAs=14> (1)
<misIz=14> (53)
<misI{z}=14> (13)
<misRs=14> (1)
<misrIs=14> (1)
<misrIz=14> (1)
<missIz=14> (1)
<missis=13> (1)
<missiz=13> (1)
<mistrIs=14> (2)
<mistrIz=14> (2)
<mizA(z)=14> (1)
<mizI(z)=14> (1)

<mizIz=14> (284)
<mizI{z}=14> (6)
<mizRz=14> (1)
<mizhA{zh}=14> (1)
<mizrIs=14> (1)
<mizrIz=14> (19)
<mizzIz=14> (7)
<mizzI{z}=14> (6)
<mi{z}Is=14> (2)
<mi{z}Iz=14> (11)
<mi{z}I{z}=14> (3)
<mi{z}zIz=14> (2)
<mi{z}{z}I{z}=14> (1)

067.7B P Cooper
{R} weakly retroflex
{t} flap
No Response (353)
<kewpR=14> (11)
<kewp[R]=14> (1)
<kewp{R}=14> (3)
<koopR=14> (145)
<koopRz=14> (2)
<koop[R]=14> (117)
<kooppR=14> (2)
<koopp[R]=14> (2)
<koopp{R}=14> (1)
<koop{R}=14> (51)
<kuepR=14> (153)
<kuepRz=14> (1)
<kuep[R]=14> (90)
<kuepp[R]=14> (1)
<kuepp{R}=14> (1)
<kuep{R}=14> (54)
<kuep{t}R=14> (1)
<kupR=14> (2)
<kup[R]=14> (1)
<kuppR=14> (1)
<kyewp{R}=14> (1)

067.8 L jackleg
No Response (262)
A   alley lawyer (1)
B   amateur (4)
C   apprentice (carpenter/preacher) (3)
D   assistant (minister/preacher) (2)
E   backwoods preacher (2)
F   bad preacher (1)
G   badger [preacher] (1)
H   banister preacher (1)
I   beginner (1)
J   Bible beater (1)
K   bootleg lawyer (1)
L   bootleg preacher (1)
M   botch (carpenter) (3)
N   botcher [carpenter] (2)
O   bum [carpenter] (1)
P   cake eater [preacher] (1)
Q   CC rider [preacher] (2)
R   chicken [preacher] (1)

S   chicken healer [preacher] (1)
T   chimley-cornered lawyer (1)
U   circuit (preacher) (3)
V   circuit rider (preacher) (7)
W   cobbler (3)
X   coffeepot preacher (1)
Y   common carpenter (1)
Z   country preacher (2)
aa   crooked lawyer (1)
ab   daddle-do [carpenter] (1)
ac   drugstore quarterback (1)
ad   Dummkopf [G] (1)
ae   entered apprentice (1)
af   evangelist (11)
ag   exalted, the (1)
ah   exhorter (2)
ai   fake (1)
aj   fieldworker [preacher] (1)
ak   fill-in preacher (1)
al   fill-out [preacher] (1)
am   flunky [carpenter] (1)
an   fly-by-night carpenter (1)
ao   footlog preacher (1)
ap   free-lance preacher (1)
aq   get-by [carpenter] (1)
ar   greenhorn [mechanic] (1)
as   hack [carpenter] (1)
at   half-ass (1)
au   half-ass carpenter (1)
av   half-ass lawyer (1)
aw   half-ass mechanic (1)
ax   half-ass preacher (2)
ay   half-assed (2)
az   half-assed [mechanic] (1)
ba   half-assed preacher (1)
bb   half-handed man [builder] (1)
bc   half-handed mechanic (1)
bd   half-handed preacher (2)
be   hammer-and-saw carpenter (1)
bf   handyman (4)
bg   haphazard carpenter (1)
bh   hard-call preacher (1)
bi   hard-time [preacher] (1)
bj   hatchet and hammer [carpenter] (1)
bk   helper [carpenter] (2)
bl   henpeck preacher (1)
bm   hick [carpenter] (1)
bn   hillbilly (preacher) (2)
bo   Holy Roller (preacher) (2)
bp   hypocrite (5)
bq   inexperienced preacher (1)
br   infidel [preacher] (1)
bs   interim pastor (1)
bt   intern (1)
bu   intern preacher (1)
bv   itinerant (carpenter) (1)
bw   itinerant minister (1)
bx   itinerant (preacher) (10)

by   jack (2)
bz   jack [preacher] (1)
ca   jack at all trades (3)
cb   jack carpenter (2)
cc   jack-of-all-trades (man) (35)
cd   jackass (1)
ce   jackass at all trades (1)
cf   jackass carpenter (1)
cg   jackass preacher (1)
ch   jackleg (116)
ci   jackleg at all jobs (1)
cj   jackleg at all trades (1)
ck   jackleg blacksmith (1)
cl   jackleg bricklayer/mason (3)
cm   jackleg builder (1)
cn   jackleg car repairman (1)
co   jackleg (carpenter) (221)
cp   jackleg (doctor) (32)
cq   jackleg (electrician) (3)
cr   jackleg farmer (4)
cs   jackleg (governor) (4)
ct   jackleg horse (1)
cu   jackleg (lawyer) (91)
cv   jackleg man (1)
cw   jackleg (mechanic) (38)
cx   jackleg of a carpenter (5)
cy   jackleg of a preacher (6)
cz   jackleg of all trades (4)
da   jackleg (painter) (3)
db   jackleg plow-hand (1)
dc   jackleg (plumber) (11)
dd   jackleg (politician) (2)
de   jackleg (preacher) (286)
df   jackleg president (1)
dg   jackleg singer (1)
dh   jackleg (teacher) (14)
di   jacklegged (1)
dj   jacklegged carpenter (2)
dk   jacklegged lawyer (2)
dl   jacklegged preacher (10)
dm   jacklegged teacher (1)
dn   jailhouse (lawyer) (1)
do   jake leg (2)
dp   jake leg (carpenter) (4)
dq   jake leg [cobbler] (1)
dr   jake leg (mechanic) (1)
ds   jake leg [preacher] (2)
dt   jerk water (1)
du   lay minister (2)
dv   lay preacher (23)
dw   lay reader (1)
dx   lay speaker (1)
dy   layman (21)
dz   lousy preacher (1)
ea   makeshift [carpenter] (2)
eb   makeshift [preacher] (1)
ec   misfit (1)
ed   missionary [preacher] (1)
ee   monkey wrench [handyman] (1)

ef   nail bender [carpenter] (1)
eg   ne'er-do-well [tradesman] (1)
eh   no-(ac)count preacher (1)
ei   oak tree mechanic (1)
ej   one-horse (preacher) (2)
ek   outlaw preacher (1)
el   part-time minister (1)
em   part-time pastor (1)
en   part-time preacher (13)
eo   peckerwood (2)
ep   pickup [carpenter] (1)
eq   piece away [carpenter] (1)
er   piece of a doctor (1)
es   pillroller [doctor] (1)
et   poor preacher (3)
eu   pot-liquor preacher (1)
ev   quack (2)
ew   quack (doctor) (15)
ex   quack [preacher] (3)
ey   quack [teacher] (1)
ez   quasi (carpenter) (1)
fa   rinky-dink carpenter (1)
fb   roadside mechanic (1)
fc   rough carpenter (1)
fd   sawmill mechanic (1)
fe   scab (3)
ff   scab on the trade [carpenter] (1)
fg   shade tree (3)
fh   shade-tree (carpenter) (1)
fi   shade-tree (mechanic) (42)
fj   shade tree [painter] (1)
fk   shade-tree (preacher) (8)
fl   shyster (lawyer) (7)
fm   sidewalk preacher (1)
fn   slack preacher (1)
fo   sloppy carpenter (1)
fp   sorry [carpenter] (2)
fq   sorry preacher (2)
fr   street preacher (1)
fs   striker [preacher] (1)
ft   stump leg [preacher] (1)
fu   stump preacher (2)
fv   stumpknocker (preacher) (6)
fw   substitute (preacher) (2)
fx   supply pastor (1)
fy   supply (preacher) (3)
fz   table tapper [preacher] (1)
ga   tinker (1)
gb   traveling preacher (2)
gc   tree-stump preacher (1)
gd   two-bit carpenter (1)
ge   two-bit lawyer (1)
gf   two-by-four (carpenter) (2)
gg   uneducated (preacher) (2)
gh   unordained minister (1)
gi   untrained minister (1)
gj   wagon-tail [preacher] (1)
gk   wish-washy [preacher] (1)
gl   wood bee [carpenter] (1)

gm   wood butcher [carpenter] (3)
gn   wood butcherer (1)
go   yard ax [preacher] (2)

067.8 S lawyer

No Response (733)
|JJHeaa| (1)
|JJHmaj| (3)
|JSCeac| (1)
|QAFeaa| (1)
|QAFjjl| (1)
|QCHead| (1)
|QFAdaj| (1)
|QFAeaa| (1)
|QFAeac| (1)
|QFAjjc| (1)
|QFAjjd| (1)
|QFAlfa| (1)
|QFAmab| (2)
|QFAqfb| (1)
|QFB| (1)
|QFBeaa| (5)
|QFBeac| (5)
|QFBeaj| (6)
|QFBjjc| (5)
|QFBjjcmaj| (1)
|QFBjjl| (6)
|QFBmaa| (1)
|QFBmab| (2)
|QFBmaj| (2)
|QFBmak| (4)
|QFBmfk| (1)
|QFC| (1)
|QFCeaa| (4)
|QFCeac| (3)
|QFCeah| (1)
|QFCjjc| (1)
|QFCmaa| (2)
|QFCqfa| (1)
|QFCqfb| (34)
|QFCqfbeaj| (4)
|QFCqfj| (1)
|QFCqfk| (1)
|QFFeaa| (3)
|QFFeaj| (1)
|QFFeam| (1)
|QFFmaj| (2)
|QFH| (1)
|QFHeaj| (1)
|QFHqfb| (5)
|QFHqff| (1)
|QMA| (2)
|QMAeaj| (1)
|QMAmal| (1)
|QMBeaa| (2)
|QMBeab| (1)
|QMBeac| (4)
|QMBeaj| (1)
|QMBmab| (1)
|QMBqfb| (1)

|QMCdab| (1)
|QMCeaa| (2)
|QMCeac| (1)
|QMCeaj| (2)
|QMCmaj| (2)
|QMCmak| (2)
|QMCqfb| (6)
|QMCqfbeaj| (1)
|QMCqfj| (1)
|QMCqfk| (2)
|QMHeac| (1)
|QMHqfb| (2)
|QMHqff| (1)
|SAGjjh| (1)
|SAGmaj| (1)
|SAGqfj| (2)
|TCA| (1)
|TCAeaj| (1)
|TCG| (1)
|TFAqfa| (2)
|TFBeaa| (1)
|TFBeaj| (1)
|TFBqfa| (1)
|TFBqfb| (1)
|TFBqfj| (2)
|TFBqfl| (1)
|TMBqfk| (1)
|qfcQMB| (2)

067.9 P your aunt

{a}   low-front
{o}   low-back
{oe}   lowered onset
{R}   weakly retroflex
{r}   weakly retroflex
{t}   flap
{?}   glottal
No Response (96)
<(y)oo[r]aint=31> (1)
<a[n]tI=14> (1)
<a[n]{t}I=14> (1)
<ain(t)> (3)
<ain(t)I=14> (1)
<aint> (48)
<aintI=14> (1)
<aints> (5)
<ain{t}I=14> (1)
<an(t)> (4)
<an(t)I=14> (4)
<ant> (178)
<antI=14> (6)
<antIz=14> (1)
<antee=13> (1)
<antee=31> (1)
<ants> (8)
<anttee=13> (1)
<an{t}I=14> (2)
<awnt> (2)
<awntee=13> (1)
<ent> (5)

<o[n]t> (1)
<ont> (60)
<ontI=14> (8)
<ontee=13> (7)
<ontee=31> (2)
<onttI=14> (1)
<onttee=13> (2)
<yRaint=41> (10)
<yRant=41> (37)
<yRantI=414> (1)
<yRent=41> (1)
<yRont=41> (1)
<yR{a}nt=41> (7)
<y[R]a[n](t)=41> (1)
<y[R]aint=41> (9)
<y[R]ain{t}I=414> (1)
<y[R]ant=41> (17)
<y[R]antee=412> (1)
<y[R]ont=41> (3)
<y[R]ontee=413> (1)
<y[R]ontee=431> (1)
<y[R]{a}n(t)I=414> (1)
<y[R]{a}nt=41> (6)
<yaw(r)ant=31> (1)
<yaw(r)o[n]t=31> (1)
<yaw(r)ont=31> (1)
<yaw(r){a}nt=21> (1)
<yawrant=21> (1)
<yawrant=31> (1)
<yawr{a}nt=21> (1)
<yew(r)ont=13> (1)
<yew(r)ontI=314> (1)
<yiraint=31> (1)
<yirant=31> (1)
<yi{r}ant=31> (1)
<yoe(r)aint=31> (4)
<yoe(r)ant=21> (2)
<yoe(r)ant=31> (8)
<yoe(r)antee=321> (1)
<yoe(r)ont=31> (4)
<yoe(r)ontI=214> (1)
<yoe(r){a}nt=21> (1)
<yoe(r){a}nt=31> (2)
<yoe(r){a}ntI=314> (2)
<yoe[r]aint=31> (1)
<yoe[r]an(t)I=314> (1)
<yoe[r]ant=21> (2)
<yoe[r]ant=31> (4)
<yoe[r]{a}nt=31> (3)
<yoeraint=21> (1)
<yoerant=31> (2)
<yoerent=11> (1)
<yoeront=21> (1)
<yoero{r}nt=21> (1)
<yoer{a}nt=13> (1)
<yoer{a}nt=21> (1)
<yoer{a}nt=31> (3)
<yoe{r}ant=31> (1)
<yoe{r}ont=31> (1)

<yoe{r}{a}nt=31> (1)
<yoo(r)ant=31> (4)
<yoo(r)ont=31> (2)
<yoo(r){a}nt=31> (2)
<yoo[r]aint=31> (1)
<yoo[r]an(t)=31> (2)
<yoo[r]an(t)I=314> (1)
<yoo[r]ant=13> (2)
<yoo[r]ant=21> (8)
<yoo[r]ant=31> (10)
<yoo[r]antI=214> (3)
<yoo[r]antee=113> (1)
<yoo[r]antee=213> (1)
<yoo[r]o(n)t=31> (1)
<yoo[r]ont=21> (5)
<yoo[r]ont=31> (9)
<yoo[r]ontI=214> (1)
<yoo[r]ontI=314> (2)
<yoo[r]{a}nt=21> (2)
<yoo[r]{a}nt=31> (4)
<yooraint=13> (1)
<yooraint=31> (5)
<yooran(t)I=214> (1)
<yoorant=11> (4)
<yoorant=13> (10)
<yoorant=21> (11)
<yoorant=31> (59)
<yooront=21> (4)
<yooront=31> (2)
<yoororntI=314> (1)
<yoor{a}nt=13> (1)
<yoor{a}nt=21> (5)
<yoor{a}nt=31> (7)
<yoor{o}nt=13> (1)
<yoor{o}nt=31> (1)
<yoo{r}aint=31> (1)
<yoo{r}ant=13> (1)
<yoo{r}ant=31> (8)
<yoo{r}{a}nt=13> (1)
<yoo{r}{a}nt=31> (7)
<yoo{r}{o}nt=21> (1)
<yor{a}nt=31> (1)
<yu[r]aint=31> (8)
<yu[r]ant=31> (6)
<yu[r]antI=314> (1)
<yu[r]ont=31> (1)
<yu[r]ontI=314> (1)
<yu[r]{a}nt=31> (5)
<yu[r]{a}n{t}I=314> (1)
<yue(r)ont=31> (1)
<yue[r]ant=31> (2)
<yue[r]awnt=31> (1)
<yuraint=31> (3)
<yurant=11> (2)
<yurant=13> (2)
<yurant=21> (3)
<yurant=31> (42)
<yurant=41> (1)
<yuront=31> (3)

<yur{a}nt=21> (1)
<yur{a}nt=31> (9)
<yu{r}aint=31> (1)
<yu{r}ant=31> (2)
<yu{r}ont=31> (4)
<yu{r}o{r}nt=13> (1)
<yu{r}{a}nt=31> (1)
<y{R}aint=41> (2)
<y{R}ant=41> (5)
<y{R}ont=41> (1)
<y{R}ontI=414> (1)
<y{R}{a}nt=41> (5)
<y{oe}(r)aint=31> (1)
<y{oe}(r)ant=31> (1)
<y{oe}[r]ontI=314> (1)
<y{oe}r{a}nt=31> (1)
<y{oe}{r}ant=31> (2)
<y{oe}{r}ont=31> (1)
<y{o}raint=13> (1)
<{a}[n]t=31> (1)
<{a}n(t)I=14> (2)
<{a}nt> (85)
<{a}ntI=14> (7)
<{a}ntee=13> (1)
<{a}nts> (3)
<{a}n{?}> (1)
<{a}n{t}I=14> (1)
<{o}nt> (1)
<{o}ntI=14> (1)
<{o}ntee=13> (1)

068.1 P Sarah
{ai} lowered onset/upglide
{r} weakly retroflex
{t} flap
No Response (309)
<sai(r)A=14> (2)
<sairA=14> (295)
<sairI=14> (4)
<sair{t}A=14> (1)
<sai{r}A=14> (3)
<sarA=14> (13)
<sa{r}(A)> (1)
<se[r]A=14> (1)
<ser(A)> (2)
<serA=14> (231)
<serI=14> (13)
<serR=14> (1)
<seree=13> (1)
<seroe=13> (1)
<se{r}(A)> (2)
<se{r}A=14> (3)
<sir(A)> (1)
<sirA=14> (2)
<si{r}(A)> (1)
<sorA=14> (1)
<surA=14> (10)
<surI=14> (3)
<s{ai}rA=14> (28)
068.2A P uncle

<L> dark
<l> dark
{L} clear
{n} palatal
{oo} unrounded
{z} devoiced
No Response (221)
<awnkL=14> (2)
<oenk[L]=14> (1)
<oenk{L}=14> (1)
<onkL=14> (12)
<onkLz=14> (1)
<onk{L}=14> (1)
<oonkL=14> (1)
<u(n)kL=14> (1)
<u[n]k[L]=14> (1)
<u[n]k{L}=14> (1)
<ung(k)L=14> (3)
<unk(L)> (2)
<unkL=14> (457)
<unkLz=14> (5)
<unkL{z}=14> (2)
<unk[L]=14> (119)
<unk[L]z=14> (1)
<unkool=13> (1)
<unk{L}=14> (172)
<unk{L}z=14> (1)
<u{n}kL=14> (1)
<{oo}ng(k)[L]=14> (1)
<{oo}nkL=14> (2)
<{oo}nkLz=14> (1)

068.2B P William
<l> dark
{l} clear
{t} flap
{z} devoiced
No Response (425)
<vilyM=14> (1)
<wee(1)yM=14> (6)
<weelyM=14> (1)
<we{1}yM=14> (1)
<wi(1)yM=14> (87)
<wi(1)yMz=14> (1)
<wi(1)yM{z}=14> (1)
<wi[1](yM)> (4)
<wi[1]yM=14> (31)
<wil(yM)> (14)
<wilyM=14> (49)
<wily[M]=14> (1)
<wi{1}(yM)> (8)
<wi{1}I=14> (9)
<wi{1}IM=144> (1)
<wi{1}yM=14> (292)
<wi{1}yM{z}=14> (1)
<wi{1}y[M]=14> (1)
<wi{1}yum=13> (1)
<wi{t}yM=14> (1)
068.2C P John
{aw} unrounded onset/upglide

{o}   low-back
{z}   devoiced
No Response (326)
<jaw[n]> (1)
<jawn> (34)
<jo[n]> (9)
<joen> (3)
<jon> (461)
<jonI=14> (9)
<jonnI=14> (6)
<jonz> (2)
<jon{z}> (1)
<j{aw}n> (12)
<j{o}[n]> (1)
<j{o}n> (63)
<j{o}nI=14> (1)

068.2 S John

No Response (3)
|PAA| (4)
|PAC| (5)
|PACmaj| (1)
|PAG| (2)
|PAI| (2)
|PCA| (5)
|PCAmaj| (1)
|PCC| (4)
|PCCmaj| (1)
|PCEqfj| (1)
|PDAmdj| (1)
|PDC| (1)
|PDD| (2)
|PDE| (1)
|PDEmdj| (1)
|PDI| (1)
|PFEqfa| (1)
|PKC| (2)
|PKEmdj| (1)
|QFFjjq| (1)
|QXH| (1)
|RKBrda| (1)
|RKEmda| (1)
|SAA| (5)
|SAAmaj| (3)
|SAB| (21)
|SABmaj| (11)
|SAD| (5)
|SAE| (99)
|SAEmaj| (85)
|SAEqfj| (1)
|SAEsab| (7)
|SAEtaj| (1)
|SAF| (7)
|SAFsab| (1)
|SAG| (24)
|SAGmaj| (9)
|SAGqfj| (1)
|SBB| (1)
|SCA| (35)
|SCAmaj| (17)

|SCB| (17)
|SCBmaj| (5)
|SCD| (5)
|SCDmaj| (1)
|SCDpaj| (1)
|SCE| (95)
|SCEmaa| (2)
|SCEmaj| (104)
|SCEmak| (1)
|SCEmdj| (1)
|SCEmfj| (1)
|SCEpaj| (5)
|SCEsab| (2)
|SCEtaa| (2)
|SCF| (3)
|SCFmaj| (1)
|SCG| (10)
|SCGmaj| (8)
|SCGmfj| (1)
|SCGqfa| (1)
|SCGqfj| (2)
|SCGtaj| (1)
|SDA| (2)
|SDAmdj| (2)
|SDB| (6)
|SDBmda| (1)
|SDBmdj| (2)
|SDD| (1)
|SDE| (17)
|SDEmdj| (16)
|SDF| (2)
|SDFmdj| (1)
|SDG| (5)
|SDGmdj| (2)
|SFA| (1)
|SFE| (3)
|SFEmaj| (1)
|SFEmfj| (3)
|SFG| (1)
|SKA| (8)
|SKAmda| (2)
|SKAmdj| (12)
|SKB| (6)
|SKBmdj| (3)
|SKD| (3)
|SKDmdj| (1)
|SKE| (16)
|SKEmda| (1)
|SKEmdj| (31)
|SKG| (1)
|SME| (1)
|SMEmaj| (5)
|SMEqfj| (1)
|SOE| (1)
|SOEloj| (1)
|SOEmdj| (1)
|SXEmdj| (2)
|TAAtfk| (1)
|TABqfj| (1)

|TAD| (14)
|TADmaj| (15)
|TADmfj| (2)
|TADqfj| (1)
|TADtab| (1)
|TADtaf| (2)
|TADtfj| (1)
|TAF| (2)
|TAFpak| (1)
|TCA| (6)
|TCAmaj| (4)
|TCAqfj| (1)
|TCAqfk| (1)
|TCBmaj| (2)
|TCD| (3)
|TCDmaj| (9)
|TCDmfj| (1)
|TCF| (1)
|TCFmaj| (1)
|TDA| (1)
|TDDmdj| (3)
|TDF| (1)
|TFA| (3)
|TFB| (1)
|TFBmaa| (1)
|TFBqfj| (1)
|TFD| (1)
|TFFqfj| (1)
|TKA| (3)
|TKAmda| (2)
|TKDtoj| (1)
|TMAmaj| (2)
|TMAmfj| (1)
|TMB| (1)
|TMD| (2)
|TMDmaj| (1)
|TMFmaj| (2)
|TOA| (1)
|TOBqoa| (1)
|TOE| (1)
|TXA| (1)
|TXBmdj| (1)
|TXF| (1)
|TXFqof| (1)
|edjSKBsdj| (1)

068.3 P general

{R}   weakly retroflex
{r}   weakly retroflex
{t}   flap
{z}   devoiced
{?}   glottal
No Response (173)
<gyin(r)L=14> (1)
<janArL=144> (1)
<je(n)rL=14> (2)
<je(n){?}L=14> (1)
<je[n](r)L=14> (1)
<je[n](r)[L]=14> (1)
<je[n](r)l> (4)

<je[n]R[L]=144> (1)
<je[n]rL=14> (4)
<jeen(r)L=14> (1)
<jeenArL=144> (1)
<jeenRL=144> (1)
<jeenr[L]=14> (1)
<jen(r)L=14> (56)
<jen(r)[L]=14> (2)
<jenArL=144> (62)
<jenAr[L]=144> (6)
<jenA{t}L=144> (1)
<jenIrL=144> (6)
<jenIrL{z}=144> (1)
<jenRL=144> (47)
<jenRLz=144> (1)
<jenR[L]=144> (3)
<jenRl=14> (7)
<jenRu[1]=143> (1)
<jenRul=143> (3)
<jenn(r)L=14> (3)
<jenrL=14> (233)
<jenrLz=14> (4)
<jenrL{z}=14> (1)
<jenr[L]=14> (6)
<jenruel=13> (1)
<jenrul=13> (2)
<jenurL=134> (1)
<jenu{r}l=13> (2)
<jen{R}L=144> (5)
<jen{R}l=14> (10)
<jen{R}lz=14> (2)
<jen{R}rL=144> (1)
<jen{t}L=14> (3)
<ji(n)RL=144> (2)
<ji(n)r[L]=14> (1)
<ji[n]RL=144> (1)
<ji[n]rL=14> (2)
<ji[n]rR=14> (1)
<ji[n]r[L]=14> (1)
<jin(r)L=14> (18)
<jin(r)[L]=14> (2)
<jinArL=144> (38)
<jinArLz=144> (1)
<jinAr[L]=144> (2)
<jinIrL=144> (1)
<jinRL=144> (35)
<jinR[L]=144> (3)
<jinRl=14> (16)
<jinRrL=144> (4)
<jinn(r)L=14> (5)
<jinnRl=14> (1)
<jinn{R}Rl=144> (1)
<jinrL=14> (121)
<jinrL{z}=14> (1)
<jinr[L]=14> (8)
<jinrul=13> (2)
<jinurL=134> (1)
<jin{R}L=144> (2)
<jin{R}l=14> (6)

<jin{t}L=14> (2)
<joonRl=14> (1)
<jun(r)L=14> (1)
<junRl=14> (1)
<junrL=14> (3)
<ju{r}nrL=14> (1)
<zhenIrol=341> (1)
<zhenrL=14> (1)
<zhoonrL=14> (1)

068.4 P colonel
{o}   low-back
{R}   weakly retroflex
{t}   flap
{z}   devoiced
{?}   glottal
No Response (214)
<kaw(r)nL=14> (1)
<kaw[r]nL=14> (1)
<kawr(n)[L]=14> (1)
<kernL=14> (1)
<kirnL=14> (1)
<ko(r)lN=14> (1)
<ko(r)nL=14> (1)
<ko[r]nL=14> (1)
<koo(r)n[L]=14> (1)
<kornL=14> (1)
<ku[r][n]L=14> (1)
<ku[r]n(L)> (1)
<ku[r]nL=14> (136)
<ku[r]nLz=14> (2)
<ku[r]n[L]=14> (9)
<ku[r]nnL=14> (1)
<ku[r]{t}[n]L=14> (2)
<kui(r)nL=14> (1)
<kurnL=14> (404)
<kurnLz=14> (6)
<kurnL{z}=14> (1)
<kurn[L]=14> (31)
<kurn[L]s=14> (1)
<kur{?}L=14> (1)
<kur{t}(n)L=14> (3)
<kur{t}[n]L=14> (2)
<ku{r}nL=14> (95)
<ku{r}nLd=14> (1)
<ku{r}nLz=14> (1)
<ku{r}n[L]=14> (5)
<k{o}(r)nL=14> (1)

068.5 P captain
{?}   glottal
No Response (180)
<kab(t)M=14> (2)
<kap(t)M=14> (85)
<kap(t)N=14> (6)
<kappN=14> (1)
<kappin=13> (1)
<kappun=13> (1)
<kaptIg=14> (1)
<kaptM=14> (1)
<kaptN=14> (615)

<kaptNG=14> (4)
<kaptNs=14> (1)
<kaptNz=14> (5)
<kapt[N]=14> (3)
<kapten=13> (2)
<kaptin=13> (17)
<kapzM=14> (1)
<kap{?}M=14> (3)
<kap{?}N=14> (2)
<kep(t)M=14> (1)
<keptN=14> (39)
<koptN=14> (1)
<kyaptN=14> (13)
<kyeptN=14> (3)
<kyeptNz=14> (1)
<kyoptN=14> (1)

068.6 P judge
{d}   devoiced
{j}   devoiced
{oo}   unrounded
{r}   weakly retroflex
{u}   up/back glide
{ui}   unrounded/upglide
{zh}   devoiced
No Response (115)
<chuch> (1)
<jej> (13)
<je{j}> (1)
<jij> (1)
<ji{j}> (1)
<joj> (1)
<jooj> (4)
<juch> (12)
<jud> (2)
<juij> (5)
<jui{j}> (1)
<juj> (487)
<jujlz=14> (9)
<jurj> (7)
<juzh> (1)
<ju{d}> (1)
<ju{j}> (91)
<ju{r}j> (13)
<ju{r}{j}> (2)
<ju{zh}> (1)
<j{oo}j> (17)
<j{oo}{j}> (5)
<j{ui}d> (2)
<j{ui}j> (24)
<j{ui}{j}> (9)
<j{u}j> (88)
<j{u}{j}> (9)
<{j}uch> (2)
<{j}uj> (3)
<{j}u{j}> (8)
<{j}u{r}{j}> (1)

068.7 L student
No Response (144)
A   cadet (1)

B   co-ed (5)
C   college-bound student (1)
D   college boy (1)
E   college co-ed (1)
F   college kid (1)
G   college pupil (1)
H   college student (26)
I   collegian (1)
J   collegiate (1)
K   day scholar (1)
L   day student (1)
M   grade kid (1)
N   grade-school student (1)
O   graduate student (2)
P   grammar-school student (1)
Q   high-school scholar (3)
R   high-school student (3)
S   kid (1)
T   normal (2)
U   pupil (194)
V   scholar (92)
W   school kid (3)
X   school scholar (2)
Y   school student (1)
Z   schoolboy (9)
aa   schoolchild (19)
ab   schoolgirl (3)
ac   seven-grade scholar (1)
ad   student (679)

068.7 P student

{t}   flap
{z}   devoiced
{?}   glottal
No Response (216)
<stewd[N](t)=14> (1)
<stewd[N]t=14> (1)
<stewdeent=13> (1)
<stewdent=13> (1)
<stewdiNt=134> (1)
<stewdint=13> (2)
<stewdINt=144> (1)
<stewdN(t)s=14> (3)
<stewdN(t)=14> (13)
<stewdNG(t)=14> (1)
<stewdNts=14> (13)
<stewdNt=14> (169)
<stewdN{?}=14> (1)
<stew{t}Nt=14> (2)
<stew{t}unt=13> (1)
<stoedNt=14> (1)
<stoodN(t)=14> (1)
<stuedINts=144> (1)
<stuedINt=144> (2)
<stuedIint=143> (1)
<stuedIstN=144> (1)
<stuedN(t)s=14> (2)
<stuedN(t)=14> (25)
<stuedN(t){z}=14> (1)
<stuedNts=14> (23)

<stuedNt=14> (277)
<stuedN{?}=14> (5)
<stuedN{t}=14> (1)
<stued[N]t=14> (1)
<stuedent=13> (1)
<stuediNts=134> (1)
<stuedin(:)=13> (1)
<stuedint=13> (2)
<stuedunt=13> (2)
<stue{t}N(t)=14> (1)
<stue{t}Nt=14> (8)
<stue{t}[N](t)=14> (1)
<stue{t}unt=13> (1)
<styewdN(t)=14> (1)
<styewdNts=14> (3)
<styewdNt=14> (18)
<styood[N](t)=14> (1)
<styuedents=13> (1)
<styuedi(nt)=13> (1)
<styuedINts=144> (1)
<styuedint=13> (2)
<styuedN(t)=14> (6)
<styuedNts=14> (8)
<styuedNt=14> (99)
<styuejNt=14> (1)
<thewdNt=14> (1)
<thewdN{?}=14> (1)

068.8 P secretary

{ai}   lax onset/upglide
{R}   weakly retroflex
{r}   weakly retroflex
{t}   flap
{z}   devoiced
No Response (162)
<seg(r)ItirI=1434> (1)
<sek(r)AtairI=1434> (4)
<sek(r)AtairIz=1434> (1)
<sek(r)Ate(r)I=1434> (1)
<sek(r)Ate(rI)=143> (1)
<sek(r)Ate[r](I)=143> (2)
<sek(r)Ater(I)=143> (1)
<sek(r)AterI=1424> (1)
<sek(r)AterI=1434> (113)
<sek(r)AterI=3414> (1)
<sek(r)AterIz=1434> (2)
<sek(r)AterI{z}=1434> (1)
<sek(r)Ate{r}(I)=143> (1)
<sek(r)Ate{r}A=1434> (1)
<sek(r)Ate{r}I=1434> (5)
<sek(r)Atu[r]I=1434> (1)
<sek(r)AturI=1434> (6)
<sek(r)AturrI=1434> (1)
<sek(r)Atu{r}(I)=143> (1)
<sek(r)Atu{r}I=1434> (1)
<sek(r)Atu{r}rI=1434> (1)
<sek(r)At{ai}(rI)=143> (1)
<sek(r)Itai(rI)=143> (2)
<sek(r)ItarI=1434> (3)
<sek(r)Ite(r)I=1434> (1)

<sek(r)Ite[r]I=1434> (1)
<sek(r)Itee(rI)=143> (1)
<sek(r)Iter(I)=143> (1)
<sek(r)IterI=1424> (1)
<sek(r)IterI=1434> (118)
<sek(r)IterIz=1434> (2)
<sek(r)Ite{r}I=1434> (2)
<sek(r)Ite{r}ee=1423> (1)
<sek(r)Itu[r]I=1434> (1)
<sek(r)IturI=1434> (8)
<sek(r)Itu{r}(I)=143> (1)
<sek(r)Itu{r}I=1434> (1)
<sek(r)Itu{r}rI=1434> (2)
<sek(r)It{ai}(rI)=143> (3)
<sek(rI)terI=134> (7)
<sekRterI=1434> (11)
<sekrAtairI=1434> (1)
<sekrAter(I)=143> (1)
<sekrAterA=1434> (1)
<sekrAterI=1424> (1)
<sekrAterI=1434> (75)
<sekrAterIz=1434> (2)
<sekrAtirI=1434> (1)
<sekrAturI=1434> (2)
<sekrA{t}erI=1434> (1)
<sekrIta(r)I=1434> (1)
<sekrItarI=1434> (4)
<sekrIte(rI)=143> (1)
<sekrIter(I)=143> (1)
<sekrIterI=1424> (3)
<sekrIterI=1434> (219)
<sekrIterI=3414> (3)
<sekrIterIz=1434> (5)
<sekrIterI{z}=1434> (1)
<sekrIteree=1423> (6)
<sekrIteree=3413> (1)
<sekrIte{r}(I)=143> (3)
<sekrIte{r}I=1434> (10)
<sekrIte{r}I=3414> (1)
<sekrIte{t}I=1434> (1)
<sekrIte{t}I=3414> (1)
<sekrItirI=1434> (1)
<sekrIturI=1434> (20)
<sekrIturIz=1434> (1)
<sekrItu{r}(I)=143> (2)
<sekrItu{r}I=1434> (4)
<sekrItu{r}rI=1434> (12)
<sekrIt{ai}(rI)=143> (1)
<sekrRterIz=1434> (1)
<sekreeterI=3214> (1)
<sekriterI=1324> (2)
<sekr{R}terI=1434> (1)
<sekr{R}tu{r}rI=1434> (1)
<seks(rI)terI=134> (2)
<sekyAterI=1434> (1)
<sekyAteree=1423> (1)
<sekyIt{ai}(rI)z=143> (1)
<sek{R}terI=1424> (2)
<sek{R}terI=1434> (8)

<sek{R}te{r}rI=1434> (1)
<set(r)NterI=1434> (1)
<shek(r)Atai(rI)=143> (1)
<shek(r)AterI=1434> (1)
<sig(r)AtirI=1434> (1)
<sik(r)IterI=1434> (1)
<sik(r)IturI=1434> (1)
<sikrIter(I)=143> (1)
<sikrIteree=1432> (1)
<suk(r)IterIz=1434> (1)
<suk(r)IterI{z}=1434> (1)
<suk(r)IturI=1434> (1)
<sukrAterI=1434> (1)
<sukrIterI=1434> (2)
<sukrIturI=1434> (2)
<sukrIturIz=1434> (1)
<s{ai}g(r)ItairI=1434> (1)
<s{ai}k(r)Ater(I)=143> (1)
<s{ai}k(r)AterI=1434> (15)
<s{ai}k(r)AterIz=1434> (1)
<s{ai}k(r)Ate{r}I=1434> (2)
<s{ai}k(r)At{ai}rI=1434> (1)
<s{ai}kRterI=1434> (1)
<s{ai}krAt(e)rIz=144> (1)
<s{ai}krAterI=1434> (5)
<s{ai}krIterI=1434> (4)
<thek(r)Atee(rI)=143> (1)

069.1 L actress

No Response (289)
A   actor (48)
B   actor lady (1)
C   actor star (1)
D   actress (562)
E   entertainer (2)
F   movie actress (2)
G   movie star (30)
H   moving star (1)
I   performer (1)
J   show actor (1)
K   show woman (2)
L   star (19)
M   star of the movie (1)

069.1 P actress

{a}   upglide
{ai}   lax onset
{R}   weakly retroflex
{t}   flap
{z}   devoiced
No Response (339)
<a(k)trIs=14> (2)
<a(k)tris=13> (2)
<ak(tr)Is=14> (1)
<ak(tr)sI=14> (1)
<akchrIs=14> (1)
<akt(r)A{z}=14> (1)
<akt(r)Is=14> (4)
<aktArAs=144> (1)
<aktRs=14> (11)
<aktrA(s)=14> (1)

<aktrAs=14> (24)
<aktrI(s)=14> (2)
<aktrId{z}=14> (1)
<aktrIs=14> (441)
<aktrIsIz=144> (3)
<aktrIst=14> (1)
<aktree(s)=13> (1)
<aktres=13> (5)
<aktres=31> (6)
<aktrest=13> (1)
<aktris=13> (44)
<aktris=21> (4)
<aktris=31> (2)
<aktrist=13> (1)
<aktr{ai}(s)=13> (1)
<aktshrIs=14> (1)
<akt{R}s=14> (1)
<akt{t}Is=14> (2)
<ak{t}{R}s=14> (1)
<ektrAs=14> (1)
<ektrIs=14> (3)
<ektris=13> (1)
<haktrIs=14> (1)
<{a}ktrIs=14> (3)
<{a}ktres=13> (1)

069.2 P American

{ai}   lax onset
{r}   weakly retroflex
{t}   flap
{z}   devoiced
No Response (166)
<(A)ma[r](I)kN=14> (1)
<(A)marAkN=144> (1)
<(A)marIkN=144> (3)
<(A)me(r)IkN=144> (1)
<(A)me[r](I)kN{z}=14> (1)
<(A)me[r]AkN=144> (1)
<(A)me[r]IkN=144> (1)
<(A)mer(I)kN=14> (1)
<(A)merAkN=144> (13)
<(A)merIkN=144> (55)
<(A)merIkNz=144> (8)
<(A)merIkN{z}=144> (1)
<(A)me{r}(I)kN=14> (1)
<(A)me{r}AkN=144> (2)
<(A)mu[r](I)kN=14> (1)
<(A)mur(I)kN=14> (3)
<(A)murAkN=144> (1)
<(A)murIkN=144> (6)
<(A)mu{r}(I)kN=14> (3)
<(A)mu{r}AkN=144> (1)
<(A)mu{r}IkN=144> (4)
<(A)mu{r}rIkN=144> (1)
<Ama(r)IkN=4144> (1)
<Amai(rI)kN=414> (1)
<Amai[r](I)kN=414> (1)
<AmairIkN=4144> (1)
<Amar(I)kN=414> (2)
<AmarAkN=4144> (5)

<AmarIkN=4144> (8)
<AmarikN=4134> (1)
<Ama{r}(I)kN=414> (1)
<Ama{r}rIkN=4144> (1)
<Ame(r)AkNz=4144> (1)
<Ame(r)IkN=4144> (3)
<Ame[r](I)kN=414> (5)
<Ame[r](I)kNz=414> (1)
<Ame[r]AkN=4144> (1)
<Ame[r]IkN=4144> (4)
<Ame[r]rIkN=4144> (3)
<Amer(I)kN=414> (8)
<Amer(I)kN{z}=414> (2)
<AmerAkN=4144> (64)
<AmerAkNz=4144> (4)
<AmerAkN{z}=4144> (3)
<AmerAkun=4143> (1)
<AmerAkurn{z}=4143> (1)
<AmerIkN=4144> (328)
<AmerIkNz=4144> (26)
<AmerIkN{z}=4144> (7)
<AmerIk[N]=4144> (3)
<AmerikN=4134> (42)
<AmerikN{z}=4134> (1)
<Ame{r}(I)kN=414> (9)
<Ame{r}AkN=4144> (1)
<Ame{r}IkN=4144> (8)
<Ame{t}IkN=4144> (1)
<Ame{t}IkNz=4144> (1)
<AmirAkN=4144> (1)
<AmirIkN=4144> (4)
<AmirikN=4134> (1)
<Amu[r](I)kN=414> (1)
<Amu[r]IkN=4144> (1)
<Amu[r]rIkN=4144> (2)
<Amur(I)kN=414> (2)
<AmurAkN=4144> (1)
<AmurIgN=4144> (1)
<AmurIkN=4144> (38)
<AmurIkNz=4144> (3)
<AmurIkN{z}=4144> (1)
<AmurIk[N]z=4144> (1)
<AmurikN=4134> (7)
<Amu{r}(I)kN=414> (2)
<Amu{r}IkN=4144> (4)
<Amu{r}Ik{R}(n)=4144> (1)
<Amu{r}rAkN=4144> (1)
<Amu{r}rIkN=4144> (6)
<Am{ai}(rI)kN=414> (2)
<Am{ai}rAkN=4144> (3)
<ImarIkN=4144> (1)
<ImerAkN=4144> (1)
<ImerIkN=4144> (2)
<Imu[r](I)kN=414> (1)
<ImurIkN=4144> (3)
<Imu{r}(I)kN=414> (1)
<Imu{r}IkN=4144> (1)
<Imu{r}rIkN=4144> (2)
<MerIkN=4144> (1)

<MmurIkN=4144> (1)
<MurIkN=4144> (2)
<aime{r}IkN=3144> (1)
<amerIkN=3144> (1)
<amerIkN{z}=3144> (1)
<hAmerIkN=4144> (1)
<omerAkN=3144> (1)
<omurIkN=3144> (2)
<omu{r}rIkN=3144> (1)
<ume[r](I)kN=314> (1)
<umerAkN=3144> (2)
<umerIkN=3144> (1)
<umurIkN=3144> (2)
<umu{r}(I)kN=314> (1)
<umu{r}rIkN=3144> (3)

069.3 L Negro

No Response (30)
A   ace of spades (1)
B   African (29)
C   Afro (3)
D   Afro-American (17)
E   Afro-American engineer (1)
F   alligator bait (1)
G   (alli)gator bait (4)
H   American Indian (1)
I   ape (3)
J   Aunt (8)
K   Auntie (4)
L   auntie (2)
M   bad nigger (1)
N   big black buck nigger (1)
O   big fat nigger (1)
P   big nigger (3)
Q   bigeye nigger (1)
R   black (350)
S   black African (2)
T   black American (3)
U   black ape (4)
V   black-ass so-and-so (1)
W   black bastard (4)
X   black bitch (2)
Y   black boy (12)
Z   black children (1)
aa   black coon (2)
ab   black crow (1)
ac   black dude (1)
ad   black folk(s) (16)
ae   black girl (3)
af   black guy (1)
ag   black heel (1)
ah   black kid (1)
ai   black lady (3)
aj   black mammy (3)
ak   black man (48)
al   black MF (1)
am   black Negro (1)
an   black nigger (14)
ao   black person/people (120)
ap   black polecat (1)

aq   black race (21)
ar   black rascal (2)
as   black so-and-so (1)
at   black son of a bitch (7)
au   black spook (1)
av   black thing (4)
aw   black trash (3)
ax   black woman (11)
ay   blackbird (3)
az   blackie(s) (3)
ba   blacks (3)
bb   blood (1)
bc   blue (1)
bd   blue(-)gum(s) (3)
be   blue-gum nigger (3)
bf   boll weevil (1)
bg   bone (1)
bh   bonehead (1)
bi   booger (1)
bj   boogies (1)
bk   boot (1)
bl   Bosco bunny (1)
bm   Boy (2)
bn   boy (12)
bo   bro (1)
bp   brother (2)
bq   brown-skin nigger (1)
br   brown-skin people (1)
bs   buck nigger (4)
bt   bucks (2)
bu   buckwheat nigger (1)
bv   bugaboo (1)
bw   bunnies (1)
bx   burr head (13)
by   burrheaded colored people (1)
bz   burrheaded son[N-i] of a bitches (1)
ca   buzzard (2)
cb   carrion crow (1)
cc   chocolate (1)
cd   chocolate drop (1)
ce   chocolate motherfucker (1)
cf   coal-black nigger wench (1)
cg   color folk(s) (3)
ch   color people(s) (4)
ci   colored(s) (247)
cj   colored boy (19)
ck   colored dude (1)
cl   colored fellow (14)
cm   colored folk(s) (55)
cn   colored gal (1)
co   colored girl (10)
cp   colored guy (3)
cq   colored kids (1)
cr   colored lady (7)
cs   colored mammy (1)
ct   colored man (59)
cu   colored nigger (1)
cv   colored person/people (261)

cw   colored race (6)
cx   colored trash (1)
cy   colored woman (25)
cz   Congo cookie (1)
da   coon (69)
db   cotton-picking nigger (1)
dc   country colored (1)
dd   country nigger (1)
de   cracker (1)
df   crow (1)
dg   damn nigger (6)
dh   damn shit-assy nigger (1)
di   dang nigger (1)
dj   dark (2)
dk   dark folks (1)
dl   dark person (1)
dm   darky (79)
dn   descendant of Ham (1)
do   devil (1)
dp   dimbo (1)
dq   dirty nigger (1)
dr   donkey (1)
ds   dragger (1)
dt   dusky (1)
du   E-Eighty (1)
dv   East Texas nigger (1)
dw   Englishman (1)
dx   Ethiopia (1)
dy   Ethiopian (3)
dz   Ethiopian race (1)
ea   ex-slaves (1)
eb   free man/person of color (2)
ec   Geechee (4)
ed   Geech(ee) nigger (1)
ee   gentlemen of color (1)
ef   gig (1)
eg   girl (1)
eh   gingersnap (1)
ei   good black people (1)
ej   good nigger (5)
ek   good-old darky (1)
el   granny (1)
em   Ham's children (1)
en   head (1)
eo   immigrant (1)
ep   jig (9)
eq   jigaboo (16)
er   Jim Crow (2)
es   jive-ass nigger (1)
et   jungle bunny (18)
eu   kinky head (1)
ev   ladies of color (1)
ew   lint head (1)
ex   little black girl (1)
ey   Little Black Sambo (1)
ez   little colored boy (2)
fa   little nigger (4)
fb   low-down good-for-nothing nigger (1)

fc   low-down nigger (2)
fd   low-down no-good nigger (1)
fe   Mammy (1)
ff   mammy (1)
fg   man of color (1)
fh   mean nigger (1)
fi   melon eater (1)
fj   Mobile nigger (1)
fk   monkey (2)
fl   natives (2)
fm   Neger [G] (1)
fn   Negress (1)
fo   negrette (1)
fp   Neg(ro) (1)
fq   Neg(roes) (1)
fr   Negro (632)
fs   negro [S] (1)
ft   Negro boy (1)
fu   Negro girl (1)
fv   Negro mammy (1)
fw   Negro man (5)
fx   Negro people (2)
fy   Negro race (9)
fz   Negro woman (9)
ga   Negroid(s) (4)
gb   Negroid race (3)
gc   Nelda (1)
gd   nig (4)
ge   nigaroo (1)
gf   nigger (667)
gg   nigger boy (12)
gh   nigger cracker (1)
gi   nigger girl (3)
gj   nigger kids (1)
gk   nigger mammy (1)
gl   nigger man (8)
gm   nigger people (2)
gn   nigger race (4)
go   nigger slave (2)
gp   nigger straight out (1)
gq   nigger woman (27)
gr   niggeress (1)
gs   night fighter (1)
gt   nigritos [S] (1)
gu   nits (1)
gv   nivada (1)
gw   no-(ac)count nigger (3)
gx   no-good (1)
gy   Northern nigger (1)
gz   Number Two [military] (1)
ha   old black boy (1)
hb   old black lady (1)
hc   old colored darky (1)
hd   old colored fellow (1)
he   old colored lady (1)
hf   old colored man (2)
hg   old colored woman (3)
hh   old coon (1)
hi   old cornfield niggers (1)

hj   old darky (8)
hk   old Geechee (1)
hl   old nigger (16)
hm   old nigger woman (7)
hn   old slave nigger woman (1)
ho   old slavery nigger (1)
hp   Old Uncle (1)
hq   old woolly-head nigger (1)
hr   Oreos (4)
hs   pickaninny (8)
ht   plain nigger (2)
hu   polecat (1)
hv   poor black trash (1)
hw   poor blacks (1)
hx   poor colored (1)
hy   poor colored folks (1)
hz   poor Negro (1)
ia   Preacher (1)
ib   pure nigger (1)
ic   rascal (1)
id   raspberry colored folks (1)
ie   Red Bone (4)
if   rogue (1)
ig   saltwater Geech(ee) (1)
ih   Sambo (4)
ii   Schwartze [G] (1)
ij   scoundrel (1)
ik   shine (3)
il   shoeshine boy (1)
im   Schwartzer [G] (1)
in   slaveries (1)
io   slaves (3)
ip   smokies (1)
iq   smutty buddy (1)
ir   son of a bitch (1)
is   sooboo (1)
it   sorry nigger (6)
iu   soul brother (1)
iv   Southern nigger (1)
iw   spade (32)
ix   spliv (1)
iy   spear carrier (1)
iz   spear thrower (1)
ja   spook (11)
jb   stupid nigger (1)
jc   sunburn American (1)
jd   Swahilis (1)
je   swamp nigger (2)
jf   tadpole (2)
jg   tar baby (1)
jh   Tom, a (1)
ji   trifling nigger (1)
jj   Two (1)
jk   Uncle (19)
jl   Uncle Joe (1)
jm   Uncle Tom (6)
jn   uncles (1)
jo   uppity nigger (1)
jp   walking, talking Tootsie Roll (1)

jq   weird-ass nigger (1)
jr   white man's nigger (1)
js   woollies (1)
jt   woolly heads (1)
ju   yard ape (2)

069.3 P Negro
{ai}   lax onset
{t}   flap
{z}   devoiced
No Response (308)
<naigroez=13> (2)
<neeg(r)oe=13> (1)
<neeg(roe)> (1)
<neegrA=14> (19)
<neegrAs=14> (1)
<neegrAz=14> (17)
<neegrA{z}=14> (1)
<neegroe=13> (157)
<neegroe=31> (2)
<neegroedh=13> (1)
<neegroes=13> (1)
<neegroez=13> (50)
<neegroe{z}=13> (3)
<neeg{t}oe=13> (3)
<negrA=14> (1)
<negroe=13> (1)
<neg{t}oe=13> (1)
<niAgroe=143> (1)
<nig(r)oez=13> (1)
<nigAroe=341> (1)
<nigAroez=143> (1)
<niggroe=31> (1)
<nigrA=14> (100)
<nigrAz=14> (59)
<nigrAzh=14> (1)
<nigrA{z}=14> (3)
<nigrI=14> (2)
<nigrIz=14> (1)
<nigroe=13> (165)
<nigroe=31> (1)
<nigroedh=13> (1)
<nigroez=13> (56)
<nigroe{z}=13> (2)
<nigroz=13> (1)
<nig{t}oe=13> (1)
<nyeegroe=13> (1)
<n{ai}grA=14> (1)

069.4 L Caucasian
No Response (151)
A   American (3)
B   American-born man (1)
C   Anglo-American (1)
D   Anglo-Saxon (10)
E   Anglo-Sax(on) (1)
F   Anglo-Saxon race (2)
G   Anglos (21)
H   aristocrat (1)
I   Aryan (2)
J   barbarian (1)

K   bleached white (1)
L   buck (1)
M   buckra (2)
N   Caucasian (169)
O   Caucasian race (3)
P   Caucasoid (1)
Q   common white people (1)
R   cracker (43)
S   cracker honky (1)
T   cracker neck (1)
U   crackerjack (1)
V   delta red (1)
W   devil (2)
X   dirty white (1)
Y   Dixie (1)
Z   English-American people (1)
aa Gentiles (2)
ab Georgia Cracker (5)
ac good-old white man (1)
ad gringo/gringa [S] (11)
ae hick (1)
af high rent (1)
ag hillbilly (12)
ah hokies (1)
ai honky (99)
aj hoosier (7)
ak hootchy (1)
al hunky (3)
am Jim Crow (1)
an lazy cracker (1)
ao little-old white boy (1)
ap longneck (1)
aq low-down (1)
ar Man, the (2)
as Mongolian (1)
at motherfucker (1)
au mothers (1)
av nasty-ass red-neck (1)
aw nasty cracker (1)
ax nigger (1)
ay nutcracker (1)
az ofay (5)
ba old cracker (1)
bb old hunky (1)
bc old hoosier (1)
bd old red-neck (1)
be old red peckerwood (1)
bf old scamp (1)
bg old white fellow (1)
bh ordinary people (1)
bi ornery sapsucker (1)
bj Paddies (1)
bk paleface (5)
bl peck (10)
bm pecker (1)
bn peckerwood (56)
bo pig (1)
bp poor cracker (1)
bq poor white cracker (1)

br poor white folks (1)
bs potato head (1)
bt pure white person (1)
bu quacker (1)
bv racist (1)
bw red (1)
bx red-neck (46)
by red-neck cracker (1)
bz red-neck white folk (1)
ca red pecker (1)
cb redhead peckerwood (1)
cc resin chewer (1)
cd sager (1)
ce saltine (1)
cf sandhill red-neck (1)
cg snowball (1)
ch soda cracker (4)
ci stone cracker (1)
cj straight-out honky (1)
ck stringneck (1)
cl stupid cracker (1)
cm Supreme Being, the (1)
cn surf eaters (1)
co swine (1)
cp tallow face (1)
cq ugly-ass cracker (1)
cr unsleek bull (1)
cs WASP (1)
ct white [adj.] (401)
cu white bastard (1)
cv white boy (15)
cw white cracker (3)
cx white folk(s) (74)
cy white hoosier (1)
cz white man (82)
da white MF (1)
db white ones (2)
dc white peck (1)
dd white person/people (218)
de white population (1)
df white race (43)
dg white son-of-a-bitch (1)
dh white trash (4)
di Whitecap (1)
dj whiteface (1)
dk whites (85)
dl Whitey (41)
dm Yankee (2)
dn yaps (3)
do yellow woman (1)
dp yellowbelly (1)

069.5 L mulatto

No Response (411)
A   (a)dulterated up (1)
B   Afro-Cuban white (1)
C   alabaster (1)
D   albino (10)
E   bastard (9)
F   bastard nigger (1)

G   biracial (4)
H   black (1)
I   blond niggers (1)
J   blue-eyed nigger (1)
K   breed (1)
L   bright [adj.] (18)
M   bright [n.] (1)
N   bright girl (1)
O   bright man (1)
P   bright people (1)
Q   bright-skinned (1)
R   brighter (1)
S   brown (2)
T   brown baby (1)
U   brown skin (1)
V   brown-skin nigger (1)
W   cafe au lait [F] (1)
X   Cajun (12)
Y   Cajun folks (1)
Z   Cajun people (1)
aa chinch (1)
ab chocolates (1)
ac colored (2)
ad coon (3)
ae coonass (5)
af coony (4)
ag cream in the coffee (1)
ah Creole (27)
ai Creole man (1)
aj Creole people (2)
ak cross (2)
al crossbreed (13)
am crossed between (two races) (1)
an cuarteron [S] (1)
ao dead nigger in the woodpile (1)
ap duke's mixture (1)
aq ethnic, a (1)
ar fay (1)
as free jack (11)
at French (1)
au French Creole (1)
av Frenchman (2)
aw Geech(ee) nigger (1)
ax generation gap, a (1)
ay ginger cake (2)
az ginger-cake color (3)
ba ginger-cake nigger (1)
bb got nigger blood (1)
bc griffe [F] (2)
bd gypsy (1)
be half (1)
bf half-and-half (7)
bg half black (3)
bh half black and half white (1)
bi half-black kid (1)
bj half-breed (89)
bk half colored and half white (1)
bl half nigger [adj.] (2)
bm half nigger [n.] (3)

bn half nigger and half white (2)
bo half nigger [J-0] half white (1)
bp half white (16)
bq half white and half nigger (1)
br half white [J-0] half black (1)
bs half-white child (2)
bt half-white Negro (1)
bu half-white nigger (2)
bv half-yellow so-and-so (1)
bw (her)maphrodite (1)
bx high brown (3)
by high yellow (64)
bz high-yellow girl (1)
ca illegitimate child (1)
cb integrated (1)
cc interbreed (1)
cd intermarriage (1)
ce interrace[N-i] (1)
cf interracial (2)
cg kind of yellow (1)
ch kind of yellow-like skin (1)
ci light (2)
cj light-colored (1)
ck light-colored Negro (1)
cl light nigger (1)
cm light-skin darky (1)
cn light-skinned (1)
co light-skinned Negro (1)
cp Louisiana Cajun (1)
cq malabaster (1)
cr Maroon (1)
cs mellow yellow (1)
ct Melungeons (2)
cu mix, a (4)
cv mix-blooded (4)
cw mix breed (44)
cx mix-breeded (1)
cy mix child/children (3)
cz mix colored (1)
da mix colors (1)
db mix folks (1)
dc mix man (1)
dd mix-marriage baby (1)
de mix people (1)
df mix race (8)
dg mixblood (7)
dh mixed [adj.] (37)
di mixed [n.] (3)
dj mixed blood (8)
dk mixed-blooded (1)
dl mixed breed (24)
dm mixed child (1)
dn mixed nigger (1)
do mixed race (6)
dp mixed tumor (1)
dq mixed-up child (2)
dr mixed-up people (1)
ds mixed-up race (3)
dt mixture (3)

du Mongol (1)
dv mongrel (1)
dw mulateral (1)
dx mulato [S] (1)
dy mulatre, le [F] (3)
dz (mu)latto (2)
ea mulatto (233)
eb mulatto folks (1)
ec mulatto man (1)
ed mulatto Negro (1)
ee mulatto nigger (6)
ef mulatto race (1)
eg mulatto woman (1)
eh mulattress (1)
ei mule (1)
ej Negro (3)
ek nigger (4)
el nigger in the woodpile (4)
em no nation (1)
en octoroon (28)
eo of mixed blood (1)
ep old red nigger (1)
eq Oreo (1)
er paper-sack brown (1)
es partly colored, partly Negro (1)
et passovers (1)
eu pure half-breed (1)
ev quadroon (21)
ew quarter black (1)
ex quarter breeds (2)
ey quarteroon (1)
ez real bright (2)
fa Red Bone (4)
fb Scuffletoni(an) (1)
fc stray one (1)
fd three-quarter breeds (1)
fe white (1)
ff white nigger (5)
fg white-skinned (1)
fh woods colt (1)
fi wrong cat on that line (1)
fj yellow [adj.] (6)
fk yellow [n.] (3)
fl yellow mulatto (1)
fm yellow Negro (3)
fn yellow nigger (12)
fo yellow person (3)
fp yellow race (1)
fq yellowish (1)
fr zebra (2)

069.6 L employer

No Response (457)
A Big Boss (1)
B big boss (1)
C Big Master (1)
D big shot (1)
E Boss (23)
F boss (245)
G Boss Man (3)

H boss man (80)
I Cap (18)
J Captain (25)
K captain (43)
L Chief (1)
M chief (5)
N dona [S] (1)
O employer (21)
P foreman (8)
Q general (1)
R general boss (1)
S gov (1)
T Governor (1)
U Grandpa (1)
V headman (1)
W horse master (1)
X jefe [S] (1)
Y judge (1)
Z king bee (1)
aa kingpin (1)
ab Little Boss (1)
ac little boss (1)
ad Little Master (1)
ae main boss (1)
af Major (2)
ag Man, the (5)
ah Marse (5)
ai marse (7)
aj Massa (6)
ak massa (11)
al Master (7)
am master (98)
an mill boss (1)
ao Miss (7)
ap Missy (1)
aq missy (1)
ar Mist(er) (1)
as Mister (130)
at Mister Boss (3)
au Mistress (1)
av mistress (3)
aw Mrs. (4)
ax old boss (4)
ay old man (1)
az old marse (2)
ba old massa (2)
bb Old Master (2)
bc old master (11)
bd Old Miss (1)
be old miss (4)
bf old mistress (1)
bg overseer (6)
bh patron [F] (1)
bi patron [S] (3)
bj plantation owner (1)
bk road foreman (1)
bl sir (10)
bm straw boss (2)
bn superior officer (1)

bo sup(ervisor) (1)
bp supervisor (4)
bq young captain (1)
br young master (1)

069.7 L poor whites [white usage]

No Response (323)
A bastard (1)
B boll weevil (1)
C bones (1)
D bums (24)
E chufa bellies (1)
F common (2)
G common people (3)
H common trash (2)
I common white trash (1)
J commoner (1)
K Conchs (1)
L country crackers (2)
M country hicks (1)
N country sager (1)
O country trash (1)
P cracker neck (1)
Q crackerjacks (2)
R crackers (20)
S dagos (1)
T damn lazy white folks (1)
U deadbeats (6)
V didn't have no get-up-and-get-it (1)
W dirt (1)
X dirty people (1)
Y do-nothing (1)
Z drifters (1)
aa drone (1)
ab drunkard (2)
ac drunks (1)
ad dullard (1)
ae dumb bunnies (1)
af Florida Crackers (2)
ag Georgia Crackers (16)
ah good-for-nothing (14)
ai good-for-nothing and don't care (1)
aj good-for-nothings (2)
ak hard-luck folks (1)
al hicks (2)
am hillbillies (4)
an hippies (3)
ao hoboes (2)
ap hoodlums (1)
aq hoosier (5)
ar ignorant (2)
as illiterates (4)
at indigent (1)
au kicker (1)
av kind of trashy people (1)
aw lazy (46)
ax lazy as a nigger (1)
ay lazy bastards (1)

az lazy bum (1)
ba lazy folks (2)
bb lazy good-for-nothing bums (1)
bc lazy good-for-nothing person (1)
bd lazy hammer knocker (1)
be lazy loafer (1)
bf lazy, low-down white trash (1)
bg lazy no-good thing (1)
bh lazy man (1)
bi lazy people (10)
bj lazy white folks (1)
bk lazybones (1)
bl little-old dirt-land farmers (1)
bm loafers (7)
bn longneck (1)
bo low class (2)
bp low class of people (2)
bq low-class people (2)
br low-class trash (1)
bs low-class white man (1)
bt low-class whites (1)
bu low-down (6)
bv low-down class of people (1)
bw low-down folks (1)
bx low-down people (2)
by low-down, sorry white folks (1)
bz low-down trash (1)
ca low-down white trash (1)
cb low-grade white people (1)
cc low-life (1)
cd lower class (3)
ce lower-class people (2)
cf lower-class white people (1)
cg lower whites (1)
ch Mississippi Cracker (1)
ci nasty and slouchy (1)
cj nasty low class (1)
ck ne'er-do-wells (2)
cl neglector, a (1)
cm no-(ac)count (15)
cn no-(ac)count bastard (1)
co no (ac)count for anything (1)
cp no-(ac)count people (2)
cq no-(ac)counters (1)
cr no-(ac)counts (1)
cs no-account (6)
ct no better than a nigger (2)
cu no-good (25)
cv no-good for nothing (3)
cw no-good people (3)
cx no-good residents (1)
cy no-good trash (1)
cz no-good white (1)
da no-worm peckerwoods (1)
db not much good (1)
dc old common trash (2)
dd old sorry nothing (1)
de old sorry white folks (1)
df old trash (1)

dg old trashy something (1)
dh old white cracker (1)
di ornery (3)
dj other-side-of-the-street people (1)
dk paupers (5)
dl peckerwood farmers (1)
dm peckerwoods (19)
dn pickings (1)
do piney woods (1)
dp poor (10)
dq poor class of people (2)
dr poor crackers (3)
ds poor devils (1)
dt poor dunks (1)
du poor folks (9)
dv poor people (22)
dw poor trash (11)
dx poor trashy people (2)
dy poor white people (11)
dz poor white trash (120)
ea poor whites (30)
eb pure sorry (1)
ec pure trash (3)
ed pure white trash (1)
ee PWTs [=poor white trash] (1)
ef rascals (1)
eg real backward (1)
eh real poor (2)
ei real sorry people (1)
ej real sorry, trashy white people (1)
ek red-neck hippie (1)
el red-necks (36)
em red-necky (1)
en regular hoosier (1)
eo regular peckerwood (1)
ep riffraff (1)
eq sans le prix [F] (1)
er scalawag (1)
es scum (3)
et scum of the earth (1)
eu sharecrop (1)
ev sharecroppers (3)
ew shiftless (9)
ex shiftless people (2)
ey shit kicker (2)
ez shysters (1)
fa slouch (2)
fb sluggish (1)
fc slum people (1)
fd so sorry (1)
fe sorriest (1)
ff sorriness (1)
fg sorry (22)
fh sorry as old chicken fertilizer (1)
fi sorry class of people (2)
fj sorry class of white people (1)
fk sorry fellow (2)
fl sorry folks (1)

fm   sorry man (1)
fn   sorry no-(ac)count (1)
fo   sorry peckerwood (1)
fp   sorry people (11)
fq   sorry son[N-i] of bitches (1)
fr   sorry trash (1)
fs   sorry-type folks (1)
ft   sorry white folks (2)
fu   sorry white man (1)
fv   sorry white person (1)
fw   sorry white trash (3)
fx   stringneck (1)
fy   Tobacco Road (1)
fz   too sorry to work (1)
ga   tramps (10)
gb   trash (88)
gc   trash of the country (1)
gd   trash of the world (1)
ge   trashy (11)
gf   trashy people (13)
gg   trashy white folks (1)
gh   trashy whites (1)
gi   trifle (2)
gj   trifling (14)
gk   trifling as a nigger (1)
gl   trifling good-for-nothing scoundrel
      (1)
gm   trifling people (3)
gn   underprivilege (1)
go   underprivileged (1)
gp   vagabonds (1)
gq   vagrants (1)
gr   wayfar(er) (1)
gs   welfare recipients (1)
gt   welfarers (1)
gu   white cracker (1)
gv   white niggers (1)
gw   white poor people (1)
gx   white trash (162)
gy   wino (1)
gz   woodpecker (1)
ha   woolhatter (1)
hb   worthless (3)
hc   worthless white man (1)
hd   wouldn't hit a lick at a snake
      (1)

069.8 L poor whites [black usage]

No Response (623)
A   buckra (2)
B   buckra folks (1)
C   bunch of bums (1)
D   cheap (1)
E   coon neck (1)
F   country hick (1)
G   country people (1)
H   cracker (35)
I   dirty cracker (1)
J   dirty poor white person (1)
K   dirty white folks (1)

L   hick (3)
M   hillbilly (3)
N   honky (9)
O   hoodgy (1)
P   hoodlum (2)
Q   hoosier (3)
R   last class (1)
S   lazy (6)
T   lazy good-for-nothing (1)
U   lazy peckerwood (1)
V   lazy people (1)
W   low class (3)
X   low-class people (1)
Y   low-down person (1)
Z   low-down white folks (1)
aa   low-grade white folks (1)
ab   low grades (1)
ac   mean peckerwood (1)
ad   mean white person (1)
ae   misfit (1)
af   no-(ac)count people (1)
ag   no-(ac)count white folks (1)
ah   no-good folks (1)
ai   old cracker (1)
aj   old honky (1)
ak   old peckerwood (1)
al   old white pecker (1)
am   old white trash (2)
an   old Whitey (1)
ao   peck (3)
ap   pecker(3)
aq   peckerwood (41)
ar   pitiful (1)
as   poor (5)
at   poor buckra (1)
au   poor class (of people) (3)
av   poor-class white people (1)
aw   poor cracker (4)
ax   poor fellow (1)
ay   poor honky (1)
az   poor hoosier (3)
ba   poor man (1)
bb   poor peck (4)
bc   poor pecker (1)
bd   poor peckerwood (1)
be   poor people (5)
bf   poor trash (14)
bg   poor white (14)
bh   poor white cracker (1)
bi   poor white folks (7)
bj   poor white man (3)
bk   poor white people (11)
bl   poor white trash (59)
bm   puds (1)
bn   razorback (1)
bo   red-neck (29)
bp   red-neck cracker (1)
bq   resin chawer (1)
br   resin chewer (1)

bs   rogue (2)
bt   roughneck (1)
bu   sager (3)
bv   sapsucker (1)
bw   shiftless (1)
bx   shit kicker (1)
by   slummy person (1)
bz   sorry (5)
ca   sorry class of white peoples (1)
cb   sorry no-good (1)
cc   sorry trash (1)
cd   sorry white (1)
ce   sorry white trash (1)
cf   Southern cracker (1)
cg   trash (32)
ch   trashy (1)
ci   trashy no-good, a (1)
cj   trashy person/people (3)
ck   trashy white folks (1)
cl   trifling (3)
cm   underprivilege white (1)
cn   white cracker (1)
co   white folks (1)
cp   white motherfuckers (1)
cq   white trash (71)
cr   Whitey (5)
cs   woodpecker (1)
ct   yellow (1)
cu   yellowbelly (1)
cv   yokel (1)

069.9 L rustic

No Response (175)
A   alligator catcher (1)
B   Arkansas Hoosier (1)
C   back in the sticks (1)
D   back-in-the-woods folks (1)
E   backcountry folks (1)
F   backcountry man (1)
G   backcountry nigger (1)
H   backheels (1)
I   backward (2)
J   backward folks (1)
K   backwards (1)
L   backwood countryman (1)
M   backwood cracker (1)
N   backwood folks (1)
O   backwood hoosier (2)
P   backwood people (1)
Q   backwoods (9)
R   backwoods cracker (4)
S   backwoods hick (1)
T   backwoods hoosier (1)
U   backwoods people (1)
V   backwoodser (2)
W   backwoodsman (18)
X   backwoodsy (5)
Y   bayou red-neck (1)
Z   billy (1)
aa   bon rien [F] (1)

gw piney-woods peckerwood (1)
gx piney-woods rooter (2)
gy plain-old country person (1)
gz plowboy (1)
ha Podunk (1)
hb podunk (1)
hc poor codger (1)
hd poor countryman (1)
he poor cracker (1)
hf poor dunk (1)
hg quasi-hillbilly (1)
hh rascal (3)
hi razorback (1)
hj recluse (2)
hk Red Bone (3)
hl red-hill people (1)
hm red-neck (79)
hn regular mountain hoosier (1)
ho regular peckerwood (1)
hp resin chawer (1)
hq resin chewer (1)
hr Resinite (1)
hs ridge runner (7)
ht right out of the corn patch (1)
hu river boomer (1)
hv river rat (9)
hw riverman (2)
hx road runner (1)
hy rogue (1)
hz roughneck (4)
ia rube (5)
ib ruffian (1)
ic rural dweller (1)
id rural person (4)
ie rustic (2)
if sager (1)
ig sandhill red-neck (1)
ih sauvage [F] (1)
ii scalawag (1)
ij seed (1)
ik shinny maker (1)
il snuff chewer (1)
im sodbuster (2)
in sourbone (1)
io Southern cracker (1)
ip Southern Frenchmen (1)
iq Southern hick (1)
ir squatter (1)
is stranger (1)
it stump jumper (4)
iu sucker (1)
iv swamp angel (1)
iw swamp nigger (2)
ix swamp rat (3)
iy swamp stomper (1)
iz sweet-gum smacker (1)
ja tarheel (1)
jb Tennessee hillbilly (1)
jc tickite (1)

jd tobacco chewer (1)
je tramp (9)
jf uncivilize (1)
jg valley pud (1)
jh webfeet (1)
ji webs between the toes (1)
jj wetback (1)
jk white hick (1)
jl wild people (1)
jm wood rat (1)
jn woodpecker (2)
jo Yahoo (3)
jp yokel (3)
jq yokes (1)

070.1 G almost (midnight)
No Response (304)
A   (a)bout (16)
B   (a)bout near (1)
C   approaching (2)
D   (al)most (374)
E   (a)long about (1)
F   anytime nearabout (1)
G   (a)round (3)
H   (a)round (a)bout (2)
I   close (to) (43)
J   coming on (1)
K   damn near (1)
L   damn nigh (2)
M   darn near (1)
N   getting (around) close (to) (13)
O   getting near (3)
P   getting on to (1)
Q   getting to be (1)
R   getting [P-0] (1)
S   going on (3)
T   just (a)bout (26)
U   just before (3)
V   little before, a (1)
W   might near (24)
X   might nearly (1)
Y   might nigh to (1)
Z   mighty close to (1)
aa mighty near (4)
ab near (44)
ac nearabout (35)
ad nearabout about (1)
ae nearer (1)
af nearing (2)
ag nearly (141)
ah nearly (a)bout (2)
ai nigh (1)
aj nigh onto (3)
ak not quite (2)
al onto (1)
am plague nigh (1)
an practically (6)
ao pretty close (to) (8)
ap pret(ty) near (31)
aq pretty nearly (1)

ar pret(ty) nigh (1)
as right close (2)
at right near (1)
au right nigh (1)
av soon (to) be (3)
aw soon will be (2)
ax very near (2)
ay very nearly (1)
az well near (1)
ba well nigh (1)

070.2 G almost (fell)
No Response (277)
A   (a)bout (3)
B   about to [X-0] (1)
C   (al)most (324)
D   almost like to (1)
E   damn near (1)
F   damn nigh (1)
G   dang near (1)
H   darn nigh (1)
I   just (a)bout (8)
J   like to (261)
K   like to have (80)
L   like to [X-0] (9)
M   like to've/(ha)ve (7)
N   liked (1)
O   liken to [X-0] (1)
P   might near (22)
Q   might nearly (1)
R   might nigh (4)
S   mighty near (1)
T   nearabout (18)
U   nearly (79)
V   nearly (a)bout (2)
W   practically (1)
X   pret(ty) near (7)
Y   pret(ty) nearly (2)
Z   very near (1)

070.3 P just
{d} palatal
{i} central
{oo} central
{?} glottal
No Response (334)
<(j){i}s(t)> (1)
<(j){i}sht> (1)
<chust> (1)
<des(t)> (2)
<dest> (1)
<dhis(t)> (1)
<dis(t)> (7)
<disht> (1)
<dist> (5)
<doos(t)> (1)
<dus(t)> (2)
<dust> (4)
<dzus(t)> (1)
<dz{i}s(t)> (1)
<dz{i}st> (1)

<d{i}s(t)> (12)
<d{i}st> (2)
<jes(t)> (19)
<jesh(t)> (1)
<jesht> (2)
<jest> (29)
<jetht> (1)
<jez(t)> (1)
<jis(t)> (26)
<jist> (47)
<jith(t)> (1)
<joost> (9)
<jost> (2)
<jus(t)> (66)
<just> (245)
<j{i}s(t)> (117)
<j{i}sh(t)> (2)
<j{i}sht> (1)
<j{i}st> (113)
<j{oo}s(t)> (3)
<j{oo}st> (23)
<yus(t)> (1)
<yust> (1)
<y{i}s(t)> (1)
<zush(t)> (1)
<{?}dist> (1)
<{d}esh> (1)
<{d}esh(t)> (1)
<{d}est> (2)
<{d}isht> (1)
<{d}ist> (1)
<{d}ust> (1)
<{d}{i}s(t)> (1)

070.4 P far
{aw}   lower low-back
{f}   bilabial
{o}   lower low-back
{r}   weakly retroflex
No Response (214)
<f(o)r> (1)
<faw(r)> (2)
<faw[r]> (3)
<fawr> (13)
<faw{r}> (4)
<fo(r)> (21)
<fo[r]> (29)
<foe(r)> (2)
<foer> (2)
<for> (230)
<fo{r}> (42)
<fu[r]> (49)
<fur> (87)
<fu{r}> (25)
<fwawr> (1)
<f{aw}(r)> (13)
<f{aw}[r]> (20)
<f{aw}r> (55)
<f{aw}{r}> (7)
<f{o}(r)> (16)

<f{o}[r]> (48)
<f{o}r> (122)
<f{o}{r}> (6)
<{f}aw(r)> (1)
<{f}awr> (2)
<{f}o[r]> (1)
<{f}or> (3)
<{f}u{r}> (1)
<{f}{o}[r]> (2)
<{f}{o}r> (1)

070.5 G look here
No Response (580)
A   look (81)
B   look at (this) (53)
C   look here (79)
D   look out (there) (2)
E   look over here (2)
F   look over there (25)
G   look over thisaway (1)
H   look over yonder (2)
I   look right here (2)
J   look right (over) there (6)
K   look right yonder (there) (2)
L   look there (11)
M   look this way (1)
N   look yonder (6)
O   look-a-here (47)
P   look-a-there (12)
Q   look-a-yonder (3)
R   lookee (3)
S   lookee there (1)
T   lookee yonder (4)

071.1 P often
{aw}   unrounded onset
{f}   bilabial
{o}   low-back
{oe}   lowered onset
{t}   flap
{?}   glottal
No Response (178)
<aw(f)tN=14> (1)
<awfM=14> (1)
<awfN=14> (255)
<awffN=14> (2)
<awftN=14> (369)
<awfthN=14> (1)
<awftin=13> (2)
<awfun=13> (1)
<awf{?}N=14> (2)
<awf{t}N=14> (2)
<aw{f}N=14> (2)
<aw{f}tN=14> (2)
<oefN=14> (31)
<oeftN=14> (38)
<oeftin=13> (1)
<oe{f}tN=14> (2)
<ofN=14> (11)
<oftN=14> (12)
<of{t}N=14> (1)

<orfN=14> (1)
<owfN=14> (1)
<{aw}fN=14> (39)
<{aw}ftN=14> (36)
<{aw}f{t}N=14> (1)
<{oe}fN=14> (1)
<{o}fN=14> (5)
<{o}ftN=14> (5)

071.2 P either/neither
{R}   weakly retroflex
{t}   flap
No Response (164)
<eedR=14> (1)
<eed[R]=14> (5)
<eedhR=14> (129)
<eedh[R]=14> (221)
<eedh{R}=14> (57)
<idh[R]=14> (1)
<iedhR=14> (3)
<iedh[R]=14> (3)
<nee(dhR)> (1)
<needR=14> (3)
<need[R]=14> (8)
<needhR=14> (138)
<needh[R]=14> (153)
<needhu[r]=13> (2)
<needh{R}=14> (39)
<need{R}=14> (1)
<neet[R]=14> (1)
<nee{t}R=14> (1)
<nee{t}[R]=14> (3)
<nidhR=14> (2)
<niedhR=14> (4)
<niedh[R]=14> (2)
<ni{t}[R]=14> (1)
<nudhR=14> (1)
<nudh[R]=14> (1)

071.3 P forehead
{ai}   lax onset
{aw}   unrounded onset
{d}   devoiced
{f}   bilabial
{o}   low-back
{R}   weakly retroflex
{r}   weakly retroflex
{?}   glottal
No Response (130)
<far(h)Ad=14> (1)
<faw(rh)Ad=14> (1)
<faw(rh)Id=14> (9)
<faw(rh)I{d}=14> (2)
<faw(r)hed=13> (2)
<faw(r)wAd=14> (2)
<faw(r)wId=14> (1)
<faw(r)wIj=14> (1)
<faw(r)wRd=14> (2)
<faw(r)w{R}d=14> (1)
<faw[r](h)Id=14> (1)
<faw[r](he)d> (2)

<faw[r]hed=13> (5)
<faw[r]rId=14> (1)
<faw[r]red=13> (1)
<faw[r]wAd=14> (1)
<fawr(h)Ad=14> (3)
<fawr(h)Id=14> (32)
<fawr(h)I{d}=14> (1)
<fawr(he)d> (3)
<fawrhed=13> (8)
<fawrheed=13> (1)
<fawrhet=13> (1)
<fawrh{ai}d=13> (1)
<faw{r}(h)Id=14> (2)
<faw{r}(he)d> (2)
<faw{r}hed=13> (2)
<fo(rh)Ad=14> (1)
<fo(rh)Id=14> (3)
<fo(rhe)d> (1)
<fo(r)hed=13> (1)
<fo(r)wId=14> (3)
<fo[r](h)Id=14> (1)
<fo[r](h)id=13> (1)
<fo[r](he)d> (2)
<fo[r](he){d}> (1)
<fo[r]hed=13> (1)
<fo[r]rAd=14> (1)
<fo[r]rId=14> (8)
<fo[r]rI{d}=14> (1)
<fo[r]wAd=14> (2)
<fo[r]wId=14> (1)
<foe(rh)Ad=14> (1)
<foe(rh)Id=14> (12)
<foe(rh)aid=13> (1)
<foe(rh)ed=13> (3)
<foe(r)hed=11> (1)
<foe(r)hed=13> (45)
<foe(r)hid=13> (1)
<foe(r)hit=13> (1)
<foe(r)h{ai}d=13> (12)
<foe(r)wAd=14> (1)
<foe[r](h)Ad=14> (3)
<foe[r](h)Id=14> (4)
<foe[r](h)id=13> (1)
<foe[r](he)d> (3)
<foe[r]had=13> (1)
<foe[r]hed=11> (1)
<foe[r]hed=13> (77)
<foe[r]he{d}=13> (1)
<foe[r]hid=13> (3)
<foe[r]h{ai}d=13> (19)
<foe[r]h{ai}{d}=13> (2)
<foe[r]rId=14> (8)
<foe[r]wAd=14> (1)
<foe[r]wId=14> (2)
<foe[r]{?}Ad=14> (1)
<foer(h)Ad=14> (3)
<foer(h)Id=14> (46)
<foer(h)I{d}=14> (2)
<foer(h)N=14> (1)

<foer(h)ed=13> (9)
<foer(h)id=13> (2)
<foer(he)d> (6)
<foerhId=14> (4)
<foerhed=13> (152)
<foerhet=13> (1)
<foerhe{d}=13> (3)
<foerhid=11> (1)
<foerh{ai}d=13> (28)
<foerh{ai}{d}=13> (2)
<foerrAd=14> (1)
<foerwAd=14> (1)
<foe{r}(h)Ad=14> (3)
<foe{r}(h)Id=14> (4)
<foe{r}(h)I{d}=14> (1)
<foe{r}(h)ed=13> (1)
<foe{r}(he)d> (2)
<foe{r}hed=13> (45)
<foe{r}he{d}=13> (2)
<foe{r}h{ai}d=13> (5)
<for(h)Ad=14> (10)
<for(h)Id=14> (116)
<for(h)I{d}=14> (7)
<for(h)ed=13> (1)
<for(h)id=13> (1)
<for(he)d> (6)
<forhed=13> (4)
<forrId=14> (1)
<fo{r}(h)Ad=14> (5)
<fo{r}(h)At=14> (1)
<fo{r}(h)Id=14> (11)
<fo{r}(h){R}d=14> (1)
<fo{r}(he)d> (2)
<fo{r}(he){d}> (1)
<fo{r}hed=13> (5)
<fo{r}he{d}=13> (1)
<fo{r}rId=14> (3)
<fo{r}wAd=14> (1)
<fo{r}wId=14> (1)
<fur(h)Id=14> (1)
<furhId=14> (1)
<furhed=13> (1)
<f{aw}(r)wAd=14> (1)
<f{aw}(r)wRd=14> (1)
<f{aw}r(h)Id=14> (4)
<f{aw}{r}(h)Id=14> (1)
<f{o}(rh)Id=14> (3)
<f{o}[r](h)Id=14> (1)
<f{o}r(h)Ad=14> (1)
<f{o}r(h)Id=14> (19)
<f{o}r(h)Is=14> (1)
<f{o}r(he)d> (4)
<f{o}rhed=13> (1)
<f{o}rhi{d}=13> (1)
<f{o}rh{ai}d=13> (1)
<f{o}rwRd=14> (1)
<f{o}{r}(h)Id=14> (1)
<f{o}{r}(he)d> (2)
<{f}aw(r)hid=13> (1)

<{f}aw[r]hed=13> (1)
<{f}awr(h)Id=14> (4)
<{f}awr(h)I{d}=14> (1)
<{f}awrhi{d}=13> (1)
<{f}oe(r)haid=13> (1)
<{f}oe(r)hed=13> (1)
<{f}oe(r)hid=13> (2)
<{f}oerhed=13> (1)
<{f}or(h)Id=14> (1)
<{f}or(h)R{d}=14> (1)
<{f}o{r}(h)Id=14> (1)

071.4A P hair
{a} upglide
{ai} lax onset
{r} weakly retroflex
No Response (90)
<ha(r)> (40)
<ha[r]> (176)
<ha[R]=14> (1)
<hai(r)> (1)
<hai[r]> (1)
<hair> (7)
<haiyR=14> (1)
<hai{r}> (2)
<har> (342)
<ha{r}> (99)
<he(r)> (3)
<he[r]> (35)
<her> (117)
<he{r}> (26)
<hir> (2)
<hor> (13)
<ho{r}> (2)
<hur> (2)
<hyar> (1)
<h{ai}[r]> (1)
<h{ai}r> (6)
<h{ai}{r}> (1)
<h{a}(r)> (1)
<h{a}[r]> (4)
<h{a}r> (4)
<h{a}{r}> (3)

071.4B P beard
{d} devoiced
{r} weakly retroflex
{z} devoiced
No Response (199)
<be[r]d> (4)
<be[r]{d}> (1)
<bee(r)d> (1)
<bee[r]d> (11)
<bee[r]{d}> (2)
<beer(d)> (1)
<beerd> (42)
<beerd{z}> (1)
<beer{d}> (5)
<beer{d}{z}> (1)
<beeu[r]d=13> (1)
<bee{r}(d)> (1)

<bee{r}d> (9)
<bee{r}{d}> (1)
<ber(d)> (1)
<berd> (5)
<bewwI(d)=14> (1)
<be{r}d> (2)
<be{r}dz> (1)
<bi(r)d> (2)
<bi[r](d)> (2)
<bi[r]d> (81)
<bi[r]dz> (7)
<bi[r]d{z}> (1)
<bi[r]j> (1)
<bi[r]t> (1)
<bi[r]ts> (1)
<bi[r]{d}> (9)
<bi[r]{d}{z}> (1)
<bir(d)> (2)
<birId=14> (1)
<bird> (313)
<birdz> (2)
<bird{z}> (3)
<bir{d}> (19)
<bi{r}(d)> (2)
<bi{r}d> (72)
<bi{r}dz> (1)
<bi{r}d{z}> (2)
<bi{r}{d}> (4)
<byai(r){d}> (1)
<bye[r]d> (1)
<byee[r]d> (1)
<byee[r]d{z}> (1)
<byeerd> (4)
<byerd> (2)
<byer{d}> (1)
<bye{r}d> (3)
<byi[r]d> (21)
<byi[r]{d}> (4)
<byird> (50)
<byir{d}> (4)
<byi{r}d> (15)
<byurd> (1)

071.4 S beard

No Response (16)
|AAImea| (1)
|ABAmea| (1)
|ABBmej| (1)
|ABCmaa| (2)
|ABCmea| (6)
|ABCmej| (1)
|ABE| (1)
|ABElfj| (1)
|ABEmea| (3)
|ABImaa| (1)
|ABImaj| (2)
|ABImea| (4)
|AGAeaa| (1)
|AGAmaa| (1)
|AGAmea| (10)

|AGAmeb| (1)
|AGAmed| (1)
|AGCmaa| (1)
|AGCmea| (5)
|AGEeajmea| (1)
|AGEmaa| (1)
|AGEmaj| (1)
|AGEmea| (4)
|AGEmej| (2)
|AGIeaj| (1)
|AGImaa| (1)
|AGImak| (1)
|AGImea| (2)
|AQAmna| (1)
|BBCmea| (1)
|BBHmaa| (1)
|BGAmea| (7)
|BGAmeb| (1)
|BGAmed| (1)
|BGAmpa| (3)
|BJAmea| (1)
|DAA| (1)
|DAAmaa| (5)
|DAAmaj| (1)
|DAAmajmea| (1)
|DAAmea| (27)
|DABdac| (1)
|DABdacmea| (1)
|DABdbjmaa| (1)
|DABkacmea| (1)
|DABmaa| (22)
|DABmaj| (17)
|DABmajmea| (2)
|DABmea| (107)
|DABmej| (12)
|DABmfa| (1)
|DABmfj| (1)
|DABmla| (1)
|DACmaa| (1)
|DACmea| (9)
|DADmea| (1)
|DADmej| (1)
|DAE| (1)
|DAEeaj| (1)
|DAEmaa| (11)
|DAEmaj| (11)
|DAEmea| (78)
|DAEmej| (11)
|DAEmfj| (1)
|DAFmaa| (6)
|DAFmea| (4)
|DAFmej| (1)
|DAGmaa| (5)
|DAGmaj| (9)
|DAGmajmea| (1)
|DAGmea| (33)
|DAGmej| (1)
|DAHmea| (3)
|DAImaa| (5)

|DAImaj| (7)
|DAImea| (15)
|DBAmej| (1)
|DBBmej| (1)
|DBEmea| (1)
|DBFmaj| (1)
|DCA| (1)
|DCAmaa| (4)
|DCAmac| (1)
|DCAmaj| (6)
|DCAmea| (7)
|DCAmej| (1)
|DCAmejmab| (1)
|DCBeaa| (1)
|DCBeaj| (1)
|DCBmaa| (9)
|DCBmaj| (23)
|DCBmajmea| (1)
|DCBmea| (93)
|DCBmej| (11)
|DCBmfj| (2)
|DCCmaj| (1)
|DCCmea| (7)
|DCDmaj| (1)
|DCEeaj| (2)
|DCEmaa| (7)
|DCEmaj| (8)
|DCEmea| (62)
|DCEmeb| (1)
|DCEmej| (8)
|DCFmaj| (2)
|DCFmea| (5)
|DCGeaamea| (1)
|DCGeaj| (2)
|DCGmaa| (4)
|DCGmaj| (2)
|DCGmajmea| (1)
|DCGmea| (18)
|DCGmej| (2)
|DCHmea| (1)
|DCImaj| (3)
|DCImea| (7)
|DCImej| (1)
|DDAmdj| (1)
|DDBmda| (1)
|DDBmdj| (1)
|DDImdj| (1)
|DFBmea| (1)
|DFBmpj| (1)
|DFEmfj| (1)
|DGAmea| (1)
|DGAmej| (1)
|DGBmaj| (1)
|DGBmea| (1)
|DGBmej| (1)
|DGEeal| (1)
|DGFmaj| (1)
|DGGmea| (1)
|DKBmda| (1)

|DMBmej| (1)
|EABeah| (1)
|EABeahmea| (1)
|EABmea| (6)
|EABmfa| (1)
|EACmea| (2)
|EACmej| (1)
|EAEmea| (3)
|EAGmaa| (1)
|EAGmea| (1)
|EAHmaa| (1)
|EAImea| (2)
|ECBmea| (4)
|ECCmea| (1)
|ECDmea| (1)
|ECEmea| (1)
|ECFmea| (1)
|ECGmea| (1)
|ECHmea| (3)
|EMHmaa| (1)
|GGA| (1)
|KABmaj| (1)
|KABmea| (2)
|KAEmea| (2)
|KAFmaj| (1)
|KAFmea| (2)
|KCAmea| (1)
|KCBmea| (1)
|KCEmea| (1)
|KCFmaj| (3)
|KCFmea| (2)
|KCFmej| (1)
|KCGmea| (1)
|KCImaa| (1)
|MEA| (1)
|daaABAmea| (1)
|daaABJmaa| (1)
|daaBBJmea| (1)
|daaBBJmej| (1)
|dabABJ| (1)
|dabABJmaa| (2)
|dabABJmea| (5)
|dabBBJmaj| (1)
|dabBBJmea| (2)
|dadBBJmea| (1)
|daeABJmaa| (1)
|dahDAAmea| (1)
|eaaBJA| (1)
|eadBBMmea| (1)
|eadEAFmea| (1)
|eaeEAFmea| (1)
|eajKCBmea| (1)

071.5A P left ear
{ai}   lax onset
{e}   inglide
{r}   weakly retroflex
{f}   bilabial
{?}   glottal
No Response (112)

<a[r]z> (1)
<ai[r]> (1)
<air> (1)
<ai{r}> (1)
<e[r]> (1)
<e[r]z> (5)
<ee[r]> (1)
<eer> (1)
<ee{r}> (1)
<er> (6)
<erz> (1)
<i[r]> (14)
<i[r]z> (5)
<ir> (22)
<irz> (10)
<ir{z}> (2)
<i{r}> (4)
<i{r}z> (2)
<lai{f}(t)> (1)
<lef(t)> (17)
<lef(t)e[r]=11> (1)
<lef(t)e[r]=13> (5)
<lef(t)ee[r]=13> (2)
<lef(t)eer=13> (1)
<lef(t)ee{r}=13> (2)
<lef(t)i[r]=13> (23)
<lef(t)ir=13> (9)
<lef(t)ir=21> (1)
<lef(t)i{r}=13> (4)
<lef(t)ye{r}=31> (1)
<lef(t)yi[r]=13> (5)
<lef(t)yi[r]=21> (1)
<lefchir=13> (1)
<left> (36)
<leftR=14> (1)
<leftai[r]=13> (1)
<leftair=13> (1)
<leftchi{r}=13> (1)
<lefte[r]=13> (9)
<lefte[r]=21> (1)
<lefte[r]=31> (1)
<leftee[r]=13> (1)
<lefteer=12> (1)
<lefteer=13> (10)
<lefteer=31> (2)
<leftee{r}=13> (1)
<lefter=11> (1)
<lefter=13> (14)
<lefter=21> (1)
<lefte{r}=13> (1)
<lefte{r}=21> (2)
<lefthir=11> (1)
<lefti(r)=13> (2)
<lefti[r]=11> (4)
<lefti[r]=13> (63)
<lefti[r]=21> (4)
<lefti[r]=31> (2)
<leftir=11> (14)
<leftir=13> (180)

<leftir=21> (23)
<leftir=31> (10)
<lefti{r}=13> (48)
<lefti{r}=21> (2)
<lefti{r}=31> (4)
<leftur=13> (1)
<leftye{r}=13> (1)
<leftyi[r]=13> (1)
<leftyi[r]=31> (1)
<leftyir=13> (3)
<leftyir=31> (1)
<leftyi{r}=13> (3)
<left{ai}r=13> (1)
<lef{?}ir=13> (2)
<lef{?}i{r}=13> (1)
<le{f}te(r)=31> (1)
<le{f}teer=13> (2)
<le{f}ter=13> (1)
<le{f}ti(r)=13> (1)
<lif(t)ee(r)=13> (1)
<lif(t)ee[r]=13> (1)
<liftee[r]=13> (2)
<lifteer=13> (1)
<lifti[r]=13> (1)
<luf(t)> (1)
<lufti[r]=13> (1)
<luftir=13> (1)
<l{ai}f(t)> (1)
<l{ai}ft> (2)
<l{ai}fti[r]=13> (2)
<l{ai}ftir=13> (5)
<l{ai}fti{r}=13> (1)
<l{e}f(t)> (11)
<l{e}f(t)e[r]=13> (1)
<l{e}f(t)ee[r]=13> (1)
<l{e}f(t)i[r]=13> (5)
<l{e}f(t)ir=11> (2)
<l{e}f(t)ir=13> (9)
<l{e}f(t)i{r}=13> (2)
<l{e}f(t)yi[r]=13> (2)
<l{e}f(t)yi[r]=21> (1)
<l{e}ft> (29)
<l{e}fte[r]=13> (1)
<l{e}fter=13> (2)
<l{e}fter=21> (1)
<l{e}fte{r}=13> (2)
<l{e}fti[r]=11> (1)
<l{e}fti[r]=13> (11)
<l{e}fti[r]=21> (1)
<l{e}fti[r]=31> (1)
<l{e}ftir=11> (8)
<l{e}ftir=13> (48)
<l{e}ftir=21> (5)
<l{e}ftir=31> (1)
<l{e}fti{r}=13> (6)
<l{e}ftyi[r]=13> (1)
<l{e}ftyir=13> (5)
<l{e}f{?}ir=11> (1)
<l{e}v(t)> (1)

<l{e}{f}teer=13> (1)
<yi[r]> (3)
<yi[r]z> (1)
<yir> (5)
<yirz> (1)

071.5B P right ear

{ai}   lax onset
{ie}   monophthong/short upglide
{r}   weakly retroflex
{t}   flap
{z}   devoiced
{?}   glottal

No Response (106)
<a[r]z> (1)
<ai{r}> (1)
<e[r]> (2)
<e[r]z> (5)
<eer> (1)
<er> (5)
<erz> (1)
<e{r}> (1)
<e{r}z> (2)
<i[r]> (16)
<i[r]z> (3)
<i[r]{z}> (2)
<ir> (17)
<irz> (11)
<ir{z}> (1)
<i{r}> (6)
<i{r}z> (3)
<riechee[r]=13> (1)
<riet> (66)
<rietair=13> (1)
<riete[r]=11> (1)
<riete[r]=13> (14)
<rietee[r]=13> (5)
<rieteer=11> (1)
<rieteer=13> (8)
<rieteer=31> (1)
<rieter=13> (8)
<rieter=21> (1)
<riete{r}=31> (1)
<rieti[r]=11> (4)
<rieti[r]=13> (108)
<rieti[r]=21> (6)
<rieti[r]=31> (2)
<rietir=11> (10)
<rietir=13> (200)
<rietir=21> (9)
<rietir=31> (4)
<rieti{r}=11> (1)
<rieti{r}=13> (42)
<rieti{r}=21> (1)
<rieti{r}=31> (1)
<rietyer=13> (1)
<rietyi[r]=11> (1)
<rietyi[r]=13> (3)
<rietyi[r]=21> (1)
<rietyi[r]=31> (1)

<rietyi[r]z=13> (1)
<rietyir=13> (3)
<rietyi{r}=13> (5)
<rie{?}> (1)
<rie{?}yi(r)=13> (1)
<rie{t}ee[r]=13> (5)
<rie{t}eer=13> (8)
<rie{t}i[r]=13> (1)
<rie{t}i[r]=31> (1)
<rie{t}ir=13> (2)
<rie{t}i{r}=13> (1)
<r{ie}t> (32)
<r{ie}tai[r]=21> (1)
<r{ie}te[r]=13> (2)
<r{ie}teer=13> (1)
<r{ie}tee{r}=13> (1)
<r{ie}ter=13> (13)
<r{ie}te{r}=11> (1)
<r{ie}te{r}=13> (3)
<r{ie}ti(r)=13> (1)
<r{ie}ti[r]=13> (13)
<r{ie}tir=11> (7)
<r{ie}tir=13> (77)
<r{ie}tir=21> (7)
<r{ie}tir=31> (1)
<r{ie}ti{r}=11> (1)
<r{ie}ti{r}=13> (14)
<r{ie}ti{r}=21> (1)
<r{ie}tur=13> (1)
<r{ie}tye[r]=13> (1)
<r{ie}tyi[r]=13> (1)
<r{ie}tyi[r]=21> (1)
<r{ie}tyir=13> (6)
<r{ie}tyir=21> (2)
<r{ie}tyi{r}=13> (2)
<r{ie}t{ai}r=13> (1)
<r{ie}{t}ee[r]=13> (1)
<r{ie}{t}ir=13> (1)
<yi[r]> (4)
<yi[r]z> (1)
<yir> (5)
<yirz> (1)

071.5 S ear

No Response (0)
|ABCmaa| (2)
|ABCmea| (1)
|ABEmaa| (1)
|ABEmea| (1)
|ABImea| (1)
|AGAeaa| (1)
|AGAmaa| (4)
|AGAmea| (1)
|AGCmaa| (1)
|AGCmea| (5)
|AGCmed| (1)
|AGEmaa| (1)
|AGSmea| (3)
|AGUmea| (1)
|BGAmaa| (1)

|BGAmea| (2)
|DAAbbamea| (1)
|DAAeakmea| (1)
|DAAmaa| (6)
|DAAmaj| (3)
|DAAmea| (20)
|DAAmej| (4)
|DABbbjmea| (1)
|DABmaa| (62)
|DABmaj| (11)
|DABmea| (174)
|DABmej| (5)
|DABmfa| (1)
|DABmfj| (1)
|DACbbamaa| (1)
|DACdabmea| (1)
|DACmaj| (1)
|DACmea| (18)
|DADmaj| (1)
|DADmea| (1)
|DAEmaa| (41)
|DAEmaj| (9)
|DAEmajmea| (1)
|DAEmea| (115)
|DAEmej| (6)
|DAFmaa| (3)
|DAGmaa| (13)
|DAGmaj| (2)
|DAGmea| (44)
|DAGmej| (1)
|DAHdabmea| (1)
|DAHmea| (4)
|DAImaa| (26)
|DAImaj| (7)
|DAImea| (39)
|DATmea| (2)
|DATmfa| (1)
|DAWmea| (1)
|DAYmea| (1)
|DBBmea| (1)
|DC1maa| (1)
|DCAkae| (1)
|DCAkaj| (1)
|DCAmaa| (5)
|DCAmaj| (3)
|DCAmea| (5)
|DCAmej| (3)
|DCBeaamea| (1)
|DCBeaj| (1)
|DCBeajmea| (1)
|DCBkaj| (1)
|DCBmaa| (17)
|DCBmaj| (5)
|DCBmea| (48)
|DCBmpa| (1)
|DCC| (1)
|DCCmaa| (2)
|DCCmea| (6)
|DCE| (1)

|DCEmaa| (9)
|DCEmaj| (1)
|DCEmea| (25)
|DCFmaa| (1)
|DCFmaj| (1)
|DCGabemea| (1)
|DCGmaa| (3)
|DCGmea| (9)
|DCHmea| (1)
|DCImaa| (4)
|DCImaj| (1)
|DCImea| (6)
|DCTmaa| (1)
|DCTmea| (1)
|DCTmpa| (1)
|DCUabamea| (1)
|DCWmea| (1)
|DDBmda| (1)
|DDBmdj| (1)
|DGBmea| (1)
|DGEmea| (1)
|DGFmea| (1)
|DKAmda| (1)
|DKBkda| (1)
|DKEmda| (1)
|EAAbbamea| (1)
|EABmaa| (1)
|EABmea| (6)
|EACmea| (1)
|EADmaa| (1)
|EADmea| (1)
|EAGmaa| (1)
|EAHeabmea| (1)
|EAHmaa| (3)
|EAHmea| (3)
|EAImea| (1)
|EATmea| (1)
|EAZmea| (1)
|ECBmaa| (2)
|ECBmea| (3)
|ECCmea| (1)
|ECDmea| (1)
|ECFmea| (1)
|ECHmaa| (1)
|ECHmea| (3)
!GBAmea| (1)
|GBFeajmaa| (1)
|KAAmaa| (1)
|KAAmaj| (1)
|KAAmea| (1)
|KAAmej| (1)
|KABmaj| (1)
|KABmea| (5)
|KADmaj| (1)
|KAEmaa| (1)
|KAEmaj| (1)
|KAEmea| (3)
|KAFmaa| (2)
|KAFmaj| (1)

|KAFmea| (3)
|KAFmej| (2)
|KAGmea| (1)
|KAImaj| (1)
|KAImea| (1)
|KBAmea| (1)
|KBEmea| (1)
|KCAmaa| (1)
|KCAmaj| (1)
|KCBmea| (1)
|KCCmaa| (1)
|KCCmaj| (1)
|KCCmea| (1)
|KCFmea| (1)
|KCImaa| (1)
|KGAmaa| (1)
|KGFmea| (1)
|LAAmea| (1)
|OABmaa| (1)

071.6 P mouth
{dh}   devoiced
{f}   bilabial
{z}   devoiced
<ow> variants:
{ou}   raised onset/unrounded offset
o{u}   unrounded offset
{ow}   raised onset/rounded offset
{uw}   mid-central onset
No Response (107)
<math> (3)
<mow(th)> (7)
<mowf> (23)
<mows> (1)
<mowt> (11)
<mowth> (347)
<mo{u}(th)> (1)
<mo{u}f> (1)
<mo{u}s> (1)
<mo{u}t> (2)
<mo{u}th> (80)
<m{ou}(th)> (1)
<m{ou}th> (46)
<m{ow}(th)> (4)
<m{ow}f> (8)
<m{ow}s> (2)
<m{ow}t> (2)
<m{ow}th> (288)
<m{ow}{dh}{z}> (1)
<m{ow}{f}> (2)
<m{uw}f> (3)
<m{uw}th> (7)

071.7A P neck
{ai}   lax onset
{e}   inglide
No Response (156)
<naik> (2)
<nak> (4)
<neg> (1)
<nek> (462)

<neks> (8)
<nik> (16)
<nuk> (2)
<ny{ai}k> (1)
<n{ai}k> (96)
<n{e}k> (173)
<n{e}ks> (2)

071.7 S neck
No Response (0)
|DCA| (3)
|DCAeaj| (2)
|DCC| (2)
|DCE| (1)
|DDH| (1)
|DKA| (2)
|ECAeaj| (1)
|GBCeaj| (2)
|GCCeaj| (1)
|KAA| (129)
|KAAeaj| (21)
|KAAmaa| (2)
|KAAmaj| (18)
|KAB| (67)
|KABeaa| (1)
|KABeaj| (23)
|KABgbj| (2)
|KABmaj| (81)
|KABmak| (7)
|KAC| (5)
|KACmaj| (5)
|KAD| (2)
|KAE| (121)
|KAEeaj| (8)
|KAEgbj| (3)
|KAEkab| (1)
|KAEmaj| (43)
|KAEmak| (5)
|KAF| (52)
|KAFeaa| (2)
|KAFeaj| (30)
|KAFmaj| (3)
|KAG| (9)
|KAGmaj| (5)
|KAGmak| (2)
|KAI| (9)
|KAImaj| (5)
|KBA| (17)
|KBAeaj| (2)
|KBAmaj| (1)
|KBB| (2)
|KBBmaj| (2)
|KBC| (1)
|KBE| (2)
|KBEmaj| (1)
|KBF| (3)
|KBFmaj| (1)
|KCA| (61)
|KCAdaj| (1)
|KCAeaj| (3)

|KCAeal| (3)
|KCAkaa| (1)
|KCAmaj| (5)
|KCB| (18)
|KCBeaj| (1)
|KCBmaj| (14)
|KCBmak| (1)
|KCC| (6)
|KCD| (2)
|KCE| (19)
|KCEeaj| (2)
|KCEmaj| (6)
|KCEmak| (4)
|KCF| (2)
|KCFeaj| (1)
|KCG| (1)
|KCGkaj| (1)
|KCT| (1)
|KDA| (5)
|KDB| (2)
|KDBmdj| (3)
|KDC| (1)
|KDCmdj| (1)
|KDD| (2)
|KDE| (4)
|KDEmdj| (1)
|KDEmdk| (1)
|KDF| (2)
|KDFmdj| (1)
|KFBmaj| (1)
|KFE| (1)
|KFEmaj| (1)
|KGA| (4)
|KGB| (2)
|KGBmaj| (1)
|KGF| (1)
|KKA| (5)
|KKAmdj| (1)
|KKB| (1)
|KKBedj| (1)
|KKE| (3)
|KKEmdj| (1)
|KKG| (1)
|LAD| (1)
|NADmaj| (1)
|OABkaj| (1)
|OCB| (1)
|OCBkaj| (1)
|ODF| (1)

071.7B P throat
{r}   weakly retroflex
{t}   flap
{?}   glottal
No Response (135)
<froet> (1)
<hroet> (1)
<sroet> (3)
<s{t}oet> (1)
<th(r)oet> (63)

<throe(t)> (1)
<throek> (1)
<throet> (203)
<throe{?}> (1)
<thruet> (1)
<th{r}oet> (209)
<th{t}oet> (305)
<th{t}oets> (2)
<th{t}roet> (1)
<troet> (5)
<troets> (1)
<t{r}oet> (5)

071.7C P goozle
{R}   weakly retroflex
No Response (476)
<geezL=14> (1)
<gewzL=14> (29)
<gewzLpiep=143> (2)
<gewzh[L]=14> (1)
<giz[R]d=14> (1)
<gogLpiep=143> (1)
<golIt=14> (1)
<goozL=14> (2)
<gruezL=14> (1)
<guegL=14> (6)
<guegLboen=143> (1)
<guegLpiep=143> (1)
<gueg[L]z=14> (1)
<gueglIbain=341> (1)
<guegl{R}=14> (1)
<guesL=14> (2)
<gues(L)piep=13> (1)
<guez(L)piep=13> (2)
<guezL=14> (320)
<guezLM=144> (1)
<guezLR=144> (1)
<guezLbain=143> (2)
<guezLbief=143> (1)
<guezLboen=143> (1)
<guezLpiep=143> (15)
<guezLport=143> (1)
<guezLtheng=143> (1)
<guezLz=14> (1)
<guezR=14> (1)
<guez[L]=14> (18)
<guez[L]piep=143> (7)
<guezhL=14> (5)
<guezh[L]=14> (2)
<guezlNpiep=143> (1)
<guezlR=14> (2)
<guezuel=13> (1)
<guez{R}=14> (1)
<gulIt=14> (6)
<guzL=14> (6)
<guzul=13> (1)
<juegl[R]z=14> (1)
<kuezL=14> (1)

071.8 P tooth/teeth
S: singular

P: plural
{f}   bilabial
No Response (92)
<P:tueth> (4)
<S:teef> (2)
<S:teesh> (1)
<S:teet> (1)
<S:teeth> (12)
<taith> (1)
<tee(th)> (2)
<teech> (2)
<teef> (20)
<teefIz=14> (4)
<teesIz=14> (1)
<teet> (9)
<teeth> (774)
<teethIz=14> (7)
<teets> (2)
<teez> (2)
<tee{f}> (1)
<tewth> (58)
<tooth> (4)
<tue(th)> (1)
<tuef> (21)
<tuefs> (1)
<tues> (4)
<tuet> (10)
<tueth> (609)
<tuethIz=14> (1)
<tue{f}> (2)
<tue{f}is=13> (1)
<tush> (1)
<tushIz=14> (1)

071.8 S tooth
No Response (1)
|BJA| (4)
|BJAmaj| (1)
|BJE| (1)
|BJEefj| (1)
|BSA| (1)
|BSE| (1)
|CJD| (3)
|CSA| (1)
|CSD| (4)
|EFAmaj| (1)
|FADmaj| (1)
|FAF| (2)
|FFDmaj| (4)
|FFF| (1)
|FFFmaj| (1)
|FFH| (1)
|FMD| (2)
|FMDmaj| (4)
|bbaBJA| (1)
|bjaBJK| (2)
|bscBJA| (1)
|csdBJA| (1)
|daiBJA| (2)
|eaaBBA| (5)

|eaaBJA| (70)
|eaaBSA| (1)
|eaaFFD| (1)
|eacBBA| (1)
|eacBJA| (3)
|eadCBD| (1)
|eadCJD| (1)
|eaeBJA| (1)
|eafBJA| (1)
|ecaBJA| (4)
|ecbBJA| (1)
|eccBJA| (2)
|efaBJA| (451)
|efaBJC| (1)
|efaBJE| (3)
|efaBJS| (1)
|efaBSA| (14)
|efaCJD| (1)
|efbBJA| (2)
|efbBJB| (1)
|efcBJA| (20)
|efcBJC| (2)
|efcBJJ| (2)
|efcBSA| (2)
|efcCJD| (1)
|efdBJA| (2)
|efdBJD| (1)
|efeBJA| (3)
|efeBJE| (3)
|efhBJA| (1)
|efhBJJ| (2)
|efiBJA| (1)
|efiBJE| (1)
|efiBJJ| (2)
|ejaBJA| (2)
|emaBJA| (5)
|emaCJA| (1)
|emdBJA| (3)
|emdCJA| (1)
|eoaBUA| (1)
|faaCJD| (1)
|fadBJA| (2)
|fadCBD| (1)
|fadCJD| (6)
|ffaBJA| (5)
|ffaBJC| (1)
|ffaBJJ| (2)
|ffaCJA| (7)
|ffaCJD| (2)
|ffbBJA| (3)
|ffbBJJ| (1)
|ffbCJB| (1)
|ffbCJD| (1)
|ffcBJA| (7)
|ffcBJJ| (1)
|ffdBJA| (27)
|ffdBJJ| (2)
|ffdCJA| (1)
|ffdCJD| (154)

|ffdCJH| (1)
|ffdCJM| (2)
|ffdCSD| (5)
|ffdFFF| (1)
|fffBJF| (1)
|fffCJM| (1)
|ffhBJA| (1)
|ffhCJD| (2)
|ffhCJG| (1)
|ffhCJH| (1)
|ffhFFD| (1)
|fmaBJA| (4)
|fmdBJJ| (1)
|fmdCJD| (3)

071.9 P gums
{aw} inglide
{b} devoiced
{g} devoiced
{m} devoiced
{o} raised
{oo} unrounded
{u} inglide/upglide
{z} devoiced
{zh} devoiced
No Response (143)
<gom> (2)
<gomz> (1)
<goomz> (2)
<goom{z}> (1)
<guemz> (1)
<gum> (64)
<gum(z)> (2)
<gums> (1)
<gumsh> (1)
<gumz> (160)
<gum{zh}> (1)
<gum{z}> (75)
<gu{m}s> (1)
<g{aw}m{z}> (1)
<g{oo}m> (6)
<g{oo}mz> (6)
<g{oo}m{z}> (9)
<g{o}m> (17)
<g{o}m(z)> (1)
<g{o}mz> (44)
<g{o}m{z}> (10)
<g{u}[m]> (1)
<g{u}m> (110)
<g{u}m(z)> (7)
<g{u}mz> (190)
<g{u}m{b}{z}> (3)
<g{u}m{zh}> (1)
<g{u}m{z}> (55)
<{g}um{z}> (1)

072.1 P palm
{ai} lax onset
{aw} unrounded onset
{o} low-back
No Response (129)

<pa[1][m]> (1)
<pa[1]m> (4)
<pa[1]n> (1)
<pa[m]> (1)
<pal(m)> (1)
<palm> (1)
<pam> (18)
<pan> (39)
<panL=14> (7)
<pan[L]=14> (1)
<paw[1]m> (19)
<pawlm> (7)
<pawm> (24)
<po[1][m]> (3)
<po[1]m> (266)
<po[1]mz> (1)
<po[1]n> (1)
<poem> (1)
<pol(m)> (1)
<polm> (33)
<pom> (212)
<pomz> (3)
<pon> (1)
<prom> (1)
<p{ai}n> (1)
<p{aw}m> (10)
<p{o}[1][m]> (1)
<p{o}[1]m> (50)
<p{o}lm> (33)
<p{o}m> (61)
<p{o}mL=14> (1)
<p{o}nd> (1)

072.2 P fist/fists
{f} bilabial
{z} devoiced
{?} glottal
No Response (115)
<fees(ts)> (2)
<feest(s)> (1)
<feest> (1)
<fi(s)t> (1)
<fi(s)th(s)> (1)
<fis(t)> (132)
<fis(t)Is=14> (1)
<fis(t)Iz=14> (8)
<fis(t)I{?}=14> (1)
<fis(t)I{z}=14> (4)
<fis(ts)> (216)
<fisk(s)> (1)
<fiskt> (1)
<fist(s)> (336)
<fist> (578)
<fistA(s)=14> (1)
<fistA=14> (1)
<fistI(s)=14> (3)
<fistIz=14> (37)
<fistI{z}=14> (3)
<fists> (109)
<fitht(s)> (1)

<vi(s)th> (1)
<{f}is(t)> (3)
<{f}is(t)Iz=14> (1)
<{f}is(ts)> (2)
<{f}ist(s)> (8)
<{f}ist> (11)
<{f}ists> (2)

072.3 P joints

{ie} monophthong/short upglide
{oe} lowered monophthong
{oy} inglide
{r} weakly retroflex
No Response (165)
<jawnt> (1)
<jaw{r}nts> (1)
<jient> (6)
<jients> (19)
<joyn(t)> (2)
<joynt> (219)
<joyntch> (1)
<joynts> (330)
<ju[r]nts> (3)
<jurnt> (2)
<ju{r}nts> (2)
<j{ie}nt> (2)
<j{ie}nts> (6)
<j{oe}nt> (1)
<j{oy}nt(s)> (3)
<j{oy}nt> (61)
<j{oy}nts> (104)

072.3 S joint

No Response (62)
|J2Aeda| (1)
|J2Ceda| (5)
|J2Cedj| (4)
|J2Cmdj| (4)
|J2Deda| (1)
|J2Dmdj| (1)
|J2Hedj| (4)
|J2Hmda| (1)
|J2Hmdj| (2)
|JBHeab| (1)
|JJCeaa| (6)
|JJCeab| (2)
|JJCeac| (4)
|JJCeaj| (2)
|JJCmaa| (1)
|JJCmab| (2)
|JJCmaj| (1)
|JJDeaj| (1)
|JJFeaa| (1)
|JJH| (1)
|JJHeaa| (12)
|JJHeab| (10)
|JJHeaj| (4)
|JJHefj| (1)
|JJHmab| (2)
|JJHmaj| (1)
|JSCbbj| (1)

|JSCeaa| (5)
|JSCeac| (2)
|JSHeaa| (1)
|JSHeab| (1)
|JSHeac| (1)
|JSHmaa| (1)
|JUCbhc| (1)
|JUCeda| (2)
|JUCkdb| (1)
|JUCmdb| (1)
|JUHeda| (2)
|JUHmda| (1)
|KFAeaj| (1)
|KKCmda| (1)
|LFAeaa| (1)
|LFAeaj| (2)
|LFAeej| (2)
|LFEeaa| (1)
|LFGeaa| (1)
|LFGeak| (1)
|LHEeda| (1)
|LND| (1)
|MEA| (1)
|MIA| (1)
|MKAeda| (1)
|NADkak| (1)
|PAAeaa| (2)
|PAEeaa| (2)
|PAEeak| (1)
|PAHkab| (1)
|PAIeaa| (1)
|PAIeaj| (1)
|PDEeda| (1)
|PDGeda| (1)
|PFAeaj| (1)
|PFEeaa| (1)
|PKAmdj| (1)
|QADeaa| (1)
|QADeaj| (1)
|QAFeaa| (1)
|QAHeaj| (1)
|QAHmab| (1)
|QCHeac| (1)
|QDCedc| (1)
|QDF| (1)
|QDHedj| (1)
|QFAeaa| (3)
|QFAeab| (1)
|QFAeac| (3)
|QFAeaj| (14)
|QFAeak| (2)
|QFAeal| (1)
|QFAeam| (1)
|QFAmab| (3)
|QFAmaj| (4)
|QFAmak| (1)
|QFBeaa| (122)
|QFBeab| (23)
|QFBeac| (36)

|QFBead| (1)
|QFBeaj| (36)
|QFBeal| (5)
|QFBefjkab| (1)
|QFBkaa| (1)
|QFBkab| (5)
|QFBkaj| (1)
|QFBkak| (1)
|QFBmaa| (17)
|QFBmab| (62)
|QFBmaj| (11)
|QFBmak| (3)
|QFBqfaeaj| (1)
|QFCeaa| (14)
|QFCeab| (2)
|QFCeac| (2)
|QFCeaj| (2)
|QFCkab| (1)
|QFCkak| (1)
|QFCmab| (3)
|QFCmaj| (1)
|QFCqfbeaa| (1)
|QFCqfbeaj| (8)
|QFCqfbeal| (1)
|QFDdaa| (1)
|QFDdan| (1)
|QFDeaa| (14)
|QFDeab| (1)
|QFDeaj| (1)
|QFDeam| (1)
|QFFeaa| (9)
|QFFeab| (9)
|QFFeaj| (7)
|QFFeak| (2)
|QFFmaj| (1)
|QFFmak| (1)
|QFHeaa| (2)
|QFHeab| (2)
|QFHeaj| (2)
|QFHmaj| (1)
|QFHmajeaa| (1)
|QFHmak| (1)
|QMA| (1)
|QMAeaa| (11)
|QMAeac| (1)
|QMAead| (1)
|QMAeah| (1)
|QMAeaj| (2)
|QMAeal| (1)
|QMAmaa| (1)
|QMAmaj| (1)
|QMBeaa| (11)
|QMBeab| (3)
|QMBeac| (8)
|QMBeaj| (3)
|QMBmaa| (5)
|QMBmab| (8)
|QMBmaj| (1)
|QMBmak| (1)

|QMCeaa| (4)
|QMCeac| (3)
|QMCeaj| (1)
|QMCmab| (2)
|QMDdal| (1)
|QMDeaa| (1)
|QMDeaj| (5)
|QMDeal| (1)
|QMDeam| (1)
|QMDmaj| (1)
|QMFeaa| (1)
|QMFmak| (1)
|QMHeaa| (1)
|QMHeab| (1)
|QMHmak| (1)
|QOAeda| (6)
|QOAedj| (9)
|QOAmdb| (2)
|QOB| (1)
|QOBeda| (39)
|QOBedb| (1)
|QOBedc| (6)
|QOBedj| (4)
|QOBeoj| (1)
|QOBeojeda| (1)
|QOBeojkdb| (1)
|QOBkdb| (5)
|QOBmda| (2)
|QOBmdb| (6)
|QOBmdj| (4)
|QOCeda| (5)
|QOCedc| (4)
|QOCedj| (1)
|QOCkdb| (1)
|QOCmdb| (3)
|QOCqobeda| (1)
|QOCqobedl| (1)
|QOCqobkda| (2)
|QOCqobkdk| (1)
|QODeda| (7)
|QODmdj| (1)
|QOFeda| (2)
|QOFedb| (1)
|QOFedj| (1)
|QOFkda| (1)
|QOFkdb| (1)
|QOFkdk| (1)
|QOHeda| (1)
|QOHedl| (1)
|QOHkdk| (1)
|QXAbhj| (1)
|QXAeda| (3)
|QXAedj| (5)
|QXAmdj| (2)
|QXBeda| (6)
|QXBedc| (1)
|QXBedl| (1)
|QXCedj| (1)
|QXCmdj| (1)

|QXDeda| (1)
|QXDmdj| (1)
|RABeaj| (1)
|RABkaj| (1)
|RAEeaa| (2)
|RAEeaj| (3)
|RAGeaj| (1)
|RCAeaj| (1)
|RCBeaj| (1)
|RCEeaa| (1)
|RCEeaj| (1)
|RDAeda| (1)
|RDIedj| (1)
|ROEmdj| (1)
|SAFeaj| (1)
|SCGeaj| (1)
|SFEeaa| (1)
|SODeda| (1)
|SOEedj| (1)
|TDDqobkdj| (1)
|TFBeaa| (1)
|TFBeaj| (1)
|TFFeaj| (1)
|TKAeda| (4)
|TKAedjmda| (1)
|TKBeda| (1)
|TXAeda| (3)
|eajQFBeaa| (1)

072.4A P chest
{ai} lax onset
{e} inglide
{i} inglide
No Response (188)
<chaist> (2)
<ches(t)> (62)
<chesh(t)> (1)
<chest> (289)
<chish(t)> (1)
<chist> (7)
<chitht> (1)
<chust> (2)
<ch{ai}s(t)> (11)
<ch{ai}st> (101)
<ch{e}(st)> (1)
<ch{e}s(t)> (38)
<ch{e}sk> (1)
<ch{e}st> (213)
<ch{i}st> (4)

072.4B P shoulders
{R} weakly retroflex
{t} flap
{z} devoiced
{zh} devoiced
No Response (170)
<choeldR=14> (1)
<choeldRz=14> (5)
<choeld[R]=14> (1)
<choeld[R]z=14> (2)
<shoe(1)dR=14> (1)

<shoe(1)dRsh=14> (1)
<shoe(1)dRz=14> (5)
<shoe(1)dR{z}=14> (8)
<shoe(1)d[R]z=14> (2)
<shoe(1)d[R]{z}=14> (1)
<shoe(1)d{R}=14> (2)
<shoe(1)d{R}z=14> (1)
<shoe(1){t}Rz=14> (1)
<shoe[1]dR(z)=14> (1)
<shoe[1]dR=14> (4)
<shoe[1]dRz=14> (7)
<shoe[1]dRzh=14> (1)
<shoe[1]dR{z}=14> (5)
<shoe[1]d[R]=14> (4)
<shoe[1]d[R]z=14> (3)
<shoe[1]d[R]{zh}=14> (2)
<shoe[1]d[R]{z}=14> (6)
<shoe[1]d{R}=14> (1)
<shoe[1]d{R}z=14> (2)
<shoel(d)R=14> (1)
<shoel(d)R{z}=14> (1)
<shoel(d)[R]=14> (2)
<shoel(d)[R]s=14> (1)
<shoel(d)[R]z=14> (4)
<shoeldR(z)=14> (1)
<shoeldR=14> (39)
<shoeldRs=14> (1)
<shoeldRz=14> (186)
<shoeldR{z}=14> (69)
<shoeld[R](z)=14> (4)
<shoeld[R]=14> (66)
<shoeld[R]z=14> (166)
<shoeld[R]{z}=14> (36)
<shoeldurz=13> (1)
<shoeld{R}=14> (20)
<shoeld{R}z=14> (68)
<shoeld{R}{z}=14> (20)
<shoel{t}[R]=14> (2)
<shueld[R](z)=14> (1)

072.5 P hand/hands
{a} upglide
{ai} lax onset
{d} devoiced
{dh} devoiced
{z} devoiced
{?} glottal
No Response (59)
<(h)an(d)> (1)
<(h)an(d)z> (2)
<ha(nd)> (1)
<ha[n](d)> (4)
<ha[n](d){z}> (3)
<ha[n](dz)> (4)
<ha[n]d> (1)
<hain(d)> (12)
<hain(d)z> (5)
<hain(d){z}> (3)
<hain(dz)> (2)
<haind> (2)

<haindz> (2)
<haind{z}> (1)
<hain{dh}(z)> (1)
<hain{d}> (2)
<hain{d}{z}> (2)
<han(d)> (467)
<han(d)s> (3)
<han(d)z> (409)
<han(d){z}> (143)
<han(dz)> (40)
<hand(z)> (4)
<hand> (211)
<handz> (38)
<hand{z}> (17)
<hant> (1)
<hants> (3)
<hant{z}> (1)
<han{?}> (1)
<han{d}> (67)
<han{d}s> (1)
<han{d}{z}> (14)
<hen(d)> (12)
<hen(d)z> (8)
<hend> (6)
<hendz> (1)
<hend{z}> (1)
<hents> (1)
<hen{d}> (3)
<hen{d}{z}> (1)
<h{ai}n(d)> (2)
<h{ai}n(d)z> (3)
<h{ai}n(d){z}> (3)
<h{ai}nd(z)> (1)
<h{ai}nd> (2)
<h{a}n(d)> (58)
<h{a}n(d)z> (40)
<h{a}n(d){z}> (4)
<h{a}n(dz)> (10)
<h{a}nd> (27)
<h{a}ndz> (13)
<h{a}nd{z}> (1)
<h{a}n{d}> (1)
<h{a}n{d}{z}> (2)
<{?}an(d){z}> (1)
<{?}ang(d){z}> (1)

072.6A P leg

{a}   upglide
{ai}   lax onset
{e}   inglide
{g}   devoiced
{i}   inglide
{l}   labial
{z}   devoiced
{?}   glottal
No Response (97)
<daig> (1)
<lag> (9)
<lagz> (1)
<lag{z}> (2)

<lai(g)> (2)
<laig> (88)
<laigz> (9)
<laig{z}> (4)
<lai{?}> (1)
<lai{g}> (4)
<lai{g}{z}> (1)
<leg> (139)
<legs> (1)
<legz> (15)
<legzh> (1)
<leg{z}> (10)
<le{g}> (8)
<le{g}{z}> (1)
<lig> (2)
<li{?}> (1)
<li{g}> (1)
<l{ai}(g)> (1)
<l{ai}g> (353)
<l{ai}gdh> (1)
<l{ai}gz> (32)
<l{ai}g{z}> (5)
<l{ai}{?}> (2)
<l{ai}{g}> (18)
<l{ai}{g}{z}> (2)
<l{a}g> (29)
<l{a}gz> (2)
<l{e}g> (73)
<l{e}gz> (12)
<l{e}g{z}> (2)
<l{e}{g}> (3)
<l{i}g> (1)
<l{i}{g}> (1)
<{l}{ai}{g}{z}> (1)

072.6 S leg

No Response (0)
|DCA| (1)
|DCAeaj| (2)
|DCE| (1)
|DKI| (1)
|GBAdae| (1)
|GBAeaa| (4)
|GBAead| (1)
|GBBeaa| (1)
|GBBeas| (1)
|GBC| (2)
|GBCeaa| (32)
|GBCeaj| (14)
|GBEeaa| (4)
|GBEeaj| (1)
|GBEmaj| (1)
|GBIeaa| (9)
|GCCeaa| (1)
|GGAeaj| (1)
|GGC| (3)
|GGCeaa| (10)
|GGCeaj| (8)
|GGCeak| (1)
|GGEeaj| (3)

|GGIeaa| (1)
|GGIeaj| (2)
|KAA| (32)
|KAAeaa| (1)
|KAAeaj| (33)
|KAAmaj| (4)
|KAB| (22)
|KABeaa| (10)
|KABeab| (1)
|KABeac| (1)
|KABeaj| (109)
|KABeak| (1)
|KABeal| (2)
|KABgbj| (1)
|KABmaj| (2)
|KABmak| (7)
|KAC| (4)
|KACeaa| (1)
|KACeaj| (23)
|KACkab| (2)
|KACmaj| (1)
|KAD| (4)
|KAE| (39)
|KAEeaa| (2)
|KAEeab| (1)
|KAEeaj| (14)
|KAEgbj| (3)
|KAEkab| (1)
|KAEmaj| (8)
|KAEmak| (26)
|KAF| (5)
|KAFea2| (1)
|KAFeaa| (3)
|KAFeaj| (23)
|KAG| (2)
|KAGeaa| (1)
|KAGeaj| (3)
|KAGmaj| (1)
|KAGmak| (2)
|KAI| (3)
|KAIeaj| (5)
|KBA| (9)
|KBAeaj| (4)
|KBB| (3)
|KBBeaj| (5)
|KBBmak| (3)
|KBCeaj| (2)
|KBCebj| (1)
|KBEeaj| (1)
|KBF| (1)
|KCA| (35)
|KCAeaa| (12)
|KCAeaj| (75)
|KCAeak| (1)
|KCAeal| (1)
|KCAkaamaj| (1)
|KCAmaj| (8)
|KCB| (16)
|KCBeaa| (4)

|KCBeaj| (35)
|KCBeal| (1)
|KCBkaa| (1)
|KCBmaj| (3)
|KCBmak| (6)
|KCC| (3)
|KCCeaa| (1)
|KCCeaj| (17)
|KCCeal| (1)
|KCCgbj| (1)
|KCCkaj| (1)
|KCCmaj| (1)
|KCD| (5)
|KCDmaj| (3)
|KCE| (22)
|KCEeaa| (3)
|KCEeaj| (16)
|KCEeal| (1)
|KCEgbj| (2)
|KCEmaj| (9)
|KCEmak| (10)
|KCF| (3)
|KCFeaj| (6)
|KCFmaj| (1)
|KCG| (2)
|KCGmak| (1)
|KCI| (1)
|KCImaj| (2)
|KGA| (6)
|KGAeaj| (15)
|KGBeaj| (4)
|KGBmaj| (2)
|KGBmak| (1)
|KGEeaa| (1)
|KGEeaj| (1)
|KGF| (2)
|KKA| (1)
|KKAedj| (2)
|OAAeaa| (1)
|OAAeaj| (2)
|OAAkak| (1)
|OABeaa| (2)
|OABeaj| (7)
|OABkaj| (5)
|OBB| (1)
|OBFeaj| (1)
|OCAeaj| (2)
|OCAgbj| (1)
|OCBeaj| (2)
|OCBkaj| (4)

072.6B P foot/feet

P: plural
S: singular
{f} bilabial
{oo} inglide
{t} flap
{?} glottal
No Response (61)
<P:foot> (6)

<P:f{oo}t> (2)
<S:feet> (4)
<feet> (740)
<feets> (19)
<fee{?}> (1)
<foot> (506)
<foots> (25)
<foo{t}> (2)
<fuet> (2)
<fuit> (1)
<fut> (8)
<f{oo}t> (267)
<f{oo}ts> (8)
<{f}eet> (14)
<{f}oot> (8)
<{f}{oo}t> (12)

072.7 L shin

No Response (228)
A blade bone (1)
B chick bone (1)
C crazy bone (4)
D devant [D-0] jambe [F] (1)
E funny bone (5)
F humor bone (1)
G leg bone (7)
H shank(s) (44)
I shank bone (12)
J shank portion (1)
K shin(s) (521)
L shinbone (120)
M shine bone (1)
N shinny (2)
O shunkles (1)
P tibia (1)

072.8 L haunches

No Response (366)
A ass (1)
B back of the leg (8)
C back of the thigh (6)
D backside (2)
E behind (1)
F benders (1)
G biceps (1)
H bongers (1)
I bottom (3)
J butt (11)
K buttocks (7)
L calf (of the leg) (33)
M chamorra [S] (1)
N dewclaws (1)
O fanny (6)
P feet (3)
Q flank (3)
R fleshy part of the leg (1)
S ham (6)
T hanger (1)
U haunchers (1)
V haunches (222)
W heel(s) (10)

X hind legs (2)
Y hind part of the leg (1)
Z hips (27)
aa honkies (1)
ab horses (1)
ac hunkers (173)
ad hunks (2)
ae legs (7)
af muscle of the leg (2)
ag pones (1)
ah posterior (1)
ai rear (3)
aj rear end (4)
ak rump (6)
al seat (2)
am setter (1)
an squatter (1)
ao thigh(s) (142)

072.9 L peaked

No Response (250)
A ailing (3)
B anemic (2)
C awful (1)
D bad (103)
E bad off (1)
F badly (1)
G beat out (1)
H cagou [F] (1)
I colorless (1)
J creepy (1)
K cupid (1)
L debilitated (1)
M down (1)
N down in the dumps (2)
O down in the mouth (1)
P down in the weathers (1)
Q down-and-out (3)
R drawn (3)
S dreary (1)
T drooped up (1)
U droopy (2)
V drowsy and no-good (1)
W emaciated (2)
X feeble (11)
Y frail (8)
Z gaunt (3)
aa green around the gills (1)
ab haggard (1)
ac hallowed (1)
ad ill (21)
ae in low cotton (1)
af jaggedy (1)
ag like a walking corpse (1)
ah listless (2)
ai miserable well (1)
aj not up to par (3)
ak not up to snuff (1)
al not well (2)
am off (1)

an   old and stiff (1)
ao   ornery (1)
ap   out of it (1)
aq   pale (204)
ar   pale-looking (1)
as   palish (1)
at   pallid (4)
au   peak (4)
av   peaked (342)
aw   peaked-like (1)
ax   peakedy (2)
ay   peakish (6)
az   peaky (1)
ba   pepid (1)
bb   pert (1)
bc   picky (1)
bd   pink (2)
be   pinked around the gills (1)
bf   pinky (1)
bg   pitiful (2)
bh   poor (11)
bi   poorly (25)
bj   puny (177)
bk   puny, puny (1)
bl   queasy (1)
bm   rough (2)
bn   run-down (1)
bo   sallow (2)
bp   sallow-looking (2)
bq   scrawngy (1)
br   scrawny (2)
bs   shabby (1)
bt   shaky (3)
bu   shitty-looking (1)
bv   sick (47)
bw   sickly (60)
bx   sickly-looking (2)
by   skinny (1)
bz   sorry-looking (1)
ca   spindly (1)
cb   stupid (2)
cc   swarthy (3)
cd   tallow (1)
ce   tepid (1)
cf   terrible (1)
cg   thin (11)
ch   timid (1)
ci   tired (4)
cj   tough (2)
ck   under the cover (1)
cl   under the weather (17)
cm   wan (4)
cn   weak (103)
co   weakened (1)
cp   weaker (1)
cq   weakly (6)
cr   weary (1)
cs   weaselly (1)
ct   white (1)

cu   whitish (1)
cv   wobbly (1)
cw   worn out (1)
cx   worried (2)
cy   worser (1)
cz   yellow (1)

073.1 L strong

No Response (158)
A   able (2)
B   able-bodied (2)
C   athletic (5)
D   big (25)
E   big-old (2)
F   bowed up (1)
G   brawny (5)
H   broad (1)
I   built (5)
J   built-up (2)
K   bulky (1)
L   bully (1)
M   cut up (1)
N   developed (1)
O   dumpy (1)
P   fat (9)
Q   fine (3)
R   fit (1)
S   great big (1)
T   hale (2)
U   hale and hardy (4)
V   hardy (6)
W   heavy (8)
X   heavy-built (2)
Y   heavyset (5)
Z   heavysot (1)
aa   hefty (12)
ab   huge (1)
ac   husky (90)
ad   husky-built (1)
ae   husky-looking (1)
af   in fine fettle (1)
ag   in good shape (1)
ah   large (3)
ai   large-sized (1)
aj   lot of bulk (1)
ak   masculine (4)
al   much of a man (6)
am   muscle-built (1)
an   muscled (1)
ao   muscled up (3)
ap   muscular (40)
aq   physically fit (2)
ar   pink like a prizefighter (1)
as   plenty of oompower (1)
at   powerful (7)
au   powerful built (1)
av   right smart of a man (1)
aw   robust (49)
ax   robusty (1)
ay   solid (2)

az   stocky (16)
ba   stocky-built (1)
bb   stout (324)
bc   stout-built (1)
bd   stout-looking (2)
be   strapping (2)
bf   strong (642)
bg   strong-looking (1)
bh   strongly (1)
bi   sturdy (2)
bj   tough (1)
bk   vigorous (1)
bl   virile (1)
bm   well-built (8)

073.1 P strong

{aw}   upglide
{g}   devoiced
{ng}   devoiced
{o}   upglide
{ow}   raised onset
{r}   devoiced
{s}   palatal
{t}   flap

No Response (247)
<s(t){r}{aw}ng> (1)
<sh(t)r{aw}ng> (1)
<shtr{aw}ng> (5)
<shtr{o}ng> (1)
<st(r){aw}ng> (1)
<strawng> (51)
<strawnk> (1)
<stroe{ng}> (1)
 (24)
<strowng> (1)
<str{aw}(ng)> (1)
<str{aw}[n]{g}> (1)
<str{aw}[ng]> (3)
<str{aw}ng> (251)
<str{aw}ng[R]=14> (2)
<str{aw}nggIs(t)=14> (1)
<str{aw}ng{g}> (1)
<str{o}[ng]> (1)
<str{o}ng> (30)
<str{o}ngg> (1)
<st{r}aw[ng]> (1)
<st{r}awng> (12)
<st{r}oeng> (3)
<st{r}ong> (12)
<st{r}owng> (1)
<st{r}ung> (1)
<st{r}{aw}[ng]> (9)
<st{r}{aw}ng> (121)
<st{r}{aw}ngg> (1)
<st{r}{aw}nggR=14> (1)
<st{r}{aw}ng{g}> (3)
<st{r}{ow}ng> (2)
<st{r}{o}[ng]> (7)
<st{r}{o}ng> (41)
<st{r}{o}ng{g}> (1)

<s{t}r{aw}ng> (1)
<thrawng> (1)
<thr{aw}ng> (1)
<thr{o}ng> (1)
<{s}(t)r{aw}ng> (2)
<{s}trangg> (1)
<{s}trawng> (12)
<{s}trong> (3)
<{s}tr{aw}ng> (52)
<{s}tr{aw}ng[R]=14> (1)
<{s}tr{aw}nk> (1)
<{s}tr{o}ng> (3)
<{s}t{r}{aw}[ng]> (1)
<{s}t{r}{aw}ng> (5)
<{s}t{r}{o}ng> (1)

073.2 L good-natured

No Response (273)

A admirable (2)
B affable (4)
C agile (1)
D agreeable (20)
E amenable (1)
F amiable (7)
G animated (1)
H average (1)
I beautiful (1)
J best-natured (1)
K bright (1)
L calm (11)
M caring (1)
N charming (1)
O cheerful (17)
P chickenhearted (1)
Q chipper (1)
R clever (2)
S compatible (4)
T congenial (26)
U considerate (1)
V contented (1)
W cool (5)
X cooperative (4)
Y cordial (3)
Z courteous (3)
aa delightful (1)
ab easy (3)
ac easy to agree with (1)
ad easy to get along with (25)
ae easy-tempered (9)
af easygoing (86)
ag even (1)
ah even-dispositioned (1)
ai even-keeled (1)
aj even-tempered (13)
ak fine (6)
al friendly (94)
am friendly-natured (1)
an full of life (1)
ao gay (2)
ap genial (1)

aq genteel (1)
ar gentle (16)
as good (29)
at good-dispositioned (1)
au good-hearted (2)
av good-humored (4)
aw good-natured (181)
ax good-tempered (5)
ay good to get along with (3)
az gracious (1)
ba hail fellow well met (1)
bb happy (43)
bc happy dispositione(d) (1)
bd happy-go-lucky (14)
be harmonious (1)
bf helpful (1)
bg humble (2)
bh humorous (1)
bi (in) good humor (5)
bj in jolly foot (1)
bk jokal (1)
bl jolly (36)
bm jolly good (3)
bn jolly good-natured (1)
bo jovial (8)
bp joyful (1)
bq kind (34)
br kindhearted (3)
bs level-headed (1)
bt lighthearted (1)
bu likable (15)
bv likely (1)
bw lively (1)
bx lovely (4)
by meek (2)
bz merry (1)
ca mild-mannered (6)
cb mild-tempered (5)
cc nice (54)
cd not hard to get along with (1)
ce of a good nature (1)
cf optimistic (1)
cg outgoing (2)
ch patient (4)
ci peaceful (1)
cj pleasant (116)
ck pleasing (2)
cl polite (4)
cm popular (1)
cn quiet (1)
co quiet-tempered (1)
cp reasonable (1)
cq smooth (1)
cr smooth-tempered (8)
cs sociable (6)
ct sweet (10)
cu temperamental (1)
cv tenderhearted (1)
cw too good a natured (1)

cx well thought of (1)
cy well-tempered (1)
cz well-turned (1)
da with a good turn (1)
db wonderful (1)

073.3 L awkward

No Response (267)

A a-gangling (1)
B a-gawking (1)
C accident-prone (1)
D all arms (1)
E all arms and legs (1)
F all legs (1)
G all thumbs (3)
H awkward (185)
I awkward as a ox (1)
J awkward-like (1)
K awkward-looking (2)
L awkwards (1)
M bad (1)
N bad boy (2)
O big fumbler (1)
P big scoundrel (1)
Q big-old gosling (1)
R blind mule in a rail pile (1)
S blunderbuss (1)
T blundering (around) (2)
U boisterous (1)
V bull in a china shop (1)
W bumble-fisted (1)
X bumblefooted (1)
Y bumbling (1)
Z bungler (1)
aa butterfingers (2)
ab careless (6)
ac clumsy (441)
ad clumsy and awkward (1)
ae clumsy and helpless (1)
af clumsy as a ox (1)
ag Clumsy Claude (1)
ah clumsy foot (1)
ai clumsy ox (1)
aj clumsy rascal (1)
ak coltish (1)
al couple doub(le) long (1)
am cumbersome (1)
an devilish kind of fellow (1)
ao dumb (4)
ap dummy (1)
aq dupey (1)
ar emplatre, un [F] (1)
as feeble (1)
at fidgety (1)
au flimsy (1)
av flustrated (1)
aw fumble-fisted (2)
ax fumbler (1)
ay fumblified (1)
az fumbling (1)

ba fumbly (1)
bb gaga (1)
bc gangling (19)
bd gangling [n.] (1)
be gangly (32)
bf gawky (58)
bg giant (1)
bh goofball (1)
bi goofy (1)
bj growed up like a bad weed (1)
bk grown up like a bean pole (1)
bl headlonging (1)
bm horse-limb(ed) (1)
bn ignorant (3)
bo klutz (5)
bp klutzy (2)
bq lanky (28)
br lean and lanky (1)
bs left-legged (1)
bt leggy (1)
bu long and skinny (1)
bv long-arm(ed) (1)
bw long-legged (3)
bx loose-jointed (1)
by lopsided (1)
bz mischievous (1)
ca muddler (1)
cb must have but(ter) in his hand (1)
cc nervous (4)
cd not very coordinated (1)
ce oafish (1)
cf octopus (1)
cg out of fashion (1)
ch outgrow his strength (1)
ci outgrown himself (1)
cj overgrown (5)
ck pear-toed (1)
cl pitiful (1)
cm pole (1)
cn Ralph, a (1)
co rambunctious (3)
cp rangy (1)
cq rawbony (1)
cr reckless (1)
cs rough (5)
ct rowdy (1)
cu rude (1)
cv scrawny (1)
cw skinny (6)
cx skinny and awkward (1)
cy slender (1)
cz slouchy (2)
da sluggish (2)
db spastic (1)
dc spider (1)
dd spider legs (1)
de staggery (1)
df straggly (1)

dg string bean (1)
dh stringy (1)
di stumble (1)
dj stumblebum (1)
dk stumbling (2)
dl stumbly (3)
dm stupid (5)
dn tall and gangling (1)
do tall and linky (1)
dp tall, lean, and lanky (1)
dq thumble-fisted (1)
dr two left feet (1)
ds unbalanced (1)
dt uncoordinated (7)
du weak-kneed (1)
dv wild (1)

073.4 L fool
No Response (365)
A baboso [S] (1)
B bad boy (1)
C blunderbuss (1)
D braque [F] (1)
E bumbler (2)
F bungler (1)
G clown (1)
H complete ass (1)
I crack (1)
J crackbrain (1)
K crank (1)
L crazy boy (1)
M crazy guy (2)
N crazy person (1)
O cuckoo (2)
P cutup (1)
Q dimwit (2)
R dodo (1)
S doofus (2)
T dope (4)
U dud (1)
V dumb ass (2)
W dumb bunny (2)
X dumb Dora (1)
Y dumb fool (2)
Z dumb ox (1)
aa dumb person (1)
ab dumb-dumb (1)
ac dumbbell (6)
ad dumbhead (2)
ae Dumbo (1)
af dummox (1)
ag dummy (40)
ah dunce (6)
ai fathead (1)
aj flake (1)
ak fogy (1)
al fool (429)
am fool man (1)
an freak (2)
ao fumbler (1)

ap goof (5)
aq goof-up (1)
ar gooney (1)
as goose (1)
at ham skin (1)
au hardhead (1)
av idiot (106)
aw ignoramus (2)
ax imbecile (4)
ay jackass (3)
az jerk (2)
ba jinx (1)
bb klutz (3)
bc knothead (1)
bd knucklehead (3)
be kook (3)
bf loco bobo [S] (1)
bg loony [n.] (1)
bh loose screw (1)
bi lunatic (3)
bj maniac (3)
bk misfit (1)
bl monkey (1)
bm moron (3)
bn mutt (1)
bo nerd (2)
bp nincompoop (1)
bq nitwit (4)
br nuisance (1)
bs numb [n.] (1)
bt numbskull (4)
bu nut (70)
bv nut head (1)
bw pain in the neck (1)
bx pendejo [S] (3)
by pest (2)
bz pill (1)
ca pumpkin head (1)
cb sap (1)
cc scatterbrain (3)
cd schmuck (1)
ce screw-up (1)
cf screwball (1)
cg silly [n.] (1)
ch simp (1)
ci simpleton (3)
cj space cadet (1)
ck stumblebum (1)
cl stupe (3)
cm stupid fellow (1)
cn tomfool (1)
co turkey (1)
cp weirdball (1)
cq weirdo (4)
cr witch (1)
cs zafado [S] (1)
ct zip fool (1)

073.5 L tightwad
No Response (213)

A   a-misering (1)
B   austere person (1)
C   beat [n.] (2)
D   bulge pockets (1)
E   cautious (1)
F   cheap (15)
G   cheap screw (1)
H   cheapo (1)
I   cheapskate (10)
J   chiche, le [F] (1)
K   chinch [n.] (1)
L   chinchy (6)
M   chintzy (5)
N   close (27)
O   close as bark to a tree (1)
P   close as the bark on a hickory (1)
Q   close fellow (1)
R   close one (1)
S   closefisted (2)
T   closewad (1)
U   conservative (2)
V   crab apple (1)
W   dago (1)
X   dollar hoarder (1)
Y   don't want to get up off their cash (1)
Z   driver (1)
aa frugal (5)
ab geyser (1)
ac good manager (1)
ad good saver (1)
ae got the first dime he ever made (1)
af grasping (1)
ag greedy (3)
ah greedy gut (2)
ai griper (2)
aj griping (3)
ak gritty (1)
al grouch (1)
am grouchy (1)
an hidebound (1)
ao hoarder (3)
ap Jew (3)
aq live close to [D-0] hog (1)
ar malin, un [F] (1)
as mean (1)
at meany (1)
au miser (282)
av miserly (7)
aw Mister Scrooge (1)
ax money lover (5)
ay money miser (3)
az money pincher (1)
ba (money) worshiper (1)
bb niggardly (2)
bc nit (2)
bd nitty (2)
be old bag (1)

bf overbearing (1)
bg penny grabber (1)
bh penny pincher (40)
bi penny-pinching (1)
bj penurious (1)
bk persimmon (1)
bl pinchpenny (4)
bm poor mouth (1)
bn progressive (1)
bo pure stinginess (1)
bp rank (1)
bq rascal (2)
br real tight one (1)
bs rich fool (1)
bt saver (1)
bu saving (2)
bv saving with his money (1)
bw Scot (1)
bx Scotch (2)
by Scotchman (1)
bz Scotsman (1)
ca Scrooge (16)
cb selfish (7)
cc selfish fellow (1)
cd selfish person (2)
ce short (2)
cf sissy (1)
cg skinflint (44)
ch slave driver (2)
ci slave master (1)
cj smart (1)
ck spendthrift (9)
cl spinster (1)
cm squeaks when he walks (1)
cn stinge [n.] (1)
co stinger [n.] (1)
cp stingy (287)
cq stingy [n.] (6)
cr stingy folks (1)
cs stingy gut (3)
ct stingy guy (1)
cu stingy like a Jew (1)
cv stingy man (7)
cw stingy old cuss (1)
cx stingy old goat (1)
cy stingy person (8)
cz stingy rascal (3)
da stingy sapsucker (1)
db stingy thing (1)
dc stingy wart (1)
dd thrifty (5)
de thrifty person (1)
df tight (99)
dg tight [n.] (1)
dh tight as bark on a tree (1)
di tight as paper on the wall (1)
dj tight ass (1)
dk tight boss (1)
dl tight character (1)

dm tight guy (1)
dn tight head (1)
do tight man (1)
dp tight with (his) money (2)
dq tight-fisted person (1)
dr tightfist (1)
ds tightfisted (5)
dt tightwad (364)
du too tight to spend it (1)
dv wad (2)
dw would pinch a nickel to try to make a dime out of it (1)
[gets money from others]
dx beat [n.] (2)
dy beater (2)
dz bum (4)
ea bummer (1)
eb cheat [n.] (2)
ec cheater (1)
ed chiseler (6)
ee city slicker (1)
ef con man (1)
eg crook (1)
eh deadbeat (2)
ei deadbeater (1)
ej finagler (1)
ek freeloader (1)
el grafter (1)
em hustler (1)
en leech (4)
eo manipulator (1)
ep mooch [n.] (1)
eq moocher (7)
er natural-born sponge (1)
es parasite (1)
et regular bum (1)
eu schemer (1)
ev slick talker (1)
ew slicker (2)
ex snitcher (1)
ey sponger (1)
ez swindle [n.] (1)
fa swindler (3)
fb thief (1)

073.6 L common
No Response (245)
A   complimentary (77)
B   derogatory (297)
C   neutral (334)
D   widespread/everyday (148)
E   undefined (11)

074.1 L lively [of older people]
No Response (199)
A   able (2)
B   active (294)
C   agile (30)
D   alert (25)
E   amazing (1)
F   ambitious (1)

G   apt (1)
H   bright (2)
I   brisk (1)
J   busy (2)
K   busy as a beaver (1)
L   busy as a bee (1)
M   capable (3)
N   chipper (12)
O   chippy (2)
P   clever (1)
Q   competent (1)
R   conscious (1)
S   energetic (30)
T   feisty (11)
U   fine (2)
V   fit (3)
W   fresh (5)
X   frisky (17)
Y   full of energy (3)
Z   full of life (7)
aa   full of pep (7)
ab   full of pep and energy (1)
ac   full of spirit (2)
ad   full of vinegar (2)
ae   funny (1)
af   game (2)
ag   glib (11)
ah   good (9)
ai   graceful (1)
aj   hale (1)
ak   hale and hardy (1)
al   handy (1)
am   hardy (1)
an   healthy (15)
ao   healthy as a buck (1)
ap   in control (1)
aq   in good shape (2)
ar   independent (2)
as   jolly (1)
at   liberal (1)
au   limber (6)
av   lively (79)
aw   manly (1)
ax   mobile (1)
ay   movable (1)
az   nervy (1)
ba   nimble (1)
bb   outgoing (3)
bc   peppy (33)
bd   perky (5)
be   pert (43)
bf   pertly (1)
bg   perty (1)
bh   prissy (2)
bi   proud (1)
bj   quick (5)
bk   radiant (1)
bl   ready (1)
bm   robust (1)

bn   self-sufficient (2)
bo   sharp as a brier (1)
bp   sharp as a tack (1)
bq   smart (9)
br   spirited (1)
bs   sprightly (2)
bt   sprucy (4)
bu   spry (348)
bv   spry as a chicken (1)
bw   spry as a cricket (3)
bx   spunky (4)
by   steady (1)
bz   stout (4)
ca   strong (20)
cb   strong-looking (1)
cc   sturdy (1)
cd   suitable (1)
ce   super (4)
cf   supple (6)
cg   swift (2)
ch   thrifty (1)
ci   tireless (1)
cj   tough (1)
ck   unusual (4)
cl   up and at them (1)
cm   vigorous (2)
cn   virile (2)
co   vivacious (2)
cp   well (4)
cq   well-blessed (1)
cr   well-kept (1)
cs   well-preserved (9)
ct   wide awake (1)
cu   young (27)
cv   young at heart (1)
cw   young-looking (7)
cx   youthful (5)

074.1 P pert
{r}   weakly retroflex
No Response (871)
<pert> (1)
<pi[r]t> (1)
<pirt> (18)
<pi{r}t> (2)
<pu[r]t> (2)
<purt> (9)
<pu{r}t> (2)
<pyi[r]t> (1)
<pyirt> (8)

074.2 P un- [prefix]
{oo}   unrounded
No Response (375)
<[N]-> (37)
<aw[n]-> (1)
<awn-> (8)
<h[N]-> (1)
<hun-> (1)
<o[n]-> (1)
<oen-> (2)

<on-> (11)
<u[n]-> (2)
<un-> (481)
<{oo}n-> (1)

074.3 L afraid
No Response (93)
A   (a)feared (1)
B   afeared (5)
C   (a)fraid (163)
D   afraid (493)
E   ascared (20)
F   fearful (3)
G   fright (1)
H   frighten (6)
I   frightened (50)
J   panicky (1)
K   petrified (2)
L   scare (3)
M   scared (542)
N   shot-scared (1)

074.4 P used to be
{b}   fricative
{t}   flap
{z}   devoiced
No Response (274)
<yeestAbee=143> (1)
<yews(t)Abee=143> (1)
<yews(t)Ibee=143> (1)
<yewsh(t)Abee=143> (1)
<yewshtAbai=143> (1)
<yewshtAbee=143> (2)
<yewstAbee=141> (1)
<yewstAbee=143> (62)
<yewstAbee=341> (1)
<yewstIbee=143> (18)
<yewstoobee=132> (1)
<yewstuebee=132> (2)
<yews{t}Abee=143> (1)
<yewztIbee=143> (5)
<yew{z}tIbee=141> (1)
<yew{z}tIbee=143> (3)
<yistAbee=143> (1)
<yue(s)tAbee=143> (2)
<yues(t)Abee=143> (2)
<yues(tA)bee=13> (1)
<yueshtAbee=143> (1)
<yuessAbee=143> (2)
<yuesstIbee=241> (1)
<yuest(A)bee=13> (2)
<yuestAbee=141> (1)
<yuestAbee=143> (341)
<yuestAbee=241> (15)
<yuestAbee=341> (14)
<yuestA{b}ee=143> (1)
<yuestIbee=143> (38)
<yuestuebee=132> (2)
<yues{t}Abee=143> (1)
<yueztAbee=143> (6)
<yueztIbee=143> (40)

<yueztIbee=341> (2)
<yueztoobee=132> (1)
<yueztuebee=231> (1)
<yue{z}tAbee=143> (6)
<yue{z}tA{b}ee=143> (1)
<yue{z}tIbee=141> (1)
<yue{z}tIbee=143> (57)

074.5 G didn't use to
No Response (465)
A   ain't use to (1)
B   did not use to (2)
C   didn't use to (215)
D   never did use to (1)
E   never used to (14)
F   not used to (2)
G   used not to (21)
H   used not [P-0] (2)
I   used to be not (2)
J   used to couldn't (6)
K   used to did not (2)
L   used to didn't (80)
M   used to don't (1)
N   used to never (2)
O   used to not (63)
P   used to wasn't (10)
Q   used to wouldn't (10)
R   used [P-0] didn't (3)
S   used [P-0] not (2)
T   usen't to (1)

074.6 P careless
{r}   weakly retroflex
{t}   flap
No Response (230)
<ka(r)lAs=14> (3)
<ka(r)lIs=14> (47)
<ka(r)lIst=14> (1)
<ka[r]lAs=14> (1)
<ka[r]lIs=14> (43)
<ka[r]les=21> (2)
<kairlIs=14> (2)
<karlIs=14> (131)
<karles=13> (1)
<karles=31> (1)
<karlis=13> (2)
<ka{r}lAs=14> (2)
<ka{r}lIs=14> (43)
<ka{r}lis=13> (1)
<ke(r)lIs=14> (21)
<ke[r]lAs=14> (4)
<ke[r]lIs=14> (60)
<ke[r]lIth=14> (1)
<ke[r]les=13> (1)
<kerlAs=14> (10)
<kerlIs=14> (208)
<kerlIsh=14> (2)
<kerlIth=14> (1)
<kerles=13> (3)
<kerlis=13> (6)
<ke{r}lAs=14> (2)

<ke{r}lIs=14> (29)
<ke{t}(1)Is=14> (1)
<ki(r)lIs=14> (2)
<ki[r]lIs=14> (4)
<kirlAs=14> (1)
<kirlIs=14> (18)
<ki{r}lIs=14> (1)
<ko{r}lIs=14> (1)
<kurlAs=14> (1)
<kurlIs=14> (4)
<kya(r)lIs=14> (1)
<kyarlIs=14> (3)
<kya{r}lIs=14> (1)
<kye(r)lIs=14> (2)
<kye[r]lIs=14> (10)
<kyerlAs=14> (1)
<kyerlIs=14> (8)
<kye{r}lIs=14> (1)
<kyirlIs=14> (6)
<kyurlIs=14> (1)

074.7 L queer
No Response (178)
A   absentminded (2)
B   addlebrained (1)
C   addled (1)
D   ain't/not (quite) all there (5)
E   ain't real (1)
F   ain't screwed up tight (1)
G   ain't tight (1)
H   backwoodsman (1)
I   backwoodsy (1)
J   balmy (1)
K   barmy (1)
L   bashful (1)
M   batty (2)
N   beside herself (1)
O   bizarre (2)
P   bread ain't done (2)
Q   childish (2)
R   contrary (3)
S   cracked (1)
T   cracked up (1)
U   cracking up (1)
V   cranky (8)
W   crazy (132)
X   crazy in her old age (1)
Y   crazy-like (2)
Z   cuckoo (4)
aa   curious (22)
ab   different (9)
ac   doesn't have all his marbles (1)
ad   don't act right (2)
ae   don't percolate right (1)
af   dressed slouchy (1)
ag   dubious (1)
ah   dumb (7)
ai   dummy (1)
aj   eccentric (16)
ak   fag (3)

al   fairy (3)
am   far-out (1)
an   feeble (1)
ao   feeblemind (1)
ap   flaky (1)
aq   flighty (1)
ar   foggy (2)
as   foolish (29)
at   freak (1)
au   freaky (1)
av   frizzy (1)
aw   fruit [n.] (1)
ax   fruity (1)
ay   funny (133)
az   funny boy (1)
ba   funny-acting (1)
bb   funny-looking [of clothes] (2)
bc   gay [adj.] (12)
bd   gay [n.] (1)
be   goofball (1)
bf   goofy (31)
bg   got odd ways (1)
bh   gripy (1)
bi   hermit (2)
bj   homo (1)
bk   homosexual [n.] (18)
bl   homosexuality (1)
bm   hot in the pants (1)
bn   indifferent (1)
bo   insane (1)
bp   irrational (1)
bq   joto [S] (2)
br   kind of curious (2)
bs   kind/sort of funny (6)
bt   kind of/kindly off (7)
bu   kind of old (1)
bv   kind of queer (8)
bw   kooky (1)
bx   lacking some of her marbles (1)
by   lacks something (1)
bz   lame-brained (1)
ca   leery (1)
cb   left-hander (1)
cc   Lesbian (3)
cd   like an imbecile (1)
ce   little shaky (1)
cf   looks odd (1)
cg   loony (5)
ch   losing her marbles (1)
ci   mentally (1)
cj   mindless (3)
ck   mixed-up in the head (2)
cl   moody (2)
cm   nervous (1)
cn   neurotic (1)
co   not all there (1)
cp   not bright (1)
cq   not (just) right (2)
cr   not together (1)

cs   nut (1)
ct   nuts (2)
cu   nutty (20)
cv   odd (70)
cw   odd person (1)
cx   odd-acting (1)
cy   oddball (9)
cz   off (51)
da   off a little/a little (bit) off (10)
db   off balance (1)
dc   off (her/the) rocker(s) (10)
dd   off in their brains (1)
de   off the course (1)
df   offbeat (2)
dg   old fogy (1)
dh   old-fashion (1)
di   on the dumb side (1)
dj   on the off side (1)
dk   on the queer side (1)
dl   out (of) the way (1)
dm   pansy (1)
dn   peculiar (90)
do   peculiar nut (1)
dp   pervert (1)
dq   plumb queer (1)
dr   puto [S] (2)
ds   quaint (1)
dt   queer [see glosses at fy below]
     (568)
du   queer duck (3)
dv   queer in the head (3)
dw   queer mind (1)
dx   queer money (1)
dy   queer person (12)
dz   queer to blind (1)
ea   queer ways (6)
eb   queer-acting (4)
ec   queer-like (1)
ed   queer-looking (1)
ee   queer-thinking (1)
ef   queer-turned (1)
eg   queerish (2)
eh   queery (2)
ei   quiet (1)
ej   retarded (1)
ek   right queer (1)
el   screw loose, a (1)
em   screwball (1)
en   screwy (2)
eo   senile (11)
ep   set in his/their ways (2)
eq   sickly (1)
er   silly (44)
es   silly-like (1)
et   simple (2)
eu   slowful (1)
ev   snobby (1)
ew   so-called fellow (1)
ex   spacy (2)

ey   spastic (1)
ez   spooky (3)
fa   squirrelly (1)
fb   standoffish (1)
fc   strange (113)
fd   strange-acting (1)
fe   strange-looking thing (1)
ff   stuck-up (1)
fg   stupid (15)
fh   superstitious (1)
fi   tacky [of clothes] (3)
fj   tooky (1)
fk   tooky-acting (1)
fl   touched (6)
fm   touched in the head (3)
fn   unaware (1)
fo   unbalanced (1)
fp   uncanny (1)
fq   unfamiliar (1)
fr   unusual (7)
fs   wacky-wacky (1)
ft   weird (85)
fu   weird old people (1)
fv   weirdo (4)
fw   worried (1)
fx   zany (1)

[queer glosses]
fy   queer [=antisocial/recluse] (9)
fz   queer [=counterfeit] (1)
ga   queer [=crazy/mentally off] (18)
gb   queer [=curious] (8)
gc   queer [=different] (49)
gd   queer [=eccentric] (17)
ge   queer [=foolish] (4)
gf   queer [=forgetful] (1)
gg   queer [=funny] (22)
gh   queer [=homosexual] [n.] (74)
gi   queer [=homosexual] [adj.]
     (174)
gj   queer [=not bright] (2)
gk   queer [=old-fashioned] (2)
gl   queer [of old maid/bachelor] (1)
gm   queer [=a little off] (24)
gn   queer [=obstinate] (1)
go   queer [=opinionated] (1)
gp   queer [=out of the ordinary] (2)
gq   queer [=peculiar/odd] (125)
gr   queer [=quaint/odd] (2)
gs   queer [=shy] (1)
gt   queer [=quiet/not talkative] (2)
gu   queer [=senile] (11)
gv   queer [=silly] (2)
gw   queer [=strange] (65)
gx   queer [=unfriendly] (1)
gy   queer [=unusual] (11)
gz   queer [=nervous] (1)
ha   queer [=short-tempered] (1)
hb   queer [=worried] (2)

074.7 P queer

{b} devoiced
{k} postvelar/fricative
{r} weakly retroflex
{w} devoiced
No Response (345)
<kvir> (1)
<kwa(r)> (2)
<kwa[r]> (8)
<kwair> (1)
<kwar> (21)
<kwa{r}> (5)
<kwe[r]> (14)
<kwee[r]> (13)
<kweer> (21)
<kwee{r}> (3)
<kwer> (21)
<kwerR=14> (1)
<kwe{r}> (5)
<kwi[r]> (101)
<kwir> (258)
<kwirI=14> (2)
<kwi{r}> (79)
<kwor> (5)
<kwo{r}> (1)
<kwur> (5)
<k{b}ir> (1)
<k{w}a(r)> (1)
<k{w}i[r]> (13)
<k{w}ir> (20)
<k{w}i{r}> (4)
<{k}wir> (1)

074.8 L obstinate
No Response (210)
A   acorn head (1)
B   adamant (2)
C   argumentry (1)
D   arrogant (1)
E   awful (1)
F   bad (1)
G   balky (1)
H   belligerent (2)
I   bigheaded (3)
J   blockheaded (2)
K   boisterous (1)
L   bold (1)
M   boneheaded (1)
N   bossy (3)
O   brash (1)
P   bullhead (1)
Q   bullheaded (140)
R   bumptious (1)
S   butt-headed (4)
T   cantankerous (3)
U   close-minded (5)
V   closed (1)
W   cocksure (1)
X   cocky (1)
Y   conceited (4)
Z   contentious (1)

aa contrarious (1)
ab contrary (32)
ac crabby (2)
ad cranky (7)
ae crazy (8)
af curious (1)
ag dead set (4)
ah determine (1)
ai determined (9)
aj difficult (1)
ak disagreeable (1)
al doggy bullheaded (1)
am dogmatic (4)
an domineering (1)
ao dullheaded (1)
ap dumb (3)
aq dumbheaded (1)
ar dummy (2)
as easy (4)
at eccentric (1)
au egotistical (1)
av finicky (1)
aw firm (1)
ax fixed (1)
ay fool (1)
az foolish (4)
ba funny (1)
bb fussy (1)
bc goat-headed (2)
bd grouchy (3)
be hard head (2)
bf hard to change (1)
bg hard to understand (1)
bh hard-boil (1)
bi hard-nose (2)
bj hard-nosed (1)
bk hard-shell (1)
bl hardhead (9)
bm hardheaded (171)
bn hardheaded as a mule (1)
bo hardheaded as a rock (1)
bp hardheaded as mischief (1)
bq hardhearted (1)
br hateful (1)
bs head-set (2)
bt headlong (5)
bu headstrong (18)
bv hen-house ways (1)
bw high-minded (1)
bx high-strung (1)
by high-tempered (1)
bz hotheaded (2)
ca humblish (1)
cb ignorant (3)
cc independent (1)
cd infidel (1)
ce ironheaded (1)
cf ivory (1)
cg jackal-headed (1)

ch knotheaded (1)
ci know-it-all (1)
cj knucklehead (1)
ck loner (1)
cl long head (1)
cm longheaded (1)
cn loud (1)
co low-down (1)
cp mean (10)
cq mind of his own (1)
cr mulehead (1)
cs muleheaded (49)
ct muleheadedy (1)
cu muley (1)
cv muleyheaded (1)
cw mulish (1)
cx narrow-minded (2)
cy nasty (2)
cz no sense (1)
da nubbin head (1)
db obnoxious (3)
dc obstinate (26)
dd obstreperous (2)
de old maid (1)
df old-fashioned (1)
dg old-timey (1)
dh one-minded (1)
di one-track mind (5)
dj one-way (3)
dk opinionated (4)
dl optimistic (1)
dm ornery (21)
dn particular (3)
do peckerwood (1)
dp peculiar (2)
dq persistent (2)
dr pig head (1)
ds pigheaded (18)
dt pompous (1)
du positive (3)
dv queer (5)
dw quick (1)
dx rebellious (1)
dy recalcitrant (1)
dz sarcastic (1)
ea self-assured (1)
eb self-centered (1)
ec self-conceited (1)
ed self-determined (1)
ee selfish (3)
ef set (15)
eg set in his ways (120)
eh set-willed (1)
ei silly (4)
ej smart (2)
ek sot (2)
el sot in his head (1)
em sot in his mind (1)
en sot in his ways (6)

eo sourpuss (1)
ep staunch (3)
eq steadfast (2)
er stick-in-the-mud (1)
es stiff (1)
et stiff-necked (1)
eu straitlaced (2)
ev strong (1)
ew strong-minded (5)
ex strong-will (1)
ey strong-willed (6)
ez strong-willed as a mule (1)
fa strongheaded (4)
fb stubborn (379)
fc stubborn as a bluenose mule (1)
fd stubborn as a donkey (1)
fe stubborn as a Missouri mule (1)
ff stubborn as a mule (7)
fg stubborn as an ox (1)
fh stubborn as hell (1)
fi stubborn-headed (1)
fj stubborn-minded (1)
fk stuck in his ways (4)
fl stuck-up (1)
fm stupid (13)
fn sure of yourself (4)
fo thick skull (1)
fp thickheaded (2)
fq unyielding (2)
fr warp-minded (1)
fs well-made-up mind (1)

075.1 L touchy

No Response (246)
A aggressive (2)
B anger [adj.] (1)
C bad (1)
D bad-tempered (1)
E cantankerous (3)
F childish (1)
G contrary (1)
H crabbish (1)
I crabby (4)
J cranky (6)
K crazy (5)
L crochety (1)
M cross (5)
N crutchous (1)
O curious (5)
P difficult (1)
Q disagreeable (6)
R disturbed (1)
S easily/easy offended (4)
T easily provoked (1)
U easily upset (1)
V easy irritated (1)
W easy made mad (1)
X easy to fly off the handle (1)
Y easy to get mad (6)
Z easy to get upset (2)

aa   easy to lose his temper (2)
ab   easy to make mad (3)
ac   easy (to) touch (2)
ad   edgy (5)
ae   fanatic (1)
af   feisty (9)
ag   fiery (4)
ah   fighty (1)
ai   finicky (2)
aj   foolish (1)
ak   fractious (28)
al   fretful (6)
am   fretted (1)
an   funny (3)
ao   goofy (1)
ap   grouchy (8)
aq   grumpy (1)
ar   hard to get along with (6)
as   hard to handle (1)
at   hardheaded (2)
au   harebrained (1)
av   headstrong (1)
aw   high nervous (1)
ax   high-headed (2)
ay   high-minded (1)
az   high-strung (24)
ba   high-temper(ed) (103)
bb   horsey (1)
bc   hostile (1)
bd   hot (1)
be   hot-tempered (13)
bf   hotheaded (26)
bg   humorless (1)
bh   ignorant (1)
bi   ill (2)
bj   ill-disposed (1)
bk   ill-natured (1)
bl   ill-tempered (9)
bm   immature (1)
bn   impatient (2)
bo   independent (1)
bp   irritable (16)
bq   irritated (1)
br   jump(y) (3)
bs   leery (2)
bt   low-down (1)
bu   mean (15)
bv   moody (3)
bw   nar(row)-minded (2)
bx   nervous (13)
by   nettly (1)
bz   obnoxious (1)
ca   on edge (1)
cb   on offsides (1)
cc   ornery (1)
cd   out of line (1)
ce   oversensitive (1)
cf   paranoid (1)
cg   particular (2)

ch   peculiar (3)
ci   pissy (1)
cj   possessed (1)
ck   prickly (1)
cl   puckered mouth (1)
cm   put out (1)
cn   queer (5)
co   quick (1)
cp   quick on the draw (1)
cq   quick to get mad (3)
cr   quick to get upsetted over nothing (1)
cs   quick to shoot off (1)
ct   quick-temper(ed) (50)
cu   radical (1)
cv   rough (1)
cw   selfish (2)
cx   sensitive (80)
cy   serious (7)
cz   serious-minded (1)
da   shaky (1)
db   short (1)
dc   short patience (1)
dd   short patient (4)
de   short-minded (1)
df   short-tempered (15)
dg   shy (1)
dh   silly (1)
di   skittish (1)
dj   soft-skinned (1)
dk   sore (3)
dl   sorry (1)
dm   standoffish (1)
dn   straitlaced (1)
do   strong-minded (1)
dp   strong-tempered (1)
dq   stubborn (2)
dr   stupid (2)
ds   sullen (1)
dt   super-sensitive (1)
du   taciturn (1)
dv   teeky (1)
dw   temperamental (16)
dx   temperous (1)
dy   tender (1)
dz   tenderhearted (1)
ea   tense (2)
eb   terrible (1)
ec   testy (5)
ed   thin-skin(ned) (6)
ee   ticky (1)
ef   timid (1)
eg   tore up (1)
eh   touchous (76)
ei   touchy (321)
ej   ugly (1)
ek   unstable (1)
el   upset (4)
em   uptight (4)

en   volatile (1)
eo   weak (1)
ep   wild (2)

075.2 L angry

No Response (154)
A   aggravated (8)
B   all to pieces (2)
C   angry (231)
D   annoyed (1)
E   bad (1)
F   bent out of shape (1)
G   boiled up (1)
H   bothered (2)
I   burned (1)
J   burned up (1)
K   cranky (1)
L   crazy (2)
M   cross (3)
N   disgusted (1)
O   disturbed (6)
P   embarrassed (1)
Q   emotional (2)
R   excited (3)
S   fanatic (1)
T   fired up (5)
U   flustered (1)
V   flustrated (4)
W   flying mad (1)
X   foul (1)
Y   fractious (2)
Z   fretted (3)
aa   fuffed up (1)
ab   furious (11)
ac   furious mad (1)
ad   fussy (1)
ae   hateful (1)
af   heated (1)
ag   het up (3)
ah   hostile (1)
ai   hot (9)
aj   hot as a firecracker (1)
ak   hot under the collar (2)
al   huffy (3)
am   hurt (2)
an   ill (1)
ao   impatient (1)
ap   insulted (1)
aq   irate (2)
ar   irritated (4)
as   lit up (1)
at   livid with rage (1)
au   mad (591)
av   mad as a hornet (1)
aw   mad as fire (1)
ax   mad as get-out (1)
ay   mad as hell (2)
az   mad as the devil (1)
ba   mad as the dickens (1)
bb   mad enough to die (1)

bc   mean (5)
bd   nasty (1)
be   offended (11)
bf   on edge (1)
bg   ornery (1)
bh   out of his mind (1)
bi   out of sorts (1)
bj   peeled (1)
bk   peeved (3)
bl   perturbed (2)
bm   pissed off (6)
bn   provoked (1)
bo   put out (1)
bp   riled (6)
bq   riled up (19)
br   rude (1)
bs   serious (1)
bt   shook up (2)
bu   silly (1)
bv   skunked (1)
bw   sore (4)
bx   steamed up (1)
by   stirred up (2)
bz   teed off (2)
ca   ticked off (1)
cb   touchous (1)
cc   ugly (5)
cd   unglued (1)
ce   unruly (1)
cf   upset (131)
cg   uptight (9)
ch   vexed (4)
ci   vigorous (1)
cj   wide open (1)
ck   wild up (1)
cl   worked up (1)
cm   worried (1)
cn   wrought up (1)

075.3 P calm
{aw}   unrounded onset
{o}   low-back
{?}   glottal
No Response (357)
<ka(1)m> (12)
<ka(1)mN=14> (1)
<ka(1)mz> (1)
<ka[1]m> (8)
<kaw(1)m> (21)
<kaw[1]m> (16)
<kawlm> (2)
<ke(1)m> (1)
<ko(1)m> (128)
<ko(1)mN=14> (2)
<ko[1][m]> (1)
<ko[1]m> (251)
<ko[1]mN=14> (4)
<kolm> (26)
<ku(1)m> (1)
<kya(1)m> (2)

<k{aw}(1)m> (4)
<k{aw}[1]m> (1)
<k{o}(1)m> (30)
<k{o}[1]m> (57)
<k{o}lm> (13)
<k{o}{?}(m)> (1)

075.4 L tired
No Response (120)
A   all in (9)
B   all out (2)
C   all to pieces (1)
D   beat (18)
E   beat down (1)
F   beat out (1)
G   beat to a pulp (1)
H   bone tired (2)
I   broke down (5)
J   burnt out (3)
K   bushed (18)
L   dead (5)
M   dead tired (1)
N   dog tired (5)
O   down-and-out (1)
P   drained (1)
Q   exasperated (2)
R   exhausted (102)
S   fagged (3)
T   fagged out (11)
U   fatigue [F] (1)
V   fatigued (18)
W   frazzled (1)
X   frazzled out (1)
Y   fried out (1)
Z   gave/give(n) out (74)
aa   give slam out (1)
ab   jaded (1)
ac   jaded out (1)
ad   just out (1)
ae   knocked out (2)
af   out (1)
ag   petered out (5)
ah   played out (6)
ai   poofed (1)
aj   pooped (60)
ak   pooped out (13)
al   puckered (1)
am   pumped out (1)
an   punked out (1)
ao   ready to fall out (1)
ap   rest-broken (1)
aq   retired (2)
ar   run-down (7)
as   sluggish (1)
at   slumped (1)
au   spent (1)
av   stove up (1)
aw   tired (734)
ax   tired out (19)
ay   tucked out (1)

az   tuckered (1)
ba   tuckered out (21)
bb   used up (1)
bc   washed out (1)
bd   wasted (2)
be   weak (1)
bf   wearied (1)
bg   weary (21)
bh   whipped (8)
bi   wiped out (1)
bj   wore/worn out (18)
bk   worked down (2)
bl   worry (1)

075.5 G wear
<!>   infinitive
<*>   preterit
<#>   past participle
No Response (269)
<!war> (2)
<!wa{r}> (1)
<!we[r]> (1)
<!wer> (2)
<*waw[r]> (2)
<*woe(r)> (1)
<*woe[r]> (1)
<*woer> (4)
<*woe{r}> (1)
<#waw(r)> (4)
<#waw(r)N=14> (1)
<#waw(r)d> (1)
<#waw(r)n> (6)
<#waw[r]> (23)
<#waw[r]n> (48)
<#waw[r]nd> (1)
<#wawr> (29)
<#wawrn> (115)
<#wawrnt> (1)
<#waw{r}> (16)
<#waw{r}d> (1)
<#waw{r}n> (19)
<#wa{r}d> (1)
<#wo[r]n> (1)
<#woe(r)> (39)
<#woe(r)d> (1)
<#woe(r)n> (8)
<#woe[r]> (24)
<#woe[r]n> (78)
<#woer> (63)
<#woerd> (2)
<#woern> (145)
<#woewN=14> (1)
<#woe{r}> (19)
<#woe{r}d> (1)
<#woe{r}n> (31)
<#wurn> (2)
<#wu[r]> (1)

076.1 G got sick
No Response (264)
A   became ill (50)

B became sick (22)
C caught sick (1)
D fell ill (2)
E fell sick (2)
F gave sick (1)
G got ill (6)
H got sick (453)
I took ill (17)
J took sick (207)
K turned sick (1)

076.2 G by and by

No Response (673)
A after (a) while (12)
B before (too) long (4)
C by and by (96)
D by the time you know it (1)
E by time (1)
F directly (6)
G eventually (7)
H (in a little) while (10)
I in plenty [P-0] time (1)
J in time (2)
K later (on) (7)
L little bit, a (1)
M little by little (1)
N pretty soon (12)
O real soon (3)
P right away (1)
Q right short (1)
R right soon (1)
S shortly (9)
T sometime (soon) (8)
U sometimes (1)
V soon (84)
W soon enough (1)
X soon to be (1)
Y sooner or later (18)

076.3 G caught a cold

No Response (282)
A caught a cold (293)
B caught cold (111)
C caught that cold (2)
D caught the cold (4)
E got a cold (51)
F got cold (5)
G took a cold (140)
H took cold (95)
I took this cold (1)

076.3 S cold

No Response (1)
|IJAefjcba| (1)
|J2Heoj| (1)
|JJA| (1)
|JJAefa| (6)
|JJAefacba| (1)
|JJAefacbj| (1)
|JJAefj| (24)
|JJAffa| (1)
|JJAffacba| (1)

|JJAffd| (25)
|JJAffdcba| (1)
|JJAffdmaj| (1)
|JJAffj| (1)
|JJAjjb| (25)
|JJAjjf| (2)
|JJAjjk| (1)
|JJAjjm| (1)
|JJAlfj| (6)
|JJBefj| (2)
|JJC| (1)
|JJCcba| (1)
|JJCcjc| (1)
|JJCefa| (9)
|JJCefj| (23)
|JJCffd| (3)
|JJCjja| (1)
|JJCjjb| (4)
|JJCjjk| (2)
|JJCjsb| (1)
|JJClfj| (1)
|JJD| (5)
|JJDefa| (266)
|JJDefacba| (9)
|JJDefacbj| (14)
|JJDefamaj| (1)
|JJDefj| (31)
|JJDefjcba| (3)
|JJDefjcbj| (2)
|JJDema| (2)
|JJDffa| (2)
|JJDffc| (1)
|JJDffd| (54)
|JJDffdcba| (1)
|JJDffj| (2)
|JJDffm| (13)
|JJDfmd| (1)
|JJDlfj| (2)
|JJDlfk| (1)
|JJFefa| (4)
|JJFefacba| (2)
|JJFefj| (6)
|JJGefa| (1)
|JJGefj| (2)
|JJHefa| (7)
|JJHefacba| (1)
|JJHefj| (8)
|JJHefjcba| (1)
|JJHffd| (1)
|JJHffm| (1)
|JJHjjo| (1)
|JJIefj| (1)
|JSA| (2)
|JSAefa| (2)
|JSAefj| (7)
|JSAffacba| (2)
|JSAffj| (2)
|JSAjjb| (8)
|JSAjjk| (1)

|JSAlfa| (1)
|JSAlfj| (5)
|JSAmaj| (1)
|JSBffa| (1)
|JSCcbj| (1)
|JSCefa| (5)
|JSCefj| (23)
|JSCefjmaj| (1)
|JSCffd| (1)
|JSCffjcba| (1)
|JSCmaj| (1)
|JSD| (2)
|JSDcba| (4)
|JSDeaa| (1)
|JSDefa| (104)
|JSDefacba| (2)
|JSDefacbj| (3)
|JSDefamaj| (1)
|JSDefj| (29)
|JSDefjcba| (1)
|JSDema| (1)
|JSDffacba| (1)
|JSDffd| (11)
|JSDffdcba| (1)
|JSDffdmaj| (1)
|JSDffj| (1)
|JSDffjcba| (1)
|JSDffm| (4)
|JSDlfk| (1)
|JSDmaj| (1)
|JSFefa| (3)
|JSFefj| (2)
|JSGefa| (1)
|JSHefa| (6)
|JSHefj| (5)
|JSHefjcbj| (1)
|JSHffd| (1)
|JSHffm| (1)
|JSSffa| (1)
|JUDeoa| (1)
|KMAefjcba| (2)
|LAAfaacbj| (1)
|LCAfaacbj| (1)
|LFAefa| (9)
|LFAffjcba| (1)
|LFEefa| (3)
|LFEefj| (3)
|LFEffd| (2)
|LFGefa| (2)
|LFGefj| (1)
|LMAefa| (2)
|LMAefj| (1)
|LMAefjcbj| (1)
|LMAfajcba| (1)
|LMAffa| (4)
|LMAffacba| (5)
|LMAffamaa| (1)
|LMAffj| (3)
|LMAffjcba| (9)

|LMDefa| (1)

|LMDffacba| (1)

|LMDffj| (1)

|LMGefj| (1)

|LXAfoj| (1)

|QFBjjccba| (1)

|QFHefa| (1)

|QFHjjb| (1)

|QMHefj| (1)

076.4 P hoarse

{oe}   lowered onset

{r}   weakly retroflex

No Response (156)

<haw[r]s> (4)

<hawrs> (7)

<hawrth> (1)

<haw{r}s> (1)

<hoe(r)s> (21)

<hoe[r]s> (96)

<hoe[r]sh> (3)

<hoers> (153)

<hoersh> (1)

<hoe{r}s> (60)

<hors> (2)

<horsh> (1)

<h{oe}(r)s> (12)

<h{oe}(r)th> (1)

<h{oe}[r]s> (95)

<h{oe}[r]sh> (1)

<h{oe}[r]th> (1)

<h{oe}rs> (247)

<h{oe}rsh> (1)

<h{oe}{r}s> (55)

076.4 S hoarse

No Response (1)

|J2Beoj| (1)

|J2Cmdj| (2)

|J2Fmda| (1)

|JBCefj| (1)

|JJAbjn| (1)

|JJAeaj| (1)

|JJAefj| (5)

|JJAffamea| (1)

|JJAmaa| (1)

|JJAmaj| (3)

|JJAmea| (4)

|JJAmej| (6)

|JJBefjmea| (1)

|JJBmaa| (1)

|JJC| (3)

|JJCeaa| (1)

|JJCeac| (1)

|JJCefa| (3)

|JJCefamaj| (1)

|JJCefamea| (1)

|JJCefj| (4)

|JJCefjeea| (1)

|JJCefjmaa| (3)

|JJCefjmea| (48)

|JJCffamea| (1)

|JJCffmeac| (1)

|JJCjja| (1)

|JJCmaa| (12)

|JJCmaj| (7)

|JJCmakmea| (1)

|JJCmea| (62)

|JJCmej| (2)

|JJCmfj| (1)

|JJCmpa| (1)

|JJDeaa| (1)

|JJDeaj| (1)

|JJDefa| (10)

|JJDefamea| (1)

|JJDefj| (11)

|JJDefjmaa| (1)

|JJDefjmea| (1)

|JJDffd| (2)

|JJDffdmaj| (3)

|JJDffdmea| (6)

|JJDffdmej| (4)

|JJDffm| (1)

|JJDmaa| (22)

|JJDmaj| (14)

|JJDmea| (86)

|JJDmeb| (1)

|JJDmej| (8)

|JJDmek| (3)

|JJDmfa| (2)

|JJFefjmea| (2)

|JJFmaa| (1)

|JJFmea| (3)

|JJHeab| (1)

|JJHeal| (1)

|JJHefamea| (1)

|JJHefj| (1)

|JJHefjmaa| (1)

|JJHefjmea| (1)

|JJHmaa| (4)

|JJHmaj| (7)

|JJHmak| (1)

|JJHmea| (25)

|JJHmej| (1)

|JJHmfa| (1)

|JSAeaj| (2)

|JSAeal| (1)

|JSAefa| (1)

|JSAefj| (1)

|JSAffamaa| (1)

|JSAffj| (1)

|JSAffjmea| (1)

|JSAlfj| (1)

|JSAmaa| (7)

|JSAmaj| (3)

|JSAmak| (1)

|JSAmea| (6)

|JSAmej| (11)

|JSBffamaa| (1)

|JSBffamea| (2)

|JSBffjmaa| (1)

|JSBmaa| (2)

|JSBmea| (2)

|JSBmej| (1)

|JSC| (5)

|JSCcjjmaa| (1)

|JSCeal| (1)

|JSCefa| (1)

|JSCefamea| (1)

|JSCefj| (1)

|JSCefjmea| (1)

|JSCffj| (1)

|JSClfj| (1)

|JSCmaa| (18)

|JSCmab| (1)

|JSCmaj| (18)

|JSCmak| (3)

|JSCmea| (101)

|JSCmej| (2)

|JSCmfa| (1)

|JSCmfp| (1)

|JSD| (1)

|JSDeaa| (1)

|JSDefa| (4)

|JSDefamea| (1)

|JSDefj| (4)

|JSDffamea| (1)

|JSDffjmaa| (1)

|JSDffjmea| (2)

|JSDmaa| (24)

|JSDmab| (1)

|JSDmaj| (12)

|JSDmak| (1)

|JSDmea| (77)

|JSDmej| (4)

|JSDmpa| (1)

|JSFmaa| (1)

|JSFmea| (1)

|JSFmpa| (1)

|JSHeaj| (1)

|JSHefj| (1)

|JSHffamea| (1)

|JSHffjmea| (1)

|JSHmaa| (7)

|JSHmab| (1)

|JSHmaj| (4)

|JSHmea| (15)

|JSHmfb| (1)

|JSHmfj| (1)

|JUCmdj| (1)

|JUCmna| (2)

|LFDmaa| (1)

|LMAffamea| (1)

|LMAffjmea| (1)

|QABmpa| (1)

|QFAmea| (1)

|QFBefamea| (1)

|QFBefj| (1)

|QFBefjmaa| (1)

|QFBefjmea| (15)
|QFBjjjmea| (1)
|QFBjjmmea| (1)
|QFBmaa| (4)
|QFBmaj| (3)
|QFBmajmea| (2)
|QFBmea| (23)
|QFBmej| (1)
|QFBmek| (1)
|QFCefjmaa| (1)
|QFCefjmea| (1)
|QFCjjcmaa| (1)
|QFCmea| (1)
|QFFefjmea| (1)
|QFFmea| (4)
|QFFmej| (1)
|QFHmea| (1)
|QMAmea| (2)
|QMBmaa| (7)
|QMBmaj| (11)
|QMBmak| (1)
|QMBmea| (15)
|QMBmej| (3)
|QMBmek| (1)
|QMBmfj| (2)
|QMCmea| (3)
|QMFmea| (1)
|QOBjua| (1)
|QOCqob| (1)
|SAEmea| (1)
|TMAmaj| (1)
|TMAmea| (1)
|TMBmea| (1)

076.5 P cough
{aw} unrounded onset
{f} bilabial
{o} low-back
{oe} unrounded onset
No Response (180)
<kaw(f)> (1)
<kawf> (484)
<kawfN=14> (33)
<kawfNG=14> (1)
<kawfin=13> (2)
<kawfs> (2)
<kawft> (4)
<kaw{f}> (5)
<kaw{f}[N]=14> (1)
<koef> (1)
<kof> (24)
<kofNG=14> (1)
<k{aw}f> (105)
<k{aw}fN=14> (2)
<k{aw}fNG=14> (1)
<k{aw}fs> (1)
<k{aw}{f}> (1)
<k{oe}f> (55)
<k{oe}fN=14> (5)
<k{oe}{f}> (2)

<k{o}f> (7)
<k{o}{f}> (1)
076.6 L sleepy
No Response (437)
A bad (2)
B bozy (1)
C disgusted (1)
D draggy (1)
E droopy (2)
F drowsy (103)
G fagged out (1)
H foggy (1)
I gappy (1)
J groggy (3)
K jade(d) (4)
L lazy (1)
M let down (1)
N low (1)
O moody (1)
P noddy (1)
Q petered out (1)
R poorly (1)
S queasy (1)
T sleepy (400)
U sleepyheaded (3)
V sluggish (2)
W stretchified (1)
X stretchy (1)
Y stupid (2)
Z tired (26)
aa tough (2)
ab weary (8)
ac woozy (1)
ad wore/worn out (2)
ae yawny (1)
076.7 L wake up
No Response (457)
A arise (11)
B awake [v.] (6)
C awake up (1)
D awaken (5)
E get out (1)
F get out of bed (1)
G get right up (1)
H get up (203)
I get up and stir (1)
J get woke up (2)
K hit the floor (1)
L pop awake (1)
M rise (4)
N rouse (4)
O rouse up (4)
P stir around (1)
Q wake (10)
R wake up (284)
S waken (2)
076.8 L wake him up
No Response (498)
A arise him (1)

B arouse him (1)
C awake him (9)
D awake him up (2)
E awaken him (6)
F call him (3)
G get him out (1)
H get him out of bed (2)
I get him up (27)
J hurry him up (1)
K rouse him (10)
L rouse him up (5)
M roust him out of bed (1)
N shake him (2)
O shake him up (2)
P wake him (94)
Q wake him up (281)
R wake (him) up out of bed (1)
S waken him (4)

077.1 G take
<!> infinitive
<&> present 3rd singular
<@> present participle
<*> preterit
<#> past participle
{k} flap
{?} glottal
No Response (22)
<!taig> (2)
<!taik> (775)
<!taiks> (1)
<!tait> (1)
<!tai{k}> (1)
<!tek> (38)
<!took> (1)
<!traik> (1)
<&taik> (2)
<&taiks> (21)
<@taikN=14> (16)
<@taikNG=14> (3)
<@tekN=14> (1)
<*dook> (1)
<*t(oo)[1]k> (1)
<*tai(k)N=14> (1)
<*taigN=14> (1)
<*taik> (3)
<*taikId=14> (1)
<*taikN=14> (106)
<*taikNd=14> (8)
<*taikNG=14> (12)
<*taikNGd=14> (1)
<*taikt> (2)
<*tait> (1)
<*taitN=14> (9)
<*tai{k}N=14> (3)
<*tek> (2)
<*tekN=14> (1)
<*tekt> (1)
<*tetN=14> (1)
<*tik> (5)

<*toog> (1)
<*toogN=14> (1)
<*took> (665)
<*tuek> (2)
<*tuk> (64)
<#oev[R]took=341> (1)
<#tai(k)N=14> (3)
<#taig> (1)
<#taigN=14> (3)
<#taigun=13> (1)
<#taik> (2)
<#taikId=14> (1)
<#taik[N]=14> (1)
<#taikN=14> (536)
<#taikNd=14> (4)
<#taikNG=14> (3)
<#taikun=13> (1)
<#taitN=14> (8)
<#tai{?}N=14> (2)
<#tek[N]=14> (1)
<#tekN=14> (11)
<#took> (123)
<#tooken=13> (1)
<#tookN=14> (5)
<#tookNG=14> (1)
<#tuk> (10)
<#tukN=14> (1)

077.2 L deaf
No Response (154)
A　deaf (745)
B　deaf as a badger (1)
C　deaf as a doornail (1)
D　deaf as a post (3)
E　deaf as a stump (1)
F　deafy (1)
G　hard of hearing (86)
H　stone-deaf (18)

077.2 P deaf
{ai}　lax onset
{d}　devoiced
{e}　inglide
{f}　bilabial
{i}　inglide
{r}　weakly retroflex
No Response (160)
<daf> (4)
<daif> (6)
<dai{f}> (4)
<deef> (149)
<deeth> (1)
<dee{f}> (3)
<def> (159)
<de{r}f> (1)
<dif> (2)
<d{ai}f> (41)
<d{ai}{f}> (1)
<d{e}(f)> (1)
<d{e}f> (421)
<d{e}{f}> (1)

<d{i}f> (13)
<{d}ee{f}> (1)
<{d}e{f}> (1)
<{d}{e}{f}> (1)

077.3 G sweat
<!>　infinitive
<&>　present 3rd singular
<@>　present participle
<*>　preterit
<#>　past participle
No Response (258)
<!shwit> (1)
<!swat> (1)
<!swet> (97)
<!swit> (1)
<&swet> (3)
<&swets> (16)
<@AswetN=414> (1)
<@swedN=14> (1)
<@swetN=14> (50)
<@swetNG=14> (15)
<@switN=14> (1)
<*shwetId=14> (1)
<*svetId=14> (1)
<*swed> (2)
<*swedId=14> (53)
<*swet> (136)
<*swetAd=14> (1)
<*swetI(d)=14> (3)
<*swetId=14> (292)
<*swetIt=14> (2)
<*swetI{?}=14> (2)
<*swit> (5)
<*switId=14> (3)
<*switid=13> (1)
<*swutId=14> (2)
<#swedId=14> (3)
<#swet> (16)
<#swetId=14> (53)
<#switId=14> (1)
<#swutId=14> (1)

077.3 L sweated
No Response (368)
A　perspirated (1)
B　perspire (2)
C　perspired (154)
D　perstrated (1)
E　sweat (138)
F　sweated (403)

077.4 L boil [n.]
No Response (160)
A　abscess (13)
B　blackhead (6)
C　blood boil (7)
D　boil (620)
E　bulge (1)
F　bump (18)
G　canker (4)
H　carbuncle (142)

I　cat boil (3)
J　double-headed rising (1)
K　fester (3)
L　hickey (2)
M　knot (1)
N　knot on your arm (1)
O　lump (1)
P　pimple (58)
Q　pip (3)
R　pip jenny (2)
S　pone (1)
T　rising (354)
U　running sore (1)
V　skin boil (1)
W　sore (25)
X　sunspot (1)
Y　wasp[N-k] nest (1)
Z　whelp (1)
aa　whitehead (4)
ab　zit (3)

077.4 P boil
{aw}　unrounded onset
{b}　fricative
{ie}　centered onset
{L}　dark
{l}　dark
{oy}　inglide/unrounded
{z}　devoiced
{?}　glottal
No Response (275)
<bawl> (2)
<baw{?}L=14> (1)
<baw{?}{L}=14> (1)
<baw{l}> (3)
<biel> (2)
<boe[1]> (1)
<boel> (1)
<boe{l}> (1)
<boy(1)> (2)
<boyL=14> (3)
<boy[1]> (9)
<boy[1]{z}> (1)
<boyl> (118)
<boylN=14> (1)
<boyld> (1)
<boylz> (13)
<boyl{z}> (4)
<boy{l}> (162)
<boy{l}z> (5)
<bur{l}> (1)
<bw{oy}l> (1)
<b{aw}[1]> (1)
<b{aw}l> (1)
<b{aw}rl> (1)
<b{aw}{l}> (3)
<b{ie}{l}> (2)
<b{oy}(1)> (1)
<b{oy}[1]> (5)
<b{oy}[1]{z}> (1)

<b{oy}l> (103)
<b{oy}lz> (12)
<b{oy}l{z}> (4)
<b{oy}{l}> (161)
<b{oy}{l}z> (13)
<b{oy}{l}{z}> (4)
<{b}oy{l}> (1)
<{b}{oy}{l}> (1)

077.5 L pus

No Response (186)
A bloody corruption (1)
B core (80)
C core corruption (1)
D cored stuff (1)
E corruption (206)
F dead white cells (1)
G discharge (2)
H drainage (2)
I fester (7)
J festering (1)
K fluid (3)
L goop (1)
M head (1)
N infection (8)
O inflammation (6)
P matter (27)
Q mucus (4)
R old stuff (1)
S poison (6)
T puff (2)
U pus (543)
V pus bag (1)
W pus-like (1)
X refuse [n.] (1)
Y running pus (1)
Z secretion (1)
aa white stuff (1)

077.6 G swell

<!> infinitive
<&> present 3rd singular
<@> present participle
<*> preterit
<#> past participle
{?} glottal
No Response (246)
<!shwail> (1)
<!shwil> (1)
<!svel> (1)
<!swa[l]> (1)
<!swai[l]> (1)
<!swal> (1)
<!swe[l]> (13)
<!swel> (395)
<!sweld> (1)
<!swe{?}> (1)
<!swi[l]> (1)
<!swil> (2)
<!swoe[l]> (1)
<!swoel> (3)

<!swul> (1)
<!unswel=31> (1)
<&swel> (1)
<&swe[l]z> (3)
<&swelz> (20)
<&swoelz> (1)
<@sweling=13> (1)
<@swelN=14> (27)
<@swelNG=14> (10)
<@swilN=14> (1)
<*s(w)old> (1)
<*shwel> (1)
<*shwild> (1)
<*shwoel> (1)
<*swail> (2)
<*swaild> (3)
<*swawl> (1)
<*swe[l]> (2)
<*swe[l]d> (4)
<*swel> (15)
<*sweld> (276)
<*sweldId=14> (1)
<*swelt> (3)
<*swil> (1)
<*swild> (1)
<*swoe[l]> (11)
<*swoel> (107)
<*swoeld> (19)
<*swoelN=14> (24)
<*swool> (1)
<*swuld> (3)
<#shwil> (1)
<#swawlN=14> (9)
<#swe[l]> (1)
<#swel> (7)
<#sweld> (73)
<#swelN=14> (1)
<#swoe[l]> (5)
<#swoe[l]N=14> (3)
<#swoel> (24)
<#swoeld> (4)
<#swoeldN=14> (1)
<#swoelN=14> (444)
<#swoelNd=14> (1)
<#swoelNG=14> (1)
<#swoelun=13> (1)
<#swolN=14> (1)
<#swulN=14> (2)

077.7 L water [in blister]

No Response (423)
A acid (1)
B blister water (2)
C body fluid (1)
D clear fluid (1)
E clear liquid (3)
F clear stuff (1)
G clear water (1)
H corruption (6)
I fester [n.] (5)

J fluid (34)
K hot water (3)
L humor (2)
M juice (4)
N liquid (6)
O matter (4)
P mucus (1)
Q poison (1)
R pus (33)
S serum (1)
T thin fluid (1)
U thin, watery pus (1)
V water (408)
W water-like (substance) (1)
X watery-like (substance) (2)
Y watery liquid (1)
Z watery matter (1)
aa watery stuff (2)
ab watery substance (3)
ac watery-type substance (1)
ad white mucus (1)
ae yellow liquid (1)

078.1 P wound

{aw} unrounded onset
{d} devoiced
{z} devoiced
{?} glottal
No Response (171)
<wewn(d)> (5)
<wewnd> (6)
<wewn{d}> (1)
<woen(d)> (1)
<woend> (2)
<woon(d)> (1)
<woond> (1)
<woondId=14> (1)
<wown(d)> (1)
<wownd> (4)
<wue[n](d)> (9)
<wuen(d)> (337)
<wuen(d)z> (3)
<wuen(d){z}> (2)
<wuend> (317)
<wuendId=14> (14)
<wuendIt=14> (2)
<wuendI{d}=14> (4)
<wuend{z}> (1)
<wuents> (1)
<wuen{d}> (41)
<w{aw}n(d)> (1)
<{?}uend> (1)

078.1 S wound

No Response (0)
|B2E| (1)
|BJAefj| (1)
|BJEbjj| (1)
|BSA| (1)
|BSAefa| (2)
|BSAmaj| (1)

|BSE| (1)
|BSEefa| (1)
|C2Dmdj| (1)
|CJH| (1)
|CSA| (1)
|CSD| (1)
|CUC| (1)
|CUCmdj| (1)
|EMA| (1)
|EMG| (1)
|FMFmaj| (1)
|FOB| (1)
|FOBfoi| (1)
|JJBcsa| (1)
|JJFbja| (1)
|JUAeoj| (1)
|JUFeoj| (1)
|RAGefa| (1)
|RKFjub| (1)
|RKGfod| (1)
|SDBqod| (1)
|bhaBUA| (1)
|bjcBJA| (1)
|c2cCUD| (1)
|cucCUD| (1)
|cudBUA| (1)
|cudCUA| (1)
|eaaBBA| (4)
|eaaBJA| (18)
|eaaBSA| (10)
|eaaCSD| (1)
|eacBJA| (2)
|eahEFB| (1)
|eajBSA| (1)
|ecbBJA| (1)
|edaB2A| (1)
|edaBHA| (1)
|edaBUA| (17)
|edaCHA| (1)
|eddB2A| (1)
|ediBUA| (1)
|edjfobBUA| (1)
|efaBJA| (108)
|efaBJAmaj| (1)
|efaBSA| (58)
|efaBSE| (1)
|efaCJD| (2)
|efaCSD| (1)
|efbBJA| (7)
|efbBSA| (1)
|efcBJA| (6)
|efcBSA| (9)
|efcCJD| (2)
|efdCJD| (1)
|efeBJA| (2)
|efhCJD| (1)
|ekaBUA| (5)
|ekaBUC| (1)
|ekcBUA| (2)

|emaBJA| (4)
|emaCJD| (1)
|embBJA| (1)
|emcBJA| (2)
|emcBJJ| (1)
|emcBSA| (1)
|emcCSD| (1)
|emdBJA| (2)
|emhCJD| (1)
|eoaB2A| (33)
|eoaB2Amdj| (1)
|eoaB2E| (1)
|eoaBUA| (71)
|eoaBUC| (1)
|eoaBUD| (1)
|eoaBUJ| (2)
|eobBUA| (3)
|eocB2A| (1)
|eocBUA| (1)
|eocC2A| (1)
|eocCUD| (1)
|eodCUD| (1)
|eoeBUA| (1)
|eoeBUE| (1)
|eogBUJ| (1)
|eohBUA| (1)
|eosBUA| (1)
|exaB2A| (1)
|exaBUA| (17)
|excBUA| (9)
|excBUE| (1)
|excBUJ| (1)
|exdBUA| (1)
|exeCUJ| (1)
|exfBUA| (2)
|exgCUA| (1)
|exhBUA| (3)
|exhBUC| (1)
|exhCUD| (1)
|exiBUA| (2)
|exiBUJ| (4)
|exiBUN| (1)
|exiCUA| (1)
|exiCUD| (1)
|exiCUJ| (1)
|faaBJA| (2)
|facBJA| (1)
|facEFA| (1)
|fadBJA| (1)
|fadCJD| (1)
|fadCSD| (1)
|fahBJA| (1)
|fcaBJA| (1)
|fccCJD| (1)
|fcfCJD| (1)
|fdaBUA| (1)
|fdaCUA| (1)
|fddBUA| (1)
|fddCUD| (3)

|fdfCUF| (1)
|fdiBUA| (1)
|ffaBJA| (5)
|ffaBJJ| (1)
|ffaCJA| (2)
|ffaCSD| (2)
|ffaFFB| (1)
|ffbBJA| (4)
|ffbCJD| (1)
|ffdBJA| (10)
|ffdBJJ| (2)
|ffdBSA| (6)
|ffdBSD| (1)
|ffdCJD| (61)
|ffdCJF| (3)
|ffdCJM| (7)
|ffdCSD| (50)
|ffdCSF| (1)
|ffdCUD| (2)
|fffBJA| (1)
|fffCJD| (2)
|fffCJF| (1)
|ffhBJA| (4)
|ffhCJD| (7)
|ffhCJH| (1)
|ffhCSD| (3)
|ffiFFB| (1)
|fjaBJA| (2)
|fjdCJD| (1)
|fkdCUD| (1)
|fkdCUH| (1)
|fkhCUD| (1)
|fmaBJA| (11)
|fmaCJA| (1)
|fmaEFA| (1)
|fmbBJA| (1)
|fmcBJA| (1)
|fmcCJC| (1)
|fmdBJJ| (1)
|fmdBSA| (1)
|fmdCJD| (9)
|fmdCSD| (3)
|fmfBJA| (1)
|fmhCJD| (1)
|foaBUA| (1)
|foaCUA| (8)
|fobBUA| (2)
|fobBUJ| (1)
|fobCUD| (1)
|focB2A| (1)
|focBUA| (3)
|focBUJ| (1)
|focCUA| (2)
|focCUC| (1)
|focCUD| (2)
|focCUH| (1)
|focFOB| (1)
|fodB2A| (4)
|fodB2D| (2)

|fodBUA| (13)
|fodC2A| (1)
|fodC2D| (11)
|fodCHF| (1)
|fodCUA| (2)
|fodCUD| (39)
|fodCUDmdj| (1)
|fodCUF| (3)
|fodCUH| (3)
|fodc2aC2A| (1)
|fofCUA| (2)
|fofCUD| (1)
|fofcudCUB| (1)
|fohBUA| (2)
|fohC2A| (1)
|fohC2D| (3)
|fohCUB| (1)
|fohCUD| (8)
|fohCUH| (1)
|foiBUA| (2)
|foiFOA| (1)
|foiFOB| (2)
|fubBUA| (1)
|fxaBUA| (2)
|fxaCUA| (3)
|fxbBUA| (2)
|fxbCUA| (1)
|fxbCUJ| (2)
|fxcBUJ| (2)
|fxcCUA| (4)
|fxcCUC| (2)
|fxcCUD| (4)
|fxdBUA| (7)
|fxdC2D| (1)
|fxdCUA| (1)
|fxdCUD| (8)
|fxgBUJ| (1)
|fxhBUA| (1)
|fxhC2A| (1)
|fxhCUD| (2)
|fxhCUH| (1)
|fxiBUJ| (5)
|fxiCUJ| (2)
|laeBJJ| (1)
|lkdEOK| (1)
|nddEOK| (1)
|nfaBJA| (1)
|nfbBJA| (1)

078.2 L proud flesh

No Response (355)
A   bad flesh (1)
B   cold flesh (1)
C   dead flesh (10)
D   dead skin (5)
E   died flesh (1)
F   gristle (2)
G   plowed flesh (28)
H   plowed flush (2)
I   plowed fresh (15)

J   prodded flesh (1)
K   proud corruption (1)
L   proud flesh (493)
M   proud flush (2)
N   proud fresh (23)
O   proud skin (1)
P   quick flesh (2)
Q   scar tissue (8)
R   wild flesh (2)

078.2 P proud flesh

{a}   lower low-front/monophthong
{ai}   lax onset
{d}   devoiced
{e}   inglide
{f}   bilabial
{l}   devoiced
{ow}   inglide
{r}   devoiced
{t}   flap
{u}   central offglide
{w}   labial retroflex
{?}   glottal

No Response (352)
<p(r)ow(d)fl{ai}sh=13> (1)
<p(r)ow(d)f{l}esh=13> (1)
<p(r)owdflesh=13> (1)
<p(r)owdflesh=31> (1)
<p(r)owdfl{e}sh=11> (2)
<p(r)owdfresh=13> (1)
<plowdflush=21> (1)
<plowdfl{ai}sh=31> (1)
<plowdfl{u}sh=31> (1)
<plowdfresh=31> (1)
<plowdf{l}esh=13> (1)
<plowdf{r}ish=21> (1)
<pl{ow}dfl{ai}sh=31> (1)
<prow(d)flesh=13> (1)
<prow(d)f{l}esh=13> (1)
<prowd> (2)
<prowdflash=11> (1)
<prowdflesh=11> (22)
<prowdflesh=12> (2)
<prowdflesh=13> (23)
<prowdflesh=21> (5)
<prowdflesh=31> (21)
<prowdflish=13> (2)
<prowdflish=21> (1)
<prowdfl{ai}sh=13> (20)
<prowdfl{ai}sh=21> (3)
<prowdfl{ai}sh=31> (19)
<prowdfl{e}(sh)=13> (1)
<prowdfl{e}sh=11> (25)
<prowdfl{e}sh=13> (9)
<prowdfl{e}sh=31> (2)
<prowdfl{e}t=13> (1)
<prowdfl{u}sh=13> (1)
<prowdfresh=11> (2)
<prowdfresh=13> (2)
<prowdfresh=31> (1)

<prowdfr{ai}sh=13> (1)
<prowdf{l}esh=11> (4)
<prowdf{l}esh=13> (2)
<prowdf{l}esh=31> (1)
<prowdf{l}ush=13> (1)
<prowdf{l}{ai}sh=13> (1)
<prowdf{l}{ai}sh=31> (1)
<prowdf{l}{e}sh=11> (2)
<prowdf{l}{e}sh=13> (1)
<prowdf{r}esh=31> (2)
<prowdf{w}{e}sh=11> (1)
<prowdmlf{r}esh=141> (1)
<prowd{f}lish=13> (1)
<prowd{f}rish=13> (1)
<prowtflesh=13> (1)
<prow{d}flesh=12> (1)
<prow{d}flesh=13> (1)
<prow{d}flesh=21> (1)
<pr{a}dflesh=13> (2)
<pr{a}dflesh=31> (2)
<pr{ow}dflash=11> (1)
<pr{ow}dflash=13> (1)
<pr{ow}dflesh=11> (2)
<pr{ow}dflesh=12> (1)
<pr{ow}dflesh=13> (8)
<pr{ow}dflesh=31> (2)
<pr{ow}dfl{ai}sh=13> (1)
<pr{ow}dfl{ai}sh=31> (3)
<pr{ow}dfl{e}sh=11> (4)
<pr{ow}dfresh=11> (1)
<pr{ow}df{l}esh=11> (1)
<pr{ow}df{l}esh=13> (1)
<pr{ow}df{l}{e}sh=13> (1)
<pr{ow}d{f}lesh=21> (1)
<pr{ow}{d}f{w}esh=13> (1)
<p{l}owd> (2)
<p{l}owdflash=13> (1)
<p{l}owdflesh=11> (2)
<p{l}owdflesh=13> (1)
<p{l}owdflesh=31> (3)
<p{l}owdfl{ai}sh=13> (1)
<p{l}owdfl{ai}sh=31> (1)
<p{l}owdfl{e}sh=31> (1)
<p{l}owdfresh=13> (1)
<p{l}owdfr{e}sh=13> (2)
<p{l}owdfwesh=13> (1)
<p{l}owdf{l}ash=11> (1)
<p{l}owdf{l}esh=13> (1)
<p{l}owdf{l}esh=21> (2)
<p{l}owdf{l}esh=31> (1)
<p{l}owdf{l}oosh=21> (1)
<p{l}owdf{l}ush=21> (2)
<p{l}owdf{l}{e}sh=11> (2)
<p{l}owdf{l}{e}sh=13> (1)
<p{l}owdf{l}{e}sh=31> (2)
<p{l}owdf{r}esh=11> (1)
<p{l}owdf{r}esh=13> (1)
<p{l}owdf{r}ush=21> (1)
<p{l}owsf{r}esh=31> (1)

<p{l}{ow}dflesh=31> (1)
<p{l}{ow}dfresh=31> (1)
<p{r}odIf{l}{e}sh=143> (1)
<p{r}ow(d)f{l}esh=11> (1)
<p{r}owd> (2)
<p{r}owdAf{l}esh=143> (1)
<p{r}owdflash=13> (2)
<p{r}owdflash=21> (1)
<p{r}owdflash=31> (1)
<p{r}owdfle(sh)=11> (1)
<p{r}owdflesh=11> (19)
<p{r}owdflesh=13> (28)
<p{r}owdflesh=21> (3)
<p{r}owdflesh=31> (8)
<p{r}owdflursh=31> (1)
<p{r}owdflush=11> (1)
<p{r}owdflush=13> (2)
<p{r}owdfl{ai}sh=13> (2)
<p{r}owdfl{e}sh=11> (11)
<p{r}owdfl{e}sh=12> (2)
<p{r}owdfl{e}sh=13> (7)
<p{r}owdfl{e}sh=21> (2)
<p{r}owdfl{e}sh=31> (3)
<p{r}owdfl{u}sh=13> (1)
<p{r}owdfresh=11> (1)
<p{r}owdfresh=13> (2)
<p{r}owdfresh=31> (2)
<p{r}owdfr{e}(sh)=13> (1)
<p{r}owdfr{e}sh=11> (2)
<p{r}owdfr{e}sh=13> (1)
<p{r}owdfr{e}sh=21> (1)
<p{r}owdf{l}ash=11> (1)
<p{r}owdf{l}esh=11> (10)
<p{r}owdf{l}esh=13> (55)
<p{r}owdf{l}esh=21> (44)
<p{r}owdf{l}esh=31> (6)
<p{r}owdf{l}ush=11> (1)
<p{r}owdf{l}ush=13> (2)
<p{r}owdf{l}ush=21> (4)
<p{r}owdf{l}{ai}sh=21> (2)
<p{r}owdf{l}{e}sh=11> (3)
<p{r}owdf{l}{e}sh=12> (1)
<p{r}owdf{l}{e}sh=13> (1)
<p{r}owdf{l}{e}sh=21> (5)
<p{r}owdf{l}{e}sh=31> (1)
<p{r}owdf{r}esh=13> (3)
<p{r}owdf{r}esh=21> (2)
<p{r}owdf{r}ush=13> (3)
<p{r}owdf{r}{e}sh=13> (1)
<p{r}owdf{w}esh=13> (1)
<p{r}owdslesh=13> (1)
<p{r}owd{f}{r}esh=13> (1)
<p{r}ow{?}flesh=11> (1)
<p{r}ow{d}flesh=11> (2)
<p{r}ow{d}flesh=13> (1)
<p{r}ow{d}f{l}esh=11> (1)
<p{r}{ow}dflesh=13> (3)
<p{r}{ow}dflesh=31> (3)
<p{r}{ow}dfl{e}sh=13> (1)

<p{r}{ow}df{e}sh=31> (1)
<p{r}{ow}df{l}esh=11> (1)
<p{r}{ow}df{l}esh=13> (7)
<p{r}{ow}df{l}esh=21> (1)
<p{r}{ow}df{l}ush=21> (1)
<p{r}{ow}df{l}{e}sh=11> (1)
<p{r}{ow}df{r}{e}sh=13> (1)
<p{t}owdflesh=11> (1)
<p{t}owdflesh=13> (1)
<p{w}owdflash=11> (1)
<p{w}owdflesh=11> (6)
<p{w}owdflesh=13> (5)
<p{w}owdflesh=21> (1)
<p{w}owdflesh=31> (6)
<p{w}owdfl{ai}sh=13> (1)
<p{w}owdfl{e}sh=11> (2)
<p{w}owdfl{e}sh=13> (4)
<p{w}owdfl{e}sh=21> (2)
<p{w}owdfl{e}sh=31> (1)
<p{w}owdfrish=13> (1)
<p{w}owdf{l}esh=11> (1)
<p{w}owdf{l}esh=13> (1)
<p{w}owdf{l}{e}sh=13> (1)
<p{w}{ow}dflesh=13> (1)
<p{w}{ow}dflesh=31> (1)
<{f}lowdflesh=31> (1)
<{f}rowdfl{e}sh=13> (1)

078.3 P iodine

{d}   devoiced
{ie}   monophthong/inglide
{R}   weakly retroflex
{r}   weakly retroflex
{t}   flap
{z}   devoiced
No Response (182)
<ar(A)d{ie}n=31> (1)
<arAdien=143> (1)
<a{r}(A)dien=13> (1)
<eAdien=341> (1)
<eAd{ie}n=143> (1)
<er(A)deen=13> (1)
<erId{ie}n=143> (1)
<hieAd{ie}n=143> (1)
<ie(A)dN=14> (1)
<ie(A)deen=13> (25)
<ie(A)deen=31> (1)
<ie(A)die[n]=13> (4)
<ie(A)dien=11> (1)
<ie(A)dien=13> (50)
<ie(A)dien=31> (7)
<ie(A)d{ie}[n]=13> (1)
<ie(A)d{ie}n=13> (14)
<ieAdN=144> (3)
<ieAdee[n]=143> (1)
<ieAdeen=143> (21)
<ieAdeen=341> (4)
<ieAdie[n]=143> (2)
<ieAdiem=143> (1)
<ieAdien=143> (106)

<ieAdien=241> (2)
<ieAdien=341> (7)
<ieAdown=143> (1)
<ieAd{ie}n=142> (1)
<ieAd{ie}n=143> (22)
<ieIdeen=143> (2)
<ieId{ie}n=142> (1)
<ier(A)dien=13> (1)
<ierIdien=341> (1)
<ieyAdeen=143> (1)
<ieyAdien=143> (2)
<ieyoedien=231> (1)
<irIdien=143> (1)
<oRd{ie}n=143> (1)
<orIdien=143> (2)
<{ie}(A)dN=14> (4)
<{ie}(A)dain=13> (1)
<{ie}(A)dan=13> (2)
<{ie}(A)deen=13> (54)
<{ie}(A)deen=31> (10)
<{ie}(A)deen{z}=13> (1)
<{ie}(A)die[n]=13> (3)
<{ie}(A)dien=12> (3)
<{ie}(A)dien=13> (25)
<{ie}(A)dien=31> (1)
<{ie}(A)din=13> (2)
<{ie}(A)d{ie}[n]=13> (3)
<{ie}(A)d{ie}n=12> (1)
<{ie}(A)d{ie}n=13> (75)
<{ie}(A)d{ie}n=21> (1)
<{ie}(A)d{ie}n=31> (4)
<{ie}(A){t}N=14> (1)
<{ie}(A){t}een=13> (1)
<{ie}(A){t}{ie}[n]=13> (1)
<{ie}(A){t}{ie}n=13> (1)
<{ie}AdN=144> (12)
<{ie}Adee(n)=143> (1)
<{ie}Adee[n]=143> (1)
<{ie}Adeen=142> (1)
<{ie}Adeen=143> (44)
<{ie}Adeen=341> (2)
<{ie}Adeen{d}=143> (1)
<{ie}Adie[n]=143> (1)
<{ie}Adien=143> (55)
<{ie}Adien=241> (1)
<{ie}Adien=341> (2)
<{ie}Adiezd=143> (1)
<{ie}Adin=143> (3)
<{ie}Ad{ie}[n]=143> (2)
<{ie}Ad{ie}d=143> (1)
<{ie}Ad{ie}m=143> (1)
<{ie}Ad{ie}n=142> (1)
<{ie}Ad{ie}n=143> (122)
<{ie}Ad{ie}n=241> (2)
<{ie}Ad{ie}n=341> (7)
<{ie}Ajeen=143> (1)
<{ie}Id{ie}n=143> (1)
<{ie}Rdeen=143> (2)
<{ie}Rdien=143> (1)

<{ie}Rd{ie}n=143> (3)
<{ie}Rd{ie}n=341> (1)
<{ie}odien=132> (1)
<{ie}oedeen=231> (1)
<{ie}oed{ie}n=132> (1)
<{ie}r(A)dien=13> (1)
<{ie}r(A)d{ie}n=13> (1)
<{ie}rAd{ie}n=143> (1)
<{ie}rId{ie}n=143> (1)
<{ie}yAd{ie}n=143> (1)
<{ie}{R}d{ie}n=143> (2)
<{ie}{r}(A)deen=13> (1)
<{ie}{r}(A)deen=31> (1)
<{ie}{r}(A)d{ie}n=13> (2)

078.4 P quinine

{ie}   monophthong/inglide
{k}   fricative
{o}   low-back
{w}   devoiced

No Response (239)
<kwAnien=41> (1)
<kwAn{ie}n=41> (1)
<kwI[n]{ie}[n]=41> (1)
<kwIn{ie}n=41> (1)
<kwa[n]{ie}n=13> (1)
<kwanien=13> (2)
<kwan{ie}n=13> (2)
<kweenien=13> (1)
<kween{ie}n=13> (1)
<kwenien=13> (5)
<kwenyA=14> (1)
<kwen{ie}[n]=13> (1)
<kwen{ie}n=13> (3)
<kwieAn{ie}n=143> (1)
<kwie[n]ien=13> (1)
<kwienN=14> (1)
<kwieneen=13> (1)
<kwienie(n)=13> (3)
<kwienie[n]=13> (5)
<kwienien=12> (1)
<kwienien=13> (174)
<kwienien=21> (1)
<kwien{ie}[n]=13> (1)
<kwien{ie}n=13> (29)
<kwinN=14> (1)
<kwindeen=13> (1)
<kwinie[n]=13> (1)
<kwinie[n]=31> (1)
<kwinien=13> (83)
<kwinien=31> (3)
<kwinin=13> (1)
<kwinnien=13> (2)
<kwin{ie}[n]=13> (4)
<kwin{ie}n=12> (2)
<kwin{ie}n=13> (104)
<kwin{ie}n=21> (1)
<kwin{ie}n=31> (3)
<kwon{ie}n=13> (1)
<kwunien=13> (1)

<kw{ie}nN=14> (2)
<kw{ie}nie[n]=13> (1)
<kw{ie}nien=12> (2)
<kw{ie}nien=13> (30)
<kw{ie}n{ie}[n]=13> (1)
<kw{ie}n{ie}n=12> (1)
<kw{ie}n{ie}n=13> (190)
<kw{ie}n{ie}n=31> (3)
<kw{ie}rnien=13> (1)
<kw{o}n{ie}n=13> (1)
<k{w}ienien=13> (3)
<k{w}in{ie}n=13> (9)
<k{w}{ie}n{ie}[n]=13> (1)
<k{w}{ie}n{ie}n=13> (8)
<{k}wienien=13> (1)

078.5 L died [neutral/veiled]

No Response (36)
A   called to his reward (1)
B   (de)cease(d) (67)
C   (de)ceaseded (4)
D   demised (1)
E   departed (this life) (13)
F   descended (1)
G   didn't make it (6)
H   didn't recover (1)
I   died (822)
J   drop(ped) dead (7)
K   dropped out (2)
L   (e)xpired (56)
M   fell dead (4)
N   gave out (1)
O   gave up the ghost (8)
P   gone (37)
Q   gone above (1)
R   gone home (1)
S   gone on (to the other side) (7)
T   gone to another world (1)
U   gone to his final resting place (1)
V   gone to rest (2)
W   gone to sleep (2)
X   got dead (1)
Y   left (us) (18)
Z   met his glory (2)
aa   met his Maker (8)
ab   moved on (1)
ac   moved to the happy hunting
       ground (3)
ad   out of his troubles (1)
ae   pass(ed) (116)
af   passed away (462)
ag   passed into the great beyond (2)
ah   passed on (108)
ai   passed out (24)
aj   passed over (the hill) (3)
ak   resigned (1)
al   slept (away) (2)
am   slipped away (1)
an   succumb(ed) (9)
ao   taken by his Creator (1)

ap   took a trip (1)
aq   transpired (1)
ar   up and died (2)
as   went away (3)
at   went on (2)
au   went over (1)
av   went right on out (1)
aw   went to heaven (2)
ax   went to his eternal rest (1)
ay   went to his future home (1)
az   went to his reward (8)
ba   went to meet his Father (1)
bb   went to (meet) his Maker (4)
bc   went to the great beyond (2)
bd   with the angels now (1)

078.6 L died [crude/humorous]

No Response (444)
A   bit the dirt (2)
B   bit the dust (5)
C   bought the farm (2)
D   bumped off (1)
E   cashed in (his chips) (7)
F   checked out (2)
G   conked out (4)
H   conked over (3)
I   cooked (2)
J   cranked out (1)
K   croaked (out) (58)
L   died dead (1)
M   dominoed (1)
N   flaked off (1)
O   flaked out (1)
P   flipped the bucket (1)
Q   gave it up (4)
R   gave up the ghost (5)
S   gone gosling [n.] (1)
T   gone to hell (3)
U   gone west (1)
V   gone where he's supposed to (1)
W   got his just deserts (1)
X   got off (1)
Y   got out of the way (5)
Z   got smeared (1)
aa   got what he deserved (2)
ab   gypped away (1)
ac   handed in his checks (1)
ad   heeled up (1)
ae   hit the bucket (1)
af   hit the grit (1)
ag   hung up his spurs (1)
ah   keeled over (16)
ai   kicked (off) (15)
aj   kicked out (11)
ak   kicked the bucket (over) (389)
al   kicked the can (1)
am   kicked the light out (1)
an   knocked off (4)
ao   left the scene (1)
ap   left town (1)

aq looking at the stars (1)
ar made it (1)
as paid his debt (1)
at pegged out (10)
au piped out (1)
av played out (1)
aw punched the big time clock (1)
ax pushing up daisies (2)
ay quit (1)
az quit breathing (1)
ba ripped off (1)
bb shoved off (1)
bc shuffled off (1)
bd split (1)
be stopped ticking (1)
bf threw in his cards (1)
bg took the bus (2)
bh took the journey (1)
bi turned up his toes (2)
bj up and kicked the bucket (1)
bk went right on to hell (2)
bl went to the big pool hall (1)
bm went up Swift Creek (1)
bn woke up in hell (1)

078.7 G (died) of

No Response (234)
A from (188)
B of (273)
C with (294)

078.8 L cemetery

No Response (82)
A bone orchard (2)
B boneyard (5)
C boot hill (6)
D burial ground(s) (18)
E burial lot (1)
F burial place (4)
G burial plot (5)
H burial spot (1)
I burying ground (28)
J burying place (2)
K burying plot (1)
L burying yard (1)
M cemetery (759)
N cemetery lot (2)
O cemetery plot (1)
P church burying ground (1)
Q church cemetery (11)
R church graveyard (2)
S church ground (1)
T church plot (1)
U churchyard (16)
V churchyard cemetery (2)
W cimetiere [F] (1)
X city cemetery (2)
Y community cemetery (1)
Z country cemetery (1)
aa country graveyard (3)
ab family burial ground (3)

ac family burial place (1)
ad family burying ground (5)
ae family burying plot (1)
af family cemetery (29)
ag family graveyard (19)
ah family lot (2)
ai family plot (25)
aj family's cemetery (1)
ak final resting place (1)
al free burial ground (1)
am garden (2)
an grave lot (1)
ao grave site (1)
ap graveside (2)
aq graveyard (517)
ar graveyard hill (1)
as graveyard plot (1)
at home burial (2)
au home cemetery (1)
av lot (4)
aw mausoleum (7)
ax memorial garden (4)
ay memorial park (4)
az military cemetery (1)
ba Negro cemetery (1)
bb nigger cemetery (1)
bc old sage field (1)
bd park (2)
be pauper's field (1)
bf plot (18)
bg potter's field (4)
bh private cemetery (8)
bi private graveyard (2)
bj private plot (1)
bk public burying ground (1)
bl resting place (3)
bm skull orchard (2)
bn slavery graveyard (1)
bo white cemetery (1)
bp wooded graveyard (1)

079.1 L casket

No Response (105)
A aluminum box (1)
B black box (4)
C box (45)
D burial box (1)
E cajon [S] (1)
F casket (569)
G casket box (2)
H coffin (542)
I coffin box (2)
J couch (1)
K grave (1)
L homemade coffin (1)
M lead coffin (1)
N metal casket (2)
O pine box (25)
P pinewood box (1)
Q pinto (3)

R plain wooden box (1)
S rosewood coffin (1)
T rough box (1)
U sharpshooter (2)
V sharpshooter casket (1)
W shotgun coffin (1)
X steel casket (1)
Y wood box (2)
Z wooden box (13)
aa wooden casket (2)
ab wooden coffin (2)
ac wooden overcoat (1)

079.2 L funeral

No Response (136)
A burial (36)
B burial ceremony (6)
C burial service(s) (3)
D burying (3)
E bye-bye, the (1)
F ceremony (4)
G church ceremony (1)
H church funeral (1)
I close-casket funeral (1)
J double funeral (1)
K funeral (729)
L funeral ceremony (1)
M funeral rites (1)
N funeral service (33)
O funeral time (1)
P grave rites (1)
Q graveside (1)
R graveside burial (2)
S graveside ceremony (3)
T graveside rites (1)
U graveside service(s) (10)
V interment (3)
W last rites (6)
X laying to rest (1)
Y memorial service (1)
Z nigger funeral (1)
aa obsequies (1)
ab planting (1)
ac requiem (1)
ad rite(s) (4)
ae ritual (1)
af service(s) (14)

079.2 P funeral

{f} bilabial
{n} nasalized flap
{R} weakly retroflex
{r} weakly retroflex
{z} devoiced
No Response (114)
<f(y)i[n]AwL=144> (1)
<f(y)oonArL=144> (1)
<f(y)uenArL=144> (1)
<f(y)uenrL=14> (1)
<f(y)urnArL=144> (1)
<f(y)urnRL=144> (1)

<few[n]r[L]=14> (1)
<fewn(r)L=14> (23)
<fewn(r)Lz=14> (1)
<fewn(r)[L]=14> (2)
<fewnArL=144> (17)
<fewnArLz=144> (1)
<fewnArL{z}=144> (1)
<fewnAr[L]=144> (1)
<fewnIrL=144> (2)
<fewnRL=144> (18)
<fewnRl=14> (7)
<fewnirL=134> (1)
<fewnn(r)L=14> (1)
<fewnrL=14> (44)
<fewnrL{z}=14> (1)
<fewnrRl{z}=14> (1)
<fewn{R}L=144> (3)
<fewn{R}l=14> (4)
<few{n}(r)L=14> (1)
<fruenrL=14> (1)
<fyeenrL=14> (1)
<fyewR[L]=144> (1)
<fyewn(r)L=14> (5)
<fyewn(r)[L]=14> (1)
<fyewnArL=144> (1)
<fyewnArul=143> (1)
<fyewnIrL=144> (2)
<fyewnRL=144> (2)
<fyewnRl=14> (2)
<fyewnrL=14> (24)
<fyewnr[L]=14> (3)
<fyewnrul=13> (1)
<fyewn{R}L=144> (2)
<fyewn{R}l=14> (3)
<fyewn{r}L=14> (1)
<fyewn{r}Lz=14> (1)
<fyinArL=144> (1)
<fyinRL=144> (1)
<fyinR[L]=144> (1)
<fyoon(r)L=14> (2)
<fyoonArL=144> (1)
<fyoonIrL=144> (1)
<fyoonRL=144> (3)
<fyoonrL=14> (5)
<fyoonrul=13> (1)
<fyue(n)Rl=14> (1)
<fyue(n)rL=14> (1)
<fyue[n](r)L=14> (5)
<fyue[n](r)[L]=14> (1)
<fyue[n]IrL=144> (1)
<fyue[n]rL=14> (11)
<fyue[n]rLz=14> (1)
<fyue[n]yL=14> (1)
<fyuen(r)L=14> (111)
<fyuen(r)L{z}=14> (1)
<fyuen(r)[L]=14> (6)
<fyuen(rL)> (1)
<fyuenArL=144> (53)
<fyuenArLz=144> (3)

<fyuenArL{z}=144> (1)
<fyuenAr[L]=144> (1)
<fyuenIrL=144> (35)
<fyuenIrLz=144> (1)
<fyuenIr[L]=144> (1)
<fyuenRL=144> (24)
<fyuenRL{z}=144> (1)
<fyuenR[L]=144> (2)
<fyuenRl=14> (33)
<fyuenRrL=144> (5)
<fyuenrL=14> (274)
<fyuenrLs=14> (1)
<fyuenrLz=14> (5)
<fyuenr[L]=14> (5)
<fyuenue(r)l=13> (1)
<fyuenyL=14> (2)
<fyuen{R}L=144> (2)
<fyuen{R}l=14> (12)
<fyue{n}(r)L=14> (2)
<fyue{n}IrL=144> (1)
<fyun(r)L=14> (2)
<fyunRL=144> (1)
<fyunR[L]=144> (1)
<fyunrL=14> (2)
<fyunrL{z}=14> (1)
<fyu{r}nIrL=144> (1)
<{f}yeenr[L]=14> (1)
<{f}yewn(r)[L]=14> (3)
<{f}yewnRL=144> (2)
<{f}yewnR[L]=144> (1)
<{f}yewnr[L]=14> (2)
<{f}yin(r)[L]=14> (1)
<{f}yinAR[l]=144> (1)
<{f}yinR[L]=144> (1)
<{f}yoonr[L]=14> (1)
<{f}yuen(r)[L]=14> (1)
<{f}yuenR[L]=144> (1)
<{f}yuen[R][L]=144> (1)

079.3 L (in) mourning
No Response (179)
A acting a fool (2)
B all in black (1)
C all shooken up (1)
D all up in the air (1)
E bemoaning (1)
F bereaved (1)
G breaking down (2)
H broken up (2)
I carried away (2)
J carrying on (27)
K crying (2)
L disturbed (1)
M dressed in black (3)
N falling out (2)
O getting carried away (1)
P getting hysterical (3)
Q giving away (1)
R (going) all to pieces (3)
S going haywire (1)

T going into hysterics (1)
U going on (1)
V going to fall out (1)
W going to pieces (1)
X grief-stricken (1)
Y grieved (3)
Z grieving (4)
aa heartbroken (1)
ab hurt over it (1)
ac hysterical (19)
ad in a frenzy (1)
ae (in) bereavement (2)
af in black (2)
ag (in) deep mourning (1)
ah (in) full mourning (1)
ai (in) grief (1)
aj (in) grieving (1)
ak in hysterics (1)
al (in) mourning (684)
am (in) second mourning (1)
an in shock (1)
ao (in) sorrow (3)
ap in sympathy (1)
aq in the mourning clothes (2)
ar mourn (12)
as mourn(ing) (around) (1)
at nerves [X-0] stirred up (1)
au nervous (1)
av overcome with grief (1)
aw putting on (4)
ax putting on a show (1)
ay putting on mourning (1)
az shook up (1)
ba sobbing (1)
bb sorrowing (1)
bc taking it (mighty) hard (15)
bd taking it serious (1)
be taking on (a lot) (25)
bf turning loose (1)
bg upset (3)
bh wailing (1)
bi weeping (5)

079.3 P mourning
{aw} unrounded onset
{o} low-back
{oe} lowered onset
{r} weakly retroflex
<(NG)> unmarked participle
No Response (207)
<maw(r)nN=14> (12)
<maw(r)nNG=14> (1)
<maw[r]nN=14> (8)
<maw[r]nNG=14> (3)
<maw[r]ning=13> (1)
<mawrn(NG)> (1)
<mawrnN=14> (20)
<mawrnNG=14> (16)
<maw{r}nN=14> (2)
<moe(r)n(NG)> (1)

<moe(r)nN=14> (7)
<moe(r)nNG=14> (6)
<moe[r]nN=14> (19)
<moe[r]nNG=14> (16)
<moe[r]ning=13> (1)
<moernN=14> (16)
<moernNG=14> (58)
<moe{r}n(NG)> (1)
<moe{r}nN=14> (14)
<moe{r}nNG=14> (13)
<moo[r]nNG=14> (1)
<mowrn(NG)> (1)
<mwaw{r}nN=14> (1)
<m{aw}(r)n(NG)> (1)
<m{aw}rnN=14> (1)
<m{aw}rnNG=14> (1)
<m{oe}(r)[n](NG)> (1)
<m{oe}(r)n(NG)> (2)
<m{oe}(r)nN=14> (32)
<m{oe}(r)nNG=14> (7)
<m{oe}(r)n[N]=14> (1)
<m{oe}[r][n](NG)> (1)
<m{oe}[r][n]N=14> (1)
<m{oe}[r]n(NG)> (1)
<m{oe}[r]nN=14> (67)
<m{oe}[r]nNG=14> (50)
<m{oe}[r]nNz=14> (1)
<m{oe}rn(NG)> (3)
<m{oe}rnN=14> (84)
<m{oe}rnNG=14> (168)
<m{oe}rn[N]=14> (1)
<m{oe}rning=13> (2)
<m{oe}{r}[n](NG)> (1)
<m{oe}{r}n(NG)> (1)
<m{oe}{r}nN=14> (32)
<m{oe}{r}nNG=14> (35)
<m{o}rnNG=14> (1)

079.4 G pretty well

No Response (298)

A   able to get along (1)
B   (a)bout (as) usual (3)
C   (about) average (4)
D   (a)bout like common (1)
E   (a)bout like I've been (1)
F   ain't doing so good (1)
G   all right (76)
H   as usual (2)
I   awful droopy (1)
J   bad (2)
K   better (5)
L   bitter (1)
M   blowing and a-going (1)
N   doing nicely (1)
O   don't feel so hot (1)
P   don't feel too well (2)
Q   don't feel up to par (1)
R   droopy (2)
S   fair (24)
T   fair enough (1)

U   fair to middling (13)
V   fair to moderate (1)
W   fair well (2)
X   fairly (2)
Y   fairly good (6)
Z   fairly middling (1)
aa   fairly well (13)
ab   feeling like hell (1)
ac   fine (269)
ad   getting (a)long all right (2)
ae   getting along fine (1)
af   getting along pretty good (1)
ag   good (13)
ah   good enough (1)
ai   hadn't been feeling too well (1)
aj   hadn't got a worry in the world (1)
ak   hanging on (1)
al   have felt better (2)
am   I ain't well, I ain't down (1)
an   I don't know (1)
ao   I wish I knew (1)
ap   I'll do (1)
aq   I'll pass (1)
ar   I'm here (1)
as   just (a)bout like I [X-0] been (1)
at   just ain't much (1)
au   just barely here (1)
av   just commonly well (1)
aw   just dragging along (1)
ax   just fair (2)
ay   just fine (20)
az   just getting by (1)
ba   just great (2)
bb   just middling (1)
bc   just only (1)
bd   just so-so (3)
be   just tolerable (1)
bf   kicking but not high (1)
bg   kind of blah (1)
bh   kind of down and out (1)
bi   kind of middling (1)
bj   kind of salty (1)
bk   kind of so-so (1)
bl   making it (1)
bm   medinar(y) (1)
bn   medium (3)
bo   middling (9)
bp   middling considering (1)
bq   middling fair (1)
br   mighty fine (1)
bs   no complaints (1)
bt   no-good (1)
bu   not at all (1)
bv   not doing (1)
bw   not feeling so good (1)
bx   not feeling too good (1)
by   not kicking very high (1)

bz   not so well (3)
ca   not too good (3)
cb   not up to par (1)
cc   OK (73)
cd   on a mighty low limb (1)
ce   on a pass (1)
cf   only tolerable (1)
cg   poorly (2)
ch   pretty bum (1)
ci   pretty fair (6)
cj   pretty good (152)
ck   pretty poorly (2)
cl   pretty tough (1)
cm   pretty well (42)
cn   punk (1)
co   puny (1)
cp   quite well (1)
cq   same as usual (1)
cr   seen better days (1)
cs   so-and-so (3)
ct   so good (1)
cu   so-so (31)
cv   still living (1)
cw   supposed to be up (1)
cx   think I'll make it (1)
cy   tolerable (24)
cz   tolerable well (4)
da   tolerably well (2)
db   up to par (1)
dc   very common (2)
dd   very well (43)
de   well (1)
df   wonderful (1)

079.5 P worry

{d}   devoiced
{oo}   unrounded
{r}   weakly retroflex
{t}   flap

No Response (182)

<wawrI=14> (1)
<werI=14> (10)
<weree=13> (1)
<werrI=14> (1)
<we{r}I=14> (1)
<wirI=14> (2)
<woerI=14> (2)
<woorI=14> (2)
<worI=14> (4)
<wu[r](I)> (4)
<wu[r](I)d> (2)
<wu[r]I=14> (14)
<wu[r]Id=14> (1)
<wu[r]eed=13> (1)
<wu[r]id=13> (1)
<wu[r]{t}I=14> (1)
<wue(r)Id=14> (1)
<wur(I)> (6)
<wurA=14> (3)
<wurI=14> (462)

<wurId=14> (32)
<wurIz=14> (6)
<wurI{d}=14> (4)
<wuree=13> (16)
<wureed=13> (1)
<wurrI=14> (105)
<wurrai=13> (1)
<wurree=13> (2)
<wu{r}(I)> (2)
<wu{r}A=14> (1)
<wu{r}I=14> (16)
<wu{r}Id=14> (1)
<wu{r}rI=14> (36)
<wu{r}rId=14> (2)
<w{oo}rI=14> (1)

079.5 S worry

No Response (38)
|DAEmea| (1)
|DAImea| (1)
|EACmea| (1)
|ECAmea| (1)
|FDAmza| (1)
|FFC| (1)
|JJHmea| (2)
|KABmea| (1)
|KAEmea| (4)
|KAGmea| (1)
|KCA| (1)
|KCCmea| (1)
|KCE| (1)
|KCEmea| (1)
|KCI| (1)
|KFA| (1)
|LAA| (8)
|LAAeaj| (1)
|LAAmaj| (1)
|LAAmea| (28)
|LAAmej| (1)
|LAB| (1)
|LABmea| (8)
|LABmej| (1)
|LAC| (3)
|LACmea| (6)
|LAD| (4)
|LADmea| (12)
|LADmej| (1)
|LAE| (10)
|LAEmaj| (3)
|LAEmea| (23)
|LAEmej| (1)
|LAEmpa| (1)
|LAFmea| (1)
|LAG| (1)
|LAGmea| (8)
|LAH| (2)
|LAHmea| (1)
|LAImea| (2)
|LCA| (40)
|LCAeaa| (3)

|LCAmaa| (1)
|LCAmaj| (2)
|LCAmea| (18)
|LCC| (1)
|LCD| (6)
|LCDmaj| (1)
|LCDmea| (2)
|LCDmej| (1)
|LCE| (4)
|LCEmaj| (3)
|LCEmea| (7)
|LCEmej| (1)
|LCF| (1)
|LCG| (1)
|LCGmea| (1)
|LCHmaj| (1)
|LEA| (9)
|LEAmes| (1)
|LEB| (1)
|LEDmea| (1)
|LEE| (3)
|LEEmaj| (1)
|LFA| (14)
|LFAeaj| (2)
|LFAmaj| (11)
|LFAmea| (8)
|LFB| (2)
|LFBmaj| (1)
|LFBmea| (5)
|LFBmej| (1)
|LFCmea| (1)
|LFDmea| (1)
|LFDmej| (1)
|LFE| (3)
|LFEmaj| (1)
|LFEmea| (3)
|LFEmej| (1)
|LFGmaj| (1)
|LFGmea| (1)
|LGA| (1)
|LLA| (7)
|LLE| (1)
|LLEmaj| (1)
|LMA| (51)
|LMAeaj| (3)
|LMAmaj| (14)
|LMAmak| (1)
|LMAmea| (6)
|LMAmfj| (1)
|LMBmea| (2)
|LMD| (1)
|LME| (1)
|LMEmea| (1)
|LMEmej| (1)
|LPA| (2)
|LYA| (3)
|LYE| (1)
|MAE| (2)
|MCA| (1)

|MCDmea| (1)
|MCE| (1)
|MEA| (218)
|MEAeal| (1)
|MEB| (8)
|MEC| (2)
|MED| (21)
|MEE| (5)
|MEH| (1)
|MIA| (1)
|MLA| (110)
|MLAbba| (1)
|MLB| (7)
|MLD| (8)
|MLE| (3)
|MLF| (1)
|MMA| (1)
|MPA| (8)
|MPB| (1)
|MPD| (1)
|MWA| (1)
|MWE| (1)
|MYA| (5)
|MYD| (1)
|NAA| (1)
|NABmea| (2)
|NAD| (4)
|NADmaj| (3)
|NADmea| (10)
|NAF| (3)
|NAHmaj| (3)
|NAHmea| (1)
|NAImaj| (1)
|NCD| (2)
|NCDmaj| (1)
|NCDmea| (1)
|NCFmaj| (1)
|NCH| (2)
|NCHmaj| (1)
|NCHmea| (1)
|NCImea| (1)
|NFA| (1)
|NFG| (1)
|NFHmaj| (1)
|NMA| (1)
|NMD| (2)
|NMDmaj| (2)
|NMDmea| (1)
|NMG| (1)
|PAA| (1)
|PABmea| (1)
|PAI| (1)
|fmaCJA| (1)

079.6 L rheumatism

No Response (158)
A aches and pains (1)
B arthri(tis) (1)
C arthrit(is) (1)
D arthritis (591)

E arthritis [not rheumatism] (7)
F Arthur (1)
G buritis (1)
H bursitis (42)
I cramp, the (1)
J cramps (1)
K creaking joints (1)
L gout (11)
M joint ache (1)
N lumbago (9)
O miseries (1)
P misery (1)
Q neural(gia) (1)
R neuralgia (8)
S neuritis (6)
T old age (1)
U old Arthur(s) (2)
V pain in the joints (1)
W pains in the bones (1)
X rheumatic pains (2)
Y rheumatic(s) (5)
Z (rheuma)tism (1)
aa rheumatis(m) (17)
ab rheumatism(s) (506)
ac rheumatoid (1)
ad rheumatoid arthritis (3)
ae sciatic rheumatism (1)
af stiff joints (2)
ag tendonitis (1)

079.7 P diphtheria

{p} fricative
{R} weakly retroflex
{r} weakly retroflex
{t} flap
No Response (178)
<dIkthirIA=4144> (1)
<dIptherIA=4144> (1)
<dIpthirI(A)=414> (2)
<dIpthirIA=4144> (9)
<dIpthireeA=4134> (1)
<dIpthiriA=4134> (1)
<dItthirIA=4144> (1)
<dI{p}thirIA=4144> (2)
<deptireeyA=3134> (1)
<di(p)therIyA=3144> (1)
<di(p)thirI(A)=314> (1)
<dibthiriA=2134> (1)
<die(p)thirIA=3144> (1)
<dif(th)irI(A)=314> (1)
<diftheerIA=3144> (1)
<difthirIA=2144> (1)
<difthirIA=3144> (6)
<difthirIR=3144> (1)
<difthirIyA=3144> (1)
<difthireeA=3134> (4)
<difthireeyA=1234> (3)
<difthireeyA=3134> (3)
<difthiriA=2134> (1)
<difthiriA=3134> (1)

<difthi{r}(I)yA=314> (1)
<dikthirIA=3144> (1)
<dip(th)irI(A)=314> (1)
<dipNthi{r}(I)A=3414> (1)
<dipdhirIA=3144> (1)
<dipftheer(I)yA=314> (1)
<dipfthir(I)A=134> (1)
<dipfthirIyA=1344> (1)
<dippir(I)A=314> (1)
<dipseer(I)A=314> (1)
<dipterIA=1244> (1)
<dipterIA=3144> (1)
<dipthai[r]I(A)=314> (1)
<dipthe(r)I(A)=134> (1)
<dipthee(rI)yA=134> (1)
<diptheer(I)A=124> (1)
<diptheer(I)A=314> (1)
<diptheerI(A)=314> (2)
<diptheerIA=3144> (1)
<diptheerIyA=1344> (1)
<diptheeree(A)=123> (1)
<diptheeree(A)=313> (1)
<diptheereeA=2134> (1)
<diptheereeA=3134> (1)
<diptheereeyA=1234> (1)
<dipther(I)yA=314> (2)
<diptherI(A)=134> (3)
<diptherI(A)=214> (1)
<diptherI(A)=314> (13)
<diptherIA=2144> (4)
<diptherIA=3144> (9)
<diptherI{R}=1144> (1)
<dipteree(A)=123> (1)
<diptereeA=3134> (1)
<dipthe{r}r(I)A=314> (1)
<dipthi(r)I(A)=124> (1)
<dipthi(rI)A=134> (1)
<dipthi(rI)A=314> (1)
<dipthi(rI)yA=314> (1)
<dipthir(I)A=124> (1)
<dipthir(I)A=134> (5)
<dipthir(I)A=314> (7)
<dipthir(I)R=214> (1)
<dipthir(I)yA=134> (7)
<dipthir(I)yA=314> (10)
<dipthir(IA)=12> (1)
<dipthir(IA)=31> (1)
<dipthirI(A)=124> (3)
<dipthirI(A)=134> (31)
<dipthirI(A)=214> (17)
<dipthirI(A)=314> (89)
<dipthirIA=1244> (10)
<dipthirIA=1344> (17)
<dipthirIA=2144> (29)
<dipthirIA=3144> (201)
<dipthirIR=2144> (1)
<dipthirIR=3144> (1)
<dipthirIyA=1344> (7)
<dipthirIyA=2144> (1)

<dipthirIyA=3144> (16)
<dipthiree(A)=123> (11)
<dipthiree(A)=213> (1)
<dipthiree(A)=313> (4)
<dipthireeA=1234> (7)
<dipthireeA=2134> (6)
<dipthireeA=2314> (1)
<dipthireeA=3134> (25)
<dipthireeyA=1234> (11)
<dipthireeyA=2134> (1)
<dipthireeyA=3134> (20)
<dipthiriA=2134> (4)
<dipthiriA=3134> (13)
<dipthiriyA=1234> (1)
<dipthiriyA=3134> (3)
<dipthiri{R}=3134> (1)
<dipthirriA=3134> (1)
<dipthiryI(A)=314> (1)
<dipthi{r}(I)A=134> (1)
<dipthi{r}(I)A=314> (6)
<dipthi{r}(I)yA=314> (12)
<dipthi{r}(IA)=13> (1)
<dipthi{r}(IA)=21> (1)
<dipthi{r}I(A)=134> (2)
<dipthi{r}I(A)=214> (1)
<dipthi{r}I(A)=314> (6)
<dipthi{r}IA=3144> (4)
<dipthi{r}eeyA=1234> (1)
<dipthi{r}r(I)A=314> (1)
<dipthi{r}rIA=3144> (5)
<dipthi{r}rIyA=3144> (1)
<dipthi{r}yI(A)=314> (1)
<dipthlirIA=1144> (1)
<dipthur(I)yA=134> (1)
<dipthurI(A)=134> (3)
<dipthurIA=3144> (2)
<dipthuree(A)=123> (2)
<dipthureeyA=1334> (1)
<dipth{t}(ir)I(A)=14> (1)
<dipth{t}i(rIA)=31> (1)
<diptirI(A)=314> (2)
<diptirIA=1344> (1)
<diptirIA=3144> (3)
<diptirIyA=3144> (1)
<diptireeA=2134> (1)
<diptireeyA=3134> (1)
<dipti{R}A=3144> (1)
<dipti{r}(I)yA=314> (1)
<dipti{r}rIA=3144> (1)
<dip{p}irI(A)=134> (1)
<divthirIA=1344> (1)
<di{p}thirI(A)=214> (1)
<di{p}thirIA=3144> (3)
<di{p}thireeyA=3134> (1)

079.8 L yellow jaundice

No Response (174)
A bilious (1)
B Black John (1)
C cirrhosis of (the) liver (2)

D   hepatitis (52)
E   infected liver (1)
F   jaundice (228)
G   jaundiced [adj.] (1)
H   jaundiced eye (1)
I   liver trouble (1)
J   malaria (21)
K   malarial (2)
L   malaria(1) fever (2)
M   swamp fever (1)
N   yellow chills (1)
O   yellow fe(ver) (1)
P   yellow fever (40)
Q   yellow-fever epidemic (1)
R   yellow jaun(dice) (2)
S   yellow jaundice (523)

079.8 P jaundice
{aw}   unrounded onset
{d}   devoiced
{j}   devoiced
{o}   low-back
{R}   weakly retroflex
{r}   weakly retroflex
{t}   flap
{z}   devoiced
No Response (185)
<dam(d)Azh=14> (1)
<dondAs=14> (1)
<gandIz=14> (1)
<jamnAz=14> (1)
<jan(d)As=14> (7)
<jan(d)Is=14> (2)
<jandA(s)=14> (5)
<jandAs=14> (27)
<jandAz=14> (21)
<jandA{z}=14> (5)
<jandIs=14> (27)
<jandIz=14> (2)
<jandR(z)=14> (1)
<jandRz=14> (20)
<jandR{z}=14> (6)
<jandurz=13> (1)
<jand{R}(z)=14> (2)
<jand{R}z=14> (22)
<jand{R}{z}=14> (3)
<janj{R}z=14> (1)
<jan{t}As=14> (1)
<jan{t}Is=14> (1)
<jaw(n)dIs=14> (1)
<jawn(d)As=14> (2)
<jawn(d)Is=14> (5)
<jawnd(Is)> (1)
<jawndA(s)=14> (1)
<jawndAs=14> (43)
<jawndAz=14> (1)
<jawndA{z}=14> (1)
<jawndIs=14> (138)
<jawndIth=14> (1)
<jawndRs=14> (1)

<jawndRz=14> (8)
<jawndR{z}=14> (5)
<jawndis=13> (3)
<jawndrIs=14> (1)
<jawnd{R}(s)=14> (1)
<jawnd{R}s=14> (1)
<jawnd{R}z=14> (7)
<jawnd{R}{z}=14> (1)
<jawnnIs=14> (2)
<jawntIs=14> (5)
<jawnvIs=14> (1)
<jawn{t}As=14> (1)
<jawn{t}Is=14> (1)
<jendR{z}=14> (1)
<jenj{R}(z)=14> (1)
<jien(d)A(s)=14> (1)
<jien(d)As=14> (4)
<jien(d)Is=14> (1)
<jien(d){R}s=14> (1)
<jiendAs=14> (3)
<jiendIs=14> (1)
<jientIs=14> (1)
<jien{d}Is=14> (1)
<jien{t}A{z}=14> (1)
<jo[n](d)Is=14> (1)
<jon(d)As=14> (4)
<jon(d)Is=14> (6)
<jon(dIs)> (1)
<jondA(s)=14> (4)
<jondAs=14> (59)
<jondAz=14> (7)
<jondA{z}=14> (10)
<jondI(s)=14> (1)
<jondIs=14> (139)
<jondIz=14> (2)
<jondI{z}=14> (2)
<jondRs=14> (1)
<jondRz=14> (10)
<jondR{z}=14> (2)
<jondis=13> (1)
<jondrI{z}=14> (1)
<jondurz=13> (1)
<jondu{r}z=13> (1)
<jond{R}s=14> (2)
<jond{R}z=14> (9)
<jond{R}{z}=14> (7)
<jonjIs=14> (1)
<jontAs=14> (2)
<jon{d}As=14> (2)
<jon{t}As=14> (1)
<jon{t}Is=14> (2)
<jowndIs=14> (1)
<joyndAs=14> (1)
<jo{r}ndAs=14> (1)
<j{aw}ndAs=14> (13)
<j{aw}ndAz=14> (1)
<j{aw}ndIs=14> (22)
<j{aw}ndIst=14> (1)
<j{aw}ndRz=14> (3)

<j{aw}ndR{z}=14> (1)
<j{aw}n{d}Is=14> (1)
<j{aw}n{t}Is=14> (1)
<j{o}n(d)Is=14> (2)
<j{o}ndAs=14> (7)
<j{o}ndIs=14> (17)
<j{o}ndRz=14> (4)
<j{o}n{d}e(s)=13> (1)
<sand{R}z=14> (1)
<zandA{z}=14> (1)
<zawndRz=14> (1)
<zhawn(d)Is=14> (1)
<zhawndAs=14> (1)
<zhawndIs=14> (1)
<zhawndis=31> (1)
<zhon(d)Is=14> (1)
<zhondAs=14> (2)
<{j}ondAsh=14> (1)
<{j}ondIs=14> (1)

080.1 L appendicitis
No Response (167)
A   abscess (1)
B   acid (1)
C   acute indigestion (1)
D   (ap)pendicitis (364)
E   appendicitis (339)
F   (ap)pendix (26)
G   appendix (20)
H   appendix attack (5)
I   (ap)pendix trouble (1)
J   (ap)pendix was bad (1)
K   attack of (ap)pendicitis (2)
L   attack of appendix (4)
M   attack of colic (1)
N   bad appendix (1)
O   bellyache (2)
P   blind gut (1)
Q   burst appendix (1)
R   bursted (ap)pendix (1)
S   busted appendix (1)
T   case of appendix (1)
U   colic (14)
V   cramp colic (20)
W   cramps (2)
X   inflamed appendix (1)
Y   kidney colic (2)
Z   lock bowels (2)
aa   packed bowels (1)
ab   pleurisy (1)
ac   pleurisy of the side (1)
ad   pneumonia from your side (1)
ae   renal colic (1)
af   rupture appendix (3)
ag   ruptured (ap)pendix (3)
ah   ruptured appendix (3)
ai   side ache (1)
aj   side pleurisy (1)
ak   stomach colic (2)
al   stomachache (1)

080.1 P appendicitis

{R}   weakly retroflex

{t}   flap

No Response (216)

<(A)pIn(d)AsietIs=4414> (1)

<(A)pIn(dI)sietAs=414> (1)

<(A)pIndAsiedAs=4414> (1)

<(A)pe[n]dAsietA(s)=3414> (1)

<(A)pe[n]{t}IsietIs=3414> (1)

<(A)peen(d)IsietIs=3414> (1)

<(A)peendIsietIs=3414> (1)

<(A)pen(d)AseetAs=3414> (1)

<(A)pen(d)Asie(t)Is=3414> (1)

<(A)pen(d)AsiedIs=3414> (1)

<(A)pen(d)AsietAs=3414> (3)

<(A)pen(d)AsietIs=3414> (8)

<(A)pen(d)IntsietAs=3414> (1)

<(A)pen(d)IsiedI(s)=3414> (1)

<(A)pen(d)IsiedIs=2414> (1)

<(A)pen(d)IsiedIs=3414> (8)

<(A)pen(d)IsietA(s)=3414> (1)

<(A)pen(d)IsietAs=3414> (2)

<(A)pen(d)IsietIs=1434> (1)

<(A)pen(d)IsietIs=3414> (2)

<(A)pen(d)Isie{t}Ath=3414> (1)

<(A)pen(d)Isie{t}Is=3414> (2)

<(A)pendAshsie{t}Ish=3414> (1)

<(A)pendAsiedAs=3414> (1)

<(A)pendAsietA(s)=3414> (1)

<(A)pendAsietAs=1424> (1)

<(A)pendAsietAs=3414> (28)

<(A)pendAsietI(s)=3414> (1)

<(A)pendAsietIs=3414> (30)

<(A)pendAsie{t}As=1434> (1)

<(A)pendAsie{t}As=3414> (2)

<(A)pendAsie{t}Is=3414> (1)

<(A)pendI(sietIs)=14> (1)

<(A)pendIksiedIs=1414> (1)

<(A)pendIshiedAs=3414> (1)

<(A)pendIsie(t)Is=3414> (1)

<(A)pendIsie(tIs)=341> (1)

<(A)pendIsiedIs=1434> (3)

<(A)pendIsiedIs=2414> (1)

<(A)pendIsiedIs=3414> (46)

<(A)pendIsielNt=3414> (1)

<(A)pendIsietAs=3414> (9)

<(A)pendIsietI(s)=3414> (2)

<(A)pendIsietIs=3414> (45)

<(A)pendIsie{t}Is=2414> (1)

<(A)pendIsie{t}Is=3414> (3)

<(A)pendIsie{t}Ith=1434> (1)

<(A)pend{R}sietIs=3414> (1)

<(A)pennAsiedIs=3414> (1)

<(A)pennIsietAs=3414> (1)

<(A)pennIsietIs=3414> (1)

<(A)pennIsie{t}Is=3414> (1)

<(A)pentAsietIs=3414> (1)

<(A)pen{t}AsiedAs=3414> (1)

<(A)pen{t}AsietAs=3414> (1)

<(A)pen{t}AsietIs=3414> (1)

<(A)pen{t}IsietAs=3414> (1)

<(A)pen{t}IsietIs=3414> (2)

<(A)pen{t}Isie{t}As=1434> (1)

<(A)pi[n](dI)sie{t}Is=314> (1)

<(A)pin(d)AsietAs=3414> (6)

<(A)pin(d)AsietIs=3414> (2)

<(A)pin(d)IsiedA(s)=3414> (1)

<(A)pin(d)IsiedIs=3414> (1)

<(A)pin(d)IsietAs=3414> (5)

<(A)pin(d)IsietIs=3414> (2)

<(A)pin(d)Isie{t}As=3414> (1)

<(A)pin(d)Isie{t}Is=3414> (1)

<(A)pindAsiedAs=1424> (1)

<(A)pindAsiedAs=3414> (1)

<(A)pindAsiedIs=1434> (1)

<(A)pindAsietAs=3414> (17)

<(A)pindAsietIs=3414> (16)

<(A)pindAsie{t}As=3414> (1)

<(A)pindIsie(tIs)=341> (1)

<(A)pindIsiedIs=2414> (1)

<(A)pindIsiedIs=3414> (5)

<(A)pindIsietAs=1434> (1)

<(A)pindIsietAs=3414> (21)

<(A)pindIsietIs=3414> (16)

<(A)pindIsiet{R}(s)=3414> (1)

<(A)pindIsie{t}As=3414> (1)

<(A)pindIsie{t}Is=1434> (1)

<(A)pindIsie{t}Is=3414> (3)

<(A)pinnIsiedA(s)=3414> (1)

<(A)pinnIsiedIs=3414> (1)

<(A)pin{t}AsietAs=3414> (2)

<(A)pin{t}AsietIs=3414> (1)

<(A)pin{t}Isied(Is)=341> (1)

<(A)pin{t}IsiedIs=3414> (1)

<(A)pin{t}IsietAs=3414> (8)

<(A)pin{t}IsietIs=3414> (1)

<(A)pin{t}Isie{t}As=3414> (1)

<(A)pin{t}Isie{t}Is=3414> (1)

<Apen(d)AsietAs=43414> (2)

<Apen(d)AsietIs=42414> (1)

<Apen(d)AsietIs=43414> (2)

<Apen(d)IsiedIs=43414> (1)

<Apen(d)IsietI(s)=43414> (1)

<Apen(d)IsietIs=41434> (1)

<Apen(d)IsietIs=43414> (1)

<Apend(I)sietA(s)=4314> (1)

<ApendAsie(tIs)=4341> (1)

<ApendAsietAs=43414> (15)

<ApendAsietIs=43414> (36)

<ApendAsie{t}As=43414> (2)

<ApendAsotAz=43414> (1)

<ApendIksietIs=43414> (1)

<ApendIksie{t}Is=43414> (1)

<ApendIsiedAs=43414> (1)

<ApendIsiedIs=42414> (6)

<ApendIsiedIs=43414> (39)

<ApendIsietA(s)=43414> (1)

<ApendIsietAs=43414> (10)

<ApendIsietIs=41414> (1)

<ApendIsietIs=42414> (2)

<ApendIsietIs=43414> (36)

<ApendIsie{t}As=43414> (2)

<ApendIsie{t}Is=43414> (4)

<ApendIthiedIs=43414> (1)

<ApennIsietIs=42414> (1)

<Apen{t}IsietAs=41414> (1)

<Apen{t}IsietIs=43414> (1)

<Apen{t}Isie{t}As=43414> (1)

<Apin(d)Asie{t}Is=41424> (1)

<Apin(d)IsietIs=43414> (1)

<Apin(d)Isie{t}As=43414> (2)

<Apind(Isiet)As=414> (1)

<ApindAseetAs=43414> (1)

<ApindAsiedIs=43414> (1)

<ApindAsietA(s)=43414> (1)

<ApindAsietAs=41424> (1)

<ApindAsietAs=42414> (1)

<ApindAsietAs=43414> (13)

<ApindAsietIs=43414> (26)

<ApindAsietIz=43414> (1)

<ApindAsieyAs=43414> (1)

<ApindIshsietAs=42414> (1)

<ApindIsiedIs=43414> (5)

<ApindIsietAs=42414> (3)

<ApindIsietAs=43414> (51)

<ApindIsietIs=41414> (1)

<ApindIsietIs=43414> (26)

<ApindIsie{t}As=41424> (1)

<ApindIsie{t}As=42414> (1)

<ApindIsie{t}As=43414> (1)

<ApindIsie{t}Is=42414> (2)

<ApindIsie{t}Is=43414> (4)

<ApindIthie{t}Ith=41414> (1)

<Apin{t}IsietAs=43414> (6)

<Apin{t}IsietIs=43414> (1)

<Appin{t}IsietIs=43414> (1)

<Ipen(d)IsietIs=43414> (1)

<IpendAsietIs=43414> (6)

<IpendIsietIs=43414> (2)

<IppendAsietIs=43414> (1)

<apendAsietIs=32414> (1)

<apendIsietIs=21424> (1)

<apendIsietIs=33414> (1)

<apindIsie{t}Is=31414> (1)

<apindIsie{t}Is=32414> (1)

<eppindAsie{t}As=32414> (1)

<ipindIsietAs=32414> (1)

080.2 L vomit [neutral]

No Response (147)

A   barf (5)

B   be ill (2)

C   be nauseated (13)

D   be nauseous (3)

E   be/get sick (5)

F   belch it (2)

G   belch it up (3)

H   belch up (1)

I   bring it up (2)
J   bring up (2)
K   bulk it up (1)
L   burp (2)
M   burp it (1)
N   burp it up (1)
O   come up (2)
P   cough it up (1)
Q   expell (1)
R   gag (5)
S   gag it up (1)
T   get rid of the food (1)
U   have a action (1)
V   have a sick stomach (3)
W   have a sour stomach (2)
X   have a vomiting stomach (1)
Y   have an upset stomach (2)
Z   have indigestion (1)
aa have nausea (1)
ab have the bellyache (3)
ac have the stomachache (1)
ad have the vomits (1)
ae heave (22)
af heave it up (1)
ag heave up (4)
ah let it come back (1)
ai let it up (1)
aj lose (one's) breakfast (2)
ak lose (one's) dinner (5)
al lose (one's) lunch (1)
am lose (one's) meal (1)
an puke (23)
ao regurgitate (51)
ap (re)gurgitate (4)
aq resuscitate (1)
ar retch (5)
as spit it up (5)
at spit out (one's) food (1)
au spit up (26)
av throw back (one's) food (1)
aw throw it back up (1)
ax throw it out (1)
ay throw it up (38)
az throw (one's) food up (1)
ba throw up (366)
bb throw up (one's) food (1)
bc toss (one's) cookies (2)
bd up [v.] (1)
be up it up (1)
bf up-swallow (1)
bg urp (18)
bh urp it up (1)
bi urp up (1)
bj upchuck (70)
bk vomit (640)
bl vomit it up (16)
bm vomit (one's) food up (1)
bn vomit up (5)

080.3 L vomit [crude]

No Response (409)
A   barf (23)
B   blow groceries (1)
C   blow lunch (3)
D   bring (one's) shoe soles and all
    up (1)
E   call Monroe (1)
F   call Ralph (2)
G   cascade (1)
H   chuck up (1)
I   chuck-a-luck (1)
J   crack (one's) lunch (1)
K   crap (1)
L   drunk throw-up, a (1)
M   feed the fish (1)
N   flash (2)
O   gag (2)
P   going to Europe (1)
Q   heave (19)
R   heave up (1)
S   holler for Ralph (1)
T   holler for the dinosaurs (1)
U   hug the toilet (1)
V   let her rip (1)
W   lose it all (1)
X   lose (one's) biscuits (1)
Y   lose (one's) cookies (1)
Z   lose (one's) groceries (1)
aa lose (one's) lunch (4)
ab mess (1)
ac pitch (one's) cookies (3)
ad puke (316)
ae puke it up (8)
af puke like a buzzard (1)
ag puke like a horse (1)
ah puke (one's) guts out (1)
ai puke (one's) guts up (2)
aj puke (one's) insides out (1)
ak puke up (6)
al Ralph (3)
am (re)gurgitate (4)
an regurgitate (9)
ao shit it all up (1)
ap spew (4)
aq spew up (1)
ar spill (one's) cookies (1)
as spill (one's) guts (1)
at spill (one's) supper (1)
au spit up (2)
av throw it out (2)
aw throw it up (9)
ax throw (one's) stomach upside
    down inside out (1)
ay throw (one's) toes up (1)
az throw up (93)
ba throw up (one's) guts (1)
bb throw up (one's) socks (1)
bc toss (one's) cookies (7)
bd upchoke (1)

be upchuck (51)
bf upswallow (1)
bg url (1)
bh urp (13)
bi urp it up (3)
bj urp (one's) toes up (1)
bk urp up (1)
bl vomir [F] (1)
bm vomit (44)
bn vomit up (1)

080.4 G (sick) at his stomach

No Response (167)
A   at her stomach (1)
B   at his belly (1)
C   at his stomach (211)
D   at his tummy (2)
E   at my stomach (47)
F   at stomach (1)
G   at the belly (1)
H   at the stomach (102)
I   at their stomach[N-i] (13)
J   at your stomach (23)
K   at [D-0] stomach (4)
L   at [D-0] [N-0] (1)
M   from his stomach (1)
N   from the stomach (1)
O   in his belly (2)
P   in his stomach (79)
Q   in my stomach (13)
R   in the belly (1)
S   in the bottom of your stomach
    (3)
T   in the gut (1)
U   in the pit of his stomach (1)
V   in the stomach (77)
W   in your belly (1)
X   in your stomach (15)
Y   in [D-0] stomach (1)
Z   of a stomach (1)
aa of his stomach (6)
ab of my stomach (1)
ac of the stomach (8)
ad on his stomach (54)
ae on my stomach (5)
af on the stomach (21)
ag on their stomach[N-i] (1)
ah on your stomach (1)
ai on [D-0] stomach (1)
aj soured on his stomach (1)
ak to his stomach (46)
al to my stomach (10)
am to the stomach (10)
an to their stomach[N-i] (5)
ao to your stomach (3)
ap to [D-0] stomach (1)
aq to [M-0] stomach (1)
ar upset in the stomach (1)
as with his stomach (2)
at with my stomach (1)

au with the stomach (1)
av with their stomach[N-i] (1)
aw [P-0] his stomach (5)
ax [P-0] the stomach (1)
ay [P-0] [D-0] stomach (1)

080.5 G for to (+ inf.)

No Response (588)
A for (1)
B for to (31)
C to (197)
D [P-0] (4)

081.1 G I shall (be disappointed)

No Response (517)
A I shall (41)
B I will (228)
C I [X-0] (22)
D I'll (188)
E shall I (5)
F will I (2)

081.2A G we shall (be glad)

No Response (739)
A shall we (1)
B we shall (9)
C we will (66)
D we [X-0] (11)
E we'll (72)

081.2B G glad (to see you)

No Response (680)
A delighted (4)
B glad (192)
C great (1)
D happy (20)
E pleased (4)
F proud (96)
G thrilled (1)
H welcome (1)

081.3 G go and/take and [+ verb]

No Response (644)
A go and (94)
B take and (42)
C up and (2)

081.4 L courting

No Response (173)
A a-courting (11)
B a-courting pretty heavy (1)
C a-dating (1)
D a-going with (her) (1)
E a-sparking (2)
F being with (her) (1)
G booing (1)
H chasing (her) (2)
I corresponding (1)
J courting (571)
K courting along (1)
L courting heavy (6)
M courting (her) mighty close (1)
N courting (her) pretty (1)
O courting on (her) (1)
P courting pretty close (1)

Q courting pretty heavy (4)
R courting right along (1)
S courting steadily/steady (1)
T dating (168)
U dating pretty heavy (1)
V dating steadily/steady (5)
W dining (her) (1)
X dogging (1)
Y escorting (2)
Z falling in love (8)
aa fixing to marry/get married (1)
ab fooling around with (1)
ac galing (1)
ad getting close (2)
ae getting down to gritty (1)
af getting engaged (2)
ag getting in love (3)
ah getting (pretty) thick (5)
ai getting serious (13)
aj getting steady (1)
ak getting too thick (1)
al going after her (1)
am going out (with) (10)
an going out a lot (5)
ao going out courting (1)
ap going regular (3)
aq going steady (with) (153)
ar going to see (her) (4)
as going together (51)
at going with (61)
au hanging around after (her) (2)
av hanging his hat there (a lot) (1)
aw having intercourse with (1)
ax having relations with (her) (1)
ay he-ing and she-ing (1)
az heavy dating (2)
ba him-ing and her-ing (1)
bb interested in (her) (6)
bc keeping (her) company (9)
bd knocking around (1)
be making dates with (her) (1)
bf making love (2)
bg on the make (1)
bh paying attention to (her) (1)
bi playing up to (her) (1)
bj plug knuckling (1)
bk romancing (3)
bl rushing (her) (4)
bm seeing (her/each other) (11)
bn seeing (her) a lot (2)
bo seeing (her) regular (1)
bp setting up to (her) (1)
bq shining up to (her) (2)
br smelling around (1)
bs sniffing around the bushes (1)
bt sparking (151)
bu sparking courting (1)
bv sparking heavy (1)
bw sparkling (1)

bx spooking (1)
by spooning (4)
bz sprucing (1)
ca squiring (1)
cb steady dating (4)
cc stepping out with (1)
cd sweeping her off her feet (1)
ce sweethearting (1)
cf taking (her) out (3)
cg talking (to) (4)
ch waiting on her (2)
ci willing (her) (1)
cj wising up (1)
ck wooing (4)

081.5 L boyfriend

No Response (173)
A beau (167)
B beau, le [F] (1)
C best beau (1)
D best boyfriend (3)
E best friend (1)
F Boy Friday (1)
G boyfriend (561)
H company (1)
I courter (1)
J date (13)
K dude (2)
L fellow (62)
M fianc(e) (2)
N fiance (70)
O finance (3)
P financier (1)
Q flame (1)
R flapper (1)
S flirt (1)
T friend (11)
U friend boy (2)
V gentleman friend (1)
W grand sweetheart (1)
X guy (3)
Y high-school sweetheart (1)
Z honey (4)
aa honey breeches (1)
ab honey pie (1)
ac intended husband (1)
ad lover (24)
ae lover boy (1)
af main man (1)
ag main nigger (1)
ah main squeeze (1)
ai main thing (1)
aj man (12)
ak man friend (1)
al old man (8)
am one boy (1)
an puppy lover (1)
ao regular (2)
ap regular boyfriend (1)
aq regular date (1)

ar right-hand man (1)
as Schatz [G] (1)
at special boyfriend (2)
au standby (2)
av steady (34)
aw steady beau (3)
ax steady boyfriend (4)
ay steady date (3)
az sucker (1)
ba sugar baby (1)
bb sugar daddy (1)
bc sugar lump (1)
bd suitor (14)
be sweetheart (176)
bf sweetie (4)
bg to-be husband (1)
bh young man (2)

081.6 L girl friend

No Response (205)
A baby doll (1)
B belle (2)
C belle, la [F] (1)
D best girl (3)
E best girl friend (3)
F bitch (1)
G bride (2)
H bride to be (1)
I broad (1)
J chick (5)
K companion (1)
L date (4)
M dear (1)
N dearest (1)
O fianc(ee) (2)
P fiancee (33)
Q finance (1)
R first love (1)
S friend (3)
T friend girl (1)
U future wife (2)
V gal (11)
W gal friend (1)
X girl (103)
Y girl friend (518)
Z heartthrob (1)
aa honey (5)
ab honeybunch (1)
ac intended (1)
ad intended wife (1)
ae lady (4)
af lady friend (5)
ag lady love (1)
ah little girl (1)
ai lover (8)
aj lover girl (1)
ak main girl (2)
al main squeeze (1)
am old lady (8)
an old standby (1)

ao pal (2)
ap paramour (1)
aq patootie (1)
ar pet (1)
as prospective bride (1)
at regular girl (1)
au romance (1)
av special girl (1)
aw steady (16)
ax steady date (1)
ay steady girl (4)
az steady girl friend (4)
ba sucker (1)
bb sugar babe (1)
bc sweet mama (1)
bd sweet patootie (1)
be sweetheart (198)
bf sweetie (8)
bg sweetie pie (1)
bh wife to be (1)
bi woman (11)

081.7 L kissing

No Response (320)
A bussing (22)
B canoodling (2)
C caressing (1)
D carrying on (1)
E catting (1)
F courting (12)
G cuddling (1)
H flirting (2)
I fooling around (3)
J fooling with (1)
K Frenching (2)
L getting down (1)
M getting it on (1)
N getting/giving some sugar (2)
O grubbing (1)
P hanky-pankying (1)
Q having fun (1)
R hugging (16)
S hugging and kissing (7)
T kissing (379)
U kissing and hugging (1)
V kissing and loving (1)
W kissing around (1)
X loving (14)
Y loving up (2)
Z making love (7)
aa making out (37)
ab making whoopee (1)
ac messing (2)
ad messing around (5)
ae messing up (1)
af misbehaving (1)
ag mooching (1)
ah moonlighting (1)
ai mugging (1)
aj necking (131)

ak parking (6)
al petting (21)
am picking huckleberries (1)
an pitching woo (1)
ao playing around (1)
ap playing kissy face (1)
aq scooter pooping (1)
ar screwing around (1)
as scrunching (1)
at smacking (9)
au smirking (2)
av smooching (220)
aw smooching around (1)
ax snoofing (1)
ay sparking (6)
az spooking (1)
ba spooning (23)
bb spooning around (1)
bc squeezing (1)
bd swapping slobber (1)
be sweethearting (1)

082.1 L turned him down

No Response (199)
A ain't going to date him no more (1)
B axed him (1)
C backed down (1)
D backed out (13)
E backed out of the marriage (1)
F backed out on him (3)
G beached him (1)
H broke away (1)
I broke her promise (2)
J broke his heart (5)
K broke his neck (1)
L broke it (off) (34)
M broke it up (5)
N broke off (the engagement) (24)
O broke off with him (10)
P broke the engagement (68)
Q broke the gate (1)
R broke up the wedding (2)
S broke up (with him) (104)
T brushed him off (2)
U bumped him (4)
V busted up (6)
W called it off (3)
X called off the wedding (1)
Y canned him (1)
Z cast him off (1)
aa changed her mind (6)
ab cooled him down (1)
ac cut him off (5)
ad cut him out (1)
ae cut off from him (1)
af declined (4)
ag denied him (2)
ah deserted him at the altar (5)
ai did him wrong (2)

aj didn't do right (1)

ak didn't treat him right (1)

al didn't want (to marry) him (12)

am disappointed him (6)

an discarded him (1)

ao discarded the fool out of him (1)

ap ditched him (11)

aq dropped him (28)

ar dropped him like a hot potato (3)

as dropped him like a hotcake (1)

at ducked him (1)

au dumped him (9)

av dumped on him (1)

aw failed on him (1)

ax fell out with him (1)

ay fluffed him off (1)

az flushed him (1)

ba fooled him (1)

bb froze him out (1)

bc gave him back his ring (1)

bd gave him her sack (1)

be gave him his walking papers (3)

bf gave him the air (6)

bg gave him the ax (1)

bh gave him the brush-off (4)

bi gave him the cold foot (1)

bj gave him the cold shoulder (4)

bk gave him the dodge (1)

bl gave him the door (1)

bm gave him the gate (6)

bn gave him the GB [=good-bye] (1)

bo gave him the go-by (1)

bp gave him the heigh-ho (1)

bq gave him the mitten (1)

br gave him the "no" sign (1)

bs gave him the runaround (1)

bt gave him the shaft (3)

bu gave him the slip (2)

bv gave his ring back (2)

bw got a new guy (1)

bx got out of notion (1)

by got rid of him (1)

bz got tired and quit (1)

ca gypped him (2)

cb had a falling out with him (2)

cc hurt his feelings (1)

cd ignored him (1)

ce is through with him (5)

cf jilted him (161)

cg jolted him (3)

ch jumped him (1)

ci kicked him (14)

cj kicked him out (3)

ck knocked him cold (1)

cl knocked him flat (1)

cm left him (5)

cn left him at the altar (2)

co left him at the church (1)

cp left him flat (1)

cq let him down (5)

cr let him go (1)

cs let him out (1)

ct looked for higher bushes and sweeter berries (1)

cu lost interest (1)

cv made a fool out of him (1)

cw messed him up (2)

cx passed him by (1)

cy put him down (15)

cz put him in the sack (1)

da put him off (1)

db put him on the road (1)

dc put him out in the cold (1)

dd put him (up) on the shelf (2)

de quit dating him (1)

df quit going with him (2)

dg quit him (67)

dh quit seeing him (1)

di ran him off (3)

dj ran off and left him (2)

dk ran out on him (2)

dl refused him (188)

dm refused his proposal (7)

dn rejected him (48)

do reneged (1)

dp rotted him (1)

dq sacked him (4)

dr said no (and forget it) (20)

ds sat him down (1)

dt set him up (1)

du shafted him (2)

dv shifted him (1)

dw shit on him (1)

dx shot him down (1)

dy shot him out of the saddle (1)

dz showed him the door (2)

ea showed him the gate (1)

eb sidetracked him off (1)

ec slighted him (12)

ed split (1)

ee spurned him (3)

ef stood him up (15)

eg stopped seeing him (4)

eh stopped the engagement (1)

ei stuck him up (1)

ej threw him (1)

ek threw him back (1)

el threw him off (1)

em threw him out (1)

en threw him over (5)

eo threw him overboard (2)

ep tired of him (3)

eq told him no (4)

er told him to bug off (1)

es told him to hit the road (1)

et told him to take a walk (1)

eu turned against him (1)

ev turned down his offer (1)

ew turned down his proposal (1)

ex turned him away (1)

ey turned him down (302)

ez turned him off (for good) (5)

fa undid it (1)

fb turned him out (3)

fc turned it down (1)

fd walked away (1)

fe went back on him (1)

ff went off (and left him) (2)

fg wouldn't accept (1)

fh wouldn't have him (4)

fi wrote him a Dear John letter (1)

fj wrote him his walking papers (1)

082.2 L got married

No Response (21)

A broke her/the neck (8)

B caught (2)

C chained together (1)

D clamped on the ball and chain (1)

E collar tied around your neck (1)

F committed suicide (1)

G coupled (1)

H cut her throat (1)

I eloped (5)

J finally made up (1)

K got a life sentence (1)

L got double harness (1)

M got the letter (1)

N got the neck broke (1)

O got/had the knot tied (5)

P hitched (187)

Q hitched them up (1)

R hitched up (13)

S hooked (13)

T hooked for life (1)

U hooked up (16)

V hopped the broomstick (1)

W in a tangle (1)

X joined right hands (1)

Y joined up (1)

Z jumped over the broomstick (1)

aa jumped the broom (25)

ab jumped the broomstick (18)

ac jumped the broomstick backward (1)

ad jumped the bucket (1)

ae jumped the log (1)

af jumped the rope (1)

ag jumped the stick (1)

ah just got in trouble (1)

ai knot's been tied (1)

aj locked up (1)

ak lost his happiness (1)

al made a mistake (1)

am made it legal (2)

an   married (891)
ao   married (her) off (2)
ap   messed up (1)
aq   murdered (1)
ar   put the halter on (1)
as   put the noose on (1)
at   remarried (9)
au   ruined their life(s) (1)
av   sauter balai [F] (1)
aw   screwed up (his life) (2)
ax   sentenced (1)
ay   slipped off (1)
az   spliced (3)
ba   tied (2)
bb   tied down (1)
bc   tied for life (1)
bd   tied the knot (40)
be   tied the rope (1)
bf   tied together (5)
bg   tied up (9)
bh   took up (1)
bi   wed (6)
bj   went to bed with his shoes off
    (1)

082.2 P married

{d}   devoiced
{R}   weakly retroflex
{r}   weakly retroflex
{t}   flap
No Response (30)
<ma(r)Ad=14> (1)
<ma(r)A{d}=14> (1)
<ma(r)Id=14> (37)
<ma(r)ed=13> (1)
<ma(r)eed=13> (4)
<ma(rI)d> (2)
<ma[r](I)d> (8)
<ma[r]I{d}=14> (1)
<ma[r]eed=13> (2)
<mai(r)Id=14> (1)
<mairId=14> (4)
<mai{r}Id=14> (1)
<mar(I)d> (1)
<mar(I){d}> (1)
<marAd=14> (2)
<marI(d)=14> (1)
<marI=14> (4)
<marId=14> (590)
<marIt=14> (11)
<marIz=14> (1)
<marI{d}=14> (84)
<mared=13> (1)
<mareed=13> (7)
<maree{d}=13> (2)
<marid=13> (2)
<mari{d}=13> (1)
<marrId=14> (7)
<maw(r)Id=14> (1)
<ma{r}(I)d> (16)

<ma{r}Id=14> (21)
<ma{r}eed=13> (1)
<ma{r}rId=14> (6)
<ma{r}rI{d}=14> (2)
<ma{t}Id=14> (3)
<me(r)I{d}=14> (1)
<me(r)ed=13> (1)
<mer(I)d> (2)
<merAd=14> (1)
<merI(d)=14> (1)
<merId=14> (161)
<merI{d}=14> (21)
<mereed=13> (1)
<merid=13> (1)
<merrId=14> (1)
<me{R}d=14> (1)
<me{r}(I)d> (1)
<me{r}Id=14> (5)
<mo(r)Id=14> (1)
<morId=14> (5)
<morI{d}=14> (1)
<mo{t}I{d}=14> (1)
<murId=14> (13)
<murIt=14> (1)
<mureed=13> (1)
<murrI=14> (1)
<mu{r}Id=14> (1)

082.2 S married

No Response (1)
|DAB| (1)
|GCC| (1)
|GCCmea| (1)
|GGCmea| (1)
|KAAmea| (3)
|KAB| (2)
|KABeajmea| (1)
|KABmea| (3)
|KACmaj| (1)
|KACmea| (23)
|KACmej| (1)
|KAE| (2)
|KAEmaj| (1)
|KAEmea| (11)
|KAFmea| (1)
|KAGmej| (1)
|KAI| (1)
|KAImaj| (1)
|KAImea| (10)
|KBCmea| (1)
|KBImea| (1)
|KCA| (1)
|KCAmea| (2)
|KCAmpa| (1)
|KCB| (2)
|KCBmea| (1)
|KCC| (11)
|KCCmaj| (1)
|KCCmea| (18)
|KCCmej| (1)

|KCCmpa| (2)
|KCE| (4)
|KCEmea| (3)
|KCGmea| (1)
|KCI| (1)
|KCImea| (2)
|KDC| (1)
|KDCmna| (1)
|KDEmea| (1)
|KDEmna| (1)
|KDImna| (1)
|KFA| (1)
|KGCmea| (1)
|KKC| (1)
|KKCmna| (4)
|KKEmna| (1)
|KQCmna| (1)
|LADmea| (1)
|LAEmea| (1)
|LAHmaj| (1)
|MLA| (1)
|OAA| (6)
|OAAkaj| (3)
|OAAkajmea| (7)
|OAAmaj| (1)
|OAAmea| (55)
|OAAmej| (5)
|OAAmek| (2)
|OAB| (19)
|OABeajmea| (1)
|OABkaj| (13)
|OABkajmea| (4)
|OABkajmpa| (1)
|OABkan| (1)
|OABmaj| (2)
|OABmea| (83)
|OABmej| (1)
|OABmla| (1)
|OABmpa| (2)
|OAC| (11)
|OACkaj| (1)
|OACkajmea| (3)
|OACmea| (25)
|OACmej| (2)
|OAE| (5)
|OAEkaj| (3)
|OAEkan| (1)
|OAEmaj| (2)
|OAEmak| (1)
|OAEmea| (23)
|OAEmej| (1)
|OAEmpa| (1)
|OAF| (3)
|OAFmea| (1)
|OAG| (2)
|OAGmea| (12)
|OAI| (2)
|OAIkajmea| (1)
|OAImaj| (1)

|OAImea| (11)
|OBAmea| (2)
|OBBmea| (2)
|OBBmpa| (1)
|OBEmea| (1)
|OCA| (76)
|OCAeaj| (1)
|OCAeajmea| (1)
|OCAgbjmea| (1)
|OCAkaamea| (1)
|OCAkaj| (24)
|OCAkajmea| (4)
|OCAlaj| (1)
|OCAmaa| (1)
|OCAmaj| (14)
|OCAmea| (93)
|OCAmej| (17)
|OCAmek| (1)
|OCAmpa| (3)
|OCAmpj| (2)
|OCAmps| (1)
|OCB| (55)
|OCBkaj| (5)
|OCBkajmea| (3)
|OCBmaj| (5)
|OCBmea| (32)
|OCBmfj| (1)
|OCBmpa| (3)
|OCC| (5)
|OCCkaj| (1)
|OCCmea| (2)
|OCE| (9)
|OCEkaj| (4)
|OCEmaj| (1)
|OCEmea| (11)
|OCEmpa| (1)
|OCF| (1)
|OCG| (1)
|OCGkaj| (1)
|OCGmea| (9)
|OCGmej| (1)
|OCI| (1)
|OCIkaj| (1)
|OCImea| (7)
|ODAmej| (1)
|ODAmna| (1)
|ODBmea| (1)
|ODBmna| (3)
|ODCmna| (1)
|OGAmaj| (1)
|OGAmea| (2)
|OGBeaj| (1)
|OGEmea| (1)
|OKA| (7)
|OKAkdj| (3)
|OKAmdj| (2)
|OKAmea| (1)
|OKAmej| (1)
|OKAmna| (7)

|OKAmnj| (1)
|OKB| (2)
|OKBmna| (2)
|OKCmna| (1)
|OKEkdj| (1)
|OMB| (1)
|PADmea| (1)
|RABmea| (1)
|RAG| (1)
|RAGmea| (1)
|RCG| (1)
|RKG| (1)
|SCAmea| (1)
|SCD| (1)
|SKF| (1)

082.3 L best man
No Response (299)
A   another outside man (1)
B   attendant (1)
C   best friend (1)
D   best man (568)
E   boy of honor (1)
F   broom (1)
G   groom's maid (2)
H   groom[N-k] maid (1)
I   groom's waiter (1)
J   groomsman (29)
K   man groom (1)
L   ring man (1)
M   wait man (6)
N   waiter (16)
O   waiting man (1)
P   waitings man (1)
Q   wed man (1)
R   witness (2)

082.4 L bridesmaid
No Response (321)
A   attendant (9)
B   best girl (10)
C   best lady (6)
D   best maid (5)
E   best woman (7)
F   best-man girl (1)
G   bridal maid (1)
H   bridemaid (30)
I   brides maiden (2)
J   brides matron (2)
K   bridesmaid (360)
L   flower girl (1)
M   girl (1)
N   girl friend (2)
O   girl of honor (1)
P   girl wed man (1)
Q   groom (1)
R   helper (1)
S   honor maid (1)
T   honor matron (1)
U   lady-in-waiting (2)
V   leading maid (1)

W   maid (12)
X   maid and/or matron of honor (1)
Y   maid bride (1)
Z   maid of honor (202)
aa maid or (the) matron of honor (9)
ab matron (6)
ac matron of honor (93)
ad wait man (3)
ae waiter (9)
af waiter girl (2)
ag waiting woman (1)
ah waitress (2)
ai witness (1)

082.5 L shivaree
No Response (329)
A   celebrate (them) (2)
B   celebrating (16)
C   celebration (6)
D   charivari [F] (13)
E   charivari wedding (1)
F   cheering (them) (1)
G   chivalry (3)
H   cowbellion (1)
I   harass(ing) (4)
J   hasseling [v.] (2)
K   hazing [v.] (2)
L   horning (1)
M   initiate (them) (3)
N   Katzen [G] (1)
O   pull(ing) pranks (3)
P   razzing [v.] (1)
Q   reception (1)
R   send-off (2)
S   send-off party (1)
T   serenade [n.] (102)
U   serenade [v.] (112)
V   serenading [n.] (2)
W   setting up (with them) (1)
X   shivaree [n.] (181)
Y   shivaree [v.] (72)
Z   shivaree dance (1)
aa shivareeing [n.] (1)
ab soiree (1)
ac storm party (1)
ad storming [v.] (1)
ae surprise [n.] (1)

082.6 G up in (place-name)
No Response (189)
A   about in (1)
B   above (15)
C   around (1)
D   at (12)
E   back down near (1)
F   back in (1)
G   back to (2)
H   below (20)
I   down around (2)
J   down at (30)

K down below (12)
L down from (1)
M down in (128)
N down into (1)
O down near (to) (2)
P down to (104)
Q down toward (1)
R down [P-0] (10)
S in (65)
T out at (6)
U out in (26)
V out into (1)
W out to (11)
X out [P-0] (1)
Y over around (1)
Z over at (24)
aa over in (104)
ab over to (84)
ac over [P-0] (7)
ad past (1)
ae to (10)
af up above (6)
ag up around (11)
ah up at (27)
ai up by (1)
aj up from (2)
ak up in (121)
al up into (2)
am up near (3)
an up to (104)
ao up [P-0] (6)

082.6 S down

No Response (0)
|OAAefa| (1)
|OAAjja| (1)
|OAAjjd| (13)
|OAAjjf| (2)
|OAAjjh| (2)
|OAAjsa| (1)
|OAAmaa| (2)
|OAAmaj| (1)
|OABefa| (1)
|OABefj| (1)
|OABjjd| (6)
|OACeaa| (1)
|OACefa| (24)
|OACefc| (2)
|OACefj| (13)
|OACffa| (1)
|OACffd| (2)
|OACffm| (11)
|OACjbd| (3)
|OACjbm| (1)
|OACjja| (7)
|OACjjb| (3)
|OACjjd| (77)
|OACjjh| (1)
|OACjjj| (1)
|OACjjk| (2)

|OACjjl| (4)
|OACjjm| (3)
|OACjjo| (2)
|OACmaj| (5)
|OACmfa| (10)
|OACmfj| (4)
|OADeaa| (1)
|OAGjjd| (2)
|OAIeaa| (4)
|OAIefa| (8)
|OAIjjd| (1)
|OAImaa| (1)
|OAImfa| (1)
|OCAffj| (1)
|OCAlfa| (1)
|OCAlfg| (1)
|OCAlfj| (1)
|OCAmfa| (1)
|OCCefa| (4)
|OCCefj| (5)
|OCCffd| (1)
|OCCjjd| (4)
|OCCjjm| (1)
|OCCmfa| (2)
|ODAlda| (1)
|ODCeda| (2)
|ODCedjjud| (1)
|ODCeoa| (3)
|ODCjhd| (1)
|ODCjud| (4)
|ODCjum| (2)
|ODCmda| (2)
|ODEfoq| (1)
|ODHjuh| (1)
|OKAfoa| (2)
|OKAfoj| (5)
|OKAjhj| (1)
|OKAjuj| (2)
|OKAjuk| (1)
|OKAloa| (2)
|OKAmda| (1)
|OKCeda| (1)
|OKCeoa| (3)
|OKCfoa| (1)
|OKCfxa| (1)
|OKCjuj| (1)
|OKCloa| (2)
|PACffd| (1)
|RAAefa| (1)
|RAAffa| (9)
|RAAffc| (1)
|RAAffd| (1)
|RAAjja| (3)
|RAAjjb| (5)
|RAAjjc| (1)
|RAAjjd| (1)
|RAAlfj| (1)
|RAAmaj| (1)
|RABeaa| (27)

|RABeac| (1)
|RABefa| (114)
|RABefc| (7)
|RABefj| (4)
|RABffa| (5)
|RABffd| (12)
|RABffh| (1)
|RABffm| (3)
|RABjbd| (1)
|RABjja| (11)
|RABjjb| (29)
|RABjjd| (93)
|RABjjf| (2)
|RABjjj| (1)
|RABjjm| (4)
|RABjsd| (1)
|RABlfe| (1)
|RABmaa| (9)
|RABmab| (2)
|RABmaj| (1)
|RABmfa| (6)
|RACefa| (1)
|RACjjb| (1)
|RACjjd| (1)
|RADjja| (1)
|RAEefa| (4)
|RAEefc| (1)
|RAEffa| (1)
|RAEffd| (1)
|RAEjjb| (14)
|RAEjjd| (5)
|RAEjjf| (1)
|RAEjjh| (1)
|RAEmaa| (1)
|RAEmab| (1)
|RAEman| (1)
|RAFeaa| (9)
|RAFefa| (23)
|RAFffd| (1)
|RAFjja| (3)
|RAFjjd| (6)
|RAFmaa| (1)
|RAGefa| (10)
|RAGefc| (1)
|RAGefe| (2)
|RAGffd| (3)
|RAGjja| (1)
|RAGjjb| (1)
|RAGjjd| (4)
|RAGlfa| (1)
|RCAffa| (1)
|RCAffc| (1)
|RCAlfj| (2)
|RCBeaa| (3)
|RCBefa| (17)
|RCBefc| (1)
|RCBefe| (1)
|RCBffd| (3)
|RCBjja| (1)

|RCBjjb| (1)

|RCBjjd| (10)

|RCBlfa| (1)

|RCBmfa| (3)

|RCBmfj| (1)

|RCCmaj| (1)

|RCEjja| (1)

|RCEjjd| (1)

|RCFeaa| (1)

|RCFjjc| (2)

|RCGefa| (2)

|RDAjub| (3)

|RDAjum| (1)

|RDBeda| (3)

|RDBeoa| (10)

|RDBeoc| (4)

|RDBfod| (2)

|RDBfoh| (1)

|RDBjhm| (2)

|RDBjua| (4)

|RDBjub| (7)

|RDBjuc| (2)

|RDBjud| (7)

|RDBjuf| (3)

|RDBjum| (7)

|RDBjuo| (1)

|RDBmda| (6)

|RDEjuf| (2)

|RDEjum| (1)

|RDEjuo| (1)

|RDFjua| (2)

|RDFjub| (1)

|RDFjud| (3)

|RDGjhm| (1)

|RDGjub| (1)

|RDGjud| (1)

|RDIeoa| (1)

|RKAfoa| (4)

|RKAfoj| (2)

|RKAmda| (1)

|RKBeoa| (6)

|RKBeoc| (1)

|RKBfod| (1)

|RKBfoj| (1)

|RKBjhd| (1)

|RKBjud| (3)

|RKBjuh| (1)

|RKBloa| (1)

|RKBmda| (1)

|RKFjha| (1)

|RKFjud| (1)

|RKGeoa| (1)

|SADjjb| (1)

|SKAfoa| (1)

|SKAfoj| (2)

|SKAjuj| (1)

|SKBfoj| (1)

|SKDfom| (1)

082.7 G up at (the Browns')

No Response (423)

A at (15)

B down at (11)

C down to (5)

D down [P-0] (1)

E in (1)

F out at (2)

G over at (38)

H over by (1)

I over to (12)

J over with (1)

K over [P-0] (2)

L up at (15)

M up (there) with (2)

N up [P-0] (1)

O with (24)

082.8 L (whole) crowd

No Response (238)

A all (4)

B audience (1)

C bang (1)

D batch (1)

E block (2)

F bunch (374)

G business (3)

H caboodle (2)

I camp (1)

J capush (1)

K city (1)

L community (7)

M congregation (1)

N country (6)

O county (2)

P Coxey's Army (1)

Q crew (13)

R crowd (174)

S deal (1)

T dirty crowd (1)

U drove (2)

V everybody (5)

W everybody and his brother (1)

X family (13)

Y flock (1)

Z gang (134)

aa gathering (5)

ab group (118)

ac heap (3)

ad hell raisers (1)

ae herd (1)

af house (7)

ag household (1)

ah kit and caboodle (11)

ai kit and caboose (1)

aj lawless bunch (1)

ak lot (35)

al mass (1)

am mob (20)

an mob crowd (1)

ao neighborhood (2)

ap outfit (4)

aq pack (2)

ar party (14)

as party group (1)

at passel (6)

au place (3)

av posse (1)

aw push (4)

ax push and caboodle (1)

ay set-up (1)

az shebang (14)

ba shooting match (7)

bb sight, a (1)

bc slew (2)

bd squad (1)

be thing (18)

bf throng (1)

bg town (5)

bh tribe (1)

bi troop (2)

bj troublemakers (3)

bk universe (1)

bl wild bunch (1)

bm wilder bunch (1)

bn works (2)

bo world (5)

bp young bunch (2)

082.8 P whole

{aw} unrounded onset

{l} dark

No Response (241)

<(h)oel> (2)

<(h)oe{l}> (1)

<hoe(1)> (32)

<hoe[1]> (101)

<hoel> (236)

<hoeld> (1)

<hoe{l}> (328)

<hool> (1)

<h{aw}{l}> (1)

083.1 L dance

No Response (216)

A accordeon, un [F] (1)

B accordion dance (1)

C after-hours dance (1)

D apple peeling (3)

E baile [S] (1)

F bal [F] (2)

G bal de maison, un [F] (1)

H ball (27)

I ballroom dance (2)

J banco (1)

K banquet (1)

L barbeque (1)

M barn dance (11)

N barn party (1)

O barn raising (1)

P bash (2)

Q bean hulling (1)

R   bean stringing (3)
S   big dance (3)
T   big folk's dance (1)
U   blast (1)
V   blowout (1)
W   boy-girl party (1)
X   breakdown (12)
Y   breakdown dance (1)
Z   candy drawing (1)
aa   candy making (1)
ab   candy pulling (7)
ac   chaperoned dance (1)
ad   chimley daubing (1)
ae   community dance (1)
af   community social (1)
ag   corn shucking (6)
ah   cotillion (4)
ai   country dance (7)
aj   cowboy dance (1)
ak   dance (586)
al   dance party (4)
am   dancing party (2)
an   debutante ball (1)
ao   dinner dance (2)
ap   dinner-and-dance party (1)
aq   fais-dodo [F] (8)
ar   family dance (1)
as   fiddle down (1)
at   fish fry (1)
au   folly (1)
av   football dance (1)
aw   formal (8)
ax   formal dance (2)
ay   frolic (20)
az   get-together (7)
ba   hang dang (1)
bb   harvest festival (1)
bc   hoedown (26)
bd   hoedown dance (2)
be   home dance (2)
bf   home party (2)
bg   hootenanny (1)
bh   hop (6)
bi   house dance (3)
bj   house party (5)
bk   housewarming (1)
bl   inaugural ball (1)
bm   informal dance (1)
bn   jam (1)
bo   juke jam (2)
bp   jump Josie party (1)
bq   junior prom (1)
br   king-and-queen ball (1)
bs   log rolling (3)
bt   matinee dance (1)
bu   party (39)
bv   pea hulling (1)
bw   peanut boiling (1)
bx   peanut parching (1)

by   peanut shelling (2)
bz   play (1)
ca   play-party (5)
cb   program dance (1)
cc   prom (14)
cd   public dance (2)
ce   pull candy (1)
cf   railroad dance (1)
cg   round dance (36)
ch   ruckus (1)
ci   school dance (5)
cj   school hop (1)
ck   scrip dance (1)
cl   senior prom (1)
cm   shakedown (1)
cn   shindig (36)
co   shivaree dance (1)
cp   showdown (1)
cq   social (4)
cr   sock hop (12)
cs   soiree (2)
ct   square dance (143)
cu   street dance (4)
cv   tea dance (2)
cw   Valentine dance (1)
cx   watermelon cutting (2)
cy   wedding dance (1)
cz   young people's party (1)

083.1 P dance

{a}   upglide
{ai} lax onset
{z}   devoiced
No Response (125)
<da[n]s> (1)
<da[n]sN=14> (1)
<da[n]ts> (1)
<dai[n]s> (1)
<dai[n]sN=14> (1)
<dains> (9)
<dainsIz=14> (1)
<dainsN=14> (4)
<dainth> (1)
<daints> (11)
<daintsAz=14> (1)
<daintsIz=14> (2)
<daintsN=14> (2)
<dan(s)> (1)
<dans> (75)
<dansAs=14> (1)
<dansIz=14> (13)
<dansI{z}=14> (1)
<dansN=14> (18)
<dansNG=14> (8)
<danst> (3)
<dants> (334)
<dantsAz=14> (1)
<dantsIz=14> (46)
<dantsI{z}=14> (4)
<dantsN=14> (39)

<dantsNG=14> (14)
<dantsin=13> (1)
<dantst> (1)
<danz> (1)
<dens> (2)
<densN=14> (1)
<dents> (7)
<dentsN=14> (2)
<dients> (1)
<dientsN=14> (1)
<d{ai}ns> (3)
<d{ai}nts> (7)
<d{ai}ntsN=14> (1)
<d{a}[n]ts> (1)
<d{a}nch> (1)
<d{a}ns> (32)
<d{a}nsAz=14> (1)
<d{a}nsIz=14> (9)
<d{a}nsN=14> (8)
<d{a}nt(s)> (1)
<d{a}nth> (1)
<d{a}nts> (111)
<d{a}ntsIz=14> (11)
<d{a}ntsN=14> (9)

083.2 L (school) lets out

No Response (282)
A   (about to) end (1)
B   adjourn(s) (5)
C   broke up (1)
D   close(s/ed) (68)
E   closing time (1)
F   disbands (1)
G   dismiss them (1)
H   dismiss(es/ed) (43)
I   end(s/ed) (22)
J   ends over (1)
K   excused (1)
L   finish(es) (2)
M   get(s/ing)/got out (50)
N   gets over (1)
O   give on out (1)
P   go out (3)
Q   is about out (1)
R   is called (1)
S   is/was over (16)
T   is/was/will be out (233)
U   lay out (1)
V   leaves out (1)
W   lets them out (1)
X   let(s/ing) out (141)
Y   out (19)
Z   over (4)
aa recess(ed) (2)
ab releases (1)
ac (school) held till four (1)
ad (school) is turned out (2)
ae start turning out (1)
af terminated (2)
ag time for school to be out (1)

ah turn me out (1)
ai turn up (1)
aj turn(ed) (us) out (3)
ak turn(s/ing/ed) out (166)
al turned out of school (1)
am turned the school out (1)
an turning-out time (1)
ao vacates (1)
ap we're out of school (2)
aq we/they get out of school (3)
ar would close school (1)
as wound up (1)

083.3 L (when does school) start?
No Response (324)
A begin (145)
B commence (9)
C convene (1)
D go in (2)
E lets in (1)
F open (62)
G open up (9)
H start (388)
I start in (8)
J start up (3)
K take in (32)
L take up (33)

083.4 L skipped class
No Response (211)
A absent (12)
B absent from school (1)
C acting rookie (1)
D AWOL (1)
E bagging (1)
F being/was truant (5)
G broke class(es) (2)
H copping(ed) out (2)
I cut a/the class (7)
J cut school (5)
K cuts it (1)
L cut(ting) (21)
M cut(ting) (his) class(es) (56)
N dart school (1)
O deserted the school (1)
P didn't go (2)
Q didn't go to class (1)
R didn't report (1)
S didn't show up for class (1)
T disappeared (1)
U do a hook (1)
V dropped out (1)
W dropped out of school today (1)
X ducked school (1)
Y escape(d) school (1)
Z flew the coop (1)
aa goofed/ing off (5)
ab he was a fallout (1)
ac hooked school (1)
ad hooky (19)
ae jump(ed) class (1)

af kidnapped (1)
ag laid off (1)
ah laid out from school (1)
ai lay out till school time (1)
aj lay(s/ing)/laid out (39)
ak lay(s/ing)/laid out of school (17)
al laying out on the teacher (1)
am loafing (1)
an lying out (1)
ao miss(ed) (1)
ap missed his class (1)
aq miss(ed) school (1)
ar miss(ed) (the) class (3)
as out of school (1)
at play hookies (1)
au play(s/ed/ing) hooky (559)
av (played) a slacker (1)
aw played around (1)
ax played hide (1)
ay played hooky from school (3)
az played out (2)
ba played out of school (1)
bb played the hooky (1)
bc played the truant (1)
bd played truant (2)
be pretended to be sick (1)
bf reneged (1)
bg (re)neged on his class (1)
bh rookie (1)
bi run off from school (1)
bj run/ran away (6)
bk run/ran off (5)
bl runned away (1)
bm shoot/shot the hook (2)
bn shoot(ing)/shot hooky (6)
bo shot so much of hooky (1)
bp shot/shooting a hook (1)
bq skip a class (2)
br skip(ed/ing) (47)
bs skip(ed/ing) (his) class(es) (56)
bt skip(ed/ing) school (60)
bu skipped a certain class (1)
bv skipped out (6)
bw slackered (1)
bx slept in (2)
by slipped around (1)
bz snuck off (1)
ca stayed out (2)
cb stayed out of school (4)
cc threw a hook (1)
cd truancy (1)
ce truant (7)
cf walked out (1)
cg was a truant (1)
ch was absent of school (1)
ci was crooked (1)
cj went truant (1)

083.5 L education
No Response (111)
A book learning (6)
B common-school education (1)
C country-school education (1)
D education (779)
E eighth-grade education (1)
F elementary education (1)
G first learning (1)
H formal education (1)
I formal schooling (1)
J fourth-grade education (1)
K learn(ing) (3)
L learning (36)
M ordinary learning (1)
N plantation education (1)
O schooling (44)
P teaching (1)

083.5 P education
{a} upglide
{ai} lax onset
{j} devoiced
{u} advanced
{z} devoiced
No Response (138)
<IjAgaishN=4414> (1)
<ai{j}Ak{ai}shN=3414> (1)
<ajAkaishN=1434> (1)
<ajIkaishN=3414> (1)
<e(d)zhAkaishN=1424> (1)
<e(d)zhAkaishN=2414> (1)
<e(d)zhAk{ai}shN=3414> (1)
<e(d)zhuekaishN=2314> (1)
<e(d)zhuekaishun=2312> (1)
<echAkaishN=3414> (3)
<echIkaishN=3414> (3)
<echuekaishN=1324> (2)
<echyIkyaishN=3414> (1)
<ed(zh)AkaishN=3414> (7)
<ed(zh)IkaishN=1434> (1)
<ed(zh)IkaishN=3414> (7)
<eddIkaishN=3414> (1)
<edjIkaishN=3414> (1)
<edshuekaishN=2314> (1)
<edyAkaishN=3414> (12)
<edyAk{ai}shN=3414> (1)
<edyIkaishN=2414> (2)
<edyIkaishN=3414> (26)
<edyookaishN=2314> (1)
<edyuekaishN=2314> (2)
<ej(I)kaishN=314> (2)
<ej(I)k{ai}shN=314> (3)
<ejAkaichN=3414> (1)
<ejAkaishN=1414> (1)
<ejAkaishN=1424> (3)
<ejAkaishN=1434> (5)
<ejAkaishN=2414> (1)
<ejAkaishN=3414> (140)
<ejAkaishNz=3414> (1)

<ejAkaizhN=1434> (1)
<ejAkaizhN=3414> (1)
<ejAkeeshN=3414> (1)
<ejAkeshN=3414> (1)
<ejAkishN=2414> (1)
<ejAkyaishN=3414> (1)
<ejAk{ai}shN=1424> (1)
<ejAk{ai}shN=1434> (1)
<ejAk{ai}shN=2414> (1)
<ejAk{ai}shN=3414> (15)
<ejIkaishN=1434> (3)
<ejIkaishN=2414> (1)
<ejIkaishN=3414> (381)
<ejIkaizhN=3414> (1)
<ejIkeshN=3414> (4)
<ejIkyaishN=3414> (1)
<ejIk{ai}shN=2414> (1)
<ejIk{ai}shN=3414> (5)
<ejIk{a}shN=3414> (1)
<ejikaishN=2314> (2)
<ejookaishN=2314> (3)
<ejook{ai}shN=2314> (2)
<ejuekaishN=1324> (17)
<ejuekaishN=2314> (19)
<ejuekaishN=3214> (1)
<ejuekyaishN=2314> (1)
<ejuek{ai}shN=2314> (1)
<ejyAkaishN=1434> (1)
<ejyAkaishN=2414> (1)
<ejyAkaishN=3414> (2)
<ejyIkaishN=3414> (2)
<ejyuekaishN=2314> (3)
<ejyuekaishN=3214> (1)
<e{j}AkaishN=3414> (1)
<e{j}Ak{ai}shN=1434> (1)
<e{j}Ak{ai}shN=3414> (2)
<e{j}IkaishN=3414> (21)
<e{j}IkeshN=1434> (1)
<e{j}uekaishN=1324> (2)
<e{j}uekaishN=2314> (2)
<hechuekaishN=1324> (1)
<i(d)zhuekaishN=2314> (1)
<ijAkaishN=2414> (1)
<ijAk{ai}shN=1434> (1)
<ijAk{ai}shN=3414> (4)
<ijIkaishNz=3414> (1)
<ijuek{ai}shN=2314> (1)
<i{j}uek{ai}shN=2314> (1)
<ujIkaishN=3414> (1)
<{ai}jAkaishN=3414> (6)
<{ai}jAkaizhN=3414> (1)
<{ai}jIkaishN=3414> (1)
<{u}dewkaishN=2314> (1)
<{u}jAkaishN=3414> (2)
<{u}jIkaishN=2414> (1)
<{u}jIkaishN=3414> (41)
<{u}jIkaishN{z}=3414> (1)
<{u}jIkeshN=3414> (3)
<{u}jIk{ai}shN=3414> (1)

<{u}juekaishN=2314> (5)
<{u}{j}IkaishN=3414> (5)

083.6 P college

{aw}   unrounded onset
{d}   devoiced
{j}   devoiced
{l}   clear
{o}   low-back
{r}   weakly retroflex
{z}   devoiced
{zh}   devoiced
{?}   glottal

No Response (118)
<kalIj=14> (1)
<kawlI(d)zh=14> (1)
<kawlId(zh)=14> (1)
<kawlIj=14> (16)
<kawlI{j}=14> (1)
<kawle{j}=13> (1)
<kawlij=13> (3)
<ko(1)I(d)sh=14> (1)
<ko[1]I{j}=14> (2)
<kolAch=14> (1)
<kolAj=14> (3)
<kolAs=14> (1)
<kolAt(zh)=14> (1)
<kolI(d)zh=14> (5)
<kolI(d){zh}=14> (4)
<kolI(j)=14> (3)
<kolIch=14> (38)
<kolId(zh)=14> (13)
<kolIj=14> (404)
<kolIjIz=144> (1)
<kolIt(zh)=14> (2)
<kolI{?}=14> (2)
<kolI{d}(zh)=14> (2)
<kolI{j}=14> (221)
<kolI{zh}=14> (1)
<kolej=13> (1)
<kolet(zh)=13> (1)
<kole{j}=13> (1)
<kolij=13> (29)
<kolijIz=134> (1)
<kolijI{z}=134> (1)
<koli{j}=13> (4)
<kolyI{j}=14> (1)
<ko{l}I(d)sh=14> (1)
<ko{l}I(d)zh=14> (1)
<ko{l}Ich=14> (2)
<ko{l}Id(zh)=14> (1)
<ko{l}Ij=14> (32)
<ko{l}IjIz=144> (1)
<ko{l}It(zh)=14> (2)
<ko{l}I{j}=14> (29)
<ko{l}ij=13> (1)
<ko{l}i{j}=13> (2)
<ko{r}lIj=14> (1)
<k{aw}lij=13> (1)
<k{o}lI(j)=14> (1)

<k{o}lIch=14> (2)
<k{o}lId(zh)=14> (1)
<k{o}lIj=14> (30)
<k{o}lI{j}=14> (17)
<k{o}lijI{z}=134> (1)
<k{o}{l}Ij=14> (1)
<k{o}{l}I{j}=14> (1)

083.6 S college

No Response (26)
|PAA| (34)
|PAC| (11)
|PAG| (1)
|PAI| (2)
|PCA| (16)
|PCC| (8)
|PCI| (1)
|PFE| (1)
|PFI| (1)
|QFH| (1)
|RCA| (5)
|RCE| (6)
|RCG| (1)
|SAA| (32)
|SAAmaj| (1)
|SAAsaamaj| (1)
|SAB| (44)
|SABmaj| (3)
|SAD| (21)
|SAE| (259)
|SAEma2| (1)
|SAEmaj| (35)
|SAEmej| (1)
|SAEtaj| (1)
|SAF| (18)
|SAFmaj| (1)
|SAG| (37)
|SAGmaj| (1)
|SCA| (85)
|SCAcba| (1)
|SCAmaj| (5)
|SCB| (11)
|SCBmaj| (3)
|SCD| (10)
|SCE| (86)
|SCEmaj| (40)
|SCF| (1)
|SCG| (3)
|SCGmaj| (3)
|SDE| (2)
|SFA| (1)
|SFB| (1)
|SFE| (8)
|SFEmaj| (2)
|SGA| (1)
|SGE| (1)
|SKA| (1)
|SKE| (1)
|SMA| (1)
|SME| (2)

|SMEmaj| (1)
|TAA| (3)
|TAAmaj| (1)
|TAB| (3)
|TABmaj| (1)
|TAD| (22)
|TADmaj| (7)
|TADtfj| (1)
|TAE| (1)
|TAF| (4)
|TAG| (1)
|TCA| (2)
|TCD| (3)
|TCDmaj| (1)
|TCEmaj| (1)
|TFA| (3)
|TFAmaj| (1)
|TFB| (1)
|TFBqfb| (1)
|TFD| (11)
|TFDtfb| (1)
|TFF| (3)
|TMD| (1)
|TMDmaj| (1)

083.7 L first grade
No Response (245)
A   ABC (class) (2)
B   beginner(s) (9)
C   big school (1)
D   catechism (1)
E   chart [before 1st grade] (2)
F   chart class (1)
G   chart class [before 1st reader]
      (3)
H   elementary (35)
I   elementary grade (1)
J   elementary school (35)
K   first (14)
L   first class (3)
M   first grade (542)
N   first learning (1)
O   first primary (1)
P   first reader (28)
Q   first school (1)
R   first speller (1)
S   first year (2)
T   first-grade school (1)
U   free school (2)
V   grade (2)
W   grade school (52)
X   grammar (4)
Y   grammar school (51)
Z   literary school (1)
aa   primary (44)
ab   primary [before 1st grade] (2)
ac   primary class (3)
ad   primary department (2)
ae   primary grade (16)

af   primary grade [before 1st grade]
      (1)
ag   primary school (14)
ah   primer (105)
ai   primer [before 1st grade] (26)
aj   primer class (3)
ak   primer grade (3)
al   real school (1)
am   regular school (3)
an   school (5)

083.8 P desk/desks
{ai}   lax onset
{z}   devoiced
No Response (127)
\<dais(k)\> (1)
\<daisk\> (4)
\<daisk(s)\> (5)
\<daisks\> (1)
\<das(ks)\> (2)
\<dask\> (2)
\<dask(s)\> (1)
\<dast\> (1)
\<des(k)\> (84)
\<des(k)Iz=14\> (11)
\<des(k)I{z}=14\> (5)
\<des(ks)\> (84)
\<desh(ks)\> (1)
\<desk\> (448)
\<desk(s)\> (243)
\<deskIz=14\> (37)
\<deskI{z}=14\> (5)
\<desks\> (115)
\<dest\> (48)
\<dest(s)\> (33)
\<destI(s)=14\> (1)
\<destIs=14\> (1)
\<destIz=14\> (16)
\<destI{z}=14\> (2)
\<dests\> (7)
\<deth(ks)\> (1)
\<dethk\> (1)
\<dis(k)\> (3)
\<disk\> (4)
\<disk(s)\> (4)
\<disks\> (2)
\<dissI(s)=14\> (1)
\<dist\> (1)
\<dith(ks)\> (1)
\<d{ai}s(k)\> (19)
\<d{ai}s(ks)\> (31)
\<d{ai}sk\> (114)
\<d{ai}sk(s)\> (67)
\<d{ai}skA(s)=14\> (1)
\<d{ai}skIz=14\> (4)
\<d{ai}sks\> (16)
\<d{ai}st\> (7)
\<d{ai}st(s)\> (9)
\<d{ai}stIz=14\> (2)
\<d{ai}sts\> (2)

084.1 P library
{b}   fricative
{ie}   monophthong/short glide
{R}   weakly retroflex
{r}   weakly retroflex
{t}   flap
{z}   devoiced
{?}   glottal
No Response (142)
\<fl{ie}brerI=134\> (1)
\<lieb(r)RI=144\> (3)
\<lieb(r)RrI=144\> (1)
\<lieb(r)arI=134\> (1)
\<lieb(r)e(r)A=134\> (1)
\<lieb(r)ee(rI)=13\> (1)
\<lieb(r)er(I)=13\> (1)
\<lieb(r)erA=134\> (1)
\<lieb(r)erI=124\> (1)
\<lieb(r)erI=134\> (99)
\<lieb(r)erI{z}=134\> (1)
\<lieb(r)eree=123\> (2)
\<lieb(r)e{r}I=134\> (2)
\<lieb(r)irI=134\> (1)
\<lieb(r)urI=134\> (17)
\<lieb(r)urrI=134\> (1)
\<lieb(r)u{r}I=134\> (5)
\<lieb(r)u{r}rI=134\> (3)
\<lieb(r)u{r}wI=134\> (1)
\<liebr(er)I=14\> (23)
\<liebr(er)ee=13\> (2)
\<liebrai(rI)=13\> (10)
\<liebrairI=134\> (3)
\<liebrarI=134\> (1)
\<liebre(r)I=134\> (3)
\<liebre[r]I=134\> (1)
\<liebrerI=124\> (2)
\<liebrerI=134\> (148)
\<liebrerI=314\> (2)
\<liebrerIz=134\> (2)
\<liebreree=123\> (1)
\<liebre{r}I=134\> (3)
\<liebre{r}rI=134\> (1)
\<liebrirI=134\> (3)
\<liebri{t}I=134\> (1)
\<liebru[r](I)=13\> (1)
\<liebru[r]I=134\> (2)
\<liebrurA=134\> (1)
\<liebrurI=134\> (47)
\<liebru{r}I=134\> (4)
\<liebru{r}I=314\> (1)
\<liebru{r}rI=134\> (8)
\<liebru{r}{t}I=134\> (1)
\<lieb{t}e{t}I=134\> (1)
\<lie{b}rerI=134\> (1)
\<lie{b}rurI=134\> (1)
\<l{ie}b(r)RI=144\> (2)
\<l{ie}b(r)RrI=144\> (1)
\<l{ie}b(r)arI=134\> (1)
\<l{ie}b(r)e(r)I=134\> (1)

<l{ie}b(r)e(r)I=314> (1)
<l{ie}b(r)e[r]I=134> (1)
<l{ie}b(r)erA=134> (1)
<l{ie}b(r)erI=134> (85)
<l{ie}b(r)erI=314> (4)
<l{ie}b(r)eree=123> (1)
<l{ie}b(r)e{r}(I)=13> (4)
<l{ie}b(r)e{r}I=134> (2)
<l{ie}b(r)irI=124> (1)
<l{ie}b(r)ur(I)=13> (1)
<l{ie}b(r)urI=134> (10)
<l{ie}b(r)urI=314> (1)
<l{ie}b(r)urrI=134> (1)
<l{ie}b(r)u{r}(I)=13> (2)
<l{ie}b(r)u{r}I=134> (7)
<l{ie}b(r)u{r}rI=134> (6)
<l{ie}b(r)u{r}wI=134> (1)
<l{ie}br(er)I=14> (23)
<l{ie}br(er)ee=13> (4)
<l{ie}brai(rI=13> (8)
<l{ie}brairI=134> (1)
<l{ie}brarI=124> (1)
<l{ie}brawrI=134> (1)
<l{ie}bre(r)I=134> (6)
<l{ie}bre[r](I)=13> (1)
<l{ie}brer(I)=13> (3)
<l{ie}brerA=134> (1)
<l{ie}brerI=124> (2)
<l{ie}brerI=134> (135)
<l{ie}brerI=314> (1)
<l{ie}brerIz=134> (2)
<l{ie}breree=123> (6)
<l{ie}brerrI=134> (1)
<l{ie}bre{?}I=134> (1)
<l{ie}bre{r}I=134> (5)
<l{ie}brirI=134> (3)
<l{ie}brur(I)=13> (1)
<l{ie}brurA=134> (2)
<l{ie}brurI=134> (11)
<l{ie}brurrI=134> (1)
<l{ie}bru{r}(I)=13> (1)
<l{ie}bru{r}I=134> (9)
<l{ie}bru{r}rI=124> (1)
<l{ie}bru{r}rI=134> (5)
<l{ie}br{R}(I)=14> (1)
<l{ie}b{t}urI=134> (1)
<l{ie}{b}(re)rI=14> (1)
<l{ie}{b}rer(I)=13> (1)
<l{ie}{b}rerI=124> (1)

084.2 P post office
{aw} unrounded onset
{d} devoiced
{f} bilabial
No Response (101)
<awfIs=14> (4)
<awfIsIz=144> (2)
<ofIs=14> (5)
<pAst{aw}fIs=414> (1)
<poes(t)awfIs=134> (3)

<poes(t)oefIs=134> (3)
<poesdawfIs=134> (1)
<poeshtawfIs=134> (3)
<poeshtawfIsh=134> (1)
<poeshtawfIth=134> (1)
<poeshtawffIs=134> (1)
<poeshtawffIth=134> (1)
<poeshtawffIzh=134> (1)
<poeshtawvI(s)=134> (1)
<poeshtaw{f}Is=134> (3)
<poeshtoefIth=134> (2)
<poeshto{f}Is=134> (1)
<poesht{aw}fIs=134> (1)
<poesht{aw}fIth=134> (1)
<poesht{aw}ffIs=134> (1)
<poestAofIs=1434> (1)
<poestawf(I)s=13> (1)
<poestawf(Is=13> (1)
<poestawfA(s)=134> (2)
<poestawfAs=134> (30)
<poestawfAs=314> (1)
<poestawfI(s)=134> (4)
<poestawfIsIz=1344> (1)
<poestawfIs=114> (11)
<poestawfIs=134> (366)
<poestawfIs=214> (3)
<poestawfIs=314> (7)
<poestawfIth=134> (1)
<poestawfIz=134> (3)
<poestawffIs=134> (7)
<poestawfis=123> (1)
<poestaw{f}Is=134> (3)
<poestaw{f}Is=214> (1)
<poestdawfIs=134> (1)
<poesthawfIs=134> (1)
<poestoefAs=134> (1)
<poestoefI(s)=134> (2)
<poestoefIs=114> (10)
<poestoefIs=134> (97)
<poestoefIsIz=1344> (1)
<poestoefIth=134> (1)
<poestoeffI(s)=134> (1)
<poestofA(s)=134> (1)
<poestofAs=134> (3)
<poestofAs=214> (1)
<poestofIs=124> (1)
<poestofIs=134> (159)
<poestofIs=214> (2)
<poestoffIs=134> (2)
<poestovI(s)=134> (1)
<poestovIs=134> (1)
<poestowfIs=134> (1)
<poesto{f}Ith=134> (1)
<poest{aw}fIs=134> (65)
<poest{aw}fIth=134> (1)
<poest{aw}ffIs=124> (1)
<poest{aw}ffIs=134> (4)
<poest{aw}f{f}Is=134> (1)
<poest{aw}vIs=134> (2)

<poes{d}awfIz=134> (1)
<poes{d}owfIs=134> (1)
<pustoefIs=134> (1)
<{f}oestawfIs=134> (1)

084.3 P hotel
{ai} lax onset
{h} velar
{l} dark
{z} devoiced
No Response (167)
<(h)oete[l]=31> (1)
<(h)oete[l]dz=13> (1)
<(h)oetel=13> (1)
<hawte[l]=13> (1)
<hawtel=31> (1)
<hoetai[l]=31> (1)
<hoetail=13> (3)
<hoetail=31> (3)
<hoetai{l}=13> (3)
<hoete(1)=31> (2)
<hoete[1]=13> (68)
<hoete[1]=21> (4)
<hoete[1]=31> (13)
<hoete[1]{z}=13> (1)
<hoetel=12> (1)
<hoetel=13> (188)
<hoetel=21> (7)
<hoetel=31> (70)
<hoetelz=13> (8)
<hoetelz=31> (5)
<hoetel{z}=31> (2)
<hoete{l}=12> (2)
<hoete{l}=13> (252)
<hoete{l}=21> (15)
<hoete{l}=31> (91)
<hoete{l}z=13> (6)
<hoete{l}z=31> (3)
<hoete{l}{z}=13> (1)
<hoeti[l]=13> (2)
<hoet{ai}l=13> (1)
<hoet{ai}l=31> (1)
<hoet{ai}{l}=13> (1)
<hoet{ai}{l}=31> (1)
<{h}awte{l}=31> (1)

084.4 L theater
No Response (147)
A auditorium (8)
B cinema (7)
C coliseum (1)
D concert hall (1)
E drive-in (10)
F drive-in movie (1)
G drive-in theater (7)
H hall, the (1)
I motion-picture house (1)
J motion pictures (1)
K movie (40)
L movie building (1)
M movie house (34)

N   movie picture show (1)
O   movie show (5)
P   movie theater (10)
Q   movies (23)
R   moving picture(s) (3)
S   moving-picture house (3)
T   moving-picture show (15)
U   opera (3)
V   opera house (24)
W   outdoor theater (1)
X   picture cinema (1)
Y   picture show (133)
Z   picture theater (1)
aa   pictures (1)
ab   playhouse (3)
ac   show (53)
ad   showhouse (1)
ae   theater (700)
af   walk-in theater (1)

084.4 P theater

{ai}   lax onset
{d}   tense
{R}   weakly retroflex
{t}   flap
{z}   devoiced

No Response (202)
<feeai{d}{R}=134> (1)
<tIai{t}[R]=414> (1)
<teeA{d}R=144> (1)
<teeai{d}R=134> (1)
<teeai{d}[R]=134> (4)
<teeai{d}[R]=314> (2)
<teeai{d}{R}=314> (1)
<thIaid[R]=414> (1)
<thIait{R}=414> (1)
<thIai{d}[R]=414> (1)
<thIai{d}{R}=414> (2)
<thIai{t}R=414> (4)
<thIai{t}[R]=414> (2)
<thIa{t}[R]=414> (1)
<thIyait{R}=414> (1)
<thIyai{d}{R}=414> (1)
<thI{ai}{t}R=414> (2)
<thI{ai}{t}[R]=414> (1)
<thai(A){d}[R]=14> (1)
<theA{d}R=144> (1)
<theai{d}R=134> (1)
<thee(A){d}R=14> (10)
<thee(A){d}Rz=14> (1)
<thee(A){d}[R]=14> (7)
<thee(A){d}[R]z=14> (1)
<thee(A){d}{R}=14> (4)
<thee(A){t}R=14> (5)
<thee(A){t}[R]=14> (3)
<theeA(tR)=14> (1)
<theeAt[R]=144> (2)
<theeA{d}R=144> (34)
<theeA{d}Rz=144> (1)
<theeA{d}[R]=144> (15)

<theeA{d}ur=143> (2)
<theeA{d}{R}=144> (4)
<theeA{t}R=144> (7)
<theeA{t}[R]=144> (8)
<theeId[R]=144> (1)
<theeI{d}R=144> (3)
<theeI{d}[R]=144> (3)
<theeI{d}{R}=144> (2)
<theeI{t}R=144> (2)
<theeI{t}[R]=144> (1)
<theeI{t}{R}=144> (1)
<theeaidR=134> (1)
<theeait[R]=134> (3)
<theeait{R}=134> (1)
<theeai{d}R=124> (1)
<theeai{d}R=134> (180)
<theeai{d}R=214> (4)
<theeai{d}R=314> (16)
<theeai{d}Rz=134> (1)
<theeai{d}R{z}=134> (2)
<theeai{d}[R]=124> (2)
<theeai{d}[R]=134> (121)
<theeai{d}[R]=214> (2)
<theeai{d}[R]=314> (23)
<theeai{d}[R]z=124> (1)
<theeai{d}[R]z=134> (1)
<theeai{d}[R]z=314> (3)
<theeai{d}u[r]=123> (1)
<theeai{d}ur=213> (1)
<theeai{d}{R}=134> (39)
<theeai{d}{R}=214> (1)
<theeai{d}{R}=314> (12)
<theeai{d}{R}{z}=134> (1)
<theeai{t}R=134> (5)
<theeai{t}R=214> (1)
<theeai{t}R=314> (5)
<theeai{t}[R]=134> (5)
<theeai{t}[R]=214> (1)
<theeai{t}[R]=314> (1)
<theeai{t}{R}=134> (5)
<theeai{t}{R}=314> (1)
<theeetR=134> (1)
<theee{d}R=134> (5)
<theee{d}R=314> (2)
<theee{d}[R]=134> (3)
<theee{d}[R]=314> (1)
<theee{d}{R}=314> (1)
<theee{t}[R]=134> (2)
<theee{t}{R}=134> (1)
<theeo{d}R=134> (1)
<theeu{d}[R]=134> (2)
<theeyA{d}R=144> (1)
<theeyait{R}=134> (1)
<theeyai{d}[R]=134> (3)
<theeyai{d}{R}=134> (2)
<theey{ai}{d}[R]=134> (1)
<thee{ai}{d}R=134> (2)
<thee{ai}{d}[R]=134> (3)
<thee{ai}{d}{R}=134> (2)

<thee{ai}{t}R=134> (1)
<thee{ai}{t}R=214> (1)
<thee{ai}{t}[R]=314> (1)
<thee{ai}{t}{R}=314> (1)
<thi(A)t[R]=14> (2)
<thi(A){d}R=14> (22)
<thi(A){d}[R]=14> (19)
<thi(A){d}{R}=14> (4)
<thi(A){t}R=14> (1)
<thi(A){t}[R]=14> (1)
<thiA{d}R=144> (11)
<thiA{d}[R]=144> (8)
<thiA{d}{R}=144> (6)
<thiA{t}R=144> (1)
<thiI{d}R=144> (2)
<thiI{d}[R]=144> (3)
<thiI{d}{R}=144> (2)
<thiaitR=314> (1)
<thiait[R]=134> (1)
<thiai{d}R=134> (7)
<thiai{d}R=314> (1)
<thiai{d}[R]=134> (2)
<thiai{d}[R]=314> (3)
<thiai{d}[R]z=134> (1)
<thiai{d}{R}=134> (2)
<thiai{t}R=314> (1)
<thie{d}[R]=134> (2)
<thiyA{d}ur=143> (1)
<thiyai{d}{R}=314> (1)
<thi{ai}{d}R=134> (1)
<thi{ai}{d}{R}=134> (1)
<thuai{d}[R]=314> (1)

084.5 P hospital

{aw}   unrounded onset
{b}   devoiced
{d}   tense
{o}   low-back
{p}   voiced
{R}   weakly retroflex
{r}   weakly retroflex
{t}   flap
{z}   devoiced
{?}   glottal

No Response (103)
<(h)ospI(tL)=14> (1)
<(h)os{p}I{d}L=144> (2)
<hawsbi{d}L=134> (3)
<hawsbi{t}L=134> (2)
<hawsh{b}i(tI)lz=13> (1)
<hawspItol=143> (1)
<hawspI{d}L=144> (11)
<hawspI{d}[L]=144> (4)
<hawspI{t}L=144> (3)
<hawspI{t}[L]=144> (1)
<hawspi(tI)l=13> (2)
<hawspid[L]=134> (1)
<hawspitL=134> (1)
<hawspi{d}L=134> (14)
<hawspi{t}L=134> (2)

<hawspi{t}[L]=134> (2)
<haws{p}I{d}L=144> (1)
<haws{p}I{t}L=144> (1)
<haw{r}spI{d}L=144> (1)
<hosbI(t)[L]=144> (1)
<hosbI(ti)l=14> (1)
<hosbIdoo[l]=143> (1)
<hosbI{d}L=144> (9)
<hosbI{d}[L]=144> (8)
<hosbI{d}u[l]=143> (1)
<hosbI{t}L=144> (5)
<hosbI{t}[L]=144> (9)
<hosbi(t)L=134> (1)
<hosbi(t)[L]z=134> (1)
<hosbi(tI)l=13> (4)
<hosbi(tI)lz=13> (1)
<hosbidL=134> (1)
<hosbitL=134> (1)
<hosbit[L]=134> (1)
<hosbi{d}L=134> (57)
<hosbi{d}Lz=134> (1)
<hosbi{d}[L]=134> (13)
<hosbi{d}[L]{z}=134> (1)
<hosbi{d}u[l]=123> (2)
<hosbi{d}u[l]z=123> (1)
<hosbi{t}L=134> (25)
<hosbi{t}L=314> (1)
<hosbi{t}Lz=134> (1)
<hosbi{t}[L]=134> (11)
<hosbi{t}u[l]=123> (1)
<hoshpitL=134> (1)
<hoshpi{t}L=134> (2)
<hoshpi{t}[L]=134> (1)
<hosh{p}i{t}[L]=134> (1)
<hosp(It)L=14> (2)
<hospA{t}[L]=144> (1)
<hospI(t)L=144> (2)
<hospI(tI)l=14> (3)
<hospId(L)=14> (1)
<hospIdL=144> (12)
<hospId[L]=144> (2)
<hospItLz=144> (1)
<hospItul=143> (1)
<hospIz[L]=144> (1)
<hospI{d}L=144> (184)
<hospI{d}Lz=144> (4)
<hospI{d}[L]=144> (3)
<hospI{t}L=144> (62)
<hospI{t}Lz=144> (2)
<hospI{t}[L]=144> (11)
<hospI{t}ul=143> (1)
<hospI{t}{R}=144> (1)
<hospee{d}[L]=134> (1)
<hospi(tI)l=13> (1)
<hospidL=134> (1)
<hospitL=134> (4)
<hospi{d}L=124> (1)
<hospi{d}L=134> (173)
<hospi{d}L=214> (1)

<hospi{d}Lz=134> (5)
<hospi{d}[L]=134> (15)
<hospi{d}u[l]=123> (1)
<hospi{d}ul=123> (2)
<hospi{d}ul=133> (1)
<hospi{t}L=134> (46)
<hospi{t}L=214> (1)
<hospi{t}L{z}=134> (1)
<hospi{t}[L]=134> (10)
<hospi{t}ul=123> (3)
<hospoo{d}L=134> (1)
<hosppi{d}L=134> (1)
<hosspi{t}L=134> (1)
<hos{b}i{d}L=134> (1)
<hos{b}i{d}[L]=134> (1)
<hos{b}i{t}L=134> (4)
<hos{p}I(t)L=144> (1)
<hos{p}IdL=144> (5)
<hos{p}IdLz=144> (1)
<hos{p}Id[L]=144> (1)
<hos{p}I{d}L=144> (29)
<hos{p}I{t}L=144> (12)
<hos{p}I{t}[L]=144> (1)
<hos{p}i{d}L=134> (5)
<hos{p}i{t}L=134> (3)
<hos{p}u{t}L=134> (1)
<hothpI{t}[L]=144> (1)
<hothpi{t}L=134> (1)
<ho{r}sp(It)L=14> (1)
<ho{r}spI{?}(L)=14> (1)
<huspI{d}L=144> (1)
<h{aw}sbI{d}L=144> (1)
<h{aw}sbI{t}L=144> (1)
<h{aw}spI{d}L=144> (1)
<h{aw}spi{d}L=134> (2)
<h{o}sbI{d}L=144> (1)
<h{o}sbi{d}L=134> (3)
<h{o}sbi{d}[L]=134> (1)
<h{o}spIdL=144> (2)
<h{o}spI{d}L=144> (11)
<h{o}spI{t}L=144> (5)
<h{o}spI{t}[L]=144> (3)
<h{o}spi(tI)[l]=13> (1)
<h{o}spi{d}L=134> (5)
<h{o}spi{t}L=134> (2)
<h{o}s{b}i(tI)l=13> (1)
<h{o}s{p}IdL=144> (1)
<h{o}s{p}I{d}Lz=144> (1)
<h{o}s{p}I{t}L=144> (2)
<h{o}s{p}i{d}[L]=134> (1)

084.6 P nurse
{r}   weakly retroflex
{z}   devoiced
No Response (143)
<ne(r)sIz=14> (1)
<nersIz=14> (1)
<ne{r}s> (1)
<ne{r}sIz=14> (1)
<nirs> (2)

<noors> (1)
<no{r}s> (1)
<nu[r]s> (123)
<nu[r]sIz=14> (31)
<nu[r]sI{z}=14> (3)
<nu[r]shIz=14> (1)
<nurs> (458)
<nursAz=14> (2)
<nursI(z)=14> (1)
<nursIz=14> (50)
<nursIzh=14> (1)
<nursI{z}=14> (4)
<nursh> (2)
<nurshIz=14> (1)
<nu{r}s> (83)
<nu{r}sI(z)=14> (1)
<nu{r}sIz=14> (7)
<nu{r}sh> (1)
<nu{r}sk> (1)

084.7 L railroad station
No Response (217)
A   depot (524)
B   depot station (3)
C   flag stop (1)
D   rail depot (1)
E   rail junction (1)
F   rail station (13)
G   rail terminal (1)
H   railhead (2)
I   railroad depot (19)
J   railroad junction (3)
K   railroad office (2)
L   railroad shed (1)
M   railroad (station) (12)
N   railroad station (269)
O   railroad stop (1)
P   railroad terminal (1)
Q   railway depot (3)
R   railway (station) (2)
S   railway station (52)
T   sitting room (1)
U   station (175)
V   station depot (1)
W   station house (2)
X   stop (1)
Y   terminal (10)
Z   terminal station (3)
aa   train depot (7)
ab   train station (145)
ac   train stop (1)
ad   train terminal (2)
ae   waiting room (3)
af   waiting station (1)

084.7 S rail
No Response (16)
|GACeaj| (1)
|GAI| (1)
|GBAbbl| (1)
|GBAdae| (2)

|GBAeaamaj| (2)
|GBAeaa| (17)
|GBAeac| (2)
|GBAeajmaa| (1)
|GBAeajmaj| (2)
|GBAeajmfacba| (1)
|GBAeaj| (20)
|GBAkab| (1)
|GBAkae| (1)
|GBAkan| (1)
|GBAmaj| (3)
|GBBeajmaa| (1)
|GBBeaj| (9)
|GBBmaj| (3)
|GBCdaa| (1)
|GBCdae| (1)
|GBCeaa| (14)
|GBCeae| (1)
|GBCeaj| (20)
|GBCmaa| (1)
|GBCmaj| (11)
|GBDabjcbj| (1)
|GBDeajmaj| (1)
|GBDeaj| (1)
|GBEdae| (2)
|GBEdag| (1)
|GBEeaacba| (2)
|GBEeaamaa| (1)
|GBEeaamaj| (47)
|GBEeaa| (98)
|GBEeab| (1)
|GBEeacmaa| (1)
|GBEeac| (1)
|GBEeajcba| (2)
|GBEeajmaa| (3)
|GBEeajmaj| (3)
|GBEeaj| (40)
|GBEeal| (4)
|GBEmaacbj| (1)
|GBEmaa| (8)
|GBEmajcba| (3)
|GBEmajcbj| (1)
|GBEmaj| (98)
|GBEmak| (2)
|GBE| (1)
|GBFeaa| (1)
|GBFeaj| (1)
|GBFmajcba| (1)
|GBFmaj| (4)
|GBFmak| (1)
|GBGeajmaj| (1)
|GBGeaj| (6)
|GBGmaj| (1)
|GBG| (1)
|GBHeaj| (1)
|GBIeaamaj| (7)
|GBIeaa| (29)
|GBIeajmaa| (3)
|GBIeaj| (9)

|GBIebj| (1)
|GBImajcba| (1)
|GBImaj| (14)
|GBI| (2)
|GGAeaamaj| (1)
|GGAeaa| (2)
|GGAeajmaacba| (4)
|GGAeajmaa| (1)
|GGAeajmabcba| (1)
|GGAeaj| (10)
|GGAkaj| (1)
|GGAmajcba| (2)
|GGAmaj| (43)
|GGAmamcba| (1)
|GGA| (1)
|GGBeaamaa| (1)
|GGBeaj| (3)
|GGBmaj| (1)
|GGCdac| (1)
|GGCeaamcj| (1)
|GGCeajmdacha| (1)
|GGCeaj| (10)
|GGCmaj| (9)
|GGCmfjcha| (1)
|GGEeaamaa| (1)
|GGEeaamaj| (8)
|GGEeaamca| (1)
|GGEeaa| (20)
|GGEeac| (1)
|GGEeajcba| (1)
|GGEeajeaa| (1)
|GGEeajmaacba| (1)
|GGEeajmaa| (2)
|GGEeajmaj| (3)
|GGEeaj| (18)
|GGEeal| (1)
|GGEkajcba| (1)
|GGEmaa| (9)
|GGEmajcba| (2)
|GGEmaj| (110)
|GGEmak| (7)
|GGEmfjcba| (1)
|GGEmfj| (1)
|GGFmaa| (1)
|GGFmaj| (8)
|GGGeaamaj| (1)
|GGGeaj| (1)
|GGGmaj| (1)
|GGIbbjcba| (1)
|GGIeaamaj| (2)
|GGIeaa| (2)
|GGIeac| (1)
|GGIeajmaa| (2)
|GGIeajmaj| (1)
|GGIeaj| (8)
|GGImaj| (9)
|HCCeaamaj| (1)
|KABeaa| (3)
|KABeaj| (4)

|KABmaj| (2)
|KABmak| (1)
|KAB| (2)
|KADmaj| (2)
|KAEmaj| (2)
|KAFeaj| (3)
|KAF| (1)
|KAGeaj| (1)
|KAIeaa| (1)
|KAImaj| (1)
|KBBmajcba| (1)
|KBBmak| (1)
|KBB| (1)
|KCAeaamaacba| (1)
|KCAeaamaa| (1)
|KCAeaa| (4)
|KCAmajcba| (1)
|KCBeaakaa| (1)
|KCBeaamaacba| (2)
|KCBeaamaa| (1)
|KCBeaa| (2)
|KCBmaj| (2)
|KCEkaa| (1)
|KCFeaa| (1)
|KCIeaamaacha| (1)
|KGA| (1)
|kabGBA| (4)
|kabGBC| (1)

085.1 L public square
No Response (401)
A   center of town (1)
B   circle (3)
C   city commons (1)
D   city park (1)
E   city square (1)
F   common (1)
G   county courthouse square (1)
H   county square (3)
I   court lawn (2)
J   court park (1)
K   court square (34)
L   courthouse (71)
M   courthouse greens (1)
N   courthouse grounds (6)
O   courthouse lawn (26)
P   courthouse lot (1)
Q   courthouse property (1)
R   courthouse square (79)
S   courthouse square park (1)
T   courthouse yard (14)
U   courtyard (36)
V   courtyard square (1)
W   esplanade (1)
X   grass (2)
Y   green (2)
Z   grounds (1)
aa   heart of town (1)
ab   lawn (31)
ac   lot (1)

ad   mall (4)
ae   middle of town (1)
af   open place (1)
ag   park (180)
ah   plaza (10)
ai   plazuela [S] (1)
aj   public park (5)
ak   public square (10)
al   recreation area (1)
am   recreation park (1)
an   rest area (1)
ao   square (155)
ap   town park (2)
aq   town square (24)
ar   village green (1)
as   wagonyard (1)
at   yard(s) (5)

085.2 L cater-cornered

No Response (221)
A   across a catercorner (11)
B   adjacent (1)
C   angle sided (1)
D   angled (15)
E   angling (across) (15)
F   angly (1)
G   angular (2)
H   antigodlin (79)
I   at an angle (5)
J   biased (2)
K   biasin (1)
L   biasy (1)
M   cat walk [v.] (1)
N   catawampus(ed) (52)
O   catechism (2)
P   cater (1)
Q   cater bias (6)
R   cater crooked (1)
S   cater cross (1)
T   cater cut (1)
U   cater ranging (1)
V   cater way (1)
W   cater-corner(ed) (548)
X   cater-mac-bias (1)
Y   catergodlin (1)
Z   catering across (1)
aa   cockeyed (1)
ab   cornerwise (1)
ac   cross (16)
ad   cross (the) corner (2)
ae   crosscut (1)
af   crossway(s) (31)
ag   crosswise (5)
ah   cut a corner (3)
ai   cut (a)cross (23)
aj   cut the butter (1)
ak   cutting the corners (8)
al   cutting through (2)
am   cutting through the cabbage (1)
an   cutting through the middle (1)

ao   Denver crossing (1)
ap   diagonal(ly) (across) (78)
aq   diangling (1)
ar   going through (1)
as   haphazard (1)
at   horizontal (2)
au   jackleg (1)
av   jay horsing (1)
aw   jaywalk (106)
ax   jig-jag (1)
ay   jigzag (1)
az   mighty godlin (1)
ba   narrow cut (1)
bb   near cut (8)
bc   near shoot (1)
bd   near(er) way (3)
be   nigh cut (1)
bf   oblique (1)
bg   oblong (2)
bh   overcross (1)
bi   quartered (1)
bj   right angling (1)
bk   short path (1)
bl   short way (1)
bm   shortcut (28)
bn   sideways (1)
bo   sigodlin (1)
bp   skigoglin (1)
bq   slantwise (2)
br   snaggler diagonal (1)
bs   straight across (11)
bt   straight cut (2)
bu   took a path (1)
bv   triangle (5)
bw   whompy-jawed (1)
bx   whopper-jawed (1)
by   woppy-jawed (1)
bz   wrong-sided (1)
ca   zigzag (14)

085.3 L streetcar

No Response (245)
A   bus (1)
B   cable car (20)
C   electric car (15)
D   electric coach (1)
E   electric streetcar (1)
F   electric train (2)
G   electric trolley (2)
H   streetcar (519)
I   taxi (2)
J   trackless trolley (3)
K   train (2)
L   tram (6)
M   tranvia [S] (2)
N   trolley (144)
O   trolley bus (2)
P   trolley car (107)

085.4 G (where I) want to get off

No Response (107)

[of person on streetcar]

A   be let off (1)
B   be let out (1)
C   get down (1)
D   getting off (1)
E   going to get off (4)
F   (going to) get off at (1)
G   going to get out (1)
H   got off (1)
I   let me off (4)
J   like to get off (2)
K   want off (112)
L   (want) off at (2)
M   (want) out (4)
N   (want to) be off (1)
O   want to get down (2)
P   want to get off (330)
Q   (want to) get off at (14)
R   (want) to get out (6)
S   (want) to stop (12)
T   wants to stop off (1)
U   (where I) get/got off (180)
V   (where I/you) get off at (3)
W   (where I) get out (3)
X   where I stop at (1)
Y   would get off (2)

[of cat at door]

aa   get out (2)
ab   has to go out (1)
ac   is/was wanting out (2)
ad   needs out (2)
ae   wants out (45)
af   wants to get out (20)
ag   wants to go out (8)
ah   would want out (1)

085.5 L county seat

No Response (249)
A   capital (23)
B   capital center (1)
C   capital of the county (2)
D   capital of this parish (1)
E   center (1)
F   county chair (1)
G   county city (1)
H   county seat (551)
I   county seat town (1)
J   county site (7)
K   county town (2)
L   headquarters (5)
M   home seat (1)
N   main city (1)
O   parish capital (1)
P   parish seat (31)
Q   seat (41)
R   seat of the county (2)
S   site (2)
T   town capital (1)
U   town seat (1)
V   trading center (1)

085.6 P government

{ai}　lax onset
{b}　fricative
{g}　devoiced
{oo}　unrounded
{R}　weakly retroflex
{t}　flap
{v}　devoiced
{?}　glottal

No Response (140)
\<gawv(Rnm)Nt=14> (1)
\<gawv{R}n(mN)t=14> (1)
\<go(vRn)mN(t)=14> (1)
\<gob[R](n)mNt=144> (2)
\<goov(Rn)mNt=14> (1)
\<goov(Rn)ment=13> (1)
\<goov[R](n)mNt=144> (1)
\<goov{R}(n)mNt=144> (1)
\<govR(n)mNt=144> (2)
\<govR(n)mont=143> (1)
\<gov[R](n)mNt=144> (6)
\<gov[R](n)men(t)=143> (1)
\<gov[R](n)mint=143> (1)
\<gu(vR)[n]mN(t)=14> (1)
\<gu(vR)mm[N]t=14> (1)
\<gu(vRn)mNt=14> (5)
\<gu(vRn)mint=13> (1)
\<gub(R)M(m)Nt=144> (1)
\<gub(R)MmNt=144> (3)
\<gub(R)Mment=143> (1)
\<gub(Rn)mN(t)=14> (6)
\<gub(Rn)mNt=14> (16)
\<gub(Rn)ment=13> (2)
\<gub(Rn)mint=13> (2)
\<gub(Rn)munt=13> (1)
\<gub[R](n)mN(t)=144> (1)
\<gub[R](n)mNt=144> (3)
\<gub[R](n)ment=143> (1)
\<gum(Rn)mNt=14> (1)
\<gun[R](n)ment=143> (1)
\<guv(R)M(m)Nt=144> (5)
\<guv(R)M(m)e[n]t=143> (1)
\<guv(R)MmNt=144> (9)
\<guv(R)Mment=143> (5)
\<guv(R)Mmint=143> (2)
\<guv(R)NmNt=144> (1)
\<guv(R)Nmint=143> (1)
\<guv(R)Nmunt=143> (3)
\<guv(Rn)mN(t)=14> (10)
\<guv(Rn)mNt=14> (138)
\<guv(Rn)mNts=14> (1)
\<guv(Rn)m[N]t=14> (9)
\<guv(Rn)me[n]t=13> (1)
\<guv(Rn)ment=13> (4)
\<guv(Rn)mi[n]t=13> (1)
\<guv(Rn)min(t)=13> (1)
\<guv(Rn)mint=13> (24)
\<guv(Rn)munt=13> (4)
\<guv(Rnm)Nt=14> (1)

\<guv(Rnm)[N]t=14> (1)
\<guvR(n)mN(t)=144> (1)
\<guvR(n)mNt=144> (69)
\<guvR(n)m[N]t=144> (11)
\<guvR(n)ment=142> (1)
\<guvR(n)ment=143> (9)
\<guvR(n)mi[n]t=143> (1)
\<guvR(n)mint=143> (17)
\<guvR(n)munt=143> (1)
\<guvR(n)m{ai}nt=143> (1)
\<guvRn(mN)t=14> (1)
\<guvRnmNt=144> (14)
\<guvRnm[N]t=144> (3)
\<guvRnment=143> (3)
\<guvRnmint=143> (1)
\<guv[R](n)mN(t)=144> (14)
\<guv[R](n)mNt=144> (184)
\<guv[R](n)mNts=144> (1)
\<guv[R](n)mN{?}=144> (1)
\<guv[R](n)m[N]t=144> (29)
\<guv[R](n)men(t)=143> (1)
\<guv[R](n)ment=143> (19)
\<guv[R](n)ment=341> (3)
\<guv[R](n)mi(n)t=143> (1)
\<guv[R](n)mi[n](t)=143> (1)
\<guv[R](n)mint=142> (1)
\<guv[R](n)mint=143> (50)
\<guv[R](n)moont=143> (1)
\<guv[R](n)munt=143> (7)
\<guv[R]nmNt=144> (3)
\<guve(r)nment=132> (1)
\<guvrNme[n]{t}=143> (1)
\<guvur(n)mNt=134> (1)
\<guv{R}(n)mN(t)=144> (1)
\<guv{R}(n)mNt=144> (31)
\<guv{R}(n)ment=143> (5)
\<guv{R}(n)mint=143> (7)
\<gu{?}[R](n)ment=143> (1)
\<gu{b}(Rn)mN(t)=14> (5)
\<gu{b}(Rn)mNt=14> (12)
\<gu{b}(Rn)me[n]t=13> (1)
\<gu{b}(Rn)ment=13> (2)
\<gu{b}[R](n)M(n)t=144> (1)
\<gu{b}[R](n)mNt=144> (4)
\<gu{b}v[R](n)ment=143> (1)
\<gu{v}(Rn)mint=13> (1)
\<gu{v}R(n)mint=143> (1)
\<gu{v}[R](n)ment=143> (2)
\<gyuv[R](n)mNt=144> (1)
\<g{oo}b(Rn)mN(t)=14> (1)
\<g{oo}b[R](n)ment=143> (1)
\<g{oo}v(R)M(m)Nt=144> (1)
\<g{oo}v(Rn)mN(t)=14> (1)
\<g{oo}v(Rn)mNt=14> (13)
\<g{oo}v(Rn)m[N](t)=14> (1)
\<g{oo}v(Rn)mint=13> (2)
\<g{oo}v(Rn)munt=13> (1)
\<g{oo}vR(n)mNt=144> (2)
\<g{oo}vR(n)mint=143> (1)

\<g{oo}v[R](n)mNt=144> (4)
\<g{oo}v[R](n)mNts=144> (1)
\<g{oo}v[R](n)ment=143> (2)
\<g{oo}v[R](n)mint=143> (2)
\<{g}um(Rn)m[N]t=14> (1)
\<{g}uv(Rn)mNt=14> (2)
\<{g}uv(Rn)mN{t}=14> (1)
\<{g}u{v}[R](n)mNt=144> (1)

085.7 P law and order

{aw}　unrounded onset
{d}　devoiced
{o}　low-back
{R}　weakly retroflex
{r}　weakly retroflex
{t}　flap

No Response (323)
\<[l]awN(d)oerdR=3414> (1)
\<glawN(d)oerdR=3414> (1)
\<law(Nd)aw{r}d[R]=134> (1)
\<law(Nd)oe{r}d[R]=114> (1)
\<law(a)n(d)oerdR=114> (1)
\<lawA(nd)aw[r]d[R]=3414> (1)
\<lawN(d)aw(r)d(R)=143> (1)
\<lawN(d)aw(r)d(R)=341> (1)
\<lawN(d)aw(r)dR=3414> (1)
\<lawN(d)aw(r)d[R]=1414> (4)
\<lawN(d)aw(r)d[R]=1434> (5)
\<lawN(d)aw(r)d[R]=2414> (1)
\<lawN(d)aw(r)d[R]=3414> (16)
\<lawN(d)aw(r)d[R]z=3414> (1)
\<lawN(d)aw(r)d{R}=1434> (1)
\<lawN(d)aw(r)d{R}=3414> (3)
\<lawN(d)aw(r){t}[R]=1434> (1)
\<lawN(d)aw[r]d[R]=1414> (5)
\<lawN(d)aw[r]d[R]=1434> (6)
\<lawN(d)aw[r]d[R]=2414> (6)
\<lawN(d)aw[r]d[R]=3414> (27)
\<lawN(d)aw[r]d{R}=3414> (1)
\<lawN(d)aw[r]{t}R=1414> (1)
\<lawN(d)aw[r]{t}[R]=1424> (1)
\<lawN(d)aw[r]{t}{R}=1434> (1)
\<lawN(d)awrdR=1414> (2)
\<lawN(d)awrdR=1434> (8)
\<lawN(d)awrdR=2414> (5)
\<lawN(d)awrdR=3414> (25)
\<lawN(d)awrd[R]=2414> (1)
\<lawN(d)awrdur=2413> (2)
\<lawN(d)awrd{R}=2414> (1)
\<lawN(d)awrd{R}=3414> (4)
\<lawN(d)aw{r}dR=1434> (1)
\<lawN(d)aw{r}dR=3414> (1)
\<lawN(d)aw{r}d[R]=1414> (1)
\<lawN(d)aw{r}d[R]=1434> (3)
\<lawN(d)aw{r}d[R]=2414> (1)
\<lawN(d)aw{r}d[R]=3414> (5)
\<lawN(d)aw{r}d{R}=1434> (1)
\<lawN(d)aw{r}d{R}=3414> (8)
\<lawN(d)o(r)dR=3414> (1)
\<lawN(d)oe(r)dR=1434> (1)

<lawN(d)oe(r)dR=3414> (1)
<lawN(d)oe(r)d[R]=1434> (2)
<lawN(d)oe(r)d[R]=2414> (1)
<lawN(d)oe(r)d[R]=3414> (9)
<lawN(d)oe(r)d{R}=3414> (3)
<lawN(d)oe(r){t}[R]=1424> (1)
<lawN(d)oe(r){t}[R]=1434> (1)
<lawN(d)oe[r](dR)=241> (1)
<lawN(d)oe[r]dR=1424> (1)
<lawN(d)oe[r]dR=3414> (3)
<lawN(d)oe[r]d[R]=1414> (4)
<lawN(d)oe[r]d[R]=1434> (4)
<lawN(d)oe[r]d[R]=2414> (9)
<lawN(d)oe[r]d[R]=3414> (28)
<lawN(d)oe[r]d{R}=1434> (1)
<lawN(d)oe[r]d{R}=2414> (1)
<lawN(d)oe[r]d{R}=3414> (1)
<lawN(d)oe[r]{d}[R]=3414> (1)
<lawN(d)oe[r]{t}R=1424> (1)
<lawN(d)oe[r]{t}[R]=1414> (1)
<lawN(d)oerdR=1414> (18)
<lawN(d)oerdR=1424> (1)
<lawN(d)oerdR=1434> (23)
<lawN(d)oerdR=2414> (20)
<lawN(d)oerdR=3414> (78)
<lawN(d)oerdur=2413> (1)
<lawN(d)oerd{R}=1414> (1)
<lawN(d)oerd{R}=2414> (2)
<lawN(d)oer{t}R=3414> (2)
<lawN(d)oe{r}dR=1414> (1)
<lawN(d)oe{r}dR=1434> (2)
<lawN(d)oe{r}dR=2414> (1)
<lawN(d)oe{r}dR=3414> (5)
<lawN(d)oe{r}d[R]=2414> (1)
<lawN(d)oe{r}d[R]=3414> (3)
<lawN(d)oe{r}d{R}=1424> (1)
<lawN(d)oe{r}d{R}=1434> (2)
<lawN(d)oe{r}d{R}=2414> (1)
<lawN(d)oe{r}d{R}=3414> (7)
<lawN(d)oe{t}d[R]=1434> (1)
<lawN(d){aw}(r)d[R]=3414> (1)
<lawN(d){aw}rdR=3414> (1)
<lawN(d){o}[r]d[R]=3414> (1)
<lawN(d){o}rdR=2414> (1)
<lawN(d){o}rd{R}=1434> (1)
<lawN(d){o}r{t}R=1424> (1)
<lawN(d){o}r{t}R=1434> (2)
<lawN{t}oerdR=3414> (1)
<law[N](d)oe[r]d[R]=3414> (1)
<lawa[n](d)oerd[R]=3214> (1)
<lawan(d)aw(r)d[R]=1324> (1)
<lawan(d)aw(r)d[R]=2314> (2)
<lawan(d)aw(r)d{R}=1324> (1)
<lawan(d)aw(r)d{R}=2314> (2)
<lawan(d)aw[r]d[R]=1114> (1)
<lawan(d)aw[r]d[R]=1314> (2)
<lawan(d)aw[r]d[R]=2314> (1)
<lawan(d)awrdR=1214> (1)
<lawan(d)awrdR=2314> (1)

<lawan(d)aw{r}d[R]=1314> (1)
<lawan(d)aw{r}d{R}=2314> (3)
<lawan(d)oe(r)d[R]=2314> (1)
<lawan(d)oe(r)d{R}=3314> (1)
<lawan(d)oe[r]d[R]=1314> (3)
<lawan(d)oe[r]d[R]=2314> (8)
<lawan(d)oe[r]d[R]z=3214> (1)
<lawan(d)oerdR=1314> (1)
<lawan(d)oerdR=1324> (4)
<lawan(d)oerdR=2314> (14)
<lawan(d)oerdR=3114> (1)
<lawan(d)oerd{R}=1314> (1)
<lawan(d)oe{r}dR=1324> (1)
<lawan(d)oe{r}dR=2314> (3)
<lawan(d)oe{r}dR=3314> (1)
<lawan(d)oe{r}d{R}=1114> (1)
<lawan(d)oe{r}d{R}=1324> (1)
<lawan(d)oe{r}d{R}=2314> (1)
<lawandoerdR=1314> (1)
<lawen(d)aw(r)d[R]=1314> (1)
<lawen(d)oe(r)d{R}=3314> (1)
<lawen(d)oe[r]d[R]=1314> (2)
<lawen(d)oe[r]d[R]=2314> (2)
<lawen(d)oerdR=1314> (1)
<lawen(d)oerdR=2314> (1)
<lawen(d)oerdR=3314> (1)
<lawen(d)oerd{R}=2314> (1)
<lawen(d)oe{r}d[R]=1324> (1)
<lawen(d)oe{r}d{R}=3314> (1)
<lawen(d)ordR=1314> (1)
<lawrN(d)oerdR=1434> (1)
<lawun(d)oe[r]d{R}=2314> (2)
<lawun(d)oerdR=2314> (1)
<lawzN(d)oerdR=1434> (1)
<law{r}N(d)aw{r}d[R]=3414> (1)
<law{r}N(d)aw{r}d{R}=1434> (1)
<law{r}N(d)oe[r]d[R]=3414> (1)
<law{r}an(d)oe{r}dR=2314> (1)
<loN(d)aw[r]d[R]=3414> (1)
<loN(d)awrdR=1434> (1)
<loN(d)aw{r}d[R]=1434> (1)
<loN(d)aw{r}d{R}=3434> (1)
<loN(d)oerdR=1434> (1)
<loN(d)oerdR=3414> (2)
<loeN(d)aw(r)d[R]=3414> (1)
<loeN(d)awrdR=2414> (1)
<loeN(d)oe(r)d[R]=3414> (1)
<loeN(d)oe[r]{t}[R]=1424> (1)
<loeN(d)oerdR=3414> (1)
<loean(d)o[r]d[R]=1324> (1)
<loeun(d)awrdR=1324> (1)
<lowN(d)awrdR=1414> (1)
<lowN(d)awrd[R]=1434> (1)
<l{aw}N(d)aw(r)dR=1414> (1)
<l{aw}N(d)aw(r)dR=3414> (1)
<l{aw}N(d)aw(r)d[R]=3414> (1)
<l{aw}N(d)awrdR=1414> (1)
<l{aw}N(d)awrdR=1424> (1)
<l{aw}N(d)awrdR=1434> (1)

<l{aw}N(d)awrdR=3414> (2)
<l{aw}N(d)awrd[R]=2414> (1)
<l{aw}N(d)awr{t}R=1434> (1)
<l{aw}N(d)aw{r}dR=3414> (1)
<l{aw}N(d)aw{r}d{R}=1414> (1)
<l{aw}N(d)aw{r}d{R}=3414> (1)
<l{aw}N(d)oe(r)d[R]=1414> (1)
<l{aw}N(d)oe[r]dR=3414> (2)
<l{aw}N(d)oe[r]d[R]=3414> (2)
<l{aw}N(d)oerdR=1414> (2)
<l{aw}N(d)oerdR=1424> (1)
<l{aw}N(d)oerdR=1434> (2)
<l{aw}N(d)oerdR=3414> (17)
<l{aw}N(d)oerd[R]=3414> (1)
<l{aw}N(d)oerd{R}=3414> (2)
<l{aw}N(d)oer{t}ur=1423> (1)
<l{aw}N(d)oe{r}dR=1434> (1)
<l{aw}N(d)oe{r}dR=3414> (6)
<l{aw}N(d)oe{r}d[R]=1434> (1)
<l{aw}N(d)oe{r}d{R}=3414> (2)
<l{aw}N(d){aw}(r)dR=3414> (2)
<l{aw}N(d){aw}(r)d[R]=1424> (1)
<l{aw}N(d){aw}(r){t}[R]=1424>
        (1)
<l{aw}N(d){aw}rdR=3414> (1)
<l{aw}an(d)oe(r)d[R]=2314> (1)
<l{aw}an(d)oe(r)d{R}=3314> (1)
<l{aw}an(d)oe[r]d[R]=1314> (1)
<l{aw}an(d)oe[r]d[R]=2314> (1)
<l{aw}an(d)oerdR=2134> (1)
<l{aw}an(d)oerdR=2314> (4)
<l{aw}an(d)oe{r}dR=2314> (2)
<l{aw}an(d)oe{r}dR=3314> (1)
<l{aw}an(d)oe{r}d[R]=2314> (1)
<l{aw}an(d){aw}[r]d{R}=2314>
        (1)
<l{aw}en(d)oe{r}d{R}=2314> (1)
<l{aw}endoe[r]d[R]=2314> (1)
<l{o}N(d)aw(r){t}R=1434> (1)
<l{o}N(d)awrdR=1414> (1)
<l{o}N(d)oerdR=3414> (1)
<l{o}N(d){o}(r){t}[R]=1434> (1)
<l{o}N(d){o}r{t}R=1424> (1)

085.8 L Civil War

No Response (137)
A American Civil War (2)
B Blue and the Gray (2)
C Blue-Gray War (1)
D Civil Right(s) (2)
E Civil War (704)
F Civil War between the States (1)
G Confederate War (66)
H Conflict, the (1)
I Conflict between the North and the South (1)
J Federal War (4)
K Fight between the Rebels and the Yankees (1)
L First War (1)

M Freedom War (1)
N Great War (1)
O Late Unpleasantness, the (1)
P Lincoln's War (1)
Q Lost Cause (1)
R North and South (War) (4)
S Old War (2)
T Republican and Democrat War (1)
U Republicans and Democrats (1)
V Rebellion (3)
W Revolution (7)
X Revolution War (2)
Y Secession War (1)
Z Second Revolutionary War (1)
aa Second War for Independence (1)
ab Southern War (1)
ac Terrible War (1)
ad United States War (1)
ae War, the (6)
af War against the State(s) (2)
ag War among the States (1)
ah War between the Nations (1)
ai War between (the) North (and) South (21)
aj War between the Northern States and the Southern States (1)
ak War between the State(s) (253)
al War between the Two States (2)
am War betwixt the State[N-i] (1)
an War for Independence (1)
ao War for Southern Independence (1)
ap War for the Confederacy (1)
aq War in the States (1)
ar War of Hate (1)
as War of Northern Aggression (5)
at War of Rebellion (2)
au War of Secession (2)
av War of Slavery (2)
aw War of the Divided Nation (1)
ax War of the Northern Aggression (1)
ay War of the Rebellion (2)
az War of the Revolution (1)
ba War of the South (1)
bb War of the States (4)
bc War of Yankee Aggression (2)
bd War to Free the Slaves (1)
be War with State[N-i] (1)
bf War with the Yankees (1)
bg Yankee War (2)
bh Yankees against the Southerners (1)
bi Yankees and the Confederates (1)
bj Yankees and the Rebels (2)

085.8 P Civil War

{aw}   unrounded onset
{o}   low-back
{oe}   lowered onset
{r}   weakly retroflex
{v}   bilabial
No Response (218)
<saivLw{oe}r=143> (1)
<seevLwaw(r)=143> (1)
<seevLwaw[r]=143> (1)
<seevLwawr=143> (1)
<seevLwawr=341> (1)
<seevLw{oe}[r]=341> (1)
<sevLwawr=141> (1)
<sevLwawr=143> (2)
<sevLw{oe}[r]=241> (1)
<sevLw{oe}r=142> (1)
<sevLw{oe}r=143> (1)
<sevLw{oe}r=341> (1)
<sevLw{o}r=143> (1)
<sev[L]w{oe}r=341> (1)
<shiv[L]waw[r]=143> (1)
<si(v)Lw{oe}r=143> (1)
<sib[L]waw{r}=341> (1)
<silvAw{o}[r]=141> (1)
<silvRwawr=341> (1)
<sivLdw{oe}[r]=143> (1)
<sivLwaw(r)=141> (17)
<sivLwaw(r)=143> (45)
<sivLwaw(r)=241> (6)
<sivLwaw(r)=341> (13)
<sivLwaw[R]=1434> (1)
<sivLwaw[R]=3414> (1)
<sivLwaw[r]=141> (29)
<sivLwaw[r]=142> (1)
<sivLwaw[r]=143> (58)
<sivLwaw[r]=241> (5)
<sivLwaw[r]=341> (16)
<sivLwawr=141> (35)
<sivLwawr=143> (116)
<sivLwawr=241> (17)
<sivLwawr=341> (56)
<sivLwawrd=143> (1)
<sivLwawwaw(r)=2413> (1)
<sivLwaw{r}=141> (2)
<sivLwaw{r}=143> (45)
<sivLwaw{r}=241> (4)
<sivLwaw{r}=341> (23)
<sivLwo[r]=141> (1)
<sivLwo[r]=143> (1)
<sivLwo[r]=341> (1)
<sivLwoer=143> (1)
<sivLwoer=341> (1)
<sivLwor=142> (1)
<sivLwor=143> (14)
<sivLwor=341> (3)
<sivLwo{r}=143> (2)
<sivLwo{r}=341> (1)
<sivLw{aw}(r)=341> (1)
<sivLw{aw}r=143> (2)

<sivLw{aw}r=341> (3)
<sivLw{oe}(r)=143> (1)
<sivLw{oe}(r)=341> (1)
<sivLw{oe}[r]=141> (1)
<sivLw{oe}[r]=143> (10)
<sivLw{oe}[r]=341> (2)
<sivLw{oe}r=141> (2)
<sivLw{oe}r=143> (35)
<sivLw{oe}r=241> (5)
<sivLw{oe}r=341> (36)
<sivLw{oe}{r}=143> (7)
<sivLw{oe}{r}=341> (4)
<sivLw{o}(r)=143> (6)
<sivLw{o}(r)=241> (1)
<sivLw{o}[r]=141> (3)
<sivLw{o}[r]=143> (10)
<sivLw{o}[r]=341> (7)
<sivLw{o}r=142> (1)
<sivLw{o}r=143> (10)
<sivLw{o}r=341> (5)
<sivLw{o}w[R]=2414> (1)
<sivRwaw[r]=143> (1)
<siv[L]wa[r]=241> (1)
<siv[L]waw(r)=143> (3)
<siv[L]waw(r)=241> (1)
<siv[L]waw[r]=143> (2)
<siv[L]waw[r]=341> (2)
<siv[L]waw[r]z=341> (1)
<siv[L]wawr=143> (1)
<siv[L]waw{r}=143> (1)
<siv[L]waw{r}=341> (2)
<siv[L]w{aw}(r)=143> (1)
<siv[L]w{oe}[r]=142> (1)
<siv[L]w{oe}[r]=143> (1)
<siv[L]w{oe}r=143> (1)
<siv[L]w{oe}r=341> (1)
<siv[L]w{o}r=143> (1)
<siv[L]w{o}r=241> (1)
<sivilwawr=231> (1)
<sivu[l]waw(r)=132> (1)
<si{v}Lwaw[r]=141> (1)
<si{v}Lwawr=142> (1)
<si{v}[L]wawr=143> (1)
<si{v}[L]w{oe}{r}=142> (1)

085.9 G hang
<!> infinitive
<@> present participle
<*> preterit
<#> past participle
No Response (276)
<!haing> (7)
<!hang> (78)
<@haingN=14> (1)
<@hangN=14> (6)
<*haing> (2)
<*haingd> (12)
<*hang> (10)
<*hangd> (121)
<*hanggd> (3)

<me[r](I)lN(d)=14> (11)
<me[r](I)lNd=14> (2)
<me[r](I)l[N](d)=14> (2)
<me[r]AlN(d)=144> (7)
<me[r]IlN(d)=144> (1)
<me[r]IlNd=144> (1)
<mer(I)lN(d)=14> (47)
<mer(I)lNd=14> (6)
<merAlN(d)=144> (93)
<merAlNd=144> (20)
<merAl[N](d)=144> (2)
<merAlun(d)=143> (2)
<merAlund=143> (1)
<merIlN(d)=144> (231)
<merIlNd=144> (99)
<merIlNt=144> (1)
<merIl[N](d)=144> (1)
<merIlund=143> (1)
<merLN(d)=144> (2)
<merRlN(d)=144> (3)
<mirAlN(d)=144> (1)
<mirAlNd=144> (2)
<mirIlN(d)=144> (6)
<mirIlNd=144> (2)
<mur(I)lN(d)=14> (6)
<mur(I)lNd=14> (1)
<murAlN(d)=144> (3)
<murAlNd=144> (1)
<murIlN(d)=144> (11)
<murIlNd=144> (3)
<murLN(d)=144> (2)
<murLNd=144> (1)
<myerIlN(d)=144> (1)

086.2A P Virginia
No Response (225)
<(vur)jinyA=14> (2)
<fRjinyA=414> (4)
<fRjinyI=414> (1)
<f[R]jinjA=414> (1)
<f[R]jinyA=414> (21)
<f[R]jinyI=414> (1)
<f[R]jinyi=413> (2)
<furjinyA=314> (8)
<m[R]jeenyA=414> (1)
<v(ur)jinyA=14> (1)
<vRjeenyA=414> (3)
<vRjenyA=414> (10)
<vRjenyR=414> (1)
<vRjin(y)I=414> (1)
<vRjinIA=4144> (2)
<vRjineeyA=4134> (1)
<vRjiniA=4134> (1)
<vRjinjA=414> (2)
<vRjinyA=414> (114)
<vRjinyI=414> (13)
<vRjinyR=414> (4)
<vRjinyi=413> (1)
<vRjinyo=413> (1)
<v[R]jee[n]yA=414> (1)

<v[R]jeenyA=414> (7)
<v[R]jenyA=414> (13)
<v[R]jenyR=414> (2)
<v[R]jin(y)A=414> (2)
<v[R]jinIA=4144> (3)
<v[R]jinIR=4144> (1)
<v[R]jiniA=4134> (1)
<v[R]jinjA=414> (10)
<v[R]jinjAz=414> (1)
<v[R]jinjI=414> (1)
<v[R]jinyA=414> (266)
<v[R]jinyI=414> (23)
<v[R]jinyN=414> (1)
<v[R]jinyR=414> (12)
<v[R]zhinyA=414> (1)
<ve(r)jinyA=314> (1)
<vi(r)jinyA=314> (4)
<vo(r)jinyA=314> (1)
<vrIjinIA=4144> (1)
<vu[r]jinIA=3144> (1)
<vu[r]jinyA=314> (24)
<vu[r]jinyI=314> (4)
<vurjeenjA=314> (1)
<vurjeenyA=314> (3)
<vurjenyA=314> (7)
<vurjinIA=3144> (1)
<vurjineeyA=3134> (2)
<vurjinjI=314> (1)
<vurjinjN=314> (1)
<vurjinyA=134> (3)
<vurjinyA=314> (119)
<vurjinyI=314> (8)
<vurjinyR=314> (1)
<vurjinzhA=314> (1)
<vurzhinyA=214> (1)
<wes(t)fu[r]jinyA=1324> (1)
<wes(t)vRjinyA=1414> (1)
<wes(t)vRjinyA=1434> (1)
<wes(t)vRjinyA=3414> (4)
<wes(t)vRzhinyA=1424> (1)
<wes(t)v[R]jenyA=2414> (1)
<wes(t)v[R]jinjA=1414> (1)
<wes(t)v[R]jinjA=1434> (1)
<wes(t)v[R]jinyA=1414> (1)
<wes(t)v[R]jinyA=2414> (1)
<wes(t)v[R]jinyA=3414> (2)
<wes(t)vurjinyA=1324> (1)
<wes(t)vurjinyA=2314> (1)
<wes(t)vurjinyA=3314> (1)
<wes(t)vurzinyA=2314> (1)
<westv[R]jinyA=2414> (1)
<westv[R]jinyA=3414> (2)
<westvurjinyA=1324> (1)
<wi(r)jinyA=314> (1)
<wis(t)v[R]jinyI=1424> (1)
<wurjinyA=314> (2)

086.2B P North Carolina
No Response (235)
<(noerth)ke(rA)lienA=314> (1)

<(noerth)ke[r](A)lienA=314> (1)
<(noerth)ker(A)lienA=314> (1)
<maw(r)thka[r](A)lienA=3214> (1)
<naw(r)thk(arA)LienA=1434> (2)
<naw(r)thk(arA)lienA=214> (1)
<naw(r)thkI(rA)lienA=3414> (1)
<naw(r)thkR(A)lienA=1434> (1)
<naw(r)thkR(A)lienA=3414> (1)
<naw(r)thk[R](A)lienA=1414> (1)
<naw(r)thk[R](A)lienA=1424> (3)
<naw(r)thk[R](A)lienA=1434> (14)
<naw(r)thk[R](A)lienA=2414> (6)
<naw(r)thk[R](A)lienA=3414> (9)
<naw(r)thka(r)AlienA=13424> (1)
<naw(r)thka(r)AlienA=23414> (1)
<naw(r)thka(rA)lienA=1234> (1)
<naw(r)thka(rA)lienA=1314> (1)
<naw(r)thka(rA)lienA=1324> (3)
<naw(r)thka(rA)lienA=2314> (2)
<naw(r)thka[r](A)lInA=1344> (1)
<naw(r)thka[r](A)lienA=1324> (1)
<naw(r)thka[r](A)lienA=1334> (1)
<naw(r)thka[r](A)lienA=2314> (1)
<naw(r)thkar(A)lienA=1234> (1)
<naw(r)thkarAlien(A)=1243> (1)
<naw(r)thkarAlienA=13424> (1)
<naw(r)thkarAlienA=21434> (1)
<naw(r)thkarAlienA=23414> (8)
<naw(r)thkarAlienA=32414> (2)
<naw(r)thkarIlienA=13424> (1)
<naw(r)thke(r)AlienA=23414> (1)
<naw(r)thke(rA)lienA=1314> (2)
<naw(r)thke(rA)lienA=1324> (1)
<naw(r)thke(rA)lienA=2314> (1)
<naw(r)thke(rA)lienA=3314> (1)
<naw(r)thkeRlienA=23414> (1)
<naw(r)thke[r](A)lienA=1324> (1)
<naw(r)thker(A)lienA=1234> (1)
<naw(r)thker(A)lienA=1314> (1)
<naw(r)thker(A)lienA=1324> (3)
<naw(r)thker(A)lienA=2314> (2)
<naw(r)thker(A)lienA=3314> (1)
<naw(r)thkerAlienA=12434> (1)
<naw(r)thkerAlienA=13414> (4)
<naw(r)thkerAlienA=13424> (3)
<naw(r)thkerAlienA=23414> (6)
<naw(r)thkerAlienA=32414> (2)
<naw(r)thkir(A)lienA=1314> (1)
<naw(r)thkir(A)lienA=1324> (1)
<naw(r)thkir(A)lienA=2314> (1)
<naw(r)thkurAlienA=23414> (1)
<naw(r)thkurIlienA=23414> (1)
<naw(rth)k[R](A)lienA=1434> (1)
<naw[r](th)karAlienA=23414> (1)
<naw[r]fk[R](A)lienA=1434> (1)
<naw[r]sker(A)lienA=1324> (1)
<naw[r]thk(ar)LienA=3414> (1)
<naw[r]thkR(A)lienA=3414> (1)
<naw[r]thk[R](A)lienA=1414> (1)

<noerthkarAlienA=33414> (1)
<noerthkarIlienA=11434> (1)
<noerthkarIlienA=13414> (2)
<noerthkarIlienA=23414> (1)
<noerthkarIlienA=32414> (1)
<noerthke(r)AlienA=23414> (1)
<noerthke[r](A)lienA=1314> (1)
<noerthke[r](A)lienA=3314> (1)
<noerthke[r]IlienA=23414> (1)
<noerthker(A)lienA=1234> (1)
<noerthker(A)lienA=1314> (3)
<noerthker(A)lienA=1324> (8)
<noerthker(A)lienA=2314> (6)
<noerthker(A)lienA=3314> (2)
<noerthker(IlienA)=13> (1)
<noerthkerAlienA=12414> (1)
<noerthkerAlienA=12434> (2)
<noerthkerAlienA=13414> (7)
<noerthkerAlienA=13424> (5)
<noerthkerAlienA=21434> (1)
<noerthkerAlienA=23414> (29)
<noerthkerAlienA=32414> (3)
<noerthkerAlienA=33414> (4)
<noerthkerAlienR=13414> (1)
<noerthkerIlienA=11434> (2)
<noerthkerIlienA=12414> (2)
<noerthkerIlienA=13414> (14)
<noerthkerIlienA=13424> (8)
<noerthkerIlienA=21424> (1)
<noerthkerIlienA=21434> (1)
<noerthkerIlienA=23414> (7)
<noerthkerIlienR=13414> (2)
<noerthku[r](A)lienA=1334> (1)
<noerthkur(A)lienA=1314> (6)
<noerthkur(A)lienA=2314> (7)
<noerthkurAlienA=13414> (2)
<noerthkurAlienA=13424> (2)
<noerthkurAlienA=23414> (2)
<noerthkurAlienR=13414> (1)
<noerthkurIlienA=13424> (1)
<noerthky[R](A)lienA=1424> (1)
<noertkarAlienA=23414> (1)
<noertku[r](A)lienA=1324> (1)
<northkR(A)lienA=1434> (1)
<northka(rA)lienA=1334> (1)
<northkarAlienA=23414> (1)
<northkerAlienA=12434> (1)
<northkerAlienA=13414> (2)
<northkerAlienA=13424> (3)
<northkerAlienA=23414> (3)
<nu[r]thk[R](A)lienA=3414> (1)

086.3A P South Carolina
No Response (238)
<(sowth)k[R](A)lienA=414> (1)
<(sowth)ka[r](A)lienA=314> (1)
<(sowth)karAlienA=3414> (1)
<(sowth)ke[r](A)lienR=314> (1)
<(sowth)kerAlienA=3414> (1)
<sow(th)k[R](A)lienA=3414> (2)

<sow(th)ka[r]AlieN=23414> (1)
<sow(th)kerAlienA=23414> (2)
<sowfkR(A)lienA=2414> (1)
<sowfkR(A)lienA=3414> (1)
<sowfk[R](A)lienA=3414> (2)
<sowfkar(A)lienA=1324> (1)
<sowfke(rA)lienA=2314> (1)
<sowsk[R](A)lienA=1414> (1)
<sowsk[R](A)lienA=3414> (1)
<sowska[r](A)lienA=1324> (1)
<sowskarIlienA=11434> (1)
<sowske[r]AlienA=13414> (1)
<sowthk(er)LienA=1424> (2)
<sowthk(er)LienA=1434> (2)
<sowthk(er)LienA=l424> (1)
<sowthkR(A)lienA=1414> (4)
<sowthkR(A)lienA=1424> (1)
<sowthkR(A)lienA=1434> (10)
<sowthkR(A)lienA=2414> (3)
<sowthkR(A)lienA=3414> (10)
<sowthkR(A)lienR=1434> (2)
<sowthk[R](A)lien(A)=143> (1)
<sowthk[R](A)lienA=1414> (25)
<sowthk[R](A)lienA=1424> (2)
<sowthk[R](A)lienA=1434> (82)
<sowthk[R](A)lienA=2414> (12)
<sowthk[R](A)lienA=3414> (25)
<sowthk[R](A)lienI=1434> (1)
<sowthk[R](A)lienR=1414> (1)
<sowthk[R](A)lienR=1434> (3)
<sowthk[R](A)lienR=3414> (2)
<sowthka(rA)lienA=1314> (1)
<sowthka(rA)lienA=1324> (10)
<sowthka(rA)lienA=2314> (6)
<sowthka(r)AlienA=12414> (1)
<sowthka(r)AlienA=13424> (1)
<sowthka(r)AlienA=33414> (1)
<sowthka[r](A)lien(A)=132> (1)
<sowthka[r](A)lienA=1134> (1)
<sowthka[r](A)lienA=1314> (4)
<sowthka[r](A)lienA=1324> (5)
<sowthka[r]AlienA=13414> (1)
<sowthkairIlienA=23414> (1)
<sowthkar(A)lie[n](A)=132> (1)
<sowthkar(A)lien(A)=123> (1)
<sowthkar(A)lienA=1214> (1)
<sowthkar(A)lienA=1234> (1)
<sowthkar(A)lienA=1314> (2)
<sowthkar(A)lienA=1324> (17)
<sowthkar(A)lienA=2314> (11)
<sowthkar(A)lienA=3314> (1)
<sowthkarAlien(A)=1243> (1)
<sowthkarAlien(A)=1342> (1)
<sowthkarAlien(A)=2143> (1)
<sowthkarAlienA=12414> (2)
<sowthkarAlienA=13414> (11)
<sowthkarAlienA=13424> (28)
<sowthkarAlienA=13434> (1)
<sowthkarAlienA=21434> (1)

<sowthkarAlienA=23414> (28)
<sowthkarAlienA=33414> (2)
<sowthkarIlienA=11434> (3)
<sowthkarIlienA=13414> (7)
<sowthkarIlienA=13424> (2)
<sowthkarIlienA=23414> (2)
<sowthke(rA)lienA=1324> (14)
<sowthke(r)AlienA=11434> (1)
<sowthke(r)AlienA=13414> (1)
<sowthke(r)AlienA=13424> (1)
<sowthke(r)AlienA=23414> (2)
<sowthke(r)AlienA=32414> (1)
<sowthkeRlienA=13414> (1)
<sowthke[r](A)lienA=1134> (1)
<sowthke[r](A)lienA=1314> (7)
<sowthke[r](A)lienA=1324> (6)
<sowthke[r](A)lienA=2314> (2)
<sowthke[r](A)lienA=3314> (1)
<sowthke[r]AlienA=23414> (1)
<sowthker(A)lie[n](A)=131> (1)
<sowthker(A)lienA=1134> (1)
<sowthker(A)lienA=1214> (1)
<sowthker(A)lienA=1234> (2)
<sowthker(A)lienA=1314> (9)
<sowthker(A)lienA=1324> (23)
<sowthker(A)lienA=2314> (9)
<sowthker(A)lienA=3214> (1)
<sowthker(A)lienA=3314> (2)
<sowthker(A)lienR=1314> (1)
<sowthkerAlie[n](A)=1343> (1)
<sowthkerAlien(A)=1341> (2)
<sowthkerAlienA=12434> (9)
<sowthkerAlienA=13414> (22)
<sowthkerAlienA=13424> (51)
<sowthkerAlienA=13434> (2)
<sowthkerAlienA=21434> (1)
<sowthkerAlienA=23414> (31)
<sowthkerAlienA=32414> (5)
<sowthkerAlienA=33414> (5)
<sowthkerAlienR=13414> (1)
<sowthkerAlienR=23414> (1)
<sowthkerIlienA=11434> (4)
<sowthkerIlienA=12414> (1)
<sowthkerIlienA=13414> (27)
<sowthkerIlienA=13424> (15)
<sowthkerIlienA=13434> (1)
<sowthkerIlienA=23414> (8)
<sowthkerIlienA=33414> (1)
<sowthkerIlienR=13414> (1)
<sowthkerIlienR=13424> (1)
<sowthki[r](A)lienA=1314> (1)
<sowthki[r](A)lienA=2314> (1)
<sowthkir(A)lienR=2314> (1)
<sowthkorAlienA=13424> (1)
<sowthku[r](A)lienA=1314> (1)
<sowthku[r](A)lienA=2314> (3)
<sowthku[r](A)lienR=1314> (1)
<sowthkur(A)lienA=1314> (5)
<sowthkur(A)lienA=1324> (3)

<sowthkur(A)lienA=2314> (5)
<sowthkurAlienA=13414> (4)
<sowthkurAlienA=13424> (8)
<sowthkurAlienA=23414> (4)
<sowthkurIlienA=13414> (1)
<sowthkurIlienA=13424> (2)
<sowthkye(rA)lienA=1324> (1)
<sowthkye[r](A)lienA=1324> (1)
<sowthkye[r](A)lienA=2314> (1)
<sowthkyer(A)lienA=1314> (1)
<sowthkyerAlienA=23414> (1)
<sowtka[r]AlienA=13414> (1)
<sowtkar(A)lienA=1324> (1)
<sowtkarIlienA=13414> (1)
<sowtkerAlienA=13424> (1)
<sowtkir(A)lienA=1324> (1)

086.3B P Georgia

{R}   weakly retroflex
{r}   weakly retroflex
No Response (109)
<jaw(r)jA=14> (41)
<jaw(r)jI=14> (16)
<jaw(r)jo=13> (1)
<jaw(r)yA=14> (1)
<jaw[r]jA=14> (53)
<jaw[r]jI=14> (22)
<jaw[r]jR=14> (1)
<jaw[r]zhA=14> (1)
<jawj{R}=14> (1)
<jawrjA=14> (58)
<jawrjI=14> (21)
<jawrji=13> (2)
<jawrjie=13> (1)
<jawrj{R}=14> (1)
<jaw{r}jA=14> (26)
<jaw{r}jI=14> (12)
<jaw{r}jR=14> (1)
<jaw{r}j{R}=14> (3)
<jo(r)jA=14> (3)
<jo[r]jA=14> (2)
<jo[r]jI=14> (1)
<joe(r)jA=14> (22)
<joe(r)jI=14> (6)
<joe[r]chA=14> (1)
<joe[r]chI=14> (1)
<joe[r]jA=14> (159)
<joe[r]jI=14> (44)
<joe[r]ji=13> (1)
<joe[r]njA=14> (1)
<joe[r]yI=14> (2)
<joerjA=14> (213)
<joerjI=14> (80)
<joerjR=14> (3)
<joerje=13> (1)
<joerji=13> (1)
<joerjie=13> (2)
<joerj{R}=14> (3)
<joerzhI=14> (1)
<joe{r}chA=14> (1)

<joe{r}jA=14> (41)
<joe{r}jI=14> (11)
<joe{r}j{R}=14> (1)
<joo[r]jA=14> (1)
<jorjA=14> (9)
<jorjI=14> (1)
<joy(r)jA=14> (8)
<joy(r)jI=14> (8)
<zhoe[r]jA=14> (1)

086.4A P Florida

No Response (160)
<f[l]aw(r)AdA=144> (1)
<f[l]awrIdA=144> (1)
<f[l]oe[r](I)dA=14> (2)
<f[l]or(I)dA=14> (1)
<flaw(I)dI=14> (1)
<flaw(r)AdA=144> (3)
<flaw(r)AdR=144> (1)
<flaw(r)IdA=144> (11)
<flaw(r)IdI=144> (1)
<flaw(rI)dA=14> (1)
<flaw(rIdA)> (1)
<flawRdA=144> (2)
<flaw[r](I)dA=14> (12)
<flaw[r](I)dI=14> (1)
<flaw[r](I)du=13> (1)
<flaw[r]AdA=144> (1)
<flaw[r]IdA=144> (3)
<flawr(I)dA=14> (8)
<flawr(I)dI=14> (1)
<flawr(I)dR=14> (2)
<flawrAdA=144> (13)
<flawrIdA=144> (66)
<flawrIdR=144> (3)
<flawridA=134> (1)
<flo(r)AdA=144> (4)
<flo(r)IdA=144> (14)
<flo(r)idA=134> (1)
<flo(r)wIdA=144> (1)
<flo(rI)dA=14> (3)
<floRdA=144> (8)
<floRdI=144> (1)
<flo[r](I)dA=14> (34)
<flo[r](I)dI=14> (2)
<flo[r]AdA=144> (1)
<flo[r]IdA=144> (2)
<floe(r)AdA=144> (5)
<floe(r)IdA=144> (4)
<floe(r)idA=134> (1)
<floe(rId)A=14> (1)
<floeRdA=144> (1)
<floe[r](I)dA=14> (15)
<floe[r](I)dI=14> (1)
<floe[r]AdA=144> (3)
<floe[r]IdA=144> (5)
<floer(I)dA=14> (6)
<floer(I)dI=14> (1)
<floerAdA=144> (6)
<floerIdA=144> (98)

<floerIdAs=144> (1)
<floerIdI=144> (2)
<floerIdR=144> (1)
<floeridA=134> (1)
<flor(I)dA=14> (64)
<flor(I)dI=14> (5)
<flor(I)dR=14> (2)
<flor(Id)A=14> (1)
<flor(Id)I=14> (1)
<florAdA=144> (61)
<florAdI=144> (2)
<florI(d)A=144> (1)
<florI(dA)=14> (1)
<florId(A)=14> (1)
<florIdA=144> (261)
<florIdI=144> (11)
<florIdR=144> (11)
<florIdee=143> (2)
<floridA=134> (21)
<flurIdA=144> (1)
<fra[r](I)dA=14> (1)

086.4B P Alabama

No Response (140)
<(alA)bamA=14> (1)
<a(l)AbamA=1434> (1)
<a(l)AbamA=3414> (1)
<a(l)IbamA=2414> (1)
<a[l](A)bamA=134> (1)
<a[l](A)bamA=314> (1)
<a[l]AbamA=1424> (1)
<a[l]AbamA=2414> (1)
<a[l]AbamA=3414> (8)
<a[l]AbamR=2414> (1)
<a[l]IbamA=1434> (1)
<a[l]IbamA=3414> (7)
<al(A)bamA=114> (1)
<al(A)bamA=314> (5)
<al(A)bamee=123> (1)
<alAba(m)A=3414> (1)
<alAbam(A)=341> (2)
<alAbamA=1424> (6)
<alAbamA=1434> (18)
<alAbamA=2414> (17)
<alAbamA=3414> (426)
<alAbamI=3414> (2)
<alAbamR=2414> (1)
<alAbamR=3414> (23)
<alAbamo=3413> (1)
<alAbamu=2413> (3)
<alAbawmA=3414> (1)
<alAbomA=3414> (1)
<alIbaimA=3414> (1)
<alIbam(A)=341> (3)
<alIbamA=1434> (3)
<alIbamA=2414> (5)
<alIbamA=3414> (237)
<alIbamI=3414> (3)
<alIbamR=3414> (9)
<alIbambA=3414> (1)

<alIbamee=1423> (1)
<alIbemA=3414> (1)
<alIbomA=3414> (1)
<elAbamA=1414> (1)
<elAbamA=3414> (17)
<elIbamA=3414> (5)
<helIbamA=3414> (1)
<olAbamA=3414> (1)
<olAbomA=3414> (1)

086.5A P Louisiana

No Response (183)
<lAweez(ee)yanA=4214> (1)
<lAweezIanA=41434> (3)
<lAweezIanA=43414> (17)
<lAweezIanu=41423> (1)
<lAweezIenA=41434> (1)
<lAweezIennA=42414> (1)
<lAweezIennA=43414> (1)
<lAweezeeanA=41324> (2)
<lAweezeeanA=42314> (8)
<lAweezeeanA=43314> (1)
<lAweezeeanR=42314> (1)
<lAwiz(ee)anA=4214> (1)
<lIweezIanA=41434> (1)
<lIweezIanA=42414> (2)
<lIweezIanA=43414> (5)
<lew(ee)z(ee)anA=314> (2)
<lew(ee)z(ee)yanA=314> (1)
<lew(ee)zAanA=3414> (1)
<lew(ee)zIanA=1424> (1)
<lew(ee)zIanA=1434> (4)
<lew(ee)zIanA=2414> (1)
<lew(ee)zIanA=3414> (24)
<lew(ee)zIenA=2414> (1)
<lew(ee)zianA=1324> (1)
<lewIz(ee)anA=3414> (1)
<lewIzIanA=34414> (1)
<leweezIanA=32414> (2)
<leweezIanR=32414> (1)
<loo(ee)zIanA=3414> (3)
<loo(ee)zeeanA=2314> (1)
<looIz(ee)anA=3414> (1)
<looIzIanA=34414> (4)
<looIzeeanA=24314> (1)
<looIzhIanA=34414> (1)
<looeezIanA=31414> (1)
<looeezIanA=32414> (4)
<looeezIinA=32414> (1)
<looizIanA=13414> (1)
<looizIanA=23414> (1)
<looweez(ee)anA=3214> (1)
<looweezIanA=21434> (1)
<looweezIanA=23414> (2)
<looweezIanA=31434> (1)
<looweezIanA=32414> (9)
<looweezIenA=32414> (1)
<looweezIennA=32414> (1)
<looweezeeanA=23214> (1)
<looweezeeanA=32314> (7)

<lue(ee)dh(ee)anA=134> (1)
<lue(ee)dh(ee)anA=214> (1)
<lue(ee)dhIanA=1424> (1)
<lue(ee)sIanA=3414> (1)
<lue(ee)th(ee)anA=314> (1)
<lue(ee)z(ee)anA=214> (1)
<lue(ee)z(ee)anA=314> (15)
<lue(ee)z(ee)anR=314> (1)
<lue(ee)z(ee)yanA=314> (1)
<lue(ee)zAanA=3414> (3)
<lue(ee)zIanA=1414> (2)
<lue(ee)zIanA=1424> (4)
<lue(ee)zIanA=1434> (36)
<lue(ee)zIanA=2414> (5)
<lue(ee)zIanA=2434> (1)
<lue(ee)zIanA=3414> (296)
<lue(ee)zIanR=2414> (1)
<lue(ee)zIanR=3414> (30)
<lue(ee)zIanee=3413> (1)
<lue(ee)zIannA=3414> (5)
<lue(ee)zIenA=3414> (3)
<lue(ee)zIenR=3414> (1)
<lue(ee)zIennA=1434> (1)
<lue(ee)zIennA=3414> (1)
<lue(ee)zIenu=1423> (1)
<lue(ee)zIyanA=3414> (2)
<lue(ee)zeean(A)=132> (1)
<lue(ee)zeeanA=1324> (6)
<lue(ee)zeeanA=2314> (17)
<lue(ee)zeeanAz=2314> (1)
<lue(ee)zeeanR=2314> (1)
<lue(ee)zh(ee)anA=314> (2)
<lue(ee)zh(ee)anR=314> (1)
<lue(ee)zhIanA=1434> (2)
<lue(ee)zi(a)nR=134> (1)
<lue(ee)zianA=1324> (4)
<lue(ee)zianA=2314> (3)
<lueAzIanA=34414> (1)
<lueAzeeanA=14324> (1)
<lueIz(ee)anA=3414> (1)
<lueIzAanA=34414> (1)
<lueIzIanA=14414> (1)
<lueIzIanA=14434> (2)
<lueIzIanA=24414> (2)
<lueIzIanA=34414> (32)
<lueIzIanR=34414> (2)
<lueIzIeenA=14434> (2)
<lueIzIenA=34414> (2)
<lueIzIyanA=34414> (1)
<lueIzeeanA=14324> (5)
<lueIzeeanA=14334> (1)
<lueIzeeanA=24314> (10)
<lueIzeeanA=34314> (4)
<lueIzeeanI=24314> (1)
<lueIzeeanR=24314> (1)
<lueIzeeenA=34314> (1)
<lueIzeeonA=24314> (1)
<lueeezIanA=13434> (2)
<lueeezIanA=23414> (9)

<lueeezIanA=31414> (1)
<lueeezIanA=31434> (4)
<lueeezIanA=32414> (34)
<lueeezIanA=33414> (1)
<lueeezIanR=32414> (2)
<lueeezIenA=32414> (1)
<lueeezIennA=32414> (1)
<lueeezeeanA=13234> (1)
<lueeezeeanA=13324> (1)
<lueeezeeanA=23214> (1)
<lueeezeeanA=23314> (1)
<lueeezeeanA=31324> (1)
<lueeezeeanA=32314> (3)
<lueeezeeannA=32314> (1)
<lueeezianA=32314> (1)
<lueizIanA=32414> (2)
<lueizeeanR=32314> (1)
<lueoozIanA=23414> (1)
<luewAzIanA=34414> (1)
<luewAzeeanA=14324> (1)
<luewAzianA=14324> (1)
<luewAzianA=24314> (1)
<luewIzIanA=14434> (1)
<luewIzIanA=34414> (1)
<luewIzeeanA=14324> (5)
<luewIzeeanA=24314> (8)
<luewIzheeanA=14234> (1)
<lueweesIanA=32414> (1)
<lueweezIanA=13424> (1)
<lueweezIanA=13434> (1)
<lueweezIanA=23414> (15)
<lueweezIanA=32414> (17)
<lueweezIenA=32414> (1)
<lueweezIennA=32414> (1)
<lueweezeeanA=12324> (1)
<lueweezeeanA=13324> (2)
<lueweezeeanA=23214> (1)
<lueweezeeanA=23314> (7)
<lueweezeeanA=32314> (11)
<lueweezeeanR=32314> (1)
<lueweezeeinno=23213> (1)
<lui(ee)sIanA=3414> (1)
<lui(ee)zIanA=1424> (1)
<lui(ee)zIanA=1434> (1)
<lui(ee)zIanA=3414> (5)
<luwIz(ee)yanA=1434> (1)

086.5B P Kentucky

No Response (232)
<kNdukI=414> (1)
<kNtookI=414> (1)
<kNtukI=414> (386)
<kNtukee=413> (5)
<k[N]tukI=414> (6)
<k[N]tukee=413> (1)
<kaintukI=314> (6)
<kantukI=314> (2)
<ke(n)tukee=313> (1)
<keentukI=314> (1)
<kentukA=314> (1)

<kentukI=124> (3)
<kentukI=134> (7)
<kentukI=214> (3)
<kentukI=314> (49)
<kentukee=313> (3)
<ki[n]tukI=314> (1)
<kintAkee=143> (1)
<kintukI=134> (4)
<kintukI=214> (1)
<kintukI=314> (184)
<kintukee=123> (2)
<kintukee=313> (10)
<koontukI=314> (1)
<kuntukI=314> (17)
<kyNtukI=414> (1)
<kyintukI=134> (1)

086.6A P Tennessee
No Response (136)
<tNIsee=441> (1)
<ten(I)see=13> (2)
<ten(I)see=31> (3)
<tenAsI=144> (4)
<tenAsee=142> (7)
<tenAsee=143> (59)
<tenAsee=241> (6)
<tenAsee=341> (98)
<tenIsI=144> (3)
<tenIsee=142> (3)
<tenIsee=143> (143)
<tenIsee=241> (7)
<tenIsee=341> (171)
<tennAsee=142> (3)
<tennAsee=143> (8)
<tennAsee=341> (8)
<tennIsI=144> (2)
<tennIsee=142> (1)
<tennIsee=143> (4)
<tennIsee=241> (3)
<tennIsee=341> (9)
<tent(I)see=21> (1)
<tin(I)see=31> (1)
<tinAsI=144> (4)
<tinAsee=142> (7)
<tinAsee=143> (36)
<tinAsee=241> (4)
<tinAsee=341> (48)
<tinIsI=144> (4)
<tinIsee=143> (54)
<tinIsee=241> (3)
<tinIsee=341> (79)
<tinisee=231> (1)
<tinnAsee=143> (6)
<tinnAsee=341> (8)
<tinnIsI=144> (1)
<tinnIsee=143> (23)
<tinnIsee=241> (1)
<tinnIsee=341> (28)
086.6B P Missouri
No Response (263)

<mAjoorA=414> (1)
<mAroorA=414> (1)
<mAzhoorA=414> (1)
<mAzhurI=414> (1)
<mAzirI=414> (1)
<mAzoeree=413> (1)
<mAzoo(r)I=414> (1)
<mAzooR=414> (2)
<mAzoolI=414> (1)
<mAzoor(I)=41> (6)
<mAzoorA=414> (109)
<mAzoorI=414> (183)
<mAzooree=413> (3)
<mAzuerI=414> (2)
<mAzurI=414> (3)
<mAzyoorI=414> (1)
<mItzoorA=414> (1)
<mIzewrI=414> (1)
<mIzhoorI=414> (1)
<mIzirI=414> (3)
<mIzoor(I)=41> (1)
<mIzoorA=414> (23)
<mIzoorI=414> (77)
<mIzooree=413> (3)
<mIzooryA=414> (1)
<mIzoowI=414> (1)
<mIzuer(I)=41> (1)
<mIzurI=414> (3)
<mezoorI=314> (1)
<miszoorI=314> (1)
<mizoerI=314> (1)
<mizoo(r)I=314> (1)
<mizoor(I)=31> (2)
<mizoorA=214> (1)
<mizoorA=314> (93)
<mizoorI=314> (111)
<mizooree=213> (1)
<mizooree=313> (12)
<mizuerA=314> (1)
<mizuerI=314> (2)
<mizurI=314> (2)
<mizuree=313> (1)
<mizyoorI=314> (1)
<moozuerA=314> (1)
<muzoo(r)I=314> (1)
<muzoorA=314> (8)
<muzoorI=214> (1)
<muzoorI=314> (9)

086.7A P Arkansas
No Response (206)
<a(r)kNsaw=143> (1)
<a[r]kNso=143> (1)
<aw(r)kNsaw=142> (2)
<aw(r)kNsaw=143> (8)
<aw(r)kinsaw=132> (2)
<aw(r)ksNsaw=143> (1)
<aw[r]kNsaw=143> (2)
<awrkNsaw=143> (25)
<o(r)kNsaw=143> (84)

<o(r)kNso=142> (1)
<o(r)kNso=143> (3)
<o(r)k[N]saw=143> (2)
<o(r)kansAs=314> (1)
<o(r)kanzAs=134> (1)
<o(r)kinsaw=132> (3)
<o[r]kNsA=144> (1)
<o[r]kNsaw=142> (2)
<o[r]kNsaw=143> (49)
<o[r]kNsaw=341> (1)
<o[r]kNso=143> (2)
<o[r]k[N]so=143> (1)
<o[r]kanzA=124> (1)
<o[r]kanzIs=314> (1)
<o[r]kinsA=134> (1)
<o[r]kinsaw=132> (1)
<o[r]kyanzIs=134> (1)
<oerkNsaw=143> (1)
<orgNso=143> (1)
<orkN(saw)=14> (1)
<orkNGsaw=143> (1)
<orkNsA=144> (3)
<orkNsaw=141> (1)
<orkNsaw=142> (9)
<orkNsaw=143> (446)
<orkNsaw=341> (4)
<orkNsawz=143> (1)
<orkNso=143> (23)
<orkNthaw=143> (2)
<ork[N]saw=143> (7)
<orkansAs=314> (1)
<orkanzAs=314> (1)
<orkanzAz=314> (2)
<orkanzIs=314> (5)
<orkanzIz=314> (2)
<orke(n)saw=132> (1)
<orkensaw=123> (1)
<orkensaw=132> (3)
<orkinsaw=123> (1)
<orkinsaw=132> (8)
<orkinso=313> (1)
<orkunsaw=132> (4)

086.7B P Mississippi
No Response (162)
<(misI)sipI=14> (1)
<m(is)IsipI=414> (1)
<mA(sI)sipI=414> (2)
<mI(sI)sipI=414> (1)
<mIs(I)sipI=414> (2)
<mIs(I)sipee=413> (1)
<mIsIsippI=4414> (2)
<mesAsipee=2413> (1)
<messIsippI=3414> (1)
<mi(sI)sIpee=143> (1)
<mi(sI)sip(I)=31> (1)
<mi(sI)sipI=134> (8)
<mi(sI)sipI=214> (8)
<mi(sI)sipI=314> (117)
<mi(sI)sipee=313> (3)

<mi(sI)sippI=314> (4)
<mi(sI)zip(I)=31> (1)
<mibIsippI=1434> (1)
<mid(I)sipI=134> (1)
<mis(I)sIpee=143> (1)
<mis(I)shipI=314> (1)
<mis(I)sipI=114> (1)
<mis(I)sipI=124> (1)
<mis(I)sipI=134> (11)
<mis(I)sipI=214> (9)
<mis(I)sipI=314> (124)
<mis(I)sipee=123> (1)
<mis(I)sipee=213> (1)
<mis(I)sipee=313> (2)
<mis(I)sippI=134> (3)
<mis(I)sippI=314> (6)
<mis(I)zipI=134> (1)
<misAsipI=1424> (2)
<misAsipI=1434> (5)
<misAsipI=2414> (3)
<misAsipI=3414> (83)
<misAsipee=1432> (1)
<misAsipee=3412> (1)
<misAsipee=3413> (1)
<misAsippI=3414> (3)
<misI(si)pee=143> (1)
<misIsip(I)=341> (2)
<misIsipI=1414> (1)
<misIsipI=1424> (2)
<misIsipI=1434> (15)
<misIsipI=2414> (11)
<misIsipI=3414> (214)
<misIsipee=1423> (4)
<misIsipee=3413> (7)
<misIsippI=1434> (1)
<misIsippI=2414> (1)
<misIsippI=3414> (8)
<misIssipI=3414> (1)
<misIthipI=3414> (1)
<misIzsipI=3414> (1)
<misIzsipee=1423> (1)
<mish(I)sipI=214> (1)
<misisipI=2314> (3)
<misisipee=2313> (1)
<missAsipI=1424> (1)
<missAsipI=1434> (1)
<missAsipI=3414> (24)
<missAsipee=3413> (2)
<missAsippI=2414> (1)
<missAsippI=3414> (1)
<missIsaipI=3414> (1)
<missIsepI=3414> (1)
<missIsipI=1434> (1)
<missIsipI=3414> (44)
<missIsipee=2413> (1)
<missIsipee=3413> (2)
<missIsippI=1424> (1)
<missIsippI=2414> (1)
<missIsippI=3414> (18)

<missIsippee=1423> (1)
<missIsippee=2413> (1)
<mistIsipI=3414> (1)
<miz(I)chipI=314> (1)
<miz(I)sIpI=144> (1)
<miz(I)sIpee=143> (1)
<miz(I)sipI=134> (6)
<miz(I)sipI=314> (28)
<miz(I)sipee=123> (2)
<miz(I)sipee=313> (1)
<mizAsipI=3414> (2)
<mizIsipI=2414> (1)
<mizIsipI=3414> (4)
<moossAsipI=3414> (1)

086.8A P Texas
No Response (161)
<taiksIs=14> (6)
<taksIs=14> (1)
<te(k)sIth=14> (1)
<tekfIs=14> (1)
<teksA(s)=14> (1)
<teksAs=14> (23)
<teksAz=14> (11)
<teksI(s)=14> (2)
<teksIk=14> (1)
<teksIs=14> (492)
<teksIsh=14> (1)
<teksIz=14> (201)
<tekshIsh=14> (1)
<teksis=13> (7)
<teksiz=12> (1)
<teksiz=13> (1)
<tekthIth=14> (3)
<tekzAs=14> (7)
<tekzAz=14> (1)
<tekzI(s)=14> (1)
<tekzIs=14> (14)
<tekzIz=14> (3)
<tekzus=13> (1)
<tuksIs=14> (1)
<tyeksIs=14> (1)

086.8B P Oklahoma
No Response (274)
<awklAhoemA=3414> (1)
<hoeklAhoemA=3414> (1)
<oe(k)LIhoemA=34414> (1)
<oe(k)lIhoemA=3414> (1)
<oek(1)AhoemA=1434> (1)
<oek(1)AhoemA=3414> (12)
<oek(1)IhoemA=3414> (5)
<oek(1)IhoemI=3414> (1)
<oek(1A)hoemA=314> (1)
<oeklAhoe[m](A)=241> (1)
<oeklAhoe[m](A)=341> (1)
<oeklAhoemA=1424> (7)
<oeklAhoemA=1434> (21)
<oeklAhoemA=2414> (14)
<oeklAhoemA=3414> (289)
<oeklAhoemI=1434> (1)

<oeklAhoemR=3414> (3)
<oeklAhoemmA=3414> (1)
<oeklIhoemA=1434> (1)
<oeklIhoemA=2414> (6)
<oeklIhoemA=3414> (263)
<oeklIhoemR=3414> (3)
<oeklIhoemmA=3414> (1)
<oeklIhumA=3414> (2)
<oekleehoemI=2314> (1)
<oeklihoemA=1314> (1)
<oeklihoemA=1324> (1)
<oeklihoemA=2314> (1)
<oekrAhoemA=3414> (1)

086.9A P Massachusetts
No Response (302)
<mas(I)chewsI(t)s=314> (1)
<mas(I)chewsIts=314> (4)
<mas(I)chewzAts=314> (1)
<mas(I)choosIts=314> (1)
<mas(I)chuesAts=314> (1)
<mas(I)chuesI(t)s=134> (2)
<mas(I)chuesI(t)s=214> (1)
<mas(I)chuesI(t)s=314> (2)
<mas(I)chuesI(ts)=314> (1)
<mas(I)chuesIts=134> (2)
<mas(I)chuesIts=214> (2)
<mas(I)chuesIts=314> (5)
<mas(I)chuesets=313> (1)
<mas(I)shuesIts=314> (1)
<mas(I)stuesI(ts)=314> (1)
<mas(I)tewsAts=314> (1)
<mas(I)tewsI(t)s=214> (1)
<mas(I)tewsI(t)s=314> (7)
<mas(I)tewsI(ts)=314> (2)
<mas(I)tewsIts=134> (1)
<mas(I)tewsIts=214> (3)
<mas(I)tewsIts=314> (7)
<mas(I)tewshI(t)sh=314> (1)
<mas(I)tewshIts=314> (1)
<mas(I)toosI(t)s=314> (1)
<mas(I)tuesAt(s)=134> (1)
<mas(I)tuesAts=314> (1)
<mas(I)tuesI(t)s=214> (2)
<mas(I)tuesI(t)s=314> (4)
<mas(I)tuesIt(s)=314> (1)
<mas(I)tuesIts=214> (1)
<mas(I)tuesIts=314> (5)
<mas(I)tueshIts=314> (1)
<masAchewsAts=3414> (1)
<masAchewsI(t)s=3414> (1)
<masAchewsIts=1434> (1)
<masAchewsIts=2414> (2)
<masAchewsIts=3414> (6)
<masAchewshI(t)z=3414> (1)
<masAchoosI(ts)=2414> (1)
<masAchues(Its)=341> (1)
<masAchuesA(t)z=3414> (1)
<masAchuesAt(s)=3414> (1)
<masAchuesAts=1424> (2)

<masAchuesAts=1434> (3)
<masAchuesI(t)s=3414> (4)
<masAchuesI(ts)=3414> (1)
<masAchuesIts=1424> (2)
<masAchuesIts=2414> (2)
<masAchuesIts=3414> (34)
<masAchueshA(t)s=1434> (1)
<masAchueshA(ts)=3414> (1)
<masAchueshI(t)sh=3414> (1)
<masAchuesits=2413> (1)
<masAchuesuts=3413> (1)
<masAjuesIts=3414> (1)
<masAschuesAts=2414> (1)
<masAshuesI(ts)=3414> (1)
<masAshuesets=3413> (1)
<masAstewsIts=3414> (1)
<masAtewsA(t)s=3414> (2)
<masAtewsAts=3414> (2)
<masAtewsI(t)s=3414> (26)
<masAtewsI(ts)=3414> (6)
<masAtewsIt(s)=3414> (2)
<masAtewsIts=1424> (2)
<masAtewsIts=2414> (2)
<masAtewsIts=3414> (33)
<masAtewshA(ts)=3414> (2)
<masAtewshI(t)s=3414> (2)
<masAtewshI(ts)=3414> (2)
<masAtewsits=3413> (2)
<masAtoosIts=3414> (1)
<masAtuesA(t)s=2414> (1)
<masAtuesA(t)s=3414> (2)
<masAtuesA(ts)=3414> (1)
<masAtuesAts=1414> (1)
<masAtuesAts=1434> (2)
<masAtuesI(t)s=3414> (15)
<masAtuesI(t)z=3414> (1)
<masAtuesI(ts)=3414> (2)
<masAtuesIj=3414> (1)
<masAtuesIt(s)=1434> (1)
<masAtuesIt(s)=3414> (4)
<masAtuesIts=1414> (1)
<masAtuesIts=1424> (1)
<masAtuesIts=1434> (1)
<masAtuesIts=3414> (20)
<masAtueshA(t)s=3414> (1)
<masAtueshI(t)s=3414> (1)
<masAtueshI(t)z=3414> (1)
<masAtueshItsh=3414> (1)
<masAtueshi(t)s=3413> (1)
<masAtuesits=1423> (1)
<masIchewsAts=1434> (1)
<masIchewsI(t)s=1434> (1)
<masIchewsI(t)s=3414> (9)
<masIchewsI(ts)=2414> (1)
<masIchewsI(ts)=3414> (2)
<masIchewsIt(s)=1434> (1)
<masIchewsIts=1424> (1)
<masIchewsIts=3414> (10)
<masIchewsets=3413> (2)

<masIchewthAts=3414> (1)
<masIchoosI(t)s=3414> (1)
<masIchoosIts=3414> (1)
<masIchuesAts=1434> (1)
<masIchuesI(t)s=1434> (3)
<masIchuesI(t)s=3414> (28)
<masIchuesI(t)z=1434> (1)
<masIchuesI(t)z=3414> (2)
<masIchuesI(ts)=3414> (3)
<masIchuesIt(s)=2414> (1)
<masIchuesIt(s)=3414> (3)
<masIchuesIts=1424> (1)
<masIchuesIts=1434> (7)
<masIchuesIts=2414> (1)
<masIchuesIts=3414> (26)
<masIchuesets=3413> (1)
<masIchueshI(ts)=3414> (1)
<masIchuesits=1423> (1)
<masIchuesits=2413> (1)
<masIkewsIks=3414> (1)
<masIstuesI(ts)=3414> (1)
<masItchuesits=1413> (1)
<masItewsA(t)s=3414> (1)
<masItewsI(t)s=1434> (1)
<masItewsI(t)s=2414> (1)
<masItewsI(t)s=3414> (17)
<masItewsI(ts)=2314> (1)
<masItewsI(ts)=3414> (7)
<masItewsIts=1424> (1)
<masItewsIts=1434> (3)
<masItewsIts=3414> (17)
<masItewsets=3413> (1)
<masItewshA(ts)=3414> (1)
<masItewshI(t)s=3414> (1)
<masItewsits=2413> (1)
<masItewzI(t)s=3414> (1)
<masItoosI(t)s=3414> (2)
<masItues(Its)=341> (1)
<masItuesAts=3414> (1)
<masItuesI(t)s=2414> (3)
<masItuesI(t)s=3414> (18)
<masItuesI(ts)=3414> (1)
<masItuesIj=3414> (2)
<masItuesIts=1434> (2)
<masItuesIts=2414> (4)
<masItuesIts=3414> (19)
<masItuesee(ts)=3413> (1)
<masItueshA(ts)=3414> (1)
<masItueshI(t)s=3414> (1)
<masItueshI(ts)=3414> (1)
<masItueshits=2413> (1)
<masItueshits=3413> (1)
<masItuesits=3413> (1)
<masNchuesets=3413> (1)
<mashIchusI(t)s=3414> (1)
<mashItewshI(t)s=3414> (1)
<mass(I)tewsI(t)s=214> (1)
<mass(I)tewsIts=314> (1)
<massAchewsIt(s)=3414> (1)

<massAchewsIts=3414> (4)
<massAchoosIt(s)=3414> (2)
<massAchoosIts=3414> (1)
<massAchuesI(t)s=3414> (3)
<massAchuesI(ts)=3414> (1)
<massAchuesIt(s)=3414> (1)
<massAchuesIts=1434> (1)
<massAchuesIts=3414> (34)
<massAchueshIts=3414> (1)
<massAtewsAts=3414> (2)
<massAtewsI(t)s=3414> (2)
<massAtewsI(ts)=3414> (1)
<massAtewsIt(s)=3414> (1)
<massAtewsIts=3414> (18)
<massAtewshA(t)s=1414> (1)
<massAtewshA(t)s=3414> (1)
<massAtewsits=2413> (1)
<massAtewzI(t)s=3414> (1)
<massAtuesA(t)s=3414> (1)
<massAtuesAts=3414> (1)
<massAtuesI(t)s=3414> (2)
<massAtuesI(ts)=3414> (2)
<massAtuesIts=3414> (4)
<massAtueshIts=3414> (1)
<massAtuesits=2413> (1)
<massIchewsI(t)s=3414> (1)
<massIchuesI(t)s=3414> (2)
<massIchuesIts=3414> (1)
<massItewsI(t)s=3414> (3)
<massItuesIts=3414> (1)
<mastAtewsI(t)s=3414> (1)
<math(I)chuesI(ts)=214> (1)
<mathAtuesI(t)s=3414> (1)
<mathIchuesI(t)s=3414> (1)
<mazAchyusA(ts)=3414> (1)
<mes(I)chuesI(t)s=314> (1)
<mes(I)tewsI(t)s=314> (1)
<mesAchuesIts=3414> (1)
<mesAtewshI(t)s=3414> (1)
<mesAtoochA(t)s=3414> (1)
<mesItewsI(t)s=3414> (1)
<mezAtewsI(t)z=3414> (1)
<misIchuezI(t)z=3414> (1)
<musItuesI(t)s=3414> (1)
<pwas(I)chuesIts=134> (1)

086.9B P New England States
No Response (423)
<(new)englN(d)staits=141> (1)
<(new)inglN(d)staits=241> (1)
<[n]yAinglN(d)staits=4141> (1)
<newanglN(d)staits=3241> (1)
<neweenglN(d)staits=2141> (1)
<newengAlN(d)staits=21443> (1)
<newengglN(d)staits=2143> (2)
<newengglN(d)staits=3143> (1)
<newengglNd=314> (1)
<newengglNdstaits=2143> (1)
<newenglN(d)=114> (1)
<newenglN(d)=134> (1)

<newenglN(d)=214> (1)
<newenglN(d)=314> (2)
<newenglN(d)stait(s)=1341> (1)
<newenglN(d)staits=1342> (1)
<newenglN(d)staits=2143> (2)
<newenglN(d)staits=3141> (1)
<newenglNd=314> (1)
<newenglNdstait=2143> (1)
<newenglNdstaits=2143> (1)
<newengl[N](d)staits=2143> (1)
<newing(l)N(d)=314> (1)
<newing(l)N(d)thtaitsh=3142> (1)
<newing(l)NG(d)=314> (1)
<newing(l)[N](d)staits=2143> (1)
<newing(lNd=31> (1)
<newinggAlN(d)staits=21442> (1)
<newingglN(d)=114> (1)
<newingglN(d)=214> (2)
<newingglN(d)=314> (5)
<newingglN(d)staits=1341> (1)
<newingglN(d)staits=1342> (1)
<newingglN(d)staits=1343> (1)
<newingglN(d)staits=2141> (1)
<newingglN(d)staits=2142> (1)
<newingglN(d)staits=2143> (2)
<newingglN(d)staits=3141> (3)
<newingglN(d)staits=3142> (11)
<newingglN(d)staits=3143> (2)
<newingglNd=314> (3)
<newingglNdstaits=2143> (1)
<newingglNdstaits=3141> (2)
<newingglNdstaits=3142> (2)
<newinglN(d)=114> (2)
<newinglN(d)=134> (1)
<newinglN(d)=214> (14)
<newinglN(d)=314> (52)
<newinglN(d)stai(t)s=2143> (1)
<newinglN(d)stait=1142> (1)
<newinglN(d)stait=1342> (1)
<newinglN(d)stait=3141> (1)
<newinglN(d)stait=3142> (2)
<newinglN(d)staith=3142> (1)
<newinglN(d)staits=1141> (1)
<newinglN(d)staits=1143> (1)
<newinglN(d)staits=1341> (6)
<newinglN(d)staits=1342> (4)
<newinglN(d)staits=2141> (15)
<newinglN(d)staits=2142> (1)
<newinglN(d)staits=2143> (65)
<newinglN(d)staits=2341> (3)
<newinglN(d)staits=3141> (51)
<newinglN(d)staits=3142> (38)
<newinglN(d)staits=3143> (44)
<newinglN(d)staits=3241> (4)
<newinglNd=134> (1)
<newinglNd=214> (2)
<newinglNd=314> (5)
<newinglNdstaits=1141> (1)
<newinglNdstaits=1342> (1)

<newinglNdstaits=2141> (3)
<newinglNdstaits=2143> (2)
<newinglNdstaits=3141> (6)
<newinglNdstaits=3142> (3)
<newinglNdstaits=3143> (1)
<newinglNdstaits=3241> (1)
<newingl[N](d)staits=2143> (1)
<newingl[N](d)staits=3143> (1)
<newinglind=213> (1)
<nooinglN(d)staits=3142> (1)
<nueengglN(d)staits=2143> (1)
<nueenglN(d)staits=2143> (1)
<nueenglN(d)staits=3142> (1)
<nueing[1]N(d)=314> (1)
<nueinggAlN(d)staits=21443> (1)
<nueingglN(d)=314> (1)
<nueingglN(d)staits=2143> (1)
<nueingglN(d)staits=3142> (4)
<nueingglN(d)staits=3143> (1)
<nueingglNd=314> (1)
<nueingglNdstaits=2143> (1)
<nueinglN(d)=214> (2)
<nueinglN(d)=314> (13)
<nueinglN(d)s=214> (1)
<nueinglN(d)stai(t)s=3142> (2)
<nueinglN(d)staits=1243> (1)
<nueinglN(d)staits=1341> (1)
<nueinglN(d)staits=2141> (2)
<nueinglN(d)staits=2142> (1)
<nueinglN(d)staits=2143> (7)
<nueinglN(d)staits=2341> (1)
<nueinglN(d)staits=3141> (5)
<nueinglN(d)staits=3142> (10)
<nueinglN(d)staits=3143> (11)
<nueinglN(d)staits=3241> (3)
<nueinglNd=214> (1)
<nueinglNd=314> (2)
<nueinglNdstaits=1342> (2)
<nueinglNdstaits=3141> (1)
<nueinglNdstaits=3143> (1)
<nueinglind=213> (1)
<nuewinglN(d)staits=2143> (1)
<nylinglN(d)=414> (1)

087.1A P Baltimore
No Response (353)
<baltAmoe[r]=143> (1)
<baltAmoer=143> (1)
<baw(l)tAmoe(r)=143> (1)
<baw(l)tImoe[r]=143> (4)
<baw(l)tImoer=143> (8)
<baw[1](t)Amoer=143> (1)
<baw[1]dAmoe[r]=143> (1)
<baw[1]tAmawr=143> (1)
<baw[1]tAmoe(r)=143> (1)
<baw[1]tAmoer=143> (1)
<baw[1]tImoe(r)=143> (2)
<baw[1]tImoe[r]=143> (2)
<baw[1]tImoer=143> (3)
<bawl(t)Amoe[r]=143> (1)

<bawl(t)Imoer=143> (2)
<bawldAmoer=143> (1)
<bawldImaw[r]=143> (1)
<bawldImoe(r)=143> (1)
<bawldImoer=143> (3)
<bawlt(I)maw[r]=13> (1)
<bawlt(I)moe(r)=13> (1)
<bawlt(I)moe[r]=13> (2)
<bawlt(I)moer=13> (6)
<bawltAmaw(r)=143> (2)
<bawltAmaw[r]=143> (1)
<bawltAmawr=143> (1)
<bawltAmoe(r)=143> (8)
<bawltAmoe[r]=143> (22)
<bawltAmoer=143> (64)
<bawltIm[R]=144> (1)
<bawltImR=144> (1)
<bawltImaw(r)=143> (2)
<bawltImaw[r]=143> (3)
<bawltImawr=143> (1)
<bawltImer=143> (1)
<bawltImoe(r)=143> (27)
<bawltImoe[r]=143> (123)
<bawltImoer=143> (229)
<bawltImoewA=1434> (1)
<bawltImur=143> (1)
<boe[1]tAmaw[r]=143> (1)
<boeltAmoer=143> (1)
<boeltImoe[r]=143> (2)
<boeltImoer=143> (1)
<boltAmoer=143> (2)
<boltImoe(r)=143> (2)
<boltImoe[r]=143> (5)
<boltImoer=143> (18)

087.1B P Washington, DC
No Response (167)
<washNGtN=144> (1)
<washNGtNdeesee=14432> (1)
<washNGtNdeesee=24431> (1)
<washNtN=144> (1)
<washNtNdeesee=14431> (1)
<washNtNdeesee=24431> (1)
<wash[NG]tN=144> (1)
<waw(sh)NtNdeesee=14411> (1)
<wawrshNGtN=144> (11)
<wawrshNGtNdeesee=14411> (7)
<wawrshNGtNdeesee=14431> (4)
<wawrshNGtNdeesee=14432> (1)
<wawrshNdNdeesee=14413> (1)
<wawrshNtN=144> (5)
<wawrshNtNdeesee=14431> (1)
<wawrsh[NG]tN=144> (1)
<wawsNGtNdeesee=14421> (1)
<wawshN(t)N=144> (1)
<wawshN(t)Ndeesee=14431> (1)
<wawshN(t)Ndeesee=14432> (1)
<wawshNGtN=144> (33)
<wawshNGtNdeesai=14431> (1)
<wawshNGtNdeesee=14411> (43)

<wawshNGtNdeesee=14412> (1)
<wawshNGtNdeesee=14413> (5)
<wawshNGtNdeesee=14421> (1)
<wawshNGtNdeesee=14423> (1)
<wawshNGtNdeesee=14431> (13)
<wawshNGtNdeesee=14432> (2)
<wawshNGtNdeesee=24413> (1)
<wawshNGtNdeesee=24431> (7)
<wawshNGtNdeesee=34431> (1)
<wawshNGtun=143> (1)
<wawshNdNdeesee=14423> (1)
<wawshNdNdeesee=14431> (1)
<wawshNdNdeesee=24431> (1)
<wawshNtN=144> (5)
<wawshNtNdeesee=14411> (2)
<wawshNtNdeesee=14413> (2)
<wawshNtNdeesee=14421> (1)
<wawshNtNdeesee=14423> (1)
<wawshNtNdeesee=14431> (5)
<wawshNtNdeesee=14432> (3)
<wawshNtNdeesee=24431> (1)
<wawshNtNdeesee=34431> (1)
<wawsh[NG](tN)deesee=1413> (1)
<wawsh[NG]dN=144> (1)
<wawsh[NG]tN=144> (2)
<wawshingtN=134> (4)
<wawshingtNdIsee=13443> (1)
<wawshingtNdeesee=13411> (5)
<wawshingtNdeesee=13412> (1)
<wawshingtNdeesee=13413> (1)
<wawshingtNdeesee=13431> (2)
<wawshintNdeesee=13432> (1)
<wawzhNG(tN)deesee=1411> (1)
<whoshNGtN=144> (1)
<whoshNGtNdeesee=14431> (1)
<whoshNtNdeesee=24431> (1)
<wochNGtNdeesee=14431> (1)
<woch[NG]tNdeesee=14432> (1)
<woershNGtN=144> (1)
<woeshNGtN=144> (1)
<woorshNGtN=144> (1)
<worshNGtN=144> (2)
<worshNGtNdeesee=14411> (5)
<worshNGtNdeesee=14431> (2)
<worshNdNdIsee=24441> (1)
<worshNtN=144> (3)
<worshNtNdeesee=14431> (3)
<worsh[NG]tNdeesee=14421> (1)
<worshingtNdeesee=13423> (1)
<worshingtNdeesee=13431> (3)
<wosh(NG)dNdeesee=1431> (1)
<wosh(NG)tN=14> (3)
<wosh(NG)tNdeesee=1411> (1)
<wosh(NG)tNdeesee=1432> (1)
<wosh(NG)tNdeesee=2431> (1)
<wosh(NGt)Ndeesee=1432> (1)
<wosh(NGtN)> (1)
<woshN(t)N=144> (1)
<woshN(t)NdIsee=14442> (1)

<woshN(t)NdIsee=14443> (1)
<woshN(t)Ndeesee=14421> (1)
<woshN(t)Ndeesee=14431> (1)
<woshN(tN)dIsI=1444> (1)
<woshN(tN)dIsee=1441> (1)
<woshN(tN)deesee=1413> (1)
<woshN(tN)deesee=2431> (2)
<woshN(tN)deesee=3413> (1)
<woshN(tN)deesee=3421> (1)
<woshNG(tN)=14> (1)
<woshNG(tN)deesee=1431> (2)
<woshNG(tN)deesee=1432> (1)
<woshNGdN=144> (2)
<woshNGdNdeesee=14432> (1)
<woshNGdNdeesee=24431> (1)
<woshNGtN=144> (111)
<woshNGtNdIsee=14441> (3)
<woshNGtNdIsee=14443> (1)
<woshNGtNdeesee=14411> (56)
<woshNGtNdeesee=14413> (18)
<woshNGtNdeesee=14421> (4)
<woshNGtNdeesee=14423> (4)
<woshNGtNdeesee=14431> (53)
<woshNGtNdeesee=14432> (8)
<woshNGtNdeesee=14433> (2)
<woshNGtNdeesee=24413> (1)
<woshNGtNdeesee=24421> (1)
<woshNGtNdeesee=24431> (21)
<woshNGtun=143> (1)
<woshNGtundeesee=24331> (1)
<woshNdI(n)=144> (1)
<woshNdN=144> (4)
<woshNdNdeesee=14423> (1)
<woshNdNdeesee=14431> (1)
<woshNdNdeesee=14432> (1)
<woshNdNdeesee=24413> (1)
<woshNdNdeesee=34431> (1)
<woshNktN=144> (1)
<woshNtN=144> (62)
<woshNtNdIsee=14441> (1)
<woshNtNdeesee=14411> (6)
<woshNtNdeesee=14413> (6)
<woshNtNdeesee=14421> (3)
<woshNtNdeesee=14423> (2)
<woshNtNdeesee=14431> (29)
<woshNtNdeesee=14432> (11)
<woshNtNdeesee=24413> (1)
<woshNtNdeesee=24431> (22)
<woshNtun=143> (1)
<woshNtundeesee=14313> (2)
<woshNtundeesee=14321> (1)
<woshNtundeesee=14331> (1)
<woshNtundeesee=14332> (1)
<woshNz(tN)=14> (1)
<wosh[NG]tN=144> (11)
<wosh[NG]tNdIsee=14442> (1)
<wosh[NG]tNdeesee=14411> (10)
<wosh[NG]tNdeesee=14413> (4)
<wosh[NG]tNdeesee=14421> (2)

<wosh[NG]tNdeesee=14431> (4)
<wosh[NG]tNdeesee=24431> (2)
<wosh[NG]tun=143> (1)
<woshi(ng)tNdeesee=13413> (1)
<woshi(ng)tNdeesee=13431> (1)
<woshin(t)Ndeesee=23413> (1)
<woshindNdeesee=23431> (1)
<woshingtN=134> (9)
<woshingtNdeesee=13411> (4)
<woshingtNdeesee=13413> (5)
<woshingtNdeesee=13421> (3)
<woshingtNdeesee=13431> (12)
<woshingtNdeesee=13433> (1)
<woshingtNdeesee=23413> (1)
<woshingtNdeesee=23431> (1)
<woshintN=134> (2)
<woshintNdeesee=13421> (2)
<woshintNdeesee=13431> (2)
<woshintNdeesee=13433> (1)
<woshintNdeesee=23413> (1)
<woshuntN=134> (1)

087.1C P St. Louis

No Response (319)
<(saint)lueI=14> (1)
<(saint)lueIs=14> (1)
<sN(t)lueI=414> (1)
<sN(t)lueIs=414> (1)
<sNtlueAs=414> (1)
<sNtlueIs=414> (1)
<sNtlueIsh=414> (1)
<sNtlueee=413> (1)
<sai[n](t)lueIs=314> (1)
<sai[n]tlueIs=134> (1)
<sai[n]tlueIs=214> (1)
<sain(t)looIs=314> (3)
<sain(t)lueI=134> (1)
<sain(t)lueI=214> (2)
<sain(t)lueI=314> (3)
<sain(t)lueIs=214> (4)
<sain(t)lueIs=314> (3)
<sain(t)luewIs=314> (1)
<saindlueIs=124> (1)
<saintlewIs=114> (1)
<saintlewIs=124> (1)
<saintlewIs=134> (1)
<saintlewIs=314> (1)
<saintlooAs=314> (1)
<saintlooI=214> (1)
<saintlooIs=114> (1)
<saintlooIs=134> (4)
<saintlooIs=214> (5)
<saintlooIs=314> (14)
<saintlueAs=124> (1)
<saintlueAs=214> (10)
<saintlueI=114> (2)
<saintlueI=134> (1)
<saintlueI=214> (2)
<saintlueI=314> (8)
<saintlueIs=114> (58)

<saintlueIs=124> (7)
<saintlueIs=134> (38)
<saintlueIs=214> (94)
<saintlueIs=314> (262)
<saintlueeee=123> (1)
<saintlueeee=213> (1)
<saintluewAs=314> (2)
<saintluewI=114> (1)
<saintluewIs=124> (2)
<saintluewIs=214> (2)
<saintluewIs=314> (2)
<san(t)lueIs=114> (1)
<santlooI=314> (1)
<santlueAs=214> (1)
<santlueI=214> (1)
<santlueIs=114> (1)
<santlueIs=214> (4)
<santlueIs=314> (7)
<santluewIs=314> (2)
<sen(t)lue(I)s=31> (1)
<sendlueIs=314> (1)
<sentlewIs=314> (1)
<sentlooIs=134> (1)
<sentlueIs=114> (2)
<sentlueIs=134> (1)
<sentlueIs=214> (1)
<sentlueIs=314> (17)
<sentluewAs=314> (1)
<sin(t)lueIs=314> (2)
<sintloowIs=214> (1)
<sintlueIs=314> (2)
<sunglueIs=314> (1)

087.2A P Charleston
No Response (389)
<cha[r]lstN=14> (1)
<chaw(r)ls(t)N=14> (1)
<chaw(r)lstN=14> (7)
<chaw(r)lztN=14> (2)
<chaw(rl)stN=14> (2)
<chaw[r](l)stN=14> (1)
<chaw[r]lstN=14> (8)
<chawrl(s)tN=14> (1)
<chawrlstN=14> (17)
<chawrlztN=14> (1)
<cho(r)[l]s(t)N=14> (1)
<cho(r)[l]stN=14> (3)
<cho(r)ls(t)N=14> (1)
<cho(r)lstN=14> (38)
<cho(r)lztN=14> (10)
<cho(rl)stN=14> (3)
<cho(rl)zsNt=14> (1)
<cho(rl)ztN=14> (9)
<cho[R](l)stN=144> (1)
<cho[r](l)shN=14> (1)
<cho[r](l)stN=14> (9)
<cho[r](l)z(t)N=14> (1)
<cho[r](l)ztN=14> (9)
<cho[r](l)zt[N]=14> (1)
<cho[r]ls(t)N=14> (2)

<cho[r]lstN=14> (100)
<cho[r]ltstN=14> (1)
<cho[r]lztN=14> (14)
<chor(l)stN=14> (10)
<chor(l)ztN=14> (12)
<chorL(s)tN=144> (1)
<chorLshtN=144> (1)
<chorLstN=144> (2)
<chorLstun=143> (1)
<chor[l]stN=14> (1)
<chor[l]ztN=14> (1)
<chorls(t)N=14> (3)
<chorlstN=14> (204)
<chorlstu(n)=13> (1)
<chorlztN=14> (40)
<sho[r]lstN=14> (1)
<shorl(s)tN=14> (1)
<shorlstN=14> (1)

087.2B P Birmingham
No Response (290)
<boo(r)mingham=132> (1)
<bu[r](m)Nham=143> (1)
<bu[r](mi)nham=13> (1)
<bu[r]mNG(h)[M]=144> (1)
<bu[r]mNG(h)am=143> (2)
<bu[r]mNGha[m]=143> (2)
<bu[r]mNGham=142> (1)
<bu[r]mNGham=143> (54)
<bu[r]mNGhem=143> (2)
<bu[r]mNham=143> (11)
<bu[r]mNham=341> (1)
<bu[r]mi[ng]ham=132> (1)
<bu[r]mingham=123> (1)
<bu[r]mingham=132> (30)
<bu[r]mingham=312> (1)
<bu[r]mingham=321> (1)
<bu[r]minham=132> (1)
<bu[r]minham=231> (1)
<bu[r]nNGha[m]=143> (1)
<bu[r]nNGham=241> (1)
<bu[r]nNham=143> (4)
<bu[r]nNham=341> (1)
<bu[r]ninghM=134> (1)
<burb[NG]ham=143> (1)
<burm(ing)ham=13> (2)
<burmMham=143> (1)
<burmN(h)am=143> (1)
<burmNG(h)a[m]=143> (1)
<burmNG(h)am=142> (1)
<burmNGham=142> (11)
<burmNGham=143> (237)
<burmNGham=241> (3)
<burmNGham=341> (2)
<burmNGhem=143> (6)
<burmNGhum=143> (2)
<burmNGtN=143> (1)
<burmNha[m]=143> (1)
<burmNham=142> (1)
<burmNham=143> (46)

<burmNham=341> (2)
<burm[NG]ham=143> (6)
<burmi[ng]ham=132> (1)
<burmingham=123> (3)
<burmingham=132> (147)
<burmingham=133> (6)
<burmingham=231> (7)
<burmingham=321> (1)
<burminham=132> (2)
<burminham=231> (1)
<burn(ing)ham=13> (1)
<burnMham=143> (1)
<burnNGham=143> (7)
<burnNham=143> (6)

087.2C P Chicago
No Response (270)
<(shI)kogoe=13> (1)
<ch(I)kogoe=13> (4)
<chAkogoe=413> (1)
<chIkawgoe=413> (3)
<chIkogoe=412> (1)
<chIkogoe=413> (47)
<chIkorgoe=413> (3)
<cheekogoe=313> (1)
<chikawgoe=313> (2)
<chikogA=314> (1)
<chikogoe=313> (12)
<jIkogoe=413> (1)
<sIkogoe=413> (4)
<sIkorgoe=413> (1)
<sh(I)kawgoe=13> (3)
<sh(I)kogoe=13> (16)
<sh(I)korgoe=13> (2)
<shAgogoe=413> (1)
<shAkawgoe=413> (6)
<shAkawrgoe=413> (2)
<shAkogoe=413> (32)
<shAkorgoe=413> (5)
<shIkawgoe=412> (1)
<shIkawgoe=413> (33)
<shIkawrgoe=413> (4)
<shIko(g)oe=413> (1)
<shIkog(oe)=41> (1)
<shIkogA=414> (5)
<shIkogoe=412> (3)
<shIkogoe=413> (277)
<shIkogoe=421> (1)
<shIkorgA=414> (1)
<shIkorgoe=412> (1)
<shIkorgoe=413> (45)
<sheekogoe=213> (1)
<sheekogoe=313> (2)
<sheekorgoe=313> (1)
<shikagoe=213> (1)
<shikawgoe=213> (1)
<shikawgoe=313> (9)
<shikawrgoe=213> (1)
<shikawrgoe=313> (1)
<shiko(g)oe=313> (1)

<shikogA=314> (2)
<shikogR=314> (1)
<shikogoe=213> (4)
<shikogoe=312> (2)
<shikogoe=313> (95)
<shikorgoe=313> (7)
<shookogoe=313> (1)
<sikawgoe=313> (1)
<sikogoe=313> (4)

087.3A P Montgomery
No Response (321)
<(mont)gumrI=14> (1)
<mN(t)gumrI=414> (12)
<mN(t)gunrI=414> (1)
<mNG(t)gumrI=414> (1)
<mNdgumrI=414> (3)
<mNtgumr(I)=41> (1)
<mNtgumrI=414> (45)
<mNtgumri=413> (2)
<m[N](t)gumrI=414> (1)
<m[N]tgumrI=414> (1)
<mawn(t)gumrI=214> (1)
<mawntgumrI=314> (1)
<mo(nt)gumrI=314> (1)
<mo(nt)gumri=213> (1)
<mo[n](t)gumrI=314> (2)
<mo[n]tgumrI=314> (1)
<mompgumrI=314> (1)
<mon(t)gomrI=314> (1)
<mon(t)gumRI=2144> (1)
<mon(t)gumRI=3144> (1)
<mon(t)gumrI=134> (2)
<mon(t)gumrI=314> (45)
<mondgumrI=214> (1)
<mong(t)gumRI=3144> (1)
<mong(t)gumrI=314> (1)
<montgumRI=3144> (8)
<montgumbrI=314> (1)
<montgumrA=314> (1)
<montgumrI=124> (2)
<montgumrI=134> (2)
<montgumrI=214> (5)
<montgumrI=314> (76)
<montgumri=123> (1)
<montgumri=313> (3)
<montgunrI=314> (1)
<moon(t)gumrI=314> (1)
<moontgumrI=314> (2)
<mowntgumrI=214> (1)
<mu[n](t)gumrI=314> (4)
<mu[n]tgumRI=3144> (1)
<mu[n]tgumrI=314> (4)
<mun(t)gomrI=314> (1)
<mun(t)grumrI=314> (1)
<mun(t)gu[m]rI=314> (1)
<mun(t)gumRI=3144> (2)
<mun(t)gumrI=134> (4)
<mun(t)gumrI=214> (6)
<mun(t)gumrI=314> (169)

<mun(t)gumri=313> (2)
<mundgumrI=314> (1)
<mung(t)gumrA=314> (1)
<mung(t)gumrI=314> (4)
<muntgum(r)I=314> (2)
<muntgumRI=3144> (6)
<muntgumbrI=314> (1)
<muntgumrI=134> (2)
<muntgumrI=214> (7)
<muntgumrI=314> (146)
<muntgumri=123> (1)
<muntgumri=313> (2)

087.3B P Mobile
No Response (348)
<mAbeel=41> (6)
<moebL=14> (12)
<moebee[l]=12> (1)
<moebee[l]=13> (7)
<moebee[l]=21> (5)
<moebee[l]=31> (15)
<moebeel=12> (13)
<moebeel=13> (165)
<moebeel=21> (31)
<moebeel=31> (257)
<moebi[l]=12> (1)
<moebi[l]=13> (8)
<moebi[l]=21> (1)
<moebi[l]=31> (3)
<moebil=12> (4)
<moebil=13> (13)
<moebil=21> (2)
<moebil=31> (29)
<moetL=14> (1)
<mubeel=21> (1)
<mubeel=31> (2)

087.4A P Asheville
No Response (539)
<ash(vL)> (1)
<ashAvul=143> (1)
<ashvL=14> (248)
<ashveel=13> (2)
<ashvil=11> (1)
<ashvil=13> (121)
<ashvil=21> (4)
<ashvil=31> (1)
<ashvul=11> (1)
<ashvul=12> (1)
<hashvL=14> (1)

087.4B P Knoxville
No Response (399)
<nawksvL=14> (7)
<nawksvil=13> (3)
<nawksvul=13> (1)
<nawktvL=14> (1)
<nawt(s)vL=14> (1)
<nogAvul=143> (1)
<nogzvil=13> (1)
<nok(s)vil=13> (1)
<noksAvL=144> (1)

<noksfL=14> (5)
<noksvL=14> (333)
<noksv[L]=14> (1)
<noksveel=13> (1)
<noksvel=21> (1)
<noksvi[l]=13> (2)
<noksvil=11> (2)
<noksvil=13> (152)
<noksvil=21> (2)
<notsvL=14> (1)
<notsvil=13> (1)

087.4C P Chattanooga
No Response (337)
<(ch)adNuegA=3414> (1)
<chadAnuegA=3414> (2)
<chadInuegA=3414> (1)
<chadNewgA=3414> (1)
<chadNuegI=1434> (1)
<chadNueyA=3414> (1)
<chagAnuegA=3414> (2)
<chagInuegA=3414> (1)
<chat(I)newgA=314> (1)
<chat(I)newgI=134> (1)
<chat(I)noogI=214> (1)
<chat(I)nuegA=124> (1)
<chat(I)nuegA=134> (4)
<chat(I)nuegA=314> (19)
<chat(I)nuegee=123> (1)
<chatAnewgA=1424> (1)
<chatAnewgA=1434> (1)
<chatAnewgA=2414> (3)
<chatAnewgA=3414> (8)
<chatAnoogA=1424> (1)
<chatAnoogA=1434> (1)
<chatAnoogA=3414> (5)
<chatAnoogI=3414> (1)
<chatAnue(g)A=3414> (1)
<chatAnuedA=3414> (1)
<chatAnuegA=1424> (9)
<chatAnuegA=1434> (2)
<chatAnuegA=2414> (3)
<chatAnuegA=3414> (220)
<chatAnuegI=3414> (10)
<chatAnuegR=3414> (1)
<chatAnuegee=1423> (1)
<chatAnuejI=3414> (2)
<chatAnugA=3414> (1)
<chatInewgA=1424> (1)
<chatInewgA=2414> (1)
<chatInewgA=3414> (17)
<chatInewgI=3414> (7)
<chatInewgee=1423> (1)
<chatInoogA=1434> (2)
<chatInoogA=3414> (4)
<chatInoogI=3414> (3)
<chatInuedA=3414> (1)
<chatInuegA=1424> (3)
<chatInuegA=1434> (15)
<chatInuegA=2414> (7)

<chatInuegA=3414> (146)
<chatInuegI=3414> (23)
<chatInuegR=3414> (5)
<chatInuego=3413> (1)
<chatInuejI=3414> (1)
<chatInuekI=1434> (1)
<chatNewgA=2414> (1)
<chatNnuegA=1434> (1)
<chatNnuegA=3414> (13)
<chatNnuegI=3414> (1)
<chatNuegA=1434> (1)
<chatNuegA=2414> (1)
<chatNuegI=3414> (1)
<chatinuegA=1314> (1)
<chetAnoogA=3414> (1)
<chetAnuegA=3414> (7)
<chetAnuego=1413> (1)
<chetAnugA=3414> (1)
<chetInuegA=3414> (3)
<chotAnuegA=3414> (1)
<chotInuegA=3414> (1)
<sedAnuegA=3414> (1)
<shatAnue(g)A=3414> (1)
<shatAnuegA=3414> (1)
<shatInuegA=3414> (3)

087.5A P Memphis
No Response (266)
<mamfIs=14> (1)
<me(m)fIs=14> (1)
<me[m]fIs=14> (14)
<me[m]pfIs=14> (2)
<membrIth=14> (1)
<memfAs=14> (19)
<memfI(s)=14> (1)
<memfIs=14> (195)
<memfis=13> (1)
<memp(f)Is=14> (2)
<mempfAs=14> (13)
<mempfI(s)=14> (3)
<mempfIs=14> (186)
<mempfis=13> (1)
<menfIs=14> (1)
<mentchAs=14> (1)
<mentfIs=14> (1)
<mi(m)fIs=14> (2)
<mi[m]fAs=14> (1)
<mi[m]fIs=14> (15)
<mimfAs=14> (12)
<mimfI(s)=14> (2)
<mimfIs=14> (132)
<mimpfAs=14> (3)
<mimpfIs=14> (54)
<minfAs=14> (1)
<mintfAs=14> (1)
<mumfIs=14> (1)
<myemfIs=14> (1)

087.5B P Nashville
No Response (253)
<nachvL=14> (2)

<nash(v)[L]=14> (1)
<nash(v)il=13> (1)
<nashNvil=143> (1)
<nashfL=14> (1)
<nashvL=14> (420)
<nashv[L]=14> (4)
<nashval=13> (1)
<nashveel=13> (2)
<nashvil=11> (1)
<nashvil=13> (224)
<nashvil=31> (1)
<nashvul=13> (1)
<nasvL=14> (1)
<nasvil=13> (1)
<nazhvil=13> (3)
<neshvL=14> (1)
<noshvL=14> (1)

087.6A P Atlanta
No Response (226)
<(a)tlantA=14> (1)
<(a)tlanto=13> (1)
<(at)lan(t)A=14> (6)
<(at)lantA=14> (8)
<(at)lantI=14> (2)
<(at)lantR=14> (1)
<A(t)lan(t)A=414> (11)
<A(t)lan(t)Ik=414> (1)
<A(t)lantA=414> (7)
<A(t)lantR=414> (1)
<Atlan(t)A=414> (15)
<Atlan(t)R=414> (1)
<AtlantA=414> (32)
<AtlantIk=414> (1)
<AtlantR=414> (2)
<I(t)lan(t)A=414> (4)
<Idlan(t)A=414> (3)
<IdlandA=414> (1)
<IdlantA=414> (1)
<Iglan(t)A=414> (1)
<Itla[n]tA=414> (1)
<Itlan(t)A=414> (79)
<Itlan(t)Ik=414> (1)
<Itlan(t)R=414> (3)
<ItlandA=414> (1)
<ItlantA=414> (81)
<ItlantIk=414> (1)
<ItlantR=414> (2)
<Itlen(t)A=414> (1)
<ItlentA=414> (1)
<Itlon(t)I=414> (1)
<Iv(1)an(t)A=414> (1)
<a(t)lan(t)A=314> (1)
<a(t)lantA=314> (2)
<adlan(t)R=214> (1)
<atAlantA=1434> (1)
<atlan(t)A=114> (1)
<atlan(t)A=134> (2)
<atlan(t)A=214> (8)
<atlan(t)A=314> (88)

<atlan(t)I=314> (1)
<atlan(t)R=134> (1)
<atlan(t)R=314> (3)
<atlandA=314> (1)
<atlandR=314> (1)
<atlantA=124> (1)
<atlantA=134> (7)
<atlantA=214> (5)
<atlantA=314> (118)
<atlantI=314> (1)
<atlantIk=314> (2)
<atlantR=134> (1)
<atlantR=214> (1)
<atlantR=314> (4)
<atlen(t)A=314> (1)
<atlentA=314> (3)
<e(t)landA=314> (1)
<edlan(t)A=314> (1)
<eglan(t)A=314> (1)
<eklan(t)I=314> (1)
<etla(n)tA=314> (1)
<etla[n]tA=314> (1)
<etlan(t)A=214> (2)
<etlan(t)A=314> (73)
<etlan(t)R=214> (1)
<etlan(t)R=314> (2)
<etlantA=214> (1)
<etlantA=314> (109)
<etlantR=314> (5)
<etlen(t)A=314> (1)
<etlentA=314> (2)
<hatlan(t)A=314> (1)
<hetlantA=314> (1)
<i(t)lan(t)A=314> (1)
<i(t)lantA=314> (3)
<itlan(t)A=314> (22)
<itlantA=314> (13)
<itlantR=314> (2)
<lotlan(t)A=314> (1)
<utlan(t)A=314> (3)
<utlantA=314> (7)
<utlantR=314> (1)

087.6B P Savannah
No Response (385)
<(sa)vanA=14> (1)
<dAvanA=414> (1)
<sAvainA=414> (1)
<sAvanA=414> (368)
<sAvanI=414> (1)
<sAvanR=414> (13)
<sAvenA=414> (4)
<sAvonA=414> (2)
<sIsanA=414> (1)
<sIvanA=414> (129)
<sIvanR=414> (8)
<sIvenA=414> (1)
<saivanA=314> (1)
<savIno=143> (1)
<savanA=314> (1)

<sevanA=314> (1)
<suvanA=214> (1)

087.7A P Macon

No Response (470)
<maikLn=14> (1)
<maikM=14> (1)
<maikN=14> (409)
<maikNG=14> (11)
<maik[N]=14> (7)
<maingN=14> (1)
<mekM=14> (1)
<mekN=14> (13)

087.7B P Columbus

No Response (417)
<k(A)lum(b)As=14> (1)
<k(A)lumbAs=14> (34)
<k(A)lumbAth=14> (1)
<k(A)lumbIs=14> (4)
<kAlombAs=414> (3)
<kAlum(b)As=414> (9)
<kAlumIoos=4143> (1)
<kAlumb(As)=41> (1)
<kAlumbA(s)=414> (4)
<kAlumbAs=414> (378)
<kAlumbAth=414> (2)
<kAlumbAz=414> (1)
<kAlumbIs=414> (7)
<kAlumboos=413> (2)
<kIlombIs=414> (1)
<kIlum(b)As=414> (1)
<kIlum(b)Is=414> (1)
<kIlumbAs=414> (32)
<kIlumbIs=414> (12)
<kLlumbIs=414> (1)
<kLumbAs=414> (5)
<kLumbIs=414> (1)
<kNlumbAs=414> (1)
<kawlum(b)As=314> (1)
<kolumbAs=314> (2)
<kulumbIs=314> (1)

087.8A P New Orleans

No Response (231)
<n(ue)aw(r)linz=13> (1)
<n(ue)awrlNz=14> (1)
<n(ue)awrlinz=13> (1)
<nAawrlINz=4144> (1)
<nAwaw(r)lN(z)=414> (1)
<nAwo(r)lNz=414> (1)
<nIaw(r)linth=413> (1)
<nIaw[r]lNz=414> (1)
<nIwaw(r)lNz=414> (1)
<nIwoe(r)lNz=414> (1)
<neeawrlNz=314> (1)
<newA(r)leenz=341> (2)
<newaw(r)lINz=2144> (2)
<newaw(r)lINz=3144> (3)
<newaw(r)lN(z)=214> (1)
<newaw(r)lN(z)=314> (4)
<newaw(r)lNz=134> (2)

<newaw(r)lNz=214> (4)
<newaw(r)lNz=314> (45)
<newaw(r)l[N]z=314> (1)
<newaw(r)leeNz=3134> (2)
<newaw(r)leen(z)=231> (1)
<newaw(r)leenz=231> (1)
<newaw(r)leenz=313> (3)
<newaw(r)liNz=3134> (1)
<newaw(r)linz=213> (1)
<newaw(r)linz=313> (1)
<newaw[r]lINz=3144> (3)
<newaw[r]lN(z)=214> (1)
<newaw[r]lN(z)=314> (5)
<newaw[r]lNs=134> (1)
<newaw[r]lNth=124> (1)
<newaw[r]lNz=114> (7)
<newaw[r]lNz=134> (7)
<newaw[r]lNz=214> (5)
<newaw[r]lNz=314> (50)
<newaw[r]l[N](z)=134> (1)
<newaw[r]l[N](z)=314> (1)
<newaw[r]leeNz=1134> (1)
<newaw[r]leeNz=2134> (1)
<newaw[r]leeNz=3134> (4)
<newaw[r]leen(z)=331> (1)
<newaw[r]leenz=113> (1)
<newaw[r]leenz=213> (2)
<newaw[r]leenz=231> (4)
<newaw[r]leenz=313> (2)
<newaw[r]linz=113> (1)
<newaw[r]linz=213> (1)
<newawrlINz=2144> (3)
<newawrlINz=3144> (13)
<newawrlN(z)=214> (1)
<newawrlN(z)=314> (3)
<newawrlNth=134> (1)
<newawrlNth=314> (1)
<newawrlNz=114> (4)
<newawrlNz=134> (4)
<newawrlNz=214> (12)
<newawrlNz=314> (65)
<newawrleeNts=2134> (1)
<newawrleeNz=1234> (3)
<newawrleeNz=2134> (4)
<newawrleeNz=3134> (8)
<newawrleen(z)=231> (1)
<newawrleenz=132> (3)
<newawrleenz=213> (7)
<newawrleenz=231> (13)
<newawrleenz=313> (9)
<newawrleenz=321> (3)
<newawrleenz=331> (1)
<newawrlenz=231> (1)
<newawrliNz=1134> (1)
<newawrliNz=2134> (1)
<newawrliNz=3134> (2)
<newawrlinz=213> (2)
<newawrlinz=313> (4)
<newo(r)lINz=2144> (1)

<newo(r)lINz=3144> (1)
<newo(r)lNz=314> (3)
<newo(r)lainz=231> (1)
<newo(r)leeNz=3134> (1)
<newo(r)leenz=313> (1)
<newoe(r)lNz=214> (2)
<newoe(r)lNz=314> (4)
<newoe[r]lINz=2144> (1)
<newoe[r]lINz=3144> (1)
<newoe[r]lNz=114> (3)
<newoe[r]lNz=134> (6)
<newoe[r]lNz=214> (5)
<newoe[r]lNz=314> (14)
<newoe[r]leeNz=1134> (1)
<newoe[r]leen(z)=221> (1)
<newoe[r]leenz=113> (1)
<newoe[r]leenz=213> (1)
<newoe[r]leenz=231> (3)
<newoerlINz=1244> (1)
<newoerlINz=2144> (1)
<newoerlINz=3144> (1)
<newoerlN(z)=214> (1)
<newoerlN(z)=314> (1)
<newoerlNz=114> (4)
<newoerlNz=134> (1)
<newoerlNz=214> (15)
<newoerlNz=314> (45)
<newoerleeNz=1134> (3)
<newoerleeNz=1234> (1)
<newoerleeNz=2134> (7)
<newoerleeNz=3134> (5)
<newoerleenz=131> (3)
<newoerleenz=132> (1)
<newoerleenz=213> (2)
<newoerleenz=221> (1)
<newoerleenz=231> (10)
<newoerleenz=313> (4)
<newoerleenz=331> (1)
<newoerlinz=213> (1)
<newoerlinz=313> (1)
<neworlINz=3144> (1)
<neworlN(z)=214> (1)
<neworlNz=214> (1)
<neworlNz=314> (6)
<neworleen(z)=231> (1)
<neworleenz=231> (2)
<neworleenz=313> (1)
<neworleenz=321> (1)
<neworliN(z)=3134> (1)
<neworliNz=3134> (1)
<newu[r]leenz=212> (1)
<newwaw(r)lNz=314> (1)
<niaw[r]lNz=314> (1)
<nioe[r]lNz=314> (1)
<nue(awr)lainz=31> (1)
<nue(awr)leenz=31> (1)
<nueA(r)leenz=341> (1)
<nueaw(r)lINz=2144> (1)
<nueaw(r)lINz=3144> (1)

<nueaw(r)lIinz=3143> (1)
<nueaw(r)lN(z)=314> (1)
<nueaw(r)lNz=214> (2)
<nueaw(r)lNz=314> (16)
<nueaw(r)l[N]z=314> (1)
<nueaw(r)leeNz=2134> (3)
<nueaw(r)leeNz=3134> (1)
<nueaw(r)leenz=231> (4)
<nueaw(r)leenz=312> (1)
<nueaw(r)leenz=321> (1)
<nueaw(r)linz=313> (1)
<nueaw[r]lIINz=3144> (1)
<nueaw[r]lNdz=314> (1)
<nueaw[r]lNz=214> (5)
<nueaw[r]lNz=314> (10)
<nueaw[r]leen(z)=231> (1)
<nueaw[r]leenz=213> (1)
<nueaw[r]leenz=313> (1)
<nueawrl(Nz)=31> (1)
<nueawrlIINts=3144> (1)
<nueawrlIINz=3144> (2)
<nueawrlNGz=214> (1)
<nueawrlNth=314> (1)
<nueawrlNz=134> (1)
<nueawrlNz=214> (6)
<nueawrlNz=314> (19)
<nueawrleenz=231> (4)
<nueawrleenz=313> (1)
<nueawrlinz=312> (1)
<nueo(r)lNz=314> (3)
<nueo(r)leenz=231> (1)
<nueo(r)liNz=2134> (1)
<nueo[r]lNz=214> (1)
<nueo[r]lNz=314> (1)
<nueo[r]l[N](z)=314> (1)
<nueoe(r)lIINz=3144> (1)
<nueoe(r)lNz=214> (1)
<nueoe(r)lNz=314> (2)
<nueoe(r)leeNz=3134> (1)
<nueoe(r)linz=213> (1)
<nueoe[r]lNz=214> (1)
<nueoe[r]lNz=314> (3)
<nueoerlIINz=2144> (2)
<nueoerlIINz=3144> (2)
<nueoerlNz=214> (5)
<nueoerlNz=314> (13)
<nueoerleeNz=2134> (2)
<nueoerleeNz=3134> (3)
<nueoerleeinz=1223> (1)
<nueoerleeinz=2123> (1)
<nueoerleenz=213> (2)
<nueoerleenz=231> (3)
<nueoerleenz=313> (1)
<nueoerlinz=213> (1)
<nueorlIINz=2144> (1)
<nueorlNz=214> (1)
<nueorlNz=314> (6)
<nueorleenz=213> (1)
<nueorliNz=3134> (1)

<nueurleenz=132> (1)
<nuyawrlNz=314> (1)
<ny(ue)aw(r)lIINz=144> (1)
<ny(ue)aw(r)lN(z)=14> (1)
<ny(ue)aw(r)lNz=14> (26)
<ny(ue)aw(r)leenz=31> (1)
<ny(ue)aw[r]lNz=14> (3)
<ny(ue)aw[r]leenz=31> (1)
<ny(ue)awrlNz=14> (4)
<ny(ue)o(r)lNz=14> (1)
<ny(ue)oe(r)lNz=14> (1)
<ny(ue)oe(r)linz=13> (1)
<ny(ue)oe[r]lN(z)=14> (1)
<ny(ue)oerlNz=14> (1)
<nyAaw(r)lIINz=4144> (1)
<nyAaw(r)lN(z)=414> (1)
<nyAaw(r)lNz=414> (1)
<nyAawrlIINz=4144> (1)
<nyAawrlNz=414> (3)
<nyAawrlinz=413> (1)
<nyAo(r)lNz=414> (1)
<nyAoerlNz=414> (1)
<nyAorlunz=413> (1)
<nyIaw[r]leenz=431> (1)
<nyIaw[r]lunz=413> (1)
<nyIawrleenz=412> (1)
<nyIoe[r]lNz=414> (1)
<nyewawrlindz=213> (1)
<nyiaw(r)lNz=314> (1)
<nyuaw[r]lNz=314> (2)
<nyuawrlNz=314> (1)
<nyuawrleeNz=3134> (1)
<nyuoe(r)lNz=314> (1)

087.8B P Baton Rouge
No Response (329)
<badNruej=143> (1)
<badNruezh=143> (1)
<badNruezh=341> (1)
<baik[N]ruej=141> (1)
<baitNrewj=143> (1)
<baitNruej=141> (1)
<baitNruej=143> (7)
<baitNruej=241> (2)
<baitNruej=341> (4)
<baitNruezh=143> (1)
<bat(N)rooj=31> (1)
<batN(r)uej=341> (1)
<batNrewj=141> (2)
<batNrewj=142> (2)
<batNrewj=143> (1)
<batNrewj=241> (1)
<batNrewzh=141> (2)
<batNrewzh=143> (3)
<batNrewzh=241> (4)
<batNrewzh=341> (3)
<batNrij=341> (1)
<batNrooj=143> (3)
<batNrooj=341> (1)
<batNroozh=141> (1)

<batNroozh=241> (1)
<batNroozh=341> (2)
<batNrue(zh)=141> (2)
<batNrue(zh)=143> (2)
<batNrue(zh)=341> (8)
<batNrueAzh=1434> (1)
<batNrueIj=1414> (1)
<batNrueIzh=1414> (1)
<batNrueach=2413> (1)
<batNruech=143> (1)
<batNruech=341> (1)
<batNrued=141> (2)
<batNrued=341> (1)
<batNrueg=143> (1)
<batNruej=141> (32)
<batNruej=142> (1)
<batNruej=143> (50)
<batNruej=241> (21)
<batNruej=341> (157)
<batNrues=341> (1)
<batNruesh=141> (1)
<batNruesh=241> (1)
<batNruesh=341> (2)
<batNruez=341> (4)
<batNruezh=141> (30)
<batNruezh=142> (1)
<batNruezh=143> (42)
<batNruezh=241> (22)
<batNruezh=341> (123)
<batNrui(zh)=341> (1)
<batNruich=241> (2)
<batNruich=341> (1)
<batNruij=141> (1)
<batNruij=143> (2)
<batNruij=241> (1)
<batNruij=341> (14)
<batNruish=141> (1)
<batNruish=241> (1)
<batNruizh=141> (3)
<batNruizh=143> (3)
<batNruizh=241> (1)
<batNruizh=341> (3)
<batanruezh=231> (1)
<batunrozh=231> (1)
<betNrue(zh)=241> (1)
<betNruej=241> (1)
<betNruej=341> (5)
<betNruij=341> (1)

087.9A P Cincinnati
No Response (368)
<sensAnatA=3414> (3)
<sensAnatI=3414> (13)
<sensInatA=3414> (3)
<sensInatI=1434> (1)
<sensInatI=3414> (2)
<sentsAnatA=3414> (5)
<sentsAnatI=3414> (1)
<sentsInatA=1434> (1)
<sentsInatI=3414> (7)

<si(n)sInatA=3414> (1)
<si(n)sInatI=3414> (2)
<si[n]sAnatI=3414> (3)
<si[n]sInatI=3414> (2)
<si[n]tsAnatA=3414> (1)
<sins(I)natI=314> (2)
<sinsAnatA=3414> (58)
<sinsAnatI=1424> (3)
<sinsAnatI=2414> (2)
<sinsAnatI=3414> (96)
<sinsAnatR=3414> (1)
<sinsIn(at)I=144> (1)
<sinsInanI=3414> (1)
<sinsInatA=1424> (1)
<sinsInatA=2414> (1)
<sinsInatA=3414> (37)
<sinsInatI=1424> (3)
<sinsInatI=1434> (5)
<sinsInatI=2414> (5)
<sinsInatI=3414> (127)
<sinsInatee=1423> (1)
<sinsInatee=2413> (1)
<sinsInatee=3413> (10)
<sinsInetI=3414> (2)
<sinsNatI=2414> (1)
<sinsNatI=3414> (1)
<sinsinatI=2314> (1)
<sinsunatA=3214> (1)
<sints(I)natI=214> (1)
<sintsAnatA=3414> (11)
<sintsAnatI=3414> (21)
<sintsAnatR=3414> (1)
<sintsIna(t)I=3414> (1)
<sintsIna(tI)=341> (1)
<sintsInatA=2414> (2)
<sintsInatA=3414> (23)
<sintsInatI=3414> (82)

087.9B P Louisville

No Response (390)
<lew(I)v[L]=14> (1)
<lewAvL=144> (1)
<lewAv[L]=144> (1)
<lewIsvL=144> (1)
<lewIsvi[1]=143> (1)
<lewIvL=144> (2)
<lewIvi(1)=143> (1)
<lewIvi[1]=143> (2)
<lewIvil=143> (1)
<loeIvil=143> (2)
<looAvL=144> (1)
<looAvil=143> (2)
<looIsvil=143> (1)
<looIvL=144> (2)
<looIvil=143> (1)
<looIzvL=144> (1)
<looeevil=132> (1)
<looivL=134> (1)
<luIvL=144> (1)
<lue(I)svil=13> (1)

<lue(I)vi[1]=11> (1)
<lue(I)vi[1]=13> (1)
<lue(I)wL=14> (1)
<lueAsvL=144> (5)
<lueAsvil=143> (2)
<lueAvL=144> (35)
<lueAv[L]=144> (1)
<lueAvil=143> (2)
<lueIsvL=144> (26)
<lueIsvi[1]=141> (1)
<lueIsvi[1]=143> (2)
<lueIsvil=143> (32)
<lueIsvil=341> (1)
<lueIvL=144> (159)
<lueIv[L]=144> (7)
<lueIveel=143> (1)
<lueIvi[1]=143> (12)
<lueIvil=142> (1)
<lueIvil=143> (131)
<lueIvul=143> (2)
<lueIwi[1]=143> (1)
<lueIzvL=144> (4)
<lueIzv[L]=144> (1)
<lueIzvil=142> (1)
<lueIzvil=143> (5)
<lueIzvil=341> (1)
<lueisvL=134> (1)
<lueisvil=132> (1)
<lueivL=134> (12)
<lueivi[1]=132> (2)
<lueivil=123> (1)
<lueivil=132> (5)
<lueizvL=134> (1)
<luewAsvil=143> (1)
<luewAvL=144> (3)
<luewAvil=143> (1)
<luewAvul=143> (1)
<luewIsvL=144> (1)
<luewIsvil=143> (2)
<luewIvL=144> (18)
<luewIvil=143> (24)
<luewIvil=341> (1)
<lueweevL=134> (2)
<lueweevil=132> (1)
<lueweevil=231> (1)
<luewivL=134> (5)
<luewivil=132> (2)
<luewivil=133> (1)
<luezIvil=143> (1)
<luivL=14> (1)

087.9C P Ireland

No Response (548)
<awrlN(d)=14> (1)
<ie(r)lN(d)=14> (6)
<ieRlN(d)=144> (3)
<ie[R]lN(d)=144> (3)
<ie[R]lNd=144> (1)
<ie[r]lN(d)=14> (19)
<ierAlNd=144> (1)

<ierlN(d)=14> (259)
<ierlNd=14> (69)
<ierlNt=14> (1)
<ieurlNs=124> (1)
<orlN(d)=14> (3)

087.9D P France

No Response (497)
<f(r)ants> (1)
<fra[n](s)> (1)
<frains> (1)
<fraints> (5)
<frans> (39)
<fransh> (1)
<frants> (357)
<frents> (13)

087.9E P Russia

No Response (540)
<rooshA=14> (7)
<roshA=14> (1)
<rueshI=14> (1)
<ruishI=14> (1)
<rushA=14> (335)
<rushI=14> (16)
<rushM=14> (1)
<rushR=14> (9)
<rushu=13> (3)
<rushyA=14> (1)

088.1 G miles

No Response (126)
A   mile[N-i] (173)
B   miles (703)
C   mileses (1)

088.1 S miles

No Response (13)
|OAAmaj| (1)
|PAHmaj| (1)
|PKAmda| (1)
|RAA| (5)
|RAAdab| (2)
|RAAeaa| (2)
|RAAeaamaj| (1)
|RAAeaj| (10)
|RAAkaj| (1)
|RAAkak| (1)
|RAAmaj| (3)
|RABcba| (1)
|RABeaa| (4)
|RABeaj| (6)
|RABeajcba| (1)
|RABkaj| (4)
|RABmaj| (16)
|RAE| (14)
|RAEcba| (4)
|RAEcbj| (3)
|RAEdaj| (1)
|RAEeaa| (4)
|RAEeaamaj| (1)
|RAEeaj| (36)
|RAEeajmaj| (1)

|RAEeal| (2)
|RAEkab| (1)
|RAEkaj| (93)
|RAEkak| (1)
|RAEkan| (1)
|RAEmaa| (2)
|RAEmaj| (69)
|RAEmajcba| (8)
|RAEmak| (4)
|RAEmam| (1)
|RAG| (3)
|RAGcba| (4)
|RAGeaa| (1)
|RAGeaj| (27)
|RAGeal| (1)
|RAGkaj| (2)
|RAGmaj| (41)
|RAGmajcba| (2)
|RAIeaj| (1)
|RAImaj| (2)
|RCA| (38)
|RCAeaj| (22)
|RCAeajmaa| (1)
|RCAhaj| (1)
|RCAkaj| (26)
|RCAkak| (1)
|RCAmaa| (7)
|RCAmaacba| (2)
|RCAmaj| (32)
|RCAmajcba| (1)
|RCB| (17)
|RCBcbj| (1)
|RCBeaa| (4)
|RCBeaj| (9)
|RCBeajcba| (1)
|RCBkaj| (9)
|RCBmaa| (1)
|RCBmaj| (14)
|RCBmajcba| (1)
|RCBmajcbj| (1)
|RCDmaj| (1)
|RCE| (41)
|RCEeaa| (4)
|RCEeaamaj| (1)
|RCEeaj| (16)
|RCEeajmaj| (1)
|RCEeal| (1)
|RCEkaj| (38)
|RCEkan| (1)
|RCEmaa| (7)
|RCEmab| (1)
|RCEmaj| (78)
|RCEmajcba| (4)
|RCEmak| (2)
|RCG| (2)
|RCGcba| (3)
|RCGcbj| (1)
|RCGeaamaj| (1)
|RCGeaj| (10)

|RCGeal| (1)
|RCGkaj| (2)
|RCGkan| (1)
|RCGmaa| (2)
|RCGmaj| (37)
|RDE| (1)
|RDEedj| (2)
|RDEkdj| (1)
|RDEmdj| (3)
|RDEmdm| (1)
|RKA| (2)
|RKAmda| (1)
|RKAmdj| (3)
|RKBmda| (1)
|RKBmdb| (1)
|RKEedj| (1)
|RKEkdj| (1)
|RKEkdn| (2)
|RKEmdj| (2)
|RKEmdk| (1)
|RKGeda| (1)
|RKGkdn| (1)
|RKGmdj| (3)
|SAAeajmaj| (1)
|SAD| (2)
|SADmaj| (3)
|SAEmaj| (2)
|SAFcba| (1)
|SAFeaa| (1)
|SAFmaj| (7)
|SCA| (1)
|SCAmaj| (5)
|SCAmajcba| (2)
|SCBmaj| (3)
|SCBmajcba| (1)
|SCD| (1)
|SCDmaj| (1)
|SCEmaa| (1)
|SCG| (1)
|SKAmdjcha| (2)
|SKAmojcha| (1)
|SKBmdj| (1)
|SKDmdjcha| (1)

088.2 G (I don't know) if
No Response (323)
A   as (14)
B   as to whether (2)
C   do[V-p] (1)
D   if (183)
E   that (10)
F   whether (460)

088.3 G (seems) as though
No Response (597)
A   [J-0]/[P-0] (11)
B   as (2)
C   as if (21)
D   as though (19)
E   if (1)
F   like (234)

G   like that (2)
H   likely (2)
I   so (1)
J   that (58)
K   to be (2)

088.4 G unless
No Response (399)
A   lest (1)
B   nolessen (1)
C   or not (1)
D   (u)nless (2)
E   (un)less (35)
F   unless (427)
G   (un)lessen (19)
H   unlessen (25)
I   (wi)thout (3)
J   without (48)

088.5 G instead of
No Response (384)
A   beside (1)
B   in lieu of (1)
C   in place of (18)
D   in preference (to) (2)
E   in spite of (2)
F   (in)stead of (36)
G   instead of (479)
H   other than (1)
I   rather than (21)
J   to keep from (1)
K   without (19)

088.5 P instead
{ai}   lax onset
{d}   devoiced
{e}   inglide
{i}   inglide
{t}   flap
No Response (427)
<(in)sted> (14)
<(in)stid> (8)
<(in)stud> (1)
<(in)st{e}d> (4)
<(in)st{i}d> (1)
<N(s)ted=41> (1)
<Ns(t)ed=41> (1)
<Nstaid=41> (1)
<Nsted=41> (86)
<Nsteed=41> (1)
<Nste{t}=41> (1)
<Nstid=41> (23)
<Nsti{t}=41> (2)
<Nstud=41> (16)
<Nst{ai}d=41> (12)
<Nst{e}d=41> (29)
<Nst{e}{d}=41> (1)
<Nst{e}{t}=41> (1)
<Nst{i}d=41> (2)
<[N]sted=41> (7)
<[N]stid=41> (2)
<[N]st{e}d=41> (1)

<i[n]sted=31> (1)
<ins(t){e}d=31> (1)
<instAd=14> (1)
<instId=14> (1)
<instai(d)=31> (1)
<instaid=31> (2)
<insted=11> (1)
<insted=12> (1)
<insted=13> (8)
<insted=21> (2)
<insted=31> (135)
<inste{d}=13> (1)
<inste{d}=31> (2)
<inste{t}=31> (3)
<instid=13> (1)
<instid=31> (21)
<instud=31> (2)
<inst{ai}d=31> (27)
<inst{ai}{d}=31> (1)
<inst{e}d=31> (82)
<inst{e}t=31> (2)
<inst{i}d=31> (2)
<u[n]st{e}d=31> (1)
<unsted=31> (3)
<unst{ai}d=31> (1)
<unst{e}d=31> (1)
<winst{i}d=31> (1)
<{i}nsteed=31> (1)
<{i}nst{e}d=13> (1)
<{i}nst{e}d=31> (2)

088.6 G because
No Response (143)
A (be)cause (310)
B because (642)
C due to (5)
D for some cause (1)
E on a cause (1)
F on (ac)count of (9)
G on account of (107)
H on (ac)count [P-0] (1)
I on account [P-0] (1)
J on that account (2)
K on the (ac)count of (1)
L on the account of (1)
M on the strength of (1)
N [P-0] (ac)count of (1)
O [P-0] account of (2)

089.1 P Baptist
{a} upglide
{b} devoiced
{d} devoiced
{e} inglide
{i} inglide
{p} voiced
{s} voiced
{t} voiced
No Response (92)
<ba(b)tIs(t)=14> (1)
<bab(d)As(t)=14> (1)

<bab(d)Is(t)=14> (2)
<babdAs(t)=14> (2)
<babdAst=14> (1)
<babdI(st)=14> (1)
<babdIs(t)=14> (269)
<babdIs(t)Iz=144> (1)
<babdIsh(t)=14> (2)
<babdIst=14> (55)
<babdIsts=14> (1)
<babdIz(t)=14> (1)
<babdI{s}(t)=14> (1)
<babdes(t)=13> (1)
<babdis(t)=13> (7)
<babdist=13> (10)
<babd{i}s(t)=13> (3)
<bablIs(t)=14> (1)
<babtI(st)=14> (1)
<babtIs(t)=14> (131)
<babtIs(ts)=14> (1)
<babtIsh(t)=14> (1)
<babtIst=14> (29)
<babtIsts=14> (1)
<babthIs(t)=14> (1)
<babtis(t)=13> (6)
<babtist=13> (3)
<babt{i}s(t)=13> (6)
<bab{d}Is(t)=14> (8)
<bab{d}Ist=14> (2)
<bab{d}ist=13> (1)
<bab{t}Is(t)=14> (65)
<bab{t}Ist=14> (4)
<bab{t}is(t)=13> (2)
<bab{t}ist=13> (1)
<baibdIs(t)=14> (2)
<baiptIs(t)=14> (1)
<bapdIs(t)=14> (2)
<bapdIst=14> (1)
<baptAs(t)=14> (1)
<baptAst=14> (2)
<baptI(st)=14> (2)
<baptIs(t)=14> (86)
<baptIsh(t)=14> (1)
<baptIst=14> (17)
<baptis(t)=13> (8)
<baptist=13> (7)
<bapt{i}s(t)=13> (4)
<bapt{i}st=13> (2)
<bap{d}is(t)=13> (1)
<bap{d}Is(t)=14> (1)
<bap{t}is(t)=13> (1)
<bap{t}Is(t)=14> (16)
<bap{t}Ist=14> (2)
<ba{b}dIs(t)=14> (4)
<ba{b}dist=13> (1)
<ba{b}tAs(t)=14> (1)
<ba{b}tIs(t)=14> (15)
<ba{b}tIst=14> (5)
<ba{b}teest=13> (1)
<ba{b}tist=13> (1)

<ba{b}{d}Is(t)=14> (4)
<ba{b}{d}Ist=14> (1)
<ba{b}{t}Is(t)=14> (2)
<ba{p}dIs(t)=14> (2)
<ba{p}tAs(t)=14> (1)
<ba{p}tIs(t)=14> (23)
<ba{p}tIst=14> (3)
<ba{p}t{i}s(t)=13> (3)
<ba{p}{d}Is(t)=14> (1)
<ba{p}{t}As(t)=14> (5)
<ba{p}{t}Is(t)=14> (7)
<ba{p}{t}is(t)=13> (1)
<bebdIs(t)=14> (3)
<bebdIst=14> (1)
<bebtIs(t)=14> (1)
<beb{t}Is(t)=14> (1)
<bestI(st)=14> (1)
<boptIs(t)=14> (1)
<b{a}bdAs(t)=14> (1)
<b{a}bdAst=14> (1)
<b{a}bdIs(t)=14> (1)
<b{a}b{t}Ist=14> (1)
<b{e}bdIs(t)=14> (1)
<b{e}{b}tIs(t)=14> (1)
<{b}aptIs(t)=14> (1)
<{b}aptIst=14> (1)

089.2A P joined
{ai} monophthong/short glide
{aw} unrounded onset
{d} devoiced
{j} devoiced
{oe} inglide
{r} weakly retroflex
{t} flap
<oy> variants:
{oi} unrounded onset/upglide
{ou} low-central/inglide
{oy} inglide
No Response (189)
<jain> (4)
<jaind> (6)
<jawn(d)> (1)
<jawn> (1)
<jawrnd> (2)
<joenNG=14> (1)
<joyn(d)> (33)
<joyn> (136)
<joynN=14> (6)
<joynd> (296)
<joynz> (4)
<joyn{d}> (17)
<joyn{t}> (2)
<jo{r}nd> (1)
<jund> (1)
<jurn> (1)
<jurnd> (1)
<ju{r}n> (1)
<ju{r}nd> (2)
<j{ai}n(d)> (2)

<j{ai}n> (6)
<j{ai}nd> (2)
<j{aw}n(d)> (1)
<j{oe}n(d)> (1)
<j{oe}n> (1)
<j{oe}nd> (1)
<j{oi}n(d)> (1)
<j{oi}n> (3)
<j{oi}nd> (5)
<j{ou}n(d)> (1)
<j{ou}n> (2)
<j{ou}nd> (1)
<j{oy}n(d)> (9)
<j{oy}n> (46)
<j{oy}nN=14> (1)
<j{oy}nNG=14> (3)
<j{oy}nd> (122)
<j{oy}nz> (3)
<j{oy}n{d}> (1)
<zh{oy}n> (1)
<{j}oyn(d)> (2)
<{j}oynd> (6)
<{j}oynz> (1)
<{j}oyn{d}> (1)
<{j}yoynd> (1)
<{j}{aw}n(d)> (1)
<{j}{oi}n(d)> (1)
<{j}{oi}nd> (1)
<{j}{oy}nd> (1)

089.2B P church

{r}　weakly retroflex
No Response (75)
<che(r)ch> (3)
<cherch> (2)
<che{r}ch> (1)
<chi[r](ch)> (1)
<chi[r]ch> (1)
<chirch> (7)
<chu[r]ch> (238)
<chu[r]chIz=14> (3)
<chu[r]t> (1)
<chur(ch)> (1)
<church> (498)
<churchAz=14> (1)
<churchIz=14> (2)
<churt> (2)
<chu{r}(ch)> (1)
<chu{r}ch> (142)
<chu{r}t> (1)
<ju[r]ch> (1)
<shu[r]ch> (1)
<shurch> (1)
<sursh> (1)
<turch> (1)

089.2 S church

No Response (0)
|DCIeaj| (1)
|DFImea| (1)
|EAAmea| (1)

|ECAmea| (2)
|HCA| (1)
|KADmeaeaj| (1)
|KFEmaj| (1)
|LAA| (18)
|LAAeaa| (1)
|LAAeaj| (7)
|LAAeal| (2)
|LAAmaj| (5)
|LAAmak| (2)
|LAAmea| (33)
|LAAmej| (3)
|LABeej| (1)
|LABmaj| (1)
|LABmea| (3)
|LABmeakaj| (1)
|LABmej| (1)
|LACmea| (8)
|LACmej| (1)
|LADeaa| (1)
|LADmea| (3)
|LADmeaeaj| (1)
|LAEeaa| (1)
|LAEeaj| (1)
|LAEmak| (1)
|LAEmea| (9)
|LAEmej| (1)
|LAFmea| (1)
|LAGmak| (1)
|LAGmea| (3)
|LCA| (5)
|LCAeaj| (2)
|LCAmaj| (2)
|LCAmea| (1)
|LCAmej| (2)
|LCDmea| (1)
|LCDmej| (1)
|LEA| (18)
|LEAeaj| (2)
|LEAmaj| (6)
|LEAmej| (6)
|LEB| (1)
|LEBmak| (1)
|LED| (1)
|LEDmaj| (1)
|LEE| (2)
|LEG| (1)
|LFA| (4)
|LFAeaj| (51)
|LFAeal| (2)
|LFAefj| (1)
|LFAkaj| (2)
|LFAmaj| (27)
|LFAmak| (15)
|LFAmea| (4)
|LFAmej| (8)
|LFAmek| (1)
|LFAmfj| (1)
|LFAmfk| (1)

|LFBeaj| (7)
|LFBmaj| (3)
|LFBmak| (5)
|LFCeaj| (3)
|LFDeaj| (2)
|LFDmaj| (1)
|LFDmeaeaj| (1)
|LFEmaj| (1)
|LFEmea| (5)
|LFGeaj| (1)
|LFHeaj| (2)
|LLA| (1)
|LMA| (3)
|LMAeaj| (9)
|LMAmaj| (18)
|LMAmak| (9)
|LMAmej| (3)
|LMAmfk| (1)
|LMDmea| (1)
|LME| (1)
|LMEmea| (2)
|LPA| (12)
|LPAeaj| (3)
|LPAefj| (1)
|LPAmaj| (1)
|LPAmak| (1)
|LPAmfk| (1)
|LPB| (1)
|LPD| (1)
|LPE| (1)
|LYA| (1)
|LYAeaj| (1)
|LYAmej| (1)
|LYBmaj| (1)
|MCAeaa| (3)
|MCAeaj| (1)
|MCAeea| (1)
|MCAmeb| (1)
|MEA| (276)
|MEAeal| (1)
|MEAmaj| (3)
|MEB| (4)
|MEC| (1)
|MED| (31)
|MEDmaj| (1)
|MEE| (10)
|MEF| (2)
|MEH| (2)
|MLA| (107)
|MLAmaj| (4)
|MLAmea| (1)
|MLB| (3)
|MLD| (7)
|MLE| (2)
|MLH| (1)
|MLI| (1)
|MPA| (22)
|MPAmaj| (1)
|MPB| (1)

|MPD| (2)
|MYA| (5)
|MYAmaj| (1)
|MYB| (1)
|MYE| (1)
|NAAmej| (1)
|NABmea| (1)
|NADmea| (11)
|NADmej| (1)
|NAFmea| (4)
|NAGmea| (1)
|NFAmea| (1)
|NFDmaj| (1)
|NFDmea| (1)
|NFDmeb| (1)
|NFFmea| (1)

089.3 P God

{aw}   unrounded
{d}   devoiced
{g}   devoiced
{o}   low-back
{z}   devoiced
{?}   glottal
No Response (160)
<dod> (1)
<gaw(d)> (1)
<gawd> (43)
<go(d)> (1)
<god> (611)
<godz> (2)
<god{z}> (3)
<go{?}> (3)
<go{d}> (26)
<gyod> (1)
<g{aw}d> (7)
<g{o}d> (84)
<g{o}t> (1)
<g{o}{d}> (2)
<{g}od> (4)
<{g}o{d}> (3)

089.4 L sermon

No Response (178)
A   God's Word (1)
B   gospel (20)
C   gospel message (2)
D   gospel of the Lord (1)
E   lecture (2)
F   message (70)
G   preaching service (2)
H   sermon (727)
I   Word (of God) (5)

089.4 P sermon

{d}   devoiced
{r}   weakly retroflex
{z}   devoiced
{?}   glottal
No Response (185)
<churmN=14> (1)
<saw(r)mNt=14> (1)

<se(r)mN=14> (2)
<sermN=14> (5)
<se{r}mN=14> (3)
<shurmN=14> (1)
<su[r]mN=14> (113)
<su[r]mNt=14> (5)
<su[r]m[N]=14> (1)
<surmAt=14> (1)
<surmN=14> (474)
<surmNd=14> (1)
<surmNs=14> (2)
<surmNt=14> (20)
<surmNts=14> (1)
<surmNz=14> (4)
<surmN{?}=14> (2)
<surmN{d}=14> (1)
<surmN{z}=14> (1)
<surm[N]t=14> (3)
<surmmN=14> (1)
<surmun=13> (6)
<su{r}mN=14> (85)
<su{r}mNt=14> (2)
<su{r}mNz=14> (2)
<su{r}m[N]=14> (1)

089.5 L church music

No Response (187)
A   a capella singing (1)
B   anthem (2)
C   ballad (1)
D   choir song (1)
E   gospel music (2)
F   gospel song (1)
G   hymn (8)
H   music (717)
I   organ music (3)
J   Sacred Harp sing (1)
K   singing (32)
L   singing choir (1)
M   song (2)
N   song service (2)
O   spiritual hymn (1)
P   spiritual song (1)

089.5 P music

{g}   devoiced
{z}   devoiced
{?}   glottal
No Response (186)
<m(y)eezIk=14> (1)
<m(y)uezIk=14> (7)
<m(y)uezik=13> (1)
<mewsIk=14> (1)
<mewzI(k)=14> (1)
<mewzIk=14> (151)
<mew{z}Ik=14> (3)
<mew{z}ik=13> (1)
<myewdhIk=14> (1)
<myewzAk=14> (1)
<myewzIk=14> (48)
<myewzI{g}=14> (1)

<myewzhIk=14> (2)
<myewzik=13> (5)
<myew{z}Ik=14> (1)
<myew{z}ik=13> (1)
<myoozIk=14> (3)
<myuesIk=14> (7)
<myuez(Ik)> (1)
<myuezAk=14> (7)
<myuezI(k)=14> (6)
<myuezIk=14> (449)
<myuezIt=14> (1)
<myuezI{?}=14> (4)
<myuezhIk=14> (3)
<myuezik=13> (17)
<myuezsIk=14> (2)
<myue{z}I(k)=14> (1)
<myue{z}Ik=14> (26)
<myue{z}I{?}=14> (1)
<myue{z}ik=13> (2)

089.6 P beautiful

{d}   tense
{f}   bilabial
{R}   weakly retroflex
{t}   flap
{v}   bilabial
{?}   glottal
No Response (210)
<b(y)ee{t}A{f}[L]=144> (1)
<b(y)ee{t}I{f}L=144> (1)
<b(y)uedAfL=144> (1)
<b(y)uetifL=134> (1)
<b(y)ue{d}AfL=144> (1)
<b(y)ue{d}IfL=144> (1)
<bewdIfL=144> (24)
<bewdIf[L]=144> (1)
<bewdifL=134> (3)
<bewtAfL=144> (1)
<bewtIful=143> (1)
<bewtifL=134> (2)
<bew{d}(I)fL=14> (1)
<bew{d}AfL=144> (5)
<bew{d}IfL=144> (76)
<bew{d}If[L]=144> (5)
<bew{d}Ifool=143> (12)
<bew{d}Iful=143> (1)
<bew{d}ifL=134> (8)
<bew{t}AfL=144> (2)
<bew{t}IfL=144> (7)
<bew{t}I{f}L=144> (1)
<boo{d}Af[L]=144> (1)
<brue{d}IfL=144> (1)
<byee{t}A{f}[L]=144> (1)
<byee{t}IfL=144> (1)
<byew(t)Iv[L]=144> (1)
<byew(t)I{v}[L]=144> (1)
<byewdIfL=144> (1)
<byewtAfL=144> (2)
<byewtIfL=144> (2)
<byew{d}AfL=144> (21)

<byew{d}Aful=143> (2)
<byew{d}IfL=144> (13)
<byew{d}Iful=143> (3)
<byew{t}AfL=144> (3)
<byew{t}A{f}oo[1]=143> (1)
<byew{t}IfL=144> (6)
<byew{t}If[L]=144> (3)
<byew{t}Iful=143> (1)
<byew{t}I{f}L=144> (1)
<byew{t}I{f}[L]=144> (1)
<byew{t}I{v}[L]=144> (1)
<byi(t)I{f}[L]=144> (1)
<byi{t}Af[L]=144> (1)
<byi{t}IfL=144> (2)
<byi{t}If[L]=144> (1)
<byi{t}Ifu[1]=143> (1)
<byi{t}I{f}L=144> (1)
<byi{t}I{f}[L]=144> (1)
<byoodIfL=144> (1)
<byoo{d}IfL=144> (3)
<byoo{t}AfL=144> (1)
<byoo{t}A{f}L=144> (1)
<byuedAfL=144> (2)
<byuedIfL=144> (57)
<byuedIf[L]=144> (3)
<byuedIfoo[1]=143> (2)
<byuedIfool=143> (2)
<byuedIfu[1]=143> (1)
<byuedifL=134> (3)
<byuetAfL=144> (1)
<byuetIfL=144> (7)
<byuetIful=341> (1)
<byue{?}IfL=144> (1)
<byue{d}AfL=144> (95)
<byue{d}Af[L]=144> (2)
<byue{d}Afool=143> (3)
<byue{d}Aful=143> (4)
<byue{d}IfL=144> (244)
<byue{d}If[L]=144> (12)
<byue{d}Ifoo(1)=143> (1)
<byue{d}Ifoo[1]=143> (3)
<byue{d}Ifool=143> (18)
<byue{d}Ifu[1]=143> (2)
<byue{d}Ifuel=143> (1)
<byue{d}Iful=143> (5)
<byue{d}eefL=134> (4)
<byue{d}ifL=134> (9)
<byue{d}if[L]=134> (2)
<byue{d}iful=132> (1)
<byue{t}AfL=144> (2)
<byue{t}Aful=143> (1)
<byue{t}AvL=144> (1)
<byue{t}IfL=144> (10)
<byue{t}If[L]=144> (9)
<byue{t}Ifaw[1]=143> (1)
<byue{t}Ifu[1]=143> (1)
<byue{t}Iful=143> (1)
<byue{t}I{f}[L]=144> (1)
<byue{t}{R}fool=143> (1)

089.7 G by the time
No Response (533)
A   afore (2)
B   (be)fore (39)
C   before (204)
D   by [D-0] time (15)
E   by the time (114)
F   from (1)
G   when (38)
H   [P-0] the time (1)
I   [P-0] [D-0] time (17)

090.1 L devil
No Response (107)
A   adversary (3)
B   Asteroff (1)
C   bad boy (1)
D   bad man (92)
E   beast (1)
F   Beelzebub (12)
G   black angel (1)
H   booger (2)
I   booger bear (2)
J   boogerman (190)
K   boogers (1)
L   boogeyman (33)
M   deceiver (1)
N   demon (13)
O   DEVIL (1)
P   devil (760)
Q   diab(le) [F] (1)
R   diable [F] (1)
S   Diabolo (1)
T   diabolo, el [S] (1)
U   dickens (1)
V   Dragon (1)
W   dragon (6)
X   evil one (1)
Y   evil spirit (1)
Z   false prophet (1)
aa   Gable (1)
ab   heathen (1)
ac   imp (2)
ad   infern (1)
ae   infidel (1)
af   infierno [S] (1)
ag   Lucifer (58)
ah   Lucius (1)
ai   man with a horn over his head (1)
aj   man with the horns (1)
ak   man with the pitchfork (1)
al   Mister Bad Man (1)
am   old bad man (4)
an   old booger (1)
ao   old boogerman (7)
ap   old boogeyman (1)
aq   old boy (1)
ar   old deluder (1)
as   old devil (9)

at   old dragon (1)
au   Old Haggy (1)
av   Old Haggy Bill (1)
aw   Old Harry (3)
ax   old imp (1)
ay   Old Jack (1)
az   old man (1)
ba   Old Nick (9)
bb   old Satan (18)
bc   Old Scratch (22)
bd   old Scrooge (1)
be   old serpent (1)
bf   Prince of Darkness (1)
bg   red devil (2)
bh   red man (1)
bi   Saint Lucifer (1)
bj   Saint Nick (1)
bk   Sat(an) (1)
bl   Satan (381)
bm   serpent (2)
bn   Tataille [F] (1)
bo   wicked one (1)

090.1 P devil
{ai}   lax onset
{b}   fricative
{d}   devoiced
{v}   devoiced
{z}   devoiced
No Response (146)
<daivL=14> (1)
<davL=14> (2)
<de(v)l> (1)
<debL=14> (2)
<deb[L]=14> (1)
<devL=14> (692)
<devLz=14> (6)
<devL{z}=14> (1)
<dev[L]=14> (23)
<dev[L]{z}=14> (1)
<devul=13> (1)
<de{b}L=14> (7)
<de{b}[L]=14> (6)
<de{v}L=14> (3)
<divL=14> (5)
<div[L]=14> (2)
<di{b}Ap=14> (1)
<duvL=14> (1)
<d{ai}vL=14> (16)
<d{ai}{b}L=14> (1)
<{d}evL=14> (1)
<{d}ev[L]=14> (1)

090.2 L spooks
No Response (147)
A   angels (2)
B   apparitions (3)
C   bad booger (1)
D   bad spirits (2)
E   banshees (1)
F   booger (19)

G booger bear (2)
H boogey bear (2)
I boogerman (23)
J boogeyman (13)
K dead, the (1)
L dead people (2)
M dead things (1)
N demons (1)
O diable [F] (1)
P evil spirits (3)
Q fairy (1)
R ghost people (1)
S ghostly troll (1)
T ghosts (623)
U ghouls (2)
V goblins (37)
W haunts (250)
X hobgoblins (2)
Y hoodlums (2)
Z hoodoos (2)
aa little devils (1)
ab old goblin (1)
ac old spooks' witch (1)
ad phantoms (2)
ae pocket haunts, a (1)
af poltergeist (1)
ag rawhead and bloodybones (1)
ah revenant [F] (1)
ai scarecrow (2)
aj shades (1)
ak shadows (1)
al skeleton (3)
am specters (2)
an spirits (98)
ao spirits from dead people (1)
ap spiritual spirit (1)
aq spooks (134)
ar will-o'-[D-0]-wisp (1)
as witch (13)
at wraiths (1)
au Yahoo (1)
av zombi (1)

090.3 L haunted house

No Response (520)
A booger house (1)
B camp (1)
C creepy house (1)
D deserted house (2)
E empty house (2)
F ghost house (32)
G ghosty house (4)
H haunt house (2)
I haunted homestead (1)
J haunted house (346)
K haunted place (3)
L haunting house (1)
M haunty house (2)
N horror house (1)
O house full of boogers (1)

P house of ghost[N-i] (1)
Q house of goblins (1)
R old haunted house (2)
S old house (2)
T old spooky house (1)
U scary house (2)
V spook house (10)
W spooked house (1)
X spooky house (11)
Y witch house (2)

090.3 P haunted

{a} upglide
{ai} lax
{aw} unrounded onset
{d} devoiced
{o} low-back
{oe} lowered onset
{r} weakly retroflex
{t} voiced
{?} glottal
No Response (178)
<hai[n]{?}Id=14> (4)
<hain(t)I(d)=14> (4)
<hain(t)Id=14> (31)
<hain(t)I{d}=14> (5)
<haintId=14> (13)
<hain{?}Ad=14> (1)
<hain{?}I(d)=14> (1)
<hain{?}Id=14> (18)
<hain{t}I(d)=14> (1)
<hain{t}Id=14> (24)
<hain{t}I{d}=14> (3)
<han(t)I(d)=14> (5)
<han(t)Id=14> (10)
<han(t)I{d}=14> (1)
<hantId=14> (14)
<hantI{d}=14> (1)
<han{?}I(d)=14> (1)
<han{?}Id=14> (9)
<han{?}I{d}=14> (1)
<han{t}I(d)=14> (3)
<han{t}Id=14> (29)
<han{t}I{d}=14> (2)
<haw(n){?}Id=14> (3)
<haw[n](t)Id=14> (2)
<haw[n]tId=14> (1)
<haw[n]{?}Id=14> (9)
<haw[n]{?}I{d}=14> (1)
<haw[n]{t}Id=14> (2)
<haw[n]{t}I{d}=14> (1)
<hawn(t)Id=14> (141)
<hawn(t)It=14> (2)
<hawn(t)I{d}=14> (20)
<hawnnId=14> (2)
<hawntId=14> (56)
<hawntIt=14> (1)
<hawntI{d}=14> (6)
<hawntid=13> (1)
<hawn{?}Id=14> (37)

<hawn{?}I{d}=14> (2)
<hawn{?}id=13> (1)
<hawn{t}Id=14> (132)
<hawn{t}I{d}=14> (4)
<haw{r}n{?}Id=14> (1)
<he{r}n{t}I{d}=14> (1)
<hien(t)I{d}=14> (1)
<ho[n]{?}Id=14> (1)
<ho[n]{t}Id=14> (1)
<hoen(t)Id=14> (2)
<hoentId=14> (1)
<hoen{t}Id=14> (1)
<hon(t)Id=14> (24)
<hon(t)I{d}=14> (3)
<honchId=14> (1)
<hontId=14> (19)
<hontI{d}=14> (2)
<hon{?}Id=14> (17)
<hon{t}Id=14> (10)
<hown(t)I{d}=14> (1)
<hown{?}Id=14> (1)
<hoyn{t}I{d}=14> (1)
<huen(t)I{d}=14> (1)
<huntId=14> (1)
<hun{t}Id=14> (1)
<h{ai}ntId=14> (1)
<h{ai}n{?}Id=14> (2)
<h{aw}(n){?}Id=14> (1)
<h{aw}n(t)Id=14> (20)
<h{aw}n(t)It=14> (1)
<h{aw}n(t)I{d}=14> (6)
<h{aw}ntId=14> (6)
<h{aw}ntI{d}=14> (1)
<h{aw}n{?}Id=14> (4)
<h{aw}n{?}I{d}=14> (1)
<h{aw}n{?}id=13> (1)
<h{aw}n{t}Id=14> (11)
<h{a}n(t)I(d)=14> (1)
<h{a}n(t)Id=14> (9)
<h{a}ntId=14> (7)
<h{a}ntI{d}=14> (1)
<h{a}n{?}Id=14> (8)
<h{a}n{?}I{d}=14> (1)
<h{a}n{t}I(d)=14> (1)
<h{a}n{t}Id=14> (8)
<h{oe}n(t)Id=14> (6)
<h{oe}n(t)I{d}=14> (4)
<h{oe}ntId=14> (1)
<h{oe}n{t}Id=14> (4)
<h{o}n(t)Id=14> (3)
<h{o}ntId=14> (6)
<h{o}n{?}Id=14> (1)
<h{o}n{t}Id=14> (4)
<h{o}n{t}I{d}=14> (2)

090.4 G rather [=quite]

No Response (235)
A a bit (2)
B (a) little (20)
C a little bit (2)

D   a mite (2)
E   fairly (27)
F   kind of (359)
G   kindly (111)
H   kindly rather (1)
I   middling (1)
J   moderately (3)
K   pretty (256)
L   pretty much (6)
M   pretty tolerable (2)
N   pretty well (6)
O   quite (29)
P   reasonable (1)
Q   rather (139)
R   right (65)
S   right quite (1)
T   somewhat (2)
U   somewhat rather (1)
V   sort of (164)
W   sort [X-0] (1)
X   tad (1)
Y   tolerable (1)

090.4 P rather [=quite]
{o}   low-back
{R}   weakly retroflex
No Response (777)
<radR=14> (1)
<radhR=14> (37)
<radh[R]=14> (42)
<radh{R}=14> (11)
<rath{R}=14> (1)
<redhR=14> (9)
<redh[R]=14> (17)
<redh{R}=14> (3)
<rodhR=14> (3)
<rodh[R]=14> (3)
<rodh{R}=14> (1)
<rudhR=14> (2)
<rudh[R]=14> (9)
<rudh{R}=14> (1)
<r{o}dh[R]=14> (1)

090.5 P rather [=prefer]
{dh}   devoiced
{o}   low-back
{R}   weakly retroflex
{r}   devoiced
{t}   flap
{th}   voiced
No Response (279)
<d(r)udh[R]=14> (1)
<dradhR=14> (2)
<dradh[R]=14> (2)
<dra{dh}[R]=14> (1)
<dredhR=14> (3)
<dredh[R]=14> (1)
<dredh{R}=14> (1)
<drodh[R]=14> (1)
<drudhR=14> (8)
<drudh[R]=14> (11)

<drudh{R}=14> (2)
<d{r}odh[R]=14> (1)
<radR=14> (1)
<rad[R]=14> (2)
<radhR=14> (122)
<radh[R]=14> (126)
<radh{R}=14> (43)
<rawdh[R]=14> (1)
<ra{th}[R]=14> (1)
<ra{t}[R]=14> (2)
<red[R]=14> (2)
<redhR=14> (70)
<redh[R]=14> (92)
<redh{R}=14> (31)
<ret[R]=14> (1)
<reth[R]=14> (1)
<revR=14> (1)
<re{dh}R=14> (1)
<re{dh}[R]=14> (1)
<re{t}[R]=14> (1)
<ridh{R}=14> (1)
<rodhR=14> (15)
<rodh[R]=14> (30)
<rodh{R}=14> (11)
<rudhR=14> (16)
<rudh[R]=14> (81)
<rudh{R}=14> (14)
<ru{dh}[R]=14> (1)
<r{o}dh[R]=14> (2)

090.6 G mighty glad
No Response (484)
[I'm...to see you]
A   all glad (1)
B   awful glad (6)
C   awful happy (1)
D   awful proud (1)
E   awfully glad (6)
F   awfully happy (1)
G   delighted (10)
H   glad (222)
I   happy (27)
J   mighty glad (18)
K   mighty pleased (1)
L   mighty proud (7)
M   pleased (6)
N   plowed (1)
O   pretty proud (1)
P   proud (103)
Q   real glad (4)
R   real proud (4)
S   really glad (6)
T   really proud (1)
U   right glad (1)
V   so glad (64)
W   so happy (6)
X   so proud (8)
Y   super glad (1)
Z   sure (am) glad (13)
aa   sure (am) proud (3)

ab   sure happy (1)
ac   tickle (2)
ad   tickle to death (1)
ae   tickled (1)
af   very glad (10)
ag   very happy (4)
ah   very please (1)
ai   very pleased (1)
[it's...to see you]
aj   awfully good (1)
ak   good (20)
al   great (2)
am   mighty fine (2)
an   mighty good (5)
ao   mighty nice (3)
ap   nice (6)
aq   real nice (1)
ar   so good (7)
as   so nice (2)
at   sure good (1)
au   sure (is) good (3)
av   wonderful (1)

090.6 P proud
{a}   inglide
{d}   devoiced
{l}   devoiced
{ow}   inglide
{r}   devoiced
{t}   flap
No Response (788)
<prowd> (69)
<prow{d}> (1)
<pr{a}d> (3)
<pr{ow}d> (10)
<pr{ow}{d}> (1)
<p{l}owd> (1)
<p{r}owd> (39)
<p{r}ow{d}> (1)
<p{r}{ow}d> (3)
<p{t}owd> (1)

090.7 G right smart
No Response (298)
A   right smart [adj.] (52)
B   right smart [adv.] (90)
C   right smart (of) [n.] (247)
D   right smart [usage unclear] (82)
E   right smarter (1)

091.1 G certainly
No Response (467)
A   absolutely (17)
B   amen (2)
C   and how (1)
D   by all means (1)
E   by George (1)
F   certainly (126)
G   certainly right (1)
H   certainly so (1)
I   course (6)
J   damn right (5)

K   damn right, shit (1)
L   damn straight (2)
M   darn right (5)
N   definite (1)
O   definitely (8)
P   definitely so (1)
Q   doggone right (3)
R   exactly (3)
S   for certain (1)
T   for sure (9)
U   honest to gosh (1)
V   I can tell you (1)
W   I declare (1)
X   I don't mean maybe (1)
Y   I mean (5)
Z   I should say (3)
aa I should say so (1)
ab I tell you (3)
ac I tell you for a fact (1)
ad I tell you that (1)
ae I tell you what (1)
af I'd say so (1)
ag I'll bet (2)
ah I'll say (1)
ai I'm sure (6)
aj I'm telling you (6)
ak (in)deed (1)
al indeed (31)
am most certainly (2)
an of course (33)
ao positively (2)
ap really and truly (1)
aq right (15)
ar right on (2)
as right so (1)
at sure (133)
au sure as hell (2)
av sure as the world (3)
aw sure as you're born (1)
ax sure (e)nough (17)
ay sure enough (15)
az sure indeed (1)
ba sure thing (1)
bb sure will (1)
bc surely (12)
bd that was right (1)
be that's all right (1)
bf that's exactly right (1)
bg that's for sure (6)
bh that's it (1)
bi that's it, partner (1)
bj (that's) no joke (2)
bk that's right (33)
bl that's the truth (2)
bm that's true (2)
bn there you are (1)
bo there you are, brother (1)
bp there you go (2)
bq to be sure (2)

br too sure (1)
bs true (1)
bt well, I guess (1)
bu without a doubt (1)
bv yes, ma'am (19)
bw yes, sir (83)
bx yes, sir, ma'am (1)
by yes sirree (18)
bz yes sirree bob (1)
ca you bet (14)
cb you bet you (6)
cc you bet your boots (1)
cd (you) bet your life (2)
ce you got something (1)
cf you know it (1)
cg you [C-0] damn right (3)
ch you [C-0] darn right (3)
ci you [C-0] doggone right (2)
cj you [X-0] better believe it (2)
ck you [X-0] better know (1)
cl you're darn right (2)
cm you're right (2)

091.2 P sure
{oo}   high central
{r}   weakly retroflex
No Response (246)
<choe(r)> (1)
<shaw(r)> (2)
<shaw[r]> (1)
<shawr> (3)
<shaw{r}> (1)
<shew(r)> (2)
<shew[r]> (3)
<shewr> (2)
<shi[r]> (1)
<shir> (15)
<shi{r}> (1)
<shoe(r)> (119)
<shoe[r]> (50)
<shoer> (34)
<shoe{r}> (18)
<shoo(r)> (14)
<shoo[r]> (93)
<shoor> (199)
<shoo{r}> (52)
<shu[r]> (3)
<shue(r)> (10)
<shue[r]> (4)
<shuer> (8)
<shue{r}> (2)
<shur> (65)
<shu{r}> (7)
<sh{oo}(r)> (4)
<sh{oo}[r]> (39)
<sh{oo}r> (92)
<sh{oo}{r}> (18)

091.3 G yes
No Response (92)
A   all right (17)

B   GRUNT(A) (10)
C   GRUNT(H) (1)
D   oh, yeah (106)
E   oh, yes (68)
F   OK (142)
G   right (80)
H   that's correct (2)
I   that's OK (2)
J   that's right (96)
K   there you go (1)
L   (this is) true (2)
M   yeah (621)
N   yep (30)
O   yes (446)
P   yes, indeed (4)
Q   yes, sir (7)
R   you bet (2)
S   you bet you (1)
T   you're right (1)

091.4 G yes, sir/ma'am
No Response (465)
A   no, (ma'a)m/y(es), (m)a'am
    [polite] (25)
B   sir ?/ma'am ? (5)
C   yeah, sir (1)
D   yes/no, sir/ma'am [polite] (394)
E   yes/no, sir/ma'am [emphatic]
    (94)

091.5 P hesitation
{r}   weakly retroflex
{?}   glottal
No Response (329)
<(1)e(t)ssee=13> (1)
<(1)e(t)sseeu=311> (1)
<AwelA=414> (1)
<Awelum=411> (1)
<Mhum=41> (1)
<[M]wel=41> (1)
<a[m]> (1)
<aigosh=31> (1)
<aindu=13> (1)
<an(d)A=14> (1)
<an(d)o=13> (1)
<an(d)u=13> (5)
<an(d)u[m]=13> (1)
<an(d)um=13> (2)
<andd[M]=14> (1)
<andom=13> (1)
<andoo=13> (1)
<andu=13> (16)
<andu[m]=13> (3)
<andum=13> (1)
<anno=13> (5)
<annu=13> (27)
<annu{?}=13> (1)
<an{?}u=13> (1)
<awlA(ts)see=143> (1)
<endom=11> (1)

<endu=13> (2)
<enno=13> (1)
<ennu=13> (4)
<gawlee=13> (1)
<haw[m]> (1)
<hu> (2)
<hu[m]> (2)
<hum> (4)
<hwai> (3)
<inum=13> (1)
<lMmeeseenow=4313> (1)
<le(t)mIsee=341> (2)
<le(t)meesee=231> (1)
<le(t)ssee=31> (7)
<le(t)sseehi{r}=313> (1)
<le(t)sseenow=313> (1)
<le(ts)shee=21> (1)
<lemmIsee=143> (1)
<lemmIsee=341> (1)
<letmeeseenow=2313> (1)
<letssee=13> (1)
<letssee=31> (5)
<li(t)ssee=13> (1)
<litssee=31> (1)
<mwe[1]> (1)
<nAuwel=431> (1)
<nowletmisee=3231> (1)
<nwel> (1)
<o> (16)
<o[m]A=14> (1)
<o[m]{?}> (1)
<oe> (6)
<oejee=31> (1)
<oekaile(t)ssee=3123> (1)
<oele(ts)see=231> (1)
<oelet(s)see=313> (1)
<oeletmIsee=2341> (1)
<oeu=13> (1)
<oew[L]no=143> (1)
<oletmeesee=1321> (1)
<oletssee=131> (1)
<om> (9)
<owel=11> (1)
<owel=31> (1)
<u> (66)
<u[m]> (13)
<u[m]letmeesee=1331> (1)
<u[m]o[m]=11> (1)
<ue> (1)
<um> (33)
<ump> (1)
<umwel=11> (1)
<umwel=31> (2)
<umwoe=11> (1)
<un> (1)
<unnu=13> (1)
<unu=13> (1)
<uoe=11> (1)
<uu=11> (1)

<uwel=31> (2)
<uwelu=111> (1)
<uwelu=113> (1)
<vel> (2)
<wa[1]> (1)
<wai[1]> (3)
<wail> (11)
<wail{?}u[m]=13> (1)
<wal> (11)
<walle(t)ssee=131> (1)
<we(1)> (9)
<we(1)sI=14> (1)
<weL=14> (1)
<we[1]> (26)
<we[1]A=14> (1)
<we[1]{?}> (1)
<we[1]{?}or=13> (1)
<wel> (407)
<welA=14> (4)
<wel[M]=14> (1)
<wellA(t)ssee=143> (1)
<welle(t)ssI=134> (1)
<welle(t)ssee=231> (1)
<welle(ts)seenow=2313> (1)
<welletssee=313> (1)
<wellu=13> (1)
<welno=13> (1)
<welnow=11> (3)
<welnow=13> (2)
<welnow=31> (1)
<welo=11> (1)
<welo=13> (3)
<welo=31> (1)
<welo[m]=13> (1)
<welom=11> (1)
<welsR=14> (1)
<welsur=13> (2)
<welu=11> (8)
<welu=13> (23)
<welu=21> (2)
<welu[m]=11> (1)
<welu[m]=13> (1)
<welum=11> (1)
<welum=13> (4)
<wel{?}> (2)
<wel{?}o=11> (1)
<wel{?}u=11> (1)
<wel{?}u=13> (1)
<wel{?}um=13> (1)
<we{?}> (1)
<wi(1)> (1)
<wi[1]> (4)
<wiel> (1)
<wil> (19)
<wilnow=13> (1)
<wilu=13> (1)
<wil{?}> (1)
<wil{?}oe=12> (1)
<wu[1]> (1)

<wul> (25)
<wul{?}> (1)
<wu{r}> (1)
<{?}Awel=41> (1)
<{?}air> (1)
<{?}aw> (1)
<{?}i[m]> (1)
<{?}o> (1)
<{?}o[m]> (1)
<{?}oe> (1)
<{?}oe[m]> (1)
<{?}oehoe=13> (1)
<{?}om> (2)
<{?}orla(ts)see=132> (1)
<{?}u> (14)
<{?}u[m]> (8)
<{?}ue[m]> (1)
<{?}um> (16)
<{?}uuuu=1111> (1)
<{?}uwel=11> (1)
<{?}wel> (1)
<{?}wil> (1)

091.6 G really (dreaded)
No Response (387)
A   absolutely (5)
B   certainly (2)
C   clear (1)
D   damn well (1)
E   downright (1)
F   flat (3)
G   just (5)
H   just pinely (1)
I   just plain (1)
J   just really (3)
K   low-down (1)
L   pinely (1)
M   plain (3)
N   plumb (21)
O   pure (1)
P   purely (17)
Q   really (478)
R   really and truly (5)
S   simply (1)
T   sure (16)
U   sure (e)nough (2)
V   surely (6)
W   truly (1)

091.7A P real
{ee} lax
{r} labial
No Response (321)
<hril> (1)
<rail> (6)
<re[1]> (1)
<ree[1]> (20)
<reel> (279)
<rel> (4)
<ri[1]> (47)
<ril> (279)

<r{ee}[l]> (1)
<r{ee}l> (9)
<{r}ee[l]> (1)
<{r}eel> (1)
<{r}i[l]> (1)
<{r}{ee}l> (1)

091.7B P really

{ee} lax
{r} labial
No Response (390)
<railI=14> (4)
<ralI=14> (1)
<reelI=14> (136)
<reelII=14> (1)
<relI=14> (12)
<ri[l]I=14> (2)
<ri[l]lI=14> (1)
<rilI=14> (363)
<rilII=14> (2)
<rillee=13> (1)
<rulII=14> (1)
<r{ee}lI=14> (43)
<{r}i[l]I=14> (1)
<{r}ilI=14> (3)

092.1 G damn

No Response (707)
A   by damn (1)
B   dad blame (1)
C   dad drat it (1)
D   dad gum (it) (15)
E   dad shum it (1)
F   dag nab it (1)
G   damn (it) (85)
H   damn it to hell (2)
I   damn the luck (1)
J   damnation (2)
K   damn(ed), I('ll) be (12)
L   dang (7)
M   darn (it) (34)
N   darn your hide (1)
O   darn(ed), I('ll) be (11)
P   dog (2)
Q   dog(ged), I('ll) be (13)
R   doggone, I('ll) be (6)
S   doggone (it) (24)
T   doggone the luck (1)
U   drat (it) (1)
V   God damn, I('ll) be (2)
W   God damn (it/you) (31)
X   God dang (3)
Y   God darn (3)
Z   God dog (it) (5)
aa   golly bum (1)
ab   golly (gosh)/gosh darn (3)
ac   golly/gosh dog (2)
ad   hot damn (2)
ae   hot dog (1)

092.2 G land's sakes

No Response (319)

A   Albert and Jesus (1)
B   Almighty God (1)
C   bless my soul (1)
D   blow me down (1)
E   boy (26)
F   boy, howdy (3)
G   boy, oh, boy (2)
H   brother (1)
I   by dog (1)
J   by George (6)
K   by God (6)
L   by gollies (4)
M   by golly (21)
N   by gosh (2)
O   by Jackson (1)
P   by jingoes (1)
Q   by jinks (1)
R   by Jove (1)
S   Christ (2)
T   dear Gussy (1)
U   deary (1)
V   double wow (1)
W   for Christ's sake (1)
X   for crying out loud (2)
Y   for God[N-k] sake (1)
Z   for goodness' sake(s) (13)
aa   for heaven('s) sake(s) (7)
ab   for land('s) sake(s) (2)
ac   for Lord('s) sake(s) (2)
ad   for Pete('s) sake (2)
ae   for pity's sake (1)
af   gad (1)
ag   gee (34)
ah   gee whillikins (1)
ai   gee whiz (15)
aj   glory (3)
ak   glory be (2)
al   God, (oh,) (18)
am   God Almighty (8)
an   God Almighty[N-k] sake (1)
ao   God dog (3)
ap   golly (39)
aq   golly bum (1)
ar   golly darn (1)
as   golly dog (1)
at   golly Moses (1)
au   golly Pete (1)
av   good God (5)
aw   good God Almighty (4)
ax   good golly (2)
ay   good gosh (3)
az   good gosh almighty (1)
ba   good gracious (22)
bb   good grac(ious) alive (1)
bc   good gracious alive (9)
bd   good grannies/granny (2)
be   good grief (14)
bf   good heavens (7)
bg   good land (1)

bh   good Lord (8)
bi   good Lordy (1)
bj   good night (7)
bk   good night, boy (1)
bl   goodness (49)
bm   goodness alive (3)
bn   goodness gracious (10)
bo   goodness gracious alive (1)
bp   goodness me (1)
bq   goodness' sake(s) (3)
br   goodness' sakes alive (1)
bs   gosh (93)
bt   gosh almighty (1)
bu   gosh darn (1)
bv   gosh dog (2)
bw   gosh sakes (1)
bx   gracious (13)
by   gracious goodness me (1)
bz   gracious me (1)
ca   gracious sakes (1)
cb   great balls of fire (1)
cc   great day (2)
cd   great day in the morning (1)
ce   great God (2)
cf   great goodness (5)
cg   great goodness alive (3)
ch   heavenly days (1)
ci   heavens (13)
cj   heavens above (1)
ck   heavens to Betsy (1)
cl   heaven[N-k] sake(s) (2)
cm   Himmel [G] (1)
cn   holy cow (2)
co   holy mackerel (2)
cp   holy shit (1)
cq   holy smokes (1)
cr   I can't/don't believe it (3)
cs   I declare (43)
ct   I do declare (1)
cu   I never (1)
cv   I say, well, (1)
cw   I swan (1)
cx   I swanny (4)
cy   I swear (2)
cz   I swear to goodness (1)
da   I'll declare (4)
db   I'll say, well, (2)
dc   I'll swan (1)
dd   I'll swanny (3)
de   I'm telling you (1)
df   jeez (3)
dg   Jehosophat (1)
dh   Jesus (5)
di   Jesus Christ (7)
dj   Jesus Christ Almighty (1)
dk   Jesus God (1)
dl   land (2)
dm   land of Goshen (2)
dn   land of rest (1)

do land sakes alive (1)
dp land('s) sake(s) (17)
dq law (17)
dr law me (1)
ds laws (1)
dt Lord, (oh,) (117)
du Lord, child (1)
dv Lord God (2)
dw Lord, gosh (1)
dx Lord, have mercy (56)
dy Lord, help my soul (1)
dz Lord, help us (2)
ea Lord, I reckon (1)
eb Lord whillikins (1)
ec Lord's sakes (1)
ed Lordy (13)
ee Lordy mercy (6)
ef love of Pete (1)
eg man (19)
eh man alive (3)
ei man, oh, man (1)
ej merciful kingdom (1)
ek mercy (23)
el mercy alive (2)
em mercy goodness (1)
en mercy, Lord (1)
eo mercy me (1)
ep my (2)
eq my God (30)
er my God Almighty (2)
es my goodness (91)
et my goodness alive (11)
eu my goodness gracious (2)
ev my gosh (17)
ew my gracious (2)
ex my gracious alive (1)
ey my heavens (3)
ez my Jesus (1)
fa my land(s) (2)
fb my law (1)
fc my Lord (18)
fd my Lord, have mercy (2)
fe my Lordy (1)
ff my, my, (my) (2)
fg my soul (2)
fh my stars (7)
fi my stars above (2)
fj my word (4)
fk no (4)
fl oh (26)
fm oh, boy (31)
fn oh, brother (3)
fo oh, dear (23)
fp oh, man (13)
fq oh, me (9)
fr oh, my (30)
fs oh, my child (1)
ft oh, wee (1)
fu oh, wow (7)

fv really (11)
fw sakes alive (1)
fx son (of) [D-0] bitch (2)
fy son of a bitch (10)
fz son of a booger (1)
ga son of a gun (6)
gb sure (e)nough (2)
gc sweet Lucy (1)
gd that beats all/it (2)
ge what? (2)
gf what (in) the devil (2)
gg what (in) the hell (5)
gh what in the world (1)
gi what the dickens (1)
gj what [X-0] you talking (a)bout?
    (1)
gk what/who (in) the heck (7)
gl who on earth (1)
gm whoa (2)
gn woo (3)
go wow (17)
gp wowee (1)
gq ye gods (2)

092.3 G shucks
No Response (702)
A bull (1)
B bullshit (2)
C crap (8)
D holy shit (1)
E pshaw (11)
F shit (13)
G shit fire (2)
H shoot (98)
I shoot fire (1)
J shucks (84)
K shuck[N-i] (13)
L shucks fire (1)
M shut (1)

092.4 P idea
{ee} lax
{ie} monophthong/short glide
{R} weakly retroflex
{r} weakly retroflex
{t} flap
{z} devoiced
No Response (315)
<Adee(A)=41> (1)
<ied(ee)A=14> (7)
<ied(ee)I=14> (53)
<ied(ee){R}=14> (1)
<iedIA=144> (7)
<iedIyA=144> (1)
<iedee(A)=13> (13)
<iedee(A)=21> (1)
<iedee(A)=31> (7)
<iedee(A)z=13> (1)
<iedeeA=134> (23)
<iedeeA=214> (3)
<iedeeA=314> (35)

<iedeeAsh=124> (1)
<iedeeAz=134> (1)
<iedeeAz=314> (1)
<iedeeR=134> (1)
<iedeeyA=134> (5)
<iedeeyA=214> (1)
<iedeeyA=314> (16)
<iedee{R}=214> (1)
<iedi(A)r=21> (1)
<iedi(A)r=31> (8)
<iedi(A)z=31> (1)
<iedi(A){r}=13> (1)
<iedi(A){r}=31> (2)
<iediA=214> (1)
<iediA=314> (1)
<iedi{R}=314> (1)
<ied{ee}(A)=12> (1)
<ied{ee}(A)=13> (57)
<ied{ee}(A)=21> (12)
<ied{ee}(A)=31> (55)
<ied{ee}(A)z=13> (1)
<ied{ee}(A)z=31> (1)
<ied{ee}(A){r}=31> (1)
<ied{ee}(A){z}=13> (1)
<ied{ee}A=134> (12)
<ied{ee}A=214> (11)
<ied{ee}A=314> (55)
<ied{ee}A{z}=134> (1)
<ied{ee}{R}=314> (1)
<ie{t}(ee)I=14> (2)
<ie{t}eeA=134> (1)
<{ie}d(ee)A=14> (7)
<{ie}d(ee)I=14> (44)
<{ie}d(ee)Iz=14> (1)
<{ie}d(ee)R=14> (1)
<{ie}dIA=144> (17)
<{ie}dee(A)=13> (23)
<{ie}dee(A)=31> (2)
<{ie}dee(A)r=31> (1)
<{ie}dee(A)rz=13> (1)
<{ie}deeA=124> (1)
<{ie}deeA=134> (20)
<{ie}deeA=214> (5)
<{ie}deeA=314> (20)
<{ie}deeAz=134> (1)
<{ie}deeR=314> (2)
<{ie}deeyA=134> (7)
<{ie}deeyA=314> (21)
<{ie}deeyAz=314> (1)
<{ie}dee{R}=214> (1)
<{ie}di(A)r=13> (2)
<{ie}di(A)r=31> (6)
<{ie}di(A){r}=13> (1)
<{ie}di(A){r}=21> (1)
<{ie}di(A){r}=31> (2)
<{ie}dirz=31> (1)
<{ie}dye(A){r}=31> (1)
<{ie}d{ee}(A)=13> (19)
<{ie}d{ee}(A)=21> (1)

<{ie}d{ee}(A)=31> (28)
<{ie}d{ee}(A)r=31> (1)
<{ie}d{ee}(A){r}=31> (1)
<{ie}d{ee}A=134> (5)
<{ie}d{ee}A=214> (3)
<{ie}d{ee}A=314> (30)
<{ie}d{ee}Az=134> (1)
<{ie}d{ee}[R]=134> (1)
<{ie}d{ee}yA=314> (1)
<{ie}{t}IA=144> (1)
<{ie}{t}eeA=214> (1)
<{ie}{t}eeA=314> (1)

092.5 G how are you?

No Response (295)
A   are you feeling good? (2)
B   are you getting along nicely? (1)
C   are you in good health? (1)
D   did you sleep well? (1)
E   glad to see you (11)
F   good morning/evening (18)
G   good morning, ma'am/sir (1)
H   good to see you (again) (4)
I   got any complaints? (1)
J   hello (60)
K   hello there (11)
L   hey (19)
M   hey, boy (1)
N   hey, man (2)
O   hey, there (4)
P   hi (38)
Q   hi, neighbor (1)
R   hi, there (2)
S   hi, you old rascal (1)
T   how are y'all? (1)
U   how are you (today/this morning)? (259)
V   how are you coming on? (1)
W   how are you doing? (17)
X   how are you feeling (today/this morning)? (28)
Y   how are you getting (a)long? (12)
Z   how are you going? (1)
aa   how are you making out? (1)
ab   how do you do? (10)
ac   how do you feel (today/this morning)? (15)
ad   how do you feeling? (1)
ae   how have you been? (8)
af   how have you been doing? (4)
ag   how, hello there (1)
ah   how in the world are you getting along? (1)
ai   how in the world [X-0] you doing? (1)
aj   how is everybody out home? (1)
ak   how is things with you this morning? (1)
al   how is your health? (1)

am   how the hell are you? (1)
an   how [C-0] everybody? (1)
ao   how [C-0] y'all? (1)
ap   how [C-0] you (today/this morning)? (22)
aq   how [C-0] your health? (1)
ar   how [X-0] you be doing? (1)
as   how [X-0] you been? (8)
at   how [X-0] you been doing (lately)? (9)
au   how [X-0] you been feeling? (3)
av   how [X-0] you been getting (a)long? (5)
aw   how [X-0] you been making it? (1)
ax   how [X-0] you come[V-s] on? (1)
ay   how [X-0] you coming on? (1)
az   how [X-0] you do? (15)
ba   how [X-0] you doing (today/this morning)? (78)
bb   how [X-0] you doing here/there? (2)
bc   how [X-0] you doing, neighbor? (1)
bd   how [X-0] you feel (this morning)? (14)
be   how [X-0] you feeling (today/this morning)? (52)
bf   how [X-0] you getting (a)long? (33)
bg   how [X-0] you getting on? (1)
bh   how [X-0] you going (a)long? (2)
bi   how [X-0] you making it? (2)
bj   how [X-0] [M-0] do? (3)
bk   how [X-0] [M-0] doing? (1)
bl   how're you (this morning)? (8)
bm   how're you doing? (8)
bn   how're you feeling (today/this morning)? (11)
bo   how're you getting along? (2)
bp   how's everything going? (1)
bq   how's everything percolating down there? (1)
br   how's it going? (3)
bs   how's my boyfriend? (1)
bt   how's the world been treating you? (1)
bu   how's the world serving you? (1)
bv   how's things? (1)
bw   how's y'all's family? (1)
bx   how's you getting (a)long? (1)
by   how's your health? (3)
bz   how've you been? (5)
ca   how've you been doing? (1)
cb   howdy (16)

cc   howdy, Aunt/Uncle (1)
cd   howdy do? (8)
ce   howdy doody (2)
cf   I hope you're well (1)
cg   I'm mighty happy to see you (1)
ch   I'm (so) glad to see you (again) (7)
ci   I'm so proud to see you (1)
cj   I'm sure glad to see you looking well (1)
ck   it's mighty good to see you (1)
cl   long time, no see (2)
cm   long time, [M-0] haven't seen you (1)
cn   mighty proud to see you (1)
co   morning, neighbor (1)
cp   nice seeing you (1)
cq   nice to see you (1)
cr   not that I give a damn, but how [X-0] you feeling? (1)
cs   so happy to see you (2)
ct   what are you a-doing down here? (1)
cu   what [C-0] you (a)bout to do? (1)
cv   what [X-0] you been doing? (2)
cw   what [X-0] you been doing with yourself? (1)
cx   what [X-0] you doing? (1)
cy   what [X-0] you know? (2)
cz   what [X-0] [M-0] say? (1)
da   what's going on? (1)
db   what's happening? (6)
dc   where [X-0] you been? (1)
dd   [X-0] you doing all right? (1)
de   [X-0] you feeling all right? (1)
df   [X-0] you feeling good? (1)
dg   [X-0] [M-0] doing OK? (1)

092.6 G how do you do?

No Response (421)
A   certainly a pleasure meeting you (1)
B   comment ca va? [F] (1)
C   delighted to meet you (1)
D   glad I met you (2)
E   glad to be acquainted with you (1)
F   glad to (have) met you (3)
G   glad to have you here (1)
H   glad to know you (22)
I   glad to make your acquaintance (3)
J   glad to meet you (86)
K   glad to see you (6)
L   good afternoon/evening/morning (15)
M   good morning to you (1)
N   good to know you (1)

O good to meet you (4)
P good to see you (1)
Q happy to have met you (1)
R happy to know you (1)
S happy to meet you (5)
T hello (33)
U hello, brother (1)
V hello there (1)
W hello there, friend (1)
X hey, how [X-0] you doing? (2)
Y hi (13)
Z hi, there (1)
aa how are you? (73)
ab how are you coming on? (1)
ac how are you do[V-s]? (1)
ad how are you doing? (6)
ae how are you feeling (today?) (3)
af how are you today/this morning? (3)
ag how are you getting (a)long? (1)
ah how d(o) you do? (2)
ai how do you do? (112)
aj how d(o) [M-0] do? (1)
ak how do you feel? (3)
al how have you been? (1)
am how have you been doing? (1)
an how [C-0] you? (3)
ao how [X-0] you been? (1)
ap how [X-0] you been doing? (1)
aq how [X-0] you been getting along? (2)
ar how [X-0] you do? (26)
as how [X-0] you doing? (20)
at how [X-0] you feeling? (6)
au how [X-0] you getting (a)long? (5)
av how [X-0] you going (a)long? (1)
aw how [X-0] you making it? (1)
ax how [X-0] [M-0] do? (1)
ay howdy (8)
az howdy do? (11)
ba how're you today/this morning? (2)
bb how's it going? (2)
bc how's things going? (1)
bd how's your family? (1)
be I [C-0] please to meet you (1)
bf I'm awful glad to meet you (1)
bg I'm glad I met you (3)
bh I'm glad to know you (8)
bi I'm glad to meet you (16)
bj I'm glad to see you (2)
bk I'm glad to shake your hand (1)
bl I'm happy to know you (1)
bm I'm happy to meet you (2)
bn I'm honored to meet you (1)

bo I'm please to meet you (1)
bp I'm pleased to meet you (10)
bq I'm proud to meet you (4)
br I'm so glad to know you (1)
bs I'm so glad to meet you (3)
bt I'm sure glad to meet you (1)
bu I'm very glad to have met you (1)
bv I'm very glad to know you (2)
bw I'm very glad to meet you (1)
bx I'm very happy to meet you (2)
by it's a pleasure (1)
bz it's a pleasure to meet you (1)
ca it's been nice to know you (1)
cb it's good to know you (2)
cc it's good to meet you (1)
cd it's nice meeting you (3)
ce it's nice to meet you (3)
cf it's very nice to meet you (2)
cg mighty glad to meet you (2)
ch my compliment (1)
ci my pleasure (1)
cj nice meeting you (4)
ck nice to know you (3)
cl nice to make your acquaintance (1)
cm nice to meet you (28)
cn nice to see you (5)
co please to meet you (1)
cp pleased to meet you (30)
cq pleased to see you (1)
cr pleasure meeting you (1)
cs pleasure to meet you, (a) (3)
ct proud to meet you (1)
cu so glad to meet you (2)
cv so nice to have met you (1)
cw very glad to know you (2)
cx very glad to meet you (1)
cy what's happening? (5)

093.1 P again
{ai} lax onset
{e} inglide
{i} inglide
{y} devoiced
No Response (216)
<(A)g{e}n> (1)
<(A)g{i}n> (1)
<Again=41> (30)
<Agan=41> (6)
<Agee[n]=41> (1)
<Ageen=41> (19)
<Agen=41> (145)
<Agi[n]=41> (6)
<Agin=41> (136)
<Agyen=41> (1)
<Agy{i}n=41> (1)
<Ag{ai}n=41> (36)
<Ag{e}[n]=41> (2)
<Ag{e}n=41> (189)

<Ag{i}[n]=41> (2)
<Ag{i}n=41> (210)
<A{y}en=41> (1)
<Igen=41> (3)
<Igin=41> (2)
<Ig{i}n=41> (2)
<ugan=31> (1)

093.2 G Merry Christmas
No Response (112)
A Big Christmas (1)
B Christmas Aid (1)
C Christmas Cheer (2)
D Christmas Eve Gift (21)
E Christmas Gift (265)
F Christmas Gifts (1)
G Christmas Give (41)
H Christmas Gives (2)
I Christmas Greeting (5)
J Christmas Greetings (10)
K Christmas Kiss (1)
L Christmas Present (1)
M Christmas Treat (1)
N Feliz Navidad [S] (4)
O Good Christmas (5)
P Good Holiday (1)
Q Good Wishes (1)
R Happy Christmas (68)
S Happy Christmas Day (2)
T Happy Christmas Give (1)
U Happy Greeting (1)
V Happy Holiday (5)
W Happy Holidays (10)
X Happy, Merry Christmas (2)
Y Happy Noel (1)
Z Happy Yule (1)
aa Happy Yuletide (2)
ab Holiday Wishes (1)
ac Joyous Christmas (1)
ad Joyous Noel (1)
ae Merry Christmas (724)
af Merry Christmas Gift (1)
ag Nice Christmas (1)
ah Noel (1)
ai Season's Greetings (2)
aj Wonderful Christmas (2)

093.2 P merry
{ai} lax onset
{r} weakly retroflex
{t} flap
No Response (187)
<mAerI=414> (1)
<ma(r)I=14> (1)
<ma[r](I)> (2)
<mairI=14> (13)
<marI=14> (5)
<maree=13> (2)
<me(r)I=14> (11)
<me[r]I=14> (5)
<mer(I)> (5)

<merA=14> (4)
<merI=14> (552)
<meree=13> (9)
<merrI=14> (9)
<me{r}(I)> (4)
<me{r}I=14> (16)
<me{r}ee=13> (1)
<me{r}rI=14> (6)
<me{t}I=14> (1)
<mirI=14> (9)
<miree=13> (1)
<mi{r}I=14> (1)
<mu[r](I)> (1)
<mu[r]I=14> (1)
<murA=14> (1)
<murI=14> (44)
<muree=13> (1)
<murrI=14> (3)
<mu{r}(I)> (3)
<mu{r}I=14> (7)
<mu{r}rI=14> (11)
<m{ai}rI=14> (4)
<m{ai}{r}I=14> (1)

093.2 S merry

No Response (16)
|AJCmej| (1)
|DAAmea| (1)
|DAEmea| (2)
|DAI| (4)
|DAImea| (2)
|DCAmea| (2)
|DCAmpa| (1)
|DCBmej| (1)
|DCEmpa| (1)
|EABmpa| (1)
|GAImea| (1)
|GBCmaj| (1)
|GBE| (1)
|GBEmaj| (1)
|GBEmajmea| (1)
|GBIeaj| (1)
|GBImea| (2)
|GGA| (2)
|GGAmea| (1)
|GGC| (1)
|KAA| (13)
|KAAeaj| (1)
|KAAmaj| (4)
|KAAmea| (41)
|KAAmed| (1)
|KAAmfj| (1)
|KAAmpa| (1)
|KAB| (25)
|KABeaj| (1)
|KABmaa| (2)
|KABmaj| (6)
|KABmea| (15)
|KABmej| (2)
|KAC| (28)

|KACmaamea| (1)
|KACmea| (14)
|KACmej| (1)
|KAD| (2)
|KAE| (107)
|KAEeaa| (1)
|KAEmaj| (27)
|KAEmea| (188)
|KAEmej| (11)
|KAEmpa| (1)
|KAF| (12)
|KAFeaj| (1)
|KAFeajmea| (1)
|KAFgbjmea| (2)
|KAFmea| (37)
|KAFmej| (1)
|KAG| (4)
|KAGmaj| (2)
|KAGmea| (9)
|KAI| (8)
|KAImaj| (3)
|KAImea| (15)
|KBAmea| (9)
|KBB| (1)
|KBBmea| (4)
|KBE| (1)
|KBEmaj| (1)
|KBEmea| (6)
|KBFmea| (1)
|KCA| (18)
|KCAeaj| (1)
|KCAmaj| (4)
|KCAmea| (10)
|KCAmej| (4)
|KCB| (7)
|KCBmaj| (1)
|KCBmea| (8)
|KCBmej| (1)
|KCC| (10)
|KCCma2| (1)
|KCCmea| (9)
|KCCmpj| (1)
|KCE| (19)
|KCEeab| (1)
|KCEmaj| (6)
|KCEmajmea| (1)
|KCEmea| (20)
|KCEmej| (2)
|KCF| (1)
|KCFbbj| (1)
|KCFmea| (2)
|KCGmea| (1)
|KCI| (5)
|KCImaj| (1)
|KCImea| (6)
|KDB| (3)
|KDE| (3)
|KDEmna| (1)
|KEAmea| (1)

|KEE| (1)
|KFE| (1)
|KGA| (1)
|KGAeaj| (1)
|KGAmea| (6)
|KGB| (1)
|KGC| (1)
|KKBmda| (1)
|KKBmna| (1)
|KKC| (1)
|KKEmna| (1)
|KMA| (1)
|KME| (1)
|KMEmea| (1)
|KPA| (1)
|KQCmda| (1)
|LAA| (1)
|LAAmea| (2)
|LAD| (2)
|LADmea| (22)
|LAE| (1)
|LAHmea| (3)
|LCA| (2)
|LCAeaj| (1)
|LCAeak| (1)
|LDD| (1)
|LFAmej| (1)
|LFDmea| (1)
|MCA| (1)
|MEA| (19)
|MED| (3)
|MLA| (21)
|OAAmaj| (1)
|OAAmea| (1)
|OAB| (1)
|OABmea| (2)
|OCEmea| (1)

093.3 G Happy New Year

No Response (185)
A Bonne Annee [F] (1)
B Feliz Ano Nuevo [S] (1)
C Gross Neu Jahr [G] (1)
D Happy and Prosperous New Year (1)
E Happy New Year (610)
F Happy New Year's (87)
G Happy New Year's Day (2)
H Happy New Year's Eve (1)
I Merry New Year (2)
J Merry New Year's (2)
K New Year Gift (1)
L New Year's Eve Gift (4)
M New Year's Gift (53)
N New Year's Give (7)
O New Year's Greeting (5)
P Properous New Year (3)
Q Prosperous New Year's (1)

093.3 P New Year

{r} weakly retroflex

{z}   devoiced
{zh} devoiced
No Response (157)
<[n]yueyir=13> (1)
<nAyee[r]=41> (1)
<neeyi(r)=12> (1)
<neeyi[r]=12> (1)
<neeyir=13> (2)
<newye[r]=13> (3)
<newye[r]z=13> (1)
<newye[r]{z}=13> (1)
<newyee[r]=13> (1)
<newyeer=12> (1)
<newyeer=13> (2)
<newyer=13> (3)
<newyerz=13> (1)
<newyer{z}=13> (1)
<newye{r}=13> (2)
<newyi[r]=13> (82)
<newyi[r]=31> (1)
<newyi[r]dh=13> (1)
<newyi[r]z=13> (14)
<newyir=11> (4)
<newyir=12> (1)
<newyir=13> (115)
<newyir=21> (4)
<newyirz=11> (1)
<newyirz=13> (31)
<newyirz=31> (1)
<newyir{z}=13> (2)
<newyi{r}=11> (1)
<newyi{r}=13> (26)
<newyi{r}z=13> (5)
<newyi{r}{z}=13> (1)
<newyurz=13> (2)
<newyur{z}=13> (1)
<newyu{r}=13> (1)
<newyu{r}{zh}=13> (1)
<niy[R]=14> (1)
<niyir=13> (2)
<nooyeer=13> (1)
<nooyi[r]=12> (1)
<nooyi[r]=13> (1)
<nooyir=13> (2)
<nooyir=21> (1)
<nueyR=14> (1)
<nueye[r]=13> (5)
<nueyee[r]=12> (1)
<nueyee[r]=13> (1)
<nueyeer=13> (1)
<nueyer=13> (2)
<nueyerz=13> (2)
<nueyi(r)dh=13> (1)
<nueyi[r]=13> (68)
<nueyi[r]=21> (1)
<nueyi[r]=31> (2)
<nueyi[r]z=13> (5)
<nueyi[r]z=31> (1)
<nueyi[r]{z}=13> (6)

<nueyir=12> (2)
<nueyir=13> (102)
<nueyirz=13> (6)
<nueyir{zh}=13> (1)
<nueyir{z}=13> (4)
<nueyi{r}=12> (1)
<nueyi{r}=13> (22)
<nueyi{r}=31> (1)
<nueyi{r}z=13> (1)
<nueyi{r}{z}=13> (1)
<nueyurz=13> (1)
<nueyu{r}=13> (1)
<nyewye[r]=13> (1)
<nyewye[r]z=13> (1)
<nyewye{r}=13> (1)
<nyewye{r}z=13> (1)
<nyewyi[r]=13> (2)
<nyewyi[r]z=13> (1)
<nyewyir=13> (3)
<nyewyir=31> (1)
<nyewyirz=13> (2)
<nyewyirzh=13> (1)
<nyewyi{r}=13> (4)
<nyewyi{r}z=13> (1)
<nyuey[R]z=14> (1)
<nyueyarz=13> (1)
<nyueye[r]=13> (3)
<nyueyer=13> (3)
<nyueyerz=13> (2)
<nyueye{r}=13> (1)
<nyueye{r}z=13> (3)
<nyueyi(r)z=13> (2)
<nyueyi[r]=13> (41)
<nyueyi[r]=31> (1)
<nyueyi[r]z=13> (8)
<nyueyir=12> (6)
<nyueyir=13> (51)
<nyueyirz=13> (13)
<nyueyir{z}=13> (2)
<nyueyi{r}=13> (33)
<nyueyi{r}z=13> (6)
<nyueyi{r}{z}=13> (1)
<nyueyu[r]=13> (1)
<nyueyur=13> (1)
<nyueyurz=13> (1)
<nyuyirz=13> (1)
<yueyi{r}=13> (1)

093.4 P obliged

{b}   devoiced
{d}   devoided
{ie} monophthong/short glide
{j}   devoiced
{z}   devoiced
{zh} devoiced
No Response (494)
<(A)bliej(d)> (2)
<(A)bl{ie}j(d)> (1)
<(A)bl{ie}jd> (2)
<(A)b{ie}lzhd> (1)

<A(b)liejd=41> (1)
<Ab(1)iejd=41> (1)
<Ab(1)ie{j}{d}=41> (2)
<Ab(1){ie}j(d)=41> (1)
<Ablajt=41> (1)
<Ablee{d}sh(d)=41> (1)
<Ablie(j)d=41> (5)
<Ablie(jd)=41> (8)
<Abliecht=41> (2)
<Ablieg(d)=41> (1)
<Abliej(d)=41> (44)
<Abliejd=41> (62)
<Abliejt=41> (1)
<Abliej{d}=41> (24)
<Abliej{d}t=41> (1)
<Ablienzh(d)=41> (1)
<Abliez(d)=41> (1)
<Abliezh(d)=41> (3)
<Abliezh{d}=41> (1)
<Ablie{j}(d)=41> (18)
<Ablie{j}d=41> (1)
<Ablie{j}t=41> (1)
<Ablie{j}{d}=41> (29)
<Ablie{zh}(d)=41> (1)
<Ablie{zh}{d}=41> (1)
<Abl{ie}(j)d=41> (1)
<Abl{ie}(jd)=41> (1)
<Abl{ie}ch(d)=41> (2)
<Abl{ie}cht=41> (6)
<Abl{ie}j(d)=41> (38)
<Abl{ie}jd=41> (118)
<Abl{ie}j{d}=41> (12)
<Abl{ie}sh(d)=41> (1)
<Abl{ie}z(d)=41> (1)
<Abl{ie}zh(d)=41> (2)
<Abl{ie}zhd=41> (1)
<Abl{ie}{j}(d)=41> (3)
<Abl{ie}{j}t=41> (1)
<Abl{ie}{j}{d}=41> (2)
<Abl{ie}{zh}(d)=41> (2)
<Abl{ie}{z}(d)=41> (1)
<Abrie{j}{d}=41> (1)
<A{b}lie{j}(d)=41> (1)
<oblie(jd)=31> (1)
<obliej(d)=31> (1)
<oebliej(d)=31> (2)
<oebliej{d}=31> (2)
<oeblie{j}(d)=31> (1)
<oebl{ie}jd=31> (2)
<oobl{ie}{j}{d}=31> (1)
<ubliej{d}=31> (1)
<ubl{ie}{zh}(d)=31> (1)

094.1 G I think

No Response (104)
A   I assume (5)
B   I believe (262)
C   I believe so (3)
D   I calculate (1)
E   I daresay (1)

F   I don't believe (5)
G   I don't believe so (1)
H   I don't expect (3)
I   I don't guess (4)
J   I don't imagine (2)
K   I don't reckon (27)
L   I don't reckon so (1)
M   I don't suppose (3)
N   I don't think (12)
O   I doubt (1)
P   I expect (36)
Q   I expect so (2)
R   I figure(d) (15)
S   I gather (2)
T   I guess (460)
U   I guess not (2)
V   I guess so (19)
W   I imagine (139)
X   I imagine so (4)
Y   I presume (8)
Z   I reckon (357)
aa I reckon not (2)
ab I reckon so (6)
ac I suppose (79)
ad I suppose so (2)
ae I suspect (4)
af I think (434)
ag I think so (10)
ah I thinks (1)
ai I would imagine (3)
aj I would think (2)
ak I'd suppose (1)
al I'm believing (1)

094.2 L shopping
No Response (213)
A   dealing and wheeling (1)
B   going to market (2)
C   going to the store (1)
D   making groceries (2)
E   marketing (1)
F   shopping (659)
G   swapping (2)
H   trading (97)

094.3 P wrapped
{d}   devoiced
{o}   low-back
No Response (150)
<rap> (165)
<rap(t)> (1)
<rapd> (3)
<raps> (20)
<rapt> (544)
<rap{d}> (1)
<rep> (3)
<reps> (1)
<rept> (9)
<rop> (6)
<rop(t)> (1)
<rops> (1)

<ropt> (14)
<rowpt> (1)
<r{o}pt> (2)

094.4 P unwrapped
{aw}   lower low-back
No Response (292)
<Nrapt=41> (13)
<anrapt=13> (1)
<aw[n]rap=31> (1)
<awnrap=13> (1)
<awnrapt=13> (1)
<awnrapt=31> (2)
<hunrap=13> (1)
<oenrapt=13> (1)
<oenrapt=21> (1)
<onrap=13> (5)
<onrap=21> (1)
<onrap=31> (2)
<onrapt=13> (5)
<onrapt=31> (6)
<oonrapt=13> (1)
<oonrapt=31> (1)
<u[n]rapt=13> (1)
<unra(p)t=13> (1)
<unrap(t)=31> (1)
<unrap=12> (3)
<unrap=13> (85)
<unrap=21> (2)
<unrap=31> (64)
<unrapN=114> (1)
<unrapN=314> (1)
<unrapNG=314> (1)
<unraps=13> (1)
<unraps=31> (2)
<unrapt=12> (11)
<unrapt=13> (254)
<unrapt=21> (8)
<unrapt=31> (130)
<unrawpt=13> (1)
<unrep=31> (1)
<unrept=13> (1)
<unrop=13> (1)
<unrop=31> (1)
<unropt=13> (3)
<unropt=31> (3)
<unr{aw}pt=31> (1)
<unwap=13> (1)
<{aw}nrapt=13> (1)

094.5 P loss
{aw}   unrounded onset
{o}   low-back
No Response (394)
<laws> (405)
<lawsh> (1)
<lawst> (15)
<loes> (3)
<loesh> (1)
<los> (8)
<lost> (1)

<l{aw}s> (83)
<l{aw}st> (2)
<l{o}s> (2)

094.6 G cost
<!>   infinitive
<&>   present 3rd singular
<@>   present participle
<*>   preterit
<#>   past participle
No Response (275)
<!kaws(t)> (20)
<!kawsh(t)> (1)
<!kawsht> (1)
<!kawst> (47)
<!koest> (1)
<!kos(t)> (1)
<!kost> (1)
<&kaw(st)> (1)
<&kaws(t)> (488)
<&kaws(t)Is=14> (1)
<&kaws(t)Iz=14> (4)
<&kawsh(t)> (1)
<&kawsht> (1)
<&kawst> (40)
<&kawstIs=14> (2)
<&kawstIz=14> (10)
<&kawsts> (17)
<&kawth(t)> (1)
<&koes(t)> (7)
<&koesh(t)> (1)
<&kos(t)> (12)
<&kost> (3)
<@kawstN=14> (2)
<*kast> (1)
<*kaws(t)> (16)
<*kawst> (19)
<*kosht> (1)
<#kaws(t)> (2)
<#kawst> (2)

094.7 P due
No Response (271)
<dew> (315)
<due> (172)
<dyew> (41)
<dyue> (120)
<jue> (2)

094.8 P dues
{d}   devoiced
{dh} devoiced
{z}   devoiced
{zh} devoiced
No Response (287)
<dew(z)> (5)
<dewd> (1)
<dewdh> (1)
<dews> (2)
<dewz> (269)
<dew{dh}> (2)
<dew{zh}> (2)

<dew{z}> (41)
<duez> (135)
<duezh> (1)
<due{z}> (20)
<dyewz> (25)
<dyew{dh}> (1)
<dyew{z}> (2)
<dyuez> (115)
<dyue{z}> (7)
<jewz> (1)
<juez> (1)
<{d}ew{z}> (1)

095.1 P borrow
{aw}   unrounded onset
{b}   devoiced
{o}   low-back
{R}   weakly retroflex
{r}   weakly retroflex
{t}   flap
{v}   bilabial
No Response (176)
<baw(r)A=14> (1)
<baw(r)I=14> (1)
<baw[r](A)> (1)
<bawr(A)> (5)
<bawrA=14> (25)
<bawrAd=14> (1)
<bawrI=14> (21)
<bawrId=14> (1)
<bawree=13> (1)
<bawroe=13> (11)
<bawroed=13> (1)
<bawrrA=14> (1)
<bawrrI=14> (1)
<bawrroe=13> (1)
<bawr{R}=14> (1)
<baw{r}A=14> (1)
<bo(rA)> (1)
<bo[r](A)> (2)
<bo[r]I=14> (1)
<boe(r)I=14> (1)
<boer(A)> (1)
<boerA=14> (2)
<boerI=14> (2)
<boeroe=13> (2)
<bor(A)> (22)
<bor(A)d> (1)
<borA=14> (172)
<borAd=14> (4)
<borI=14> (136)
<borId=14> (5)
<borR=14> (1)
<boree=13> (7)
<boroe=13> (69)
<borrA=14> (27)
<borrI=14> (12)
<borroe=13> (6)
<boru=13> (1)
<borue=13> (1)

<boryI=14> (1)
<bo{r}(A)> (10)
<bo{r}A=14> (4)
<bo{r}Ad=14> (1)
<bo{r}I=14> (4)
<bo{r}rA=14> (8)
<bo{r}rI=14> (5)
<bo{t}A=14> (1)
<bo{t}oe=13> (1)
<burA=14> (1)
<b{aw}rA=14> (3)
<b{aw}roe=13> (3)
<b{o}(r)A=14> (1)
<b{o}[r](A)> (1)
<b{o}r(A)> (4)
<b{o}rA=14> (71)
<b{o}rI=14> (54)
<b{o}rId=14> (2)
<b{o}ree=13> (4)
<b{o}roe=13> (23)
<b{o}rrA=14> (7)
<b{o}rrI=14> (4)
<b{o}rree=13> (1)
<b{o}rroe=13> (1)
<b{o}{R}=14> (1)
<b{o}{r}(A)> (1)
<b{o}{r}I=14> (1)
<{b}or(A)> (1)
<{v}orA=14> (1)

095.2 P scarce
{a}   upglide
{ai}   lax onset
{r}   weakly retroflex
No Response (214)
<ska(r)s> (9)
<ska[r]s> (36)
<skai(r)s> (36)
<skai[r]s> (10)
<skairs> (7)
<skairz> (1)
<skai{r}s> (1)
<skars> (88)
<ska{r}As=14> (1)
<ska{r}s> (21)
<ske(r)s> (5)
<ske[r]s> (75)
<skers> (292)
<skersh> (4)
<skerth> (1)
<skerts> (1)
<ske{r}s> (54)
<ski(r)s> (1)
<ski[r]s> (6)
<skirs> (29)
<ski{r}s> (4)
<skurs> (2)
<skya[r]s> (1)
<skye[r]s> (1)
<skyers> (9)

<skyi[r]s> (1)
<skyirs> (4)
<skyi{r}s> (1)
<sk{ai}(r)s> (10)
<sk{ai}rs> (5)
<sk{ai}{r}s> (4)
<sk{a}(r)s> (3)

095.3 G dive
<!>   infinitive
<&>   present 3rd singular
<@>   present participle
<*>   preterit
<#>   past participle
No Response (178)
<!diev> (495)
<!dov> (4)
<&dievz> (27)
<@AdievN=414> (2)
<@dievN=14> (42)
<@dievNG=14> (14)
<@dovN=14> (1)
<*diebd> (1)
<*diev> (39)
<*dievd> (365)
<*dievt> (1)
<*div> (39)
<*divd> (2)
<*doe(v)> (1)
<*doev> (257)
<*dovd> (2)
<*dowvd> (1)
<*droev> (1)
<#die(v)d> (1)
<#diebd> (1)
<#diev> (15)
<#dievd> (281)
<#div> (24)
<#divd> (2)
<#divN=14> (17)
<#doev> (103)
<#doevd> (1)
<#doevN=14> (1)
<#dovd> (2)

095.4 L belly flop
No Response (369)
A   bang, a (1)
B   belly bath (1)
C   belly burst (3)
D   belly bust (42)
E   belly buster (406)
F   belly bustering (1)
G   belly busting (3)
H   belly dive (17)
I   belly diving (1)
J   belly flip (1)
K   belly flop (38)
L   belly flopper (4)
M   belly hit (1)
N   belly land (3)

O   belly landing (7)
P   belly loop (1)
Q   belly plop (1)
R   belly something (2)
S   belly splash (4)
T   belly splasher (2)
U   belly stroke (1)
V   belly washer (2)
W   belly whopper (12)
X   burst (2)
Y   bust (2)
Z   buster (5)
aa   busting the water (1)
ab   devil's dive (1)
ac   flop (1)
ad   pancake (2)
ae   skinning (1)
af   slap diving (1)
ag   splash, a (8)
ah   splashdown (1)
ai   splatter, a (1)
aj   stomach buster (2)

095.5 L somersault
No Response (223)
A   backwards somerset (1)
B   barrel roll (1)
C   canover (1)
D   cut a somerset (1)
E   cut somersaults (1)
F   double somersault (2)
G   double somerset (3)
H   flip (113)
I   flip over (1)
J   flip-flop (5)
K   flop-flip (1)
L   forward roll (2)
M   head over heels (2)
N   keel over (1)
O   loop-[D-0]-loop (1)
P   roll [n.] (4)
Q   roll [v.] (5)
R   roll over [n.] (2)
S   sloosh over [v.] (1)
T   somersault (415)
U   somersaulting (2)
V   somerset (200)
W   sumblesault (3)
X   sumbleset (5)
Y   tomersault (1)
Z   tumble (9)
aa   tumble over [v.] (2)
ab   tumbler up (1)
ac   tumblesault (33)
ad   tumbleset (58)
ae   tumbleset [v.] (1)
af   tumbling (6)
ag   tummy set (1)
ah   tummy up (1)
ai   turnover (1)

aj   wheelbarrow (2)

095.6 G swim
<!>   infinitive
<&>   present 3rd singular
<@>   present participle
<*>   preterit
<#>   past participle
No Response (166)
<!shwim> (5)
<!svim> (1)
<!swam> (5)
<!swem> (10)
<!swim> (590)
<!swi[m]> (1)
<!swum> (1)
<!twim> (1)
<&sweemz> (1)
<&swim> (1)
<&swimz> (12)
<@AswimN=414> (1)
<@swamN=14> (1)
<@sweemNG=14> (1)
<@swemN=14> (1)
<@swimN=14> (91)
<@swimNG=14> (14)
<*fwum> (1)
<*shwam> (1)
<*shwim> (1)
<*shwum> (1)
<*svam> (1)
<*swaim> (1)
<*swam> (399)
<*swamd> (5)
<*swa[m]> (2)
<*swem> (6)
<*swemd> (1)
<*swim> (45)
<*swimd> (27)
<*swom> (2)
<*swum> (90)
<*swumd> (2)
<*thwam> (1)
<#sfum> (1)
<#shwum> (2)
<#svam> (1)
<#swam> (147)
<#swamd> (5)
<#swa[m]> (1)
<#swem> (9)
<#swemd> (2)
<#swim> (39)
<#swimd> (43)
<#swi[m]> (1)
<#swom> (1)
<#swum> (222)
<#swumd> (2)
<#swu[m]> (2)

095.7 L lagniappe
No Response (531)

A   appreciation (9)
B   appreciation gift (3)
C   baker's dozen (1)
D   boneless (1)
E   bonus (97)
F   bonus gift (1)
G   boot (2)
H   countra (2)
I   courtesy gift (1)
J   extra bonus (1)
K   extra gift (1)
L   for free (1)
M   free gift (1)
N   free prize (1)
O   gift (69)
P   good-will gesture (1)
Q   gravy (1)
R   handout (4)
S   lagniappe (86)
T   leftover (1)
U   little appreciation, a (1)
V   little bit extra, a (1)
W   little bonus (1)
X   little donation (1)
Y   little extra (2)
Z   little extra bonus (1)
aa   little gift (9)
ab   little knock-off (1)
ac   little present (1)
ad   little something extra (1)
ae   little token (1)
af   little-old merchant gift (1)
ag   love gift (1)
ah   love-offering (1)
ai   on the house (3)
aj   patronage (1)
ak   pilon (18)
al   premium (10)
am   present (21)
an   prize (6)
ao   recompense (1)
ap   something extra (1)
aq   special gift (1)
ar   token (14)
as   token of appreciation (1)
at   token of good will (1)
au   treat (5)

096.1 G drown
<!>   infinitive
<&>   present 3rd singular
<@>   present participle
<*>   preterit
<#>   past participle
{d}   flap
No Response (190)
<!dran> (1)
<!drown> (398)
<!drownd> (63)
<!drowndId=14> (1)

<!drow[n]> (7)
<!frown> (1)
<&drown> (1)
<&drownz> (3)
<@AdrowndN=414> (1)
<@drownd> (1)
<@drowndN=14> (8)
<@drowndNG=14> (12)
<@drowning=13> (1)
<@drownN=14> (16)
<@drownNG=14> (13)
<@drown[NG]=14> (1)
<@grownNG=14> (1)
<*d(r)owndId=14> (1)
<*drand> (1)
<*drown> (103)
<*drownd> (307)
<*drowndI(d)=14> (1)
<*drowndId=14> (119)
<*drowndIt=14> (1)
<*drownId=14> (4)
<*drown{d}Id=14> (1)
<*drow[n]> (1)
<*dwown> (1)
<*frown> (1)
<*jowndId=14> (1)
<#AdrowndId=414> (1)
<#droend> (1)
<#drown> (70)
<#drownd> (263)
<#drowndI(d)=14> (1)
<#drowndId=14> (162)
<#drowndid=21> (1)
<#drowndN=14> (1)
<#drownId=14> (8)
<#drownnI(d)=14> (1)
<#drown{d}Id=14> (5)
<#drow[n]> (2)
<#drow[n]Id=14> (1)
<#dwowndId=14> (1)

096.2 L crawls

No Response (220)
A crawls (691)
B creeps (22)
C scoots (2)

096.3 G climb

<!> infinitive
<&> present 3rd singular
<@> present participle
<*> preterit
<#> past participle
{r} weakly retroflex
No Response (196)
<!kAliem=41> (1)
<!klam> (20)
<!klie(m)> (1)
<!kliem> (575)
<!kliemb> (2)
<!kliemd> (1)

<!kliengg> (1)
<!klie[m]> (3)
<!klom> (6)
<&klamz> (1)
<&kliemz> (14)
<&klomz> (1)
<@klamN=14> (3)
<@kliemN=14> (14)
<@kliemNG=14> (6)
<*kAliemd=41> (2)
<*klam> (19)
<*klamd> (11)
<*klemd> (1)
<*kliem> (35)
<*kliemb> (2)
<*kliembd> (5)
<*kliemd> (450)
<*kliemt> (1)
<*klim> (22)
<*kloem> (3)
<*klom> (2)
<*klomd> (6)
<*klowm> (1)
<*klum> (62)
<*klumd> (2)
<*kriem> (1)
<#klam> (13)
<#klamd> (8)
<#kliem> (19)
<#kliemb> (2)
<#kliembd> (2)
<#kliemd> (380)
<#klie[m]> (1)
<#klim> (12)
<#klimd> (1)
<#kloem> (1)
<#klom> (2)
<#klomd> (3)
<#klo{r}m> (1)
<#kluem> (1)
<#klum> (38)

096.4 L crouch

No Response (222)
A bend (5)
B bend down (14)
C bend over (7)
D clunch down (1)
E creep down (1)
F croop (1)
G crouch (69)
H crouch down (27)
I crump up (1)
J crumple (1)
K crunch (2)
L crunch down (2)
M crush up (1)
N cuddle up (1)
O dodge (1)
P dodge down (1)

Q down on his dewclaws (1)
R down on his haunches (5)
S down on his hunkers (6)
T draw up (2)
U duck (16)
V duck down (5)
W dunk (1)
X dunk down (1)
Y (es)condileto [S] (1)
Z get down (2)
aa get down on (his) all fours (2)
ab haunch down (1)
ac hide (24)
ad huddle up (1)
ae hump (1)
af hump down (1)
ag hump over (3)
ah hump up (2)
ai hunch (3)
aj hunch down (9)
ak hunk down (1)
al hunker (30)
am hunker around (4)
an hunker down (153)
ao hunker over (3)
ap hunker up (2)
aq hunker way over (1)
ar in a haunch (1)
as peeping down (1)
at scoot down (3)
au scootch (1)
av screech up (1)
aw scrinch down (2)
ax scrooch (4)
ay scrooch down (19)
az scrooch up (9)
ba scrouch (4)
bb scrouge down (2)
bc scrout down (1)
bd scrum up (1)
be scrunch (3)
bf scrunch down (7)
bg scrunch up (2)
bh set (2)
bi sit back on his haunches (1)
bj sit down on his hunkers (1)
bk sit on his haunches (3)
bl sit on his heels (1)
bm slumber over (1)
bn slump down (1)
bo squat (283)
bp squat down (204)
bq squat down on his feet (1)
br squat down on his haunches (1)
bs squat down on his hunkers (1)
bt squat on his heels (1)
bu squeech down (1)
bv squish down (1)
bw stoop (117)

bx   stoop down (51)
by   stoop over (16)

096.5 G kneel
<!>   infinitive
<&>   present 3rd singular
<@>   present participle
<*>   preterit
<#>   past participle
No Response (261)
<!neel> (127)
<!nee[l]> (8)
<!nil> (1)
<!nyee[l]> (1)
<&neelz> (18)
<&nee[l]z> (1)
<@neelN=14> (14)
<@neelNG=14> (8)
<*nailt> (1)
<*neel> (66)
<*neeld> (148)
<*neelt> (1)
<*nee[l]> (1)
<*nee[l]d> (8)
<*nel(t)> (10)
<*nelt> (283)
<*ne[l]t> (20)
<*nil> (1)
<*nild> (7)
<*nilt> (4)
<*nul> (1)
<*nyel(t)> (1)
<*nyelt> (2)
<*nye[l]t> (1)
<#neel> (1)
<#neeld> (1)
<#nelt> (2)

096.6-097.1 G lie
<!>   infinitive
<&>   present 3rd singular
<@>   present participle
<*>   preterit
<#>   past participle
No Response (261)
<!lai> (360)
<!le> (3)
<!lie> (373)
<!lo> (7)
<&lai> (1)
<&laiz> (16)
<&lie> (1)
<&liez> (2)
<@AlaiN=414> (3)
<@AlaiyN=414> (2)
<@laiN=14> (53)
<@laiNG=14> (2)
<@lain> (1)
<@laiyN=14> (9)
<@laiyNG=14> (1)
<@lieN=14> (2)

<@lieNG=14> (2)
<@lieyN=14> (7)
<@lieyNG=14> (1)
<@lo(NG)> (1)
<@loN=14> (1)
<*lai> (239)
<*laid> (217)
<*lait> (1)
<*lie> (7)
<*lied> (21)
<*lod> (2)
<#lai> (3)
<#laid> (2)
<#lain> (4)
<#lien> (1)

097.2 G dream
<!>   infinitive
<&>   present 3rd singular
<@>   present participle
<*>   preterit
<#>   past participle
No Response (235)
<!dreem> (483)
<!dreemz> (1)
<!dree[m]> (1)
<!dre[m]> (1)
<!drim> (2)
<&dreemz> (5)
<&greemz> (1)
<@AdreemN=414> (1)
<@dreemN=14> (34)
<@dreemNG=14> (6)
<@greemN=14> (1)
<*d(r)impt> (1)
<*draim> (2)
<*dreem> (32)
<*dreemd> (438)
<*dreemp> (1)
<*dreemt> (4)
<*drem> (1)
<*dremp> (51)
<*drempt> (36)
<*dremt> (7)
<*drimd> (5)
<*drimp> (21)
<*drimpt> (13)
<*drimt> (18)
<*treemd> (1)
<#dReem=41> (1)
<#dreem> (31)
<#dreemd> (272)
<#dreemt> (2)
<#drem> (2)
<#dremp> (25)
<#drempt> (36)
<#drempth> (1)
<#dremt> (9)
<#drimd> (2)
<#drimp> (14)

<#drimpt> (11)
<#drimt> (17)
<#drumd> (1)

097.3 G wake
<!>   infinitive
<&>   present 3rd singular
<@>   present participle
<*>   preterit
<#>   past participle
No Response (198)
<!Awaik=41> (23)
<!AwaikN=414> (10)
<!Awek=41> (4)
<!vaik> (1)
<!waig> (1)
<!waik> (429)
<!waikN=14> (7)
<!weg> (1)
<!wek> (27)
<&waiks> (5)
<&weks> (1)
<@waikN=14> (2)
<*aiwoek=31> (2)
<*Awaik=41> (2)
<*AwaikN=414> (1)
<*AwaikNd=414> (21)
<*Awaikt=41> (4)
<*Awawk=41> (1)
<*AwekNd=414> (2)
<*Awoek=41> (48)
<*Awuk=41> (1)
<*awwaikt=13> (1)
<*vaik> (1)
<*waik> (2)
<*waikd> (3)
<*waikN=14> (4)
<*waikNd=14> (2)
<*waikt> (73)
<*wawk> (6)
<*wawkN=14> (1)
<*wekt> (1)
<*woek> (488)
<*woekN=14> (2)
<*woekt> (2)
<*wook> (1)
<*wuek> (1)
<*wuk> (3)
<#AwaikNd=414> (3)
<#waikNd=14> (1)
<#woek> (8)

097.4 P stamp
{aw}   lower low-back
{o}   lower low-back
No Response (235)
<shtamp> (1)
<stamp> (34)
<stampN=14> (4)
<stampNG=14> (6)
<stamp[N]=14> (1)

<stampt> (16)
<staw[m]p> (1)
<stawm(p)t> (6)
<stawmp> (204)
<stawmpN=14> (57)
<stawmpNG=14> (9)
<stawmpd> (1)
<stawmps> (1)
<stawmpt> (72)
<sto[m](p)> (1)
<sto[m]pN=14> (1)
<stoemp> (8)
<stoempN=14> (5)
<stom(p)t> (1)
<stomp> (105)
<stompN=14> (31)
<stompNG=14> (12)
<stompd> (1)
<stomping=13> (3)
<stomps> (2)
<stompt> (46)
<stump> (4)
<stumpN=14> (1)
<stumpt> (4)
<st{aw}mp> (32)
<st{aw}mpN=14> (4)
<st{aw}mpt> (7)
<st{o}mp> (23)
<st{o}mpNG=14> (1)
<st{o}mpt> (7)

097.5 L (may I) take you home?

No Response (205)
A   accept your company (2)
B   accompany her/you (back) home (15)
C   assist you (in going home) (2)
D   be glad to carry you (2)
E   be your escort (1)
F   bring me/you (home) (6)
G   carry [=transport a person] (86)
H   carry [=transport a large animal/-object] (17)
I   carry [literal] (29)
J   carry(ing/ed) (her back home) (171)
K   carry her along (1)
L   carry her to [D-0] picture show (1)
M   carry me/your girl on home (2)
N   catch a ride (1)
O   come by (1)
P   come with you (2)
Q   do you need a lift? (1)
R   do you need a ride (home)? (4)
S   (do you) want a ride? (4)
T   drive you (home) (69)
U   drop you by your house (1)
V   drop you off (1)

W   escort(ing) her/you (home) (107)
X   fetch you home (1)
Y   get a lift (1)
Z   give him/you a ride (home) (49)
aa give me/you a lift or a ride (6)
ab give you a ride or a lift (1)
ac give you/them a lift (home) (61)
ad go along for a ride (1)
ae go (along) with you (15)
af go home with you (10)
ag haul(s) her/me/you (3)
ah have her/my/your company (3)
ai have the pleasure of accompanying you home (1)
aj have the pleasure of taking you home (1)
ak have the pleasure [P-0] escorting you home (1)
al help you home (1)
am how about walking you home? (1)
an if I wanted a lift or a ride (1)
ao if I wanted a ride home (1)
ap join you (2)
aq lift, a (2)
ar offer you a lift (1)
as offer you a ride home (2)
at pick her/him/you up (10)
au pick her up and take her to school (1)
av picked me up and carried me (1)
aw picked up someone (1)
ax ride, a (1)
ay ride (home) with me/you (2)
az ride with me/you (home) (6)
ba ride you a piece (1)
bb ride you (home) (15)
bc see her/you (back) home (82)
bd see you (safe) to the house (2)
be show you home (1)
bf take a walk with you (1)
bg take you for a ride (1)
bh take you in the car and carry you home (1)
bi take/took her/you (back home) (341)
bj walk her/them/you (back home) (118)
bk walk her to church (1)
bl walk(ing) home with her/you (17)
bm walk with me/them/you (home) (16)
bn walk you over there (1)
bo walk you to home (1)
bp walk you to the door (1)
bq walked home (1)

br walking along with you home (1)
bs would you accept my company home? (1)

097.6 P pull

{d}   devoiced
{oo} inglide
{p}   fricative
{u}   unrounded/high-back
No Response (63)
<poo(1)z> (1)
<poo[1]> (22)
<poo[1]N=14> (1)
<poo[1]d> (1)
<pool> (613)
<poolN=14> (6)
<poolNG=14> (2)
<poold> (20)
<poolz> (2)
<pool{d}> (2)
<poot> (1)
<pu[1]> (1)
<puel> (15)
<pueld> (1)
<puil> (5)
<pul> (12)
<p{oo}[1]> (8)
<p{oo}l> (191)
<p{oo}lN=14> (1)
<p{oo}ld> (6)
<p{u}[1]> (3)
<p{u}l> (7)
<p{u}lz> (1)
<{p}ool> (1)

097.6 S pull

No Response (3)
|BJA| (1)
|BJCmaj| (1)
|CJH| (1)
|EAA| (2)
|EAC| (1)
|ECA| (2)
|ECAmaa| (1)
|ECAmaj| (1)
|EFA| (36)
|EFAbjj| (1)
|EFAcba| (1)
|EFAmaj| (6)
|EFB| (11)
|EFBmaj| (3)
|EFC| (5)
|EFCmaj| (2)
|EFD| (3)
|EFE| (5)
|EFF| (2)
|EFG| (2)
|EFH| (1)
|EFI| (4)
|EMA| (12)

|EMAmaa| (2)
|EMAmaj| (1)
|EMB| (2)
|EMBmaj| (1)
|EMBmajcba| (1)
|EMC| (5)
|EMCmaj| (2)
|EMCmajcba| (1)
|EME| (1)
|EMI| (3)
|EMImaj| (1)
|EXAmdjcha| (1)
|FAA| (6)
|FAAmaj| (1)
|FAC| (3)
|FAD| (9)
|FADmaj| (3)
|FAH| (6)
|FAHcbj| (1)
|FCA| (4)
|FCC| (1)
|FCDcbj| (1)
|FCDmaj| (1)
|FCHmaj| (1)
|FCImaj| (1)
|FFA| (49)
|FFAefj| (2)
|FFAfaj| (2)
|FFAmaa| (1)
|FFAmaj| (1)
|FFB| (27)
|FFBcba| (2)
|FFBmaa| (1)
|FFBmaj| (5)
|FFC| (18)
|FFD| (272)
|FFDbjj| (3)
|FFDcba| (7)
|FFDcbj| (4)
|FFDfaj| (1)
|FFDmaj| (91)
|FFDmak| (1)
|FFDmas| (1)
|FFF| (58)
|FFFmaj| (14)
|FFG| (3)
|FFGcba| (1)
|FFGmaj| (1)
|FFH| (37)
|FFHmaj| (8)
|FFI| (2)
|FKD| (1)
|FMA| (21)
|FMAmaj| (1)
|FMAmajcba| (1)
|FMB| (6)
|FMBcba| (1)
|FMBmaj| (4)
|FMBmajcba| (2)

|FMC| (3)
|FMD| (28)
|FMDcba| (1)
|FMDcbj| (4)
|FMDmaj| (40)
|FMF| (4)
|FMFcba| (1)
|FMFmaj| (5)
|FMH| (1)
|FMHmaj| (4)
|FMI| (1)
|FSA| (1)
|MCB| (1)
|NAAfaj| (1)
|NAB| (1)
|NABefj| (1)
|NAE| (1)
|NFAfaj| (1)

097.7 P push

{oo}   inglide
{p}   fricative
{u}   unrounded
No Response (122)
<pish> (3)
<pishIzh=14> (1)
<poorsh> (1)
<poosh> (518)
<pooshIz=14> (3)
<pooshN=14> (14)
<pooshNG=14> (4)
<poosht> (21)
<puesh> (25)
<puesht> (1)
<puish> (69)
<puisht> (1)
<push> (10)
<p{oo}s> (1)
<p{oo}sh> (161)
<p{oo}shIz=14> (1)
<p{oo}sht> (1)
<p{u}sh> (2)
<{p}oosh> (3)

097.7 S push

No Response (0)
|BJCmaj| (1)
|BSC| (1)
|CJB| (1)
|DFE| (1)
|EAA| (3)
|EACmaj| (1)
|EAD| (1)
|ECA| (3)
|ECAmaj| (1)
|ECD| (1)
|EFA| (28)
|EFAeaj| (2)
|EFAmaj| (6)
|EFAmak| (3)
|EFB| (24)

|EFBeaj| (4)
|EFBmaj| (8)
|EFBmam| (1)
|EFBmbk| (1)
|EFC| (5)
|EFCeaj| (3)
|EFCefb| (1)
|EFCffa| (1)
|EFCmaj| (1)
|EFD| (4)
|EFE| (2)
|EFEmaj| (1)
|EFFeaj| (1)
|EFG| (3)
|EFGefk| (1)
|EFGmaj| (1)
|EFH| (2)
|EFIeaj| (1)
|EJH| (1)
|EMA| (14)
|EMAmaj| (8)
|EMAmak| (1)
|EMB| (4)
|EMC| (1)
|EMCeaj| (1)
|EMCmaj| (1)
|EMD| (3)
|FAA| (2)
|FAC| (2)
|FAD| (16)
|FADeaj| (1)
|FADmaj| (2)
|FAH| (1)
|FCA| (2)
|FCC| (1)
|FCD| (2)
|FFA| (31)
|FFAeaj| (3)
|FFAkaj| (2)
|FFAmaj| (1)
|FFAqfj| (1)
|FFB| (26)
|FFBcjj| (1)
|FFBeaj| (4)
|FFBmaa| (1)
|FFBmaj| (4)
|FFBmak| (4)
|FFC| (12)
|FFCeaj| (1)
|FFCffd| (1)
|FFCmaj| (2)
|FFCmej| (1)
|FFD| (240)
|FFDbjj| (2)
|FFDcjm| (2)
|FFDeaj| (14)
|FFDeal| (2)
|FFDefj| (1)
|FFDmaj| (52)

|FFDmak| (6)
|FFF| (99)
|FFFbjj| (2)
|FFFcjm| (2)
|FFFeaj| (7)
|FFFefj| (1)
|FFFmaj| (28)
|FFFmak| (3)
|FFG| (3)
|FFGbjj| (1)
|FFGmaj| (3)
|FFGmak| (1)
|FFH| (11)
|FFHeal| (1)
|FFHmaj| (3)
|FFI| (1)
|FFIffk| (1)
|FMA| (40)
|FMAeaj| (3)
|FMAmaj| (3)
|FMB| (16)
|FMBeaj| (1)
|FMBmaj| (2)
|FMBmak| (1)
|FMD| (24)
|FMDefj| (1)
|FMDfaj| (1)
|FMDmaj| (19)
|FMDmak| (4)
|FMF| (17)
|FMFbjj| (1)
|FMFeaj| (2)
|FMFeal| (1)
|FMFmaj| (3)
|FMFmak| (1)
|FMH| (1)
|HCA| (1)
|LAB| (1)
|LACeaj| (1)
|LACefj| (1)
|LAEmaj| (1)
|LFGmaj| (1)
|NAAean| (1)
|NAB| (1)
|NABeaj| (1)
|NABkaj| (1)
|NFB| (1)

098.1 L lug
No Response (200)
A   bring (3)
B   carry (227)
C   fetch (1)
D   haul (16)
E   hoist (1)
F   lag (1)
G   lug (157)
H   pack (83)
I   shoulder (3)
J   tote (518)

K   tug (3)
L   wag (4)
M   waggle (1)

098.2 P touch
{e}   inglide
{oo}   unrounded
{r}   weakly retroflex
{u}   inglide
No Response (263)
<tech> (27)
<techN=14> (1)
<toch> (4)
<tooch> (3)
<tuch> (510)
<tuchIz=14> (1)
<turch> (1)
<tush> (2)
<tu{r}ch> (1)
<t{e}ch> (2)
<t{oo}ch> (25)
<t{u}ch> (90)

098.3 L (go) bring
No Response (284)
A   bring (199)
B   fetch (57)
C   get (135)
D   go and bring (14)
E   go and fetch (1)
F   go and get (18)
G   go bring (91)
H   go fetch (20)
I   go find (7)
J   go get (233)
K   go to fetch (1)
L   go to get (1)
M   run and get (4)
N   run bring (2)
O   run fetch (1)
P   run get (8)

098.4 L goal [children's games]
No Response (375)
A   base (345)
B   dare base (1)
C   free base (1)
D   goal (57)
E   home (91)
F   home base (112)
G   home free (6)
H   home place (1)
I   home plate (8)
J   home-plate tree (1)
K   home tree (1)
L   pigpen (1)
M   pole (1)
N   post (3)
O   safe (place) (2)
P   safety (1)
Q   station (2)

098.5 G catch

<!>   infinitive
<&>   present 3rd singular
<@>   present participle
<*>   preterit
<#>   past participle
No Response (67)
<!kach> (149)
<!kes> (1)
<!kesh> (2)
<!ked> (1)
<!kets> (3)
<!kech> (673)
<!kechIz=14> (2)
<!kits> (1)
<!kich> (23)
<!krech> (1)
<!kuch> (4)
<!kyach> (1)
<!kyesh> (1)
<!kyech> (2)
<&kachIz=14> (3)
<&kechIz=14> (16)
<@AkechN=414> (1)
<@kech> (1)
<@kechId=14> (1)
<@kechN=14> (20)
<@kechNG=14> (1)
<@kichN=14> (1)
<*kaw(t)> (2)
<*kawd> (2)
<*kawt> (658)
<*kech> (7)
<*kechd> (1)
<*kecht> (10)
<*kicht> (2)
<*koet> (6)
<*koech> (1)
<*kot> (33)
<*koch> (2)
<*kocht> (1)
<*kuch> (1)
<#kaw(t)> (1)
<#kawd> (1)
<#kawt> (528)
<#kech> (2)
<#kecht> (5)
<#koet> (4)
<#kot> (25)
<#kocht> (1)

099.1 G (wait) for
No Response (257)
A   for (509)
B   on (154)

099.2 P chance
{a}   upglide
{ai}   lax onset
No Response (178)
<cha[n](s)> (1)
<cha[n]ts> (2)

<chain(s)> (1)
<chainch> (2)
<chains> (6)
<chaints> (41)
<chan(s)> (2)
<chanch> (8)
<chans> (56)
<chansh> (3)
<chanst> (1)
<chant(s)> (1)
<chants> (428)
<chantsIz=14> (2)
<chanz> (1)
<cheens> (1)
<chench> (1)
<chens> (3)
<chenth> (1)
<chents> (31)
<chints> (1)
<chonts> (1)
<chonz> (1)
<ch{ai}[n]s> (1)
<ch{ai}ns> (2)
<ch{ai}nts> (17)
<ch{a}[n](s)> (1)
<ch{a}[n]ts> (1)
<ch{a}nch> (4)
<ch{a}ns> (23)
<ch{a}nst> (3)
<ch{a}nts> (122)
<shants> (2)

099.3 P humor
{h}   weakly realized
{R}   weakly retroflex
No Response (298)
<(h)ewmR=14> (2)
<(h)ewm[R]=14> (3)
<(h)juemR=14> (1)
<(h)yewmR=14> (13)
<(h)yewm[R]=14> (11)
<(h)yewm{R}=14> (7)
<(h)yoomR=14> (3)
<(h)yoom[R]=14> (3)
<(h)yoom[R]t=14> (1)
<(h)yoom{R}=14> (1)
<(h)yue[m]bR=14> (1)
<(h)yuemR=14> (107)
<(h)yuem[R]=14> (118)
<(h)yuem{R}=14> (34)
<h(y)uemR=14> (2)
<h(y)uem[R]=14> (1)
<hewmR=14> (26)
<hewm[R]=14> (16)
<hewm{R}=14> (4)
<hyewmR=14> (7)
<hyewm[R]=14> (5)
<hyewm{R}=14> (8)
<hyoo[m]R=14> (1)
<hyoomR=14> (7)

<hyoom[R]=14> (4)
<hyue[m][R]=14> (1)
<hyuemR=14> (113)
<hyuem[R]=14> (77)
<hyuem[R]d=14> (1)
<hyuem[R]z=14> (1)
<hyuemaw(r)=13> (1)
<hyuem{R}=14> (43)
<newm[R]=14> (1)
<nyewm[R]=14> (1)
<nyuem[R]=14> (1)
<{h}yuemR=14> (6)
<{h}yuem[R]=14> (3)
<{h}yuem{R}=14> (1)

099.4 G get rid of
No Response (224)
A   get rid of (633)
B   get shed of (5)
C   get shut of (134)
D   get through with (1)
E   make way with (1)

100.1 G acted as if
No Response (561)
A   acted (13)
B   acted as (1)
C   acted as if (26)
D   acted as though (5)
E   acted like (139)
F   acted [J-0] if (3)
G   as if (3)
H   came off (1)
I   claims to (1)
J   faked like (1)
K   let on (2)
L   let on like (4)
M   like (2)
N   likes like (1)
O   looked like (2)
P   made as if (2)
Q   made believe (2)
R   made like (15)
S   made on like (1)
T   made out (11)
U   made out like (71)
V   made out [J-0] (2)
W   played like (8)
X   pretended (42)
Y   pretended like (3)
Z   put on (1)
aa   seem[V-r] like (1)
ab   talked like (3)
ac   thinks/thought (60)
ad   would make like (1)

100.2 L swiped
No Response (366)
A   absconded (2)
B   borrowed (7)
C   carried off (1)
D   copped (5)

E   filched (4)
F   glommed on (1)
G   got (65)
H   grabbed (1)
I   heisted (2)
J   hocked (1)
K   hooked (13)
L   latched onto (2)
M   lifted (11)
N   made off with (1)
O   nabbed (1)
P   nixed (1)
Q   picked up (12)
R   pilfered (2)
S   pinched (3)
T   purloined (1)
U   ran off with (1)
V   relieved of (1)
W   ripped off (41)
X   rogued (1)
Y   rooked (1)
Z   slipped (1)
aa   snatched (10)
ab   sniped (1)
ac   snitched (57)
ad   snooked (1)
ae   snuck (1)
af   stole (345)
ag   stoled (62)
ah   swiped (152)
ai   taked (2)
aj   takened (1)
ak   thieved (1)
al   took (151)
am   walked off with (1)

100.3 L remember
No Response (220)
A   call (2)
B   recall (17)
C   recollect (24)
D   remember (621)
E   (re)member (99)
F   think of (3)

100.4 L (I) don't remember
No Response (127)
A   can't bring it out (1)
B   can't bring it to mind (2)
C   can't call (105)
D   can't recall (57)
E   can't recollect (4)
F   can't remember (206)
G   can't (re)member (8)
H   can't say (1)
I   can't tell (2)
J   can't think (of) (13)
K   disremember (15)
L   don't disremember (1)
M   don't get (1)
N   don't have any recollection (1)

    O   don't recall (50)
    P   don't (re)call (2)
    Q   don't recollect (17)
    R   don't remember (492)
    S   don't (re)member (45)
    T   don't think of (1)
    U   forget (124)
    V   let it slip my mind (2)
    W   never remember (1)
    X   wouldn't remember (1)

100.5 G write

    <!>   infinitive
    <&>   present 3rd singular
    <@>   present participle
    <*>   preterit
    <#>   past participle
    {t}   flap
    {?}   glottal
    No Response (96)
    <!rie(t)> (4)
    <!riet> (701)
    <!ro(t)> (1)
    <!rod> (1)
    <!rot> (10)
    <&riets> (6)
    <@rietN=14> (12)
    <@rietNG=14> (11)
    <@rie{t}NG=14> (1)
    <*rid> (1)
    <*riet> (2)
    <*rit> (9)
    <*ritN=14> (13)
    <*ri{?}N=14> (1)
    <*roet> (644)
    <#reetN=14> (2)
    <#ridN=14> (3)
    <#riet> (1)
    <#rit> (3)
    <#ritN=14> (371)
    <#ri{?}N=14> (1)
    <#ri{t}N=14> (4)
    <#roe(t)> (1)
    <#roet> (169)
    <#roetN=14> (3)
    <#{t}oet> (1)

100.5 S write

    No Response (0)
    |PAHeaa| (1)
    |PCAeaa| (2)
    |PCAeaj| (2)
    |RAA| (2)
    |RAAeaa| (16)
    |RAAeab| (1)
    |RAAead| (2)
    |RAAeaj| (24)
    |RAAeak| (1)
    |RAAkaj| (5)
    |RAB| (7)
    |RABdaa| (1)

|RABdab| (1)
|RABeaa| (6)
|RABeaj| (66)
|RABkaj| (11)
|RACeaj| (1)
|RADeaa| (1)
|RAE| (3)
|RAEdaa| (2)
|RAEeaa| (36)
|RAEeab| (4)
|RAEeac| (1)
|RAEead| (1)
|RAEeaj| (178)
|RAEeak| (5)
|RAEeal| (5)
|RAEeaq| (1)
|RAEkab| (1)
|RAEkaj| (30)
|RAEkak| (7)
|RAEkal| (1)
|RAEkan| (1)
|RAEmaj| (4)
|RAEmak| (1)
|RAFeaj| (1)
|RAG| (23)
|RAGbbj| (1)
|RAGeaa| (14)
|RAGeaj| (78)
|RAGeak| (9)
|RAGeal| (1)
|RAGkaj| (1)
|RAGkak| (1)
|RAGmaj| (1)
|RAGmam| (1)
|RCA| (17)
|RCAbbj| (1)
|RCAdaj| (2)
|RCAeaa| (21)
|RCAeab| (2)
|RCAeaf| (1)
|RCAeaj| (63)
|RCAeal| (1)
|RCAeam| (1)
|RCAeas| (1)
|RCAkaj| (16)
|RCAkak| (1)
|RCAkan| (1)
|RCAkap| (1)
|RCAmaj| (8)
|RCAmak| (1)
|RCB| (3)
|RCBeaa| (5)
|RCBeaj| (17)
|RCBkaj| (1)
|RCBmak| (1)
|RCE| (14)
|RCEeaa| (23)
|RCEeab| (2)
|RCEeac| (1)

|RCEead| (1)
|RCEeaj| (50)
|RCEeak| (1)
|RCEeal| (2)
|RCEkaj| (39)
|RCEkak| (2)
|RCEkan| (1)
|RCEmaj| (1)
|RCEmak| (1)
|RCG| (1)
|RCGdaj| (2)
|RCGeaa| (6)
|RCGeaj| (23)
|RCGmaj| (1)
|RGAeaa| (1)
|RKAmdj| (1)
|RKEedj| (1)
|SABeaj| (1)
|SCAdaj| (1)
|SCDeaj| (8)
|SCEeaa| (1)
|SKAedj| (1)
|SKDmdj| (1)

100.6 P answer

    {a}   upglide
    {ai}   lax onset
    {R}   weakly retroflex
    {r}   weakly retroflex
    {t}   flap
    {z}   devoiced
    No Response (195)
    <a[n]sR=14> (2)
    <a[n]s[R]=14> (9)
    <a[n]s{R}=14> (1)
    <a[n]ts[R]=14> (1)
    <ai[n]stR=14> (1)
    <ainsR=14> (2)
    <ainsR{z}=14> (1)
    <ains[R]=14> (1)
    <aintsR=14> (5)
    <aintsRd=14> (1)
    <aints[R]=14> (2)
    <aints{R}=14> (1)
    <ansR=14> (155)
    <ansRN=144> (2)
    <ansRd=14> (2)
    <ans[R]=14> (113)
    <ans[R]d=14> (3)
    <ans[R]z=14> (3)
    <anstR=14> (10)
    <anst[R]=14> (1)
    <ansur=13> (1)
    <ansu{r}=13> (1)
    <ans{R}=14> (48)
    <ans{R}d=14> (1)
    <ans{R}{z}=14> (1)
    <anth[R]=14> (1)
    <ants(R)N=14> (2)
    <antsR=14> (148)

<antsR{z}=14> (2)
<ants[R]=14> (84)
<ants[R]d=14> (1)
<ants[R]z=14> (2)
<antsrA=14> (1)
<ants{R}=14> (26)
<an{t}s[R]=14> (1)
<an{z}R=14> (1)
<e[n]sR=14> (1)
<ensR=14> (2)
<ens[R]=14> (5)
<entsR=14> (7)
<ents[R]=14> (1)
<onsR=14> (1)
<ons[R]=14> (1)
<ons{R}d=14> (1)
<{ai}nsR=14> (2)
<{ai}ntsR=14> (1)
<{a}[n]s[R]=14> (1)
<{a}nsR=14> (26)
<{a}nsRd=14> (1)
<{a}ns[R]=14> (18)
<{a}ns[R]z=14> (2)
<{a}ns{R}=14> (14)
<{a}ntsR=14> (11)
<{a}nts[R]=14> (12)
<{a}nts{R}=14> (12)
<{a}nts{R}z=14> (1)

100.7 P address [v.]
{ai}   lax onset
No Response (301)
<(a)dres> (3)
<(a)dresN=14> (1)
<(a)dris> (1)
<Addres=41> (1)
<Adres=41> (241)
<AdresN=414> (8)
<AdresNG=414> (2)
<Adresh=41> (1)
<AdressNG=414> (1)
<Adrest=41> (6)
<Adris=41> (6)
<Adrus=41> (2)
<Adr{ai}s=41> (21)
<Ajres=41> (2)
<Idres=41> (6)
<addres=13> (17)
<addres=31> (5)
<addrest=13> (1)
<addrith=13> (1)
<addr{ai}s=13> (1)
<addr{ai}s=21> (1)
<adres=12> (5)
<adres=13> (139)
<adres=21> (8)
<adres=31> (73)
<adresN=134> (2)
<adresN=314> (4)
<adresNG=314> (2)

<adrest=13> (1)
<adrest=21> (1)
<adrest=31> (2)
<adris=13> (3)
<adris=31> (1)
<adrith=31> (1)
<adr{ai}s=13> (2)
<adr{ai}s=31> (5)
<ajres=13> (3)
<eddres=31> (2)
<eddr{ai}s=31> (1)
<edres=13> (2)
<edres=31> (20)
<edrest=31> (1)
<odres=31> (6)
<udras=31> (1)
<udres=11> (1)
<udres=31> (8)
<udr{ai}s=13> (1)
<ujres=31> (1)

100.8 P address [n.]
{ai}   lax onset
No Response (245)
<(A)dres> (3)
<Adrais=41> (1)
<Adras=41> (2)
<Adre(s)=41> (1)
<Adres=41> (170)
<AdresIz=414> (2)
<Adreth=41> (1)
<Adris=41> (3)
<Adr{ai}s=41> (19)
<Ajres=41> (1)
<Iddr{ai}s=41> (1)
<Idres=41> (7)
<Idrith=41> (1)
<Idr{ai}s=41> (1)
<addres=11> (1)
<addres=13> (33)
<addres=31> (4)
<addrith=13> (1)
<addr{ai}s=13> (15)
<adrAs=14> (1)
<adrIs=14> (1)
<adraith=13> (1)
<adre(s)=13> (4)
<adres=12> (1)
<adres=13> (321)
<adres=21> (9)
<adres=31> (35)
<adris=13> (7)
<adris=31> (1)
<adrish=13> (1)
<adr{ai}s=13> (22)
<adr{ai}s=31> (5)
<ajres=13> (3)
<eddres=13> (1)
<eddres=31> (1)
<edres=13> (3)

<edres=31> (9)
<odres=31> (1)
<udres=31> (4)
<udr{ai}s=31> (1)

101.1 G teach/learn
<!>   infinitive
<&>   present 3rd singular
<@>   present participle
<*>   preterit
<#>   past participle
{r}   weakly retroflex
{?}   glottal
No Response (193)
<!larn> (1)
<!lorn> (1)
<!lurn> (16)
<!lu[r]n> (15)
<!lu{r}n> (9)
<!tawk> (1)
<!teech> (16)
<&lurnz> (1)
<&teechIz=14> (1)
<@lurnN=14> (1)
<@lu[r]nN=14> (3)
<@lu{r}nN=14> (1)
<*lurn> (5)
<*lurnd> (35)
<*lurnt> (42)
<*lu[r]n> (8)
<*lu[r]nd> (17)
<*lu[r]nt> (41)
<*lu{r}n> (3)
<*lu{r}nd> (11)
<*lu{r}nt> (3)
<*taw(t)> (3)
<*tawt> (529)
<*taw{?}> (1)
<*teech> (4)
<*teecht> (6)
<*toet> (4)
<*tot> (22)
<*tut> (1)
<#lurnd> (4)
<#lurnt> (5)
<#lu[r]n> (2)
<#lu{r}nt> (1)
<#tawt> (42)
<#teech> (1)
<#teecht> (1)

101.2 L intending to
No Response (416)
A   about to (5)
B   (a)bout to (2)
C   aiming on (3)
D   aiming to (71)
E   arranging to (1)
F   expecting to (16)
G   (e)xpecting to (2)
H   figuring on (5)

I   fixing to (285)
J   fixing up to (1)
K   getting all ready to (1)
L   getting ready to (92)
M   going to (37)
N   gwine to (1)
O   hoping to (8)
P   intending to (50)
Q   (in)tending to (1)
R   looking to (1)
S   meaning to (9)
T   planning on (25)
U   planning to (143)
V   preparing to (10)
W   ready to (8)
X   threatening to (1)

101.3 L tattletale

No Response (291)
A   backbiter (1)
B   big mouth (1)
C   blabbermouth (4)
D   blabbermouth gabber (1)
E   blat (1)
F   bong toter (1)
G   brownnoser (1)
H   busy bee (1)
I   busy mouth (1)
J   busybody (6)
K   carrier of tales (1)
L   crybaby (1)
M   fibber (3)
N   fink (2)
O   fuss maker (1)
P   gabber (1)
Q   gossip (105)
R   gossip box (1)
S   gossip lady (1)
T   gossip people (1)
U   gossiper (29)
V   gossipy kind (1)
W   gossipy old lady (1)
X   hot breath (1)
Y   informer (1)
Z   liar (8)
aa   meddler (3)
ab   meddlesome butt (1)
ac   mess maker (1)
ad   moocher (1)
ae   news carrier (1)
af   news dispatcher (1)
ag   news toter (1)
ah   newspaper (1)
ai   noser (1)
aj   nosy [n.] (2)
ak   nuisance (1)
al   peacebreaker (3)
am   PI [=pimp] (1)
an   pigeon (1)
ao   pimp (21)

ap   rat (1)
aq   rat fink (2)
ar   shit (1)
as   sissy (1)
at   smart [n.] (1)
au   smart aleck (1)
av   sneak (1)
aw   snitch (13)
ax   snitcher (9)
ay   snooper (1)
az   squealer (6)
ba   stool pigeon (14)
bb   stoolie (1)
bc   storyteller (5)
bd   tale carrier (1)
be   tale-teller (4)
bf   tale-tolder (1)
bg   talebear(er) (5)
bh   taletattler (3)
bi   tattle [n.] (1)
bj   tattle box (5)
bk   tattle butt (1)
bl   tattle tattler (1)
bm   tattler (102)
bn   tattletale (508)
bo   tattletale lady (1)
bp   tattletale tit (1)
bq   tattletaler (4)
br   tattling child (1)
bs   tattly box (1)
bt   telephone gossiper (2)
bu   teller (1)
bv   telltale (2)
bw   tongue tattler (1)
bx   two-face (1)
by   Uncle Tom (1)
bz   wagtail (1)
ca   white mouth (1)
cb   windjammer (1)

101.4 L pick (flowers)

No Response (362)
A   break (12)
B   break off (1)
C   clip (6)
D   collect (3)
E   crop (1)
F   cut (159)
G   gather (99)
H   gather up (1)
I   get (39)
J   get up (1)
K   pick (328)
L   pick off (1)
M   pick up (2)
N   pluck (16)
O   pull (15)
P   snatch (1)
Q   snip (1)

101.4 P flowers

{a}   raised onset/short glide
{f}   bilabial
{o}   advanced/monophthong/short
       glide
{ow}   raised onset
{R}   weakly retroflex
{r}   weakly retroflex
{z}   devoiced
{zh}   devoiced
No Response (196)
<f[1]{ow}Rs=14> (1)
<flaRz=14> (1)
<flaiw[R]z=14> (1)
<flar> (2)
<flarz> (20)
<flar{z}> (3)
<flawRz=14> (1)
<flo(w)Rz=14> (1)
<flow(r)z> (1)
<flowR(z)=14> (1)
<flowR=14> (6)
<flowRs=14> (1)
<flowRz=14> (83)
<flowR{zh}=14> (1)
<flowR{z}=14> (28)
<flow[R](z)=14> (1)
<flow[R]=14> (14)
<flow[R][z]=14> (1)
<flow[R]dh=14> (1)
<flow[R]s=14> (1)
<flow[R]z=14> (99)
<flow[R]zh=14> (1)
<flow[R]{z}=14> (27)
<flow[r]> (1)
<flow[r]z> (2)
<flowr> (1)
<flowrz> (18)
<flowr{z}> (4)
<flowurz=13> (3)
<flow{R}=14> (5)
<flow{R}z=14> (39)
<flow{R}{z}=14> (11)
<flow{r}z> (6)
<fl{a}Rz=14> (1)
<fl{a}r{z}> (1)
<fl{a}wRz=14> (4)
<fl{a}w[R]=14> (3)
<fl{a}w[R]z=14> (8)
<fl{a}w[R]{zh}=14> (1)
<fl{a}w{R}=14> (1)
<fl{a}w{R}z=14> (5)
<fl{a}w{R}{z}=14> (1)
<fl{a}{R}z=14> (1)
<fl{ow}R(z)=14> (1)
<fl{ow}R=14> (5)
<fl{ow}Rz=14> (23)
<fl{ow}R{z}=14> (13)
<fl{ow}[R]=14> (2)
<fl{ow}[R]z=14> (22)

|RABjjjmea| (1)
|RABjjm| (8)
|RABjsa| (1)
|RABkaj| (1)
|RABkajmea| (2)
|RABlfa| (1)
|RABlfjmea| (1)
|RABmaa| (1)
|RABmaemea| (1)
|RABmaj| (6)
|RABmea| (4)
|RABmfa| (4)
|RABmfj| (1)
|RACjjamea| (1)
|RACjjd| (2)
|RAE| (8)
|RAEefa| (8)
|RAEefc| (4)
|RAEefj| (1)
|RAEffa| (4)
|RAEffbmea| (1)
|RAEffd| (2)
|RAEjjb| (8)
|RAEjjc| (1)
|RAEjjd| (6)
|RAEjjq| (1)
|RAEkaj| (1)
|RAEmab| (1)
|RAEmaj| (2)
|RAEmea| (1)
|RAEmfa| (1)
|RAF| (4)
|RAFeaa| (2)
|RAFefa| (3)
|RAFefamea| (1)
|RAFffd| (2)
|RAFjja| (2)
|RAFjjamea| (1)
|RAFjjb| (1)
|RAFjjbmaa| (1)
|RAFjjd| (2)
|RAFjjm| (1)
|RAFlfjmea| (3)
|RAG| (1)
|RAGefa| (1)
|RAGefamaa| (1)
|RAGefc| (1)
|RAGffcmea| (1)
|RAGffd| (3)
|RAGjbamea| (1)
|RAGjja| (1)
|RAGjjd| (8)
|RAGjjdmaj| (1)
|RAGjjm| (3)
|RAGjjq| (1)
|RAGmaamea| (1)
|RAGmaj| (1)
|RCA| (6)
|RCAefa| (2)

|RCAefj| (3)
|RCAffa| (6)
|RCAffd| (2)
|RCAffj| (1)
|RCAjja| (2)
|RCAjjamea| (1)
|RCAjjbmaa| (1)
|RCAjjdmaa| (1)
|RCAlfa| (4)
|RCAlfj| (1)
|RCAlfjmea| (1)
|RCAmaj| (3)
|RCAmajcba| (1)
|RCAmea| (1)
|RCAqfj| (1)
|RCB| (52)
|RCBeaa| (1)
|RCBeaamaa| (2)
|RCBeal| (1)
|RCBefa| (20)
|RCBefamaa| (3)
|RCBefamea| (3)
|RCBefj| (7)
|RCBefjmea| (1)
|RCBffa| (1)
|RCBffd| (2)
|RCBffm| (1)
|RCBjbo| (1)
|RCBjja| (6)
|RCBjjc| (1)
|RCBjjd| (8)
|RCBjjf| (3)
|RCBjjm| (2)
|RCBjsd| (1)
|RCBlfa| (4)
|RCBmaa| (1)
|RCBmaamea| (1)
|RCBmaj| (10)
|RCBmea| (8)
|RCBmfj| (1)
|RCE| (12)
|RCEffa| (1)
|RCEffd| (2)
|RCEjja| (1)
|RCEjjb| (2)
|RCElfa| (1)
|RCEmaj| (3)
|RCEmea| (3)
|RCF| (2)
|RCFefa| (1)
|RCFjja| (2)
|RCFjjd| (1)
|RCFlfn| (1)
|RCFmea| (3)
|RCG| (3)
|RCGefa| (1)
|RCGefj| (2)
|RCGffd| (1)
|RCGjjd| (1)

|RCGmaj| (1)
|RCGmea| (2)
|RCSmaj| (1)
|RDBjud| (1)
|RDG| (1)
|RKGmna| (1)
|SAD| (1)
|SADefc| (1)
|SADjjb| (2)
|SADjjm| (1)
|SAF| (2)
|SAFjjd| (1)
|SCAfaj| (1)
|SCAffa| (1)
|SCAffj| (2)
|SCBffj| (1)
|SCDffj| (3)
|SCDmea| (1)
|cbaOKCloa| (1)
|cbaPCAffj| (1)

101.5 L toy

No Response (196)
A baby toy (1)
B baby's play-pretty (1)
C bought toy (1)
D broken toy (2)
E children's play-pretty (1)
F Christmas toy (2)
G gadget (1)
H homemade toy (6)
I junk (3)
J little-old toy (2)
K makeshift [n.] (1)
L play toy (36)
M play-pretty (340)
N plaything (147)
O pretty [n.] (14)
P pretty play toy (1)
Q pretty-pretty (1)
R something to play with (1)
S stuff (1)
T stuffed toy (1)
U toy (628)
V trash (1)
W trinket (4)

101.6 G know

<!> infinitive
<*> preterit
<#> past participle
No Response (278)
<!naw> (1)
<!new> (1)
<!noe> (17)
<!nyue> (1)
<*new> (259)
<*newd> (2)
<*noe> (3)
<*noed> (192)
<*noen> (4)

<*noo> (1)
<*nu> (1)
<*nue> (125)
<*nued> (1)
<*nyew> (18)
<*nyue> (110)
<*nyued> (2)
<#new> (5)
<#noe> (1)
<#noed> (25)
<#noen> (14)
<#nyue> (1)

102.1 G give

<!> infinitive
<&> present 3rd singular
<@> present participle
<*> preterit
<#> past participle
No Response (84)
<!gaiv> (1)
<!geb> (1)
<!gee(v)> (1)
<!geev> (7)
<!gev> (1)
<!gi(v)> (42)
<!gib> (16)
<!giv> (629)
<!givz> (1)
<&gibz> (1)
<&givz> (14)
<@Agiv[N]=414> (1)
<@givN=14> (3)
<@givNG=14> (2)
<*gai(v)> (23)
<*gaib> (6)
<*gaiv> (516)
<*geev> (4)
<*gev> (7)
<*gi(v)> (34)
<*gi(v)d> (1)
<*gib> (9)
<*gibN=14> (1)
<*giv> (247)
<*givd> (1)
<*givN=14> (1)
<#gai(v)> (1)
<#gaiv> (22)
<#gaivd> (1)
<#gaivN=14> (2)
<#geev> (2)
<#geevN=14> (3)
<#gev> (1)
<#gevN=14> (1)
<#gi(v)> (4)
<#gib> (4)
<#gibM=14> (3)
<#gibN=14> (1)
<#giv> (88)
<#givd> (1)

<#givN=14> (388)
<#givun=13> (1)

102.2 G begin

<!> infinitive
<&> present 3rd singular
<@> present participle
<*> preterit
<#> past participle
No Response (314)
<!(bI)gin> (3)
<!b(I)gin> (1)
<!b(Ig)in> (1)
<!bAgan=41> (3)
<!bAgen=41> (7)
<!bAgin=41> (41)
<!bIgan=41> (10)
<!bIge[n]=41> (1)
<!bIgeen=41> (4)
<!bIgen=41> (25)
<!bIgi[n]=41> (2)
<!bIgin=41> (269)
<!bIginz=41> (1)
<!beegin=31> (4)
<!bigan=31> (1)
<!bigen=31> (1)
<!bigin=31> (23)
<!boogin=31> (2)
<&bAgin=41> (2)
<&bAgints=41> (1)
<&bAginz=41> (4)
<&bIgan=41> (1)
<&bIganz=41> (1)
<&bIgeenz=41> (1)
<&bIgi[n]z=41> (1)
<&bIginz=41> (18)
<&biginz=31> (2)
<@bAginN=414> (4)
<@bAginNG=414> (1)
<@bIgenNG=414> (1)
<@bIginN=414> (9)
<@bIginNG=414> (10)
<@biginN=314> (2)
<*(b)Agin=41> (1)
<*(bI)gan> (1)
<*(bI)gin> (2)
<*bAgan=41> (9)
<*bAgen=41> (5)
<*bAgin=41> (11)
<*bAgun=41> (6)
<*bIgain=41> (1)
<*bIgan=41> (230)
<*bIgand=41> (1)
<*bIgen=41> (98)
<*bIgend=41> (1)
<*bIgi[n]=41> (1)
<*bIgin=41> (88)
<*bIgind=41> (2)
<*bIgindId=414> (1)
<*bIgon=41> (2)

<*bIgun=41> (41)
<*beegan=31> (4)
<*bigan=31> (13)
<*bigin=31> (8)
<*bigun=31> (3)
<*boogan=31> (1)
<#(bI)gun> (1)
<#bAgan=41> (3)
<#bAgen=41> (2)
<#bAgin=41> (5)
<#bAgun=41> (14)
<#bIga[n]=41> (2)
<#bIgain=41> (1)
<#bIgan=41> (44)
<#bIgen=41> (23)
<#bIgin=41> (25)
<#bIgind=41> (1)
<#bIgon=41> (5)
<#bIgu(n)=41> (1)
<#bIgu[n]=41> (3)
<#bIgun=41> (188)
<#beegon=31> (2)
<#beegun=31> (2)
<#bigan=31> (1)
<#bigin=31> (5)
<#bigun=31> (10)
<#boogin=31> (1)
<#boogun=31> (1)

102.3 G run

<!> infinitive
<&> present 3rd singular
<@> present participle
<*> preterit
<#> past participle
No Response (75)
<!rain> (1)
<!ran> (2)
<!rawn> (2)
<!ren> (1)
<!rin> (1)
<!ron> (3)
<!roon> (3)
<!rud> (1)
<!ru(n)d> (1)
<!ru(n)t> (1)
<!run> (688)
<!runz> (3)
<!ru[n]> (3)
<&roon> (1)
<&run> (3)
<&runz> (31)
<&ru[n]dz> (1)
<@ArunN=414> (4)
<@ronN=14> (2)
<@ronNG=14> (1)
<@runin=13> (1)
<@runN=14> (31)
<@runNG=14> (6)
<*rain> (4)

<*ran> (458)
<*rand> (1)
<*rant> (1)
<*ra[n]> (1)
<*ren> (2)
<*ron> (3)
<*run> (319)
<*rund> (11)
<*ru[n]> (1)
<#ran> (75)
<#ron> (1)
<#run> (360)
<#rund> (3)
<#ru[n]> (5)

102.4 G come
   <!>   infinitive
   <&>   present 3rd singular
   <@>   present participle
   <*>   preterit
   <#>   past participle
   No Response (34)
<!kaim> (1)
<!kem> (1)
<!kom> (8)
<!kum> (706)
<!kumz> (2)
<!ku[m]> (2)
<&komz> (2)
<&kum> (5)
<&kumz> (57)
<@komN=14> (1)
<@komNG=14> (1)
<@kuming=13> (1)
<@kumN=14> (24)
<@kumNG=14> (14)
<*kaim> (592)
<*kai[m]> (2)
<*kam> (3)
<*kem> (9)
<*kiem> (1)
<*klum> (1)
<*kom> (5)
<*kum> (461)
<*kumd> (2)
<*ku[m]> (1)
<#kaim> (37)
<#kom> (2)
<#kum> (338)
<#ku[m]> (1)

102.5 G see
   <!>   infinitive
   <&>   present 3rd singular
   <@>   present participle
   <*>   preterit
   <#>   past participle
   No Response (18)
<!saw> (1)
<!see> (778)
<!seez> (1)

<!shee> (3)
<&seez> (3)
<@seeN=14> (9)
<@seeNG=14> (1)
<@seey[N]=14> (1)
<*saw> (615)
<*sawd> (1)
<*see> (3)
<*seed> (41)
<*seen> (216)
<*seend> (1)
<*shaw> (1)
<*so> (13)
<*soe> (4)
<*sow> (1)
<*thaw> (2)
<*tho> (1)
<#saw> (96)
<#sawd> (1)
<#see> (1)
<#seed> (44)
<#seeN=14> (1)
<#seen> (753)
<#seend> (1)
<#seez> (1)
<#sheen> (1)

102.6 G tear
   <!>   infinitive
   <&>   present 3rd singular
   <@>   present participle
   <*>   preterit
   <#>   past participle
   No Response (312)
<!ta(r)> (1)
<!ta[r]> (2)
<!tar> (7)
<!ta{r}> (1)
<!te[r]> (4)
<!ter> (5)
<!toe[r]> (1)
<!toe{r}> (1)
<&terz> (1)
<@terN=14> (1)
<*tard> (1)
<*taw(r)> (1)
<*taw[r]> (5)
<*tawr> (6)
<*tawrd> (1)
<*taw{r}> (1)
<*te[r]d> (1)
<*terd> (1)
<*toe(r)> (14)
<*toe[r]> (13)
<*toer> (39)
<*toern> (1)
<*toe{r}> (5)
<#taw(r)> (3)
<#taw(r)[n]> (1)
<#taw(r)n> (5)

<#taw[r]> (11)
<#taw[r]d> (1)
<#taw[r]n> (37)
<#tawr> (7)
<#tawrd> (1)
<#tawrn> (79)
<#taw{r}> (9)
<#taw{r}n> (16)
<#toe(r)> (36)
<#toe(r)N=14> (1)
<#toe(r)d> (1)
<#toe(r)n> (8)
<#toe[r]> (22)
<#toe[r][n]> (1)
<#toe[r]n> (87)
<#toer> (73)
<#toern> (145)
<#toe{r}> (29)
<#toe{r}n> (18)

102.7 P put it on
   {aw}   unrounded onset
   {o}   low-back
   {oo}   inglide
   {p}   fricative
   {t}   flap
   No Response (161)
<awn> (35)
<oen> (16)
<pAtIton=441> (1)
<pA{t}I{t}oen=441> (3)
<pA{t}I{t}on=441> (1)
<pI{t}Idoen=441> (1)
<pI{t}I{t}awn=441> (1)
<pI{t}I{t}oen=441> (1)
<pI{t}I{t}on=441> (1)
<poo(t)I{t}oen=341> (1)
<poodIdoen=143> (1)
<poodI{t}oen=143> (1)
<poot> (79)
<poot(I)toen=31> (1)
<poot(I)ton=13> (1)
<poot(It)awn=13> (2)
<poot(It)awn=21> (1)
<poot(It)awn=31> (1)
<pootAtawn=341> (1)
<pootIdawn=241> (1)
<pootId{o}n=241> (1)
<pootItaw[n]=341> (2)
<pootItawn=141> (2)
<pootItawn=143> (21)
<pootItawn=241> (29)
<pootItawn=341> (131)
<pootItoe[n]=341> (3)
<pootItoen=142> (1)
<pootItoen=143> (15)
<pootItoen=241> (5)
<pootItoen=341> (99)
<pootIton=143> (1)
<pootIton=241> (1)

<pootIton=341> (12)
<pootItun=341> (1)
<pootIt{aw}[n]=341> (2)
<pootIt{aw}n=143> (1)
<pootIt{aw}n=341> (23)
<pootIt{o}n=143> (3)
<pootIt{o}n=241> (2)
<pootIt{o}n=341> (10)
<pootI{t}awn=241> (1)
<pootI{t}awn=341> (3)
<pootI{t}oen=141> (1)
<pootMawn=143> (1)
<pootMawn=241> (5)
<pootMawn=341> (6)
<pootMoen=341> (4)
<pootMon=143> (1)
<pootMon=241> (1)
<pootMon=341> (2)
<pootNG=14> (1)
<pootNGIt{aw}n=3441> (1)
<pootNGoen=143> (1)
<pootNItoen=3441> (1)
<pootNawn=341> (1)
<pootNitawn=2431> (2)
<pootawn=12> (1)
<pootawn=13> (2)
<pootawn=21> (2)
<pootawn=31> (9)
<pootdMawn=341> (1)
<pootdM{o}n=341> (1)
<pootdhatawn=231> (1)
<pootdheezon=231> (1)
<pootdhisawn=231> (1)
<pootdhisawn=321> (1)
<pootdhisoen=231> (1)
<pootitawn=131> (2)
<pootitawn=132> (3)
<pootitawn=213> (1)
<pootitawn=231> (36)
<pootitawn=331> (1)
<pootitoen=131> (1)
<pootitoen=132> (1)
<pootitoen=133> (1)
<pootitoen=231> (1)
<pootitoen=312> (1)
<pootitoen=321> (1)
<pootitoen=331> (7)
<pootiton=132> (1)
<pootiton=231> (5)
<pootiton=331> (1)
<pootit{aw}n=231> (1)
<pootit{o}n=231> (2)
<pooti{t}awn=231> (2)
<pootoen=13> (8)
<pootoen=21> (2)
<pootoen=31> (10)
<pooton=13> (1)
<pooton=31> (1)
<pootsItawn=341> (1)

<pootsawn=13> (1)
<pootthisawn=331> (1)
<poot{o}n=13> (1)
<poo{t}I(t)oen=341> (1)
<poo{t}Idoen=143> (1)
<poo{t}Itawn=143> (1)
<poo{t}Itawn=241> (1)
<poo{t}Itawn=341> (2)
<poo{t}Itoen=143> (1)
<poo{t}Itoen=341> (2)
<poo{t}It{aw}n=341> (2)
<poo{t}I{t}awn=143> (1)
<poo{t}I{t}awn=241> (1)
<poo{t}I{t}awn=341> (3)
<poo{t}I{t}oe[n]=143> (2)
<poo{t}I{t}oen=143> (4)
<poo{t}I{t}oen=241> (1)
<poo{t}I{t}on=143> (2)
<poo{t}I{t}on=341> (1)
<poo{t}I{t}{o}n=143> (1)
<poo{t}awn=13> (1)
<poo{t}itawn=131> (1)
<poo{t}itawn=231> (1)
<poo{t}i{t}oen=132> (1)
<poo{t}i{t}oen=331> (1)
<poo{t}oen=13> (1)
<pudItawn=341> (1)
<pudI{t}oen=341> (1)
<put> (9)
<put(It)oen=13> (1)
<putItawn=143> (2)
<putItawn=241> (4)
<putItawn=341> (8)
<putItoen=143> (1)
<putItoen=341> (7)
<putIton=143> (2)
<putIton=241> (1)
<putIton=341> (1)
<putIt{aw}n=341> (1)
<putMawn=241> (1)
<putMawn=341> (1)
<putNGawn=341> (1)
<putawn=13> (1)
<putdhMawn=341> (1)
<putitawn=231> (3)
<putiton=231> (2)
<putit{o}n=231> (1)
<putoen=31> (2)
<pu{t}I{t}awn=143> (1)
<pu{t}I{t}oen=241> (2)
<pu{t}I{t}oen=341> (2)
<pu{t}I{t}on=143> (1)
<pu{t}Nitawn=2431> (1)
<pu{t}i{t}oen=231> (1)
<p{oo}t> (1)
<{aw}n> (1)
<{o}n> (1)
<{p}ootItawn=341> (1)
<{p}ootIt{o}n=143> (1)

102.8 G do
<!> infinitive
<&> present 3rd singular
<@> present participle
<*> preterit
<#> past participle
No Response (49)
<!dew> (39)
<!doo> (5)
<!due> (747)
<!duz> (3)
<!dyue> (1)
<&due> (3)
<&du(z)> (1)
<&duz> (24)
<@dewN=14> (1)
<@dueing=13> (1)
<@dueN=14> (10)
<@dueNG=14> (2)
<*ded> (1)
<*deed> (4)
<*di(d)> (2)
<*did> (660)
<*dit> (2)
<*don> (1)
<*due> (2)
<*dued> (1)
<*duez> (1)
<*dun> (331)
<*du[n]> (4)
<*dyun> (1)
<#did> (70)
<#don> (2)
<#dued> (1)
<#dun> (593)
<#du[n]> (3)

103.1 P nothing
{d} devoiced
{dh} devoiced
{oo} unrounded
{p} fricative
{t} flap
{?} glottal
No Response (105)
<nathN=14> (1)
<nethN=14> (3)
<nithN=14> (1)
<notN=14> (1)
<nothN=14> (15)
<nothNG=14> (4)
<noth[N]=14> (3)
<no{p}M=14> (1)
<nu(th)N=14> (1)
<nu(th)n> (1)
<nudN=14> (2)
<nudhN=14> (7)
<nudhNG=14> (2)
<nufN=14> (5)
<nutN=14> (52)

<nutNG=14> (1)
<nuthN=14> (655)
<nuthNG=14> (147)
<nuthNd=14> (1)
<nuthNz=14> (3)
<nuth[N]=14> (2)
<nutheng=13> (1)
<nuthin=13> (10)
<nuthing=13> (14)
<nut{?}N=14> (1)
<nu{dh}NG=14> (1)
<nu{d}N=14> (1)
<nu{t}N=14> (10)
<n{oo}thN=14> (6)

103.2 P something
{b}   fricative
{oo} unrounded
{?}   glottal
No Response (50)
<sampN=14> (1)
<sawmthin=13> (1)
<so[m]{?}M=14> (1)
<som(th)M=14> (1)
<sompM=14> (8)
<sompthN=14> (2)
<sompthNG=14> (1)
<somp{?}M=14> (1)
<somtNG=14> (1)
<somthN=14> (12)
<somthNG=14> (5)
<somthing=13> (2)
<su(m)bM=14> (1)
<su(m)pM=14> (1)
<su(m)pthN=14> (1)
<su(m)thin=13> (1)
<su(m){?}M=14> (6)
<su(m){?}N=14> (2)
<su(mth)M=14> (1)
<su[m](th)M=14> (1)
<su[m]pM=14> (2)
<su[m]thN=14> (8)
<su[m]thNG=14> (1)
<su[m]thing=13> (1)
<su[m]{?}M=14> (2)
<sum(th)M=14> (7)
<sum(th)N=14> (2)
<sum(thNG)> (7)
<sumbM=14> (1)
<sumdhN=14> (2)
<sumdhing=13> (1)
<sumfN=14> (1)
<sump(th)N=14> (1)
<sumpM=14> (323)
<sumpN=14> (25)
<sumpbM=14> (1)
<sumpdhN=14> (1)
<sumptNG=14> (1)
<sumpthN=14> (114)
<sumpthNG=14> (38)

<sumptheeng=13> (1)
<sumpthin=13> (3)
<sumpthing=13> (10)
<sumptin=13> (1)
<sump{?}M=14> (52)
<sump{?}N=14> (14)
<sumtN=14> (2)
<sumtNG=14> (1)
<sumteen=13> (1)
<sumthN=14> (316)
<sumthNG=14> (146)
<sumth[N]=14> (1)
<sumtheeng=13> (2)
<sumthen=13> (1)
<sumtheng=13> (2)
<sumthin=13> (10)
<sumthing=13> (73)
<sumting=13> (1)
<sum{?}M=14> (7)
<sum{?}N=14> (3)
<sum{?}NG=14> (1)
<sum{b}M=14> (1)
<suntN=14> (1)
<sunthN=14> (1)
<surthNG=14> (1)
<su{?}thN=14> (1)
<s{oo}bM=14> (1)
<thomthN=14> (2)

103.3 P such
{oo} unrounded
No Response (405)
<sech> (21)
<shuch> (2)
<sich> (95)
<sish> (1)
<soch> (1)
<sooch> (2)
<such> (432)
<sush> (2)
<sut> (2)
<suts> (2)
<s{oo}ch> (2)
<zush> (1)

103.4 P always
{ai} lax onset
{aw} unrounded onset
{dh} devoiced
{o}   low-back
{z}   devoiced
{zh} devoiced
No Response (127)
<aw(1)wA(z)=14> (1)
<aw(1)wAz=14> (4)
<aw(1)wIz=14> (15)
<aw(1)wI{dh}=14> (1)
<aw(1)wI{z}=14> (3)
<aw(1)waiz=13> (208)
<aw(1)waiz=31> (4)
<aw(1)wai{z}=13> (5)

<aw(1)weez=13> (1)
<aw(1)wesh=13> (1)
<aw(1)wez=13> (10)
<aw(1)wiz=13> (1)
<aw(1)w{ai}z=13> (15)
<aw(1)w{ai}z=31> (1)
<aw(1)w{ai}zh=13> (1)
<aw(1)w{ai}{z}=13> (2)
<aw(1w)Iz=14> (1)
<aw[1]vaiz=13> (1)
<aw[1]wAz=14> (1)
<aw[1]wIz=14> (1)
<aw[1]waidh=13> (1)
<aw[1]waiz=13> (35)
<aw[1]waiz=31> (1)
<aw[1]waizh=13> (1)
<aw[1]wai{dh}=13> (1)
<aw[1]wai{z}=13> (2)
<aw[1]wee{z}=13> (1)
<aw[1]wez=31> (1)
<aw[1]we{z}=13> (1)
<aw[1]wis=13> (1)
<aw[1]wiz=13> (1)
<aw[1]wi{z}=13> (1)
<aw[1]w{ai}z=13> (1)
<aw[1]w{ai}zh=13> (1)
<aw[1]w{ai}{zh}=13> (1)
<aw[1]w{ai}{z}=13> (2)
<awl(w)Az=14> (11)
<awl(w)A{z}=14> (3)
<awl(w)I{z}=14> (1)
<awl(wA)s> (1)
<awlwAz=14> (48)
<awlwIz=14> (21)
<awlwI{z}=14> (2)
<awlwai(z)=13> (2)
<awlwaiz=11> (1)
<awlwaiz=12> (1)
<awlwaiz=13> (311)
<awlwaiz=31> (3)
<awlwaizh=13> (1)
<awlwai{z}=13> (12)
<awlweez=13> (1)
<awlwez=13> (24)
<awlwe{z}=13> (1)
<awlwiz=13> (2)
<awlwi{z}=13> (1)
<awlw{ai}dh=13> (1)
<awlw{ai}z=13> (12)
<awlw{ai}{z}=13> (1)
<o(1)waiz=13> (5)
<o[1]wAz=14> (1)
<o[1]wIz=14> (1)
<o[1]wI{z}=14> (2)
<o[1]waiz=13> (2)
<o[1]wez=13> (2)
<o[1]w{ai}{z}=13> (1)
<oe(1)wIz=14> (2)
<oe(1)waiz=13> (7)

<oe(1)weez=13> (1)
<oe(1)w{ai}z=13> (1)
<oe[1]waiz=13> (2)
<oe[1]w{ai}z=13> (1)
<oelwAz=14> (1)
<oelwIz=14> (2)
<oelwaiz=13> (2)
<oelwai{z}=13> (1)
<oelwez=13> (1)
<oelwe{z}=13> (1)
<olwaiz=13> (3)
<olwai{z}=13> (2)
<ow(1)wIz=14> (1)
<{aw}(1)wAz=14> (8)
<{aw}(1)wIz=14> (1)
<{aw}(1)waiz=13> (42)
<{aw}(1)wai{z}=13> (2)
<{aw}(1)wez=13> (2)
<{aw}(1)w{ai}(z)=13> (1)
<{aw}(1)w{ai}dh=13> (1)
<{aw}(1)w{ai}v=13> (1)
<{aw}(1)w{ai}z=13> (5)
<{aw}(1)w{ai}{z}=13> (3)
<{aw}[1]waiz=13> (1)
<{aw}lwAz=14> (4)
<{aw}lwai(z)=13> (1)
<{aw}lwaiz=11> (1)
<{aw}lwaiz=13> (46)
<{aw}lwai{z}=13> (2)
<{aw}lweezh=13> (1)
<{aw}lwez=13> (2)
<{aw}lw{ai}(z)=13> (1)
<{aw}lw{ai}z=13> (2)
<{o}(1)wI{z}=14> (1)
<{o}(1)w{ai}{z}=13> (2)
<{o}[1]wIz=14> (1)
<{o}[1]waiz=13> (1)
<{o}[1]wee{z}=13> (1)
<{o}[1]wez=13> (1)
<{o}[1]w{ai}z=13> (1)
<{o}lwAz=14> (1)
<{o}lwI(z)=14> (1)
<{o}lwI{z}=14> (3)
<{o}lwai(z)=13> (1)
<{o}lwaiz=13> (12)
<{o}lwai{z}=13> (2)
<{o}lw{ai}dh=13> (1)
<{o}lw{ai}z=13> (9)
<{o}lw{ai}{z}=13> (4)

103.5 P since
{ai}   lax onset
{z}   devocied
No Response (139)
<dins> (1)
<se[n]s> (1)
<se[n]ts> (1)
<seents> (3)
<sens> (9)
<sents> (77)

<sets> (1)
<si(n)s> (1)
<si[n]s> (3)
<si[n]th> (1)
<si[n]ts> (6)
<si[n]{z}> (1)
<sin(s)> (3)
<sinch> (3)
<sins> (100)
<sint(s)> (4)
<sinth> (4)
<sints> (608)
<sinz> (1)
<sin{z}> (2)
<sunts> (2)
<s{ai}nts> (2)
<thinsh> (1)

103.6 G on purpose
No Response (422)
A   apurpose (41)
B   deliberately (11)
C   for a purpose (6)
D   for purpose (4)
E   for that/the purpose (4)
F   in person (1)
G   in purpose (1)
H   intention (1)
I   intentionally (14)
J   on apurpose (3)
K   on person (1)
L   on purpose (367)
M   purposely (27)
N   unthoughtedly (1)
O   with purpose (1)
P   [P-0] purpose (13)

103.7 P affirmation
{?}   glottal
No Response (341)
<(dh)a(t)sriet=31> (1)
<Aho[m]=41> (2)
<Ahu=41> (2)
<Ahu[m]=41> (6)
<Ahu{?}=41> (2)
<Mhum=41> (25)
<Mhump=41> (1)
<Mhum{?}=41> (1)
<Mum=41> (3)
<Mye=41> (1)
<N{?}hun=41> (1)
<[M]hoo[m]=41> (1)
<[M]hu=41> (1)
<[M]hu[m]=41> (6)
<a[m]ha[m]=31> (1)
<a[m]ho[m]=13> (1)
<a[m]hu[m]=31> (1)
<aw[m]haw[m]=13> (1)
<aw[m]ho[m]=31> (1)
<aw[m]hu[m]=13> (1)
<aw[m]hu[m]=31> (1)

<awhu[m]=31> (1)
<awhum=31> (1)
<e[m]> (1)
<e[m]hA=14> (1)
<e[m]ho[m]=13> (1)
<e[m]{?}e[m]=31> (1)
<hoho=13> (1)
<hu[m]hu[m]=31> (1)
<hu[m]u[m]=12> (1)
<hum> (1)
<humhM=14> (1)
<humum=31> (1)
<mun{?}hun=31> (1)
<nu[m]hu[m]=13> (1)
<o[m]h[M]=14> (2)
<o[m]ho[m]=13> (2)
<o[m]ho[m]=21> (1)
<o[m]ho[m]=31> (22)
<o[m]hu[m]=13> (4)
<o[m]hu[m]=31> (3)
<o[m]u[m]=31> (1)
<o[m]{?}o[m]=31> (1)
<o[m]{?}u[m]=13> (1)
<ohA=14> (1)
<oho=13> (1)
<oho=31> (5)
<oho[m]=13> (1)
<ohu=13> (1)
<ohu=21> (1)
<ohu=31> (5)
<ohum=31> (1)
<oo[m]hoo[m]=31> (1)
<oo[m]{?}oo[m]=31> (1)
<o{?}ho{?}=31> (1)
<o{?}hu=31> (1)
<riet> (1)
<u[m]> (2)
<u[m]hA=14> (4)
<u[m]h[M]=14> (4)
<u[m]ho=31> (1)
<u[m]ho[m]=13> (1)
<u[m]ho[m]=31> (6)
<u[m]hon=31> (1)
<u[m]hu=11> (1)
<u[m]hu=21> (3)
<u[m]hu=31> (10)
<u[m]hu[m]=13> (18)
<u[m]hu[m]=21> (4)
<u[m]hu[m]=31> (69)
<u[m]hum=13> (3)
<u[m]hum=31> (5)
<u[m]um=31> (1)
<u[m]{?}hu=11> (1)
<u[m]{?}hu[m]=13> (1)
<u[m]{?}hu[m]=31> (1)
<u[m]{?}hu[m]{?}=31> (1)
<u[m]{?}u[m]=13> (2)
<u[m]{?}u[m]=31> (1)
<uhA=14> (6)

<uh[M]=14> (1)
<uha[m]=31> (1)
<uhaw[m]=31> (1)
<uhu=13> (8)
<uhu=21> (8)
<uhu=31> (40)
<uhu[m]=13> (2)
<uhu[m]=31> (14)
<uhum=31> (2)
<uhu{?}=21> (1)
<um> (13)
<umM=14> (3)
<umMhum=143> (2)
<umMhum=241> (1)
<umM{?}=14> (1)
<um[M]=14> (1)
<umhA=14> (6)
<umhM=14> (12)
<umh[M]=14> (2)
<umhu=31> (13)
<umhu[m]=13> (2)
<umhu[m]=31> (27)
<umhum=11> (1)
<umhum=13> (42)
<umhum=21> (8)
<umhum=31> (254)
<umhump=31> (1)
<umhumum=133> (1)
<umhum{?}=31> (2)
<umhun=21> (1)
<umhun=31> (2)
<umhu{?}=31> (1)
<ump> (1)
<umu[m]=31> (2)
<umum=13> (5)
<umum=31> (7)
<um{?}M=14> (1)
<um{?}hum=13> (1)
<um{?}hum=21> (1)
<um{?}hum=31> (4)
<um{?}hum{?}=13> (1)
<um{?}hum{?}=31> (1)
<um{?}um=13> (3)
<um{?}um=31> (3)
<um{?}um{?}=31> (1)
<unhu[m]=31> (1)
<unhum=31> (1)
<unhun=13> (1)
<unhun=31> (1)
<u{?}A=14> (1)
<u{?}hu=31> (1)
<ya> (2)
<ya[m]> (1)
<yaum{?}um=133> (1)
<ye> (7)
<yeA=14> (1)
<ye[m]> (4)
<yes> (6)
<yip> (1)

<yu> (1)
<{?}Ahaw=41> (1)
<{?}Aho[m]=41> (1)
<{?}Ahu=41> (4)
<{?}Ahu[m]=41> (1)
<{?}Mhum=41> (12)
<{?}Mum=41> (1)
<{?}[M]hu[m]=41> (4)
<{?}aw[m]h[M]=14> (1)
<{?}aw[m]haw[m]=13> (1)
<{?}o[m]ho[m]=13> (2)
<{?}o[m]ho[m]=31> (2)
<{?}oho[m]=13> (3)
<{?}u[m]> (1)
<{?}u[m][M]=14> (1)
<{?}u[m]h[M]=14> (1)
<{?}u[m]haw[m]=31> (1)
<{?}u[m]hu=31> (1)
<{?}u[m]hu[m]=13> (10)
<{?}u[m]hu[m]=21> (2)
<{?}u[m]hu[m]=31> (13)
<{?}u[m]hun=31> (1)
<{?}u[m]u[m]=13> (1)
<{?}u[m]u[m]=31> (1)
<{?}u[m]{?}[M]=14> (1)
<{?}uhA=14> (1)
<{?}uh[M]=14> (1)
<{?}uho=31> (1)
<{?}uhoe[m]=31> (1)
<{?}uhu=13> (2)
<{?}uhu=21> (3)
<{?}uhu=31> (8)
<{?}uhu[m]=13> (3)
<{?}uhum=31> (1)
<{?}um> (4)
<{?}umM=14> (2)
<{?}umhM=14> (5)
<{?}umhum=12> (1)
<{?}umhum=13> (28)
<{?}umhum=21> (4)
<{?}umhum=31> (18)
<{?}umhun=13> (1)
<{?}umkai=31> (1)
<{?}ump{?}A=14> (1)
<{?}umum=13> (1)
<{?}umum=31> (1)
<{?}um{?}> (1)
<{?}um{?}hum=31> (4)
<{?}um{?}um=31> (1)
<{?}u{?}hu=31> (1)
<{?}u{?}u=31> (1)
<{?}yaA=14> (1)

103.8 P negation
{R}   weakly retroflex
{r}   weakly retroflex
{?}   glottal
No Response (245)
<M{?}um{?}=41> (1)
<[M]hu[m]=41> (2)

<aw[m]noe=21> (1)
<aw[m]u=13> (1)
<awnaw=13> (1)
<e{?}e{?}=31> (1)
<goshnoe=13> (1)
<heknoe=11> (1)
<heknoe=31> (2)
<helnaw=13> (1)
<helnoe=13> (1)
<helnoe=21> (2)
<hnaw> (1)
<huA=14> (1)
<hu[m]u[m]=13> (1)
<hu[m]{?}A=14> (1)
<hu[m]{?}[M]=14> (2)
<hu[m]{?}u=13> (1)
<hu[m]{?}u[m]=13> (12)
<hu[m]{?}u[m]=31> (1)
<hu[m]{?}u[m]{?}=13> (1)
<hu[m]{?}{?}u[m]=21> (1)
<humM=14> (1)
<hum{?}M=14> (3)
<hum{?}um=13> (2)
<hu{?}A=14> (1)
<hu{?}[M]=14> (1)
<hu{?}u=13> (1)
<hu{?}u[m]=13> (1)
<mun{?}N=14> (1)
<mun{?}um{?}=31> (1)
<na> (5)
<naw> (141)
<naw[n]> (1)
<nawman=13> (1)
<nawnaw=11> (1)
<nawnoe=13> (1)
<naws[R]=14> (2)
<nawsu[r]=13> (1)
<nawsu{r}=31> (1)
<naws{R}=14> (1)
<nie> (1)
<no> (19)
<no[m]{?}A=14> (1)
<noe> (394)
<noeM=14> (3)
<noeNdeed=341> (1)
<noehu[m]{?}u[m]=113> (2)
<noeindeed=231> (1)
<noeindeed=321> (1)
<noem> (1)
<noemam=21> (1)
<noemam=31> (2)
<noeman=11> (1)
<noeman=13> (1)
<noenoe=11> (6)
<noenoe=13> (5)
<noenoe=21> (1)
<noenoe=31> (2)
<noenoeumpA=1114> (1)
<noep> (23)

<noesR=14> (3)
<noes[R]=14> (2)
<noeso[r]=13> (1)
<noesu[r]=11> (1)
<noesu[r]=13> (1)
<noesur=31> (4)
<noesu{r}=13> (1)
<noeu=13> (1)
<noeu[m]{?}u[m]=113> (6)
<noeu[m]{?}{?}u[m]=113> (1)
<noeum=11> (1)
<noeum{?}{?}um=113> (1)
<noeu{?}u=131> (1)
<noewai=31> (1)
<noe{?}u[m]u[m]=113> (1)
<noo> (2)
<nosu{r}=13> (1)
<nowai=31> (1)
<no{?}A=14> (1)
<nu> (2)
<nu[m]u[m]=13> (3)
<nu[m]{?}[M]=14> (2)
<nu[m]{?}u=13> (2)
<nu[m]{?}u[m]=13> (9)
<nu[m]{?}u[m]=31> (1)
<nu[m]{?}{?}u[m]=13> (1)
<nue> (3)
<nup> (1)
<nu{?}u=13> (5)
<nu{?}u[m]=13> (1)
<nu{r}> (1)
<o[m]hu[m]=31> (1)
<o[m]o[m]=13> (2)
<o[m]u[m]=13> (1)
<o[m]{?}A=14> (5)
<o[m]{?}[M]=14> (4)
<o[m]{?}o[m]=13> (6)
<o[m]{?}u[m]=13> (1)
<o[m]{?}{?}o[m]=13> (2)
<o[n]{?}o[m]=13> (1)
<oehelnoe=311> (1)
<oelaw[r]dnoe=213> (1)
<oenoe=11> (1)
<oenoe=13> (2)
<oenoe=21> (1)
<oenoe=31> (2)
<om{?}um=13> (1)
<oo[m]{?}oo[m]=13> (1)
<o{?}A=14> (3)
<o{?}o=11> (1)
<o{?}o=13> (1)
<o{?}o{?}=11> (1)
<o{?}o{?}=31> (1)
<o{?}u=13> (2)
<o{?}u{?}=13> (1)
<uA=14> (3)
<u[m]> (3)
<u[m]hu[m]=13> (1)
<u[m]nu[m]=13> (1)

<u[m]o[m]=31> (1)
<u[m]p{?}A=14> (1)
<u[m]u=13> (1)
<u[m]u[m]=13> (11)
<u[m]u[m]=21> (1)
<u[m]u[m]=31> (3)
<u[m]{?}A=14> (3)
<u[m]{?}[M]=14> (2)
<u[m]{?}o[m]=13> (1)
<u[m]{?}u=13> (4)
<u[m]{?}u=31> (2)
<u[m]{?}u[m]=12> (1)
<u[m]{?}u[m]=13> (30)
<u[m]{?}u[m]=21> (1)
<u[m]{?}u[m]=31> (3)
<u[m]{?}u[m]{?}=31> (1)
<u[m]{?}{?}u=13> (2)
<u[m]{?}{?}u[m]=13> (16)
<u[m]{?}{?}u[m]=31> (1)
<um> (5)
<umM=14> (1)
<um[M]=14> (1)
<umhu=31> (1)
<umhu[m]=31> (1)
<umnoe=11> (1)
<umnoe=31> (1)
<umnu[m]=31> (1)
<ump> (1)
<umpA=14> (6)
<umpM=14> (4)
<ump[M]=14> (5)
<umpmA=14> (1)
<umpu[m]=13> (1)
<umpum=13> (2)
<ump{?}A=14> (3)
<ump{?}[M]=14> (1)
<ump{?}u=31> (1)
<umu[m]=13> (1)
<umum=11> (1)
<umum=13> (6)
<umum=31> (2)
<um{?}> (1)
<um{?}A=14> (2)
<um{?}M=14> (3)
<um{?}[M]=14> (1)
<um{?}pM=14> (1)
<um{?}p[M]=14> (2)
<um{?}pu[m]=31> (1)
<um{?}um=12> (1)
<um{?}um=13> (50)
<um{?}um=31> (10)
<um{?}um{?}=13> (2)
<um{?}um{?}=31> (1)
<um{?}{?}um=13> (40)
<um{?}{?}um=21> (2)
<um{?}{?}um=31> (3)
<un{?}N=14> (2)
<un{?}u[m]=13> (1)
<un{?}un=13> (1)

<uu=13> (1)
<uump=31> (1)
<u{?}A=14> (9)
<u{?}mpM=14> (1)
<u{?}o[m]=31> (1)
<u{?}u=12> (1)
<u{?}u=13> (15)
<u{?}u=31> (3)
<u{?}u[m]=13> (1)
<u{?}u{?}=13> (3)
<u{?}{?}u=13> (2)
<u{?}{?}u=31> (1)
<u{r}[m]u{r}[m]=13> (1)
<welnoe=21> (1)
<welnoe=31> (1)
<{?}A{?}u[m]=41> (1)
<{?}M{?}um=41> (1)
<{?}a[m]{?}a[m]=13> (1)
<{?}humum=13> (1)
<{?}noe> (1)
<{?}o[m]{?}A=14> (2)
<{?}o[m]{?}[M]=14> (1)
<{?}o[m]{?}o[m]=13> (2)
<{?}o[m]{?}u[m]=31> (1)
<{?}oo[m]u[m]=13> (1)
<{?}oo[m]{?}u=13> (1)
<{?}o{?}A=14> (3)
<{?}o{?}o=13> (1)
<{?}o{?}o=21> (1)
<{?}o{?}o=31> (1)
<{?}o{?}u=31> (1)
<{?}u[m]> (1)
<{?}u[m][M]=14> (1)
<{?}u[m]u[m]=13> (2)
<{?}u[m]{?}A=14> (1)
<{?}u[m]{?}[M]=14> (7)
<{?}u[m]{?}u=13> (1)
<{?}u[m]{?}u[m]=13> (20)
<{?}u[m]{?}u[m]=31> (3)
<{?}u[m]{?}um=13> (1)
<{?}u[m]{?}um=31> (1)
<{?}umM=14> (1)
<{?}umhum=31> (1)
<{?}umnA=14> (1)
<{?}umpA=14> (2)
<{?}umpum=13> (1)
<{?}ump{?}M=14> (1)
<{?}umum=13> (2)
<{?}um{?}A=14> (1)
<{?}um{?}M=14> (22)
<{?}um{?}um=11> (2)
<{?}um{?}um=13> (42)
<{?}um{?}um=21> (1)
<{?}um{?}um=31> (1)
<{?}um{?}um{?}=13> (2)
<{?}um{?}um{?}=31> (1)
<{?}um{?}un=13> (1)
<{?}unt{?}un=13> (1)
<{?}un{?}u[m]=13> (1)

<{?}un{?}un=13> (1)
<{?}un{?}un=31> (1)
<{?}upM=14> (1)
<{?}uu=13> (1)
<{?}uu=31> (1)
<{?}u{?}A=14> (5)
<{?}u{?}pM=14> (1)
<{?}u{?}u=11> (1)
<{?}u{?}u=13> (26)
<{?}u{?}u=21> (1)
<{?}u{?}u=31> (1)
<{?}u{?}u[m]=13> (2)
<{?}u{?}u[m]=31> (1)

103.9 G I think so
No Response (408)
A I believe (5)
B I believe not (1)
C I believe so (18)
D I do believe so (1)
E I don't believe (7)
F I don't believe so (17)
G I don't guess (6)
H I don't guess so (2)
I I don't reckon (15)
J I don't think (20)
K I don't/didn't think so (158)
L I expect so (1)
M I feel so (1)
N I figure (1)
O I guess (39)
P I guess not (2)
Q I guess so (113)
R I imagine so (18)
S I reckon (7)
T I reckon not (2)
U I reckon so (47)
V I should imagine so (1)
W I suppose (1)
X I suppose so (16)
Y I think (16)
Z I think maybe so (1)
aa I think not (3)
ab I think/thought so (195)
ac I would guess so (2)
ad I would imagine so (1)
ae I would presume so (1)
af I would think so (9)
ag I'd guess so (1)
ah I'd think (1)
ai I'd think so (4)
aj I wouldn't think so (6)

104.1 G ask
<!> infinitive
<&> present 3rd singular
<@> present participle
<*> preterit
<#> past participle
No Response (106)
<!a(s)k> (3)

<!a(s)t> (3)
<!a(sk)> (2)
<!ais(k)> (2)
<!aisk> (3)
<!aist> (1)
<!aith(k)> (1)
<!aks> (40)
<!as(k)> (211)
<!ash(k)> (2)
<!ashk> (1)
<!ask> (464)
<!ast> (79)
<!ath(k)> (2)
<!athk> (1)
<!eks> (1)
<!eksh> (1)
<!es(k)> (10)
<!esk> (9)
<!est> (4)
<!ieisk=13> (1)
<!osk> (1)
<&aks> (1)
<&as(k)> (1)
<&as(k)Iz=14> (1)
<&ask> (2)
<&asks> (1)
<&asts> (1)
<@aks> (1)
<@aksN=14> (8)
<@as(k)N=14> (1)
<@askN=14> (20)
<@askNG=14> (6)
<@ask[N]=14> (1)
<@astN=14> (8)
<@astNG=14> (1)
<@ekshN=14> (1)
<@eskN=14> (1)
<@eskNG=14> (2)
<*a(s)k> (1)
<*a(s)kt> (1)
<*a(sk)t> (1)
<*aiskt> (2)
<*aks> (18)
<*akst> (15)
<*as(k)> (102)
<*as(k)t> (221)
<*as(k)tId=14> (1)
<*ash(k)t> (1)
<*ask> (257)
<*asks> (1)
<*askst> (1)
<*askt> (94)
<*ath(k)> (1)
<*athk> (1)
<*ath(k)t> (1)
<*eksh> (1)
<*es(k)> (2)
<*es(k)t> (2)
<*esk> (5)

<*eskt> (2)
<*ieIs(k)t=14> (1)
<#aks> (8)
<#akst> (12)
<#as(k)> (66)
<#as(k)t> (121)
<#as(k)tId=14> (1)
<#ask> (162)
<#askId=14> (1)
<#askd> (1)
<#askt> (55)
<#ath(k)> (2)
<#esk> (3)
<#eskt> (2)

104.2 G fight
<!> infinitive
<&> present 3rd singular
<@> present participle
<*> preterit
<#> past participle
{t} flap
No Response (220)
<!fiet> (581)
<!fot> (5)
<!fut> (1)
<&fiet> (1)
<&fiets> (6)
<@AfietN=414> (1)
<@fiedN=14> (2)
<@fietN=14> (62)
<@fietNG=14> (26)
<@fietnN=14> (1)
<@fie{t}N=14> (1)
<@fie{t}NG=14> (2)
<@fotN=14> (1)
<*fawt> (419)
<*fiet> (3)
<*fietId=14> (2)
<*fit> (18)
<*foet> (1)
<*fot> (14)
<*fowt> (13)
<*tawt> (1)
<#fawt> (347)
<#fawtN=14> (1)
<#fiet> (10)
<#fietId=14> (2)
<#fietN=14> (1)
<#fit> (9)
<#foet> (1)
<#fot> (17)
<#fowt> (10)

104.3 G stab
<!> infinitive
<&> present 3rd singular
<@> present participle
<*> preterit
<#> past participle
No Response (365)

<!sdob> (1)
<!stab> (80)
<!stabz> (1)
<!stawb> (1)
<!steb> (2)
<!stob> (16)
<&stabz> (3)
<@AstobN=414> (1)
<@stabN=14> (5)
<*stab> (10)
<*stabd> (389)
<*stabt> (3)
<*staibd> (1)
<*stawb> (1)
<*stawbd> (1)
<*stebd> (6)
<*stiebd> (1)
<*sto(b)> (1)
<*sto(b)d> (1)
<*stob> (5)
<*stobd> (46)
<#stabd> (18)
<#staibd> (1)

104.4 G draw
<!> infinitive
<&> present 3rd singular
<@> present participle
<*> preterit
<#> past participle
No Response (231)
<!d(r)aw> (1)
<!draw> (203)
<!dro> (1)
<!droe> (1)
<!withdraw=31> (1)
<&drawz> (13)
<@drawN=14> (7)
<@drawNG=14> (5)
<@drawwun=13> (1)
<*d(r)ue> (1)
<*draw> (10)
<*drawd> (209)
<*drawn> (2)
<*drew> (27)
<*dri> (1)
<*drod> (1)
<*droo> (1)
<*dru> (1)
<*drue> (377)
<*withdrew=31> (1)
<*withdrue=21> (1)
<*withdrue=31> (5)
<*wIthdrue=41> (2)
<#drawd> (61)
<#drawn> (33)
<#drue> (4)

104.5 P hoist
{aw} unrounded onset
{ie} monophthong/centering glide

{oy} centering glide
{r} weakly retroflex
{t} flap
No Response (437)
<hais(t)> (1)
<hais(t)N=14> (1)
<haist> (4)
<hawrst> (1)
<hawst> (8)
<haw{r}st> (1)
<hies(t)> (5)
<hies(t)N=14> (1)
<hiest> (64)
<hiestId=14> (1)
<hiestN=14> (7)
<hietht> (1)
<hoest> (7)
<hoe{r}s(t)> (1)
<hoys(t)> (10)
<hoys(t)NG=14> (1)
<hoyst> (266)
<hoystId=14> (3)
<hoystN=14> (8)
<hoystNG=14> (2)
<hoys{t}I{t}=14> (1)
<h{aw}st> (1)
<h{aw}wIst=14> (1)
<h{ie}st> (21)
<h{ie}stN=14> (1)
<h{oy}s(t)> (3)
<h{oy}s(t)N=14> (1)
<h{oy}st> (86)
<h{oy}stN=14> (1)

105.1 major sections of the city
105.2 U financial district
No Response (29)
A business area (2)
B business district (9)
C business section (2)
D business section of town (1)
E CBD (2)
F central business district (6)
G downtown (83)
H downtown area (4)
I downtown section (1)
J downtown (specific city) (2)
K financial center (1)
L financial district (5)
M heart of the city (1)
N heart of the town (1)
O main business district (1)
P town (2)
Q uptown (6)

105.3 U shopping district
No Response (21)
A center of town (1)
B crosstown (2)
C downtown (91)
D downtown area (3)

E downtown store (1)
F downtown (specific city) (8)
G heart of (specific city) (1)
H in town (1)
I inner city (1)
J mall (10)
K midtown (1)
L on the square (2)
M plaza (1)
N shopping center (14)
O shopping mall (1)
P square (1)
Q subdivision (1)
R suburban shopping center (1)
S suburbs (1)
T town (2)
U up in town (1)
V uptown (19)
W uptown area (1)

105.4 ethnic neighborhoods
105.5 ethnic neighborhoods [stratified]
105.6 ethnic commerce centers
106.1 upper-class neighborhoods
106.2 middle-class neighborhoods
106.3 lower-class neighborhoods
106.4 local landmarks
106.5 U municipal airport
No Response (6)
A air terminal (1)
B airfield (20)
C airport (71)
D airstrip (2)
E big airport (1)
F Continental (1)
G downtown airport (2)
H field (2)
I Intercontinental (1)
J Intercontinental Airport (1)
K International (3)
L International Airport (6)
M landing field (1)
N Metro Airport (2)
O Metropolitan Airport (2)
P Municipal (1)
Q Municipal Airport (13)
R naval air station (1)
S old airport (2)

107.1 U interstate highway
No Response (21)
A beltline (1)
B bypass (3)
C causeway (1)
D east-west freeway (1)
E express (1)
F express turnpike (1)
G expressway (23)
H federal highway (1)
I four-lane (3)
J four-lane highway (2)

K   freeway (23)
L   highway (52)
M   interstate (72)
N   interstate highway (6)
O   parkway (1)
P   state highway (1)
Q   state road (1)
R   superhighway (4)
S   superslab (1)
T   thoroughfare (1)
U   toll road (1)
V   turnpike (4)
W   turnpike road (1)
X   two-lane highway (1)

107.2 U rest and service area

No Response (15)
A   comfort station (3)
B   emergency area (1)
C   emergency stop (1)
D   filling station (5)
E   gas station (1)
F   information center (1)
G   joint (1)
H   park (2)
I   park coverage (1)
J   picnic area (5)
K   picnic grounds (1)
L   pit stop (1)
M   pull off (1)
N   pull-off place (1)
O   recreation area (1)
P   rest area (76)
Q   rest camp (1)
R   rest halt (1)
S   rest park (1)
T   rest period (1)
U   rest place on the highway (1)
V   rest room (2)
W   rest spot (1)
X   rest station (2)
Y   rest stop (32)
Z   road stop (1)
aa   roadside (1)
ab   roadside park (16)
ac   roadside table (1)
ad   scenic overlook (1)
ae   service area (3)
af   service station (7)
ag   service stop (1)
ah   side rest area (1)
ai   snack bar (1)
aj   state rest area (1)
ak   stop (2)
al   stop area (1)
am   stop on the road (1)
an   stopover (1)
ao   stopping place (1)
ap   tourist information center (1)
aq   truck stop (3)

ar   truckers' stop (2)
as   wayside park (2)
at   welcome center (2)
au   welcome station (3)

107.3 U lane markers

No Response (7)
A   arrow (2)
B   Azalea Trail (1)
C   banisters (1)
D   boulevard (1)
E   boundary (1)
F   brick wall (1)
G   broken white line (1)
H   buffer (2)
I   bulkhead (1)
J   car line (1)
K   caution strip (2)
L   center line (13)
M   center stripe (4)
N   concrete divider (1)
O   concrete wall (1)
P   curb (1)
Q   divided esplanade (1)
R   divided lane (1)
S   divider (10)
T   divider line (1)
U   divider strip (1)
V   dividing line (14)
W   division line (2)
X   dots (1)
Y   double line (1)
Z   double yellow line (1)
aa   esplanade (2)
ab   grass median (1)
ac   grassland (1)
ad   guardrail (4)
ae   guideline (2)
af   highway divider (1)
ag   highway line (1)
ah   highway marker (1)
ai   highway marking (1)
aj   highway striping (1)
ak   island (2)
al   knots (1)
am   lane (2)
an   lane barrier (1)
ao   lane divider (3)
ap   lane marker (3)
aq   line (40)
ar   line in the middle of the road (1)
as   line in the road (2)
at   line marking (1)
au   margin (2)
av   marker (3)
aw   median (44)
ax   median strip (7)
ay   medium (8)
az   meridian (1)
ba   middle line (1)

bb   neutral ground (2)
bc   neutral strip (2)
bd   no-passing line (1)
be   number line (1)
bf   painted line (1)
bg   pink one (1)
bh   plat (1)
bi   railing (1)
bj   reflectors (4)
bk   retaining wall (1)
bl   road line (2)
bm   road marker (2)
bn   road markings (1)
bo   safety line (1)
bp   shoulder line (1)
bq   side road strip (1)
br   single stripe (1)
bs   slab of concrete (1)
bt   solid yellow (1)
bu   solid yellow line (1)
bv   street divider (1)
bw   strip (1)
bx   strip of grass (1)
by   stripe (14)
bz   traffic lane (1)
ca   wall (1)
bc   white and yellow lines (1)
cc   white center line (1)
cd   white line (12)
ce   white marking (1)
cf   white one (1)
cg   white streak (1)
ch   white stripe (2)
ci   yellow (1)
cj   yellow and white lines (1)
ck   yellow divider (1)
cl   yellow line (26)
cm   yellow mark (1)
cn   yellow strip (1)
co   yellow stripe (3)
cp   zone line (1)

107.4 U entrance/exit ramp

No Response (14)
A   access (6)
B   access ramp (1)
C   access road (3)
D   approach (3)
E   approach ramp (1)
F   cloverleaf (3)
G   conjunction (1)
H   curve (1)
I   egress (1)
J   enter (2)
K   enter point (1)
L   entering ramp (1)
M   entrance (27)
N   entrance ramp (19)
O   entry (2)
P   entry ramp (1)

Q   exit (79)
R   exit feeder (1)
S   exit ramp (32)
T   exit road (1)
U   exit route (1)
V   feeder road (1)
W   feeder street (1)
X   interchange (4)
Y   intersection (3)
Z   merge [n.] (1)
aa off ramp (8)
ab off road (1)
ac on and off ramps (1)
ad on ramp (11)
ae outlet (1)
af overpass (2)
ag plank (1)
ah ramp (28)
ai road (1)
aj service road (1)
ak slant (1)
al turnoff (2)
am underpass (2)
an yield [n.] (1)

107.5 U limited-access road

No Response (58)
A   access road (3)
B   boulevard (21)
C   bridge (2)
D   bypass (3)
E   causeway (17)
F   crossroad (1)
G   crosstown expressway (2)
H   elevated highway (1)
I   expressway (13)
J   four-lane (1)
K   freeway (6)
L   frontage road (1)
M   highway (6)
N   interchange (1)
O   interloop (1)
P   interstate (1)
Q   limited access (1)
R   limited-access highway (1)
S   limited-access road (3)
T   main road (2)
U   main street (1)
V   major thoroughfare (1)
W   median (1)
X   one-way (1)
Y   one-way street (15)
Z   parkway (1)
aa thoroughfare (1)
ab through street (1)
ac thruway (2)
ad toll (1)
ae toll bridge (1)
af toll road (4)
ag turnpike (2)

ah two-way street (2)

107.6 main streets in the city
107.7 neighborhood streets
107.8 U underpass

No Response (18)
A   bridge (22)
B   bypass (1)
C   crossing (4)
D   dip (1)
E   extension (1)
F   over and underpass (1)
G   overhead (2)
H   overhead bridge (1)
I   overhead ramp (1)
J   overpass (66)
K   overpath (1)
L   rail crossing (1)
M   railroad crossing (14)
N   railroad overpass (3)
O   railroad pass (2)
P   railroad stopping (1)
Q   train crossing (1)
R   trains' overpass (1)
S   trestle (17)
T   tunnel (9)
U   underpass (72)
V   underpath (1)
W   viaduct (42)

108.1 U parallel parking

No Response (23)
A   curb parking (3)
B   forward (1)
C   male parking (1)
D   next to the curb (1)
E   on the side of the road (1)
F   parallel (40)
G   parallel park (7)
H   parallel parking (55)
I   parallel to the curb (4)
J   parallel-park [v.] (3)
K   parallel-parks [v.] (1)
L   park parallel to the curb (2)
M   park up behind each other (1)
N   parking (2)
O   parking next to [D-0] curb (1)
P   parking parallel (1)
Q   parking straight (1)
R   parking to the curb (1)
S   sidewards (1)
T   straight parallel to the curb (1)
U   straight parking (2)
V   street parking (2)

108.2 U fire hydrant

No Response (12)
A   fire faucet (1)
B   fire hydrant (83)
C   fire steamer (1)
D   fireplug (31)
E   hydrant (31)

F   plug (4)
G   water hydrant (3)
H   water plug (3)

108.3 U angle parking

No Response (49)
A   across parking (1)
B   adjacent (1)
C   angle (5)
D   angle in (1)
E   angle-in parking (1)
F   angle parking (21)
G   angling (1)
H   angular parking (1)
I   at an angle (1)
J   diagonal (6)
K   diagonal parking (5)
L   female parking (1)
M   head to head (1)
N   head-in parking (3)
O   head-on parking (4)
P   horizontal (2)
Q   horizontal park (1)
R   horizontal parking (1)
S   just parking (1)
T   off-street parking (3)
U   on an angle (1)
V   parallel (1)
W   parallel or diagonal on the street (1)
X   parallel park (1)
Y   parallel parking (6)
Z   parallel to the next car (1)
aa park in the lines (1)
ab parking (2)
ac parking in there straight (1)
ad perpendicular (1)
ae pull in (1)
af pull-in parking (1)
ag pull into that place (1)
ah pull right in (1)
ai pull straight in (1)
aj regular parking (1)
ak side by side (1)
al side parking (1)
am slant parking (3)
an slanted (1)
ao slanted parking (1)
ap square parking (1)
aq straight in (3)
ar straight-in parking (3)
as straight parking (3)
at triangle parking (1)
au vertical (4)
av vertical parking (3)

108.4 U parking ramp

No Response (22)
A   building (1)
B   car storage (1)
C   deck (1)

D   drive and park (1)
E   drive-in (1)
F   garage (16)
G   high-rise parking (2)
H   indoor parking (1)
I   inside parking (2)
J   lot (1)
K   motor inn (1)
L   park and drive (1)
M   park and ride (1)
N   parking (1)
O   parking area (6)
P   parking building (4)
Q   parking complex (2)
R   parking deck (21)
S   parking facilities (1)
T   parking garage (42)
U   parking high-rise (1)
V   parking house (1)
W   parking levels (1)
X   parking lot (44)
Y   parking ramp (4)
Z   parking site (1)
aa   parking space (2)
ab   parking station (1)
ac   parking-lot building (1)
ad   pigeonhole parking lot (1)
ae   public parking garage (1)
af   ramp (4)
ag   storage garage (1)
ah   two-story garage (1)
ai   upper-story parking lot (1)
aj   upstairs (1)

108.5 U skyscraper
No Response (19)
A   apartment (4)
B   apartment building (1)
C   apartment complex (4)
D   bank (4)
E   bank building (4)
F   big building (3)
G   building (2)
H   business building (1)
I   complex (1)
J   condominium (1)
K   dorm (1)
L   federal building (1)
M   high-rise (56)
N   high-rise apartment (8)
O   high-rise apartment building (3)
P   high-rise building (5)
Q   high-rise dormitory (1)
R   high-rise housing (1)
S   hotel (2)
T   huge building (1)
U   large building (2)
V   multistoried building (1)
W   multistory building (2)
X   office building (9)

Y   old-age building (1)
Z   skyline (1)
aa   skyliner (1)
ab   skyscraper (88)
ac   tall building (3)
ad   tower apartment (1)
ae   town house (1)

108.6 U alley
No Response (14)
A   alley (126)
B   alleyway (4)
C   back alley (1)
D   back road (1)
E   back street (1)
F   breezeway (1)
G   catwalk (1)
H   driveway (7)
I   easement (1)
J   lane (2)
K   passage sidewalk (1)
L   passageway (1)
M   path (3)
N   public alley (1)
O   public drive (1)
P   road (1)
Q   service alley (1)
R   side alley (1)
S   walkway (4)

108.7 U vacant lot
No Response (17)
A   abandon lot (1)
B   building site (1)
C   condemned land (1)
D   construction site (2)
E   demolition site (1)
F   empty lot (12)
G   empty space (1)
H   fallen-down section (1)
I   field (1)
J   land (1)
K   little-old sandlot (1)
L   lot (21)
M   mess (1)
N   open field (1)
O   open lot (2)
P   park (2)
Q   parking lot (7)
R   playground (2)
S   playground area (1)
T   raw land (1)
U   rec(reation) area (1)
V   renovated (1)
W   sandlot (1)
X   under construction (1)
Y   unimproved property (1)
Z   unrestored (1)
aa   urban renewal (2)
ab   urban-renewal area (1)
ac   vacant (2)

ad   vacant area (1)
ae   vacant field (1)
af   vacant land (3)
ag   vacant lot (101)
ah   vacant place (1)
ai   vacant space (2)
aj   vacant yard (1)
ak   vacated (1)
al   yard (1)

108.8 U drinking fountain
No Response (12)
A   cooler (2)
B   drinking fountain (19)
C   faucet (1)
D   fountain (41)
E   spicket (2)
F   spigot (2)
G   sprinkler (1)
H   trough (1)
I   water cooler (8)
J   water faucet (3)
K   water fountain (88)
L   water hydrant (2)

109.1 U coupe
No Response (19)
A   bug (4)
B   car with just two seats (1)
C   club cab (1)
D   club coupe (2)
E   compact (6)
F   compact car (8)
G   coupe (50)
H   coupe convertible (1)
I   economy car (4)
J   foreign car (4)
K   four-wheel drive (1)
L   hardtop (1)
M   hatchback (3)
N   hot rod (2)
O   one-seat car (1)
P   racer (1)
Q   racy car (1)
R   roadster (8)
S   shrimp (1)
T   small car (2)
U   small compact car (1)
V   sport car (6)
W   sport model (1)
X   sports car (48)
Y   sports coupe (3)
Z   sports model (1)
aa   subcompact (2)
ab   T-top (1)
ac   town coupe (1)
ad   two-seat (1)
ae   two-seater (3)

109.2 U two-door sedan
No Response (22)
A   car (1)

B   coupe (12)
C   family car (2)
D   family sports car (1)
E   hardtop (9)
F   ice wagon (1)
G   jeep (2)
H   medium-size car (1)
I   middle-size car (1)
J   one-door (1)
K   passenger car (1)
L   sedan (29)
M   sedan car (1)
N   sports family car (1)
O   two (2)
P   two-door (42)
Q   two-door car (18)
R   two-door coupe (2)
S   two-door hardtop (1)
T   two-door hardtop sedan (1)
U   two-door sedan (24)
V   two-door thing (1)
W   two doors (7)
X   vinyl top (2)

109.3 U four-door sedan
No Response (29)
A   big car (1)
B   coupe (3)
C   family car (8)
D   four (2)
E   four-door (37)
F   four-door car (16)
G   four-door hardtop (1)
H   four-door sedan (21)
I   four doors (7)
J   four-passenger (1)
K   four seater (1)
L   full-size (1)
M   hardtop (6)
N   joy wagon (1)
O   lift back (1)
P   passenger car (3)
Q   regular car (1)
R   sedan (42)
S   touring car (4)
T   two-seated car (1)

109.4 U limousine
No Response (44)
A   bad car (1)
B   bad ride (2)
C   Batmobile (2)
D   big nigger's car (1)
E   big-shot car (1)
F   blunderbuss (1)
G   boat (3)
H   brougham (2)
I   cabriolet (1)
J   Caddy (4)
K   Cadillac (7)
L   chariot (1)

M   coach (1)
N   convertible (2)
O   deuce (2)
P   deuce and a quarter (9)
Q   deuce wagon (1)
R   dice mobile (1)
S   dreamboat (1)
T   El Dog (2)
U   expensive car (1)
V   flashy car (1)
W   gangster ride (1)
X   gas burner (1)
Y   gas drinker (1)
Z   gas guzzler (13)
aa   gas hog (12)
ab   gaudy (1)
ac   gaudy car (1)
ad   got rocks (1)
ae   guzzler (2)
af   hearse (4)
ag   hog (20)
ah   hunchback (1)
ai   junky car (1)
aj   Kitty Cat (1)
ak   limousine (33)
al   luxury car (14)
am   luxury model (1)
an   machine (2)
ao   money car (1)
ap   nigger (1)
aq   nigger car (2)
ar   pimp car (2)
as   pimp's car (1)
at   pimped up (1)
au   pimpmobile (15)
av   pussy wagon (1)
aw   ride (2)
ax   ritzy car (1)
ay   road hog (4)
az   Rolls Royce (1)
ba   sedan (3)
bb   ship (1)
bc   short (1)
bd   slick (1)
be   snazzy car (1)
bf   Stanley Steamer (1)
bg   sweat hog (1)
bh   T-Bird (1)
bi   T-top (1)
bj   tank (1)
bk   too much (1)
bl   town car (2)
bm   wagon (1)
bn   welfare Cadillac (1)

109.5 U station wagon
No Response (21)
A   airplane (1)
B   camper (1)
C   estate wagon (1)

D   fastback (1)
E   hatchback (4)
F   ranch wagon (1)
G   runabout (1)
H   square back (2)
I   station wagon (122)
J   suburban bus (1)
K   suburban sedan (1)
L   wagon (4)

109.6 U van
No Response (17)
A   army truck (1)
B   bread truck (2)
C   bus (1)
D   camper (4)
E   camper truck (1)
F   camper van (1)
G   car truck (1)
H   delivery (3)
I   delivery truck (24)
J   delivery van (2)
K   dray (1)
L   family van (1)
M   florist's truck (1)
N   flower truck (1)
O   four-by-four panel wagon (1)
P   grocery truck (1)
Q   jeep (1)
R   mail truck (4)
S   milk truck (2)
T   minibus (1)
U   package truck (1)
V   panel (2)
W   panel car (1)
X   panel truck (31)
Y   panel wagon (1)
Z   pickup with a camper top (1)
aa   postal truck (1)
ab   sedan delivery (1)
ac   service truck (1)
ad   step van (1)
ae   truck (11)
af   truck car (1)
ag   vacant truck (1)
ah   van (82)
ai   van truck (2)
aj   van type (1)

109.7 U pickup truck
No Response (18)
A   big pickup (1)
B   camper (1)
C   car truck (1)
D   city truck (1)
E   compact pickup (1)
F   delivery truck (1)
G   department truck (1)
H   farmer's truck (1)
I   flat body (1)
J   flat truck (1)

K   flatbed (9)
L   flatbed truck (4)
M   four-by-four (1)
N   half ton (3)
O   half-ton pickup (2)
P   half-ton truck (1)
Q   haul truck (1)
R   mini-pickup (1)
S   open bed (1)
T   pickup (48)
U   pickup truck (67)
V   produce truck (1)
W   regular truck (1)
X   sleeper truck (1)
Y   small pickup (1)
Z   small truck (1)
aa stake truck (1)
ab storage truck (1)
ac three-quarter ton (1)
ad ton pickup (1)
ae truck (9)
af two ton (1)
ag two-ton pickup (1)
ah two-ton truck (1)
ai wagon (1)

109.8 U airport limousine
No Response (27)
A   airline limousine (1)
B   airport bus (4)
C   airport limousine (16)
D   airport limousine service (1)
E   bus (4)
F   cab (4)
G   Cadillac (1)
H   courtesy bus (1)
I   funeral car (1)
J   hauler (1)
K   hunky bus (1)
L   jitney (1)
M   limo (2)
N   limousine (93)
O   limousine service (5)
P   minibus (2)
Q   passenger car (1)
R   scuttle service (1)
S   shuttle bus (1)
T   shuttle service (1)
U   small bus (2)
V   taxi (9)
W   taxicab (2)
X   van (3)

109.9 U public transportation
No Response (10)
A   big yellow bus (1)
B   bus (110)
C   bus line (1)
D   bus service (4)
E   bus system (1)
F   bus transportation (1)

G   cab (18)
H   city bus (8)
I   city bus line (1)
J   City Line bus (1)
K   commuter train (1)
L   express bus service (1)
M   ferry (1)
N   Greyhound bus (2)
O   jitney (5)
P   Liberty City jitney (1)
Q   local bus (1)
R   MARTA bus (1)
S   minibus (1)
T   monorail system (1)
U   motor bus (1)
V   rapid transit (2)
W   school bus (2)
X   senior-citizen bus (1)
Y   streetcar (7)
Z   subway (2)
aa subway system (1)
ab taxi (29)
ac taxicab (5)
ad train (2)
ae transit bus (1)
af trolley (1)
ag van (2)

110.1 U dashboard
No Response (11)
A   dash (31)
B   dashboard (107)
C   face board (1)
D   instrument panel (8)
E   operating buttons (1)
F   panel (3)
G   panel board (1)

110.2 U glove compartment
No Response (13)
A   car pocket (2)
B   compartment (2)
C   dash box (1)
D   dash pocket (1)
E   glove box (5)
F   glove compartment (118)
G   glove department (2)
H   glove pocket (1)
I   inside pocket (1)
J   locker (1)
K   map compartment (1)
L   map pocket (2)
M   parcel shelf (1)
N   pocket (6)
O   pocket of the car (2)
P   utility compartment (1)

110.3 U rubber band
No Response (12)
A   band (3)
B   elastic (4)
C   elastic band (2)

D   elastic rubber (1)
E   rubber (13)
F   rubber band (126)

110.4 U paper clip
No Response (13)
A   clamp (4)
B   clip (20)
C   fastener (1)
D   Gem (1)
E   Gem clip (40)
F   Jimmy clip (1)
G   little clamp (1)
H   little clip (1)
I   paper clamp (1)
J   paper clip (100)

110.5 U trunk
No Response (10)
A   back of the car (1)
B   back part (1)
C   back trunk (1)
D   boot (1)
E   compartment (1)
F   hatchback (1)
G   luggage compartment (1)
H   truck (1)
I   trunk (131)
J   turtle (1)
K   turtle shell (2)

110.6 U accelerator
No Response (10)
A   accelerator (94)
B   accelerator pedal (3)
C   foot feed (2)
D   foot speed (1)
E   gas (24)
F   gas pedal (43)
G   gas throttle (1)
H   gasoline feed (1)
I   pedal (6)
J   throttle (1)

110.7 U gearshift
No Response (12)
A   automatic (14)
B   automatic gearshift (1)
C   automatic shift (2)
D   automatic transmission (1)
E   column shift (2)
F   column-mounted shift (1)
G   conventional shift (1)
H   five forwards (1)
I   five on the floor (2)
J   five-speed (5)
K   floor (1)
L   floor shift (8)
M   floor stick (1)
N   four forwards (1)
O   four in the floor (13)
P   four on the floor (24)
Q   four-speed (12)

R   gear change (1)
S   gear stick (4)
T   gear(s) (9)
U   gearshift (57)
V   gearshift lever (3)
W   hand gears (1)
X   hand shift (2)
Y   in the column (1)
Z   in the floor (4)
aa in the tree (1)
ab lot of gears, a (1)
ac manual (5)
ad manual shift (1)
ae manual transmission (4)
af on the column (3)
ag on the floor (4)
ah on the steering wheel (1)
ai post shift (1)
aj regular shift (1)
ak shift (14)
al shift lever (1)
am shifter(s) (3)
an shiftgear (2)
ao shifting lever (1)
ap standard (9)
aq standard gear (1)
ar standard shift (14)
as standard transmission (5)
at steering-column shift (1)
au stick (19)
av stick in the floor (3)
aw stick shift (50)
ax straight shift (6)
ay three forwards (1)
az three on the column (1)
ba three on the floor (1)
bb three on the tree (2)
bc three shift (1)
bd three-speed (10)
be upright (1)

110.8 U speed breaker
No Response (34)
A   automobile killer (1)
B   bastard (1)
C   breaker (3)
D   built-in bump (1)
E   bump (15)
F   bump in the road (3)
G   bumper (1)
H   dam (1)
I   dip (5)
J   hump (9)
K   hump in the road (2)
L   little bump (1)
M   little hump (2)
N   road breaker (1)
O   rumble strip (1)
P   safety bump (1)
Q   shock buster (1)

R   slow bump (1)
S   speed blocker (1)
T   speed break (1)
U   speed breaker (46)
V   speed bump (28)
W   speed control (1)
X   speed hump (4)
Y   speed reducer (1)
Z   speed stopper (1)
aa speed trap (1)
ab stop (2)
ac stopper (1)
ad strip (1)
ae tooth jostler (1)
af topes [S] (1)
ag traffic break (1)
ah traffic bump (2)
ai warning device (1)

111.1 U fire truck
No Response (17)
A   basic engine (1)
B   basic fire truck (1)
C   diesel engine (1)
D   engine (5)
E   fire engine (49)
F   fire truck (94)
G   fire wagon (5)
H   gas job (1)
I   pumper (1)
J   tanker (1)
K   truck (2)

111.2 U pumper truck
No Response (77)
A   daddy truck (1)
B   engine (1)
C   engine truck (1)
D   fire engine (6)
E   fire pumper (2)
F   fire truck (4)
G   fire wagon (1)
H   head truck (1)
I   hose truck (4)
J   pump (3)
K   pump and ladder (1)
L   pump engine (2)
M   pumper (23)
N   pumper truck (7)
O   pumping system (1)
P   regular pumper (1)
Q   tank (1)
R   tank truck (1)
S   tanker (2)
T   truck (1)
U   wagon (1)
V   water carrier (1)
W   water truck (8)
X   water wagon (1)

111.3 U hook-and-ladder truck
No Response (62)

A   aerial truck (2)
B   big truck (1)
C   extension truck (1)
D   fire truck (4)
E   hook and ladder (38)
F   hook-and-ladder fire truck (1)
G   hook-and-ladder truck (9)
H   ladder (5)
I   ladder on a fire truck (1)
J   ladder one (1)
K   ladder thing (1)
L   ladder truck (20)
M   ladder-and-hook rig (1)
N   long fire truck (1)
O   swinging-ladder one (1)
P   truck (1)
Q   truck and ladder (1)

111.4 U snorkel truck
No Response (90)
A   aerial fire-fighter truck (1)
B   aerial ladder (2)
C   aerial truck (2)
D   boom (1)
E   boom and bucket (1)
F   boom truck (1)
G   bucket (2)
H   bucket truck (2)
I   cherry picker (7)
J   crane (1)
K   electric truck (1)
L   elevator truck (1)
M   fire truck with a snorkel (1)
N   gasoline truck (1)
O   hose truck (1)
P   hydrolift (1)
Q   ladder truck (2)
R   lift (2)
S   pea picker (1)
T   rescue unit (1)
U   snorkel (22)
V   Snorkel (1)
W   snorkel truck (7)
X   telephone truck (1)
Y   telescopic boom (1)
Z   utility truck (1)

111.5 U emergency truck
No Response (15)
A   ambulance (68)
B   ambulance truck (1)
C   bone wagon (1)
D   cardiac care unit (1)
E   EMA ambulance (1)
F   emergency (2)
G   emergency ambulance (2)
H   emergency call (1)
I   emergency car (2)
J   emergency medical something (1)
K   Emergency Medical Technician
    (2)

L emergency squad (3)
M emergency truck (9)
N emergency unit (3)
O emergency van (1)
P emergency vehicle (10)
Q EMO (1)
R EMS truck (1)
S EMT (2)
T fire bus (1)
U fire-department ambulance (2)
V first aid (1)
W first aid truck (1)
X for the rescue (1)
Y little truck for the paramedics (1)
Z meat wagon (1)
aa medic truck (1)
ab medical (1)
ac mercy vehicle (1)
ad module (1)
ae paramedic truck (2)
af paramedic(s) (11)
ag paramedics' truck (2)
ah pickup truck (1)
ai rescue (3)
aj rescue squad (15)
ak rescue squad car (1)
al rescue truck (13)
am rescue unit (6)
an rescue vehicle (1)
ao rescue wagon (2)
ap small pickup (1)
aq station wagon (1)
ar truck (2)
as van (5)
at van truck (1)
au van-type truck (1)
av vehicle (1)

111.6 U chief's car
No Response (30)
A car (27)
B chief's car (37)
C chief[N-k] car (3)
D cruiser (1)
E custom car (1)
F fire car (7)
G fire chief (3)
H fire-chief's car (26)
I fire-chief[N-k] car (3)
J fire-department car (2)
K fire-marshall's car (1)
L fireman's car (1)
M his car (1)
N lead car (1)
O little red car (4)
P ordinary car (1)
Q passenger car (2)
R pickup truck (1)
S red (2)
T red car (7)

U red fire car (1)
V red-and-white car (1)
W regular car (2)
X sedan (4)
Y station wagon (4)

111.7 U police sedan
No Response (13)
A black and white (6)
B blue and gray (1)
C blue and white (4)
D blue-and-white car (1)
E car (9)
F cherry top (1)
G city kitty (1)
H cop car (11)
I county Mountie (1)
J cruiser (13)
K emergency car (1)
L fuzzmobile (1)
M grasshopper (1)
N interceptor (1)
O Metro (1)
P passenger car (1)
Q patrol car (27)
R peanut wagon (1)
S pig car (1)
T pig's car (1)
U plainclothes car (1)
V police car (86)
W police cruiser (1)
X police vehicle (1)
Y police-chief's car (1)
Z private car (1)
aa prowl car (2)
ab prowler (2)
ac roach (1)
ad scout car (3)
ae sedan (4)
af sheriff's car (2)
ag sheriff's patrol (1)
ah Smokey (1)
ai squad car (35)
aj trooper's car (1)
ak unmark car (1)

111.8 U police van
No Response (28)
A accident-investigation vehicle (1)
B Black Maria (17)
C boogerman (1)
D carryall (1)
E hoodlum box (1)
F hoodlum wagon (2)
G Maria (1)
H paddy bus (1)
I paddy wagon (95)
J patrol (1)
K patrol wagon (10)
L police bus (1)
M police patrol (1)

N police truck (2)
O police van (9)
P police wagon (3)
Q tank (1)
R truck (2)
S van (7)
T wagon (6)

111.9 U helicopter
No Response (9)
A chopper (16)
B copter (3)
C eggbeater (3)
D gyro (1)
E helicopter (131)
F hoppyclopter (1)
G police helicopter (3)
H whirlybird (14)
I whirlygig (2)

111.9 P helicopter
{o} low-back
{R} weakly retroflex
{z} devoiced
{?} glottal
No Response (779)
<(helI)kopt{R}=14> (1)
<halIkoptR=1434> (1)
<halIkopt[R]=1434> (1)
<hanIkopt[R]=1434> (1)
<he[1](I)koptRz=134> (1)
<he[1]IkoptR=1434> (2)
<heelIAkoptR=14434> (1)
<heelIkoptR=1434> (1)
<hel(I)kawpt[R]=134> (1)
<hel(I)koptRz=134> (1)
<hel(I)kopt[R]z=134> (1)
<helAkop(tR)=143> (1)
<helAkoptR=1434> (13)
<helAkoptRs=1434> (1)
<helAkoptRz=1424> (1)
<helAkoptRz=1434> (4)
<helAkoptR{z}=1434> (3)
<helAkopt[R]=1434> (4)
<helAkopt[R]z=1434> (1)
<helAkopt[R]{z}=1434> (1)
<helAkopt{R}=1434> (6)
<helI(koptR)=14> (1)
<helIko(ptR)=143> (1)
<helIkop(t)[R]=1434> (1)
<helIkopp[R]=1434> (1)
<helIkoptR=1434> (33)
<helIkoptR=3414> (1)
<helIkoptRz=1434> (9)
<helIkoptR{z}=1434> (2)
<helIkopt[R]=1434> (20)
<helIkopt[R]z=1434> (4)
<helIkopt[R]z=3414> (1)
<helIkopt[R]{z}=1434> (1)
<helIkoptrA=1434> (1)
<helIkopt{R}=1434> (6)

‹hellkopt{R}z=1434› (1)
‹hellkopt{R}{z}=1434› (1)
‹hellko{?}d[R]=1424› (1)
‹hellkropt[R]=1434› (1)
‹hellk{o}ptR=1434› (1)
‹heloekoptR=1324› (1)
‹hillkopt[R]=1434› (2)
‹hillkopt[R]z=1434› (1)
‹hollkopt[R]=1434› (1)
‹hopIkloptR=1434› (1)
‹hullkoptR=1434› (1)
‹hullkopt[R]=1434› (1)
‹hullkopt[R]z=1434› (1)

112.1 U hurricane

No Response (18)
A blue norther (1)
B cyclone (2)
C depression (1)
D electric storm (1)
E gale (3)
F gulf wind (1)
G gust (1)
H hailstorm (1)
I hurricane (124)
J monsoon (1)
K sea spout (1)
L spout (1)
M storm (2)
N strong wind (1)
O thunderstorm (1)
P tidal wave (2)
Q tornado (2)
R tropical storm (5)
S turbulent wind (1)
T twister (1)
U typhoon (8)
V waterspout (3)
W windstorm (3)

112.2 U tornado

No Response (12)
A cyclone (23)
B cyclone of wind (1)
C funnel (3)
D funnel cloud (5)
E funnel-like thing (1)
F hail (1)
G monsoon (2)
H northeaster (1)
I norther (1)
J storm (2)
K tornado (126)
L tornado storm (1)
M tropical depression (1)
N twister (11)
O typhoon (2)
P waterspout (9)
Q whirling dervish (1)
R whirlwind (4)
S windstorm (2)

112.3 U ice storm

No Response (46)
A big freeze (1)
B blizzard (3)
C cold front (1)
D freeze [n.] (7)
E freeze storm (1)
F freezing rain (6)
G freezing storm (1)
H frost (1)
I hail [n.] (21)
J hailstorm (9)
K hard freeze (2)
L heavy freeze (1)
M hoarfrost (1)
N ice (5)
O ice slick (1)
P ice storm (51)
Q rain (1)
R sleet (29)
S sleet storm (5)
T slush (1)
U snow (5)
V snowstorm (5)
W winter storm (2)

112.4 U fireman

No Response (32)
A assistant engineer (1)
B chief (1)
C engineer (2)
D fire chief (1)
E fire-eater (1)
F fire fighter (22)
G fire freak (1)
H fireman (105)
I forty thieves (1)
J hot papa (1)
K Law, the (1)
L Man, the (1)
M paramedic (1)
N pipeman (1)
O rookie (1)
P smoke eater (2)
Q smoky (1)

112.5 U policeman

No Response (6)
A bacon (1)
B bastard (1)
C bear (1)
D bicycle policeman (1)
E black dude (1)
F blue boy (1)
G bluecoat (1)
H boogerman (1)
I bull (1)
J capitan, el [S] (1)
K Charley (1)
L chief (1)
M city kitty (2)
N constable on patrol (1)
O cop (100)
P copper (5)
Q county Mountie (2)
R deputy (2)
S detective (3)
T dick (1)
U do-right boy (2)
V dog (2)
W fat pig (1)
X finger (1)
Y flatfoot (12)
Z foot patrolman (1)
aa full-grown bear (1)
ab fuzz (50)
ac gooseneck (1)
ad gray boy (1)
ae head knocker (1)
af heat, the (9)
ag highway patrolman (1)
ah hog (1)
ai hopper (1)
aj Jason (1)
ak Jerry (1)
al jive law (1)
am Johnny Law (1)
an Law, the (9)
ao law-enforcement officer (1)
ap lawman (2)
aq little-old nosy cop (1)
ar local (1)
as man in the blue (1)
at Man, the (11)
au Mickey Metro (1)
av Mister Charley (1)
aw Mister Do-Right (1)
ax Mister Policeman (1)
ay motor cop (1)
az nab John (1)
ba narc (2)
bb officer (12)
bc oink-oink (1)
bd patrolman (3)
be peace officer (2)
bf pig (96)
bg pig dog (1)
bh police lady (1)
bi police officer (5)
bj policeman (80)
bk red-neck (1)
bl roller (3)
bm rookie (3)
bn screw (1)
bo sheriff (1)
bp Smokey (4)
bq Smokey Bear (2)
br SOB (1)
bs squad-car man (1)
bt star (1)

bu   swiller (1)
bv   trooper (1)
bw   white honky (1)
bx   Whitey (1)

112.6 U fire station

No Response (8)
A   central fire station (1)
B   chief fire station (1)
C   enginehouse (3)
D   fire department (17)
E   fire depot (1)
F   fire headquarters (1)
G   fire station (77)
H   fire-department garage (1)
I   fire-department house (1)
J   firehall (12)
K   firehouse (53)
L   firemen's home (1)
M   fireplace (1)
N   station (8)

112.7 U police station

No Response (13)
A   central lockup (2)
B   central police station (1)
C   city hall (6)
D   cop shop (1)
E   court building (1)
F   courthouse (2)
G   headquarters (4)
H   jail (2)
I   jailhouse (4)
J   joint (1)
K   office (1)
L   police building (1)
M   police department (10)
N   police headquarters (10)
O   police house (2)
P   police palace (1)
Q   police station (94)
R   precinct (11)
S   precinct station (1)
T   sheriff[N-k] office (1)
U   station (6)
V   station house (1)

112.8 U jail

No Response (5)
A   bedroom (1)
B   Big House (6)
C   bullpen (1)
D   caboose (1)
E   calaboose (8)
F   can (3)
G   carcel [S] (1)
H   cell (7)
I   central lockup (2)
J   city jail (14)
K   clincher (1)
L   clink (6)
M   clinker (3)

N   cooler (2)
O   coop (1)
P   county jail (14)
Q   county workhouse (1)
R   detoxification center (1)
S   downtown (1)
T   drunk tank (39)
U   drying out (1)
V   drying room (1)
W   drying tank (1)
X   drying-out tank (1)
Y   DTs [=drunk tank] (1)
Z   federal prison (1)
aa   free hotel (1)
ab   guardhouse (1)
ac   High Five (1)
ad   hole (1)
ae   hoosegow (5)
af   house of correction (1)
ag   house of detention (1)
ah   jail (113)
ai   jailhouse (12)
aj   joint (1)
ak   jug (2)
al   lockup (2)
am   low-class motel (1)
an   main place (1)
ao   parish prison (2)
ap   pen (8)
aq   penitentiary (7)
ar   pig pen (1)
as   pit (1)
at   poke (1)
au   pokey (7)
av   prison (13)
aw   safety building (1)
ax   sheriff's office (1)
ay   slammer (17)
az   sobering-up place (1)
ba   state prison (2)
bb   station (2)
bc   station house (1)
bd   stockade (3)
be   substation (2)
bf   tank (12)
bg   terminal city (1)
bh   under the jail (1)
bi   walls, the (1)
bj   where the birds don't fly (1)

113.1 U pistol

No Response (7)
A   automatic (10)
B   automatic pistol (1)
C   bad piece (1)
D   Betsy (1)
E   caliber thirty-eight (1)
F   cannon (1)
G   Colt forty-five (3)
H   derringer (4)

I   dueling pistol (1)
J   equalizer (1)
K   forty-eight (1)
L   forty-five (6)
M   forty-five Colt (1)
N   German Luger (1)
O   gun (91)
P   handgun (16)
Q   heat (4)
R   heater (1)
S   Luger (3)
T   magnum (2)
U   midnight special (3)
V   piece (7)
W   pistol (77)
X   police special (1)
Y   protection (1)
Z   rascal (1)
aa   revolver (35)
ab   rod (3)
ac   Roscoe (1)
ad   Saturday night special (15)
ae   service revolver (1)
af   shit (2)
ag   sidearm (4)
ah   six-shooter (3)
ai   Smith and Wesson (1)
aj   snub nose (1)
ak   stuff (1)
al   thirty-eight (7)
am   thirty-eight Remington (1)
an   thirty-eight Smith and Wesson (1)
ao   thirty-eight Smith and Wesson special gun (1)
ap   thirty-eight special (2)
aq   thirty-thirty (2)
ar   thirty-two (2)
as   thirty-two caliber (1)
at   thirty-two special (1)
au   three-fifty magnum (1)
av   three-fifty-seven magnum (3)
aw   twenty-five (1)
ax   twenty-two (6)
ay   twenty-two caliber (2)
az   twenty-two pistol (1)
ba   twenty-two Saturday night special (1)
bb   weapon (3)
bc   zip gun (1)

113.2 U nightstick

No Response (8)
A   bar (1)
B   bat (2)
C   baton (2)
D   billy (20)
E   billy club (44)
F   billy stick (12)
G   blackjack (36)

H   bully stick (1)
I   club (26)
J   flapjack (1)
K   head whipper (1)
L   headache stick (1)
M   jack (1)
N   mallet (1)
O   nigger knocker (3)
P   nigger stick (1)
Q   nightstick (50)
R   pencil (1)
S   police club (1)
T   police stick (1)
U   riot stick (1)
V   sap (1)
W   slapjack (2)
X   slapper (2)
Y   slapstick (1)
Z   stick (14)
aa   swipy stick (1)
ab   tire knocker (1)
ac   ugly stick (1)
ad   walking stick (1)

113.3 U prostitute

No Response (19)
A   B-girl (1)
B   bad bird broad (1)
C   bad woman (1)
D   bee (1)
E   bitch (6)
F   broad (2)
G   call girl (21)
H   chick (1)
I   chippy (3)
J   cutie (1)
K   dressed lady (1)
L   floozy (2)
M   freak (1)
N   girl (1)
O   good-time girl (1)
P   harlot (2)
Q   high-class call girl (1)
R   HO (1)
S   hooker (44)
T   horny (1)
U   hustler (4)
V   Jane (2)
W   kept woman (2)
X   lady (1)
Y   lady in red (1)
Z   lady of evils (1)
aa   lady of ill fame (1)
ab   lady of ill repute (2)
ac   lady of leisure (1)
ad   lady of the evening (18)
ae   lady of the night (12)
af   Lizzy (1)
ag   madam (1)
ah   madame (1)

ai   mademoiselle (1)
aj   masseuse (1)
ak   mistress (1)
al   night woman (1)
am   nympho (1)
an   old gal (1)
ao   piece (1)
ap   pink lady (1)
aq   pro (2)
ar   promiscuous (1)
as   prostitute (64)
at   red lady (1)
au   riverbank whore (1)
av   shady lady (1)
aw   slut (12)
ax   sporting lady (1)
ay   street lady (1)
az   street person (1)
ba   street whore (1)
bb   street woman (3)
bc   street worker (1)
bd   streetwalker (26)
be   trick baby (1)
bf   two-bit whore (1)
bg   wench (1)
bh   whore (84)
bi   witch (1)
bj   woman of the street (1)

113.4 U whorehouse

No Response (31)
A   assignation house (1)
B   block (1)
C   blue light (2)
D   boardinghouse (1)
E   bordello (3)
F   brothel (8)
G   cathouse (16)
H   crib (1)
I   fancy house (1)
J   health studio (1)
K   home (1)
L   honky-tonk heaven (1)
M   hooker shop (1)
N   hotel (5)
O   hothouse (1)
P   house (6)
Q   house of flowers (1)
R   house of ill fame (1)
S   house of ill repute (21)
T   house of prostitution (9)
U   house of the evening (1)
V   house with a red light on (1)
W   in the street (1)
X   joy house (1)
Y   La Strip (1)
Z   lewd house (1)
aa   love house (1)
ab   madam's house (1)
ac   massage parlor (3)

ad   message parlor (1)
ae   motel (1)
af   pad (1)
ag   parlor (1)
ah   pink house (1)
ai   prostitute house (1)
aj   prostitutes' house (1)
ak   prostitution house (3)
al   red-light district (17)
am   red-light house (3)
an   red lights (1)
ao   rooming house (1)
ap   shack (1)
aq   sleazy joint (1)
ar   spot (1)
as   stable (1)
at   strip joint (1)
au   transit house (2)
av   whoop shack (1)
aw   whoopee house (1)
ax   whorehouse (84)

113.5 U pimp/madam

No Response (25)
A   businessman (1)
B   dagger (1)
C   dynamite (1)
D   he she (1)
E   headman (1)
F   her him (1)
G   house lady (1)
H   housemother (3)
I   hustler (1)
J   john (1)
K   lady (1)
L   lady manager (1)
M   Mac (1)
N   madam (43)
O   main man (1)
P   main whore (1)
Q   mamma (2)
R   Man, the (1)
S   manager (2)
T   master (1)
U   matron (1)
V   Mrs. so-and-so (1)
W   Nupe (1)
X   owner (1)
Y   panderer (1)
Z   pimp (110)
aa   procurer (2)
ab   public nuisance (1)
ac   solicitor (2)
ad   street pimp (3)
ae   whoremonger (1)
af   woman (1)

113.6 U drunk

No Response (11)
A   alcoholic (82)
B   alky (5)

C   Bay Street cadet (1)
D   beer hound (1)
E   boozehound (1)
F   boozer (4)
G   bum (19)
H   closet (1)
I   destitute alcoholic (1)
J   drinker (1)
K   drunk (84)
L   drunkard (22)
M   drunken (1)
N   drunken bum (1)
O   DWI (1)
P   funky drunk (1)
Q   gin head (1)
R   grogger (1)
S   heavy drinker (2)
T   lush (6)
U   lush head (2)
V   parasite (1)
W   rummy (1)
X   social drinker (1)
Y   sot (7)
Z   souse (1)
aa splo drinker (1)
ab wine head (1)
ac wino (69)
ad wino type (1)
ae winola (1)

113.7 U derelict

No Response (38)
A   beggar (1)
B   bum (53)
C   degenerate (1)
D   derelict (40)
E   deviate (1)
F   down-and-out (2)
G   down-and-outer (1)
H   drifter (2)
I   flunky (1)
J   guttersnipe (1)
K   hobo (55)
L   hood (1)
M   hoodlum (2)
N   hustler (1)
O   itinerant (1)
P   loaf (1)
Q   loafer (5)
R   loiterer (1)
S   ne'er-do-well (1)
T   no-good loafer (1)
U   panhandler (1)
V   peddler (1)
W   riffraff (1)
X   rogue (1)
Y   skid-row bum (2)
Z   street bum (1)
aa street guy (1)
ab street person (2)

ac thug (1)
ad tramp (13)
ae transient (2)
af unemployed (1)
ag vagabond (2)
ah vagrant (8)

113.8 U cheap hotel

No Response (39)
A   boardinghouse (4)
B   bunkhouse (1)
C   cheap (1)
D   cheap hotel (15)
E   cheap motel (1)
F   cheap rooming house (1)
G   court (1)
H   crash house (1)
I   crummy cheap hotel (1)
J   derelict house (1)
K   dive (5)
L   doghouse (1)
M   down-and-out hotel (1)
N   drink house (1)
O   dump (6)
P   Fifth Avenue hotel (1)
Q   flat (1)
R   fleabag (11)
S   fleabag hotel (3)
T   fleabag joint (1)
U   flop (1)
V   flophouse (55)
W   ghetto (2)
X   Grenada Arden (1)
Y   gutter section (1)
Z   halfway house (3)
aa hangout (1)
ab highway hotel (1)
ac low-class hotel (1)
ad mission (4)
ae no-tell motel (1)
af old hotel (1)
ag pink house (1)
ah rat den (1)
ai rat trap (1)
aj rathole (1)
ak roach palace (1)
al rooming house (1)
am run-down hotel (1)
an run-down hotel or motel (1)
ao Salvation Army (1)
ap second-rate hotel (1)
aq shabby hotel (1)
ar shack (3)
as slum hotel (1)
at slum motel or hotel (1)
au transit (1)
av transit house (1)

114.1 U marijuana

No Response (13)
A   Acapulco Gold (7)

B   Acapulco Green (1)
C   African (1)
D   black Colombian (1)
E   black dog (1)
F   Black Gold (1)
G   bush (2)
H   cali (1)
I   Colombia weed (1)
J   Colombian (8)
K   Colombian Gold (3)
L   Colombian Red (2)
M   dope (21)
N   drugs (1)
O   evil weed (1)
P   fingers (1)
Q   ganja (1)
R   garbage (1)
S   gold (4)
T   good stuff (1)
U   grass (51)
V   hash (5)
W   hashish (2)
X   herb (2)
Y   homegrown (1)
Z   Howie Maui (1)
aa Jamaican (5)
ab Jamaican Gold (1)
ac Jane (1)
ad Jays/J's (2)
ae joint (23)
af lid (8)
ag locoweed (1)
ah marijuana (107)
ai marijuana cigarette (1)
aj Mary Jane (22)
ak Maui Wowie (1)
al Me Jane (1)
am Mexican (3)
an Mexican Gold (1)
ao Mexican marijuana (1)
ap Mexican-grown (1)
aq muggles (1)
ar mushroom (1)
as narcotic (1)
at no-name cigarette (1)
au Panama Red (2)
av pot (58)
aw red (2)
ax redbud (1)
ay reed (1)
az reefer (20)
ba roach (3)
bb rope (1)
bc shit (7)
bd skag (1)
be sleepy woman (1)
bf smoke (2)
bg soaper (1)
bh stick (1)

bi   stuff (3)
bj   Texas shit (1)
bk   Thai stick (2)
bl   Tijuana Gold (1)
bm   toke (2)
bn   weed (33)

114.2 U hard drugs

No Response (19)
A   acid (20)
B   amphetamines (26)
C   angel dust (9)
D   barbiturates (23)
E   barbs (1)
F   barcotics (1)
G   bennies (5)
H   Benzedrine (1)
I   big H (1)
J   black angels (1)
K   Black Beauties (3)
L   Black Mollies (3)
M   black RJS (1)
N   blue devils (2)
O   blue heavens (1)
P   blues (1)
Q   boy (1)
R   cannabis (1)
S   Christmas trees (5)
T   cocaine (72)
U   codeine (3)
V   coke (23)
W   cross tops (1)
X   crystal meth (1)
Y   Darvon (1)
Z   Dexamyl (1)
aa   Dexedrine (1)
ab   dope (13)
ac   downers (38)
ad   downs (3)
ae   drugs (4)
af   dust (1)
ag   East Coast West Coast (1)
ah   glue (2)
ai   greens (1)
aj   H (7)
ak   hallucinogenics (1)
al   hallucinogens (2)
am   happy dust (1)
an   happy pills (1)
ao   hard dope (1)
ap   hard drugs (3)
aq   hard stuff (3)
ar   hash (12)
as   hashish (6)
at   heroin (78)
au   hits (1)
av   horse (13)
aw   juice (1)
ax   junk (1)
ay   libras (1)

az   LSD (42)
ba   lucky ladies (1)
bb   mescaline (9)
bc   Mister Fantastic (1)
bd   Mister Natural (1)
be   morphine (8)
bf   mushrooms (1)
bg   narcotic (1)
bh   narcotics (1)
bi   No-Doze (1)
bj   opium (6)
bk   orange sunshine (1)
bl   PCP (4)
bm   pennies (1)
bn   pep pills (2)
bo   peyote (1)
bp   peyote buttons (2)
bq   peyote weed (1)
br   phenobarbitol (2)
bs   pills (12)
bt   pink and blues (1)
bu   pinks (1)
bv   poppers (1)
bw   powder (1)
bx   psilocybin (2)
by   psychedelic drugs (1)
bz   Quaaludes (11)
ca   rainbows (1)
cb   red devils (4)
cc   red jackets (1)
cd   red pill (1)
ce   redbirds (1)
cf   reds (6)
cg   reducing pills (1)
ch   RJS (1)
ci   Seconals (1)
cj   seven-fourteens (1)
ck   skag (4)
cl   sleepers (1)
cm   sleeping pill (1)
cn   sleepy ladies (1)
co   smack (14)
cp   snow (6)
cq   Snow White (1)
cr   speed (30)
cs   STP (1)
ct   sugar (1)
cu   supers (1)
cv   TAC (1)
cw   tetrahydro (1)
cx   TFC (1)
cy   THC (5)
cz   Thorazine (1)
da   tranquilizers (1)
db   truck-driving speed (1)
dc   TSC (1)
dd   TSH (1)
de   Tuinal(s) (2)
df   Turkish hash (1)

dg   two-hundred-proof alcohol (1)
dh   uppers (35)
di   ups (2)
dj   Valium(s) (2)
dk   white cross (2)
dl   White Gold (1)
dm   white stuff (1)
dn   windowpane (1)
do   yellow jackets (6)
dp   yellows (2)

114.3 U drug addict

No Response (24)
A   addict (50)
B   addicted (3)
C   coke freak (1)
D   coke head (1)
E   coke-sniffing set (1)
F   cool (1)
G   dope (1)
H   dope addict (20)
I   dope fiend (8)
J   dopehead (6)
K   doper (2)
L   dopey (1)
M   drug addict (30)
N   druggie (3)
O   fiend (1)
P   freak (1)
Q   freaked out (1)
R   gone (1)
S   have the monkey on your back (1)
T   head (2)
U   hip (1)
V   hippie (1)
W   hooked (2)
X   hooked on drugs (1)
Y   hooked on it (1)
Z   hookee (1)
aa   hophead (4)
ab   junkie (23)
ac   knocked up (1)
ad   mainliner (1)
ae   out of it (1)
af   pill popper (1)
ag   pothead (1)
ah   speed freak (3)
ai   strung out (1)
aj   user (1)
ak   weed head (1)
al   zonked-out person (1)

114.4 U drug seller

No Response (19)
A   big boss (1)
B   booster (1)
C   dealer (32)
D   dope dealer (2)
E   dope peddler (5)
F   dope pusher (2)

G   dope seller (1)
H   drug dealer (2)
I   drug pusher (6)
J   drug seller (1)
K   drug vendor (1)
L   Dude, the (1)
M   fence (1)
N   handler (2)
O   hustler (2)
P   junkie (5)
Q   Man, the (1)
R   marijuana pusher (1)
S   narcotic agent (1)
T   narcotics dealer (1)
U   offender (1)
V   peddler (6)
W   pot dealer (1)
X   push (1)
Y   pusher (94)
Z   salesman (2)
aa street dealer (1)
ab supplier (5)

114.5 U money

No Response (23)
A   berries (1)
B   bills (13)
C   bones (1)
D   bread (64)
E   breed (1)
F   brownies (1)
G   buck (13)
H   cabbage (1)
I   capital (1)
J   case dime (1)
K   case quarter (1)
L   cash (45)
M   cents (1)
N   change (12)
O   chomp (1)
P   coin of the realm (1)
Q   coin(s) (15)
R   cold hard cash (1)
S   collard green (1)
T   collateral (1)
U   consideration (1)
V   coppers (1)
W   corn (1)
X   crinkles (1)
Y   currency (2)
Z   cush (1)
aa dime (1)
ab dinero [S] (3)
ac dirty devil (1)
ad dough (51)
ae duckies (1)
af dust (2)
ag fast buck (1)
ah federal green (1)
ai filthy lucre (3)

aj fin (4)
ak five cents [=$5] (1)
al folding money (1)
am funds (1)
an G (1)
ao George Washington (2)
ap gold (2)
aq grand (2)
ar Green Stamps (1)
as green stuff (7)
at green(s) (25)
au greenback (16)
av hard cash (1)
aw jack (5)
ax kale (1)
ay legal tender (1)
az lettuce (3)
ba life (1)
bb lines (1)
bc long green (2)
bd loot (3)
be lucre (1)
bf mazuma (4)
bg mean green (1)
bh money (17)
bi moola (18)
bj nickel [=$5] (1)
bk notes (1)
bl paper (2)
bm pesos [S] (1)
bn sass (1)
bo sawbuck (4)
bp scratch (3)
bq shank (1)
br silver (4)
bs six bits (1)
bt snatch (1)
bu spare change (1)
bv stash (1)
bw ten cent(s) [=$10] (3)
bx twenty-five cent[N-i] [=$25]
     (1)
by two bits (1)
bz wad (1)
ca Washington (1)
cb what makes the mare go (1)
cc William (2)

114.6 U pawnshop

No Response (19)
A   flea market (1)
B   hock house (2)
C   hock shop (21)
D   loan office (1)
E   loan shark (1)
F   loan shop (4)
G   pawn dealer (1)
H   pawnbroker (4)
I   pawnshop (118)
J   secondhand store (1)

K   swap shop (1)
L   trading post (1)

114.7 U wine

No Response (50)
A   Annie Green Springs (2)
B   apple wine (1)
C   applejack (1)
D   Bali Hai (2)
E   belly buster (1)
F   berries (1)
G   berry wine (1)
H   blackberry wine (3)
I   blood (2)
J   Boone's Farm (2)
K   cheap wine (5)
L   cherry wine (2)
M   Crimson Tide (1)
N   dollar wine (1)
O   embalming fluid (1)
P   fight your mammy [n.] (1)
Q   firewater (2)
R   fruit of the vine (2)
S   Gold Seal (1)
T   grape, the (2)
U   grape juice (1)
V   grapes (2)
W   gut rot (1)
X   headache juice (1)
Y   home brew (1)
Z   homemade wine (1)
aa formaldehyde (1)
ab juice (2)
ac Kool-Aid (1)
ad Mad Dog (5)
ae Mad Dog Twenty-Twenty (1)
af MD Twenty-Twenty (1)
ag Mogen David Twenty-Twenty
     (1)
ah muscadine wine (1)
ai nigger wine (1)
aj pluck (1)
ak Red Dagger (2)
al Red Label (1)
am red something or other (1)
an Ripple (11)
ao river water (1)
ap rotgut (1)
aq rotgut wine (1)
ar rubbing alcohol (1)
as scuppernong wine (1)
at sterno (1)
au Sweet Lucy (3)
av T-Bird (1)
aw Thunderbird (4)
ax vino (3)
ay walnut wine (1)
az wild-cherry wine (1)
ba wine (49)

114.8 U skid row

No Response (42)
A   bad section (1)
B   bottoms, the (1)
C   bowery/Bowery (4)
D   buzzard's roost (1)
E   dead end (1)
F   down by the mission or blood
     bank (1)
G   downtown (4)
H   dregs (1)
I   drift track (1)
J   dump (1)
K   ghetto (11)
L   gutter section (1)
M   hobo jungle (1)
N   hoodlum territory (1)
O   low end of town (1)
P   lower end of town (1)
Q   mission (1)
R   off limits (1)
S   old beer joint (1)
T   other side of the tracks (1)
U   outskirts of town (1)
V   over the tracks (1)
W   parks (1)
X   pimp town (1)
Y   plasma center (1)
Z   projects (2)
aa railroad yard (1)
ab riverfront (1)
ac run-down [adj.] (1)
ad skid row (47)
ae slum(s) (23)
af slum area (6)
ag sorry part of town (1)
ah strip/Strip (2)
ai town (1)
aj welfare trade (1)
ak wharfs, the (1)
al wino or derelict street (1)
am wino street (1)

114.9 U X-rated movie theater

No Response (44)
A   adult center (1)
B   adult cinema (1)
C   adult films (1)
D   adult movie house (1)
E   adult movie theater (2)
F   adult movies (2)
G   adult store (1)
H   adult theater (14)
I   art theater (1)
J   awful pictures (1)
K   bathhouse (1)
L   blue films (1)
M   blue movies (3)
N   cheap theater (1)
O   cheap thrills (1)
P   dirty (1)

Q   dirty house (1)
R   dirty-movie theater (1)
S   dirty movies (6)
T   drive-in (1)
U   film flick (1)
V   filth (1)
W   flaming flickers (1)
X   flick house (1)
Y   flicks (3)
Z   fuck film (1)
aa funky films (1)
ab get-down films (1)
ac girlie house (1)
ad girlie show (1)
ae good flick (1)
af hard-core porn (1)
ag hornies (1)
ah hot movies (1)
ai movie house (3)
aj movie theater (2)
ak movies (2)
al nasty pictures (1)
am nut theaters (1)
an obscene movies (1)
ao passion palace (1)
ap peek show (1)
aq peeking theater (1)
ar peep show (2)
as peep-show place (1)
at porn (1)
au porn flick (1)
av porn house (4)
aw porn movie house (1)
ax porn movie theater (1)
ay porn palace (2)
az porno films (3)
ba porno flicks (3)
bb porno house (6)
bc porno movie house (1)
bd porno movie theater (1)
be porno movies (3)
bf porno palace (1)
bg porno place (1)
bh porno shop (4)
bi porno theater (2)
bj pornographic bookstore (1)
bk pornographic film shop (1)
bl pornographic films (1)
bm pornographic movie (1)
bn pornographic shows (1)
bo pornographic theater (2)
bp pornography (3)
bq pornos (2)
br rated-X theater (2)
bs restricted (1)
bt sex movies (2)
bu skin flicks (21)
bv smut (1)
bw stag films (3)

bx stag shop (1)
by theater (7)
bz triple X (1)
ca vulgar pictures (1)
cb X and double X (1)
cc X one (1)
cd X-rated (13)
ce X-rated cinema (1)
cf X-rated movie house (6)
cg X-rated movie theater (5)
ch X-rated movies (17)
ci X-rated place (1)
cj X-rated shop (1)
ck X-rated theater (7)

115.1 U mailman

No Response (7)
A   letter carrier (3)
B   mail carrier (7)
C   mail person (1)
D   mail woman (3)
E   mailman (96)
F   postal worker (1)
G   postman (77)
H   postwoman (2)

115.2 U garbage man

No Response (9)
A   engineer (1)
B   garbage collector (16)
C   garbage-disposal people (1)
D   garbage (man) (3)
E   garbage man (107)
F   garbologist (1)
G   maintenance man (1)
H   people with the garbage
     department (1)
I   refuse (man) (1)
J   sanitary engineer (1)
K   sanitary man (1)
L   sanitary worker (1)
M   sanitation-department worker (1)
N   sanitation engineer (4)
O   sanitation man (1)
P   sanitation worker (5)
Q   trash collector (3)
R   trash man (27)
S   trash people (1)

115.3 U political influence

No Response (25)
A   authority (1)
B   bought the inside track (1)
C   can pull strings (1)
D   carries a lot of weight (1)
E   clout (20)
F   connection (1)
G   connection[N-i] (1)
H   connections (16)
I   contacts (2)
J   cronyism (2)
K   friends (1)

L   good connections (1)
M   got somebody in there (1)
N   graft (2)
O   great influence (1)
P   influence (26)
Q   inside contact (1)
R   inside pull (1)
S   know the right people (1)
T   knows somebody (2)
U   leverage (1)
V   lot of influence (1)
W   lot of pull (2)
X   lot of weight (1)
Y   money (2)
Z   nepotism (1)
aa   on the in (1)
ab   patronage (2)
ac   political authori(ty) (1)
ad   political influence (9)
ae   political pull (6)
af   political pull, a (1)
ag   political savvy (1)
ah   position (1)
ai   power (3)
aj   powerful (1)
ak   prestige (2)
al   pull (53)
am   pull, a (1)
an   special privileges (1)
ao   weight (1)

115.4 U pay-roller
No Response (62)
A   boss's son-in-law (1)
B   bum (6)
C   bureaucrat (3)
D   carpetbagger (1)
E   cheat (1)
F   city flunky (1)
G   crook (3)
H   counselor (1)
I   deadbeat (1)
J   deadhead (3)
K   do-nothing (1)
L   excess baggage (1)
M   fat cat (1)
N   feather bedder (2)
O   figurehead (2)
P   floating (1)
Q   flunky (4)
R   free rider (2)
S   freeloader (7)
T   fuck off [n.] (1)
U   get overs (1)
V   goldbrick (3)
W   goldbricker (1)
X   good-for-nothing (1)
Y   goof-off (2)
Z   grafter (1)
aa   lackey (2)

ab   leech (4)
ac   loafer (4)
ad   lucky sucker (1)
ae   malingerer (1)
af   moocher (2)
ag   nigger token (1)
ah   on the payroll (4)
ai   paid flunky (1)
aj   parasite (3)
ak   part of the bureaucracy (1)
al   patsy (1)
am   pay-roller (1)
an   payroll (1)
ao   political appointee (1)
ap   political bum (1)
aq   political hack (1)
ar   politician (3)
as   rider on the city payroll (1)
at   scab (1)
au   slough [n.] (1)

116.1 U large food store
No Response (7)
A   chain food store (2)
B   chain grocery (2)
C   chain grocery store (1)
D   chain (store) (1)
E   chain store (10)
F   chains (1)
G   exchange store (1)
H   food market (1)
I   food store (9)
J   general store (2)
K   grocer store (1)
L   grocery (2)
M   groc(ery) store (1)
N   grocery store (66)
O   large chain stores (1)
P   large food store (1)
Q   market (4)
R   meat market (1)
S   public store (1)
T   shopping-center grocery store (1)
U   store (2)
V   supermarket (81)
W   supermarket-type store (1)
X   superstore (2)

116.2A U neighborhood grocery
No Response (47)
A   convenience store (1)
B   convenient corner store (1)
C   corner, the (1)
D   corner grocery (4)
E   corner grocery store (5)
F   corner market (1)
G   corner neighborhood store (1)
H   corner store (13)
I   family grocery store (1)
J   food store (3)
K   grocery (4)

L   grocery and barroom (1)
M   grocery store (39)
N   independent grocer (1)
O   independent grocery (1)
P   independent neighborhood store (1)
Q   independent store (1)
R   little grocery (1)
S   little grocery store (2)
T   little neighborhood store (1)
U   little-old neighborhood grocery (1)
V   market (3)
W   mom and pop (1)
X   mom-and-pop store (1)
Y   neighborhood grocer (1)
Z   neighborhood grocery (7)
aa   neighborhood grocery store (2)
ab   neighborhood store (9)
ac   private-owned store (1)
ad   small grocery (1)
ae   small neighborhood store (1)
af   small store (1)
ag   store (7)
ah   supermarket (2)
ai   supermart (1)

116.2B U convenience store
No Response (45)
A   all-night food store (1)
B   all-night grocery (2)
C   all-night store (1)
D   chain store (1)
E   convenience (store) (2)
F   convenience store (42)
G   convenient food market (1)
H   convenient food store (1)
I   drive-in (5)
J   drive-in market (2)
K   drive-in store (2)
L   emergency store (1)
M   fast-food store (2)
N   graveyard store (1)
O   gyppy mart (1)
P   handy shop (1)
Q   handy store (1)
R   icehouse (3)
S   Jiffy Store (1)
T   Majik Market (1)
U   mini-market (1)
V   mini-mart (1)
W   miniature store (1)
X   Minute Market (3)
Y   Minute Mart (1)
Z   min(ute) savers (1)
aa   package store (1)
ab   quick, late-hour-type (1)
ac   quick shop (1)
ad   quickie (store) (1)
ae   rip-off mart (1)

af rippy marts (1)
ag serve and go (1)
ah Seven-Eleven (7)
ai Shop and Go (1)
aj shopping stores (1)
ak store (1)
al Time Saver (1)
am Tote-Sum (1)

116.3 U delicatessen

No Response (28)
A deli (20)
B delicatessen (103)
C delicatessen section (1)
D delicatessen type (1)
E Jew store (1)
F Jewish store (2)
G Kosher market (1)
H Kosher store (2)
I meat market (2)
J meat store (1)
K import store (2)
L sandwich shop (2)
M special market (1)
N specialty food store (1)
O specialty shop (2)
P specialty store (1)

116.4A U electric frying pan

No Response (60)
A camp fryer (1)
B (e)lectric fryer (1)
C (e)lectric frying pan (7)
D electric frying pan (13)
E (electric) frypan (1)
F (e)lectric frypan (1)
G electric frypan (8)
H electric pan (1)
I (e)lectric skillet (11)
J electric skillet (35)
K fryer (1)
L frying pan (7)
M frypan (1)
N skillet (11)
O skillet deal (1)

116.4B U microwave oven

No Response (60)
A (e)lectrowave oven (1)
B micro (1)
C micro oven (2)
D microwave (32)
E microwave oven (45)
F radar oven (5)
G Radarange (5)
H radium oven (1)
I ultraviolet (1)
J ultraviolet-ray oven (1)
K ultrawave (1)

116.4C U toaster oven

No Response (89)
A baker (1)

B broiler (7)
C broiler oven (2)
D Dutch oven (1)
E (e)lectric baker (1)
F (e)lectric broiler (1)
G electric broiler (1)
H electric heater (1)
I (e)lectric oven (1)
J electric oven (1)
K electric oven cooker (1)
L (e)lectric stove (1)
M electric toaster (2)
N little-bitty toaster-oven-type thing
    (1)
O little (e)lectric oven (1)
P Muncie oven (1)
Q oven (4)
R oven toaster (2)
S roaster (1)
T rotisserie (1)
U small oven (2)
V toaster (17)
W toaster [=oven] (2)
X toaster and oven (1)
Y toaster oven (14)
Z warmer (3)
aa warming oven (1)

116.5 U Laundromat

No Response (8)
A automatic laundry (1)
B cleaner (1)
C coin laundry (11)
D coin-op (1)
E coin-operated launderette (1)
F coin-operated laundry (4)
G coin-operated self-service laundry
    (1)
H launderette (12)
I Laundromat (89)
J laundry (10)
K laundry room (2)
L self-service laundry (1)
M wash arena (1)
N washater(ia) (3)
O washateri(a) (1)
P washateria (40)
Q washer (3)
R washerette (6)
S washhouse (8)
T wishy-washy (3)

116.6 U laundry hamper

No Response (10)
A basket (5)
B bin (1)
C clothes basket (8)
D clothes bin (3)
E clothes hamper (41)
F dirty clothes (4)
G dirty-clothes basket (9)

H dirty-clothes box (1)
I dirty-clothes bucket (1)
J dirty-clothes hamper (23)
K dirty-clothes pail (1)
L hamper (70)
M laundry basket (7)
N laundry box (1)
O laundry hamper (4)

116.7 U vacuum cleaner

No Response (10)
A Airway (1)
B carpet cleaner (1)
C carpet sweeper (9)
D (e)lectric sweeper (2)
E electric sweeper (2)
F floor sweeper (2)
G Hoover (2)
H Hoover sweeper (1)
I hooving iron (1)
J sweeper (6)
K vacuum (29)
L vacuum [v.] (2)
M vacuum cleaner (100)
N vacuum sweeper (4)
O vacuuming cleaner (1)

116.8 U vacuum bag

No Response (14)
A bag (83)
B catcher (2)
C cleaner bag (1)
D collector's bag (1)
E dirt bag (1)
F dirt catcher (1)
G disposable vacuum-cleaner bag
    (1)
H dust bag (21)
I dust catcher (1)
J dust collect(or) (1)
K filter (1)
L garbage bag (1)
M liner (1)
N lint catcher (1)
O lint filter (1)
P paper bag (1)
Q paper insert filter (1)
R plastic bag (1)
S sack (3)
T suction bag (1)
U sweeper bag (1)
V trash bag (2)
W waste bag (1)
X vacuum bag (17)
Y vacuum-cleaner bag (12)

116.9 U plastic pail

No Response (18)
A bucket (78)
B mop bucket (12)
C mop pail (5)
D pail (44)

E plastic (bucket) (2)
F plastic bucket (20)
G (plastic) pail (1)
H plastic (pail) (1)
I plastic pail (7)
J sand pail (2)
K scrub bucket (3')
L water bucket (1)

117.1 U trash presser
No Response (18)
A compact garbage disposal (1)
B compac(tor) (1)
C compact(or) (3)
D compactor (42)
E compressor (9)
F crusher (1)
G decomposer (1)
H disposal (1)
I garbage compac(tor) (1)
J garbage compactor (7)
K garbage compressor (7)
L garbage disposal (13)
M garbage (di)sposer (1)
N garbage disposer (3)
O garbage presser (1)
P garbage smasher (1)
Q grinder (1)
R packer (1)
S presser (1)
T smasher (1)
U trash compactor (42)
V trash compressor (4)
W trash contractor (1)
X trash disposal (1)
Y trash masher (10)
Z trash presser (2)
aa trash smasher (1)
ab trash squeezer (1)
ac waste compactor (1)

117.2 U large garbage can
No Response (18)
A big garbage can (1)
B bigger garbage can (1)
C can (4)
D container (1)
E drum (1)
F garbage (1)
G garbage bin (1)
H garbage can (99)
I garbage disposer (1)
J garbage trash can (1)
K large garbage can (1)
L outside garbage can (1)
M outside trash can (1)
N trash bin (1)
O trash can (31)
P tin can (1)
Q waste can (1)

117.3 U large garbage bin

No Response (30)
A big garbage box (1)
B bin (8)
C container (1)
D Dempsey (1)
E Dempsey Dumpster (6)
F Dempster (2)
G Dempster dump (1)
H Dempster Dumpster (26)
I Dempsty Dumpster (1)
J Demsty Dumpster (1)
K Dipster Dumpster (1)
L Dipsty Dumpster (2)
M Dipsy Dumpster (4)
N Dipsy Dumpsy (1)
O dump (3)
P dump can (1)
Q dumpster (32)
R Dumpster (1)
S garbage bin (16)
T garbage can (5)
U garbage collector (1)
V garbage container (2)
W garbage disposal (3)
X garbage disposal bin (1)
Y garbage dump (3)
Z garbage dumpster (1)
aa hopper (1)
ab jumbo (1)
ac refuse container (1)
ad trash barrel (1)
ae trash bin (8)
af trash box (1)
ag trash can (1)
ah trash composer (1)
ai trash container (4)
aj trash dispenser (1)
ak underground garbage can (2)
al waste collector (1)
am waste-control container (1)

117.4 U undertaker
No Response (18)
A caretaker (2)
B dead-man filler (1)
C director (2)
D embalmer (13)
E funeral attendant (1)
F funeral director (34)
G fun(eral) director (1)
H funeral-home director (3)
I mortician (58)
J people [R-0] embalm people (1)
K undertake (1)
L undertaker (79)
M zombie (1)

117.5 U hearse
No Response (20)
A ambulance (10)
B coffin car (1)

C dead wagon (2)
D death wagon (2)
E funeral car (8)
F funeral-home limosine (1)
G hack (1)
H hearse (113)
I limousine (9)
J meat wagon (3)

117.6 U mausoleum
No Response (38)
A above-the-ground grave (1)
B aboveground vault (1)
C crematorium (1)
D crematory (2)
E crypt (11)
F dead house (1)
G drawers (1)
H grave (1)
I mausoleum (79)
J monastery (1)
K monument (2)
L mortuary (8)
M mosque (1)
N Muslim (1)
O pyramid (1)
P receiving vault (1)
Q tomb (10)
R vault (23)

117.7 U cigarettes
No Response (43)
A butt (8)
B cancer stick (34)
C cancer twig (1)
D cancer weed (2)
E cig (5)
F cigaboo (1)
G cigarette (26)
H coffin nail (6)
I coffin tack (2)
J evil weed (1)
K fag (14)
L faggot (1)
M gasper (1)
N pack-a-days (1)
O pill (1)
P puff (1)
Q ready roll (2)
R short (1)
S smoke (16)
T square (7)
U stick (4)
V stickweed (1)
W stogie (1)
X stump (1)
Y tobacco stick (3)
Z weed (22)

118.1 U sun-room
No Response (23)
A atrium (3)

B   breakfast room (1)
C   Florida room (21)
D   flower room (1)
E   foyer (1)
F   garden room (1)
G   indoor patio (1)
H   patio (3)
I   porch (7)
J   screened-in porch (2)
K   sleeping porch (4)
L   solar room (1)
M   solarium (18)
N   studio (1)
O   sun deck (4)
P   sun parlor (10)
Q   sun porch (18)
R   sun-room (55)
S   sun-room porch (1)
T   veranda (1)

118.2 U den
No Response (12)
A   den (107)
B   family Florida room (1)
C   family room (36)
D   Florida room (12)
E   fun room (1)
F   game room (7)
G   living room (10)
H   parlor (1)
I   playroom (14)
J   rec room (1)
K   recreation room (10)
L   rumpus room (2)
M   sitting room (2)
N   TV room (6)

118.3 U half bath
No Response (13)
A   bath (1)
B   bath and a half (7)
C   bathroom (20)
D   boudoir (1)
E   closet (1)
F   downstairs bath (1)
G   dressing room (4)
H   half a bath (7)
I   half a bathroom (1)
J   half bath (77)
K   half bathroom (5)
L   john (1)
M   lavatory (6)
N   powder room (11)
O   rest room (9)
P   spare bathroom (1)
Q   toilet (2)
R   toilet room (1)
S   walk-in half bath (1)
T   washroom (9)
U   water closet (1)

118.4 U stoves/furnaces

No Response (30)
A   airtight heater (1)
B   big furnace (1)
C   big gas stove (1)
D   big-old wood stove (1)
E   boiler (1)
F   butane (heater) (1)
G   cast-iron stove (1)
H   central furnace (1)
I   circulating heater (1)
J   circulator (1)
K   coal burner (1)
L   coal furnace (3)
M   coal heater (2)
N   coal stove (11)
O   coal-oil stove (2)
P   coal-stoked furnace (1)
Q   cookstove (2)
R   electric furnace (1)
S   electric heater (12)
T   electric range (1)
U   (e)lectric space heater (1)
V   electric stove (11)
W   (electric) unit (1)
X   electrical furnace (1)
Y   electrical (stove) (1)
Z   fireplace (17)
aa   floor furnace (15)
ab   floor heater (2)
ac   forced-air furnace (1)
ad   fuel-oil heater (2)
ae   furnace (20)
af   furnace heater (1)
ag   gas circulator (1)
ah   gas floor furnace (1)
ai   gas furnace (5)
aj   gas heater (19)
ak   gas stove (18)
al   gas-fired central-heating furnace (1)
am   gas-fired floor furnace (1)
an   heat pump (3)
ao   heat roller (1)
ap   heater (19)
aq   heating pump (1)
ar   heating stove (1)
as   heating unit (1)
at   kerosene heater (5)
au   large wood range (1)
av   main heater (1)
aw   oil circulator (1)
ax   oil furnace (1)
ay   oil heater (3)
az   oil stove (2)
ba   oil-burning furnace (2)
bb   older wood deal (1)
bc   panel ray (heater) (1)
bd   portable plug-in heater (1)
be   potbellied stove (4)

bf   potbelly stove (1)
bg   radiators (3)
bh   range (2)
bi   small floor heater (1)
bj   small unit heater (1)
bk   space heater (10)
bl   steam heater (1)
bm   stove (15)
bn   tin heater (1)
bo   tin stove (1)
bp   wall heater (4)
bq   wall unit (1)
br   warm-morning heater (2)
bs   wood-burning furnace (1)
bt   (wood-burning) heater (1)
bu   wood cookstove (1)
bv   wood heater (4)
bw   wood stove (17)
bx   wooden stove (4)

118.5 U circulation systems
No Response (19)
A   air-condition [central] (1)
B   air-condition [wall] (2)
C   air-conditioner [central] (1)
D   air-conditioner [window] (3)
E   air-conditioning system (1)
F   air-conditioning unit (2)
G   air-conditioning vents (1)
H   air ducts (2)
I   air handler (1)
J   attic fan (1)
K   blower (3)
L   blower system (1)
M   ceiling fan (1)
N   ceiling heat (1)
O   ceiling vents (1)
P   central (6)
Q   central air (18)
R   central air and heat (4)
S   central air condition (1)
T   central air conditioning (7)
U   central air heating (1)
V   central by air ducts (1)
W   central ducts (1)
X   central gas heat and air (1)
Y   central heat (16)
Z   central heat and air (3)
aa   central heating (14)
ab   central heating air (1)
ac   central heating and air (2)
ad   central heating and air conditioning (1)
ae   central heating and cooling (1)
af   central heating furnace (1)
ag   central heating system (2)
ah   central system (1)
ai   central unit (2)
aj   circulating heater (1)
ak   climate-control unit (1)

al ducts (7)
am ductwork (4)
an electric fan (2)
ao fan (16)
ap fan blower (1)
aq floor, from the (1)
ar floor fan (1)
as floor furnace (5)
at floor heaters (1)
au floor vents (1)
av forced air (3)
aw forced-air heating (1)
ax gas circulator (1)
ay gravity fed (1)
az heat pump (3)
ba heating pump (1)
bb hot-water heat (1)
bc panel (1)
bd radiant (1)
be radiant heat (4)
bf radiators (1)
bg registers (2)
bh seal heat (1)
bi sealed heat (1)
bj solar heat (1)
bk steam heat (1)
bl vents (17)
bm wall air-conditioning (1)
bn wall heater (2)
bo wall units (1)
bp window air-conditioner (2)
bq window air conditioning (1)
br window box (1)
bs window fan (3)
bt window-type air-conditioner (1)
bu window unit (4)

118.6 U shotgun house
No Response (58)
A chicken-coop house (1)
B cracker box (1)
C duplex (3)
D gun-barrel house (1)
E gunshot house (1)
F linear house (1)
G long house (1)
H railroad (apartments) (1)
I railroad flat (1)
J rifle house (1)
K shack (1)
L shotgun (23)
M shotgun doubles (1)
N shotgun house (53)
O shotgun shack (1)
P straight house (1)
Q straight shoot (1)
R straight shotgun house (1)
S tenant house (1)
T three-room shotgun house (2)
U walk-through (1)

118.7 U dogtrot house
No Response (101)
A dog pen house (1)
B dog-run house (1)
C dogtrot (4)
D dogtrot house (5)
E double-tenant house (1)
F double tenement (1)
G duplex (10)
H rooming house (1)
I shotgun house (2)

[passageway]
J breezeway (10)
K dogtrot (5)
L hall (1)
M hallway (4)
N porch (1)
O runway (1)

118.8 U hall-and-parlor house
No Response (121)
A ell (1)
B ell house (2)
C hall and parlor (2)
D L (1)
E L-shape(d) (3)
F L-shape(d) house (6)
G parlor house (1)

118.9 U house designs
No Response (52)
A A-frame (house) (11)
B airplane (1)
C antebellum (home/mansion) (3)
D antebellum-type (home) (2)
E atrium (1)
F barny house (1)
G bay-window house (1)
H beach house (2)
I Bermudan (1)
J blockhouse (1)
K bungalow (14)
L cabin (3)
M camelback (house) (2)
N cap house (1)
O Cape Cod (2)
P carriage house (1)
Q CBS (house) (3)
R Colonial (home/house) (11)
S cottage (7)
T cottage-type house (1)
U cracker box (house) (4)
V creole cottage (1)
W double house (1)
X double-pen house (1)
Y double-tenant house (1)
Z duplex (house) (8)
aa ell house (1)
ab English (1)
ac farmhouse (1)
ad flattop (1)

ae four-room house (1)
af frame box house (1)
ag French (1)
ah high-built house (1)
ai lean-to (1)
aj log cabin (2)
ak mansion (2)
al matchbox (house) (1)
am Mediterranean (3)
an millhouse (1)
ao modern (2)
ap old bungalow style (1)
aq Old English (1)
ar one-family (1)
as one-room house (2)
at one-story (1)
au palmetto shack (1)
av plantation house (1)
aw railroad house (1)
ax ranch (house) (4)
ay ranch-style (house) (9)
az ranch-type house (2)
ba roundhouse (1)
bb saltbox (house) (2)
bc shack (9)
bd shanty (5)
be single (1)
bf single story (1)
bg ski-lodge house (1)
bh Spanish (house) (8)
bi Spanish-type (1)
bj split-level (house) (20)
bk spreading house (1)
bl stor(y)-and-a-half (1)
bm T-shape (1)
bn tenant house (1)
bo three-room house (1)
bp three-story (1)
bq town house (2)
br tri-level (2)
bs Tudor (1)
bt two-part house (1)
bu two-story (house) (11)
bv Tudor (2)
bw Victorian (2)

119.1 U row house
No Response (88)
A attached housing (1)
B row house (31)
C row of houses (3)
D together apartments (1)
E town house (28)

119.2 U apartment building
No Response (14)
A apartment building (25)
B apartment complex (21)
C (a)partment hotel (1)
D apartment house (39)
E apartment project (1)

F   apartments (41)
G   boardinghouse (4)
H   complex (8)
I   condominium (2)
J   development (1)
K   double tenants (1)
L   duplex (25)
M   duplex apartments (1)
N   four plex (1)
O   garage apartment (1)
P   garden apartments (3)
Q   government apartment building
    (1)
R   government apartments (1)
S   government project (1)
T   high-rise (17)
U   high-rise apartment building (2)
V   high-rise apartments (3)
W   high-rise building (1)
X   housing apartments (1)
Y   housing complex (1)
Z   housing project (6)
aa multi-unit dwelling (1)
ab multi-units (1)
ac multifamily dwelling (1)
ad one-story apartment house (1)
ae project (9)
af proj(ect) (1)
ag rooming house (3)
ah row house (3)
ai slum(s) (2)
aj tenement(s) (23)
ak tenement building (1)
al tenement house (7)
am tenement housing (2)
an towers (1)
ao town house (13)
ap triplex (5)
aq two-story apartments (1)
ar walk-up (1)

119.3 U condominium
No Response (27)
A   apartment (2)
B   apartment houses (2)
C   co-op (6)
D   commune (1)
E   condo (13)
F   condomini(um) (1)
G   condominium (111)
H   duplexes (1)
I   family house (1)
J   high-rise community (1)
K   town houses (9)

119.4 U flat
No Response (62)
A   apartment (7)
B   apartment floor (1)
C   duplex (2)
D   duplex apartment (1)

E   flat (33)
F   flat apartment (1)
G   garden apartment (1)
H   ground floor (1)
I   one-level (1)
J   one-level apartments (1)
K   one-story apartment house (1)
L   penthouse (29)
M   straight-through flat (1)
N   suite (8)
O   triplex (1)
P   two-room flat (1)

119.5 U superintendent
No Response (13)
A   agent (1)
B   apartment manager (3)
C   assistant manager (2)
D   attendant (1)
E   building engineer (1)
F   building man (1)
G   building manager (3)
H   building supervisor (1)
I   caretaker (8)
J   construction (1)
K   custodian (16)
L   engineer (1)
M   handyman (10)
N   head resident (1)
O   jack-of-trades (1)
P   janitor (43)
Q   landlord (15)
R   maintenance (5)
S   maintenance engineer (1)
T   maintenance man (52)
U   maintenance person (1)
V   maintenance personnel (1)
W   maintenance upkeeper (1)
X   manager (44)
Y   rent-office man (1)
Z   repairman (8)
aa resident manager (20)
ab service worker (1)
ac serviceman (1)
ad super (5)
ae superintendent (15)
af supervisor (1)
ag upkeeper (1)
ah utility man (1)

120.1 U manual lawn mower
No Response (15)
A   armstrong (1)
B   do-it-yourself lawn mower (1)
C   hand lawn mower (1)
D   hand mower (10)
E   hand-powered mower (1)
F   lawn mow(er) (5)
G   lawn mower (90)
H   lawn mower without a motor (1)
I   lawn mower you push (1)

J   man-powered lawn mower (1)
K   manual (3)
L   manual lawn mower (2)
M   manual one (1)
N   manual-type (1)
O   mower (9)
P   old-fashion mower (1)
Q   old hand-push thing (1)
R   plain lawn mower (1)
S   push it yourself (1)
T   push lawn mower (5)
U   push mow(er) (2)
V   push mower (39)
W   push reel type (1)
X   pushing mower (1)
Y   pushing one [n.] (2)
Z   reel mower (2)
aa reel type (1)
ab reel-type lawn mower (1)
ac rotary mower (1)

120.2 U gas/electric lawn mower
No Response (22)
A   blade mower (1)
B   chain drive (1)
C   electric lawn mower (4)
D   (e)lectric mow(er) (2)
E   electric mower (8)
F   (e)lectric one (2)
G   electric push mower (1)
H   gas-driven lawn mower (1)
I   gas lawn mower (1)
J   gas mower (2)
K   gas power, a (1)
L   gas-power mower (1)
M   gas-powered (1)
N   gasoline lawn mow(er) (1)
O   gasoline mower (1)
P   lawn mow(er) (5)
Q   lawn mower (57)
R   motor-driven (lawn mower) (1)
S   motor lawn mow(er) (1)
T   motor mower (1)
U   motorized (mower) (1)
V   mower (7)
W   non-riding rotary mower (1)
X   one with the motor (1)
Y   one you push (1)
Z   power grass mower (1)
aa power lawn mower (1)
ab pow(er) mower (1)
ac power mow(er) (1)
ad power mower (34)
ae powered (1)
af pull lawn mower (1)
ag push, a (1)
ah push lawn mower (1)
ai push mow(er) (2)
aj push mower (14)
ak remote-control lawn mower (1)

al   rotary (3)
am   rotary mower (1)
an   rotary type (1)
ao   self-propel (1)
ap   self-propelled (9)
aq   self-propelled lawn mower (2)
ar   self-propelled mow(er) (1)
as   self-propelled mower (1)
at   self-propelling (1)
au   walking mower (1)

120.3 U riding lawn mower
No Response (35)
A   (e)lectric lawn mower (1)
B   grass cutter (1)
C   lawn mow(er) (1)
D   lawn mower (8)
E   lawn tractor (1)
F   Mister Dupont's mower (1)
G   mower (1)
H   one that you drive (1)
I   one that you sit on (1)
J   one you ride (1)
K   power mower (1)
L   reel-type mower (1)
M   ride lawn mower (1)
N   ride mower (1)
O   ride-and-guide (1)
P   rider (1)
Q   rider lawn mower (1)
R   rider mower (2)
S   riding (2)
T   riding kind (1)
U   riding lawn mow(er) (2)
V   riding lawn mower (29)
W   riding mow(er) (3)
X   riding mower (51)
Y   riding one (2)
Z   riding rotary mower (1)
aa   seated mower (1)
ab   sitting lawn mower (1)
ac   some that you ride on (1)
ad   tractor (3)
ae   tractor mower (2)

120.4 U tiller
No Response (51)
A   cultivator (3)
B   disking machine (1)
C   garden cultivator (1)
D   garden plow (3)
E   gasoline-driven plow (1)
F   grass grinder (1)
G   grinder (1)
H   hand plow (2)
I   motorized plow (1)
J   plow (13)
K   portable plow (1)
L   power tiller (1)
M   push plow (1)
N   roto (1)

O   Roto-Rooter (1)
P   Rototiller (15)
Q   soil tiller (1)
R   soil tilter (1)
S   tiller (63)
T   tractor (12)
U   weeder (1)

120.5 U hand trowel
No Response (53)
A   bricklayer (1)
B   cement finisher (1)
C   dandelion digger (1)
D   digger (2)
E   flower scoop (1)
F   flower-bed shovel (1)
G   flowering tool (1)
H   garden hand tool (1)
I   garden shovel (2)
J   garden trowel (1)
K   gardening shovel (1)
L   hand shovel (7)
M   hand spade (3)
N   hand tool (3)
O   hand trowel (3)
P   hole digger (1)
Q   little garden tool (1)
R   little shovel (1)
S   little shovel-like, a (1)
T   little spade (2)
U   little spatula (1)
V   little-old garden shovel (1)
W   miniature hand shovel (1)
X   potting tool (1)
Y   scoop (4)
Z   sharpshooter (1)
aa   shovel (18)
ab   smoother (1)
ac   spade (26)
ad   spade-like tool (1)
ae   spatula (2)
af   spoon (1)
ag   trowel (34)

120.6 U hand fork
No Response (92)
A   claw (3)
B   cultivating tool (1)
C   digger (1)
D   flower fork (1)
E   fork (19)
F   garden fork (5)
G   garden pick (1)
H   grader (1)
I   hand cultivator (1)
J   hand digger (1)
K   hand fork (13)
L   hand rake (5)
M   hand trowel (1)
N   little fork (1)
O   little rake-like tool (1)

P   pitchfork (1)
Q   prongs (1)
R   pruning fork (1)
S   rake (1)
T   scraper (1)
U   scratcher (1)
V   small fork (1)
W   trowel (1)

120.7 U rake
No Response (11)
A   bamboo rake (3)
B   broom (1)
C   broom rake (3)
D   dirt rake (7)
E   fan rake (1)
F   field rake (1)
G   flat rake (1)
H   garden rake (24)
I   grass broom (1)
J   grass rake (8)
K   grass sweeper (1)
L   hand rake (3)
M   hard rake (1)
N   hay rake (1)
O   heavy [n.] (1)
P   heavy rake (2)
Q   hoe rake (1)
R   iron rake (6)
S   iron-tooth rake (1)
T   lawn rake (11)
U   leaf rake (37)
V   lightweight rake (1)
W   little rake (1)
X   metal one (1)
Y   metal rake (1)
Z   mud rake (1)
aa   potato rake (1)
ab   prong rake (1)
ac   pull rake (1)
ad   pulling rake (1)
ae   rake (103)
af   real rake (1)
ag   regular rake (1)
ah   rock rake (1)
ai   spider fingers (1)
aj   steel rake (2)
ak   stiff rake (1)
al   sweep [n.] (1)
am   sweeping rake (1)
an   wide-tooth rake (1)
ao   wire broom (1)
ap   wire rake (2)
aq   yard broom (6)
ar   yard rake (17)

120.8 U hedge trimmer
No Response (13)
A   big clippers (1)
B   clipper(s) (51)
C   cutters (1)

D   edge cutter (1)
E   edger(s) (14)
F   edger trimmer (1)
G   electric clippers (8)
H   electric grass clippers (1)
I   electric hedge clippers (5)
J   electric hedge cutter (1)
K   electric hedge shears (2)
L   electric hedge trimmer(s) (2)
M   electric hedger (1)
N   electric shears (3)
O   electric trimmer (1)
P   electrical shears (1)
Q   electricity clippers (1)
R   garden shears (1)
S   grass cutters (1)
T   hand shears (1)
U   hand trimmer(s) (4)
V   hedge clipper(s) (39)
W   hedge cutter(s) (12)
X   hedge shear(s) (9)
Y   hedge snips (1)
Z   hedge trimmer(s) (30)
aa   hedger(s) (8)
ab   hedging clippers (1)
ac   little clippers (1)
ad   loppers (1)
ae   manual hedge trimmer (1)
af   power clippers (2)
ag   power cutters (1)
ah   power hedge trimmer (1)
ai   pruner(s) (3)
aj   pruning shears (7)
ak   scissors (2)
al   shears (19)
am   snipper nose (1)
an   snips (2)
ao   tree trimmer (1)
ap   trimmer(s) (4)
aq   yard scissors (2)

120.9 U chain saw
No Response (15)
A   chain saw (82)
B   chain-link saw (1)
C   electric handsaw (1)
D   electric saw (21)
E   electrical saw (5)
F   gas saw (1)
G   gasoline saw (1)
H   gassed saw (1)
I   high-powered saw (1)
J   motor-operated (saw) (1)
K   pop saw (1)
L   power blade (1)
M   power chain saw (1)
N   power saw (42)
O   powered saw (1)
P   rotary saw (1)
Q   saw (27)

R   tree saw (1)

121.1 U beefsteak
No Response (10)
A   beef (3)
B   beefsteak (8)
C   boneless steak (1)
D   Chateaubriand (1)
E   chop (1)
F   chop steak (4)
G   chopped steak (1)
H   chuck (2)
I   chuck steak (9)
J   club (1)
K   club steak (6)
L   country rib eye (1)
M   cube (1)
N   cube steak (5)
O   Delmonico (6)
P   Delmonico steak (1)
Q   Delmonico strip (1)
R   eye of the round (4)
S   filet mignon (18)
T   fillet (9)
U   fillet steak (2)
V   flank (2)
W   flank steak (8)
X   hamburger steak (1)
Y   Kansas City (steak) (2)
Z   Kansas City strip steak (1)
aa   KC strip steak (1)
ab   loin (2)
ac   loin steak (1)
ad   London broil (5)
ae   minute (1)
af   minute steak (2)
ag   New York (steak) (2)
ah   New York steak (1)
ai   New York strip (6)
aj   New York strip steak (2)
ak   New York stripper (1)
al   New Yorker (1)
am   plank steak (1)
an   porter (something) (1)
ao   porterhouse (22)
ap   porterhouse steak (6)
aq   quarterhouse (1)
ar   rib (2)
as   rib eye (25)
at   rib-eye steak (5)
au   rib steak (6)
av   round (7)
aw   round (steak) (2)
ax   round steak (40)
ay   rump (3)
az   Salisbury steak (2)
ba   seven steak (3)
bb   shoulder steak (3)
bc   sirloin (60)
bd   sirloin steak (17)

be   sirloin strip (2)
bf   sirloin tip (7)
bg   sirloin-tip steak (1)
bh   skirt steak (1)
bi   steak (48)
bj   strip (6)
bk   strip steak (2)
bl   T-bone (60)
bm   T-bone steak (24)
bn   tenderloin (9)
bo   tenderloin steak (1)
bp   veal steak (1)

121.2 U cuts of beef
No Response (24)
A   backbone (1)
B   bacon (1)
C   beef liver (2)
D   beef neck bones (1)
E   beef ribs (4)
F   beef roast (7)
G   beef tip (1)
H   beef tongue (2)
I   beef tripe (1)
J   boneless rump (1)
K   Boston roll (2)
L   brisket (6)
M   brisket meat (1)
N   brisket of beef (1)
O   butt ends (1)
P   calf liver (2)
Q   chopped (1)
R   chops (3)
S   chuck (3)
T   chuck beef (1)
U   chuck roast (19)
V   cow beef (1)
W   cow brain (1)
X   cow tongue (2)
Y   English cut (2)
Z   English-cut roast (2)
aa   eye (1)
ab   eye of the round (3)
ac   eye round (1)
ad   flank (1)
ae   ground (1)
af   ground beef (20)
ag   ground chuck (9)
ah   ground meat (2)
ai   ground round (6)
aj   ground-up meat (1)
ak   hamburg(er) (1)
al   hamburger (42)
am   hamburger meat (3)
an   hamburger patties (1)
ao   hindquarter of beef (1)
ap   hindquarters (1)
aq   kidney (1)
ar   liver (2)
as   liver beef (1)

at London broil (5)
au loin (6)
av loin tip roast (2)
aw oxtails (1)
ax pot roast (4)
ay prime rib (2)
az prime rib roast (1)
ba prime roast (1)
bb rib beef (2)
bc rib roast (11)
bd ribs (20)
be roast (40)
bf roast made from the round (1)
bg roll roast (1)
bh rolled roast (1)
bi round (1)
bj round roast (5)
bk rump (9)
bl rump roast (29)
bm sausage (1)
bn shank (1)
bo short ribs (3)
bp shoulder (6)
bq shoulder beef (2)
br shoulder meat (1)
bs shoulder roast (12)
bt side of beef (1)
bu sirloin patties (1)
bv sirloin tip (5)
bw sirloin-tip roast (1)
bx soup bones (2)
by soup meat (1)
bz standing rib roast (2)
ca stew beef (1)
cb stew meat (9)
cc tongue (5)
cd tripe (4)
ce veal chops (1)
cf veal cutlet (2)
cg veal liver (1)

121.3 U cuts of pork
No Response (10)
A backbone(s) (10)
B bacon (36)
C boiling meat (1)
D Boston butt(s) (3)
E breakfast chop (1)
F Canadian bacon (2)
G center cut(s) (2)
H center-cut pork chops (2)
I chitlins (3)
J chitterlings (1)
K chops (4)
L country bacon (1)
M cracklings (1)
N dinner chop (1)
O ears (3)
P end cut(s) (2)
Q fatback (3)

R feet (4)
S flank (1)
T half a ham (1)
U ham(s) (87)
V ham hock(s) (7)
W ham roast (2)
X ham steak(s) (5)
Y hambone (1)
Z hindquarter (1)
aa hocks (1)
ab hog (1)
ac hog bone (1)
ad hog brains (2)
ae hog jaw (1)
af hog jowl(s) (5)
ag hog liver (1)
ah hog neck bones (1)
ai hog tail(s) (1)
aj hog's feet (1)
ak hog's head (1)
al jowls (2)
am little picnic hams (1)
an liver (3)
ao loin(s) (8)
ap loin chops (2)
aq neck bone(s) (5)
ar picnic [=ham] (1)
as picnic [=shoulder] (1)
at picnic ham(s) (14)
au picnic shoulders (1)
av pig ears (9)
aw pig feet (16)
ax pig knuckles (2)
ay pig legs (1)
az pig tail(s) (13)
ba pig tongue (2)
bb pigs' brains (1)
bc pigs' feet (14)
bd pork (11)
be pork chop(s) (96)
bf pork liver (1)
bg pork loin(s) (8)
bh pork loin roast(s) (3)
bi pork meat (ground) (1)
bj pork neck bones (1)
bk pork ribs (4)
bl pork roast(s) (26)
bm pork round (1)
bn pork shoulder (6)
bo pork shoulder roast (1)
bp pork steak(s) (7)
bq quarter cuts (1)
br quarter loin (1)
bs rear end (1)
bt rib chops (1)
bu rib pork (1)
bv ribs (23)
bw roast (6)
bx round (1)

by rump(s) (2)
bz salt meat (1)
ca shanks (2)
cb shoulder(s) (18)
cc shoulder cuts (1)
cd shoulder ham (2)
ce shoulder loin (1)
cf shoulder roast (2)
cg side meat (1)
ch souse meat (1)
ci spareribs (14)
cj steak pork (1)
ck streak of lean (1)
cl tenderloin(s) (6)
cm tongue (1)
cn white meat (1)
[ham]
co baked ham (2)
cp boil ham (1)
cq boiled ham (1)
cr boneless ham (1)
cs can ham (1)
ct canned ham (1)
cu city ham (1)
cv cooked ham (1)
cw country-fried ham (1)
cx country ham (14)
cy country smoked ham (1)
ca country style (1)
da cure ham (2)
db cured ham (13)
dc diced ham (1)
dd fresh ham (2)
de fried ham (1)
df hickory ham (1)
dg little picnic hams (1)
dh picnic (1)
di picnic ham(s) (14)
dj raw ham (1)
dk ready-cooked ham (1)
dl roast ham (1)
dm salt-cured ham (1)
dn salted ham (2)
do shoulder ham (2)
dp sliced ham (1)
dq smoke ham (2)
dr smoked ham (22)
ds sugar-cure ham (1)
dt sugar-cured ham (7)
du sweet ham (1)
dv Tennessee country ham (1)
dw Virginia ham (3)
dx whole ham (4)
121.4 U cuts of lamb
No Response (38)
A breast of (the) lamb (3)
B brisket (1)
C chops (5)
D crown roast (2)

S   poor boy sandwich (10)
T   Reuben (1)
U   sub (6)
V   sub sandwich (3)
W   submarine (41)
X   submarine sandwich (25)
Y   super sub (1)
Z   yogi (1)

121.8 U soft drinks
No Response (4)
A   beverage (1)
B   carbonated drink (2)
C   chocolate Coke (1)
D   Coca-Cola (1)
E   Coke [=cola drink] (26)
F   Coke [=soft drink] (35)
G   cola (8)
H   cola drink (1)
I   cold drink (13)
J   cool drink (2)
K   dope [=Coke] (2)
L   dope [=cola drinks] (1)
M   dope [=soft drinks] (1)
N   drink (11)
O   grape Coke (1)
P   orange Coke (1)
Q   pop (31)
R   sarsaparilla (1)
S   soda (24)
T   soda pop (11)
U   soda water (10)
V   soft drink (61)
W   soft drink [=fruit drink] (2)
X   soft drink beverage (1)
Y   soft pop (1)

121.9 U beer
No Response (22)
A   ale (4)
B   backwater (1)
C   beer (109)
D   bock beer (1)
E   bottle beer (1)
F   brew (24)
G   bubbly (1)
H   chilly cool (1)
I   cola (1)
J   cold one (1)
K   Colorado Kool-Aid (1)
L   dark (1)
M   draft (3)
N   draft beer (4)
O   Gatorade (1)
P   grog (1)
Q   heavy beer (1)
R   home brew (2)
S   keg beer (1)
T   Kool-Aid (1)
U   lager beer (1)
V   light (1)

W   light beer (3)
X   loose juice (1)
Y   malt liquor (1)
Z   mucky beer (1)
aa   pearl pop with foam on top (1)
ab   suds (33)
ac   three point two (1)
ad   three-two beer (1)
ae   weak beer (1)

122.1 U coffee cake
No Response (36)
A   cake (14)
B   cheese cake (1)
C   coffee cake (83)
D   coffee ring (2)
E   crumb cake (1)
F   Danish (6)
G   Danish ring (1)
H   Danish-type thing (1)
I   ginger breakfast cake (1)
J   nutcake (2)
K   pastry (4)
L   pastry cake (1)
M   streusel (1)
N   strudel (1)
O   sweet bread (3)
P   tea cake (2)

122.2 U sweet roll
No Response (22)
A   almond Danish (1)
B   bear claw (1)
C   breakfast roll (5)
D   cherry Danish (1)
E   chokers (1)
F   cinnam(on) bun (1)
G   cinnamon bun (4)
H   cinnamon Danish (1)
I   cinnamon roll (34)
J   cinnamon sweet roll (1)
K   cinnamon-type roll (1)
L   coffee cake (6)
M   coffee roll (7)
N   Danish (34)
O   Danish bun (1)
P   Danish go-(a)rounds (1)
Q   Danish pastry (12)
R   Danish roll (12)
S   finger roll (1)
T   French roll (1)
U   fruit Danish (1)
V   honey bun (3)
W   hope hearts (1)
X   jelly Danish (1)
Y   jelly roll (2)
Z   melt aways (1)
aa   pastry (8)
ab   pecan Danish (1)
ac   pecan roll (2)
ad   prune Danish (1)

ae   raspberry Danish (1)
af   snails (1)
ag   strawberry Danish (1)
ah   streusel (1)
ai   strudel (1)
aj   sugar bun (1)
ak   Swedish pastry (1)
al   sweet bread (1)
am   sweet bun (1)
an   sweet cake (1)
ao   sweet roll (56)
ap   tea cake (1)

122.3 U frosting
No Response (22)
A   frosting (45)
B   glaze (60)
C   glazing (3)
D   glossing (1)
E   icing (98)
F   topping (2)

122.4 U frosted doughnut
No Response (85)
A   chocolate doughnut (1)
B   chocolate-coated doughnut (2)
C   chocolate-covered doughnut (6)
D   chocolate-frosted (2)
E   crispy doughnut (1)
F   dipped (1)
G   frosted doughnut (6)
H   glaze doughnut (26)
I   glazed doughnut (21)
J   iced doughnut (4)
K   plain glazed (1)
L   sugar-dipped doughnut (1)
M   sugar-frosted (1)
N   sugar-glaze doughnut (1)

122.5 U long john
No Response (98)
A   beignets [F] (3)
B   doughnut (1)
C   dunking doughnut (1)
D   French-cut doughnut (1)
E   frosted doughnut (1)
F   long john (11)
G   square one (1)

122.6 U bismarck
No Response (29)
A   Bavarian cream (1)
B   bismarck (3)
C   cherry-filled doughnut (1)
D   cream doughnut (4)
E   cream-fill doughnut (5)
F   cream-filled doughnut (10)
G   cream fills (1)
H   cream puff (6)
I   fill doughnut (2)
J   filled doughnut (5)
K   fruit-filled doughnut (1)
L   jellied doughnut (1)

M   jellies (2)
N   jelly bun (2)
O   jelly doughnut (53)
P   jelly-fill doughnut (8)
Q   jelly-filled doughnut (18)
R   jelly puff (1)
S   jelly roll (18)
T   lemon doughnut (1)
U   lemon-filled doughnut (2)
V   lemon puff (4)
W   powder doughnut (1)
X   puff (2)
Y   raspberry lemon puff (1)
Z   raspberry puff (1)

122.7 U cruller
No Response (68)
A   cinnamon stick (1)
B   cinnamon twist (5)
C   coffee doughnut (1)
D   crul(ler) (2)
E   cruller (20)
F   curl doughnut (1)
G   curler (2)
H   doughnut (1)
I   doughnut [twisted] (1)
J   doughnut twist (6)
K   French curl (1)
L   French twist (2)
M   squirrel (1)
N   sugar doughnut (1)
O   sugar twist (1)
P   sugar twisted doughnut (1)
Q   swirl (1)
R   twirl (2)
S   twist (21)
T   twist doughnut (1)
U   twisted (1)
V   twisted cinnamon roll (1)
W   twisted doughnut (16)
X   twisted roll (1)
Y   twisted-up doughnut (1)
Z   twister (5)

123.1 U finger ring
No Response (19)
A   amethyst (1)
B   bauble (1)
C   big rock (1)
D   big sparkler (1)
E   birthday ring (1)
F   birthstone (ring) (10)
G   black onyx (1)
H   cameo ring (1)
I   class ring (12)
J   club ring (1)
K   clunker (1)
L   cluster (3)
M   cocktail ring (3)
N   costume jewelry/ring (8)
O   diamond (16)

P   diamond (ring) (12)
Q   dinner ring (23)
R   egg (1)
S   engagement (ring) (18)
T   eye-catcher (1)
U   fashion ring (1)
V   finger ring (1)
W   friendship (ring) (4)
X   gewgaw (1)
Y   glittering glass (1)
Z   graduation ring (1)
aa   huge ring (1)
ab   hunk of ice (2)
ac   hunk of rock (1)
ad   ice (5)
ae   life ring (1)
af   light bulb (1)
ag   Masonic ring (1)
ah   mood ring (1)
ai   Mother's ring (1)
aj   nigger (1)
ak   pagoda ring (1)
al   party ring (2)
am   piece of ice (1)
an   pinky ring (1)
ao   princess ring (1)
ap   promise (1)
aq   ring (77)
ar   rock [=ring] (1)
as   rock [=stone] (19)
at   ruby (1)
au   service ring (1)
av   shiny stuff (1)
aw   Shrine ring (1)
ax   solitaire (1)
ay   sparkler (1)
az   star (1)
ba   stone (3)
bb   stone [=ring] (1)
bc   tacky ring (1)
bd   turquoise ring (1)

123.2 U knee-length shorts
No Response (20)
A   (Ber)muda shorts (1)
B   Bermuda shorts (57)
C   Bermudas (16)
D   bloomers (1)
E   calypso stuff (1)
F   city shorts (1)
G   culottes (4)
H   cutoffs (2)
I   gauchos (1)
J   knee knockers (8)
K   knee pants (2)
L   knee shorts (2)
M   knee-high shorts (1)
N   knee-length pants (1)
O   knee-length shorts (1)
P   knee-length walking shorts (1)

Q   knickerbockers (5)
R   knickerbottoms (1)
S   knickers (10)
T   knockers (1)
U   long shorts (2)
V   outside shorts (1)
W   pedal pushers (11)
X   regular shorts (1)
Y   short pants (7)
Z   shorts (26)
aa   walking shorts (25)

123.3 U below-the-knee shorts
No Response (46)
A   ankle wipers (1)
B   Bermuda shorts (3)
C   bloomers (1)
D   breeches (1)
E   calypso pants (1)
F   clam diggers (6)
G   culottes (4)
H   cutoff pants (1)
I   cutoffs (2)
J   gaucho pants (1)
K   gauchos (3)
L   golf pants (1)
M   high waters (5)
N   knee knockers (1)
O   knickerbockers (3)
P   knickers (22)
Q   Liederhosen (1)
R   long shorts (2)
S   maxis (1)
T   middy (1)
U   midways (1)
V   pantaloons (1)
W   pants (7)
X   pedal pushers (46)
Y   short pair of breeches (1)
Z   short pants (2)
aa   shorts (1)
ab   surfers (1)

123.4 U above-the-knee shorts
No Response (23)
A   Bermuda shorts (5)
B   Bermudas (1)
C   bikini shorts (1)
D   bikinis (1)
E   briefs (1)
F   cutoff shorts (1)
G   cutoffs (8)
H   gym shorts (7)
I   hiking shorts (1)
J   hot pants (39)
K   Jamaica shorts (1)
L   jogging shorts (2)
M   mid-thigh shorts (1)
N   middy shorts (1)
O   minishorts (2)
P   short shorts (78)

Q   shorts (37)
R   tennis shorts (4)
S   tights (1)
T   too-short shorts (1)
U   trunks (1)
V   walking shorts (3)

123.5 U used clothes

No Response (11)
A   castoffs (5)
B   charity (1)
C   cheap clothing (1)
D   donations (1)
E   givaways (3)
F   hand-me-downs (119)
G   hand-me-outs (1)
H   hand-me-overs (1)
I   hand-you-downs (2)
J   hand-[M-0]-downs (1)
K   handouts (1)
L   leftovers (2)
M   old clothes (5)
N   pass-me-downs (1)
O   reclaimed clothing (1)
P   recycled (1)
Q   retreads (1)
R   rummage (1)
S   rummage clothes (1)
T   salvage (1)
U   secondhand clothes/clothing/
      garments (45)
V   secondhanded clothes (3)
W   secondhands (5)
X   seconds (2)
Y   thrift clothes (1)
Z   thrift-store clothes (1)
aa   throw-offs (1)
ab   throwaways (1)
ac   use clothes/clothing (5)
ad   used clothes/clothing (20)
ae   worn-over clothes (1)

123.6 U fashionable clothes

No Response (38)
A   bad (1)
B   bad rags (3)
C   beautiful rags (1)
D   best clothes (1)
E   chic (11)
F   classy (1)
G   contemporary clothing (1)
H   cool (2)
I   cool studs (1)
J   courtiers (1)
K   couturier (1)
L   designer clothes (2)
M   designer fashions (1)
N   drags (1)
O   dress clothes (2)
P   dress like a pimp (1)
Q   dress[V-t] to kill (1)

R   dress[V-t] to the hilt (1)
S   duds (6)
T   expensive clothes (7)
U   faddish (1)
V   fancy (1)
W   fancy duds (1)
X   fancy Toms (1)
Y   far-out (1)
Z   fashion (1)
aa   fashionable clothes (6)
ab   fashionable things (1)
ac   fast (1)
ad   fine clothes (3)
ae   fine, fashionable clothes (1)
af   flashy clothes (5)
ag   funky-wearing clothes (1)
ah   glitter stuff (1)
ai   good clothes (1)
aj   good-looking clothes (3)
ak   GQ (1)
al   high-class (1)
am   high fashion (3)
an   high style (1)
ao   in (1)
ap   in good taste (1)
aq   in style (5)
ar   jive (1)
as   jive clothes (1)
at   late-model (1)
au   looks sharp (1)
av   loud colors (1)
aw   mod (1)
ax   modern (1)
ay   neat clothes (2)
az   neat threads (1)
ba   new clothes (1)
bb   nice clothes/clothing (2)
bc   nice dress (1)
bd   nice threads (1)
be   nice-looking (1)
bf   on the scene (1)
bg   out of sight (1)
bh   pimp clothes (2)
bi   pimp shirt (1)
bj   pimp stuff (1)
bk   popular (1)
bl   preppy (1)
bm   pretty clothes (1)
bn   rags (7)
bo   real sharp-looking clothes (1)
bp   really skintight (1)
bq   ritzy (1)
br   sharp clothes/clothing (8)
bs   sharp dresser (1)
bt   sharp suit (1)
bu   sharp threads (1)
bv   slick (3)
bw   smart (3)
bx   sophisticated (1)

by   spiffy (1)
bz   spiffy duds (1)
ca   spiffy threads (1)
cb   stud clothes (1)
cc   studs (1)
cd   stylish clothes (8)
ce   suave (1)
cf   Sunday clothes (2)
cg   Sunday-go-to-meeting clothes (1)
ch   super fly (1)
ci   super toggery (1)
cj   super togs (1)
ck   swank (1)
cl   swanky togs (1)
cm   tailor-made (1)
cn   tailored (1)
co   threads (20)
cp   toggery (1)
cq   tweeds (1)
cr   uptown (1)
cs   very becoming (1)
ct   vogue (1)
cu   wealthy clothes (1)
cv   with it (1)

123.7 U garment bag

No Response (22)
A   bag (13)
B   boot bag (1)
C   canvas bag (1)
D   carry-on bag (1)
E   carryall (1)
F   cedar closet (1)
G   cellophane bag (7)
H   cleaner bag (2)
I   cleaners bag (4)
J   cleaning bag (1)
K   cloth bag (1)
L   clothes bag (29)
M   clothes case (1)
N   clothes container (1)
O   clothes hanger (1)
P   clothing bag (5)
Q   coat bag (1)
R   cover (2)
S   dress bag (1)
T   film bag (1)
U   flight bag (3)
V   fold-over bag (1)
W   garment bag (30)
X   green plastic bag (1)
Y   handbag (2)
Z   hang-up bag (2)
aa   hanger (1)
ab   hanger bag (1)
ac   hanging bag (7)
ad   laundry bag (5)
ae   little storage thing (1)
af   luggage bag (1)
ag   moth bag (8)

ah   mothball bag (4)
ai   mothproof bag (9)
aj   nylon bag (1)
ak   overnight bag (2)
al   plastic bag (57)
am   plastic cleaner bag (1)
an   plastic cover (1)
ao   proof bag (1)
ap   protective bag (1)
aq   protector (1)
ar   rat pack (1)
as   sack (2)
at   storage bag (22)
au   stretch bag (1)
av   suit bag (17)
aw   suiter (1)
ax   tote bag (1)
ay   travel bag (9)
az   traveling bag (4)
ba   two-suiter (1)
bb   weekend bag (1)
bc   winter bag (1)
bd   wrapper (1)
be   zip bag (1)
bf   zipper bag (2)

123.8 U shoes

No Response (8)
A   alligators (1)
B   ankle boots (1)
C   ankle straps (1)
D   baby dolls (1)
E   ballerina (shoes) (1)
F   ballet-type (shoes) (1)
G   baseball shoes (1)
H   basketball shoes (1)
I   Bass Weejuns (1)
J   beach shoes (2)
K   bedroom shoes (4)
L   bedroom slippers (4)
M   black-and-white oxfords (1)
N   blucher shoes (3)
O   boat shoes (1)
P   boots (46)
Q   box toes (1)
R   brogans (4)
S   brogues (2)
T   bucks (4)
U   bum-around shoes (1)
V   butterfies (1)
W   button shoes (2)
X   Candies (1)
Y   casual shoes (12)
Z   cheerleader shoes (1)
aa   chukkas (1)
ab   clam diggers (1)
ac   cleats (1)
ad   clobblers (1)
ae   clodhoppers (1)
af   clods (1)

ag   clogs (7)
ah   close-toed shoes (1)
ai   closed-in shoes (1)
aj   closed shoe (1)
ak   combat boots (2)
al   cork shoes (1)
am   cowboy boots (6)
an   crutches (1)
ao   cutout sandals (1)
ap   cutouts (1)
aq   deck shoes (3)
ar   desert boots (2)
as   dress boots (3)
at   dress shoes (33)
au   dress-up shoes (1)
av   dressed-up shoes (1)
aw   dressy shoes (4)
ax   E. Z. Walkers (2)
ay   Earth shoes (7)
az   espadrilles (1)
ba   evening (shoes) (1)
bb   everyday shoes (2)
bc   flat sandals (1)
bd   flat shoes (1)
be   flat walking shoes (1)
bf   flats (11)
bg   flip-flops (12)
bh   flip ons (1)
bi   flops (1)
bj   football shoes (2)
bk   formal dress shoes (1)
bl   formal shoes (2)
bm   fuzzies (1)
bn   galoshes (1)
bo   go-go boots (1)
bp   golf shoes (2)
bq   gym shoes (2)
br   hard-sole shoes (1)
bs   hard soles (1)
bt   heels (11)
bu   high boots (1)
bv   high-button shoes (1)
bw   high-heel dress shoes (1)
bx   high-heel shoes (11)
by   high-heel spike shoes (1)
bz   high-heel things (1)
ca   high heels (37)
cb   high-lace shoes (1)
cc   high shoes (1)
cd   high-top shoes (3)
ce   high tops (3)
cf   hiking boots (4)
cg   hippie shoes (1)
ch   horseback-riding shoes (1)
ci   house shoes (7)
cj   house slippers (1)
ck   huaraches (2)
cl   hunting boots (4)
cm   Hush Puppies (6)

cn   Hustlers (1)
co   Indian shoes (1)
cp   insurance shoes (1)
cq   Jap slaps (1)
cr   Jesus sandals (1)
cs   jogging shoes (1)
ct   Keds (2)
cu   kicks (1)
cv   knockabouts (1)
cw   lace shoes (1)
cx   lace-up shoes (3)
cy   lace-ups (3)
cz   laced shoes (2)
da   lacing-up shoes (1)
db   leather shoes (4)
dc   lifts (1)
dd   lizard (shoes) (1)
de   loafers (54)
df   low-cut shoes (1)
dg   low-heel pumps (1)
dh   low-heel shoes (2)
di   low heels (8)
dj   low quarters (2)
dk   low shoes (1)
dl   medium heels (1)
dm   military heels (1)
dn   mini-boots (1)
do   moccasins (10)
dp   mukluks (1)
dq   mules (1)
dr   nigger shoes (1)
ds   open-toed pumps (1)
dt   open-toed shoes (4)
du   open toes (1)
dv   oxfords (21)
dw   partying shoes (1)
dx   patent-leather pumps (1)
dy   patent-leather shoes (2)
dz   penny loafers (1)
ea   plain-toe shoes (1)
eb   plain toes (1)
ec   platform heels (1)
ed   platform shoes (6)
ee   platforms (12)
ef   plowshoes (1)
eg   pointed (1)
eh   pointed toes (1)
ei   pointy toes (1)
ej   pump shoes (1)
ek   pumps (31)
el   rain shoes (1)
em   reptile (1)
en   riding boots (2)
eo   rubber boots (1)
ep   running shoes (1)
eq   saddle oxfords (3)
er   sandals (88)
es   sandals-like (1)
et   scare-off boots (1)

eu   shit kickers (1)
ev   shit shoes (1)
ew   shit stompers (1)
ex   shoes (7)
ey   skiing shoes (1)
ez   slides (3)
fa   sling backs (1)
fb   sling pumps (1)
fc   slip-ons (6)
fd   slipover shoes (1)
fe   slipper shoes (1)
ff   slippers (17)
fg   sneakers (27)
fh   snow boots (1)
fi   snowshoes (1)
fj   sole-frame shoes (1)
fk   spike heels (4)
fl   spiked heels (2)
fm   spikes (3)
fn   sports (1)
fo   square heels (1)
fp   square toes (1)
fq   stabbers (1)
fr   stack heels (5)
fs   stacks (9)
ft   stilts (1)
fu   straight pair of shoes (1)
fv   straps (1)
fw   street shoes (1)
fx   stump kickers (1)
fy   suede shoes (3)
fz   support shoes (1)
ga   suppository stabbers (1)
gb   surfer shoes (1)
gc   T straps (2)
gd   tennies (1)
ge   tennis (6)
gf   tennis shoes (72)
gg   tennises (2)
gh   tenny shoes (1)
gi   thick soles (1)
gj   thongs (7)
gk   tie shoes (3)
gl   tie-up shoes (1)
gm   Topsiders (4)
gn   track shoes (1)
go   traps (1)
gp   truckers (1)
gq   uppers (1)
gr   walking shoes (1)
gs   Wallabys (1)
gt   wedge-heel sandals (1)
gu   wedge heels (7)
gv   wedged heel (shoes) (1)
gw   wedges (5)
gx   wedgies (4)
gy   Weejuns (3)
gz   Western boots (1)
ha   wing-tip shoes (2)

hb   wing tips (14)
hc   winkle-picker shoes (1)
hd   work boots (1)
he   work shoes (4)
hf   working boots (1)
hg   working shoes (1)
hh   yo-yos (1)
hi   zip-up boots (1)
hj   zip-up shoes (1)

123.9 U hairstyles
No Response (22)
A   African (2)
B   (A)fro (8)
C   Afro (75)
D   Afro hair (1)
E   Afro look (1)
F   Afro style (1)
G   angel wings (2)
H   army cut (1)
I   artichoke (1)
J   Balboa (1)
K   ball (1)
L   bangs (3)
M   barrow white (1)
N   beehive (9)
O   blow back (1)
P   blow cut (1)
Q   blow out [n.] (1)
R   blowout Afro (1)
S   blunt cut (1)
T   bob (3)
U   bobbed (2)
V   bopeep (1)
W   bouffant (14)
X   bouffant style (1)
Y   box style (1)
Z   boy greasy look (1)
aa   boy look (1)
ab   boyish bob (1)
ac   braid(s) (14)
ad   braided (8)
ae   braided look (1)
af   braiding (2)
ag   brush back (1)
ah   bubble (1)
ai   buckwheat (1)
aj   bumblebee (1)
ak   bun (3)
al   burr (2)
am   burr cut (3)
an   burr haircut (3)
ao   bush (6)
ap   bushwhack (1)
aq   Buster Brown (1)
ar   butch (6)
as   butch cut (2)
at   buzz (1)
au   California curls (1)
av   calvo [S] (1)

aw   cavani haircut (1)
ax   chili bowl (1)
ay   cluster curls (1)
az   coiffures (1)
ba   completely natural (1)
bb   conked (1)
bc   cooter cage (1)
bd   cornrows (26)
be   cornstalks (1)
bf   crew cut (38)
bg   croquignole (1)
bh   curl(s) (2)
bi   curled (2)
bj   curly [n.] (2)
bk   curly (A)fro (1)
bl   curly Afro (1)
bm   curly look (1)
bn   curly top (2)
bo   DA (1)
bp   dried up (1)
bq   duck's ass (1)
br   ducktail (5)
bs   ducktail haircut (1)
bt   Dutch boy (3)
bu   Dutch-boy cut (1)
bv   English [n.] (1)
bw   falloff (1)
bx   Farah Fawcet (1)
by   feathercut (3)
bz   feathered (1)
ca   feathered back (1)
cb   flattop (20)
cc   flip (6)
cd   fluffed (1)
ce   freak (1)
cf   freedom (A)fro (1)
cg   French braids (2)
ch   French style (1)
ci   French twist (2)
cj   frizzy [n.] (2)
ck   frosted (1)
cl   garcon haircut (1)
cm   GI (2)
cn   GI Joe (1)
co   gypsy (1)
cp   haystack (1)
cq   hippie cut (1)
cr   hippie haircut (1)
cs   hippie style (2)
ct   honey-dripper style (1)
cu   honeycomb (1)
cv   ironed-[J-0]-pressed look (1)
cw   Isaac Hayes (1)
cx   jelly roll (1)
cy   Jerry curl (1)
cz   Joe Namath look (1)
da   kinked (1)
db   kinky (1)
dc   knotty haircut (1)

dd layer (1)
de layer cut (1)
df layered (1)
dg long (hair) (16)
dh long and straight (2)
di long curls (1)
dj long shag (1)
dk long style (1)
dl long-haired hippie (1)
dm love knots (1)
dn low Afro (1)
do low cut (2)
dp Marcel (1)
dq Marine haircut (2)
dr military cut (1)
ds mini-Afro (1)
dt mod (2)
du mod cut (1)
dv Mohawk (3)
dw Mohican (1)
dx natural [n.] (10)
dy neckline (haircut) (1)
dz non-teased (1)
ea old-country look (1)
eb old-lady style (1)
ec page (1)
ed pageboy (15)
ee perm (1)
ef permanent (10)
eg permanent process (1)
eh pigtail(s) (11)
ei pixie (6)
ej pixie cut (1)
ek plain (1)
el plaited (5)
em plaited in rows (1)
en plaited up (1)
eo plaiting (1)
ep plaits (4)
eq pompadour (7)
er pompano (1)
es ponytail (25)
et poodle perms (1)
eu pressed (2)
ev process (2)
ew Psyche (1)
ex pyramid (1)
ey Quo Vadis (1)
ez razor cut (1)
fa rich man (1)
fb rolled (1)
fc rows (2)
fd Satsuma (2)
fe shag (32)
ff shag cut (2)
fg shag haircut (1)
fh shingle cut (1)
fi shingled (1)
fj Shirley Temple (1)

fk short (hair) (9)
fl short and sassy (1)
fm short shag (1)
fn skinny (1)
fo soup bowl (1)
fp square haircut (1)
fq straight (3)
fr straight look (1)
fs straightened (1)
ft taper cut (1)
fu teased (3)
fv teased head (1)
fw teasing (1)
fx Tenille (1)
fy underbraid (1)
fz underbraid and overbraid (1)
ga updo (1)
gb Washington haircut (1)
gc wave the hair (1)
gd waves (1)
ge wedge (2)
gf wedge cut (1)
gg whitewalls (1)
gh windblown (1)
gi wings (2)

124.1 U effeminate male

No Response (28)
A candy (1)
B drag queen (1)
C duck (1)
D effeminate (25)
E effeminate guy (1)
F effeminate type (1)
G effete (2)
H fag (14)
I faggot (5)
J faggy (1)
K fairy (4)
L female impersonator (1)
M feminine (8)
N feminine man (1)
O feminist (2)
P fly-by-night (1)
Q freak (4)
R funny (4)
S funny boy (1)
T gay (3)
U gay boy (2)
V gay person (1)
W girl (1)
X girlified (1)
Y girlish (3)
Z he she (2)
aa he squats to pee (1)
ab homo (2)
ac kook (1)
ad left-handed people (1)
ae Lesbian (1)
af lightweight (1)

ag limp-wristed (1)
ah mamma's boy (2)
ai odd (1)
aj old-maidish (1)
ak on the gay side (1)
al pansy (2)
am pimp (1)
an pretty boy (2)
ao punk (9)
ap puss (1)
aq queen (2)
ar queer (12)
as shaky (1)
at sweet (2)
au sweet guy (1)
av sweet thing (1)
aw sweetie (1)
ax sissified (1)
ay sissy (61)
az sissy [of child] (5)
ba strange (1)
bb transvestite (1)
bc weird (1)
bd weirdo (1)
be womanish (2)

124.2 U male homosexual

No Response (43)
A AC/DC (1)
B bisexual (1)
C closet queen (3)
D cocksucker (1)
E drag queen (4)
F drag set, the (1)
G fag (44)
H faggish (1)
I faggot (14)
J fairy (12)
K flower people (1)
L freak (4)
M Frederick Fruit (1)
N fruit (9)
O fruitcake (1)
P funnies (1)
Q funny (1)
R funny boy (1)
S gay (46)
T gay dude (1)
U gay girl (1)
V girl (1)
W he she (2)
X heemajeema (1)
Y homo (11)
Z homosexular (1)
aa homosex(ual) (1)
ab homosexual (38)
ac homosexual person (1)
ad it (1)
ae kook (1)
af male homosexual (1)

ag   Mary (1)
ah   mother (1)
ai   pansy (3)
aj   patsy (1)
ak   pervert (1)
al   princess (1)
am   punk (7)
an   queen (8)
ao   queer (62)
ap   queer person (2)
aq   quint (1)
ar   shakies (1)
as   she (1)
at   sickie (1)
au   sissy (16)
av   spaceman (1)
aw   star (1)
ax   stupid (1)
ay   sweet boy (1)
az   sweetie (1)
ba   weird (2)
bb   weirdo (2)

124.3 U masculine female
No Response (55)
A   Amazon (1)
B   boyish (3)
C   brute (1)
D   butch (11)
E   domineering woman (1)
F   dyke (1)
G   funny (1)
H   half and half (1)
I   hermaphrodite (1)
J   independent (1)
K   Lesbian (2)
L   mannish (8)
M   mannish girl (1)
N   masculine (14)
O   masculine (female) (1)
P   masculine type (1)
Q   masculine ways (1)
R   queer (2)
S   queer women (1)
T   she he (1)
U   strange (2)
V   tomboy (28)
W   tomboy [of any age] (3)
X   tomboy [of child] (23)
Y   tomboyish (3)
Z   tough gal (1)
aa   weird (2)

124.4 U female homosexual
No Response (47)
A   AC/DC (2)
B   bull (1)
C   bull dagger (16)
D   bull dyke (4)
E   bull dyker (4)
F   bulldog (1)

G   butch (16)
H   dagger (3)
I   dyke (22)
J   dude (1)
K   fag (1)
L   female homosexual (1)
M   female queer (1)
N   flat (1)
O   freak (1)
P   frigid women (1)
Q   funnies (1)
R   funny (1)
S   gay (10)
T   he she (1)
U   hermaphrodite (1)
V   homo (1)
W   homosexual (1)
X   it (1)
Y   knife (1)
Z   Les (1)
aa   Lesbian (73)
ab   Lesbo (1)
ac   Lez (4)
ad   Lezzie (4)
ae   lukewarm Lizzie (1)
af   man, the (1)
ag   odd (1)
ah   pervert (1)
ai   queer (14)
aj   red (1)
ak   slim (1)
al   tomboy (1)

124.5 U sexually overactive male
No Response (69)
A   aggressive (1)
B   animal (2)
C   buck (1)
D   Casanova (2)
E   CJ Throbber (1)
F   cock hound (1)
G   cocksman (2)
H   cool dude (1)
I   Don (1)
J   Don Juan (4)
K   dude (1)
L   excited (1)
M   fruitcake (1)
N   gigolo (1)
O   good cocksman (1)
P   got a whole lot of women (1)
Q   got it together (1)
R   hard dick (1)
S   hard up (3)
T   hornet (1)
U   horny (12)
V   hot papa (1)
W   hot to spot (1)
X   jock (1)
Y   ladies' man (2)

Z   lady-killer (1)
aa   lover (3)
ab   madman (1)
ac   maniac (4)
ad   normal (2)
ae   normal man (1)
af   nuisance (1)
ag   nympho (2)
ah   nymphomaniac (2)
ai   obsessed (1)
aj   on the move (1)
ak   overly sexed (1)
al   overly-sexed male (1)
am   oversexed (8)
an   pervert (4)
ao   pervert [facetious] (1)
ap   pleasure pleaser (1)
aq   promiscuous (1)
ar   rock (1)
as   Romeo (1)
at   Romeo (type) (1)
au   satyr (1)
av   sex-crazed (1)
aw   sex fiend (1)
ax   sex maniac (8)
ay   stud (21)
az   studhorse (2)
ba   virile (1)
bb   whore hopper (1)
bc   whoremonger (2)
bd   wolf (1)
be   womanizer (1)

124.6 U sexually overactive female
No Response (71)
A   (ag)gressive (1)
B   aggressive (1)
C   ass (1)
D   bad bird broad (1)
E   bitch (1)
F   broad (1)
G   cool (1)
H   easy (3)
I   easy lady (1)
J   easy lay (1)
K   fast (2)
L   freak (1)
M   fruitcake (2)
N   gigoless (1)
O   has men (1)
P   horny (2)
Q   hot (2)
R   hot mama (2)
S   hot-to-go bitch (1)
T   hot to trot (3)
U   hyper (1)
V   lame (1)
W   loose (2)
X   maniac (1)
Y   nymph (7)

ag look[V-p] like your mom [X-0] been whip[V-t] with a ugly stick (1)
ah looks like a piece of shit (1)
ai looks like he caught afire and got beat[V-t] out with a baseball shoe (1)
aj looks like hell (2)
ak looks like he's been run over with track shoes (1)
al looks like shit (1)
am loser (3)
an messed up (2)
ao monkey (1)
ap monkey face (1)
aq monster (1)
ar moon face (1)
as mugly (1)
at nerd (2)
au not good-looking (1)
av not handsome (1)
aw ogre (1)
ax old dog (1)
ay pain (1)
az pill (1)
ba plain ugly (1)
bb pure ugly (1)
bc rat (1)
bd ruined (1)
be runt (1)
bf skank (1)
bg slob (1)
bh so ugly (1)
bi stink dog (1)
bj terrible-looking (1)
bk throw him in the lake; you'll skim ugly for two weeks (1)
bl tore up (1)
bm troll (1)
bn turkey (1)
bo uglier than a bull's butt (1)
bp ugliest thing I've ever seen (1)
bq ugly (28)
br Ugly (1)
bs ugly-ass man (1)
bt ugly boy (4)
bu ugly duckling (1)
bv ugly dude (1)
bw ugly man (3)
bx ugly person (1)
by unhandsome man (1)
bz weirdo (1)
ca wrong (1)
cb yoogly (1)
cc zit face (1)

125.2 U ugly female
No Response (43)
A bad (1)
B bag (1)

C bat (3)
D bear rug (1)
E beast (3)
F been beaten by the ugly stick (1)
G Big Bertha (1)
H bird (1)
I bitch (2)
J booger bear (1)
K brace face (1)
L canine (1)
M crater face (1)
N creature (1)
O creep (2)
P critter (1)
Q didn't look good (1)
R dodo bird (1)
S dog (34)
T fag (1)
U fat women (1)
V gag of maggot[N-i] (1)
W girl goblin (1)
X gorilla (1)
Y got a face like concrete (1)
Z got a mug (1)
aa Gravel Gertie (1)
ab groovie goomies (1)
ac gross (2)
ad hag (2)
ae hog (3)
af homely (14)
ag homely as a mud fence (1)
ah homemade soap (1)
ai horrid (1)
aj horse (1)
ak horseface (1)
al kind of fat (1)
am lizard lips (1)
an look like your mom [X-0] been whip[V-t] with a ugly stick (1)
ao look[V-p] like a monkey (1)
ap looks like a hag (1)
aq looks like a mule eating briars (1)
ar looks like hell (1)
as mongoose (1)
at monk (1)
au monk(ey) (1)
av monkey (1)
aw monster (4)
ax moose (1)
ay needs an operation (1)
az no-good bitch (1)
ba not attractive (1)
bb old dog (1)
bc pain (1)
bd pathetic (1)
be pig (5)
bf pitiful (1)
bg pitiful sight (1)

bh plain (2)
bi plain Jane (1)
bj plain ugly (1)
bk porpoise face (1)
bl put a paper bag over her face (1)
bm raunchy-looking (1)
bn real dog (3)
bo real loser (1)
bp rough (1)
bq ruined (1)
br sconions (1)
bs scuzzy (1)
bt sea monster (1)
bu sick-looking (1)
bv skag (3)
bw skank (2)
bx slut (2)
by snag lightning (1)
bz snake lips (1)
ca so ugly she could dip her face in dough and make gorilla cookies (1)
cb so ugly she has to cover herself up at night so sleep can creep up on her (1)
cc so ugly their mamma had to tie a pork chop around their neck[N-i] to make the dog play with them (1)
cd tacky (1)
ce tangle face (1)
cf tarantula (1)
cg toot [n.] (1)
ch trash (1)
ci ugly (22)
cj ugly as homemade sin (1)
ck ugly as the back road to Richmond Heights (1)
cl ugly bitch (1)
cm ugly girl (1)
cn unattractive (1)
co wallflower (1)
cp warehouse (1)
cq witch (4)
cr zit face (1)

125.3 U attractive male
No Response (41)
A absolute hunk (1)
B Adonis (2)
C appealing (1)
D attractive (3)
E bad (1)
F bad dude (1)
G beautiful (2)
H bowed up (1)
I brute (1)
J Casanova (2)
K cool (2)
L cool cat (1)

M   cute (9)
N   cutie (2)
O   doll (2)
P   Don Juan (2)
Q   dap (1)
R   dapper (1)
S   dream (1)
T   dude (3)
U   easy on the eye (1)
V   fine (1)
W   fox (6)
X   good-looking (24)
Y   good-looking dude (3)
Z   good-looking man (1)
aa   got a nice body (1)
ab   handsome (58)
ac   handsome fellow (1)
ad   handsome stud (1)
ae   he'll keep (1)
af   hunk (12)
ag   hunk of man (1)
ah   hunk of meat (1)
ai   jock (1)
aj   lady-killer (1)
ak   lady's man (1)
al   living doll (1)
am   looking good (1)
an   macho (2)
ao   natural man (1)
ap   neat (1)
aq   Nelda (1)
ar   nice (1)
as   nice body (1)
at   nice-looking (7)
au   nice-looking boy (1)
av   nice-looking fellow (1)
aw   nice-looking guy (1)
ax   pimp (1)
ay   pretty boy (2)
az   pretty dude (1)
ba   real (at)tractive man (1)
bb   real hunk (1)
bc   real looker (1)
bd   Romeo (1)
be   rondo [S] (1)
bf   sexy (1)
bg   sharp (5)
bh   slick dude (1)
bi   smart (1)
bj   spik (1)
bk   Stan the man (1)
bl   stud (6)
bm   very attractive (1)
bn   very handsome (2)

125.4 U attractive female
No Response (34)
A   angel (1)
B   attractive (10)
C   bad (1)

D   bad freak (1)
E   bad-looking girl (1)
F   beaut, a (2)
G   beautiful (29)
H   beautiful doll (1)
I   beautiful girl (1)
J   beautiful woman (1)
K   beauty, a (5)
L   belle, a (1)
M   box (1)
N   brick (1)
O   broad (1)
P   built like a brick outhouse (1)
Q   charming (1)
R   cheesecake (1)
S   chic (1)
T   chick (3)
U   comely (1)
V   cute (10)
W   cute as a doll (1)
X   cute chick (1)
Y   dame (1)
Z   debutante (1)
aa   dish (1)
ab   doll (10)
ac   fine (4)
ad   fine as a brick shit house (1)
ae   fine babe (1)
af   fine broad (1)
ag   fine chick (1)
ah   fine piece of ass (1)
ai   fox (27)
aj   foxy (8)
ak   foxy chick (1)
al   foxy lady (1)
am   foxy little lady (1)
an   gem (1)
ao   go neat all the time (1)
ap   good-looker (3)
aq   good-looking (13)
ar   good-looking bitch (1)
as   good-looking broad (1)
at   good-looking chick (1)
au   good-looking woman (1)
av   gorgeous (2)
aw   great looker (1)
ax   hammer (1)
ay   handsome (1)
az   honey, a (1)
ba   hot (1)
bb   hunk (1)
bc   knock you out (1)
bd   knockout (3)
be   little doll (1)
bf   looker (2)
bg   looks good (1)
bh   lovely (5)
bi   mellow (1)
bj   model (1)

bk   mother's daughter (1)
bl   movie star (1)
bm   nice (3)
bn   nice broad (1)
bo   nice-looking (5)
bp   nice-looking lady (2)
bq   pert (1)
br   piece (2)
bs   pleasing (1)
bt   precious (1)
bu   pretty (34)
bv   pretty woman (1)
bw   queen (3)
bx   real beauty (1)
by   real cheese (1)
bz   real cute (1)
ca   real doll (1)
cb   real fox (1)
cc   real hunk of pussy (1)
cd   real pie (1)
ce   real piece (1)
cf   real piece of cheese (1)
cg   regular Venus (1)
ch   sensuous (1)
ci   sexpot (1)
cj   sexy (3)
ck   sharp (1)
cl   sharp chick (1)
cm   sharp-looking (1)
cn   slick (2)
co   slick bitch (1)
cp   slick chick (1)
cq   slick freak (1)
cr   slim (1)
cs   stacked (1)
ct   stacked like a brick shit house (2)
cu   stacked woman (1)
cv   stallion (2)
cw   stylish (1)
cx   sweet thing (1)
cy   tree (1)
cz   very attractive (1)
da   very pretty (1)
db   winner (1)

125.5 U bookish person
No Response (28)
A   Bomar brain (1)
B   book freak (1)
C   bookish (1)
D   bookish person (1)
E   bookworm (97)
F   bore (1)
G   brain (7)
H   brain head (1)
I   brainiac (1)
J   brainy (1)
K   bright (1)
L   computer (1)

M crud (1)
N egghead (7)
O erudite (1)
P fanatic (1)
Q genius (2)
R grind (1)
S he love[V-p] to read (1)
T hermit (1)
U home boy (1)
V honor student (1)
W intellect (3)
X intellectual (2)
Y intelligent (1)
Z intelligent person (1)
aa ivory-tower intellectual (1)
ab lizard (1)
ac magazine freak (1)
ad mama's boy (1)
ae Miss Intelligent (1)
af Mister Intelligent (1)
ag nerd (5)
ah pointy head (1)
ai pointy-headed intellectual (1)
aj professor (1)
ak scholar (2)
al scholarly (2)
am scholarly person (1)
an Sergeant Four-Oh (1)
ao smart (5)
ap smart aleck (1)
aq smart-alecky (1)
ar smart girl (1)
as smart person (1)
at snob (1)
au straight (1)
av stuck to books (1)
aw studious (5)
ax studious person (1)
ay too smart for his pants (1)
az trickster (1)
ba turkey (1)
bb very studious person (1)
bc weirdo (1)
bd whiz kid (1)
be worm (1)

125.6 U brownnose
No Response (32)
A apple-polisher (9)
B ass kiss (1)
C ass kisser (9)
D attention getter (1)
E (at)tention seeker (1)
F attention seeker (1)
G baby (1)
H back stabber (1)
I bootlicker (2)
J boss's flunky (1)
K boss's pet (2)
L braggadocious (1)

M braggart (1)
N brat (2)
O brownie (1)
P brownnose (13)
Q brownnoser (18)
R brownnosing (9)
S brownnosing the boss (1)
T bully (1)
U butt kisser (2)
V butt licker (2)
W cheese eater (6)
X class clown (1)
Y clown (2)
Z cocky (1)
aa crack licker (1)
ab dunce (1)
ac eager beaver (1)
ad eating cheese (1)
ae egomaniac (1)
af favorite [n.] (1)
ag flunky (2)
ah get over [n.] (1)
ai getting over (1)
aj glory hound (1)
ak goody-goody (2)
al ham (2)
am home boy (1)
an jerk (1)
ao jester (1)
ap joker (1)
aq kiss ass [n.] (1)
ar kiss ass (3)
as kissing ass (1)
at looking for Brownie points (1)
au looking for praise (1)
av make Brownie points (1)
aw mama's boy (1)
ax nerd (1)
ay nuisance (2)
az obnoxious (1)
ba pain in the ass (1)
bb pain in the neck (1)
bc pest (4)
bd pet (14)
be pimp (2)
bf polish the apple (1)
bg punk (1)
bh put on (1)
bi self-conceited (1)
bj sharp show (1)
bk show-off (10)
bl smart aleck (3)
bm smart ass (2)
bn snitcher (1)
bo spoiled brat (1)
bp spoiled children (1)
bq status climber (1)
br status seeker (1)
bs stoolie (1)

bt stuck on himself (1)
bu suck ass (1)
bv suck up (1)
bw teacher's pet (58)
bx toadies up to the teacher (1)
by twerp (1)
bz Uncle Tom (1)
ca winning Brownie points (1)
cb worrisome person (1)
cc yes-man (1)

125.7 U grade school
No Response (14)
A elementary school (90)
B grade school (34)
C grammar school (35)
D intermediate (1)
E junior high (1)
F kindergarten (12)
G lower school (1)
H middle school (17)
I prep school (1)
J primary (1)
K primary grades (1)
L primary school (8)
M primer (1)

125.8 U junior high school
No Response (37)
A junior high (79)
B junior high school (29)
C junior school (3)
D mid school (1)
E middle school (22)
F prep (1)
G secondary school (2)

125.9 U high school
No Response (19)
A high (4)
B high school (110)
C normal school (1)
D senior high (22)
E senior high school (7)
F upper school (1)

126.1 U woven-wire fence
No Response (26)
A all-weather fence (1)
B bar fence (1)
C barbwire (1)
D barbwire fence (1)
E chain fence (2)
F chain link (21)
G chain link (fence) (6)
H chain link fence (24)
I chain link wire fence (1)
J chance length (1)
K chance lengths fence (1)
L chicken wire (2)
M chicken-wire fence (1)
N cock fence (1)
O Cook's fence (1)

P   Cox fence (1)
Q   Cox's fence (1)
R   crisscross (fence) (1)
S   Cyclone (3)
T   Cyclone (fence) (3)
U   Cyclone fence (9)
V   fence (4)
W   fence with the little X's (1)
X   galvanize fencing (1)
Y   galvanized fence (1)
Z   high fence (1)
aa   Hurricane (fence) (2)
ab   Hurricane fence (2)
ac   iron (1)
ad   iron fence (3)
ae   link (1)
af   link fence (1)
ag   mesh (2)
ah   mesh wire (1)
ai   metal (1)
aj   metal fence (2)
ak   normal fence (1)
al   Page chain fence (1)
am   Page fence (1)
an   pivot fence (1)
ao   prong fence (1)
ap   real heavy wire (1)
aq   Rio Grande (1)
ar   silver-mesh-looking (1)
as   steel (1)
at   steel (fence) (1)
au   stone fence (1)
av   storm fence (2)
aw   Ten-Forty-Seven (1)
ax   weaving fence (1)
ay   wire (6)
az   wire (fence) (1)
ba   wire fence (28)
bb   wire iron fence (1)
bc   wire Page (1)
bd   wire-mesh fence (1)
be   woven (1)
bf   woven-wire (fence) (1)
bg   woven-wire fence (2)

126.2 U gymnasium
No Response (16)
A   athletic building (1)
B   athletic complex (1)
C   basketball court (2)
D   boys' gym (2)
E   coliseum (2)
F   court (2)
G   field house (1)
H   girls' gym (2)
I   gym (95)
J   gym room (1)
K   gymnasium (69)
L   gymnatorium (1)
M   indoor court (1)

N   recreation cent(er) (1)
O   spa (1)

126.3 U lavatory
No Response (16)
A   bath (1)
B   bathroom (71)
C   boys' room (5)
D   can (2)
E   closet (1)
F   crapper (1)
G   dressing room (2)
H   girls' room (5)
I   guesthouse (1)
J   head (4)
K   jane (1)
L   john (20)
M   la la (1)
N   ladies' room (6)
O   latrine (5)
P   lavatory (26)
Q   little-boys' room (1)
R   little-girls' room (1)
S   lounge (1)
T   men's (1)
U   men's room (7)
V   outhouse (1)
W   piss house (1)
X   privy (1)
Y   rest room (82)
Z   school bathroom (1)
aa   toilet (16)
ab   toilet room (2)
ac   washroom (2)
ad   women's (1)

126.4 U Orientals
No Response (28)
A   aliens (1)
B   Asians (2)
C   Charleys [=Vietnamese] (2)
D   Chinamen (11)
E   Chinee people (1)
F   Chinese (24)
G   Chinese boy (1)
H   Ching-Ching Chinaman (1)
Ia   Chinks (29)
Ib   Chinks [=Orientals] (15)
Ic   Chinks [=Chinese] (20)
Id   Chinks [=Japanese] (2)
J   Cong [=Vietnamese] (1)
K   coolie [=Chinese] (1)
L   dinks (1)
M   Filipino (1)
N   gong [=Vietnamese] (1)
Oa   gooks (1)
Ob   gooks [=Orientals] (3)
Oc   gooks [=Chinese] (1)
Od   gooks [=Vietnamese] (7)
Oe   gooks [=Vietnamese/Korean]
        (2)

Pa   Japs (31)
Pb   Japs [=Orientals] (3)
Pc   Japs [=Japanese] (24)
Q   Japanese (22)
R   Japans (1)
S   Kamikazes (1)
T   Korean (11)
U   Nips [=Japanese] (2)
V   Orientals (6)
W   pineapple [=Hawaiian/
        Philippino] (1)
X   running dog (1)
Y   Sampan Sam (1)
Z   slant-eyed so-and-so [=Japanese]
        (1)
aa-a   slant-eyes (7)
aa-b   slant-eyes [=Orientals] (5)
aa-c   slant-eyes [=Chinese] (1)
aa-d   slant-eyes [=Japanese] (1)
ab   slanties (1)
ac   slants (2)
ad   slope heads (1)
ae   slopes (2)
af   squinch eyes [=Orientals] (1)
ag   squinchies (1)
ah   squint eyes (1)
ai   Tojos [=Japanese] (1)
aj   VC [=Vietnamese] (1)
ak   Vietnamese (6)
al   Vietnams (1)
am   wetbacks (1)
an-a   wops (1)
an-b   wops [=Orientals] (1)
ao   Yangs [=Chinese/Japanese] (1)
ap   yellow backs (1)
aq   yellow dogs (1)
ar   yellow men (1)
as   yellow people (1)
at   yellow skins (2)

126.5 U Roman Catholics
No Response (89)
A   bead feelers (1)
B   bead rattlers (1)
C   beast (1)
D   cat licker (1)
E   Catholics (25)
F   cross-backs (4)
G   Father worshipers (1)
H   fish eaters (6)
I   Friday fish eaters (1)
J   holy rollers (1)
K   idol worshipers (1)
L   mackerel snappers (3)
M   Papist (1)
N   Pope lovers (1)
O   Popers (1)
P   Roman Catholics (7)
Q   Romans (1)

126.6 U Protestants

No Response (82)
A   alcoholic (E)piscopalian (1)
B   Baptists (3)
C   Bible bangers (1)
D   Bible Belters (1)
E   Bible thumpers (1)
F   Campbellites (1)
G   charismatics (1)
H   Christians (1)
I   Church of Christ (1)
J   Church of God (1)
K   drinking Methodists (1)
L   drunk Catholics (1)
M   fanatics (1)
N   foot-washing Baptists (2)
O   Freewill Baptists (1)
P   glory rollers (1)
Q   God Squad (2)
R   hard down (1)
S   Hard-Shell (Baptists) (4)
T   Hard-Shell Baptists (4)
U   Holy Joes (1)
V   Holy Rollers (29)
W   Holy Rollies (1)
X   Jehovah people (1)
Y   Jehovah[N-k] Witnesses (1)
Z   Jehovah's Witnesses (1)
aa   Jehovahs (1)
ab   Jesus freaks (1)
ac   Methodists (2)
ad   Mover of God (1)
ae   Presbyterians (2)
af   Primitive Baptists (1)
ag   Protestant groups (1)
ah   Protestants (6)
ai   Quakers (2)
ag   red-necks (1)
ak   Sanctified (3)
al   Sanctify (1)
am   Seven Days Adventist (1)
an   snake handlers (1)
ao   Soft-Shell (Baptists) (1)
ap   Southern Baptists (1)
aq   tongue wagglers (1)
ar   WASPs (7)
as   White Anglo-Saxon Protestants
       (1)

126.7 U Jews
No Response (52)
A   big nose (1)
B   chosen people (1)
C   Christ killers (1)
D   conservative (1)
E   dirty Hebes (1)
F   dirty Jews (1)
G   dirty kikes (1)
H   goddamn kikes (1)
I   Hebes (6)
J   Hebrews (1)

K   hook noses (1)
L   Jew (17)
M   Jew baby (3)
N   Jew boys (4)
O   Jewbirds (1)
P   Jewish (14)
Q   Jewish children (1)
R   Jewish family (1)
S   Jewish girl (1)
T   Jewish people (10)
U   Jewish population (1)
V   Jews (35)
W   kikes (18)
X   Kosher Jews (1)
Y   mockies (1)
Z   moneybags (1)
aa   moneylenders (1)
ab   non-Kosher Jews (1)
ac   old bags (1)
ad   Orthodox (2)
ae   Orthodox Jews (1)
af   penny pinchers (3)
ag   pinchpennies (1)
ah   Polacks (1)
ai   poor Jews (1)
aj   rab (1)
ak   rabbi (1)
al   Reformed (1)
am   Reformed Jews (1)
an   Russian Jews (1)
ao   sheenies (3)
ap   Shylocks (1)
aq   stupid-ass Jews (1)
ar   super Jew (1)
as   tight [adj.] (1)
at   tightwads (2)
au   wops (1)
av   Yiddish (1)
aw   Yids (2)
ax   yips (1)

126.8 U American Indians
No Response (110)
A   American Indians (2)
B   Cherokee Indians (2)
C   half-breeds (1)
D   Indians (19)
E   Northern Indians (1)
F   Red Men (6)
G   red sticks (1)
H   Reds (2)
I   redskins (5)
J   parrakeets (1)
K   squaws (1)
L   squaws [=females] (1)

127.1 U Germans
No Response (62)
A   Bavarians (1)
B   Boche (1)
C   Deutsch [G] (1)

D   Dutch (4)
E   Dutch Germans (1)
F   Dutchmen (2)
G   Fritz (2)
H   German (23)
I   German people (1)
J   gypsy (1)
K   Hans (1)
L   hardheads (1)
M   High German (1)
N   highlanders (1)
O   hinklebonger (1)
P   Hitlerites (2)
Q   Hunkies (1)
R   Huns (5)
S   jerks (1)
T   Jerries (5)
U   Katzenjammers (1)
V   knockers (1)
W   kraut eaters (1)
X   kraut heads (2)
Y   Krauts (41)
Z   lettuce (1)
aa   love Hitlers (1)
ab   Low Germans (1)
ac   Nazis (14)
ad   squareheads (1)

127.2 U Low Germans
No Response (133)
A   Bavarians (1)
B   Deutsch [G] (1)
C   Dutch (4)
D   Dutch [=German] (1)
E   Dutch [=Hollanders] (2)
F   Dutch Germans (1)
G   Dutchman (1)
H   Dutchman [=Dutch] (1)
I   highlanders (1)
J   Hollanders (2)
K   Hunkies (1)
L   Low Germans (1)

127.3 U Italians
No Response (47)
A   dago (45)
B   Eyetie (1)
C   goombas (1)
D   greaser (2)
E   greasies (1)
F   guinea (1)
G   guinea wop (1)
H   Ike (1)
I   Italian (32)
J   Italian [pejorative] (1)
K   Italian motherfucker (1)
L   Italy wop (1)
M   meatball (1)
N   oils (1)
O   peppies (1)
P   pizza lover (1)

Q slick hairs (1)
R spaghetti eater (1)
S spaghetti people (1)
T spik (9)
U wop (54)
V woppo (1)

127.4 U Poles

No Response (49)
A dumb Polack (2)
B Pokes (1)
C Polack [adj.] (2)
D Polacks (78)
E Poles (15)
F Polish (4)
G Polish people (2)
H tight tongue (1)
I Warsaw winner (1)
J wops (2)

127.5 U Russians

No Response (95)
A Commies (3)
B Communists (6)
C Cossack (1)
D Red Russians (1)
E Reds (17)
F relics (1)
G Russians (15)
H Russkies (16)
I spies (1)

127.6 U Czechs

No Response (96)
A Bohemian (3)
B Bohunks (4)
C Czech [adj.] (1)
D Czechoslovakian (2)
E Czechs (42)
F Slavs (1)
G Slovaks (1)

127.7 U Lithuanians

No Response (138)
A foot peddlers (1)
B Jews (1)
C Lithos (2)
D Lithuanians (5)
E Wanians (1)

127.8 U Englishmen

No Response (91)
A beefeaters (1)
B blimeys (1)
C bloody, blooming, dirty so-and-sos (1)
D British (6)
E Britoners (1)
F Britons (2)
G chaps (1)
H Cockney (1)
I Englanders (1)
J English (7)
K Englishmen (8)

L Englishwoman (1)
M Limeys (26)
N queen's kids (1)
O saws (1)
P stiff-neck Limey (1)
Q stimy (1)
R stuff shirts (1)

127.9 U Irishmen

No Response (97)
A billy-goat Irish (1)
B bog trotters (1)
C dirty Irish (1)
D drunkards (1)
E greenies (1)
F honkies (1)
G Idaho potato (1)
H Irish (14)
I Irish brawlers (1)
J Irishmen (15)
K mickey (2)
L micks (15)
M old Pat (1)
N Paddy (3)
O potato eaters (1)
P potato heads (1)
Q potato man (1)
R red [n.] (1)
S shantyboats (1)

128.1 U Scots

No Response (112)
A Highlander (1)
B kilt wearers (1)
C kilties (1)
D Royal Scot (1)
E Scotch (3)
F Scotch-Irish (2)
G Scotch people (2)
H Scotch tightwads (1)
I Scotchmen (2)
J Scots (9)
K Scotsmen (1)
L Scotties (2)
M Scottish (6)
N tartans (1)
O tightwads (1)
P women from hell (1)

128.2 U French

No Response (97)
A French (9)
B French people (1)
C French whore (1)
D Frenchies (8)
E Frenchmen (8)
F frogs (14)
G Gascon (1)
H gigolos (1)
I hoolios (1)
J oui-oui (1)
K queers (1)

L wogs (1)

128.3 U Cajuns

No Response (80)
A bayou (people) (1)
B black Cajuns (1)
C Cajun coons (1)
D Cajuns (48)
E coonasses (14)
F coonies (1)
G coons (4)
H Creoles (13)
I French people (1)
J Geechees (1)
K half-and-half (1)
L half-breeds (3)
M light-skin darky (1)
N messieurs [F] (1)
O mixbloods (1)
P mudfoots (1)
Q red-neck (1)
R Southies (1)
S swamp people (1)

128.4 U Greeks

No Response (118)
A big daddies (1)
B dagos (1)
C dirty Greek (1)
D dumb Greek (1)
E greasers (1)
F Grecians (1)
G Greek (5)
H Greekos (1)
I Greeks (10)
J ski nose (1)
K wops (2)

128.5 U Cubans

No Response (105)
A Chicanos (3)
B crazy-driver Cuban (1)
C Cuban [adj.] (3)
D Cuban fellow (1)
E Cuban motherfucker (1)
F Cubana (1)
G Cubanos (2)
H Cubans (18)
I dagos (2)
J damn niggers (1)
K greasers (2)
L Jose (1)
M Latinos (1)
N no-good-ass Cuban (1)
O no-good Cuban (1)
P po-pos (1)
Q Puerto Ricans (2)
R Reds (1)
S Ricans (1)
T Spanish (1)
U Spanish people (1)
V spiks (17)

W   stupid-ass Cuban (1)
X   weird-ass Cuban (1)

128.6 U Puerto Ricans

No Response (93)
A   Chicanos (4)
B   geese (1)
C   greasers (5)
D   Latinos (1)
E   po-pos (1)
F   PRs (5)
G   (Puerto) Ricans (1)
H   Puerto Ricans (21)
I   Ricans (1)
J   Spanish (1)
K   Spanish people (1)
L   Spiko Ricans (1)
M   spiks (23)
N   stupid-ass Puerto Rican (1)
O   wetbacks (1)
P   wops (1)

128.7 U Mexicans

No Response (49)
A   bandoleros (1)
B   bay niggers (1)
C   brownies (1)
D   browns (2)
E   Chicago (1)
F   Chicanos (23)
G   dagos (1)
H   dumb-ass Mexicans (1)
I   greaseballs (1)
J   greasers (9)
K   greasy bellies (1)
L   half-breeds (1)
M   hot tamales (1)
N   Indians (1)
O   jumping beans (1)
P   Latin kinds (1)
Q   Latin-American (4)
R   Latins (2)
S   Mex (5)
T   Mexican (34)
U   Mexican-Americans (15)
V   Mexicanos (1)
W   Mexis (1)
X   pepper bellies (5)
Y   Puerto Ricans (2)
Z   Spanian (1)
aa   Spaniards (2)
ab   Spanish (5)
ac   Spanish-Americans (2)
ad   specks (1)
ae   spiks (26)
af   sweat hogs (1)
ag   taco benders (2)
ah   taco eaters (1)
ai   Tex-Mex (1)
aj   tortillas (2)
ak   wetbacks (42)

al   wops (1)

128.8 U Scandinavians

No Response (128)
A   big Swede (1)
B   blockheads (1)
C   blondies (1)
D   Danes (1)
E   Norwegians (2)
F   palefaces (1)
G   Scandinavians (7)
H   squareheads (1)
I   Swedes (7)

128.9 U Canadians

No Response (129)
A   Canadians (6)
B   Canucks (7)
C   French C's (1)
D   French Canadians (1)
E   northerners (1)

129.1 U Democrat

No Response (53)
A   big spenders (1)
B   Catholic lovers (1)
C   demigodger (1)
D   Democratic (10)
E   Democrats (72)
F   Demos (2)
G   donkeys (15)
H   goddamn jackass (1)
I   jackasses (3)
J   liberals (1)
K   pinkos (1)
L   yellow-dog Democrats (1)

129.2 U Republican

No Response (53)
A   bloody shirt Republican (1)
B   conservatives (3)
C   elephants (11)
D   Elk (1)
E   GOP (4)
F   GOPer (1)
G   GOPs (1)
H   Grand Old Party (4)
I   Grand Old Party people (1)
J   John Bircher (1)
K   Nazi (1)
L   Nixonites (1)
M   Republic(an) (1)
N   Republican (76)
O   Republican Party (1)
P   republics (2)
Q   right-wing (1)
R   rock-hard Republican (1)
S   Tory (1)
T   Willkieite (1)

129.3 U hippie

No Response (25)
A   beatnik (3)
B   Bohemian (1)

C   bomb chucker (1)
D   bum (1)
E   Commie hippie bomb thrower (1)
F   damn hippie (1)
G   dropout (2)
H   dugs (1)
I   flower child (11)
J   freak (16)
K   freaky people (1)
L   greaser (1)
M   hippie (109)
N   hippie radical (1)
O   Jesus freak (1)
P   Jesus people (1)
Q   junkie (1)
R   kook (1)
S   left-wing radical (1)
T   long-haired (1)
U   long-haired, bearded, no-good
      scoundrel (1)
V   long-haired hick (1)
W   long-haired hippie (1)
X   longhair (5)
Y   no-good (1)
Z   nonconformist (1)
aa   Northern people (1)
ab   pervert (1)
ac   rip-off (1)
ad   sissy (1)
ae   weirdo (3)
af   yippie (3)

129.4 U best friend

No Response (14)
A   ace boon coon (1)
B   amigo [S] (1)
C   asshole buddy (1)
D   best (1)
E   best buddy (2)
F   best friend (63)
G   best girl friend (1)
H   best pal (1)
I   bosom buddy (1)
J   bosom friend (1)
K   brother (3)
L   buddy (44)
M   bunk buddy (1)
N   chum (5)
O   close brother (1)
P   close friend (3)
Q   closest (1)
R   dear friend (1)
S   devoted friend (1)
T   favorite (1)
U   friend (35)
V   girl friend (13)
W   good buddy (5)
X   good friend (11)
Y   good-old buddy (1)
Z   intimate (1)

aa   kid friend (1)
ab   lady friend (1)
ac   little buddy (1)
ad   main man (4)
ae   my boy (1)
af   my cut pea (1)
ag   my man (1)
ah   my nigger (2)
ai   my right arm (1)
aj   my type (1)
ak   nicest (1)
al   nigger (1)
am   pal (28)
an   partner (6)
ao   platonic friend (1)
ap   play partner (1)
aq   play sister (1)
ar   playmate (1)
as   rap partner (1)
at   road partner (1)
au   room doom (1)
av   sister (1)
aw   very best friend (1)
ax   very personal friend (1)

129.5 U surrogate parent
No Response (72)
A   aunt (2)
B   Aunt so-and-so (1)
C   big brother (7)
D   Big Brothers (4)
E   big sister (3)
F   Big Sisters (2)
G   chaperon (1)
H   foster (1)
I   foster-mother (1)
J   foster parent (8)
K   godfather (9)
L   godmother (5)
M   godparent (6)
N   guardian (8)
O   guide (1)
P   honorary aunt (1)
Q   nanny (2)
R   play dad (1)
S   play daddy (7)
T   play father (5)
U   play mamma (9)
V   play mother (10)
W   play papa (1)
X   play parent (1)
Y   play sister (1)
Z   second father (1)
aa   second mother (1)
ab   step dad (1)
ac   stepfather (5)
ad   stepmother (4)
ae   stepparent (1)
af   supervisor (1)
ag   surrogate father (2)

ah   surrogate mother (2)
ai   Uncle (1)
aj   uncle (3)

129.6 U peer groups
No Response (33)
A   associates (1)
B   best friends (1)
C   boys (1)
D   buddies (14)
E   bunch (3)
F   bunch of boys (1)
G   chums (1)
H   clan (2)
I   classmates (1)
J   clique (8)
K   close friends (1)
L   club (3)
M   cohorts (2)
N   contemporaries (1)
O   cronies (1)
P   crowd (3)
Q   fellows (2)
R   friends (41)
S   gang (46)
T   grade-school friends (1)
U   group (12)
V   guys (2)
W   ingroup (1)
X   kids (3)
Y   neighborhood friends (1)
Z   nuclear peer group (1)
aa   pals (9)
ab   peer group (3)
ac   peers (2)
ad   play children (1)
ae   play group (1)
af   playmates (18)
ag   school buddies (1)
ah   schoolmates (1)
ai   social crowd (1)
aj   troop (1)

129.7 U playing the dozens
No Response (88)
A   argument (1)
B   bad-mouthing (1)
C   breaking peace (1)
D   confusion (1)
E   cracks (1)
F   cursing (2)
G   cut them down (1)
H   cutdown (1)
I   cutting down (1)
J   cutting someone down (1)
K   dirty dozen (1)
L   dirty dozens (1)
M   dozen (2)
N   dozens (8)
O   feud (1)
P   fighting (1)

Q   funning around (1)
R   get down in signifying a case (1)
S   get down on your case (1)
T   getting on your case (1)
U   harassments (1)
V   hassling (1)
W   hurrah (1)
X   insultation (1)
Y   insulting each other (1)
Z   joining (1)
aa   jokes (1)
ab   kid fight (1)
ac   kidding (1)
ad   meddling (1)
ae   mocking (1)
af   name-calling (1)
ag   naming (1)
ah   one-upmanship (2)
ai   picking at me (1)
aj   play the dozen (1)
ak   playing dozens (1)
al   playing the dozen (7)
am   playing the doz(ens) (1)
an   playing the dozens (15)
ao   put-down (1)
ap   putting down (1)
aq   putting in the dozen (1)
ar   putting in the dozens (1)
as   putting them in a dozens (1)
at   ranking (6)
au   ranking on me (1)
av   reading each other (1)
aw   reading you (1)
ax   ribbing (1)
ay   riding your case (1)
az   signifying (1)
ba   sticks-and-stones-type stuff (1)
bb   talking for my mama, he's (1)
bc   teasing (1)
bd   trying to embarrass one another
     (1)
be   verbal exchange (1)
bf   war march (1)

129.8 U initiation rites
No Response (108)
A   challenge me (1)
B   cold-shoulder treatment (1)
C   fight (somebody), had to (2)
D   fighting (1)
E   fraternity initiation (2)
F   gang fight (1)
G   gang up around him (1)
H   get him lost (1)
I   get up and sing a song at lunch
     (1)
J   give them a hard way to go (1)
K   go kiss some girl on the cheek
     (1)
L   good in sports, had to be (1)

M   hazed/hazing (3)
N   holler "uncle" (1)
O   initiate (them) (8)
P   (i)nitiation (3)
Q   initiation (5)
R   lead them around blindfolded (1)
S   look for the lost lady (1)
T   pass inspection (1)
U   pick on (them) (1)
V   polar-bear races (1)
W   prank him (1)
X   prove himself, had to (1)
Y   razing (1)
Z   rock them out (1)
aa   snipe hunt(ing) (3)
ab   step in dog do (1)
ac   tease him (1)
ad   test him (1)
ae   test him out (1)
af   threw grapefruits at him (1)
ag   trial period (1)
ah   whip him, see if I could (1)
ai   whip me (1)

130.1 U hiding games

No Response (21)
A   blindman's bluff (6)
B   blindman's buff (2)
C   cops and robbers (3)
D   fox and hounds (2)
E   gorilla (2)
F   Grandma Gray (1)
G   hide-and-go-get-it (1)
H   hide-and-go-seek (47)
I   hide-and-seek (69)
J   hide-go-get-them (1)
K   hide-go-seek (4)
L   hiding (1)
M   hiding-and-seek (1)
N   honey honey bee ball (2)
O   hunt the hay (2)
P   hunter hunter hero (1)
Q   hunting honeybee ball (1)
R   hunting the bee ball (1)
S   hy spy (2)
T   I spy (1)
U   kick the can (7)
V   peekaboo (1)
W   red light (1)
X   red light green light (1)
Y   ring around detective (1)
Z   sardines (2)
aa   seek-and-hide (2)
ab   sharks and the minnows (1)
ac   tag (3)
ad   there ain't no boogers out tonight
     (1)

130.2 U line/running games

No Response (34)
A   across the river (1)

B   antony over (1)
C   bacon (1)
D   bloody murder (1)
E   British bulldog(s) (2)
F   capture the flag (2)
G   catch the bacon (1)
H   catch the flag (1)
I   chase (8)
J   cheekbone (1)
K   Chinese chase (1)
L   cops and robbers (7)
M   cowboys and Indians (7)
N   crack-the-whip (3)
O   follow-the-leader (2)
P   four-forty relay (1)
Q   fox and the geese (1)
R   fox and the hounds (1)
S   freeze tag (5)
T   giant step(s) (4)
U   goosey goosey gander (1)
V   green light (1)
W   jail (1)
X   kick the can (1)
Y   king and queen (1)
Z   king of the mountain (1)
aa   Mamma, may I? (1)
ab   may I? (4)
ac   Mother, may I ? (5)
ad   old witch (1)
ae   one, two, three, red light (1)
af   pop the rope (1)
ag   pop-the-whip (3)
ah   popping the whip (2)
ai   potato race (1)
aj   race(s)/racing (5)
ak   race from corner to corner (1)
al   rag tag (1)
am   rallies (1)
an   red light (6)
ao   red light green light (2)
ap   red roses (1)
aq   red rover (25)
ar   red rover, red rover (3)
as   relay races (2)
at   relays (6)
au   roly-poly (1)
av   rover, red rover (1)
aw   run, sheep, run (1)
ax   sack races (2)
ay   sidewalk tag (1)
az   Simon says (2)
ba   soldiers (1)
bb   spies (1)
bc   stoplight (1)
bd   tag (29)
be   tag bicycle (1)
bf   tag games (1)
bg   tag out of jail (1)
bh   tag with a home base (1)

bi   tip the icebox (1)
bj   tug-of-war (5)
bk   whip, the (1)
bl   whip over the river (1)
bm   wolf across the river (1)
bn   wolf on the river, catch all you
     can (1)
bo   wolf over the river (1)

[jumping games]

bp   devil in the ditch (1)
bq   hoppy scotch (1)
br   hopscotch (31)
bs   jump so far (1)
bt   leapfrog (3)

130.3 U ring games

No Response (63)
A   (a)tisket (a)tasket (1)
B   (a)tisket atasket (1)
C   atisket atasket (1)
D   battle ball (1)
E   bluebird, bluebird through my
     window (1)
F   bull in the ring (3)
G   cat and mouse (1)
H   dodge ball (5)
I   drop my handkerchief (2)
J   drop[V-r] my handkerchief
     yesterday, found it today (1)
K   drop the handkerchief (21)
L   dropping the handkerchief (2)
M   duck duck goose (5)
N   elephant giraffe (1)
O   farmer in the dell (6)
P   going in and out the windows (1)
Q   heavy, heavy hangs over your
     head (1)
R   here we go (a)round the mulberry
     bush (1)
S   hokey-pokey (1)
T   let the bluebird out (1)
U   Little Sally Salter (1)
V   Little Sally Saucer (1)
W   Little Sally Walker (12)
X   Little Sally Walker, sitting in a
     saucer (3)
Y   London Bridge (2)
Z   London Bridge is falling down
     (3)
aa   London Bridges (3)
ab   Maypole (2)
ac   merry-go-round (1)
ad   mulberry bush (1)
ae   musical chairs (5)
af   policeman [J-0] robber[N-i] (1)
ag   ring around detective (1)
ah   ring-around-a-rosy (2)
ak   ring-around-the-roses (12)
al   ring-around-the-roses, pocket full
     of posies (1)

am ring-around-the-rosy (16)
ai ring-around-[D-0]-roses (1)
aj ring-around-[D-0]-rosy (3)
an ring play (2)
ao Sally, go (a)round sunshine (1)
ap Sally, go (a)round the sunshine (1)
aq Sally in the saucer (1)
ar Sally Walker (1)
as smile if you love me (1)
at spin the bottle (7)
au thread follows the needle, the (1)
av yardbirds (1)
aw your mama's bread is burning (1)

130.4 U ball/puck/tin can games

No Response (19)
A Annie Annie over (1)
B antony over (2)
C badminton (2)
D ball (5)
E baseball (59)
F basketball (42)
G battle ball (1)
H battling (1)
I bombardment (1)
J bowling (1)
K break ball (1)
L burn-down baseball (1)
M capture the flag (1)
N cat ball (1)
O catch ball (1)
P coming through (1)
Q court ball (1)
R croquet (2)
S dodge ball (30)
T field hockey (3)
U fliers (1)
V football (51)
W foursquare (5)
X fumble (1)
Y golf (1)
Z gorilla ball (1)
aa gym hockey (1)
ab half rubber (1)
ac hand grenade (1)
ad handball (3)
ae hockey (11)
af hot ball (1)
ag hot box (1)
ah jai alai (1)
ai jail (1)
aj keep away (3)
ak kick cans to school (1)
al kick soccer (1)
am kick the can (21)
an kick the stick (1)
ao kick the tin can (1)

ap kick tin cans (1)
aq kickball (22)
ar kicking a can (1)
as kill (1)
at kill the man with the ball (4)
au killer ball (1)
av kitty (2)
aw knocking a can with a stick (1)
ax nuke them (1)
ay paddle ball (2)
az passe (1)
ba Ping-Pong (1)
bb pitch (1)
bc polo (1)
bd pop fly (1)
be racket ball (1)
bf rag tag (1)
bg roll old golf balls into tin cans (1)
bh roly-poly (1)
bi roughhouse (1)
bj run the bases (1)
bk sandlot baseball (1)
bl sandlot football (1)
bm shinny (2)
bn shuffleboard (1)
bo slag (1)
bp slaughter ball (1)
bq smear (1)
br smear the queer with the ball (1)
bs soccer (6)
bt soccer ball (1)
bu softball (29)
bv spud (2)
bw stickball (4)
bx sting (1)
by stingaree (1)
bz stinger Marie (1)
ca suicide football (1)
cb table tennis (1)
cc tackle (2)
cd tackle and smear (1)
ce tackle basketball (1)
cf tackle football (4)
cg tackle the man with the ball (1)
ch tag football (2)
ci telephone (1)
cj tennis (10)
ck tetherball (4)
cl throwing the ball in the furnace (1)
cm tin-can hy spy (1)
cn tippy (1)
co Tom Walkers (1)
cp toss (1)
cq touch (1)
cr touch football (4)
cs volleyball (14)
ct water basketball (1)

cu whiffle ball (1)

130.5 U rough games

No Response (82)
A army (6)
B BB-gun battles (1)
C BB-gun wars (2)
D bombardment (1)
E box(ing) (6)
F bull in the ring (1)
G car games (1)
H chicken fighting (1)
I Chinese red light (1)
J coming through (1)
K cowboys and Indians (4)
L dirt-clod battles (1)
M dodge ball (2)
N dodging (1)
O dragging (1)
P field hockey (1)
Q football (7)
R gator (1)
S general horsing around (1)
T gorilla ball (1)
U grapefruit wars (1)
V hand grenade (1)
W hockey (1)
X horseback riding (1)
Y hot potato (1)
Z jai alai (1)
aa joust (1)
ab junior commanders (1)
ac keep away (1)
ad kill (1)
ae kill the man with the ball (4)
af killer ball (1)
ag king of the mountain (1)
ah murder in the dark (1)
ai Oklahoma drill (1)
aj orange wars (1)
ak passe (1)
al persimmon wars (1)
am pom-pom-pull-away (1)
an pop the rope (1)
ao pop-the-whip (1)
ap popgun wars (1)
aq prizefight (1)
ar red rover (2)
as redbelly (1)
at ring-around-[D-0]-rosy (1)
au rock battles (1)
av rock fights (2)
aw rock throwing (1)
ax roughhouse (1)
ay Russian roulette (1)
az sandlot football (1)
ba sardines (1)
bb sharks and fishes (1)
bc slaughter ball (1)
bd slingshot wars (2)

be   smear (1)
bf   smear the queer with the ball (1)
bg   squirt-gun wars (1)
bh   sting (1)
bi   stinger Marie (1)
bj   suicide football (1)
bk   swing the statue (1)
bl   tackle (2)
bm   tackle and smear (1)
bn   tackle basketball (1)
bo   tackle football (4)
bp   tackle the man with the ball (1)
bq   tackling (1)
br   tag football (1)
bs   throw rocks at the sign (1)
bt   thump (1)
bu   tie each other up (1)
bv   touch football (3)
bw   tug-of-war (2)
bx   war (4)
by   water basketball (1)
bz   wrestle/wrestling (12)
ca   wrestling games (1)

130.6A U knife games
No Response (89)
A   chicken (8)
B   dare (1)
C   daredevil (1)
D   darts (3)
E   eat a root (1)
F   jackknife game, a (1)
G   lawn darts (1)
H   mammy-peg (1)
I   mumble peg (13)
J   mumblety-peg (18)
K   mumbly-peg (4)
L   pop the chicken neck (1)
M   root the peg (1)
N   rope the pig (1)
O   Russian roulette (1)
P   split(s) (3)
Q   stretch (4)
R   target practice (1)
S   throw knives (1)
T   throw the knife in the ground (1)
U   throwing the knife (1)

130.6B U rope games
No Response (59)
A   cowboys and Indians (4)
B   horse (1)
C   jump rope (55)
D   jump(ed/ing) a/the rope (4)
E   jumped/ing rope (11)
F   jumpy rope (1)
G   lasso (1)
H   skip(ing) rope (6)
I   skip(ing) the rope (2)
J   tie-up game (1)
K   tug-of-war (17)

L   tug-the-war (1)
[jump-rope games]
M   bluebells cockleshells (1)
N   Chinese jump rope (1)
O   Cinderella (1)
P   down in the valley (1)
Q   eeby iby over (1)
R   hop, skip, and jump (1)
S   hot pepper (1)
T   suffocation (1)
U   vaccination (1)
V   where the green grass grows (1)
[jump-rope terms]
W   back door (1)
X   eggbeater, a (1)
Y   fire hot-pepper ropes (1)
Z   front door (1)
aa   popping (1)
ab   throwing the rope (1)

130.6C U marble games
No Response (47)
A   big ring (1)
B   Boston (1)
C   china (1)
D   dead man (1)
E   for keeps (1)
F   funs (1)
G   granny (1)
H   hole (1)
I   keepers (1)
J   marble game (1)
K   marbles (73)
L   play(ing) marbles (4)
M   ringers (1)
N   roll marbles into egg cartons (1)
O   roly-poly (2)
P   shoot(ing) (a/the) marble(s) (14)
Q   squaring (1)
[marble types]
R   agate (2)
S   aggie (2)
T   Bohunk (1)
U   bum roller (1)
V   cat eye (2)
W   cat's eye (2)
X   chalkies (1)
Y   glass marbles (1)
Z   hunchy (1)
aa   jaw (1)
ab   jeet (1)
ac   logroller (1)
ad   magnetic marbles (1)
ae   shooter (3)
af   steeler (1)
ag   steelie (1)
ah   taw (2)
ai   toy (1)
[terms]

aj   fats (1)
ak   inching (1)
al   lagged (1)
am   play for keeps (1)
an   puke them up (1)
ao   scrambles (1)
ap   slippers (1)
aq   threesies (1)
ar   uppers (1)

130.6D U jacks games
No Response (68)
A   (a)round the moon (1)
B   around the world (2)
C   ball and jacks (1)
D   cow jumped over the fence (1)
E   jack game (1)
F   jack rocks (2)
G   jack toy (1)
H   jacks (65)
I   jackstones (8)
J   merry-go-round (1)
K   pigs (1)
[terms]
L   foursies (1)
M   onesies (3)
N   threesies (1)
O   twosies (2)

130.7 U parties
No Response (36)
A   affair (1)
B   alcoholic party (1)
C   anniversary party (2)
D   baby shower (2)
E   bachelor party (2)
F   backyard party (2)
G   ball (2)
H   band party (1)
I   banquet (1)
J   barbecue (1)
K   bash (1)
L   basketball party (1)
M   beach party (2)
N   beer bust (7)
O   beer party (1)
P   bingo party (2)
Q   birthday party (61)
R   blast (1)
S   booze party (1)
T   boy-girl party (1)
U   bridal shower (1)
V   bridge party (1)
W   bring your own steak party (1)
X   brunch (1)
Y   bunking party (3)
Z   card party (1)
aa   choir party (1)
ab   Christmas party (6)
ac   church party (5)
ad   class party (2)

ae   club party (1)

af   cocktail party (3)

ag   coffee (1)

ah   come-as-you-are party (1)

ai   coming-home party (1)

aj   coming-out party (1)

ak   cookout (2)

al   costume party (3)

am   covered-dish party (1)

an   dam party (1)

ao   dance (9)

ap   dance party (3)

aq   dinner (2)

ar   dinner party (3)

as   divorce party (1)

at   dope party (1)

au   drinking party (2)

av   engagement party (1)

aw   field party (1)

ax   formal (1)

ay   formal dance (1)

az   Fourth of July party (4)

ba   fraternity party (1)

bb   garage party (1)

bc   get-down party (1)

bd   get-drunk-and-chase-women party (1)

be   get-together (10)

bf   get-together party (2)

bg   going-away party (3)

bh   graduation party (2)

bi   Halloween party (8)

bj   hamburger fry (1)

bk   hayride (1)

bl   hell-raising party (1)

bm   holiday party (1)

bn   hot-dog party (1)

bo   house party (2)

bp   housewarming (1)

bq   ice-cream party (2)

br   ice-cream social (1)

bs   informal dance (1)

bt   jam (3)

bu   keg party (3)

bv   lawn party (1)

bw   luncheon (2)

bx   Mad Dog party (1)

by   make-out party (1)

bz   Mexican party (1)

ca   mixer (1)

cb   neighborhood party (1)

cc   New Year's party (1)

cd   orgy (1)

ce   oyster roast (1)

cf   pajama party (1)

cg   parlor party (1)

ch   party (33)

ci   picnic (4)

cj   play-party (1)

ck   pot party (6)

cl   potluck supper (1)

cm   progressive dinner party (1)

cn   prom party (1)

co   reception party (1)

cp   record party (1)

cq   reefer party (1)

cr   school party (1)

cs   school picnic (1)

ct   school's-out party (1)

cu   sherries (1)

cv   shower (4)

cw   skating party (1)

cx   slumber party (10)

cy   small party (1)

cz   smash bash (1)

da   snap social (1)

db   social (1)

dc   social party (1)

dd   sock hop (1)

de   sorority party (1)

df   spend-the-night party (2)

dg   sports party (1)

dh   square dance (1)

di   stag party (2)

dj   stag-film party (1)

dk   summer party (1)

dl   Sunday-school party (1)

dm   Sunday-school picnic (1)

dn   surprise party (2)

do   swimming party (3)

dp   tacky party (1)

dq   taffy pulling party (1)

dr   tea (1)

ds   thing (1)

dt   toga party (1)

du   trip-around-the-world party (1)

dv   Valentine party (1)

dw   watermelon party (1)

dx   wedding party (1)

dy   wedding shower (1)

dz   wienie roast (2)

ea   wild party (1)

eb   wine-and-cheese party (2)

ec   wine-tasting party (1)

ed   yard party (1)

130.8 U recorded music

No Response (22)

A   acid rock (music) (9)

B   acoustic (1)

C   ballads (4)

D   band (1)

E   Beatle music (1)

F   bebop music (1)

G   big band (era/music) (6)

H   black rock (1)

I   bluegrass (music) (10)

J   blues (13)

K   boogie-woogie (2)

L   Broadway music (1)

M   bubble gum (music) (2)

N   bump the bump (1)

O   C and W (1)

P   chamber music (1)

Q   Chicago blues (1)

R   choirs (1)

S   choral music (1)

T   Christian music (1)

U   Christmas carols (1)

V   church music/records/singing (5)

W   classic(al) (music) (43)

X   concert music (1)

Y   contemporary (3)

Z   contemporary classic (1)

aa   contemporary rock (1)

ab   country (music) (30)

ac   country (and) western (15)

ad   country rock (7)

ae   country singing (1)

af   country soul (1)

ag   dance/dancing music (3)

ah   disco (music) (7)

ai   Dixieland jazz (1)

aj   drifty music (1)

ak   easy(-)listening (music) (5)

al   easy-listening rock (1)

am   fast music (3)

an   folk (music) (9)

ao   folk-rock (2)

ap   fox-trot (1)

aq   glitter rock (1)

ar   good, clean, pretty music (1)

as   good music (1)

at   gospel (7)

au   Grand Ole Opry (1)

av   groups (1)

aw   hard acid rock (1)

ax   hard rock (12)

ay   hardcore Nashville country (1)

az   harmonious (1)

ba   hick music (2)

bb   hillbilly (music) (6)

bc   hits (1)

bd   instrumental (2)

be   jazz (music) (44)

bf   jazz festival (1)

bg   large choral works (1)

bh   long(-)hair(ed) music (2)

bi   love song (1)

bj   lullabies (1)

bk   marches (1)

bl   medium rock (1)

bm   mellow (music) (2)

bn   melodic (music) (1)

bo   Mississippi Delta blues (1)

bp   modern (1)

bq   modern jazz (2)

br   modern-day stuff (1)

bs   mood music (1)
bt   Moog synthesizer (1)
bu   movie scores (2)
bv   old standards (1)
bw   old-time music (1)
bx   old-timey rinky-dink stuff (1)
by   opera (6)
bz   orchestra (music) (2)
ca   organ (music) (2)
cb   patriotic songs (1)
cc   piano music (1)
cd   polkas (2)
ce   pop (music) (11)
cf   pop country (1)
cg   pop rock (2)
ch   pops-type music (1)
ci   popular music/tunes (5)
cj   progressive (1)
ck   progressive country (3)
cl   progressive jazz (1)
cm   progressive rock (1)
cn   punk funk (1)
co   punk rock (1)
cp   pure music (1)
cq   rag(time) (2)
cr   religious music/records (4)
cs   rhythm (and blues) (6)
ct   rock (music)/rock 'n' roll (65)
cu   sacred (music) (2)
cv   schottische (1)
cw   sea chanteys (1)
cx   semiclassical (music) (3)
cy   sentimental (songs) (2)
cz   show music/tunes (2)
da   slow (music) (4)
db   slow black music (1)
dc   slow motion (1)
dd   slow rock (1)
de   soft dinner music (1)
df   soft music (2)
dg   soft rock (4)
dh   soul (music) (20)
di   soul rock (1)
dj   Southern boogie (1)
dk   Southern rock ('n' roll) (2)
dl   Spanish music (1)
dm   spiritual music (1)
dn   spirituals (1)
do   straight ballads (1)
dp   swing bands/music (1)
dq   Switched-On Bach (1)
dr   symphonic/symphony (music) (4)
ds   top forty (music) (3)
dt   twist (1)
du   two-step (1)
dv   waltzes (2)
dw   western (2)
dx   Western Hillbilly (1)

dy   whooping and hollering (1)
dz   wire grass (1)

131.1 local culture

131.2 secondary responses to language

Appendix I

001.1AP	one	001A.6S	May	005.7L	(going to) clear up	
001.1BP	two	001A.6FP	June	006.1L	heavy rain	
001.1S	two	001A.6GP	July	006.2L	thunderstorm	
001.2AP	three	001A.6HP	August	006.3G	blow	
001.2S	three	001A.6IP	September	006.4G	(the wind's) from (the south)	
001.2BP	four	001A.6JP	October			
001.3AP	five	001A.6KP	November	006.5L	winds	
001.3S	five	001A.6LP	December	006.6L	drizzle	
001.3BP	six	002.1AP	Sunday	006.7AP	fog	
001.4AP	seven	002.1BP	Sabbath	006.7BP	foggy	
001.4BP	eight	002.1CP	Monday	007.1L	drought	
001.4S	eight	002.1DP	Tuesday	007.1P	drought	
001.5AP	nine	002.1EP	Wednesday	007.2L	(the wind is) picking up	
001.5AS	nine	002.1FP	Thursday	007.3L	(the wind is) letting up	
001.5BP	ten	002.1GP	Friday	007.4L	snappy	
001.5BS	ten	002.1HP	Saturday	007.5L	frost	
001.6AP	eleven	002.2P	morning	007.6L	froze over	
001.6BP	twelve	002.3L	afternoon	007.7G	freeze	
001.7AP	thirteen	002.4G	good day	007.8L	sitting room	
001.7BP	fourteen	002.5P	evening	007.9G	(nine) feet (high)	
001.8AP	twenty	003.1G	good night	008.1L	chimney	
001.8BP	twenty-seven	003.2L	sunrise	008.1P	chimney	
001A.1AP	thirty	003.2S	sun	008.2P	hearth	
001A.1BP	forty	003.3G	rise	008.3L	andirons	
001A.2AP	seventy	003.4L	sunset	008.4L	mantel	
001A.2BP	hundred	003.5P	yesterday	008.5L	backlog/forestick	
001A.2CP	thousand	003.6G	Sunday a week [past]	008.5P	log	
001A.2DP	million	003.7G	Sunday a week [future]	008.6L	lightwood	
001A.3AP	first	003.8L	fortnight	008.6S	wood	
001A.3BP	second	003.8P	fortnight	008.7AP	soot	
001A.3CP	third	004.1P	tomorrow	008.7BP	white	
001A.3S	third	004.2G	what time is it?	008.7CP	ashes	
001A.3DP	fourth	004.3P	watch	008.8P	chair	
001A.3EP	fifth	004.4G	half past (seven)	009.1L	sofa	
001A.3FP	sixth	004.4P	half (past)	009.1P	sofa	
001A.3GP	seventh	004.5G	quarter of (eleven)	009.2L	chest of drawers/dresser	
001A.3HP	eighth	004.5P	quarter	009.3L	bedroom	
001A.3IP	ninth	004.6L	(for quite a) while	009.3P	bedroom	
001A.3JP	tenth	004.7P	this year	009.4L	furniture	
001A.4P	once	005.1G	years (old)	009.4P	furniture	
001A.5P	twice	005.2P	a year ago	009.5L	window shades	
001A.6AP	January	005.2S	ago	009.5P	window	
001A.6BP	February	005.3P	clouds	009.6L	clothes closet	
001A.6CP	March	005.4L	nice day	009.7L	wardrobe	
001A.6DP	April	005.5L	gloomy day	009.8L	attic	
001A.6EP	May	005.6L	(the weather is) changing	009.9L	kitchen	

010.1L	pantry	015.4L	hogpen	019.7L	tow sack
010.2L	junk	015.5AL	dairy [storage place]	019.8L	turn (of corn/wood)
010.3L	junk room	015.5P	dairy	019.9L	light bulb
010.4L	clean up (the house)	015.5BL	potato house	019.9P	bulb
010.5G	behind	015.6L	barnyard	019.9S	bulb
010.5P	broom	015.7L	pasture	020.1L	clothes basket
010.6L	laundry	015.7P	pasture	020.1P	basket
010.7L	stairway	015.8L	chop cotton	020.2P	keg
010.7P	stairs	015.9L	grass types	020.3P	hoops
010.8L	porch	016.1L	field/patch	020.4L	cork
010.8P	porch	016.1P	field	020.4P	cork
011.1L	shut the door	016.1S	field	020.5L	harmonica
011.1AP	shut	016.2L	picket fence	020.6L	Jew's harp
011.1S	shut	016.3L	wire fence	020.7P	hammer
011.1BP	door	016.3S	wire	020.7S	hammer
011.2L	weatherboards	016.4L	rail fence	020.8L	tongue [of wagon]
011.3G	drive	016.5P	post/posts	020.9L	shafts [of buggy]
011.4P	roof	016.6L	stone wall	021.1L	rim/felly
011.5L	eaves troughs	017.1AP	china	021.2L	singletree
011.6L	valley [of roof]	017.1L	china egg	021.3L	doubletree
011.6S	valley	017.1BP	china egg	021.4L	hauling
011.7L	shed	017.2L	bucket [wooden]	021.5G	drag
012.1L	outhouse	017.3L	pail [metal]	021.6L	plow
012.2G	have/got	017.4L	slop bucket	021.6P	plow
012.3G	hear	017.5L	frying pan	021.7L	harrow
012.4G	heard (tell) of	017.6L	kettle	021.7P	harrow
012.5G	ain't	017.6P	kettle	021.8L	axle
012.6G	interrogative [negative]	017.7L	vase	022.1L	sawhorse
012.7G	do [various inflections]	017.7P	vase	022.2P	brush
012.8G	does	017.8AP	spoon	022.3P	strap
013.1G	doesn't	017.8BP	knife/knives	022.4P	cartridge
013.2G	interrogative [affirmative]	017.8CP	fork	022.5L	seesaw
013.3G	(don't I) know (it?)	018.1P	wash	022.6L	joggling board
013.4G	not sure	018.2P	rinses	022.7L	flying jenny
013.4S	sure	018.3L	dishcloth	022.8L	seesawing
013.5G	aux. verb + pres. part.	018.4L	dish towel	022.9L	swing
013.6G	(what) makes (him do it?)	018.5L	washcloth	023.1L	coal scuttle
013.7G	people think/they say	018.6L	bath towel	023.2L	stovepipe/flue
014.1P	house/houses	018.6P	towel	023.3L	wheelbarrow
014.1S	house	018.7L	faucet	023.3P	wheelbarrow
014.2P	barn	018.8G	burst	023.4L	whetstone
014.3L	corncrib	019.1P	barrel	023.5L	grindstone
014.3S	crib	019.2L	stand	023.6L	car
014.4P	granary	019.3L	funnel	023.6P	car
014.5L	loft	019.4L	whip	023.6S	car
014.6L	haystack	019.4P	whip	023.7G	grease
014.7L	hay barrack	019.4S	whip	023.8P	greasy
014.8L	haycock	019.5L	paper bag	024.1P	oil
015.1L	cow barn	019.5P	paper	024.1S	oil
015.2L	stable	019.5S	bag	024.2L	kerosene
015.3L	milk gap	019.6L	cloth sack	024.3L	makeshift lamp

024.4P	tube	029.2L	pallet	033.3L	mongrel
024.5P	launch	029.3P	fertile	033.3P	feist
024.6L	rowboat	029.4L	bottomland	033.4G	bite
024.7G	aux. verb + going	029.5L	meadow	033.5L	bull
024.8G	am I/are they (going)	029.6L	swamp	033.6P	cow
024.9G	inceptives	029.6P	swamp	033.6S	cow
025.1G	here are (your clothes)	029.7L	marsh	033.7L	pair
025.2G	there are (many people)	029.8L	soil types	033.7AP	pair
025.3G	I am not (going to hurt you)	029.8P	loam	033.7BP	mules
025.4G	am I not?	030.1P	draining	033.7S	mule
025.5G	we were (going anyway)	030.2L	canal	033.8P	calf
025.6G	those were (the good-old	030.3L	creek [tidal]	033.9L	calve
	days)	030.4L	ravine	034.1L	stallion
025.7G	(it wasn't) I	030.5L	gully	034.2AP	horse/horses
025.8G	deletions	030.6L	creek	034.2S	horse
026.1G	be [finite]	030.6P	creek	034.2BP	mare
026.2L	sample	030.8L	hill	034.3G	ride
026.2P	sample	030.8AP	hill	034.4G	fell off (the horse)
026.3AP	pretty	030.8S	hill	034.5AG	fell out of bed
026.3BP	prettier	030.8BP	knob	034.5BG	fall
026.4L	apron	030.9P	Gulf of Mexico	034.6P	horseshoes
026.4P	apron	031.1P	mountain	034.7P	hoof/hoofs
026.5AP	pen	031.2L	cliff	034.8L	quoits
026.5BP	pin	031.2P	cliff/cliffs	034.9L	ram
026.6AP	ten cents	031.3L	notch	035.1L	ewe
026.6BP	tin	031.3P	notch	035.1P	ewe
026.6S	tin	031.4L	wharf	035.2P	wool
027.1P	coat	031.5L	waterfall	035.3L	boar
027.1S	coat	031.6L	road materials/surfaces	035.4L	barrow
027.2G	(buttons) on it	031.6AP	tar	035.4P	barrow
027.3L	vest	031.6BP	dirt	035.5P	hogs
027.4L	trousers	031.6CP	gravel	035.6P	bristles
027.4P	overalls	031.7L	byway	035.7P	tusks
027.5G	bring	031.8L	lane	035.8P	trough/troughs
027.6G	fit	031.9AL	sidewalk	035.9L	wild hog
027.7P	new suit	031.9BL	parkway	036.1L	castrate
027.8L	bulge	032.1AL	rock	036.2L	bawl [of calf]
027.8P	bulge	032.1G	throw	036.3L	low [of cow]
027.9G	shrink	032.1BL	threw	036.4L	whinny [of horse]
028.1L	dress up	032.2G	(not) at home	036.5L	cattle
028.2L	purse	032.2S	home	036.6L	fowls
028.2P	purse	032.3L	black coffee	036.7L	setting hen
028.3P	bracelet	032.3P	without	036.8L	chicken coop
028.4L	string of beads	032.4P	with	036.8P	coop
028.5L	suspenders	032.5G	(coming) toward	037.1L	wishbone
028.6L	umbrella	032.5P	toward	037.2L	haslet
028.6P	umbrella	032.6G	(ran) across	037.3L	chitterlings
028.7L	bedspread	032.7G	(named) for	037.3P	chitterlings
028.8P	pillow	033.1P	dog	037.4L	feeding time
028.9G	all the way (across)	033.1S	dog	037.5G	calls to cows
029.1L	quilt	033.2G	calls to dogs to attack	037.6G	calls to calves

037.7G	gee/haw	043.4EG	hers	049.1G	drink
037.8G	calls to horses	043.5G	you-all	049.2G	sit down
038.1G	get up [to horse]	043.6G	you-all's	049.3G	sit
038.2AG	whoa [to horse]	043.7AG	who-all	049.4G	help yourself
038.2BG	back up [to horse]	043.7BG	who-all's	049.5G	help
038.3G	calls to pigs	043.8G	what-all	049.6G	I don't care for any
038.4G	calls to sheep	044.1G	themselves	050.1L	warmed-over
038.5G	calls to chickens	044.2G	himself	050.2P	chew
038.6L	harness [v.]	044.3L	loaf bread	050.3L	mush
038.6P	harness	044.4L	other flour breads	050.4P	vegetables
039.1L	lines	044.5-6L	corn breads	050.5L	garden
039.2L	reins	045.1L	store-bought bread	050.5P	garden
039.3P	stirrups	045.2L	doughnut	050.6AL	grits
039.4L	lead horse	045.3L	pancakes	050.6BL	hominy
039.5G	a little way	045.4G	pounds	050.7P	rice
040.1G	a long way	045.5P	yeast	050.8L	moonshine
040.2G	anywhere	045.5S	yeast	051.1G	smell (that)
040.3P	backward	045.6L	yolk	051.2G	molasses is
040.4P	forward	045.7P	yellow	051.2L	molasses
040.5G	ne'er (a one)	046.1P	eggs	051.2P	molasses
040.5P	ne'er (a)	046.2L	poached egg	051.3L	syrup
040.6G	(didn't do) anything	046.3L	salt pork	051.3P	syrup
040.7G	(didn't like it) anyway	046.4L	side (of bacon)	051.4P	genuine
040.8G	(didn't give me) any	046.5L	smoked meat	051.5P	bulk
040.9G	duratives	046.6L	bacon rind	051.6P	jelly
041.1G	like as not	046.7L	bacon	051.7P	salt/pepper
041.2P	furrows	046.8AP	sausage	051.7S	salt
041.3P	crop	046.8BP	butcher	051.8G	a/an (apple)
041.3S	crop	046.9L	spoiled [meat]	052.1G	those (boys)
041.4L	cleared (the land)	046.9P	spoiled	052.2G	over there
041.5L	second cutting	047.1L	headcheese	052.3G	this way
041.6L	sheaf	047.2L	liver sausage	052.4G	what's that?
041.7L	shock	047.3L	blood sausage	053.1P	poor
041.8G	bushels	047.4L	scrapple	053.1S	poor
042.1G	oats are	047.5L	rancid [butter]	053.2P	orchard
042.1P	thrashed	047.6L	curdled milk	053.3G	whose father (is rich)
042.2G	you and I	048.1L	cottage cheese	054.1L	cherry seed
042.3G	both of us	048.2AP	strain	054.2L	peach seed
042.4G	he and I	048.2S	strain	054.3L	cling peach
042.5AG	(it's) I	048.2BP	milk	054.4L	freestone peach
042.5BG	(it's) he	048.3L	cobbler	054.5L	apple core
042.5CG	(it's) she	048.4L	food	054.6L	snits
042.5DG	(it's) they	048.5L	sweet sauce	054.7L	peanuts
042.6G	(as tall) as I am	048.6L	snack	054.8AL	shell [hard/inner]
043.1G	(as tall) as he is	048.7G	eat	054.8BL	hull [soft/outer]
043.2G	(better) than I can	048.8L	make (some coffee)	054.8P	walnut
043.3G	the farthest	048.8P	coffee	054.9AP	almonds
043.4AG	yours	048.9G	break	054.9BP	pecans
043.4BG	ours	048.9AP	glass	055.1AP	oranges
043.4CG	theirs	048.9S	glass	055.1BP	all gone
043.4DG	his	048.9BP	water	055.1S	gone

055.2P	radishes	059.3L	woodpecker	063.2L	wife
055.3L	cherry tomato	059.4L	skunk	063.3L	widow
055.3P	tomatoes	059.5L	varmint	063.3P	widow
055.4L	potatoes	059.5P	varmints	063.3S	woman
055.5L	sweet potatoes	059.6L	gray squirrel	063.4-5L	father
055.6P	onions	059.7L	fox squirrel	063.4P	father
055.7L	spring onions	059.8L	chipmunk	063.4S	father
055.7P	shallots	059.9L	fish	063.6-7L	mother
055.8P	okra	060.1P	oysters	063.6P	mother
055.9P	shriveled	060.1S	oysters	063.8P	parents
055A.1G	cabbages	060.2L	bullfrog	064.1L	grandfather
055A.2L	shell [v.]	060.3L	spring frog	064.2L	grandmother
055A.3L	butter bean	060.4L	toad	064.3L	children
055A.3S	bean	060.5L	earthworm	064.4L	pet name
055A.4L	green beans	060.5S	worm	064.5L	baby carriage
055A.5L	greens	060.6L	turtle	064.6L	wheel (the baby)
055A.6P	heads	060.7L	terrapin	064.7G	most grown up
055A.7G	heads (of children)	060.8L	crawfish	064.8P	daughter
055A.8P	passel	060.9P	shrimp	064.8S	daughter
056.1L	shuck	060A.1L	moth	064.9P	girl
056.2L	roasting ears	060A.2P	moth/moths	064.9S	girl
056.3P	tassel	060A.3L	firefly	065.1L	pregnant
056.4L	corn silk	060A.4L	dragonfly	065.2L	midwife
056.5P	pumpkin	060A.5L	hornet/bee	065.3L	resembles (his father)
056.6P	squash	060A.6L	wasp/dirt dauber	065.4L	reared
056.7L	muskmelon	060A.6P	wasps	065.5L	whipping
056.8L	mushroom	060A.7L	yellow jacket/fly	065.6G	grow
056.8P	mushroom	060A.8P	mosquito	065.7L	bastard
056.9L	watermelon	060A.9L	chigger	066.1G	more loving
057.1L	toadstool	061.1L	grasshopper	066.2P	nephew
057.2P	swallow (it)	061.2L	minnow	066.3L	orphan
057.3AP	cigars	061.3L	spider web	066.3P	orphan
057.3BP	cigarettes	061.4P	roots	066.4L	guardian
057.4G	a-(+ pres. part.)	061.5L	maple	066.4P	guardian
057.5L	obligated	061.6L	grove	066.5L	relatives
057.6P	can [v./stressed]	061.7L	sycamore	066.6L	no kin
057.7P	can't	061.7P	sycamore	066.7L	stranger
057.8G	done [+ v.]	061.8L	trees	067.1P	Mary
057.9G	done [+ adj./adv.]	062.1P	cherry	067.1S	Mary
058.1G	should	062.2L	sumac	067.2P	Martha
058.2G	dare not	062.2P	sumac	067.3P	Nelly
058.3G	ought	062.3L	poison ivy	067.3S	Nelly
058.4G	ought not	062.3S	poison	067.4P	Billy
058.5P	won't	062.4P	strawberries	067.5P	Matthew
058.6G	might have	062.5P	raspberries	067.6L	woman teacher
058.7G	might could	062.6P	poisonous	067.7AP	Mrs.
059.1L	screech owl	062.7L	mountain laurel	067.7BP	Cooper
059.1P	screech owl	062.8L	rhododendron	067.8L	jackleg
059.2L	hoot owl	062.9L	magnolia	067.8S	lawyer
059.2P	owl	063.1L	husband	067.9P	your aunt
059.2S	owl	063.1S	husband	068.1P	Sarah

068.2AP	uncle	072.6AP	leg	078.2P	proud flesh
068.2BP	William	072.6S	leg	078.3P	iodine
068.2CP	John	072.6BP	foot/feet	078.4P	quinine
068.2S	John	072.7L	shin	078.5L	died [neutral/veiled]
068.3P	general	072.8L	haunches	078.6L	died [crude/humorous]
068.4P	colonel	072.9L	peaked	078.7G	(died) of
068.5P	captain	073.1L	strong	078.8L	cemetery
068.6P	judge	073.1P	strong	079.1L	casket
068.7L	student	073.2L	good-natured	079.2L	funeral
068.7P	student	073.3L	awkward	079.2P	funeral
068.8P	secretary	073.4L	fool	079.3L	(in) mourning
069.1L	actress	073.5L	tightwad	079.3P	mourning
069.1P	actress	073.6L	common	079.4G	pretty well
069.2P	American	074.1L	lively [of older people]	079.5P	worry
069.3L	Negro	074.1P	pert	079.5S	worry
069.3P	Negro	074.2P	un- [prefix]	079.6L	rheumatism
069.4L	Caucasian	074.3L	afraid	079.7P	diphtheria
069.5L	mulatto	074.4P	used to be	079.8L	yellow jaundice
069.6L	employer	074.5G	didn't use to	079.8P	jaundice
069.7L	poor whites [white usage]	074.6P	careless	080.1L	appendicitis
069.8L	poor whites [black usage]	074.7L	queer	080.1P	appendicitis
069.9L	rustic	074.7P	queer	080.2L	vomit [neutral]
070.1G	almost (midnight)	074.8L	obstinate	080.3L	vomit [crude]
070.2G	almost (fell)	075.1L	touchy	080.4G	(sick) at his stomach
070.3P	just	075.2L	angry	080.5G	for to (+ inf.)
070.4P	far	075.3P	calm	081.1G	I shall (be disappointed)
070.5G	look here	075.4L	tired	081.2AG	we shall (be glad)
071.1P	often	075.5G	wear	081.2BG	glad (to see you)
071.2P	either/neither	076.1G	got sick	081.3G	go and/take and [+ verb]
071.3P	forehead	076.2G	by and by	081.4L	courting
071.4AP	hair	076.3G	caught a cold	081.5L	boyfriend
071.4BP	beard	076.3S	cold	081.6L	girl friend
071.4S	beard	076.4P	hoarse	081.7L	kissing
071.5AP	left ear	076.4S	hoarse	082.1L	turned him down
071.5BP	right ear	076.5P	cough	082.2L	got married
071.5S	ear	076.6L	sleepy	082.2P	married
071.6P	mouth	076.7L	wake up	082.2S	married
071.7AP	neck	076.8L	wake him up	082.3L	best man
071.7S	neck	077.1G	take	082.4L	bridesmaid
071.7BP	throat	077.2L	deaf	082.5L	shivaree
071.7CP	goozle	077.2P	deaf	082.6G	up in (place-name)
071.8P	tooth/teeth	077.3G	sweat	082.6S	down
071.8S	tooth	077.3L	sweated	082.7G	up at (the Browns')
071.9P	gums	077.4L	boil [n.]	082.8L	(whole) crowd
072.1P	palm	077.4P	boil	082.8P	whole
072.2P	fist/fists	077.5L	pus	083.1L	dance
072.3P	joints	077.6G	swell	083.1P	dance
072.3S	joint	077.7L	water [in blister]	083.2L	(school) lets out
072.4AP	chest	078.1P	wound	083.3L	(when does school) start?
072.4BP	shoulders	078.1S	wound	083.4L	skipped class
072.5P	hand/hands	078.2L	proud flesh	083.5L	education

083.5P	education	087.4BP	Knoxville	091.7AP	real
083.6P	college	087.4CP	Chattanooga	091.7BP	really
083.6S	college	087.5AP	Memphis	092.1G	damn
083.7L	first grade	087.5BP	Nashville	092.2G	land's sakes
083.8P	desk/desks	087.6AP	Atlanta	092.3G	shucks
084.1P	library	087.6BP	Savannah	092.4P	idea
084.2P	post office	087.7AP	Macon	092.5G	how are you?
084.3P	hotel	087.7BP	Columbus	092.6G	how do you do?
084.4L	theater	087.8AP	New Orleans	093.1P	again
084.4P	theater	087.8BP	Baton Rouge	093.2G	Merry Christmas
084.5P	hospital	087.9AP	Cincinnati	093.2P	merry
084.6P	nurse	087.9BP	Louisville	093.2S	merry
084.7L	railroad station	087.9CP	Ireland	093.3G	Happy New Year
084.7S	rail	087.9DP	France	093.3P	New Year
085.1L	public square	087.9EP	Russia	093.4P	obliged
085.2L	cater-cornered	088.1G	miles	094.1G	I think
085.3L	streetcar	088.1S	miles	094.2L	shopping
085.4G	(where I) want to get off	088.2G	(I don't know) if	094.3P	wrapped
085.5L	county seat	088.3G	(seems) as though	094.4P	unwrapped
085.6P	government	088.4G	unless	094.5P	loss
085.7P	law and order	088.5G	instead of	094.6G	cost
085.8L	Civil War	088.5P	instead	094.7P	due
085.8P	Civil War	088.6G	because	094.8P	dues
085.9G	hang	089.1P	Baptist	095.1P	borrow
086.1AP	New York State	089.2AP	joined	095.2P	scarce
086.1BP	Maryland	089.2BP	church	095.3G	dive
086.2AP	Virginia	089.2S	church	095.4L	belly flop
086.2BP	North Carolina	089.3P	God	095.5L	somersault
086.3AP	South Carolina	089.4L	sermon	095.6G	swim
086.3BP	Georgia	089.4P	sermon	095.7L	lagniappe
086.4AP	Florida	089.5L	church music	096.1G	drown
086.4BP	Alabama	089.5P	music	096.2L	crawls
086.5AP	Louisiana	089.6P	beautiful	096.3G	climb
086.5BP	Kentucky	089.7G	by the time	096.4L	crouch
086.6AP	Tennessee	090.1L	devil	096.5G	kneel
086.6BP	Missouri	090.1P	devil	096.6G	lie
086.7AP	Arkansas	090.2L	spooks	097.1G	lie
086.7BP	Mississippi	090.3L	haunted house	097.2G	dream
086.8AP	Texas	090.3P	haunted	097.3G	wake
086.8BP	Oklahoma	090.4G	rather [=quite]	097.4P	stamp
086.9AP	Massachusetts	090.4P	rather [=quite]	097.5L	(may I) take you home?
086.9BP	New England States	090.5P	rather [=prefer]	097.6P	pull
087.1AP	Baltimore	090.6G	mighty glad	097.6S	pull
087.1BP	Washington, DC	090.6P	proud	097.7P	push
087.1CP	St. Louis	090.7G	right smart	097.7S	push
087.2AP	Charleston	091.1G	certainly	098.1L	lug
087.2BP	Birmingham	091.2P	sure	098.2P	touch
087.2CP	Chicago	091.3G	yes	098.3L	(go) bring
087.3AP	Montgomery	091.4G	yes, sir/ma'am	098.4L	goal [children's games]
087.3BP	Mobile	091.5P	hesitation	098.5G	catch
087.4AP	Asheville	091.6G	really (dreaded)	099.1G	(wait) for

099.2P	chance	108.1U	parallel parking	114.1U	marijuana
099.3P	humor	108.2U	fire hydrant	114.2U	hard drugs
099.4G	get rid of	108.3U	angle parking	114.3U	drug addict
100.1G	acted as if	108.4U	parking ramp	114.4U	drug seller
100.2L	swiped	108.5U	skyscraper	114.5U	money
100.3L	remember	108.6U	alley	114.6U	pawnshop
100.4L	(I) don't remember	108.7U	vacant lot	114.7U	wine
100.5G	write	108.8U	drinking fountain	114.8U	skid row
100.5S	write	109.1U	coupe	114.9U	X-rated movie theater
100.6P	answer	109.2U	two-door sedan	115.1U	mailman
100.7P	address [v.]	109.3U	four-door sedan	115.2U	garbage man
100.8P	address [n.]	109.4U	limousine	115.3U	political influence
101.1G	teach/learn	109.5U	station wagon	115.4U	pay-roller
101.2L	intending to	109.6U	van	116.1U	large food store
101.3L	tattletale	109.7U	pickup truck	116.2AU	neighborhood grocery
101.4L	pick (flowers)	109.8U	airport limousine	116.2BU	convenience store
101.4P	flowers	109.9U	public transportation	116.3U	delicatessen
101.4S	flower	110.1U	dashboard	116.4AU	electric frying pan
101.5L	toy	110.2U	glove compartment	116.4BU	microwave oven
101.6G	know	110.3U	rubber band	116.4CU	toaster oven
102.1G	give	110.4U	paper clip	116.5U	Laundromat
102.2G	begin	110.5U	trunk	116.6U	laundry hamper
102.3G	run	110.6U	accelerator	116.7U	vacuum cleaner
102.4G	come	110.7U	gearshift	116.8U	vacuum bag
102.5G	see	110.8U	speed breaker	116.9U	plastic pail
102.6G	tear	111.1U	fire truck	117.1U	trash presser
102.7P	put it on	111.2U	pumper truck	117.2U	large garbage can
102.8G	do	111.3U	hook-and-ladder truck	117.3U	large garbage bin
103.1P	nothing	111.4U	snorkel truck	117.4U	undertaker
103.2P	something	111.5U	emergency truck	117.5U	hearse
103.3P	such	111.6U	chief's car	117.6U	mausoleum
103.4P	always	111.7U	police sedan	117.7U	cigarettes
103.5P	since	111.8U	police van	118.1U	sun-room
103.6G	on purpose	111.9P	helicopter	118.2U	den
103.7P	affirmation	111.9U	helicopter	118.3U	half bath
103.8P	negation	112.1U	hurricane	118.4U	stoves/furnaces
103.9G	I think so	112.2U	tornado	118.5U	circulation systems
104.1G	ask	112.3U	ice storm	118.6U	shotgun house
104.2G	fight	112.4U	fireman	118.7U	dogtrot house
104.3G	stab	112.5U	policeman	118.8U	hall-and-parlor house
104.4G	draw	112.6U	fire station	118.9U	house designs
104.5P	hoist	112.7U	police station	119.1U	row house
105.2U	financial district	112.8U	jail	119.2U	apartment building
105.3U	shopping district	113.1U	pistol	119.3U	condominium
106.5U	municipal airport	113.2U	nightstick	119.4U	flat
107.1U	interstate highway	113.3U	prostitute	119.5U	superintendent
107.2U	rest and service area	113.4U	whorehouse	120.1U	manual lawn mower
107.3U	lane markers	113.5U	pimp/madam	120.2U	gas/electric lawn mower
107.4U	entrance/exit ramp	113.6U	drunk	120.3U	riding lawn mower
107.5U	limited-access road	113.7U	derelict	120.4U	tiller
107.8U	underpass	113.8U	cheap hotel	120.5U	hand trowel

120.6U	hand fork	126.6U	Protestants
120.7U	rake	126.7U	Jews
120.8U	hedge trimmer	126.8U	American Indians
120.9U	chain saw	127.1U	Germans
121.1U	beefsteak	127.2U	Low Germans
121.2U	cuts of beef	127.3U	Italians
121.3U	cuts of pork	127.4U	Poles
121.4U	cuts of lamb	127.5U	Russians
121.5U	poultry	127.6U	Czechs
121.6U	sausage	127.7U	Lithuanians
121.7U	hero sandwich	127.8U	Englishmen
121.8U	soft drinks	127.9U	Irishmen
121.9U	beer	128.1U	Scots
122.1U	coffee cake	128.2U	French
122.2U	sweet roll	128.3U	Cajuns
122.3U	frosting	128.4U	Greeks
122.4U	frosted doughnut	128.5U	Cubans
122.5U	long john	128.6U	Puerto Ricans
122.6U	bismarck	128.7U	Mexicans
122.7U	cruller	128.8U	Scandinavians
123.1U	finger ring	128.9U	Canadians
123.2U	knee-length shorts	129.1U	Democrat
123.3U	below-the-knee shorts	129.2U	Republican
123.4U	above-the-knee shorts	129.3U	hippie
123.5U	used clothes	129.4U	best friend
123.6U	fashionable clothes	129.5U	surrogate parent
123.7U	garment bag	129.6U	peer groups
123.8U	shoes	129.7U	playing the dozens
123.9U	hairstyles	129.8U	initiation rites
124.1U	effeminate male	130.1U	hiding games
124.2U	male homosexual	130.2U	line/running games
124.3U	masculine female	130.3U	ring games
124.4U	female homosexual	130.4U	ball/puck/tin can games
124.5U	sexually overactive male	130.5U	rough games
124.6U	sexually overactive female	130.6AU	knife games
124.7U	sexually indiscreet male	130.6BU	rope games
124.8U	sexually indiscreet female	130.6CU	marble games
125.1U	ugly male	130.6DU	jacks games
125.2U	ugly female	130.7U	parties
125.3U	attractive male	130.8U	recorded music
125.4U	attractive female		
125.5U	bookish person		
125.6U	brownnose		
125.7U	grade school		
125.8U	junior high school		
125.9U	high school		
126.1U	woven-wire fence		
126.2U	gymnasium		
126.3U	lavatory		
126.4U	Orientals		
126.5U	Roman Catholics		

Appendix II

a-(+ pres. part.)	057.4G	April	001A.6DP	bastard	065.7L
a/an (apple)	051.8G	apron	026.4L	bath, half	118.3U
above-the-knee shorts	123.4U	apron	026.4P	bath towel	018.6L
accelerator	110.6U	are they/am I (going)	024.8G	Baton Rouge	087.8BP
across, (ran)	032.6G	Arkansas	086.7AP	bawl [of calf]	036.2L
acted as if	100.1G	as he is	043.1G	be [finite]	026.1G
actress	069.1L	as I am	042.6G	beads, string of	028.4L
actress	069.1P	(as tall) as he is	043.1G	bean	055A.3S
addict, drug	114.3U	(as tall) as I am	042.6G	bean, butter	055A.3L
address [n.]	100.8P	as though, (seems)	088.3G	beans, green	055A.4L
address [v.]	100.7P	ashes	008.7CP	beard	071.4BP
affirmation	103.7P	Asheville	087.4AP	beard	071.4S
afraid	074.3L	ask	104.1G	beautiful	089.6P
afternoon	002.3L	at his stomach, (sick)	080.4G	because	088.6G
again	093.1P	at home, (not)	032.2G	bedroom	009.3L
ago	005.2S	Atlanta	087.6AP	bedroom	009.3P
ago, a year	005.2P	attic	009.8L	bedspread	028.7L
ain't	012.5G	attractive female	125.4U	bee/hornet	060A.5L
airport, municipal	106.5U	attractive male	125.3U	beef, cuts of	121.2U
airport limousine	109.8U	August	001A.6HP	beefsteak	121.1U
Alabama	086.4BP	aux. verb + going	024.7G	beer	121.9U
all gone	055.1BP	aux. verb + pres. part.	013.5G	begin	102.2G
all the way (across)	028.9G	awkward	073.3L	behind	010.5G
alley	108.6U	axle	021.8L	belly flop	095.4L
almonds	054.9AP	baby carriage	064.5L	below-the-knee shorts	123.3U
almost (fell)	070.2G	back up [to horse]	038.2BG	best friend	129.4U
almost (midnight)	070.1G	backlog/forestick	008.5L	best man	082.3L
always	103.4P	backward	040.3P	(better) than I can	043.2G
am I not?	025.4G	bacon	046.7L	Billy	067.4P
am I/are they (going)	024.8G	bacon rind	046.6L	Birmingham	087.2BP
am not (going to hurt you), I	025.3G	bag	019.5S	bismarck	122.6U
		bag, garment	123.7U	bite	033.4G
American	069.2P	bag, paper	019.5L	black coffee	032.3L
American Indians	126.8U	bag, vacuum	116.8U	blood sausage	047.3L
andirons	008.3L	ball/puck/tin can games	130.4U	blow	006.3G
angle parking	108.3U	Baltimore	087.1AP	boar	035.3L
angry	075.2L	Baptist	089.1P	board, joggling	022.6L
answer	100.6P	barn	014.2P	boil	077.4P
any, (didn't give me)	040.8G	barn, cow	015.1L	boil [n.]	077.4L
anything, (didn't do)	040.6G	barnyard	015.6L	bookish person	125.5U
anyway, (didn't like it)	040.7G	barrack, hay	014.7L	borrow	095.1P
anywhere	040.2G	barrel	019.1P	both of us	042.3G
apartment building	119.2U	barrow	035.4L	bottomland	029.4L
appendicitis	080.1L	barrow	035.4P	boyfriend	081.5L
appendicitis	080.1P	basket	020.1P	bracelet	028.3P
apple core	054.5L	basket, clothes	020.1L	bread, loaf	044.3L

county seat	085.5L	(died) of	078.7G
coupe	109.1U	diphtheria	079.7P
courting	081.4L	dirt	031.6BP
cow	033.6P	dirt dauber/wasp	060A.6L
cow	033.6S	dish towel	018.4L
cow barn	015.1L	dishcloth	018.3L
cows, calls to	037.5G	dive	095.3G
crawfish	060.8L	do	102.8G
crawls	096.2L	do [various inflections]	012.7G
creek	030.6L	does	012.8G
creek	030.6P	doesn't	013.1G
creek [tidal]	030.3L	dog	033.1P
crib	014.3S	dog	033.1S
crop	041.3P	dogtrot house	118.7U
crop	041.3S	dogs, calls to, to attack	033.2G
crouch	096.4L	done [+ adj./adv.]	057.9G
crowd, (whole)	082.8L	done [+ v.]	057.8G
cruller	122.7U	don't care for any, I	049.6G
Cubans	128.5U	(don't I) know (it?)	013.3G
curdled milk	047.6L	don't remember, (I)	100.4L
cuts of beef	121.2U	door	011.1BP
cuts of lamb	121.4U	doubletree	021.3L
cuts of pork	121.3U	doughnut	045.2L
cutting, second	041.5L	doughnut, frosted	122.4U
Czechs	127.6U	down	082.6S
dairy	015.5P	dozens, playing the	129.7U
dairy [storage place]	015.5AL	drag	021.5G
damn	092.1G	dragonfly	060A.4L
dance	083.1P	draining	030.1P
dance [n.]	083.1L	draw	104.4G
dare not	058.2G	dream	097.2G
dashboard	110.1U	dress up	028.1L
daughter	064.8P	dresser/chest of drawers	009.2L
daughter	064.8S	drink	049.1G
deaf	077.2L	drinking fountain	108.8U
deaf	077.2P	drinks, soft	121.8U
December	001A.6LP	drive	011.3G
deletions	025.8G	drizzle	006.6L
delicatessen	116.3U	drought	007.1L
Democrat	129.1U	drought	007.1P
den	118.2U	drown	096.1G
derelict	113.7U	drug addict	114.3U
desk/desks	083.8P	drug seller	114.4U
devil	090.1L	drugs, hard	114.2U
devil	090.1P	drunk	113.6U
(didn't do) anything	040.6G	due	094.7P
(didn't give me) any	040.8G	dues	094.8P
(didn't like it) anyway	040.7G	duratives	040.9G
didn't use to	074.5G	ear	071.5S
died [crude/humorous]	078.6L	ear, left	071.5AP
died [neutral/veiled]	078.5L	ear, right	071.5BP

ears, roasting	056.2L		
earthworm	060.5L		
eat	048.7G		
eaves troughs	011.5L		
education	083.5L		
education	083.5P		
effeminate male	124.1U		
egg, china	017.1L		
egg, china	017.1BP		
egg, poached	046.2L		
eggs	046.1P		
eight	001.4BP		
eight	001.4S		
eighth	001A.3HP		
either/neither	071.2P		
electric frying pan	116.4AU		
electric/gas lawn mower	120.2U		
eleven	001.6AP		
emergency truck	111.5U		
employer	069.6L		
Englishmen	127.8U		
entrance/exit ramp	107.4U		
evening	002.5P		
ewe	035.1L		
ewe	035.1P		
exit/entrance ramp	107.4U		
fall	034.5BG		
far	070.4P		
farthest, the	043.3G		
fashionable clothes	123.6U		
father	063.4L		
father	063.4P		
father	063.4S		
faucet	018.7L		
February	001A.6BP		
feeding time	037.4L		
feet (high), (nine)	007.9G		
feist	033.3P		
fell off (the horse)	034.4G		
fell out of bed	034.5AG		
felly/rim	021.1L		
female, attractive	125.4U		
female, masculine	124.3U		
female, sexually	124.8U		
indiscreet			
female, sexually	124.6U		
overactive			
female, ugly	125.2U		
female homosexual	124.4U		
fence, picket	016.2L		
fence, rail	016.4L		

fence, wire	016.3L	fourth	001A.3DP	girl	064.9P
fence, woven-wire	126.1U	fowls	036.6L	girl	064.9S
fertile	029.3P	fox squirrel	059.7L	girl friend	081.6L
field	016.1P	France	087.9DP	give	102.1G
field	016.1S	freestone peach	054.4L	glad, mighty	090.6G
field/patch	016.1L	freeze	007.7G	glad (to see you)	081.2BG
fifth	001A.3EP	French	128.2U	glass	048.9AP
fight	104.2G	Friday	002.1GP	glass	048.9S
financial district	105.2U	friend, best	129.4U	gloomy day	005.5L
finger ring	123.1U	friend, girl	081.6L	glove compartment	110.2U
fire hydrant	108.2U	frog, spring	060.3L	go and/take and [+ verb]	081.3G
fire station	112.6U	from (the south), (wind's)	006.4G	(go) bring	098.3L
fire truck	111.1U	frost	007.5L	goal [children's games]	098.4L
firefly	060A.3L	frosted doughnut	122.4U	God	089.3P
fireman	112.4U	frosting	122.3U	(going to) clear up	005.7L
first	001A.3AP	froze over	007.6L	gone	055.1S
first grade	083.7L	frying pan	017.5L	gone, all	055.1BP
fish	059.9L	frying pan, electric	116.4AU	good day	002.4G
fist/fists	072.2P	funeral	079.2L	good night	003.1G
fit	027.6G	funeral	079.2P	good-natured	073.2L
five	001.3AP	funnel	019.3L	goozle	071.7CP
five	001.3S	furnaces/stoves	118.4U	got married	082.2L
flat	119.4U	furniture	009.4L	got sick	076.1G
flesh, proud	078.2L	furniture	009.4P	got/have	012.2G
flesh, proud	078.2P	furrows	041.2P	government	085.6P
Florida	086.4AP	games, ball/puck/tin can	130.4U	grade school	125.7U
flour breads, other	044.4L	games, hiding	130.1U	granary	014.4P
flower	101.4S	games, jacks	130.6DU	grandfather	064.1L
flowers	101.4P	games, knife	130.6AU	grandmother	064.2L
flue/stovepipe	023.2L	games, line/running	130.2U	grass types	015.9L
flying jenny	022.7L	games, marble	130.6CU	grasshopper	061.1L
fog	006.7AP	games, ring	130.3U	gravel	031.6CP
foggy	006.7BP	games, rope	130.6BU	gray squirrel	059.6L
food	048.4L	games, rough	130.5U	grease	023.7G
food store, large	116.1U	gap, milk	015.3L	greasy	023.8P
fool	073.4L	garbage bin, large	117.3U	Greeks	128.4U
foot/feet	072.6BP	garbage can, large	117.2U	green beans	055A.4L
(for quite a) while	004.6L	garbage man	115.2U	greens	055A.5L
for to (+ inf.)	080.5G	garden	050.5L	grindstone	023.5L
forehead	071.3P	garden	050.5P	grits	050.6AL
forestick/backlog	008.5L	garment bag	123.7U	grocery, neighborhood	116.2AU
fork	017.8CP	gas/electric lawn mower	120.2U	grove	061.6L
fork, hand	120.6U	gearshift	110.7U	grow	065.6G
fortnight	003.8L	gee/haw	037.7G	grown up, most	064.7G
fortnight	003.8P	general	068.3P	guardian	066.4L
forty	001A.1BP	genuine	051.4P	guardian	066.4P
forward	040.4P	Georgia	086.3BP	Gulf of Mexico	030.9P
fountain, drinking	108.8U	Germans	127.1U	gully	030.5L
four	001.2BP	Germans, Low	127.2U	gums	071.9P
four-door sedan	109.3U	get rid of	099.4G	gymnasium	126.2U
fourteen	001.7BP	get up [to horse]	038.1G	hair	071.4AP

joints	072.3P	lie	096.6G	married	082.2S
judge	068.6P	light bulb	019.9L	married, got	082.2L
July	001A.6GP	lightwood	008.6L	marsh	029.7L
June	001A.6FP	like as not	041.1G	Martha	067.2P
junior high school	125.8U	limited-access road	107.5U	Mary	067.1P
junk	010.2L	limousine	109.4U	Mary	067.1S
junk room	010.3L	limousine, airport	109.8U	Maryland	086.1BP
just	070.3P	line/running games	130.2U	masculine female	124.3U
keg	020.2P	lines	039.1L	Massachusetts	086.9AP
Kentucky	086.5BP	Lithuanians	127.7U	Matthew	067.5P
kerosene	024.2L	little way, a	039.5G	mausoleum	117.6U
kettle	017.6L	lively [of older people]	074.1L	May	001A.6EP
kettle	017.6P	liver sausage	047.2L	May	001A.6S
kin, no	066.6L	loaf bread	044.3L	(may I) take you home?	097.5L
kissing	081.7L	loam	029.8P	meadow	029.5L
kitchen	009.9L	loft	014.5L	meat, smoked	046.5L
knee-length shorts	123.2U	log	008.5P	Memphis	087.5AP
kneel	096.5G	long john	122.5U	merry	093.2P
knife games	130.6AU	long way, a	040.1G	merry	093.2S
knife/knives	017.8BP	look here	070.5G	Merry Christmas	093.2G
knob	030.8BP	loss	094.5P	Mexicans	128.7U
know	101.6G	lot, vacant	108.7U	Mexico, Gulf of	030.9P
know (it?), (don't I)	013.3G	Louisiana	086.5AP	microwave oven	116.4BU
Knoxville	087.4BP	Louisville	087.9BP	midwife	065.2L
lagniappe	095.7L	loving, more	066.1G	might could	058.7G
lamb, cuts of	121.4U	low [of cow]	036.3L	might have	058.6G
lamp, makeshift	024.3L	Low Germans	127.2U	mighty glad	090.6G
land's sakes	092.2G	lug	098.1L	miles	088.1G
lane	031.8L	Macon	087.7AP	miles	088.1S
lane markers	107.3U	madam/pimp	113.5U	milk	048.2BP
large food store	116.1U	magnolia	062.9L	milk, curdled	047.6L
large garbage bin	117.3U	mailman	115.1U	milk gap	015.3L
large garbage can	117.2U	make (some coffee)	048.8L	million	001A.2DP
launch	024.5P	makes (him do it?), (what)	013.6G	minnow	061.2L
Laundromat	116.5U	makeshift lamp	024.3L	Mississippi	086.7BP
laundry	010.6L	male, attractive	125.3U	Missouri	086.6BP
laundry hamper	116.6U	male, effeminate	124.1U	Mobile	087.3BP
laurel, mountain	062.7L	male, sexually indiscreet	124.7U	molasses	051.2L
lavatory	126.3U	male, sexually overactive	124.5U	molasses	051.2P
law and order	085.7P	male, ugly	125.1U	molasses is	051.2G
lawn mower, gas/electric	120.2U	male homosexual	124.2U	Monday	002.1CP
lawn mower, manual	120.1U	man, best	082.3L	money	114.5U
lawn mower, riding	120.3U	mantel	008.4L	mongrel	033.3L
lawyer	067.8S	manual lawn mower	120.1U	Montgomery	087.3AP
lead horse	039.4L	maple	061.5L	moonshine	050.8L
learn/teach	101.1G	marble games	130.6CU	more loving	066.1G
left ear	071.5AP	March	001A.6CP	morning	002.2P
leg	072.6AP	mare	034.2BP	mosquito	060A.8P
leg	072.6S	marijuana	114.1U	most grown up	064.7G
letting up, (wind is)	007.3L	markers, lane	107.3U	moth	060A.1L
library	084.1P	married	082.2P	moth/moths	060A.2P

poor whites [black usage]	069.8L	ramp, entrance/exit	107.4U	Russians	127.5U
poor whites [white usage]	069.7L	ramp, parking	108.4U	rustic	069.9L
porch	010.8L	(ran) across	032.6G	Sabbath	002.1BP
porch	010.8P	rancid [butter]	047.5L	sack, cloth	019.6L
pork, cuts of	121.3U	raspberries	062.5P	sack, tow	019.7L
pork, salt	046.3L	rather [=prefer]	090.5P	salt	051.7S
post office	084.2P	rather [=quite]	090.4G	salt pork	046.3L
post/posts	016.5P	rather [=quite]	090.4P	salt/pepper	051.7P
potato house	015.5BL	ravine	030.4L	sample	026.2L
potatoes	055.4L	real	091.7AP	sample	026.2P
potatoes, sweet	055.5L	really	091.7BP	sandwich, hero	121.7U
poultry	121.5U	really (dreaded)	091.6G	Sarah	068.1P
pounds	045.4G	reared	065.4L	Saturday	002.1HP
pregnant	065.1L	recorded music	130.8U	sauce, sweet	048.5L
prettier	026.3BP	reins	039.2L	sausage	046.8AP
pretty	026.3AP	relatives	066.5L	sausage	121.6U
pretty well	079.4G	remember	100.3L	sausage, blood	047.3L
prostitute	113.3U	Republican	129.2U	sausage, liver	047.2L
Protestants	126.6U	resembles (his father)	065.3L	Savannah	087.6BP
proud	090.6P	rest and service area	107.2U	saw, chain	120.9U
proud flesh	078.2L	rheumatism	079.6L	sawhorse	022.1L
proud flesh	078.2P	rhododendron	062.8L	Scandinavians	128.8U
public square	085.1L	rice	050.7P	scarce	095.2P
public transportation	109.9U	rid of, get	099.4G	school, grade	125.7U
puck/ball/tin can games	130.4U	ride	034.3G	school, high	125.9U
Puerto Ricans	128.6U	riding lawn mower	120.3U	school, junior high	125.8U
pull	097.6P	right ear	071.5BP	(school) lets out	083.2L
pull	097.6S	right smart	090.7G	Scots	128.1U
pumper truck	111.2U	rim/felly	021.1L	scrapple	047.4L
pumpkin	056.5P	rind, bacon	046.6L	screech owl	059.1L
purpose, on	103.6G	ring, finger	123.1U	screech owl	059.1P
purse	028.2L	ring games	130.3U	scuttle, coal	023.1L
purse	028.2P	rinses	018.2P	seat, county	085.5L
pus	077.5L	rise	003.3G	second	001A.3BP
push	097.7P	road, limited-access	107.5U	second cutting	041.5L
push	097.7S	road materials/surfaces	031.6L	secretary	068.8P
put it on	102.7P	roasting ears	056.2L	sedan, four-door	109.3U
quarter	004.5P	rock	032.1AL	sedan, police	111.7U
quarter of (eleven)	004.5G	roll, sweet	122.2U	sedan, two-door	109.2U
queer	074.7L	Roman Catholics	126.5U	see	102.5G
queer	074.7P	roof	011.4P	seed, cherry	054.1L
quilt	029.1L	room, junk	010.3L	seed, peach	054.2L
quinine	078.4P	room, sitting	007.8L	(seems) as though	088.3G
quoits	034.8L	roots	061.4P	seesaw	022.5L
radishes	055.2P	rope games	130.6BU	seesawing	022.8L
rail	084.7S	rough games	130.5U	seller, drug	114.4U
rail fence	016.4L	row house	119.1U	September	001A.6IP
railroad station	084.7L	rowboat	024.6L	sermon	089.4L
rain, heavy	006.1L	rubber band	110.3U	sermon	089.4P
rake	120.7U	run	102.3G	setting hen	036.7L
ram	034.9L	Russia	087.9EP	seven	001.4AP

seventh	001A.3GP	sixth	001A.3FP	storm, ice	112.3U
seventy	001A.2AP	skid row	114.8U	stovepipe/flue	023.2L
sexually indiscreet female	124.8U	skipped class	083.4L	stoves/furnaces	118.4U
		skunk	059.4L	strain	048.2AP
sexually indiscreet male	124.7U	skyscraper	108.5U	strain	048.2S
sexually overactive female	124.6U	sleepy	076.6L	stranger	066.7L
		slop bucket	017.4L	strap	022.3P
sexually overactive male	124.5U	smell (that)	051.1G	strawberries	062.4P
shades, window	009.5L	smoked meat	046.5L	streetcar	085.3L
shafts [of buggy]	020.9L	snack	048.6L	string of beads	028.4L
shall (be disappointed), I	081.1G	snappy	007.4L	strong	073.1L
		snits	054.6L	strong	073.1P
shall (be glad), we	081.2AG	snorkel truck	111.4U	student	068.7L
shallots	055.7P	sofa	009.1L	student	068.7P
she, (it's)	042.5CG	sofa	009.1P	such	103.3P
sheaf	041.6L	soft drinks	121.8U	sumac	062.2L
shed	011.7L	soil types	029.8L	sumac	062.2P
sheep, calls to	038.4G	somersault	095.5L	sun	003.2S
shell [hard/inner]	054.8AL	something	103.2P	sun-room	118.1U
shell [v.]	055A.2L	soot	008.7AP	Sunday	002.1AP
shin	072.7L	South Carolina	086.3AP	Sunday a week [future]	003.7G
shivaree	082.5L	speed breaker	110.8U	Sunday a week [past]	003.6G
shock	041.7L	spider web	061.3L	sunrise	003.2L
shoes	123.8U	spoiled	046.9P	sunset	003.4L
shopping	094.2L	spoiled [meat]	046.9L	superintendent	119.5U
shopping district	105.3U	spooks	090.2L	sure	013.4S
shorts, above-the-knee	123.4U	spoon	017.8AP	sure	091.2P
shorts, below-the-knee	123.3U	spring frog	060.3L	sure, not	013.4G
shorts, knee-length	123.2U	spring onions	055.7L	surrogate parent	129.5U
shotgun house	118.6U	square, public	085.1L	suspenders	028.5L
should	058.1G	squash	056.6P	swallow (it)	057.2P
shoulders	072.4BP	squirrel, fox	059.7L	swamp	029.6L
shrimp	060.9P	squirrel, gray	059.6L	swamp	029.6P
shrink	027.9G	St. Louis	087.1CP	sweat	077.3G
shriveled	055.9P	stab	104.3G	sweated	077.3L
shuck	056.1L	stable	015.2L	sweet potatoes	055.5L
shucks	092.3G	stairs	010.7P	sweet roll	122.2U
shut	011.1AP	stairway	010.7L	sweet sauce	048.5L
shut	011.1S	stallion	034.1L	swell	077.6G
shut the door	011.1L	stamp	097.4P	swim	095.6G
(sick) at his stomach	080.4G	stand	019.2L	swing	022.9L
sick, got	076.1G	start?, (when does school)	083.1L	swiped	100.2L
side (of bacon)	046.4L			sycamore	061.7L
sidewalk	031.9AL	station, fire	112.6U	sycamore	061.7P
silk, corn	056.4L	station, police	112.7U	syrup	051.3L
since	103.5P	station, railroad	084.7L	syrup	051.3P
singletree	021.2L	station wagon	109.5U	take	077.1G
sit	049.3G	stirrups	039.3P	take and/go and [+ verb]	081.3G
sit down	049.2G	stone wall	016.6L	take you home?, (may I)	097.5L
sitting room	007.8L	store, convenience	116.2BU	tar	031.6AP
six	001.3BP	store-bought bread	045.1L	tassel	056.3P

tattletale	101.3L	tooth	071.8S	up in (place-name)	082.6G
teach/learn	101.1G	tooth/teeth	071.8P	used clothes	123.5U
teacher, woman	067.6L	tornado	112.2U	used to be	074.4P
tear	102.6G	touch	098.2P	vacant lot	108.7U
ten	001.5BP	touchy	075.1L	vacuum bag	116.8U
ten	001.5BS	tow sack	019.7L	vacuum cleaner	116.7U
ten cents	026.6AP	toward	032.5P	valley	011.6S
Tennessee	086.6AP	toward, (coming)	032.5G	valley [of roof]	011.6L
tenth	001A.3JP	towel	018.6P	van	109.6U
terrapin	060.7L	towel, bath	018.6L	van, police	111.8U
Texas	086.8AP	towel, dish	018.4L	varmint	059.5L
than I can, (better)	043.2G	toy	101.5L	varmints	059.5P
theater	084.4L	transportation, public	109.9U	vase	017.7L
theater	084.4P	trash presser	117.1U	vase	017.7P
theater, X-rated movie	114.9U	trees	061.8L	vegetables	050.4P
theirs	043.4CG	trimmer, hedge	120.8U	vest	027.3L
themselves	044.1G	trough/troughs	035.8P	Virginia	086.2AP
there are (many people)	025.2G	troughs, eaves	011.5L	vomit [crude]	080.3L
they, (it's)	042.5DG	trousers	027.4L	vomit [neutral]	080.2L
they say/people think	013.7G	trowel, hand	120.5U	(wait) for	099.1G
third	001A.3CP	truck, emergency	111.5U	wake	097.3G
third	001A.3S	truck, fire	111.1U	wake him up	076.8L
thirteen	001.7AP	truck, hook and ladder	111.3U	wake up	076.7L
thirty	001A.1AP	truck, pickup	109.7U	wall, stone	016.6L
this way	052.3G	truck, pumper	111.2U	walnut	054.8P
this year	004.7P	truck, snorkel	111.4U	want to get off, (where	085.4G
those (boys)	052.1G	trunk	110.5U	I)	
those were (the good-old	025.6G	tube	024.4P	War, Civil	085.8L
days)		Tuesday	002.1DP	War, Civil	085.8P
thousand	001A.2CP	turn (of corn/wood)	019.8L	wardrobe	009.7L
thrashed	042.1P	turned him down	082.1L	warmed-over	050.1L
three	001.2AP	turtle	060.6L	wash	018.1P
three	001.2S	tusks	035.7P	washcloth	018.5L
threw	032.1BL	twelve	001.6BP	Washington, DC	087.1BP
throat	071.7BP	twenty	001.8AP	wasp/dirt dauber	060A.6L
throw	032.1G	twenty-seven	001.8BP	wasps	060A.6P
thunderstorm	006.2L	twice	001A.5P	watch	004.3P
Thursday	002.1FP	two	001.1BP	water	048.9BP
tightwad	073.5L	two	001.1S	water [in blister]	077.7L
tiller	120.4U	two-door sedan	109.2U	waterfall	031.5L
tin	026.6BP	ugly female	125.2U	watermelon	056.9L
tin	026.6S	ugly male	125.1U	we shall (be glad)	081.2AG
tin can/ball/puck games	130.4U	umbrella	028.6L	we were (going anyway)	025.5G
tired	075.4L	umbrella	028.6P	wear	075.5G
toad	060.4L	un- [prefix]	074.2P	(weather is) changing	005.6L
toadstool	057.1L	uncle	068.2AP	weatherboards	011.2L
toaster oven	116.4CU	underpass	107.8U	web, spider	061.3L
tomato, cherry	055.3L	undertaker	117.4U	Wednesday	002.1EP
tomatoes	055.3P	unless	088.4G	wharf	031.4L
tomorrow	004.1P	unwrapped	094.4P	(what) makes (him do	013.6G
tongue [of wagon]	020.8L	up at (the Browns')	082.7G	it?)	

what time is it?	004.2G
what's that?	052.4G
what-all	043.8G
wheel (the baby)	064.6L
wheelbarrow	023.3L
wheelbarrow	023.3P
(when does school) start?	083.3L
(where I) want to get off	085.4G
whetstone	023.4L
while, (for quite a)	004.6L
whinny [of horse]	036.4L
whip	019.4L
whip	019.4P
whip	019.4S
whipping	065.5L
white	008.7BP
whites, poor [black usage]	069.8L
whites, poor [white usage]	069.7L
who-all	043.7AG
who-all's	043.7BG
whoa [to horse]	038.2AG
whole	082.8P
(whole) crowd	082.8L
whorehouse	113.4U
whose father (is rich)	053.3G
widow	063.3L
widow	063.3P
wife	063.2L
wild hog	035.9L
William	068.2BP
(wind is) letting up	007.3L
(wind is) picking up	007.2L
(wind's) from (the south)	006.4G
window	009.5P
window shades	009.5L
winds	006.5L
wine	114.7U
wire	016.3S
wire fence	016.3L
wishbone	037.1L
with	032.4P
without	032.3P
woman	063.3S
woman teacher	067.6L
won't	058.5P
wood	008.6S
woodpecker	059.3L
wool	035.2P
worm	060.5S

worry	079.5P
worry	079.5S
wound	078.1P
wound	078.1S
woven-wire fence	126.1U
wrapped	094.3P
write	100.5G
write	100.5S
X-rated movie theater	114.9U
year ago, a	005.2P
years (old)	005.1G
yeast	045.5P
yeast	045.5S
yellow	045.7P
yellow jacket/fly	060A.7L
yellow jaundice	079.8L
yes	091.3G
yes, sir/ma'am	091.4G
yesterday	003.5P
yolk	045.6L
you and I	042.2G
you-all	043.5G
you-all's	043.6G
your aunt	067.9P
yours	043.4AG